WILEY PLUS +

for *Financial Accounting: Tools for Business Decision-Making,* Third Canadian Edition

Check with your instructor to find out if you have access to *WileyPLUS!*

Study More Effectively with a Multimedia Text

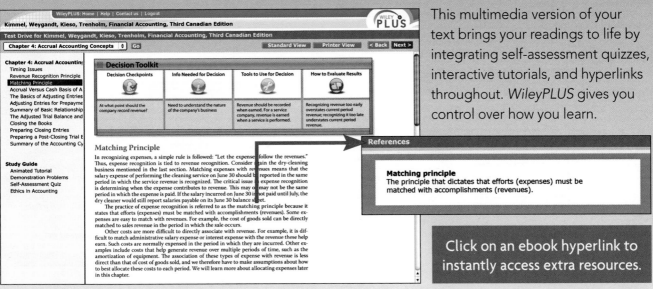

This multimedia version of your text brings your readings to life by integrating self-assessment quizzes, interactive tutorials, and hyperlinks throughout. *WileyPLUS* gives you control over how you learn.

Click on an ebook hyperlink to instantly access extra resources.

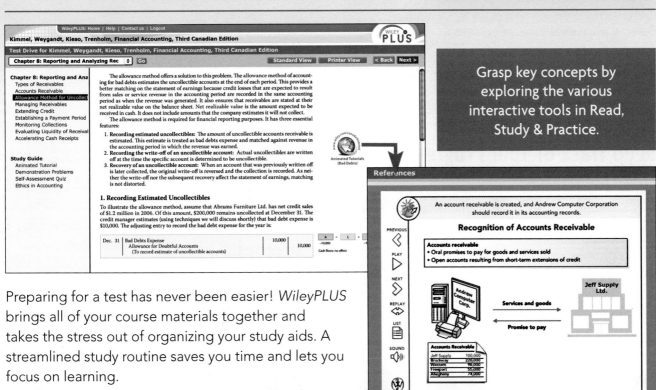

Grasp key concepts by exploring the various interactive tools in Read, Study & Practice.

Preparing for a test has never been easier! *WileyPLUS* brings all of your course materials together and takes the stress out of organizing your study aids. A streamlined study routine saves you time and lets you focus on learning.

John Wiley & Sons Canada, Ltd.

WILEY PLUS

for *Financial Accounting: Tools for Business Decision-Making,* Third Canadian Edition

Complete and Submit Assignments Online Efficiently

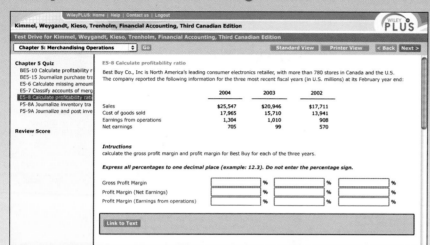

Your instructor can assign homework online for automatic grading and you can keep up-to-date on your assignments with your assignment list.

Your homework questions contain links to the relevant section of the multimedia text, so you know exactly where to go to get help solving each problem. In addition, use the Assignment area of *WileyPLUS* to monitor all of your assignments and their due dates.

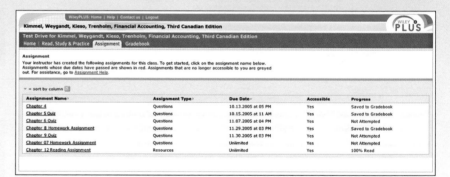

Keep Track of Your Progress

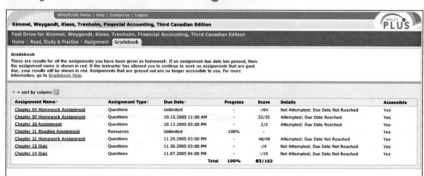

Your personal Gradebook lets you review your answers and results from past assignments as well as any feedback your instructor may have for you.

Keep track of your progress and review your completed questions at any time.

Technical Support: http://higheredwiley.custhelp.com
Student Resource Centre: http://www.wileyplus.com

For further information regarding *WileyPLUS* and other Wiley products, please visit www.wiley.ca

Financial Accounting
Tools for Business Decision-Making

Third Canadian Edition

Paul D. Kimmel PhD, CPA
University of Wisconsin—Milwaukee

Jerry J. Weygandt PhD, CPA
Arthur Andersen Alumni Professor of Accounting
University of Wisconsin—Madison

Donald E. Kieso PhD, CPA
KPMG Emeritus Professor of Accountancy
Northern Illinois University

Barbara Trenholm MBA, FCA
University of New Brunswick

John Wiley & Sons Canada, Ltd.

Dedicated to our students.

Library and Archives Canada Cataloguing in Publication

Financial accounting : tools for business decision-making / Paul D. Kimmel, Jerry J. Weygandt, Donald E. Kieso, Barbara Trenholm—3rd Canadian ed.

Includes index.
ISBN-13: 978-0-470-83679-8
ISBN-10: 0-470-83679-2

1. Accounting--Textbooks. I. Kimmel, Paul D

HF5635.F44 2005 fol.   657'.044   C2005-905898-6

Production Credits

Editorial Manager: Karen Staudinger
Publishing Services Director: Karen Bryan
Developmental Editor: Zoë Craig
New Media Editor: Elsa Passera
Editorial Assistant: Lindsay Humphreys and Sara Vanderwillik
Senior Marketing Manager: Isabelle Moreau
Cover Design: Interrobang Graphic Design Inc.
Design and Typesetting: OrangeSprocket Communications
Printing and Binding: Tri-Graphic Printing Limited

Printed and bound in Canada
10 9 8 7 6 5 4 3

WILEY

John Wiley & Sons Canada, Ltd.
6045 Freemont Blvd.
Mississauga, Ontario L5R 4J3

Visit our website at: www.wiley.ca

Canadian Edition

Barbara Trenholm, MBA, FCA, is a professor of accounting at the University of New Brunswick. Her teaching and educational leadership is renowned. She is a recipient of the National Post/Pricewaterhouse Coopers Leaders in Management Education Award, the Global Teaching Excellence Award, and the University of New Brunswick's Merit Award and Dr. Allan P. Stuart Award for Excellence in Teaching. Several editions of the *Maclean's Guide to Canadian Universities and Colleges* have cited her as one of the University of New Brunswick's most popular professors. In 2003, she was named a Teaching Scholar of the University of New Brunswick.

Her experience and involvement in professional accounting education is widely recognized throughout Canada. She is a past-president of the New Brunswick Institute of Chartered Accountants. She has served as chair of the Canadian Institute of Chartered Accountants Academic Research Committee, Interprovincial Education Committee, and Canadian Institute of Chartered Accountants/Canadian Academic Accounting Association Liaison Committee. She has served as a member of the Canadian Institute of Chartered Accountants Qualification Committee, International Qualifications Appraisal Board, Education Reeingineering Task Force, and the American Accounting Association's Globalization Initiatives Task Force. She has chaired and been a member of numerous other education committees at both the national and provincial levels of the profession.

Professor Trenholm is a member of the boards of many organizations, including Atomic Energy of Canada (AECL) and Plazacorp Retail Properties. She chairs the audit committee of both of these organizations. She is a member of the Institute of Corporate Directors and has had training in best practices for corporate boards. She is a past member, and co-chair, of the University of New Brunswick Pension Board of Trustees. She has also served as a member of the Canadian Institute of Chartered Accountants Board of Directors and Atlantic School of Chartered Accountancy Board of Governors.

In addition to her involvement with her profession, she has an extensive record of service in leadership roles in the university and community. She has served as acting dean of the Faculty of Business Administration and as a member of the University Senate, in addition to chairing and serving on many university and faculty committees.

She has published widely in the field of accounting standard-setting and explored various director and auditor liability issues in journals including *Accounting Horizons, International Journal of Production Economics, CAmagazine, CGA Magazine,* and *CMA Magazine.* She is also the Canadian author of the textbook Weygandt, Kieso, Kimmel, Trenholm, *Accounting Principles,* published by John Wiley & Sons Canada, Ltd.

US Edition

Paul D. Kimmel, PhD, CPA, received his bachelor's degree from the University of Minnesota and his doctorate in accounting from the University of Wisconsin. He is an Associate Professor at the University of Wisconsin—Milwaukee, and has public accounting experience with Deloitte & Touche. He was the recipient of the UWM School of Business Advisory Council Teaching Award and the Reggie Taite Excellence in Teaching Award, and is a three-time winner of the Outstanding Teaching Assistant Award at the University of Wisconsin. He is also a recipient of the Elijah Watts Sells Award for Honorary Distinction for his results on the CPA exam.

He is a member of the American Accounting Association and has published articles in *Accounting Review, Accounting Horizons, Advances in Management Accounting, Managerial Finance, Issues in Accounting Education,* and *Journal of Accounting Education,* as well as other journals. His research interests include accounting for financial instruments and innovation in accounting education. He has published papers and given numerous talks on incorporating critical thinking into accounting education, and helped prepare a catalogue of critical thinking resources for the Federated Schools of Accountancy.

Jerry J. Weygandt, PhD, CPA, is the Arthur Andersen Alumni Professor of Accounting at the University of Wisconsin—Madison. He holds a PhD in accounting from the University of Illinois. Articles by Professor Weygandt have appeared in *Accounting Review, Journal of Accounting Research, Accounting Horizons, Journal of Accountancy,* and other academic and professional journals. He is a member of the American Accounting Association, the American Institute of Certified Public Accountants, and the Wisconsin Society of Certified Public Accountants. He has served on numerous committees of the American Accounting Association and as a member of the editorial board of *Accounting Review;* he also has served as President and Secretary-Treasurer of the American Accounting Association. In addition, he has

been actively involved with the American Institute of Certified Public Accountants and has been a member of the Accounting Standards Executive Committee (AcSEC) of that organization. He has served on the FASB task force that examined the reporting issues related to accounting for income taxes and is presently a trustee of the Financial Accounting Foundation. Professor Weygandt has received the Chancellor's Award for Excellence in Teaching and the Beta Gamma Sigma Dean's Teaching Award. He is on the board of directors of M&I Bank of Southern Wisconsin and the Dean Foundation. He is the recipient of the Wisconsin Institute of CPA's Outstanding Educator's Award and the Lifetime Achievement Award. In 2001 he received the American Accounting Association's Outstanding Accounting Educator Award.

Donald E. Kieso, PhD, CPA, received his bachelor's degree from Aurora University and his doctorate in accounting from the University of Illinois. He has served as chairman of the Department of Accountancy and is currently the KPMG Emeritus Professor of Accounting at Northern Illinois University. He has public accounting experience with Price Waterhouse & Co. and Arthur Andersen & Co. and research experience with the Research Division of the American Institute of Certified Public Accountants. He has done post-doctoral work as a Visiting Scholar at the University of California at Berkeley and is a recipient of NIU's Teaching Excellence Award and four Golden Apple Teaching Awards. Professor Kieso is a member of the American Accounting Association, the American Institute of Certified

fied Public Accountants, and the Illinois CPA Society. He has served as a member of the Board of Directors of the Illinois CPA Society, the AACSB's Accounting Accreditation Committees, the State of Illinois Comptroller's Commission, as Secretary-Treasurer of the Federation of Schools of Accountancy, and as Secretary-Treasurer of the American Accounting Association. He served as a charter member of the national Accounting Education Change Commission. He is the recipient of the Outstanding Accounting Educator Award from the Illinois CPA Society, the FSA's Joseph A. Silvoso Award of Merit, the NIU Foundation's Humanitarian Award for Service to Higher Education, the Distinguished Service Award from the Illinois CPA Society, and in 2003 an honorary doctorate from Aurora University.

Our efforts to continually improve this text are driven by a few key beliefs:

"It really matters."

Since late 2002, the economy has been affected by failures in corporate governance and financial reporting, as well as by the increased regulation and other steps taken to address those failures. Consequently, there is a heightened awareness of the importance of accounting to a smoothly-running economic system. Many of our feature stories, Accounting Matters insight boxes, and Broadening Your Perspective cases have been designed to reveal accounting's critical role in society. In short, it has never been more evident that accounting really matters!

"Less is more."

Our instructional objective is to provide students with an understanding of those concepts that are fundamental to the use of accounting. Most students will forget procedural details within a short period of time. On the other hand, concepts, if well taught, should be remembered for a lifetime. Concepts are especially important in a world where the details are constantly changing.

"Don't just sit there— do something."

Students learn best when they are actively engaged. The overriding pedagogical objective of this book is to provide students with continual opportunities for active learning. One of the best tools for active learning is strategically placed questions. Our discussions are framed by questions, often beginning with rhetorical questions and ending with review questions. Even our selection of analytical devices, called Decision Tools, is referenced using key questions to emphasize the purpose of each device.

"I'll believe it when I see it."

Students are most willing to commit time and energy to a topic when they believe that it is relevant to their future career. There is no better way to demonstrate relevance than to ground discussion in the real world as we do with our feature stories and Accounting Matters insight boxes. In addition, by using high-profile companies such as Air Canada, Canadian Tire, CanWest Global, Intrawest, Loblaw, Sears, and Wyeth Consumer Healthcare to frame our discussion of accounting issues, we demonstrate the relevance of accounting while teaching students about companies with which they have daily contact. As they become acquainted with the financial successes and failures of these companies, many students will begin to follow business news more closely, making their learning a dynamic, ongoing process. We also discuss smaller companies to highlight the challenges they face as they try to grow.

"You need to make a decision."

All business people must make decisions. Decision-making involves critical evaluation and analysis of the information at hand, and this takes practice. We have integrated important analytical tools throughout the book. After each new decision tool is presented, we summarize the key features of that tool in a Decision Toolkit. At the end of each chapter, we provide a comprehensive demonstration of an analysis of a real company using the decision tools presented in the chapter. The presentation of these tools throughout the book is cumulative, sequenced to take full advantage of the tools presented in earlier chapters.

"It's a small world."

In today's global economy, few business decisions can be made without consideration of international factors. This will become even more important in the years to come as we move to a single set of high-quality, internationally accepted accounting principles. To heighten student awareness of international issues, we have increased references to international companies and provided A Global Focus case in each chapter.

Key Features of Each Chapter

Chapter 1: Introduction to Financial Statements
- Feature story about Loblaw and how accounting aids decision-making
- Describes the role of accounting in providing reliable financial information, and the importance of ethics in accounting
- Identifies the uses and users of financial accounting information
- Explains the content and purpose of each of the financial statements
- Uses the financial statements of a hypothetical company (to keep it simple), followed by those for a real company, Loblaw Companies Limited (to make it relevant)
- Using the Decision Toolkit compares Sobeys' financial statements to Loblaw's

Chapter 2: A Further Look at Financial Statements
- Feature story about Nortel Networks and the importance of reliable accounting information
- Describes the conceptual framework of accounting
- Presents the classified balance sheet
- Applies ratio analysis to Sears' and Hudson's Bay's statements of earnings (earnings per share and price-earnings ratio), balance sheet (working capital, current ratio, and debt to total assets) and cash flow statements (free cash flow)
- Using the Decision Toolkit analyzes Canadian Tire's liquidity, profitability, and solvency, and compares it to that of Sears and Hudson's Bay

Chapter 3: The Accounting Information System
- Feature story about BeaverTails Canada's experiences with an accounting information system
- Covers transaction analysis—emphasizes fundamentals while avoiding unnecessary detail
- Explains the first steps in the accounting cycle, from journalizing through the preparation of a trial balance
- Using the Decision Toolkit corrects an erroneously prepared trial balance for Prairie Grain Growers

Chapter 4: Accrual Accounting Concepts
- Feature story about revenue and expense recognition
- Explains the revenue recognition and matching principles
- Emphasizes the difference between cash and accrual accounting
- Completes the accounting cycle, from adjusting entries to the closing process
- Using the Decision Toolkit prepares financial statements for Fishery Products International Limited

Chapter 5: Merchandising Operations
- Feature story about Wal-Mart's inventory control and distribution system
- Introduces merchandising concepts using the perpetual inventory system (periodic inventory system presented in an appendix)
- Presents the multiple-step statement of earnings

- Applies ratio analysis to Wal-Mart and Hudson's Bay (gross profit margin and profit margin)
- Using the Decision Toolkit compares Wal-Mart's and Costco's profitability

Chapter 6: Reporting and Analyzing Inventory
- Feature story about Caterpillar's inventory management
- Explains how inventory quantities and ownership is determined
- Covers cost flow assumptions and implications for financial reporting. For simplification, emphasizes the periodic inventory system (perpetual inventory system covered in an appendix)
- Discusses the effects of inventory errors on financial statements
- Explains the lower of cost and market basis of valuing inventory
- Applies ratio analysis to Wal-Mart (inventory turnover and days in inventory)
- Using the Decision Toolkit reviews IPSCO's inventory performance

Chapter 7: Internal Control and Cash
- Feature story about cash control at the Granite Brewery
- Covers internal control concepts and implications of control failures
- Presents the bank reconciliation as a control device
- Explains how cash is reported on the balance sheet
- Discusses cash management, including cash budgeting
- Using the Decision Toolkit reviews some internal control issues at a local basketball association

Chapter 8: Reporting and Analyzing Receivables
- Feature story about Wyeth Consumer Healthcare's management of receivables
- Presents the basics of accounts and notes receivable and bad debt estimation
- Discusses receivables management, including methods used to accelerate cash receipts
- Applies ratio analysis to Wyeth (receivables turnover and average collection period)
- Using the Decision Toolkit compares Eli Lilly's receivables management and liquidity to that of Wyeth's

Chapter 9: Reporting and Analyzing Long-Lived Assets
- Feature story about Air Canada's long-lived assets
- Covers the acquisition and disposition of tangible and intangible assets
- Discusses the implications of alternative amortization methods (details the calculation of declining-balance and units-of-activity amortization methods in an appendix)
- Applies ratio analysis to Air Canada and WestJet Airlines (return on assets and asset turnover)
- Using the Decision Toolkit analyzes Research in Motion's accounting for its long-lived assets

Chapter 10: Reporting and Analyzing Liabilities
- Feature story about Quebecor's liabilities
- Covers current and long-term liabilities

- Presents the straight-line and effective-interest methods of amortization in appendices
- Applies ratio analysis to Quebecor (current ratio, debt to total assets, and times interest earned)
- Discusses other analysis issues, including contingencies and off–balance sheet financing
- Using the Decision Toolkit compares CanWest Global Communications' liquidity and solvency to Quebecor's

Chapter 11: Reporting and Analyzing Shareholders' Equity

- Feature story about Research in Motion's shareholders' equity
- Discusses the corporate and other forms of organization
- Covers issues related to common and preferred shares, including reacquisition of shares
- Explains cash dividends, stock dividends, stock splits, and their implications for analysis
- Describes the presentation of equity items, including accumulated other comprehensive income
- Applies ratio analysis to Research in Motion (payout ratio, dividend yield, earnings per share, and return on common shareholders' equity)
- Using the Decision Toolkit compares Research in Motion's dividend record and earnings performance to palmOne's

Chapter 12: Reporting and Analyzing Investments

- Feature story about EnCana's strategic investments
- Explains why companies purchase debt and equity investments
- Describes the accounting for short- and long-term debt investments
- Describes the accounting for equity investments, including the cost and equity methods
- Describes the accounting for, and valuation of, trading, available-for-sale, and held-to-maturity investments
- Discusses the potential for earnings management with the valuation and reporting of investments
- Explains how investments are reported on the financial statements, including the statement of comprehensive income
- Using the Decision Toolkit reviews the Royal Bank's investment portfolio

Chapter 13: Cash Flow Statement

- Feature story about Intrawest's cash flow
- Explains the purpose and format of the cash flow statement
- Splits chapter into two parts, allowing instructor to use either the indirect approach of preparing the operating activities section or the direct approach, or both
- Applies ratio analysis to Intrawest (cash current debt coverage and cash total debt coverage)
- Using the Decision Toolkit compares cash- and accrual-based measures for Intrawest and the American Skiing Company

Chapter 14: Performance Measurement

- Feature story reviews the PotashCorp.'s award-winning annual report

- Discusses sustainable earnings, and the implications of discontinued operations and changes in accounting principles
- Demonstrates horizontal and vertical analysis for Potash-Corp.
- Capstone chapter, summarizing ratio analyses introduced in previous chapters
- Discusses factors that affect the quality of earnings
- A comprehensive analysis of PotashCorp compared to Agrium is included in an appendix to reinforce analytical tools and review how the tools relate to each other

New In This Edition

The third edition of *Financial Accounting: Tools for Business Decision-Making* provides an opportunity to improve a textbook that has set high standards for quality. The feedback from reviewers and other users gave us valuable insight that helped shape this edition to better meet their, and their students', needs. We added and deleted topical coverage as suggested and increased the breadth and depth of the end-of-chapter material. In addition, we increased the number and type of interactive learning aids for students and enhanced the technological features of the text to help both instructors and students.

In the Real World, Accounting Matters!

Since we wrote the second edition of *Financial Accounting: Tools for Business Decision-Making*, we have seen a heightened awareness about the importance of accounting to society. As a result of a rash of accounting irregularities and erroneous financial reporting and other misdeeds, new regulations and laws have been passed and the structure of the accounting and auditing professions has been altered. It is now evident to the whole world that accounting really matters!

In response to these real-world events, we are emphasizing the theme "Accounting Matters" in the third edition of *Financial Accounting*. The label "Accounting Matters!" appears on our chapter-opening real-world feature stories and on the business insight boxes found in every chapter. Recent corporate scandals and steps taken to address these scandals are discussed in many of the feature stories, business insight boxes, and throughout the chapter material as appropriate.

Chapter 1, which previously included material on how to solve ethical dilemmas, now commences with a new section defending the importance of accounting and its contributions to our economic system. Ethical insights and cases in the end-of-chapter material have been thoroughly revised to inform students of the consequences of various actions on financial reporting.

Relevance to Users

This edition continues, and expands, the inclusion of user-oriented material to demonstrate the relevance of accounting to all students, no matter their area of study. Our focus companies are again Loblaw and Sobeys. They were chosen because they have high name recognition with students, operate in a single industry, and have relatively simple financial statements. We updated the chapter and end-of-chapter material to the January 3, 2004 financial statements for Loblaw and the May 1, 2004 financial statements for Sobeys.

This edition was also subject to a comprehensive updating to ensure that it continues to be relevant and fresh. All real-world examples were updated, or replaced, in the text as appropriate, including the chapter-opening feature stories, the Accounting Matters insight boxes, Using the Decision Toolkits, and other references. In addition, 43 percent of the chapter-opening feature stories were replaced with new stories, 55 percent of the Accounting Matters insight boxes are new, and all the Review It questions relating to Loblaw are new, corresponding to the January 3, 2004 financial statements.

Pedagogical Effectiveness

Our Navigator learning system continues to empower students to succeed by teaching them how to study, what to study, and why they should study. The third edition places increased emphasis, throughout the text, on the processes students go through as they learn. Our Learning Styles model, introduced in previous editions, is incorporated throughout the text to enable students with different learning approaches to better understand the material. We continue to believe that infographics help visual learners quickly assimilate difficult concepts. In response to reviewers' comments, many of these graphics were updated and redesigned.

In addition, study objectives were combined or reorganized to facilitate learning, and more summaries were added throughout the chapter to help students stop and assimilate the material they just learned. Stepped-out pedagogy was used to break down complex topics, making the material more manageable for students. Before You Go On feedback sections at the end of each major study objective were augmented in both number and content coverage to facilitate student understanding.

Simplified Presentation

We made design enhancements in response to comments made by instructors and students. These include a crisper, cleaner look along with more open margin space, which will aid readability and understanding. The text material has been thoroughly reviewed by an instructor of English as a Second Language to ensure that *Financial Accounting* continues to provide an unprecedented level of clarity and readability.

Expanded Topical Coverage

Additional topical coverage was requested by instructors to help them better prepare students for the complexities of today's world of accounting. These topics had to pass a strict test to warrant their inclusion: they were added only if they represented a major concept, issue, or procedure that an introductory accounting student needed to understand. Some of the more significant additions include the following:

- Chapter 2: A Further Look at Financial Statements—A new section was added about international accounting principles and the trend toward global convergence. The formula for earnings per share was expanded to include the weighted average number of common shares instead of the average number of common shares, which was used in the past edition for simplicity. Students are briefly introduced to the formula components in this chapter and learn how to calculate the weighted average in Chapter 11: Reporting and Analyzing Shareholders' Equity.

- Chapter 3: The Accounting Information System—The impact of transaction analysis on the financial position of the company was expanded to include each separate component of shareholders' equity (common shares, revenues, expenses, and dividends).

- Chapter 4: Accrual Accounting Concepts—The formula to calculate straight-line amortization was introduced in a simplified manner (without salvage value). An expanded explanation of closing entries and illustration of a post-closing trial balance was added.

- Chapter 5: Merchandising Operations—Reorganized the "Inventory Systems" section to add additional detail for, and better explain the differences between, a perpetual and periodic inventory system. Added information about quantity discounts. In addition, reorganized and expanded the discussion of cost of goods sold and the single- and multiple-step statements of earnings.

- Chapter 6: Reporting and Analyzing Inventory—The discussion of determining inventory quantities was expanded, and internal control features were added. An example illustrating the calculation of lower of cost and market was also added.

- Chapter 7: Internal Control and Cash—Added information about the proposed Canadian Securities Administrators expanded internal control requirements. Also, expanded the explanation of cheques and deposits.

- Chapter 8: Reporting and Analyzing Receivables—Expanded discussion of revenue recognition and matching principles. Added information about the subsidiary accounts receivable ledger, in addition to securitization of receivables.

- Chapter 9: Analyzing Long-Lived Assets—Added a brief discussion about asset retirement costs and how they affect the cost of long-lived assets. Also included a discussion about leasehold improvements and impairment losses.

- Chapter 10: Reporting and Analyzing Liabilities—Streamlined examples used in the discussion of bonds. Added more detail about how discounts and premiums affect the cost of borrowing and why companies might wish to redeem bonds before maturity. Added a statement of earnings presentation to the "Financial Statement Presentation" section.

- Chapter 11: Reporting and Analyzing Shareholders' Equity—Added a description of income trusts as an emerging form of business organization. Substantially expanded discussion of, and accounting for, reacquisition of shares. Introduced comprehensive income. Explained how the net earnings available to common shareholders and weighted average number of common shares are calculated in the earnings per share formula. Added the dividend yield ratio—a ratio frequently reported in the financial press and used by investors.

- Chapter 12: Reporting and Analyzing Investments—Added the accounting for short-term debt investments (e.g., money-market instruments) to this chapter. This chapter was substantially rewritten to incorporate the new material on financial instruments for trading, available-for-sale, and held-to-maturity securities.

Organizational Changes

Organizational changes were made to simplify chapters or to provide instructors with greater flexibility of coverage. Some of the areas most affected are as follows:

- Chapter 1: Introduction to Financial Statements—The material on assumptions and principles was moved to Chapter 2: A Further Look at Financial Statements and combined with the discussion in that chapter about the characteristics of useful information and constraints in accounting.
- Chapter 2: A Further Look at Financial Statements—Moved the cash current debt coverage and cash total debt coverage ratios to Chapter 13: Cash Flow Statement. Free cash flow, a more commonly used measure, was moved from Chapter 13 to Chapter 2.
- Chapter 3: The Accounting Information System—Reorganized the discussion of debits and credits to better follow the accounting equation.
- Chapter 5: Merchandising Operations—Moved the discussion of freight costs from Chapter 6: Reporting and Analyzing Inventory to Chapter 5.
- Chapter 6: Reporting and Analyzing Inventory—Moved the "Classifying Inventory" section to the end of the chapter. Changed the method of determining cost of goods sold from calculating both cost of goods sold and ending inventory separately to calculating ending inventory first, then determining the cost of goods sold by formula, as is more common in real life.
- Chapter 9: Analyzing Long-Lived Assets—Reorganized presentation of disclosure items into "Statement Presentation" section and added information about the statement of earnings presentation. Changed recording of the credit for the amortization of limited life intangibles from the asset account to an accumulated amortization account to be more consistent with the accounting treatment shown in intermediate accounting textbooks.
- Chapter 10: Reporting and Analyzing Liabilities—Simplified procedure for calculating property taxes. Moved discussion of notes to precede that of bonds, in keeping with the premise that students are far more likely to encounter notes than bonds in real life.
- Chapter 13: Cash Flow Statement—Reorganized material in the "Reporting of Cash Flows" section and clarified the distinction between operating, investing, and financing activities. In addition, changed steps to prepare the cash flow statement. These steps and the subsequent discussion that follows better coincides with the actual statement preparation order. As previously mentioned, moved free cash flow from this chapter to Chapter 2, and moved the cash current debt coverage and cash total debt coverage ratios from Chapter 2 to this chapter.
- Chapter 14: Performance Measurement—Replaced the section on "Improper Recognition" with one on "Professional Judgement." Replaced Molson with PotashCorp.—the 2004 winner of the corporate reporting awards. Compared PotashCorp. and Agrium and their industry in a comprehensive illustration of ratio analysis presented in appendix.

Deleted Material

We condensed or deleted concepts and procedures that are little used or are better suited to advanced courses.

- Chapter 2: A Further Look at Financial Statements—Deleted the section "Using the Statement of Retained Earnings."
- Chapter 9: Analyzing Long-Lived Assets—Deleted explanation of how revisions to amortization are calculated and the section on "Expenditures During Useful Life."
- Chapter 10: Reporting and Analyzing Liabilities—Deleted the calculation of sales on a tax inclusive basis. Expanded terminology for notes, and condensed terminology for bonds. Deleted discussion of retractable bonds and "Issuing Procedures" section. Deleted acid-test ratio.
- Chapter 11: Reporting and Analyzing Shareholders' Equity—Deleted section on forming a corporation, and condensed discussion of par and stated value shares. Deleted section on stock compensation plans and the debt vs. equity decision.
- Chapter 13: Cash Flow Statement—Condensed coverage from two years of transactions to one year of transactions for both the indirect and direct methods of preparing the operating activities section.
- Chapter 14: Performance Measurement—Reduced detail about extraordinary items (now explained but not illustrated) given their rarity in Canada.

Unparalleled End-of-Chapter Material

The third edition of *Financial Accounting: Tools for Business Decision-Making* has more end-of-chapter material than any other textbook. This material guides students through the basic levels of cognitive understanding—knowledge, comprehension, application, analysis, synthesis, and evaluation—in a step-by-step process, starting first with questions, followed by brief exercises, exercises, problems, and finally cases.

Instructors told us they wanted more breadth and depth within each of these groupings to give them more flexibility in assigning end-of-chapter material. All of the end-of-chapter material was carefully reviewed and compared to the study objectives. Topical gaps were identified and additional material added as required to facilitate progressive learning. Existing material was expanded, where relevant, to include additional transactions. Complexities were added or deleted to selected end-of-chapter material as required to increase the range and difficulty level of material available to test critical problem-solving skills. As well, an exciting new serial problem has been added to each chapter in the Broadening Your Perspectives section. The problem begins in Chapter 1 with a student who starts up a cookie-making school called "Cookie Creations." The life of the company continues in each subsequent chapter, incurring transactions and encountering situations relevant to the topical material at hand.

In total, we have added 355 new questions, brief exercises, exercises, problems, and cases to the end-of-chapter material. That's a 32 percent increase in the end-of-chapter material in the third edition over the second edition! The remaining material was updated and revised, as required.

Active Learning Supplementary Material

Financial Accounting: Tools for Business Decision-Making features a full line of learning resources. Driven by the same basic beliefs as the textbook, these supplements provide a consistent and well-integrated active learning system. This hands-on, real-world package creates an interactive learning environment that encourages students to take an active role and prepares them for decision-making in a real-world context.

The Kimmel Toolkit Website (www.wiley.com/canada/kimmel)

The Kimmel Toolkit website serves as a launching pad to numerous activities and learning materials. This comprehensive website includes resources to help students practice their analysis skills and improve upon their study skills. Animated tutorials, interactive self-test quizzes, additional demonstration problems, company links, a checklist of key figures, links to the Broadening Your Perspective web cases, profiles of real-life accountants, and many more learning aids are designed to strengthen students' understanding of financial accounting.

WileyPLUS

Also available is WileyPLUS, an online suite of resources that includes a complete multimedia version of the text that will help students come to class better prepared for lectures, and allows instructors to track student progress throughout the course more easily. Students can take advantage of tools such as self-assessment quizzes and animated tutorials to help them study more effectively. WileyPLUS is designed to provide instant feedback for students as they practice on their own. Instructors, in turn, can create assignments and automate the assigning and grading of homework or quizzes using the gradebook feature. They can also create class presentations using PowerPoint slides and interactive simulations, or they can upload their own material to create a customized presentation.

Study Guide to Accompany *Financial Accounting: Tools for Business Decision-Making*

The study guide is a comprehensive review of financial accounting that is a powerful tool when used in the classroom and in preparation for exams. It takes students through chapter content while focusing on study objectives and the decision-making process.

Each chapter includes an overview of the chapter, a review of study objectives, and a summary of key points. Students can test their knowledge and skills through multiple choice questions and problems linked to specific study objectives. Students can also apply the Decision Toolkit against two competitor companies—Domtar Inc. and Cascades Inc.—in each chapter. Detailed solutions are then presented in order to effectively provide immediate feedback.

ACKNOWLEDGMENTS

During the course of development of the third Canadian edition of *Financial Accounting: Tools for Business Decision-Making*, the author benefitted greatly from the input of reviewers, ancillary authors, contributors, and proofers. The constructive suggestions and innovative ideas of the reviewers and the creativity and accuracy of the ancillary authors and other contributors are greatly appreciated.

Reviewers

Judy Cumby, *Memorial University*
Angela Davis, *University of Winnipeg*
Chris Duff, *Royal Roads University*
Gerry Dupont, *Carleton University*
Rosemary Henriksen, *Kwantlen University College*
Ian Hutchinson, *Acadia University*

Rafik Kurji, *Mount Royal College*
Howard Leaman, *University of Guelph*
Shelley Martin, *Memorial University*
Jo-Anne Ryan, *Nipissing University*
Joy Skinner, *Assiniboine Community College*

Ancillary Authors and Contributors

Sally Anderson, *Mount Royal College*–Problem Material contributor and Solutions Manual checker
Tashia Batstone, *Memorial University*–Solutions Manual author and coordinator
Paul Berry, *Mount Allison University*–Instructor's Manual author
Peggy Coady, *Memorial University*–PowerPoint Slides author
Judy Cumby, *Memorial University*–Problem Material contributor
Gerry Dupont, *Carleton University*–Study Guide author
Ian Farmer, Solutions Manual checker
Joanne Hinton, *University of New Brunswick*–Textbook contributor and Solutions Manual checker
Pierre Hilal, *Bishop's University*–Solutions Manual Author
Jennifer Nicholson, *St. Mary's University*–Problem Material Contributor
Lori Weatherbie–Testbank and Solutions Manual author

I would like to express my appreciation to Paul Kimmel, Jerry Weygandt, and Don Kieso, co-authors of the U.S edition of this textbook, for their willingness to share their extensive teaching and writing experiences with me.

I appreciate the exemplary support and professional commitment given me by the talented team in the Wiley Canada higher education division, including John Horne, Karen Staudinger, Karen Bryan, Zoë Craig, Isabelle Moreau, Maureen Talty, Luke Curtin, Lindsay Humphreys, Sara Vanderwillik, and Elsa Passera, all of whom I worked especially closely with. I value the strong relationship we have developed over the life of this textbook. There are far too many other talented professionals involved at Wiley to name here, but each worked hard to create this book and its supplements. I am grateful for all of their efforts. I also wish to specifically thank Wiley's dedicated sales representatives who continue to work tirelessly to service your needs.

It takes many people to produce a quality textbook and supplements. I would like to thank Alison Arnot, Feature Story author; Angela Day, Word file and solutions formatter; David Schwinghamer, copyeditor; Zofia Laubitz, proofreader; Deborah Wybou, solutions formatter, and Edwin Durbin, indexer for their significant contributions.

I also wish to express my appreciation to OrangeSprocket Communications for their assistance and creativity in improving the design of this text, and for their patient and accurate typesetting efforts. In addition, they, along with folks from the company Development Box, were innovative in developing user-friendly web-based techniques to help us manage and improve our production process.

I thank Loblaw and Sobeys for permitting the use of their financial statements. I would also like to acknowledge the co-operation of the many Canadian and international companies that allowed me to include extracts from their financial statements in the text and end-of-chapter material.

It would not have been possible to write this text without the understanding of my employer, colleagues, students, friends, and family. Together, they provided a creative and supportive environment for my work.

We have tried our best to produce a text and supplement package that is error-free and that meets your specific needs. Suggestions and comments from users are encouraged and appreciated. Please don't hesitate to let us know of any improvements that we should consider for subsequent printings or editions.

Barbara Trenholm
trenholm@unb.ca
Fredericton, New Brunswick
November 2005

CHAPTER 2

A Further Look at Financial Statements

ACCOUNTING MATTERS!

Getting the Numbers Right

Many investors rely on financial statements in order to make informed decisions on when to buy and sell a company's shares.

Financial statements should provide relevant and reliable information. However, this has not always been the case. The recent accounting scandals that collapsed U.S. companies Enron and WorldCom shook investor confidence worldwide. And investors in Canadian companies have had their own cause for concern with several organizations having to restate their financials.

The most high-profile case in Canada involved Brampton, Ontario-based Nortel Networks Corporation. In January 2005, Nortel released revised financial statements for 2003, 2002, and 2001. Its net earnings for 2003 were U.S. $434 million or 10 cents a share, instead of the previously reported U.S. $732 million or 17 cents a share. Nortel also reported restated losses of 78 cents a share for 2002 and $8.08 a share for 2001.

The original results for 2003 indicated the first profitable year in seven, triggering a jump in share price and increased investor confidence. However, in March 2004, Nortel revealed that there had been accounting irregularities, with profits overstated by up to 50 percent. Nortel's chief executive officer and nine senior financial officers were soon fired "with cause," and the share price began to decline.

The restatement process that followed took nine months and cost more than $100 million. Nortel's board of directors has since committed itself to rebuilding a finance environment based on principles of transparency and integrity, and ensuring sound financial reporting and comprehensive disclosure.

Still, the company's problems are not over. Its audit committee continues to investigate the "facts and circumstances" that led to the accounting irregularities, as well as another $3.2 billion in overstated sales during 1999 and 2000. Meanwhile, Nortel is fighting several shareholders' lawsuits, and the RCMP is investigating its financial accounting situation, as are regulators in both Canada and the United States.

And—as if Nortel did not have enough problems—the focus on numbers has diverted attention away from the product. According to industry analysts, Nortel lags in product development, running 6 to 12 months behind on upgrades. This, plus the company's tarnished image resulting from its accounting problems, could affect future business.

It may take years for Nortel to regain investor confidence in its numbers—all the more reason for companies to get them right the first time round.

The **Accounting Matters!** feature story helps you picture how the topics of the chapter relate to the real world of accounting and business. References to the feature story throughout the chapter will help you put new ideas in context, organize them, and remember them.

The **Navigator** is a learning system designed to guide you through each chapter and help you succeed in learning the material. It consists of (1) a checklist at the beginning of the chapter, which outlines text features and study aids you will need, and (2) a series of check boxes that prompt you to use the learning aids in the chapter and set priorities as you study.

Intrawest: www.intrawest.com

THE NAVIGATOR

- [ ] Read *Feature Story*
- [ ] Scan *Study Objectives*
- [ ] Read *Chapter Preview*
- [ ] Read text and answer *Before You Go On*
- [ ] Work *Using the Decision Toolkit*
- [ ] Review *Summary of Study Objectives*
- [ ] Review *Decision Toolkit—A Summary*
- [ ] Work *Demonstration Problem*
- [ ] Answer *Self-Study Questions*
- [ ] Complete assignments

Study Objectives at the beginning of each chapter provide you with a framework for learning the specific concepts covered in the chapter. Each Study Objective then reappears at the point within the chapter where the concept is discussed, and all the objectives are also summarized at the end of the chapter.

STUDY OBJECTIVES

After studying this chapter, you should be able to:

1. Describe the purpose and format of the cash flow statement.
2. Prepare a cash flow statement using one of two approaches: (a) the indirect method or (b) the direct method.
3. Use the cash flow statement to evaluate a company's liquidity and solvency.

The **Preview** links the Feature Story with the major topics of the chapter. It then gives a graphic outline of major topics and subtopics that will be discussed. This narrative and visual preview help you organize the information you are learning.

Key Terms that represent essential concepts are printed in blue where they are first explained in the text. They are listed and defined again in the end-of-chapter Glossary.

Colour illustrations, such as this infographic, help you visualize and apply the information as you study. They reinforce important concepts.

Study Objectives reappear in the margins at the point where the topic is discussed. End-of-chapter questions, brief exercises, exercises, and problems are keyed to the Study Objectives.

Financial statements appear regularly throughout the book. Those from real companies are usually identified by a logo. Often, numbers or categories are highlighted in red type to draw your attention to key information.

A **Web** icon directs you to the Toolkit website, where additional learning resources are available.

PREVIEW OF CHAPTER 3

As indicated in the feature story, an accounting information system that produces timely and accurate financial information is a necessity for a company like BeaverTails. The purpose of this chapter is to explain and illustrate the features of an accounting information system. The chapter is organized as follows:

THE ACCOUNTING INFORMATION SYSTEM

Accounting Transactions	The Account	Steps in the Recording Process	The Trial Balance
▶ Analyzing transactions ▶ Summary of transactions	▶ Debits and credits ▶ Expanded accounting equation	▶ The journal ▶ The ledger ▶ Posting ▶ The recording process illustrated	▶ Limitations of a trial balance

Accounting Transactions

The system of collecting and processing transaction data and communicating financial information to decision-makers is known as the **accounting information system**. Accounting information systems vary widely. Some factors that shape these systems are the type of business and its transactions, the size of the company, the amount of data, and the information that management and others need. For example, as indicated in the feature story, BeaverTails did not need a formal accounting system when it first began. However, as the business and the number and type of transactions grew, an organized accounting information system became essential.

An accounting information system begins with determining what relevant transaction data should be collected and processed. Not all events are recorded and reported as accounting transactions. For example, suppose a new employee is hired, or a new computer purchased. Are these events entered in the company's accounting records? The first event would not be recorded, but the second event would. The hiring of an employee will lead to an accounting transaction (e.g., the payment of salary after the work has been completed), but, until that time, no accounting transaction has occurred.

An **accounting transaction** occurs when assets, liabilities, or shareholders' equity items change as a result of some economic event. Illustration 3-1 summarizes the process that is used to decide whether or not to record economic events.

Illustration 3-1 ▶

Transaction identification process

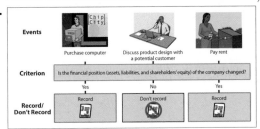

Events	Purchase computer	Discuss product design with a potential customer	Pay rent
Criterion	Is the financial position (assets, liabilities, and shareholders' equity) of the company changed?		
	Yes	No	Yes
Record/ Don't Record	Record	Don't record	Record

Using the Financial Statements   ◀   61

...ce selected examples of liquidity, profitability, and ...ment of earnings, balance sheet, and cash flow state...3 and 2002, for our intracompany comparisons. We ...vo years to those of one of its competitors, Hudson's ...clude an intercompany comparison. Finally, we will ...parisons for the retail department store industry.

...rings

...by selling merchandise. The statement of earnings ...ng this profit. It reports the amount earned during ...ed during the same period (expenses). Illustration ...of earnings.

study objective 4

Identify and calculate ratios for analyzing a company's profitability.

Illustration 2-12 ◀

Sears' statement of earnings

SEARS CANADA INC. Statement of Earnings Year Ended January 3, 2004 (in millions)		
	2003	2002
Total revenues	$6,222.7	$6,535.9
Expenses		
Cost of merchandise sold, operating, administrative, and selling expenses	5,775.9	6,107.9
Amortization	146.6	148.7
Interest	59.5	59.8
Unusual items	5.0	189.1
Total expenses	5,987.0	6,505.5
Earnings before income taxes	235.7	30.4
Income tax expense (recovery)	101.0	(21.8)
Net earnings	$ 134.7	$ 52.2

From the statement of earnings, we can see that Sears' total revenues decreased during the year. However, even though revenues decreased, net earnings increased from $52.2 million to $134.7 million. In order to increase net earnings, the company needs its revenues to increase more than its expenses, or its expenses to decline more than its revenues. The latter was the case for Sears. While its revenues declined by nearly 5%, its expenses declined by 8%.

If we remove the impact of the unusual items, expenses declined by 5%, about the same as revenues. It is important to understand the nature of expenses that are considered to be "unusual." They are not likely recurring expenses (note they declined significantly in 2003), and are unlikely to have the same impact in future years. We will learn more about unusual items in Chapter 14.

The Basics of Adjusting Entries

For revenues to be recorded in the period in which they are earned, and for expenses to be matched with the revenue they generate, **adjusting entries** are made to adjust accounts at the end of the accounting period. Adjusting entries make it possible to produce relevant financial information at the end of the accounting period. Thus, the balance sheet reports appropriate assets, liabilities, and shareholders' equity at the statement date, and the statement of earnings shows the proper revenues, expenses, and net earnings (or loss) for the period.

Adjusting entries are necessary because the trial balance—the first pulling together of the transaction data—may not contain complete and up-to-date data. This is true for several reasons:

1. Some events are not journalized daily, because it would not be useful or efficient to do so. Examples are the use of supplies and the earning of wages by employees.
2. Some costs are not journalized during the accounting period, because these costs expire with the passage of time rather than as a result of recurring daily transactions. Examples include insurance and amortization.
3. Some items may be unrecorded. An example is a utility service bill that will not be received until the next accounting period. The bill, however, covers services delivered in the current accounting period.

Animated Tutorials
(Accounting Cycle Tutorial)

...and creditors are interested in a company's profit...earnings or operating success of a company for a ...wo examples of profitability ratios in this section: ...ratio.

...(EPS) measures the net earnings for each common ...eported only for common shareholders. It is calcu...the common shareholders by the weighted average ...he year.

...ares was 107.1 million for 2003 and 106.8 million ...hares, the net earnings available to common share-

The Basics of Adjusting Entries ◀ 159

are twelve months in a year. Calculating amortization will be refined and examined in more detail in Chapter 9.

For Sierra Corporation, amortization on the office equipment is estimated to be $83 per month ($1,000 × ¹⁄₁₂). Accordingly, amortization for October is recognized by this adjusting entry:

Oct. 31	Amortization Expense	83	
	Accumulated Amortization—Office Equipment		83
	(To record monthly amortization)		

A = L + SE
   −83   −83
Cash flows: no effect

Accounting equation analyses appear in the margin next to key journal entries. They will help you understand the impact of an accounting transaction on the financial position and cash flows.

After the adjusting entry is posted, the accounts appear as follows:

Accumulated Amortization—Office Equipment		Amortization Expense	
	Oct. 31 Adj. 83	Oct. 31 Adj. 83	
	Oct. 31 Bal. 83	Oct. 31 Bal. 83	

The balance in the Accumulated Amortization account will increase by $83 each month until the asset is fully amortized in five years.

As in the case of other prepaid expenses, if this adjusting entry is not made, total assets, shareholders' equity, and net earnings will all be overstated by $83 and amortization expense will be understated by $83.

Statement Presentation. As we learned in Chapter 2, a contra account is an account that is offset against (deducted from) a related account on the statement of earnings or balance sheet. Accumulated Amortization—Office Equipment is a **contra asset account**. That means it is off-set against an asset account (Office Equipment) on the balance sheet. Its normal balance is a credit—the opposite of the normal debit balance of its related account, Office Equipment.

There is a simple reason for using a separate contra account instead of decreasing (crediting) Office Equipment: using this account discloses both the original cost of the equipment and the total estimated cost that has expired to date. In the balance sheet, Accumulated Amortization—Office Equipment is deducted from the related asset account as follows:

Office equipment	$5,000
Less: Accumulated amortization—office equipment	83
Net book value	4,917

The difference between the cost of any amortizable asset and its related accumulated amortization is referred to as the **net book value**, or book value, of that asset. In the above illustration, the book value of the office equipment at the balance sheet date is $4,917. Be sure to understand that, except at acquisition, the book value of the asset and its market value (the price at which it could be sold) are two different values. As noted earlier, the purpose of amortization is not to state an asset's value, but to allocate its cost over time.

Helpful Hint Every contra account has increases, decreases, and normal balances that are opposite to those of the account it relates to.

Helpful Hints in the margins are like having an instructor with you as you read. They help clarify concepts being discussed.

Alternative Terminology
Book value is also referred to as carrying value.

Alternative Terminology notes present synonymous terms that you may come across in practice.

Accounting Matters! insights give glimpses into how real companies make decisions using accounting information. These high-interest boxes are classified by four different points of view—*investor perspectives*, *management perspectives*, *international perspectives*, and *ethics perspectives*.

---

154   Chapter 4 ▶   Accrual Accounting Concepts

ACCOUNTING MATTERS!   Management Perspective

Suppose you work for a movie studio. Over what period should the cost of producing a movie be expensed? It should be expensed over the economic life of the movie. But what is its economic life? The filmmaker must estimate how much revenue will be earned from box office sales, DVD sales, television, and games and toys—a period that could be less than a year or many years.

Take, for example, *Harry Potter and the Prisoner of Azkaban*, released by Warner Bros. in 2004. It cost U.S. $130 million to produce this film, and the film more than recovered this cost in the first two weekends it was released. In fact, all of the *Harry Potter* movies have broken box office and product sales records. Compare this to *The Cat in the Hat*, released by Universal Studios in 2003. It cost U.S. $109 million to produce this movie but it has only recovered U.S. $100.4 million to date. These situations illustrate how difficult it can be in real life for companies to properly match expenses to revenues.

Each chapter presents decision tools that help business makers use financial statements. At the end of the text discussion, a **Decision Toolkit** summarizes the key features of a decision tool and reviews why and how you would use it.

Decision Toolkit

Decision Checkpoints	Info Needed for Decision	Tools to Use for Decision	How to Evaluate Results
At what point should the company record expenses?	Need to understand the nature of the company's business	Expenses should "follow" revenues—that is, the effort (expense) should be matched with the result (revenue).	Recognizing expenses too early overstates current period expenses; recognizing them too late understates current period expenses.

BEFORE YOU GO ON . . .

▶ Review It

1. How does a single-step statement of earnings differ
2. How are sales and contra revenue accounts reported
3. What is the significance of gross profit?
4. How do operating activities differ from non-operating
5. Does Loblaw use a single-step or multiple-step statement question is at the end of the chapter.

Loblaws
A passion for food... and a lot more!

▶ Do It

Abela Corporation reported the following selected information:

Cost of goods sold	$619,000
Income tax expense	11,500
Interest expense	2,000
Operating expenses	161,000
Rent revenue	18,000
Sales	910,000
Sales returns and allowances	85,000
Sales discounts	15,000

Calculate the following amounts for Abela Corporation: (a) net sales, (b) gross profit, (c) earnings from operations, (d) earnings before income tax, and (e) net earnings.

Action Plan

- Separate the items into operating and non-operating (other revenues and other expenses).
- Recall the formula for net sales: Sales − sales returns and allowances − sales discounts.
- Recall the formula for gross profit: Net sales − cost of goods sold.
- Recall the formula for earnings from operations: Gross profit − operating expenses.
- Recall the formula for earnings before income tax: Earnings from operations + other revenue − other expenses.
- Recall the formula for net earnings: Earnings before income tax − income tax expense.

Solution

(a) Net sales: $910,000 − $85,000 − $15,000 = $810,000
(b) Gross profit: $810,000 − $619,000 = $191,000
(c) Earnings from operations: $191,000 − $161,000 = $30,000
(d) Earnings before income tax: $30,000 + $18,000 − $2,000 = $46,000
(e) Net earnings: $46,000 − $11,500 = $34,500

Before You Go On sections follow each key topic. Review It questions prompt you to stop and review the key points you have just studied.

Review It questions marked with the Loblaw logo direct you to find information in Loblaw's financial statements, printed in Appendix A. Answers appear at the end of the chapter.

Brief **Do It** exercises ask you to put newly acquired knowledge to work in some form of financial statement preparation. They outline an **Action Plan** necessary to complete the exercise and show a **Solution**.

A **Using the Decision Toolkit** exercise follows the final set of **Review It** questions in the chapter. It asks you to use information from financial statements to make decisions. You should think through the questions related to the decision before you study the printed **Solution**.

The **Summary of Study Objectives** reviews the main points related to the Study Objectives. It provides you with another opportunity to review, as well as to see how all the key topics within the chapter are related.

At the end of each chapter, **Decision Toolkit—A Summary** reviews the contexts and useful techniques for decision-making that were covered in the chapter. A **web** icon directs you to the Toolkit website, where a comprehensive summary of the Decision Toolkits in each chapter is available.

The **Glossary** defines all the key terms and concepts introduced in the chapter. A web icon directs you to the Toolkit website, where a searchable, comprehensive glossary is available.

---

284   Chapter 6   ▶   Reporting and Analyzing Inventory

Of course, if prices are falling, the inverse relationships will result. If prices are constant, all three cost flow assumptions will yield the same results. And, finally, remember that the sum of cost of goods sold and ending inventory always equals the cost of goods available for sale, which is the same under all the cost flow assumptions.

Using the Decision Toolkit

IPSCO Inc., headquartered in Regina, Saskatchewan, manufactures and sells steel mill and fabricated products in Canada and the U.S. Selected financial information (in U.S. thousands) for IPSCO Inc. follows:

	2004	2003	2002
Inventories	$ 434,526	$ 286,159	$ 255,410
Sales	2,452,675	1,294,566	1,081,709
Cost of sales	1,660,009	1,122,625	929,140
Net earnings	438,610	16,585	20,279

Selected industry data follow:

	2004	2003
Inventory turnover	5.5 times	5.3 times
Days in inventory	66 days	69 days
Gross profit margin	23.9%	22.0%
Profit margin	8.6%	

Instructions

(a) IPSCO uses the average cost flow assumption. [...] two years in response to increased demand for [...] due to China's rapidly growing economy. If IPSC[...] would its net earnings have been higher or lowe[...]
(b) Do each of the following:
  1. Calculate the inventory turnover and days in [...]
  2. Calculate the gross profit margin and profit [...]
  3. Evaluate IPSCO's performance with invento[...] and compare its performance to that of the i[...]

Solution

(a) If IPSCO used the FIFO cost flow assumption in[...] tion during a period of rising prices, its cost of g[...] earnings higher than currently reported.

(b)

1.	Ratio	2004	
	Inventory turnover	$\dfrac{\$1,660,009}{(\$434,526 + \$286,159) \div 2}$	= 4.6 times
	Days in inventory	$\dfrac{365 \text{ days}}{4.6}$	= 79 days

2.	Ratio	2004	
	Gross profit margin	$\dfrac{\$2,452,675 - \$1,660,009}{\$2,452,675}$	= 32.3%
	Profit margin	$\dfrac{\$438,610}{\$2,452,675}$	= 17.9%

---

72   Chapter 2   ▶   A Further Look at Financial Statements

Summary of Study Objectives

1. *Describe the objective of financial reporting and apply the qualitative characteristics of accounting information to the elements of financial statements.* The objective of financial reporting is to provide information that is useful for decision-making. To be useful, information should have these qualitative characteristics: understandability, relevance, reliability, and comparability. The elements of financial statements include assets, liabilities, shareholders' equity, revenues, and expenses.

2. *Identify and apply assumptions, principles, and constraints.* Assumptions include the monetary unit assumption, economic entity assumption, time period assumption, and going concern assumption. Generally accepted accounting principles include the cost principle and full disclosure principle. The two constraints of cost-benefit and materiality can change how these principles are applied.

3. *Identify the sections of a classified balance sheet.* In a classified balance sheet, assets are classified as current assets; investments; property, plant, and equipment; and intangible assets. Liabilities are classified as either current or long-term. There is also a shareholders' equity section, which shows share capital and retained earnings.

4. *Identify and calculate ratios for analyzing a company's profitability.* Profitability ratios, such as earnings per share and the price-earnings ratio, measure a company's operating success for a specific period of time.

5. *Identify and calculate ratios for analyzing a company's liquidity and solvency.* Liquidity ratios, such as working capital and the current ratio, measure a company's short-term ability to pay its maturing obligations and meet unexpected needs for cash. Solvency ratios, such as debt to total assets and free cash flow, measure a company's ability to survive over a long period.

Decision Toolkit—A Summary

Decision Checkpoints	Info Needed for Decision	Tools to Use for Decision	How to Evaluate Results
How does the company's earnings performance compare with previous years?	Net earnings available to common shareholders and weighted average number of common shares	Earnings per share $=$ $\dfrac{\text{Net earnings available to common shareholders}}{\text{Weighted average number of common shares}}$	A higher measure suggests improved performance. Values should not be compared across companies.
How does the market see the company's prospects for future earnings?	Earnings per share and market price per share	Price-earnings ratio $=$ $\dfrac{\text{Market price per share}}{\text{Earnings per share}}$	A high ratio suggests the market expects good performance, although it may also suggest that shares are overvalued
Can the company meet its short-term obligations?	Current assets and current liabilities	Working capital $=$ Current assets − Current liabilities	A higher amount indicates liquidity.
		Current ratio $=$ $\dfrac{\text{Current assets}}{\text{Current liabilities}}$	A higher ratio suggests favourable liquidity.
Can the company meet its long-term obligations?	Total debt and total assets	Debt to total assets $=$ $\dfrac{\text{Total liabilities}}{\text{Total assets}}$	A lower value suggests favourable solvency.
	Cash provided (used) by operating activities, capital expenditures, and cash dividends	Free cash flow $=$ Cash provided (used) by operating activities − Net capital expenditures − Dividends paid	Free cash flow indicates the potential to finance new investments or pay more dividends.

(Decision Toolkit Summaries)

www.wiley.com/canada/kimmel

Study Tools (Glossary)

Glossary

Average cost flow assumption An inventory cost flow assumption that assumes that the goods available for sale are homogeneous or nondistinguishable. Each good is assumed to have the same weighted average cost per unit. (p. 275)

Consigned goods Goods shipped by a consignor, who retains ownership, to a party called the consignee, who holds the goods for sale. (p. 269)

Days in inventory A measure of the average number of days inventory is held. It is calculated as 365 divided by the inventory turnover ratio. (p. 285)

Finished goods Manufactured items that are completed and ready for sale. (p. 284)

First-in, first-out (FIFO) cost flow assumption An inventory cost flow assumption that assumes that the costs of the oldest goods acquired are the first to be recognized as the cost of goods sold. The costs of the latest goods acquired are assumed to remain in ending inventory. (p. 273)

Internal control The policies and procedures used by a company to (1) optimize resources, (2) prevent and detect errors, (3) safeguard assets, and (4) enhance the accuracy

Last-in, first-out (LIFO) cost flow assumption An inventory cost flow assumption that assumes that the costs of the latest units purchased are the first to be allocated to the cost of goods sold. The costs of the oldest goods acquired are assumed to remain in ending inventory. (p. 275)

Lower of cost and mar[...] (LCM) A basis for stating inventory at the lower of cost and mar[...] (usually defined as net realizable value) at the end of the perio[...]

Net realizable value The selling price of an inventory[...] less any costs required to make the item saleable. (p. 284)

Raw materials Basic goods that will be used in production but have not yet been sent into production. (p. 284)

Replacement cost The cost of replacing an asset. (p. 284)

Specific identification method A costing method that follows the actual physical flow of goods, and in which individual items are specifically costed to arrive at the cost of goods sold and cost of the ending inventory. (p. 271)

Weighted average unit cost Average cost that is weighted by the number of units purchased at each unit cost. It is calculated as the cost of goods available for sale divided by the

Demonstration Problem

Study Tools
(Demonstration Problems)

Action Plan
- First identify which accounts should be reported on each statement. Then determine which classification each account should be reported in.
- Prepare the statements in this order: (1) statement of earnings, (2) statement of retained earnings, and (3) balance sheet.
- The statement of earnings covers a period of time. In preparing the statement of earnings, first list revenues, and then expenses. Report income tax expense separately.
- The statement of retained earnings covers the same period of time as the statement of earnings. This statement calculates the ending retained earnings balance (which is also reported on the balance sheet) by adding net earnings (from the statement of earnings) less dividends to the opening retained earnings amount.
- The balance sheet is prepared at a specific point in time. In preparing a classified balance sheet, list items in order of their liquidity in the current classifications and in order of their permanency in the non-current classifications.

Listed here are items taken from the statement of earnings and balance sheet of Hudson's Bay Company for the year ended January 31, 2004. Certain items have been combined for simplification and all numbers are reported in thousands.

Accounts payable and accrued liabilities	$ 926,101	Long-term receivables	$ 7,052
Accounts receivable	64,811	Merchandise inventories	1,485,088
Cash	8,033	Operating expenses	7,238,917
Credit card receivables	538,734	Other long-term assets	517,715
Dividends	37,178	Other long-term liabilities	244,088
Fixed assets	1,089,334	Prepaid expenses and other current assets	78,669
Goodwill	152,294	Retained earnings,	
Income tax expense	49,243	February 1, 2003	740,853
Interest expense	42,662	Sales and revenue	7,400,051
Long-term debt	383,107	Share capital	1,657,728
Long-term debt due within one year	125,436	Short-term borrowings	1,309
		Short-term deposits	168,943

Instructions

Prepare a statement of earnings, statement of retained earnings, and classified balance sheet using the items listed

Solution to Demonstration Problem

HUDSON'S BAY COMPANY
Statement of Earnings
Year Ended January 31, 2004
(in thousands)

Sales and revenue		$7,400,051
Expenses		
Operating expenses	$7,238,917	
Interest expense	42,662	
Total expenses		7,281,579
Earnings before income taxes		118,472
Income tax expense		49,243
Net earnings		$ 69,229

HUDSON'S BAY COMPANY
Statement of Retained Earnings
Year Ended January 31, 2004
(in thousands)

Retained earnings, February 1, 2003	
Add: Net earnings	
Less: Dividends	
Retained earnings, January 31, 2004	

Common shares	$20,000	
Retained earnings	3,300	23,300
Total liabilities and shareholders' equity		$42,000

Questions

(SO 1) 1. Can a business enter into a transaction that affects only the left side of the accounting equation? If so, give an example.

(SO 1) 2. Are the following events recorded in the accounting records? Explain your answer in each case.
  (a) A major shareholder of the company dies.
  (b) Supplies are purchased on account.
  (c) An employee is fired.
  (d) The company pays a cash dividend to its shareholders.
  (e) A local lawyer agrees to provide legal services to the company for the next year.

(SO 1) 3. Indicate how each transaction affects the accounting equation:
  (a) Cash is paid for janitorial services.
  (b) Equipment is purchased on account.
  (c) Common shares are issued to investors in exchange for cash.
  (d) An account payable is paid in full.
  (e) Cash is received in advance for website hosting services.

(SO 2) 4. Why is an account referred to as a T account?

(SO 2) 5. Charles Thon, a fellow student, claims that the double-entry system means each transaction must be recorded twice. Is Charles correct? Explain.

(SO 2) 6. Natalie Boudreau, an introductory accounting student, believes debit balances are favourable and credit balances are unfavourable. Is Natalie correct? Discuss.

(SO 2) 7. State the debit and credit effects and identify the normal balance for the following types of accounts: (a) assets, (b) liabilities, (c) common shares, (d) retained earnings, (e) dividends, (f) revenues, and (g) expenses.

(SO 2) 8. Indicate the appropriate statement classification for each of the following accounts. State whether it would have a normal debit or credit balance.

  (a) Accounts R...
  (b) Accounts P...
  (c) Equipment
  (d) Dividends

9. For the follow... debited and th...
  (a) Supplies ar...
  (b) Cash is rec...
  (c) Employees...
  (d) Services ar...
  ... Cash is collected on account.

10. For ... account listed, indicate whether it generally will have debit entries only, credit entries only, or both debit and credit entries:
  (a) Cash   (d) Salaries Expense
  (b) Dividends   (e) Service Revenue
  (c) Accounts Payable

11. Should the balance in total shareholders' equity equal the balance in the Cash account? Explain why or why not.

12. A company received cash from a customer. It debited the Cash account. Name three credit accounts that the company might have used to record a cash receipt from a customer. Describe the circumstances ... you would use each of these three accounts.

13. Identify and describe the steps in the recording process.

14. An efficiency expert who was reviewing the steps in the recording process suggested dropping the general journal and recording and summarizing transactions directly into the general ledger instead. Comment on this suggestion.

15. (a) What is a general ledger?
    (b) What is a chart of accounts and why is it important?

16. Arrange the following accounts in their normal order in a chart of accounts: common shares, prepaid insur-

Self-Study Questions

Study Tools (Self-Assessment Quizzes)

(SO 1) 1. The effects on the accounting equation of receiving cash in advance of performing a service are to:
  (a) increase assets and decrease shareholders' equity.
  (b) increase assets and increase shareholders' equity.
  (c) increase assets and increase liabilities.
  (d) increase liabilities and increase shareholders' equity.

(SO 1) 2. Shareholders' equity consists of the following:
  (a) common shares, revenues, and expenses.
  (b) revenues and expenses.
  (c) liabilities, common shares, and retained earnings.
  (d) common shares and retained earnings.

(SO 2) 3. Which statement about an account is true?
  (a) In its simplest form, an account consists of two parts.
  (b) An account is an individual accounting record of increases and decreases in specific asset, liability, and shareholders' equity.
  (c) There are separate accounts for specific assets and liabilities but only one account for shareholders' equity items.

  (d) The left side of an account is the credit or decrease side.

4. Debits: (SO 2)
  (a) increase both assets and liabilities.
  (b) decrease both assets and liabilities.
  (c) increase assets and decrease liabilities.
  (d) decrease assets and increase liabilities.

5. Which accounts normally have debit balances? (SO 2)
  (a) Assets, expenses, and revenues
  (b) Assets, expenses, and retained earnings
  (c) Assets, liabilities, and dividends
  (d) Assets, dividends, and expenses

6. Which of these statements about a general journal is (SO 3) false?
  (a) It contains only revenue and expense accounts.
  (b) It provides a chronological record of transactions.
  (c) It helps to locate errors because the debit and credit amounts for each entry can be quickly compared.
  (d) It discloses the complete effect of a transaction in one place.

A **Demonstration Problem** is the final step before you begin homework. These sample problems provide you with an **Action Plan** in the margin that lists the strategies needed to approach and solve the problem. The **Solution** demonstrates both the form and content of complete answers. A **web** icon directs you to the Toolkit website, where additional demonstration problems are available.

Self-Study Questions provide a practice test that gives you an opportunity to check your knowledge of important topics. Answers appear on the last page of the chapter. A **web** icon tells you that there is a self-assessment quiz on the Toolkit website that can further help you master the material.

Questions allow you to explain your understanding of concepts and relationships covered in the chapter. Use them to help prepare for class discussion and tests.

Brief Exercises generally help you focus on one Study Objective at a time and thus help you build confidence in your basic skills and knowledge.

Brief Exercises

Journalize purchase transactions.
(SO 2)

BE5–1 Prepare the journal entries to record the following purchase transactions in Xiaoyan Ltd.'s books. The company uses a perpetual inventory system.

Jan. 3 Xiaoyan purchased $900,000 of merchandise from Feng Corp., terms 2/10, n/30, FOB destination.
      6 Xiaoyan returned $120,000 of the merchandise purchased on January 3 because it was not needed.
     12 Xiaoyan paid the balance owed to Feng.

Journalize sales transactions.
(SO 3)

BE5–2 Prepare the journal entries to record the following sale transactions in Feng Corp.'s books. Feng uses a perpetual inventory system.

Jan. 3 Feng sold $900,000 of merchandise to Xiaoyan Ltd., terms 2/10, n/30, FOB destination. The cost of the merchandise sold was $600,000.
      4 Feng paid delivery charges of $10,000 on the merchandise shipped to Xiaoyan.
      6 Xiaoyan returned $120,000 of the merchandise purchased from Feng on January 3 because it was not needed. The cost of the merchandise returned was $80,000, and it was restored to inventory.
     12 Feng received the balance due from Xiaoyan.

Match merchandising terms.
(SO 1, 2, 3)

BE5–3 Insert the number in the space beside the best definition of each of the following merchandising terms:

1. Purchase discount
2. Merchandise inventory
3. Non-operating activities
4. Purchase return
5. Quantity discount
6. FOB destination
7. FOB shipping point
8. Sales allowance
9. Contra revenue account
10. Cost of goods sold

(a) ___ Freight terms indicating that the seller will pay for the shipping costs of the goods
(b) ___ An account, such as Sales Returns and Allowances, that is offset against (deducted from) a revenue account in the statement of earnings
(c) ___ The return of unsatisfactory purchased merchandise
(d) ___ The total cost of merchandise sold during the period
(e) ___ Freight terms indicating that the buyer will pay for the shipping costs of the goods
(f) ___ A cash discount given to the buyer for volume purchases
(g) ___ The reduction in price of unsatisfactory sold merchandise
(h) ___ A cash discount given to a buyer for early payment of the balance due
(i) ___ Goods purchased for resale to customers
(j) ___ Amounts earned or incurred, such as interest, which come from activities that are not part of a company's primary operations

Determine missing amounts.
(SO 4)

BE5–4 Presented here are selected components of the multiple-step statement of earnings for three companies. Determine the missing amounts.

Company	Sales	Cost of Goods Sold	Gross Profit	Operating Expenses	Non-Operating Revenues	Inc Exp
A	$ 75,000	(b)	$ 30,000	(d)	$4,000	
B	108,000	$ 70,000	(c)	$ 23,000	(e)	
C	(a)	150,000	100,000	60,000	0	

BE5–5 Saguenay Limited reports the following information: Sales $500,000; Sales and Allowances $15,000; Sales Discounts $25,000; Cost of Goods Sold $275,000; ing Expenses $110,000; Other Revenues $18,000; Other Expenses $12,000; and In Expense $20,000. Calculate the following: (a) net sales, (b) gross profit, (c) earn operations, (d) earnings before income tax, and (e) net earnings.

BE5–6 Explain where each of the following items would appear on (1) a multiple-s ment of earnings and (2) a single-step statement of earnings: gain on sale of equip of goods sold, amortization expense, interest expense, rent revenue, sales returns a ances, sales discounts, and income tax expense.

A special icon ⚒ indicates material that asks you to use the decision tools presented in the chapter.

Calculate profitability ratios and comment.
(SO 5)
⚒

BE5–7 The Forzani Group Ltd. reports sales revenue of $968.1 million, cost of goods sold of $635.1 million, and net earnings of $28.0 million for 2004. It reported sales revenue of $923.8 million, cost of goods sold of $603.3 million, and net earnings of $30.5 million for 2003. Calculate the gross profit margin and profit margin for each of 2004 and 2003. Comment on Forzani's changing profitability.

Journalize purchase transactions.
(SO 6)

*BE5–8 From the information in BE5–1, prepare the journal entries to record the purchase transactions on Xiaoyan Ltd.'s books, assuming a periodic inventory system is used instead of a perpetual inventory system.

Journalize sales transactions.
(SO 6)

*BE5–9 From the information in BE5–2, prepare the journal entries to record the sale transactions on Feng Corp.'s books, assuming a periodic inventory system is used instead of a perpetual inventory system.

Calculate cost of goods sold and gross profit.
(SO 6)

*BE5–10 Bassing Corp. uses a periodic inventory system and reports the following information: net sales $630,000; purchases $400,000; purchase returns and allowances $11,000; purchase discounts $8,000; freight in $16,000; beginning inventory $60,000; and ending inventory $90,000. Calculate (a) net purchases, (b) cost of goods purchased, (c) cost of goods sold, and (d) gross profit.

Exercises

Journalize purchase transactions.
(SO 2)

E5–1 This information is for Olaf Corp.:

Apr. 5 Purchased merchandise from DeVito Ltd. for $18,000, terms 2/10, n/30, FOB shipping point.
      6 The appropriate party paid freight costs of $900 on the merchandise purchased from DeVito on April 5.
      7 Purchased equipment on account for $26,000.
      8 Returned $2,800 of the April 5 merchandise to DeVito.
     15 Paid the amount due to DeVito in full.

Instructions

(a) Record the transactions in the books of Olaf Corp., assuming a perpetual inventory system is used.
(b) Assume that Olaf Corp. paid the balance due to DeVito on May 4 instead of April 15. Prepare the journal entry to record this payment.

Journalize sales transactions.
(SO 3)

E5–2 Refer to the information in E5–1 for Olaf Corp. and the following additional information:

1. The cost of the merchandise sold on April 5 was $10,800.
2. The cost of the merchandise returned on April 8 was $1,680.

Instructions

Record the transactions in the books of DeVito Ltd., assuming a perpetual inventory system is used.

Journalize purchase and sales transactions.
(SO 2, 3)

E5–3 The following merchandise transactions occurred in December. Both companies use a perpetual inventory system.

Dec. 3 Pippen Ltd. sold $480,000 of merchandise to Thomas Corp., terms 2/10, n/30, FOB shipping point. The cost of the merchandise sold was $320,000.
      5 Shipping costs of $5,000 are paid.
      8 Thomas was granted a sales allowance of $25,000 for defective merchandise purchased on December 3. No merchandise was returned.
     13 Pippen received the balance due from Thomas.

Instructions

(a) Prepare the journal entries to record these transactions in the books of Pippen Ltd.
(b) Prepare the journal entries to record these transactions in the books of Thomas Corp.

Exercises that gradually increase in difficulty help you continue to build your confidence in your ability to use the material learned in the chapter.

Each **Problem** helps you pull together and apply several concepts from the chapter. Two sets of problems—**A** and **B**—are generally keyed to the same Study Objectives and provide additional opportunities to apply or expand concepts learned in the chapter.

Certain exercises or problems marked with a pencil icon help you practise written business communication, a skill much in demand among employers.

The financial results of real companies are included in the end-of-chapter material. These are indicated by the company names here in red.

Problems: Set A

P6–1A Kananaskis Limited is trying to determine the amount of its ending inventory as at February 28, 2006, the company's year end. The accountant counted everything in the warehouse, which resulted in an ending inventory value of $95,000. However, the accountant was not sure how to treat the following transactions, so he did not record them. He asked for your help in determining whether they should be included in inventory or not:

1. On February 26, Kananaskis shipped goods costing $950 to a customer and charged the customer $1,300. The goods were shipped FOB destination. The receiving report indi-

Identify items in inventory.
(SO 1)

Problems: Set B

Identify items in inventory.
(SO 1)

P6–1B Banff Limited is trying to determine the value of its ending inventory as at February 28, 2006, the company's year end. The accountant counted everything that was in the warehouse, as at February 28, which resulted in an ending inventory valuation of $48,000. However, she did not know how to treat the following transactions so she chose not to include them in inventory:

1. On February 26, Banff shipped goods costing $800 to a customer. The goods were shipped FOB shipping point. The receiving report indicates that the customer received the goods on March 2.
2. On February 26, Seller Inc. shipped goods to Banff FOB destination. The invoice price was $350 plus $25 for freight. The receiving report indicates that the goods were received by Banff on March 1.
3. Banff had $620 of inventory at a customer's warehouse "on approval." The customer was going to let Banff know whether it wanted the merchandise by the end of the week, March 5.
4. Banff also had $570 of its inventory on consignment at a Jasper craft shop.
5. On February 25, Banff ordered goods costing $750. The goods were shipped FOB shipping point on February 27. The receiving report indicates that Banff received them on March 1.
6. On February 28, Banff packaged goods and had them ready for shipping to a customer FOB destination. The invoice price was $425 plus $20 for freight; the cost of the items was $360. The receiving report indicates that the goods were received by the customer on March 2.

(a) Determine the cost of goods available for sale.
(b) Determine the cost of the ending inventory and the cost of the goods sold under each of the three cost flow assumptions: (1) FIFO, (2) average, and (3) LIFO.

P6–3A Data for Kane Ltd. were presented in P6–2A. Assume that Kane sold 850 units of product SXL for $40 each.

Prepare partial financial statements and assess financial statement effects.
(SO 3)

...ings through to gross profit for each of the three cost ...rage, and (3) LIFO.
...rted in the current assets section of the balance sheet ...mptions: (1) FIFO, (2) average, and (3) LIFO.
...lts in the highest inventory amount for the balance ...ld for the statement of earnings?

...e Inc. asks for your help in determining the compara- ...riodic inventory cost flow assumptions. For 2006, the ...selected data:

...ry 1 (10,000 units)	$ 35,000
...00,000 units sold	700,000
...ases	120,000

Apply periodic cost flow assumptions; prepare statement of earnings and memo.
(SO 2, 3)

Calculate ratios and comment on liquidity, profitability, and solvency.
(SO 4, 5)

P2–10B Selected financial data from fiscal 2004 for two forest products companies, Abitibi-Consolidated Inc. and Tembec Inc., are presented here:

(in millions, except for share price)	Abitibi	Tembec
Current assets	$1,402	$1,230
Total assets	9,787	3,921
Current liabilities	1,554	722
Total liabilities	7,061	2,724
Net earnings (loss) available to common shareholders	(36)	37
Weighted average number of common shares	440	86
Share price	8.23	8.35
Cash provided by operating activities	66	207
Net capital expenditures	381	143
Dividends paid	55	0

Instructions

(a) For each company, calculate these values and ratios. Where available, industry averages have been included in parentheses.
   1. Working capital (n/a)   4. Price-earnings ratio (26.3 times)
   2. Current ratio (1.3:1)   5. Debt to total assets (53.1%)
   3. Earnings per share (n/a)   6. Free cash flow (n/a)
(b) Compare the liquidity, profitability, and solvency of the two companies and their indust...

BROADENING YOUR PERSPECTIVE

The **Broadening Your Perspective** section helps you pull together various concepts covered in the chapter and apply them to real-world business decisions. A **web** icon tells you that there are more analysis tools available on the Toolkit website, including additional interpreting financial statement and comparative analysis problems.

Financial Reporting and Analysis

www.wiley.com/canada/weygandt
Analysis Tools

Financial Reporting Problem: *Loblaw*

BYP2–1 The financial statements of Loblaw are presented in Appendix A at the end of the book.

Instructions

(a) What were the balances of Loblaw's total current assets and total assets at the end of fiscal 2003 and 2002?
(b) Are the current assets listed in the proper order? Explain.
(c) How are Loblaw's assets classified?
(d) What were the balances of Loblaw's total current liabilities and total liabilities at the end of fiscal 2003 and 2002?

In the **Financial Reporting Problem**, you study various aspects of the financial statements of Loblaw, which are printed in Chapter 1 (in simplified form) and in Appendix A (in full).

Comparative Analysis Problem: *Loblaw and Sobeys*

BYP2–2 The financial statements of Sobeys are presented in Appendix B after the financial statements for Loblaw in Appendix A.

Instructions

(a) For each company, calculate or find the following values for the most recent fiscal year:
   1. Working capital   4. Price-earnings ratio
   2. Current ratio   5. Debt to total assets
   3. Earnings per share   6. Free cash flow
(b) Based on your findings above, discuss the relative liquidity, profitability, and solvency of the two companies.

A **Comparative Analysis Problem** offers the opportunity to compare and contrast the financial reporting of Loblaw with a competitor, Sobeys, whose financial statements are printed in Chapter 1 (in simplified form) and in Appendix B (in full).

Research Cases ask students to find a source of data, and then study or analyze the data and evaluate it.

Interpreting Financial Statements asks you to read parts of financial statements of real companies and use the decision tools presented in the chapter to interpret this information.

A **Global Focus** asks you to apply concepts presented in the chapter to specific situations faced by international companies.

Financial Reporting And Analysis ◀ 91

Research Case

BYP2–3 The May 2005 issue of *CAmagazine* includes an article by Robert Colapinto entitled "The Future Direction of Accounting Standards." This article discusses the proposed adoption of international accounting standards in Canada by the Accounting Standards Board (AcSB).

Instructions

Read the article and answer the following questions:

(a) Why is the AcSB recommending a change to international standards? What are some advantages and disadvantages of such a change?

(b) Until the proposal to change to international accounting standards, Canada was working to harmonize Canadian GAAP with U.S. GAAP. What impact do you think this change will now have on Canadian companies doing business in North America?

(c) Why is the AcSB recommending a different set of standards for publicly-traded companies than for private companies? Do you agree or disagree with this recommended course of action?

Interpreting Financial Statements

BYP2–4 The following information was reported by the Gap, Inc.:

(in U.S. millions, except share amount)	2004	2003	2002	2001	2000
Total assets	$10,048	$10,343	$9,902	$7,683	$7,013
Working capital	$4,062	$4,197	$3,014	$1,023	$(151)
Current ratio	2.8:1	2.6:1	2.1:1	1.5:1	0.9:1
Earnings per share	$1.29	$1.15	$0.55	$(0.01)	$1.03
Price-earnings ratio	18.0×	16.1×	26.3×	n/a	31.0×
Debt to total assets	28.6%	32.8%	35.5%	33.3%	18.3%
Free cash flow	$1,178	$1,899	$935	$302	$643

Instructions

(a) Comment on the change in The Gap's liquidity. Which value seems to provide a better indication of The Gap's liquidity: working capital or the current ratio? What might explain the change in The Gap's liquidity during this period?

(b) Comment on the change in The Gap's profitability during this period. Is the change in earnings per share consistent with the change in the price-earnings ratio? Explain why these two ratios might not always move in the same direction.

(c) Comment on the change in The Gap's solvency during this period.

A Global Focus

BYP2–5 Nexen Inc., headquartered in Calgary, is a globe-trotting oil and gas and chemicals company. It has exploration and production activities in Australia, Brazil, Colombia, Indonesia, Nigeria, Yemen, and the U.S., in addition to Canada.

One of the challenges global companies face is to make themselves attractive to investors from other countries. This is difficult to do when different accounting principles in other countries can blur the real impact of earnings. For example, in its statement of earnings for the year ended December 31, 2004, Nexen reported net earnings of $793 million, using Canadian GAAP. Had it reported under U.S. GAAP, its net earnings would have been $788 million.

---

92   Chapter 2   ▶   A Further Look at Financial Statements

Instructions

(a) Suppose you wish to compare Nexen to a U.S.-ba[...]
Do you believe the use of different countries' acc[...]
your comparison? If so, explain how.

(b) Suppose you wish to compare Nexen to a Canad[...]
Oil. If Imperial Oil chose to use different Canad[...]
how could this affect your comparison of the financial results?

(c) Do you see any significant difference between (1) comparing statements prepared in different countries and (2) comparing statements prepared in the same country but using different accounting principles?

Financial Analysis on the Web

Analysis Tools
(Financial Analysis on the Web)

BYP2–6 SEDAR (System for Electronic Document Analysis and Retrieval) provides access to information about, and documents of, Canadian public companies. We will use SEDAR to locate and identify recent corporate filings for Loblaw and Sobeys.

Instructions

Specific requirements of this Web case can be found on the Toolkit website.

Critical Thinking

Collaborative Learning Activity

BYP2–7 As the accountant for Soukup Inc., you have been asked to develop some key ratios from the comparative financial statements. This information will be used to convince creditors that Soukup is liquid, profitable, and solvent and therefore deserves their continued support.

Here are the data and calculations you developed from the financial statements:

	2006	2005
Current ratio	3.1:1	2.1:1
Working capital	Up 22%	Down 7%
Net earnings	Up 32%	Down 8%
Earnings per share	$2.40	$1.15
Price-earnings ratio	26 times	19 times
Debt to total assets	60%	70%
Free cash flow	Down 25%	Up 10%

Instructions

You have been asked to prepare brief comments which explain how each of these items supports the argument that Soukup's financial health is improving. The company wants to use these comments in a presentation to its creditors. Prepare the comments as requested, giving the implications and the limitations of each item separately. Then state what conclusions may be drawn from them as a whole about Soukup's financial well-being.

Communication Activity

BYP2–8 On April 1, 2003, Air Canada filed for bankr[...] protection under the *Companies' Creditors Arrangement Act* (CCAA). Filing for protection und[...] CCAA gives a company time to hold talks with its major stakeholders, such as creditors and labo[...] and to restructure its operations. During the period when Air Canada was under CCAA pro[...] tion, it issued financial statements quarterly. On September 30, 2004, Air Canada emerged from CCAA protection with a strengthened balance sheet, a reorganized corporate structure, and a strategy for sustained growth and profitability.

Financial Analysis on the Web exercises guide you to the Toolkit website where you can find and analyze information related to the chapter topic.

Critical Thinking offers additional opportunities and activities to build decision-making skills by analyzing accounting information in a less structured situation.

Collaborative Learning Activities require teams of students to evaluate a manager's decision or lead to a decision among alternative courses of action. They also give you practice in building business communication skills.

Communication Activities ask you to engage in real world business situations writing and speaking skills, including giving presentations.

Instructions

Assume the role of Air Canada's auditors and write a memo to the airline in which you discuss the appropriate basis on which Air Canada should issue its financial statements while under CCAA protection—on a going concern basis or a liquidation basis. Include in your memo an assessment of the pros and cons of each basis for Air Canada's investors and creditors.

Ethics Case

BYP2–9   When new accounting principles are issued, the required implementation date is usually 12 months or more after the date of issuance, but early implementation is encouraged.

Kathy Johnston, the accountant at Redondo Corporation, discusses with Redondo's vice-president the need for early implementation of a recently issued recommendation. She says it will result in a much fairer presentation of the company's financial condition and earnings. When the vice-president determines that early implementation would decrease reported net earnings for the year, he strongly discourages Kathy from implementing the recommendation until it is required.

Instructions

(a) Who are the stakeholders in this situation?
(b) What, if any, are the ethical considerations in this situation?
(c) What could Kathy gain by supporting early implementation? Who might be affected by the decision against early implementation?

> Through the **Ethics Cases** you will reflect on typical ethical dilemmas and decide on an appropriate course of action. A **web** icon directs you to the Toolkit website, where you will find an expanded discussion of ethical issues.

Serial Problem

(*Note*: The serial problem was started in Chapter 1 and will continue in each chapter.)

BYP2–10   After investigating the different forms of business organization, Natalie Koebel decides to operate her business as a corporation, Cookie Creations Ltd. She begins the process of getting her business running. While at a trade show, Natalie is introduced to Gerry Richards, operations manager of "Biscuits," a national food retailer. After much discussion, Gerry asks Natalie to consider being Biscuits' major supplier of oatmeal chocolate chip cookies. He provides Natalie with the most recent copy of the financial statements of Biscuits. He expects that Natalie will need to supply Biscuits' Red Deer warehouse with approximately 1,500 dozen cookies a week. Natalie is to send Biscuits a monthly invoice and she will be paid approximately 30 days from the date the invoice is received in Biscuits' Toronto office.

Natalie is thrilled with the offer; however, she has recently read in the newspaper that Biscuits has a reputation for selling cookies and donuts with high amounts of sugar and fat and, as a result, consumer demand has decreased.

Instructions

Natalie has come to you for advice and asks the following questions:

(a) Explain to me the type of information each financial statement provides.
(b) I would like to be sure that Biscuits will be able to pay my invoices. What type of information can these financial statements give that will reassure me that my invoices will be paid?
(c) Will Biscuits have enough cash to meet its current liabilities? Where can I find this information?
(d) Will Biscuits be able to survive over a long period of time? Where can I find this information?
(e) Is Biscuits profitable? Where can I find this information?
(f) Does Biscuits have any debt? Is Biscuits able to pay off both its debt and the interest on it? Where can I find this information?
(g) Does Biscuits pay any dividends? Where can I find this information?
(h) Before I seriously consider this opportunity, are there other areas of concern that I should be aware of?

> The **Serial Problem** is found in each chapter. It follows the operations of a single company, Cookie Creations Ltd. through the text.

monds at a cost of $300 per diamond.
cost of $340 each.
ach.
cost of $370 each.
ach.

ds uses the specific identification cost flow method, do

could maximize its gross profit for the month by select-
March 5 and March 25.
could minimize its gross profit for the month by select-
March 5 and March 25.
s uses the average cost flow assumption. How much
gross profit would Discount Diamonds report under this assumption?

(c) Who are the stakeholders in this situation? Is there anything unethical in choosing which diamonds to sell in a month?
(d) Which cost flow assumption should Discount Diamonds select? Explain.

Answers to Self-Study Questions

1. d   2. a   3. b   4. c   5. a   6. b   7. a   8. d   *9. c   *10. c

Answer to Loblaw Review It Question 2

Loblaw uses the FIFO (first-in, first-out) cost flow assumption to account for its inventories.

> **Answers to Self-Study Questions** provide feedback on your understanding of concepts.

> **Answers to Review It** questions based on Loblaw's financial statements appear here.

> After you complete your assignments, it is a good idea to go back to **The Navigator** checklist at the start of the chapter to see if you have used all of the chapter's study aids.

Remember to go back to the Navigator box at the beginning of the chapter to check off your completed work.

Now that you have looked at your Owner's Manual, take some time to find out how you learn best. This quiz is designed to help you find out something about your preferred learning method. Research on left brain/right brain differences and also on learning and personality differences suggests that each person has preferred ways to receive and communicate information. After taking the quiz, we will help you pinpoint the study aids in this test that will help you learn the material based on your personal learning style.

Circle the letter of the answer that best explains your preferences. If a single answer does not match your perception, please circle two or more choices. Leave blank any question that does not apply.

1. You are about to give directions to a person. She is staying in a hotel and wants to visit your house. She has a rental car. Would you
   V) draw a map on paper?
   R) write down the directions (without a map)?
   A) tell her the directions?
   K) pick her up at the hotel in your car?

2. You are staying in a hotel and have a rental car. You would like to visit friends whose address/location you do not know. Would you like them to
   V) draw a map on paper?
   R) write down the directions (without a map)?
   A) tell her the directions?
   K) pick her up at the hotel in your car?

3. You have just received a copy of your itinerary for a world trip. This is of interest to a friend. Would you
   V) call her immediately and tell her about it?
   R) send her a copy of the printed itinerary?
   A) show her on a map of the world?
   K) share what you plan to do at each place you visit?

4. You are going to cook something as a special treat for your family. Do you
   K) cook something familiar without need for instructions?
   V) thumb through the cookbook looking for ideas from the pictures?
   R) refer to a specific cookbook where there is a good recipe?
   A) ask for advice from others?

5. A group of tourists has been assigned to you to find out about national parks. Would you
   K) drive them to a national park?
   R) give them a book on national parks?
   V) show them slides and photographs?
   A) give them a talk on national parks?

6. YYou are about to purchase a new DVD player. Other than price, what would most influence your decision?
   A) The salesperson telling you what you want to know
   K) Listening to it
   R) Reading the details about it
   V) Its distinctive, upscale appearance

7. Recall a time in your life when you learned how to do something like playing a new board game. (Try to avoid choosing a very physical skill, e.g., riding a bike.) How did you learn best? By
   V) visual clues—pictures, diagrams, charts?
   A) listening to somebody explaining it?
   R) written instructions?
   K) doing it?

8. You have an eye problem. Would you prefer that the doctor
   A) tell you what is wrong?
   V) show you a diagram of what is wrong?
   K) use a model to show what is wrong?

9. You are about to learn to use a new program on a computer. Would you
   K) sit down at the keyboard and begin to experiment with the program's features?
   R) read the manual that comes with the program?
   A) telephone a friend and ask questions about it?

10. You are not sure whether a word should be spelled "dependent" or "dependant." Do you
    R) look it up in the dictionary or check the grammar software?
    V) see the word in your mind and choose the best way it looks?
    A) sound it out in your mind?
    K) write both versions down?

11. Apart from price, what would most influence your decision to buy a particular book?
    K) You have used a copy before
    R) Quickly reading parts of it
    A) A friend talking about it
    V) The way it looks is appealing

12. A new movie has arrived in town. What would most influence your decision to go or not to go?
    A) You heard a radio review of it.
    R) You read a review of it.
    V) You saw a preview of it.

13. Do you prefer an instructor who likes to use
    R) textbook, handouts, reading?
    V) flow diagrams, charts, graphics?
    K) field trips, labs, practical sessions?
    A) discussion, guest speakers?

Count your choices: ☐ ☐ ☐ ☐
                   V   A   R   K

Now match the letter or letters you have recorded most to the same letter in the Learning Styles Chart on the following page. You may have more than one learning style—many people do. Next to each letter in the chart are suggestions that will refer you to different learning aids throughout this text.

LEARNING STYLES CHART

Visual

WHAT TO DO IN CLASS	WHAT TO DO WHEN STUDYING	TEXT FEATURES THAT MAY HELP YOU	WHAT TO DO PRIOR TO EXAMS
• Pay close attention to charts, drawings, and handouts your instructor uses. • Underline and highlight. • Use different colours. • Use symbols, flow charts, graphs, different arrangements on the page, white space.	Convert your lecture notes into "page pictures." To do this: • Use the "What to do in class" strategies. • Reconstruct images in different ways. • Redraw pages from memory. • Replace words with symbols and initials. • Look at your pages.	• Accounting Matters! • The Navigator • Chapter Preview • Infographics/Illustrations • Accounting Equation Analyses in margins • Photos • Accounting Matters! insights • Decision Toolkits • Key Terms in blue • Words in bold • Demonstration Problem/Action Plan • Questions/Exercises/Problems • Financial Reporting and Analysis	• Recall your "page pictures." • Draw diagrams where appropriate. • Practise turning visuals back into words.

Aural

WHAT TO DO IN CLASS	WHAT TO DO WHEN STUDYING	TEXT FEATURES THAT MAY HELP YOU	WHAT TO DO PRIOR TO EXAMS
• Attend lectures and tutorials. • Discuss topics with students and instructors. • Explain new ideas to other people. • Use a tape recorder. • Describe overheads, pictures, and visuals to somebody who was not in class. • Leave space in your lecture notes for later recall.	You may take poor notes because you prefer to listen. Therefore: • Expand your notes by talking with others and with information from your textbook. • Put summarized notes on tape and listen. • Read summarized notes out loud. • Explain notes to another "aural" person.	• Chapter Preview • Infographics/Illustrations • Accounting Matters! insights • Review It/Do It/Action Plan • Summary of Study Objectives • Glossary • Demonstration Problem/Action Plan • Self-Study Questions • Questions/Exercises/Problems • Financial Reporting and Analysis • Critical Thinking	• Talk with the instructor. • Spend time in quiet places recalling the ideas. • Say your answers out loud. • Practise writing answers to old exam questions.

Reading/ Writing

WHAT TO DO IN CLASS	WHAT TO DO WHEN STUDYING	TEXT FEATURES THAT MAY HELP YOU	WHAT TO DO PRIOR TO EXAMS
• Use lists and headings. • Use dictionaries, glossaries and definitions. • Read handouts, textbooks , and supplemental readings. • Use lecture notes.	• Write out words again and again. • Reread notes silently. • Rewrite ideas and principles into other words. • Organize charts, diagrams, and other illustrations into statements.	• Accounting Matters! • The Navigator • Study Objectives • Chapter Preview • Accounting Equation Analyses in margins • Review It/Do It/Action Plan • Using the Decision Toolkit • Summary of Study Objectives • Glossary • Self-Study Questions • Questions/Exercises/Problems • Writing Problems • Financial Reporting and Analysis • Critical Thinking	• Practise with multiplechoice questions. • Write out lists in outline form. • Write paragraphs, beginnings, and endings. • Write exam answers. • Arrange your words into hierarchies and points.

Kinesthetic

WHAT TO DO IN CLASS	WHAT TO DO WHEN STUDYING	TEXT FEATURES THAT MAY HELP YOU	WHAT TO DO PRIOR TO EXAMS
• Use all your senses. • Go to labs and take field trips. • Use trial-and-error methods. • Listen to real-life examples. • Use hands-on approaches. • Pay attention to applications.	You may take notes poorly because topics do not seem concrete or relevant. Therefore • Put examples in note summaries. • Use pictures and photos to illustrate an idea. • Talk about notes with another "kinesthetic" person. • Use case studies and applications to help with principles and abstract concepts.	• Accounting Matters! • The Navigator • Chapter Preview • Infographics/Illustrations • Decision Toolkits • Review It/Do It/Action Plan • Using the Decision Toolkit • Summary of Study Objectives • Demonstration Problem/Action Plan • Self-Study Questions • Questions/Exercises/Problems • Financial Reporting and Analysis • Critical Thinking	• Write practice answers. • Role-play the exam situation.

BRIEF CONTENTS

CONTENTS

CHAPTER 1

Introduction to Financial Statements

ACCOUNTING MATTERS!

The **Feature Story** helps you picture how the chapter relates to the real world of accounting and business. You will find references to the story throughout the chapter.

Need Milk?

Every time you bite into President's Choice chocolate-chip cookies, or buy milk at an Independent Grocer, Loblaws, or dozens of other grocery stores, you are shopping at Canada's #1 grocery retailer and wholesaler: Loblaw Companies Limited.

How does a company become one of the biggest names in Canadian business? Through well-planned operating and financial strategies, such as owning its own real estate, reinvesting in the business, introducing non-traditional departments and services, and maintaining a strong balance sheet.

Strategic acquisitions have also played an important role. In 1956, Garfield Weston acquired a majority of shares in Toronto-based Loblaw Groceterias, and changed its name to Loblaw Companies Limited. Over the next two decades, he steadily acquired dozens of food distributors and wholesalers in both the U.S. and Canada.

When Garfield died in 1978, his son Galen took over, continuing Loblaw's expansion in the 1980s and early 1990s. In 1995 and 1996, Loblaw opened 50 new Canadian locations and moved into the Quebec market by buying the Montreal-based Provigo chain. It also bought more than 80 stores from Agora Foods in Atlantic Canada. Careful not to spread the company too thin, however, Weston let go of the company's U.S. holdings to focus on this Canadian expansion.

Another aspect of Loblaw's success has been innovation in retailing. Many new stores are massive, boasting flower shops, pharmacies, photo developers, and financial services pavilions, and some even include interior markets, restaurants, and fitness clubs.

Loblaw also introduced private labels in Canada, first with the 1978 launch of the no-name brand, then with President's Choice, G-R-E-E-N, and Too Good To Be True! In 2001, the company added President's Choice Organics, followed by President's Choice general merchandise in 2002. Some 3,500 PC products are available today.

President's Choice products are now sold in the United States, Bermuda, the Cayman Islands, Colombia, Israel, Hong Kong, Trinidad, Jamaica, and several other Caribbean islands.

Through innovation, and by ensuring cost-effective operations, the company has enjoyed long-term stable growth. Today, Loblaw Companies Limited is one of Canada's largest private employers, with nearly 1,700 stores and more than 126,000 employees.

None of this happened overnight. The path a huge corporation takes involves many decisions. Should Loblaw purchase a particular distributing operation or introduce a new frozen entrée? Should it sell groceries on-line? Exit a particular market and reallocate assets elsewhere? There are also decisions that executives do not control, such as investors choosing whether or not to purchase Loblaw shares. To make any of these financial decisions, all parties rely on one key tool—accounting.

the navigator

Loblaw Companies Limited: www.loblaw.com

The **Navigator** learning system encourages you to use the learning aids in the chapter and set priorities as you study

THE NAVIGATOR

☐ Read *Feature Story*

☐ Scan *Study Objectives*

☐ Read *Chapter Preview*

☐ Read text and answer *Before You Go On*

☐ Work *Using the Decision Toolkit*

☐ Review *Summary of Study Objectives*

☐ Review the *Decision Toolkit—A Summary*

☐ Work *Demonstration Problem*

☐ Answer *Self-Study Questions*

☐ Complete assignments

STUDY OBJECTIVES

Study Objectives give you a framework for learning specific concepts covered in the chapter.

After studying this chapter, you should be able to:

1. Explain why accounting is important.
2. Identify the uses and users of accounting.
3. Explain the three main types of business activity.
4. Describe the content and purpose of each of the financial statements.

the navigator

How do you start a business? How do you make it grow into a widely recognized brand name like Loblaw? How do you determine whether your business is making or losing money? When you need to expand your operations, where do you get money to finance the expansion— should you borrow, issue shares, or use your own funds? How do you convince lenders to lend you money or investors to buy your shares? To be successful in business, countless decisions have to be made—and decisions require financial information.

The purpose of this chapter is to show you accounting's role in providing reliable financial information. The chapter is organized as follows:

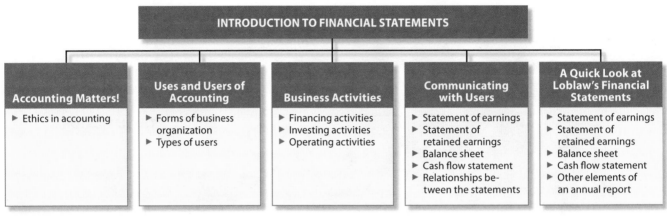

INTRODUCTION TO FINANCIAL STATEMENTS

Accounting Matters!	Uses and Users of Accounting	Business Activities	Communicating with Users	A Quick Look at Loblaw's Financial Statements
▶ Ethics in accounting	▶ Forms of business organization ▶ Types of users	▶ Financing activities ▶ Investing activities ▶ Operating activities	▶ Statement of earnings ▶ Statement of retained earnings ▶ Balance sheet ▶ Cash flow statement ▶ Relationships between the statements	▶ Statement of earnings ▶ Statement of retained earnings ▶ Balance sheet ▶ Cash flow statement ▶ Other elements of an annual report

the navigator

Accounting Matters!

study objective 1

Explain why accounting is important.

In the early 2000s, North America saw the collapse of the high-tech industry, a falling stock market, employee layoffs, and the bankruptcy of many well-known companies. Corporate scandals made headlines almost every week. The impact was staggering and it was felt around the world. For example, when the global communications company WorldCom lowered its stated earnings by U.S. $3.8 billion, this restatement contributed to investor losses of U.S. $179.3 billion and 17,000 lost jobs. As tales of fraud unfolded, WorldCom became the biggest bankruptcy in corporate history. Energy trader Enron's schemes that falsely increased its earnings by U.S. $568 million, leading to financial restatements and bankruptcy, caused investor losses of U.S. $66.4 billion and 6,100 job losses. Improper accounting practices at Nortel Networks Corporation resulted in a U.S. $434-million reduction in its earnings, and in one of Canada's most widely held shares losing most of its value.

These are only three of the many high-profile companies that in a few short years were investigated in different countries because of accusations of accounting misstatements, bogus securities trading, or misleading investors. Regulators, the investment community, and the accounting profession recommended changes to business practices, corporate governance, public oversight, and accountability. The end result of all this is that new requirements now guide business behaviour, as well as accounting and auditing practices.

One thing is very evident from all these embarrassing, illegal, and unethical business events—**accounting is important**. Good accounting is essential to sound business and investing decisions. Bad accounting will not be tolerated. If there is the slightest hint that a company's accounting practices cannot be trusted, investors sell their holdings and the company's share price falls dramatically.

The world's economic systems depend on highly transparent, reliable, and accurate financial reporting. Accounting has long been labelled "the language of business." That language must be understandable, useful, and truthful if it is to be of any value. Recent events such as these reinforce the worth of studying, understanding, and using accounting information. This textbook is your introduction to accounting as a valuable tool for business record keeping, communication, and analysis. Make the most of this course—it will serve you for a lifetime in ways you cannot now imagine.

Ethics in Accounting

The corporate scandals of the early 2000s made it very clear that reliable accounting information is essential. These scandals also highlighted the importance of ethics in accounting.

The standards of conduct by which one's actions are judged as right or wrong, honest or dishonest, fair or not fair, are **ethics**. We have seen what happens when you cannot depend on the individuals you deal with to be honest. If managers, customers, investors, co-workers, and creditors act dishonestly, effective communication and economic activity are impossible and information lacks credibility.

To help you become aware of ethical situations and to give you practice at solving ethical dilemmas, we look at ethics in a number of ways in this book: (1) Many of the feature stories, as well as other parts of the text, discuss the central importance of ethical behaviour to financial reporting. (2) Accounting Matters! boxes with an ethics perspective highlight ethics questions and issues in actual business situations. (3) In the end-of-chapter material, an ethics case asks you to put yourself in the position of a decision-maker in a particular business situation. As you analyze these ethics cases and your own ethical experiences, you should apply the three steps outlined in Illustration 1-1.

> **Essential terms** are printed in **blue** when they first appear. They are listed and defined again in the glossary at the end of the chapter.

Illustration 1-1 ▼

Steps used to analyze ethical dilemmas

1. Recognize an ethical situation and the ethical issues involved.	2. Identify and analyze the main elements in the situation.	3. Identify the alternatives, and weigh the impact of each alternative on various stakeholders.
Use your personal ethics or an organization's code of ethics to identify ethical situations and issues.	Identify the *stakeholders*—persons or groups who may be harmed or benefited. Ask the question: What are the responsibilities and obligations of the parties involved?	Select the most ethical alternative, considering all the consequences. Sometimes there will be one right answer. Other situations involve more than one possible solution. These situations require an evaluation of each alternative and the selection of the best one.

ACCOUNTING MATTERS! Ethics Perspective

Nortel Networks Corporation hired Susan Shepard, a lawyer with 30 years of experience in investigating crime and ethical behaviour, to be the new sheriff in its troubled corporate town. When Nortel's CEO, Bill Owens, announced the hiring, he described Shepard's appointment to the newly created post of chief ethics and compliance officer as tangible evidence that the company intends to set a "new tone at the top of this organization."

Recent surveys indicate that about half of North America's major corporations have ethics officers. This number is expected to rise with the introduction of new requirements that boards of directors and management must be actively involved in monitoring corporate ethics.

www.wiley.com/canada/kimmel

Ethics In Accounting

> The **Web icon** tells you there are additional resources about ethics on the Toolkit website.

Source: Shawn McCarthy, "Hiring Ethics Guru Evidence of 'New Tone' CEO Says," *The Globe and Mail*, January 12, 2005, B7.

Uses and Users of Accounting

Accounting is the information system that identifies and records the economic events of an organization, and then communicates them to interested users. There are three different types of organizations—proprietorships, partnerships, and corporations—and two types of interested users—internal users and external ones.

> **study objective 2**
>
> Identify the uses and users of accounting.

Forms of Business Organization

Suppose you open your own marketing agency. One of your first decisions is what organizational form your business should take. You have three choices—proprietorship, partnership, or corporation. A business owned by one person is a **proprietorship**. A business owned by more than one person is a **partnership**. A business organized as a separate legal entity owned by shareholders is a **corporation**.

You will probably choose the proprietorship form for your marketing agency. It is **simple to set up and gives you control over the business**. Small owner-operated businesses such as hair salons, service stations, and restaurants are often proprietorships, as are most home-based businesses.

Another possibility is for you to join forces with other individuals to form a partnership. Partnerships are often formed because one individual does not have **enough economic resources** to initiate or expand the business, or because partners bring **unique skills or resources** to the partnership. Partnerships are used to organize retail and service-type businesses, including professional practices (lawyers, doctors, architects, engineers, and accountants).

As a third alternative, you might organize as a corporation. As an investor in a corporation, you receive shares to indicate your ownership claim. Buying shares in a corporation is often more attractive than investing in a partnership because shares are easier to sell. Selling a proprietorship or partnership interest is much more complicated. Also, individuals can become shareholders by investing relatively small amounts of money. This advantage makes it is **easier for corporations to raise funds**. Successful corporations like Loblaw often have thousands of shareholders, and their shares are traded on organized stock exchanges, such as the Toronto Stock Exchange. Many businesses start as proprietorships or partnerships and eventually incorporate.

There are other factors that need to be considered when deciding which organizational form to choose. These include **legal liability** and **income taxes**. If you choose a proprietorship or partnership, you are personally liable for all debts of the business, whereas corporate shareholders are not. Proprietors and partners pay personal income tax on their respective share of the profits, while corporations pay income taxes as separate legal entities on any corporate profits. Corporations may also receive a more favourable tax treatment than other forms of business organization. We will discuss these issues in more depth in a later chapter.

Although the combined number of proprietorships and partnerships in Canada is more than the number of corporations, the revenue produced by corporations is far greater. Most of the largest companies in Canada—for example, General Motors of Canada Ltd., BCE Inc., Nortel Networks Corporation, George Weston Limited, Bombardier Inc., and Loblaw Companies Limited—are corporations. Because the majority of Canadian business is transacted by corporations, this book focuses mostly on the corporate form of organization.

Alternative Terminology
Shares are also known as *stock*.

Helpful Hint You can usually tell if a company is a corporation by looking at its name. The words *Limited (Ltd.)*, *Incorporated (Inc.)*, or *Corporation (Corp.)* normally follow its name.

Types of Users

Many people have an interest in knowing about the ongoing activities of a business organization. These people are users of accounting information. Users can be divided broadly into two types: **internal users** and **external users**.

Internal Users

Internal users of accounting information are managers who plan, organize, and run a business. These include **marketing managers**, **production supervisors**, **finance directors**, and **company officers**. In running a business, internal users must answer many important questions, as shown in Illustration 1-2.

Illustration 1-2 ◀

Questions asked by internal users

Questions Asked by Internal Users

Is there enough cash to pay bills?

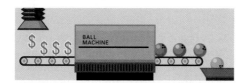

What is the cost of manufacturing each unit of product?

Can we afford to give employees pay raises this year?

Which product line is the most profitable?

To answer these and other questions, users need detailed information on a timely basis. For internal users, accounting provides internal reports, such as financial comparisons of operating alternatives, projections of earnings from new sales campaigns, and forecasts of cash needs for the next year.

External Users

There are several types of external users of accounting information. **Investors** (shareholders) use accounting information to make decisions to buy, hold, or sell their shares. **Creditors**, such as suppliers and bankers, use accounting information to evaluate the risks of granting credit or lending money. Some questions that may be asked by investors and creditors about a company are shown in Illustration 1-3.

Illustration 1-3 ◀

Questions asked by external users

Questions Asked by External Users

Is the company generating satisfactory earnings?

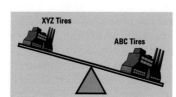

How does the company compare in size and profitability with competitors?

Will the company be able to pay its debts as they come due?

The information needs and questions of other external users vary a lot. **Taxing authorities**, such as the Canada Revenue Agency, want to know whether the company respects the tax laws. **Regulatory agencies**, such as provincial securities commissions, want to know whether the company is operating within prescribed rules. **Customers** are interested in whether a company will continue to honour product warranties and support its product lines. **Labour unions** want to know whether the company has the ability to pay increased wages and benefits. **Economic planners** use accounting information to analyze and forecast economic activity.

BEFORE YOU GO ON . . .

▶Review It

1. Why is good accounting important to decision-making?
2. Why are ethics a fundamental business concept?
3. What are the three forms of business organization and the advantages of each?
4. What are the two main types of users of accounting information? Give examples of each.

Business Activities

study objective 3

Explain the three main types of business activity.

All businesses are involved in three types of activity—**financing**, **investing**, and **operating**. For example, Galen Weston needed financing in the 1980s to revitalize and expand Loblaw. To finance this expansion, Loblaw sold shares to investors and borrowed money from outside sources, like banks. The cash obtained was then invested in new supermarkets. These new supermarkets helped increase Loblaw's operating activities of buying and selling food and other products. Let's now look at these three types of business activity in more detail.

Financing Activities

Financing Activities

It takes money to make money. The two primary ways of raising outside funds for corporations are borrowing money and issuing (selling) shares in exchange for cash.

Loblaw may borrow money in a variety of ways. For example, it can take out a loan at a bank or borrow money from other lenders. The persons or companies that Loblaw owes money to are its creditors. Amounts owed to creditors—in the form of debt and other obligations—are called liabilities.

Specific names are given to different types of liabilities, depending on their source. For instance, Loblaw may have taken funds from an operating line of credit with its bank, which results in **bank indebtedness**. Loblaw may also have a short-term **note payable** to a bank for the money borrowed to purchase its display cabinets, for example. Loblaw may also have **long-term debt**, which can include **notes payable**, **mortgages payable**, and other types of debt securities borrowed for longer periods of time.

A corporation may also obtain financing by selling shares of ownership, or share capital, to investors. As mentioned in the chapter-opening feature story, Garfield Weston purchased shares of ownership in Loblaw Groceterias, which was later renamed Loblaw Companies Limited. Loblaw has issued common shares to other interested investors over the years to raise the cash that was needed to help the business grow. **Common shares** is the term used to describe the amount paid by investors for shares of ownership in a company. Common shares are just one class or type of share capital that a company can issue.

The claims of creditors differ from those of shareholders. If you loan money to a company, you are one of its creditors. In loaning money, you specify a repayment schedule—for example, payment at the end of each month. In addition, interest is normally added to the amount due. As a creditor, you have a legal right to be paid at the agreed time. In the event of nonpayment, you may force the company to sell its property to pay its debts. The law requires that creditor claims be paid before shareholder claims.

Shareholders have no claim to corporate resources until the claims of creditors are satisfied. If you buy a company's shares instead of loaning it money, you have no legal right to expect any payments until all of its creditors are paid. Also, once shares are issued, the company has no obligation to buy them back, whereas debt obligations must be repaid. Many companies pay shareholders a return on their investment on a regular basis, as long as there is enough cash to cover required payments to creditors. Payments to shareholders are called dividends.

Investing Activities

After Loblaw raises money through financing activities, it then uses that money for investing activities. Investing activities involve the purchase of the long-lived resources—called **assets**—that a company needs to operate. For example, display cabinets, computers, delivery trucks, buildings, and land are all examples of assets that result from investing activities. Together, they are referred to as **property, plant, and equipment**.

Cash is one of the more important assets owned by Loblaw, or any other business. If a company has excess cash that it does not need for a while, it might choose to invest it in debt or equity securities of other corporations or organizations. **Investments** are another example of an asset and an investing activity.

Investing Activities

Operating Activities

Most of the company's longer-lived assets are purchased through investing activities as described above. Other assets with shorter lives, however, result from operating activities. For example, if Loblaw sells goods to a customer and does not receive cash immediately, then the company has a right to expect payment from that customer in the near future. This right to receive money in the future is called an **account receivable**. Goods available for future sales to customers are assets called **inventory**.

Operating Activities

Loblaw is in the business of selling goods such as groceries and household products. We call the amount earned from the sale of these goods **revenues**. In accounting language, revenues are increases in economic resources—normally an increase in an asset but sometimes a decrease in a liability—that result from a business's operating activities.

Revenues come from different sources and are identified by various names, depending on the nature of the business. For instance, Loblaw's main source of revenue is the money it earns from grocery sales to consumers. However, it also earns interest revenue on securities held as short-term investments. Sources of revenue that are common to many businesses are **sales revenue**, **service revenue**, and **interest revenue**.

Before Loblaw can sell any groceries, it must buy produce, meat, and other food items. It also incurs costs like salaries, utilities, and income taxes. All of these costs, referred to as expenses, are necessary to sell the product. In accounting language, expenses are the cost of assets that are consumed or services that are used in the process of generating revenues.

There are many kinds of expenses and they are identified by various names, depending on the type of asset consumed or service used. For example, Loblaw keeps track of these types of expenses: **cost of sales**, **selling and administrative expenses** (such as the cost of food products, wages of store employees, advertising costs, office supplies, and utilities), **amortization expense** (allocation of the cost of using property, plant, and equipment), **interest expense** (amounts of interest paid on various debts), and **income taxes** (corporate taxes paid to the provincial and federal governments).

Alternative Terminology *Amortization expense* is also called *depreciation expense*.

Loblaw may also have liabilities that come from these expenses. For example, it may purchase produce on credit from suppliers; the obligations to pay for these goods available for sale to its customers are called **accounts payable**. Additionally, Loblaw may have interest payable on the outstanding (unpaid) amounts owed to the bank. It may also have **wages payable**, **provincial sales taxes** and **property taxes payable** to the provincial government, and **goods and services taxes payable** to the federal government. **Income tax payable** is an example of another liability that is payable to the federal and provincial governments.

To determine whether it earned a profit, Loblaw compares the revenues of a period with the expenses of that period. When revenues are more than expenses, **net earnings** result. When expenses exceed revenues, a **net loss** results.

Alternative Terminology *Net earnings* are also commonly known as *net income*.

BEFORE YOU GO ON . . .

▶ Review It

1. What are the three types of business activity?
2. What are assets, liabilities, share capital, dividends, revenues, and expenses?

▶Do It

Classify each item first as a financing, investing, or operating activity, and then as an asset, liability, share capital, revenue, or expense:

(a) an amount paid to an employee for work performed
(b) an amount earned from providing a service
(c) an issue of shares
(d) a truck that is purchased
(e) an amount owed to a bank
(f) excess cash invested in a long-term investment

Action Plan

- Distinguish between financing, investing, and operating activities.
- Understand the distinction between assets, liabilities, share capital, revenues, and expenses.
- Classify each item based on its economic characteristics.

Solution

(a) Operating activity; expense
(b) Operating activity; revenue
(c) Financing activity; share capital

(d) Investing activity; asset
(e) Financing activity; liability
(f) Investing activity; asset

Communicating with Users

study objective 4

Describe the content and purpose of each of the financial statements.

Users of accounting information are interested in a company's assets, liabilities, shareholders' equity, revenues, and expenses. For reporting purposes, it is customary to arrange this information in four different financial statements that are the backbone of financial reporting:

- **Statement of earnings:** A statement of earnings reports revenues and expenses to show how successfully a company performed during a period of time.
- **Statement of retained earnings:** A statement of retained earnings indicates how much was distributed to you and the other shareholders of a company in the form of dividends, and how much was retained in the business to allow for future growth.
- **Balance sheet:** A balance sheet presents a picture of what a company owns (its assets), what it owes (its liabilities), and its net worth (its shareholders' equity) at a specific point in time.
- **Cash flow statement:** A cash flow statement shows where a company obtained cash during a period of time and how that cash was used.

To introduce you to these statements, in the following sections we have prepared the financial statements for a fictitious marketing agency called Sierra Corporation.

Statement of Earnings

Alternative Terminology
The *statement of earnings* is also commonly known as the *income statement*.

The **statement of earnings** reports the success or failure of the company's operations for a period of time. To indicate that Sierra's statement of earnings reports the results of operations for a **period of time**, the statement is dated "Month Ended October 31, 2006." The statement of earnings lists the company's revenues followed by its expenses. Expenses are deducted from revenues to determine earnings before income tax (commonly abbreviated as EBIT). Income tax expense is usually shown separately, immediately following earnings before income tax. Finally, the net earnings (or net loss) are determined by deducting the income tax expense.

Why are financial statement users interested in net earnings? Investors are interested in a company's past earnings because they provide information which suggests future earnings. Investors buy and sell shares based on their beliefs about the future performance of a company. If you believe that Sierra will be even more successful in the future, and that this success will translate into a higher share price, you should buy Sierra's shares. Creditors also use the statement of earnings to predict the future. When a bank loans money to a company, it does this because it believes it will be repaid in the future. If it thought it was not going to be repaid, it would not loan the money. Thus, before making the loan, the bank loan officer must try to predict whether the company will be profitable enough to repay it.

Note that the **issue of shares and distribution of dividends do not affect net earnings**. For example, if Sierra Corporation received $10,000 of cash from issuing new shares, it would not be reported as revenue in the statement of earnings. Rather, this transaction would increase cash and common shares in the balance sheet. If dividends of $500 were paid, it would not be regarded as a business expense, because it was not incurred to generate revenue. Instead, dividends are reported as a reduction of retained earnings in the statement of retained earnings.

A sample statement of earnings for Sierra Corporation is shown in Illustration 1-4.

SIERRA CORPORATION Statement of Earnings Month Ended October 31, 2006		
Revenues		
Service revenue		$10,600
Expenses		
Salaries expense	$6,800	
Supplies expense	1,500	
Rent expense	900	
Insurance expense	50	
Interest expense	25	
Amortization expense	83	
Total expense		9,358
Earnings before income tax		1,242
Income tax expense		250
Net earnings		$ 992

Illustration 1-4 ◄

Statement of earnings

Helpful Hint The heading of every statement identifies the company, the type of statement, and the time period covered by the statement. Sometimes another line is added to indicate the unit of measure. When it is used, this fourth line usually indicates that the data are presented in thousands or in millions of dollars.

Note that cents are not included in the dollar figures recorded in financial statements, such as those illustrated for Sierra Corporation. In reality, it is important to understand that cents should be and are used in recording transactions in a company's internal accounting records. In contrast, for financial reporting purposes, financial statement amounts are normally rounded to the nearest dollar, thousand dollars, or million dollars, depending on the size of the company. External reporting condenses and simplifies information so that it is easier for the reader to understand.

As well, it really does not matter whether the figures are listed in two columns, as they are for Sierra Corporation, or in one column. Companies use a variety of presentation formats, depending on their preference and what they think is easiest for the reader to understand.

Every chapter presents useful information about how decision-makers use financial statements. **Decision Toolkits** summarize discussions of key decision-making contexts and techniques.

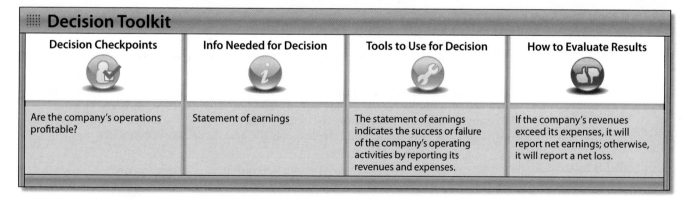

Decision Toolkit

Decision Checkpoints	Info Needed for Decision	Tools to Use for Decision	How to Evaluate Results
Are the company's operations profitable?	Statement of earnings	The statement of earnings indicates the success or failure of the company's operating activities by reporting its revenues and expenses.	If the company's revenues exceed its expenses, it will report net earnings; otherwise, it will report a net loss.

Statement of Retained Earnings

If Sierra is profitable, at the end of each period it must decide what portion of earnings to pay to shareholders in dividends. In theory, it could pay all of its current period earnings, but few companies choose to do this. Why? Because they want to retain part of the earnings or profits in the business so that the company can expand when it chooses to. **Retained earnings** are the cumulative earnings that have been retained in the corporation; in other words, they are the earnings that have not been paid out to shareholders.

The **statement of retained earnings** shows the amounts and causes of changes in retained earnings during the period. The time period is the same as for the statement of earnings. The beginning retained earnings amount is shown on the first line of the statement. Then net earnings are added and dividends (if any) are deducted to calculate the retained earnings at the end of the period. If a company has a net loss, it is deducted (rather than added) in the statement of retained earnings.

By monitoring the statement of retained earnings, financial statement users can evaluate dividend payment practices. Some investors look for companies that pay high dividends. For example, companies such as BCE, Duke Energy, Scotiabank, and Sun Life pay a high dividend rate. Other investors seek companies that pay no dividends and instead reinvest earnings to increase the company's growth. Companies such as Amazon.com, Biovail, Geac, Indigo Books & Music, and WestJet do not normally pay a dividend. Lenders monitor dividend payments because any money paid in dividends reduces a company's ability to repay its debts. Illustration 1-5 presents Sierra Corporation's sample statement of retained earnings.

Illustration 1-5 ►

Statement of retained earnings

SIERRA CORPORATION Statement of Retained Earnings Month Ended October 31, 2006	
Retained earnings, October 1	$ 0
Add: Net earnings	992
	992
Less: Dividends	500
Retained earnings, October 31	$492

Decision Toolkit

Decision Checkpoints	Info Needed for Decision	Tools to Use for Decision	How to Evaluate Results
What is the company's policy on dividends and growth?	Statement of retained earnings	How much did the company pay out in dividends to shareholders?	A company looking for rapid growth will pay no, or a low, dividend.

Balance Sheet

The **balance sheet** reports assets and claims to those assets at a specific point in time. These claims are subdivided into two categories: claims of creditors and claims of shareholders. As noted earlier, claims of creditors are called liabilities. Claims of shareholders, the owners of the company, are called **shareholders' equity**. This relationship is shown in equation form in Illustration 1-6. This equation is referred to as the basic **accounting equation**.

Illustration 1-6 ►

Basic accounting equation

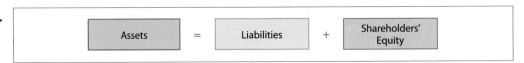

This relationship is where the name *balance sheet* comes from. Assets must be in balance with the claims to the assets. The right-hand side of the equation—the liabilities and equity—shows how the assets have been financed (borrowing from creditors, investing by shareholders, or self-financing through earnings retained in the company).

As you can see from looking at Sierra's balance sheet in Illustration 1-7, assets are listed first, followed by liabilities and shareholders' equity. Sierra's assets total $21,867 and include cash, accounts receivable, advertising supplies, prepaid insurance (insurance paid in advance but not yet used), and office equipment. Of these assets, only office equipment would be presented as an investing activity in the cash flow statement, as we will see in the next section. The others (except for cash) are examples of assets coming from operating activities.

Sierra's liabilities total $11,375 and consist of notes payable, accounts payable, interest payable, unearned revenue (cash received in advance for which the service has not yet been provided and is therefore still owed), salaries payable, and income tax payable. Of these liabilities, only the notes payable are an example of a financing activity. The others are examples of liabilities coming from operating activities.

Shareholders' equity consists of two parts: (1) **share capital** and (2) **retained earnings**. Share capital represents the shareholders' investments and includes all the classes of shares that a company has issued. If only one class of shares is issued, it is always common shares. Retained earnings are the cumulative net earnings retained in the corporation. Sierra has common shares of $10,000 and retained earnings of $492, for total shareholders' equity of $10,492.

Creditors analyze a company's balance sheet to determine the likelihood that they will be repaid. They carefully evaluate the nature of the company's assets and liabilities. For example, does the company have assets that could easily be sold, if required, to repay its debts? Managers use the balance sheet to determine whether inventory is adequate to support future sales and whether cash on hand is sufficient for immediate cash needs. Managers also look at the relationship between total liabilities and shareholders' equity to determine whether they have the best proportion of debt and equity financing.

SIERRA CORPORATION
Balance Sheet
October 31, 2006

Assets

Cash	$15,200
Accounts receivable	200
Advertising supplies	1,000
Prepaid insurance	550
Office equipment	4,917
Total assets	$21,867

Liabilities and Shareholders' Equity

Liabilities	
Notes payable	$ 5,000
Accounts payable	2,500
Interest payable	25
Unearned revenue	800
Salaries payable	2,800
Income tax payable	250
Total liabilities	11,375
Shareholders' equity	
Common shares	10,000
Retained earnings	492
Total shareholders' equity	10,492
Total liabilities and shareholders' equity	$21,867

Illustration 1-7 ◄

Balance sheet

Helpful Hint The balance sheet is dated at a *specific point in time*. The statement of earnings, statement of retained earnings, and cash flow statement cover a *period of time*.

Decision Toolkit

Decision Checkpoints	Info Needed for Decision	Tools to Use for Decision	How to Evaluate Results
Does the company rely mainly on debt or equity to finance its assets?	Balance sheet	The balance sheet reports the company's resources and claims to those resources. There are two types of claims: liabilities and shareholders' equity.	Compare the amount of liabilities versus the amount of shareholders' equity to determine whether the company relies more on creditors or shareholders for its financing.

Cash Flow Statement

The main function of a **cash flow statement** is to provide financial information about the cash receipts and cash payments of a business for a specific period of time. To help investors, creditors, and others in their analysis of a company's cash position, the cash flow statement reports the effects on cash of a company's (1) operating activities, (2) investing activities, and (3) financing activities. Operating activities are normally presented first, followed by either investing or financing activities. In addition, the statement shows the net increase or decrease in cash during the period, and the cash amount at the end of the period.

Users are interested in the cash flow statement because they want to know what is happening to a company's most important resource. The cash flow statement provides answers to these simple but important questions:

- Where did cash come from during the period?
- How was cash used during the period?
- What was the change in the cash balance during the period?

The cash flow statement for Sierra, in Illustration 1-8, shows that cash increased by $15,200 during the month. This increase resulted because operating activities (services to clients) increased cash by $5,700, and financing activities increased cash by $14,500. Investing activities used $5,000 of cash for the purchase of office equipment. Note that the positive numbers indicate cash inflows. Numbers in parentheses indicate cash outflows. Parentheses are often used in financial statements to indicate negative amounts.

For now, you should not worry too much about where the numbers came from. We will learn more about the preparation of cash flow statements in a later chapter.

Illustration 1-8 ▶

Cash flow statement

SIERRA CORPORATION
Cash Flow Statement
Month Ended October 31, 2006

Operating activities		
Cash receipts from operating activities	$11,200	
Cash payments for operating activities	(5,500)	
Cash provided by operating activities		$ 5,700
Investing activities		
Purchase of office equipment	$ (5,000)	
Cash used by investing activities		(5,000)
Financing activities		
Issue of common shares	$10,000	
Issue of note payable	5,000	
Payment of dividend	(500)	
Cash provided by financing activities		14,500
Net increase in cash		15,200
Cash, October 1		0
Cash, October 31		$15,200

Decision Toolkit

Decision Checkpoints	Info Needed for Decision	Tools to Use for Decision	How to Evaluate Results
Does the company generate enough cash from operating activities to fund its investing activities?	Cash flow statement	The cash flow statement shows the amount of cash provided or used by operating activities, investing activities, and financing activities.	Compare the amount of cash provided by operating activities with the amount of cash used by investing activities. Any deficiency in cash from operating activities must be made up with cash provided by financing activities.

Relationships Between the Statements

Because the results on some statements are used as data for other statements, the statements are said to be interrelated (related to each other). These interrelationships are evident in Sierra's financial statements:

1. The statement of retained earnings depends on the results of the statement of earnings. Sierra reported net earnings of $992 for the period, as shown in Illustration 1-4. This amount is added to the beginning amount of retained earnings as part of the process of determining ending retained earnings in Illustration 1-5.
2. The balance sheet and statement of retained earnings are interrelated because the ending amount of $492 on the statement of retained earnings in Illustration 1-5 is reported as the retained earnings amount on the balance sheet in Illustration 1-7.
3. The cash flow statement and the balance sheet are also interrelated. The cash flow statement presented in Illustration 1-8 shows how the cash account changed during the period by stating the amount of cash at the beginning of the period, the sources and uses of cash during the period, and the amount of cash at the end of the period, $15,200. The ending amount of cash shown on the cash flow statement must agree with the amount of cash on the balance sheet shown in Illustration 1-7.

Study these interrelationships carefully. To prepare financial statements, you must understand the sequence in which these amounts are determined and how each statement affects the next. Because each financial statement depends on information contained in another, financial statements must be prepared in a certain order: (1) statement of earnings; (2) statement of retained earnings; (3) balance sheet; and (4) cash flow statement.

BEFORE YOU GO ON . . .

►Review It

1. What questions might each of the following decision-makers ask that could be answered by financial information: a bank loan officer, an investor, a labour union, and a government?
2. What are the content and purpose of each statement: the statement of earnings, balance sheet, statement of retained earnings, and cash flow statement?

►Do It

CSU Corporation began operations on January 1, 2006. The following account information is available for CSU Corporation on December 31, 2006: Service Revenue $22,200; Accounts Receivable $4,000; Accounts Payable $2,000; Rent Expense $9,000; Notes Payable $5,000; Common Shares $10,000; Equipment $16,000; Insurance Expense $1,000; Supplies $1,800; Supplies Expense $200; Cash $1,400; Income Tax Expense $5,200; and Dividends $600. Using this information, prepare a statement of earnings, statement of retained earnings, balance sheet, and cash flow statement for the year.

For the operating activities section of the cash flow statement, cash receipts from operating activities were $18,200 ($22,200 − $4,000) and cash payments for operating activities were $15,200 ($9,000 + $1,000 + $200 + $5,200 + $1,800 − $2,000). You will have to determine the cash receipts and cash payments for each of the investing and financing activities sections. Assume that all transactions for these activities were cash transactions.

Action Plan

- Classify each account into the following categories: revenues, expenses, dividends, assets, liabilities, and shareholders' equity.
- Report revenues and expenses for the period in the statement of earnings.
- Show the amounts and causes (net earnings and dividends) of the changes in retained earnings for the period in the statement of retained earnings.
- Present assets and claims to those assets (liabilities and shareholders' equity) at a specific point in time in the balance sheet.
- Show the changes in cash for the period, classified as an operating, investing, or financing activity in the cash flow statement.

Solution

See facing page.

A Quick Look at Loblaw's Financial Statements

The same relationships that you observed among the financial statements of Sierra Corporation can be seen in the 2003 simplified financial statements of Loblaw Companies Limited, presented in Illustrations 1-9 through 1-12. Loblaw's actual financial statements are presented in Appendix A at the end of the book. We have simplified the financial statements to assist your learning—but they may look complicated to you anyway. Do not be alarmed by this. By the end of the book, you will have a lot of experience in reading and understanding financial statements such as these, and they will no longer look so complicated.

Before examining them, we need to explain a few points:

1. An accounting time period that is one year in length is called a **fiscal year**. Loblaw's fiscal year ends on the Saturday nearest the end of the calendar year. Consequently, its year end does not fall on the same date each year. For example, its 2003 year end was actually January 3, 2004.
2. Loblaw, like most companies, presents its financial statements for more than one year. Financial statements that report information for more than one period are called **comparative statements**. Comparative statements allow users to compare the financial position of a business at the end of one accounting period to the positions of previous periods.
3. Loblaw presents **consolidated** financial statements. This simply means that Loblaw's financial results include the results from all the companies owned by Loblaw Companies Limited—Loblaws, Atlantic Superstore, Provigo, Independent Grocer, and other companies representing the 1,700 stores Loblaw owns across Canada.
4. Note that numbers are reported in millions of dollars on Loblaw's financial statements—that is, the last six zeros (000,000) are omitted. Thus, Loblaw's net earnings in 2003 are $845,000,000 not $845.

CSU CORPORATION
Statement of Earnings
Year Ended December 31, 2006

Revenues		
Service revenue		$22,200
Expenses		
Rent expense	$9,000	
Insurance expense	1,000	
Supplies expense	200	
Total expenses		10,200
Earnings before income tax		12,000
Income tax expense		5,200
Net earnings		$ 6,800

CSU CORPORATION
Statement of Retained Earnings
Year Ended December 31, 2006

Retained earnings, January 1	$ 0
Add: Net earnings	6,800
	6,800
Less: Dividends	600
Retained earnings, December 31	$6,200

CSU CORPORATION
Balance Sheet
December 31, 2006

Assets

Cash	$ 1,400
Accounts receivable	4,000
Supplies	1,800
Equipment	16,000
Total assets	$23,200

Liabilities and Shareholders' Equity

Liabilities	
Notes payable	$ 5,000
Accounts payable	2,000
Total liabilities	7,000
Shareholders' equity	
Common shares	10,000
Retained earnings	6,200
Total shareholders' equity	16,200
Total liabilities and shareholders' equity	$23,200

CSU CORPORATION
Cash Flow Statement
Year Ended December 31, 2006

Operating activities		
Cash receipts from operating activities	$ 18,200	
Cash payments for operating activities	(15,200)	
Cash provided by operating activities		$ 3,000
Investing activities		
Purchase of equipment	$(16,000)	
Cash used by investing activities		(16,000)
Financing activities		
Issue of notes payable	$ 5,000	
Issue of common shares	10,000	
Payment of dividends	(600)	
Cash provided by financing activities		14,400
Net increase in cash		1,400
Cash, January 1		0
Cash, December 31		$ 1,400

Helpful Hint The arrows in this illustration show the relationships between the four financial statements.

Statement of Earnings

A simplified version of Loblaw's statement of earnings is presented in Illustration 1-9. Sierra is a service company: it provides services to earn its revenue. Loblaw sells a product: its main source of revenue is called sales. For 2003, Loblaw reports sales of $25,220 million. It then subtracts a variety of expenses related to operating the business. These expenses, totalling $23,949 million, include the cost of sales, selling and administrative expenses, amortization expense, and interest expense (payment of interest on debt) to arrive at earnings before income taxes of $1,271 million. After subtracting the income tax expense of $426 million, the company reports net earnings for the period of $845 million. Net earnings represent a 16-percent increase over the results of the previous year.

Illustration 1-9 ▶

Loblaw statement of earnings

LOBLAW COMPANIES LIMITED
Statement of Earnings
Year Ended January 3, 2004
(in millions)

Loblaws
A passion for food... and a lot more!

	2003	2002
Revenues		
Sales	$25,220	$23,082
Expenses		
Cost of sales, selling and administrative expenses	23,360	21,425
Amortization expense	393	354
Interest expense	196	161
Total expenses	23,949	21,940
Earnings before income taxes	1,271	1,142
Income tax expense	426	414
Net earnings	$ 845	$ 728

Statement of Retained Earnings

Loblaw presents information about its retained earnings in the statement of retained earnings in Illustration 1-10. Unlike Loblaw, some companies use a single statement to present their earnings and retained earnings. Find the line "Retained earnings, beginning of year," in Illustration 1-10 and you will see that retained earnings at the beginning of 2003 were $2,929 million. Note that this amount agrees with the end-of-year balance for 2002. The next figure for 2003 is net earnings of $845 million. This figure was taken from Loblaw's statement of earnings, presented in Illustration 1-9. Loblaw paid $165 million in dividends to its shareholders. The 2003 ending balance of retained earnings, after a $71-million adjustment for other items (which we will learn about in a later chapter), is $3,538 million. Find this amount of retained earnings in the shareholders' equity section near the bottom of Loblaw's 2003 balance sheet, presented in Illustration 1-11.

Illustration 1-10 ◄

Loblaw statement of retained earnings

LOBLAW COMPANIES LIMITED
Statement of Retained Earnings
Year Ended January 3, 2004
(in millions)

	2003	2002
Retained earnings, beginning of year	$2,929	$2,375
Add: Net earnings	845	728
	3,774	3,103
Less: Other adjustments	71	41
Dividends	165	133
Retained earnings, end of year	$3,538	$2,929

Balance Sheet

As shown in Loblaw's balance sheet in Illustration 1-11, Loblaw's assets include the types of assets mentioned in this chapter, such as cash, short-term investments, accounts receivable, inventories, and fixed assets, plus other types of assets that we will discuss in later chapters, such as prepaid expenses and goodwill.

Alternative Terminology
Fixed assets is another term for *property, plant, and equipment.*

Similarly, its liabilities include bank indebtedness, notes payable, accounts payable, income taxes payable, and long-term debt, as well as items not yet discussed, such as accrued liabilities. Loblaw's balance sheet shows that total assets increased from $11,110 million on December 28, 2002 (2002 fiscal year), to $12,177 million on January 3, 2004 (2003 fiscal year).

You can see that Loblaw relies more on debt financing than equity—it has nearly 60 percent more total liabilities than it has shareholders' equity. As you learn more about financial statements, we will discuss how to interpret the relationships and changes in financial statement items.

Illustration 1-11 ◄

Loblaw balance sheet

LOBLAW COMPANIES LIMITED
Balance Sheet
January 3, 2004
(in millions)

	2003	2002
Assets		
Cash and cash equivalents	$ 618	$ 823
Short-term investments	378	304
Accounts receivable	588	571
Inventories	1,778	1,702
Prepaid expenses and other assets	31	24
Fixed assets	6,422	5,587
Goodwill	1,607	1,599
Other assets	755	500
Total assets	$12,177	$11,110
Liabilities and Shareholders' Equity		
Liabilities		
Bank indebtedness	$ 38	$ 0
Notes payable	603	533
Accounts payable and accrued liabilities	2,227	2,336
Income taxes payable	140	179
Long-term debt	4,062	3,526
Other liabilities	375	412
Total liabilities	7,445	6,986
Shareholders' equity		
Common shares	1,194	1,195
Retained earnings	3,538	2,929
Total shareholders' equity	4,732	4,124
Total liabilities and shareholders' equity	$12,177	$11,110

Cash Flow Statement

Loblaw's cash and cash equivalents decreased by $205 million from 2002 to 2003. Cash equivalents are "near" cash items, such as highly liquid short-term investments that can be cashed quickly if there is a sudden need for cash. The reasons for Loblaw's decline in cash can be determined by examining the cash flow statement in Illustration 1-12. This statement presents Loblaw's sources and uses of cash during the period.

Illustration 1-12 ▶

Loblaw cash flow statement

LOBLAW COMPANIES LIMITED
Cash Flow Statement
Year Ended January 3, 2004
(in millions)

	2003	2002
Operating activities		
Cash receipts from operating activities	$ 25,203	$ 22,949
Cash payments for operating activities	(24,171)	(21,951)
Cash provided by operating activities	1,032	998
Investing activities		
Purchases of fixed assets	(1,271)	(1,079)
Proceeds from fixed asset sales	35	63
Sale (purchase) of investments	(114)	135
Other	(98)	(114)
Cash used by investing activities	(1,448)	(995)
Financing activities		
Issue of debt	763	447
Payment of debt	(102)	(77)
Issue of common shares	2	2
Retirement of common shares	(76)	(17)
Payment of dividends	(198)	(127)
Other	(178)	17
Cash provided by financing activities	211	245
Increase (decrease) in cash and cash equivalents	(205)	248
Cash and cash equivalents, beginning of year	823	575
Cash and cash equivalents, end of year	$ 618	$ 823

Loblaw is in expansion mode. Consequently, it spent considerable cash—$1,448 million—on investing activities. For example, it spent $1,271 million on new fixed assets in order to expand. Note that the cash provided by operating activities—$1,032 million—was enough to finance a large part of this expansion. The rest of its expansion was financed by borrowing and issuing shares. An examination of the $211 million in cash provided by financing activities shows that Loblaw received $763 million from debt financing and $2 million from equity financing. Proceeds from this financing were used to repay some of Loblaw's other debt and to retire shares. In addition, Loblaw paid $198 million of dividends to its shareholders. The net result of the sources and uses of cash during the year was a cash decrease of $205 million.

Other Elements of an Annual Report

www.wiley.com/canada/kimmel
Animated Tutorials
(Annual Report Walkthrough)

Publicly traded companies must give their shareholders an **annual report** each year. The annual report is a document that includes useful nonfinancial information about the company, as well as financial information. Nonfinancial information may include the company's mission, goals and objectives, products, and people.

Financial information normally includes a management discussion and analysis, a statement of management responsibility for the financial statements, an auditors' report, the comparative financial statements introduced in this chapter, notes to the financial statements, and a historical summary of key financial ratios and indicators. No analysis of a company's financial situation and prospects is complete without a review of each of these items.

The elements of Loblaw's annual report are reviewed in detail on the Toolkit website accompanying this text.

ACCOUNTING MATTERS! Investor Perspective

Companies preparing their annual reports have been piling on the paper lately. The reason is simple. They're trying to ease Enron-type worries on the part of investors. In Canada, Nortel Networks Corporation added an extra two dozen pages to its annual report. Other companies have done the same and annual reports today generally range from 75 to 95 pages.

The trend toward open, frank, and transparent reporting has been a long time coming. However, it is important to remember that annual reports are just one piece of the puzzle that should be scrutinized by investors.

A passion for food... *and a lot more!*

BEFORE YOU GO ON . . .

▶Review It

1. What financial information, in addition to the financial statements, might you expect to find in an annual report?
2. The basic accounting equation is: assets = liabilities + shareholders' equity. Replacing words with dollar amounts, what is Loblaw's accounting equation as at January 3, 2004? The answer to this question is at the end of this chapter.

> To answer **Review It** questions marked with this **Loblaw** icon, you need to use Loblaw's financial statements in Appendix A at the end of this book.

✔ the navigator

▦ Using the Decision Toolkit

Sobeys Inc. is Canada's second largest grocery chain, after Loblaw. Imagine that you are asking yourself if you should buy some of Sobeys' common shares as an investment.

Instructions

(a) What financial statements should you request from the company that would help you decide whether to invest or not?
(b) What should each of these financial statements tell you? Which financial statement will you likely be most interested in?
(c) Loblaw has a fiscal year end of January 3, 2004. Sobeys' fiscal year end is May 1, 2004. Is it possible to compare financial statements of these companies since they have different fiscal year ends?
(d) Simplified financial statements for Sobeys Inc. are shown below. What comparisons can you make between Sobeys and Loblaw in terms of their financial positions and results of operations?

> **Using the Decision Toolkit** exercises, which follow the final set of Review It questions in the chapter, ask you to use business information and the decision tools presented in the chapter. We encourage you to think through the questions related to the decision before you study the solution.

SOBEYS INC.
Statement of Earnings
Year Ended May 1, 2004
(in millions)

	2004	2003
Revenues		
Sales	$11,046.8	$10,414.5
Gain on sale of assets	14.6	
	11,061.4	10,414.5
Expenses		
Cost of sales, selling and administrative expenses	10,615.4	9,964.4
Amortization expense	150.9	124.0
Interest expense	42.4	41.7
Total expenses	10,808.7	10,130.1
Earnings before income taxes	252.7	284.4
Income tax expense	85.2	105.4
Net earnings	$ 167.5	$ 179.0

SOBEYS INC.
Statement of Retained Earnings
Year Ended May 1, 2004
(in millions)

	2004	2003
Balance, beginning of year	$533.4	$382.0
Add: Net earnings	167.5	179.0
	700.9	561.0
Less: Dividends	29.0	23.8
Other adjustments	4.0	3.8
Balance, end of year	$667.9	$533.4

SOBEYS INC.
Balance Sheet
May 1, 2004
(in millions)

	2004	2003
Assets		
Cash and cash equivalents	$ 164.6	$ 123.1
Short-term investments		191.4
Accounts receivable	272.4	285.4
Inventories	455.0	444.0
Prepaid expenses	40.9	30.5
Mortgages and loans receivable	165.5	150.0
Property and equipment	1,350.1	1,243.9
Goodwill	617.8	555.6
Other assets	208.4	168.6
Total assets	$3,274.7	$3,192.5
Liabilities and Shareholders' Equity		
Liabilities		
Accounts payable and accrued liabilities	$1,051.1	$ 971.9
Income taxes payable	6.7	37.4
Long-term debt	442.8	585.4
Other liabilities	198.6	161.0
Total liabilities	1,699.2	1,775.7
Shareholders' equity		
Common shares	907.6	903.4
Retained earnings	667.9	533.4
Total shareholders' equity	1,575.5	1,436.8
Total liabilities and shareholders' equity	$3,274.7	$3,192.5

	SOBEYS INC. Cash Flow Statement Year Ended May 1, 2004 (in millions)		
		2004	2003
Operating activities			
Cash receipts from operating activities		$ 11,059.8	$ 10,380.1
Cash payments for operating activities		(10,695.4)	(10,032.0)
Cash provided by operating activities		364.4	348.1
Investing activities			
Purchase of property and equipment		(316.1)	(342.3)
Proceeds from property and equipment sales		80.1	48.0
Purchase of investments		(15.5)	(9.8)
Acquisition of businesses		(53.6)	(2.5)
Other		(33.9)	(41.6)
Cash used by investing activities		(339.0)	(348.2)
Financing activities			
Issue of debt		14.9	118.6
Repayment of debt		(162.7)	(56.8)
Issue of common shares		5.4	6.7
Retirement of common shares		(6.5)	(5.9)
Payment of dividends		(29.0)	(23.8)
Other		1.3	(2.5)
Cash provided (used) by financing activities		(176.6)	36.3
Increase (decrease) in cash from continuing operations		(151.2)	36.2
Discontinued operations		1.3	3.9
Increase (decrease) in cash		(149.9)	40.1
Cash, beginning of year		314.5	274.4
Cash, end of year		$ 164.6	$ 314.5

Note: Cash is defined as cash and cash equivalents and short-term investments.

Solution

(a) Before you invest, you should investigate the statement of earnings, statement of retained earnings, cash flow statement, balance sheet, and the accompanying notes.

(b) You would probably be most interested in the statement of earnings because it shows past performance and this gives an indication of future performance. The statement of retained earnings shows the impact that current earnings and dividends have on the company's retained earnings. The cash flow statement reveals where the company is getting and spending its cash. This is especially important for a company that wants to grow. Finally, the balance sheet reveals the financial position of the company and the relationship between assets, liabilities, and shareholders' equity.

(c) Both financial statements cover a one-year period, with Loblaw's fiscal year overlapping Sobeys' for eight months (May through December 2003). If there have been no substantial changes during the periods that Loblaw's financial results cover but Sobeys' do not or vice versa, it really does not matter when each company's fiscal year ends. It is more important that we compare what each company was able to achieve within an equivalent period of time—whether it be one year, six months, or one quarter.

If, however, a major change does occur in the intervening period (the period where the statements do not overlap), such a change would likely reduce the usefulness of a comparison of the financial statements of the two companies. Say, for example, that the mad cow disease scare had happened during the non-overlapping period (it did not). The impact of this change would be reflected in Sobeys' current statements, but not in Loblaw's until the following fiscal year. It is important for users to be aware of relevant nonfinancial information such as this before they start their comparisons.

(d) Many interesting comparisons can be made between the two companies. Sobeys is much smaller, about one quarter the size of Loblaw. For example, Sobeys has total assets of $3,274.7 million versus $12,177 million for Loblaw. Also, Sobeys has lower revenue—sales of $11,046.8 million versus $25,220 million for Loblaw. Sobeys reported net earnings for its current fiscal year of $167.5 million, compared to Loblaw's net earnings of $845 million. Sobeys has a balance of $667.9 million of accumulated retained earnings, while Loblaw's retained earnings of $3,538 million are more than five times this amount. In 2003, Loblaw generated cash from operating activities of $1,032 million whereas Sobeys generated only $364.4 million.

While these comparisons are useful, these basic measures are not enough to determine whether one company will be a better investment than the other. In later chapters, you will acquire more tools to help you compare the relative profitability and financial health of these, and other, companies.

Summary of Study Objectives

1. **Explain why accounting is important.** Good accounting is necessary for making sound business and investing decisions. The world's economic systems depend on reliable and ethical accounting and financial reporting.

2. **Identify the uses and users of accounting.** The purpose of accounting is to provide useful information for decision-making. There are three types of organizations that use accounting information: proprietorships, partnerships, and corporations. A proprietorship is a business owned by one person. A partnership is a business owned by two or more people. A corporation is a separate legal entity whose shares provide evidence of ownership.

There are two types of user groups who use accounting information: internal and external users. Internal users work for the business and need accounting information to plan, organize, and run operations. The primary external users are investors and creditors. Investors (present and future shareholders) use accounting information to help decide whether to buy, hold, or sell shares. Creditors (suppliers and bankers) use accounting information to evaluate the risk of granting credit or loaning money to a business.

3. **Explain the three main types of business activity.** Financing activities involve collecting the necessary funds (through debt or equity) to support the business. Investing activities involve acquiring the resources (such as property, plant, and equipment) that are needed to run the business. Operating activities involve putting the resources of the business into action to generate a profit.

4. **Describe the content and purpose of each of the financial statements.** A statement of earnings presents the revenues and expenses of a company for a specific period of time. A statement of retained earnings summarizes the changes in retained earnings that have occurred for a specific period of time. Retained earnings are the cumulative earnings (less losses) over the company's life, less any dividends paid to shareholders. A balance sheet reports the assets, liabilities, and shareholders' equity of a business at a specific date. A cash flow statement summarizes information on the cash inflows (receipts) and outflows (payments) for a specific period of time

The **Summary of Study Objectives** repeats the main points related to the Study Objectives. It gives you an opportunity to review what you have learned.

The **Decision Toolkit—A Summary** reviews the contexts and techniques useful for decision-making that were covered in the chapter

⬚ Decision Toolkit—A Summary

Decision Checkpoints	Info Needed for Decision	Tools to Use for Decision	How to Evaluate Results
Are the company's operations profitable?	Statement of earnings	The statement of earnings indicates the success or failure of the company's operating activities by reporting its revenues and expenses.	If the company's revenues exceed its expenses, it will report net earnings; otherwise, it will report a net loss.
What is the company's policy on dividends and growth?	Statement of retained earnings	How much did the company pay out in dividends to shareholders?	A company looking for rapid growth will pay no, or a low, dividend.
Does the company rely mainly on debt or equity to finance its assets?	Balance sheet	The balance sheet reports the company's resources and claims to those resources. There are two types of claims: liabilities and shareholders' equity.	Compare the amount of liabilities versus the amount of shareholders' equity to determine whether the company relies more on creditors or shareholders for its financing.
Does the company generate enough cash from operating activities to fund its investing activities?	Cash flow statement	The cash flow statement shows the amount of cash provided or used by operating activities, investing activities, and financing activities.	Compare the amount of cash provided by operating activities with the amount of cash used by investing activities. Any deficiency in cash from operating activities must be made up with cash provided by financing activities.

Analysis Tools (Decision Toolkit Summaries)

www.wiley.com/canada/kimmel

Study Tools (Glossary)

the navigator

Glossary

Accounting The process of identifying, recording, and communicating the economic events of a business to interested users of the information. (p. 5)

Accounting equation Assets = liabilities + shareholders' equity. (p. 12)

Annual report A report prepared by management that presents financial and nonfinancial information about the company. (p. 20)

Assets The resources owned by a business. (p. 9)

Balance sheet A financial statement that reports the assets, liabilities, and shareholders' equity at a specific date. (p. 12)

Cash flow statement A financial statement that provides information about the cash inflows (receipts) and cash outflows (payments) for a specific period of time. (p. 14)

Comparative statements A presentation of the financial statements of a company for two or more years. (p. 16)

Corporation A business organized as a separate legal entity having ownership divided into transferable shares. (p. 6)

Dividends The distribution of retained earnings from a corporation to its shareholders in the form of cash or other assets. (p. 8)

Ethics The standards of conduct by which one's actions are judged as right or wrong, honest or dishonest, fair or unfair. (p. 5)

Expenses The cost of assets consumed or services used in ongoing operations to generate revenues. (p. 9)

Fiscal year An accounting period that is one year long. (p. 16)

Liabilities The debts and obligations of a business. Liabilities are claims of creditors on the assets of a business. (p. 8)

Net earnings (also known as net income) The amount by which revenues are more than expenses. (p. 9)

Net loss The amount by which expenses are more than revenues. (p. 9)

Partnership A business owned by more than one person. (p. 6)

Proprietorship A business owned by one person. (p. 5)

Retained earnings   The amount of accumulated net earnings (less losses, if any), from the prior and current periods, that has been kept in the corporation for future use and not distributed to shareholders as dividends. (p. 12)

Revenues   The economic resources that result from the operating activities of a business, such as the sale of a product or provision of a service. (p. 9)

Share capital   Shares representing the ownership interest in a corporation. If only one class of shares exists, it is known as common shares. (p. 8)

Shareholders' equity   The shareholders' claim on total assets, represented by the investments of the shareholders (share capital) and undistributed earnings (retained earnings) generated by the company. (p. 12)

Statement of earnings (also known as income state-ment)   A financial statement that presents the revenues and expenses and resulting net earnings or net loss of a company for a specific period of time. (p. 10)

Statement of retained earnings   A financial statement that summarizes the changes in retained earnings for a specific period of time. (p. 12)

Demonstration Problem

Study Tools
(Demonstration Problems)

Demonstration Problems are a final review before you begin homework. **Action Plans** that appear in the margins give you tips about how to approach the problem, and the **Solution** provided demonstrates both the form and content of complete answers.

The **Web icon** indicates there are additional demonstration problems on the Toolkit website.

Jeff Andringa, a former university hockey player, quit his job and started Ice Camp Ltd., a hockey camp for kids from ages 8 to 18. Eventually he would like to open hockey camps nationwide. Jeff has asked you to help him prepare financial statements at the end of his first year of operations. He tells you the following facts about his business activities.

In order to get the business off the ground, he decided to incorporate. He sold common shares to a few close friends and bought some of the shares himself on January 1, 2006. He initially raised $25,000 through the sale of these shares. In addition, the company borrowed $10,000 from a local bank. A used bus for transporting kids was purchased for $12,000 cash. Hockey nets and other miscellaneous equipment were purchased with $1,500 cash. The company earned camp tuition of $100,000 during the year but had collected only $80,000 of this amount. Thus, at the end of the year it was still owed $20,000. The company rents time at a local rink for $50 per hour. Total rink rental costs during the year were $8,000, insurance was $10,000, salaries were $20,000, administrative expenses totalled $9,000, and income taxes amounted to $15,000—all of which were paid in cash. The company incurred $800 in interest expense on the bank loan, which it still owed at the end of the year.

The company paid dividends during the year of $5,000 cash. The balance in the corporate bank account at December 31, 2006, was $34,500 ($25,000 + $10,000 − $12,000 − $1,500 + $80,000 − $8,000 − $10,000 − $20,000 − $9,000 − $15,000 − $5,000). Cash payments for operating activities totalled $62,000 ($8,000 + $10,000 + $20,000 + $9,000 + $15,000).

Instructions

Prepare a statement of earnings, statement of retained earnings, balance sheet, and cash flow statement for the year.

Action Plan

• On the statement of earnings, show revenues and expenses for a period of time.

• On the statement of retained earnings, show the changes in retained earnings for a period of time.

• On the balance sheet, report assets, liabilities, and shareholders' equity at a specific date.

• On the cash flow statement, report sources and uses of cash provided or used by operating, investing, and financing activities for a period of time.

Solution to Demonstration Problem

ICE CAMP LTD.
Statement of Earnings
Year Ended December 31, 2006

Revenues		
Camp tuition revenue		$100,000
Expenses		
Salaries expense	$20,000	
Insurance expense	10,000	
Administrative expense	9,000	
Rink rental expense	8,000	
Interest expense	800	
Total expenses		47,800
Earnings before income taxes		52,200
Income tax expense		15,000
Net earnings		$ 37,200

ICE CAMP LTD.
Statement of Retained Earnings
Year Ended December 31, 2006

Retained earnings, January 1	$ 0
Add: Net earnings	37,200
	37,200
Less: Dividends	5,000
Retained earnings, December 31	$32,200

ICE CAMP LTD.
Balance Sheet
December 31, 2006

Assets

Cash	$34,500
Accounts receivable	20,000
Bus	12,000
Equipment	1,500
Total assets	$68,000

Liabilities and Shareholders' Equity

Liabilities	
Bank loan payable	$10,000
Interest payable	800
Total liabilities	10,800
Shareholders' equity	
Common shares	25,000
Retained earnings	32,200
Total shareholders' equity	57,200
Total liabilities and shareholders' equity	$68,000

ICE CAMP LTD.
Cash Flow Statement
Year Ended December 31, 2006

Operating activities		
Cash receipts from operating activities	$ 80,000	
Cash payments for operating activities	(62,000)	
Cash provided by operating activities		$18,000
Investing activities		
Purchase of bus	$ (12,000)	
Purchase of equipment	(1,500)	
Cash used by investing activities		(13,500)
Financing activities		
Issue of bank loan	$ 10,000	
Issue of common shares	25,000	
Dividends paid	(5,000)	
Cash provided by financing activities		30,000
Net increase in cash		34,500
Cash, January 1		0
Cash, December 31		$34,500

the navigator

This would be a good time to return to the **Owner's Manual** at the beginning of the book (or look at it for the first time if you skipped it before) to read about the various types of assignment materials that appear at the end of each chapter. If you know the purpose of the different assignments, you will appreciate what each one contributes to your accounting skills and competencies.

Self-Study Questions

Answers are at the end of the chapter.

(SO 1) 1. Bad accounting can result in:
   (a) investors purchasing the company's shares.
   (b) the company's share price falling.
   (c) sound business and investing decisions.
   (d) reliable and accurate financial reporting.

(SO 2) 2. Ethics are the standards of conduct by which one's actions are judged to be:
   (a) decent or indecent.
   (b) successful or unsuccessful.
   (c) profitable or unprofitable.
   (d) right or wrong.

(SO 2) 3. Which is *not* one of the three forms of business organization?
   (a) Proprietorship   (c) Partnership
   (b) Creditorship   (d) Corporation

(SO 2) 4. What is an advantage of corporations compared to partnerships and proprietorships?
   (a) Harder to raise funds
   (b) Harder to transfer ownership
   (c) Harder to organize
   (d) Reduced legal liability

(SO 2) 5. Which statement about users of accounting information is incorrect?
   (a) Management is an internal user.
   (b) The Canada Revenue Agency is an external user.
   (c) Creditors are external users.
   (d) Investors are internal users.

6. Which is *not* one of the three primary business activities? (SO 3)
   (a) Financing   (c) Planning
   (b) Operating   (d) Investing

7. Which of the following is *not* an example of a financing activity? (SO 3)
   (a) Borrowing money from a bank
   (b) Repaying money to a bank
   (c) Selling goods on credit
   (d) Paying dividends

8. Net earnings will result during a time period when: (SO 3)
   (a) assets exceed liabilities.
   (b) assets exceed revenues.
   (c) expenses exceed revenues.
   (d) revenues exceed expenses.

9. Which financial statement reports assets, liabilities, and shareholders' equity? (SO 3)
   (a) Statement of earnings
   (b) Statement of retained earnings
   (c) Balance sheet
   (d) Cash flow statement

10. As at December 31, Stoneland Corporation has assets of $3,500 and shareholders' equity of $2,000. What are the liabilities for Stoneland Corporation as at December 31? (SO 4)
   (a) $1,500   (c) $3,500
   (b) $2,000   (d) $5,500

The financial results of real companies are included in the end of chapter material; these are indicated by the company names being shown in **red**.

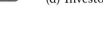

Questions

⚙ The **tool icon** means that an activity uses one of the decision tools presented in the chapter.

(SO 1) 1. "Accounting is ingrained in our society and is vital to our economic system." Do you agree? Explain.

(SO 1) 2. Why are ethics important to the accounting profession? To statement users?

(SO 1) 3. Improper accounting practices can result in stock market losses and employee layoffs. Do you agree? Explain.

(SO 2) 4. (a) What are the three basic forms of business organization?
   (b) Identify the advantages and disadvantages of each.

(SO 2) 5. (a) Who are the internal users of accounting data? Give examples.
   (b) Who are the external users? Give examples.

(SO 2) 6. Financial reporting is aimed mostly at two external user groups of accounting—investors and creditors.

Distinguish between the needs of each of these groups of users of financial information.

7. (a) Explain the differences between operating, investing, and financing activities. (SO 3)
   (b) Give two examples of each kind of activity.

8. Explain why accounts receivable, an asset, is classified as an operating activity on the cash flow statement and not as an investing activity. (SO 3)

9. ⚙ Why would a bank want to monitor the dividend payment practices of the corporation it lends funds to? (SO 3)

10. André is puzzled reading Loblaw's financial statements. He notices that the numbers have all been rounded to the nearest million. He thought financial statements were supposed to be accurate and wonders (SO 4)

what happened to the rest of the money. Respond to André's concern.

(SO 4) 11. Why do you think a balance sheet is prepared as at a specific point in time, while the other financial statements cover a period of time?

(SO 4) 12. What are retained earnings? What items increase the balance in retained earnings? What items decrease the balance in retained earnings?

(SO 4) 13. (a) What is the purpose of the cash flow statement?
(b) What are the three main categories in the cash flow statement?

(SO 4) 14. How are each of the following pairs of financial statements related?
(a) Statement of earnings and statement of retained earnings
(b) Statement of retained earnings and balance sheet
(c) Balance sheet and cash flow statement

(SO 4) 15. A company's net earnings appear directly on the statement of earnings and the statement of retained earnings. They are also included indirectly on the company's balance sheet. Do you agree? Explain.

(SO 4) 16. (a) What is the basic accounting equation?
(b) How does the accounting equation relate to the balance sheet?

(SO 4) 17. (a) Define the terms *assets*, *liabilities*, and *shareholders' equity*.

(b) What items affect shareholders' equity?

(SO 4) 18. Which of these items are liabilities for Kool Stores Inc.?
(a) Cash
(b) Accounts payable
(c) Dividends
(d) Accounts receivable
(e) Supplies
(f) Equipment
(g) Income tax payable
(h) Service revenue
(i) Rent expense
(j) Long-term debt

(SO 4) 19. Here are some items found in the financial statements of D'Anjou, Inc. Indicate in which financial statement each item would appear.
(a) Service revenue
(b) Equipment
(c) Advertising expense
(d) Accounts receivable
(e) Common shares
(f) Wages payable
(g) Cash provided by operating activities
(h) Dividends

(SO 4) 20. ⚲══⚲ Loblaw's year end is not a fixed date; rather, it can vary slightly from one year to the next. What possible problems does this pose for financial statement users?

Brief Exercises

BE1–1 The company accountant is counting the office supplies on hand at the end of the period. She realizes there are more supplies in stock than recorded in the books and decides to take some of the extra supplies home. In her own mind, this is not stealing because it will correct a book error. In addition, she is owed by the company for all the extra unpaid work she has been doing lately anyway.

Discuss ethical issues. (SO 1)

(a) Are the accountant's actions ethical? Explain why or why not.
(b) What could the company do to ensure that all employees use appropriate ethical behaviour?

BE1–2 Write the correct form of business organization—proprietorship (P), partnership (PP), or corporation (C)—beside each set of characteristics.

Describe forms of business organization. (SO 2)

(a) ___ Simple to set up; founder retains control

(b) ___ Shared control; increased skills and resources

(c) ___ Easier to transfer ownership and raise funds; no personal liability

BE1–3 The following list presents different types of evaluations made by various users of accounting information:

Identify users of accounting information. (SO 2)

1. Determining if the company respected income tax regulations
2. Determining if the company can pay its obligations
3. Determining if a marketing proposal will be cost-effective
4. Determining if the company's net earnings will result in a share price increase
5. Determining if the company should use debt or equity financing

(a) Write the number of the type of evaluation (1–5) beside the appropriate user of accounting information.
(b) Indicate if the user is internal or external.

	(a) Type of Evaluation	(b) Type of User
Investors	_____	_____
Marketing managers	_____	_____
Creditors	_____	_____
Chief financial officer	_____	_____
Canada Revenue Agency	_____	_____

Classify items by activity. (SO 3)

BE1–4 Indicate the section of the cash flow statement—operating activities (O), investing activities (I), or financing activities (F)—in which each of the following items would appear. In addition, indicate whether each item would be reported as a cash inflow (+) or cash outflow (−) on the cash flow statement.

(a) ___ Cash received from customers

(b) ___ Cash dividends paid to shareholders

(c) ___ Cash received from issuing common shares

(d) ___ Cash received from borrowing money

(e) ___ Cash paid to purchase an office building

(f) ___ Cash paid for income taxes

Determine on which financial statement items appear. (SO 4)

BE1–5 The Calgary Exhibition and Stampede Limited has the following selected accounts included in its financial statements. In each case, identify whether the item would appear on the balance sheet (BS) or statement of earnings (SE).

(a) ___ Accounts receivable

(b) ___ Inventories

(c) ___ Amortization expense

(d) ___ Common shares

(e) ___ Building

(f) ___ Stampede revenue

(g) ___ Horse racing revenue

(h) ___ Accounts payable and accrued liabilities

(i) ___ Cash and short-term deposits

(j) ___ Administration, marketing, and park services expenses

(k) ___ Interest expense

(l) ___ Prepaid expenses

Determine on which financial statement items appear. (SO 4)

BE1–6 Indicate which statement—statement of earnings (SE), balance sheet (BS), statement of retained earnings (RE), or cash flow statement (CF)—you would examine to find each of the following items:

(a) ___ Revenue earned during the period

(b) ___ Supplies on hand at the end of the year

(c) ___ Cash received from borrowing money during the period

(d) ___ Total debt at the end of the period

(e) ___ Dividends paid to shareholders during the period

Use accounting equation. (SO 4)

BE1–7 Use the accounting equation to determine the missing amounts below:

Assets	=	Liabilities	+	Shareholders' Equity
$80,000		$50,000		(a)
(b)		$45,000		$60,000
$94,000		(c)		$52,000

Use accounting equation. (SO 4)

BE1–8 Use the accounting equation to answer these questions:

(a) The shareholders' equity of Sansom Corporation is $100,000. Its total liabilities are $45,000. What is the amount of Sansom's total assets?

(b) The liabilities of Houle Corporation are $90,000. Houle's share capital is $150,000 and retained earnings $100,000. What is the amount of Houle's total assets?

(c) The total assets of Pitre Limited are $170,000. Its share capital is $35,000 and retained earnings $65,000. What is the amount of its total liabilities?

(d) The total assets of Budovitch Inc. are $500,000 and its liabilities are equal to half of its total assets. What is the amount of Budovitch's shareholders' equity?

BE1–9 At the beginning of the year, Lam Ltd. had total assets of $700,000 and total liabilities of $500,000.

Use accounting equation.
(SO 4)

(a) If total assets increased by $150,000 during the year and total liabilities decreased by $80,000, what is the amount of shareholders' equity at the end of the year?

(b) During the year, total liabilities increased by $100,000. The company reported net earnings of $50,000, sold additional shares for $10,000, and paid no dividends during the year. What is the amount of total assets at the end of the year?

(c) If total assets decreased by $90,000 during the year and shareholders' equity increased by $120,000, what is the amount of total liabilities at the end of the year?

BE1–10 Indicate whether each of these items is an asset (A), a liability (L), or shareholders' equity (SE):

Identify assets, liabilities, and shareholders' equity.
(SO 4)

(a) ___ Accounts receivable   (e) ___ Common shares

(b) ___ Salaries payable   (f) ___ Notes payable

(c) ___ Equipment   (g) ___ Retained earnings

(d) ___ Office supplies   (h) ___ Cash

BE1–11 Some transactions are presented below. Determine whether each transaction affects common shares (C), dividends (D), revenue (R), expenses (E), or has no effect on any of these shareholders' equity components (NE).

Determine effect of transactions on shareholders' equity.
(SO 4)

(a) ___ Purchase of equipment   (e) ___ Costs incurred for income tax

(b) ___ Issue of common shares   (f) ___ Amounts earned by employees

(c) ___ Services performed for cash (g) ___ Dividends paid to shareholders

(d) ___ Services performed on account (h) ___ Interest incurred on note payable

Exercises

E1–1 Here is a list of words or phrases discussed in this chapter:

Match words with descriptions.
(SO 1, 2, 3)

1. Accounts payable   5. Dividends   9. Ethics
2. Creditor   6. Corporation   10. Assets
3. Financing activities   7. Common shares
4. Retained earnings   8. Accounts receivable

Instructions

Match each word or phrase with the best description of it below:

(a) ___ A company that raises money by issuing shares

(b) ___ Amounts owed to suppliers of goods

(c) ___ Resources owned by a company

(d) ___ A party a company owes money to

(e) ___ Obtaining cash from borrowing money or issuing shares

(f) ___ Standards of conduct by which one's actions are judged as right or wrong

(g) ___ Cumulative earnings that have been retained in the company

(h) ___ The ownership interest of shareholders in the company

(i) ___ Amounts due from customers

(j) ___ Distributions of earnings to shareholders

E1–2 Indicate in which section of the cash flow statement—operating activities (O), investing activities (I), or financing activities (F)—for Fairmont Hotels & Resorts Inc. each of the

Classify items by activity.
(SO 3)

following items would appear. In addition, indicate whether each item would be reported as a cash inflow (+) or cash outflow (−) on the cash flow statement.

(a) Additions to property and equipment   (e) Issue of common shares
(b) Repurchase of common shares   (f) Sale of investments and properties
(c) Issue of long-term debt   (g) Dividends
(d) Collection of accounts receivable   (h) Repayment of long-term debt

Determine on which financial statement items appear.
(SO 4)

E1–3 Indicate on which statement—statement of earnings (SE), balance sheet (BS), statement of retained earnings (RE), or cash flow statement (CF)—you would find each of the following accounts or items:

(a) ___ Cash   (i) ___ Common shares

(b) ___ Advertising expense   (j) ___ Sales

(c) ___ Service revenue   (k) ___ Dividends

(d) ___ Inventory   (l) ___ Cash collected from customers

(e) ___ Cash paid for income tax   (m) ___ Cash received from the sale of equipment

(f) ___ Income tax expense   (n) ___ Notes payable

(g) ___ Accounts receivable   (o) ___ Equipment

(h) ___ Interest expense   (p) ___ Cash borrowed on a note payable

Use financial statement relationships to determine missing amounts.
(SO 4)

E1–4 Summaries of data from the balance sheets and statements of earnings for three corporations are presented below:

	Chiasson Corporation	Maxim Enterprises, Ltd.	K-Os Corporation
Beginning of year			
Total assets	$95,000	$125,000	$60,000
Total liabilities	80,000	(c)	25,000
Total shareholders' equity	(a)	95,000	35,000
End of year			
Total assets	160,000	180,000	(e)
Total liabilities	120,000	50,000	65,000
Total shareholders' equity	40,000	130,000	(f)
Changes in shareholders' equity during year			
Issue of shares	(b)	25,000	4,000
Dividends	24,000	(d)	30,000
Total revenues	215,000	100,000	54,000
Total expenses	175,000	85,000	40,000

Instructions

Determine the missing amounts for (a) to (f).

Classify items and prepare accounting equation.
(SO 4)

E1–5 The following items and amounts (in thousands) were taken from the January 27, 2003, balance sheet of The Forzani Group Ltd., Canada's biggest sporting goods retailer:

____ Accounts payable and accrued liabilities	$217,777
____ Accounts receivable	36,319
____ Capital assets	160,625
____ Cash	23,315
____ Goodwill and other intangibles	39,682
____ Inventory	267,221
____ Long-term debt	38,295
____ Other assets	10,105
____ Other liabilities	54,389
____ Prepaid and other expenses	11,292
____ Retained earnings	106,330
____ Share capital	131,768

Instructions

(a) Classify each item as an asset (A), liability (L), or shareholders' equity (SE) item.
(b) Determine Forzani's accounting equation by calculating the value of total assets, total liabilities, and total shareholders' equity.

E1-6 The following items and amounts (in thousands) were taken from CoolBrands International Inc.'s August 31, 2004, statement of earnings and balance sheet:

Identify financial statement components and prepare statement of earnings. (SO 4)

____	Cash and short-term		____ Receivables	$ 88,419
	investments	$ 84,700	____ Income tax expense	30,731
____	Retained earnings	123,192	____ Sales	584,951
____	Cost of goods sold	438,458	____ Income taxes payable	6,499
____	Selling, general, and		____ Accounts payable	49,384
	administrative expenses	115,131	____ Franchising revenues	4,786
____	Prepaid expenses	7,818	____ Drayage (transportation)	
____	Inventories	64,618	and other income	53,083
____	Other expenses	7,663	____ Interest expense	1,994

Instructions

(a) In each case, identify on the blank line whether the item is an asset (A), liability (L), shareholders' equity (SE), revenue (R), or expense (E) item.
(b) Prepare a statement of earnings for CoolBrands for the year ended August 31, 2004.

E1-7 This information is for Kon Inc. for the year ended December 31, 2006:

Prepare statements of earnings and retained earnings. (SO 4)

Retained earnings,		Service revenue	$58,000
January 1, 2006	$57,000	Utilities expense	2,400
Advertising expense	1,800	Salaries expense	28,000
Dividends	7,000	Income tax expense	6,000
Rent expense	10,400		

Instructions

After analyzing the data, prepare a statement of earnings and a statement of retained earnings.

E1-8 Kit Lucas is the bookkeeper for Aurora Ltd. Kit has been trying to get Aurora's balance sheet to balance. He finally managed to balance it, as shown below, and believes it to be correct but is not totally sure.

Correct incorrectly prepared balance sheet. (SO 4)

AURORA LTD.
Balance Sheet
December 31, 2006

Assets		Liabilities and Shareholders' Equity	
Cash	$18,500	Accounts payable	$16,000
Supplies	8,000	Accounts receivable	(10,000)
Equipment	40,000	Common shares	40,000
Dividends	7,000	Retained earnings	27,500
Total assets	$73,500	Total liabilities and	$73,500
		shareholders' equity	

Instructions

Prepare a correct balance sheet.

E1-9 Sea Surf Campground, Inc. is a public camping ground in Ocean National Park. It has the following financial information as at December 31, 2006:

Calculate net earnings and prepare statement of retained earnings and balance sheet. (SO 4)

Revenues—camping fees	$137,000	Dividends	$ 4,000
Revenues—general store	25,000	Notes payable	50,000
Accounts payable	11,000	Operating expenses	138,000
Cash	10,500	Supplies	2,500
Equipment	119,000	Common shares	40,000
Income tax expense	7,000	Retained earnings (Jan. 1, 2006)	18,000

Instructions

(a) Determine net earnings for the year ended December 31, 2006.
(b) Prepare a statement of retained earnings and balance sheet for the year.

Prepare cash flow statement.
(SO 4)

E1–10   This information is for Van Tran Corporation for the year ended December 31, 2006:

Cash received from customers	$65,000	Cash received from lenders	$20,000
Cash paid for new equipment	50,000	Cash paid for expenses	20,000
Cash dividends paid	6,000	Cash, January 1, 2006	12,000

Instructions

Prepare the cash flow statement for Van Tran Corporation.

Interpret financial facts.
(SO 4)

E1–11   Consider each of the following independent situations:

(a) The statement of retained earnings of Yu Corporation shows dividends of $68,000, while net earnings for the year were $75,000.
(b) The cash flow statement for Surya Corporation shows that cash provided by operating activities was $10,000; cash used by investing activities was $110,000; and cash provided by financing activities was $130,000.
(c) Naguib Ltd.'s balance sheet reports $150,000 of total liabilities and $250,000 of shareholders' equity.

Instructions

For each company, write a brief interpretation of these financial facts. For example, you might discuss the company's financial health or what seems to be its growth philosophy.

Problems: Set A

Determine forms of business organization.
(SO 2)

P1–1A   Presented below are five independent situations:

1. Three computer science professors have formed a business to sell software to reduce and control spam e-mail. Each has contributed an equal amount of cash and knowledge to the venture. While their software looks promising, they are concerned about the legal liabilities that their business might confront.
2. Joseph LeBlanc, a student looking for summer employment, has opened a bait shop in a small shed on a local fishing dock.
3. Robert Steven and Tom Cheng each owned a snow board rental business. They have decided to combine their businesses. They expect that in the coming year, they will need funds to expand their operations.
4. Darcy Becker, Ellen Sweet, and Meg Dwyer recently graduated with marketing degrees. Friends since childhood, they have decided to start a marketing consulting business.
5. Hervé Gaudet wants to rent DVD players and DVDs in airports across the country. His idea is that customers will be able to rent equipment and DVDs at one airport, watch the DVDs on their flight, and return the equipment and DVDs at their destination airport. Of course, this will require a substantial investment for equipment and DVDs, as well as employees and locations in each airport. Hervé has no savings or personal assets. He wants to maintain control over the business.

Instructions

In each case, explain what form of organization the business is likely to take: proprietorship, partnership, or corporation. Give reasons for your choice.

Identify uses and users of financial statements.
(SO 2)

P1–2A   Financial decisions often depend on one financial statement more than the others. Consider each of the following independent hypothetical situations:

1. The North Face Inc. is considering extending credit to a new customer. The terms of the credit would require the customer to pay within 30 days of receiving goods.
2. An investor is considering purchasing the common shares of Music Online, Inc. The investor plans on holding the investment for at least five years.

3. Caisse d'Économie Base Montréal is thinking about extending a loan to a small company. The company would be required to make interest payments at the end of each year for five years, and to repay the loan at the end of the fifth year.

4. The CEO of Tech Toy Limited is trying to determine whether the company is generating enough cash to increase the amount of dividends paid to investors in this, and future, years. He needs to be sure that Tech Toy will still have enough cash to buy equipment when needed.

Instructions

For each situation, state whether the individual would pay the most attention to the information provided by the statement of earnings, balance sheet, or cash flow statement. Choose only one financial statement in each case, and briefly give reasons for your choice.

P1–3A   All businesses are involved in three types of activities—operating, investing, and financing. The names and descriptions of companies in several different industries follow:

Identify business activities.
(SO 3)

Indigo Books & Music—book retailer
High Liner Foods Incorporated—processor and distributor of seafood products
Mountain Equipment Co-op—outdoor equipment retailer
Ganong Bros. Limited—maker of candy
Royal Bank—banking and financial service provider
The Gap, Inc.—casual clothing retailer

Instructions

(a) For each of the above companies, provide examples of (1) an operating activity, (2) an investing activity, and (3) a financing activity that the company likely engages in.

(b) Which of the activities that you identified in (a) are common to most businesses? Which activities are not?

P1–4A   The following accounts have been selected from the financial statements of Maple Leaf Foods Inc.:

Classify accounts.
(SO 3, 4)

	(a)	(b)
Accounts payable and accrued charges	_____	_____
Accounts receivable	_____	_____
Cash and cash equivalents	_____	_____
Common shares	_____	_____
Income and other taxes payable	_____	_____
Interest expense	_____	_____
Inventories	_____	_____
Long-term debt	_____	_____
Property and equipment	_____	_____
Sales	_____	_____

Instructions

(a) Classify each of the above accounts as an asset (A), liability (L), shareholders' equity (SE), revenue (R), or expense (E) item.

(b) Classify each of the above accounts as an operating (O), investing (I), or financing (F) activity. If you believe a particular account does not fit in any of these activities, explain why.

P1–5A   Selected information (in millions) is available for Sears Canada Inc. and Hudson's Bay Company for fiscal 2004:

Use accounting equation.
(SO 4)

	Sears	Hudson's Bay
Beginning of year		
Total assets	(i)	$4,275.7
Total liabilities	$2,414.4	(iv)
Total shareholders' equity	1,646.9	2,394.7
End of year		
Total assets	4,065.7	(v)
Total liabilities	(ii)	1,680.1
Total shareholders' equity	1,810.9	2,430.6

Changes during year in shareholders' equity		
Issue of shares	0.7	3.8
Dividends	25.6	(vi)
Total revenues	6,222.7	7,400.1
Total expenses	(iii)	7,330.8

Instructions

(a) Use the accounting equation to calculate the missing amounts for each company.
(b) At the end of fiscal 2004, which company has a higher proportion of debt financing? Of equity financing?

Prepare financial statements. (SO 4)

P1–6A   On June 1, 2006, One Planet Cosmetics Corp. was formed. Here are the assets, liabilities, and share capital of the company at June 30, and the revenues and expenses for the month of June:

Cash	$ 6,000	Service revenue	$8,000
Accounts receivable	4,000	Supplies expense	1,200
Cosmetic supplies	2,400	Gas and oil expense	900
Equipment	32,000	Advertising expense	500
Notes payable	14,000	Utilities expense	300
Accounts payable	1,375	Income tax expense	1,275
Common shares	26,200		

The company paid dividends of $1,000 in June.

Instructions

Prepare a statement of earnings, statement of retained earnings, and balance sheet for the month of June.

Prepare cash flow statement. (SO 4)

P1–7A   Presented below is selected financial information for Maison Corporation at December 31, 2006:

Cash, January 1, 2006	$ 20,000	Cash paid to purchase	
Inventory	25,000	equipment	$ 15,000
Cash paid to suppliers	100,000	Equipment	40,000
Building	200,000	Revenues	100,000
Common shares	50,000	Cash received from customers	137,000
Cash dividends paid	13,000		

Instructions

First determine which of the above items should be included in a cash flow statement. Then prepare the statement for Maison Corporation for the year ended December 31, 2006.

Use financial statement relationships to calculate missing amounts; write memo. (SO 4)

◁▦▬▭▷

◁▦▬▭▷ The **pencil icon** means that you have to write a detailed answer for an activity.

P1–8A   Here are incomplete financial statements for Baxter, Inc.:

BAXTER, INC.
Balance Sheet
November 30, 2006

Assets		Liabilities and Shareholders' Equity	
Cash	$ 5,000	Liabilities	
Accounts receivable	10,000	Notes payable	$ 69,600
Land	(ii)	Accounts payable	(iii)
Building	45,000	Total liabilities	76,500
Total assets	$ (i)	Shareholders' equity	
		Common shares	(vi)
		Retained earnings	(v)
		Total shareholders' equity	(iv)
		Total liabilities and shareholders' equity	$110,000

BAXTER, INC.
Statement of Earnings
Year Ended November 30, 2006

Revenues	$80,000
Operating expenses	(vii)
Earnings before income tax	30,000
Income tax expense	10,000
Net earnings	$ (viii)

BAXTER, INC.
Statement of Retained Earnings
Year Ended November 30, 2006

Beginning retained earnings	$12,000
Add: Net earnings	(ix)
Less: Dividends	5,000
Ending retained earnings	$ (x)

Instructions

(a) Calculate the missing amounts (i) to (x).
(b) Write a memo explaining (1) the sequence for preparing the financial statements, and (2) the interrelationships between the statement of retained earnings, statement of earnings, and balance sheet.

P1–9A   GG Corporation was formed on January 1, 2006. At December 31, 2006, Guy Géli-nas, the president and sole employee, decided to prepare a balance sheet, which appeared as follows:

Prepare corrected balance sheet. (SO 4)

GG CORPORATION
Balance Sheet
Year Ended December 31, 2006

Assets		Liabilities and Shareholders' Equity	
Cash	$ 20,000	Accounts payable	$ 40,000
Accounts receivable	55,000	Notes payable	15,000
Inventory	30,000	Boat loan payable	13,000
Boat	18,000	Shareholders' equity	55,000
	$123,000		$123,000

Guy willingly admits that he is not an accountant by training. He is concerned that his balance sheet might not be correct. He has provided you with the following additional information:

1. The boat actually belongs to Guy Gélinas, not to GG Corporation. However, because he thinks he might take customers out on the boat occasionally, he decided to list it as an asset of the corporation. To be consistent, he also listed as a liability of the corporation his personal loan that he took out at the bank to buy the boat.
2. Included in the accounts receivable balance is $10,000 that Guy Gélinas loaned to his brother two years ago. Guy included this in the receivables of GG Corporation so he would remember that his brother owes him money.

Instructions

(a) Identify any corrections that should be made to the balance sheet, and explain why.
(b) Prepare a corrected balance sheet for GG Corporation. (*Hint:* To get the balance sheet to balance, adjust shareholders' equity.)

Problems: Set B

P1–1B   Presented below are five independent situations:

1. Dawn Addington, a student looking for summer employment, has opened a vegetable stand along a busy local highway. Each morning, she buys produce from local farmers, then sells it in the afternoon as people return home from work.
2. Joseph Counsell and Sabra Surkis each own a bike shop. They have decided to combine their businesses and try to expand their operations to include skis and snowboards. They expect that in the coming year they will need funds to expand their operations.
3. Three chemistry professors have formed a business which uses bacteria to clean up toxic waste sites. Each has contributed an equal amount of cash and knowledge to the venture. The use of bacteria in this situation is experimental, and legal obligations could result.
4. Abdur Rahim has run a successful but small cooperative health and organic food store for over five years. The increased sales at his store have made him believe that the time is right to open a chain of health and organic food stores across the country. Of course, this will require a substantial investment for inventory and property, plant, and equipment, as well as for employees and other resources. Abdur has no savings or personal assets.
5. Mary Emery, Richard Goedde, and Jigme Tshering recently graduated with graduate degrees in international business. They have decided to start a consulting business aimed at helping Canadian businesses export their products internationally.

Instructions

In each case, explain what form of organization the business is likely to take: proprietorship, partnership, or corporation. Give reasons for your choice.

P1–2B   Financial decisions often depend on one financial statement more than the others. Consider each of the following independent, hypothetical situations:

1. An Ontario investor is considering purchasing the common shares of Fight Fat Ltd., which operates 13 fitness centres in the Toronto area. The investor plans on holding the investment for at least three years.
2. Comeau Ltée is considering extending credit to a new customer. The credit terms would require the customer to pay within 45 days of receipt of the goods.
3. The CEO of the Private Label Corporation is trying to determine whether the company is generating enough cash to increase the amount of dividends paid to investors in this, and future, years. He needs to ensure that there will still be enough cash to expand operations when needed.
4. The Laurentian Bank is considering extending a loan to a small company. The company would be required to make interest payments at the end of each year for five years, and to repay the loan at the end of the fifth year.

Instructions

For each situation, state whether the individual would be most interested in the statement of earnings, balance sheet, or cash flow statement. Choose only one financial statement in each case, and briefly give reasons for your choice.

P1–3B   All businesses are involved in three types of activities—operating, investing, and financing. The names and descriptions of companies in several different industries follow:

Abitibi Consolidated Inc.—manufacturer and marketer of newsprint
Wilfrid Laurier University Students' Union—university student union
Biovail Corporation—manufacturer and distributor of pharmaceutical products
Maple Leaf Sports & Entertainment Ltd.—owner of the Toronto Raptors basketball club
Grant Thornton LLP—professional accounting and business advisory firm
WestJet Airlines Ltd.—discount airline

Instructions

(a) For each of the above companies, provide examples of (1) an operating activity, (2) an investing activity, and (3) a financing activity that the company likely engages in.
(b) Which of the activities that you identified in (a) are common to most businesses? Which activities are not?

P1–4B The Mill Run Golf & Country Club details the following accounts in its financial statements:

Classify accounts.
(SO 3, 4)

	(a)	(b)
Bank overdraft	_____	_____
Capital assets	_____	_____
Income—food and beverage operations	_____	_____
Income—golf course operations	_____	_____
Inventory	_____	_____
Office and general expenses	_____	_____
Payables and accruals	_____	_____
Receivables	_____	_____
Term debt	_____	_____
Wages and benefits expense	_____	_____

Instructions

(a) Classify each of the above accounts as an asset (A), liability (L), shareholders' equity (SE), revenue (R), or expense (E) item.
(b) Classify each of the above accounts as an operating (O), investing (I), or financing (F) activity. If you believe a particular account does not fit in any of these activities, explain why.

P1–5B Selected information (in millions) is available for The Jean Coutu Group (PJC) Inc. and Shoppers Drug Mart Corporation for fiscal 2004:

Use accounting equation.
(SO 4)

	Jean Coutu	Shoppers
Beginning of year		
Total assets	$1,716.6	(iv)
Total liabilities	(i)	$1,533.6
Total shareholders' equity	1,012.9	1,597.5
End of year		
Total assets	1,837.8	(v)
Total liabilities	669.0	1,455.9
Total shareholders' equity	(ii)	(vi)
Changes during year in shareholders' equity		
Issue of shares	3.2	7.8
Dividends	(iii)	0
Total revenues	4,096.1	4,415.2
Total expenses	3,919.2	4,157.5

Instructions

(a) Use the accounting equation to calculate the missing amounts for each company.
(b) Jean Coutu's year end is May 31, 2004. Shoppers Drug Mart Corporation's year-end is January 3, 2004. If you were to compare the two companies, how would these differing year-end dates affect your assessment?

P1–6B Aero Flying School Ltd. started on May 1 with cash of $45,000 and common shares of $45,000. Here are the assets and liabilities of the company on May 31, 2006, and the revenues and expenses for the month of May, its first month of operations:

Prepare financial statements.
(SO 4)

Cash	$ 7,200	Advertising expense	$ 900
Accounts receivable	11,200	Rent expense	1,200
Equipment	60,300	Repair expense	700
Accounts payable	2,400	Fuel expense	3,400
Notes payable	27,900	Insurance expense	400
Service revenue	9,600	Income tax expense	900

Additional common shares of $1,800 were issued in May, and a cash dividend of $500 was paid.

Instructions

Prepare a statement of earnings, statement of retained earnings, and balance sheet for the month of May.

P1–7B   Presented below are selected financial statement items for Frenette Corporation at June 30, 2006:

Cash, July 1, 2005	$ 30,000	Cash dividends paid	$ 7,000
Inventory	55,000	Cash paid to buy equipment	26,000
Cash paid to suppliers	89,000	Equipment	40,000
Building	400,000	Revenues	200,000
Common shares	20,000	Cash received from customers	168,000
Cash paid for income tax	20,000		

Instructions

Determine which of the above items should be included in a cash flow statement, and then prepare the statement for Frenette Corporation for the year ended June 30, 2006.

P1–8B   Here are incomplete financial statements for Wu, Inc.:

WU, INC.
Balance Sheet
August 31, 2006

Assets		Liabilities and Shareholders' Equity	
Cash	$ (ii)	Liabilities	
Accounts receivable	20,000	Accounts payable	$15,000
Land	15,000	Shareholders' equity	
Building and equipment	40,000	Common shares	(iv)
Total assets	$ (i)	Retained earnings	(iii)
		Total liabilities and shareholders' equity	$85,000

WU, INC.
Statement of Earnings
Year Ended August 31, 2006

Service revenue	$75,000
Operating expenses	(v)
Earnings before income tax	30,000
Income tax expense	9,000
Net earnings	$ (vi)

WU, INC.
Statement of Retained Earnings
Year Ended August 31, 2006

Beginning retained earnings	$10,000
Add: Net earnings	(vii)
Less: Dividends	(viii)
Ending retained earnings	$26,000

Instructions

(a) Calculate the missing amounts (i) to (viii).
(b) Write a memo explaining (1) the sequence for preparing and presenting the financial statements, and (2) the interrelationships between the various financial statements.

P1–9B   Pam Bollinger formed the Kettle Corporation late in 2005. The company's year end is December 31. At the end of the following year, December 31, 2006, Pam prepared a statement of earnings by looking at the financial statements of other companies. Pam found it easy to prepare the statements for 2005 since it was for such a short period of time, but she found the 2006 statement much harder to prepare. She thinks she did a reasonable job but has asked you for advice. Pam's 2006 statement of earnings is as follows:

KETTLE CORPORATION
Statement of Earnings
December 31, 2006

Accounts receivable	$12,000
Service revenue	60,000
Total revenues	72,000
Rent expense	13,200
Insurance expense	5,000
Vacation expense	2,000
Total expenses	20,200
Net earnings	$51,800

Pam has also provided you with these facts:

1. Included in the revenue account is $7,000 of revenue that the company earned and received payment for in 2005. Pam forgot to include it in the 2005 statement of earnings, so she put it in this year's statement.
2. Income tax expense for Kettle Corporation for the year ended December 31, 2006, was determined to be $12,000. However, the income tax payment is not due until March 31, 2007, so Pam decided not to record the income tax expense yet.
3. Pam operates her business out of the basement of her parents' home. They do not charge her anything, but she thinks that if she paid rent it would cost her about $13,200 per year. She therefore included $13,200 of rent expense in the statement.
4. To reward herself for a year of hard work, Pam went skiing for a week at Whistler. She did not use company funds to pay for the trip, but she reported it as an expense on the statement of earnings, since it was her job that made her need the vacation.

Instructions

(a) Comment on any corrections that are needed for the four items above.
(b) Prepare a corrected statement of earnings for Kettle Corporation.

BROADENING YOUR PERSPECTIVE

Financial Reporting and Analysis

www.wiley.com/canada/kimmel

Analysis Tools

Financial Reporting Problem: *Loblaw*

BYP1–1 Actual financial statements (rather than the simplified financial statements presented in the chapter) for Loblaw are presented in Appendix A at the end of this book.

Instructions

(a) What are the dates of Loblaw's 2003 and 2002 fiscal year ends? Why do these dates differ?
(b) What were Loblaw's total assets at the end of fiscal 2003? At the end of 2002?
(c) What proportion of its assets does Loblaw finance with debt? With equity? Did this proportion change a lot between 2002 and 2003?
(d) How much cash did Loblaw generate from operating activities in fiscal 2003? In 2002? Was this amount enough to cover Loblaw's investing activities in either year? (Note that Loblaw presents the operating activities section of its cash flow statement differently than how this section was presented in the chapter. We will learn more about this in Chapter 13.)
(e) What were Loblaw's sales in 2003? In 2002? By what percentage did Loblaw's sales increase in 2003?
(f) Did Loblaw's net earnings change by roughly the same percentage as sales? If not, identify the main reason for the difference.

Comparative Analysis Problem: *Loblaw and Sobeys*

BYP1–2 The financial statements for Sobeys are presented in Appendix B, following the financial statements for Loblaw in Appendix A.

Instructions

(a) Based on the information in these financial statements, determine the following for each company:
   1. Loblaw's total assets, liabilities, and shareholders' equity at January 3, 2004, and Sobeys' total assets, liabilities, and shareholders' equity at May 1, 2004.
   2. Loblaw's and Sobeys' sales and net earnings for the most recent fiscal year.
   3. Loblaw's and Sobeys' increase or decrease in cash for the most recent fiscal year.
(b) What conclusions about the two companies can you draw from these data?

Research Case

BYP1–3 The April 1, 2002, issue of *Canadian Business* includes an article by John Grey entitled "Hide and Seek" (vol. 75, no. 6, p. 28). The article discusses how accounting tricks make it difficult for investors to get a true picture of a company's finances.

Instructions

Read the article and answer the following questions:

(a) John Grey discusses ten red flags that investors should look for to ensure that the statement of earnings reflects the company's bottom line. Name the ten red flags.
(b) Should a shareholder read the notes to the financial statements? Explain why or why not.
(c) Name a Canadian company that was involved in a corporate scandal.

Interpreting Financial Statements

BYP1–4 Gildan Activewear Inc., headquartered in Montreal, makes T-shirts, sweatshirts, and golf shirts for private label use. The company reports the following selected information (in U.S. thousands) for the years ended October 3, 2004, and October 5, 2003:

	2004	2003
Statement of earnings		
Sales	$533,368	$431,195
Cost of sales	378,696	301,341
Net earnings	60,251	53,156
Statement of retained earnings		
Dividends	0	0
Ending retained earnings	222,496	162,244
Balance sheet		
Total assets	489,004	429,663
Total liabilities	161,409	165,460
Total shareholders' equity	327,595	264,203
Cash flow statement		
Cash flows from operating activities	58,920	63,721
Cash flows from (used in) financing activities	(14,350)	411
Cash flows used in investing activities	(53,820)	(39,458)
Cash and cash equivalents, end of year	60,671	69,340

Instructions

(a) Why do you think a Canadian company such as Gildan Activewear would present its financial statements in U.S. dollars rather than Canadian dollars?
(b) Did the company's sales improve faster or slower than its net earnings? What do you think is the main reason for this?
(c) Why, in your opinion, did Gildan Activewear not pay a dividend to its shareholders in fiscal 2004 or 2003?
(d) What proportion of the company's assets is financed by debt in each fiscal year? By equity? Does this change represent an improvement or a deterioration for the company?

(e) Why, in your opinion, did the company's cash decline by U.S. $8,669 million in fiscal 2004?

(f) Why do you think net earnings increased in fiscal 2004 but cash decreased?

A Global Focus

BYP1–5   Zachary Wall is thinking about expanding the product offerings in his local store. He would like to include automobile tires. In deciding which product lines to carry, Zachary knows that it is important to consider many factors, including quality, performance rating, price, and warranty. However, he is also interested in investigating the financial health of the tire manufacturers and has obtained recent financial statements for The Goodyear Tire & Rubber Company ("Goodyear") and Compagnie Générale des Etablissements Michelin ("Michelin").

As it turns out, however, Zachary soon discovers that he is having trouble comparing the two companies' financial results. Goodyear's results are reported in US dollars and use US accounting practices. Michelin's headquarters are located in Clermont-Ferrand, France, and its financial statements use Euro dollars ("Euros") as the reporting currency. In addition, Michelin used to prepare its financial statements in accordance with French accounting practices. It was only in 2005 that certain things changed and the company was then required to follow International Financial Reporting Standards (IFRS). Zachary is confused: "I had no idea that there were so many sets of accounting practices - or languages of business!! How can this be useful to people outside the company?"

Instructions

(a) Who are the external users of accounting information?

(b) Will Zachary be able to find the information he needs about the quality, performance rating, price, and warranty in the financial statements? If not, where might he find such information?

(c) Zachary notes that Michelin explains that there are different alternatives for classifying expenses under IFRS. What are expenses and what are some examples?

(d) Zachary understands that the purpose of accounting is to provide information for decision-making. He understands that currencies change from country to country (e.g., Canadian dollars, US dollars, Euros, etc.) but he would like to know whether you think that basic decision-making changes from country-to-country. In other words, he wants to know if you think there should be different accounting practices for Goodyear, which is based in the United States, and for Michelin, which is based in France.

Financial Analysis on the Web

BYP1–6   When making decisions, no financial decision-maker should ever rely solely on the financial information reported in a company's annual report. It is important to keep abreast of financial news. This activity shows you how to search for financial news about Loblaw and Sobeys using Yahoo! Canada Finance.

Analysis Tools
(Financial Analysis on the Web)

Instructions

Specific requirements of this Web case can be found on the Toolkit website.

Critical Thinking

Collaborative Learning Activity

BYP1–7   In a recent cash flow statement, the Made-in-Canada Corporation reported a $3-million decrease in cash from its operating activities. It also reported increases in cash from investing and financing activities of $2 million and $1 million, respectively. The largest source of cash from investing activities was from the discontinuation and sale of one of the company's production facilities. The largest source of cash from financing activities was from bank borrowings. Overall, the change in cash for the year was nil, resulting in an ending cash balance of $250,000. Except for this year when the cash balance remained unchanged, cash has declined in each of the past five years.

While management believes that there are sufficient financing options to fund the company's ongoing operations and repay its obligations, the auditors have indicated concerns about the financial position and future viability of the company because of the continually declining cash position.

Instructions

With the class divided into groups, answer the following questions:

(a) If you were a creditor of Made-in-Canada, what reaction might you have to the above information?
(b) If you were an investor in Made-in-Canada, what reaction might you have to the above information?
(c) If you were evaluating the company as either a creditor or an investor, what other information would you be interested in seeing?

Communication Activity

BYP1–8   You are presented with the following information for two companies:

	Company A	Company B
Cash provided (used) by operating activities	$100	($90)
Cash provided (used) by financing activities	(30)	160
Cash used by investing activities	(10)	(10)
Net increase in cash	60	60
Cash, beginning of period	15	15
Cash, end of period	75	75

Instructions

(a) What is the main purpose of the cash flow statement?
(b) What are operating activities, financing activities, and investing activities?
(c) Which company is in better shape and why?

Ethics Case

www.wiley.com/canada/kimmel

Ethics In Accounting

BYP1–9   Chief executive officers (CEOs) and chief financial officers (CFOs) of publicly traded companies are required to personally certify that their companies' financial statements and other financial information contain no untrue statements and do not leave out any important facts. The certification requirement was introduced after numerous corporate scandals as a way to hold top executives personally responsible for the integrity of their company's financial information.

Khan Corporation just hired a new management team, and its members say they are too new to the company to know whether the most recent financial reports are accurate or not. They refuse to sign the certification.

Instructions

(a) Who are the stakeholders in this situation?
(b) Should the CEO and CFO sign the certification? Explain why or why not.
(c) What are the CEO's and CFO's alternatives?

Serial Problem

This **serial problem** starts in this chapter and continues in each chapter of the book.

BYP1–10 Natalie Koebel spent much of her childhood learning the art of cookie-making from her grandmother. They passed many happy hours mastering every type of cookie imaginable and later devised new recipes that were both healthy and delicious. Now at the start of her second year in college, Natalie is investigating various possibilities for starting her own business as part of the requirements of the Entrepreneurship program she is taking.

A long-time friend insists that Natalie has to somehow include cookies in her business plan and, after a series of brainstorming sessions, Natalie settles on the idea of operating a cookie-making school. She will start on a part-time basis and offer her services in people's homes. Now that she has started thinking about it, the possibilities seem endless. During the fall, she will concentrate on Christmas cookies. She will offer group sessions (which will probably be more entertainment than education for the participants) and individual lessons. Natalie also decides to include children in her target market. The first difficult decision is coming up with the perfect name for her business. In the end she settles on "Cookie Creations," and she then moves on to more important issues.

Instructions

(a) What form of business organization—proprietorship, partnership, or corporation—do you recommend that Natalie use for her business? Discuss the benefits and weaknesses of each form that Natalie might consider and give your reasons for choosing the form of business organization you are recommending.

(b) Will Natalie need accounting information? If yes, what information will she need and why? How often will she need this information?

(c) Identify specific asset, liability, and equity accounts that Cookie Creations will likely use to record its business transactions.

(d) Should Natalie open a separate bank account for the business? Why or why not?

(e) Natalie expects she will have to use her car to drive to people's homes and to pick up supplies, but she also needs to use her car for personal reasons. She recalls from her first-year accounting course something about keeping business and personal assets separate. She wonders what she should do for accounting purposes. What do you recommend?

Answers to Self-Study Questions

1. b   2. d   3. b   4. d   5. d   6. c   7. c   8. d   9. c   10. a

Answer to Loblaw Review It Question 2

Loblaw's accounting equation as at January 3, 2004, is (in millions):

$$\text{Assets} = \text{Liabilities} + \text{Shareholders' Equity}$$
$$\$12{,}177 = \$7{,}445 + \$4{,}732$$

Remember to go back to the Navigator box at the beginning of the chapter to check off your completed work.

CHAPTER 2

A Further Look at Financial Statements

Getting the Numbers Right

Many investors rely on financial statements in order to make informed decisions on when to buy and sell a company's shares.

Financial statements should provide relevant and reliable information. However, this has not always been the case. The recent accounting scandals that collapsed U.S. companies Enron and WorldCom shook investor confidence worldwide. And investors in Canadian companies have had their own cause for concern with several organizations having to restate their financials.

The most high-profile case in Canada involved Brampton, Ontario-based Nortel Networks Corporation. In January 2005, Nortel released revised financial statements for 2003, 2002, and 2001. Its net earnings for 2003 were U.S. $434 million or 10 cents a share, instead of the previously reported U.S. $732 million or 17 cents a share. Nortel also reported restated losses of 78 cents a share for 2002 and $8.08 a share for 2001.

The original results for 2003 indicated the first profitable year in seven, triggering a jump in share price and increased investor confidence. However, in March 2004, Nortel revealed that there had been accounting irregularities, with profits overstated by up to 50 percent. Nortel's chief executive officer and nine senior financial officers were soon fired "with cause," and the share price began to decline.

The restatement process that followed took nine months and cost more than $100 million. Nortel's board of directors has since committed itself to rebuilding a finance environment based on principles of transparency and integrity, and ensuring sound financial reporting and comprehensive disclosure.

Still, the company's problems are not over. Its audit committee continues to investigate the "facts and circumstances" that led to the accounting irregularities, as well as another $3.2 billion in overstated sales during 1999 and 2000. Meanwhile, Nortel is fighting several shareholders' lawsuits, and the RCMP is investigating its financial accounting situation, as are regulators in both Canada and the United States.

And—as if Nortel did not have enough problems—the focus on numbers has diverted attention away from the product. According to industry analysts, Nortel lags in product development, running 6 to 12 months behind on upgrades. This, plus the company's tarnished image resulting from its accounting problems, could affect future business.

It may take years for Nortel to regain investor confidence in its numbers—all the more reason for companies to get them right the first time round.

Nortel Networks Corporation: www.nortelnetworks.com

THE NAVIGATOR

☐ Read *Feature Story*

☐ Scan *Study Objectives*

☐ Read *Chapter Preview*

☐ Read text and answer *Before You Go On*

☐ Work *Using the Decision Toolkit*

☐ Review *Summary of Study Objectives*

☐ Review the *Decision Toolkit—A Summary*

☐ Work *Demonstration Problem*

☐ Answer *Self-Study Questions*

☐ Complete assignments

STUDY OBJECTIVES

After studying this chapter, you should be able to:

1. Describe the objective of financial reporting and apply the qualitative characteristics of accounting information to the elements of financial statements.

2. Identify and apply assumptions, principles, and constraints.

3. Identify the sections of a classified balance sheet.

4. Identify and calculate ratios for analyzing a company's profitability.

5. Identify and calculate ratios for analyzing a company's liquidity and solvency.

the navigator

If you are thinking of purchasing a company's shares, how can you decide what the shares are worth? If you own shares, how can you determine whether it is time to buy more or time to bail out? Your decision will be influenced by a variety of considerations, and one of these should be your careful analysis of the company's financial statements.

In this chapter, we begin by looking at the conceptual framework of accounting, which provides a general guide for financial reporting. We then take a closer look at the balance sheet and introduce some useful ways of evaluating the information provided by the financial statements. The chapter is organized as follows:

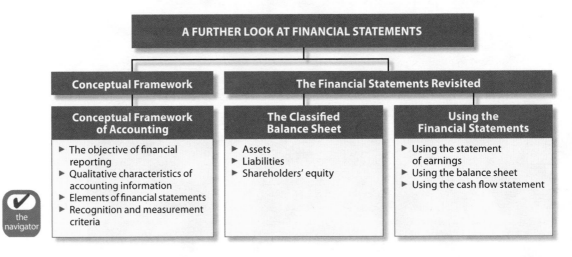

SECTION 1 ▶ CONCEPTUAL FRAMEWORK

The Financial Accounting Standards Board describes a conceptual framework as being like a constitution. It is a "…a coherent system of interrelated objectives and fundamentals that can lead to consistent standards and that prescribes the nature, function, and limits of financial accounting statements."

Conceptual Framework of Accounting

study objective 1

Describe the objective of financial reporting and apply the qualitative characteristics of accounting information to the elements of financial statements.

The **conceptual framework of accounting** guides the choice of what to present in financial statements, decisions about alternative ways of reporting economic events, and the selection of appropriate ways of communicating this information. The framework has four main sections:

1. The objective of financial reporting
2. The qualitative characteristics of accounting information
3. The elements of financial statements
4. Recognition and measurement criteria (assumptions, principles, and constraints)

The Objective of Financial Reporting

To find out the objective of financial reporting, such basic questions as these have to be answered: Who uses financial statements? Why? What information do the users need? When the answers are found, they add up to this: **the main objective of financial reporting is to provide useful information for decision-making**.

More specifically, the conceptual framework states that the objective of financial statements is to communicate information that is useful to investors, creditors, and other users when they are making investment and lending decisions and assessing management's performance. Remember that we learned in Chapter 1 that investors and creditors are the main external users of financial information.

Qualitative Characteristics of Accounting Information

To be useful for decision-making, information should have these qualitative characteristics: **understandability**, **relevance**, **reliability**, and **comparability**.

Understandability

In order for information in financial statements to be useful, all users have to be able to understand it. Financial statements cannot realistically satisfy the varied needs of all users, however. Consequently, the objective of financial reporting focuses mostly on the information needs of investors and creditors. Even within these two groups, users vary widely in the types of decisions they make and in their level of interest in the information. At one extreme is a sophisticated creditor who carefully scrutinizes all aspects of the financial information. At the other extreme is an unsophisticated investor who may only scan the text and not study the numbers.

It is therefore necessary to agree on a base level of understandability that will help both the preparer of financial information and its users. That base level is this: **the average user is assumed to have a reasonable understanding of accounting concepts and procedures, as well as of general business and economic conditions**. If this level of understanding and ability does not exist, the user is expected to rely on professionals with an appropriate level of expertise. With your study of this course, you are well on your way to becoming this average user!

Relevance

Accounting information has relevance if it will make a difference in a decision. Relevant information has predictive value or feedback value, or both. **Predictive value** helps users forecast future events. For example, when Nortel issued its restated financial statements, the information in them is considered relevant because it (hopefully) now provides a solid basis for predicting future earnings. Nortel's originally issued financial statements obviously lacked predictive value. As mentioned in the feature story, many investors are now suing Nortel because they made decisions based on these incorrect financial statements.

Feedback value confirms or corrects prior expectations. When Nortel issues financial statements, it also confirms or corrects expectations about its financial health. For accounting information to be relevant, it must also be **timely**. It must be available to decision-makers when it can still influence decisions. Nortel failed miserably on this count, releasing its December 31, 2003, financial results on January 11, 2005!

Reliability

Reliability of information means that the information can be depended on. To be reliable, accounting information must be **verifiable**—we must be able to prove that it has no errors and bias. This was obviously not the case with Nortel—which is why there was a massive investigation and restatement.

The information must also be a **faithful representation** of the economic substance, not just the legal form, of the transaction. That is, accounting information must represent what really exists or happened. To ensure reliability, external professional accountants audit financial statements. The Canadian Public Accountability Board further bolsters reliability by providing independent oversight of the auditors of public companies.

Accounting information must also be **neutral**. It cannot be selected, prepared, or presented to favour one set of interested users over another. Many accountants refer to information which is verifiable, faithfully represented, and neutral as **objective** information. This basically means that two or more people reviewing the same information would reach the same results or similar conclusions.

In situations of uncertainty, **neutrality** is affected by the use of conservatism. **Conservatism** in accounting means that when it is preparing its financial statements, a company should choose the accounting method that will be least likely to overstate assets and earnings. It does not mean, however, that a company should intentionally understate its assets or earnings.

Comparability

Imagine that you and a friend kept track of your height each year as you were growing up. If you measured your height in metres and your friend measured hers in feet, it would be difficult to compare your heights. A conversion would be necessary. In accounting, **comparability** results when companies with similar circumstances use the same accounting principles (we will learn more about accounting principles later in this chapter). This does not always happen, however, and converting the accounting numbers of companies that use different principles is not as easy as converting your height from metres to feet.

Users of accounting information also want to be able to compare a company's financial results over time. For example, to compare a company's net earnings over several years, you would need to know that the same accounting principles have been used from year to year; otherwise, you might be comparing apples to oranges. **Consistency** means that a company uses the same principles from year to year. When a company's financial information is reported on a consistent basis, the financial statements permit a meaningful analysis of trends within the company.

Elements of Financial Statements

An important part of the conceptual framework is a set of definitions that describe the basic terms used in accounting. This set of definitions is referred to as the **elements of financial statements**. They include such terms as *assets*, *liabilities*, *equity*, *revenues*, and *expenses*.

Because these elements are so important, they must be precisely defined and universally applied. We learned a few definitions in Chapter 1. We will review and expand on these definitions later in this chapter.

BEFORE YOU GO ON . . .

▶ Review It

1. What is the basic objective of financial information?
2. What qualitative characteristics make accounting information useful?

Recognition and Measurement Criteria

study objective 2

Identify and apply assumptions, principles, and constraints.

The objective of financial reporting, the qualitative characteristics of accounting information, and the elements of financial statements are very broad. Because accountants must solve practical problems, they need more detailed criteria to help them decide when items should be included in the financial statements and how they should be measured. We classify these recognition and measurement criteria as assumptions, principles, and constraints.

Illustration 2-1 outlines these recognition and measurement criteria. They are discussed in more detail in the following sections.

Illustration 2-1 ▶

Recognition and measurement criteria

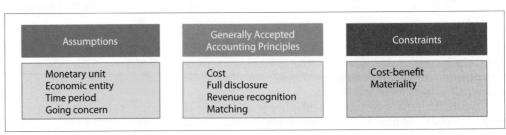

Assumptions	Generally Accepted Accounting Principles	Constraints
Monetary unit Economic entity Time period Going concern	Cost Full disclosure Revenue recognition Matching	Cost-benefit Materiality

Assumptions

Four assumptions guide when to recognize (to include) and how to measure economic events: the **monetary unit**, **economic entity**, **time period**, and **going concern** assumptions.

Monetary Unit Assumption. The **monetary unit assumption** requires that only those things that can be expressed in money be included in the accounting records. This might seem so obvious that it does not need to be mentioned, but it has important implications for financial reporting. Because the exchange of money is fundamental to business transactions, it makes sense that we measure a business in terms of money. However, it also means that some important information needed by investors and creditors is not reported in the financial statements. For example, customer satisfaction is important to every business, but it is not easily quantified in dollars; it is therefore not reported in the financial statements.

An important counterpart to the monetary unit assumption is the **assumption that the monetary unit remains stable over time**. That is, the effects of inflation (or deflation) are assumed to be minor and are therefore ignored.

Economic Entity Assumption. The **economic entity assumption** states that every economic entity must be separately identified and accounted for. Suppose you are one of Loblaw's shareholders. The amount of cash you have in your personal bank account and the balance owed on your personal car loan are not reported in Loblaw's balance sheet. This is because, for accounting purposes, you and Loblaw are separate accounting entities.

In addition, as we learned from the Chapter 1 feature story, Loblaw Companies Limited is made up of many different related companies—Loblaws, Atlantic Superstore, Provigo, Zehrs, and so on. Although the financial results of these companies have been consolidated (combined) for reporting purposes, individual accounting records and financial statements are also produced for each specific company. In order to accurately assess the performance and financial position of each company, it has to be possible to distinguish each company's activities from the transactions of any other company, related or not.

Time Period Assumption. The **time period assumption** states that the life of a business can be divided into artificial time periods and that useful reports covering those periods can be prepared for the business. All companies report at least annually. Publicly-traded companies also report to shareholders every three months (quarterly) and prepare monthly statements for internal purposes. This is known as **interim** financial reporting, which is essential for timely and relevant decision-making.

Going Concern Assumption. The **going concern assumption** states that the business will remain in operation for the foreseeable future. Of course businesses do fail, but in general, it is reasonable to assume that a business will continue operating. The going concern assumption is behind much of what we do in accounting, including the cost principle, which we will learn about in the next section. If going concern is not assumed, assets should be stated at their liquidation value (selling price less cost of disposal), not at their cost. The going concern assumption is only inappropriate when it is likely that the business will be liquidated.

Canadian Accounting Principles

Generally accepted accounting principles (GAAP) are a recognized set of principles used in financial reporting. These principles are established by the Accounting Standards Board (AcSB), an independent standard-setting body created by the Canadian Institute of Chartered Accountants. The Accounting Standards Oversight Council, with representation from business, finance, government, academe, the accounting and legal professions, and regulators, oversees the activities of the AcSB and provides input.

"Generally accepted" means that these principles have a lot of authoritative support through the Canadian and provincial business corporations acts and securities legislation. All companies whose shares or debt are publicly traded must follow GAAP. Most other companies also follow GAAP as it provides the most useful information.

While there are many accounting principles, there are four key ones that we will introduce in this text. We will learn about the **cost principle** and **full disclosure** principle in this chapter, and the **revenue recognition principle** and **matching principle** in Chapter 4.

Cost Principle.   The **cost principle** dictates that assets be recorded at their cost. This is true not only at the time an asset is purchased, but also over the time an asset is held. For example, if a company were to purchase land for $30 million, it would first be reported on the balance sheet at $30 million. But what would the company do if by the end of the next year the land had increased in value to $40 million? The answer is that under the cost principle the land would still be reported at $30 million. The land will continue to be reported at cost until either it is sold or the **going concern assumption** is no longer valid.

The cost principle is often criticized as being irrelevant. Critics say that market value would be more useful to financial decision-makers. Supporters of the cost principle counter that cost is the best measure because it is more reliable (that is, it can be easily verified). Market value, they say, is more subjective.

Full Disclosure Principle.   Some important financial information is not easily reported in the financial statements. For example, as we learned in the feature story, irate investors have filed numerous lawsuits against Nortel. Even though it is too early to tell whether these lawsuits will or will not result in losses to the company, investors and creditors need to know about this.

The **full disclosure principle** requires that all circumstances and events which would make a difference to financial statement users be disclosed. If an important item cannot be reported directly in one of the four financial statements in a reasonable way, then it should be discussed in the notes that go with the statements.

International Accounting Principles

In a global economy, many investment and credit decisions are based on an analysis of foreign financial statements. For example, one of Nortel's competitors is Alcatel in France. Unfortunately, investors interested in investing in one of these two companies find comparing their financial statements challenging. Accounting principles can differ from country to country. This lack of uniformity results from differences in legal systems, in processes for developing accounting principles, in government requirements, and in economic environments.

Until recently, the Accounting Standards Board (AcSB) had been trying to harmonize Canadian GAAP with that of both the U.S. and international GAAP. This was difficult to do, however, because international GAAP are principles-based, similar to Canadian GAAP, while U.S. GAAP are more rules-based. U.S. GAAP is based on rigid and cumbersome rules that are costly to implement, in addition to allowing loopholes that many believe leave the system open to abuse.

International GAAP, known as International Financial Reporting Standards (IFRS), are based on principles, not rules. That makes it easier to adapt to Canadian circumstances and Canadian companies. IFRS are also simpler to understand than U.S. GAAP, more flexible, and thus able to be more representative of a company's true financial condition. "When questioning whether we should be aligning ourselves closer to U.S. GAAP or to international standards, it soon became evident that the vast majority of our companies and their investors have no little or no interest in U.S. GAAP," Paul Cherry, the chair of the AcSB, said.

Consequently, the AcSB proposed that public companies adopt IFRS by 2010. Under this proposal, there will no longer be a unique set of Canadian GAAP for publicly-traded companies. Instead, adoption of the IFRS will unify global standard-setting and make it easier for multinational companies to fulfill reporting requirements.

Publicly-traded companies in Australia, Russia, and the European Union adopted the IFRS in 2005 to harmonize differing accounting principles with one international standard. IFRS are used now used as the primary basis for financial reporting in more than 90 industrialized countries, with the notable exception of the United States. Swiss pharmaceutical giant Roche, which operates in more than 100 countries, estimates that it will be able to save $100 million annually now that it can produce one set of financial statements rather than multiple sets of financial statements using different accounting principles.

The proposal sets forth different approaches for public companies, private companies, and not-for-profit organizations. This is based on the realization that one size does not necessarily fit all when it comes to standard-setting.

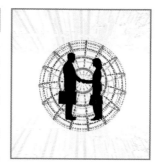

Constraints in Accounting

The goal of the qualitative characteristics we discussed earlier in this chapter is to provide users of financial statements with the most useful information for decision-making. If they are followed too rigidly, however, these characteristics can make the pursuit of useful financial information far too costly for a company. Some constraints have therefore been agreed upon to ensure that accounting principles are applied in a reasonable fashion, from the perspectives of both the company and the user. **Constraints** permit a company to make changes to generally accepted accounting principles as long as the reported information is still useful. Two constraints are cost-benefit and materiality.

Cost-Benefit. The **cost-benefit** constraint ensures that the value of the information is greater than the cost of providing it. Accountants could record or disclose every financial event that occurs and every contingency that exists. However, providing additional information increases costs, and the benefits of providing this information, in some cases, may be less than the costs.

Materiality. **Materiality** relates to a financial statement item's impact on a company's overall financial condition and operations. An item is **material** when it is likely to influence the decision of an investor or creditor. It is **immaterial** if including it will have no impact on a decision-maker. In short, if the item does not make a difference in decision-making, GAAP does not have to be followed. Determining if an item is material is a difficult decision; professional judgement has to be used and one has to understand the relative amount and importance of the item in each particular circumstance.

BEFORE YOU GO ON . . .

▶Review It

1. Describe the monetary unit, time period, economic entity, and going concern assumptions.
2. Describe the cost and full disclosure principles.
3. What are the cost-benefit and materiality constraints?

the navigator

SECTION 2 ▶ THE FINANCIAL STATEMENTS REVISITED

In Chapter 1, we introduced the four financial statements. In this section, we review the financial statements and present useful tools for evaluating them. We begin by introducing the classified balance sheet.

The Classified Balance Sheet

study objective 3

Identify the sections of a classified balance sheet.

The balance sheet presents a snapshot of a company's financial position at a point in time. To improve users' understanding of a company's financial position, companies group similar assets and similar liabilities together. This is useful because it tells the user that items in a group have similar economic characteristics. A **classified balance sheet** generally contains the standard classifications listed in Illustration 2-2.

Illustration 2-2 ▶

Standard balance sheet classifications

Assets	Liabilities and Shareholders' Equity
Current assets	Current liabilities
Long-term investments	Long-term liabilities
Property, plant, and equipment	Shareholders' equity
Intangible assets	Share capital
	Retained earnings

These groupings or classifications help readers determine such things as (1) whether the company has enough assets to pay its debts as they come due and (2) the claims of short- and long-term creditors on the company's total assets. These classifications can be seen in the balance sheet of Frenette Corporation shown in Illustration 2-3. Each grouping is explained next.

Illustration 2-3 ▶

Classified balance sheet

FRENETTE CORPORATION
Balance Sheet
October 31, 2006

Assets

Current assets			
Cash		$6,600	
Short-term investments		2,000	
Accounts receivable		7,000	
Inventories		4,000	
Supplies		2,100	
Prepaid insurance		400	
Total current assets			$ 22,100
Long-term investments			
Equity investment		$5,200	
Debt investment		2,000	
Total long-term investments			7,200
Property, plant, and equipment			
Land		$40,000	
Buildings	$75,000		
Less: Accumulated amortization	15,000	60,000	
Office equipment	$24,000		
Less: Accumulated amortization	5,000	19,000	
Total property, plant, and equipment			119,000
Intangible assets			
Goodwill			3,100
Total assets			$151,400

Liabilities and Shareholders' Equity		
Current liabilities		
Notes payable	$11,000	
Accounts payable	2,100	
Salaries payable	1,600	
Unearned revenue	900	
Interest payable	450	
Current portion of mortgage payable	1,000	
Total current liabilities		$ 17,050
Long-term liabilities		
Mortgage payable	$9,000	
Notes payable	1,300	
Total long-term liabilities		10,300
Total liabilities		27,350
Shareholders' equity		
Common shares	$74,000	
Retained earnings	50,050	
Total shareholders' equity		124,050
Total liabilities and shareholders' equity		$151,400

Assets

Assets are the resources that a company owns and that will provide future economic benefits. They include assets whose benefits will be realized within one year (current assets) and assets whose benefits will be realized over more than one year (noncurrent assets). Noncurrent assets are normally further grouped into long-term investments; property, plant, and equipment; and intangible assets. A company may also report other assets on its balance sheet, such as noncurrent receivables, future income tax assets, and property held for sale. These are usually separately reported so that users can get a better idea of their nature.

Current Assets

Current assets are assets that are expected to be converted into cash or used up by the business within one year of the balance sheet date. For example, accounts receivable are current assets because they will be converted to cash as the amounts are collected throughout the year. Supplies are a current asset because we expect that these will be used up by the business within the year.

Common types of current assets are (1) cash, including cash equivalents or near cash items such as treasury bills and money-market funds; (2) short-term investments; such as debt or equity securities; (3) receivables, such as notes receivable, accounts receivable, and interest receivable; (4) inventories; (5) supplies; and (6) prepaid expenses, such as rent and insurance. On the balance sheet, these items are listed in the order in which they are expected to be converted into cash—that is, in their order of liquidity. This arrangement is shown in Illustration 2-4 for Canada Post.

CANADA POST
Balance Sheet (partial)
December 31, 2004
(in millions)

CANADA POST   POSTES CANADA

From anywhere... to anyone

Current assets	
Cash and cash equivalents	$ 497
Short-term investments	60
Segregated cash and investments	25
Accounts receivable	477
Income tax recoverable	105
Prepaid expenses	81
Current portion of future income tax assets	42
Total current assets	1,287

Illustration 2-4 ◀

Current assets section

A company's current assets are important in assessing its liquidity—its short-term debt-paying ability—as is explained later in the chapter.

Long-Term Investments

Alternative Terminology
Long-term investments are often just referred to as *investments*.

Long-term investments are generally investments in debt (e.g., bonds) and equity (e.g., shares) of other corporations that are normally held for many years. They also include investments in property, plant, and equipment that are not currently being used in the company's operating activities. In Illustration 2-3, Frenette Corporation reported total long-term investments of $7,200 on its balance sheet. Empire Company's investments appear in the partial balance sheet in Illustration 2-5:

Illustration 2-5 ▶

Long-term investments section

EMPIRE COMPANY LIMITED
Balance Sheet (partial)
April 30, 2004
(in millions)

Investments	
Investments, at cost (quoted market value $312.6)	$278.9
Investments, at equity (realizable value $92.4)	60.8
	339.7

Property, Plant, and Equipment

Alternative Terminology
Property, plant, and equipment are sometimes called *capital assets* or *fixed assets*.

Property, plant, and equipment are assets with relatively long useful lives that are currently being used in operating the business. This category includes land, buildings, equipment, and furniture. In Illustration 2-3, Frenette Corporation reported property, plant, and equipment of $119,000.

Although the order of property, plant, and equipment items can vary among companies, these items are normally listed in the balance sheet in order of permanency. That is, land is usually listed first as it has an indefinite life, and is followed by the asset with the next longest useful life, normally buildings, and so on.

These long-lived assets, except land, have estimated useful lives over which they are expected to generate revenues. Because property, plant, and equipment benefit future periods, their cost is matched to revenues over their estimated useful life through a process called **amortization**. This is considered better than simply expensing (recording as an expense) the full purchase price of the asset and matching the cost to revenues that were generated only in the year of acquisition. Land also generates revenue, but its estimated useful life is considered to be infinite as land does not usually wear out or lose its value. Consequently, the cost of land is never amortized.

Alternative Terminology
Amortization is also commonly known as *depreciation*.

Assets that are amortized should be reported on the balance sheet at cost less the accumulated amortization. Accumulated amortization shows the amount of amortization taken so far over the *life of the asset*. It is a contra asset; that is, its balance is subtracted from the balance of the asset it relates to. The difference between cost and accumulated amortization is referred to as **net book value**. In Illustration 2-3, Frenette Corporation reported its buildings at a net book value of $60,000 and its office equipment at a net book value of $19,000.

The Forzani Group Ltd. details its property, plant, and equipment—which it calls capital assets—as shown in Illustration 2-6. Note that, except for land, all other capital assets are amortized. This includes leasehold improvements, which are long-lived additions or renovations made to leased property.

Illustration 2-6 ◀

Property, plant, and
equipment section

THE FORZANI GROUP LTD.
Balance Sheet (partial)
February 1, 2004
(in thousands)

Capital assets	Cost	Accumulated Amortization	Net Book Value
Land	$ 1,994	$ 0	$ 1,994
Buildings	16,501	1,877	14,624
Building on leased land	3,159	1,996	1,163
Furniture, fixtures, equipment, and automotive	113,495	65,490	48,005
Leasehold improvements	160,790	68,618	92,172
Construction in progress	2,667	0	2,667
Total	298,606	137,981	160,625

Intangible Assets

Many companies have assets that cannot be seen but are very valuable. **Intangible assets** are noncurrent assets that do not have physical substance and that represent a privilege or a right granted to, or held by, a company. They include goodwill, patents, copyrights, trademarks, trade names, and licences.

Intangible assets are normally divided into two groups for accounting purposes: those with definite lives and those with indefinite lives. Similar to buildings and equipment, intangible assets with definite useful lives are amortized. These include patents and copyrights. Similar to land, intangible assets with indefinite lives are not amortized. These include goodwill, trademarks, trade names, and licences.

Frenette Corporation reported goodwill of $3,100 in its intangible assets section. Goodwill is usually the largest intangible asset that appears on a company's balance sheet and is often reported separately from other intangibles. It results from the acquisition of another company when the price paid for the company is higher than the market value of the purchased company's net assets. Illustration 2-7 shows how Shaw Communications reported its intangible assets.

Illustration 2-7 ◀

Intangible assets section

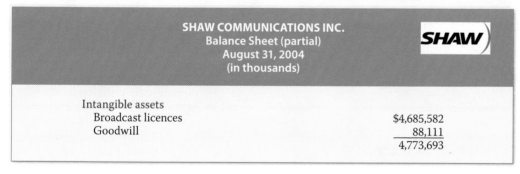

SHAW COMMUNICATIONS INC.
Balance Sheet (partial)
August 31, 2004
(in thousands)

Intangible assets	
Broadcast licences	$4,685,582
Goodwill	88,111
	4,773,693

Liabilities

Liabilities are obligations that result from past transactions. Similar to assets, they are also classified as current (due within one year) and noncurrent (due after more than one year).

Current Liabilities

Current liabilities are obligations that are to be paid in the coming year from current assets, or through the creation of other current liabilities. Common examples are accounts payable, accrued liabilities (we will learn about these in Chapter 4), wages payable, bank loans or notes payable, interest payable, taxes payable, and current maturities of long-term obligations (payments to be made in the next year on long-term obligations). In Illustration 2-3, Frenette Corporation reported six different types of current liabilities, for a total of $17,050.

Similar to current assets, current liabilities are often listed in order of liquidity. That is, the liabilities that are expected to be paid first are listed first. However, for many companies, the items in the current liabilities section are arranged according to an internal company custom rather than a prescribed rule. The current liabilities section from the balance sheet of The Jean Coutu Group is shown in Illustration 2-8.

Illustration 2-8 ▶

Current liabilities section

THE JEAN COUTU GROUP (PJC) INC. Balance Sheet (partial) May 31, 2004 (in thousands)	
Current liabilities	
Bank overdraft and bank loans	$ 20,451
Accounts payable and accrued liabilities	315,659
Income taxes payable	57,403
Current portion of long-term debt	30,773
Total current liabilities	424,286

Long-Term Liabilities

Alternative Terminology
Long-term liabilities are also called *long-term debt.*

Obligations that are expected to be paid after one year are classified as **long-term liabilities**. Liabilities in this category include bonds payable, mortgages payable, long-term notes payable, lease liabilities, pension liabilities, and future income taxes payable. Many companies report long-term debt maturing after one year as a single amount in the balance sheet and show the details of the debt in notes that go with the financial statements. In Illustration 2-3, Frenette Corporation reported long-term liabilities of $10,300. Andrés Wines reported long-term debt of $19,563 thousand on a recent balance sheet and reported the details in a note to the financial statements as shown in Illustration 2-9.

Illustration 2-9 ▶

Long-term liabilities section

ANDRÉS WINES LTD. Notes to Financial Statements (partial) March 31, 2004 (in thousands)	
5. Bank indebtedness and long-term debt	
Term bank	$21,813
Other debt	318
	22,131
Less: Current portion	2,568
	19,563

Shareholders' Equity

Shareholders' equity is divided into two parts: share capital and retained earnings. There may also be other parts to this section, such as contributed surplus or comprehensive income. We will learn more about these items in Chapter 11.

Share Capital

Alternative Terminology
Share capital is also commonly known as *capital stock.*

Shareholders' investments in a company are recorded as either common or preferred shares. If preferred shares are issued in addition to common shares, the total of all classes of shares issued is classified as, or titled, **share capital**. Quite often, companies only have one class of shares and the title is simply common shares, as shown in Illustration 2-3 for Frenette Corporation.

Retained Earnings

The cumulative earnings that have been retained for use in a company are known as **retained earnings**. Recall from Chapter 1 that ending retained earnings is reported on the end-of-period balance sheet. The amount is determined from the statement of retained earnings, which begins with the opening retained earnings amount and then adds net earnings for the period (or deducts a net loss) and deducts any dividends paid to calculate the ending retained earnings amount. In Illustration 2-3, Frenette Corporation reports an ending retained earnings balance of $50,050.

The share capital and retained earnings accounts are combined and reported as shareholders' equity on the balance sheet. The shareholders' equity section of Le Château's balance sheet is shown in Illustration 2-10.

Illustration 2-10 ◀

Shareholders' equity section

LE CHÂTEAU INC.
Balance Sheet (partial)
January 31, 2004
(in thousands)

le château

Shareholders' equity	
Capital stock	$14,774
Retained earnings	46,388
Total shareholders' equity	61,162

Sometimes, retained earnings has a negative balance. This is known as a deficit, which occurs when accumulated losses exceed earnings. If a deficit exists, it is reported as a deduction in shareholders' equity rather than an addition, as shown for retained earnings.

BEFORE YOU GO ON . . .

▶ Review It

1. What are the major sections in a classified balance sheet?
2. What factor determines whether assets should be classified as current or long-term?
3. What was Loblaw's largest current asset at January 3, 2004? The answer to this question is at the end of the chapter.
4. Where is accumulated amortization reported on the balance sheet?

▶ Do It

Ouyang Corporation recently received the following information for its December 31, 2006, balance sheet:

Accounts receivable	$11,100
Accumulated amortization—building	3,000
Accumulated amortization—office equipment	2,000
Building	75,000
Cash	1,800
Land	50,000
Office equipment	10,000
Prepaid insurance	2,300

Prepare the assets section of Ouyang Corporation's classified balance sheet.

Action Plan

- Determine which classification (current assets or property, plant, and equipment) each account should be reported in.
- Present current assets first, listing them in order of liquidity.
- List property, plant, and equipment in order of permanency.
- Subtract accumulated amortization from building and office equipment to determine the net book value.

Solution

OUYANG CORPORATION Balance Sheet (partial) December 31, 2006			
Assets			
Current assets			
Cash		$ 1,800	
Accounts receivable		11,100	
Prepaid insurance		2,300	
Total current assets			$ 15,200
Property, plant, and equipment			
Land		$50,000	
Building	$75,000		
Less: Accumulated amortization	3,000	72,000	
Office equipment	$10,000		
Less: Accumulated amortization	2,000	8,000	
Total property, plant, and equipment			130,000
Total assets			$145,200

Using the Financial Statements

In Chapter 1, we briefly discussed how the financial statements give information about a company's performance and financial position. In this chapter, we continue this discussion by showing you specific tools, such as ratio analysis, that can be used to analyze financial statements in order to make a more meaningful evaluation of a company.

    Ratio analysis expresses the relationships between selected items of financial statement data. There are three general types of ratios that are used to analyze financial statements—liquidity, profitability, and solvency—as shown in Illustration 2-11.

Illustration 2-11 ▶

Financial ratio classifications

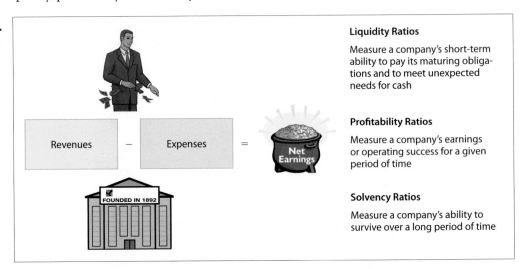

Liquidity Ratios

Measure a company's short-term ability to pay its maturing obligations and to meet unexpected needs for cash

Profitability Ratios

Measure a company's earnings or operating success for a given period of time

Solvency Ratios

Measure a company's ability to survive over a long period of time

Ratios can give clues about underlying conditions that may not be easy to see when the items of a particular ratio are examined separately. Since a single ratio by itself is not very meaningful, in this, and subsequent chapters, we will use:

1. **Intracompany comparisons** covering two years for the same company
2. **Intercompany comparisons** based on comparisons with a competitor in the same industry.
3. **Industry average comparisons** based on average ratios for particular industries

In the following sections, we will introduce selected examples of liquidity, profitability, and solvency ratios, using Sears Canada's statement of earnings, balance sheet, and cash flow statement. We will present two fiscal years, 2003 and 2002, for our intracompany comparisons. We will then compare Sears' ratios for these two years to those of one of its competitors, Hudson's Bay Company, to broaden our analysis to include an intercompany comparison. Finally, we will compare our ratios to industry average comparisons for the retail department store industry.

Using the Statement of Earnings

Sears generates a profit for its shareholders by selling merchandise. The statement of earnings reports how successful Sears is at generating this profit. It reports the amount earned during the period (revenues) and the costs incurred during the same period (expenses). Illustration 2-12 shows Sears' comparative statement of earnings.

Illustration 2-12 ◀

Sears' statement of earnings

SEARS CANADA INC.
Statement of Earnings
Year Ended January 3, 2004
(in millions)

	2003	2002
Total revenues	$6,222.7	$6,535.9
Expenses		
Cost of merchandise sold, operating, administrative, and selling expenses	5,775.9	6,107.9
Amortization	146.6	148.7
Interest	59.5	59.8
Unusual items	5.0	189.1
Total expenses	5,987.0	6,505.5
Earnings before income taxes	235.7	30.4
Income tax expense (recovery)	101.0	(21.8)
Net earnings	$ 134.7	$ 52.2

From the statement of earnings, we can see that Sears' total revenues decreased during the year. However, even though revenues decreased, net earnings increased from $52.2 million to $134.7 million. In order to increase net earnings, the company needs its revenues to increase more than its expenses, or its expenses to decline more than its revenues. The latter was the case for Sears. While its revenues declined by nearly 5%, its expenses declined by 8%.

If we remove the impact of the unusual items, expenses declined by 5%, about the same as revenues. It is important to understand the nature of expenses that are considered to be "unusual." They are not likely recurring expenses (note they declined significantly in 2003), and are unlikely to have the same impact in future years. We will learn more about unusual items in Chapter 14.

Profitability

Both investors—existing and potential—and creditors are interested in a company's profitability. **Profitability ratios** measure the earnings or operating success of a company for a specific period of time. We will look at two examples of profitability ratios in this section: earnings per share and the price-earnings ratio.

Earnings per Share.   **Earnings per share (EPS)** measures the net earnings for each common share. Accordingly, earnings per share is reported only for common shareholders. It is calculated by dividing net earnings available to the common shareholders by the weighted average number of common shares issued during the year.

Sears' weighted average number of shares was 107.1 million for 2003 and 106.8 million for 2002. Unless a company has preferred shares, the net earnings available to common shareholders will be the same as the net earnings reported on a company's statement of earnings.

We will learn more about how to calculate net earnings available to common shareholders and the weighted average number of shares in Chapter 11.

Shareholders usually think in terms of the number of shares they own—or plan to buy or sell—so reducing net earnings to a per share amount gives a useful perspective for determining the investment return. Earnings per share amounts for Sears and its competitor, Hudson's Bay, are calculated in Illustration 2-13.

Illustration 2-13 ▶

Earnings per share

EARNINGS PER SHARE =	NET EARNINGS AVAILABLE TO COMMON SHAREHOLDERS WEIGHTED AVERAGE NUMBER OF COMMON SHARES	
($ in millions except per share amounts)	2003	2002
Sears	$\frac{\$134.7}{107.1} = \$1.26$	$\frac{\$52.2}{106.8} = \$0.49$
Hudson's Bay	$0.82	$1.40
Industry average	n/a	n/a

ACCOUNTING MATTERS!   Investor Perspective

Profitability matters. When Sears missed its estimated earnings per share figure by 5 cents, its share price fell by 14 cents. Although it is not unusual for a company's share price to be affected by earnings announcements, what was unusual was that the share prices of other companies also fell as a result of the news. In this case, investors reacted because Sears' financial health is viewed as a good indicator of the strength of the economy as a whole. Investors were expressing their concern that difficult times for retailers were on the horizon.

Price-Earnings Ratio.   Comparisons of earnings per share are not very meaningful among companies, because of the wide variation in the number of shares and in the share prices. This is why there is no industry average for earnings per share in Illustration 2-13. When industry averages are not available for the ratios we calculate in this text, "n/a" (not available) appears.

In order to compare earnings across companies, we calculate the **price-earnings (P-E) ratio**. The price-earnings ratio is a frequently quoted statistic that measures the **ratio of the market price of each common share to its earnings per share**. It is calculated by dividing the market price per share by earnings per share.

The price-earnings ratio shows what investors expect of a company's future earnings. The ratio of price to earnings will be higher if investors think that current earnings levels will continue or increase; it will be lower if investors think that earnings will decline.

The market price of Sears' shares was $17.51 at the end of 2003 and $17.05 at the end of 2002. The price-earnings ratios for Sears and its competitor, Hudson's Bay, are presented in Illustration 2-14, using this information and the earnings per share amounts presented above.

Illustration 2-14 ◀

Price-earnings ratio

PRICE-EARNINGS RATIO = $\dfrac{\text{MARKET PRICE PER SHARE}}{\text{EARNINGS PER SHARE}}$		
	2003	**2002**
Sears	$\dfrac{\$17.51}{\$1.26} = 13.9$ times	$\dfrac{\$17.05}{\$0.49} = 34.8$ times
Hudson's Bay	12.6 times	6.5 times
Industry average	15.0 times	14.2 times

From 2002 to 2003, Sears' earnings per share increased. However, its price-earnings ratio decreased—in contrast to the increasing price-earnings ratios of Hudson's Bay and the industry. This decrease shows that investors were concerned about Sears' declining revenues and its ability to remain competitive against specialty and discount retailers.

▦ Decision Toolkit

Decision Checkpoints	Info Needed for Decision	Tools to Use for Decision	How to Evaluate Results
How does the company's earnings performance compare with previous years?	Net earnings available to common shareholders and weighted average number of common shares	$\text{Earnings per share} = \dfrac{\text{Net earnings available to common shareholders}}{\text{Weighted average number of common shares}}$	A higher measure suggests improved performance. Values should not be compared across companies.
How does the market perceive the company's prospects for future earnings	Earnings per share and market price per share	$\text{Price-earnings ratio} = \dfrac{\text{Market price per share}}{\text{Earnings per share}}$	A high ratio suggests the market expects good performance, although it may also suggest that shares are overvalued.

BEFORE YOU GO ON . . .

▶Review It

1. Identify three types of useful comparisons in ratio analysis.
2. Identify three types of ratios.
3. What are profitability ratios? Explain earnings per share and the price-earnings ratio.

the navigator

Using the Balance Sheet

You can learn a lot about a company's financial health by evaluating the relationships between its various assets and liabilities. A simplified balance sheet for Sears is shown in Illustration 2-15 on the following page.

study objective 5

Identify and calculate ratios for analyzing a company's liquidity and solvency.

Illustration 2-15 ▶

Sears balance sheet

Alternative Terminology
The *balance sheet* is
sometimes called the
*statement of financial
position*, as with Sears.

SEARS CANADA INC.
Statement of Financial Position
January 3, 2004
(in millions)

	2003	2002
Assets		
Current assets		
Cash and short-term investments	$ 82.6	$ 142.8
Accounts receivable	1,249.1	1,322.5
Income taxes recoverable	11.8	4.1
Inventories	801.3	754.0
Prepaid expenses and other assets	110.6	109.4
Current portion of future income tax assets	149.7	183.1
Total current assets	2,405.1	2,515.9
Investments and other assets	76.8	59.7
Capital assets	1,042.8	1,036.9
Other assets	541.0	448.8
Total assets	$4,065.7	$4,061.3
Liabilities and Shareholders' Equity		
Liabilities		
Current liabilities		
Accounts payable	$ 728.2	$ 799.0
Accrued liabilities	486.4	517.3
Income and other taxes payable	95.9	99.1
Principal payments on long-term obligations due within one year	7.3	36.2
Total current liabilities	1,317.8	1,451.6
Long-term obligations	937.0	962.8
Total liabilities	2,254.8	2,414.4
Shareholders' equity		
Capital stock	458.8	458.1
Retained earnings	1,352.1	1,188.8
Total shareholders' equity	1,810.9	1,646.9
Total liabilities and shareholders' equity	$4,065.7	$4,061.3

Liquidity

Suppose you are a furniture manufacturer interested in selling furniture on credit to Sears. You would be concerned about Sears' liquidity—its ability to pay obligations that are expected to become due within the next year. To have an idea of this, you would look closely at the relationship of its current assets to its current liabilities, using liquidity ratios. Liquidity ratios measure the short-term ability of the company to pay its maturing obligations and to meet unexpected needs for cash.

Working Capital.   One measure of liquidity is working capital, which is the difference between current assets and current liabilities. When working capital is positive, there is a greater likelihood that the company will pay its liabilities. When working capital is negative, short-term creditors may not be paid, and the company may ultimately be forced into bankruptcy.

Illustration 2-16 ◄

Working capital

WORKING CAPITAL = CURRENT ASSETS − CURRENT LIABILITIES		
($ in millions)	2003	2002
Sears	$2,405.1 − $1,317.8 = $1,087.3	$2,515.9 − $1,451.6 = $1,064.3
Hudson's Bay	$1,291.4	$1,147.7
Industry average	n/a	n/a

Industry averages are not very meaningful for working capital, because working capital is expressed in absolute dollars rather than as a ratio.

Current Ratio.   An important liquidity ratio is the current ratio, which is calculated by dividing current assets by current liabilities. The current ratio is a more dependable indicator of liquidity than working capital. Two companies with the same amount of working capital may have significantly different current ratios. The 2003 and 2002 current ratios for Sears, Hudson's Bay, and the industry average are shown in Illustration 2-17.

Illustration 2-17 ◄

Current ratio

$$\text{CURRENT RATIO} = \frac{\text{CURRENT ASSETS}}{\text{CURRENT LIABILITIES}}$$		
($ in millions)	2003	2002
Sears	$\frac{\$2,405.1}{\$1,317.8} = 1.8:1$	$\frac{\$2,515.9}{\$1,451.6} = 1.7:1$
Hudson's Bay	2.2:1	1.9:1
Industry average	2.2:1	2.1:1

What does the ratio actually mean? The 2003 current ratio of 1.8:1 means that for every dollar of current liabilities, Sears has $1.80 of current assets. Sears' current ratio has increased slightly from 2002 to 2003. However, when compared to Hudson's Bay and the industry average, Sears' short-term liquidity is not as strong.

The current ratio is only one measure of liquidity. It does not take into account the **composition** of the current assets. For example, a satisfactory current ratio does not reveal that a portion of the current assets may be tied up in uncollectible accounts receivable or slow-moving inventory. The composition of the assets matters because a dollar of cash is more easily available to pay the bills than is a dollar of inventory. For example, suppose a company's cash balance declined while its merchandise inventory increased a lot. If inventory increased because the company is having difficulty selling it, then the current ratio would not fully reflect the reduction in the company's liquidity. We will look at these effects in more detail in later chapters.

Solvency

Now suppose that instead of being a short-term creditor, you are interested in either buying Sears shares or making a long-term loan to the company. Shareholders and long-term creditors are interested in a company's long-run solvency—its ability to pay interest as it comes due and to repay the face value of the debt at maturity. Solvency ratios measure the company's ability to survive over a long period of time. The debt to total assets ratio is one source of information about debt-paying ability.

Debt to Total Assets.   The debt to total assets ratio measures the percentage of assets financed by creditors rather than by shareholders. Financing provided by creditors is riskier than financing provided by shareholders, because debt must be repaid at specific points in

Helpful Hint Some users evaluate solvency using a ratio of debt divided by shareholders' equity. The higher this ratio, the lower a company's solvency.

time, whether the company is performing well or not. Thus, the higher the percentage of debt financing, the riskier the company.

The debt to total assets ratio is calculated by dividing total debt (both current and long-term liabilities) by total assets. The higher the percentage of debt to total assets, the greater the risk that the company may be unable to pay its debts as they come due. The ratios of debt to total assets for Sears, Hudson's Bay, and the industry average are shown in Illustration 2-18.

Illustration 2-18 ▶

Debt to total assets

DEBT TO TOTAL ASSETS = $\dfrac{\text{TOTAL LIABILITIES}}{\text{TOTAL ASSETS}}$		
($ in millions)	**2003**	**2002**
Sears	$\dfrac{\$2,254.8}{\$4,065.7} = 55.5\%$	$\dfrac{\$2,414.4}{\$4,061.3} = 59.4\%$
Hudson's Bay	40.9%	44.0%
Industry average	46.8%	57.1%

The 2003 ratio of 55.5% means that 55.5 cents of every dollar Sears invested in assets has been provided by its creditors. Sears' ratio exceeds both the Hudson's Bay debt to total assets ratio of 40.9% and the industry average of 46.8%. The higher the ratio, the lower the equity "cushion" available to creditors if the company becomes insolvent (unable to pay its debts). Thus, from the creditors' point of view, a high ratio of debt to total assets is undesirable. In other words, Sears' solvency appears worse than that of either Hudson's Bay or the average company in the industry.

The significance of this ratio is often judged by looking at the company's earnings. Generally, companies with relatively stable earnings have higher debt to total assets ratios than do cyclical companies with widely fluctuating earnings.

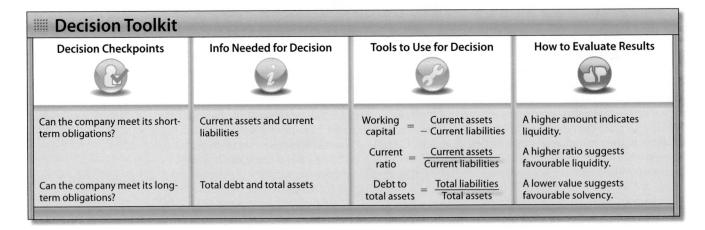

Decision Checkpoints	Info Needed for Decision	Tools to Use for Decision	How to Evaluate Results
Can the company meet its short-term obligations?	Current assets and current liabilities	Working capital = Current assets − Current liabilities	A higher amount indicates liquidity.
		Current ratio = $\dfrac{\text{Current assets}}{\text{Current liabilities}}$	A higher ratio suggests favourable liquidity.
Can the company meet its long-term obligations?	Total debt and total assets	Debt to total assets = $\dfrac{\text{Total liabilities}}{\text{Total assets}}$	A lower value suggests favourable solvency.

Decision Toolkit

BEFORE YOU GO ON . . .

▶Review It

1. What is liquidity? How can it be measured?
2. What is solvency? How can it be measured?

► Do It

Selected financial data for Drummond Inc. at January 31, 2006, are as follows: cash $60,000; accounts receivable $80,000; inventory $70,000; property, plant, and equipment $100,000. Current liabilities are $140,000 and long-term liabilities $50,000. Calculate the current ratio and debt to total assets.

Action Plan

- Use the formula for the current ratio: current assets ÷ current liabilities.
- Understand the composition of current assets (cash + receivables + inventory).
- Use the formula for debt to total assets: total liabilities ÷ total assets.
- Understand how to determine total liabilities (current liabilities + long-term liabilities) and total assets (current assets + investments + property, plant, and equipment + intangible assets).

Solution

Current ratio:

$$\frac{\$60,000 + \$80,000 + \$70,000}{\$140,000} = 1.5{:}1$$

Debt to total assets:

$$\frac{\$140,000 + \$50,000}{\$60,000 + \$80,000 + \$70,000 + \$100,000} = 61.3\%$$

the navigator

Using the Cash Flow Statement

As you learned in Chapter 1, the cash flow statement gives financial information about the sources and uses of a company's cash. Investors, creditors, and others want to know what is happening to a company's most liquid resource—its cash. In fact, it is often said that "cash is king," since a company that cannot generate cash will not survive. To help analyze cash, the cash flow statement reports the cash effects of a company's **operating activities**, **investing activities**, and **financing activities**. A simplified cash flow statement for Sears is provided in Illustration 2-19.

Illustration 2-19 ◄

Sears' cash flow statement

SEARS CANADA INC.
Cash Flow Statement
Year Ended January 3, 2004
(in millions)
Sears

	2003	2002
Operating activities		
Cash receipts from operating activities	$ 6,296.1	$ 6,023.6
Cash payments for operating activities	(6,001.9)	(5,537.6)
Cash provided by operating activities	294.2	486.0
Investing activities		
Purchases of capital assets	(196.2)	(183.6)
Proceeds from sale of capital assets	15.1	11.5
Charge account receivables	(123.1)	(492.1)
Investments and other assets	(18.0)	21.8
Cash used by investing activities	(322.2)	(642.4)
Financing activities		
Repayment of long-term obligations	(6.7)	(4.9)
Net proceeds from issue of capital stock	0.1	0.4
Dividends paid	(25.6)	(25.6)
Cash used by financing activities	(32.2)	(30.1)
Decrease in cash and short-term investments	(60.2)	(186.5)
Cash and short-term investments at beginning of year	142.8	329.3
Cash and short-term investments at end of year	$ 82.6	$ 142.8

Different users have different reasons for being interested in the cash flow statement. If you were a creditor of Sears (either short-term or long-term), you would be interested in knowing the sources of its cash in recent years. This information would give you some indication of where it might get cash to pay you. If you had a long-term interest in Sears as a shareholder, you would look to the cash flow statement for information about the company's ability to generate cash over the long run to meet its cash needs for growth.

Companies get cash from two sources: operating activities and financing activities. In the early years of a company's life, it usually cannot generate enough cash from operating activities to meet its investing needs, and so it will have to issue shares or borrow money. An established company, however, will often be able to meet most of its cash needs with the cash provided by operating activities.

Sears' cash provided by operating activities declined in 2003 to $294.2 million. Sears used a total of $322.2 million of cash for investing activities, consisting primarily of purchases of new capital assets (property, plant, and equipment) and increasing its credit card (charge) receivables. Sears used a total of $32.2 million of cash for financing activities, repaying debt, and paying dividends. Note, however, that no new borrowings occurred. Sears chose instead to finance its investing and financing activities through the cash provided by its operating activities ($294.2 million) and by reducing its cash and short-term investment balance ($60.2 million).

Free Cash Flow

Cash provided by operating activities is often adjusted to take into account the fact that a company must invest in new assets just to maintain its current level of operations. In addition, companies must also keep paying dividends to satisfy investors. The result, known as **free cash flow, is a solvency-based measure** that helps creditors and investors understand how much discretionary cash flow a company has left from its operating activities to expand operations, go after new opportunities, or pay additional dividends, among other alternatives.

Free cash flow is calculated by deducting net capital expenditures and dividends from cash provided by operating activities. Net capital expenditures—representing amounts paid for the acquisition of property, plant, and equipment less any recoveries from the sale of these assets—can be found in the investing activities section of the cash flow statement. Dividends paid, if any, are reported in the financing activities section of the cash flow statement.

Illustration 2-20 presents the free cash flow numbers for Sears and Hudson's Bay. Industry measures are not available for these ratios.

Illustration 2-20 ▶

Free cash flow

FREE CASH FLOW =	CASH PROVIDED (USED) BY OPERATING ACTIVITIES	−	NET CAPITAL EXPENDITURES	− DIVIDENDS PAID
($ in millions)	2003		2002	
Sears	$294.2 − ($196.2 − $15.1) − $25.6 = $87.5		$486.0 − ($183.6 − $11.5) − $25.6 = $288.3	
Hudson's Bay	$303.5		$60.9	
Industry average	n/a		n/a	

Sears' free cash flow declined substantially in 2003, while its larger rival's numbers increased substantially during the same period. This difference can be explained mostly by the difference in cash provided by operating activities for each company. Sears' cash flow provided by operating activities fell by nearly half in 2003 (from $486.0 million to $294.2 million), while Hudson's Bay's cash flow provided by operating activities more than doubled during the same period. In addition, Hudson's Bay's capital expenditures and dividends declined in 2003, while Sears' capital expenditures increased and its dividends remained unchanged.

Decision Toolkit

Decision Checkpoints	Info Needed for Decision	Tools to Use for Decision	How to Evaluate Results
Can the company meet its long-term obligations?	Cash provided (used) by operating activities, capital expenditures, and cash dividends	Free cash flow = Cash provided (used) by operating activities − Net capital expenditures − Dividends paid	Free cash flow indicates the potential to finance new investments or pay more dividends.

ACCOUNTING MATTERS!   Investor Perspective

Amazon.com, Inc., once the Earth's biggest bookstore, is now the Earth's biggest anything store. Amazon.com's website offers millions of books and videos (which still account for the majority of the company's sales), not to mention toys, tools, electronics, home furnishings, apparel, health and beauty goods, prescription drugs, gourmet foods, and services, including film processing.

Revenues grew by 29 percent for the 12 months ended September 30, 2004, and are expected to continue to grow more than 20 percent this year and next. Free cash flow grew 76 percent for the same period. While net earnings have not grown quite as rapidly, Lisa Ketrick, a financial analyst, is not worried. "It's not the margin number we're focused on," she says. "At the end the day, it's about free cash flow generation."

Source: Eric J. Savitaz, "Don't Bet against Jeff," *SmartMoney*, February 1, 2005, 51.

BEFORE YOU GO ON . . .

▶Review It

1. What information does the cash flow statement provide that is not available in the statement of earnings or balance sheet?
2. What is the difference between cash from operating activities and free cash flow?

the navigator

Using the Decision Toolkit

It may surprise you to learn that Canadian Tire Corporation, Limited, is one of Sears' top competitors. Don't be fooled by the modest name; Canadian Tire sells a wide array of products, including casual clothing and home, car, sports, and leisure products.

CANADIAN TIRE CORPORATION, LIMITED
Balance Sheet
January 3, 2004
(in millions)

	2003	2002
Assets		
Current assets		
Cash and cash equivalents	$ 726.6	$ 628.2
Accounts receivable	489.4	584.1
Credit charge receivables	562.8	579.8
Merchandise inventories	493.9	503.0
Prepaid expenses and deposits	27.9	19.1
Total current assets	2,300.6	2,314.2
Long-term receivables and other assets	64.1	126.7
Goodwill	40.6	32.8
Intangible assets	52.0	52.0
Property and equipment	2,443.4	2,349.7
Total assets	$4,900.7	$4,875.4
Liabilities and Shareholders' Equity		
Liabilities		
Current liabilities		
Accounts payable and other	$1,266.6	$1,294.7
Income taxes payable	96.5	80.7
Current portion of long-term debt	244.5	208.2
Total current liabilities	1,607.6	1,583.6
Long-term debt	886.2	1,125.2
Other long-term liabilities	373.6	359.7
Total liabilities	2,867.4	3,068.5
Shareholders' Equity		
Share capital	701.2	661.0
Other	(2.1)	7.9
Retained earnings	1,334.2	1,138.0
Total shareholders' equity	2,033.3	1,806.9
Total liabilities and shareholders' equity	$4,900.7	$4,875.4

CANADIAN TIRE CORPORATION, LIMITED
Statement of Earnings
Year Ended January 3, 2004
(in millions)

	2003	2002
Gross operating revenue	$6,552.8	$5,944.5
Operating expenses		
Cost of merchandise sold and operating expenses	5,916.3	5,369.5
Interest	85.0	83.0
Amortization	154.0	158.5
Other	32.4	27.3
Total operating expenses	6,187.7	5,638.3
Earnings before income taxes	365.1	306.2
Income taxes	118.5	103.8
Net earnings	$ 246.6	$ 202.4

Additional information: Canadian Tire's cash provided by operating activities was $518.6 million in 2003 and $444.3 million in 2002. Net capital expenditures and dividends paid were $238.5 million and $32.2 million in 2003, respectively, and $218.5 million and $31.6 million in 2002, respectively. Canadian Tire's net earnings are the same as its net earnings available to common shareholders. The weighted average number of shares was 80.6 million in 2003, and 79.1 million in 2002. The share price was $46.90 on January 3, 2004, and $32.45 on December 28, 2002.

Instructions

(a) Calculate Canadian Tire's current ratio for both fiscal years. Discuss its liquidity in relation to itself, Sears, and the industry.

(b) Calculate the earnings per share and price-earnings ratio for both fiscal years. Discuss Canadian Tire's profitability in relation to itself, Sears, and the industry.

(c) Calculate Canadian Tire's debt to total assets and free cash flow for both fiscal years. Discuss its solvency in relation to itself, Sears, and the industry.

Solution

(Amounts in millions)

(a) Liquidity
   Current ratio:
       2003: $2,300.6 ÷ $1,607.6 = 1.4:1
       2002: $2,314.2 ÷ $1,583.6 = 1.5:1

   Canadian Tire's liquidity appears to be reasonable although not quite as good as that of Sears or of the industry. Its current ratio declined in 2003. Still, it is above 1:1, and Canadian Tire had 1.4 times more current assets than current liabilities. Nonetheless, Canadian Tire's current ratio is still not as good as Sears' current ratio of 1.8:1. It is also below that of its industry competitors at 2.2:1.

(b) Profitability
   Earnings per share:
       2003: $246.6 ÷ 80.6 = $3.06
       2002: $202.4 ÷ 79.1 = $2.56

   Price-earnings ratio:
       2003: $46.90 ÷ $3.06 = 15.3 times
       2002: $32.45 ÷ $2.56 = 12.7 times

   Canadian Tire's profitability appears to be improving. The company's earnings per share increased in 2003, as did its price-earnings ratio, from 12.7 times to 15.3 times. This ratio is higher than that of Sears, at 13.9 times, and comparable to that of the industry, at 15.0 times. Despite Canadian Tire's lag behind Sears and the industry in liquidity investors are obviously optimistic about the future prospects of the company.

(c) Solvency
   Debt to total assets:
       2003: $2,867.4 ÷ $4,900.7 = 58.5%
       2002: $3,068.5 ÷ $4,875.4 = 62.9%

   Free cash flow:
       2003: $518.6 − $238.5 − $32.2 = $247.9
       2002: $444.3 − $218.5 − $31.6 = $194.2

   Canadian Tire's solvency improved in 2003. Based on the change in its ratio of debt to total assets, Canadian Tire's reliance on debt decreased (improved) from 2002 to 2003. Still, its reliance on debt financing is higher than that of Sears (55.5%) and the industry (46.8%). It is notable that all three—Canadian Tire, Sears, and the industry as a whole—saw an improvement in their debt to total assets ratios in 2003.

   Canadian Tire's free cash flow also improved in 2003 and is higher than that of Sears ($87.5 million). There is no industry average for this ratio.

the navigator

Summary of Study Objectives

1. *Describe the objective of financial reporting and apply the qualitative characteristics of accounting information to the elements of financial statements.* The objective of financial reporting is to provide information that is useful for decision-making. To be useful, information should have these qualitative characteristics: understandability, relevance, reliability, and comparability. The elements of financial statements include assets, liabilities, shareholders' equity, revenues, and expenses.

2. *Identify and apply assumptions, principles, and constraints.* Assumptions include the monetary unit assumption, economic entity assumption, time period assumption, and going concern assumption. Generally accepted accounting principles include the cost principle and full disclosure principle. The two constraints of cost-benefit and materiality can change how these principles are applied.

3. *Identify the sections of a classified balance sheet.* In a classified balance sheet, assets are classified as current assets; investments; property, plant, and equipment; and intangible assets. Liabilities are classified as either current or long-term. There is also a shareholders' equity section, which shows share capital and retained earnings.

4. *Identify and calculate ratios for analyzing a company's profitability.* Profitability ratios, such as earnings per share and the price-earnings ratio, measure a company's operating success for a specific period of time.

5. *Identify and calculate ratios for analyzing a company's liquidity and solvency.* Liquidity ratios, such as working capital and the current ratio, measure a company's short-term ability to pay its maturing obligations and meet unexpected needs for cash. Solvency ratios, such as debt to total assets and free cash flow, measure a company's ability to survive over a long period.

Decision Toolkit—A Summary

Decision Checkpoints	Info Needed for Decision	Tools to Use for Decision	How to Evaluate Results
How does the company's earnings performance compare with previous years?	Net earnings available to common shareholders and weighted average number of common shares	$\text{Earnings per share} = \dfrac{\text{Net earnings available to common shareholders}}{\text{Weighted average number of common shares}}$	A higher measure suggests improved performance. Values should not be compared across companies.
How does the market see the company's prospects for future earnings?	Earnings per share and market price per share	$\text{Price-earnings ratio} = \dfrac{\text{Market price per share}}{\text{Earnings per share}}$	A high ratio suggests the market expects good performance, although it may also suggest that shares are overvalued
Can the company meet its short-term obligations?	Current assets and current liabilities	Working capital = Current assets − Current liabilities	A higher amount indicates liquidity.
		$\text{Current ratio} = \dfrac{\text{Current assets}}{\text{Current liabilities}}$	A higher ratio suggests favourable liquidity.
Can the company meet its long-term obligations?	Total debt and total assets	$\text{Debt to total assets} = \dfrac{\text{Total liabilities}}{\text{Total assets}}$	A lower value suggests favourable solvency.
	Cash provided (used) by operating activities, capital expenditures, and cash dividends	Free cash flow = Cash provided (used) by operating activities − Net capital expenditures − Dividends paid	Free cash flow indicates the potential to finance new investments or pay more dividends.

**Analysis Tools
(Decision Toolkit Summaries)**

Glossary

Comparability A quality for describing accounting information that can be compared among companies in similar circumstances, because they use similar accounting principles. (p. 50)

Conservatism The approach of choosing an accounting method that will be least likely to overstate assets and net earnings. (p. 49)

Consistency Use of the same accounting principles from year to year within a company. (p. 50)

Cost-benefit The constraint that the costs of obtaining and providing information should not be higher than the benefits gained. (p. 53)

Cost principle A generally accepted accounting principle that states that assets should be recorded at their cost. (p. 52)

Current assets Cash and other resources that it is reasonable to expect will be realized in cash, or will be sold or used up by the business, within one year. (p. 55)

Current liabilities Obligations that will be paid from existing current assets or through the creation of other current liabilities, within the next year. (p. 57)

Current ratio A measure used to evaluate a company's liquidity and short-term debt-paying ability. It is calculated by dividing current assets by current liabilities. (p. 65)

Debt to total assets A measure of solvency showing the percentage of total financing provided by creditors. It is calculated by dividing total liabilities by total assets. (p. 65)

Deficit A debit (negative) balance in retained earnings. (p. 59)

Economic entity assumption An assumption that economic events can be separately identified and accounted for. (p. 51)

Earnings per share (EPS) A measure of the net earnings earned by each common share. It is calculated by dividing net earnings available to common shareholders by the weighted average number of common shares during the year. (p. 61)

Free cash flow A solvency measure that indicates the amount of cash generated during the current year that is available for expansion or for the payment of additional dividends. It is calculated by deducting net capital expenditures and dividends from cash provided by operating activities. (p. 68)

Full disclosure principle A generally accepted accounting principle that states that circumstances and events which matter to financial statement users should be disclosed. (p. 52)

Generally accepted accounting principles (GAAP) A set of rules and practices, having substantial authoritative support, that are recognized as a general guide for financial reporting purposes. (p. 51)

Going concern assumption The assumption that the business will continue operating long enough to carry out its existing objectives and commitments. (p. 51)

Intangible assets Assets of a long-lived nature that do not have physical substance but represent a privilege or a right granted to, or held by, a company. (p. 57)

Liquidity ratios Measures of a company's short-term ability to pay its maturing obligations and to meet unexpected needs for cash. (p. 64)

Long-term investments Investments in debt and equity of other companies that are normally held for many years. Also includes long-term assets, such as land and buildings, that are not currently being used in the company's operations. (p. 56)

Long-term liabilities Obligations not expected to be paid within one year. (p. 58)

Materiality The constraint of determining whether an item is likely to influence the decision of an investor or creditor. (p. 53)

Monetary unit assumption An assumption stating that only transaction data that can be expressed in terms of money should be included in the accounting records of the economic entity. (p. 51)

Price-earnings (P-E) ratio A profitability measure of the ratio of the market price of each common share to the earnings per share. It reflects the stock market's belief about a company's future earnings potential. (p. 62)

Profitability ratios Measures of a company's earnings or operating success for a specific period of time. (p. 61)

Property, plant, and equipment Assets of a long-lived nature that are being used in the business and are not intended for resale. (p. 56)

Relevance A quality for describing information that makes a difference in a decision. (p. 49)

Reliability A quality for describing information that has no errors or bias. (p. 49)

Solvency ratios Measures of a company's ability to survive over a long period of time. (p. 65)

Time period assumption An accounting assumption that the economic life of a business can be divided into artificial time periods. (p. 51)

Understandability A quality for describing information provided in the financial statements that is understandable for users and therefore useful. (p. 49)

Working capital The excess of current assets over current liabilities. (p. 64)

Demonstration Problem

**Study Tools
(Demonstration Problems)**

Listed here are items taken from the statement of earnings and balance sheet of Hudson's Bay Company for the year ended January 31, 2004. Certain items have been combined for simplification and all numbers are reported in thousands.

Accounts payable and accrued liabilities	$ 926,101	Long-term receivables	$ 7,052
Accounts receivable	64,811	Merchandise inventories	1,485,088
Cash	8,033	Operating expenses	7,238,917
Credit card receivables	538,734	Other long-term assets	517,715
Dividends	37,178	Other long-term liabilities	244,088
Fixed assets	1,089,334	Prepaid expenses and other current assets	78,669
Goodwill	152,294	Retained earnings, February 1, 2003	740,853
Income tax expense	49,243	Sales and revenue	7,400,051
Interest expense	42,662	Share capital	1,657,728
Long-term debt	383,107	Short-term borrowings	1,309
Long-term debt due within one year	125,436	Short-term deposits	168,943

Instructions

Prepare a statement of earnings, statement of retained earnings, and classified balance sheet using the items listed

Action Plan

- First identify which accounts should be reported on each statement. Then determine which classification each account should be reported in.

- Prepare the statements in this order: (1) statement of earnings, (2) statement of retained earnings, and (3) balance sheet.

- The statement of earnings covers a period of time. In preparing the statement of earnings, first list revenues, and then expenses. Report income tax expense separately.

- The statement of retained earnings covers the same period of time as the statement of earnings. This statement calculates the ending retained earnings balance (which is also reported on the balance sheet) by adding net earnings (from the statement of earnings) less dividends to the opening retained earnings amount.

- The balance sheet is prepared at a specific point in time. In preparing a classified balance sheet, list items in order of their liquidity in the current classifications and in order of their permanency in the non-current classifications.

Solution to Demonstration Problem

**HUDSON'S BAY COMPANY
Statement of Earnings
Year Ended January 31, 2004
(in thousands)**

Sales and revenue		$7,400,051
Expenses		
Operating expenses	$7,238,917	
Interest expense	42,662	
Total expenses		7,281,579
Earnings before income taxes		118,472
Income tax expense		49,243
Net earnings		$ 69,229

**HUDSON'S BAY COMPANY
Statement of Retained Earnings
Year Ended January 31, 2004
(in thousands)**

Retained earnings, February 1, 2003	$740,853
Add: Net earnings	69,229
	810,082
Less: Dividends	37,178
Retained earnings, January 31, 2004	$772,904

HUDSON'S BAY COMPANY
Balance Sheet
January 31, 2004
(in thousands)

Assets

Current assets		
Cash	$ 8,033	
Short-term deposits	168,943	
Accounts receivable	64,811	
Credit card receivables	538,734	
Merchandise inventories	1,485,088	
Prepaid expenses and other current assets	78,669	
Total current assets		$2,344,278
Long-term receivables		7,052
Fixed assets		1,089,334
Goodwill		152,294
Other long-term assets		517,715
Total assets		$4,110,673

Liabilities and Shareholders' Equity

Liabilities		
Current liabilities		
Short-term borrowings	$ 1,309	
Accounts payable and accrued liabilities	926,101	
Long-term debt due within one year	125,436	
Total current liabilities		$1,052,846
Long-term liabilities		
Long-term debt	$383,107	
Other long-term liabilities	244,088	
Total long-term liabilities		627,195
Total liabilities		1,680,041
Shareholders' equity		
Share capital	$1,657,728	
Retained earnings	772,904	
Total shareholders' equity		2,430,632
Total liabilities and shareholders' equity		$4,110,673

the navigator

www.wiley.com/canada/kimmel

Self-Study Questions

Study Tools (Self-Assessment Quizzes)

(SO 1) 1. What is the main criterion that can be used to judge accounting information?
(a) Consistency
(b) Usefulness for decision-making
(c) Materiality
(d) Comparability

(SO 1) 2. What accounting characteristic refers to the tendency of accountants to resolve uncertainty by doing what is least likely to overstate assets and earnings?
(a) Comparability   (c) Conservatism
(b) Relevance   (d) Understandability

(SO 2) 3. The cost principle states that:
(a) assets should be recorded at cost and adjusted when the market value changes.
(b) the activities of a company should be kept separate and distinct from those of its shareholders.

(c) only transaction data that can be expressed in terms of money should be included in the accounting records.
(d) assets should be recorded at their original cost.

4. An item is considered material when: (SO 2)
(a) it is more than $1,000.
(b) it occurs infrequently.
(c) its omission would influence or change a decision.
(d) it affects net earnings.

5. In a classified balance sheet, assets are usually classi- (SO 3) fied as:
(a) current assets; long-term investments; property, plant, and equipment; and intangible assets.
(b) current assets and property, plant, and equipment.
(c) current assets, long-term investments, and share capital.
(d) current assets and noncurrent assets.

(SO 3) 6. Current assets are listed:
   (a) by importance.   (c) by liquidity.
   (b) by permanence.   (d) alphabetically.

(SO 4) 7. ⚬━━⊂ Which is not an indicator of profitability?
   (a) Current ratio   (c) Net earnings
   (b) Earnings per share   (d) Price-earnings ratio

(SO 4) 8. Breau Corporation reported net earnings available to common shareholders $24,000; common shares $400,000; weighted average number of common shares 6,000; and a share market value of $60. What was its earnings per share?

(a) $0.06   (c) $15.00
(b) $4.00   (d) $16.67

9. ⚬━━⊂ Which of these measures is an evaluation of a (SO 5) company's ability to pay current liabilities?
   (a) Price-earnings ratio (c) Debt to total assets
   (b) Current ratio   (d) Free cash flow

10. ⚬━━⊂ Which of these measures is an evaluation of a (SO 5) company's ability to survive over the long-term?
   (a) Price-earnings ratio (c) Debt to total assets
   (b) Current ratio   (d) Working capital

Questions

(SO 1) 1. (a) What is the basic objective of financial reporting?
   (b) Identify the qualitative characteristics of accounting information.

(SO 1) 2. Ray Aldag, the president of Raynard Corporation, is pleased. Raynard substantially increased its net earnings in 2006, while keeping its unit inventory almost the same. Chief accountant Tom Erhardt is not as optimistic as Aldag, however. Erhardt says that since Raynard changed its method of inventory costing, there is a consistency problem and it is difficult to determine whether Raynard is better off. Is Erhardt correct? Why or why not?

(SO 1) 3. What is the difference between comparability and consistency?

(SO 2) 4. Explain the following assumptions: (a) monetary unit, (b) economic entity, (c) time period, and (d) going concern.

(SO 2) 5. How do the going concern assumption and cost principle influence the asset values reported on the balance sheet?

(SO 2) 6. Why is the full disclosure principle important to investors and creditors?

(SO 2) 7. Your roommate believes that accounting principles are the same around the world. Is your roommate correct? Explain.

(SO 2) 8. Describe the two constraints that affect the presentation of accounting information.

(SO 3) 9. Distinguish between current and noncurrent assets. What basis is used for ordering individual items in each of these sections on the balance sheet?

(SO 3) 10. Distinguish between (a) long-term investments and intangible assets and (b) property, plant, and equipment and intangible assets.

(SO 3) 11. How do current liabilities differ from long-term liabilities?

12. Identify the two parts of shareholders' equity in a corporation and indicate the purpose of each. (SO)

13. Is the opening balance or ending balance of retained earnings reported in the shareholders' equity section of the balance sheet? Explain why. (SO)

14. ⚬━━⊂ The Bank of Montreal has a price-earnings ratio of 12.2, while Scotiabank has a price-earnings ratio of 13.9. Which company do investors appear to favour? (SO)

15. ⚬━━⊂ Name some ratios that are useful in assessing (a) liquidity, (b) solvency, and (c) profitability. (SO)

16. ⚬━━⊂ What do each of these classes of ratios measure: (a) liquidity, (b) profitability, and (c) solvency? (SO)

17. Are short-term creditors, long-term creditors, and shareholders mostly interested in the same ratios when they analyze a company? Explain. (SO)

18. ⚬━━⊂ In your opinion, which ratio(s) from this chapter should be of greatest interest to: (SO)
   (a) a pension fund considering investing in a corporation's 20-year bonds?
   (b) a bank evaluating if it should give a short-term loan?
   (c) a common shareholder?

19. ⚬━━⊂ Assuming that all other factors stay the same, indicate whether each of the following generally signals good or bad news about a company: (SO)
   (a) An increase in the earnings per share
   (b) An increase in the current ratio
   (c) An increase in debt to total assets
   (d) A decrease in free cash flow

20. ⚬━━⊂ Dong Corporation has a debt to total assets ratio of 45%, while its competitor, Du Ltd., has a debt to total assets ratio of 65%. Based on this information, which company is more solvent? (SO)

Brief Exercises

BE2–1 Here are some qualitative characteristics of accounting information:

1. Predictive value
2. Neutrality
3. Verifiability
4. Timeliness
5. Faithful representation
6. Comparability
7. Feedback value
8. Consistency
9. Conservatism
10. Understandability

Match each qualitative characteristic to one of the following statements, using numbers 1 to 10:

(a) ___ Accounting information cannot be selected, prepared, or presented to favour one set of interested users over another.

(b) ___ Accounting information must be available to decision-makers before it loses its capacity to influence their decisions.

(c) ___ Accounting information is prepared on the assumption that users have a reasonable understanding of accounting and general business and economic conditions.

(d) ___ Accounting information provides a basis to evaluate a previously made decision.

(e) ___ Accounting information reports the economic substance, not the legal form, of the transaction.

(f) ___ Accounting information helps users make predictions about the outcome of past, present, and future events.

(g) ___ Accounting information about one company can be evaluated by comparing it to accounting information from another company.

(h) ___ Accounting information is prepared using the method that is least likely to overstate assets and net earnings when there is uncertainty.

(i) ___ Accounting information is free of error and bias.

(j) ___ Accounting information in a company is prepared using the same principles from year to year.

BE2–2 Presented below are the accounting assumptions, principles, and constraints discussed in this chapter:

1. Economic entity assumption
2. Going concern assumption
3. Monetary unit assumption
4. Time period assumption
5. Cost principle
6. Full disclosure principle
7. Cost-benefit constraint
8. Materiality constraint

Match the number of the most relevant assumption, principle, or constraint that describes each situation below:

(a) ___ A company is assumed to continue its business indefinitely.

(b) ___ Changes in market value after an asset is acquired are not recorded.

(c) ___ All relevant financial information should be reported.

(d) ___ The dollar is the "measuring stick" for reporting economic events.

(e) ___ The value of the information should be greater than the cost of providing it.

(f) ___ Personal and business affairs should be kept separate.

(g) ___ Items that would not likely influence a decision do not have to be disclosed.

(h) ___ Financial information is reported periodically, normally each quarter.

BE2–3 The following are the major balance sheet classifications:

1. Current assets
2. Long-term investments
3. Property, plant, and equipment
4. Intangible assets
5. Current liabilities
6. Long-term liabilities
7. Share capital
8. Retained earnings

Match each of the following accounts to its proper balance sheet classification:

(a) ___ Accounts payable   (g) ___ Income tax payable

(b) ___ Accounts receivable   (h) ___ Debt investment

(c) ___ Accumulated amortization   (i) ___ Land

(d) ___ Building   (j) ___ Merchandise inventory

(e) ___ Cash   (k) ___ Patent

(f) ___ Goodwill   (l) ___ Supplies

Prepare current assets section of balance sheet.
(SO 3)

BE2–4 A list of financial statement items for Swann Limited includes the following: accounts receivable $12,500; prepaid insurance $3,900; cash $18,400; supplies $5,200; and short-term investments $8,200. Prepare the current assets section of the balance sheet, listing the items in the proper sequence.

Prepare property, plant, and equipment section of balance sheet.
(SO 3)

BE2–5 A list of financial statement items for Shum Corporation includes the following: accumulated amortization—building $40,000; accumulated amortization—equipment $28,000; building $100,000; equipment $70,000; and land $65,000. Prepare the property, plant, and equipment section of the balance sheet, listing the items in the proper sequence.

Identify items affecting shareholders' equity.
(SO 3)

BE2–6 For each of the following events affecting the shareholders' equity of Wu Corporation, indicate whether the event would increase share capital (+), decrease share capital (−), increase retained earnings (+), or decrease retained earnings (−). Write "NE" if there is no effect.

	Share Capital	Retained Earnings
(a) Issued common shares	_____	_____
(b) Paid a cash dividend	_____	_____
(c) Reported net earnings	_____	_____
(d) Paid cash to creditors	_____	_____
(e) Reported a net loss	_____	_____
(f) Bought back common shares	_____	_____

Calculate ratios and evaluate profitability.
(SO 4)

BE2–7 The following information is available for Leon's Furniture Limited for the year ended December 31 (in thousands, except for share price):

	2004	2003
Net earnings available to common shareholders	$46,104	$38,438
Weighted average number of common shares	18,485	19,278
Share price	$35.00	$27.38

(a) Calculate the earnings per share and the price-earnings ratio for each year.
(b) Indicate whether profitability improved or decreased in 2004.

Calculate ratios and evaluate liquidity.
(SO 5)

BE2–8 Indigo Books & Music Inc. reported the following selected information for its years ended April 3, 2004, and March 29, 2003 (in thousands):

	2004	2003
Total current assets	$231,440	$221,694
Total current liabilities	267,473	249,249

(a) Calculate its working capital and current ratio for 2004 and 2003.
(b) Was Indigo's liquidity stronger or weaker in 2004 than in 2003?

Calculate ratios and evaluate solvency.
(SO 5)

BE2–9 Teddy Bear Valley Mines, Limited reported the following selected information for March 31 of each year (in thousands):

	2005	2004
Total assets	$ 1,258.0	$ 4,266.9
Total liabilities	12,894.8	11,742.6
Cash provided by operating activities	171.1	434.1
Net capital expenditures	434.1	302.9
Dividends paid	0.0	0.0

(a) Calculate the debt to total assets ratio and free cash flow for 2005 and 2004.
(b) Was the company's solvency stronger or weaker in 2005 than in 2004?

Exercises

E2–1 In January 2005, Hollinger Inc.—one of the largest newspaper groups in the world—announced that it would have to delay the release of its December 31, 2003, audited financial statements. Hollinger has a 67% voting interest in Hollinger International, which is currently battling Hollinger Inc. for control of the company. Apparently, Hollinger's 2003 annual financial statements cannot be completed and audited until an independent review of related transactions for Hollinger International is completed.

Comment on objective and qualitative characteristics of financial reporting.
(SO 1)

Instructions

Comment on how the delay in the release of Hollinger's financial statements meets, or does not meet, the objective of financial reporting and qualitative characteristics of accounting information.

E2–2 Marietta Corp. had the following reporting issues during the year:

Identify the assumption, principle, or constraint violated.
(SO 2)

1. Land with a cost of $208,000 was reported at its market value of $260,000.
2. The president of Marietta, Deanna Durnford, purchased a truck for personal use and charged it to her expense account.
3. Marietta wanted to make its net earnings look better, so it added two more weeks to the year, creating a 54-week year. Previous years were 52 weeks.
4. The president wanted to make sure that the company was not accused of hiding anything from its shareholders, so she instructed the chief financial officer to disclose everything that happened during the year in the notes to the financial statements. The notes ended up being 95 pages long.

Instructions

In each situation, identify the assumption, principle, or constraint that has been violated, if any, and explain what should have been done.

E2–3 The following are the major balance sheet classifications:

Classify accounts on balance sheet.
(SO 3)

1. Current assets
2. Long-term investments
3. Property, plant, and equipment
4. Intangible assets

5. Current liabilities
6. Long-term liabilities
7. Share capital
8. Retained earnings

Instructions

Classify each of the following selected accounts taken from TELUS Corporation's balance sheet:

(a) ___ Accounts payable and accrued liabilities
(b) ___ Accounts receivable
(c) ___ Accumulated amortization
(d) ___ Buildings
(e) ___ Cash and temporary investments
(f) ___ Dividends payable
(g) ___ Goodwill
(h) ___ Income and other taxes receivable

(i) ___ Inventories
(j) ___ Investments
(k) ___ Land
(l) ___ Long-term debt
(m) ___ Office equipment and furniture
(n) ___ Common shares
(o) ___ Prepaid expenses and other

E2–4 The assets shown below were taken from Big Rock Brewery's December 31, 2004, balance sheet:

Prepare assets section of balance sheet.
(SO 3)

Accounts receivable	$ 2,758,246
Accumulated amortization—buildings	2,814,682
Accumulated amortization—furniture and fixtures	998,431
Accumulated amortization—production equipment	10,840,095
Accumulated amortization—vehicles	258,269
Buildings	12,228,828
Cash	2,093,695
Deferred charges and other assets	323,714

Furniture and fixtures	$ 1,437,242
Goodwill	727,218
Inventories	4,667,950
Investments	33,008
Land	2,396,234
Prepaid expenses and other	427,169
Production equipment	28,160,142
Vehicles	586,499

Instructions

Prepare the assets section of the balance sheet.

Prepare balance sheet.
(SO 3)

E2–5 These items are taken from the financial statements of Summit's Bowling Alley Ltd. at December 31, 2006:

Cash	$ 18,040	Accounts payable	$12,300
Accounts receivable	13,780	Interest payable	2,600
Supplies	740	Mortgage payable	94,780
Prepaid insurance	390	Common shares	75,000
Investments	50,000	Retained earnings, January 1	66,520
Land	64,000	Bowling revenues	64,180
Building	128,800	Interest expense	2,600
Accumulated amortization—building	45,600	Income tax expense	8,000
Equipment	62,400	Operating expenses	30,000
Accumulated amortization—equipment	17,770		

Instructions

(a) Calculate net earnings and the ending balance of retained earnings at December 31, 2006. Formal statements do not need to be prepared.

(b) Prepare a balance sheet. Assume that $13,600 of the mortgage payable will be paid in 2007.

Prepare balance sheet.
(SO 3)

E2–6 The following items were taken from the March 31, 2004, balance sheet of Vincor International Inc. (in thousands):

Accounts payable and accrued liabilities	$ 66,898	Income taxes payable	$ 3,839
Accounts receivable	64,910	Inventories	220,322
Accumulated amortization—buildings	10,205	Land	18,334
Accumulated amortization—storage		Long-term debt	107,790
tanks, machinery, and equipment	55,241	Prepaid expenses	4,841
Accumulated amortization—vineyards	7,074	Other assets	8,233
Bank indebtedness	19,686	Other intangible assets	45,408
Buildings	62,868	Other long-term liabilities	3,482
Capital stock	479,434	Retained earnings	161,448
Current portion of long-term debt	24,603	Short-term investments	166,086
Future income taxes receivable (current)	1,890	Storage tanks, machinery,	
Future income taxes payable (long-term)	18,277	and equipment	134,168
Goodwill	167,354	Vineyards	63,563

Instructions

Prepare a balance sheet.

Prepare financial statements.
(SO 3)

E2–7 These financial statement items are for Batra Corporation at year end, July 31, 2006:

Salaries expense	$34,700	Supplies expense	$ 900
Utilities expense	2,600	Dividends	2,500
Equipment	15,900	Amortization expense	3,000
Accounts payable	4,220	Retained earnings, August 1, 2005	17,940
Commission revenue	61,100	Rent expense	10,800
Rent revenue	8,500	Income tax expense	5,000
Common shares	16,000	Supplies	1,500
Cash	1,560	Short-term investments	40,000
Accounts receivable	17,100	Note payable	
Accumulated amortization	6,000	(due December 31, 2006)	21,800
Interest payable	1,000	Interest expense	1,000

Instructions

Prepare a statement of earnings, statement of retained earnings, and balance sheet for the year.

E2–8 The following information is available for Cameco Corporation for the year ended December 31 (in thousands, except share price):

Calculate ratios and evaluate profitability.
(SO 4)

	2004	2003
Net earnings available for common shareholders	$278,785	$208,163
Weighted average number of common shares	171,445	168,359
Share price	$41.95	$24.39

Instructions

(a) Calculate the earnings per share and price-earnings ratio for each year.
(b) Based on your calculations above, how did the company's profitability change from 2003 to 2004?
(c) Would your answer in (b) above change if you were evaluating profitability for a potential investor, rather than an existing shareholder?

E2–9 Wal-Mart Stores, Inc. is a competitor of Sears and The Bay. Wal-Mart reported the following information for fiscal 2003 and 2002 (in U.S. millions):

Calculate ratios and comment on liquidity.
(SO 5)

	2003	2002
Current assets	$34,421	$30,483
Current liabilities	37,418	32,617

Instructions

(a) Calculate the working capital and current ratio for each fiscal year.
(b) Did Wal-Mart's liquidity improve or worsen during the year?
(c) Using the data in the chapter, compare Wal-Mart's liquidity with that of Sears, The Bay, and the industry.

E2–10 The following data were taken from the April 30 financial statements of the Québec Winter Carnival:

Calculate ratios and comment on solvency.
(SO 5)

	2004	2003
Total assets	$1,804,437	$1,589,710
Total liabilities	878,890	604,718
Cash used by operating activities	379,782	93,833
Net capital expenditures	85,957	32,820
Dividends paid	0	0

Instructions

(a) Calculate the debt to total assets ratio and free cash flow for 2004 and 2003.
(b) Discuss the Carnival's solvency in 2004 versus 2003.

Problems: Set A

P2–1A Dimethaid Research Inc. reported a deficit of US$96.3 million on its May 31, 2004, balance sheet. It has reported only net losses over the last decade. In spite of these losses, Dimethaid's common shares have traded anywhere from a high of $12.50 to a low of $0.30 on the Toronto Stock Exchange (TSX).

Comment on objective and qualitative characteristics of accounting information.
(SO 1)

Until 2003, Dimethaid's financial statements were prepared in Canadian dollars. As of May 31, 2003, the company adopted the U.S. dollar as its reporting currency.

Instructions

(a) What is the objective of financial reporting? Do you believe that Dimethaid has likely met this objective?
(b) Why would investors want to buy Dimethaid's shares if the company has consistently reported losses? Include in your answer an assessment of the relevance and reliability of the information reported on Dimethaid's financial statements.
(c) Comment on how the change in reporting information from Canadian dollars to U.S. dollars likely affected the readers of Dimethaid's financial statements. Why do you think the company probably made this change in its reporting currency?

Comment on constraints of accounting.
(SO 2)

P2–2A   A friend of yours, Ryan Konotopsky, has come to you looking for some answers about financial statements. Ryan tells you that he is thinking about opening a movie theatre in his home town. Before doing so, he wants to find out how much sales he could expect to make from food concessions as opposed to ticket sales. He wants to know what proportion of ticket sales he could expect for children, youth, and seniors, who pay less, versus adults, who pay the highest admission rate. He also wants to know how much profit he would make on ticket sales versus sales at the concession stands, and he would like to know the average wage per employee.

Ryan downloaded the financial statements of Empire Company Limited, which operates 27 Empire Theatres in Atlantic Canada. He noticed that the company's statement of earnings reported revenues for the year ended April 30, 2004, of $11,284 million and cost of sales, selling, and administrative expenses of $10,704.3 million. He read through Empire's annual report and learned that Empire Theatres is just one part of the Investments and Theatre Operations division of the company. There are food distribution and real estate divisions as well.

Ryan is disillusioned because he cannot find many details about Empire Theatres in the financial statements. He has come to you looking for explanations.

Instructions

What are two constraints in accounting? What impact have these constraints had on the financial reporting by Empire Company Limited?

Classify accounts.
(SO 3)

P2–3A   You are provided with the following selected balance sheet accounts for Leon's Furniture Limited:

Accounts payable and accrued liabilities   Future income tax liabilities
Accounts receivable   Income taxes recoverable
Buildings   Inventory
Cash and cash equivalents   Land
Common shares   Leasehold improvements
Computer hardware and software   Marketable securities
Customers' deposits   Retained earnings
Dividends payable   Vehicles
Equipment

Instructions

Identify the balance sheet category for classifying each account. For example, Accounts Payable and Accrued Liabilities should be classified as current liabilities on the balance sheet.

Prepare balance sheet.
(SO 3)

P2–4A   The following items are taken from the July 31, 2004, balance sheet of the Saskatchewan Wheat Pool (in thousands):

Cash	$ 17,169
Cash in trust	1,176
Short-term investments	25,999
Accounts receivable	164,234
Inventories	104,887
Prepaid expenses and deposits	9,810
Other current assets	1,198
Investments	5,051
Property, plant, and equipment	302,486
Accumulated amortization—property, plant, and equipment	35,644
Other long-term assets	103,784
Bank indebtedness	29,805
Accounts payable and accrued liabilities	150,745
Short-term borrowings	1,501
Members' demand loans	20,474
Long-term debt due within one year	7,893
Long-term debt	251,930
Other long-term liabilities	46,924
Share capital	210,099
Deficit	(19,221)

Instructions

Prepare a balance sheet.

P2–5A These items are taken from the financial statements of Mbong Corporation for December 31, 2006:

Prepare financial statements. (SO 3)

Retained earnings, January 1	$60,000	Amortization expense	$ 6,200
Utilities expense	2,000	Accounts receivable	14,200
Equipment	66,000	Insurance expense	2,200
Accounts payable	13,300	Salaries expense	37,000
Building	72,000	Accumulated	
Cash	5,200	amortization—equipment	17,600
Salaries payable	3,000	Income tax expense	12,000
Common shares	39,500	Supplies	200
Dividends	2,000	Supplies expense	1,000
Service revenue	81,200	Note payable, due 2009	65,000
Prepaid insurance	3,500	Investments—long-term	22,300
Repair expense	1,800	Accumulated	
Land	50,000	amortization—building	18,000

Instructions

Prepare a statement of earnings, statement of retained earnings, and balance sheet for the year.

P2–6A You are provided with the following information for Cheung Corporation for its April 30, 2006, year end:

Prepare financial statements and discuss relationships. (SO 3)

Accounts payable	$ 6,000	Income tax expense	$ 3,500
Accounts receivable	7,800	Income taxes payable	875
Accumulated amortization	9,220	Interest expense	450
Amortization expense	4,610	Notes payable, due 2009	5,700
Cash	20,200	Prepaid rent	750
Common shares	20,000	Rent expense	9,000
Dividends	2,500	Retained earnings, May 1, 2005	14,065
Equipment	23,050	Salaries expense	8,000
Fees earned	35,000	Short-term investments	11,000

Instructions

(a) Prepare a statement of earnings, statement of retained earnings, and balance sheet for the year.

(b) Explain how each financial statement is related to the others.

P2–7A Here are the statements of Johannsen Inc.:

Calculate liquidity, profitability, and solvency ratios. (SO 4, 5)

JOHANNSEN INC.
Statement of Earnings
Year Ended December 31

Sales		$2,218,500
Expenses		
Cost of goods sold	$1,012,400	
Operating	906,000	
Interest	98,000	2,016,400
Earnings before income taxes		202,100
Income tax expense		60,630
Net earnings		$ 141,470

JOHANNSEN INC.
Balance Sheet
December 31

Assets

Current assets		
Cash and cash equivalents	$ 60,100	
Short-term investments	54,000	
Accounts receivable	207,800	
Inventory	125,000	$ 446,900
Property, plant, and equipment		625,300
Total assets		$1,072,200

Liabilities and Shareholders' Equity

Liabilities		
Current liabilities		
Accounts payable	$100,000	
Income taxes payable	15,000	
Current portion of mortgage payable	27,500	$ 142,500
Mortgage payable		310,000
Total liabilities		452,500
Shareholders' equity		
Common shares	$307,630	
Retained earnings	312,070	619,700
Total liabilities and shareholders' equity		$1,072,200

Additional information:

1. Net earnings available to common shareholders was $141,470.
2. The weighted average number of shares was 5,000.
3. The share price at December 31 was $30.
4. Cash provided by operating activities was $90,800.
5. Net capital expenditures were $75,000.
6. No dividends were paid.

Instructions

Calculate these values and ratios:

(a) Working capital
(b) Current ratio
(c) Earnings per share
(d) Price-earnings ratio
(e) Debt to total assets
(f) Free cash flow

Calculate ratios and comment on liquidity, profitability, and solvency.
(SO 4, 5)

P2–8A   Financial statement data for a recent year for Chen Corporation and Caissie Corporation, two competitors, are as follows:

	Chen	Caissie
Current assets	$425,000	$190,000
Property, plant, and equipment	525,000	140,000
Current liabilities	66,000	35,000
Long-term liabilities	108,500	30,000
Net earnings available to common shareholders	325,000	115,000
Weighted average number of common shares	100,000	50,000
Share price	25	15
Cash provided by operating activities	165,000	25,000
Net capital expenditures	90,000	10,000
Dividends paid	10,000	0

Instructions

(a) Calculate the current ratio for each company. Comment on their relative liquidity.
(b) Calculate earnings per share and the price-earnings ratio of each company. Comment on their relative profitability.
(c) Calculate the debt to total assets ratio and free cash flow for each company. Comment on their relative solvency.

P2–9A Condensed balance sheet and other data for Pitka Corporation are presented here:

Calculate ratios and comment on liquidity, profitability, and solvency.
(SO 4, 5)

PITKA CORPORATION
Balance Sheet
December 31

	2006	2005
Assets		
Current assets	$185,000	$155,000
Investments	75,000	60,000
Property, plant, and equipment	500,000	470,000
Total assets	$760,000	$685,000
Liabilities and Shareholders' Equity		
Current liabilities	$ 75,000	$ 80,000
Long-term liabilities	85,000	110,000
Shareholders' equity	600,000	495,000
Total liabilities and shareholders' equity	$760,000	$685,000

Additional information:

1. Net earnings available to common shareholders were $105,000 for 2006 and $94,500 for 2005.
2. The weighted average number of common shares was 30,000 in 2006 and 30,000 in 2005.
3. The share price at December 31, 2006, was $15; it was $12 at the end of 2005.
4. Cash provided by operating activities was $75,000 in 2006 and $60,000 in 2005.
5. Net capital expenditures were $30,000 in 2006 and $25,000 in 2005.
6. No dividends were paid in either year.

Instructions

(a) Calculate these values and ratios for 2006 and 2005:
   1. Working capital
   2. Current ratio
   3. Earnings per share
   4. Price-earnings ratio
   5. Debt to total assets
   6. Free cash flow
(b) Based on the ratios and other values calculated, briefly discuss Pitka Corporation's change in liquidity, profitability, and solvency.

P2–10A Selected financial data as at March 31, 2004, of two competitors, Andrés Wines Ltd. and Vincor International Inc., are presented here:

Calculate ratios and comment on liquidity, profitability, and solvency.
(SO 4, 5)

(in thousands, except share price)	Andrés Wines	Vincor
Current assets	$ 68,493	$458,049
Total assets	146,974	885,457
Current liabilities	38,612	115,026
Total liabilities	65,666	244,575
Net earnings available to common shareholders	7,804	46,270
Weighted average number of common shares	3,882	27,738
Share price	28.05	30.65
Cash provided by operating activities	4,151	29,623
Net capital expenditures	7,792	20,998
Dividends paid	3,057	0

Instructions

(a) For each company, calculate the following values and ratios. Where available, industry averages are included in parentheses.
   1. Working capital (n/a)
   2. Current ratio (1.7:1)
   3. Earnings per share (n/a)
   4. Price-earnings ratio (18.6 times)
   5. Debt to total assets (58.8%)
   6. Free cash flow (n/a)
(b) Compare the liquidity, profitability, and solvency of the two companies and their industry.

Problems: Set B

Comment on objective and
qualitative characteristics of
accounting information.
(SO 1)

P2–1B   Except for the current fiscal year, Research In Motion (RIM) Limited has reported net losses since its inception. The company's share price has been as high as $202 per share in February 2000 and as low as $15 in September 2002.

Until 1999, RIM's financial statements were prepared in Canadian dollars. As of September 1, 1999, the company adopted the U.S. dollar as its reporting currency.

Instructions

(a) What is the objective of financial reporting? Do you believe that RIM has likely met this objective?

(b) Why would investors want to buy RIM's shares if the company has consistently reported losses until this year? Include in your answer an assessment of the relevance and reliability of the information reported on RIM's financial statements.

(c) Comment on how the change in reporting information from Canadian dollars to U.S. dollars likely affected the readers of RIM's financial statements. Why do you think the company probably made this change in its reporting currency?

Comment on constraints of
accounting.
(SO 2)

P2–2B   Under GAAP, no separate disclosure is required on the statement of earnings for the cost of goods sold (the cost of merchandise sold to customers). Because this disclosure is not specifically required, less than half of reporting companies disclose their cost of goods sold separately on their statements of earnings. Most companies include it with other expenses in their reporting of this item, as Sears Canada Inc. did in its statement of earnings shown in Illustration 2-12 presented in the chapter.

Instructions

(a) What are the two constraints in accounting?

(b) Why do you think Sears does not report the cost of goods sold separately on its statement of earnings? Does either of the accounting constraints likely have an impact on Sears' reporting policy for cost of goods sold? Explain.

Classify accounts.
(SO 3)

P2–3B   You are provided with the following alphabetical list of accounts:

Accounts payable	Income tax expense
Accounts receivable	Income taxes payable
Accumulated amortization—building	Interest expense
Accumulated amortization—equipment	Inventories
Amortization expense	Land
Building	Long-term debt
Cash	Prepaid expenses
Common shares	Retained earnings, beginning of year
Cost of goods sold	Sales
Current portion of long-term debt	Selling and administrative expenses
Dividends	Short-term investments
Equipment	Supplies
Goodwill	Wages payable

Instructions

Identify the financial statement and category for classifying each account. For example, Accounts Payable should be classified as a current liability on the balance sheet.

Prepare balance sheet.
(SO 3)

P2–4B   The following items are taken from Intrawest Corporation's June 30, 2004, balance sheet (in U.S. thousands):

Capital stock	$463,485	Bank and other indebtedness,	
Amounts payable	209,037	current portion	$109,685
Other noncurrent assets	65,306	Other current liabilities	87,649
Other current assets	112,743	Retained earnings	323,824
Amounts receivable	142,427	Cash and cash equivalents	109,816
Investments	50,899	Resort properties under	
Land	49,166	development and held for sale	780,652
Bank and other indebtedness,		Accumulated amortization—	
noncurrent portion	849,132	other resort assets	65,768
Buildings	307,000	Accumulated amortization—	
Ski lifts and area improvements	479,664	buildings	63,764
Automotive, helicopters, and		Accumulated amortization—	
other equipment	143,429	ski lifts and area improvements	157,134
Leased vehicles	4,740	Accumulated amortization—	
Other resort assets	339,703	automotive, helicopters,	
Amounts receivable		and other equipment	93,503
(noncurrent)	52,958	Accumulated amortization—	
Other long-term liabilities	212,938	leased vehicles	2,584

Instructions

Prepare a balance sheet.

P2–5B These items are taken from the December 31, 2006, financial statements of Beau-lieu Limited:

Prepare financial statements. (SO 3)

Cash	$ 8,000	Retained earnings, January 1	$ 34,000
Building	80,000	Dividends	3,500
Accumulated amortization—		Service revenue	82,000
building	12,000	Repair expense	3,200
Accounts receivable	7,500	Amortization expense	10,400
Prepaid insurance	250	Insurance expense	2,400
Equipment	32,000	Salaries expense	36,000
Accumulated amortization—		Utilities expense	3,700
equipment	19,200	Income tax payable	1,750
Accounts payable	12,000	Land	50,000
Salaries payable	3,000	Mortgage payable	100,000
Common shares	20,000	Current portion of	
Income tax expense	7,000	mortgage payable	10,000
Investments	50,000		

Instructions

Prepare a statement of earnings, statement of retained earnings, and balance sheet for the year.

P2–6B You are provided with the following information for Crusaders Inc., effective as at its January 31, 2006, year end:

Prepare financial statements and discuss relationships. (SO 3)

Accounts payable	$ 9,000	Equipment	$12,000
Accounts receivable	18,100	Income tax expense	1,000
Accumulated amortization—		Income taxes payable	250
building	4,500	Interest expense	4,000
Accumulated amortization—		Inventories	9,700
equipment	4,800	Land	60,000
Amortization expense	4,000	Mortgage payable	55,000
Building	45,000	Operating expenses	6,000
Cash	5,700	Prepaid expenses	1,200
Common shares	29,000	Retained earnings, February 1, 2005	43,150
Cost of goods sold	20,000	Sales	44,000
Current portion of mortgage		Short-term investments	12,000
payable	14,500	Wages expense	7,000
Dividends	500	Wages payable	2,000

Instructions

(a) Prepare a statement of earnings, statement of retained earnings, and balance sheet for the year.
(b) Explain how each financial statement is related to the others.

P2–7B   The statements of the Fast Corporation are presented here:

FAST CORPORATION
Statement of Earnings
Year Ended December 31

Sales		$712,000
Expenses		
Cost of goods sold	$420,000	
Operating expenses	144,000	
Interest	10,000	574,000
Earnings before income taxes		138,000
Income tax expense		41,400
Net earnings		$ 96,600

FAST CORPORATION
Balance Sheet
December 31

Assets

Current assets		
Cash	$ 23,100	
Short-term investments	34,800	
Accounts receivable	106,200	
Inventory	129,750	$293,850
Property, plant, and equipment		465,300
Total assets		$759,150

Liabilities and Shareholders' Equity

Liabilities		
Current liabilities		
Accounts payable	$134,200	
Income taxes payable	10,350	$144,550
Mortgage payable		132,000
Total liabilities		276,550
Shareholders' equity		
Common shares	$140,000	
Retained earnings	342,600	482,600
Total liabilities and shareholders' equity		$759,150

Additional information:

1. Net earnings available to common shareholders were $96,600.
2. The weighted average number of common shares was 7,000.
3. The share price at December 31 was $34.
4. Cash provided by operating activities was $42,300.
5. Net capital expenditures were $7,500.
6. Dividends paid were $5,000.

Instructions

Calculate these values and ratios:

(a) Current ratio
(b) Earnings per share
(c) Price-earnings ratio

(d) Debt to total assets
(e) Free cash flow

P2–8B   Comparative statement data for Belliveau Corp. and Shields Corp., two competitors, are presented here for a recent year:

Calculate ratios and comment on liquidity, profitability, and solvency.
(SO 4, 5)

	Belliveau	Shields
Current assets	$180,000	$700,000
Property, plant, and equipment	705,000	800,000
Current liabilities	60,000	250,000
Long-term liabilities	215,000	200,000
Net earnings available to common shareholders	36,000	173,000
Weighted average number of common shares	200,000	400,000
Share price	2.50	7.00
Cash provided by operating activities	20,000	185,000
Net capital expenditures	55,000	95,000
Dividends paid	10,000	25,000

Instructions

(a) Calculate the current ratio for each company. Comment on their relative liquidity.
(b) Calculate the earnings per share and the price-earnings ratio of each company. Comment on their relative profitability.
(c) Calculate debt to total assets and free cash flow for each company. Comment on their relative solvency.

P2–9B   Condensed balance sheet and other data for Giasson Corporation are presented below:

Calculate ratios and comment on liquidity, profitability, and solvency.
(SO 4, 5)

GIASSON CORPORATION
Balance Sheet
December 31

	2006	2005
Assets		
Current assets	$135,000	$128,000
Investments	50,000	40,000
Property, plant, and equipment	536,000	400,000
Total assets	$721,000	$568,000
Liabilities and Shareholders' Equity		
Current liabilities	$ 88,000	$ 75,000
Long-term liabilities	95,000	70,000
Shareholders' equity	538,000	423,000
Total liabilities and shareholders' equity	$721,000	$568,000

Additional information:

1. Net earnings available to common shareholders were $65,000 in 2006 and $84,000 in 2005.
2. The weighted average number of common shares was 76,000 in 2006 and 65,000 in 2005.
3. The share price at December 31, 2006, was $4; it was $6 at the end of 2005.
4. Cash provided by operating activities was $60,000 in 2006 and $125,000 in 2005.
5. Net capital expenditures were $100,000 in 2006 and $110,000 in 2005.
6. Dividends of $15,000 were paid in each year.

Instructions

(a) Calculate these values and ratios for 2006 and 2005:
    1. Working capital   4. Price-earnings ratio
    2. Current ratio   5. Debt to total assets
    3. Earnings per share   6. Free cash flow
(b) Based on the ratios calculated, briefly discuss Giasson's change in liquidity, profitability, and solvency.

Calculate ratios and comment on liquidity, profitability, and solvency.
(SO 4, 5)

P2–10B   Selected financial data from fiscal 2004 for two forest products companies, Abitibi-Consolidated Inc. and Tembec Inc., are presented here:

(in millions, except for share price)	Abitibi	Tembec
Current assets	$1,402	$1,230
Total assets	9,787	3,921
Current liabilities	1,554	722
Total liabilities	7,061	2,724
Net earnings (loss) available to common shareholders	(36)	37
Weighted average number of common shares	440	86
Share price	8.23	8.35
Cash provided by operating activities	66	207
Net capital expenditures	381	143
Dividends paid	55	0

Instructions

(a) For each company, calculate these values and ratios. Where available, industry averages have been included in parentheses.

    1. Working capital (n/a)   4. Price-earnings ratio (26.3 times)

    2. Current ratio (1.3:1)   5. Debt to total assets (53.1%)

    3. Earnings per share (n/a)   6. Free cash flow (n/a)

(b) Compare the liquidity, profitability, and solvency of the two companies and their industry.

BROADENING YOUR PERSPECTIVE

www.wiley.com/canada/kimmel

Analysis Tools

Financial Reporting and Analysis

Financial Reporting Problem: *Loblaw*

BYP2–1   The financial statements of Loblaw are presented in Appendix A at the end of this book.

Instructions

(a) What were the balances of Loblaw's total current assets and total assets at the end of fiscal 2003 and 2002?

(b) Are the current assets listed in the proper order? Explain.

(c) How are Loblaw's assets classified?

(d) What were the balances of Loblaw's total current liabilities and total liabilities at the end of fiscal 2003 and 2002?

Comparative Analysis Problem: *Loblaw and Sobeys*

BYP2–2   The financial statements of Sobeys are presented in Appendix B after the financial statements for Loblaw in Appendix A.

Instructions

(a) For each company, calculate or find the following values for the most recent fiscal year:

    1. Working capital   4. Price-earnings ratio

    2. Current ratio   5. Debt to total assets

    3. Earnings per share   6. Free cash flow

(b) Based on your findings above, discuss the relative liquidity, profitability, and solvency of the two companies.

Research Case

BYP2–3 The May 2005 issue of *CAmagazine* includes an article by Robert Colapinto entitled "The Future Direction of Accounting Standards." This article discusses the proposed adoption of international accounting standards in Canada by the Accounting Standards Board (AcSB).

Instructions

Read the article and answer the following questions:

(a) Why is the AcSB recommending a change to international standards? What are some advantages and disadvantages of such a change?
(b) Until the proposal to change to international accounting standards, Canada was working to harmonize Canadian GAAP with U.S. GAAP. What impact do you think this change will now have on Canadian companies doing business in North America?
(c) Why is the AcSB recommending a different set of standards for publicly-traded companies than for private companies? Do you agree or disagree with this recommended course of action?

Interpreting Financial Statements

BYP2–4 The following information was reported by the Gap, Inc.:

(in U.S. millions, except share amount)	2004	2003	2002	2001	2000
Total assets	$10,048	$10,343	$9,902	$7,683	$7,013
Working capital	$4,062	$4,197	$3,014	$1,023	$(151)
Current ratio	2.8:1	2.6:1	2.1:1	1.5:1	0.9:1
Earnings per share	$1.29	$1.15	$0.55	$(0.01)	$1.03
Price-earnings ratio	18.0×	16.1×	26.3×	n/a	31.0×
Debt to total assets	28.6%	32.8%	35.5%	33.3%	18.3%
Free cash flow	$1,178	$1,899	$935	$302	$643

Instructions

(a) Comment on the change in The Gap's liquidity. Which value seems to provide a better indication of The Gap's liquidity: working capital or the current ratio? What might explain the change in The Gap's liquidity during this period?
(b) Comment on the change in The Gap's profitability during this period. Is the change in earnings per share consistent with the change in the price-earnings ratio? Explain why these two ratios might not always move in the same direction.
(c) Comment on the change in The Gap's solvency during this period.

A Global Focus

BYP2–5 Nexen Inc., headquartered in Calgary, is a globe-trotting oil and gas and chemicals company. It has exploration and production activities in Australia, Brazil, Colombia, Indonesia, Nigeria, Yemen, and the U.S., in addition to Canada.

One of the challenges global companies face is to make themselves attractive to investors from other countries. This is difficult to do when different accounting principles in other countries can blur the real impact of earnings. For example, in its statement of earnings for the year ended December 31, 2004, Nexen reported net earnings of $793 million, using Canadian GAAP. Had it reported under U.S. GAAP, its net earnings would have been $788 million.

Instructions

(a) Suppose you wish to compare Nexen to a U.S.-based competitor, such as Exxon Mobil. Do you believe the use of different countries' accounting principles would help or hinder your comparison? If so, explain how.

(b) Suppose you wish to compare Nexen to a Canadian-based competitor, such as Imperial Oil. If Imperial Oil chose to use different Canadian accounting principles than Nexen, how could this affect your comparison of the financial results?

(c) Do you see any significant difference between (1) comparing statements prepared in different countries and (2) comparing statements prepared in the same country but using different accounting principles?

Financial Analysis on the Web

www.wiley.com/canada/kimmel

**Analysis Tools
(Financial Analysis on the Web)**

BYP2–6   SEDAR (System for Electronic Document Analysis and Retrieval) provides access to information about, and documents of, Canadian public companies. We will use SEDAR to locate and identify recent corporate filings for Loblaw and Sobeys.

Instructions

Specific requirements of this Web case can be found on the Toolkit website.

Critical Thinking

Collaborative Learning Activity

BYP2–7   As the accountant for Soukup Inc., you have been asked to develop some key ratios from the comparative financial statements. This information will be used to convince creditors that Soukup is liquid, profitable, and solvent and therefore deserves their continued support.

Here are the data and calculations you developed from the financial statements:

	2006	2005
Current ratio	3.1:1	2.1:1
Working capital	Up 22%	Down 7%
Net earnings	Up 32%	Down 8%
Earnings per share	$2.40	$1.15
Price-earnings ratio	26 times	19 times
Debt to total assets	60%	70%
Free cash flow	Down 25%	Up 10%

Instructions

You have been asked to prepare brief comments which explain how each of these items supports the argument that Soukup's financial health is improving. The company wants to use these comments in a presentation to its creditors. Prepare the comments as requested, giving the implications and the limitations of each item separately. Then state what conclusions may be drawn from them as a whole about Soukup's financial well-being.

Communication Activity

BYP2–8   On April 1, 2003, Air Canada filed for bankruptcy protection under the *Companies' Creditors Arrangement Act* (CCAA). Filing for protection under the CCAA gives a company time to hold talks with its major stakeholders, such as creditors and labour unions, and to restructure its operations. During the period when Air Canada was under CCAA protection, it issued financial statements quarterly. On September 30, 2004, Air Canada emerged from CCAA protection with a strengthened balance sheet, a reorganized corporate structure, and a strategy for sustained growth and profitability.

Instructions

Assume the role of Air Canada's auditors and write a memo to the airline in which you discuss the appropriate basis on which Air Canada should issue its financial statements while under CCAA protection—on a going concern basis or a liquidation basis. Include in your memo an assessment of the pros and cons of each basis for Air Canada's investors and creditors.

Ethics Case

BYP2–9   When new accounting principles are issued, the required implementation date is usually 12 months or more after the date of issuance, but early implementation is encouraged.

Ethics in Accounting

Kathy Johnston, the accountant at Redondo Corporation, discusses with Redondo's vice-president the need for early implementation of a recently issued recommendation. She says it will result in a much fairer presentation of the company's financial condition and earnings. When the vice-president determines that early implementation would decrease reported net earnings for the year, he strongly discourages Kathy from implementing the recommendation until it is required.

Instructions

(a) Who are the stakeholders in this situation?
(b) What, if any, are the ethical considerations in this situation?
(c) What could Kathy gain by supporting early implementation? Who might be affected by the decision against early implementation?

Serial Problem

(*Note*: This serial problem was started in Chapter 1 and will continue in each chapter.)

BYP2–10   After investigating the different forms of business organization, Natalie Koebel decides to operate her business as a corporation, Cookie Creations Ltd. She begins the process of getting her business running. While at a trade show, Natalie is introduced to Gerry Richards, operations manager of "Biscuits," a national food retailer. After much discussion, Gerry asks Natalie to consider being Biscuits' major supplier of oatmeal chocolate chip cookies. He provides Natalie with the most recent copy of the financial statements of Biscuits. He expects that Natalie will need to supply Biscuits' Red Deer warehouse with approximately 1,500 dozen cookies a week. Natalie is to send Biscuits a monthly invoice and she will be paid approximately 30 days from the date the invoice is received in Biscuits' Toronto office.

Natalie is thrilled with the offer; however, she has recently read in the newspaper that Biscuits has a reputation for selling cookies and donuts with high amounts of sugar and fat and, as a result, consumer demand has decreased.

Instructions

Natalie has come to you for advice and asks the following questions:

(a) Explain to me the type of information each financial statement provides.
(b) I would like to be sure that Biscuits will be able to pay my invoices. What type of information can these financial statements give that will reassure me that my invoices will be paid?
(c) Will Biscuits have enough cash to meet its current liabilities? Where can I find this information?
(d) Will Biscuits be able to survive over a long period of time? Where can I find this information?
(e) Is Biscuits profitable? Where can I find this information?
(f) Does Biscuits have any debt? Is Biscuits able to pay off both its debt and the interest on it? Where can I find this information?
(g) Does Biscuits pay any dividends? Where can I find this information?
(h) Before I seriously consider this opportunity, are there other areas of concern that I should be aware of?

Answers to Self-Study Questions

1. b   2. c   3. d   4. c   5. a   6. c   7. a   8. b   9. b   10. c

Answer to Loblaw Review It Question 3

Loblaw's largest current asset at January 3, 2004, is inventories ($1,778 million).

Remember to go back to the Navigator box at the beginning of the chapter to check off your completed work.

CHAPTER 3

The Accounting Information System

Learning to Handle the Dough

For generations, grandmothers in Grant Hooker's family would make a pastry of flattened, whole-wheat dough as a special treat called a BeaverTail®.

In 1978, Hooker trademarked his name for the pastry and sold the family secret to the public for the first time at a music festival near Killaloe, Ontario. The crowd loved it. The delectable dough was then served up at several Ottawa valley agricultural fairs. Encouraged by the enthusiasm for his treats, Hooker built a booth in Ottawa's Byward Market in 1980 to sell BeaverTails full-time. However, sales weren't as swift as at the fairs.

Undaunted, Hooker secured permission to sell BeaverTails on the Rideau Canal during Winterlude. Within three years, BeaverTails Canada Inc. had the contract to sell all food on the Rideau Canal and employed 450 people. BeaverTails began franchising in 1990 and now includes 120 locations across Canada, as well as several in the United States and overseas.

When the business first started, keeping track of the money simply meant staying on top of how much was owed to suppliers and staff, and in rent and utilities. Hooker got along fine simply managing the cheque book.

But this changed with franchising. "We weren't just selling products to people for cash, putting the cash in the bank, and then writing cheques for what we owed," says Hooker. "We were into receivables; people owed us money." The company also had liabilities, in the form of an operating loan from a bank.

Hooker hired a firm to set up an accounting information system, an experience he describes as a "rude awakening." One of the accounting staff was negligent, writing cheques for government remittances, but not sending them for fear the company's line of credit wouldn't cover them. Clearly, the accounts weren't balanced properly. Hooker hired another accountant to rebuild the accounting system, working closely with him to learn how it all worked.

The breakthrough point for him, he says, was understanding that "cash is a debit on the balance sheet." Assets (from the balance sheet) and expenses (from the statement of earnings) have normal debit balances. Liabilities and shareholders' equity (from the balance sheet) and revenues (from the statement of earnings) have normal credit balances. To increase the amount in an account, an entry has to be of a like sign, he adds. That is, debits increase debit accounts and credits increase credit accounts.

Hooker now insists his accountant provide "TAMFS"—timely, accurate, monthly financial statements. "That is an absolute necessity any time a business grows to where the owner puts his trust in somebody else to handle the money," he says. A lesson this entrepreneur learned the hard way.

the navigator

BeaverTails Canada Inc.: www.beavertailsinc.com

THE NAVIGATOR

☐ Read *Feature Story*

☐ Scan *Study Objectives*

☐ Read *Chapter Preview*

☐ Read text and answer *Before You Go On*

☐ Work *Using the Decision Toolkit*

☐ Review *Summary of Study Objectives*

☐ Review the *Decision Toolkit—A Summary*

☐ Work *Demonstration Problem*

☐ Answer *Self-Study Questions*

☐ Complete assignments

STUDY OBJECTIVES

After studying this chapter, you should be able to:

1. Analyze the effects of transactions on the accounting equation.
2. Define debits and credits and explain how they are used to record transactions.
3. Identify the basic steps in the recording process.
4. Prepare a trial balance.

the navigator

As indicated in the feature story, an accounting information system that produces timely and accurate financial information is a necessity for a company like BeaverTails. The purpose of this chapter is to explain and illustrate the features of an accounting information system. The chapter is organized as follows:

THE ACCOUNTING INFORMATION SYSTEM

Accounting Transactions	The Account	Steps in the Recording Process	The Trial Balance
▶ Analyzing transactions ▶ Summary of transactions	▶ Debits and credits ▶ Expanded accounting equation	▶ The journal ▶ The ledger ▶ Posting ▶ The recording process illustrated	▶ Limitations of a trial balance

the navigator

Accounting Transactions

The system of collecting and processing transaction data and communicating financial information to decision-makers is known as the **accounting information system**. Accounting information systems vary widely. Some factors that shape these systems are the type of business and its transactions, the size of the company, the amount of data, and the information that management and others need. For example, as indicated in the feature story, BeaverTails did not need a formal accounting system when it first began. However, as the business and the number and type of transactions grew, an organized accounting information system became essential.

An accounting information system begins with determining what relevant transaction data should be collected and processed. Not all events are recorded and reported as accounting transactions. For example, suppose a new employee is hired, or a new computer purchased. Are these events entered in the company's accounting records? The first event would not be recorded, but the second event would. The hiring of an employee will lead to an accounting transaction (e.g., the payment of salary after the work has been completed), but, until that time, no accounting transaction has occurred.

An **accounting transaction** occurs when assets, liabilities, or shareholders' equity items change as a result of some economic event. Illustration 3-1 summarizes the process that is used to decide whether or not to record economic events.

Illustration 3-1 ▶

Transaction identification process

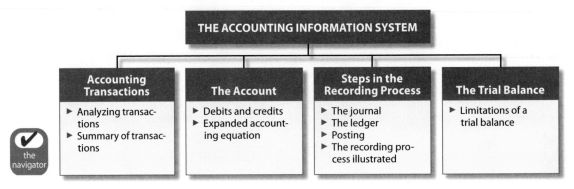

Events	Purchase computer	Discuss product design with a potential customer	Pay rent
Criterion	Is the financial position (assets, liabilities, and shareholders' equity) of the company changed?		
	Yes	No	Yes
Record/ Don't Record	Record	Don't record	Record

Analyzing Transactions

In Chapter 1, you learned about the accounting equation:

Assets	=	Liabilities	+	Shareholder's Equity

study objective 1

Analyze the effects of transactions on the accounting equation.

www.wiley.com/canada/kimmel

Animated Tutorials
(The Accounting Cycle Tutorial)

In this chapter, you will learn how to analyze transactions for their effect on each component of the accounting equation—assets, liabilities, and shareholders' equity. Remember that the accounting equation must always balance, so each transaction will have a dual (double-sided) effect on the equation. For example, if an individual asset is increased, there must be either a corresponding decrease in another asset, an increase in a specific liability, or an increase in shareholders' equity.

Chapter 1 presented the financial statements for Sierra Corporation for its first month. To illustrate the effects of economic events on the accounting equation, we will now examine the events that affected Sierra Corporation in its first month.

Transaction (1): Investment of Cash by Shareholders. On October 2, cash of $10,000 was invested in Sierra Corporation in exchange for $10,000 of common shares. This transaction results in an equal increase in assets and shareholders' equity. There is a $10,000 increase in the asset account Cash and a $10,000 increase in the shareholders' equity account Common Shares. The effect of this transaction on the accounting equation is:

	Assets	=	Liabilities	+	Shareholders' Equity
	Cash	=			Common Shares
(1)	+$10,000	=			+$10,000

Notice that the two sides of the accounting equation remain equal.

Transaction (2): Issue of Note Payable. Also on October 2, Sierra borrowed $5,000 from Scotiabank, promising to repay the note, plus 6 percent interest, in three months. This transaction results in an equal increase in assets and liabilities: Cash (an asset) increases by $5,000 and Notes Payable (a liability) increases by $5,000. The specific effect of this transaction and the cumulative effect of the first two transactions are:

	Assets	=	Liabilities	+	Shareholders' Equity
Balance	Cash	=	Notes Payable	+	Common Shares
Beginning	$10,000				$10,000
(2)	+5,000		+$5,000		
Ending	$15,000	=	$5,000	+	$10,000
			$15,000		

Total assets are now $15,000 and shareholders' equity plus the new liability also total $15,000.

Transaction (3): Purchase of Office Equipment. On October 3, Sierra acquired office equipment by paying $5,000 cash to Superior Equipment Corp. This transaction results in an equal increase and decrease in Sierra's assets. Office Equipment (an asset) increases by $5,000 and Cash (an asset) decreases by $5,000, as shown:

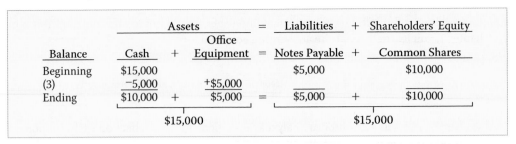

The total assets are still $15,000. Liabilities plus shareholders' equity also total $15,000.

Transaction (4): Receipt of Cash in Advance from Customer.   On October 4, Sierra received a $1,200 cash advance from R. Knox, a client, for advertising services that are expected to be completed before November 30. Revenue should not be recorded until the work has been performed. However, since cash was received before performing the advertising services, Sierra has a liability for the work due. We call this liability unearned service revenue.

Note that the word "unearned" indicates that this is a liability account rather than a revenue account. Although many liability accounts have the word "payable" in their title, not all do. Unearned service revenue is a liability account even though the word "payable" is not used.

This transaction results in an increase in Cash (an asset) of $1,200 and an increase in Unearned Service Revenue (a liability) by the same amount:

	Assets		=	Liabilities		+	Shareholders' Equity
		Office		Notes	Unearned		
Balance	Cash	Equipment		Payable	+ Service Revenue		Common Shares
Beginning	$10,000	$5,000		$5,000			$10,000
(4)	+1,200				+$1,200		
Ending	$11,200 +	$5,000	=	$5,000 +	$1,200	+	$10,000
	$16,200				$16,200		

Transaction (5): Payment of Rent.   On October 5, Sierra Corporation paid its office rent for the month of October in cash, $900. To record this transaction, Cash is decreased by $900 and Rent Expense is increased by $900. Rent is an expense incurred by Sierra in its effort to generate revenues. Expenses decrease retained earnings, which in turn decreases shareholders' equity. You will recall from earlier chapters that shareholders' equity consists of common shares (or share capital) and retained earnings. Retained earnings are increased by revenues, and decreased by expenses and dividends.

We have expanded our accounting equation to show the detailed components of retained earnings. As there is not enough room to use specific account names for each individual revenue and expense account in this illustration, they will be summarized under the column headings Revenues (abbreviated as "Rev."), Expenses (abbreviated as "Exp."), and Dividends (abbreviated as "Div."). Revenue and dividend transactions will be added later in this section.

	Assets		=	Liabilities		+	Shareholders' Equity			
		Office			Unearned		Common	Retained Earnings		
Bal.	Cash	+ Equip.	=	N/P	+ Serv. Rev.	+	Shares	+ Rev. − Exp. − Div.		
Beg.	$11,200	$5,000		$5,000	$1,200		$10,000			
(5)	−900							+$900		
End.	$10,300 +	$5,000	=	$5,000 +	$1,200	+	$10,000	− $900		
	$15,300						$15,300			

It may initially look strange to you to see $900 added to the expense column rather than subtracted from it. However, in this instance, the account Rent Expense was increased, not decreased. As we mentioned earlier, expenses reduce retained earnings and ultimately shareholders' equity.

So the final result is that assets and shareholders' equity are both decreased by $900, keeping the accounting equation in balance.

Transaction (6): Purchase of Insurance.   On October 6, Sierra paid $600 for a one-year insurance policy that will expire next year on September 30. This event is a transaction because one asset was exchanged for another. The asset Cash is decreased by $600. The asset Prepaid Insurance (abbreviated as "Pre. Ins.") is increased by $600 because the payment is for more than the current month. Payments of expenses that will benefit more than one accounting period are identified as prepaid expenses or prepayments.

As shown, the balance in total assets did not change; one asset account decreased by the same amount by which another increased.

	Assets			=	Liabilities	+		Shareholders' Equity			
		Pre.	Off.			Unearned	Com.		Retained Earnings		
Bal.	Cash +	Ins. +	Equip. =		N/P +	Serv. Rev. +	Shares +	Rev. −	Exp. −	Div.	
Beg.	$10,300		$5,000		$5,000	$1,200	$10,000		$900		
(6)	−600	+$600									
End.	$ 9,700 +	$600 +	$5,000 =		$5,000 +	$1,200 +	$10,000		− $900		

$15,300 $15,300

Transaction (7): Hiring of New Employees.   On October 6, Sierra hired four new employees to begin work on Monday, October 9. Each employee will receive a weekly salary of $500 for a five-day (Monday–Friday) work week, payable every two weeks. Employees will receive their first paycheques on Friday, October 20. There is no effect on the accounting equation because the assets, liabilities, and shareholders' equity of the company have not changed. An accounting transaction has not occurred. At this point, there is only an agreement that the employees will begin work on October 9. (See transaction 10 for the first payment.)

Transaction (8): Purchase of Supplies on Account.   On October 9, Sierra purchased a supply of advertising materials on account from Aero Supply Corp. for $2,500. The account is due in 30 days.

Assets are increased by this transaction because supplies represent a resource that will be used in the process of providing services to customers. Liabilities are increased by the amount due to Aero Supply. The asset Advertising Supplies (abbreviated as "Ad. Sup.") is increased by $2,500, and the liability Accounts Payable (abbreviated as "A/P") is increased by the same amount. The effect on the accounting equation is:

	Assets				=	Liabilities			+		Shareholders' Equity			
			Pre.	Off.				Unearned	Com.		Retained Earnings			
Bal.	Cash +	Ad. Sup. +	Ins. +	Equip. =		N/P +	A/P +	Serv. Rev. +	Shares +	Rev. −	Exp. −	Div.		
Beg.	$9,700		$600	$5,000		$5,000		$1,200	$10,000		$900			
(8)		+$2,500					+$2,500							
End.	$9,700 +	$2,500 +	$600 +	$5,000 =		$5,000 +	$2,500 +	$1,200 +	$10,000		− $900			

$17,800 $17,800

Transaction (9): Services Performed on Account.   On October 13, Sierra performed $10,000 of advertising services for Copa Ltd. Sierra sent Copa a bill for these services asking for payment before the end of the month.

Companies often provide services "on account" or "for credit." Instead of receiving cash, the company receives a different type of asset, an account receivable. Accounts receivable represent the right to receive payment at a future date.

Revenue, however, is earned when services are performed. Therefore, revenue is recorded when services are performed, even though cash has not been received. As revenue increases retained earnings—a shareholders' equity account—both assets and shareholders' equity are increased by this transaction.

In this transaction, Accounts Receivable (abbreviated as "A/R") is increased by $10,000 and Service Revenue is increased by the same amount. The new balances in the accounting equation are:

	Assets					=	Liabilities			+	Shareholders' Equity		
			Ad.		Off.				Unearned	Com.	____ Retained Earnings ____		
Bal.	Cash +	A/R +	Sup. +	Pre. Ins. +	Equip. =	N/P +	A/P +	Serv. Rev. +	Shares +	Rev. −	Exp. −	Div.
Beg.	$9,700		$2,500	$600	$5,000	$5,000	$2,500	$1,200	$10,000		$900	
(9)		+$10,000								+$10,000		
End.	$9,700 +	$10,000 +	$2,500 +	$600 +	$5,000 =	$5,000 +	$2,500 +	$1,200 +	$10,000 +	$10,000 −	$900	

$27,800 = $27,800

Transaction (10): Payment of Salaries.   Employees worked two weeks, earning $4,000 (4 employees × $500/week × 2 weeks) in salaries, and were paid on October 20. Salaries are an expense similar to rent because they are a cost of generating revenues. While the act of hiring the employees in transaction 7 did not result in an accounting transaction, the payment of the employees' salaries is a transaction because assets and shareholders' equity are affected. Cash is decreased by $4,000 and Salaries Expense is increased by $4,000:

	Assets					=	Liabilities			+	Shareholders' Equity		
			Ad.	Pre.	Off.				Unearned	Com.	____ Retained Earnings ____		
Bal.	Cash +	A/R +	Sup. +	Ins. +	Equip. =	N/P +	A/P +	Serv. Rev +	Shares +	Rev. −	Exp. −	Div.
Beg.	$9,700	$10,000	$2,500	$600	$5,000	$5,000	$2,500	$1,200	$10,000	$10,000	$ 900	
(10)	−4,000										+4,000	
End.	$5,700 +	$10,000 +	$2,500 +	$600 +	$5,000 =	$5,000 +	$2,500 +	$1,200 +	$10,000 +	$10,000 −	$4,900	

$23,800 = $23,800

Transaction (11): Payment of Dividend.   On October 25, Sierra paid a $500 cash dividend. Dividends are a distribution of retained earnings rather than an expense—they are not incurred for generating revenue. A cash dividend transaction reduces both cash (asset) and retained earnings (shareholders' equity). Cash is decreased by $500 and Dividends (abbreviated as "Div.") are increased by $500:

	Assets					=	Liabilities			+	Shareholders' Equity		
			Ad.	Pre.	Off.				Unearned	Com.	____ Retained Earnings ____		
Bal.	Cash +	A/R +	Sup. +	Ins. +	Equip. =	N/P +	A/P +	Serv. Rev. +	Shares +	Rev. −	Exp. −	Div.
Beg.	$5,700	$10,000	$2,500	$600	$5,000	$5,000	$2,500	$1,200	$10,000	$10,000	$4,900	
(11)	−500											+$500
End.	$5,200 +	$10,000 +	$2,500 +	$600 +	$5,000 =	$5,000 +	$2,500 +	$1,200 +	$10,000 +	$10,000 −	$4,900 −	$500

$23,300 = $23,300

Transaction (12): Collection of Account.   On October 30, Copa paid Sierra the amount owing on its account. Recall that an account receivable and the revenue from this transaction were recorded earlier in transaction 9, when the service was provided. Revenue should not be recorded again when the cash is collected. Rather, Cash is increased by $10,000 and Accounts Receivable is decreased by $10,000. Total assets and total liabilities and shareholders' equity are unchanged, as shown:

Bal.	Cash	+ A/R	+ Ad. Sup.	+ Pre. Ins.	+ Off. Equip.	= N/P	+ A/P	+ Unearned Serv. Rev.	+ Com. Shares	+ Rev.	− Exp.	− Div.
											Retained Earnings	
Beg.	$5,200	$10,000	$2,500	$600	$5,000	$5,000	$2,500	$1,200	$10,000	$10,000	$4,900	$500
(12)	+10,000	−10,000										
End.	$15,200 +	$ 0 +	$2,500 +	$600 +	$5,000 =	$5,000 +	$2,500 +	$1,200 +	$10,000 +	$10,000 −	$4,900 −	$500

Assets = Liabilities + Shareholders' Equity

$23,300 $23,300

ACCOUNTING MATTERS! Management Perspective

Some companies are finding that teaching their factory workers basic accounting skills can be a useful motivational tool. For example, Rhino Foods uses a financial reporting game to motivate its production line employees. Employees are taught the costs of each element of the production process, from raw materials to machinery malfunctions, so that they will make decisions that will benefit the company. The employees' bonus cheques (for managers as well as factory workers) are based on the results of the game. The owner, a former hockey coach, believes that his workers will work harder, and enjoy their work more, if they know what the score is.

Summary of Transactions

The transactions of Sierra Corporation are summarized in Illustration 3-2 to show their cumulative effect on the basic accounting equation. The transaction number, the specific effects of the transaction, and the final balances are indicated. Remember that event 7—the hiring of employees—did not result in a transaction, so no entry is included for that event.

Illustration 3-2 ▼

Tabular summary of transactions

	Cash	+ A/R	+ Ad. Sup.	+ Pre. Ins.	+ Off. Equip.	= N/P	+ A/P	+ Unearned Serv. Rev.	+ Com. Shares	+ Rev.	− Exp.	− Div.
(1)	+$10,000								+$10,000			
(2)	+5,000					+$5,000						
(3)	−5,000				+$5,000							
(4)	+1,200							+$1,200				
(5)	−900										+$ 900	
(6)	−600			+$600								
(8)			+$2,500				+$2,500					
(9)	+$10,000									+$10,000		
(10)	−4,000										+4,000	
(11)	−500											+$500
(12)	+10,000	−10,000										
	$15,200 +	$ 0 +	$2,500 +	$600 +	$5,000 =	$5,000 +	$2,500 +	$1,200 +	$10,000 +	$10,000 −	$4,900 −	$500

Assets = Liabilities + Shareholders' Equity

$23,300 $23,300

The illustration demonstrates that (1) each transaction must be analyzed for its effect on the three primary components of the accounting equation (assets, liabilities, and shareholders' equity) and (2) the two sides of the equation must always be equal.

Decision Toolkit

Decision Checkpoints	Info Needed for Decision	Tools to Use for Decision	How to Evaluate Results
Has an accounting transaction occurred?	Details of the event	Accounting equation	Determine the effect, if any, on assets, liabilities, and shareholders' equity.

BEFORE YOU GO ON . . .

▶Review It

1. Provide examples of transactions that are (a) economic events that should be recorded and (b) events that should not be recorded.
2. If an asset increases, what are the three possible effects on the accounting equation? What are the possible effects if a liability increases?

▶Do It

Transactions made by Virmari Corporation for the month of August follow:

1. Common shares were issued to shareholders for $25,000 cash.
2. Office equipment costing $7,000 was purchased on account.
3. Cash of $8,000 was received for services performed.
4. Rent was paid for the month, $850.
5. Dividends of $1,000 were paid to shareholders.

Prepare a tabular analysis which shows the effects of these transactions on the accounting equation.

Action Plan

• Analyze the effects of each transaction on the accounting equation.
• Keep the accounting equation in balance.

Solution

	Assets		=	Liabilities	+			Shareholders' Equity			
				Accounts		Common			Retained Earnings		
	Cash	+ Equipment	=	Payable	+	Shares	+	Revenue	− Expenses	− Dividends
1.	+$25,000					+$25,000				
2.		+$7,000		+$7,000						
3.	+8,000							+$8,000		
4.	−850								+$850	
5.	−1,000									+$1,000
	$31,150 +	$7,000	=	$7,000	+	$25,000	+	$8,000 −	$850 −	$1,000
	$38,150							$38,150		

the navigator

The Account

study objective 2

Define debits and credits and explain how they are used to record transactions.

Instead of using a tabular summary like the one in Illustration 3-2 for Sierra Corporation, an accounting information system uses accounts. An **account** is an individual accounting record of increases and decreases in a specific asset, liability, or shareholders' equity item. For example, Sierra Corporation has separate accounts for cash, accounts receivable, accounts payable, service revenue, salaries expense, and so on.

In its simplest form, an account consists of three parts: (1) the title of the account, (2) a left or debit side, and (3) a right or credit side. Because the alignment of these parts of an account resembles the letter T, it is referred to as a **T account**. The basic form of an account is shown in Illustration 3-3.

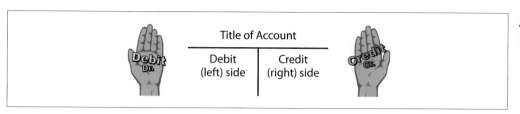

Title of Account

| Debit (left) side | Credit (right) side |

Illustration 3-3 ◄

Basic form of T account

This form of account will be used throughout the book to explain basic accounting relationships.

Debits and Credits

The term **debit** means left, and the term **credit** means right. These terms are commonly abbreviated as Dr. for debit and Cr. for credit. Debits and credits are merely directional signals used in the recording process to describe where entries are made in the accounts. For example, the act of entering an amount on the left side of an account is called **debiting** the account, and making an entry on the right side is **crediting** the account. When the totals of the two sides are compared, an account will have a debit balance if the total of the debit amounts exceeds the credits. Conversely, an account will have a credit balance if the credit amounts exceed the debits.

Each transaction affects two or more accounts in order to keep the accounting equation in balance. In other words, for each transaction, debits must equal credits. The equality of debits and credits is the basis for the **double-entry accounting system**, in which the dual (two-sided) effect of each transaction is recorded in appropriate accounts. This system provides a logical method for recording transactions and ensuring that amounts are recorded accurately. If every transaction is recorded with equal debits and credits, then the sum of all the debits to the accounts must equal the sum of all the credits.

The following diagram will help us understand how debit and credit effects apply to the accounting equation:

Debits ↑ Assets ↓ Credits = Liabilities ↑ Credits ↓ Debits + Shareholders' Equity

Helpful Hint Debits and credits do not always mean "increases" and "decreases." While debits do increase certain accounts (e.g., assets), they decrease other accounts (e.g., liabilities).

Beginning on the left-hand side of the accounting equation (asset accounts), we can see that increases in asset accounts are recorded by debits. The converse is also true: decreases in asset accounts are recorded by credits. If we cross to the right-hand side of the equation, it must follow that increases and decreases in liabilities and shareholders' equity have to be recorded *opposite from* increases and decreases in assets. Thus, increases in liabilities and shareholders' equity are recorded by credits and decreases by debits.

We will apply debit and credit procedures to T accounts for each component of the accounting equation—assets, liabilities, and shareholders' equity—in the following sections.

Assets

If we apply the accounting equation to a T account for assets, we can see that increases in assets must be entered on the left or debit side, and decreases in assets must be entered on the right or credit side. **Asset accounts normally show debit balances.** That is, debits to a specific asset account should exceed credits to that account. It was a breakthrough for Mr. Hooker in the feature story when he learned that assets, such as cash, are debits.

The diagram below shows the effects that debits and credits have on asset accounts, and the accounts' normal balance:

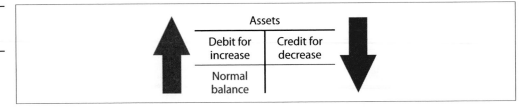

Knowing an account's normal balance may help when you are trying to identify errors. For example, a credit balance in an asset account such as Land would indicate a recording error. Occasionally, however, an abnormal balance may be correct. The Cash account, for example, will have a credit balance if a company has overdrawn its bank balance.

Liabilities and Shareholders' Equity

Liability and shareholder equity accounts are increased by credits and decreased by debits. Increases are entered on the right or credit side of the T account, and decreases are entered on the left or debit side of the T account. Just as asset accounts normally show debit balances, **liability and shareholder equity accounts normally show credit balances**.

The effects that debits and credits have on liabilities and shareholders' equity, and the normal balances are as follows:

All asset and liability accounts have the same debit/credit rule procedures. That is, all asset accounts are increased by debits and decreased by credits. All liability accounts are increased by credits and decreased by debits. However, shareholders' equity comprises different components, and they do not all move in the same direction. You will recall that shareholders' equity consists of common shares, retained earnings, revenues, expenses, and dividends. Common shares, retained earnings, and revenues all increase shareholders' equity. Dividends and expenses decrease shareholders' equity.

In the following sections, we will look at how debit and credit procedures apply to each of these equity components.

Increases in Shareholders' Equity.   Common shares and retained earnings both increase shareholders' equity. Common shares are issued in exchange for the shareholders' investments. Retained earnings are the portion of shareholders' equity that has been accumulated through the profitable operation of the company. Retained earnings are divided further into revenues and expenses (which make up net earnings) and dividends. Of these, revenues increase retained earnings, which then increases shareholders' equity.

The common shares, retained earnings, and revenue accounts are increased by credits and decreased by debits. **The normal balance in these accounts is a credit balance.** These accounts, and the effects that debits and credits have on them, are shown below:

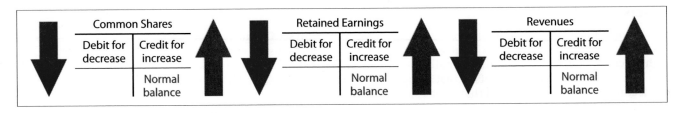

Decreases in Shareholders' Equity. Expenses and dividends both decrease retained earnings, which then decreases shareholders' equity. Since decreases in shareholders' equity are recorded by debits, it makes sense that **expense and dividend accounts would have a normal debit balance**.

Expenses, along with revenues, combine to determine net earnings. Since expenses are the negative factor in the calculation of earnings, and revenues are the positive factor, it is logical that the increase and decrease sides of expense accounts should be the reverse of revenue accounts. Thus, expense accounts are increased by debits and decreased by credits.

Dividends are a distribution to shareholders of retained earnings, which reduces retained earnings. If retained earnings are decreased by debits, it follows that increases in the dividends account are recorded with debits. Credits to the dividends account are unusual, but might be used to correct a dividend recorded in error, for example.

The normal balances in these accounts, and the effects that debits and credits have on them, are shown below:

	Expenses				Dividends	
▲	Debit for increase	Credit for decrease	▼	▲	Debit for increase	Credit for decrease	▼
	Normal balance				Normal balance	

Expanded Accounting Equation

Illustration 3-4 expands the basic accounting equation to show the types of accounts that make up shareholders' equity. Assets (on the left-hand side of the accounting equation) are increased by debits. Liabilities and shareholders' equity, on the other side of the equation, are increased by credits. Recall Mr. Hooker's comment in the feature story that increases to accounts have to be of like signs, which is a way of saying that a debit will increase a debit account and a credit will increase a credit account. Thus, the equality of the accounting equation is preserved and debits always equal credits.

As we learned above, shareholders' equity can be further divided into two components: common shares and retained earnings. Since shareholders' equity is increased by credits, both of these accounts—common shares and retained earnings—are also increased by credits.

Retained earnings can be further subdivided into revenues and expenses (revenues and expenses combine to determine net earnings) and dividends. Since revenues increase retained earnings and shareholders' equity, increases in revenue accounts are recorded by credits. Expenses and dividends decrease retained earnings, and thus shareholders' equity. Decreases in shareholders' equity are recorded by debits. Because expenses and dividends decrease shareholders' equity, increases in each of these accounts are recorded by debits.

The debit/credit rules and effects on each type of account are summarized in Illustration 3-4. Study this carefully. It will help you understand the fundamentals of the double-entry accounting system.

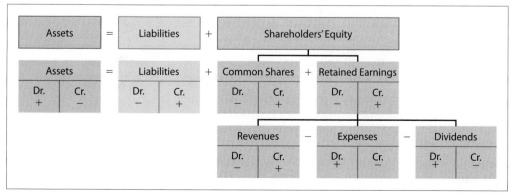

Illustration 3-4 ◀

Summary of debit and credit rules for accounting equation

BEFORE YOU GO ON . . .

▶Review It

1. What do the terms *debit* and *credit* mean?
2. What are the effects of debits and credits on assets, liabilities, and shareholders' equity?
3. What are the effects of debits and credits on dividends, revenues, and expenses?
4. What are the normal balances for Loblaw's Accounts Receivable, Long-Term Debt, Sales, and Interest Expense accounts? The answer to this question is provided at the end of the chapter.

Loblaws
A passion for food... and a lot more!

▶Do It

Lin Limited has the following selected accounts:

1. Service Revenue
2. Dividends
3. Office Equipment
4. Accounts Receivable
5. Office Supplies

6. Unearned Service Revenue
7. Accounts Payable
8. Common Shares
9. Salaries Expense
10. Cash

(a) Indicate whether each of the above accounts is an asset, liability, or shareholders' equity account. If the account is an asset or liability, indicate its balance sheet classification. If it is a shareholders' equity account, indicate what specific type it is (e.g., common shares, dividends, revenue, or expense).
(b) Indicate whether a debit would increase or decrease each account.
(c) Identify the normal balance.

Action Plan

- Classify each account into its spot in the expanded accounting equation.
- Apply the debit and credit rules. Remember that assets are increased by debits, and liabilities and shareholders' equity are increased by credits.
- Remember that the normal balance of an account is on its increase side.

Solution

Account	(a) Classification	(b) Debit Effect	(c) Normal Balance
1. Service Revenue	Shareholders' equity (revenue)	Decrease	Credit
2. Dividends	Shareholders' equity (dividends)	Increase	Debit
3. Office Equipment	Assets (property, plant, and equipment)	Increase	Debit
4. Accounts Receivable	Assets (current)	Increase	Debit
5. Office Supplies	Assets (current)	Increase	Debit
6. Unearned Service Revenue	Liabilities (current)	Decrease	Credit
7. Accounts Payable	Liabilities (current)	Decrease	Credit
8. Common Shares	Shareholders' equity (common shares)	Decrease	Credit
9. Salaries Expense	Shareholders' equity (expense)	Increase	Debit
10. Cash	Assets (current)	Increase	Debit

the navigator

Steps in the Recording Process

study objective 3

Identify the basic steps in the recording process.

Although it is possible to enter transaction information directly into the accounts, few businesses do so. Almost every business uses these basic steps in the recording process:

1. Analyze each transaction for its effect on the accounts.
2. Enter the transaction information in a general journal.
3. Transfer the journal information to the appropriate accounts in the general ledger (book of accounts).

The actual sequence of events begins with the transaction. Evidence of the transaction comes from a **source document**, such as a sales slip, cheque, bill, or cash register tape. This evidence is analyzed to determine the effect of the transaction on specific accounts. The transaction is then entered in the general journal. Finally, the journal entry is transferred to the designated accounts in the general ledger. The sequence of events in the recording process is shown in Illustration 3-5.

| Analyze each transaction | Enter transactions in a journal | Transfer journal information to ledger accounts |

Illustration 3-5 ◄

The recording process

The basic steps in the recording process occur repeatedly in every company, whether a manual or a computerized accounting system is used. However, the first two steps—the analysis and entering of each transaction—must be done by a person even when a computerized system is used. The basic difference between a manual and a computerized system is in the last step in the recording process—transferring information (and subsequent steps that we will learn about later). In a computerized system, this step is done automatically by the computer. In order to understand how this happens, we need to understand manual approaches to the recording process, which is what we will focus on in this chapter.

ACCOUNTING MATTERS! Management Perspective

Organizations of all shapes and sizes use computerized accounting systems. Cathy Love, the administrator of Bryony House, a Halifax women's shelter, agrees. "We really need our computerized system to track our accounts in detail," she says. The shelter users the popular small-business electronic accounting package *Simply Accounting*. In addition, the shelter's fundraising activities are tracked in detail using custom donation software. The shelter's staff have found that the more easily and quickly they can get the information they need, the more time they have to do their main work with the women who come for help.

The Journal

Transactions are first recorded in chronological order (i.e., by date) in a journal and then transferred to the accounts. For each transaction, the journal shows the debit and credit effects on specific accounts. Companies may use various kinds of journals, but every company has the most basic form of journal, a **general journal**.

Entering transaction data in the general journal is known as **journalizing**. To illustrate the technique of journalizing, let's look at Sierra Corporation's first transaction. On October 2, common shares were issued in exchange for $10,000 cash. In tabular equation form, this transaction appeared in our earlier discussion as follows:

	Assets	=	Liabilities	+	Shareholders' Equity
	Cash	=			Common Shares
(1)	+$10,000	=			+$10,000

This transaction would be recorded in the general journal as follows:

GENERAL JOURNAL				
Date	Account Titles and Explanation		Debit	Credit
2006 Oct. 2	Cash		10,000	
	Common shares			10,000

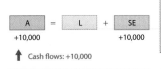

+10,000   +10,000

↑ Cash flows: +10,000

In the margins next to key journal entries are equation analyses that summarize the effects of the transaction on the accounting equation (A = L + SE) and cash flows.

Note the following features of the journal entry:

1. The date of the transaction is entered in the Date column.
2. The account to be debited is entered first at the left. The account to be credited is then entered on the next line, indented under the line above. The indentation differentiates debits from credits and decreases the chance of switching the debit and credit amounts by mistake.
3. The amounts for the debits are recorded in the Debit (left) column, and the amounts for the credits are recorded in the Credit (right) column.
4. A brief explanation of the transaction is given.

It is important to use correct and specific account titles in journalizing. Since most accounts appear later in the financial statements, inaccurate account titles lead to incorrect financial statements. There is some flexibility when account titles are first chosen. The main criterion is that each title appropriately describes the content of the account. For example, a company could use any of these account titles for recording the cost of delivery trucks: automobiles, delivery trucks, or trucks. Once the company chooses the specific account title to use (say, delivery trucks), all future transactions related to that account should be recorded in the Delivery Trucks account.

The general journal makes several contributions to the recording process:

1. It discloses the complete effect of a transaction in one place, including an explanation and, where applicable, identification of the source document.
2. It provides a chronological record of transactions.
3. It helps to prevent and locate errors, because the debit and credit amounts for each entry can be quickly compared.

The Ledger

The entire group of accounts maintained by a company is referred to as the ledger. The ledger keeps all the information about changes in specific account balances in one place.

Companies may use various kinds of ledgers, but every company has a general ledger. A **general ledger** contains all the assets, liabilities, and shareholders' equity accounts, as shown in Illustration 3-6. A company can use a looseleaf binder or card file for the ledger, with each account kept on a separate sheet or card. Most companies today, however, use a computerized accounting system where each account is kept in a separate file.

Illustration 3-6 ▶

The general ledger

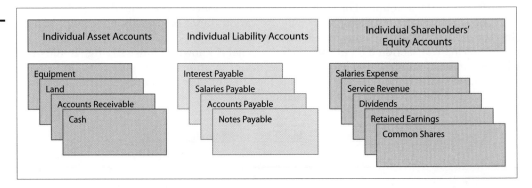

The ledger is often arranged in the order in which accounts are presented in the financial statements, beginning with the balance sheet accounts. The asset accounts come first, followed by liability accounts, and then shareholders' equity. Of course, in a computerized accounting system, the accounts can easily be rearranged in whatever order is wanted. Each account has a number so that it is easier to identify.

Most companies list their ledger accounts in a **chart of accounts**. The chart of accounts for Sierra Corporation is shown in Illustration 3-7. Accounts shown in red are used in this chapter; accounts shown in black are explained in later chapters. New accounts may be created as needed during the life of the business.

Illustration 3-7 ▼

Chart of accounts

SIERRA CORPORATION—CHART OF ACCOUNTS				
Assets	**Liabilities**	**Shareholders' Equity**	**Revenues**	**Expenses**
Cash	Notes Payable	Common Shares	Service Revenue	Salaries Expense
Accounts Receivable	Accounts Payable	Retained Earnings		Advertising Supplies Expense
Advertising Supplies	Interest Payable	Dividends		Rent Expense
Prepaid Insurance	Unearned Service Revenue			Insurance Expense
Office Equipment	Salaries Payable			Interest Expense
Accumulated Amortization—				Amortization Expense
Office Equipment				

A master chart of accounts for a sample company is included in the Study Tools section of the Toolkit website.

Study Tools (Chart of Accounts)

ACCOUNTING MATTERS! Management Perspective

The numbering system that identifies accounts in a company's chart of accounts can be quite sophisticated or pretty simple. For example, an eight-digit system is used at the Goodyear Tire & Rubber Company. The first three digits identify the account classifications as follows:

100–199	Assets	500-599	Selling, Administrative, and General Expenses
200–299	Liabilities and Shareholders' Equity	600-699	Other Revenues and Expenses
300–399	Revenues	700-799	Interest
400–499	Cost of Goods Sold	800-899	Taxes

The last five digits identify the unique account code.

Posting

The procedure of transferring journal entries to the general ledger accounts is called **posting**. This phase of the recording process accumulates the effects of journalized transactions in the individual accounts. Posting involves transferring information from the general journal to the general ledger. For example, the date and amount shown on the first line of a general journal entry is entered in the debit column of the appropriate account in the general ledger. The same is done for the credit side of the entry—the date and amount are entered in the credit column of the general ledger account.

Posting should be done on a timely basis—at least monthly—to ensure that the general ledger is up to date. In a computerized accounting system, posting usually occurs simultaneously after each journal entry is prepared.

The Recording Process Illustrated

Illustrations 3-8 through 3-19 show the basic steps in the recording process using the October transactions of Sierra Corporation. Its accounting period is a month. A basic analysis and a debit-credit analysis are done before the journalizing and posting of each transaction. Study these transaction analyses carefully. The purpose of transaction analysis is first to identify the type of account involved and then to determine whether a debit or a credit to the account is required. You should always perform this type of analysis before preparing a journal entry. Doing so will help you understand the journal entries discussed in this chapter, as well as more complex journal entries described in later chapters.

Illustration 3-8 ►

Investment of cash by shareholders

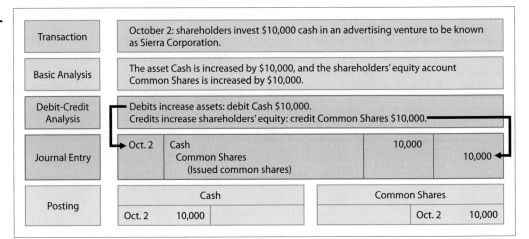

Illustration 3-9 ►

Issue of note payable

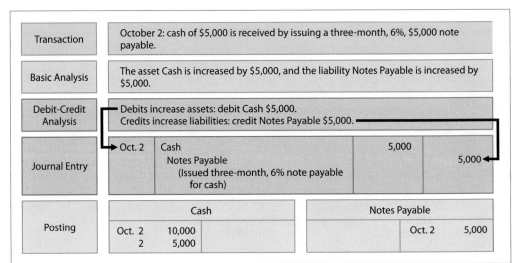

Illustration 3-10 ►

Purchase of office equipment

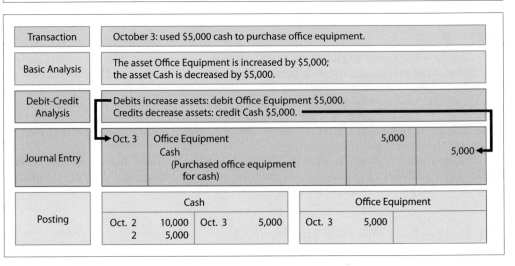

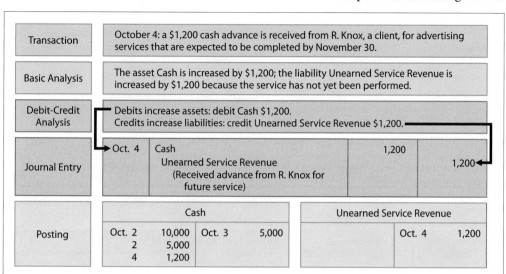

Illustration 3-11 ◀

Receipt of cash in advance from customer

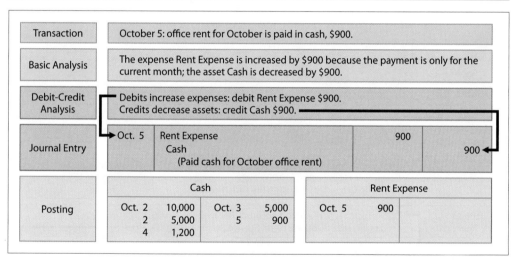

Illustration 3-12 ◀

Payment of rent

Illustration 3-13 ◀

Purchase of insurance

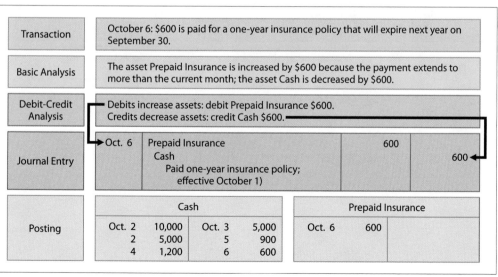

Illustration 3-14 ▶

Hiring of new employees

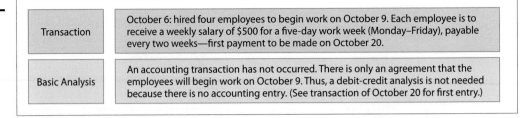

Illustration 3-15 ▶

Purchase of supplies on
account

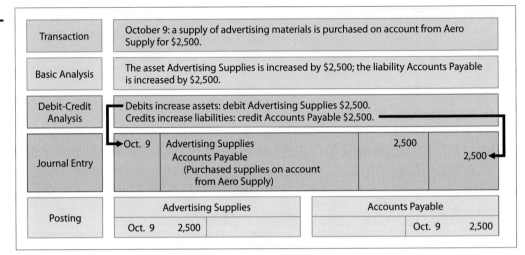

Illustration 3-16 ▶

Services performed on
account

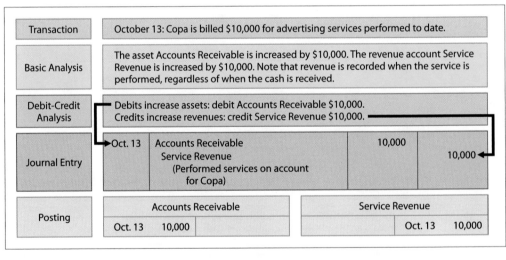

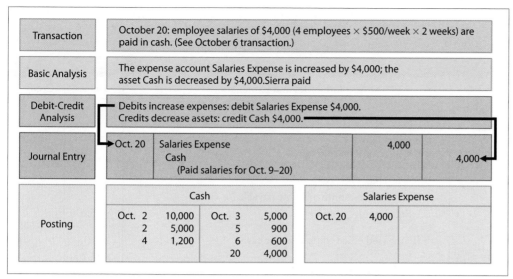

Illustration 3-17 ◀

Payment of salaries

Transaction	October 20: employee salaries of $4,000 (4 employees × $500/week × 2 weeks) are paid in cash. (See October 6 transaction.)		
Basic Analysis	The expense account Salaries Expense is increased by $4,000; the asset Cash is decreased by $4,000. Sierra paid		
Debit-Credit Analysis	Debits increase expenses: debit Salaries Expense $4,000. Credits decrease assets: credit Cash $4,000.		

Journal Entry	Oct. 20 Salaries Expense
	    Cash
	       (Paid salaries for Oct. 9–20)
		4,000	4,000

Posting		Cash				Salaries Expense	
	Oct. 2	10,000	Oct. 3	5,000	Oct. 20	4,000	
	2	5,000	5	900			
	4	1,200	6	600			
			20	4,000			

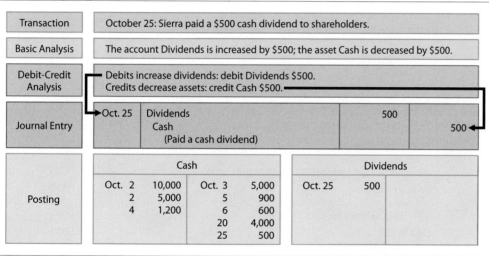

Illustration 3-18 ◀

Payment of dividend

Transaction	October 25: Sierra paid a $500 cash dividend to shareholders.		
Basic Analysis	The account Dividends is increased by $500; the asset Cash is decreased by $500.		
Debit-Credit Analysis	Debits increase dividends: debit Dividends $500. Credits decrease assets: credit Cash $500.		

Journal Entry	Oct. 25 Dividends
	    Cash
	       (Paid a cash dividend)
		500	500

Posting		Cash				Dividends	
	Oct. 2	10,000	Oct. 3	5,000	Oct. 25	500	
	2	5,000	5	900			
	4	1,200	6	600			
			20	4,000			
			25	500			

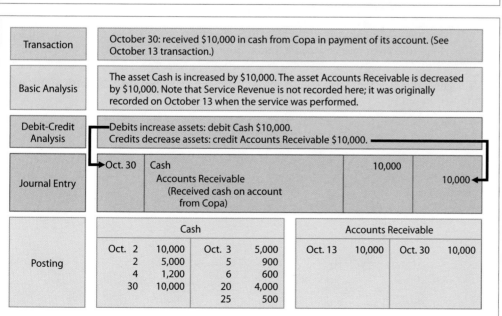

Illustration 3-19 ◀

Collection of account

Transaction	October 30: received $10,000 in cash from Copa in payment of its account. (See October 13 transaction.)		
Basic Analysis	The asset Cash is increased by $10,000. The asset Accounts Receivable is decreased by $10,000. Note that Service Revenue is not recorded here; it was originally recorded on October 13 when the service was performed.		
Debit-Credit Analysis	Debits increase assets: debit Cash $10,000. Credits decrease assets: credit Accounts Receivable $10,000.		

Journal Entry	Oct. 30 Cash
	    Accounts Receivable
	       (Received cash on account
	          from Copa)
		10,000	10,000

Posting		Cash				Accounts Receivable		
	Oct. 2	10,000	Oct. 3	5,000	Oct. 13	10,000	Oct. 30	10,000
	2	5,000	5	900				
	4	1,200	6	600				
	30	10,000	20	4,000				
			25	500				

The general journal for Sierra Corporation for the month of October is summarized in Illustration 3-20.

Illustration 3-20 ▶

Sierra Corporation general journal

Date		Account Titles and Explanations	Debit	Credit
2006				
Oct.	2	Cash	10,000	
		Common Shares		10,000
		(Issued common shares)		
	2	Cash	5,000	
		Notes Payable		5,000
		(Issued three-month, 6% note payable for cash)		
	3	Office Equipment	5,000	
		Cash		5,000
		(Purchased office equipment for cash)		
	4	Cash	1,200	
		Unearned Service Revenue		1,200
		(Received advance from R. Knox for future service)		
	5	Rent Expense	900	
		Cash		900
		(Paid cash for October office rent)		
	6	Prepaid Insurance	600	
		Cash		600
		(Paid one-year insurance policy; effective October 1)		
	9	Advertising Supplies	2,500	
		Accounts Payable		2,500
		(Purchased supplies on account from Aero Supply)		
	13	Accounts Receivable	10,000	
		Service Revenue		10,000
		(Performed services on account for Copa)		
	20	Salaries Expense	4,000	
		Cash		4,000
		(Paid salaries for Oct. 9–20)		
	25	Dividends	500	
		Cash		500
		(Paid a cash dividend)		
	30	Cash	10,000	
		Accounts Receivable		10,000
		(Received cash on account from Copa)		

The general ledger for Sierra Corporation is shown in Illustration 3-21, with all balances highlighted in red.

Illustration 3-21 ◄

Sierra Corporation general ledger

GENERAL LEDGER

Cash				
Oct. 2	10,000	Oct. 3	5,000
2	5,000	5	900
4	1,200	6	600
30	10,000	20	4,000
		25	500
Bal.	15,200		

Accounts Payable		
	Oct. 9	2,500
	Bal.	2,500

Accounts Receivable			
Oct. 13	10,000	Oct. 30	10,000
Bal.	0		

Unearned Service Revenue		
	Oct. 4	1,200
	Bal.	1,200

Common Shares		
	Oct. 2	10,000
	Bal.	10,000

Advertising Supplies	
Oct. 9	2,500
Bal.	2,500

Dividends	
Oct. 25	500
Bal.	500

Prepaid Insurance	
Oct. 6	600
Bal.	600

Service Revenue		
	Oct. 13	10,000
	Bal.	10,000

Office Equipment	
Oct. 3	5,000
Bal.	5,000

Salaries Expense	
Oct. 20	4,000
Bal.	4,000

Notes Payable		
	Oct. 2	5,000
	Bal.	5,000

Rent Expense	
Oct. 5	900
Bal.	900

BEFORE YOU GO ON . . .

► Review It

1. What is the correct sequence of steps in the recording process?
2. What does the general journal contribute to the recording process?
3. How does journalizing differ from posting?
4. Explain how a chart of accounts relates to the general ledger.

► Do It

The following events occurred during the first week of business of Hair It Is, Inc., a beauty salon:

May 1 Issued common shares to shareholders for $20,000 cash.
   3 Purchased $4,800 of equipment on account.
   5 Interviewed three people for the position of hair stylist.
   6 Purchased supplies for cash, $600.

(a) Record these transactions in the general journal.
(b) Post the transactions to the general ledger.

Action Plan

- Understand which events (the ones with economic effects) should be recorded.
- Analyze the transactions. Determine which accounts are affected and whether the transaction increases or decreases the account.
- Record the transactions in the general journal, which provides a chronological record of the transactions.
- Posting involves transferring the journalized debits and credits to specific T accounts in the general ledger.
- Ledger accounts should be arranged in statement order.

• Determine the ending balances of each ledger account by netting (calculating the difference between) the total debits and credits.

Solution

(a)

May	1	Cash	20,000	
		Common Shares		20,000
		(Issued common shares)		
	3	Equipment	4,800	
		Accounts Payable		4,800
		(Purchased equipment on account)		
	5	No entry because no transaction occurred		
	6	Supplies	600	
		Cash		600
		(Purchased supplies)		

(b)

Cash					
May	1	20,000	May	6	600
Bal.		19,400			

Supplies		
May	6	600

Equipment		
May	3	4,800

Accounts Payable		
May	3	4,800

Common Shares		
May	1	20,000

the navigator

The Trial Balance

A **trial balance** is a list of general ledger accounts and their balances at a specific time. A trial balance is normally prepared monthly, and at least at the end of each accounting period. The accounts are listed in the order in which they appear in the ledger, with debit balances listed in the left column and credit balances in the right column. The totals of the two columns must be equal.

The main purpose of a trial balance is to prove the mathematical equality of debits and credits after posting. Under the double-entry system, this equality will occur when the sum of the debit account balances equals the sum of the credit account balances. A trial balance also uncovers errors in journalizing and posting. For example, if debits do not equal credits in a journal entry, the trial balance will not balance when these unequal amounts are transferred to the general ledger. Or, if a debit or credit amount is transferred incorrectly to the general ledger from a journal entry, the trial balance will not balance. If the trial balance does not balance, then the error must be located and corrected before proceeding.

A trial balance is also useful in the preparation of financial statements, as will be explained in the next chapter. The procedure for preparing a trial balance is as follows:

1. List the account titles and their balances.
2. Total the debit column and the credit column.
3. Verify the equality of the two columns.

The trial balance prepared from the ledger of Sierra Corporation is presented in Illustration 3-22. Accounts with zero balances, such as Accounts Receivable, are normally not included in the trial balance. Note that the total debits, $28,700, equal the total credits, $28,700.

Ethics Note Auditors see errors and irregularities differently when they evaluate an accounting system. An error is the result of an unintentional mistake. As such, it is neither ethical nor unethical. An irregularity, on the other hand, is an intentional misstatement, which is generally viewed as unethical.

Illustration 3-22 ◄

Sierra Corporation trial balance

SIERRA CORPORATION
Trial Balance
October 31, 2006

	Debit	Credit
Cash	$15,200	
Advertising supplies	2,500	
Prepaid insurance	600	
Office equipment	5,000	
Notes payable		$ 5,000
Accounts payable		2,500
Unearned service revenue		1,200
Common shares		10,000
Dividends	500	
Service revenue		10,000
Salaries expense	4,000	
Rent expense	900	
	$28,700	$28,700

Limitations of a Trial Balance

A trial balance does not prove that all transactions have been recorded or that the ledger is correct. Errors may exist even though the trial balance columns agree. For example, the trial balance may balance even when (1) a transaction is not journalized, (2) a correct journal entry is not posted, (3) a journal entry is posted twice, (4) incorrect accounts are used in journalizing or posting, or (5) errors that cancel each other's effect are made in recording the amount of a transaction. In other words, as long as equal debits and credits are posted, even to the wrong account or in the wrong amount, the total debits will equal the total credits. Nevertheless, despite its limitations, the trial balance is a useful screen for finding errors.

BEFORE YOU GO ON . . .

►Review It

1. What is a trial balance and how is it prepared?
2. What is the main purpose of a trial balance?
3. What are the limitations of a trial balance?

►Do It

Koizumi Kollections Ltd. has the following alphabetical list of accounts and balances at July 31, 2006:

Account	Amount	Account	Amount
Accounts payable	$33,700	Land	$ 51,000
Accounts receivable	71,200	Machinery and equipment	35,700
Building	86,500	Notes payable	49,500
Cash	3,200	Operating expenses	105,100
Common shares	99,400	Service revenue	174,100
Dividends	4,000		

Each of the above accounts has a normal balance. Prepare a trial balance, rearranging the accounts in normal ledger (financial statement) order.

Action Plan

- Reorder the accounts as they would normally appear in the general ledger—balance sheet accounts are listed first (assets, liabilities, and equity), and then statement of earnings accounts (revenues and expenses).
- Determine whether each account has a normal debit or credit balance.
- List the amounts in the appropriate debit or credit column.
- Total the trial balance columns. Total debits must equal total credits or a mistake has been made.

Solution

KOIZUMI KOLLECTIONS LTD.
Trial Balance
July 31, 2006

	Debit	Credit
Cash	$ 3,200	
Accounts receivable	71,200	
Land	51,000	
Building	86,500	
Machinery and equipment	35,700	
Accounts payable		$ 33,700
Notes payable		49,500
Common shares		99,400
Dividends	4,000	
Service revenue		174,100
Operating expenses	105,100	
Totals	$356,700	$356,700

the navigator

▦ Decision Toolkit

Decision Checkpoints	Info Needed for Decision	Tools to Use for Decision	How to Evaluate Results
How do you determine that debits equal credits?	All general ledger account balances	Trial balance	List the account titles and their balances; total the debit and credit columns; and verify equality.

▦ Using the Decision Toolkit

Prairie Grain Growers Limited is an agri-business company. Prairie Grain Growers' trial balance (which should balance but does not) follows. Accounts are listed in alphabetical order and have normal balances.

PRAIRIE GRAIN GROWERS LIMITED
Trial Balance
July 31, 2006

	Debit	Credit
Accounts payable		$ 178,000
Accounts receivable	$ 712,000	
Accumulated amortization		147,000
Buildings	365,000	
Cash	32,000	
Cost of goods sold	2,384,000	
Current portion of long-term debt		12,000
Income tax expense	353,000	
Inventories	1,291,000	
Land	110,000	
Long-term debt		873,000
Machinery and equipment	357,000	
Notes payable		495,000
Operating expenses	651,000	
Retained earnings		822,000
Sales revenue		3,741,000
Salaries payable		62,000
	$6,255,000	$6,330,000

After checking with various people who are responsible for entering accounting data, you discover the following:

1. The purchase of a forklift, costing $7,000 and paid for with cash, was not recorded.
2. A data entry clerk accidentally deleted the account name for an account with a credit balance of $472,000, so the amount was added to the Long-Term Debt account in the trial balance.
3. July cash sales revenue of $75,000 was credited to the Sales account, but the other half of the entry was not made.
4. Operating expenses of $50,000 were mistakenly charged to Income Tax Expense.

Instructions

(a) Which mistake or mistakes have caused the trial balance to be out of balance?
(b) Should all of the items be corrected? Explain.
(c) What is the likely name of the account the data entry clerk deleted?
(d) Make the necessary corrections and balance the trial balance.
(e) On your trial balance, write "B" beside the accounts that should be shown on the balance sheet, "E" beside those that should be shown on the statement of earnings, and "RE" beside those that should be shown on the statement of retained earnings.

Solution

(a) Only mistake 3 has caused the trial balance to be out of balance.
(b) All of the items should be corrected. The misclassification error (mistake 4) in Income Tax Expense would not affect bottom-line net earnings, but it does affect the amounts reported in the two expense accounts.
(c) There is no Common Shares account, so that must be the account that was deleted by the data entry clerk.

(d) and (e)

PRAIRIE GRAIN GROWERS LIMITED
Trial Balance
July 31, 2006

	Debit	Credit	
Accounts payable		$ 178,000	B
Accounts receivable	$ 712,000		B
Accumulated amortization		147,000	B
Buildings	365,000		B
Cash ($32,000 − $7,000 + $75,000)	100,000		B
Common shares		472,000	B
Cost of goods sold	2,384,000		E
Current portion of long-term debt		12,000	B
Income tax expense ($353,000 − $50,000)	303,000		E
Inventories	1,291,000		B
Land	110,000		B
Long-term debt ($873,000 − $472,000)		401,000	B
Machinery and equipment ($357,000 + $7,000)	364,000		B
Notes payable		495,000	B
Operating expenses ($651,000 + $50,000)	701,000		E
Retained earnings		822,000	RE
Sales revenue		3,741,000	E
Salaries payable		62,000	B
	$6,330,000	$6,330,000	

Summary of Study Objectives

1. *Analyze the effects of transactions on the accounting equation.* Each business transaction has a dual effect on the accounting equation. For example, if an individual asset is increased, there must be a corresponding decrease in another asset, or increase in a specific liability, or increase in shareholders' equity.

2. *Define debits and credits and explain how they are used to record transactions.* The terms *debit* and *credit* are synonymous with *left* and *right*. Assets, dividends, and expenses are increased by debits and decreased by credits. The normal balance of these accounts is a debit balance. Liabilities, common shares, retained earnings, and revenues are increased by credits and decreased by debits. The normal balance of these accounts is a credit balance.

3. *Identify the basic steps in the recording process.* The basic steps in the recording process are (a) analyzing each transaction for its effect on the accounts, (b) entering the transaction information in a general journal, and (c) transferring the information in the general journal to the appropriate accounts in the general ledger.

4. *Prepare a trial balance.* A trial balance is a list of accounts and their balances at a specific time. The main purpose of the trial balance is to prove the mathematical equality of debits and credits after posting. A trial balance also uncovers errors in journalizing and posting and is useful in preparing financial statements.

▦ Decision Toolkit—A Summary

Decision Checkpoints	Info Needed for Decision	Tools to Use for Decision	How to Evaluate Results
Has an accounting transaction occurred?	Details of the event	Accounting equation	Determine the effect, if any, on assets, liabilities, and shareholders' equity.
How do you determine that debits equal credits?	All general ledger account balances	Trial balance	List the account titles and their balances; total the debit and credit columns; and verify equality.

Analysis Tools
(Decision Toolkit Summaries)

Glossary

Study Tools (Glossary)

Account An individual accounting record of increases and decreases in a specific asset, liability, or shareholders' equity item. (p. 104)

Accounting information system The system of collecting and processing transaction data and communicating financial information to interested parties. (p. 98)

Accounting transaction An economic event that is recorded in the financial statements because it involves an exchange that affects assets, liabilities, or shareholders' equity. (p. 98)

Chart of accounts A list of a company's accounts. (p. 111)

Credit The right side of an account. (p. 105)

Debit The left side of an account. (p. 105)

Double-entry accounting system A system that records the dual effect of each transaction in appropriate accounts. (p. 105)

General journal An accounting record in which transactions are recorded in chronological order. (p. 109)

General ledger A book or computer record that contains a company's asset, liability, and shareholders' equity accounts. (p. 110)

Posting The procedure of transferring journal entries to the ledger accounts. (p. 111)

T account The basic form of an account, with a debit (left) side and a credit (right) side showing the effect of transactions on the account. (p. 105)

Trial balance A list of general ledger accounts and their balances at a specific time. (p. 119)

Demonstration Problem

Campus Laundry Inc. opened on September 1, 2006. During the first month of operations, the following transactions occurred:

Sept. 1 Shareholders invested $20,000 cash in the business.
  3 Paid $1,000 cash for rent for the month of September.
  4 Purchased washers and dryers for $25,000, paying $10,000 in cash and signing a six-month, 8%, $15,000 note payable.
  5 Paid $1,200 for a one-year insurance policy.
  11 Paid salaries of $2,500.
  15 Performed services on account for a nearby restaurant, $6,200.
  20 Paid a $700 cash dividend to shareholders.
  29 Cash receipts for laundry services performed throughout the month were $5,000.
  30 Utilities of $1,200 and salaries of $2,500 are owed at the end of the month.

The chart of accounts for the company is the same as for Sierra Corporation except for the following two additional accounts: Laundry Equipment and Utilities Expense.

Instructions

(a) Journalize the September transactions.
(b) Open general ledger accounts and post the transactions.
(c) Prepare a trial balance.
(d) Prepare a statement of earnings, statement of retained earnings, and balance sheet.

Action Plan

- Make separate journal entries for each transaction.
- In journalizing, make sure debits equal credits.
- In journalizing, use specific account titles taken from the chart of accounts and provide an appropriate explanation of each journal entry.
- Arrange the general ledger in statement order, beginning with the balance sheet accounts.
- Prepare a trial balance which lists accounts in the order in which they appear in the ledger.
- In the trial balance, list debit balances in the left column and credit balances in the right column. Check the accuracy of your work. Total debits must equal total credits.

Solution to Demonstration Problem

(a)

GENERAL JOURNAL			
Date	Account Titles and Explanation	Debit	Credit
2006 Sept. 1	Cash	20,000	
	Common Shares		20,000
	(Issued common shares)		
3	Rent Expense	1,000	
	Cash		1,000
	(Paid September rent)		
4	Laundry Equipment	25,000	
	Cash		10,000
	Notes Payable		15,000
	(Purchased laundry equipment for cash and six-month, 8% note payable)		
5	Prepaid Insurance	1,200	
	Cash		1,200
	(Paid one-year insurance policy)		
11	Salaries Expense	2,500	
	Cash		2,500
	(Paid salaries)		
15	Accounts Receivable	6,200	
	Service Revenue		6,200
	(To record revenue for laundry services provided)		
20	Dividends	700	
	Cash		700
	(Paid a $700 cash dividend)		
29	Cash	5,000	
	Service Revenue		5,000
	(To record collection for laundry services provided)		
30	Utilities Expense	1,200	
	Salaries Expense	2,500	
	Accounts Payable		3,700
	(To record utilities and salaries due in October)		

(b)

GENERAL LEDGER

Cash

Sept. 1	20,000	Sept. 3	1,000
29	5,000	4	10,000
		5	1,200
		11	2,500
		20	700
Bal.	9,600		

Accounts Receivable

Sept. 15	6,200	

Prepaid Insurance

Sept. 5	1,200	

Laundry Equipment

Sept. 4	25,000	

Notes Payable

		Sept. 4	15,000

Accounts Payable

		Sept. 30	3,700

Common Shares

		Sept. 1	20,000

Dividends

Sept. 20	700	

Service Revenue

		Sept. 15	6,200
		29	5,000
		Bal.	11,200

Salaries Expense

Sept. 11	2,500	
30	2,500	
Bal.	5,000	

Utilities Expense

Sept. 30	1,200	

Rent Expense

Sept. 3	1,000	

(c)

CAMPUS LAUNDRY INC.
Trial Balance
September 30, 2006

	Debit	Credit
Cash	$ 9,600	
Accounts receivable	6,200	
Prepaid insurance	1,200	
Laundry equipment	25,000	
Notes payable		$15,000
Accounts payable		3,700
Common shares		20,000
Dividends	700	
Service revenue		11,200
Salaries expense	5,000	
Utilities expense	1,200	
Rent expense	1,000	
	$49,900	$49,900

(d)

CAMPUS LAUNDRY INC.
Statement of Earnings
Month Ended September 30, 2006

Revenues		
Service revenue		$11,200
Expenses		
Salaries	$5,000	
Utilities	1,200	
Rent	1,000	7,200
Net earnings		$ 4,000

CAMPUS LAUNDRY INC.
Statement of Retained Earnings
Month Ended September 30, 2006

Retained earnings, September 1		$ 0
Add: Net earnings		4,000
		4,000
Less: Dividends		700
Retained earnings, September 30		$3,300

CAMPUS LAUNDRY INC.
Balance Sheet
September 30, 2006

Assets

Current assets		
Cash	$9,600	
Accounts receivable	6,200	
Prepaid insurance	1,200	$17,000
Property, plant, and equipment		
Laundry equipment		25,000
Total assets		$42,000

Liabilities and Shareholders' Equity

Current liabilities		
Notes payable	$15,000	
Accounts payable	3,700	$18,700
Shareholders' equity		
Common shares	$20,000	
Retained earnings	3,300	23,300
Total liabilities and shareholders' equity		$42,000

the navigator

www.wiley.com/canada/kimmel

Self-Study Questions

Study Tools (Self-Assessment Quizzes)

(SO 1) 1. The effects on the accounting equation of receiving cash in advance of performing a service are to:
(a) increase assets and decrease shareholders' equity.
(b) increase assets and increase shareholders' equity.
(c) increase assets and increase liabilities.
(d) increase liabilities and increase shareholders' equity.

(SO 1) 2. Shareholders' equity consists of the following:
(a) common shares, revenues, and expenses.
(b) revenues and expenses.
(c) liabilities, common shares, and retained earnings.
(d) common shares and retained earnings.

(SO 2) 3. Which statement about an account is true?
(a) In its simplest form, an account consists of two parts.
(b) An account is an individual accounting record of increases and decreases in specific asset, liability, and shareholders' equity items.
(c) There are separate accounts for specific assets and liabilities but only one account for shareholders' equity items.

(d) The left side of an account is the credit or decrease side.

4. Debits: (SO 2)
(a) increase both assets and liabilities.
(b) decrease both assets and liabilities.
(c) increase assets and decrease liabilities.
(d) decrease assets and increase liabilities.

5. Which accounts normally have debit balances? (SO 2)
(a) Assets, expenses, and revenues
(b) Assets, expenses, and retained earnings
(c) Assets, liabilities, and dividends
(d) Assets, dividends, and expenses

6. Which of these statements about a general journal is false? (SO 3)
(a) It contains only revenue and expense accounts.
(b) It provides a chronological record of transactions.
(c) It helps to locate errors because the debit and credit amounts for each entry can be quickly compared.
(d) It discloses the complete effect of a transaction in one place.

(SO 3) 7. A general ledger:
(a) contains only asset and liability accounts.
(b) should show accounts in alphabetical order.
(c) is a collection of the entire group of accounts maintained by a company.
(d) provides a chronological record of transactions.

(SO 3) 8. Posting:
(a) normally occurs before journalizing.
(b) transfers general ledger transaction data to the general journal.
(c) is an optional step in the recording process.
(d) transfers general journal entries to general ledger accounts.

the navigator

9. A trial balance: (SO 4)
(a) is a list of accounts with their balances at a specific time.
(b) proves that transactions have been correctly journalized.
(c) will not balance if a correct journal entry is posted twice.
(d) proves that all transactions have been recorded.

10. A trial balance will not balance if: (SO 4)
(a) a journal entry to record a cash sale is posted twice.
(b) the purchase of supplies on account is debited to Supplies and credited to Cash.
(c) a $100 cash dividend is debited to Dividends for $1,000 and credited to Cash for $100.
(d) a $450 payment on account is debited to Accounts Payable for $45 and credited to Cash for $45.

Questions

(SO 1) 1. Can a business enter into a transaction that affects only the left side of the accounting equation? If so, give an example.

(SO 1) 2. Are the following events recorded in the accounting records? Explain your answer in each case.
(a) A major shareholder of the company dies.
(b) Supplies are purchased on account.
(c) An employee is fired.
(d) The company pays a cash dividend to its shareholders.
(e) A local lawyer agrees to provide legal services to the company for the next year.

(SO 1) 3. Indicate how each transaction affects the accounting equation:
(a) Cash is paid for janitorial services.
(b) Equipment is purchased on account.
(c) Common shares are issued to investors in exchange for cash.
(d) An account payable is paid in full.
(e) Cash is received in advance for website hosting services.

(SO 2) 4. Why is an account referred to as a T account?

(SO 2) 5. Charles Thon, a fellow student, claims that the double-entry system means each transaction must be recorded twice. Is Charles correct? Explain.

(SO 2) 6. Natalie Boudreau, an introductory accounting student, believes debit balances are favourable and credit balances are unfavourable. Is Natalie correct? Discuss.

(SO 2) 7. State the debit and credit effects and identify the normal balance for the following types of accounts: (a) assets, (b) liabilities, (c) common shares, (d) retained earnings, (e) dividends, (f) revenues, and (g) expenses.

(SO 2) 8. Indicate the appropriate statement classification for each of the following accounts. State whether it would have a normal debit or credit balance.

(a) Accounts Receivable (e) Supplies
(b) Accounts Payable (f) Service Revenue
(c) Equipment (g) Unearned Service Revenue
(d) Dividends (h) Income Tax Expense

9. For the following transactions, indicate the account (SO 2) debited and the account credited:
(a) Supplies are purchased on account.
(b) Cash is received on signing a note payable.
(c) Employees are paid salaries in cash.
(d) Services are performed on account.
(e) Cash is collected on account.

10. For each account listed, indicate whether it generally (SO 2) will have debit entries only, credit entries only, or both debit and credit entries:
(a) Cash (d) Salaries Expense
(b) Dividends (e) Service Revenue
(c) Accounts Payable

11. Should the balance in total shareholders' equity equal (SO 2) the balance in the Cash account? Explain why or why not.

12. A company received cash from a customer. It debited (SO 2) the Cash account. Name three credit accounts that the company might have used to record a cash receipt from a customer. Describe the circumstances where you would use each of these three accounts.

13. Identify and describe the steps in the recording process. (SO 3)

14. An efficiency expert who was reviewing the steps in (SO 3) the recording process suggested dropping the general journal and recording and summarizing transactions directly into the general ledger instead. Comment on this suggestion.

15. (a) What is a general ledger? (SO 3)
(b) What is a chart of accounts and why is it important?

16. Arrange the following accounts in their normal order (SO 3) in a chart of accounts: common shares, prepaid insur-

ance, cash, service revenue, dividends, unearned revenue, supplies, income tax expense.

(SO 3) 17. Does it matter how frequently transactions are posted from the general journal to the general ledger? Explain.

(SO 3, 4) 18. Kap Shin is confused about how accounting information flows through the accounting system. He believes information flows in the following order:
- Debits and credits are posted to the general ledger.
- An accounting transaction occurs.
- Information is entered in the general journal.
- Financial statements are prepared.
- A trial balance is prepared.

Indicate to Kap the proper flow of the information.

19. What is a trial balance? What are its purposes and (SO 4) limitations?

20. ⚒ Two students are discussing the use of a trial balance. (SO 4) ance. They wonder whether the following errors, each considered separately, would prevent the trial balance from balancing. What would you tell the students?
  (a) The bookkeeper debited Cash for $600 and credited Wages Expense for $600 for the payment of wages.
  (b) Cash collected on account was debited to Cash for $900, and Service Revenue was credited for $90.

Brief Exercises

Analyze effects of transactions.
(SO 1)

BE3–1   Presented here are six economic events. Indicate whether the event increased (+), decreased (−), or had no effect (NE) on each element of the accounting equation.

1. Purchased $250 of supplies on account.
2. Provided a service on account, $500.
3. Paid operating expenses, $300.
4. Issued common shares in exchange for cash, $5,000.
5. Paid a cash dividend to shareholders, $400.
6. Received cash from a customer who had previously been billed for services provided, $500.

Use the following format, in which the first one has been done for you as an example:

			Shareholders' Equity			
			Common	Retained Earnings		
Transaction	Assets	Liabilities	Shares	Revenues	Expenses	Dividends
1.	+$250	+$250	NE	NE	NE	NE

Indicate debit and credit effects.
(SO 2)

BE3–2   For each of the following accounts, indicate (a) the statement classification in which the account would be reported, (b) the effect of a debit or credit on the account, and (c) the normal balance:

1. Accounts payable
2. Advertising expense
3. Service revenue
4. Accounts receivable
5. Unearned service revenue

6. Dividends
7. Common shares
8. Prepaid insurance
9. Office equipment
10. Retained earnings

Identify accounts to be debited and credited.
(SO 2)

BE3–3   Transactions for Ing Corporation for the month of June are presented below. Identify the accounts to be debited and credited for each transaction.

June 1 Issued common shares to shareholders in exchange for $2,500 cash.
       2 Purchased equipment on account for $900.
       3 Paid $500 to landlord for June rent.
      12 Billed J. Kronsnoble $300 for welding work done.
      22 Received cash from J. Kronsnoble for work billed on June 12.
      25 Hired an employee to start work on July 2.
      29 Paid for equipment purchased on June 2.
      30 Paid $100 for income tax instalment.

Indicate basic debit-credit analysis.
(SO 2)

BE3–4   Riko Corporation has the following selected transactions:

1. Issued common shares to shareholders in exchange for $5,000.
2. Paid insurance in advance for six months, $2,100.
3. Received $900 from clients for services provided.

4. Paid secretary $500 salary.
5. Billed clients $1,200 for services provided.
6. Purchased $500 of supplies on account.

For each transaction, indicate (a) the basic type of account debited and credited (asset, liability, shareholders' equity), (b) the specific account debited and credited (Cash, Rent Expense, Service Revenue, etc.), and (c) whether the specific account is increased or decreased. Use the following format, in which the first one has been done for you as an example:

	Account Debited			Account Credited		
	(a)	(b)	(c)	(a)	(b)	(c)
Transaction	Basic Type	Specific Account	Effect	Basic Type	Specific Account	Effect
1.	Asset	Cash	Increase	Shareholders' equity	Common Shares	Increase

BE3–5 Journalize the transactions given in BE3–1.

Journalize transactions. (SO 3)

BE3–6 Journalize the transactions for Ing Corporation in BE3–3.

Journalize transactions. (SO 3)

BE3–7 Selected transactions are presented in journal entry form below (without explanations). Post the transactions to T accounts.

Post journal entries. (SO 3)

GENERAL JOURNAL			
Date	Account Titles	Debit	Credit
May 5	Accounts Receivable	3,200	
	Service Revenue		3,200
12	Cash	1,900	
	Accounts Receivable		1,900
15	Cash	2,000	
	Service Revenue		2,000
20	Salaries Expense	2,500	
	Cash		2,500
30	Income Tax Expense	750	
	Income Tax Payable		750

BE3–8 From the ledger balances given below, prepare a trial balance for Carland Inc. at June 30, 2006. All account balances are normal.

Prepare trial balance. (SO 4)

Accounts payable	$ 4,000	Income tax expense	$ 400
Accounts receivable	3,000	Investments	6,000
Accumulated amortization	3,600	Rent expense	1,000
Cash	4,400	Retained earnings	2,650
Common shares	20,000	Salaries expense	4,000
Dividends	1,200	Service revenue	6,600
Equipment	17,000	Unearned service revenue	150

BE3–9 Different types of posting errors are identified in the following table. For each error, indicate (a) whether the trial balance will balance, (b) the amount of the difference if the trial balance will not balance, and (c) the trial balance column that will have the larger total. Consider each error separately. Use the following form, in which error 1 is given as an example:

Identify effects of posting errors on trial balance. (SO 4)

Error	(a) In Balance	(b) Difference	(c) Larger Column
1. A $1,200 debit to Supplies was posted as a $2,100 debit.	No	$900	Debit
2. A $1,000 credit to Cash was posted twice as two credits to Cash.			
3. A $5,000 debit to Dividends was posted to the Common Shares account.			
4. A journal entry debiting Cash and crediting Service Revenue for $2,500 was not posted.			
5. The collection of $500 cash on account was posted as a debit of $500 and a credit of $5,000.			

Prepare corrected trial balance.
(SO 4)

BE3-10   An inexperienced bookkeeper prepared the following trial balance, which does not balance. Prepare a correct trial balance, assuming all account balances are normal.

BOURQUE LIMITED
Trial Balance
December 31, 2006

	Debit	Credit
Cash	$15,000	
Accounts receivable		$ 1,800
Prepaid insurance		3,500
Accounts payable		3,000
Unearned revenue	2,200	
Common shares		10,000
Retained earnings		9,500
Dividends		4,500
Service revenue		25,600
Salaries expense	18,600	
Rent expense		4,400
Insurance expense		1,300
Income tax expense	1,200	
	$37,000	$63,600

Exercises

Analyze effects of transactions.
(SO 1)

E3-1   Selected transactions for Green Lawn Care Ltd., follow:

1. Issued common shares to shareholders in exchange for cash.
2. Paid monthly rent.
3. Purchased equipment on account.
4. Billed customers for services performed.
5. Paid a dividend to shareholders.
6. Received cash from customers billed in transaction 4.
7. Incurred advertising expense on account.
8. Purchased additional equipment, issuing cash and a note payable in payment.
9. Received cash from customers when service was provided.
10. Paid cash for equipment purchased in transaction 3.
11. Paid monthly income taxes.

Instructions

Using (+) for increase, (−) for decrease, and (NE) for no effect, indicate the effect each of the transactions listed above had on the accounting equation. Use the following format, in which the first one has been done for you as an example:

				Shareholders' Equity		
			Common	Retained Earnings		
Transaction	Assets	Liabilities	Shares	Revenues	Expenses	Dividends
1.	+	NE	+	NE	NE	NE

Analyze effects of transactions.
(SO 1)

E3-2   Wang Computer Corporation entered into these transactions during the month of May:

1. Purchased a computer on account for $10,000 from Digital Equipment.
2. Paid $4,000 cash for May rent on storage space.
3. Provided computer services for $2,500 on account.
4. Paid BC Hydro $1,000 cash for utilities used in May.
5. Issued common shares to Li Wang in exchange for an additional $20,000 investment in the business.
6. Paid Digital Equipment for computers purchased in transaction 1.
7. Purchased a one-year accident insurance policy for $500 cash.
8. Received $2,500 cash in payment of the account in transaction 3.

Instructions

Using (+) for increase, (−) for decrease, and (NE) for no effect, indicate the effect each of the transactions listed above had on the accounting equation. Use the following format, in which the first one has been done for you as an example:

| | | | | Shareholders' Equity | | |
| | | | Common | | Retained Earnings | |
Transaction	Assets	Liabilities	Shares	Revenues	Expenses	Dividends
1.	+$19,000	+$19,000	NE	NE	NE	NE

E3−3 You are presented with the following alphabetical list of accounts, selected from the financial statements of Krispy Kreme Doughnuts, Inc.:

Identify statement classification and normal balance. (SO 2)

Accounts Payable
Accounts Receivable
Cash and Cash Equivalents
Common Stock
Dividends
Goodwill
Income Taxes Payable

Interest Expense
Interest Income
Inventories
Prepaid Expenses
Property and Equipment
Retained Earnings
Revenues

Instructions

(a) Indicate the financial statement—balance sheet, statement of earnings, or statement of retained earnings—where each account should be reported and its classification (e.g., current assets, long-term liabilities, revenues, etc.).
(b) Indicate the normal balance of each account.

E3−4 Selected transactions for the Decorators Mill Ltd., an interior decorator corporation in its first month of business, are as follows:

Identify debits, credits, and normal balances. (SO 2)

Mar. 3 Issued common shares for $9,000 cash.
  6 Purchased used car for $12,000 cash for use in business.
  7 Purchased supplies on account for $500.
 10 Billed customers $1,800 for services performed.
 15 Received $600 cash from a customer for services to be performed in April.
 21 Paid $250 cash to advertise business opening.
 25 Received $700 cash from customers billed on March 10.
 28 Paid creditor $300 cash on account.
 31 Paid dividends of $500 to shareholders.

Instructions

For each transaction, indicate (a) the basic type of account debited and credited (asset, liability, shareholders' equity), (b) the specific account debited and credited (Cash, Rent Expense, Service Revenue, etc.), and (c) whether the specific account is increased or decreased. Use the following format, in which transaction 1 is given as an example:

| | Account Debited | | | Account Credited | | |
| | (a) | (b) | (c) | (a) | (b) | (c) |
Transaction	Basic Type	Specific Account	Effect	Basic Type	Specific Account	Effect
March 3	Asset	Cash	Increase	Shareholders' equity	Common Shares	Increase

E3−5 Data for the Wang Computer Corporation are presented in E3−2.

Journalize transactions. (SO 3)

Instructions

Journalize the transactions.

E3−6 Data for the Decorators Mill Ltd. are presented in E3−4.

Journalize transactions. (SO 3)

Instructions

Journalize the transactions.

Analyze, journalize, and post transactions.
(SO 1, 3)

E3–7   Selected transactions for the Basler Corporation during its first month in business are presented below:

Sept. 1 Issued common shares for $25,000 cash.
       5 Purchased equipment for $12,000, paying $5,000 in cash and the balance by issuing a note payable.
      10 Purchased $500 of supplies on account.
      25 Received $4,500 cash in advance for architectural services to be provided next month.
      30 Paid a $500 dividend to shareholders.
      30 Paid amount owing for supplies (see September 10).

Instructions

(a) Prepare a tabular equation analysis of the transactions as shown in the chapter.
(b) Journalize the transactions.
(c) Post the transactions to T accounts.

Journalize transactions.
(SO 3)

E3–8   The information that follows is for Aubut Real Estate Agency Corporation:

Oct. 1 Issued common shares in exchange for $15,000 cash.
      2 Hired an administrative assistant at an annual salary of $24,000.
      3 Purchased office furniture for $1,900, paying $500 cash and the balance on account.
      6 Sold a house and lot for F. Omana. Commission due from Rollins is $5,400 (not paid by Omana at this time).
     10 Received $140 cash commission for renting an apartment.
     27 Paid $1,400 on account for the office furniture purchased on October 3.
     30 Paid the administrative assistant $2,000 salary for October.
     31 Received cash of $5,400 from F. Omana owed from October 6.

Instructions

Journalize the transactions.

Post journal entries and prepare trial balance.
(SO 3, 4)

E3–9   The journal entries for Aubut Real Estate Agency Corporation were prepared in E3–8.

Instructions

(a) Post the transactions to T accounts.
(b) Prepare a trial balance at October 31, 2006.

Post journal entries and prepare trial balance.
(SO 3, 4)

E3–10   Selected transactions from the general journal of Kang, Inc., are presented here:

GENERAL JOURNAL			
	Account Titles	Debit	Credit
Aug. 1	Cash	2,400	
	Common Shares		2,400
8	Cash	1,800	
	Service Revenue		1,800
11	Office Equipment	4,000	
	Cash		1,000
	Notes Payable		3,000
15	Accounts Receivable	1,450	
	Service Revenue		1,450
28	Cash	700	
	Accounts Receivable		700
31	Dividends	500	
	Cash		500

Instructions

(a) Post the transactions to T accounts.
(b) Prepare a trial balance at August 31, 2006.

E3–11 Here is the general ledger for Holly Corp.:

Prepare trial balance from general ledger. (SO 4)

GENERAL LEDGER

Cash

Oct.	1	1,000	Oct.	4	400
	10	650	12		1,500
	15	5,000	15		300
	20	500	30		250
	25	2,000	31		500

Accounts Receivable

Oct.	6	800	Oct.	20	500
	20	940			

Supplies

Oct.	4	400

Furniture

Oct.	3	2,000

Notes Payable

			Oct.	15	5,000

Accounts Payable

Oct.	12	1,500	Oct.	3	2,000
			28		400

Common Shares

			Oct.	1	1,000
				25	2,000

Dividends

Oct.	15	300

Service Revenue

			Oct.	6	800
				10	650
				20	940

Wages Expense

Oct.	31	500

Rent Expense

Oct.	30	250

Advertising Expense

Oct.	28	400

Instructions

Prepare a trial balance at October 31, 2006.

E3–12 The accounts in the ledger of Speedy Delivery Service, Inc., contain the following balances on July 31, 2006:

Prepare trial balance and financial statements. (SO 4)

Accounts payable	$ 7,500	Insurance expense	$ 2,400
Accounts receivable	13,500	Notes payable, due 2009	19,000
Accumulated amortization	19,400	Prepaid insurance	200
Amortization expense	19,400	Rent expense	12,000
Cash	7,000	Retained earnings	20,750
Common shares	40,000	Salaries expense	5,000
Delivery equipment	97,000	Salaries payable	800
Dividends	700	Service revenue	75,000
Gas and oil expense	750	Short-term investments	20,000
Income tax expense	4,500		

Instructions

(a) Prepare a trial balance with the accounts arranged in financial statement order.
(b) Prepare a statement of earnings, statement of retained earnings, and balance sheet.

E3–13 The bookkeeper for Castle's Equipment Repair Corporation made these errors in journalizing and posting:

Analyze errors and their effects on trial balance. (SO 4)

1. A credit posting of $400 to Accounts Receivable was omitted.
2. A debit posting of $750 for Prepaid Insurance was debited to Insurance Expense.
3. A collection on account of $100 was journalized and posted as a $100 debit to Cash and a $100 credit to Service Revenue.
4. A credit posting of $300 to Accounts Payable was made twice.
5. A cash purchase of supplies for $250 was journalized and posted as a $25 debit to Supplies and a $25 credit to Cash.
6. A debit of $465 to Advertising Expense was posted as $456.

Instructions

For each error, indicate (a) whether the trial balance will balance, (b) the amount of the difference if the trial balance will not balance, and (c) the trial balance column that will have the larger total. Consider each error separately. Use the following format, in which error 1 is given as an example:

Error	(a) In Balance	(b) Difference	(c) Larger Column
1.	No	$400	Debit

Problems: Set A

Analyze transactions and classify cash flows.
(SO 1)

P3–1A   On April 1, Seall Travel Agency, Inc., started operations. These transactions were completed during the month:

1. Issued common shares for $12,000 cash.
2. Paid $600 cash for April office rent.
3. Purchased office equipment for $5,500, paying $2,000 cash and signing a note payable for the balance.
4. Purchased $300 of advertising in the *Halifax Herald*, on account.
5. Paid $725 cash for office supplies.
6. Earned $9,000 for services performed: cash of $1,000 is received from customers, and the balance of $8,000 is billed to customers on account.
7. Paid $200 dividends to shareholders.
8. Paid *Halifax Herald* amount due in transaction 4.
9. Paid employees' salaries, $2,200.
10. Received $6,000 cash from customers billed in transaction 6.
11. Paid income tax, $1,500.

Instructions

(a) Prepare a tabular analysis of the effects of the above transactions on the accounting equation.
(b) From an analysis of the Cash column, identify where each transaction would be reported on the cash flow statement. Use "O" for operating activities, "I" for investing activities, and "F" for financing activities.

Analyze transactions and prepare financial statements.
(SO 1)

P3–2A   Ivan Izo created Ivan Izo, Inc., on July 1, 2006, which specializes in providing legal services. On July 31, the balance sheet showed Cash $4,000; Accounts Receivable $1,500; Supplies $500; Office Equipment $5,000; Accounts Payable $4,100; Common Shares $5,500; and Retained Earnings $1,400. During August the following transactions occurred:

Aug. 4 Collected $1,200 of accounts receivable due from customers.
        7 Paid $2,700 cash on accounts payable owing.
        8 Earned fees of $6,500, of which $3,000 is collected in cash and the remainder is due on account.
      12 Purchased additional office equipment for $1,200, paying $400 in cash and the balance on account.
      15 Paid salaries, $2,500, and rent, $900, for the month of August.
      18 Collected the balance of the fees earned on August 8.
      20 Paid dividends of $550 to shareholders.
      26 Received $2,000 from Laurentian Bank; the money was borrowed on a note payable.
      28 Signed a contract to provide legal services to a client in September for $4,500. The client will pay the amount owing after the work has been completed.
      29 Incurred utility expenses for the month on account, $275.
      30 Billed a client $1,000 for legal services provided.
      31 Paid income tax for the month, $1,000.

Instructions

(a) Beginning with the July 31 balances, prepare a tabular analysis of the effects of the August transactions on the accounting equation.
(b) Prepare a statement of earnings, a statement of retained earnings, and a balance sheet for the month.

P3–3A You are presented with the following alphabetical list of accounts for O'Laney's Welding Services Ltd.:

Identify normal balance and statement classification. (SO 2)

Account	(a) Normal Balance	(b) Financial Statement	(c) Classification
Accounts payable	Credit	Balance sheet	Current liabilities
Accounts receivable			
Amortization expense			
Common shares			
Cost of goods sold			
Equipment			
Goodwill			
Income tax expense			
Income taxes payable			
Insurance expense			
Interest revenue			
Inventories			
Long-term debt			
Notes payable			
Prepaid insurance			
Retained earnings			
Sales revenue			
Unearned sales revenue			

Instructions

For each account, indicate (a) whether the normal balance is a debit or a credit, (b) the financial statement where the account should be reported (e.g., balance sheet or statement of earnings), and (c) the appropriate classification (e.g., current assets, long-term liabilities, revenues, etc.). The first one has been done for you as an example.

P3–4A You are presented with the following transactions for Paddick Enterprises Ltd. for the month of February:

Identify debit and credit effects and journalize transactions. (SO 2, 3)

Feb. 1 Purchased supplies on account, $600.
   3 Purchased furniture for $10,000 by signing a note that is due in three months.
   6 Earned revenue of $90,000. Of this amount, $30,000 was received in cash. The balance was on account.
   15 Paid $1,000 in dividends to shareholders.
   20 Paid the amount owing for the supplies purchased on February 1.
   23 Collected $20,000 of the amount owing from the February 6 transaction.
   24 Paid operating expenses for the month, $12,000.
   28 Recorded wages due to employees for work performed during the month, $4,000.

Instructions

(a) For each transaction, indicate (1) the basic type of account debited and credited (asset, liability, shareholders' equity), (2) the specific account debited and credited (Cash, Service Revenue, etc.), and (3) whether the specific account is increased or decreased. Use the following format, in which the first transaction is given as an example:

	Account Debited			Account Credited		
Transaction	(1) Basic Type	(2) Specific Account	(3) Effect	(1) Basic Type	(2) Specific Account	(3) Effect
Feb. 1	Asset	Supplies	Increase	Liability	Accounts Payable	Increase

(b) Prepare journal entries to record the above transactions.

P3–5A The Bucket Club Miniature Golf and Driving Range, Inc., was opened on May 1. These selected events and transactions occurred during May:

Journalize transactions. (SO 3)

May 1 Issued common shares for $65,000 cash.
   3 Purchased Lee's Golf Land for $188,000. The price consists of land $97,000; building $53,000; and equipment $38,000. Paid cash of $50,000 and signed a mortgage payable for the balance.
   3 Advertised the opening of the driving range and miniature golf course, paying advertising expenses of $1,500.

May 5 Paid $1,800 for a one-year insurance policy.
   10 Purchased golf clubs and other equipment for $16,000 from Woods Corporation, payable in 30 days.
   18 Received $5,800 from customers for golf fees earned.
   19 Sold 100 coupon books for $35 each. Each book contains 10 coupons that each give the holder one round of miniature golf or one bucket of golf balls to hit. (*Hint*: The revenue is not earned until the customers use the coupons.)
   25 Paid dividends of $500 to shareholders.
   30 Paid salaries of $3,000.
   30 Paid Woods Corporation in full for equipment purchased on May 10.
   31 Received $4,500 from customers for golf fees earned.
   31 Paid $950 of interest on the mortgage payable.

Instructions

Journalize the May transactions.

Journalize transactions, post, and prepare trial balance.
(SO 3, 4)

P3–6A   During the first month of operations, these events and transactions occurred for Virmani Architects Inc.:

Apr. 1 Cash of $15,000 and equipment of $8,000 was invested in the company in exchange for common shares.
    1 A secretary-receptionist was hired at a monthly salary of $1,200.
    2 Paid office rent for the month, $850.
    3 Purchased architectural supplies on account from Halo Ltd., $1,700.
   10 Completed blueprints on a carport and billed client $900.
   11 Received $500 cash advance from a client for the design of a new home.
   20 Received $1,500 for services performed for a client.
   21 Received $500 from client in partial payment for work completed and billed on April 10.
   30 Paid secretary-receptionist for the month, $1,200.
   30 Paid $900 to Halo Ltd. on account (see April 3 transaction).

Instructions

(a) Journalize the transactions.
(b) Using T accounts, post the April journal entries to the ledger.
(c) Prepare a trial balance at April 30, 2006.

Journalize transactions, post, and prepare trial balance.
(SO 3, 4)

P3–7A   The Star Theatre, Inc. is unique as it shows only triple features of sequential theme movies. As at February 28, 2006, the Star's ledger showed Cash $15,000; Land $42,000; Buildings (concession stand, projection room, ticket booth, and screen) $56,000; Equipment $14,000; Accounts Payable $2,000; Mortgage Payable, $65,000; Common Shares $40,000; and Retained Earnings, $20,000. During the month of March the following events and transactions occurred:

Mar. 2 Received three Harry Potter movies to be shown during the first three weeks of March. The film rental was $27,000. Of that amount, $9,000 was paid in cash and the remainder will be paid on March 10.
    3 Ordered three Lord of the Rings movies, to be shown the last 10 days of March. The film rental cost is $300 per night.
    9 Received $16,000 from customers for admissions.
   10 Paid balance due on the Harry Potter movies rental.
   13 Paid $2,000 on accounts payable owing at the end of February.
   15 Hired M. Brewer to operate concession stand. Brewer agrees to pay Star Theatre 15% of gross receipts, payable on the last day of each month, for the right to operate the concession stand.
   17 Paid advertising expenses, $950.
   20 Received $16,600 from customers for admissions.
   21 Received the Lord of the Rings movies and paid rental fee of $3,000 ($300 × 10 nights).
   27 Received $18,400 from customers for admissions.
   31 Paid salaries of $4,200.
   31 Received statement from M. Brewer, showing gross concession receipts of $8,500, and the balance due to Star Theatre of $1,275 for March. Brewer paid $850 of the balance due and will remit the remainder on April 5.
   31 Paid $425 of interest on the mortgage.

Instructions

(a) Using T accounts, enter the beginning balances in the ledger as at March 1.
(b) Journalize the March transactions.
(c) Post the March journal entries to the ledger.
(d) Prepare a trial balance at March 31, 2006.

P3–8A You are presented with the following alphabetical list of accounts and balances (in thousands) for Taggar Enterprises Inc. at June 30, 2006:

Prepare trial balance and financial statements.
(SO 4)

Accounts receivable	$ 500	Inventories	$ 510
Accumulated amortization	600	Land	800
Cash	180	Long-term investment	495
Common shares	550	Notes payable, due 2010	1,500
Cost of goods sold	870	Operating expenses	630
Equipment	1,500	Prepaid insurance	90
Income tax expense	150	Retained earnings, July 1, 2005	525
Income tax payable	150	Sales revenue	2,500
Interest expense	100		

Instructions

(a) Prepare a trial balance, sorting each account balance into the debit column or the credit column.
(b) Prepare a statement of earnings, statement of retained earnings, and balance sheet for the year.

P3–9A The bookkeeper for Cater's Dance Studio Ltd. did the following in journalizing and posting:

Analyze errors and effect on trial balance.
(SO 4)

1. A debit posting to Supplies of $600 was omitted.
2. A credit of $500 for revenue received in advance was posted as a credit to the Service Revenue account.
3. A purchase of supplies on account of $540 was debited to Supplies for $540 and credited to Accounts Payable for $540 in the general journal.
4. A credit to Wages Payable for $1,200 was posted as a credit to the Cash account.
5. A credit posting of $250 to Cash was posted twice.
6. The debit side of the entry to record the payment of $1,200 for dividends was posted to the Dividends Expense account.
7. The collection of an account receivable of $250 was posted as a debit to the Cash account and a credit to the Accounts Payable account.
8. The sale of goods on account was debited to Accounts Receivable and credited to Sales in the general journal.

Instructions

(a) Indicate which of the above transactions are correct, and which are incorrect.
(b) For each error identified in (a), answer the following questions:
  1. Will the trial balance be in balance?
  2. Which account(s) will be incorrectly stated because of the error?
  3. State whether each of the incorrect account(s) you identified in (2) will be overstated or understated, and by how much.

P3–10A   This trial balance of Wargo Ltd. does not balance:

WARGO LTD.
Trial Balance
June 30, 2006

	Debit	Credit
Cash		$ 5,170
Accounts receivable	$ 3,230	
Supplies	800	
Equipment	3,000	
Accumulated amortization	600	
Accounts payable		2,665
Unearned revenue	1,200	
Common shares		10,000
Dividends	800	
Service revenue		4,380
Salaries expense	3,400	
Office expense	910	
Income tax expense	440	
	$14,380	$22,215

Each of the listed accounts has a normal balance per the general ledger. An examination of the general ledger and general journal reveals the following errors:

1. Cash received from a customer on account was debited for $750, and Accounts Receivable was credited for the same amount. The actual collection was for $570.
2. The purchase of a scanner on account for $360 was recorded as a debit to Supplies for $360 and a credit to Accounts Payable for $360.
3. Services were performed on account for a client for $890. Accounts Receivable was debited for $890 and Service Revenue was credited for $89.
4. A debit posting to Amortization Expense of $600 was omitted.
5. A payment made by a customer on account for $206 was debited to Cash for $206 and credited to Accounts Receivable for $602.
6. Payment of a $400 dividend to Wargo's shareholders was debited to Salaries Expense for $400 and credited to Cash for $400.
7. A transposition (reversal of digits) error was made when copying the balance in the Salaries Expense account. The correct balance should be $4,300.

Instructions

Prepare the correct trial balance.

Problems: Set B

Analyze transactions and
classify cash flows.
(SO 1)

P3–1B   Tony's Repair Shop, Inc., was started on May 1. A summary of the May transactions follows:

1. Issued common shares for $14,000 cash.
2. Purchased equipment for $8,000, paying $2,000 cash and signing a note payable for the balance.
3. Paid $840 for May office rent.
4. Purchased supplies on account, $550.
5. Received $2,100 from customers for repair services provided.
6. Paid $1,500 dividends to shareholders.
7. Provided repair services on account to customers, $800.
8. Paid for supplies purchased in transaction 4.
9. Received May telephone bill of $200.
10. Paid part-time employee salaries, $1,000.
11. Billed a customer $350 for repair services provided.

12. Collected $800 from customers for services billed in transaction 7.
13. Paid income tax of $300.

Instructions

(a) Prepare a tabular analysis of the effects of the above transactions on the accounting equation.
(b) From an analysis of the Cash column, identify where each transaction would be classified on the cash flow statement. Use "O" for operating activities, "I" for investing activities, and "F" for financing activities.

P3–2B Corso Care Corp., a veterinary business, opened on August 1, 2006. On August 31, the balance sheet showed Cash $4,500; Accounts Receivable $1,800; Supplies $350; Office Equipment $6,500; Accounts Payable $3,200; Common Shares $5,000; and Retained Earnings $4,950. During September, the following transactions occurred:

Analyze transactions and prepare financial statements. (SO 1)

Sept. 1 Paid $2,800 of the accounts payable.
  1 Paid $1,200 rent for September.
  1 Collected $1,450 of accounts receivable due from customers.
  5 Hired a part-time office assistant at $50 per day to start work the following week.
  8 Purchased additional office equipment for $2,050, paying $700 in cash and the balance on account.
 14 Billed $500 for veterinary services provided.
 15 Paid $300 for advertising expenses.
 18 Collected cash for services performed on account on September 14.
 25 Received $7,500 from Canadian Western Bank; the money was borrowed on a note payable.
 26 Sent a statement reminding a customer that he still owed the company money from August.
 28 Earned revenue of $4,300, of which $2,900 was paid in cash and the balance is due in October.
 29 Paid part-time office assistant $450 for working nine days in September.
 30 Incurred utility expenses for the month on account, $175.
 30 Paid dividends of $2,500 to shareholders.
 30 Paid income tax for the month, $650.

Instructions

(a) Prepare a tabular analysis of the September transactions beginning with the August 31 balances.
(b) Prepare a statement of earnings, statement of retained earnings, and balance sheet for the month.

P3–3B You are presented with the following alphabetical list of accounts selected from the financial statements of Reitmans (Canada) Limited:

Identify normal balance and statement classification. (SO 2)

Account	(a) Normal Balance	(b) Financial Statement	(c) Classification
Accounts payable and accrued items	Credit	Balance sheet	Current liabilities
Accounts receivable			
Capital assets			
Cash and cash equivalents			
Cost of goods sold and selling, general, and administrative expenses			
Depreciation and amortization expense			
Dividends			
Goodwill			
Income tax expense			
Income taxes payable			
Investments			
Investment income			
Merchandise inventories			
Prepaid expenses			
Retained earnings			
Sales			
Share capital			

Instructions

For each account, indicate (a) whether the normal balance is a debit or a credit, (b) the financial statement where the account should be reported (e.g., balance sheet, statement of earnings, or statement of retained earnings), and (c) the appropriate classification (e.g., current assets, long-term liabilities, revenues, etc.). The first one is done for you as an example.

Identify debit and credit effects and journalize transactions.
(SO 2, 3)

P3–4B   You are presented with the following transactions for Kailynn Corporation for the month of January:

Jan. 3 Issued $10,000 of common shares for cash.
       5 Provided services for cash, $2,500.
       7 Purchased a $35,000 SUV for use in the business. Paid cash of $10,000 and issued a note payable for the remainder.
    10 Received a $5,000 deposit from a customer for services to be provided in the future.
    12 Billed customers $20,000 for services performed during the month.
    14 Paid $4,000 salaries to employees on Friday for work done that week.
    17 Purchased $500 of supplies on account.
    20 Provided services for customers who paid in advance on January 10.
    24 Collected $10,000 owing from customers from the January 12 transaction.
    28 Paid rent for the month, $1,500.
    31 Paid income tax for the month, $4,000.

Instructions

(a) For each transaction, indicate (1) the basic type of account debited and credited (asset, liability, shareholders' equity), (2) the specific account debited and credited (Cash, Service Revenue, etc.), and (3) whether the specific account is increased or decreased. Use the following format, in which the first transaction is given as an example:

	Account Debited			Account Credited		
	(1)	(2)	(3)	(1)	(2)	(3)
Transaction	Basic Type	Specific Account	Effect	Basic Type	Specific Account	Effect
Jan. 3	Asset	Cash	Increase	Shareholders' equity	Common Shares	Increase

(b) Prepare journal entries to record the above transactions.

Journalize transactions.
(SO 3)

P3–5B   The Adventure Biking Park Corp. was formed on April 1. These selected events and transactions occurred during April:

Apr. 1 Issued common shares for $50,000 cash.
       4 Purchased an out-of-use ski hill costing $206,000, paying $30,000 cash and signing a note payable for the balance.
       8 Purchased advertising space of $2,800 on account.
    11 Paid salaries to employees, $1,500.
    12 Hired a park manager at a salary of $4,000 per month, effective May 1.
    13 Paid $4,500 for a one-year insurance policy.
    17 Paid $600 of dividends to shareholders.
    20 Received $2,700 in cash from customers for admission fees.
    25 Sold 100 coupon books for $45 each. Each book contains 10 coupons that entitle the holder to one admission to the park per coupon. (Hint: The revenue is not earned until the coupons are used.)
    30 Received $5,900 in cash for admission fees.
    30 Paid $700 for the advertising purchased on account on April 8.
    30 Paid $2,250 of interest on the note payable.

Instructions

Journalize the April transactions.

Journalize transactions, post, and prepare trial balance.
(SO 3, 4)

P3–6B   During the first month of operations, these events and transactions occurred for Astromech Accounting Services Inc.:

May 1 Common shares were issued for $26,500 cash.
      2 A secretary-receptionist was hired at a salary of $1,500 per month.
      3 Purchased $1,400 of supplies on account from Read Supply Corp.

May 5 Paid office rent of $900 for the month.
11 Completed an income tax assignment and billed client $1,175 for services provided.
12 Received $3,500 in advance on a management consulting engagement.
17 Received $1,200 for services completed for Arnold Corp.
22 Received $1,175 from client for work completed and billed on May 11.
24 Paid 60% of balance due to Read Supply Corp.
29 Received a $275 telephone bill for May, to be paid next month.
31 Paid secretary-receptionist $1,500 salary for the month.
31 Paid monthly income tax instalment, $100.

Instructions

(a) Journalize the transactions.
(b) Using T accounts, post the May journal entries to the ledger.
(c) Prepare a trial balance at May 31, 2006.

P3–7B Lake Theatre, Inc., started operations on March 31, 2006. At this time, the ledger showed Cash $6,000; Land $40,000; Buildings (concession stand, projection room, ticket booth, and screen) $60,000; Equipment $16,000; Accounts Payable $4,000; Mortgage Payable $80,000; and Common Shares $38,000. During April, the following events and transactions occurred:

Journalize transactions, post, and prepare trial balance.
(SO 3, 4)

Apr. 2 Paid film rental fee of $800 on first movie.
3 Ordered two additional films at $750 each.
9 Received $13,800 from customers for admissions.
10 Paid $2,000 on mortgage. Also paid $525 in interest on the mortgage.
11 Hired Thoms Limited to operate concession stand. Thoms agrees to pay the Lake Theatre 17% of gross concession receipts, payable monthly, for the right to operate the concession stand.
12 Paid advertising expenses, $620.
20 Received one of the films ordered on April 3 and was billed $750. The film will be shown in April.
25 Received $5,300 from customers for admissions.
29 Paid salaries, $1,900.
30 Received statement from Thoms showing gross concession receipts of $2,600 and the balance due to the Lake Theatre of $442 ($2,600 × 17%) for April. Thoms paid half of the balance due and will remit the remainder on May 5.
30 Prepaid $700 rental fee on special film to be run in May

Instructions

(a) Using T accounts, enter the beginning balances in the ledger as at April 1.
(b) Journalize the April transactions.
(c) Post the April journal entries to the ledger.
(d) Prepare a trial balance at April 30, 2006.

P3–8B The Hudson's Bay Company has the following alphabetical list of accounts and balances (in thousands) as at January 31, 2004:

Prepare trial balance and financial statements.
(SO 4)

Cash in stores	$ 8,033	Other accounts payable and	
Credit card receivables	538,734	accrued expenses	$ 510,751
Dividends	37,178	Other accounts receivable	64,811
Fixed assets	1,089,334	Other assets	524,767
Goodwill	152,294	Other long-term liabilities	244,088
Income tax expense	49,243	Prepaid expenses and other	
Interest expense	42,662	current assets	78,669
Long-term debt	383,107	Retained earnings	740,853
Long-term debt due		Sales and revenue	7,400,051
within one year	125,436	Share capital	1,657,728
Merchandise inventories	1,485,088	Short-term borrowings	1,309
Operating expenses	7,238,917	Short-term deposits	168,943
		Trade accounts payable	415,350

Instructions

(a) Prepare a trial balance, sorting each account balance into the debit column or the credit column.

(b) Prepare a statement of earnings, statement of retained earnings, and balance sheet for the year.

Analyze errors and effect on trial balance.

(SO 4)

P3–9B   A first year co-op student working for Insidz.com recorded the company's transactions for the month. He was a little unsure about the recording process, but he did the best he could. He had a few questions, however, about the following transactions:

1. Cash received from a customer on account was recorded as a debit to Cash of $560 and a credit to Accounts Receivable of $650, instead of $560.
2. A service provided for cash was posted as a debit to Cash of $2,000 and a credit to Accounts Receivable of $2,000.
3. A credit of $750 for interest earned was neither recorded nor posted. The debit was recorded correctly.
4. The debit to record $1,000 of dividends paid to shareholders was posted to the Salary Expense account.
5. The purchase, on account, of a computer that cost $2,500 was recorded as a debit to Supplies and a credit to Accounts Payable.
6. Insidz.com received advances of $500 from customers for work to be done next month. The student debited Cash for $500 but did not credit anything, as he was not sure what to credit.
7. Payment of $495 for salaries was recorded as a debit to Salary Expense and a credit to Salaries Payable.
8. Payment of rent for the month was debited to Rent Expense and credited to Cash, $850.

Instructions

(a) Indicate which of the above transactions are correct, and which are incorrect.

(b) For each error identified in (a), answer the following questions:
   1. Will the trial balance be in balance?
   2. Which account(s) will be incorrectly stated because of the error?
   3. State whether each of the incorrect account(s) you identified in (2) will be overstated or understated and by how much.

Prepare corrected trial balance.

(SO 4)

P3–10B   This trial balance of Saginaw Ltd. does not balance:

SAGINAW LTD.
Trial Balance
May 31, 2006

	Debit	Credit
Cash	$ 6,376	
Accounts receivable		$ 2,630
Equipment	9,200	
Accumulated amortization		4,200
Accounts payable		4,600
Common shares		6,900
Retained earnings		4,429
Service revenue	10,690	
Salaries expense	8,150	
Advertising expense		1,132
Amortization expense	2,100	
Insurance expense	600	
Income tax expense	200	
	$37,316	$23,891

Your review of the ledger reveals that each account has a normal balance. You also discover the following errors:

1. Prepaid Insurance, Accounts Payable, and Income Tax Expense were each understated by $100.

2. A transposition error was made in Service Revenue. Based on the posting made, the correct balance was $10,609.
3. A debit posting to Salaries Expense of $250 was omitted.
4. A $750 dividend paid to shareholders was debited to Common Shares and credited to Cash.
5. A $630 purchase of supplies on account was debited to Equipment and credited to Cash.
6. A payment of $320 for advertising was debited to Advertising Expense for $32 and credited to Cash for $32.
7. A $2,000 note payable was issued in exchange for the purchase of equipment. The transaction was neither journalized nor posted.

Instructions

Prepare the correct trial balance.

BROADENING YOUR PERSPECTIVE

Financial Reporting and Analysis

Analysis Tools

Financial Reporting Problem: *Loblaw*

BYP3–1 The 2003 financial statements of Loblaw in Appendix A at the back of this book contain the following selected accounts and amounts (in millions):

Accounts Payable and		Fixed Assets	$ 6,422
Accrued Liabilities	$2,227	Income Tax Expense	426
Accounts Receivable	588	Interest Expense	196
Depreciation Expense	393	Sales	25,220

Instructions

(a) What is the increase and decrease side for each account? What is the normal balance for each account?
(b) Identify the probable other account(s) in the transaction and the effect on that (those) account(s) when:

1. Accounts Payable is decreased.   5. Interest Expense is increased.
2. Accounts Receivable is decreased.   6. Income Tax Expense is increased.
3. Depreciation Expense is increased. 7. Sales is increased.
4. Fixed Assets is increased.

Comparative Analysis Problem: *Loblaw and Sobeys*

BYP3–2 The financial statements of Sobeys are presented in Appendix B, following the financial statements for Loblaw in Appendix A.

Instructions

(a) Using Loblaw's balance sheet, statement of retained earnings, and statement of earnings, put the accounts and amounts provided into a trial balance format as at January 3, 2004.
(b) Using Sobeys' balance sheet, statement of retained earnings, and statement of earnings, put the accounts and amounts provided into a trial balance format as at May 1, 2004.

Research Case

BYP3–3   Robert Scott's journal article "Write-Up Lives! New Companies and New Functions Hit the Market," published in the March 2005 issue of *Accounting Technology* (p. 22) discusses how computerization has changed the accounting record-keeping system.

Instructions

Read this article, and answer the following questions:
   (a) Name some of the companies which offer computerized accounting systems that are available on the market today.
   (b) Aside from basic write-up (journalizing), what are some of the other features that computerized accounting systems offer?
   (c) How does a computerized accounting system improve the accuracy of a trial balance?
   (d) Identify the similarities and differences between a manual accounting system and a computerized accounting system.

Interpreting Financial Statements

BYP3–4   Agricore United is one of Canada's leading agri-businesses. The following list of accounts and amounts were taken from Agricore United's 2004 financial statements:

AGRICORE UNITED Trial Balance October 31, 2004 (in thousands)	
Accounts receivable	$ 185,232
Accounts payable and accrued expenses	326,706
Bank and other loans payable	132,121
Cash and cash equivalents	50,214
Cost of goods sold	2,619,638
Depreciation and amortization expense	65,211
Dividends	6,541
Dividends payable	2,464
Goodwill	28,903
Income tax recovery	5,342
Intangible assets	16,502
Interest expense	52,144
Inventories	383,914
Long-term debt	361,254
Loss on disposal of assets	289
Operating, general, and administrative expense	329,912
Other assets	100,573
Other long-term liabilities	147,686
Prepaid expenses	19,888
Property, plant, and equipment	664,396
Retained earnings	38,648
Sales and revenue from services	3,048,135
Share capital	461,001

Instructions

   (a) Prepare a trial balance for Agricore United, with the accounts reorganized in financial statement order.
   (b) Present Agricore United's accounts and amounts in the form of the accounting equation: assets = liabilities + shareholders' equity.

A Global Focus

BYP3–5 XBRL (eXtensible Business Reporting Language) is an emerging technical format for publishing business reporting data after the data have been properly analyzed and recorded, according to the processes described in this chapter. XBRL is being developed by an international not-for-profit consortium of approximately 250 major companies, organisations, and government agencies. XBRL provides standards for marking financial information so that financial and other business performance data can be retrieved automatically. By using XBRL, data from different company divisions with different accounting systems can be assembled quickly, cheaply, and efficiently. It is also easy to produce different types of reports that use varying subsets of the data. A company finance division, for example, could quickly and reliably generate internal management reports, financial statements for publication, tax and other regulatory filings, as well as credit reports for lenders.

Using XBRL does not result in a forced standardisation of financial reporting. The language is flexible and is intended to support all current aspects of reporting in different countries and industries. It is already being used in several countries and implementation of XBRL is growing rapidly around the world.

Instructions

(a) If the financial information will be stored and shared through electronic media, does this mean that the concepts discussed in this chapter are out-dated?

(b) Why do you think companies are spending time and money converting accounting information into an XBRL format? Would this be more beneficial to large international companies or smaller regional ones?

Financial Analysis on the Web

BYP3–6 In this chapter, we discussed the process of recording transactions. Once this information has been accumulated by a company, the company may want to share the data with external users whose needs and preferred reporting formats may vary. XBRL, the eXtensible Business Reporting Language, is a reporting system built to accommodate the electronic preparation and exchange of business reports around the world. This case will review the benefits and uses of XBRL in communicating data produced from recording transactions to external users.

Analysis Tools
(Financial Analysis on the Web)

Instructions

Specific requirements of this Web case can be found on the Toolkit website.

Critical Thinking

Collaborative Learning Activity

BYP3–7 Andrée Boudreau operates Boudreau Riding Academy, Inc. The academy's main sources of revenue are riding fees and lesson fees, which are provided on a cash basis. The academy also boards horses and bills their owners monthly for boarding fees. In some cases, boarders pay in advance.

The academy owns 10 horses, a stable, a riding corral, riding equipment, and office equipment. It employs stable helpers and an office employee, each of whom receives a weekly salary. At the end of each month, the mail brings bills for advertising, utilities, and veterinary services. Other expenses include feed for the horses and insurance. The company also pays periodic dividends.

During the first month of operations, an inexperienced bookkeeper was employed. Andrée Boudreau asks you to review the following 8 of the 50 entries made during the month. In each case, the explanation for the entry is correct.

GENERAL JOURNAL			
Date	Account Titles and Explanations	Debit	Credit
May 1	Cash	15,000	
	Common Shares		15,000
	(Issued common shares in exchange for $15,000 cash)		
5	Cash	250	
	Riding Fees Earned		250
	(Received $250 cash for lesson fees)		
7	Cash	1,500	
	Boarding Fees Earned		1,500
	(Received $1,500 for boarding of horses beginning June 1)		
9	Hay and Feed Expense	1,200	
	Cash		1,200
	(Purchased estimated two months' supply of feed and hay for $1,200 on account)		
14	Riding Equipment	800	
	Cash		800
	(Purchased desk and other office equipment for $800 cash)		
15	Salaries Expense	400	
	Cash		400
	(Paid dividend)		
20	Cash	145	
	Riding Fees Earned		154
	(Received $154 cash for riding fees)		
31	Veterinary Expense	75	
	Accounts Payable		75
	(Received bill of $75 from veterinarian for services provided)		

Instructions

With the class divided into groups, answer the following:

(a) Identify each journal entry that is correct. For each journal entry that is incorrect, prepare the entry that should have been made by the bookkeeper.
(b) Which of the incorrect entries would prevent the trial balance from balancing?
(c) What was the correct net earnings for May, assuming the bookkeeper reported net earnings of $4,500 after posting all 50 entries?
(d) What was the correct balance for Cash at May 31, assuming the bookkeeper reported a balance of $12,475 after posting all 50 entries?

Communication Activity

BYP3–8   Your local junior hockey team sells 25-game packages of tickets for $300. On September 30, the team organizers sold 1,500 packages of tickets and collected $450,000. During October, the team played four games. Assume that the only tickets sold were part of the 25-game packages. During October, the team paid $10,000 in operating expenses.

Instructions

Write a memo to your instructor that explains and illustrates the steps in recording the transactions for September and October. Calculate the ending balance in each account at October 31. Why does the team have a liability on October 31?

Ethics Case

Ethics In Accounting

BYP3–9   Vu Hung is the assistant chief accountant at Digitech Corporation. It is the end of the first quarter and Vu is hurriedly trying to prepare a trial balance so that quarterly financial statements can be prepared and released to management and the regulatory agencies. To Vu's dismay, the total credits on the trial balance exceed the debits by $1,000.

In order to meet the 4:00 p.m. deadline, Vu decides to force the debits and credits into balancing by adding the amount of the difference to the Equipment account. She chose Equipment because it is one of the larger account balances—$250,000. Proportionally, it will be the least misstated. She wishes that she had a few more days to find the error but realizes that the financial statements are already late.

Instructions

(a) Who are the stakeholders in this situation?
(b) What ethical issues are involved?
(c) What are Vu's alternatives?

Serial Problem

(*Note:* This is a continuation of the serial problem from Chapters 1 and 2.)

BYP3-10 In November 2005 after having incorporated Cookie Creations Ltd., Natalie begins operations. After much deliberation, Natalie decides not to accept the Biscuits offer raised in Chapter 2 to supply oatmeal chocolate chip cookies. At this point in time, Natalie believes it best to focus on her cookie classes until she has more time and oven space to consider making 1,500 dozen cookies a week. The following events occur in the month of November:

Nov. 8 Natalie cashes her Canada Savings Bonds and receives $520, which she deposits in her personal bank account.
8 A bank account is opened for Cookie Creations Ltd.
8 Cookie Creations issues 500 common shares to Natalie for $500.
11 Natalie designs a brochure and a poster to advertise the company and the services available.
11 The brochures and posters are printed, at a cash cost of $95. They will be distributed as the opportunity arises.
14 Baking supplies, such as flour, sugar, butter, and chocolate chips, are purchased for $125 cash.
15 Natalie starts to gather some baking equipment to take with her when teaching the cookie classes. She has an excellent top-of-the-line food processor and mixer that originally cost her $550. Natalie decides to start using it only in her new business. She estimates that the equipment is currently worth $300 and she transfers the equipment into the business in exchange for 300 additional common shares.
16 The company needs more cash to sustain its operations. Natalie's grandmother lends the company $2,000 cash, in exchange for a two-year, 6% note payable. Interest and the principal are repayable at maturity.
17 Cookie Creations purchases more baking equipment for $900 cash.
18 Natalie books her first class for November 29 for $100. One of her mother's friends needed a novel idea for her young daughter's birthday party.
25 Natalie books a second class for December 5 for $125. As a down payment, $50 cash is received in advance.
29 Natalie teaches her first class, booked on November 18, and collects the $100 cash.
30 A one-year insurance policy is purchased for $1,200.
30 Natalie teaches a group of grade one students how to make Santa Claus cookies. At the end of the class, Natalie leaves an invoice for $250 with the school principal. The principal says that he will pass it along to head office and it will be paid sometime in December.
30 A $50 invoice for use of Natalie's cell phone is received. The cell phone is used exclusively for Cookie Creations Ltd. business. The invoice is for services provided in November and is due on December 15.

Instructions:

(a) Prepare journal entries to record the November transactions.
(b) Post the journal entries to the general ledger accounts.
(c) Prepare a trial balance at November 30, 2005.

Answers to Self-Study Questions

1. c   2. d   3. b   4. c   5. d   6. a   7. c   8. d   9. a   10. c

Answer to Loblaw Review It Question 4

Accounts Receivable (Asset-Dr.), Long-Term Debt (Liability-Cr.), Sales (Revenue-Cr.), and Interest Expense (Expense-Dr.).

 Remember to go back to the Navigator box at the beginning of the chapter to check off your completed work.

CHAPTER 4

Accrual Accounting Concepts

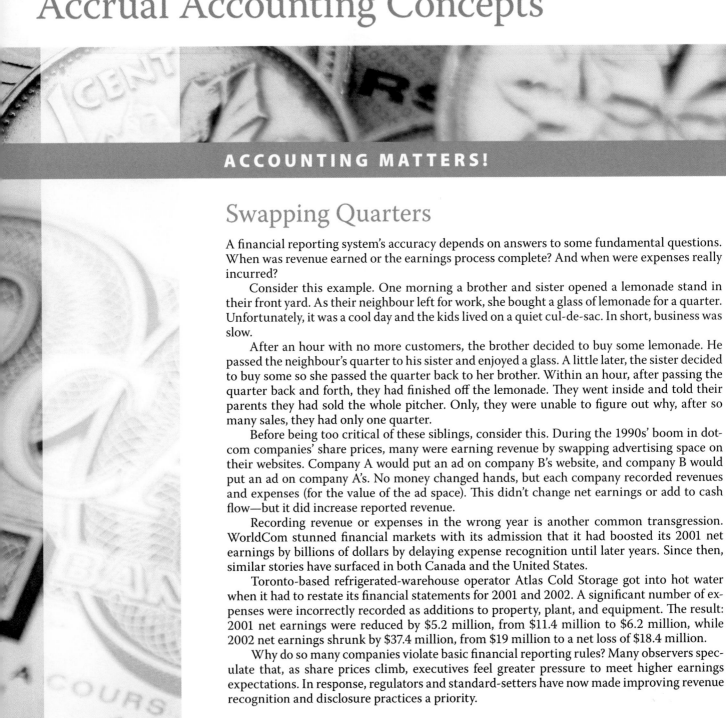

Swapping Quarters

A financial reporting system's accuracy depends on answers to some fundamental questions. When was revenue earned or the earnings process complete? And when were expenses really incurred?

Consider this example. One morning a brother and sister opened a lemonade stand in their front yard. As their neighbour left for work, she bought a glass of lemonade for a quarter. Unfortunately, it was a cool day and the kids lived on a quiet cul-de-sac. In short, business was slow.

After an hour with no more customers, the brother decided to buy some lemonade. He passed the neighbour's quarter to his sister and enjoyed a glass. A little later, the sister decided to buy some so she passed the quarter back to her brother. Within an hour, after passing the quarter back and forth, they had finished off the lemonade. They went inside and told their parents they had sold the whole pitcher. Only, they were unable to figure out why, after so many sales, they had only one quarter.

Before being too critical of these siblings, consider this. During the 1990s' boom in dot-com companies' share prices, many were earning revenue by swapping advertising space on their websites. Company A would put an ad on company B's website, and company B would put an ad on company A's. No money changed hands, but each company recorded revenues and expenses (for the value of the ad space). This didn't change net earnings or add to cash flow—but it did increase reported revenue.

Recording revenue or expenses in the wrong year is another common transgression. WorldCom stunned financial markets with its admission that it had boosted its 2001 net earnings by billions of dollars by delaying expense recognition until later years. Since then, similar stories have surfaced in both Canada and the United States.

Toronto-based refrigerated-warehouse operator Atlas Cold Storage got into hot water when it had to restate its financial statements for 2001 and 2002. A significant number of expenses were incorrectly recorded as additions to property, plant, and equipment. The result: 2001 net earnings were reduced by $5.2 million, from $11.4 million to $6.2 million, while 2002 net earnings shrunk by $37.4 million, from $19 million to a net loss of $18.4 million.

Why do so many companies violate basic financial reporting rules? Many observers speculate that, as share prices climb, executives feel greater pressure to meet higher earnings expectations. In response, regulators and standard-setters have now made improving revenue recognition and disclosure practices a priority.

the navigator

THE NAVIGATOR

- [ ] Read *Feature Story*
- [ ] Scan *Study Objectives*
- [ ] Read *Chapter Preview*
- [ ] Read text and answer *Before You Go On*
- [ ] Work *Using the Decision Toolkit*
- [ ] Review *Summary of Study Objectives*
- [ ] Review the *Decision Toolkit—A Summary*
- [ ] Work *Demonstration Problem*
- [ ] Answer *Self-Study Questions*
- [ ] Complete assignments

STUDY OBJECTIVES

After studying this chapter, you should be able to:

1. Explain the revenue recognition principle and the matching principle.
2. Prepare adjusting entries for prepayments.
3. Prepare adjusting entries for accruals.
4. Describe the nature and purpose of the adjusted trial balance.
5. Explain the purposes of closing entries.

the
navigator

Recording revenues and expenses properly is essential, as indicated in the feature story, because doing otherwise leads to a misstatement of net earnings and related accounts. In this chapter, we introduce you to the accrual accounting concepts that guide the recognition of revenue and the matching of expenses in the appropriate time period.

The chapter is organized as follows:

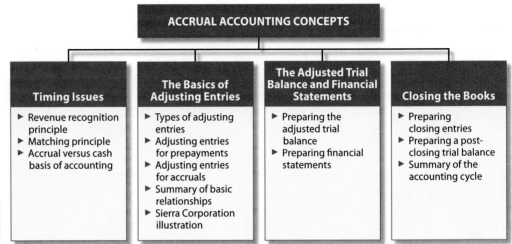

Timing Issues

study objective 1

Explain the revenue recognition principle and the matching principle.

Consider the following story:

> A grocery store owner from the old country kept his accounts payable on a spindle, accounts receivable on a notepad, and cash in a shoebox. His daughter, a CA, chided him: "I don't understand how you can run your business this way. How do you know what you've earned?"
>
> "Well," the father replied, "when I arrived in Canada 40 years ago, I had nothing but the pants I was wearing. Today your sister is a doctor, your brother is a teacher, and you are a chartered accountant. Your mother and I have a nice car, a well-furnished house, and a cottage at the lake. We have a good business and everything is paid for. So, you add all that together, subtract the pants, and there's your net earnings."

Although the old grocer may be correct in his evaluation of how to calculate earnings over his lifetime, most companies need more immediate feedback about how well they are doing. For example, management needs monthly reports on financial results, large corporations present quarterly and annual financial statements to shareholders, and the Canada Revenue Agency requires all businesses to file annual tax returns.

Consequently, **accounting divides the economic life of a business into artificial time periods**. As indicated in Chapter 2, this is the **time period assumption**. Accounting time periods are generally one month, one quarter, or one year.

Many accounting transactions affect more than one of these arbitrary time periods. For example, a new building purchased by Loblaw or a new airplane purchased by Air Canada will be used for many years. It does not make sense to expense the full cost of the building or the airplane at the time of purchase, because each will be used for many subsequent periods. Instead, we must determine the impact of each transaction on specific accounting periods.

Determining the amount of revenue and expenses to report in a particular accounting period can be difficult. Generally accepted accounting principles include two principles for recognizing revenue and expenses: the revenue recognition principle and the matching principle.

Revenue Recognition Principle

The **revenue recognition principle** states that revenue must be recognized in the accounting period in which it is earned. In a merchandising company, revenue is considered to be earned when the merchandise is sold (normally at the point of sale). In a service company, revenue is considered earned at the time the service is performed.

Revenue recognition is governed by general guidelines and there are a wide variety of interpretations. In general, though, revenue is recognized when the sales effort is substantially complete and collection reasonably assured.

To illustrate, assume a dry-cleaning business cleans clothing on June 30, but customers do not claim and pay for their clothes until the first week of July. Under the revenue recognition principle, revenue is earned in June when the service is performed, not in July when the cash is received. At June 30, the dry-cleaning service would report a receivable on its balance sheet and revenue in its statement of earnings for the service performed.

Improper use of the revenue recognition principle can have devastating consequences for investors. For example, as mentioned in the feature story for Chapter 2, Nortel Network's shares lost a significant portion of their value after investors learned about accounting irregularities related to reported revenue.

Decision Toolkit

Decision Checkpoints	Info Needed for Decision	Tools to Use for Decision	How to Evaluate Results
At what point should the company record revenue?	Need to understand the nature of the company's business	Revenue should be recorded when earned. For a service company, revenue is earned when a service is performed.	Recognizing revenue too early overstates current period revenue; recognizing it too late understates current period revenue.

Matching Principle

In recognizing expenses, a simple rule is followed: "Let the expenses follow the revenues." Thus, expense recognition is tied to revenue recognition. Consider again the dry-cleaning business mentioned in the last section. Matching expenses with revenues means that the salary expense of performing the cleaning service on June 30 should be reported in the same period in which the service revenue is recognized. The critical issue in expense recognition is determining when the expense contributes to revenue. This may or may not be the same period in which the expense is paid. If the salary incurred on June 30 is not paid until July, the dry cleaner would still report salaries payable on its June 30 balance sheet.

The practice of expense recognition is referred to as the **matching principle** because it states that efforts (expenses) must be matched with accomplishments (revenues). Some expenses are easy to match with revenues. For example, the cost of goods sold can be directly matched to sales revenue in the period in which the sale occurs.

Other costs are more difficult to directly associate with revenue. For example, it is difficult to match administrative salary expense or interest expense with the revenue these help earn. Such costs are normally expensed in the period in which they are incurred. Other examples include costs that help generate revenue over multiple periods of time, such as the amortization of equipment. The association of these types of expense with revenue is less direct than that of cost of goods sold, and we therefore have to make assumptions about how to best allocate these costs to each period. We will learn more about allocating expenses later in this chapter.

ACCOUNTING MATTERS!   Management Perspective

Suppose you work for a movie studio. Over what period should the cost of producing a movie be expensed? It should be expensed over the economic life of the movie. But what is its economic life? The filmmaker must estimate how much revenue will be earned from box office sales, DVD sales, television, and games and toys—a period that could be less than a year or many years.

Take, for example, *Harry Potter and the Prisoner of Azkaban*, released by Warner Bros. in 2004. It cost U.S. $130 million to produce this film, and the film more than recovered this cost in the first two weekends it was released. In fact, all of the *Harry Potter* movies have broken box office and product sales records. Compare this to *The Cat in the Hat*, released by Universal Studios in 2003. It cost U.S. $109 million to produce this movie but it has only recovered U.S. $100.4 million to date. These situations illustrate how difficult it can be in real life for companies to properly match expenses to revenues.

▦ Decision Toolkit

Decision Checkpoints	Info Needed for Decision	Tools to Use for Decision	How to Evaluate Results
At what point should the company record expenses?	Need to understand the nature of the company's business	Expenses should "follow" revenues—that is, the effort (expense) should be matched with the result (revenue).	Recognizing expenses too early overstates current period expenses; recognizing them too late understates current period expenses.

Accrual Versus Cash Basis of Accounting

International Note
Although different accounting principles are often used in other countries, the accrual basis of accounting is central to all these principles.

The combined application of the revenue recognition principle and the matching principle results in accrual basis accounting. **Accrual basis accounting** means that **transactions that affect a company's financial statements are recorded in the periods in which the events occur, rather than when the company actually receives or pays cash**. This means recognizing revenues when they are earned rather than when cash is received. Likewise, expenses are recognized in the period in which services or goods are used or consumed to produce these revenues, rather than when cash is paid. This results in matching revenues that have been earned with the expenses incurred to earn these same revenues.

An alternative to the accrual basis is the cash basis. Under **cash basis accounting, revenue is recorded only when cash is received, and an expense is recorded only when cash is paid**. A statement of earnings presented under the cash basis of accounting does not satisfy generally accepted accounting principles. Why not? Because it fails to record revenue that has been earned but for which cash has not yet been received, thus violating the revenue recognition principle. Similarly, a cash basis statement of earnings fails to match expenses with earned revenues, which violates the matching principle.

Illustration 4-1 compares accrual-based numbers and cash-based numbers, using a simple example. Suppose that you own a painting company and you paint a large building during year 1. In year 1, you incur and pay total expenses of $50,000, which includes the cost of the paint and your employees' salaries. You bill your customer $80,000 at the end of year 1, but you are not paid until year 2. On an accrual basis, you would report the revenue during the period earned—year 1—and the expenses would be matched to the period in which the revenues were earned. Thus, your net earnings for year 1 would be $30,000, and no revenue or expense from this project would be reported in year 2. The $30,000 of earnings reported for year 1 provides a useful indication of the profitability of your efforts during that period.

If, instead, you were reporting on a cash basis, you would report expenses of $50,000 in year 1 and revenues of $80,000 in year 2. Net earnings for year 1 would be a loss of $50,000, while net earnings for year 2 would be $80,000. While total earnings are the same over the two-year period ($30,000), cash basis measures are not very informative about the results of your efforts during year 1 or year 2.

Illustration 4-1 ◀

Accrual versus cash basis accounting

	Year 1	Year 2
Activity	Purchased paint, painted building, paid employees	Received payment for work done in year 1
Accrual basis	Revenue $ 80,000 Expense 50,000 Net earnings $ 30,000	Revenue $ 0 Expense 0 Net earnings $ 0
Cash basis	Revenue $ 0 Expense 50,000 Net loss $(50,000)	Revenue $80,000 Expense 0 Net earnings $80,000

BEFORE YOU GO ON . . .

▶Review It

1. What are the revenue recognition and matching principles?
2. What are the differences between the cash and accrual bases of accounting?

The Basics of Adjusting Entries

For revenues to be recorded in the period in which they are earned, and for expenses to be matched with the revenue they generate, **adjusting entries** are made to adjust accounts at the end of the accounting period. Adjusting entries make it possible to produce relevant financial information at the end of the accounting period. Thus, the balance sheet reports appropriate assets, liabilities, and shareholders' equity at the statement date, and the statement of earnings shows the proper revenues, expenses, and net earnings (or loss) for the period.

Adjusting entries are necessary because the trial balance—the first pulling together of the transaction data—may not contain complete and up-to-date data. This is true for several reasons:

1. Some events are not journalized daily, because it would not be useful or efficient to do so. Examples are the use of supplies and the earning of wages by employees.
2. Some costs are not journalized during the accounting period, because these costs expire with the passage of time rather than as a result of recurring daily transactions. Examples include insurance and amortization.
3. Some items may be unrecorded. An example is a utility service bill that will not be received until the next accounting period. The bill, however, covers services delivered in the current accounting period.

Adjusting entries are required every time financial statements are prepared. We first analyze each account in the trial balance to see if it is complete and up to date. The analysis requires an understanding of the company's operations and the interrelationship of accounts.

Animated Tutorials
(Accounting Cycle Tutorial)

www.wiley.com/canada/kimmel

Preparing adjusting entries is often a long process. For example, to accumulate the adjustment data, a company may need to count its remaining supplies. It may also need to prepare supporting schedules of insurance policies, rental agreements, and other commitments.

Types of Adjusting Entries

Adjusting entries can be classified as either prepayments or accruals. Each of these classes has two subcategories as shown below:

Prepayments
1. **Prepaid expenses:** Expenses paid in cash and recorded as assets before they are used or consumed
2. **Unearned revenues:** Cash received and recorded as liabilities before revenue is earned

Accruals
1. **Accrued expenses:** Expenses incurred but not yet paid in cash or recorded
2. **Accrued revenues:** Revenues earned but not yet received in cash or recorded

Specific examples and explanations of each type of adjustment are provided in the following pages. Each example is based on the October 31 trial balance of Sierra Corporation, from Chapter 3, shown again here in Illustration 4-2.

Illustration 4-2 ▶

Trial balance

SIERRA CORPORATION Trial Balance October 31, 2006		
	Debit	Credit
Cash	$15,200	
Advertising supplies	2,500	
Prepaid insurance	600	
Office equipment	5,000	
Notes payable		$ 5,000
Accounts payable		2,500
Unearned service revenue		1,200
Common shares		10,000
Dividends	500	
Service revenue		10,000
Salaries expense	4,000	
Rent expense	900	
	$28,700	$28,700

We assume that Sierra Corporation uses an accounting period of one month. Thus, monthly adjusting entries need to be made.

Adjusting Entries for Prepayments

study objective 2

Prepare adjusting entries for prepayments.

Prepayments are either prepaid expenses or unearned revenues. Adjusting entries for prepayments record the portion of the payment that applies to the current accounting period. This means that for prepaid expenses, the adjusting entry records the expenses which apply to the period. For unearned revenues, the adjusting entry records the revenues earned in the period.

Prepaid Expenses

Costs that are paid for in cash before they are used are recorded as **prepaid expenses**. When such a cost is incurred, a prepaid account should be increased (debited)—to show the service or benefit that will be received in the future—and cash should be decreased (credited). Examples of common prepayments are insurance, supplies, and rent. In addition, long-term prepayments are made when long-lived assets, such as buildings and equipment, are purchased.

Prepaid expenses are costs that expire either with the passage of time (e.g., rent and insurance) or through use (e.g., supplies). The expiration of these costs does not require daily entries, which would be impractical and unnecessary. Accordingly, we postpone recognizing these expired costs until financial statements are prepared. At each statement date, adjusting entries are made for two purposes: (1) to record the expenses (expired costs) applicable to the current accounting period, and (2) to show the remaining amounts (unexpired costs) in the asset accounts.

Until prepaid expenses are adjusted, assets are overstated and expenses are understated. If expenses are understated, then net earnings and shareholders' equity will be overstated. As shown below, **an adjusting entry for prepaid expenses results in an increase (a debit) to an expense account and a decrease (a credit) to an asset account.**

Helpful Hint A cost can be an asset or an expense. If the cost has future benefits (i.e., the benefits have not yet expired), it is an asset. If the cost has no future benefits (i.e., the benefits have expired), it is an expense.

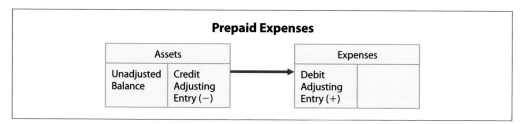

Prepaid Expenses

Let's look in more detail at some specific types of prepaid expenses, beginning with supplies.

Supplies. The purchase of supplies, such as paper, results in an increase (a debit) to an asset account. During the accounting period, supplies are used. Rather than record supplies expense as the supplies are used, supplies expense is recognized at the end of the accounting period. At that time, the company must count the remaining supplies. The difference between the balance in the supplies (asset) account and the actual cost of supplies on hand gives the supplies used (an expense) for that period.

Recall from the facts presented in Chapter 3 that Sierra Corporation purchased advertising supplies costing $2,500 on October 9. The payment was recorded by increasing (debiting) the asset account Advertising Supplies. This account shows a balance of $2,500 in the October 31 trial balance. A count at the close of business on October 31 reveals that $1,000 of supplies are still on hand. Thus, the cost of supplies used is $1,500 ($2,500 – $1,000).

This use of supplies decreases an asset, Advertising Supplies. It also decreases shareholders' equity by increasing an expense account, Advertising Supplies Expense. The use of supplies is recorded as follows:

Oct. 31	Advertising Supplies Expense	1,500	
	Advertising Supplies		1,500
	(To record supplies used)		

A	=	L	+	SE
−1,500				−1,500

Cash flows: no effect

After the adjusting entry is posted, the two supplies accounts are as follows in T account form:

Advertising Supplies				Advertising Supplies Expense		
Oct. 9	2,500	Oct. 31 Adj.	1,500	Oct. 31 Adj.	1,500	
Oct. 31 Bal.	1,000			Oct. 31 Bal.	1,500	

The asset account Advertising Supplies now shows a balance of $1,000, which is equal to the cost of supplies on hand at the statement date. In addition, Advertising Supplies Expense shows a balance of $1,500, which equals the cost of supplies used in October. If the adjusting entry is not made, October expenses will be understated and net earnings overstated by $1,500. Moreover, as the accounting equation shows, both assets and shareholders' equity will be overstated by $1,500 on the October 31 balance sheet.

Insurance.   Companies purchase insurance to protect themselves from losses caused by fire, theft, and unforeseen accidents. Insurance must be paid in advance, often for one year. Insurance payments (premiums) made in advance are normally recorded in the asset account Prepaid Insurance. At the financial statement date, it is necessary to make an adjustment to increase (debit) Insurance Expense and decrease (credit) Prepaid Insurance for the cost of insurance that has expired during the period.

On October 6, Sierra Corporation paid $600 for a one-year insurance policy. Coverage began on October 1. The payment was recorded by increasing (debiting) Prepaid Insurance when it was paid. This account shows a balance of $600 in the October 31 trial balance. An analysis of the insurance policy reveals that $50 of insurance expires each month ($600 ÷ 12 mos.). The expiration of the prepaid insurance would be recorded as follows:

A	=	L	+	SE
−50				−50

Cash flows: no effect

Oct. 31	Insurance Expense	50	
	Prepaid Insurance		50
	(To record insurance expired)		

After the adjusting entry is posted, the accounts appear as follows:

Prepaid Insurance				Insurance Expense		
Oct. 6	600	Oct. 31 Adj.	50	Oct. 31 Adj.	50	
Oct. 31 Bal.	550			Oct. 31 Bal.	50	

The asset Prepaid Insurance shows a balance of $550, which represents the cost that applies to the remaining 11 months of insurance coverage (11 × $50). At the same time, the balance in Insurance Expense is equal to the insurance cost that was used in October. If this adjustment is not made, October expenses will be understated and net earnings overstated by $50. Moreover, both assets and shareholders' equity will be overstated by $50 on the October 31 balance sheet.

Amortization.   A company typically owns a variety of assets that have long lives, such as buildings and equipment. Each is recorded as an asset, rather than as an expense, in the year it is acquired because these long-lived assets provide a service for many years. The period of service is referred to as the **useful life**.

From an accounting standpoint, the acquisition of long-lived assets is essentially a long-term prepayment for services. Similar to other prepaid expenses, there is a need to recognize the cost that has been used (an expense) during the period and to report the unused cost (an asset) at the end of the period. **Amortization** is the process of allocating the cost of a long-lived asset to expense over its useful life.

One point is very important to understand: **Amortization is an allocation concept, not a valuation concept**. That is, we amortize an asset to allocate its cost to the periods over which we use it. We are not trying to record a change in the value of the asset. We are only trying to match expenses with the revenues generated in each period.

Calculation of Amortization.   A common practice for calculating amortization expense is to divide the cost of the asset by its useful life. This is known as the **straight-line method of amortization**. Of course, at the time an asset is acquired, its useful life is not known with any certainty. It must therefore be estimated.

Sierra Corporation purchased office equipment that cost $5,000 on October 3. If its useful life is expected to be five years, annual amortization is $1,000 ($5,000 ÷ 5). In its simplest form, the formula to calculate amortization expense is as follows:

Illustration 4-3 ▶

Formula for amortization

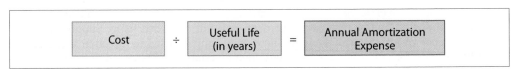

Of course, if you are calculating amortization for partial periods, the annual expense amount must be adjusted for the relevant portion of the year. For example, if we wish to determine the amortization for one month, we would multiply the annual result by one-twelfth as there are twelve months in a year. Calculating amortization will be refined and examined in more detail in Chapter 9.

For Sierra Corporation, amortization on the office equipment is estimated to be $83 per month ($1,000 × 1/12). Accordingly, amortization for October is recognized by this adjusting entry:

Oct. 31	Amortization Expense	83	
	Accumulated Amortization—Office Equipment		83
	(To record monthly amortization)		

A = L + SE
−83   −83
Cash flows: no effect

After the adjusting entry is posted, the accounts appear as follows:

Accumulated Amortization—Office Equipment			Amortization Expense		
	Oct. 31 Adj.	83	Oct. 31 Adj.	83	
	Oct. 31 Bal.	83	Oct. 31 Bal.	83	

The balance in the Accumulated Amortization account will increase by $83 each month until the asset is fully amortized in five years.

As in the case of other prepaid expenses, if this adjusting entry is not made, total assets, shareholders' equity, and net earnings will all be overstated by $83 and amortization expense will be understated by $83.

Statement Presentation. As we learned in Chapter 2, a contra account is an account that is offset against (deducted from) a related account on the statement of earnings or balance sheet. Accumulated Amortization—Office Equipment is a **contra asset account**. That means it is offset against an asset account (Office Equipment) on the balance sheet. Its normal balance is a credit—the opposite of the normal debit balance of its related account, Office Equipment.

There is a simple reason for using a separate contra account instead of decreasing (crediting) Office Equipment: using this account discloses both the original cost of the equipment and the total estimated cost that has expired to date. In the balance sheet, Accumulated Amortization—Office Equipment is deducted from the related asset account as follows:

Helpful Hint Every contra account has increases, decreases, and normal balances that are opposite to those of the account it relates to.

Office equipment	$5,000
Less: Accumulated amortization—office equipment	83
Net book value	4,917

The difference between the cost of any amortizable asset and its related accumulated amortization is referred to as the **net book value**, or book value, of that asset. In the above illustration, the book value of the office equipment at the balance sheet date is $4,917. Be sure to understand that, except at acquisition, the book value of the asset and its market value (the price at which it could be sold) are two different values. As noted earlier, the purpose of amortization is not to state an asset's value, but to allocate its cost over time.

Alternative Terminology *Book value* is also referred to as *carrying value.*

Unearned Revenues

Cash received before revenue is earned is recorded by increasing (crediting) a liability account for **unearned revenue**. Items like rent, magazine subscriptions, and customer deposits for future service may result in unearned revenues. Airlines such as Air Canada, for instance, treat receipts from the sale of tickets as unearned revenue until the flight service is provided. Similarly, tuition fees received by universities and colleges before the academic session begins are considered unearned revenue.

Unearned revenues are the opposite of prepaid expenses. Indeed, unearned revenue on the books of one company is likely to be a prepayment on the books of the company that has made the advance payment. For example, if identical accounting periods are assumed, your landlord will have unearned rent revenue when you (the tenant) have prepaid rent.

When a payment is received for services that will be provided in a future accounting period, cash should be increased (debited) and unearned revenue (a liability) should be increased (credited) to recognize the obligation that exists. Unearned revenues are later earned when the service is provided to the customer.

It is not practical to make daily journal entries as the revenue is earned. Instead, recognition of earned revenue is delayed until the adjustment process. Then an adjusting entry is made to record the revenue that has been earned during the period and to show the liability that remains at the end of the accounting period. Typically, until the adjustment is made, liabilities are overstated and revenues are understated. If revenues are understated, then net earnings and shareholders' equity are also understated. As shown below, **the adjusting entry for unearned revenues results in a decrease (a debit) to a liability account and an increase (a credit) to a revenue account**.

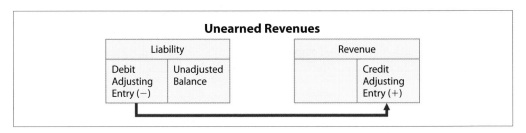

Sierra Corporation received $1,200 on October 4 from R. Knox for advertising services expected to be completed before the end of next month, November 30. The payment was credited to Unearned Service Revenue, and this liability account shows a balance of $1,200 in the October 31 trial balance. From an evaluation of the work performed by Sierra for Knox during October, it is determined that $400 worth of work was earned in October.

The following adjusting entry is made:

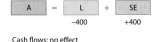

Oct. 31	Unearned Service Revenue	400	
	Service Revenue		400
	(To record revenue earned)		

After the adjusting entry is posted, the accounts appear as follows:

Unearned Service Revenue			Service Revenue		
Oct. 31 Adj. 400	Oct. 4	1,200		Oct. 13	10,000
	Oct. 31 Bal.	800		31 Adj.	400
				Oct. 31 Bal.	10,400

The liability Unearned Service Revenue now shows a balance of $800, which represents the remaining advertising services expected to be performed in the future. At the same time, Service Revenue shows total revenue earned in October of $10,400. If this adjustment is not made, revenues and net earnings will be understated by $400 in the statement of earnings. Moreover, liabilities will be overstated by $400 and shareholders' equity will be understated by that amount on the October 31 balance sheet.

BEFORE YOU GO ON . . .

▶Review It

1. What are the four types of adjusting entries?
2. What is the effect on assets, liabilities, shareholders' equity, revenues, expenses, and net earnings if an adjusting entry for a prepaid expense is not made?
3. What was the amount of Loblaw's 2003 depreciation expense? What were its accumulated depreciation and net book value as at January 3, 2004? (*Hint:* These amounts are reported in the notes to the financial statements.) The answers to these questions are provided at the end of this chapter.

4. What is the effect on assets, liabilities, shareholders' equity, revenues, expenses, and net earnings if an adjusting entry for unearned revenue is not made?

▶Do It

Hammond, Inc.'s general ledger includes these selected accounts on March 31, 2006, before adjusting entries are prepared:

	Debit	Credit
Prepaid insurance	$ 3,600	
Office supplies	2,800	
Office equipment	25,000	
Accumulated amortization—office equipment		$9,583
Unearned service revenue		9,200

An analysis of the accounts shows the following:

1. The insurance policy is a 12-month policy, effective March 1.
2. Office supplies on hand total $800.
3. The office equipment was purchased April 1, 2004, and is estimated to have a useful life of five years.
4. Half of the unearned service revenue was earned in March.

Prepare the adjusting entries for the month of March.

Action Plan

- Make sure you prepare adjustments for the appropriate time period.
- Adjusting entries for prepaid expenses require a debit to an expense account and a credit to an asset account.
- Adjusting entries for unearned revenues require a debit to a liability account and a credit to a revenue account.

Solution

			Debit	Credit
1.	Mar. 31	Insurance Expense	300	
		Prepaid Insurance		300
		(To record insurance expired: $3,600 × 1/12)		
2.	31	Office Supplies Expense	2,000	
		Office Supplies		2,000
		(To record supplies used: $2,800 − $800)		
3.	31	Amortization Expense	417	
		Accumulated Amortization—Office Equipment		417
		(To record monthly amortization: $25,000 ÷ 5 × 1/12)		
4.	31	Unearned Service Revenue	4,600	
		Service Revenue		4,600
		(To record revenue earned: $9,200 × 1/2)		

the navigator

Adjusting Entries for Accruals

The second category of adjusting entries is **accruals**. Adjusting entries for accruals are required in order to record revenues earned, or expenses incurred, in the current accounting period. Accruals have not been recognized through daily entries and thus are not yet reflected in the accounts. Until an accrual adjustment is made, the revenue account (and the related asset account), or the expense account (and the related liability account), is understated. Thus, adjusting entries for accruals will increase both a balance sheet account and a statement of earnings account.

    There are two types of adjusting entries for accruals—accrued revenues and accrued expenses. We now look at each type in more detail.

Accrued Revenues

Alternative Terminology
Accrued revenues are also
called *accrued receivables*.

Revenues earned but not yet received in cash or recorded at the statement date are **accrued revenues**. Accrued revenues may accumulate (accrue) with the passing of time, as in the case of interest revenue. Or they may result from services that have been performed but not yet billed or collected, as in the case of fees. The former are unrecorded because, as when interest is earned, they do not involve daily transactions. The latter may be unrecorded because only a portion of the total service has been provided and the clients will not be billed until the service has been completed.

An adjusting entry is required for two purposes: (1) to show the receivable that exists at the balance sheet date, and (2) to record the revenue that has been earned during the period. Until the adjustment is made, both assets and revenues are understated. Consequently, net earnings and shareholders' equity will also be understated. As shown below, **an adjusting entry for accrued revenues results in an increase (a debit) to an asset account and an increase (a credit) to a revenue account**.

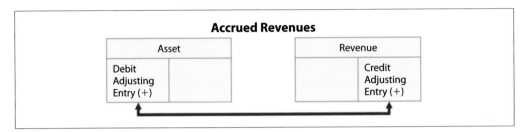

In October, Sierra Corporation earned $200 for advertising services that were not billed to clients before October 31. Because these services have not been billed, they have not been recorded. The adjusting entry would be as follows:

Oct. 31	Accounts Receivable	200	
	Service Revenue		200
	(To accrue revenue earned but not billed or collected)		

After the adjusting entry is posted, the accounts appear as below:

Accounts Receivable					Service Revenue		
Oct. 13	10,000	Oct. 30	10,000		Oct. 13	10,000
Oct. 31 Adj.	200				31 Adj.	400
Oct. 31 Bal.	200				31 Adj.	200
					Oct. 31 Bal.	10,600

The asset Accounts Receivable shows that $200 is owed by clients at the balance sheet date. The balance of $10,600 in Service Revenue represents the total revenue earned during the month. If the adjusting entry is not made, assets and shareholders' equity on the balance sheet, and revenues and net earnings on the statement of earnings, will be understated.

In the next accounting period, the clients will be billed. When this occurs, the entry to record the billing should recognize that $200 of revenue earned in October has already been recorded in the October 31 adjusting entry and should not be re-recorded. The subsequent collection of cash from clients will be recorded with an increase (a debit) to Cash and a decrease (a credit) to Accounts Receivable.

Accrued Expenses

Alternative Terminology
Accrued expenses are also
called *accrued liabilities*.

Expenses incurred but not yet paid or recorded at the statement date are called **accrued expenses**. Interest, salaries, and income taxes are common examples of accrued expenses. Accrued expenses result from the same factors as accrued revenues. In fact, an accrued expense on the books of one company is an accrued revenue to another company. For example, the

$200 accrual of service revenue for Sierra Corporation discussed above is an accrued expense for the client that received the service.

Adjustments for accrued expenses are necessary to (1) record the obligations that exist at the balance sheet date, and (2) recognize the expenses that apply to the current accounting period. Until the adjustment is made, both liabilities and expenses are understated. Consequently, net earnings and shareholders' equity are overstated. **An adjusting entry for accrued expenses results in an increase (a debit) to an expense account and an increase (a credit) to a liability account,** as shown below:

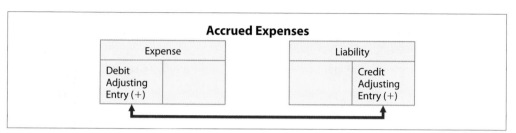

> **Helpful Hint** To make the illustration easier to understand, a simplified method of interest calculation is used. In reality, interest is calculated using the exact number of days in the interest period and year (365).

Let's look in more detail at some specific types of accrued expenses, beginning with accrued interest.

Interest. Sierra Corporation signed a three-month note payable for $5,000 on October 2. The note requires interest at an annual rate of six percent. The amount of the interest accumulation is determined by three factors: (1) the face value, or principal amount, of the note, (2) the interest rate, which is always expressed as an annual rate, and (3) the length of time the note is outstanding.

In this instance, the total interest due on the $5,000 note at its due date, three months in the future, is $75 ($5,000 × 6% × ³⁄₁₂), or $25 for one month. Note that the time period is expressed as a fraction of a year. The formula for calculating interest and how it applies to Sierra Corporation for the month of October are shown in Illustration 4-4.

Illustration 4-4 ◀

Formula for calculating interest

The accrual of interest at October 31 would be reflected in an adjusting entry as follows:

Oct. 31	Interest Expense	25	
	Interest Payable		25
	(To accrue interest on note payable)		

Cash flows: no effect

After the adjusting entry is posted, the accounts appear as follows:

Interest Expense		Interest Payable	
Oct. 31 Adj. 25			Oct. 31 Adj. 25
Oct. 31 Bal. 25			Oct. 31 Bal. 25

Interest Expense shows the interest charges for the month of October. The amount of interest owed at the statement date is shown in Interest Payable. It will not be paid until the note comes due at the end of three months. The Interest Payable account is used, instead of crediting Notes Payable, to disclose the two different types of obligations—interest and principal—in the accounts and statements. If this adjusting entry is not made, liabilities and interest expense will be understated and net earnings and shareholders' equity will be overstated.

Salaries.   Some types of expenses, such as employee salaries, are paid for after the services have been performed. At Sierra Corporation, salaries were last paid on October 20. The next payment of salaries will not occur until November 3. As shown on the calendar in Illustration 4-5, seven as yet unpaid working days remain in October (October 23–27 and October 30–31).

Illustration 4-5 ▶

Calendar showing Sierra Corporation's pay periods

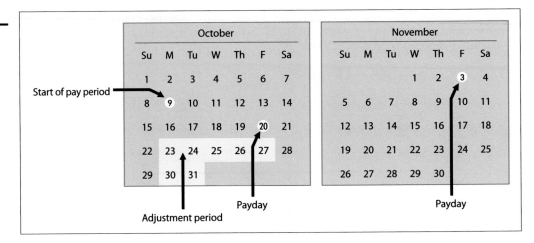

At October 31, the salaries for these seven days represent an accrued expense and a related liability to Sierra. The four employees each receive a salary of $500 a week for a five-day work week, from Monday to Friday, or $100 a day. Thus, accrued salaries at October 31 are $2,800 (7 days × $100/day × 4 employees). This accrual increases a liability, Salaries Payable, and an expense account, Salaries Expense, in the following adjusting entry:

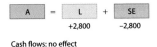

Cash flows: no effect

Oct. 31	Salaries Expense	2,800	
	Salaries Payable		2,800
	(To record accrued salaries)		

After this adjusting entry is posted, the accounts are as follows:

	Salaries Expense				Salaries Payable	
Oct. 20	4,000				Oct. 31 Adj.	2,800
31 Adj.	2,800				Oct. 31 Bal.	2,800
Oct. 31 Bal.	6,800					

After this adjustment, the balance in Salaries Expense of $6,800 (17 days × $100/day × 4 employees) is the actual salary expense for October. The balance in Salaries Payable of $2,800 is the amount of the liability for salaries owed as at October 31. If the $2,800 adjustment for salaries is not recorded, Sierra's expenses and liabilities will be understated by $2,800. Net earnings and shareholders' equity will be overstated by $2,800.

At Sierra Corporation, salaries are payable every two weeks. Consequently, the next payday is November 3, when total salaries of $4,000 will again be paid. The payment consists of $2,800 of salaries payable at October 31 plus $1,200 of salaries expense for November (3 days × $100/day × 4 employees). Therefore, the following entry is made on November 3:

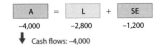

Nov. 3	Salaries Payable	2,800	
	Salaries Expense	1,200	
	Cash		4,000
	(Paid salaries for Oct. 23–Nov. 3)		

This entry eliminates the liability for salaries payable that was recorded in the October 31 adjusting entry and records the proper amount of salaries expense for the period between November 1 and November 3.

Income Taxes. For accounting purposes, corporate income taxes must be accrued based on the current period's earnings. Sierra's monthly income taxes payable are estimated to be $250. This accrual increases a liability, Income Tax Payable, and an expense account, Income Tax Expense. The adjusting entry is:

Oct. 31	Income Tax Expense	250	
	Income Tax Payable		250
	(To record accrued income taxes)		

A = L + SE
+250 −250

Cash flows: no effect

After this adjusting entry is posted, the accounts are as follows:

Income Tax Expense		Income Tax Payable	
Oct. 31 Adj. 250			Oct. 31 Adj. 250
Oct. 31 Bal. 250			Oct. 31 Bal. 250

Corporations, such as Sierra, pay corporate income taxes in monthly instalments. The payment is based on the income tax that was actually payable in the prior year. If there was no prior year, as is the case with Sierra, or if there was no tax payable in the prior year, then no income tax instalment payments are required. However, the liability must still be accrued.

If the adjustment for income taxes is not recorded, Sierra's expenses and liabilities will be understated by $250 and net earnings and shareholders' equity will be overstated by $250.

BEFORE YOU GO ON . . .

▶Review It

1. What is the effect on assets, liabilities, shareholders' equity, revenues, expenses, and net earnings if an adjusting entry for accrued revenue is not made?
2. What is the effect on assets, liabilities, shareholders' equity, revenues, expenses, and net earnings if an adjusting entry for an accrued expense is not made?

▶Do It

Micro Computer Services Inc. began operations on August 1, 2006. Management prepares monthly financial statements. This information is for August:

1. Revenue earned but unrecorded for August totalled $1,100.
2. On August 1, the company borrowed $30,000 from a local bank on a one-year note payable. The annual interest rate is 5% and interest is payable at maturity.
3. At August 31, the company owed its employees $800 in salaries that will be paid on September 1.
4. Estimated income tax payable for August totalled $275.

Prepare the adjusting entries needed at August 31.

Action Plan

- Remember that accruals are entries that were not previously recorded; therefore the adjustment pattern is different from that for prepayments.
- Adjusting entries for accrued revenues require a debit to a receivable account and a credit to a revenue account.
- Adjusting entries for accrued expenses require a debit to an expense account and a credit to a liability account.

Solution

1.	Aug. 31	Accounts Receivable	1,100	
		Service Revenue		1,100
		(To accrue revenue earned but not billed or collected)		

2.	Aug. 31	Interest Expense	125	
		Interest Payable		125
		(To record accrued interest: $30,000 \times 5\% \times \frac{1}{12}$)		
3.		Salaries Expense	800	
		Salaries Payable		800
		(To record accrued salaries)		
4.		Income Tax Expense	275	
		Income Tax Payable		275
		(To record accrued income taxes)		

Summary of Basic Relationships

The two basic types of adjusting entries—prepayments and accruals—are summarized below. Take some time to study and analyze the adjusting entries. Be sure to note that **each adjusting entry affects one balance sheet account and one statement of earnings account**.

	Type of Adjustment	Reason for Adjustment	Accounts before Adjustment	Adjusting Entry
Prepayments	Prepaid expenses	Prepaid expenses, originally recorded in asset accounts, have been used.	Assets overstated; expenses understated	Dr. Expense Cr. Asset
	Unearned revenues	Unearned revenues, initially recorded in liability accounts, have been earned.	Liabilities overstated; revenues understated	Dr. Liability Cr. Revenue
Accruals	Accrued revenues	Revenues have been earned but not yet received in cash or recorded.	Assets understated; revenues understated	Dr. Asset Cr. Revenue
	Accrued expenses	Expenses have been incurred but not yet paid.	Expenses understated; liabilities understated	Dr. Expense Cr. Liability

It is important to understand that adjusting entries never involve the Cash account (except for bank reconciliations, which we will study in Chapter 7). In the case of prepayments, cash has already been received or paid and recorded in the original journal entry. The adjusting entry simply reallocates or adjusts amounts between a balance sheet account (e.g., prepaid expenses or unearned revenues) and a statement of earnings account (e.g., expenses or revenues). In the case of accruals, cash will be received or paid in the future and recorded then. The adjusting entry simply records the receivable or payable and the related revenue or expense.

ACCOUNTING MATTERS!   Ethics Perspective

In the wake of financial scandals that are still making an impression, the Canadian Securities Administrators introduced requirements in 2005 for management to evaluate the reliability of a company's accounting system and controls. This includes a review of year-end procedures, including the procedures that are used to record recurring and nonrecurring adjusting entries.

This review will include asking such questions as the following: How are the transactions developed, authorized, and checked? What principles does the accounting department use to make adjusting entries? Do the accounting estimates and judgements reflect any biases that would consistently overstate or understate key amounts? Are the proper people involved in the year-end decision-making? All of these, and other similar questions are designed to improve the quality and reliability of financial statements.

Sierra Corporation Illustration

The journalizing and posting of the adjusting entries described in this chapter for Sierra Corporation on October 31 are shown below and on the following two pages. As you review the general ledger, notice that the adjustments are highlighted in colour.

Note also that an account for retained earnings has been added in the general ledger. Because this is Sierra's first month of operations, there is no balance in the Retained Earnings account. Although accounts with a zero balance are not normally included in the trial balance, we have added it here to make it easier to prepare the statement of retained earnings in the next section. In addition, we will again need to use this account in the section on closing entries later in this chapter.

Date	Account Titles and Explanation	Debit	Credit
GENERAL JOURNAL			
2006			
Oct. 31	Advertising Supplies Expense	1,500	
	Advertising Supplies		1,500
	(To record supplies used)		
31	Insurance Expense	50	
	Prepaid Insurance		50
	(To record insurance expired)		
31	Amortization Expense	83	
	Accumulated Amortization—Office Equipment		83
	(To record monthly amortization)		
31	Unearned Service Revenue	400	
	Service Revenue		400
	(To record revenue earned)		
31	Accounts Receivable	200	
	Service Revenue		200
	(To accrue revenue earned but not billed or collected)		
31	Interest Expense	25	
	Interest Payable		25
	(To accrue interest on note payable)		
31	Salaries Expense	2,800	
	Salaries Payable		2,800
	(To record accrued salaries)		
31	Income Tax Expense	250	
	Income Tax Payable		250
	(To record accrued income taxes)		

GENERAL LEDGER

Cash

Oct.	2	10,000	Oct.	3	5,000
	2	5,000		5	900
	4	1,200		6	600
	30	10,000		20	4,000
				25	500
Oct. 31 Bal.		15,200			

Accounts Receivable

Oct.	13	10,000	Oct.	30	10,000
	31	200			
Oct. 31 Bal.		200			

Advertising Supplies

Oct.	9	2,500	Oct.	31	1,500
Oct. 31 Bal.		1,000			

Prepaid Insurance

Oct.	6	600	Oct.	31	50
Oct. 31 Bal.		550			

Income Tax Payable

			Oct.	31	250
			Oct. 31 Bal.		250

Common Shares

			Oct.	2	10,000
			Oct. 31 Bal.		10,000

Retained Earnings

			Oct.	1	0
			Oct. 31 Bal.		0

Dividends

Oct.	25	500			
Oct. 31 Bal.		500			

Service Revenue

			Oct.	13	10,000
				31	400
				31	200
			Oct. 31 Bal.		10,600

Office Equipment		
Oct. 3	5,000	
Oct. 31 Bal.	5,000	

Salaries Expense		
Oct. 20	4,000	
31	2,800	
Oct. 31 Bal.	6,800	

Accumulated Amortization—Office Equipment		
	Oct. 31	83
	Oct. 31 Bal.	83

Advertising Supplies Expense		
Oct. 31	1,500	
Oct. 31 Bal.	1,500	

Notes Payable		
	Oct. 2	5,000
	Oct. 31 Bal.	5,000

Rent Expense		
Oct. 5	900	
Oct. 31 Bal.	900	

Accounts Payable		
	Oct. 9	2,500
	Oct. 31 Bal.	2,500

Insurance Expense		
Oct. 31	50	
Oct. 31 Bal.	50	

Interest Payable		
	Oct. 31	25
	Oct. 31 Bal.	25

Interest Expense		
Oct. 31	25	
Oct. 31 Bal.	25	

Unearned Service Revenue		
Oct. 31	400	Oct. 4	1,200
		Oct. 31 Bal.	800

Amortization Expense		
Oct. 31	83	
Oct. 31	83	

Salaries Payable		
	Oct. 31	2,800
	Oct. 31 Bal.	2,800

Income Tax Expense		
Oct. 31	250	
Oct. 31 Bal.	250	

The Adjusted Trial Balance and Financial Statements

study objective 4

Describe the nature and purpose of the adjusted trial balance.

After all adjusting entries have been journalized and posted, another trial balance is prepared from the ledger accounts. This trial balance is called an **adjusted trial balance**. It shows the balances of all accounts at the end of the accounting period, including those that have been adjusted. The purpose of an adjusted trial balance is to **prove the equality** of the total debit balances and the total credit balances in the ledger after all adjustments have been made. Because the accounts contain all the data that are needed for financial statements, the adjusted trial balance is the main source for the preparation of financial statements.

Preparing the Adjusted Trial Balance

The adjusted trial balance for Sierra Corporation presented in Illustration 4-6 has been prepared from the ledger accounts shown in the previous section. Compare the adjusted trial balance to the unadjusted trial balance presented earlier in the chapter in Illustration 4-2. The amounts affected by the adjusting entries are highlighted in colour.

Illustration 4-6 ◄

Adjusted trial balance

SIERRA CORPORATION
Adjusted Trial Balance
October 31, 2006

	Debit	Credit
Cash	$15,200	
Accounts receivable	200	
Advertising supplies	1,000	
Prepaid insurance	550	
Office equipment	5,000	
Accumulated amortization—office equipment		$ 83
Notes payable		5,000
Accounts payable		2,500
Interest payable		25
Unearned service revenue		800
Salaries payable		2,800
Income tax payable		250
Common shares		10,000
Retained earnings		0
Dividends	500	
Service revenue		10,600
Salaries expense	6,800	
Advertising supplies expense	1,500	
Rent expense	900	
Insurance expense	50	
Interest expense	25	
Amortization expense	83	
Income tax expense	250	
	$32,058	$32,058

Preparing Financial Statements

Financial statements can be prepared directly from an adjusted trial balance. The interrelationships of data in the adjusted trial balance of Sierra Corporation is presented in Illustration 4-7 on the following page.

As Illustration 4-7 shows, the statement of earnings is prepared from the revenue and expense accounts. The statement of retained earnings is prepared from the Retained Earnings account, Dividends account, and the net earnings (or net loss) shown in the statement of earnings. The balance sheet is then prepared from the asset, liability, and shareholders' equity accounts. Shareholders' equity includes the ending retained earnings as reported in the statement of retained earnings.

BEFORE YOU GO ON. . .

► Review It

1. What is the purpose of an adjusted trial balance?
2. When is an adjusted trial balance prepared?

the navigator

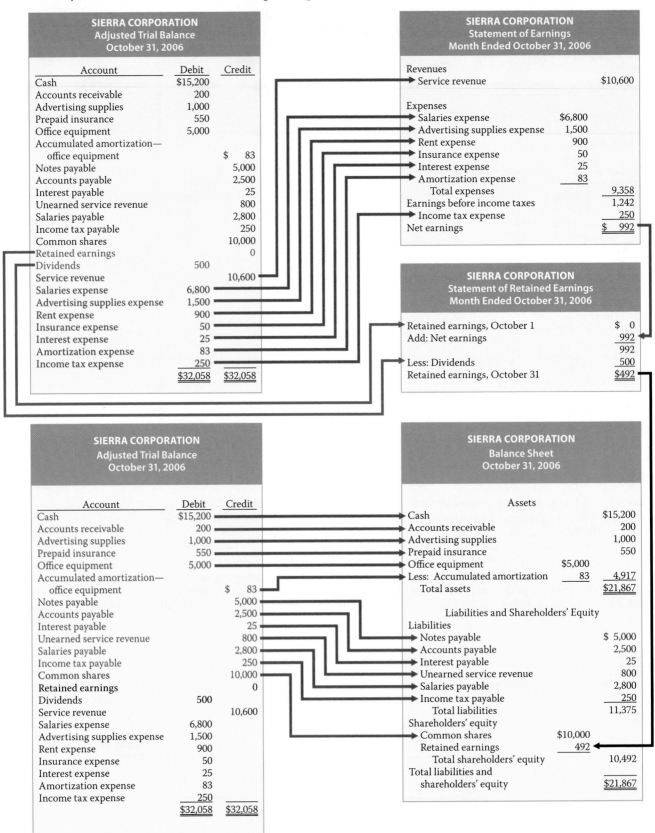

Illustration 4-7 ▲

Preparation of the financial statements from the adjusted trial balance

Closing the Books

In previous chapters, you learned that revenue and expense accounts and the dividends account are subdivisions of retained earnings, which is reported in the shareholders' equity section of the balance sheet. Because revenues, expenses, and dividends are only for a particular accounting period, they are considered **temporary accounts**. In contrast, all balance sheet accounts are considered **permanent accounts** because their balances are carried forward into future accounting periods. Illustration 4-8 identifies the accounts in each category.

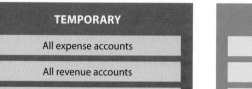

Illustration 4-8 ◀

Temporary and permanent accounts

Preparing Closing Entries

At the end of the accounting period, the temporary account balances are transferred to the permanent shareholders' equity account Retained Earnings through the preparation of closing entries. **Closing entries** formally record in the general ledger the transfer of the balances in the revenue, expense, and dividends accounts to the Retained Earnings account. In Illustration 4-6, you will note that Retained Earnings has an adjusted balance of zero. Until the closing entries are made, the balance in Retained Earnings will be its balance at the beginning of the period. For Sierra, this is zero because it is Sierra's first year of operations. After closing entries are recorded and posted, the balance in Retained Earnings will reflect its balance at the end of the period. This ending account balance will now be the same as the balance reported in the statement of retained earnings and the balance sheet.

In addition to updating retained earnings to its ending balance, closing entries produce a zero balance in each temporary account. As a result, these accounts are ready to accumulate data about revenues, expenses, and dividends in the next accounting period separately from the data in the prior periods. Permanent accounts are not closed.

When closing entries are prepared, each revenue and expense account could be closed directly to Retained Earnings. This is common in computerized accounting systems where the closing process occurs automatically when it is time to start a new accounting period. However, in manual accounting systems, this practice can result in too much detail in the Retained Earnings account. Accordingly, the revenue and expense accounts are first closed to another temporary account, **Income Summary**. Only the resulting total amount (net earnings or net loss) is transferred from this account to the Retained Earnings account. Illustration 4-9 shows the closing process.

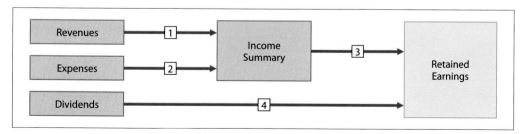

Illustration 4-9 ◀

Closing process

To prepare closing entries, four steps are necessary:

1. To close revenue accounts: Debit each individual revenue account for its balance, and credit Income Summary for total revenues.

2. To close expense accounts: Debit Income Summary for total expenses, and credit each individual expense account for its balance.

3. To close Income Summary: Debit Income Summary for the balance in the account (or credit it if there is a net loss), and credit (debit) Retained Earnings.

4. To close dividends: Debit Retained Earnings, and credit Dividends for its balance.

Closing entries can be prepared directly from the general ledger or the adjusted trial balance. If we were to prepare closing entries for Sierra Corporation, we would likely start with the adjusted trial balance presented earlier in the chapter in Illustration 4-6. In Sierra's case, all temporary accounts (Dividends, Service Revenue, and its seven different expense accounts) must be closed.

Even though Retained Earnings is not a temporary account, it will also be involved in the closing process. Remember that the balance presented in the adjusted trial balance for Retained Earnings is the beginning, not ending, balance. This permanent account is not closed but the net earnings (loss) and dividends for the period must be recorded to update the account to its ending balance.

Sierra's general journal, showing its closing entries, and its general ledger, showing the posting of the closing entries, follow:

	GENERAL JOURNAL		
Date	Account Titles and Explanation	Debit	Credit
	Closing Entries		
2006	(1)		
Oct. 31	Service Revenue	10,600	
	Income Summary		10,600
	(To close revenue account)		
	(2)		
31	Income Summary	9,608	
	Salaries Expense		6,800
	Advertising Supplies Expense		1,500
	Rent Expense		900
	Insurance Expense		50
	Interest Expense		25
	Amortization Expense		83
	Income Tax Expense		250
	(To close expense accounts)		
	(3)		
31	Income Summary	992	
	Retained Earnings		992
	(To close net earnings to retained earnings)		
	(4)		
31	Retained Earnings	500	
	Dividends		500
	(To close dividends to retained earnings)		

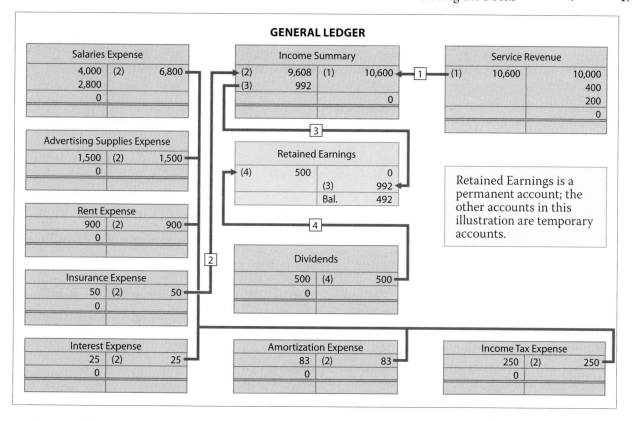

GENERAL LEDGER

Stop and check your work after the closing entries are posted: (1) The balance in the Income Summary account, immediately before the final closing entry to transfer the balance to the Retained Earnings account, should equal the net earnings (or net loss) reported in the statement of earnings. (2) All temporary accounts (dividends, revenues, expenses, and income summary) should have zero balances. (3) The balance in the Retained Earnings account should equal the ending balance reported in the statement of retained earnings and balance sheet.

ACCOUNTING MATTERS! Management Perspective

Garry Beattie, CMA and owner of HBM Integrated Technology Inc., believes that the closing process should be completed within five days of the end of the month. Accounting done in a timely, efficient manner through streamlined, computerized accounting systems can save a business time and money. "With good technology, you can provide better information faster," he says. In fact, Beattie says that studies show that posting journal entries daily can save four hours of work per week. The five-day close is possible for anyone, since many multinational companies, such as Cisco Systems, do it in less than one day.

Source: Rosemary Godin, "Five-Day Close Saves Time on Balance Sheets, Says Halifax CMA," *Bottom Line,* January 2003.

✷NOVEMBER✷

				1	2	3
4	5	6	7	8	9	10
11	12	13	14	15	16	17
18	19	20	21	22	23	24
25	26	27	28	29	30	

Preparing a Post-Closing Trial Balance

After all closing entries are journalized and posted, another trial balance, called a **post-closing trial balance,** is prepared from the ledger. We have learned about the unadjusted and adjusted trial balances so far. The last trial balance is the post-closing trial balance, which lists all permanent accounts and their balances after closing entries are journalized and posted. **The purpose of this trial balance is to prove the equality of the permanent account balances that are carried forward into the next accounting period.** Since all temporary accounts will have zero balances, the post-closing trial balance will contain only permanent—balance sheet—accounts.

Illustration 4-10 shows Sierra Corporation's post-closing trial balance on the following page.

Illustration 4-10 ▶

Post-closing trial balance

SIERRA CORPORATION Post-Closing Trial Balance October 31, 2006		
	Debit	Credit
Cash	$15,200	
Accounts receivable	200	
Advertising supplies	1,000	
Prepaid insurance	550	
Office equipment	5,000	
Accumulated amortization—office equipment		$ 83
Notes payable		5,000
Accounts payable		2,500
Interest payable		25
Unearned revenue		800
Salaries payable		2,800
Income tax payable		250
Common shares		10,000
Retained earnings		492
	$21,950	$21,950

Summary of the Accounting Cycle

The required steps in the accounting cycle are shown in Illustration 4-11. You can see that the cycle begins with the analysis of business transactions and ends with the preparation of a post-closing trial balance. The steps in the cycle are done in sequence and are repeated in each accounting period.

Steps 1 to 3 may occur daily during the accounting period, as explained in Chapter 3. Steps 4 to 7 are done on a periodic basis, such as monthly, quarterly, or annually. Steps 8 and 9, closing entries and a post-closing trial balance, are usually prepared only at the end of a company's annual accounting period.

Illustration 4-11 ▶

Required steps in the accounting cycle

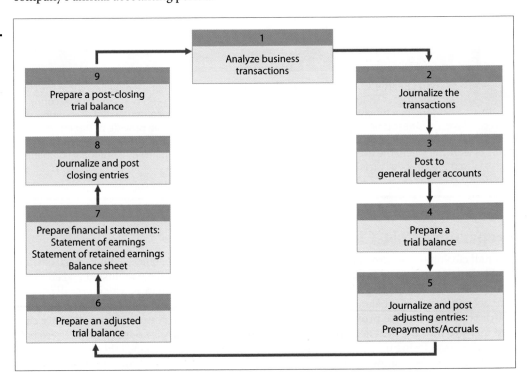

BEFORE YOU GO ON . . .

▶Review It

1. How do permanent accounts differ from temporary accounts?
2. What four different types of entries are required in closing the books?
3. What financial statement amount will the balance in the Income Summary account equal immediately before it is closed into the Retained Earnings account?
4. What are the content and purpose of a post-closing trial balance?
5. What are the required steps in the accounting cycle?

▶Do It

The adjusted trial balance for the Nguyen Corporation shows the following: Dividends $5,000; Common Shares $30,000; Retained Earnings $12,000; Service Revenue $18,000; and Operating Expenses $10,000. Prepare the closing entries at December 31.

Action Plan

- Debit each individual revenue account for its balance and credit the total to the Income Summary account.
- Credit each individual expense account for its balance and debit the total to the Income Summary account.
- Stop and check your work: Does the balance in the Income Summary account equal the reported net earnings (loss)?
- If there are net earnings, debit the balance in the Income Summary account and credit the amount to the Retained Earnings account (do the opposite if the result is a net loss).
- Credit the balance in the Dividends account and debit the amount to the Retained Earnings account. Do not close Dividends with the expenses.
- Stop and check your work: Do the temporary accounts have zero balances? Does the ending Retained Earnings balance equal the balance reported on the statement of retained earnings and balance sheet?

Solution

Dec. 31	Service Revenue	18,000	
	Income Summary		18,000
	(To close revenue account)		
31	Income Summary	10,000	
	Operating Expenses		10,000
	(To close expense account)		
31	Income Summary	8,000	
	Retained Earnings		8,000
	(To close income summary)		
31	Retained Earnings	5,000	
	Dividends		5,000
	(To close dividends)		

the navigator

▦ Using the Decision Toolkit

FPI (Fishery Products International) Limited is the world's largest seafood supplier. A simplified version of FPI's December 31, 2004, year-end adjusted trial balance is shown below.

Instructions

From the adjusted trial balance, prepare a statement of earnings, statement of retained earnings, and classified balance sheet.

FPI LIMITED
Trial Balance
December 31, 2004
(in thousands)

	Debit	Credit
Cash	$ 4,922	
Accounts receivable	88,338	
Inventories	170,624	
Prepaid expenses	9,609	
Other current assets	23	
Buildings, wharves, and land	74,799	
Machinery and equipment	128,746	
Vessels and vessel equipment	87,352	
Other long-term assets	30,628	
Accumulated amortization		
—Buildings and wharves		$ 36,823
—Machinery and equipment		79,388
—Vessels and vessel equipment		13,371
Bank indebtedness (short-term)		107,241
Accounts payable and accrued liabilities		62,042
Income tax payable		1,387
Current portion of long-term debt		7,630
Long-term debt		102,322
Share capital		121,913
Other shareholders' equity items	14,520	
Retained earnings		76,073
Dividends	3,069	
Sales		800,401
Commission income		2,575
Cost of goods sold	712,596	
Administrative and marketing expenses	52,714	
Amortization expense	13,884	
Interest expense	9,659	
Other expenses	3,837	
Income tax expense	5,846	
	$1,411,166	$1,411,166

Solution

FPI LIMITED
Statement of Earnings
Year Ended December 31, 2004
(in thousands)

Revenue		
Sales		$800,401
Commission income		2,575
Total revenue		802,976
Expenses		
Cost of goods sold	$712,596	
Administrative and marketing expenses	52,714	
Amortization expense	13,884	
Interest expense	9,659	
Other expenses	3,837	
Total expenses		792,690
Earnings before income taxes		10,286
Income tax expense		5,846
Net earnings		$ 4,440

FPI LIMITED
Statement of Retained Earnings
Year Ended December 31, 2004
(in thousands)

Retained earnings, January 1	$76,073
Add: Net earnings	4,440
Less: Dividends	3,069
Retained earnings, December 31	$77,444

FPI LIMITED
Balance Sheet
December 31, 2004
(in thousands)

Assets

Current assets			
Cash			$ 4,922
Accounts receivable			88,338
Inventories			170,624
Prepaid expenses			9,609
Other current assets			23
Total current assets			273,516
Property, plant, and equipment			
Buildings, wharves, and land	$74,799		
Less: Accumulated amortization	36,823	$37,976	
Machinery and equipment	$128,746		
Less: Accumulated amortization	79,388	49,358	
Vessels and vessel equipment	$87,352		
Less: Accumulated amortization	13,371	73,981	161,315
Other long-term assets			30,628
Total assets			$465,459

Liabilities and Shareholders' Equity

Liabilities			
Current liabilities			
Bank indebtedness		$107,241	
Accounts payable and accrued liabilities		62,042	
Income tax payable		1,387	
Current portion of long-term debt		7,630	
Total current liabilities			$178,300
Long-term debt			102,322
Total liabilities			280,622
Shareholders' equity			
Share capital		$121,913	
Other shareholders' equity items		(14,520)	
Retained earnings		77,444	
Total shareholders' equity			184,837
Total liabilities and shareholders' equity			$465,459

the navigator

Summary of Study Objectives

1. *Explain the revenue recognition principle and the matching principle.* The revenue recognition principle states that revenue must be recognized in the accounting period in which it is earned. The matching principle states that expenses must be recognized when they make their contribution to revenues.

2. *Prepare adjusting entries for prepayments.* Adjusting entries for prepayments are required in order to record the portion of the prepayment that applies to the expense incurred or revenue earned in the current accounting period. Prepayments are either prepaid expenses or unearned revenues. The adjusting entry for prepaid expenses results in an increase (a debit) to an expense account and a decrease (a credit) to an asset account. The adjusting entry for unearned revenues results in a decrease (a debit) to a liability account and an increase (a credit) to a revenue account.

3. *Prepare adjusting entries for accruals.* Adjusting entries for accruals are required in order to record the revenues and expenses that apply to the current accounting period and that have not been recognized through daily entries. Accruals are either accrued revenues or accrued expenses. The adjusting entry for accrued revenues results in an increase (a debit) to an asset account and an increase (a credit) to a revenue account. The adjusting entry for accrued expenses results in an increase (a debit) to an expense account and an increase (a credit) to a liability account.

4. *Describe the nature and purpose of the adjusted trial balance.* An adjusted trial balance is a trial balance that shows the balances of all accounts at the end of an accounting period, including those that have been adjusted. The purpose of an adjusted trial balance is to show the effects of all financial events that have occurred during the accounting period.

5. *Explain the purposes of closing entries.* One purpose of closing entries is to update the Retained Earnings account to its end-of-period balance with the results of operations for the period. A second purpose is to enable all temporary accounts (dividends, revenue, and expense accounts) to begin a new period with a zero balance. To accomplish this, entries are made to close each individual revenue and expense account to Income Summary, then Income Summary to Retained Earnings, and finally Dividends to Retained Earnings. Only temporary accounts are closed.

Decision Toolkit—A Summary

Decision Checkpoints	Info Needed for Decision	Tools to Use for Decision	How to Evaluate Results
At what point should the company record revenue?	Need to understand the nature of the company's business	Revenue should be recorded when earned. For a service company, revenue is earned when a service is performed.	Recognizing revenue too early overstates current period revenue; recognizing it too late understates current period revenue.
At what point should the company record expenses?	Need to understand the nature of the company's business	Expenses should "follow" revenues—that is, the effort (expense) should be matched with the result (revenue).	Recognizing expenses too early overstates current period expenses; recognizing them too late understates current period expenses.

Analysis Tools
(Decision Toolkit Summaries)

Glossary

www.wiley.com/canada/kimmel/
Study Tools (Glossary)

Accrual basis accounting An accounting basis in which transactions that change a company's financial statements are recorded in the periods in which the events occur, rather than in the periods in which the company receives or pays cash. (p. 154)

Accrued expenses Expenses incurred but not yet paid in cash or recorded. (p. 162)

Accrued revenues Revenues earned but not yet received in cash or recorded. (p. 162)

Adjusted trial balance A list of accounts and their balances after all adjustments have been made. (p. 168)

Adjusting entries Journal entries made at the end of an accounting period because of the time period assumption and to ensure that the revenue recognition and matching principles are followed. (p. 155)

Amortization The process of allocating the cost of a long-lived asset to expense over its useful life. (p. 158)

Cash basis accounting An accounting basis in which revenue is recorded only when cash is received, and an expense is recorded only when cash is paid. (p. 154)

Closing entries Entries at the end of an accounting period to transfer the balances of temporary accounts (dividends, revenues, and expenses) to the permanent shareholders' equity account Retained Earnings. (p. 171)

Contra asset account An account that is offset against (reduces) an asset account on the balance sheet. (p. 159)

Income summary A temporary account used in closing revenue and expense accounts. (p. 171)

Matching principle The principle that states that efforts (expenses) must be matched with accomplishments (revenues). (p. 153)

Net book value (book value) The difference between the cost of an amortizable asset and its accumulated amortization. (p. 159)

Permanent accounts Balance sheet accounts whose balances are carried forward to the next accounting period. (p. 171)

Post-closing trial balance A list of permanent accounts and their balances after closing entries have been journalized and posted. (p. 173)

Prepaid expenses Expenses paid in cash and recorded as assets before they are used or consumed. (p. 156)

Revenue recognition principle The principle that states that revenue must be recognized in the accounting period in which it is earned. (p. 153)

Straight-line method of amortization An amortization method in which amortization expense is calculated as the cost divided by the useful life. (p. 158)

Temporary accounts Revenue, expense, and dividend accounts whose balances are transferred to Retained Earnings at the end of an accounting period. (p. 171)

Unearned revenue Cash received before revenue is earned and recorded as a liability until it is earned. (p. 159)

Useful life The length of service of a productive facility. (p. 158)

Demonstration Problem

The Green Thumb Lawn Care Corporation was incorporated on April 1. At April 30, the trial balance shows the following balances for selected accounts:

www.wiley.com/canada/kimmel/
Study Tools
(Demonstration Problems)

Prepaid insurance	$ 3,600
Equipment	30,000
Note payable	20,000
Unearned service revenue	4,200
Service revenue	1,800

Analysis reveals the following additional data about these accounts:

1. Prepaid insurance is the cost of a one-year insurance policy, effective April 1.
2. The equipment is expected to have a useful life of four years.
3. The note payable is dated April 1. It is a six-month, 6% note. Interest is payable on the first of each month.
4. Seven customers paid for the company's six-month, $600 lawn service package beginning in April. These customers were serviced in April.
5. Lawn services provided to other customers but not billed at April 30 totalled $1,500.
6. Income tax expense for April is estimated to be $100.

Instructions

Prepare the adjusting entries for the month of April.

Action Plan

- Note that adjustments are being made for only one month.
- Look at what amounts are currently recorded in the accounts before determining what adjustments are necessary.
- Show your calculations.
- Select account titles carefully. Use existing titles wherever possible.
- Use T accounts to help plan, or check, your adjustments.

Solution to Demonstration Problem

	GENERAL JOURNAL		
Date	Account Titles and Explanation	Debit	Credit
	Adjusting Entries		
Apr. 30	Insurance Expense	300	
	Prepaid Insurance		300
	(To record insurance expired: $3,600 × ¹⁄₁₂)		
30	Amortization Expense	625	
	Accumulated Amortization—Equipment		625
	(To record monthly amortization: $30,000 ÷ 4 = $7,500 × ¹⁄₁₂)		
30	Interest Expense	100	
	Interest Payable		100
	(To accrue interest on note payable: $20,000 × 6% × ¹⁄₁₂)		
30	Unearned Service Revenue	700	
	Service Revenue		700
	(To record revenue earned: $600 ÷ 6 mos. × 7)		
30	Accounts Receivable	1,500	
	Service Revenue		1,500
	(To accrue revenue earned but not billed or collected)		
30	Income Tax Expense	100	
	Income Tax Payable		100
	(To accrue income taxes payable)		

Self-Study Questions

www.wiley.com/canada/kimmel

Study Tools (Self-Assessment Quizzes)

Answers are at the end of the chapter.

(SO 1) 1. Which principle or assumption states that efforts (expenses) must be recorded with accomplishments (revenues)?
   (a) Matching principle
   (b) Cost principle
   (c) Time period assumption
   (d) Revenue recognition principle

(SO 1) 2. Adjusting entries are made to ensure that:
   (a) expenses are matched to revenues in the period in which the revenue is generated.
   (b) revenues are recorded in the period in which they are earned.
   (c) balance sheet and statement of earnings accounts have correct balances at the end of an accounting period.
   (d) All of the above

(SO 2) 3. The trial balance shows Supplies $1,350 and Supplies Expense $0. If $600 of supplies are on hand at the end of the period, the adjusting entry is:

(a) Supplies	600	
Supplies Expense		600

(b) Supplies Expense	600	
Supplies		600

(c) Supplies	750	
Supplies Expense		750

(d) Supplies Expense	750	
Supplies		750

(SO 2) 4. Frontenac Corp. purchased equipment at the beginning of year 1 for $25,000, which was estimated to have a useful life of 5 years. How much is the equipment's net book value at the end of year 3?
   (a) $5,000   (c) $15,000
   (b) $10,000   (d) $25,000

(SO 2) 5. On February 1, Magazine City received $600 in advance for ten 12-month subscriptions to *Climbing Magazine*. What adjusting journal entry should Magazine City make on February 28?

(a) Subscription Revenue	550	
Unearned Subscription Revenue		550

(b) Unearned Subscription Revenue	50	
Subscription Revenue		50

(c) Unearned Subscription Revenue	550	
Subscription Revenue		550

(d) Cash	600	
Subscription Revenue		600

(SO 3) 6. A bank has a three-month, $6,000 note receivable, issued on January 1 at an interest rate of 4%. Interest is due at maturity. What adjusting entry should the bank make at the end of January?

(a) Note Receivable	20	
Interest Revenue		20
(b) Interest Receivable	60	
Interest Revenue		60
(c) Cash	20	
Interest Revenue		20
(d) Interest Receivable	20	
Interest Revenue		20

(SO 3) 7. Kathy Kiska earned a salary of $400 for the last week of September. She will be paid on October 1. The adjusting entry for Kathy's employer at September 30 is:

(a) Salaries Expense	400	
Salaries Payable		400
(b) Salaries Expense	400	
Cash		400
(c) Salaries Payable	400	
Cash		400
(d) No entry is required		

(SO 4) 8. Which statement is *incorrect* concerning the adjusted trial balance?

(a) An adjusted trial balance proves the equality of the total debit balances and the total credit balances in the ledger after all adjustments are made.

(b) The adjusted trial balance is the main source for the preparation of financial statements.

(c) The adjusted trial balance is prepared after the closing entries have been journalized and posted.

(d) The adjusted trial balance is prepared after the adjusting entries have been journalized and posted.

9. The Retained Earnings account in an unadjusted trial (SO 4) balance is $10,000. Net earnings for the period are $2,500 and dividends are $500. The Retained Earnings account balance in the adjusted trial balance will be:

(a) $9,500. (c) $12,000.

(b) $10,000. (d) $12,500.

10. Which account will have a zero balance after closing (SO 5) entries have been journalized and posted?

(a) Service Revenue

(b) Advertising Supplies

(c) Unearned Revenue

(d) Accumulated Amortization

11. Which types of accounts will appear in the post-clos- (SO 5) ing trial balance?

(a) Permanent accounts

(b) Temporary accounts

(c) Statement of earnings accounts

(d) Cash flow statement accounts

Questions

(SO 1) 1. Why are adjusting entries needed? Include in your explanation a description of the assumption and two generally accepted accounting principles that relate to adjusting the accounts.

(SO 1) 2. ⚒ Tony Galego, a lawyer, accepts a legal engagement in March, does the work in April, bills the client $8,000 in May, and is paid in June. If Galego's law firm prepares monthly financial statements, when should it recognize revenue from this engagement? Why?

(SO 1) 3. ⚒ In completing the engagement in question 2, Galego incurs $2,000 of expenses that are specifically related to this engagement in March, $2,500 in April, and none in May and June. How much expense should be deducted from revenues in the month(s) the revenue is recognized? Why?

(SO 1) 4. The Higher Education University collects tuition for the fall term from registered students in September. The fall term runs from September to December. In what month(s) should the university recognize the revenue earned from tuition fees? Explain your reasoning.

(SO 1) 5. How does the cash basis of accounting differ from the accrual basis of accounting? Which basis gives more useful information for decision-making? Why?

6. The name "prepaid expense" implies that this type of (SO 2) account is an expense account and belongs on a statement of earnings. Instead the account appears on the balance sheet as an asset. Explain why this is appropriate and why prepaid expense items require adjustment at the end of each period.

7. The name "unearned revenue" implies that this type (SO 2) of account is a revenue account and belongs on a statement of earnings. Instead the account appears on the balance sheet as a liability. Explain why this is appropriate and why unearned revenue items require adjustment at the end of each period.

8. "Amortization is a process of valuation that results in (SO 2) the reporting of the fair market value of the asset." Do you agree? Explain.

9. Explain the difference between amortization expense, (SO 2) accumulated amortization, and net book value.

10. Distinguish between the two categories of adjusting (SO 2, 3) entries and identify the types of adjustments for each category.

11. The trial balance of Hoi Inc. includes the balance sheet (SO 2, 3) accounts listed below. Identify the accounts that might

require adjustment. For each account that requires adjustment, indicate (1) the type of adjusting entry (prepaid expenses, unearned revenues, accrued revenues, and accrued expenses) and (2) the related account in the adjusting entry.
(a) Accounts Receivable
(b) Prepaid Insurance
(c) Equipment
(d) Accumulated Amortization—Equipment
(e) Notes Payable
(f) Interest Payable
(g) Unearned Service Revenue

(SO 2, 3) 12. "An adjusting entry may affect more than one balance sheet or statement of earnings account." Do you agree? Why or why not?

(SO 2, 3) 13. Adjusting entries for prepayments *always* include the Cash account, and adjusting entries for accruals *never* include the Cash account. Do you agree? Explain why or why not.

(SO 3) 14. A company has revenue earned but not yet received or recorded. Explain why it is necessary to create an adjusting entry. Which accounts are debited and which ones are credited in the adjusting entry?

(SO 3) 15. A company has a utility expense that has been incurred but not yet paid or recorded. Explain why it is necessary to create an adjusting entry. Which accounts are debited and which ones are credited in the adjusting entry?

16. A company makes an accrued revenue adjusting entry   (SO 3) for $900 and an accrued expense adjusting entry for $600. Which financial statement items were overstated or understated before these entries? Explain.

17. Why is it possible to prepare financial statements   (SO 4) directly from an adjusted trial balance?

18. How do adjusting journal entries differ from transac-   (SO 2, tion journal entries? How do closing journal entries   3, 5) differ from adjusting journal entries?

19. Explain how an unadjusted trial balance, adjusted   (SO 4) trial balance, and post-closing trial balance differ. How often should each one be prepared?

20. What items are disclosed on a post-closing trial bal-   (SO 4) ance? Why are the financial statements prepared using an adjusted trial balance instead of the post-closing trial balance?

21. Why is the account Dividends not closed with the   (SO 5) expense accounts? Why is a separate closing entry required for this account?

22. Identify the summary account(s) that are debited and   (SO 5) credited in each of the four closing entries, assuming the company has (a) net earnings for the year, and (b) a net loss for the year.

Brief Exercises

Indicate impact of transaction on cash and earnings.
(SO 1)

BE4–1   Transactions that affect earnings do not necessarily affect cash. Identify the impact, if any, of each of the following transactions on cash and net earnings. The first transaction has been completed for you as an example.

	Cash	Net Earnings
(a) Purchased supplies for cash, $100.	$(100)	$0

(b) Made an adjusting entry to record use of $50 of the above supplies.
(c) Made sales of $1,000, all on account.
(d) Received $800 from customers in payment of their accounts.
(e) Purchased equipment for cash, $2,500.
(f) Recorded amortization of equipment, $500.
(g) Borrowed $5,000 on a note payable.
(h) Made an adjusting entry to record $200 interest payable on the $5,000 note.

Prepare and post transaction and adjusting entry for supplies.
(SO 2)

BE4–2   Sain Advertising Ltd.'s opening trial balance on January 1 shows Advertising Supplies $750. On April 1, the company purchased additional supplies for $3,500 on credit. On December 31, there are $1,000 of advertising supplies on hand.

(a) Prepare the journal entry to record the purchase of advertising supplies on April 1.
(b) Prepare the adjusting entry required at December 31.
(c) Enter the opening balances in the affected advertising accounts, post the adjusting entry, and indicate the adjusted balance in each account.

Prepare transaction and adjusting entries for amortization; show statement presentation.
(SO 2)

BE4–3   On January 2, 2006, Cretien Corporation purchased a delivery truck for $45,000 cash. It estimates that the truck will have a five-year useful life. The company has a December 31 year end.

(a) Prepare the journal entry to record the purchase of the delivery truck.
(b) Prepare the adjusting entries required on December 31, 2006, 2007, and 2010.
(c) Indicate the balance sheet presentation of the delivery truck at December 31, 2006, 2007, and 2010.

BE4–4 On June 1, Bere Ltd. pays $10,000 to Marla Insurance Corp. for a one-year insurance contract. Both companies have fiscal years ending December 31.

Prepare and post transaction and adjusting entries for insurance. (SO 2, 3)

(a) Record the June 1 transaction on the books of (1) Bere and (2) Marla.
(b) Prepare the adjusting entry required on December 31 by (1) Bere and (2) Marla.
(c) Post the above entries and indicate the adjusted balance in each account.

BE4–5 The total payroll for Classic Autos Ltd. is $5,000 every Friday ($1,000 per day) for employee salaries earned during a five-day week (Monday through Friday, inclusive). Salaries were last paid on Friday, December 27. This year the company's year end, December 31, falls on a Tuesday. Salaries will be paid next on Friday, January 3, at which time employees will receive pay for the five-day work week (including the New Year's holiday). Prepare the journal entries required to record:

Prepare transaction and adjusting entries for salaries. (SO 3)

(a) the payment of the salaries on December 27.
(b) the adjustment to accrue salaries at December 31.
(c) the payment of salaries on January 3.

BE4–6 On July 1, 2006, a company purchased a truck for $40,000, paying $12,000 cash and signing a 6% note payable for the remainder. The interest and principal of the note are due on January 1, 2007. Prepare the journal entry to record the (a) purchase of the truck on July 1, 2006, (b) accrual of the interest at year end, December 31, 2006, and (c) repayment of the interest and the note on January 1, 2007.

Prepare transaction and adjusting entries for interest. (SO 3)

BE4–7 Fill in the missing amounts in the following schedule. Assume that 2005 was the company's first year of operations.

Determine missing amounts for income taxes. (SO 3)

	2005	2006	2007
Income tax expense	$2,400	$3,500	(c)
Income tax payable	(a)	500	$ 700
Income tax paid	2,200	(b)	3,300

BE4–8 The unadjusted and adjusted trial balances for Miscou Island Corporation at February 28, 2006, are as follows:

Determine missing amounts. (SO 4)

	Trial Balance Debit	Credit	Adjusted Trial Balance Debit	Credit
Cash	$ 6,000		$ 6,000	
Accounts receivable	25,000		(d)	
Supplies	(a)		1,000	
Prepaid insurance	6,000		(e)	
Equipment	22,000		22,000	
Accumulated amortization—equipment		$ 1,000		(f)
Accounts payable		13,000		$13,000
Salaries payable		0		2,000
Income tax payable		0		(g)
Common shares		20,000		20,000
Retained earnings		(b)		21,000
Dividends	(c)		4,000	
Fees earned		29,000		32,000
Salaries expense	7,000		(h)	
Rent expense	6,000		6,000	
Amortization expense	0		(i)	
Insurance expense	0		4,000	
Supplies expense	0		3,000	
Utilities expense	2,400		(j)	
Miscellaneous expense	1,600		1,600	
Income tax expense	0	0	400	0
Totals	$84,000	$84,000	$93,800	$93,800

Selected data for the year-end adjustments are as follows:

1. Revenue earned but not yet billed, $3,000
2. Supplies on hand, $1,000
3. Insurance premiums expired, $4,000
4. Amortization expense, $4,400
5. Salaries earned, but not yet paid, $2,000
6. Estimated income tax expense, $400

Determine the missing amounts.

Prepare financial statements.
(SO 4)

BE4–9   Refer to the data in BE4–8 for Miscou Island Corporation. Prepare a statement of earnings, statement of retained earnings, and balance sheet for the year.

Prepare and post closing entries.
(SO 5)

BE4–10   The statement of earnings for the Edgebrook Golf Club Ltd. for the month ended July 31 shows Green Fees Earned $16,000; Salaries Expense $8,400; Maintenance Expense $2,500; and Income Tax Expense $1,000. The statement of retained earnings shows an opening balance for Retained Earnings of $20,000 and Dividends $1,000.

(a) Prepare and post the closing journal entries.
(b) What is the ending balance in Retained Earnings?

Identify post-closing trial balance accounts.
(SO 5)

BE4–11   The following selected accounts appear in the adjusted trial balance for Atomic Energy of Canada Limited (AECL). Identify which accounts would be included in AECL's post-closing trial balance.

(a) Accounts Receivable
(b) Interest Expense
(c) Interest Earned on Short-Term Investments
(d) Inventory
(e) Amortization Expense

(f) Accounts Payable and Accrued Liabilities
(g) Cost of Sales
(h) Dividends
(i) Accumulated Amortization

List steps in accounting cycle.
(SO 5)

BE4–12   The required steps in the accounting cycle are listed below in random order. List the steps in the proper sequence by writing the numbers 1 to 9 in the blank spaces.

(a) ___ Prepare a post-closing trial balance.
(b) ___ Prepare an adjusted trial balance.
(c) ___ Journalize the transactions.
(d) ___ Journalize and post the closing entries.
(e) ___ Prepare the financial statements.

(f) ___ Analyze business transactions.
(g) ___ Prepare a trial balance.
(h) ___ Journalize and post the adjusting entries.
(i) ___ Post to the ledger accounts.

Exercises

Identify point of revenue recognition.
(SO 1)

E4–1   The following independent situations require professional judgement for determining when to recognize revenue from the transactions:

(a) WestJet Airlines sells you a non-refundable airline ticket in September for your flight home at Christmas at a special fare.
(b) Leon's Furniture sells you a home theatre on a "no money down, no interest, and no payments for one year" promotional deal.
(c) The Toronto Blue Jays sell season tickets to games in the Rogers Centre on-line. Fans can purchase the tickets at any time, although the season only begins officially in April and ends in October.
(d) The RBC Financial Group loans you money in August. The loan and the interest are re-payable in full in November.
(e) In August, you order a sweater from Sears using its on-line catalogue. It arrives in September and you charge it to your Sears credit card. You receive and pay the Sears bill in October.

Instructions

Identify when revenue should be recognized in each of the above situations.

Calculate cash basis and accrual basis earnings.
(SO 1)

E4–2   In its first year of operations, Brisson Corp. earned $26,000 in service revenue, of which $4,000 was on account. The remainder, $22,000, was collected in cash from customers.

The company incurred operating expenses of $15,000, of which $13,500 was paid in cash. Of this amount, $1,500 was still owing on account at year end. In addition, late in the year, Brisson prepaid $2,000 for insurance coverage that would not be used until its second year of operations. Brisson expects to owe $2,750 for income tax when it files its corporate income tax return after year end.

Instructions

(a) Calculate the first year's net earnings under the cash basis of accounting.
(b) Calculate the first year's net earnings under the accrual basis of accounting.
(c) Which basis of accounting (cash or accrual) gives the most useful information for decision-makers?

E4–3 The following information is available for Action Quest Games Inc. for the year ended December 31, 2006:

Prepare and post transaction and adjusting entries for prepayments.
(SO 2)

1. Purchased a one-year insurance policy on May 1, 2006, for $4,620 cash.
2. Paid $6,875 for five months' rent in advance on October 1, 2006.
3. Signed a contract for cleaning services starting December 1, 2006, for $1,050 per month. Paid for the first three months on December 1.
4. On September 15, 2006, received $3,600 cash from a corporation that sponsors a game each month for the most improved students. The $3,600 was for nine game sessions, once on the first Friday of each month starting in October. (Use the account Unearned Revenue.)
5. During the year, sold $1,500 of gift certificates. Determined that on December 31, 2006, $475 of these gift certificates had not yet been redeemed. (Use the account Unearned Gift Certificate Sales.)

Instructions

(a) For each of the above, prepare and post the journal entry required to record the initial transaction.
(b) For each of the above, prepare and post the adjusting journal entry required on December 31, 2006.
(c) Calculate the final balance in each general ledger account.

E4–4 Action Quest Games Inc. owns the following long-lived assets:

Prepare adjusting entries for amortization; calculate net book value.
(SO 2)

Asset	Date Purchased	Estimated Useful Life	Cost
Furniture	January 1, 2006	3 years	$ 9,600
Lighting equipment	January 1, 2004	8 years	18,000

Instructions

(a) Prepare amortization adjusting entries for Action Quest Games for the years ended December 31, 2006 and 2007.
(b) For each asset, calculate its accumulated amortization and net book value at December 31, 2006 and 2007.

E4–5 Action Quest Games Inc. has the following information available for accruals that must be recorded for the year ended December 31, 2006:

Prepare adjusting and subsequent entries for accruals.
(SO 3)

1. The December utility bill for $420 was unrecorded on December 31. Action Quest paid the bill on January 17, 2007.
2. Action Quest is open seven days a week and employees are paid a total of $3,360 every Thursday for a seven-day work week. December 31, 2006, is a Sunday so employees will have worked three days since their last pay day. Employees will be paid next on January 4, 2007.
3. Action Quest has a 6% note payable to its bank for $45,000. Interest is payable on the first day of each month.
4. Action Quest receives a 5% commission from its neighbour Pizza Shop for all pizzas sold to customers using Action Quest's facility. The amount owing for December is $920, which Pizza Shop will pay on January 4, 2007.
5. Action Quest sold some equipment on November 1, 2006, in exchange for an 8%, $6,000 note receivable. The principal and interest are due on February 1, 2007.

Instructions

(a) For each of the above, prepare the adjusting entry required at December 31, 2006.
(b) For each of the above, prepare the journal entry to record the subsequent cash transaction in 2007.

Prepare adjusting entries.
(SO 2, 3)

E4–6   On March 31, 2006, the trial balance of Easy Rental Agency Inc. is as follows:

	Debits	Credits
Prepaid insurance	$ 3,600	
Supplies	2,800	
Equipment	24,000	
Accumulated amortization—equipment		$ 6,000
Notes payable		20,000
Unearned rent revenue		9,300
Rent revenue		60,000
Wage expense	14,000	

An analysis of the accounts shows the following:

1. The equipment, which was purchased January 1, 2005, is estimated to have a useful life of four years.
2. One-third of the unearned rent revenue was earned during the quarter.
3. Interest accrues at a rate of 5% on the notes payable.
4. Supplies on hand total $850.
5. The insurance was purchased January 1, 2006, and expires December 31.
6. Income tax is estimated to be $5,000.

Instructions

Prepare the adjusting entries at March 31, assuming that adjusting entries are made quarterly.

Recreate transactions and adjusting entries from adjusted data.
(SO 2, 3)

E4–7   Selected accounts of Jasper Limited are shown here:

Accounts Receivable				Service Revenue		
July 31	500				July 14	1,200
					31	900
Supplies					31	500
July 1 Bal.	1,100	July 31	500			
10	200			**Salaries Expense**		
				July 15	1,200	
Unearned Service Revenue				31	500	
July 31	900	July 1 Bal.	1,500			
		20	700	**Supplies Expense**		
				July 31	500	
Salaries Payable						
		July 31	500	**Income Tax Expense**		
				July 31	600	
Income Tax Payable						
		July 31	600			

Instructions

After analyzing the accounts, journalize (a) the July transaction entries (assume all were cash transactions) and (b) the adjusting entries that were made on July 31.

Analyze adjusted data.
(SO 2, 3, 4)

E4–8   Below are selected accounts from the adjusted trial balance of Nolet Ltd., whose fiscal year began January 1:

NOLET LTD.
Adjusted Trial Balance (Partial)
January 31, 2006

	Debit	Credit
Supplies	$ 700	
Prepaid insurance	4,400	
Equipment	12,000	
Accumulated amortization—equipment		$6,000
Income tax payable		800
Unearned service revenue		750
Service revenue		2,500
Supplies expense	950	
Insurance expense	400	
Income tax expense	1,800	

Instructions

(a) If the amount in Supplies Expense is the amount of the January 31 adjusting entry, and $850 of supplies were purchased in January, what was the balance in Supplies on January 1?

(b) If the amount in Insurance Expense is the amount of the January 31 adjusting entry, and the original insurance premium was for one year, what was the total premium and when was the policy purchased?

(c) If the equipment had an estimated useful life of four years when it was originally purchased, and there have been no purchases or sales of equipment since then, how many years has it been amortized?

(d) If $2,500 of income tax was paid in January, what was the balance in Income Tax Payable on January 1?

(e) If $1,600 was received in January for services performed in January, what was the balance in Unearned Service Revenue on January 1?

E4–9 The unadjusted and adjusted trial balances for Inuit Inc. at the end of its fiscal year are shown below:

Prepare adjusting entries from analysis of trial balances. (SO 2, 3, 4)

INUIT INC.
Trial Balance
August 31, 2006

	Unadjusted Dr.	Unadjusted Cr.	Adjusted Dr.	Adjusted Cr.
Cash	$10,400		$10,400	
Accounts receivable	8,800		9,275	
Office supplies	2,450		700	
Prepaid insurance	3,775		2,355	
Office equipment	14,100		14,100	
Accumulated amortization—office equipment		$ 3,525		$ 4,700
Accounts payable		5,800		5,800
Salaries payable		0		1,125
Income tax payable		0		1,000
Unearned service revenue		1,600		700
Common shares		10,000		10,000
Retained earnings		10,600		10,600
Dividends	800		800	
Service revenue		40,800		42,175
Salaries expense	17,000		18,125	
Office supplies expense	0		1,750	
Rent expense	15,000		15,000	
Insurance expense	0		1,420	
Amortization expense	0		1,175	
Income tax expense	0		1,000	
	$72,325	$72,325	$76,100	$76,100

Instructions

Prepare the adjusting entries that were made.

E4–10 The adjusted trial balance for Inuit Inc. is given in E4–9.

Prepare financial statements. (SO 4)

Instructions

Prepare the statement of earnings, statement of retained earnings, and balance sheet for the year.

E4–11 The adjusted trial balance for Inuit Inc. is given in E4–9.

Prepare closing entries and post-closing trial balance. (SO 5)

Instructions

(a) Prepare the closing entries at August 31.
(b) Prepare a post-closing trial balance.

Problems: Set A

Prepare transaction and
adjusting entries for
prepayments.
(SO 2)

P4–1A   Ouellette Corporation began operations on January 2, 2006. Its fiscal year end is December 31, and it prepares financial statements and adjusts its accounts annually. Selected transactions during 2006 follow:

1. On January 2, purchased office supplies for $4,100 cash. A physical count at December 31 revealed that $900 of supplies were still on hand.
2. Purchased a truck for $35,000 cash on March 1. The truck is estimated to have a useful life of five years.
3. Purchased a $3,780, one-year insurance policy for cash on August 1.
4. On November 15, Ouellette received a $1,200 advance cash payment from a client for services to be provided in the future. As at December 31, half of these services had been completed.
5. On December 15, the company rented out excess office space for a six-month period starting on this date and received a $540 cheque for two months of rent.

Instructions

For each of the above situations, prepare the journal entry for the original transaction and any adjusting journal entry required at December 31.

Prepare adjusting and
subsequent entries for accruals.
(SO 3)

P4–2A   Zheng Corporation had the following selected transactions in the month of February:

1. Zheng has five employees who each earn $100 a day. Salaries are normally paid on Fridays for work completed Monday through Friday of the same week. Salaries were last paid Friday, February 24, and will be paid next on Friday, March 3.
2. The company has a 6%, $12,000 note payable due in one year. Interest is payable the first of each month. It was last paid on February 1, and will be paid next on March 1.
3. At the end of February, Zheng has earned $2,500 that it has not yet billed. It bills its clients on March 3, and collects $1,500 of the amount due on March 30.
4. At the end of February, the company earned $200 interest on its investments. The bank deposited this amount in Zheng's bank account on March 1.
5. At the end of February, the company owed the utility company $550 and the telephone company $200 for services received during the month. These bills were paid on March 10.

Instructions

(a) For each of the above situations, prepare the monthly adjusting journal entry required at February 28.
(b) Prepare any subsequent transaction entries that occur in the month of March.

Prepare transaction and
adjusting entries.
(SO 2, 3)

P4–3A   The New Age Theatre Ltd. had the following selected transactions during the year ended November 30, 2006:

1. On June 1, the theatre borrowed $5,000 from the Bank of Montreal at an interest rate of 6%. The principal is to be repaid in two years' time. The interest is payable the first of each month.
2. The theatre has eight plays each season. This year's season started October 2006 and ends in May 2007 (one play per month). Season tickets sell for $160 each. On September 1, 150 tickets were sold for the 2006–07 season.
3. Office supplies on hand amounted to $500 at the beginning of the year. During the year, additional office supplies were purchased for cash at a cost of $1,550. At the end of the year, a physical count showed that supplies on hand amounted to $300.
4. On December 1, 2005, the theatre purchased a truck for $39,000 cash. The estimated useful life of the truck is four years.
5. Upon reviewing its books on November 30, the theatre noted that the utility bill for the month of November had not yet been received. A call to Hydro-Québec determined that the amount owed was $1,350. The bill was paid on December 10.
6. The total payroll is $3,000 every Monday for employee wages earned during a six-day week (Tuesday to Sunday). This year, November 30 falls on a Thursday.

Instructions

(a) Prepare the journal entries to record the original transactions for items 1, 2, 3, and 4.
(b) Prepare the year-end adjusting entries required for each of the above.

(c) Journalize the subsequent cash transaction for the (1) interest paid on December 1 (item 1); (2) payment of the utility bill on December 10 (item 5); and (3) payment of the payroll on December 4 (item 6).

P4–4A A review of the ledger of Come-By-Chance Corporation at December 31, 2006, produces the following account and other data for the preparation of annual adjusting entries:

Prepare adjusting entries.
(SO 2, 3)

1. Note Receivable $8,000: The note was issued on September 1, 2006, at an annual interest rate of 7.75%, and matures on June 1, 2007. Interest and principal are to be paid at maturity.
2. Prepaid Insurance $13,100: The company has separate insurance policies on its building and its motor vehicles. Policy B4564 on the building was purchased on September 1, 2005, for $10,320. The policy has a term of two years. Policy A2958 on the vehicles was purchased on January 1, 2006, for $4,500. This policy has a term of 18 months.
3. Buildings $190,250: The company owns two buildings. The first was purchased on September 1, 1995, for $125,250 and has an estimated 30-year useful life. The second was purchased on May 1, 2003, for $165,000 and has an estimated 40-year useful life.
4. Unearned Subscription Revenue $61,200: Come-by-Chance produces a monthly magazine. The selling price of a magazine subscription is $60 for 12 issues. A review of subscription contracts reveals the following:

Subscription Date	Number of Subscriptions
October 1	220
November 1	310
December 1	490
	1,020

5. Salaries Payable $0: There are nine salaried employees. Salaries are paid every Monday for the previous five-day work week (Monday to Friday). Six employees receive a salary of $625 each per week, and three employees earn $750 each per week. December 31 is a Sunday.

Instructions

(a) Prepare a calculation to show why the balance (before adjustment) in the Prepaid Insurance account is $13,100 and why the balance (before adjustment) in the Unearned Subscription Revenue account is $61,200.
(b) Prepare the adjusting journal entries required at December 31, 2006.

P4–5A During the first week of January 2006, Creative Designs Ltd. began operations. Although the company kept no formal accounting records, it did maintain a record of cash receipts and disbursements and had a cash balance of $7,580 at the end of December 2006. Creative Designs approached the local bank for a $10,000 loan and was asked to submit financial statements prepared on an accrual basis.

Convert earnings from cash to accrual basis; prepare financial statements.
(SO 1, 2, 3, 4)

The following information is available for the year ended December 31, 2006:

	Cash Receipts	Cash Payments
Issue of common shares	$18,500	
Equipment		$17,700
Supplies		8,400
Rent		9,900
Income tax		4,000
Insurance		1,920
Advertising		3,400
Wages		29,900
Telephone		1,000
Dividends		5,000
Design revenue	70,300	
	$88,800	$81,220

Additional information:

1. The equipment has an estimated five-year life.
2. Supplies on hand on December 31 were $1,630.
3. Rent payments included a $750 per month rental fee and a $900 deposit that is refundable at the end of the two-year lease.
4. The insurance was paid for a one-year period expiring on March 31, 2007.
5. Wages earned for the last week in December and to be paid in January 2007 amounted to $525.

6. Design revenue earned but not yet collected amounted to $3,950.
7. The company manager used her personal automobile for business purposes: 10,000 km at 35 cents per kilometre. She was not paid for the use of her car but would like to be.

Instructions

Prepare an accrual basis statement of earnings, statement of retained earnings, and balance sheet for the year.

Prepare and post adjusting entries; prepare adjusted trial balance.
(SO 2, 3, 4)

P4−6A   Scenic Tours Limited's unadjusted trial balance is presented below.

SCENIC TOURS LIMITED
Trial Balance
June 30, 2006

	Debit	Credit
Cash	$ 3,000	
Accounts receivable	2,640	
Prepaid insurance	7,320	
Supplies	965	
Equipment	13,440	
Accumulated amortization—equipment		$ 3,300
Buses	140,400	
Accumulated amortization—buses		46,800
Accounts payable		1,985
Notes payable		54,000
Unearned revenue		14,000
Common shares		30,000
Retained earnings		15,000
Tour revenue		17,110
Salaries expense	9,560	
Advertising expense	825	
Rent expense	2,175	
Gas and oil expense	1,170	
Income tax expense	700	
	$182,195	$182,195

Additional information:

1. The insurance policy has a one-year term beginning June 1, 2006.
2. The equipment has an estimated useful life of eight years. The buses have an estimated useful life of six years.
3. A physical count shows $240 of supplies on hand at June 30.
4. The note payable has a 7% interest rate. Interest is paid at the beginning of each month.
5. Deposits of $1,400 each were received for advanced tour reservations from 10 school groups. At June 30, three of these deposits have been earned.
6. Bus drivers are paid a combined total of $425 per day. At June 30, three days' salaries are unpaid.
7. A senior citizens' organization that had not made an advance deposit took a scenic tour on June 30 for $1,150. This group was not billed for the services provided until July.
8. Additional advertising costs of $620 have been incurred, but the bills have not been received by June 30.
9. Income taxes payable are estimated to be $65.

Instructions

(a) Prepare a general ledger and enter the trial balance amounts.
(b) Prepare and post the adjusting journal entries for the month of June.
(c) Prepare an adjusted trial balance at June 30, 2006.

P4–7A   On October 31, 2006, the Alou Equipment Repair Corp.'s post-closing trial balance was as follows:

Complete accounting cycle through to preparation of financial statements. (SO 2, 3, 4)

ALOU EQUIPMENT REPAIR CORP.
Post-Closing Trial Balance
October 31, 2006

	Debit	Credit
Cash	$ 2,790	
Accounts receivable	2,910	
Supplies	2,000	
Equipment	9,000	
Accumulated amortization—equipment		$ 1,800
Accounts payable		2,300
Unearned service revenue		500
Salaries payable		400
Common shares		10,000
Retained earnings		1,700
	$16,700	$16,700

During November, the following transactions were completed:

Nov. 11 Paid $1,100 for salaries due employees, of which $700 is for November and $400 is for October salaries payable.
   12 Received $1,200 cash from customers in payment of accounts receivable.
   14 Received $5,700 cash for services performed in November.
   17 Purchased supplies on account, $1,300.
   20 Paid creditors $2,500 of accounts payable due.
   22 Paid November rent, $300.
   25 Paid salaries, $1,100.
   27 Performed services on account, $1,900.
   29 Received $550 from customers for services to be provided in future.

Adjustment data:

1. Supplies on hand are valued at $1,000.
2. Accrued salaries payable are $500.
3. The equipment has an estimated useful life of five years.
4. Unearned service revenue of $400 was earned during the month.
5. Income taxes payable are estimated to be $200.

Instructions

(a) Prepare a general ledger and enter the opening balances.
(b) Prepare and post the November transaction entries.
(c) Prepare a trial balance at November 30.
(d) Prepare and post the adjusting journal entries for the month of November.
(e) Prepare an adjusted trial balance.
(f) Prepare a statement of earnings, statement of retained earnings, and balance sheet for the month.

Prepare adjusting entries and
financial statements; assess
financial performance.
(SO 2, 3, 4)

P4–8A   The unadjusted and adjusted trial balances of Ozaki Corp. at the end of its first quarter of operations are shown below:

OZAKI CORP.
Trial Balance
September 30, 2006

	Unadjusted		Adjusted	
	Debit	Credit	Debit	Credit
Cash	$ 3,250		$ 3,250	
Accounts receivable	6,335		7,435	
Prepaid rent	1,500		0	
Supplies	1,750		1,265	
Equipment	15,040		15,040	
Accumulated amortization—equipment		$ 0		$ 750
Note payable		6,000		6,000
Accounts payable		4,250		4,460
Salaries payable		0		840
Interest payable		0		90
Income tax payable		0		1,000
Unearned commission revenue		775		550
Common shares		11,000		11,000
Dividends	700		700	
Commission revenue		20,160		21,485
Salaries expense	13,000		13,840	
Rent expense	0		1,500	
Amortization expense	0		750	
Supplies expense	0		485	
Utilities expense	610		820	
Interest expense	0		90	
Income tax expense	0		1,000	
	$42,185	$42,185	$46,175	$46,175

Instructions

(a) Prepare the quarterly adjusting journal entries that were made.
(b) Prepare a statement of earnings, statement of retained earnings, and balance sheet for the quarter.
(c) A friend of yours is considering investing in the company and asks you to comment on the results of operations and financial position. Is the company performing well or not? Does the financial position look healthy or weak? Use specific information from the financial statements to support your answer.

Prepare and post closing entries;
prepare post-closing trial
balance.
(SO 5)

P4–9A   The adjusted trial balance for Ozaki Corp. is presented in P4–8A. The company closes its books quarterly.

Instructions

(a) Prepare a general ledger and enter the adjusted trial balance amounts.
(b) Prepare and post the closing entries.
(c) Prepare a post-closing trial balance at September 30.

P4–10A The unadjusted trial balance for River Run Motel Ltd. is presented below:

Prepare and post adjusting entries; prepare adjusted trial balance and financial statements; prepare and post closing entries; prepare post-closing trial balance.
(SO 2, 3, 4, 5)

RIVER RUN MOTEL LTD.
Trial Balance
May 31, 2006

	Debit	Credit
Cash	$ 3,200	
Accounts receivable	5,900	
Prepaid insurance	5,460	
Supplies	2,440	
Land	50,000	
Lodge	84,000	
Accumulated amortization—lodge		$ 29,400
Furniture	16,800	
Accumulated amortization—furniture		6,880
Accounts payable		4,700
Unearned rent revenue		8,750
Mortgage payable		53,000
Common shares		30,000
Retained earnings		10,500
Dividends	1,000	
Rent revenue		100,160
Salaries expense	49,350	
Interest expense	4,620	
Insurance expense	1,820	
Utilities expense	13,300	
Advertising expense	500	
Income tax expense	5,000	
	$243,390	$243,390

Additional information:

1. The annual insurance policy was purchased on May 1 for $5,460.
2. A count of supplies shows $670 of supplies on hand on May 31.
3. The lodge has an estimated useful life of 20 years. The furniture has an estimated useful life of 5 years.
4. Customers must pay a $50 deposit if they want to book a room in advance during the peak period. An analysis of these bookings indicates that 175 deposits were received and credited to Unearned Rent Revenue. By May 31, 65 of the deposits were earned.
5. The mortgage interest rate is 8%. Interest has been paid to May 1; the next payment is due June 1.
6. The May utility bill of $1,210 has not yet been recorded or paid.
7. Salaries of $975 are unpaid at May 31.
8. On May 28, a local business contracted with the River Run Motel to rent one of its rooms for four months, starting June 1, at a rate of $1,400 per month. An advance payment equal to one month's rent was paid on May 28 and credited to Rent Revenue.
9. On May 31, the River Run Motel has earned $980 of rent revenue from customers who are currently staying in the motel. The customers will only pay the amount owing when they check out in early June.
10. Additional income taxes are estimated to be $500.

Instructions

(a) Prepare a general ledger and enter the trial balance amounts.
(b) Prepare and post the adjusting journal entries for the month of May.
(c) Prepare an adjusted trial balance at May 31.
(d) Prepare a statement of earnings, statement of retained earnings, and balance sheet for the month.
(e) Prepare and post the closing journal entries.
(f) Prepare a post-closing trial balance.

Complete all steps in accounting
cycle.
(SO 2, 3, 4, 5)

P4–11A   Corellian Window Washing Inc. opened on July 1, 2006. During July, the following transactions occurred:

July 1 Issued $24,000 of common shares for cash.
     1 Purchased a used truck for $36,000, paying $16,000 cash and the balance with a one-year, 8% note payable. Interest is due the first of each month.
     3 Purchased cleaning supplies for $800 on account.
     5 Paid $1,200 cash for a one-year insurance policy effective July 1.
    12 Billed customers $4,500 for cleaning services.
    18 Paid $500 on amount owed on cleaning supplies.
    20 Paid $1,600 cash for employee salaries.
    21 Collected $2,500 cash from customers billed on July 12.
    25 Billed customers $2,000 for cleaning services.
    31 Paid $250 for gas and oil used in the truck during the month.
    31 Declared and paid a $600 cash dividend.

Instructions

(a) Open general ledger accounts as required. Prepare and post the July transaction entries.
(b) Prepare a trial balance at July 31.
(c) Prepare and post the following adjustments:
    1. Services provided but unbilled and uncollected at July 31 were $1,400.
    2. An inventory count shows $600 of cleaning supplies on hand at July 31.
    3. Expired insurance needs to be recorded.
    4. The truck is expected to have an estimated useful life of five years.
    5. Accrued but unpaid employee salaries were $400.
    6. Interest on the note payable needs to be accrued.
    7. Income taxes payable is estimated to be $1,500.
(d) Prepare an adjusted trial balance at July 31.
(e) Prepare a statement of earnings, statement of retained earnings, and a balance sheet for the month.
(f) Prepare and post the closing journal entries.
(g) Prepare a post-closing trial balance at July 31.

Problems: Set B

Prepare transaction and
adjusting entries for
prepayments.
(SO 2)

P4–1B   Bourque Corporation began operations on January 1, 2006. Its fiscal year end is December 31, and it prepares financial statements and adjusts its accounts annually. Selected transactions during 2006 follow:

1. On January 2, purchased office supplies for $3,100 cash. A physical count at December 31 revealed that $670 of supplies were still on hand.
2. Purchased office equipment for $12,000 cash on March 1. The office equipment is estimated to have a useful life of three years.
3. Purchased a one-year, $5,040 insurance policy for cash on June 1.
4. On November 15, Bourque received a $1,275 advance cash payment from three clients for services to be provided in the future. As at December 31, services had been performed for two of the clients ($425 each).
5. On December 15, the company paid $4,500 rent in advance for the month of January 2007.

Instructions

For each of the above events, prepare the journal entry for the original transaction and any adjusting journal entry required at December 31.

Prepare adjusting and
subsequent entries for accruals.
(SO 3)

P4–2B   Hangzhou Corporation had the following selected transactions in the month of November:

1. Hangzhou has a biweekly payroll of $6,000. Salaries are normally paid every second Monday for work completed for the two preceding weeks. Employees work a five-day

week, Monday through Friday. Salaries were last paid Monday, November 28 for the ten days worked during the weeks of November 14 and 21. They will be paid next on Monday, December 12.

2. The company has a 6%, $120,000 mortgage payable due in five years. Interest is payable the first of each month. It was last paid on November 1, and will be paid next on December 1.

3. At the end of November, Hangzhou has $500 of invoices that have not yet been sent to customers. It mails these invoices on December 1, and collects the amounts due on December 20.

4. At the end of November, the company earned $20 interest on the cash in its bank account. The bank deposited this amount in the company's bank account on November 30, but the company did not learn of the interest until it received its bank statement on December 5.

5. At the end of November, it was estimated that the company owed $1,000 of income tax. This amount was paid on December 18.

Instructions

(a) For each of the above situations, prepare the monthly adjusting journal entry required at November 30.

(b) Prepare any subsequent transaction entries that occur in the month of December.

P4–3B The Repertory Theatre Ltd. had the following selected transactions during the year ended December 31, 2006:

Prepare transaction and adjusting entries.
(SO 2, 3)

1. Supplies on hand amounted to $460 at the beginning of the year. During the year, additional supplies were purchased for $1,720 cash. At the end of the year, a physical count showed that supplies on hand amounted to $990.

2. On January 2, 2006, the theatre purchased a used truck for $23,500 cash. The estimated useful life of the truck is five years.

3. On March 1, the theatre borrowed $10,000 from La Caisse Populaire Desjardins at an interest rate of 6.5%. The principal is to be repaid in one year. The interest is paid at the beginning of each month.

4. Repertory Theatre Ltd. has nine plays each season, which starts in September 2006 and ends in May 2007 (one play per month). Season tickets sell for $135 each. On August 1, 200 tickets were sold for the upcoming 2006–07 season.

5. Every Monday, the total payroll for the theatre is $3,000 for wages earned during a six-day work week (Tuesday–Sunday). This year, December 31 falls on a Sunday. Wages were last paid (and recorded) on Monday, December 25.

6. Upon reviewing its books on December 31, the theatre noted that a telephone bill for the month of December had not yet been received. A call to Aliant determined that the telephone bill was $375. The bill was paid on January 12.

Instructions

(a) Prepare the journal entries to record the original transactions for items 1, 2, 3, and 4.

(b) Prepare the year-end adjusting entries required for each of the above.

(c) Journalize the subsequent cash transaction for the (1) interest paid on January 1 (item 3); (2) payment of the payroll on January 1 (item 5); and (3) payment of the telephone bill on January 12 (item 6).

Prepare adjusting entries.
(SO 2, 3)

P4–4B   A review of the ledger of Greenberg Corporation at January 31, 2006, produces the following data for the preparation of annual adjusting entries:

1. Prepaid Advertising $14,160: This balance consists of payments on two advertising contracts. The contracts provide for monthly advertising in two trade magazines and the first advertisement runs in the month in which the contract is signed. The terms of the contracts are as follows:

Contract	Date	Amount	Number of Magazine Issues
A650	May 1	$ 6,240	12
B974	Sept. 1	7,920	24
		$14,160	

2. Salaries Payable $0: There are eight salaried employees. Salaries are paid every Saturday for a six-day work week (Monday–Saturday). Six employees receive a salary of $750 each per week, and two employees earn $550 each per week. January 31 is a Tuesday.

3. Unearned Rent Revenue $351,000: The company began subleasing office space in its new building on December 1. At January 31, the company had the following rental contracts that are paid in full for the entire term of the lease:

Date	Term (in months)	Monthly Rent	Number of Leases	Rent Paid
Dec. 1	6	$4,500	5	$135,000
Jan. 1	6	9,000	4	216,000
				$351,000

4. Note Payable $85,000: This balance consists of a one-year, 8% note issued on June 1. Interest is payable at maturity.

Instructions

Prepare the adjusting journal entries at January 31, 2006.

Convert earnings from cash to accrual basis; prepare financial statements.
(SO 1, 2, 3, 4)

P4–5B   The Radical Edge Ltd., a ski tuning and repair shop, opened November 1, 2005. The company carefully kept track of all its cash receipts and cash payments and had a cash balance of $5,145 at the end of its first ski season, April 30. The following information is available at April 30, 2006:

	Cash Receipts	Cash Payments
Issue of common shares	$20,000	
Repair equipment		$34,520
Rent		1,575
Advertising		460
Utility bills		950
Wages		3,600
Income tax		7,000
Ski and snowboard repair services	33,250	
	$53,250	$48,105

Additional information:

1. The repair equipment has an estimated useful life of eight years.
2. The company rents space at a cost of $225 per month on a one-year lease. The lease contract requires payment of the first and last months' rent in advance, which was done.
3. At April 30, $120 is owed for unpaid wages.
4. At the end of April, customers also owe The Radical Edge $720 for services they have received but have not yet paid for.

Instructions

Prepare an accrual basis statement of earnings, statement of retained earnings, and balance sheet for the six months ended April 30, 2006.

P4–6B Ortega Limo Service Ltd.'s unadjusted trial balance is presented below:

Prepare and post adjusting entries, prepare adjusted trial balance.
(SO 2, 3, 4)

ORTEGA LIMO SERVICE LTD.
Trial Balance
December 31, 2006

	Debit	Credit
Cash	$ 12,400	
Accounts receivable	3,200	
Prepaid insurance	3,600	
Prepaid rent	1,225	
Supplies	2,500	
Automobiles	58,000	
Accumulated amortization—automobiles		$ 14,500
Office furniture	16,000	
Accumulated amortization—office furniture		4,000
Note payable		46,000
Unearned service revenue		3,600
Common shares		10,000
Retained earnings		7,600
Dividends	8,820	
Service revenue		110,600
Salaries expense	57,000	
Interest expense	3,105	
Rent expense	14,700	
Repairs expense	6,000	
Gas and oil expense	9,300	
Income tax expense	450	
	$196,300	$196,300

Additional information:

1. Service revenue earned but unbilled is $3,000 at December 31.
2. The insurance policy has a one-year term beginning April 1.
3. The automobiles were purchased on January 2, 2005, and have an estimated useful life of four years. The office furniture was purchased on July 2, 2003, and has an estimated useful life of 10 years.
4. Interest on the 9% note payable is paid on the first day of each quarter (January 1, April 1, July 1, and October 1).
5. One of Ortega's customers paid in advance for a six-month contract at the rate of $600 per month. The contract began on November 1.
6. Drivers' salaries total $225 per day. At December 31, three days of salaries are unpaid.
7. Repairs of $650 have been incurred for automobiles, but bills have not been received prior to December 31. (Use Accounts Payable.)
8. On December 28, Ortega paid $1,225 for January 2007 rent.
9. Income taxes payable are estimated to be $50.

Instructions

(a) Prepare a general ledger and enter the trial balance amounts.
(b) Prepare and post the adjusting journal entries for the year.
(c) Prepare an adjusted trial balance at December 31, 2006.

Complete accounting cycle
through to preparation of
financial statements.
(SO 2, 3, 4)

P4–7B   On August 31, 2006, the Rijo Equipment Repair Corp.'s post-closing trial balance was as follows:

RIJO EQUIPMENT REPAIR CORP.
Post-Closing Trial Balance
August 31, 2006

	Debit	Credit
Cash	$ 4,880	
Accounts receivable	3,720	
Supplies	800	
Equipment	15,000	
Accumulated amortization—equipment		$ 1,500
Accounts payable		3,100
Unearned service revenue		400
Salaries payable		700
Common shares		10,000
Retained earnings		8,700
	$24,400	$24,400

During September, the following transactions were completed:

Sept. 8 Paid $1,100 for salaries due to employees, of which $400 is for September and $700 is for August salaries payable.
10 Received $1,200 cash from customers in payment of accounts.
12 Received $4,400 cash for services performed in September.
17 Purchased supplies on account, $1,000.
20 Paid creditors $3,500 of accounts payable due.
22 Paid September and October rent, $1,000 ($500 per month).
22 Paid salaries, $1,100.
27 Performed services on account, $800.
29 Received $650 from customers for services to be provided in the future.
30 Paid income tax for month, $600.

Adjustment data:

1. Supplies on hand total $500.
2. Accrued salaries payable are $600.
3. The equipment has a useful life of five years.
4. Unearned service revenue of $350 has been earned.

Instructions

(a) Prepare a general ledger and enter the opening balances.
(b) Prepare and post the September transaction entries.
(c) Prepare a trial balance at September 30.
(d) Prepare and post the adjusting journal entries for the month of September.
(e) Prepare an adjusted trial balance.
(f) Prepare a statement of earnings, statement of retained earnings, and balance sheet for the month.

P4–8B The unadjusted and adjusted trial balances for Grant Advertising Agency Limited as at December 31, 2006, follow:

Prepare adjusting entries and financial statements; assess financial performance.
(SO 2, 3, 4)

GRANT ADVERTISING AGENCY LIMITED
Trial Balance
December 31, 2006

	Unadjusted Debit	Unadjusted Credit	Adjusted Debit	Adjusted Credit
Cash	$ 11,000		$ 11,000	
Short-term investments	10,850		10,850	
Accounts receivable	18,650		19,750	
Art supplies	7,200		1,265	
Prepaid insurance	2,400		800	
Printing equipment	66,000		66,000	
Printing equipment—accumulated amortization		$ 26,400		$ 39,600
Accounts payable		4,200		4,800
Interest payable		0		700
Note payable		10,000		10,000
Unearned advertising revenue		7,100		6,200
Salaries payable		0		1,625
Income tax payable		0		7,000
Common shares		20,000		20,000
Retained earnings		10,400		10,400
Dividends	2,000		2,000	
Advertising revenue		58,600		60,600
Salaries expense	12,000		13,625	
Insurance expense	0		1,600	
Interest expense	0		700	
Amortization expense	0		13,200	
Art supplies expense	0		5,935	
Rent expense	6,600		7,200	
Income tax expense	0		7,000	
	$136,700	$136,700	$160,925	$160,925

Instructions

(a) Prepare the annual adjusting journal entries that were made.
(b) Prepare a statement of earnings, statement of retained earnings, and balance sheet for the year.
(c) A friend of yours is considering investing in the company and asks you to comment on the results of operations and financial position. Is the company performing well or not? Does the financial position look healthy or weak? Use specific information from the financial statements to support your answer.

P4–9B The adjusted trial balance for Grant Advertising Agency Limited is presented in P4–8B.

Prepare and post closing entries; prepare post-closing trial balance.
(SO 5)

Instructions

(a) Prepare a general ledger and enter the adjusted trial balance amounts.
(b) Prepare and post the closing entries.
(c) Prepare a post-closing trial balance at December 31.

Prepare and post adjusting
entries; prepare adjusted trial
balance and financial statements;
prepare and post closing entries;
prepare post-closing trial
balance.
(SO 2, 3, 4, 5)

P4–10B   The unadjusted trial balance for Highland Cove Resort Inc. is presented below, immediately before annual adjusting entries are made:

HIGHLAND COVE RESORT INC.
Trial Balance
August 31, 2006

	Debit	Credit
Cash	$ 18,870	
Prepaid insurance	6,360	
Supplies	3,495	
Land	25,000	
Cottages	145,000	
Accumulated amortization—cottages		$ 34,800
Furniture	28,600	
Accumulated amortization—furniture		10,725
Accounts payable		6,500
Unearned rent revenue		36,200
Mortgage payable		60,000
Common shares		35,000
Retained earnings		23,500
Dividends	5,000	
Rent revenue		247,500
Salaries expense	153,000	
Utilities expense	37,600	
Interest expense	4,400	
Repair expense	14,400	
Income tax expense	12,500	
	$454,225	$454,225

Additional information:

1. The annual insurance policy was purchased on May 31 for $6,360.
2. A count of supplies on August 31 shows $760 of supplies on hand.
3. The cottages have an estimated useful life of 25 years. The furniture has an estimated useful life of 8 years.
4. Customers must pay a $100 deposit if they want to book a cottage during the peak period. An analysis of these bookings indicates 362 deposits were received and credited to Unearned Rent Revenue. All but 45 of these deposits have been earned by August 31.
5. Salaries of $1,100 were unpaid at August 31.
6. The August utility bill of $1,840 has not yet been recorded or paid.
7. On August 25, a local business contracted with Highland Cove to rent one of the cottages for six months, starting October 1, at a rate of $1,500 per month. An advance payment equal to two months' rent was received on August 31 and credited to Rent Revenue.
8. The mortgage interest rate is 8%. Interest has been paid to August 1; the next payment is due September 1.
9. On August 31, Highland Cove has earned but not yet received $1,360 of rent revenue from customers who are currently using the cottages. The customers will pay this amount when they check out in September.
10. Additional income taxes payable are estimated to be $1,000.

Instructions

(a) Prepare a general ledger and enter the trial balance amounts.
(b) Prepare and post the adjusting journal entries for the year.
(c) Prepare an adjusted trial balance at August 31.
(d) Prepare a statement of earnings, statement of retained earnings, and balance sheet for the year.
(e) Prepare and post the closing entries.
(f) Prepare a post-closing trial balance.

P4–11B Ewok's Carpet Cleaners Ltd. opened on March 1, 2006. During March, the following transactions were completed:

Complete all steps in accounting cycle.
(SO 2, 3, 4, 5)

Mar. 1 Issued $10,000 of common shares for cash.
    1 Purchased a used truck for $26,000, paying $6,000 cash and signing a three-year, 8% note payable for the balance. Interest is due the first of each month.
    2 Paid rent for the month, $500.
    3 Purchased cleaning supplies for $1,200 on account.
    5 Paid $1,800 cash for a one-year insurance policy effective March 1.
   14 Billed customers $4,800 for cleaning services.
   18 Paid $700 on amount owed on cleaning supplies.
   20 Paid $1,500 cash for employee salaries.
   21 Collected $3,600 cash from customers billed on March 14.
   28 Billed customers $4,500 for cleaning services.
   31 Paid $400 for gas and oil for the truck during the month.
   31 Paid a $1,000 cash dividend.

Instructions

(a) Open general ledger accounts as required. Prepare and post the March transaction entries.
(b) Prepare a trial balance at March 31.
(c) Prepare and post the following adjustments:
    1. Services provided but unbilled and uncollected at March 31 were $1,600.
    2. An inventory count shows $400 of cleaning supplies on hand at March 31.
    3. Expired insurance needs to be recorded.
    4. The truck is expected to have a useful life of five years.
    5. Interest on the note needs to be accrued.
    6. Accrued but unpaid employee salaries were $700.
    7. Income tax for the month is estimated to be $1,400.
(d) Prepare an adjusted trial balance at March 31.
(e) Prepare a statement of earnings, statement of retained earnings, and a balance sheet for the month.
(f) Prepare and post the closing journal entries.
(g) Prepare a post-closing trial balance at March 31.

BROADENING YOUR PERSPECTIVE

Financial Reporting and Analysis

www.wiley.com/canada/kimmel

Analysis Tools

Financial Reporting Problem: *Loblaw*

BYP4–1 The financial statements of Loblaw are presented in Appendix A at the end of this book.

Instructions

(a) Does Loblaw report any prepayments on its balance sheet? If so, identify each item that is a prepaid expense or unearned revenue. Using the statement of earnings, indicate the other account that is likely used in preparing adjusting entries for these items.
(b) Does Loblaw report any accruals on its balance sheet? If so, identify each item that is an accrued revenue or accrued expense. Using the statement of earnings, indicate the other account that is likely used in preparing adjusting entries for these items.
(c) Reconstruct the summary closing journal entries prepared by Loblaw at January 3, 2004.

Comparative Analysis Problem: *Loblaw and Sobeys*

BYP4–2   The financial statements of Sobeys are presented in Appendix B, following the financial statements for Loblaw in Appendix A.

Instructions

(a) Identify two accounts on Sobeys' balance sheet which show that Sobeys uses accrual accounting. In each case, identify the statement of earnings account that would be affected by the adjustment process.
(b) Identify two accounts on Loblaw's balance sheet which show that Loblaw uses accrual accounting. In each case, identify the statement of earnings account that would be affected by the adjustment process.

Research Case

BYP4–3   The article "PwC Identifies Best Practices for Monthly Close" appears in the February 1, 2005, issue of the *Accounting Department Management Report*, published by the Institute of Management and Administration. In this article, PricewaterhouseCoopers (PwC) reports findings from its global best practices survey. It finds that leading companies are able to close their books in a single day.

Instructions

Read the article and answer these questions:

(a) What industry sectors are generally able to close their books in only one day? What industry sectors can take as many as 10 days to close their books?
(b) PwC identifies 11 attributes of a fast close. Identify any five of these.

Interpreting Financial Statements

BYP4–4   Google Inc. is the most used site in the world for Internet searches. An excerpt from the notes to Google's 2004 financial statements follows:

GOOGLE INC.
Notes to the Financial Statements
December 31, 2004

Note 1. The Company and Summary of Accounting Policies—Revenue Recognition

In the first quarter of 2000, the Company introduced its first advertising program through which it offered advertisers the ability to place text-based ads on Google web sites targeted to users' search queries. Advertisers paid the Company based on the number of times their ads were displayed on users' search results pages and the Company recognized revenue at the time these ads appeared. In the fourth quarter of 2000, the Company launched Google AdWords, an online self-service program that enables advertisers to place text-based ads on Google web sites. AdWords advertisers originally paid the Company based on the number of times their ads appeared on users' search results pages. In the first quarter of 2002, the Company began offering AdWords exclusively on a cost-per-click basis, so that an advertiser pays the Company only when a user clicks on one of its ads. The Company recognizes as revenue the fees charged advertisers each time a user clicks on one of the text-based ads that are displayed next to the search results on Google web sites. Effective January 1, 2004, the Company now offers a single pricing structure to all of its advertisers based on the AdWords cost-per-click model.

The Company generates fees from search services through a variety of contractual arrangements, which include per-query search fees and search service hosting fees. Revenues from set-up and support fees and search service hosting fees are recognized on a straight-line basis over the term of the contract, which is the expected period during which these services will be provided. The Company's policy is to recognize revenues from per query search fees in the period queries are made and results are delivered.

Instructions

(a) When does Google recognize the revenue from its advertising services? From its search services?

(b) When would Google likely incur the expenses related to its advertising and search services? Explain how the matching principle does, or does not, relate to Google's revenue recognition practices.

(c) Google reports U.S. $36.5 million of deferred revenue in the current liabilities section of its balance sheet. "Deferred revenue" is another name for unearned revenue. Under what circumstances should Google record unearned revenue from its advertising services? From its search services?

A Global Focus

BYP4–5   Internet Initiative Japan Inc. (IIJ) is one of Japan's leading Internet-access and comprehensive Internet solution providers. In its 2004 annual report, it reported the following selected information (in millions):

	2004	2003
Cash and cash equivalents	¥12.3	¥ 3.6
Accounts receivable	9.0	10.3
Total revenues	38.8	44.0
Net loss	0.1	16.5
Cash provided by operating activities	1.9	1.6

Instructions

(a) Explain how the company could have reported a net loss in both fiscal years and still have a positive cash flow from operating activities.

(b) Explain how the company's cash from operating activities could be ¥1.9 million in 2004, while its cash and cash equivalents balance increased by ¥8.7 million to ¥12.3 million in 2004.

(c) During 2004, the company's revenues were ¥38.8 million. At the beginning of the year, it had ¥10.3 million of accounts receivable. At the end of the year, it had ¥9 million of accounts receivable. Based on this data, determine the amount of cash collected from customers during the year.

Financial Analysis on the Web

BYP4–6   This case reviews the revenue recognition policies used by Rogers Communications Inc. and its subsidiary, the Toronto Blue Jays Baseball Club.

Instructions

Specific requirements of this Web case can be found on the Toolkit website.

Analysis Tools
(Financial Analysis on the Web)

Critical Thinking

Collaborative Learning Activity

BYP4–7   Air Canada sells tickets for airline flights that can vary a great deal in price and conditions. For example, at the low end of the pricing scheme, you can purchase a nonrefundable ticket from Fredericton to Toronto for a one-way "Tango" fare of $238. At the high end of the pricing scheme, you can purchase a fully refundable ticket from Fredericton to Toronto for a one-way "Latitude" fare of $426.

Assume that Air Canada's management team is brainstorming its options in terms of recognizing the revenue from the different categories of fares. One member of the management team says it should recognize the revenue as soon as the tickets are sold for the Tango-type fares because these tickets are nonrefundable. Another member of the management team states that revenue should be recognized when passengers pick up their tickets and pay for the flight. "What about when the boarding passes are collected at the gate?" a third asks. "Or when passengers arrive at their destinations?" a fourth adds.

Instructions

With the class divided into groups, do the following:

(a) Each group will be assigned, or should choose, one of the above fare types (Tango or Latitude). Evaluate the effect of each of the revenue recognition choices on recorded revenues, expenses, and net earnings for your assigned fare type.

(b) Determine the point at which you think Air Canada should recognize the revenue from flight ticket sales for your fare type. Explain why you believe your chosen point of revenue recognition is the best: refer to appropriate generally accepted accounting principles in your answer.

Communication Activity

BYP4–8   There are many people today who believe that cash is a better indicator of a company's future success than net earnings. This notion gained popularity after many reports of corporate financial scandals where management was apparently able to manipulate prepayments and accruals to influence net earnings.

Instructions

Write a memo discussing whether you believe cash is a more reliable performance measure than net earnings. Include in your memo the answers to the following questions:

(a) What is the difference between accrual-based net earnings and cash?

(b) Do you believe that it is possible for management to manipulate net earnings? If so, identify one way that management might be able to increase net earnings by manipulating prepayments or accruals.

(c) Do you believe that it is possible for management to manipulate cash? If so, identify one way that management might be able to increase cash flow.

Ethics Case

Ethics In Accounting

BYP4–9   Die Hard Corporation is a pesticide manufacturer. Its sales declined greatly this year because of new legislation that outlaws the sale of several Die Hard chemical pesticides. During the coming year, Die Hard will have environmentally safe and competitive chemicals to replace these discontinued products. Sales in the next year are expected to be much higher than those of any prior year. The decline in this year's sales and profits appears, therefore, to be a one-year aberration.

   Even so, the company president believes that a large dip in the current year's profits could cause a significant drop in the market price of Die Hard's shares and make the company a takeover target. To avoid this possibility, he urges Carole Denton, the company's controller, to accrue every possible revenue and to defer as many expenses as possible when making this period's year-end adjusting entries. The president says to Carole, "We need the revenues this year, and next year can easily absorb expenses deferred from this year. We can't let our share price be hammered down!" Carole did not get around to recording the adjusting journal entries until January 17, but she dated the entries December 31 as if they were recorded then. Carole also made every effort to comply with the president's request.

Instructions

(a) Who are the stakeholders in this situation?

(b) What are the ethical considerations of the president's request and Carole's dating the adjusting entries December 31?

(c) Can Carole aggressively accrue revenues and defer expenses and still be ethical?

Serial Problem

(*Note*: This serial problem started in Chapter 1 and continued in chapters 2 and 3. From the information gathered through Chapter 3, follow the instructions below using the general ledger accounts you have already prepared.)

BYP4–10 Cookie Creations is gearing up for the Christmas season. During the month of December 2005, the following transactions occur:

Dec. 1 An assistant is hired at an hourly wage of $8 to help Natalie with cookie making and some administrative duties.

5 Natalie teaches the class that was booked on November 25. The balance outstanding is received.

8 A cheque is received for the amount due from the neighbourhood school for the class given on November 30.

9 The local school board pays $625 in advance for five classes that are to be given during December and January.

15 The cell phone invoice outstanding at November 30 is paid.

19 A deposit of $50 is received on a cookie class scheduled for early January.

23 Additional revenue earned during the month for cookie-making classes amounts to $3,500. (Natalie has not had time to account for each class individually.) Cash of $3,000 has been collected and $500 is still outstanding. (This is in addition to the December 5 and December 9 transactions.)

23 Additional supplies purchased during the month for sugar, flour, and chocolate chips amount to $1,250 cash.

23 A cheque is issued to Natalie's assistant for $800. Her assistant worked approximately 100 hours from when she was hired until December 23.

23 Natalie is paid $500 cash for her salary earned to date.

28 A dividend of $100 is paid to the common shareholder (Natalie).

As at December 31, Cookie Creations' year end, the following adjusting entry data is available:

1. A count reveals that $50 of brochures and posters remains at the end of December.
2. Amortization is recorded on the baking equipment purchased in November. The baking equipment has a useful life of five years. (Assume that only one month's worth of amortization is required.)
3. Interest on the note payable is accrued. (Assume that one and a half months of interest accrued during November and December.)
4. One month's worth of insurance has expired.
5. Natalie is unexpectedly telephoned on December 28 to give a cookie class at the neighbourhood community centre. The community centre is invoiced in early January for $375.
6. A count reveals that $1,000 of baking supplies were used.
7. A cell phone invoice is received for $75. The invoice is for services provided during the month of December and is due on January 15.
8. Because the cookie-making class occurred unexpectedly on December 28 and is for such a large group of children, Natalie's assistant helps out. Her assistant worked seven hours at a rate of $8 per hour.
9. An analysis of the Unearned Revenue account reveals that two of the five classes paid for by the local school board on December 9 have still not been taught by the end of December. The $50 deposit received on December 19 for another class also remains unearned.
10. Cookie Creations Ltd. expects to pay income tax at a rate of 15% on earnings before income tax.

Instructions

(a) Journalize the above transactions.
(b) Post the December transactions. (Use the general ledger accounts that you prepared in Chapter 3.)
(c) Prepare a trial balance at December 31.
(d) Prepare and post adjusting journal entries for the month of December.
(e) Prepare an adjusted trial balance at December 31.
(f) Prepare a statement of earnings and a statement of retained earnings for the two-month period ending December 31, and a balance sheet at December 31.

(g) Prepare and post the closing entries.
(h) Prepare a post-closing trial balance at December 31.

Answers to Self-Study Questions

1. a   2. d   3. d   4. b   5. b   6. d   7. a   8. c   9. b   10. a   11. a

Answer to Loblaw Review It Question 3

Depreciation expense, $393 million (see Consolidated Statement of Earnings); accumulated depreciation, $2,588 million and net book value, $6,422 million (see note 8 in Notes to the Consolidated Financial Statements).

 Remember to go back to the Navigator box at the beginning of the chapter to check off your completed work.

CHAPTER 5

Merchandising Operations

The Right Way to Retail

Being a consumer is a basic part of life in the Western world. North America was the birthplace of consumerism, and nowhere is this consumerism more evident than in the discount retail industry led by the U.S.-based giant Wal-Mart.

Wal-Mart is the number one retailer in the world, with global sales of more than $256 billion in 2004. It entered Canada in 1994 by purchasing 122 Woolco stores. Today, Wal-Mart has 235 discount department stores and six SAM'S CLUBS across the country. These are among the more than 1,500 stores located in nine countries—Argentina, Brazil, Canada, China, Germany, Korea, Mexico, Puerto Rico, and the United Kingdom—as well as more than 3,600 Supercenters, SAM'S CLUBS, Neighborhood Markets, and Wal-Mart stores in the United States.

A key contributor to Wal-Mart's success is its inventory control and distribution system. Using satellite technology, the company receives 8.4 million updates every minute on what items customers buy and the relationship among the items sold to each person. This allows stores to keep shelves stocked with exactly what the customers want, while still keeping inventory under control.

Wal-Mart improved on this inventory control in 2004 with the introduction of electronic product codes (EPCs). Similar to bar codes, which tell a retailer the number of boxes of a specific product it has, EPCs distinguish one box of a specific product from another box. This allows retailers to better monitor product inventory from supplier to distribution centre to store.

As of January 2005, more than 130 Wal-Mart suppliers were putting EPC tags on cases and pallets being shipped to Wal-Mart. The tags use radio frequency identification (RFID) technology. The RFID tags are passed by a special reader, which receives and transmits their unique product identifier codes to an inventory control system. RFID readers installed at distribution centres will automatically let Wal-Mart's operations and merchandising teams, as well as suppliers, know that this exact shipment has arrived. The readers installed at stores will automatically confirm that the shipment is in the back room. Individual products will then be stocked as needed.

There are plans to use EPC in 13 distribution centres and 600 Wal-Mart and SAM'S CLUB stores by October 2005, with another 200 suppliers beginning to tag cases and pallets in January 2006. Wal-Mart Canada is watching developments in the United States but is not planning to introduce EPCs here just yet.

the navigator

Wal-Mart: www.walmart.com

THE NAVIGATOR

- [ ] Read *Feature Story*
- [ ] Scan *Study Objectives*
- [ ] Read *Chapter Preview*
- [ ] Read text and answer *Before You Go On*
- [ ] Work *Using the Decision Toolkit*
- [ ] Review *Summary of Study Objectives*
- [ ] Review the *Decision Toolkit—A Summary*
- [ ] Work *Demonstration Problem*
- [ ] Answer *Self-Study Questions*
- [ ] Complete assignments

STUDY OBJECTIVES

After studying this chapter, you should be able to:

1. Identify the differences between service and merchandising companies.
2. Explain the recording of purchases under a perpetual inventory system.
3. Explain the recording of sales under a perpetual inventory system.
4. Distinguish between a single-step and a multiple-step statement of earnings.
5. Calculate the gross profit margin and profit margin.
6. Explain the recording of purchases and sales under a periodic inventory system (Appendix 5A).

the navigator

The first four chapters of this text focused mostly on service companies. In this and the next chapter, we turn our attention to merchandising companies. Merchandising companies, such as Wal-Mart discussed in our feature story, buy and sell merchandise for profit rather than perform a service.

In this chapter, you will learn the basics about accounting for merchandising transactions. In addition, you will learn how to prepare and analyze a commonly used form of the statement of earnings—the multiple-step statement of earnings.

The chapter is organized as follows:

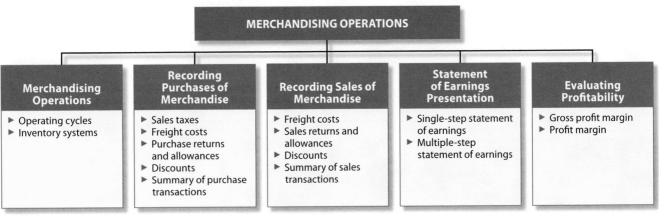

MERCHANDISING OPERATIONS

Merchandising Operations	Recording Purchases of Merchandise	Recording Sales of Merchandise	Statement of Earnings Presentation	Evaluating Profitability
▶ Operating cycles ▶ Inventory systems	▶ Sales taxes ▶ Freight costs ▶ Purchase returns and allowances ▶ Discounts ▶ Summary of purchase transactions	▶ Freight costs ▶ Sales returns and allowances ▶ Discounts ▶ Summary of sales transactions	▶ Single-step statement of earnings ▶ Multiple-step statement of earnings	▶ Gross profit margin ▶ Profit margin

the navigator

Merchandising Operations

study objective 1

Identify the differences between service and merchandising companies.

Merchandising involves purchasing products—also called merchandise inventory or just inventory—to resell to customers. Merchandising is one of the largest and most influential industries in Canada. The total value of merchandise available for sale at the end of 2004 in this country was $62.6 billion.

Measuring net earnings for a merchandising company is basically the same as for a service company. That is, net earnings (or loss) results when expenses are matched with revenues. In a merchandising company, the main source of revenue is the sale of merchandise, often referred to simply as **sales revenue**. Unlike expenses for a service company, expenses for a merchandising company are divided into two categories: (1) cost of goods sold and (2) operating expenses.

The **cost of goods sold** is the total cost of merchandise sold during the period. This expense is directly related to the revenue recognized from the sale of goods. Sales revenue less the cost of goods sold is called **gross profit**. For example, as mentioned in the feature story, Wal-Mart reported sales revenue of U.S. $256 billion in 2004. It cost Wal-Mart U.S. $195 billion to purchase this merchandise, so the company earned a gross profit of $61 billion ($256 billion – $195 billion) on these sales.

After gross profit is calculated, operating expenses are deducted to determine earnings before income tax. **Operating expenses** are expenses that are incurred in the process of earning sales revenue. The operating expenses of a merchandising company include many of the same expenses found in a service company, such as salaries, insurance, utilities, and amortization.

Then, as is done for a service company, income tax expense is deducted from earnings before income tax to determine net earnings (loss). The earnings measurement process for a merchandising company is shown in Illustration 5-1. The items in the two blue boxes are unique to a merchandising company; they are not used by a service company.

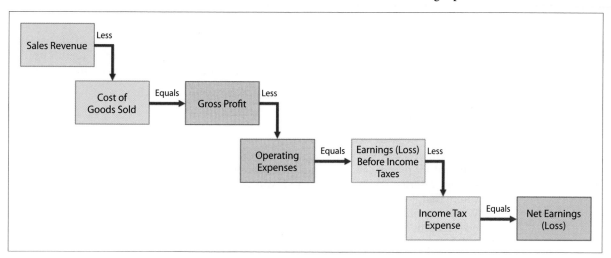

Illustration 5-1 ▲

Earnings measurement process for a merchandising company

Operating Cycles

The **operating cycle**—the time it takes to go from cash to cash in producing revenues—is usually longer for a merchandising company than it is for a service company. The purchase of merchandise inventory and the lapse of time until it is sold lengthen the cycle. The operating cycles of service and merchandising companies can be contrasted as shown in Illustration 5-2. Note that a merchandising company has an additional account: Merchandise Inventory.

Illustration 5-2 ◀

Operating cycles for service and merchandising companies

Service Company

Receive cash · Perform services · Cash · Accounts Receivable · Pay to the order of

Merchandising Company

Receive cash · Buy inventory · Cash · Sell inventory · Accounts Receivable · Merchandise Inventory · Pay to the order of

Inventory Systems

A merchandising company keeps track of its inventory to determine what is available for sale (inventory) and what has been sold (cost of goods sold). One of two kinds of systems is used to account for inventory and the cost of goods sold: a **perpetual inventory system** or a **periodic inventory system**.

Perpetual Inventory System

In a **perpetual inventory system**, detailed records of the cost of each product purchased and sold are maintained. These records continuously—perpetually—show the quantity and cost of the inventory purchased, sold, and on hand. By using the sophisticated electronic inventory system described in the feature story, Wal-Mart knows the quantity, cost, and location of every item that it buys and sells.

When inventory items are purchased under a perpetual inventory system, the item purchased is recorded by debiting (increasing) a merchandise inventory account. Not all purchases are debited to Merchandise Inventory, however. Purchases of assets that the company will use rather than resell, such as supplies and equipment, are recorded as increases to specific asset accounts rather than as increases to the Merchandise Inventory account. For example, Wal-Mart would increase the Supplies account to record the purchase of materials used to make shelf signs or for cash register receipt paper.

When merchandise inventory is later sold, the cost of the goods sold (the original purchase cost of the merchandise) is taken from the inventory records. This cost is transferred from the account Merchandise Inventory (an asset) to the account Cost of Goods Sold (an expense). Under a perpetual inventory system, the cost of goods sold and reduction in inventory—both in quantity and cost—are recorded each time a sale occurs.

Inventory is usually the largest current asset for a merchandiser. Effective control over the merchandise on hand is an important feature of a perpetual inventory system. Since the inventory records show the quantities that should be on hand, the merchandise can be counted at any time to see whether the amount of the merchandise actually on hand matches the inventory records. Any shortages that are found can be investigated. For control purposes, a physical inventory count is always taken at least once a year under the perpetual inventory system. We will learn more about physical inventory counts later in this chapter and in the next one.

Periodic Inventory System

In a **periodic inventory system**, detailed inventory records of the merchandise on hand are not kept throughout the period. The **cost of goods sold is determined only at the end of the accounting period**—that is, periodically—when a physical inventory count is done to determine the cost of the goods on hand.

Once the cost of the goods on hand (inventory) at the end of the period has been determined, we can calculate the cost of the goods sold. To determine the cost of goods sold under a periodic inventory system, the following steps are necessary:

1. Beginning inventory: Determine the cost of goods on hand at the beginning of the accounting period.
2. Cost of goods available for sale: Add the cost of goods purchased to the beginning inventory. The total is the cost of goods available for sale during the period.
3. Ending inventory: Subtract the cost of goods on hand at the end of the accounting period from the cost of goods available for sale. The result is the cost of goods sold.

Illustration 5-3 gives the formula to calculate the cost of goods sold.

Illustration 5-3 ▶

Formula for cost of goods sold

Because the perpetual inventory system is most widely used, we illustrate it in this chapter. The periodic inventory system, still used by some companies, is described in the appendix to this chapter.

ACCOUNTING MATTERS! Investor Perspective

When snowboard maker Morrow Snowboards, Inc., issued shares to the public for the first time, some investors were reluctant to invest in Morrow because of a number of internal control problems. To reduce investor concerns, Morrow began using a perpetual inventory system to improve its control over inventory. It promised that it would perform a physical inventory count every quarter to ensure that the perpetual inventory system was reliable.

Recording Purchases of Merchandise

Purchases of inventory can be made for cash or on account (credit). Purchases are normally recorded by the buyer when the goods are received from the seller. Every purchase should be supported by a document that provides written evidence of the transaction. In larger companies, when orders are placed with a supplier, each order is documented with a **purchase order**.

Cash purchases should be supported by a cash register receipt indicating the items purchased and amounts paid. Cash purchases are recorded by an increase (debit) in Merchandise Inventory and a decrease (credit) in Cash.

Credit purchases should be supported by a **purchase invoice** that indicates the total purchase price and other relevant information. The buyer does not prepare a separate purchase invoice. Instead, an invoice is prepared by the seller. The original copy of the invoice goes to the buyer to be used as a purchase invoice, and a copy is kept by the seller to be used as a sales invoice. In Illustration 5-4, for example, the sales invoice prepared by PW Audio Supply, Inc. (the seller) is used as a purchase invoice by Sauk Stereo Ltd. (the buyer).

study objective 2

Explain the recording of purchases under a perpetual inventory system.

Illustration 5-4 ◄

Sales/purchase invoice

INVOICE NO. 731

PW Audio Supply, Inc.
277 Wellington Street, West
Toronto, Ontario, M5V 3H2

▼

Firm name:	Sauk Stereo Ltd.	
Attention of:	James Hoover, Purchasing Agent	
Address:	21 King Street, West	
	Hamilton	Ontario	L8P 4W7
	City	Province	Postal Code

S O L D T O

Date: May 4, 2006	Salesperson: Malone	Terms 2/10, n/30	FOB shipping point

Catalogue No.	Description	Quantity	Price	Amount
X572Y9820	Printed Circuit Board-prototype	1	2,300	$2,300
A2547Z45	Production Model Circuits	5	300	1,500

IMPORTANT: ALL RETURNS MUST BE MADE WITHIN 10 DAYS	TOTAL	$3,800

The buyer, Sauk Stereo, would make the following entry to record the purchase of merchandise:

A	=	L
+3,800		+3,800

Cash flows: no effect

May 4	Merchandise Inventory	3,800	
	Accounts Payable		3,800
	(To record goods purchased on account from PW Audio Supply per invoice #731, terms 2/10, n/30)		

Sales Taxes

Sales taxes are collected by most merchandising and service companies on the goods they sell and the services they provide. Sales taxes in Canada include the Goods and Services Tax (GST) and the Provincial Sales Tax (PST). The federal GST is assessed at a rate of 7% across Canada. Provincial sales tax rates vary throughout the provinces and territories. In the Atlantic provinces (except for P.E.I.), GST and PST have been combined into one 15% tax, called the Harmonized Sales Tax (HST).

Although a company collects these sales taxes when it makes a sale, sales taxes are not revenue to the company. These amounts are collected "in trust" for the federal and provincial governments and must be periodically remitted to the Receiver General, or another collecting authority. Until then, they are a current liability of the company.

Sales taxes add much complexity to the accounting process. In addition, not all companies and not all goods and services are taxable. Accounting transactions described in this and other chapters are therefore presented without the added complication of sales taxes. That is why Invoice No. 731 in Illustration 5-4 did not include sales taxes, which would normally be added to the invoice price.

Freight Costs

The sales/purchase invoice should indicate whether the seller or the buyer must pay the cost of transporting the goods to the buyer's place of business. Freight terms may vary, but they generally say who pays the freight and who is responsible for the risk of damage to the merchandise during transit. Terms are often expressed as either FOB shipping point or FOB destination. The letters FOB mean "free on board."

FOB shipping point means that the goods are delivered to the point of shipping (normally the seller's place of business) by the seller. The buyer pays the freight costs to get the goods from the point of shipping to the destination (normally the buyer's place of business). Conversely, **FOB destination** means that the goods are delivered by the seller to their destination. The seller pays the freight to get the goods from the point of shipping to their destination.

Dell Canada normally sells its computers FOB shipping point. However, it has a temporary promotion available where it will pay the shipping costs for on-line orders of computers—changing its shipping terms to FOB destination. Illustration 5-5 illustrates these shipping terms.

Illustration 5-5 ▶

Freight terms

The purchase invoice in Illustration 5-4 indicates that the freight terms are FOB shipping point. Thus, the buyer (Sauk Stereo) pays the freight charges and merchandise inventory is increased (debited) for the additional cost. **Any freight paid by the buyer is part of the cost of the merchandise purchased.**

For example, if upon delivery of the goods on May 4, Sauk Stereo (the buyer) pays Fast Freight Corporation $150 for freight charges, the entry on Sauk's books is:

May 4	Merchandise Inventory	150	
	Cash		150
	(To record payment of freight on goods purchased)		

A = L + SE
+150
−150
↓ Cash flows: −150

Purchase Returns and Allowances

A purchaser may be dissatisfied with the merchandise received. The goods may be damaged or defective, of inferior quality, or might not fit the buyer's specifications. In such cases, the buyer may return the goods to the seller. The buyer will receive a cash refund if the purchase was made for cash. Credit is granted if the purchase was made on account.

Alternatively, the buyer may choose to keep the merchandise if the seller is willing to grant an allowance (deduction) from the purchase price. These types of transactions are known as **purchase returns and allowances**.

Assume that Sauk Stereo returned goods costing $300 to PW Audio Supply on May 8. The entry by Sauk Stereo for the returned merchandise is:

May 8	Accounts Payable	300	
	Merchandise Inventory		300
	(To record return of goods to PW Audio Supply)		

A = L + SE
−300 −300
Cash flows: no effect

Because Sauk Stereo increased Merchandise Inventory when the goods were received, Merchandise Inventory is decreased when it returns the goods, or is granted an allowance.

Discounts

The terms of a purchase may include an offer of a **quantity discount** for a bulk purchase. A quantity discount gives a reduction in price according to the volume of the purchase. Quantity discounts are not recorded or accounted for separately. For example, PW Audio Supply may offer a 10% price discount on orders of 25 or more items. So, if 25 printed circuit boards were ordered, the price per board would be $2,070 ($2,300 × 90%) rather than $2,300. Only the $2,070 amount would be recorded by Sauk Stereo.

Quantity discounts are not the same as a **purchase discount**, which is offered to customers for early payment of the balance due. A purchase discount offers advantages to both parties: the purchaser saves money, and the seller is able to shorten the operating cycle by converting accounts receivable into cash earlier.

Purchase discounts are noted on the invoice through credit terms. These terms specify the amount of the discount and the time period during which it is offered. They also indicate the date by which the purchaser is expected to pay the full invoice price. In the sales invoice in Illustration 5-4, credit terms are 2/10, n/30, which is read "two-ten, net thirty." This means that a 2% cash discount may be taken on the invoice price, less ("net of") any returns or allowances, if payment is made within 10 days of the invoice date (the discount period). Otherwise, the invoice price, less any returns or allowances, is due 30 days from the invoice date.

When the seller chooses not to offer a discount for fast payment, credit terms will specify only the maximum time period for paying the balance due. For example, the time period may be stated as n/30, meaning that the net amount must be paid in 30 days.

In contrast to quantity discounts, purchase discounts are recorded separately. When an invoice is paid within the discount period, the amount of the discount decreases the merchandise inventory account. By paying within the discount period, the merchandiser has reduced the cost of its inventory.

To illustrate, assume Sauk Stereo pays the balance due of $3,500 (gross invoice price of $3,800 less purchase returns and allowances of $300) on May 14, the last day of the discount period. Note that discounts are not taken on freight costs. The discount is $70 ($3,500 × 2%), and the amount of cash paid by Sauk Stereo is $3,430 ($3,500 − $70). The entry to record the May 14 payment by Sauk Stereo is:

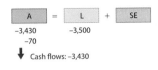

-3,430
-70

▼ Cash flows: -3,430

May 14	Accounts Payable	3,500	
	Cash		3,430
	Merchandise Inventory		70
	(To record payment to PW Audio Supply within discount period)		

A merchandising company should usually take all available purchase discounts. Passing up the discount may be viewed as paying interest for use of the money. For example, if Sauk Stereo passed up the discount, it would be paying 2% for the use of $3,500 for 20 days. This equals an annual interest rate of 36.5% (2% × 365 ÷ 20). Obviously, it would be better for Sauk Stereo to borrow at bank interest rates than to lose the discount.

Summary of Purchase Transactions

A summary of the effect of the previous transactions on merchandise inventory is provided in the following T account (with transaction descriptions in parentheses). Sauk originally purchased $3,800 worth of inventory for resale. It paid $150 in freight charges. It then returned $300 worth of goods. Finally, it received a $70 discount off the balance owed because it paid within the discount period. This results in a balance in the Merchandise Inventory account of $3,580.

		Merchandise Inventory			
(Purchase)	May 4	3,800	May 8	300	(Purchase return)
(Freight)	4	150	14	70	(Purchase discount)
	Bal.	3,580			

BEFORE YOU GO ON . . .

▶Review It

1. How does the measurement of net earnings in a merchandising company differ from its measurement in a service company?
2. How does a perpetual inventory system differ from a periodic system?
3. Under the perpetual inventory system, what entries (if any) are made to record purchases, freight costs, purchase returns and allowances, quantity discounts, and purchase discounts?

Recording Sales of Merchandise

study objective 3

Explain the recording of sales under a perpetual inventory system.

Sales revenues, like service revenues, are recorded when earned in order to comply with the revenue recognition principle. Typically, sales revenues are earned when the goods are transferred from the seller to the buyer. At this point, the sales transaction is completed and the sales price is established.

Sales may be made for cash or credit. Every sales transaction should be supported by a business document that provides written evidence of the sale. Cash register tapes provide evidence of cash sales. A **sales invoice**, like the one that was shown in Illustration 5-4, provides support for a credit sale.

Two entries are made for each sale in a perpetual inventory system. The first entry records the sales revenue: Cash or Accounts Receivable is increased by a debit and Sales is increased by a credit for the selling (invoice) price of the goods. The second entry records the cost of the merchandise sold: Cost of Goods Sold is increased by a debit and Merchandise Inventory is decreased by a credit for the cost of the goods. As a result, at all times Merchandise Inventory will show the amount of inventory that should be on hand.

To illustrate a credit sales transaction, we will use the sales invoice shown earlier in Illustration 5-4 for PW Audio Supply's sale of $3,800 of merchandise on May 4 to Sauk Stereo. Assume the merchandise cost PW Audio Supply $2,400 when it was originally purchased. The sale is recorded as follows:

May	4	Accounts Receivable	3,800	
		Sales		3,800
		(To record credit sale to Sauk Stereo per invoice #731, terms 2/10, n/30)		
	4	Cost of Goods Sold	2,400	
		Merchandise Inventory		2,400
		(To record cost of merchandise sold on invoice #731 to Sauk Stereo)		

A = L + SE
+3,800   +3,800
Cash flows: no effect

A = L + SE
−2,400   −2,400
Cash flows: no effect

For internal decision-making purposes, merchandising companies may use more than one sales account. For example, PW Audio Supply may decide to keep separate sales accounts for its sales of televisions, CD players, and DVD players. By using separate sales accounts for major product lines, rather than a single combined sales account, company management can monitor sales trends more closely and respond more strategically to changes in sales patterns. For example, if DVD player sales are increasing while CD player sales are decreasing, the company should re-evaluate both its advertising and pricing policies on each of these items to ensure that they are optimal.

On its statement of earnings presented to outside investors, a merchandising company would normally provide only a single sales figure—the sum of all of its individual sales accounts. This is done for two reasons. First, providing detail on all of its individual sales accounts would make its statement of earnings much longer. Second, companies do not want their competitors to know the details of their operating results.

Freight Costs

As discussed earlier in the chapter, freight terms on the sales invoice—FOB destination and FOB shipping point—indicate who is responsible for shipping costs. If the term is FOB destination, the seller assumes the responsibility for getting the goods to their intended destination. Freight costs incurred by the seller on outgoing merchandise are an operating expense to the seller. These costs are debited to the account Freight Out or Delivery Expense. When the freight charges are paid by the seller, the seller will usually set a higher invoice price for the goods to cover the cost of shipping.

The Freight *Out* account is used to record shipping costs paid on outgoing merchandise by the seller. Later, in the appendix to this chapter, we will learn about the account Freight *In*, which is used in a periodic inventory system to record shipping costs paid on incoming merchandise by the buyer.

In PW Audio Supply's sale of electronic equipment to Sauk Stereo, the freight terms (FOB shipping point) indicate that Sauk Stereo (the buyer) must pay the cost of shipping the goods from the shipping point to their destination. PW Audio Supply makes no journal entry to record the cost of shipping, since this cost was incurred by the buyer and not the seller.

Sales Returns and Allowances

We now look at the "flip side" of purchase returns and allowances, which are recorded as **sales returns and allowances** on the books of the seller.

Just as a sale requires two entries, so too will returns and allowances. PW Audio Supply prepares the two separate journal entries shown below to record the $300 credit for goods returned by Sauk. The first entry records an increase (debit) in Sales Returns and Allowances and a decrease (credit) in Accounts Receivable for the $300 selling price. The second entry records an increase (debit) in Merchandise Inventory (assume a $140 cost) and a decrease (credit) in Cost of Goods Sold. This second entry assumes that the merchandise is not damaged and is resalable. Otherwise, a loss account would be debited rather than an inventory account.

A	=	L	+	SE
−300				−300

Cash flows: no effect

A	=	L	+	SE
+140				+140

Cash flows: no effect

May	8	Sales Returns and Allowances	300	
		Accounts Receivable		300
		(To record return of goods by Sauk Stereo)		
	8	Merchandise Inventory	140	
		Cost of Goods Sold		140
		(To record cost of merchandise returned by Sauk Stereo)		

Sales Returns and Allowances is a **contra revenue account** to Sales. The normal balance of the Sales Returns and Allowances account is a debit. A contra account is used, instead of debiting the Sales account, to disclose the amount of sales returns and allowances. A decrease (debit) recorded directly to Sales would hide the percentage of total sales that ends up being lost through sales returns and allowances. It could also distort comparisons between total sales in different accounting periods.

This information is important to management. Excessive returns and allowances suggest inferior merchandise, inefficiencies in filling orders, errors in billing customers, or mistakes in the delivery or shipment of goods. Wal-Mart carefully monitors and streamlines its returns through the use of its electronic product codes, as described in the feature story.

ACCOUNTING MATTERS!   Management Perspective

For retailers, sales returns are a big headache—one that becomes worse during the holidays when customers return unwanted gifts. Between 5 and 30 percent of sales end up being returned. On-line retailers lean toward the higher return rate, while bricks and mortar stores lean toward the lower return rate. Retailers are trying to regain control over the return issue. Some companies have tightened their return policies, some are charging restocking fees, many are using technology to better understand and control returns, and others have turned to specialists for help.

Hudson's Bay, Canadian Tire, and Best Buy Canada, for example, ship returns to Genco Distribution Systems, which manages the returns for each of the retailers. Depending on the condition of the goods, Genco decides whether to ship them back to suppliers, sell them to discount dealers, or give them to charity. Lori DeCou, spokesperson for Best Buy Canada, speaks highly of using third-party specialists such as Genco. "It absolutely has resulted in a cost saving to the company," she says.

Source: Marina Strauss, "Retailers Tackle Thorny Problem of Returns," *The Globe and Mail*, January 19, 2004, B6.

Discounts

Quantity discounts and sales discounts given on invoice prices affect the seller, as well as the buyer. No separate entry is made to record a **quantity discount**. Sales are recorded at the invoice price—whether it is the full retail price, a sale price, or a volume discount price.

Like a purchase discount, the seller may offer the buyer a cash discount for quick payment of the balance due. From the seller's point of view, this is called a **sales discount** and is offered on the invoice price less returns and allowances, if any.

Although no new account is added to record purchase discounts in a perpetual inventory system—the discount is recorded as a reduction in the Merchandise Inventory account—a new account, called Sales Discounts, is added to record sales discounts. Like the account for sales returns and allowances, Sales Discounts is a **contra revenue account** to Sales. Its normal balance is a debit. This account is used, instead of debiting Sales, to show the amount of cash discounts taken by customers.

The entry by PW Audio Supply to record the cash receipt on May 14 from Sauk Stereo within the discount period is:

A	=	L	+	SE
+3,430				−70
−3,500				

 Cash flows: +3,430

May 14	Cash	3,430	
	Sales Discounts ($3,500 × 2%)	70	
	Accounts Receivable ($3,800 − $300)		3,500
	(To record collection from Sauk Stereo within 2/10, n/30 discount period)		

Summary of Sales Transactions

A summary of the effects of the previous transactions on Sales, and its contra accounts, is provided in the following T accounts. PW Audio Supply sold merchandise for $3,800, and $300 of it was later returned. A sales discount of $70 was granted when the invoice was paid within the discount period. In contrast to the purchase transactions illustrated on p. 220, which affected only one account, Merchandise Inventory, sales transactions are recorded in different accounts.

	Sales			Sales Returns and Allowances	
	May 4	3,800	May 8	300	

	Sales Discounts	
May 14	70	

BEFORE YOU GO ON . . .

► Review It

(a) Under a perpetual inventory system, what are the two entries that must be recorded for each sale and sales return?

(b) Why is it important to use contra revenue accounts such as Sales Returns and Allowances and Sales Discounts, rather than simply reduce the Sales account, when goods are returned or sold with a discount payment period?

► Do It

On September 5, Guerette Corp. buys merchandise on account from Lalonde Ltd., terms 1/10, n/30. The selling price of the goods is $1,500, and the cost to Lalonde was $800. On September 8, goods with a selling price of $300 and a cost of $140 are returned and restored to inventory. On September 15, Geurette pays its account in full. Record the transactions on the books of both companies.

Action Plan

• Buyer: Record purchases of inventory at cost. Reduce the Merchandise Inventory account for returned goods.

• Seller: Record two entries for the sale and return of goods: (1) record the selling price and (2) record the cost of the sale. Record the selling price of returns in the contra account Sales Returns and Allowances.

Solution

Guerette Corp. (Buyer)

Sept. 5	Merchandise Inventory		1,500	
	Accounts Payable			1,500
	(To record goods purchased on account from Lalonde Ltd., terms 1/10, n/30)			
8	Accounts Payable		300	
	Merchandise Inventory			300
	(To record return of goods to Lalonde)			
15	Accounts Payable ($1,500 − $300)		1,200	
	Merchandise Inventory ($1,500 − $300) × 1%)			12
	Cash ($1,200 − $12)			1,188
	(To record payment to Lalonde within discount period)			

Lalonde Ltd. (Seller)

Sept. 5	Accounts Receivable		1,500	
	Sales			1,500
	(To record credit sale to Guerette Corp., terms 1/10, n/30)			
5	Cost of Goods Sold		800	
	Merchandise Inventory			800
	(To record cost of goods sold to Guerette)			

Sept. 8	Sales Returns and Allowances	300	
	Accounts Receivable		300
	(To record credit granted for receipt of returned goods from Guerette)		
8	Merchandise Inventory	140	
	Cost of Goods Sold		140
	(To record cost of goods returned from Guerette)		
15	Cash ($1,200 − $12)	1,188	
	Sales Discounts ($1,500 − $300) × 1%)	12	
	Accounts Receivable ($1,500 − $300)		1,200
	(To record collection from Guerette within discount period)		

Statement of Earnings Presentation

Merchandisers use the classified balance sheet introduced in Chapter 2. In addition, two forms of the statement of earnings are widely used by merchandising companies. One is the **single-step statement of earnings**. It has this name because only one step—subtracting total expenses from total revenues—is required for determining earnings before income tax. A second form of the statement of earnings is the **multiple-step statement of earnings**. This statement gets its name because it shows multiple steps in determining earnings before income tax. We will look at each of these statement forms in the following sections.

Single-Step Statement of Earnings

In a **single-step statement of earnings**, all data are classified into two categories: (1) revenues and (2) expenses. The revenues category includes operating revenues (e.g., sales) and non-operating revenues (e.g., interest revenue and a gain on sale of equipment). The expenses category includes cost of goods sold, operating expenses, and non-operating expenses (e.g., interest expense and a loss on the sale of equipment). Income tax expense is usually disclosed separately from the other expenses.

A condensed single-step statement of earnings for PW Audio Supply, Inc., using assumed data, is shown in Illustration 5-6.

Illustration 5-6 ▶

Single-step statement of earnings

PW AUDIO SUPPLY, INC. Statement of Earnings Year Ended December 31, 2006		
Revenues		
Net sales	$460,000	
Interest revenue	3,000	
Gain on sale of equipment	600	$463,600
Expenses		
Cost of goods sold	$316,000	
Operating expenses	114,000	
Interest expense	1,800	
Casualty loss from vandalism	200	432,000
Earnings before income tax		31,600
Income tax expense		6,300
Net earnings		$ 25,300

The single-step statement of earnings is the form we have used in the text so far. There are two main reasons for using the single-step form: (1) a company does not realize any type of profit or earnings until total revenues exceed total expenses, so it makes sense to divide the statement into these two categories; and (2) the single-step form is simple and easy to read.

Multiple-Step Statement of Earnings

The **multiple-step statement of earnings** shows several steps in determining net earnings (or loss). It is often considered more useful because it separately highlights the components of net earnings and the majority of Canadian companies use this format, or a modified version of it.

The multiple-step statement of earnings shows five main steps:

1. Net sales: Sales returns and allowances and sales discounts are subtracted from gross sales to determine net sales.
2. Gross profit: Cost of goods sold is subtracted from net sales to determine gross profit.
3. Earnings from operations: Operating expenses are deducted from gross profit to determine earnings from operations.
4. Non-operating activities: The results of activities that are not related to operations are added (as other revenue) or subtracted (as other expenses) to determine earnings before income tax.
5. Net earnings: Income tax expense is subtracted from earnings before income tax deducted to determine net earnings (loss).

The first three steps involve the company's principal operating activities. The fourth step distinguishes between **operating** and **non-operating activities**. The last step is the same step shown in a single-step statement. We will now look more closely at the components of a multiple-step statement of earnings.

Net Sales

The multiple-step statement of earnings for a merchandising company begins by presenting sales revenues. As contra revenue accounts, sales returns and allowances and sales discounts are deducted from gross sales in the statement of earnings to arrive at **net sales**. The sales revenues section of the statement of earnings for PW Audio Supply, using assumed data, is as follows:

Sales revenues			
Sales			$480,000
Less:	Sales returns and allowances	$12,000	
	Sales discounts	8,000	20,000
Net sales			460,000

This presentation shows the key aspects of the company's main revenue-producing activities. Many companies condense this information and report only the net sales figure in their statement of earnings.

Gross Profit

From Illustration 5-1, you learned that the cost of goods sold is deducted from net sales to determine **gross profit**. Based on the sales data presented above (net sales of $460,000) and an assumed cost of goods sold amount of $316,000, the gross profit for PW Audio Supply is $144,000, calculated as follows:

Alternative Terminology
Gross profit is sometimes referred to as *gross margin*.

Net sales	$460,000
Cost of goods sold	316,000
Gross profit	144,000

Earnings from Operations

Operating expenses are the next component in measuring net earnings for a merchandising company. As indicated earlier, these expenses are similar in merchandising and service companies. **Earnings from operations**, or the results of the company's normal operating activities, are calculated by subtracting operating expenses from gross profit.

At PW Audio Supply, operating expenses are assumed to be $114,000. Thus, its earnings from operations are $30,000, as shown below:

Gross profit	$144,000
Operating expenses	114,000
Earnings from operations	30,000

Sometimes operating expenses are subdivided into selling expenses and administrative expenses. **Selling expenses** are associated with making sales. They include advertising expenses as well as the expenses of completing the sale, such as delivery and shipping expenses. **Administrative expenses** relate to general operating activities such as management, accounting, and legal matters.

Non-Operating Activities

Non-operating activities consist of other revenues and expenses that are unrelated to the company's main operations. When a company has non-operating activities, they are presented in the statement of earnings right after "earnings from operations." The distinction between operating and non-operating activities is crucial to many external users of financial data. Earnings from operations are viewed as sustainable and therefore long-term, and non-operating activities are viewed as nonrecurring and therefore short-term.

Examples of non-operating activities, separated into two sections—other revenues and other expenses—are shown in Illustration 5-7:

Illustration 5-7 ▶

Non-operating activities

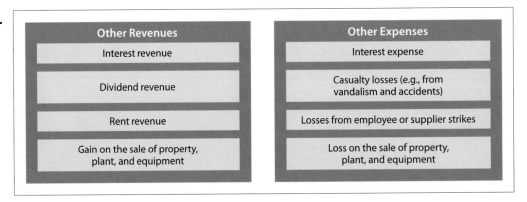

PW Audio Supply's non-operating activities, using assumed data, are presented below. Depending on whether the non-operating activities result in a net increase (other revenues exceed other expenses) or net decrease (other expenses exceed other revenues), they are added or deducted from the earnings from operations. The result is earnings before income tax.

Earnings from operations		$30,000
Other revenues		
Interest revenue	$3,000	
Gain on sale of equipment	600	
Total non-operating revenues	3,600	
Other expenses		
Interest expense	$1,800	
Casualty loss from vandalism	200	
Total non-operating expenses	2,000	
Net non-operating revenue		1,600
Earnings before income tax		31,600

If there are no non-operating activities, earnings from operations will be the same as earnings before income tax.

Net Earnings

Net earnings is the final outcome of all the company's operating and non-operating activities. PW Audio Supply's net earnings are $25,300 after deducting its income tax expense of $6,300:

Earnings before income tax	$31,600
Income tax expense	6,300
Net earnings	$25,300

In Illustration 5-8, we bring together all the steps above in a comprehensive multiple-step statement of earnings for PW Audio Supply. Note that the net earnings in Illustrations 5-8 (multiple-step) and 5-6 (single-step) are the same. The differences between the two statements of earnings concern the amount of detail displayed and the order of presentation.

PW AUDIO SUPPLY, INC.
Statement of Earnings
Year Ended December 31, 2006

Sales revenues		
Sales		$480,000
Less: Sales returns and allowances	$12,000	
Sales discounts	8,000	20,000
Net sales		460,000
Cost of goods sold		316,000
Gross profit		144,000
Operating expenses		
Salaries expense	$45,000	
Rent expense	19,000	
Utilities expense	17,000	
Advertising expense	16,000	
Amortization expense	8,000	
Freight out	7,000	
Insurance expense	2,000	
Total operating expenses		114,000
Earnings from operations		30,000
Other revenues		
Interest revenue	$ 3,000	
Gain on sale of equipment	600	
	3,600	
Other expenses		
Interest expense	$ 1,800	
Casualty loss from vandalism	200	
	2,000	1,600
Earnings before income tax		31,600
Income tax expense		6,300
Net earnings		$ 25,300

Illustration 5-8 ◄

Multiple-step statement of earnings

ACCOUNTING MATTERS! Ethics Perspective

Things couldn't be stickier for Krispy Kreme Doughnuts Inc. A class action lawsuit by shareholders alleges that the company tried to hide a declining sales demand by shipping more doughnuts than customers ordered at the end of the quarter. Unsold doughnuts were then shipped back after the quarter ended, the suit alleges. This had the impact of temporarily increasing sales and net earnings and leading investors to believe that the company would continue to grow. Instead, it is now believed that Krispy Kreme is suffering from poor sales performance because of the trend toward low-fat, low-carbohydrate diets, such as the South Beach and Atkins diets.

Source: Barrie McKenna, "Krispy Kreme Hires Corporate Fixer," *Globe and Mail*, January 5, 2005, B9.

BEFORE YOU GO ON . . .

▶Review It

1. How does a single-step statement of earnings differ from a multiple-step statement?
2. How are sales and contra revenue accounts reported in the statement of earnings?
3. What is the significance of gross profit?
4. How do operating activities differ from non-operating activities?
5. Does Loblaw use a single-step or multiple-step statement of earnings? The answer to this question is at the end of the chapter.

▶Do It

Abela Corporation reported the following selected information:

Cost of goods sold	$619,000
Income tax expense	11,500
Interest expense	2,000
Operating expenses	161,000
Rent revenue	18,000
Sales	910,000
Sales returns and allowances	85,000
Sales discounts	15,000

Calculate the following amounts for Abela Corporation: (a) net sales, (b) gross profit, (c) earnings from operations, (d) earnings before income tax, and (e) net earnings.

Action Plan

- Separate the items into operating and non-operating (other revenues and other expenses).
- Recall the formula for net sales: Sales − sales returns and allowances − sales discounts.
- Recall the formula for gross profit: Net sales − cost of goods sold.
- Recall the formula for earnings from operations: Gross profit − operating expenses.
- Recall the formula for earnings before income tax: Earnings from operations + other revenue − other expenses.
- Recall the formula for net earnings: Earnings before income tax − income tax expense.

Solution

(a) Net sales: $910,000 − $85,000 − $15,000 = $810,000
(b) Gross profit: $810,000 − $619,000 = $191,000
(c) Earnings from operations: $191,000 − $161,000 = $30,000
(d) Earnings before income tax: $30,000 + $18,000 − $2,000 = $46,000
(e) Net earnings: $46,000 − $11,500 = $34,500

Evaluating Profitability

study objective 5

Calculate the gross profit margin and profit margin.

In Chapter 2, we learned about two profitability ratios: earnings per share and the price-earnings ratio. We add two more examples of profitability ratios in this chapter: the gross profit margin and the profit margin.

Gross Profit Margin

A company's gross profit may be expressed as a percentage, called the **gross profit margin**. This is done by dividing the amount of gross profit by net sales. For PW Audio Supply, the gross profit margin is 31.3% ($144,000 ÷ $460,000). The gross profit *margin* is generally considered more informative than the gross profit *amount*, because it expresses a more meaningful relationship between gross profit and net sales. For example, a gross profit amount of $1 million may sound impressive. But if it is the result of sales of $100 million, the company's gross profit margin is only 1%.

Gross profit represents the merchandising profit of a company. It is not a measure of the overall profit of a company, because operating expenses have not been deducted. Nevertheless, the amount and trend of gross profit are closely watched by management and other interested parties. Comparisons of current gross profit with past amounts and margins, and with those in the industry, indicate the effectiveness of a company's purchasing and pricing policies.

The gross profit margin for Wal-Mart and the retail industry for two recent fiscal years is presented in Illustration 5-9.

GROSS PROFIT MARGIN = $\dfrac{\text{GROSS PROFIT}}{\text{NET SALES}}$		
(in U.S. millions)	2004	2003
Wal-Mart	$\dfrac{\$57,582}{\$256,329} = 22.5\%$	$\dfrac{\$51,317}{\$229,616} = 22.3\%$
Industry average	24.6%	37.3%

Illustration 5-9 ◀

Gross profit margin

Wal-Mart's gross profit margin improved marginally in 2004, from 22.3% to 22.5%. The company explains the reason for this change in its Management Discussion and Analysis (MD&A): "This increase in gross margin occurred primarily due to a favorable shift in mix of products sold and our global sourcing efforts (which resulted in lower cost for merchandise sold), offset by increased apparel markdowns (price reductions) in the second half of the year."

At first glance, it might seem surprising that Wal-Mart has a lower gross profit margin than the industry average. It is likely, however, that this can be explained by the fact that grocery products are becoming an increasingly large component of Wal-Mart's sales. In fact, in its MD&A, Wal-Mart says, "we expect that food sales will increase as a percentage of our total net sales. Because food items generally carry a lower gross margin than our other merchandise, increasing food sales tends to have an unfavorable impact on our total gross margin."

Normally, we would compare Wal-Mart's gross profit margin to that of a competitor, such as Hudson's Bay. However, The Bay, like many Canadian companies, does not report gross profit separately on its statement of earnings. Rather, it combines the cost of goods sold with its operating expenses for reporting purposes. Gross profit is considered sensitive information that some companies do not want to make available to their competitors. In fact, less than half of the publicly traded companies in Canada report a separate cost of goods sold figure on their statement of earnings.

Decision Toolkit

Decision Checkpoints	Info Needed for Decision	Tools to Use for Decision	How to Evaluate Results
Is the price of goods keeping pace with changes in the cost of inventory?	Gross profit and net sales	$\text{Gross profit margin} = \dfrac{\text{Gross profit}}{\text{Net sales}}$	A higher ratio suggests the average margin between the selling price and inventory cost is increasing. Too high a margin may result in lost sales.

Profit Margin

Like gross profit, net earnings is often expressed as a percentage of sales. The **profit margin** measures the percentage of each dollar of sales that results in net earnings. It is calculated by dividing net earnings by net sales for the period.

How do the gross profit margin and profit margin differ? The gross profit margin measures the amount by which the selling price is greater than the cost of goods sold. The profit margin measures the extent by which the selling price covers all expenses (including the cost of goods sold). A company can improve its profit margin by increasing its gross profit margin or by controlling its operating expenses (or by doing both).

Profit margins for Wal-Mart and Hudson's Bay, and the industry average, are presented in Illustration 5-10.

Illustration 5-10 ▶

Profit margin

$$\text{PROFIT MARGIN} = \frac{\text{NET EARNINGS}}{\text{NET SALES}}$$

(in U.S. millions)	2004	2003
Wal-Mart	$\frac{\$9,054}{\$256,329} = 3.5\%$	$\frac{\$7,955}{\$229,616} = 3.5\%$
Hudson's Bay	0.9%	1.5%
Industry average	3.5%	2.1%

Wal-Mart generated 3.5 cents on each dollar of sales in both fiscal years. Its profit margin remained unchanged from 2003 to 2004. Although its sales increased, its net earnings increased proportionately, so its cost of goods sold and operating expenses therefore kept the same relationship to its sales revenue.

How does Wal-Mart compare to its competitors? Its profit margin is much higher than that of the Hudson's Bay Company. Although higher than that of the industry in 2003, in 2004 Wal-Mart's profit margin of 3.5 percent was comparable to that of the industry.

The gross profit margin and profit margin are **profitability measures** that both vary according to the specific industry. Businesses with a high turnover of inventory, such as food stores (e.g., Loblaw), generally experience lower gross profit and profit margins. Low-turnover businesses, such as computer services (e.g., Microsoft), have higher gross profit and profit margins. Gross profit margins and profit margins from a variety of industries are shown in Illustration 5-11.

Illustration 5-11 ▼

Gross profit and profit margins by industry

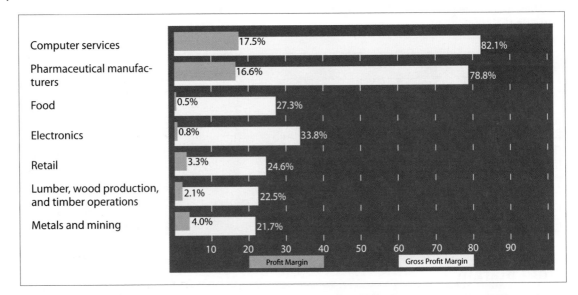

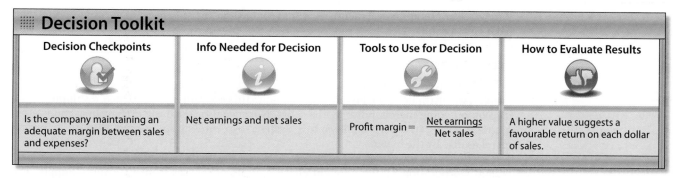

Decision Toolkit

Decision Checkpoints	Info Needed for Decision	Tools to Use for Decision	How to Evaluate Results
Is the company maintaining an adequate margin between sales and expenses?	Net earnings and net sales	$\text{Profit margin} = \dfrac{\text{Net earnings}}{\text{Net sales}}$	A higher value suggests a favourable return on each dollar of sales.

BEFORE YOU GO ON . . .

▶Review It

1. Distinguish between the gross profit margin and profit margin.
2. What is the effect on the profit margin when a company makes its operations more efficient?

the navigator

APPENDIX 5A ▶ PERIODIC INVENTORY SYSTEM

As described in this chapter, there are two basic systems of accounting for inventories: (1) the perpetual inventory system and (2) the periodic inventory system. In the chapter, we focused on the characteristics of the perpetual inventory system. In this appendix, we discuss and illustrate the periodic inventory system.

Explain the recording of purchases and sales under a periodic inventory system.

One key difference between the two systems is when the cost of goods sold is calculated. In a periodic inventory system, revenues from the sale of merchandise are recorded when sales are made, in the same way as in a perpetual inventory system, but on the date of sale the cost of the merchandise sold is not recorded. Instead, a physical inventory count is done at the end of the period to determine the cost of the merchandise on hand. This figure and other information are then used to calculate the cost of the goods sold during the period.

There are other differences between the perpetual and periodic inventory systems. Under a periodic system, purchases of merchandise are recorded in the expense account Purchases rather than the asset account Merchandise Inventory. In addition, freight costs paid by the buyer, purchase returns and allowances, and purchase discounts are all recorded in separate expense and contra expense accounts.

To illustrate the recording of merchandise transactions under a periodic inventory system, we will use purchase and sale transactions between PW Audio Supply, Inc. (the seller), and Sauk Stereo Ltd. (the buyer), as illustrated for the perpetual inventory system earlier in this chapter.

Recording Purchases of Merchandise

Based on the purchase invoice (invoice No. 731 in Illustration 5-4) and receipt of the merchandise ordered from PW Audio Supply, Sauk Stereo records the $3,800 purchase as follows:

May 4	Purchases	3,800	
	Accounts Payable		3,800
	(To record goods purchased on account per invoice #731, terms 2/10, n/30)		

A	=	L	+	SE
		+3,800		−3,800

Cash flows: no effect

Purchases is a temporary expense account reported on the statement of earnings. Its normal balance is a debit.

Freight Costs

When the buyer pays for the freight costs, the account Freight In is debited. Earlier in the chapter, we introduced the Freight *Out* account. This account is used to record shipping costs paid on outgoing merchandise by the seller. Now, we introduce the Freight *In* account. This account is used in a periodic inventory system to record shipping costs paid on incoming merchandise by the buyer.

To illustrate the recording of freight costs by the buyer, assume, Sauk Stereo pays Fast Freight Corporation $150 for freight charges on its purchases from PW Audio Supply. The entry on Sauk Stereo's books is as follows:

May 4	Freight In		150	
	Cash			150
	(To record payment of freight on goods purchased)			

Like Purchases, Freight In is a temporary expense account whose normal balance is a debit. Just as freight was part of the cost of the merchandise inventory in a perpetual inventory system, **freight is part of the cost of goods purchased** in a periodic inventory system. In accordance with the cost principle, the cost of goods purchased should include any freight charges incurred in bringing the goods to the buyer. As a result, freight in is added to net purchases to determine the cost of goods purchased.

Purchase Returns and Allowances

When $300 of merchandise is returned to PW Audio Supply, Sauk Stereo prepares the following entry to recognize the return:

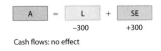

May 8	Accounts Payable		300	
	Purchase Returns and Allowances			300
	(To record return of goods to PW Audio Supply)			

Purchase Returns and Allowances is a temporary account whose normal balance is a credit. It is a contra expense account, whose balance is deduced from the Purchases account.

Purchase Discounts

On May 14, Sauk Stereo pays the balance due on account to PW Audio Supply, taking the 2% cash discount allowed by PW Audio Supply for payment within 10 days. Note that freight costs are not subject to a purchase discount. Purchase discounts apply on the invoice cost of the merchandise purchased, less any returns.

The payment and discount are recorded by Sauk Stereo as follows:

May 14	Accounts Payable ($3,800 − $300)		3,500	
	Purchase Discounts ($3,500 × 2%)			70
	Cash			3,430
	(To record payment to PW Audio Supply within discount period)			

Purchase Discounts is a temporary account whose normal balance is a credit. Like Purchase Returns and Allowances, it is a contra expense account subtracted from the Purchases account.

In each of the above cases, to record purchases of merchandise a temporary expense account was used instead of the Merchandise Inventory account used in a perpetual inventory system. The Purchases and Freight In accounts were debited rather than Merchandise Inventory in the first two entries, and Purchases Returns and Allowances and Purchase Discounts were credited in the last two entries rather than Merchandise Inventory. As we will see later in this appendix, these temporary accounts are needed for calculating the cost of goods purchased at the end of the period.

Recording Sales Of Merchandise

The sale of $3,800 of merchandise to Sauk Stereo on May 4 is recorded by the seller, PW Audio Supply, as follows:

May 4	Accounts Receivable	3,800	
	Sales		3,800
	(To record credit sale to Sauk Stereo per invoice #731)		

A	=	L	+	SE
+3,800				+3,800

Cash flows: no effect

Freight Costs

Freight costs incurred by the seller on outgoing merchandise are an operating expense to the seller. There is no distinction between accounting for these costs in a perpetual and periodic inventory system. Under both systems, these costs are debited to the Freight Out or Delivery Expense account.

You will recall that Sauk Stereo (the buyer) paid the shipping costs in our sales illustration, so no journal entry is required by PW Audio Supply (the seller) at this point in time.

Sales Returns and Allowances

When Sauk Stereo returns merchandise on May 8, PW Audio Supply records the $300 sales return as follows:

May 8	Sales Returns and Allowances	300	
	Accounts Receivable		300
	(To record return of goods by Sauk Stereo)		

A	=	L	+	SE
−300				−300

Cash flows: no effect

Sales Discounts

On May 14, PW Audio Supply receives a payment of $3,430 on account from Sauk Stereo. PW Audio Supply honours the 2% cash discount and records the payment of Sauk Stereo's account receivable in full as follows:

May 14	Cash	3,430	
	Sales Discounts ($3,500 × 2%)	70	
	Accounts Receivable ($3,800 − $300)		3,500
	(To record collection from Sauk Stereo within 2/10, n/30		
	discount period)		

A	=	L	+	SE
+3,430				−70
−3,500				

⬆ Cash flows: +3,430

The sales entries illustrated in this section are exactly the same as those illustrated earlier in the chapter for a perpetual inventory system, with one exception. In a perpetual inventory system, two journal entries are made for each transaction. The first entry records the accounts receivable and sales revenue (or return), as illustrated above. The second journal entry records the cost of the sale by transferring the inventory to the Cost of Goods Sold account (or the opposite in the case of a return).

In a periodic inventory system, there is only one journal entry made at the time of the sale (the entry to record the sales revenue) and only one at the time of the return (the entry to record the sales return). The cost of the sale is not recorded. Instead, the cost of goods sold is determined by calculation at the end of the period.

Calculating Cost of Goods Sold

Calculating the cost of goods sold is different in a periodic inventory system than in a perpetual inventory system. When a company uses a perpetual inventory system, all transactions that affect inventory (such as purchases, freight cost, returns, and discounts) are recorded directly to the Merchandise Inventory account. In addition, at the time of each sale, the perpetual inventory system requires a reduction (credit) in Merchandise Inventory and an increase (debit) in the Cost of Goods Sold account.

Under a periodic inventory system, there is no running account (continuous updating) of changes in inventory. The balance in ending inventory, as well as the cost of goods sold for the period, is calculated at the end of the period. This balance becomes the beginning inventory of the next period. To calculate the cost of goods sold, three steps are required:

1. Calculate the cost of goods purchased.
2. Determine the cost of goods on hand at the beginning and end of the accounting period.
3. Calculate the cost of goods sold.

We will discuss each of these steps in the following sections.

Cost of Goods Purchased

Earlier in this appendix, we used four accounts—Purchases, Freight In, Purchase Returns and Allowances, and Purchase Discounts—to record the purchase of inventory. These four accounts combine to determine the cost of goods purchased. First, purchase returns and allowances and purchase discounts are deducted from purchases to determine **net purchases**. Second, freight in is added to net purchases to arrive at the **cost of goods purchased**.

Using the assumed data for PW Audio Supply, the calculation of net purchases and the cost of goods purchased is as follows:

Purchases		$325,000
Less: Purchase returns and allowances	$10,400	
Purchase discounts	6,800	17,200
Net purchases		307,800
Add: Freight in		12,200
Cost of goods purchased		320,000

Cost of Goods on Hand

To determine the cost of the inventory on hand, PW Audio Supply must take a physical inventory. Taking a physical inventory involves these procedures:

1. Count the units on hand for each item of inventory.
2. Apply unit costs to the total units on hand for each item of inventory (we will learn more about how to do this in the next chapter).
3. Total the costs for each item of inventory to determine the total cost of goods on hand.

The total cost of goods on hand is known as the ending inventory. PW Audio Supply's physical inventory count on December 31, 2006, determines that the cost of its goods on hand, or ending inventory, is $40,000. This ending inventory amount will be used to calculate the cost of goods sold shown in the next section.

Cost of Goods Sold

There are two steps in calculating the cost of goods sold:

1. Add the cost of goods purchased to the cost of goods on hand at the beginning of the period (beginning inventory). The result is the **cost of goods available for sale**.
2. Subtract the cost of goods on hand at the end of the period (ending inventory) from the cost of goods available for sale. The result is the cost of goods sold.

Illustration 5A-1 reproduces the cost of goods sold formula first shown in Illustration 5-3, and inserts the relevant data for PW Audio Supply.

Illustration 5A-1 ◀

Formula for cost of goods sold

For PW Audio Supply, the cost of goods available for sale is $356,000 and the cost of goods sold is $316,000.

Comparison of Entries—Perpetual vs. Periodic

The periodic inventory system entries for purchases and sales are shown in Illustration 5A-2 next to those that were illustrated earlier in the chapter under the perpetual inventory system. Having these entries side by side should help you compare the differences. The entries that are different in the two inventory systems are highlighted.

Illustration 5A-2 ▼

Comparison of journal entries under perpetual and periodic inventory systems

	ENTRIES ON SAUK STEREO'S BOOKS (BUYER)				
Transaction	Perpetual Inventory System			Periodic Inventory System	
May 4 Purchase of merchandise on credit	Merchandise Inventory	3,800		Purchases	3,800	
	Accounts Payable		3,800	Accounts Payable		3,800
4 Freight costs on purchases	Merchandise Inventory	150		Freight In	150	
	Cash		150	Cash		150
8 Purchase returns and allowances	Accounts Payable	300		Accounts Payable	300	
	Merchandise Inventory		300	Purchase Returns and Allowances		300
14 Payment on account with a discount	Accounts Payable	3,500		Accounts Payable	3,500	
	Cash		3,430	Cash		3,430
	Merchandise Inventory		70	Purchase Discounts		70

	ENTRIES ON PW AUDIO SUPPLY'S BOOKS (SELLER)				
Transaction	Perpetual Inventory System			Periodic Inventory System	
May 4 Sale of merchandise on credit	Accounts Receivable	3,800		Accounts Receivable	3,800	
	Sales		3,800	Sales		3,800
	Cost of Goods Sold	2,400		No entry		
	Merchandise Inventory		2,400			
8 Return of merchandise sold	Sales Returns and Allowances	300		Sales Returns and Allowances	300	
	Accounts Receivable		300	Accounts Receivable		300
	Merchandise Inventory	140		No entry		
	Cost of Goods Sold		140			
14 Cash received on account with a discount	Cash	3,430		Cash	3,430	
	Sales Disounts	70		Sales Discounts	70	
	Accounts Receivable		3,500	Accounts Receivable		3,500

Statement of Earnings

Using the periodic inventory system does not affect the content of the balance sheet. As under the perpetual system, merchandise inventory is reported in the current assets section, and at the same amount. In a perpetual inventory system, the ending inventory balance can be obtained from the general ledger. In a periodic inventory system, the ending inventory balance has to be determined from the physical count of the goods on hand.

The key distinction between the two inventory systems is in the calculation and presentation of the cost of goods sold in the statement of earnings. In a perpetual inventory system, a multiple-step income statement uses only one line to report the cost of goods sold, as was shown in Illustration 5-7 in the chapter. In a periodic inventory system, the cost of goods sold section is detailed as shown in Illustration 5A-3.

PW AUDIO SUPPLY, INC.
Statement of Earnings
Year Ended December 31, 2006

Sales revenues			
Sales			$480,000
Less: Sales returns and allowances		$12,000	
Sales discounts		8,000	20,000
Net sales			460,000
Cost of goods sold			
Inventory, January 1			36,000
Purchases		$325,000	
Less: Purchase returns and allowances	$10,400		
Purchase discounts	6,800	17,200	
Net purchases		307,800	
Add: Freight in		12,200	
Cost of goods purchased			320,000
Cost of goods available for sale			356,000
Inventory, December 31			40,000
Total cost of goods sold			316,000
Gross profit			144,000
Operating expenses			
Salaries expense		$45,000	
Rent expense		19,000	
Utilities expense		17,000	
Advertising expense		16,000	
Amortization expense		8,000	
Freight out		7,000	
Insurance expense		2,000	
Total operating expenses			114,000
Earnings from operations			30,000
Other revenues			
Interest revenue		$ 3,000	
Gain on sale of equipment		600	
		3,600	
Other expenses			
Interest expense		$ 1,800	
Casualty loss from vandalism		200	
		2,000	1,600
Earnings before income taxes			31,600
Income tax expense			6,300
Net earnings			$ 25,300

▦ Using the Decision Toolkit

The Costco Wholesale Corporation operates wholesale clubs in Canada, the U.S., Japan, Mexico, South Korea, Taiwan, and the UK. It competes head to head with Wal-Mart, offering discount prices on 4,000 different products. The following financial data (in U.S. millions) is available for Costco:

	2004	2003
Net sales	$47,146	$41,693
Cost of goods sold	42,092	37,235
Net earnings	882	721

Instructions

(a) Wal-Mart is more than five times larger than Costco. Can a comparison of the financial results of these two companies be meaningful?

(b) Calculate the gross profit margin and profit margin for Costco for the 2004 and 2003 fiscal years.

(c) Using the ratios calculated in (b), compare Costco's profitability to Wal-Mart's, which was given in the chapter.

Solution

(a) It does not matter that Wal-Mart is more than five times larger than Costco. Ratio analysis puts both companies' financial information into the same perspective for a comparison. It is the relationship between the figures that is meaningful.

(b)

(in U.S. millions)	2004	2003
Gross profit margin	$\dfrac{(\$47{,}146 - \$42{,}092)}{\$47{,}146} = 10.7\%$	$\dfrac{(\$41{,}693 - \$37{,}235)}{\$41{,}693} = 10.7\%$
Profit margin	$\dfrac{\$882}{\$47{,}146} = 1.9\%$	$\dfrac{\$721}{\$41{,}693} = 1.7\%$

(c) Costco's gross profit margin remained unchanged from 2003 to 2004, while its profit margin increased slightly. Wal-Mart's gross profit margin of 22.5% in 2004 and 22.3% in 2003, and its profit margin of 3.5% in 2004 and 3.5% in 2003, are also are relatively unchanged.

Wal-Mart's gross profit margin is significantly better than Costco's. Comparing Wal-Mart's gross profit margin to Costco's, it appears that Wal-Mart has a much higher markup on its goods. This is not surprising since Costco sells only discounted goods, which would have a lower gross profit margin, and Wal-Mart sells a mix of discounted and nondiscounted goods.

Wal-Mart's profit margin is also much higher than Costco's. This could be an indication that Wal-Mart is better able to control its operating costs—which is not surprising because it has the advantage of being much larger than Costco.

the navigator

Summary of Study Objectives

1. **Identify the differences between service and merchandising companies.** A service company performs services. It has service or fee revenue and operating expenses. A merchandising company sells goods. It has sales revenue, cost of goods sold, and gross profit in addition to operating expenses. Both types of company also report income tax expense.

2. **Explain the recording of purchases under a perpetual inventory system.** The Merchandise Inventory account is debited for all purchases of merchandise, and for freight costs, if they are paid by the buyer. It is credited for purchase discounts, and purchase returns and allowances.

3. **Explain the recording of sales under a perpetual inventory system.** When inventory is sold, two entries are required: (1) Accounts Receivable (or Cash) is debited and Sales is credited for the selling price of the merchandise, and (2) Cost of Goods Sold is debited and Merchandise Inventory is credited for the cost of inventory items sold. Contra accounts are used to record sales returns and allowances and sales discounts. Two journal entries are also required for sales returns, to record both the selling price and the cost of the returned merchandise.

4. **Distinguish between a single-step and a multiple-step statement of earnings.** In a single-step statement of earnings, all data (except for income tax expense) are classified under two categories—revenues or expenses—and earnings before income tax is determined in one step. Income tax expense is separated from the other expenses and reported separately after earnings before income tax to determine net earnings (loss).

A multiple-step statement of earnings shows several steps in determining net earnings. Step 1 deducts sales returns and allowances and sales discounts from gross sales to determine net sales. Step 2 deducts the cost of goods sold from net sales to determine gross profit. Step 3 deducts operating expenses from gross profit to determine earnings from operations. Step 4 adds or deducts any non-operating items to determine earnings before income tax. Finally, step 5 deducts income tax expense to determine net earnings (loss).

5. **Calculate the gross profit margin and profit margin.** The gross profit margin, calculated by dividing gross profit by net sales, measures the gross profit earned for each dollar of sales. The profit margin, calculated by dividing net earnings by net sales, measures the net earnings (total profit) earned for each dollar of sales. Both are measures of profitability that are closely watched by management and other interested parties.

6. **Explain the recording of purchases and sales under a periodic inventory system (Appendix 5A).** In contrast to recording purchases in a perpetual inventory system, separate temporary accounts are used to record (a) purchases, (b)

purchase returns and allowances, (c) purchase discounts, and (d) freight costs that are paid by the buyer. Similarly, temporary accounts are used to record (a) sales, (b) sales returns and allowances, and (c) sales discounts. Sales are recorded as they are in a perpetual inventory system, except that the cost of goods sold is not recorded throughout the period. Instead, the cost of goods sold is determined and recorded at the end of the period.

To determine the cost of goods sold, first calculate the cost of goods purchased by adjusting purchases for returns, allowances, discounts, and freight in. Then, calculate the cost of goods sold by adding the cost of goods purchased to beginning inventory and subtracting ending inventory.

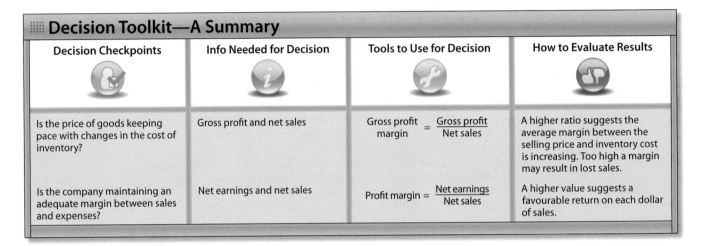

Decision Toolkit—A Summary

Decision Checkpoints	Info Needed for Decision	Tools to Use for Decision	How to Evaluate Results
Is the price of goods keeping pace with changes in the cost of inventory?	Gross profit and net sales	$\text{Gross profit margin} = \dfrac{\text{Gross profit}}{\text{Net sales}}$	A higher ratio suggests the average margin between the selling price and inventory cost is increasing. Too high a margin may result in lost sales.
Is the company maintaining an adequate margin between sales and expenses?	Net earnings and net sales	$\text{Profit margin} = \dfrac{\text{Net earnings}}{\text{Net sales}}$	A higher value suggests a favourable return on each dollar of sales.

Analysis Tools
(Decision Toolkit Summaries)

Study Tools (Glossary)

Glossary

Cost of goods available for sale   Term used in a periodic inventory system. It is calculated as the sum of beginning inventory and the cost of goods purchased. (p. 230)

Cost of goods purchased   Term used in a periodic inventory system. It is calculated as the sum of net purchases and freight in. (p. 230)

Cost of goods sold   The total cost of merchandise sold during the period. In a perpetual inventory system, it is recorded. In a periodic inventory system, it is calculated by deducting ending inventory from the cost of goods available for sale. (p. 210)

Earnings from operations   The results of a company's normal operating activities. It is calculated as gross profit less operating expenses. (p. 221)

FOB (free on board) destination   Freight terms indicating that the seller will pay for the shipping costs of the goods. (p. 214)

FOB (free on board) shipping point   Freight terms indicating that the seller is responsible for the goods only until they reach their shipping point (normally the seller's place of business). The buyer will pay for the shipping costs of the goods from the shipping point to the destination. (p. 214)

Gross profit   Sales revenue less cost of goods sold. (p. 210)

Gross profit margin   Gross profit expressed as a percentage of sales. It is calculated by dividing gross profit by net sales. (p. 224)

Net purchases   Term used in a periodic inventory system. It is calculated as purchases less purchase returns and allowances and purchase discounts. (p. 230)

Net sales   Sales less sales returns and allowances and sales discounts. (p. 221)

Operating cycle   The time required to go from cash to cash in producing revenues. (p. 211)

Operating expenses   Expenses incurred in the process of earning sales revenue. They are deducted from gross profit to arrive at earnings from operations. (p. 210)

Periodic inventory system   An inventory system in which detailed records are not maintained and the ending inventory and cost of goods sold are determined only at the end of an accounting period. (p. 212)

Perpetual inventory system   A detailed inventory system in which the quantity and cost of each inventory item is maintained. The records continuously show the inventory that should be on hand and the cost of the items sold. (p. 212)

Profit margin   Net earnings expressed as a percentage of net sales. It is calculated by dividing net earnings by net sales. (p. 225)

Purchase discount   A price reduction, based on the invoice price less any returns and allowances, claimed by a buyer for early payment of a credit purchase. (p. 215)

Purchase returns and allowances   A return of goods for cash or credit, or a deduction granted by the seller on the selling price of unsatisfactory merchandise. (p. 215)

Quantity discount   A price reduction that reduces the invoice price and is given to the buyer for volume purchases. (p. 215)

Sales discount   A price reduction that is based on the invoice price less any returns and allowances and is given by a seller for early payment of a credit sale. (p. 218)

Sales returns and allowances   A return of goods, or reduction in price, of unsatisfactory merchandise. (p. 217)

Sales revenue   The main source of revenue in a merchandising company. (p. 210)

Demonstration Problem

The adjusted trial balance at December 31, 2006, for Dykstra Inc. follows:

Study Tools
(Demonstration Problems)

DYKSTRA INC.
Adjusted Trial Balance
December 31, 2006

	Debit	Credit
Cash	$ 4,500	
Accounts receivable	11,100	
Merchandise inventory	29,000	
Prepaid insurance	2,500	
Land	150,000	
Building	500,000	
Accumulated amortization—building		$ 40,000
Equipment	95,000	
Accumulated amortization—equipment		18,000
Notes payable		25,000
Accounts payable		10,600
Property tax payable		4,000
Mortgage payable—currently due		21,000
Mortgage payable—long-term		530,000
Common shares		70,000
Retained earnings		61,000
Dividends	10,000	
Sales		536,800
Sales returns and allowances	6,700	
Sales discounts	5,000	
Cost of goods sold	363,400	
Freight out	7,600	
Advertising expense	12,000	
Salaries expense	56,000	
Utilities expense	18,000	
Rent expense	24,000	
Amortization expense	9,000	
Insurance expense	4,500	
Interest expense	4,600	
Interest revenue		2,500
Income tax expense	6,000	
	$1,318,900	$1,318,900

Instructions

Prepare a multiple-step statement of earnings, statement of retained earnings, and balance sheet for the year.

Action Plan

• Prepare the statement of earnings first, followed by the statement of retained earnings, and then the classified balance sheet.

• Remember the major subtotal headings in the statement of earnings: net sales, gross profit, earnings from operations, earnings before income tax, and net earnings.

Solution to Demonstration Problem

DYKSTRA INC.
Statement of Earnings
Year Ended December 31, 2006

Sales		$536,800
Less: Sales returns and allowances	$6,700	
Sales discounts	5,000	11,700
Net sales		525,100
Cost of goods sold		363,400
Gross profit		161,700
Operating expenses		
Salaries expense	$56,000	
Rent expense	24,000	
Utilities expense	18,000	
Advertising expense	12,000	
Amortization expense	9,000	
Freight out	7,600	
Insurance expense	4,500	
Total operating expenses		131,100
Earnings from operations		30,600
Other revenues		
Interest revenue	$2,500	
Other expenses		
Interest expense	4,600	
Net non-operating expense		2,100
Earnings before income tax		28,500
Income tax expense		6,000
Net earnings		$ 22,500

DYKSTRA INC.
Statement of Retained Earnings
Year Ended December 31, 2006

Retained earnings, January 1	$61,000
Add: Net earnings	22,500
	83,500
Less: Dividends	10,000
Retained earnings, December 31	$73,500

DYKSTRA INC.
Balance Sheet
December 31, 2006

Assets

Current assets
Cash — $ 4,500
Accounts receivable — 11,100
Merchandise inventory — 29,000
Prepaid insurance — 2,500
  Total current assets — $ 47,100
Property, plant, and equipment
Land — $150,000
Building — $500,000
Less: Accumulated amortization — 40,000 — 460,000
Equipment — $ 95,000
Less: Accumulated amortization — 18,000 — 77,000
  Total property, plant, and equipment — 687,000
Total assets — $734,100

Liabilities and Shareholders' Equity

Current liabilities
Notes payable — $25,000
Accounts payable — 10,600
Property tax payable — 4,000
Mortgage payable — 21,000
  Total current liabilities — $ 60,600
Long-term liabilities
Mortgage payable — 530,000
  Total liabilities — 590,600

Shareholders' equity
Common shares — $70,000
Retained earnings — 73,500 — 143,500
Total liabilities and shareholders' equity — $734,100

Note: All questions, exercises, and problems below with an asterisk (*) relate to material in Appendix 5A.

Self-Study Questions

Study Tools (Self-Assessment Quizzes)

(SO 1) 1. Which of the following statements about a perpetual inventory system is true?
(a) Cost of goods sold is only determined at the end of the accounting period.
(b) Detailed records of the cost of each inventory purchase and sale are kept continuously.
(c) The periodic system provides better control over inventories than a perpetual system.
(d) A physical inventory count is not performed in a perpetual inventory system.

(SO 2) 2. Under a perpetual inventory system, which of the following items does not result in an entry to the Merchandise Inventory account?
(a) A purchase of merchandise
(b) A return of merchandise inventory to the supplier

(c) Payment of freight costs by the buyer
(d) Payment of freight costs by the seller

3. Which sales accounts normally have a debit balance? (SO 3)
(a) Sales
(b) Sales Returns and Allowances
(c) Sales Discounts
(d) Both (b) and (c)

4. A credit sale of $750 is made on June 13, terms 2/10, (SO 3) n/30, on which a return of $50 is given on June 16. What amount is received as payment in full on June 22?
(a) $686 (c) $735
(b) $700 (d) $750

5. Sales revenues are $400,000; cost of goods sold is (SO 4) $310,000; operating expenses are $60,000; other

revenue is $10,000; and income tax expense is $8,000. What is the gross profit?
(a) $30,000   (c) $90,000
(b) $32,000   (d) $100,000

(SO 4) 6. Which of the following appears on both a single-step and a multiple-step statement of earnings?
(a) Gross profit
(b) Earnings from operations
(c) Non-operating activities
(d) Earnings before income tax

(SO 5) 7.  Which of the following would affect the gross profit margin?
(a) An increase in advertising expense
(b) A decrease in amortization expense
(c) An increase in cost of goods sold
(d) A decrease in insurance expense

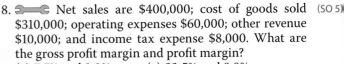

8. Net sales are $400,000; cost of goods sold $310,000; operating expenses $60,000; other revenue $10,000; and income tax expense $8,000. What are the gross profit margin and profit margin?   (SO 5)
(a) 7.5% and 8.0%   (c) 22.5% and 8.0%
(b) 8.0% and 22.5%   (d) 25.0% and 8.0%

*9. When goods are purchased for resale by a company using a periodic inventory system: (SO 6)
(a) purchases are debited to Merchandise Inventory.
(b) purchases are debited to Purchases.
(c) purchase returns are debited to Purchase Returns and Allowances.
(d) freight costs are debited to Purchases.

*10. Beginning inventory is $60,000; purchases are $400,000; purchase returns and allowances are $25,000; freight in is $5,000; and ending inventory is $50,000. What is the cost of goods sold?   (SO 6)
(a) $380,000   (c) $435,000
(b) $390,000   (d) $440,000

Questions

(SO 1) 1. What are the differences in the main activities of a merchandising company and a service company?

(SO 1) 2. How do revenues and expenses differ between a merchandising company and a service company?

(SO 1) 3. What is meant by the term "operating cycle"? Why is the normal operating cycle for a merchandising company likely to be longer than that of a service company?

(SO 1) 4. Distinguish between a perpetual and a periodic inventory system.

(SO 1) 5. Song Yee wonders why a physical inventory count is necessary in a perpetual inventory system. After all, the accounting records show how much inventory is on hand. Explain why a physical inventory count is required in a perpetual inventory system.

(SO 2) 6. Why are purchases of merchandise for resale recorded in a separate account from the purchases of other items, such as supplies or equipment? Would it not be better to use one account to record all these purchases?

(SO 2) 7. Distinguish between FOB shipping point and FOB destination. What freight term will result in a debit to Merchandise Inventory by the buyer? A debit to Freight Out by the seller?

(SO 2) 8. The Fukushima Corporation received an invoice for $16,000, terms 1/10, n/30. It will have to borrow from the bank to pay this invoice within the 10-day discount period. The interest rate Fukushima pays on its bank loans is 7%. Should it take advantage of the purchase discount offered or not? Explain.

(SO 2, 3) 9. Inventory was purchased on credit in April and paid for in May. It was sold in June. In which month(s) should the company record the revenue and expense from these transactions?

10. Explain why purchase returns are credited directly to the Merchandise Inventory account but sales returns are not debited directly to the Sales account.   (SO 2,

11. Using Xs for amounts, give the journal entries to record (a) a cash sale and (b) a credit sale for both the buyer and the seller, assuming a perpetual inventory system.   (SO 2

12. Distinguish between a quantity discount and a sales discount. Explain how each discount is recorded.   (SO 3

13. Distinguish between a single-step and a multiple-step statement of earnings for a merchandising company.   (SO 4

14. Identify the sections of a multiple-step statement of earnings that relate to (a) operating activities, and (b) non-operating activities.   (SO 4

15. Why is interest expense reported as a non-operating expense and not as an operating expense on a multiple-step statement of earnings?   (SO 4

16. How do the gross profit margin and profit margin differ?   (SO 5

17. What factors affect a company's gross profit margin—that is, what can cause the gross profit margin to increase and what can cause it to decrease?   (SO 5

*18. How is the cost of goods sold calculated and recorded in a periodic inventory system? In a perpetual inventory system?   (SO 6

*19. Using Xs for amounts, prepare the journal entries to record (a) a cash sale and (b) a cash purchase, assuming (1) a periodic inventory system is used, and (2) a perpetual inventory system is used.   (SO 6

*20. Identify the accounts that are added to or deducted from purchases to determine the cost of goods purchased. For each account, indicate (a) whether its balance is added or deducted and (b) what its normal balance is.   (SO 6

Brief Exercises

BE5–1 Prepare the journal entries to record the following purchase transactions in Xiaoyan Ltd.'s books. The company uses a perpetual inventory system.

Journalize purchase transactions.
(SO 2)

Jan. 3 Xiaoyan purchased $900,000 of merchandise from Feng Corp., terms 2/10, n/30, FOB destination.

6 Xiaoyan returned $120,000 of the merchandise purchased on January 3 because it was not needed.

12 Xiaoyan paid the balance owed to Feng.

BE5–2 Prepare the journal entries to record the following sale transactions in Feng Corp.'s books. Feng uses a perpetual inventory system.

Journalize sales transactions.
(SO 3)

Jan. 3 Feng sold $900,000 of merchandise to Xiaoyan Ltd., terms 2/10, n/30, FOB destination. The cost of the merchandise sold was $600,000.

4 Feng paid delivery charges of $10,000 on the merchandise shipped to Xiaoyan.

6 Xiaoyan returned $120,000 of the merchandise purchased from Feng on January 3 because it was not needed. The cost of the merchandise returned was $80,000, and it was restored to inventory.

12 Feng received the balance due from Xiaoyan.

BE5–3 Insert the number in the space beside the best definition of each of the following merchandising terms:

Match merchandising terms.
(SO 1, 2, 3)

1. Purchase discount
2. Merchandise inventory
3. Non-operating activities
4. Purchase return

5. Quantity discount
6. FOB destination
7. FOB shipping point
8. Sales allowance

9. Contra revenue account
10. Cost of goods sold

(a) ____ Freight terms indicating that the seller will pay for the shipping costs of the goods

(b) ____ An account, such as Sales Returns and Allowances, that is offset against (deducted from) a revenue account in the statement of earnings

(c) ____ The return of unsatisfactory purchased merchandise

(d) ____ The total cost of merchandise sold during the period

(e) ____ Freight terms indicating that the buyer will pay for the shipping costs of the goods

(f) ____ A cash discount given to the buyer for volume purchases

(g) ____ The reduction in price of unsatisfactory sold merchandise

(h) ____ A cash discount given to a buyer for early payment of the balance due

(i) ____ Goods purchased for resale to customers

(j) ____ Amounts earned or incurred, such as interest, which come from activities that are not part of a company's primary operations

BE5–4 Presented here are selected components of the multiple-step statement of earnings for three companies. Determine the missing amounts.

Determine missing amounts.
(SO 4)

Company	Sales	Cost of Goods Sold	Gross Profit	Operating Expenses	Non-Operating Revenues	Income Tax Expense (20%)	Net Earnings
A	$ 75,000	(b)	$ 30,000	(d)	$4,000	$3,200	$12,800
B	108,000	$ 70,000	(c)	$ 23,000	(e)	4,300	17,200
C	(a)	150,000	100,000	60,000	0	(f)	(g)

BE5–5 Saguenay Limited reports the following information: Sales $500,000; Sales Returns and Allowances $15,000; Sales Discounts $25,000; Cost of Goods Sold $275,000; Operating Expenses $110,000; Other Revenues $18,000; Other Expenses $12,000; and Income Tax Expense $20,000. Calculate the following: (a) net sales, (b) gross profit, (c) earnings from operations, (d) earnings before income tax, and (e) net earnings.

Calculate amounts from
statement of earnings.
(SO 4)

BE5–6 Explain where each of the following items would appear on (1) a multiple-step statement of earnings and (2) a single-step statement of earnings: gain on sale of equipment, cost of goods sold, amortization expense, interest expense, rent revenue, sales returns and allowances, sales discounts, and income tax expense.

Identify placement of items on
statement of earnings.
(SO 4)

Calculate profitability ratios and comment.
(SO 5)

BE5–7   The Forzani Group Ltd. reports sales revenue of $968.1 million, cost of goods sold of $635.1 million, and net earnings of $28.0 million for 2004. It reported sales revenue of $923.8 million, cost of goods sold of $603.3 million, and net earnings of $30.5 million for 2003. Calculate the gross profit margin and profit margin for each of 2004 and 2003. Comment on Forzani's changing profitability.

Journalize purchase transactions.
(SO 6)

*BE5–8   From the information in BE5–1, prepare the journal entries to record the purchase transactions on Xiaoyan Ltd.'s books, assuming a periodic inventory system is used instead of a perpetual inventory system.

Journalize sales transactions.
(SO 6)

*BE5–9   From the information in BE5–2, prepare the journal entries to record the sale transactions on Feng Corp.'s books, assuming a periodic inventory system is used instead of a perpetual inventory system.

Calculate cost of goods sold and gross profit.
(SO 6)

*BE5–10   Bassing Corp. uses a periodic inventory system and reports the following information: net sales $630,000; purchases $400,000; purchase returns and allowances $11,000; purchase discounts $8,000; freight in $16,000; beginning inventory $60,000; and ending inventory $90,000. Calculate (a) net purchases, (b) cost of goods purchased, (c) cost of goods sold, and (d) gross profit.

Exercises

Journalize purchase transactions.
(SO 2)

E5–1   This information is for Olaf Corp.:

Apr. 5 Purchased merchandise from DeVito Ltd. for $18,000, terms 2/10, n/30, FOB shipping point.
    6 The appropriate party paid freight costs of $900 on the merchandise purchased from DeVito on April 5.
    7 Purchased equipment on account for $26,000.
    8 Returned $2,800 of the April 5 merchandise to DeVito.
  15 Paid the amount due to DeVito in full.

Instructions

(a) Record the transactions in the books of Olaf Corp., assuming a perpetual inventory system is used.
(b) Assume that Olaf Corp. paid the balance due to DeVito on May 4 instead of April 15. Prepare the journal entry to record this payment.

Journalize sales transactions.
(SO 3)

E5–2   Refer to the information in E5–1 for Olaf Corp. and the following additional information:

1. The cost of the merchandise sold on April 5 was $10,800.
2. The cost of the merchandise returned on April 8 was $1,680.

Instructions

Record the transactions in the books of DeVito Ltd., assuming a perpetual inventory system is used.

Journalize purchase and sales transactions.
(SO 2, 3)

E5–3   The following merchandise transactions occurred in December. Both companies use a perpetual inventory system.

Dec. 3 Pippen Ltd. sold $480,000 of merchandise to Thomas Corp., terms 2/10, n/30, FOB shipping point. The cost of the merchandise sold was $320,000.
    5 Shipping costs of $5,000 are paid.
    8 Thomas was granted a sales allowance of $25,000 for defective merchandise purchased on December 3. No merchandise was returned.
  13 Pippen received the balance due from Thomas.

Instructions

(a) Prepare the journal entries to record these transactions in the books of Pippen Ltd.
(b) Prepare the journal entries to record these transactions in the books of Thomas Corp.

E5–4 On September 1, Campus Office Supply Ltd. had an inventory of 10 pocket calculators at a cost of $24 each. The company uses a perpetual inventory system. During September these transactions occurred:

Journalize and post purchase and sales transactions.
(SO 2, 3)

Sept. 6 Purchased 60 calculators at $24 each from Digital Corp. on account, terms 2/10, n/30.
   10 Returned two calculators to Digital for $48 credit because they did not meet specifications.
   12 Sold 26 calculators for $30 each to Campus Book Store, terms 2/10, n/30.
   14 Granted credit of $30 to Campus Book Store for the return of one calculator that was not ordered. The calculator was restored to inventory.
   15 Paid Digital Corp. amount owing.
   20 Sold 30 calculators for $30 each to Student Card Shop, terms 2/10, n/30.
   21 Received payment in full from Campus Book Store.
   30 Counted the inventory and determined that there were actually 12 calculators on hand.

Instructions

(a) Journalize the September transactions.
(b) Post the appropriate entries to the Merchandise Inventory and Cost of Goods Sold accounts. Determine the ending balances in both dollars and quantities.

E5–5 The following list of accounts is from the adjusted trial balance for Swirsky Corporation:

Classify accounts.
(SO 4)

Accounts payable
Accounts receivable
Accumulated amortization—building
Accumulated amortization—equipment
Advertising expense
Amortization expense
Building
Cash
Common shares

Dividends
Equipment
Freight out
Insurance expense
Interest expense
Interest payable
Land
Merchandise inventory
Mortgage payable

Prepaid insurance
Property tax payable
Salaries expense
Salaries payable
Sales
Sales discounts
Sales returns and allowances
Unearned sales revenue
Utilities expense

Instructions

For each account, identify whether it should be reported on the balance sheet, statement of retained earnings, or statement of earnings. Please specify where the account should be classified. For example, Accounts Payable would be classified under current liabilities on the balance sheet.

E5–6 Gildan Activewear Inc., headquartered in Montreal, makes customized T-shirts, sweatshirts, and golf shirts for private-label use. The company reports the following condensed data (in U.S. millions) for the year ended October 3, 2004:

Prepare statements of earnings.
(SO 4)

Cost of sales	$378.7
Income tax expense	3.1
Interest expense	6.2
Sales	533.4
Selling, general, and administrative expenses	85.2

Instructions

(a) Prepare a single-step statement of earnings.
(b) Prepare a multiple-step statement of earnings.

E5–7 Financial information is presented here for two companies:

Determine missing amounts and calculate profitability ratios.
(SO 4, 5)

	Young Ltd.	Rioux Ltée
Sales	$90,000	$ (f)
Sales returns and allowances	(a)	5,000
Net sales	81,000	95,000
Cost of goods sold	52,650	(g)
Gross profit	(b)	38,000
Operating expenses	18,250	(h)
Earnings from operations	(c)	16,750
Non-operating revenues	0	500
Earnings before income tax	(d)	(i)
Income tax expense	2,000	(j)
Net earnings	(e)	14,250

Instructions

(a) Calculate the missing amounts.
(b) Calculate the gross profit margin and profit margin for each company.

Calculate profitability ratios and comment.
(SO 5)

E5–8   Best Buy Co., Inc. is North America's leading consumer electronics retailer, with more than 780 stores in Canada and the U.S. The company reported the following selected information (in U.S. millions) at its February year end:

	2004	2003	2002
Net sales	$24,547	$20,946	$17,711
Cost of goods sold	17,965	15,710	13,941
Earnings from operations	1,304	1,010	908
Net earnings	705	99	570

Instructions

(a) Calculate the gross profit margin and profit margin for Best Buy for each of the three years.
(b) Recalculate the profit margin for the three years using earnings from operations instead of net earnings. Does this result in a different trend than you saw in (a)? If yes, what might be the reason for this change?
(c) Comment on whether the ratios have improved or deteriorated over the last three years.

Journalize purchase and sales transactions.
(SO 6)

*E5–9   Data for Olaf Corp. are presented in E5–1 and E5–2.

Instructions

Repeat the requirements for E5–1 and E5–2, assuming a periodic inventory system is used instead of a perpetual inventory system.

Journalize purchase and sales transactions.
(SO 6)

*E5–10   On June 10, Duvall Ltd. sold $10,000 of merchandise to Pele Ltd., terms 2/10, n/30, FOB shipping point. The merchandise cost Duvall $6,000. Freight costs of $350 are paid on June 11. Duvall receives damaged goods totalling $500 on June 12—the goods were returned by Pele for credit. The cost of the returned merchandise was $300. It was repaired and returned to inventory. On June 19, Pele pays Duvall in full.

Instructions

(a) Prepare journal entries for each transaction in the books of Pele Ltd., assuming (1) a perpetual inventory system is used, and (2) a periodic inventory system is used.
(b) Prepare journal entries for each transaction for Duvall Ltd., assuming (1) a perpetual inventory system is used, and (2) a periodic inventory system is used.

Determine missing amounts.
(SO 6)

*E5–11   Below are the cost of goods sold sections for four companies:

	Co. 1	Co. 2	Co. 3	Co. 4
Beginning inventory	$ 250	$ 120	$1,000	(m)
Purchases	1,500	1,080	(i)	$43,600
Purchase returns and allowances	50	(e)	300	700
Purchase discounts	30	20	150	(n)
Net purchases	(a)	1,030	7,210	42,100
Freight in	110	(f)	(j)	2,250
Cost of goods purchased	(b)	1,230	7,900	(o)
Cost of goods available for sale	(c)	(g)	(k)	49,550
Ending inventory	300	(h)	1,450	(p)
Cost of goods sold	(d)	1,230	(l)	43,300

Instructions

Fill in the lettered blanks to complete the cost of goods sold sections.

Prepare statement of earnings.
(SO 6)

*E5–12   The following selected information is presented for the Okanagan Corporation for the year ended February 28, 2006:

Freight in	$10,000	Purchases	$200,000
Freight out	7,000	Purchase discounts	20,000
Insurance expense	12,000	Purchase returns and allowances	6,000
Interest expense	6,000	Rent expense	20,000
Merchandise inventory,		Salaries expense	61,000
March 1, 2005	42,000	Sales	315,000
Merchandise inventory,		Sales discounts	31,000
February 28, 2006	61,000	Sales returns and allowances	13,000

Instructions

Prepare a statement of earnings for the year.

Problems: Set A

P5–1A Phantom Book Warehouse Ltd. distributes hardcover books to retail stores and extends credit terms of n/30 to all of its customers. It also purchases merchandise on credit terms of n/30. At the end of May, Phantom's inventory consists of 240 books purchased at $6 each. It uses a perpetual inventory system. During the month of June, the following merchandise transactions occurred:

Journalize purchase and sales transactions.
(SO 2, 3)

June 1 Purchased 160 books on account for $5 each from Reader's World Publishers.
    3 Sold 120 books on account to the Book Nook for $10 each. The cost of the books sold was $720.
    6 Received $50 credit for 10 books returned to Reader's World Publishers.
    7 Sold 120 books on account to Read-A-Lot Bookstore for $10 each. The cost of the books sold was $720.
    8 Issued a $50 credit memorandum to Read-A-Lot Bookstore for the return of five damaged books. The books were determined to be no longer saleable and were destroyed.
  12 Purchased 110 books on account for $5 each from Read More Publishers.
  27 Sold 110 books on account to Readers Bookstore for $10 each. The total cost of the books sold was $550.
  28 Granted Readers Bookstore $150 credit for 15 books returned. These books were restored to inventory.
  28 Received payment in full from Read-A-Lot Bookstore.
  29 Paid Reader's World Publishers in full.
  30 Received payment in full from the Book Nook.

Instructions

Journalize the June transactions.

P5–2A Presented here are selected transactions for Norlan Inc. during September of the current year. Norlan uses a perpetual inventory system.

Journalize purchase and sales transactions.
(SO 2, 3)

Sept. 2 Purchased delivery equipment on account for $28,000, terms n/30, FOB destination.
    3 Freight charges of $500 were paid by the appropriate party on the Sept. 2 purchase of delivery equipment.
    4 Purchased merchandise on account from Hillary Corp. at a cost of $60,000, terms 2/10, n/30, FOB shipping point.
    5 Freight charges of $1,000 were paid by the appropriate party on the Sept. 4 purchase of merchandise.
    6 Returned damaged goods costing $8,000 received from Hillary Corp. on September 4.
    9 Sold merchandise costing $15,000 to Fischer Limited on account for $20,000, terms 1/10, n/30, FOB shipping point.
  10 Freight charges of $250 were paid by the appropriate party on the Sept. 9 sale of merchandise.
  14 Paid Hillary the balance due.
  15 Purchased supplies for $4,000 cash.
  16 Received balance due from Fischer Limited.
  18 Purchased merchandise for $6,000 cash.
  22 Sold inventory costing $20,000 to Where's Waldo Inc. on account for $27,000, terms 1/10, n/30, FOB shipping point.
  23 Freight charges of $300 were paid by the appropriate party on the Sept. 22 sale of merchandise.
  28 Where's Waldo returned merchandise sold for $10,000 that cost $7,500. The merchandise was restored to inventory.

Instructions

Journalize the September transactions.

Journalize, post, and prepare trial balance and partial statement of earnings.
(SO 2, 3, 4)

P5–3A   At the beginning of the current golf season, on April 1, the ledger of Weir's Pro Shop showed Cash $2,500; Merchandise Inventory $3,500; Common Shares $5,000; and Retained Earnings $1,000. The company uses a perpetual inventory system.

The following transactions are for April 2006:

Apr. 5 Purchased golf bags, clubs, and balls on account from Balata Corp. for $1,700, terms 2/10, n/30, FOB shipping point.
     7 Freight of $80 was paid by the appropriate party on the April 7 purchase from Balata.
     9 Received $150 credit from Balata for merchandise returned.
    10 Sold merchandise on account to members for $950, terms n/30. The merchandise had a cost of $600.
    12 Purchased golf shoes, sweaters, and other accessories on account from Arrow Sportswear for $770, terms 1/10, n/30.
    14 Paid Balata in full.
    17 Received $75 credit from Arrow Sportswear for merchandise returned.
    20 Made sales on account to members for $790, terms n/30. The cost of the merchandise sold was $500.
    21 Paid Arrow Sportswear in full.
    27 Granted a $50 sales allowance to members for soiled clothing. No merchandise was returned.
    30 Received payments on account from members, $1,250.

Instructions

(a) Prepare a general ledger and enter the opening balances.
(b) Journalize and post the April transactions.
(c) Prepare a trial balance as at April 30, 2006.
(d) Prepare a statement of earnings through to gross profit.

Journalize, post, and prepare partial financial statements.
(SO 2, 3, 4)

P5–4A   Eagle Hardware Store Ltd. completed the following merchandising transactions in the month of May. At the beginning of May, Eagle's ledger showed Cash $4,000; Accounts Receivable $5,000; Common Shares $5,000; and Retained Earnings $4,000.

May 1 Purchased merchandise on account from Depot Wholesale Supply for $5,800, terms 2/10, n/30, FOB shipping point.
     2 Freight charges of $200 were paid by the appropriate party on the merchandise purchased on May 1.
     4 Sold merchandise on account for $2,250, terms 2/10, n/30, FOB destination. The cost of the merchandise sold was $1,500.
     5 Freight charges of $100 were paid by the appropriate party on the May 4 sale.
     7 Received $200 credit from Depot Wholesale Supply for merchandise returned.
    10 Paid Depot Wholesale Supply in full.
    11 Purchased supplies for $600 cash.
    12 Purchased merchandise for $2,400 cash.
    13 Received payment in full from customers billed for merchandise sold on account on May 4.
    15 Received cash refund of $230 from supplier for return of poor-quality merchandise.
    17 Purchased merchandise from Harlow Distributors for $1,900, terms 2/10, n/30, FOB shipping point.
    19 Freight of $250 was paid by the appropriate party on the May 17 purchase of merchandise.
    24 Sold merchandise for $6,200 cash. The cost of the merchandise was $4,600.
    25 Purchased merchandise from Horicon Inc. for $1,000, terms 2/10, n/30, FOB destination.
    27 Paid Harlow Distributors in full.
    29 Paid $100 cash refund to customers for returned merchandise. The cost of the returned merchandise was $70. It was restored to inventory.
    31 Sold merchandise on account for $1,600, terms n/30, FOB shipping point. The cost of the merchandise was $1,000.

Instructions

(a) Prepare a general ledger and enter the opening balances.

(b) Journalize and post the May transactions, assuming a perpetual inventory system is used.

(c) Prepare a statement of earnings through to gross profit and the current assets section of the balance sheet.

P5–5A The following list of accounts has been selected from the financial statements of Leon's Furniture Limited:

Classify accounts.
(SO 4)

Accounts payable and accrued liabilities	Income tax payable
Accounts receivable	Interest income
Accumulated amortization	Inventory
Advertising expense	Land
Amortization expense	Leasehold improvements
Buildings	Marketable securities
Cash and cash equivalents	Rent and property tax expense
Common shares	Retained earnings
Cost of sales	Salaries and commissions expense
Dividends	Salaries payable
Dividends payable	Sales
Equipment	Vehicles
Income tax expense	

Instructions

For each account, identify whether the account should be reported on the balance sheet, statement of earnings, or statement of retained earnings. Also specify where the account should be classified. For example, Accounts Payable and Accrued Liabilities would be classified as a current liability on the balance sheet.

P5–6A The unadjusted trial balance of Mesa Inc. at the company's fiscal year end of December 31 follows:

Journalize, post, and prepare adjusted trial balance and financial statements.
(SO 4)

MESA INC.
Trial Balance
December 31, 2006

	Debit	Credit
Cash	$ 13,000	
Accounts receivable	31,700	
Merchandise inventory	28,750	
Supplies	2,940	
Prepaid insurance	1,980	
Land	30,000	
Building	150,000	
Accumulated amortization—building		$ 18,000
Equipment	45,000	
Accumulated amortization—equipment		13,500
Accounts payable		35,600
Unearned sales revenue		4,000
Mortgage payable		157,600
Common shares		20,000
Retained earnings		21,425
Dividends	2,000	
Sales		263,770
Sales returns and allowances	2,500	
Sales discounts	3,275	
Cost of goods sold	171,225	
Salaries expense	30,950	
Utilities expense	5,100	
Interest expense	9,975	
Income tax expense	5,500	
	$533,895	$533,895

Adjustment data:

1. The 12-month insurance policy was purchased on February 1, 2006.
2. There were $650 of supplies on hand on December 31.
3. Amortization expense for the year is $6,000 for the building and $4,500 for the equipment.
4. Salaries of $940 are accrued and unpaid at December 31.
5. Accrued interest expense at December 31 is $1,000.
6. Unearned sales revenue of $975 is still unearned at December 31. On the sales that were earned, the cost of goods sold was $2,000.
7. Of the mortgage payable, $9,000 is payable next year.
8. Income tax of $500 is due and unpaid.

Instructions

(a) Prepare a general ledger and enter the trial balance amounts.
(b) Journalize and post the adjusting entries for the year.
(c) Prepare an adjusted trial balance.
(d) Prepare a statement of earnings, statement of retained earnings, and balance sheet for the year.

Calculate missing amounts and assess profitability.
(SO 2, 4, 5)

P5–7A Psang Inc. purchases all merchandise inventory on credit and uses a perpetual inventory system. The Accounts Payable account is used for recording merchandise inventory purchases only; all other current liabilities are accrued in separate accounts. You are provided with the following selected information for the fiscal years 2004 through 2006:

	2006	2005	2004
Statement of Earnings Data			
Net sales	$82,000	$ (v)	$96,900
Cost of goods sold	26,500	27,000	(ix)
Gross profit	(i)	61,500	69,300
Operating expenses	52,100	(vi)	63,500
Net earnings	$ (ii)	$ 4,500	$ (x)
Balance Sheet Data			
Merchandise inventory	(iii)	$14,700	$11,000
Accounts payable	(iv)	4,600	6,500
Additional Information			
Purchase of merchandise inventory on account	$22,000	(vii)	$25,900
Cash payments to suppliers	24,000	(viii)	24,000

Instructions

(a) Calculate the missing amounts.
(b) Calculate the gross profit margin and profit margin for each year.
(c) Sales declined over the three-year period 2004 to 2006. Does this mean that profitability also had to decline? Refer to the gross profit margin and profit margin to explain and support your answer.

Calculate ratios and comment.
(SO 5)

P5–8A Danier Leather Inc., headquartered in Toronto, is the second largest specialty leather apparel retailer in the world. The following selected information (in thousands) is available for three recent fiscal years:

	2004	2003	2002
Current assets	$ 54,579	$ 46,223	$ 44,154
Current liabilities	10,377	9,350	10,522
Net sales	178,115	175,487	179,977
Cost of sales	90,060	88,788	92,098
Net earnings (loss)	(7,097)	5,394	10,725

Instructions

(a) Calculate the current ratio, gross profit margin, and profit margin for each year. Comment on whether the ratios have improved or deteriorated over the three years.
(b) Compare the 2004 ratios to the following industry averages: current ratio 2.5:1; gross profit margin 38.1%; and profit margin 5.0%. Are Danier Leather's ratios better or worse than those of its industry?

Consider impact of transactions on ratios.
(SO 5)

P5–9A You are presented with the following information for La Crosse Inc. as at May 24, 2006. The company's year end is May 31.

LA CROSSE INC.
Balance Sheet
May 24, 2006

Current assets	$ 60,000
Noncurrent assets	50,000
Total assets	$110,000
Current liabilities	$ 25,000
Long-term liabilities	35,000
Total liabilities	60,000
Shareholders' equity	50,000
Total liabilities and shareholders' equity	$110,000

LA CROSSE INC.
Statement of Earnings
Year Ended May 24, 2006

Net sales	$25,000
Cost of goods sold	18,000
Gross profit	7,000
Operating expenses	5,000
Earnings before income tax	2,000
Income tax expense	400
Net earnings	$ 1,600

The company has debt covenants with the bank which require it to maintain a current ratio greater than 2 to 1, a gross profit margin of 25%, a profit margin of 4%, and a debt to total assets ratio which cannot be more than 60%. The company wants to boost its financial performance by year end, as it may be going back to the bank to finance the purchase of some equipment.

The sales manager has come to you with a proposal. She says that she can purchase inventory on account for $13,500. She has a customer who she can sell the inventory to, also on account, for $18,000. "I know the gross profit on the deal is not as high as usual. But the beauty of this is that we should be able to collect the cash from our customer early next month, in time to pay the supplier. And the bank will be impressed by the $4,500 increase in earnings! So we can boost our profit without having to pay out any cash, which I know we're short of anyway!"

Instructions

(a) Calculate the following, based on the financial data presented as at May 24:
   1. Current ratio   3. Gross profit margin
   2. Debt to total assets   4. Profit margin
(b) If you followed the sales manager's proposal, what would be the impact on each of the ratios you calculated in (a)? Ignore any income tax effects. Do you recommend that the company go with the sales manager's suggestion?

*P5–10A   Data for Phantom Book Warehouse Ltd. are presented in P5–1A.

Instructions

Journalize the June transactions, assuming a periodic inventory system is used instead of a perpetual inventory system.

*P5–11A   Data for Norlan Inc. are presented in P5–2A.

Instructions

Journalize the September transactions, assuming a periodic inventory system is used instead of a perpetual inventory system.

*P5–12A   Data for Weir's Pro Shop are presented in P5–3A. A physical inventory count determined that $4,687 of inventory was on hand at April 30.

Instructions

(a) Prepare a general ledger and enter the opening balances.

Journalize purchase and sales transactions.
(SO 6)

Journalize purchase and sales transactions.
(SO 6)

Journalize, post, and prepare trial balance and partial statement of earnings.
(SO 6)

(b) Journalize and post the April transactions, assuming a periodic inventory system is used instead of a perpetual inventory system.

(c) Prepare a trial balance as at April 30, 2006.

(d) Prepare a statement of earnings through to gross profit.

Prepare financial statements.
(SO 6)

*P5–13A   Beaupré Ltée's adjusted trial balance appears as follows on December 31, 2006, the end of its fiscal year:

Accounts payable	$ 86,300	Land	$ 75,000
Accounts receivable	49,200	Merchandise inventory	40,500
Accumulated amortization—		Mortgage payable	155,000
building	51,800	Prepaid insurance	2,400
Accumulated amortization—		Property tax expense	4,800
equipment	42,900	Property tax payable	4,800
Amortization expense	23,400	Purchases	441,600
Building	190,000	Purchase discounts	22,500
Cash	23,000	Purchase returns and allowances	6,400
Common shares	95,000	Retained earnings	68,600
Dividends	8,000	Salaries expense	122,500
Equipment	110,000	Salaries payable	3,500
Freight in	5,600	Sales	623,000
Freight out	7,500	Sales discounts	15,000
Income tax expense	5,000	Sales returns and allowances	8,000
Insurance expense	7,200	Unearned sales revenue	2,300
Interest expense	5,400	Utilities expense	18,000

Additional information:

1. **Beaupré** uses a periodic inventory system.
2. A physical inventory count determined that merchandise inventory on December 31, 2006, is $72,600.

Instructions

Prepare a statement of earnings, statement of retained earnings, and balance sheet for the year.

Problems: Set B

Journalize purchase and sales transactions.
(SO 2, 3)

P5–1B   Travel Warehouse Ltd. distributes suitcases to retail stores and extends credit terms of n/30 to all of its customers. At the end of June, Travel Warehouse's inventory consisted of 40 suitcases purchased at $30 each. It uses a perpetual inventory system. During the month of July, the following merchandising transactions occurred:

July 1 Purchased 50 suitcases on account for $30 each from Trunk Manufacturers, terms n/30.

3 Sold 40 suitcases on account to Satchel World for $55 each.

4 Issued a $55 credit memorandum to Satchel World for the return of a damaged suitcase. The suitcase was determined to be no longer saleable and was destroyed.

7 Sold 30 suitcases on account to The Going Concern for $55 each.

18 Purchased 60 suitcases on account for $1,800 from Holiday Manufacturers, terms n/30.

20 Received $300 credit for 10 suitcases returned to Holiday Manufacturers.

21 Sold 40 suitcases on account to Fly-By-Night for $55 each.

23 Granted Fly-By-Night $275 credit for five suitcases returned costing $150. The suitcases were in good condition and were restored to inventory.

27 Received payment in full from The Going Concern.

29 Paid Trunk Manufacturers in full.

31 Received balance owing from Satchel World.

Instructions

Journalize the July transactions.

Journalize purchase and sales transactions.
(SO 2, 3)

P5–2B   Presented here are selected transactions for Shaoshi Inc. during October of the current year. Shaoshi uses a perpetual inventory system.

Oct. 1 Purchased merchandise on account from Microcell Ltd. at a cost of $60,000, terms 2/10, n/30, FOB shipping point.

1 Freight charges of $2,000 were paid by the appropriate party on the October 1 purchase of merchandise.

5 Returned for credit $7,000 of damaged goods purchased from Microcell on October 1.

8 Sold the remaining merchandise purchased from Microcell to Guidant Corp. on account for $90,000, terms 2/10, n/30, FOB shipping point.

8 Freight charges of $3,000 were paid by the appropriate party on the October 8 sale of merchandise.

9 Guidant returned some of the merchandise purchased on October 8 for a $4,000 credit on account. The merchandise originally cost $2,400 and was restored to inventory.

10 Paid Microcell the balance owing.

12 Made cash purchase of supplies costing $5,000.

15 Made cash purchase of merchandise for $7,500.

17 Received the balance owing from Guidant.

20 Purchased delivery equipment on account for $45,000.

28 Sold on account $30,000 of merchandise, costing $18,000, to Deux Ltée, terms 2/10, n/30, FOB destination.

28 Freight charges of $1,000 were paid by the appropriate party on the October 28 sale of merchandise.

Instructions

Journalize the October transactions.

P5–3B   At the beginning of the current tennis season, on April 1, the ledger of the Kicked-Back Tennis Shop showed Cash $2,500; Merchandise Inventory $1,700; Common Shares $3,000; and Retained Earnings $1,200. The company uses a perpetual inventory system. The following transactions are for April 2006:

Journalize, post, and prepare trial balance and partial statement of earnings.
(SO 2, 3, 4)

Apr. 4 Purchased racquets and balls from Robert Corp. for $1,460, terms 2/10, n/30, FOB shipping point.

6 The appropriate party paid $60 freight on the April 4 purchase of merchandise.

8 Sold merchandise to members for $950, terms n/30. The merchandise cost $640.

10 Received credit of $35 from Robert Corp. for a damaged racquet that was returned.

11 Purchased tennis shoes from Niki Sports for $460 cash.

12 Purchased supplies for $650 cash from Discount Supplies.

13 Paid Robert Corp. in full.

14 Purchased tennis shirts and shorts from Martina's Sportswear for $725, terms 2/10, n/30, FOB shipping point.

15 The appropriate party paid freight on the April 14 purchase of merchandise, $30.

16 Received $55 cash refund from Niki Sports for damaged merchandise that was returned.

17 Returned $60 of the supplies purchased on April 12 and received a cash refund.

18 Sold merchandise to members for $850, terms n/30. The cost of the merchandise was $570.

20 Received $500 in cash from members in settlement of their accounts.

21 Paid Martina's Sportswear in full.

25 Purchased equipment for use in the business from DomCo Ltd. for $1,800, terms n/30.

27 Granted a $50 sales allowance to members for slightly torn tennis clothing. No merchandise was returned.

30 Received cash payments on account from members, $600.

Instructions

(a) Prepare a general ledger and enter the opening balances.
(b) Journalize and post the April transactions.
(c) Prepare a trial balance as at April 30, 2006.
(d) Prepare a statement of earnings through to gross profit.

Journalize, post, and prepare
partial financial statements.
(SO 2, 3, 4)

P5–4B   Nisson Distributing Ltd. completed the following merchandising transactions in the month of April. At the beginning of April, Nisson's ledger showed Cash $4,000; Accounts Receivable $5,000; Common Shares $5,000; and Retained Earnings $4,000.

Apr. 2 Purchased merchandise on account from Kai Supply Corp. for $8,900, terms 2/10, n/30, FOB shipping point.

    3 The appropriate party paid $100 freight on the April 2 purchase of merchandise.

    4 Sold $10,800 of merchandise on account to Kananaskis Supply Ltd., terms 2/10, n/30, FOB destination. The cost of the merchandise was $9,000.

    5 The appropriate party paid $200 freight on the April 4 sale of merchandise.

    6 Issued $540 credit for merchandise returned by Kananaskis Supply. The returned merchandise had a cost of $460 and was restored to inventory for future resale.

  11 Paid Kai Supply in full.

  13 Received balance owing from Kananaskis Supply.

  14 Purchased merchandise for $3,800 cash.

  16 Received $500 refund from supplier for returned merchandise on cash purchase of April 14.

  18 Purchased merchandise from Pigeon Distributors for $4,200, terms 2/10, n/30, FOB destination.

  19 The appropriate party paid $100 freight on the April 18 purchase.

  20 Received $300 credit for merchandise returned to Pigeon Distributors.

  23 Sold merchandise for $6,400 cash. The cost of the merchandise was $5,200.

  26 Purchased merchandise for $2,300 cash.

  27 Paid Pigeon Distributors in full.

  29 Made cash refunds of $90 to customers for returned merchandise. The returned merchandise had a cost of $60 and was restored to inventory for future resale.

  30 Sold merchandise on account to Yeung Limited for $3,700, terms n/30, FOB shipping point. The cost of the merchandise was $2,800.

Instructions

(a) Prepare a general ledger and enter the opening balances.

(b) Journalize and post the April transactions, assuming a perpetual inventory system is used.

(c) Prepare a statement of earnings through to gross profit and the current assets section of the balance sheet.

Classify accounts.
(SO 4)

P5–5B   The following list of accounts has been selected from the financial statements of Scott Paper Limited:

Accounts payable and accrued liabilities	Inventories
Accumulated amortization	Land
Amortization expense	Machinery and equipment
Buildings	Long-term debt
Cash and cash equivalents	Operating expenses
Common shares	Other intangible assets
Cost of products sold	Prepaid expenses
Current portion of long-term debt	Retained earnings
Goodwill	Sales less discounts, rebates, and allowances
Income tax expense	Trade and other accounts receivable
Income tax payable	Trademarks
Interest expense	

Instructions

For each account, indicate whether the account was reported on Scott Paper's balance sheet, statement of earnings, or statement of retained earnings. Also specify where the account was most likely classified. For example, Accounts Payable and Accrued Liabilities would be classified as a current liability on the balance sheet.

Journalize, post, and prepare
adjusted trial balance and
financial statements.
(SO 4)

P5–6B   The unadjusted trial balance of Fashion Centre Ltd. contained the following accounts at November 30, the company's fiscal year end:

FASHION CENTRE LTD.
Trial Balance
November 30, 2006

	Debit	Credit
Cash	$ 14,000	
Accounts receivable	30,600	
Merchandise inventory	27,500	
Supplies	1,650	
Prepaid insurance	1,800	
Investments	37,000	
Furniture and equipment	26,800	
Accumulated amortization—furniture and equipment		$ 10,720
Leasehold improvements	42,000	
Accumulated amortization—leasehold improvements		8,400
Accounts payable		34,400
Unearned sales revenue		3,000
Note payable		35,000
Common shares		50,000
Retained earnings		30,000
Dividends	10,000	
Sales		238,500
Sales discounts	4,520	
Sales returns and allowances	4,600	
Cost of goods sold	157,000	
Salaries expense	31,600	
Rent expense	13,850	
Miscellaneous expenses	6,100	
Income tax expense	1,000	
	$410,020	$410,020

Adjustment data:

1. The 12-month insurance policy was purchased on August 1.
2. There are $750 of supplies on hand at November 30.
3. Amortization expense for the year is $5,360 on the furniture and equipment, and $4,200 on the leasehold improvements.
4. Salaries of $1,210 are accrued and unpaid at November 30.
5. Accrued interest expense at November 30 is $2,100.
6. Of the unearned sales revenue, $1,950 has been earned by November 30. The cost of goods sold incurred in earning this revenue is $1,275.
7. Of the note payable, $6,000 is to be paid during 2007.
8. Income tax of $100 is due and unpaid.

Instructions

(a) Prepare a general ledger and enter the trial balance amounts.
(b) Journalize and post the adjusting entries for the year.
(c) Prepare an adjusted trial balance.
(d) Prepare a statement of earnings, statement of retained earnings, and balance sheet for the year.

P5–7B MacLean Corp. purchases all merchandise inventory on credit and uses a perpetual inventory system. The Accounts Payable account is used for recording merchandise inventory purchases only; all other current liabilities are accrued in separate accounts. The following selected information is for the fiscal years 2004 through 2006:

Calculate missing amounts and assess profitability.
(SO 2, 4, 5)

	2006	2005	2004
Merchandise inventory (ending)	$ 11,300	$ 14,700	$ 12,200
Net sales	225,700	227,600	219,500
Purchase of merchandise inventory on account	141,000	150,000	132,000
Cash payments to suppliers	135,000	161,000	127,000

Additional information:

1. The balance in Merchandise Inventory at the beginning of 2004 was $13,000.
2. The balance in Accounts Payable at the beginning of 2004 was $20,000.

Instructions

(a) Calculate cost of goods sold for each year.
(b) Calculate the ending balance of Accounts Payable for each year.
(c) Calculate the gross profit and gross profit margin for each year.
(d) Sales declined in 2006. Does this mean that profitability also had to decline? Refer to the gross profit margin to explain and support your answer.

Calculate ratios and comment.
(SO 5)

P5−8B IPSCO Inc., headquartered in Regina, produces steel products. The following selected information (in U.S. thousands) is available for three recent fiscal years:

	2004	2003	2002
Current assets	$1,181,615	$ 649,302	$ 476,270
Current liabilities	344,850	198,181	171,458
Net sales	2,452,675	1,294,566	1,081,709
Cost of sales	1,660,009	1,122,625	976,392
Net earnings	438,610	16,585	20,279

Instructions

(a) Calculate the current ratio, gross profit margin, and profit margin for each year. Comment on whether the ratios have improved or deteriorated over the three years.
(b) Compare the 2004 ratios to the following industry averages: current ratio 1.7:1; gross profit margin 20.8%; and profit margin 3.9%. Are IPSCO's ratios better or worse than those of its industry?

Consider impact of transactions on ratios.
(SO 5)

P5−9B You are presented with the following statement of earnings for Merigomish Mariners Inc. for the year ended July 31, 2006:

MERIGOMISH MARINERS INC.
Statement of Earnings
Year Ended July 31, 2006

Net sales		$450,000
Cost of goods sold		315,000
Gross profit		135,000
Operating expenses		
Salaries expense	$65,000	
Utilities expense	10,500	
Amortization expense	6,700	
Advertising expense	5,600	
Freight out	1,500	
Insurance expense	1,200	
Total operating expenses		90,500
Earnings from operations		44,500
Other expense		
Interest expense		7,000
Earnings before income tax		37,500
Income tax expense		15,000
Net earnings		$ 22,500

The sales manager has come to the company president with a proposal. He wants to increase advertising expense and salaries by 10% each. He also wants to cut the gross profit margin by three percentage points (that is, if the gross profit margin is 30%, it would have to be cut to 27%). The sales manager says that marketing research shows that net sales will increase by 12% if this is done. The sales manager is really excited about this new proposal: "This increase in sales will be great!"

Instructions

(a) Calculate the gross profit margin and profit margin.

(b) Recalculate the ratios in (a), assuming that the sales manager's proposed changes are implemented. Assume that income tax expense is 40% of earnings before income tax.

(c) The president wants to make sure that the company's profit margin will not deteriorate if she follows the sales manager's proposal. Should the president agree to the sales manager's proposal?

*P5–10B   Data for Travel Warehouse Ltd. are presented in P5–1B.

Journalize purchase and sales transactions. (SO 6)

Instructions

Journalize the July transactions, assuming a periodic inventory system is used instead of a perpetual inventory system.

*P5–11B   Data for Shaoshi Inc. are presented in P5–2B.

Journalize purchase and sales transactions. (SO 6)

Instructions

Journalize the October transactions, assuming a periodic inventory system is used instead of a perpetual inventory system.

*P5–12B   Data for the Kicked-Back Tennis Shop are presented in P5–3B. A physical inventory count determined that $3,091 of inventory was on hand at April 30.

Journalize, post, and prepare trial balance and partial statement of earnings. (SO 6)

Instructions

(a) Prepare a general ledger and enter the opening balances.

(b) Journalize and post the April transactions, assuming a periodic inventory system is used instead of a perpetual inventory system.

(c) Prepare a trial balance as at April 30, 2006.

(d) Prepare a statement of earnings through to gross profit.

*P5–13B   The Goody Shop Ltd.'s adjusted trial balance appears as follows on November 30, 2006, the end of its fiscal year:

Prepare financial statements. (SO 6)

Accounts payable	$ 32,310	Land	$ 85,000
Accounts receivable	13,770	Merchandise inventory	34,360
Accumulated amortization—		Mortgage payable	146,000
building	61,200	Prepaid insurance	4,500
Accumulated amortization—		Property tax expense	3,500
equipment	19,880	Property tax payable	3,500
Amortization expense	14,000	Purchases	630,700
Building	175,000	Purchase discounts	12,000
Cash	8,500	Purchase returns and allowances	3,315
Common shares	56,000	Retained earnings	40,800
Dividends	5,000	Salaries expense	122,000
Equipment	57,000	Salaries payable	8,500
Freight in	5,060	Sales	849,000
Freight out	8,200	Sales discounts	15,000
Income tax expense	4,000	Sales returns and allowances	10,000
Insurance expense	9,000	Unearned sales revenue	3,000
Interest expense	11,315	Utilities expense	19,600

Additional information:

1. The Goody Shop uses a periodic system.

2. A physical inventory count determined that merchandise inventory on November 30, 2006, is $37,350.

Instructions

Prepare a statement of earnings, statement of retained earnings, and balance sheet for the year.

BROADENING YOUR PERSPECTIVE

Financial Reporting and Analysis

Analysis Tools

Financial Reporting Problem: *Loblaw*

BYP5–1   The financial statements for Loblaw are presented in Appendix A at the end of this book.

Instructions

(a) Is Loblaw a service company or a merchandising company?
(b) Are any non-operating revenues and non-operating expenses included in Loblaw's statement of earnings? If so, identify the accounts included.
(c) Using "cost of sales, selling and administrative expenses" in place of cost of goods sold, calculate Loblaw's gross profit margin for the two fiscal years presented.
(d) Calculate Loblaw's profit margin for the two fiscal years presented in the annual report.
(e) Comment on the trend in Loblaw's gross profit margin and profit margin.

Comparative Analysis Problem: *Loblaw and Sobeys*

BYP5–2   The financial statements of Sobeys are presented in Appendix B following the financial statements for Loblaw in Appendix A.

Instructions

(a) Based on the information contained in these financial statements, determine the following values for each company for each of the two most recent years presented in their financial statements:
    1. Percentage change in sales
    2. Percentage change in operating income
    3. Gross profit margin (use "cost of sales, selling and administrative expenses" in place of cost of goods sold)
    4. Profit margin
(b) What conclusions about the relative profitability of the two companies can be drawn from these data?

Research Case

BYP5–3   The article "The Future Is Still Smart," published on page 63 of the June 26, 2004, issue of *The Economist*, discusses smart-tag technology. Smart tags are radio frequency identification microchips which, when attached to inventory items, provide the tagged item with a unique identification code. When prompted by a reader, the tag broadcasts the information on the microchip.

Instructions

Read the article and answer the following questions:

(a) Why are smart tags considered to be a significant improvement over bar codes?
(b) Why will smart tags result in savings of hundreds of billions of dollars a year?
(c) How is Marks & Spencer using the smart tags for its inventory items?
(d) What are some uses of smart tags other than for inventory?

Interpreting Financial Statements

BYP5–4 Big Rock Brewery is a western producer and marketer of premium quality beers. On January 3, 2003, Big Rock Brewery Ltd. reorganized as an income trust (a corporation with a different form of equity section). Its year end had been March 31. After the reorganization, it chose a new year end of December 31.

Information from Big Rock's statement of earnings for the current year, and the preceding nine months since it formed as an income trust follows:

	Year ended December 31, 2004	Nine months ended December 31, 2003
Net sales	$38,789,564	$28,503,840
Cost of sales	13,696,549	10,298,575
Operating expenses	17,397,249	12,757,866
Income tax expense	928,858	891,543

Instructions

(a) Calculate the gross profit and gross profit margin for each of the two periods. Comment on any trend in this percentage.

(b) Calculate the net earnings and profit margin for each of the two periods. Comment on any trend in this percentage.

(c) How well has Big Rock managed its operating expenses over the two-year period?

A Global Focus

BYP5–5 Carrefour, headquartered in Paris, is the world's second largest retailer—second only to Wal-Mart. Although Wal-Mart is still the world's #1 retailer, its international sales are far lower than Carrefour's. This is a concern for Wal-Mart, since its primary opportunity for future growth lies outside of North America.

Below are selected financial data for Carrefour (in euros) and Wal-Mart (in U.S. dollars). Even though their results are presented in different currencies, by employing ratios we can make some basic comparisons.

	Carrefour (in billions)	Wal-Mart (in billions)
Sales	€70.5	$256.3
Cost of goods sold	54.6	198.7
Net earnings	1.7	9.1
Total assets	39.1	104.9
Current assets	14.5	34.4
Current liabilities	13.7	37.4
Total liabilities	29.4	61.3

Instructions

(a) Calculate the gross profit margin for each company. Discuss their relative profitability and ability to control their cost of goods sold.

(b) Calculate the profit margin for each company. Discuss their relative profitability and ability to control their operating expenses.

(c) Calculate the current ratio and the debt to total assets ratio for each company. Discuss their relative liquidity and solvency.

(d) What concerns might you have in relying on this comparison?

Financial Analysis on the Web

BYP5–6 Fishery Products International (FPI) Limited is a Newfoundland and Labrador-based seafood company. This case investigates how FPI analyzes changes in its gross profit and communicates this information to external users.

Instructions

Specific requirements for this Web case can be found on the Toolkit website.

Analysis Tools
(Financial Analysis on the Web)

Critical Thinking

Collaborative Learning Activity

BYP5–7   Wu Department Store Ltd. opened three years ago. For the first two years, business was good, but the following results for the current year, 2006, were disappointing:

WU DEPARTMENT STORE LTD. Statement of Earnings Year Ended December 31, 2006	
Net sales	$700,000
Cost of goods sold	560,000
Gross profit	140,000
Operating expenses	120,000
Earnings before income tax	20,000
Income tax expense	4,000
Net earnings	$ 16,000

The controller, Kathy, believes the problem is the relatively low gross profit margin of 20%. The store manager, John, believes the problem is that operating expenses are too high.

Kathy thinks the gross profit margin can be improved by making the following changes:

1. Increase average selling prices by 17%. This increase is expected to lower the sales volume so that total sales will increase by only 8%.
2. Buy merchandise in larger quantities to get quantity discounts and take all purchase discounts. These changes are expected to increase the gross profit margin by 3%. Kathy does not expect these changes to have any effect on operating expenses.

John thinks expenses can be cut by making these changes:

1. Cut the sales salaries of $60,000 in half and give sales personnel a commission of 2% of net sales.
2. Reduce store deliveries to one day per week rather than twice a week. This change will reduce delivery expenses of $40,000 by 40%. John feels that these changes will not have any effect on net sales.

Kathy and John come to you for help in deciding the best way to improve net earnings.

Instructions

With the class divided into groups, do the following:

(a) Prepare a projected statement of earnings for 2007 assuming (1) Kathy's changes are implemented and (2) John's ideas are adopted. The income tax rate is expected to be 20% of earnings before income tax in 2007.
(b) Prepare a projected statement of earnings for 2007, assuming both sets of proposed changes are made.
(c) What is your recommendation to Kathy and John?
(d) Discuss the impact that other factors might have. For example, would increasing the quantity of inventory increase costs? Would a salary cut affect employee morale? Would decreased morale affect sales? Would decreased store deliveries decrease customer satisfaction? What other suggestions might be considered?

Communication Activity

BYP5–8   Consider the following events:

Sept. 23 Dexter Maersk decides to buy a custom-made snowboard and calls the Great Canadian Snowboard Corporation to inquire about its products.

28 Dexter asks Great Canadian Snowboard to manufacture a custom board for him.

Oct. 3 The company sends Dexter a purchase order to fill out, which he immediately completes, signs, and sends back with a required 25% down payment.

7 Great Canadian Snowboard receives Dexter's purchase order and down payment, and begins working on the board.

Dec. 31 Great Canadian Snowboard has its fiscal year end. At this time, Dexter's board is 75% completed.

Jan. 28 The company completes the snowboard for Dexter and notifies him that he can take delivery.

Feb. 3 Dexter picks up his snowboard from the company and takes it home.

4 Dexter tries the snowboard out and likes it so much that he carves his initials in it.

21 Great Canadian Snowboard bills Dexter for the cost of the snowboard, less the 25% down payment.

28 The company receives partial payment (another 25%) from Dexter.

Mar. 18 The company receives payment of the remaining amount due from Dexter.

Instructions

(a) In a memo to the president of Great Canadian Snowboard, outline the alternatives and recommend when the company should record the revenue and expense related to the snowboard.

(b) If Dexter had not been required to make a down payment with his purchase order, would your answer to part (a) be different?

Ethics Case

BYP5–9 Rita Pelzer was just hired as the assistant controller of Zaz Stores Ltd., a specialty chain store company that has nine retail stores concentrated in one city. Among other things, the payment of all invoices is centralized in one of the departments Rita will manage. Her main responsibility is to keep the company's high credit rating by paying all bills when they are due and to take advantage of all cash discounts.

Ethics In Accounting

Jamie Caterino, the former assistant controller who has been promoted to controller, is training Rita in her new duties. He instructs Rita that she is to continue the practice of preparing all cheques for the amount due less the discount and to date the cheques the last day of the discount period. "But," Jamie continues, "we always hold the cheques at least four days beyond the discount period before mailing them. That way we get another four days of interest on our money. Most of our creditors need our business and don't complain. And, if they scream about our missing the discount period, we blame it on Canada Post. We've only lost one discount out of every hundred we take that way. I think everybody does it. By the way, welcome to our team!"

Instructions

(a) What are the ethical considerations in this case?

(b) What stakeholders are harmed or benefited?

(c) Should Rita continue the practice started by Jamie? Does she have any choice?

Serial Problem

(*Note*: This serial problem was started in Chapter 1 and continued in Chapters 2 through 4. From the information gathered through Chapter 4, follow the instructions below using the general ledger accounts you have already prepared.)

BYP5–10 Cookie Creations, after experiencing a successful initial operating period, is considering other opportunities to develop business. One opportunity is the sale of deluxe European mixers. The sales manager of Mixer Deluxe has approached Cookie Creations to become the exclusive Canadian distributor of these mixers. The current cost of the European mixer is approximately $525 Canadian, and the company would sell each one for $1,050.

Natalie, struggling to do the accounting for the company, comes to you for advice on how to account for these mixers. Each appliance has a serial number and can easily be identified. Natalie asks you the following questions:

1. "Would you consider these mixers to be inventory? Or, should they be classified as supplies or equipment?"
2. "I've learned a little about keeping track of inventory using both the perpetual and periodic inventory systems. Which system do you think is better? Which one would you recommend for the type of inventory that Cookie Creations wants to sell?"
3. "How often should the company count inventory if the perpetual inventory system is used? Does it need to count inventory at all?"

In the end, Cookie Creations decides to use the perpetual inventory system, and the following transactions occur during the month of January:

Jan. 4 The company buys five deluxe mixers on account from Kzinski Supply Co. for $2,625, terms n/30, FOB shipping point.
       5 $100 freight is paid on the January 4 purchase.
       7 One of the mixers is returned to Kzinski because it was damaged during shipping. Kzinski issues a credit note to Cookie Creations for the cost of the mixer plus $20 for the cost of freight that was paid on January 6 for one mixer.
       8 The amount due from the neighbourhood community centre that was accrued at the end of December is collected.
      12 Three deluxe mixers are sold to various customers on account for $3,150, terms 1/10, n/30, FOB destination.
      13 $75 of freight charges are paid for the three mixers that were sold on January 12.
      14 The cellphone bill previously accrued in the December adjusting journal entries is paid.
      15 Four deluxe mixers are purchased on account from Kzinski Supply Co. for $2,100, terms n/30, FOB shipping point.
      16 $80 freight is paid on the January 15 purchase.
      19 1,000 new common shares are issued for $1,000 cash.
      20 Two deluxe mixers are sold for $2,100 cash.
      21 Amounts due from customers for the January 12 transaction are collected.
      28 The assistant's wages are paid. She worked 20 hours in January and is also paid for amounts owing at December 31, 2005.
      31 Kzinski is paid all amounts due.
      31 $750 of dividends are paid to shareholders.

As at January 31, the following adjusting entry data is available:

1. A count of brochures and posters reveals that none were used in January.
2. A count of baking supplies reveals that none were used in January.
3. Another month's worth of amortization needs to be recorded on the baking equipment bought in November. (Recall that the baking equipment has a useful life of five years or 60 months.)
4. An additional month's worth of interest on the bank loan needs to be accrued. (The interest rate is 6%.)
5. One month's worth of insurance has expired.
6. The cellphone bill is received, $75. The bill is for services provided in January and is due February 15. (Recall that the cellphone is only used for business purposes.)
7. An analysis of the unearned revenue account reveals that no lessons have been taught this month because Natalie has been so busy selling mixers. As a result, there is no change to the unearned revenue account. Natalie hopes to book the outstanding lessons in February.
8. An inventory count of mixers at the end of January reveals that three mixers are remaining.
9. Recall that Cookie Creations' income tax rate is 15% of earnings before tax.

Instructions

Using the information that you have gathered through Chapter 4, and the new information above, do the following:

(a) Answer Natalie's questions.
(b) Record and post the January 2006 transactions.
(c) Prepare a trial balance.
(d) Record and post the adjusting journal entries required.
(e) Prepare an adjusted trial balance.
(f) Prepare a statement of earnings, statement of retained earnings, and balance sheet for the month.

Answers to Self-Study Questions

1. b   2. d   3. d   4. a   5. c   6. d   7. c   8. c   *9. b   *10. b

Answer to Loblaw Review It Question 5

Loblaw uses a multiple-step statement of earnings and reports its non-operating interest expense separate from operating income. However, the first portion of its statement of earnings is not the same as the multiple-step statements presented in this chapter. For competitive reasons, Loblaw does not report its cost of sales or its gross profit separately.

Remember to go back to the Navigator box at the beginning of the chapter to check off your completed work.

CHAPTER 6

Reporting and Analyzing Inventory

How Many Dump Trucks Did You Want?

Let's talk inventory-BIG inventory. Illinois-based Caterpillar Inc. is the world's largest manufacturer of construction and mining products. It produces more than 300 machines at 50 facilities in the United States and 63 other locations worldwide. In Canada, Caterpillar has manufacturing operations in Edmonton and Montreal, logistics operations in Guelph and Saskatoon, financial services in Calgary and Toronto, and a training and demonstration centre in Toronto.

The world's largest dump truck, the Caterpillar 797B, is as tall as a three-storey building and has a 345-tonne capacity. In 1998, Caterpillar sent six of its predecessor Cat 797s to Fort McMurray, Alberta-no easy feat, since many highways and bridges can't take their weight-to be tested at Syncrude Canada, the world's largest producer of crude oil from oil sands. Syncrude evaluated the Cat 797 for long-term production capability, durability, and maintenance in an oil sands mine, one of the toughest mining environments. The trucks scored top marks. By 2005, Syncrude had 33 Cat 797s and another nine on order.

A Cat 797B can cost millions of dollars and requires one heck of a big garage for storage. Obviously, Caterpillar needs to avoid having too much of this kind of inventory sitting around. Still, it has to have enough to meet its customers' demands. In short, Caterpillar has big inventory challenges.

And big sales. Caterpillar enjoys record sales, profits, and growth. In fact, 2004 was a banner year, with $30.25 billion in revenues and a record profit of $2.03 billion, an 85 percent increase from 2003. Expectations for 2005 were even better.

Effective inventory management is key to this success. From 1993 to 2003, Caterpillar's sales increased by more than 97 percent, while its inventory increased by only 49 percent. To achieve this inventory reduction, Caterpillar used a two-pronged approach. First, a factory modernization program increased production efficiency, reducing the time required to manufacture a part by 75 percent. Second, an improved distribution system allows Caterpillar to fill more than 180 million order lines annually from 19 distribution centres located on six continents. It can now ship an order in less than 24 hours more than 99 percent of the time.

In fact, Caterpillar is so well known for its parts distribution expertise, it formed a wholly-owned subsidiary in 1987 to market integrated supply chain solutions to other companies. Caterpillar Logistics Services now serves more than 50 global corporations in a variety of industries.

Caterpillar's inventory management and accounting practices make a crucial contribution to its own and other companies' profitability.

the navigator

Caterpillar Inc.: www.caterpillar.com

THE NAVIGATOR

☐ Read *Feature Story*

☐ Scan *Study Objectives*

☐ Read *Chapter Preview*

☐ Read text and answer *Before You Go On*

☐ Work *Using the Decision Toolkit*

☐ Review *Summary of Study Objectives*

☐ Review the *Decision Toolkit—A Summary*

☐ Work *Demonstration Problem*

☐ Answer *Self-Study Questions*

☐ Complete assignments

STUDY OBJECTIVES

After studying this chapter, you should be able to:

1. Describe the steps in determining inventory quantities.
2. Apply the inventory cost flow assumptions under a periodic inventory system.
3. Explain the financial statement effects of the inventory cost flow assumptions and inventory errors.
4. Demonstrate the presentation and analysis of inventory.
5. Apply the inventory cost flow assumptions under a perpetual inventory system (Appendix 6A).

the navigator

In the previous chapter, we discussed the accounting for merchandise inventory using a perpetual inventory system. In this chapter, we explain the procedures for determining inventory quantities. We then discuss the cost flow assumptions used to calculate the cost of goods sold during the period and the cost of inventory on hand at the end of the period. We also discuss the effects of inventory errors on a company's financial statements, and we conclude by illustrating methods to report and analyze inventory.

The chapter is organized as follows:

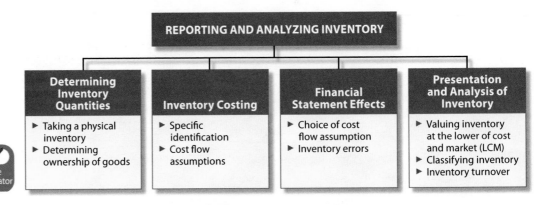

Determining Inventory Quantities

Whether they are using a perpetual inventory system or a periodic one, all companies need to determine inventory quantities at the end of the accounting period. When they use a perpetual inventory system, companies take a physical inventory (i.e., count all the inventory) at year end for two purposes: (1) to check the accuracy of their perpetual inventory records and (2) to determine the amount of inventory lost due to shrinkage or theft. Recall that you learned in Chapter 5 that in a perpetual inventory system, the accounting records continuously—perpetually—show the quantity of inventory that *should* be on hand, not necessarily what *is* on hand.

In a periodic inventory system, inventory quantities are not updated on a continuous basis. Companies that use a periodic inventory system must take a physical inventory to determine the inventory on hand at the balance sheet date. Once the ending inventory amount is determined, this amount is then used to calculate the cost of goods sold for the period.

Determining inventory quantities involves two steps: (1) taking a physical inventory of goods on hand and (2) determining the ownership of goods.

Taking a Physical Inventory

Taking a physical inventory involves actually counting, weighing, or measuring each kind of inventory on hand. In many companies, taking an inventory is a formidable task. For example, retailers such as Loblaw have thousands of different inventory items. An inventory count is generally more accurate when goods are not being sold or received during the counting. Consequently, companies often take inventory when the business is closed or when business is slow.

To make fewer errors in taking the inventory, a company should ensure that it has a good system of internal control in place. **Internal control** consists of policies and procedures to optimize resources, prevent and detect errors, safeguard assets, and enhance the accuracy and reliability of accounting records. Some internal control procedures for counting inventory include the following:

1. The counting should be done by employees who do not have responsibility for the custody or recordkeeping for the inventory.
2. Each counter should establish the validity of each inventory item: this means checking that the items actually exist, how many there are of them, and what condition they are in.

3. There should be a second count by another employee or auditor. Counting should take place in teams of two.
4. Prenumbered inventory tags should be used to ensure that all inventory items are counted and that none are counted more than once.

We will learn more about internal controls in Chapter 7.

After the physical inventory is taken, the quantity of each kind of inventory is listed on inventory summary sheets. To ensure accuracy, the listing should be verified by a second employee, or auditor. Unit costs are then applied to the quantities in order to determine the total cost of the inventory—this will be explained later in the chapter when we discuss inventory costing.

Determining Ownership of Goods

Before we can begin to calculate the cost of inventory, we need to consider the ownership of goods. To determine who owns what inventory, two questions must be answered: (1) Do all of the goods included in the count belong to the company? (2) Does the company own any goods that were not included in the count?

Goods in Transit

Goods in transit at the end of the period (on board a truck, train, ship, or plane) make determining ownership a bit more complicated. The company may have purchased goods that have not yet been received, or it may have sold goods that have not yet been delivered. To arrive at an accurate count, ownership of these goods must be determined.

Goods in transit should be included in the inventory of the company that has legal title to the goods. As we learned in Chapter 5, legal title, or ownership, is determined by the terms of the sale as follows:

1. **FOB (free on board) shipping point:** Legal title (ownership) of the goods passes to the buyer when the public carrier accepts the goods from the seller.
2. **FOB destination:** Legal title (ownership) of the goods remains with the seller until the goods reach the buyer.

If the shipping terms are FOB shipping point, the buyer is responsible for paying the shipping costs and has legal title to the goods while they are in transit. If the shipping terms are FOB destination, the seller is responsible for paying the shipping costs and has legal title to the goods while they are in transit. These terms will be important in determining the exact date that a purchase or sale should be recorded and what items should be included in inventory, even if the items are not physically present at the time of the inventory count.

For example, publishers normally ship textbooks to campus bookstores on FOB shipping point terms. This means that the bookstores (and ultimately the students) pay the cost of shipping. This also means that if the bookstore has a December 31 year end, it must adjust its inventory count for any textbooks still in transit for the beginning of the winter term. The bookstore also accepts the risk of damage or loss when the books are in transit.

The following table summarizes who pays the shipping costs, and who has legal title to (owns) the goods, while they are in transit between the seller's location (the shipping point) and the buyer's location (the destination):

Shipping Terms	Shipping Costs	Legal Title
FOB shipping point	Buyer	Buyer
FOB destination	Seller	Seller

Consigned Goods

In some lines of business, it is customary to hold goods belonging to other parties and sell them, for a fee, without ever taking ownership of the goods. These are called **consigned goods**. Under a consignment arrangement, the holder of the goods (called the *consignee*) does not own the goods. Ownership remains with the shipper of the goods (called the *consignor*) until the goods are actually sold to a customer. Because consigned goods are not owned by the consignee, they should not be included in the consignee's physical inventory count. Conversely, the consignor should include in its inventory any of the consignor's merchandise that is being held by the consignee.

For example, artists often display their paintings and other works of art at galleries on consignment. In such cases, the art gallery does not take ownership of the art—it still belongs to the artist. Therefore, if an inventory count is taken, any art on consignment should not be included in the art gallery's inventory. When the art sells, the gallery then takes a commission and pays the artist the remainder. Many craft stores, second-hand clothing stores, sporting goods stores, and antique dealers sell goods on consignment to keep their inventory costs down and to avoid the risk of purchasing an item they will not be able to sell.

Other Situations

Sometimes goods are not physically on the premises because they have been taken home *on approval* by a customer. Goods on approval should be added to the physical inventory count because they still belong to the seller. The customer will either return the item or decide to buy it at some point in the future.

In other cases, goods are sold but the seller is holding them for alteration, or until they are picked up or delivered to the customer. These goods should not be included in the physical count, because legal title to ownership has passed to the customer. Damaged or unsaleable goods should also be separated from the physical count, and any loss should be recorded.

ACCOUNTING MATTERS!   Ethics Perspective

Over the years, inventory has played a role in many fraud cases. A classic one involved salad oil. Management filled storage tanks mostly with water, and since oil rises to the top, the auditors thought the tanks were full of oil. In this instance, management also said the company had more tanks than it really did—numbers were repainted on the tanks to confuse the auditors.

Today, inventory theft is a serious problem for companies, estimated to amount to around $60 billion a year. Surprisingly, a significant amount of this theft takes place from the inside out. A 2002 Ipsos-Reid survey found that 20 percent of Canadians were personally aware of employees stealing from their companies. A physical inventory count helps identify inventory losses, which then enables a company to put preventive security measures into place.

Source: Kira Vermond, "From the Inside Out," *CMA Management*, May 2003, p. 36.

BEFORE YOU GO ON . . .

▶Review It

1. What steps are involved in determining inventory quantities?
2. How is ownership determined for goods in transit?
3. Who has title to consigned goods?

▶Do It

The Too Good To Be Threw Corporation completed its inventory count. It arrived at a total inventory amount of $200,000, counting everything currently on hand in its warehouse. Discuss how the following additional information will affect the reported cost of the inventory.

1. Goods costing $15,000 and held on consignment were included in the inventory.
2. Purchased goods of $10,000 were in transit (terms FOB shipping point) and not included in the count.
3. Sold inventory with a cost of $12,000 was in transit (terms FOB shipping point) and not included in the count.

Action Plan

- Apply the rules of ownership to goods held on consignment.
- Apply the rules of ownership to goods in transit:
  - ° FOB shipping point: Goods sold or purchased and shipped FOB shipping point belong to the buyer.
  - ° FOB destination: Goods sold or purchased and shipped FOB destination belong to the seller until they reach their destination.

Solution

1. The goods held on consignment should be deducted from Too Good To Be Threw's inventory count ($200,000 − $15,000 = $185,000).
2. The goods in transit purchased FOB shipping point should be added to the company's inventory count ($185,000 + $10,000 = $195,000).
3. The goods in transit sold FOB shipping point were correctly excluded from Too Good To Be Threw's ending inventory, since title passed when the goods were handed over to the shipping company.

The correct inventory total is $195,000, and not $200,000 as originally reported.

the navigator

Inventory Costing

study objective 2

Apply the inventory cost flow assumptions under a periodic inventory system.

After the number of units of inventory has been determined, unit costs are applied to those quantities to determine the total cost of the goods sold and cost of the ending inventory. When all inventory items have been purchased at the same unit cost, this calculation is simple. However, when items have been purchased at different costs during the period, it can be difficult to determine what the unit costs are of the items that remain in inventory and what the unit costs are of the items that were sold.

For example, assume that throughout the calendar year Wynneck Electronics Ltd. buys at different prices 1,000 Astro Condenser units for resale. Some Astro Condensers cost $10 when originally purchased last year. Units purchased in April cost $11, those purchased in August cost $12, and those acquired in November cost $13. Now suppose Wynneck Electronics has 450 Astro Condensers remaining in inventory at the end of December. Should these inventory items be assigned a cost of $10, $11, $12, $13, or some combination of all four?

To determine the cost of goods sold as well as the cost of ending inventory, we need a way of allocating the purchase cost to each item in inventory and each item that has been sold. One allocation method—specific identification—uses the actual physical flow of the goods to determine cost. We will look at this method next.

www.wiley.com/canada/kimmel/

Animated Tutorials (Inventory Cost Flow)

Specific Identification

The **specific identification method** tracks the actual physical flow of the goods. Each item of inventory is marked, tagged, or coded with its specific unit cost. Items still in inventory at the end of the year are specifically costed to determine the total cost of the ending inventory.

Assume, for example, that Wynneck Electronics buys three DVD recorder/players at costs of $700, $750, and $800. During the year, two are sold at a selling price of $1,200 each. At December 31, the company determines that the $750 DVD recorder/player is still on hand. The ending inventory is $750 and the cost of goods sold is $1,500 ($700 + $800).

Illustration 6-1 ▶

Specific identification

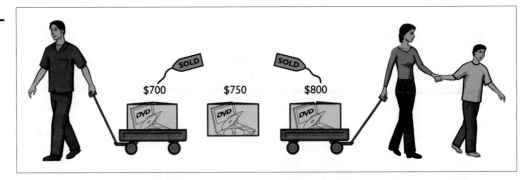

Specific identification is the ideal method for determining cost. This method reports ending inventory at actual cost and matches the actual cost of goods sold against sales revenue. However, there are also disadvantages to this method. For example, specific identification may allow management to manipulate net earnings. To see how, assume that Wynneck Electronics wants to maximize its net earnings just before its year end. When selling one of the three DVD recorder/players referred to earlier, management could choose the recorder/player with the lowest cost ($700) to match against revenues ($1,200). Or, it could minimize net earnings by selecting the highest-cost ($800) recorder/player.

Specific identification is most practical to use when a company sells a limited number of items that have a high unit cost and that can be clearly identified from purchase through to sale. Automobiles are a good example of a type of inventory that works well with the specific identification method as they can easily be distinguished by serial number. On the other hand, automobile dealers also sell hundreds of relatively low-unit-cost items as parts. These are often identical to each other, so it may not be possible to track the cost of each item separately.

Today, with bar coding, it is theoretically possible to use specific identification with nearly any type of product. The reality is, however, that this practice is still relatively expensive and rare. Instead, rather than keep track of the cost of each particular item sold, most companies make assumptions—called **cost flow assumptions**—about which units are sold. Even Caterpillar, in the feature story, uses a cost flow assumption instead of specific identification to track its sales of the Cat 797.

Cost Flow Assumptions

Cost flow assumptions differ from specific identification as they assume flows of costs that may not be the same as the actual physical flow of goods. There are three commonly used cost flow assumptions:

1. First-in, first-out (FIFO)
2. Average
3. Last-in, first-out (LIFO)

These three cost flow assumptions can be used in both the perpetual inventory system and the periodic inventory system. Under a perpetual inventory system, the cost of goods available for sale (beginning inventory plus the cost of goods purchased) is allocated to the cost of goods sold and ending inventory as each item is sold. Under a periodic inventory system, the allocation is made only at the end of the period.

The periodic inventory system will be used to illustrate cost flow assumptions in this chapter. We have several reasons for doing this. First, many companies that use a perpetual inventory system use it only to keep track of *quantities* on hand. When they determine the cost of goods sold at the end of the period, they use one of the three cost flow assumptions under a periodic inventory system. Second, most companies that use the average cost flow assumption use it under a periodic inventory system. Third, the FIFO cost flow assumption gives the same results under the periodic and perpetual systems. Finally, it is simpler to demonstrate the cost flow assumptions under the periodic inventory system, which makes them easier to understand. (The chapter appendix explains how these cost flow assumptions are used under a perpetual inventory system.)

To illustrate these three inventory cost flow assumptions in a periodic inventory system, we will assume that Wynneck Electronics Ltd. has the following information for one of its products, the Astro Condenser:

WYNNECK ELECTRONICS LTD.
Astro Condensers

Date	Explanation	Units	Unit Cost	Total Cost
Jan. 1	Beginning inventory	100	$10	$ 1,000
Apr. 15	Purchase	200	11	2,200
Aug. 24	Purchase	300	12	3,600
Nov. 27	Purchase	400	13	5,200
	Total	1,000		$12,000

The company had a total of 1,000 units available for sale during the period. The total cost of these units was $12,000. A physical inventory count at the end of the year determined that 450 units remained on hand at the end of the year. Consequently, it can be calculated that 550 (1,000 − 450) units were sold during the year.

The question to be answered next is this: as the 1,000 units available for sale had different unit costs, how does Wynneck determine which unit costs to allocate to the 450 units remaining so that it can determine the cost of the ending inventory? Once this question is answered and the cost of the ending inventory is determined, we can then calculate the cost of goods sold.

The total cost (or "pool of costs") of the 1,000 units available for sale was $12,000. We will demonstrate the allocation of this pool of costs, using FIFO, average, and LIFO in the next sections. Note that, throughout these sections, the total cost of goods available for sale will remain the same under all three inventory cost flow assumptions. The pool of costs does not change with the choice of cost flow assumption—only the allocation of these costs between the ending inventory and the cost of goods sold changes, as shown in Illustration 6-2.

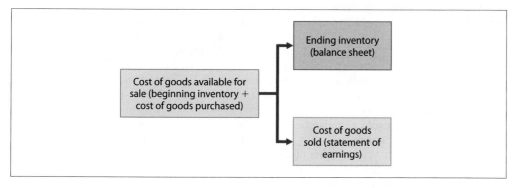

Illustration 6-2 ◀

Allocation of cost of goods available for sale

First-In, First-Out (FIFO)

The **first-in, first-out (FIFO) cost flow assumption** assumes that the earliest (oldest) goods purchased are the first ones to be sold. This does not necessarily mean that the oldest units are sold first, only that the cost of the oldest units is recognized first. Note that there is no accounting requirement for the cost flow assumption to match the actual physical movement of goods. Nonetheless, FIFO often matches the actual physical flow of merchandise, because it is generally good business practice to sell the oldest units first.

In the periodic inventory system, we ignore the different dates of each of the sales. Instead we make the allocation **at the end of a period** and assume that the entire pool of costs is available for allocation at that time. The allocation of the cost of goods available for sale at Wynneck Electronics under FIFO is shown in Illustration 6-3 on the following page.

Illustration 6-3 ▶

Periodic system—FIFO

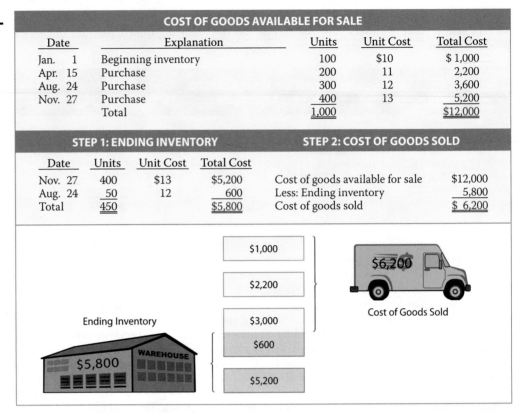

COST OF GOODS AVAILABLE FOR SALE				
Date	Explanation	Units	Unit Cost	Total Cost
Jan. 1	Beginning inventory	100	$10	$ 1,000
Apr. 15	Purchase	200	11	2,200
Aug. 24	Purchase	300	12	3,600
Nov. 27	Purchase	400	13	5,200
	Total	1,000		$12,000

STEP 1: ENDING INVENTORY

Date	Units	Unit Cost	Total Cost
Nov. 27	400	$13	$5,200
Aug. 24	50	12	600
Total	450		$5,800

STEP 2: COST OF GOODS SOLD

Cost of goods available for sale	$12,000
Less: Ending inventory	5,800
Cost of goods sold	$ 6,200

Ending Inventory — $5,800 — WAREHOUSE

$1,000
$2,200
$3,000
$600
$5,200

Cost of Goods Sold — $6,200

The cost flow assumption—FIFO in this case—always indicates the order of selling. In other words, with FIFO the order in which the goods are assumed to be sold is first in, first out. The cost of the ending inventory is determined by taking the unit cost of the most recent purchase and working backward until all units of inventory have been costed. In this example, the 450 units of ending inventory must be costed using the most recent purchase costs. The last purchase was 400 units at $13 on November 27. The remaining 50 units are costed at the price of the second most recent purchase, $12, on August 24.

Once the cost of the ending inventory is determined, the cost of goods sold is calculated by subtracting the cost of the units not sold (ending inventory) from the cost of all goods available for sale (the pool of costs).

The cost of goods sold can also be separately calculated or proven as shown below. To determine the cost of goods sold, simply start at the first item of beginning inventory and count forward until the total number of units sold (550) is reached. Note that of the 300 units purchased on August 24, only 250 units are assumed sold. This agrees with our calculation of the cost of the ending inventory, where 50 of these units were assumed unsold and thus included in ending inventory.

Date	Units	Unit Cost	Cost of Goods Sold
Jan. 1	100	$10	$1,000
Apr. 15	200	11	2,200
Aug. 24	250	12	3,000
Total	550		$6,200

Because of the potential for calculation errors, we recommend that the cost of goods sold amounts be separately calculated and proven in your assignments. The ending inventory and cost of goods sold total can then be compared to the cost of goods available for sale to check the accuracy of the calculations, which would be as follows for Wynneck: $5,800 + $6,200 = $12,000.

Average

The **average cost flow assumption** assumes that the goods available for sale are homogeneous or nondistinguishable. Under this assumption, the allocation of the cost of goods available for sale is made based on the weighted average unit cost incurred. Note that this average cost is not calculated by taking a simple average [($10 + $11 + $12 + $13) ÷ 4 = $11.50 per unit], but by weighting the quantities purchased at each unit cost.

The formula and calculation of the **weighted average unit cost** are given in Illustration 6-4.

Illustration 6-4 ◄

Calculation of weighted average unit cost

The weighted average unit cost is then applied to the units on hand to determine the cost of the ending inventory. The allocation of the cost of goods available for sale at Wynneck Electronics using average cost is shown in Illustration 6-5.

Illustration 6-5 ◄

Periodic system—Average

COST OF GOODS AVAILABLE FOR SALE				
Date	Explanation	Units	Unit Cost	Total Cost
Jan. 1	Beginning inventory	100	$10	$ 1,000
Apr. 15	Purchase	200	11	2,200
Aug. 24	Purchase	300	12	3,600
Nov. 27	Purchase	400	13	5,200
	Total	1,000		$12,000

STEP 1: ENDING INVENTORY			STEP 2: COST OF GOODS SOLD	
$12,000 ÷ 1,000 = $12.00			Cost of goods available for sale	$12,000
Units	Unit Cost	Total Cost	Less: Ending inventory	5,400
450	$12.00	$5,400	Cost of goods sold	$ 6,600

$$\frac{\$12,000}{1,000 \text{ units}} = \$12 \text{ per unit}$$

450 units X $12 = $5,400

WAREHOUSE

Ending Inventory

550 units X $12 = $6,600

Cost of Goods Sold

We can verify the cost of goods sold under the average cost flow assumption by multiplying the units sold by the weighted average unit cost (550 × $12 = $6,600). And, again, we can prove our calculations by ensuring that the total of the ending inventory and cost of goods sold equals the cost of goods available for sale ($5,400 + $6,600 = $12,000).

Last-In, First-Out (LIFO)

The **last-in, first-out (LIFO) cost flow assumption** assumes that the most recent (latest) goods purchased are the first ones to be sold. For most companies, LIFO rarely matches the actual physical flow of inventory. Only for goods stored in piles, such as sand, gravel, or hay, where goods are removed from the top of the pile when they are sold, would LIFO match the actual physical flow of goods. But, as explained earlier, this does not mean that the LIFO cost flow assumption cannot be used in other cases. It is the flow of costs that is important, not the physical flow of goods.

The allocation of the cost of goods available for sale at Wynneck Electronics under LIFO is shown in Illustration 6-6.

Illustration 6-6 ▶

Periodic system—LIFO

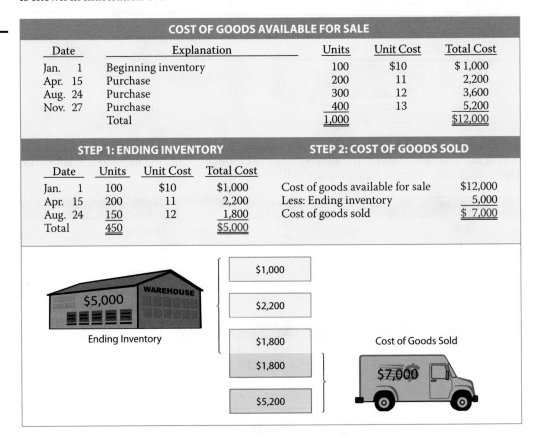

	COST OF GOODS AVAILABLE FOR SALE			
Date	Explanation	Units	Unit Cost	Total Cost
Jan. 1	Beginning inventory	100	$10	$ 1,000
Apr. 15	Purchase	200	11	2,200
Aug. 24	Purchase	300	12	3,600
Nov. 27	Purchase	400	13	5,200
	Total	1,000		$12,000

STEP 1: ENDING INVENTORY				STEP 2: COST OF GOODS SOLD	
Date	Units	Unit Cost	Total Cost		
Jan. 1	100	$10	$1,000	Cost of goods available for sale	$12,000
Apr. 15	200	11	2,200	Less: Ending inventory	5,000
Aug. 24	150	12	1,800	Cost of goods sold	$ 7,000
Total	450		$5,000		

Under LIFO, since it is assumed that the goods that are sold first are the ones that are purchased most recently, ending inventory is based on the costs of the oldest units purchased. That is, the cost of the ending inventory is determined by taking the unit cost of the earliest goods available for sale and working forward until all units of inventory have been costed.

In our example, therefore, the 450 units of ending inventory must be costed using the earliest purchase prices. The first purchase was 100 units at $10 in the January 1 beginning inventory. Then 200 units were purchased at $11. The remaining 150 units are costed at $12 per unit, the August 24 purchase price.

Under LIFO, the cost of the last goods in is the first cost to assign to the cost of goods sold. We can prove the cost of goods sold in our example by starting at the end of the period and counting backwards until we reach the total number of units sold (550). The result is that 400 units from the last purchase (November 27) are assumed to be sold first, and only 150 units from the next purchase (August 24) are needed to reach the total 550 units sold.

Date	Units	Unit Cost	Cost of Goods Sold
Nov. 27	400	$13	$5,200
Aug. 24	150	12	1,800
Total	550		$7,000

When the ending inventory and cost of goods sold amounts are then added together, they should equal the cost of goods available for sale, which is as follows for Wynneck: $5,000 + $7,000 = $12,000.

Remember that, under a periodic inventory system, all goods purchased during the period are assumed to be available for allocation, regardless of when they were purchased. Note also that because goods that are purchased late in a period are assumed to be available for the first sale, earnings could be manipulated in LIFO by a last minute end-of-period purchase of inventory.

BEFORE YOU GO ON . . .

▶Review It

1. Why is the specific identification method not practical to use in all circumstances?
2. Distinguish between the three cost flow assumptions—FIFO, average, and LIFO.
3. Which inventory cost flow assumption best approximates the actual physical flow of goods?
4. Which inventory method and cost flow assumption can be manipulated?

▶Do It

The accounting records of Ag Implement Inc. show the following data:

Beginning inventory	4,000 units at $3
Purchases	6,000 units at $4
Sales	8,000 units at $8

Determine the cost of ending inventory and cost of goods sold under a periodic inventory system using (a) FIFO, (b) average, and (c) LIFO.

Action Plan

- Ignore the selling price in allocating cost.
- Determine the ending inventory first. Calculate the cost of goods sold by subtracting ending inventory from the cost of goods available for sale.
- For FIFO, allocate the latest costs to the goods on hand.
- For average, determine the weighted average unit cost (cost of goods available for sale ÷ number of units available for sale). Multiply this cost by the number of units on hand.
- For LIFO, allocate the earliest costs to the goods on hand.
- Prove the cost of goods sold (CGS) separately and then check that ending inventory plus the cost of goods sold equals the cost of goods available for sale.

Solution

Goods available for sale: 4,000 + 6,000 = 10,000 units
Cost of goods available for sale: (4,000 × $3) + (6,000 × $4) = $36,000
Ending inventory: 10,000 − 8,000 = 2,000 units

(a) FIFO ending inventory: 2,000 × $4 = $8,000
 FIFO cost of goods sold: $36,000 − $8,000 = $28,000
 CGS proof: (4,000 × $3) + (4,000 × $4) = $28,000
 Check: $8,000 + $28,000 = $36,000
(b) Weighted average unit cost: $36,000 ÷ 10,000 = $3.60
 Average ending inventory: 2,000 × $3.60 = $7,200
 Average cost of goods sold: $36,000 − $7,200 = $28,800
 CGS proof: 8,000 × $3.60 = $28,800
 Check: $7,200 + $28,800 = $36,000
(c) LIFO ending inventory: 2,000 × $3 = $6,000
 LIFO cost of goods sold: $36,000 − $6,000 = $30,000
 CGS proof: (6,000 × $4) + (2,000 × $3) = $30,000
 Check: $6,000 + $30,000 = $36,000

the navigator

Financial Statement Effects

Inventory affects two financial statements: (1) the balance sheet through merchandise inventory and retained earnings, and (2) the statement of earnings through cost of goods sold and net earnings. Consequently, the choice of cost flow assumption can have a significant financial effect on both financial statements. In addition, if there is an inventory error, the effects of this error on the financial statements can be extensive. We will address both of these topics in the next two sections.

Choice of Cost Flow Assumption

Companies can choose the specific identification method or any of the three inventory cost flow assumptions—FIFO, average, or LIFO. Having this many choices is necessary, because different companies have different types of **inventory and circumstances.**

Ault Foods, Canadian Tire, and Sobeys use FIFO. Abitibi-Price, Andrés Wines, and Mountain Equipment Co-op use average. Caterpillar, Cominco, and Suncor use LIFO for part or all of their inventory. Indeed, a company may use more than one cost flow assumption at the same time. Finning International, for example, uses specific identification to account for its equipment inventory, FIFO to account for about two-thirds of its inventory of parts and supplies, and average to account for the rest.

About an equal number of companies in Canada use FIFO and the average cost flow assumptions. Only a very few companies, about three percent, use LIFO. The Canadian companies that do use LIFO tend to use it to harmonize their reporting practices with the U.S., where LIFO is used more often.

Although the FIFO and average cost flow assumptions are more commonly used in Canada, in order to understand global financial reporting, students still need to have some understanding of the impact of the LIFO cost flow assumption. It is important to be able to compare the financial statement impacts of these choices when competing companies use different cost flow assumptions. For example, Hudson's Bay uses the average cost flow assumption, while its competitor Wal-Mart uses the LIFO cost flow assumption.

Statement of Earnings Effects

To understand why companies might choose a particular cost flow assumption, let's examine the effects of the different cost flow assumptions on the financial statements of Wynneck Electronics. The condensed statements of earnings in Illustration 6-7 assume that Wynneck sold its 550 units for $11,500, had operating expenses of $2,000, and has an income tax rate of 30%.

WYNNECK ELECTRONICS LTD.
Condensed Statement of Earnings

	FIFO		Average		LIFO	
Sales		$11,500		$11,500		$11,500
Beginning inventory	$ 1,000		$ 1,000		$ 1,000	
Purchases	11,000		11,000		11,000	
Cost of goods available for sale	12,000		12,000		12,000	
Ending inventory	5,800		5,400		5,000	
Cost of goods sold		6,200		6,600		7,000
Gross profit		5,300		4,900		4,500
Operating expenses		2,000		2,000		2,000
Earnings before income tax		3,300		2,900		2,500
Income tax expense (30% except for LIFO)		990		870		990
Net earnings		$ 2,310		$ 2,030		$ 1,510

For simplicity, we have assumed that the beginning inventory ($1,000) is the same under all three inventory cost flow assumptions. In reality, the cost of the beginning inventory may very well differ under each assumption. For the purposes of this illustration, since the beginning inventory is the same, the cost of goods available for sale ($12,000) is also the same under each of the three inventory cost flow assumptions. But the ending inventories and costs of goods sold are both different. This difference is because of the unit costs that are allocated under each method. Each dollar of difference in ending inventory results in a corresponding dollar difference in earnings before income tax. For Wynneck, there is an $800 difference between the FIFO and LIFO cost of goods sold.

In periods of changing prices, the choice of cost flow assumption can have a significant impact on earnings. In a period of inflation (rising prices), as is the case for Wynneck, FIFO produces higher net earnings because the lower unit costs of the first units purchased are matched against revenues. As indicated in Illustration 6-7, FIFO reports the highest net earnings ($2,310) and LIFO the lowest ($1,510). Average falls roughly in the middle ($2,030). To management, higher net earnings are an advantage: they cause external users to view the company more favourably. In addition, if management bonuses are based on net earnings, FIFO will provide the basis for higher bonuses.

If prices are falling, the results from the use of FIFO and LIFO are reversed: FIFO will report the lowest net earnings and LIFO the highest. If prices are stable, all three cost flow assumptions will report the same results.

Overall, LIFO provides the best statement of earnings valuation. It matches current costs with current revenues since, under LIFO, the cost of goods sold is assumed to be the cost of the most recently acquired goods. You will recall that the matching principle is important in accounting. The CICA recommends that in those cases "where the choice of method of inventory valuation is an important factor in determining income, the most suitable method for determining cost is that which results in charging against operations costs which most fairly match the sales revenue for the period."

However, even though LIFO may produce the best match of revenues and expenses, it can also result in distortions of earnings if beginning inventory is ever liquidated. It can also be manipulated by timing purchases. The use of LIFO is not permitted for income tax purposes in Canada and most firms do not want to maintain two sets of inventory records—one for accounting purposes and another for income tax purposes. Companies can use FIFO or average to determine their income tax, but not LIFO. That is why, in Illustration 6-7, it was assumed that the income tax expense amount was the same under both the FIFO and LIFO alternatives.

Balance Sheet Effects

A major advantage of FIFO is that in a period of inflation, the costs allocated to ending inventory will approximate their current cost. For example, for Wynneck, 400 of the 450 units in the ending inventory are costed under FIFO at the higher November 27 unit cost of $13. Since management needs to replace inventory when it is sold, a valuation that approximates the replacement cost is helpful for decision-making.

Conversely, a major limitation of LIFO is that in a period of inflation the costs that are allocated to ending inventory may be significantly understated in terms of the current cost of inventory. This is true for Wynneck, where the cost of the ending inventory includes the $10 unit cost of the beginning inventory. The understatement becomes greater over extended periods of inflation if the inventory includes goods that were purchased in one or more earlier accounting periods.

Helpful Hint LIFO may provide the best statement of earnings valuation, but FIFO provides the best balance sheet evaluation.

Summary of Financial Statement Effects

The following illustration summarizes the key financial statement differences that will result from the different choices of cost flow assumption during a period of rising prices. These effects will be the inverse if prices are falling, and equal if prices are constant. In all instances, using the average cost flow assumption will give results that fall somewhere in between the results of FIFO and LIFO.

	FIFO	LIFO
Cost of goods sold	Lowest	Highest
Gross profit/Net earnings	Highest	Lowest
Pre-tax cash flow	Same	Same
Ending inventory	Highest	Lowest

We have seen that both inventory on the balance sheet and net earnings on the statement of earnings are highest when FIFO is used in a period of inflation. Do not confuse this with cash flow. All three cost flow assumptions produce exactly the same cash flow before income taxes. Sales and purchases are not affected by the choice of cost flow assumption. The only thing affected is the allocation between ending inventory and the cost of goods sold, which does not involve cash.

It is also worth remembering that all three cost flow assumptions will give exactly the same results over the life cycle of the business or its product. That is, the allocation between the cost of goods sold and ending inventory may vary annually, but it will produce the same cumulative results over time. Although much has been written about the impact of the choice of inventory cost flow assumption on a variety of performance measures, in reality there is little real economic distinction among the assumptions over time.

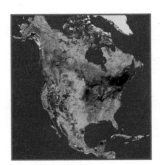

ACCOUNTING MATTERS!   International Perspective

In the U.S., unlike in Canada, use of LIFO is permitted for income tax purposes. Not surprisingly, many U.S. corporations choose LIFO because it reduces earnings and taxes when prices are rising. It also increases after-tax cash flow, since less income tax has to be paid in the short term. However, because of the impact of LIFO on the balance sheet, U.S. companies must also disclose in the notes to their statements what their inventory cost would have been if they had used FIFO.

International accounting standards have designated FIFO and average as the recommended cost flow assumptions. In some countries, such as Canada and the UK, even though LIFO may be used for financial reporting, it cannot be used for income taxes. This is why LIFO is not very popular around the world, other than in the U.S.

Inventory Errors

Unfortunately, errors occasionally occur in accounting for inventory. In some cases, errors are caused by mistakes in counting or costing the inventory. In other cases, errors occur because the transfer of legal title is not recognized properly for goods that are in transit. When errors occur, they affect both the statement of earnings and the balance sheet.

Statement of Earnings Effects

As we have learned, the cost of goods available for sale (beginning inventory plus the cost of goods purchased) is allocated between ending inventory and the cost of goods sold. This means that an error in any of these components will affect both the statement of earnings (through the cost of goods sold and net earnings) and the balance sheet (through ending inventory and retained earnings).

The dollar effects of inventory errors can be calculated by entering data in the earnings formula.

Illustration 6-8 ◀

Earnings formula

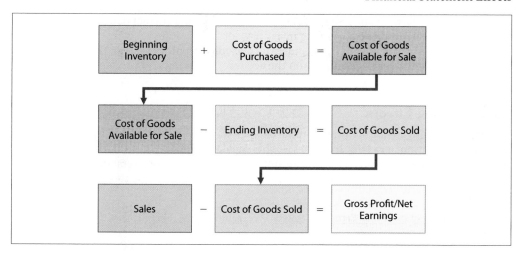

If beginning inventory is understated, cost of goods sold will be understated (assuming no other offsetting errors have occurred). On the other hand, understating ending inventory will overstate cost of goods sold. Cost of goods sold is deducted from sales to determine gross profit, and finally net earnings. An understatement in cost of goods sold will produce an overstatement in gross profit and net earnings (assuming that there are no errors in operating expenses). An overstatement in cost of goods sold will produce an understatement in gross profit and net earnings.

As you know, both the beginning and ending inventories appear in the statement of earnings for companies that use the periodic inventory system. The ending inventory of one period automatically becomes the beginning inventory of the next period. Consequently, an error in the *ending* inventory of the current period will have a **reverse effect on net earnings of the next accounting period**. This is shown in Illustration 6-9.

SAMPLE COMPANY
Statement of Earnings

	2006 Incorrect	2006 Correct	2007 Incorrect	2007 Correct
Sales	$80,000	$80,000	$90,000	$90,000
Beginning inventory	$20,000	$20,000	$12,000	$15,000
Cost of goods purchased	40,000	40,000	68,000	68,000
Cost of goods available for sale	60,000	60,000	80,000	83,000
Ending inventory	12,000	15,000	23,000	23,000
Cost of goods sold	48,000	45,000	57,000	60,000
Gross profit	32,000	35,000	33,000	30,000
Operating expenses	10,000	10,000	20,000	20,000
Earnings before income tax	22,000	25,000	13,000	10,000
Income tax expense (25%)	5,500	6,250	3,250	2,500
Net earnings	$16,500	$18,750	$ 9,750	$ 7,500

Net earnings understated
($2,250)

Net earnings overstated
$2,250

The errors cancel. Thus the combined total earnings
for the two-year period are correct.

In this illustration, ending inventory in 2006 was understated by $2,250. The understatement of ending inventory results in an overstatement of the cost of goods sold and an understatement of net earnings in the same year. It also results in an understatement of the beginning inventory and cost of goods sold in 2007 and an overstatement of net earnings for that year.

Over the two years, total net earnings are correct because the errors offset each other. Notice that total earnings using incorrect data are $26,250 ($16,500 + $9,750), which is the same as the total earnings of $26,250 ($18,750 + $7,500) using correct data. Also note in this example that an error in the beginning inventory does not result in a corresponding error in the ending inventory for that period. Under the periodic inventory system, the correctness of the ending inventory depends entirely on the accuracy of taking and costing the inventory at the balance sheet date.

Balance Sheet Effects

The effect of ending inventory errors on the balance sheet can be calculated by using the basic accounting equation: assets = liabilities + shareholders' equity. Errors in the ending inventory have the effects shown below. U is for understatement, O is for overstatement, and NE is for no effect.

Ending Inventory Error	Assets	=	Liabilities	+	Shareholders' Equity
Overstated	O		NE		O
Understated	U		NE		U

Recall from the previous section that errors in ending inventory affect net earnings. If net earnings are affected, then shareholders' equity will be affected by the same amount since net earnings are closed into the Retained Earnings account, which is part of shareholders' equity. Consequently, an error in ending inventory affects the asset account Merchandise Inventory and the shareholders' equity account Retained Earnings.

Depending on whether income tax has been paid or not, the Income Tax Payable account might also be affected. For simplicity in this chapter, we will assume that all income tax has been paid, so that the effects on assets and shareholders' equity are equal.

The effect of an error in ending inventory on the next period was shown in Illustration 6-9. Recall that if the error is not corrected, the combined total net earnings for the two periods would be correct. In the example, therefore, the assets and shareholders' equity reported on the balance sheet at the end of 2007 will be correct.

Decision Toolkit

Decision Checkpoints	Info Needed for Decision	Tools to Use for Decision	How to Evaluate Results
What is the impact of the choice of inventory cost flow assumption?	Are prices increasing, or are they decreasing?	Statement of earnings and balance sheet effects	It depends on the objective. In a period of rising prices, earnings and inventory are higher under FIFO. LIFO provides opposite results. Average can soften the impact of changing prices.

BEFORE YOU GO ON . . .

▶Review It

1. What factors should be considered by management when choosing an inventory cost flow assumption?
2. Which inventory cost flow assumption produces the highest net earnings in a period of rising prices? The highest ending inventory valuation? The highest pre-tax cash flow?
3. How do inventory errors affect the statement of earnings? How do they affect the balance sheet?

▶Do It

On July 31, 2006, Zhang Inc. counted and recorded $600,000 of inventory. This count did not include $90,000 of goods in transit that were purchased on July 29 on account and shipped to Zhang FOB shipping point. Determine the correct July 31 inventory. Identify any accounts that are in error at July 31, 2006. State the amount and direction (e.g., understated or overstated) of the error for each of these accounts. You can ignore any income tax effects.

Action Plan

- Use the earnings formula to determine the error's impact on statement of earnings accounts.
- Use the accounting equation to determine the error's impact on balance sheet accounts.

Solution

The correct inventory count should have been $690,000 ($600,000 + $90,000).

<u>Statement of earnings accounts:</u>

Purchases are understated (U) by $90,000. However, since ending inventory is also understated, the cost of goods sold, gross profit, and net earnings will be correct [beginning inventory + cost of goods purchased (U $90,000) − ending inventory (U $90,000) = cost of goods sold].

<u>Balance sheet accounts:</u>

Merchandise Inventory (ending) is understated by $90,000, as is Accounts Payable [assets (U $90,000) = Liabilities (U $90,000) + Shareholders' Equity].

Presentation and Analysis of Inventory

Presenting inventory appropriately on the financial statements is important because inventory is usually the largest current asset (merchandise inventory) on the balance sheet and the largest expense (cost of goods sold) on the statement of earnings. For example, expanding on the feature story, Caterpillar reported inventory of U.S. $4,674 million in 2004, which comprises nearly one-quarter of its total current assets. Caterpillar's cost of goods sold of U.S. $22,420 million amounts to more than 80 percent of total operating expenses on its statement of earnings.

In addition, these reported numbers are critical for analyzing a company's effectiveness in managing its inventory. In the next sections, we will discuss issues that are related to the presentation and analysis of inventory.

study objective 4

Demonstrate the presentation and analysis of inventory.

Valuing Inventory at the Lower of Cost and Market (LCM)

Before presenting inventory on the financial statements, we must first ensure that it is properly valued. Inventory sometimes decreases in value due to changes in technology or style. For example, suppose you are the owner of a retail store that sells computers. During the recent 12-month period, the cost of the computers dropped by almost 30 percent. At the end of your fiscal year, you still have some of these computers in inventory. Do you think your inventory should be stated at cost, in accordance with the cost principle, or at its lower market value?

As you probably reasoned, when this situation occurs, the cost basis of accounting is no longer followed. When the value of inventory is lower than its cost, inventory is written down to its market value. This is done by valuing the inventory at the **lower of cost and market (LCM)** in the period in which the decline occurs. LCM is an example of the accounting concept of **conservatism**. You will recall from our discussion of conservatism in Chapter 2 that the method that is least likely to overstate assets and net earnings is the one that should be used.

The term *market* in the phrase *lower of cost and market* is not specifically defined in Canada. It can mean the **replacement cost** or the **net realizable value**, among other things. The majority of Canadian companies use net realizable value to define market for LCM purposes. For a merchandising company, net realizable value is the selling price, less any costs required to make the goods ready for sale.

International Note Almost every country in the world applies the LCM rule; however, the definition of market can vary. The International Accounting Standards Board defines market as net realizable value, as do the UK, France, and Germany. The U.S., Italy, and Japan define it as the replacement cost.

LCM is applied to the inventory after specific identification or one of the cost flow assumptions (FIFO, average, or LIFO) has been used to determine the cost. Assume that Wacky World has the following lines of merchandise with costs and market values as indicated. LCM produces the following results:

	Cost	Market	Lower of Cost and Market
Television sets			
LCD	$ 60,000	$ 55,000	
Plasma	45,000	52,000	
	105,000	107,000	
Video equipment			
DVD recorder/players	48,000	45,000	
VCRs	15,000	14,000	
	63,000	59,000	
Total inventory	$168,000	$166,000	$166,000

LCM can be applied separately to each individual item, to categories of items (e.g., television sets and video equipment), or to total inventory. It is common practice to use total inventory rather than individual items or major categories when determining the LCM valuation.

Using total inventory, the journal entry to record the loss for Wacky World would be as follows under a periodic inventory system:

−2,000   −2,000

Cash flows: no effect

Loss Due to Decline in Net Realizable Value of Inventory	2,000	
Merchandise Inventory		2,000
(To record decline in inventory value from original cost of $168,000 to market value of $166,000)		

The loss would be reported as part of cost of goods sold on the statement of earnings. In a perpetual inventory system, the loss would be debited directly to the Cost of Goods Sold account.

Classifying Inventory

How a company classifies its inventory depends on whether it is a merchandiser or a manufacturer. In a **merchandising company**, such as those described in Chapter 5, the inventory includes many different items. For example, in a grocery store like Loblaw, canned goods, dairy products, meats, and produce are just a few of the inventory items on hand. In a merchandising company, inventory has two common characteristics: (1) it is owned by the company, and (2) it is in a form that is ready for sale to customers in the ordinary course of business. Thus, only one inventory classification, merchandise inventory, is needed to describe the many different items that make up the total inventory.

Helpful Hint Regardless of the classification, all inventories are reported as current assets on the balance sheet.

In a **manufacturing company**, some of its inventory may not yet be ready for sale. As a result, inventory is usually classified into three categories: finished goods, work in process, and raw materials. **Finished goods** inventory includes manufactured items that are completed and ready for sale. **Work in process** is that portion of manufactured inventory that has been placed into the production process but is not yet complete. **Raw materials** are the basic goods that will be used in production but have not yet been sent into production. For example, Caterpillar in the feature story classifies "earth-moving trucks completed and ready for sale" as finished goods. The trucks on the assembly line in various stages of production are classified as work in process. The steel, glass, tires, and other components that are on hand waiting to be used in the production of trucks are identified as raw materials.

By observing the levels of these three inventory types and changes in these levels, financial statement users can gain insight into management's production plans. For example, low levels of raw materials and high levels of finished goods could suggest that management believes it has enough inventory on hand and will slow down production—perhaps because it expects a recession. On the other hand, high levels of raw materials and low levels of finished goods probably indicate that management is planning to increase production.

In the notes to the financial statements, the following information related to inventory should be disclosed: (1) the major inventory classifications, (2) the basis of valuation (cost or lower of cost and market), and (3) the cost flow assumption (specific identification, FIFO, average, or LIFO).

Inventory Turnover

The inventory turnover and days in inventory ratios help companies manage their inventory levels. The **inventory turnover** ratio measures the number of times, on average, that inventory is sold ("turns over") during the period. It is calculated as the cost of goods sold divided by the average inventory.

Whenever a ratio compares a balance sheet figure (e.g., inventory) to a statement of earnings figure (e.g., cost of goods sold), the balance sheet figure must be averaged. Averages for balance sheet figures are determined by adding the beginning and ending balances together and then dividing the result by two. Averages are used to ensure that the balance sheet figures (which represent end-of-period amounts) cover the same period of time as the statement of earnings figures (which represent amounts for the entire period).

A complement to the inventory turnover ratio is the **days in inventory** ratio. It converts the inventory turnover into a measure of the average age of the inventory. It is calculated as 365 days divided by the inventory turnover ratio.

A low inventory turnover ratio (high days in inventory) could mean that the company has too much of its funds in inventory. It could also mean that the company has excessive carrying costs (e.g., for interest, storage, insurance, and taxes) or that it has obsolete inventory.

A high inventory turnover ratio (low days in inventory) could mean that the company has little of its funds in inventory—in other words, that it has a minimal amount of inventory on hand at any specific time. Although having minimal funds tied up in inventory suggests efficiency, too high an inventory turnover ratio may indicate that the company is losing sales opportunities because of inventory shortages. For example, investment analysts suggested recently that Office Depot had gone too far in reducing its inventory—analysts said they were seeing too many empty shelves. Management should watch this ratio closely so that it achieves the best balance between too much and too little inventory.

In Chapter 5, we discussed the increasingly competitive environment of retailers like Wal-Mart and Hudson's Bay. We noted that Wal-Mart has implemented many technological innovations to improve the efficiency of its inventory management. The following data are available for Wal-Mart (in U.S. millions):

	2004	2003	2002
Inventory	$ 26,612	$ 24,401	$ 22,614
Cost of goods sold	198,747	178,299	171,562

Illustration 6-10 presents the inventory turnover and days in inventory ratios for Wal-Mart for 2004 and 2003. No comparative information is presented for the Hudson's Bay Company because, as explained in Chapter 5, it does not separately report its cost of goods sold on its statement of earnings.

Illustration 6-10 ▶

Inventory turnover and days in inventory

	INVENTORY TURNOVER = $\dfrac{\text{COST OF GOODS SOLD}}{\text{AVERAGE INVENTORY}}$	
	DAYS IN INVENTORY = $\dfrac{\text{365 DAYS}}{\text{INVENTORY TURNOVER}}$	

(in U.S. millions)		2004	2003
Wal-Mart	Inventory turnover	$\dfrac{\$198,474}{(\$26,612 + \$24,401) \div 2} = 7.8$ times	$\dfrac{\$178,299}{(\$24,401 + \$22,614) \div 2} = 7.6$ times
	Days in inventory	$\dfrac{365 \text{ days}}{7.8} = 47$ days	$\dfrac{365 \text{ days}}{7.6} = 48$ days
Industry average	Inventory turnover	7.2 times	6.9 times
	Days in inventory	51 days	53 days

The calculations in Illustration 6-10 show that Wal-Mart improved its inventory turnover slightly from 2003 to 2004 and that it turns its inventory over more frequently than the industry in general. This suggests that Wal-Mart is more efficient in its inventory management. Wal-Mart's sophisticated inventory tracking and distribution system allows it to keep minimum amounts of inventory on hand, while still keeping the shelves full of what customers are looking for.

ACCOUNTING MATTERS!   Management Perspective

Inventory management for companies that make and sell high-tech products is very complex because the product life cycle is so short. The company wants to have enough inventory to meet demand, but does not want to have too much inventory, because the introduction of a new product can eliminate demand for the "old" product. Palm, Inc., maker of personal digital assistants (PDAs), learned this lesson the hard way in the early 2000s. Sales of its existing products had been booming, and the company was frequently faced with shortages, so it started increasing its inventories. Then sales started to slow and inventories started to grow faster than wanted. Management panicked and decided to announce that its new product—one that would make its old one obsolete—would be coming out in two weeks. Sales of the old product quickly died—leaving a mountain of inventory. As it turned out, however, the new product was not actually ready for six weeks and potential sales during those weeks were lost.

▦ Decision Toolkit

Decision Checkpoints	Info Needed for Decision	Tools to Use for Decision	How to Evaluate Results
How long is an item in inventory?	Cost of goods sold; beginning and ending inventory	Inventory turnover $=\dfrac{\text{Cost of goods sold}}{\text{Average inventory}}$ Days in inventory $=\dfrac{\text{365 days}}{\text{Inventory turnover}}$	A higher inventory turnover or lower days in inventory suggests that management is reducing the amount of inventory on hand, relative to sales.

BEFORE YOU GO ON . . .

▶Review It

1. When should inventory be reported at a value other than cost?
2. What inventory cost flow assumption does Loblaw use to account for its inventories? The answer to this question is provided at the end of the chapter
3. What is the purpose of the inventory turnover ratio? What is the relationship between the inventory turnover and days in inventory ratios?

the navigator

APPENDIX 6A ▶ INVENTORY COST FLOW ASSUMPTIONS IN PERPETUAL INVENTORY SYSTEMS

Each of the inventory cost flow assumptions described in the chapter for a periodic inventory system may be used in a perpetual inventory system. To show how to use the three cost flow assumptions (FIFO, average, and LIFO) under a perpetual system, we will use the data below, the same as what was shown earlier in the chapter for Wynneck Electronics' Astro Condenser.

study objective 5

Apply the inventory cost flow assumptions under a perpetual inventory system.

WYNNECK ELECTRONICS LTD. Astro Condensers					
Date	Explanation	Units	Unit Cost	Total Cost	Balance in Units
Jan. 1	Beginning inventory	100	$10	$ 1,000	100
Apr. 15	Purchases	200	11	2,200	300
May 1	Sales	150			150
Aug. 24	Purchases	300	12	3,600	450
Sept. 10	Sales	400			50
Nov. 27	Purchases	400	13	5,200	450
	Total			$12,000	

First-In, First-Out (FIFO)

Under perpetual FIFO, the cost of the oldest goods on hand before each sale is allocated to the cost of goods sold. The cost of goods sold on May 1 is assumed to consists of all the January 1 beginning inventory and 50 units of the items purchased on April 15. Similarly, the cost of goods sold on September 10 is assumed to consist of the remaining units purchased on April 15, and 250 of the units purchased on August 24. Illustration 6A-1, on the following page, shows the inventory under a FIFO perpetual system.

Date	Purchases Units	Cost	Total	Cost of Goods Sold Units	Cost	Total	Balance Units	Cost	Total
Jan. 1							100	$10	$1,000
Apr. 15	200	$11	$ 2,200				100 200	10 11	} 3,200
May 1				100 50	$10 11	} $1,550	150	11	1,650
Aug. 24	300	12	3,600				150 300	11 12	} 5,250
Sept. 10				150 250	11 12	} 4,650	50	12	600
Nov. 27	400	13	5,200				50 400	12 13	} 5,800
	900		$11,000	550		$6,200			

As shown, the ending inventory in this situation is $5,800, and the cost of goods sold is $6,200.

   Although the calculation format may differ, the results under FIFO in a perpetual system are the **same as in a periodic system** (see Illustration 6-3 where, similarly, the ending inventory is $5,800 and the cost of goods sold is $6,200). Under both inventory systems, the first costs in are the ones assigned to cost of goods sold.

Average

The average cost flow assumption in a perpetual inventory system is often called the **moving average cost flow assumption**. The average cost is calculated in the same manner as we calculated the weighted average unit cost in a periodic inventory system: by dividing the cost of goods available for sale by the units available for sale. The difference under the perpetual inventory system is that a new average is calculated after each purchase. The average cost is then applied (1) to the remaining units on hand, to determine the cost of the ending inventory, and (2) to the units sold, to determine the cost of goods sold. Use of the average cost flow assumption by Wynneck Electronics is shown in Illustration 6A-2.

Date	Purchases Units	Cost	Total	Cost of Goods Sold Units	Cost	Total	Balance Units	Cost	Total
Jan. 1							100	$10.00	$1,000.00
Apr. 15	200	$11.00	$ 2,200.00				300	10.67	3,200.00
May 11				150	$10.67	$1,600.00	150	10.67	$1,600.00
Aug. 24	300	12.00	3,600.00				450	11.56	5,200.00
Sept. 10				400	11.56	4,622.22	50	11.56	577.78
Nov. 27	400	13.00	5,200.00				450	12.84	5,777.78
	900		$11,000.00	550		$6,222.22			

   As indicated above, **a new average is calculated each time a purchase (or purchase return) is made**. On April 15, after 200 units are purchased for $2,200, a total of 300 units costing $3,200 ($1,000 + $2,200) is on hand. The average unit cost is $10.67 ($3,200 ÷ 300). Accordingly, the unit cost of the 150 units sold on May 1 is shown at $10.67, and the total cost of goods sold is $1,600. This unit cost is used in costing the units sold until another purchase is made, and a new unit cost must then be calculated.

   On August 24, after 300 units are purchased for $3,600, a total of 450 units costing $5,200 ($1,600 + $3,600) are on hand. This results in an average cost per unit of $11.56 ($5,200 ÷ 450), which is used to cost the September 10 sale. After the November 27 purchase of 400 units for $5,200, there are 450 units on hand costing $5,777.78 ($577.78 + $5,200), resulting in a new average cost of $12.84 ($5,777.78 ÷ 450).

   In practice, these average unit costs may be rounded to the nearest cent, or even to the nearest dollar. This illustration used the exact unit cost amounts, as would a computerized schedule, even though the unit costs have been rounded to the nearest digit for presentation in Illustration 6A-2. However, it is important to remember that this is an *assumed* cost flow, and using four digits, or even cents, suggests a false level of accuracy.

This moving average cost under the perpetual inventory system should be compared to Illustration 6-5 shown earlier in the chapter, which presents the weighted average cost under a periodic inventory system.

Last-In, First-Out (LIFO)

With the LIFO cost flow assumption under a perpetual system, the cost of the most recent purchase before a sale is allocated to the units sold. Therefore, the cost of the goods sold on May 1 is assumed to consist of the units from the latest purchase, on April 15, at the cost of $11 per unit. The cost of goods sold on September 10 counts backwards until a total of 400 units is reached, first allocating the 300 units purchased on August 24, then the 50 remaining units from the April 15 purchase, and finally the 50 units in beginning inventory.

For our example, the ending inventory under a LIFO cost flow assumption is calculated in Illustration 6A-3.

Date	Purchases			Cost of Goods Sold			Balance		
	Units	Cost	Total	Units	Cost	Total	Units	Cost	Total
Jan. 1							100	$10	$1,000
Apr. 15	200	$11	$ 2,200				100	10	3,200
							200	11	
May 1				150	$11	$1,650	100	10	1,550
							50	11	
Aug. 24	300	12	3,600				100	10	5,150
							50	11	
							300	12	
Sept. 10				300	12	4,650	50	10	500
				50	11				
				50	10				
Nov. 27	400	13	5,200				50	10	5,700
							400	13	
	900		$11,000	550		$6,300			

The ending inventory in this LIFO perpetual illustration is $5,700 and the cost of goods sold is $6,300. Compare this to the LIFO periodic example in Illustration 6-6, where the ending inventory is $5,000 and the cost of goods sold is $7,000.

The use of LIFO in a perpetual system will usually produce cost allocations that differ from using LIFO in a periodic system. In a perpetual system, the latest units purchased **before each sale** are allocated to the cost of goods sold. In a periodic system, the latest units purchased **during the period** are allocated to the cost of goods sold. When a purchase is made after the last sale, the LIFO periodic system will apply this purchase to the previous sale. See Illustration 6-6 where the 400 units at $13 purchased on November 27 are all allocated to the sale of 550 units. As shown under the LIFO perpetual system, the 400 units at $13 purchased on November 27 are all applied to the ending inventory.

A comparison of the cost of goods sold and ending inventory figures for each of these cost flow assumptions under a perpetual inventory system gives the same proportionate outcomes that we saw in the application of cost flow assumptions under a periodic system. That is, in a period of rising prices (prices rose from $10 to $13 in this example), FIFO will always result in the highest ending inventory valuation and LIFO in the lowest. On the other hand, LIFO will always result in the highest cost of goods sold figure (and lowest net earnings), and FIFO in the lowest. Average results fall somewhere in between FIFO and LIFO. The following table summarizes these effects under a perpetual inventory system:

	FIFO	Average	LIFO
Cost of goods sold	$ 6,200	$ 6,222	$ 6,300
Ending inventory	5,800	5,778	5,700
Cost of goods available for sale	$12,000	$12,000	$12,000

Of course, if prices are falling, the inverse relationships will result. If prices are constant, all three cost flow assumptions will yield the same results. And, finally, remember that the sum of cost of goods sold and ending inventory always equals the cost of goods available for sale, which is the same under all the cost flow assumptions.

▒ Using the Decision Toolkit

IPSCO Inc., headquartered in Regina, Saskatchewan, manufactures and sells steel mill and fabricated products in Canada and the U.S. Selected financial information (in U.S. thousands) for IPSCO Inc. follows:

	2004	2003	2002
Inventories	$ 434,526	$ 286,159	$ 255,410
Sales	2,452,675	1,294,566	1,081,709
Cost of sales	1,660,009	1,122,625	929,140
Net earnings	438,610	16,585	20,279

Selected industry data follow:

	2004	2003
Inventory turnover	5.5 times	5.3 times
Days in inventory	66 days	69 days
Gross profit margin	23.9%	22.0%
Profit margin	8.6%	5.9%

Instructions

(a) IPSCO uses the average cost flow assumption. Steel prices have risen over the last two years in response to increased demand for steel and its raw materials, largely due to China's rapidly growing economy. If IPSCO had used FIFO instead of average, would its net earnings have been higher or lower than currently reported?

(b) Do each of the following:
1. Calculate the inventory turnover and days in inventory for 2004 and 2003.
2. Calculate the gross profit margin and profit margin for each of 2004 and 2003.
3. Evaluate IPSCO's performance with inventories over the most recent two years and compare its performance to that of the industry.

Solution

(a) If IPSCO used the FIFO cost flow assumption instead of the average cost flow assumption during a period of rising prices, its cost of goods sold would be lower and its net earnings higher than currently reported.

(b)

1.

Ratio	2004	2003
Inventory turnover	$\dfrac{\$1,660,009}{(\$434,526 + \$286,159) \div 2} = 4.6$ times	$\dfrac{\$1,122,625}{(\$286,159 + \$255,410) \div 2} = 4.1$ times
Days in inventory	$\dfrac{365 \text{ days}}{4.6} = 79$ days	$\dfrac{365 \text{ days}}{4.1} = 89$ days

2.

Ratio	2004	2003
Gross profit margin	$\dfrac{\$2,452,675 - \$1,660,009}{\$2,452,675} = 32.3\%$	$\dfrac{\$1,294,566 - \$1,122,625}{\$1,294,566} = 13.3\%$
Profit margin	$\dfrac{\$438,610}{\$2,452,675} = 17.9\%$	$\dfrac{\$16,585}{\$1,294,566} = 1.3\%$

3. IPSCO's inventory turnover and days in inventory ratios improved in 2004, although they remain below the industry averages. That means that IPSCO has more inventory on hand and is not selling it as fast as its competitors. IPSCO's profitability ratios increased substantially in 2004. After performing below the industry average in 2003, IPSCO's profitability was better than that of the industry in 2004. IPSCO attributes this to the rising prices and demand for steel. In addition, the strong Canadian dollar also increased reported results.

Summary of Study Objectives

1. *Describe the steps in determining inventory quantities.* The steps are (1) taking a physical inventory of goods on hand and (2) determining the ownership of goods in transit, on consignment, and in similar situations.

2. *Apply the inventory cost flow assumptions under a periodic inventory system.* The cost of goods available for sale (beginning inventory plus the cost of goods purchased) may be allocated to ending inventory and the cost of goods sold by specific identification or by one of the three cost flow assumptions—FIFO (first-in, first-out), average, or LIFO (last-in, first-out).

Specific identification allocates the exact cost of each merchandise item to ending inventory and the cost of goods sold. FIFO assumes a first-in, first-out cost flow for sales. Ending inventory is determined by allocating the cost of the most recent goods purchased to the units on hand. Cost of goods sold consists of the cost of the earliest goods purchased. Average uses dollar and unit amounts for the goods available for sale to calculate a weighted average cost per unit. This unit cost is then applied to the number of units remaining to determine ending inventory and the number of units sold to prove cost of goods sold. LIFO assumes a last-in, first-out cost flow for sales. Ending inventory is determined by allocating the cost of the earliest goods purchased to the units on hand. Cost of goods sold consists of the cost of the most recent goods purchased.

3. *Explain the financial statement effects of the inventory cost flow assumptions and inventory errors.* When prices are rising, FIFO results in a lower cost of goods sold and higher net earnings than average and LIFO. The reverse is true when prices are falling. In the balance sheet, FIFO results in an ending inventory that is closest to current (replacement) value, whereas the inventory under LIFO is the furthest from current value. All three cost flow assumptions result in the same cash flow before income taxes. LIFO is not permitted for income tax purposes in Canada.

An error in beginning inventory will have a reverse effect on net earnings in the current year (e.g., an overstatement of inventory results in an understatement of net earnings). An error in ending inventory will have a similar effect on net earnings (e.g., an overstatement of inventory results in an overstatement of net earnings). If ending inventory errors are not corrected in the following period, their effect on net earnings for that period is reversed, and total net earnings for the two years will be correct. In the balance sheet, ending inventory errors will have the same effects on total assets and total shareholders' equity, and no effect on liabilities (ignoring income taxes).

4. *Demonstrate the presentation and analysis of inventory.* Ending inventory is reported as a current asset on the balance sheet. Cost of goods sold is reported as an operating expense on the statement of earnings. Additional disclosure includes information about the major inventory classifications, the cost flow assumption chosen, and the basis of valuation. Inventory is valued at the lower of cost and market (LCM), which results in a write-down when the market value (net realizable value) is less than cost.

The inventory turnover ratio is calculated as the cost of goods sold divided by average inventory. It can be converted to days in inventory by dividing 365 days by the inventory turnover ratio.

5. *Apply the inventory cost flow assumptions under a perpetual inventory system (Appendix 6A).* Under FIFO, the cost of the oldest goods on hand is allocated to the cost of goods sold. The cost of the most recent goods purchased is allocated to ending inventory. Under average, a new weighted (moving) average unit cost is calculated after each purchase and applied to the number of units sold and the number of units remaining in ending inventory. Under LIFO, the cost of the most recent purchase is allocated to the cost of goods sold. The cost of the earliest goods purchased is allocated to ending inventory.

Each of these cost flow assumptions is applied in the same cost flow order as in a periodic inventory system. The main difference is that in a perpetual inventory system the cost flow assumption is applied at the date of each sale to determine the cost of goods sold. In a periodic inventory system, the cost flow assumption is applied only at the end of the period.

▦ Decision Toolkit—A Summary

Decision Checkpoints	Info Needed for Decision	Tools to Use for Decision	How to Evaluate Results
What is the impact of the choice of inventory cost flow assumption?	Are prices increasing, or are they decreasing?	Statement of earnings and balance sheet effects	It depends on the objective. In a period of rising prices, earnings and inventory are higher under FIFO. LIFO provides opposite results. Average can soften the impact of changing prices.
How long is an item in inventory?	Cost of goods sold; beginning and ending inventory	$$\text{Inventory turnover} = \frac{\text{Cost of goods sold}}{\text{Average inventory}}$$ $$\text{Days in inventory} = \frac{365 \text{ days}}{\text{Inventory turnover}}$$	A higher inventory turnover or lower days in inventory suggests that management is reducing the amount of inventory on hand, relative to sales.

**Analysis Tools
(Decision Toolkit Summaries)**

www.wiley.com/canada/kimmel

Study Tools (Glossary)

Glossary

Average cost flow assumption   An inventory cost flow assumption that assumes that the goods available for sale are homogeneous or nondistinguishable. Each good is assumed to have the same weighted average cost per unit. (p. 269)

Consigned goods   Goods shipped by a consignor, who retains ownership, to a party called the consignee, who holds the goods for sale. (p. 263)

Days in inventory   A measure of the average number of days inventory is held. It is calculated as 365 divided by the inventory turnover ratio. (p. 279)

Finished goods   Manufactured items that are completed and ready for sale. (p. 278)

First-in, first-out (FIFO) cost flow assumption   An inventory cost flow assumption that assumes that the costs of the oldest goods acquired are the first to be recognized as the cost of goods sold. The costs of the latest goods acquired are assumed to remain in ending inventory. (p. 267)

Internal control   The policies and procedures used by a company to (1) optimize resources, (2) prevent and detect errors, (3) safeguard assets, and (4) enhance the accuracy and reliability of accounting records. (p. 262)

Inventory turnover   A measure of the number of times, on average, that inventory is sold during the period. It is calculated by dividing the cost of goods sold by the average inventory. Average inventory is calculated by adding the beginning and ending inventory balances and dividing the result by two. (p. 279)

Last-in, first-out (LIFO) cost flow assumption   An inventory cost flow assumption that assumes that the costs of the latest units purchased are the first to be allocated to the cost of goods sold. The costs of the oldest goods acquired are assumed to remain in ending inventory. (p. 269)

Lower of cost and market (LCM)   A basis for stating inventory at the lower of cost and market values (usually defined as net realizable value) at the end of the period. (p. 277)

Net realizable value   The selling price of an inventory item, less any costs required to make the item saleable. (p. 277)

Raw materials   Basic goods that will be used in production but have not yet been sent into production. (p. 278)

Replacement cost   The cost of replacing an asset. (p. 277)

Specific identification method   A costing method that follows the actual physical flow of goods, and in which individual items are specifically costed to arrive at the cost of goods sold and cost of the ending inventory. (p. 265)

Weighted average unit cost   Average cost that is weighted by the number of units purchased at each unit cost. It is calculated as the cost of goods available for sale divided by the number of units available for sale. (p. 269)

Work in process   Manufactured inventory that has begun the production process but is not yet complete. (p. 278)

Demonstration Problem

Englehart Ltd. has the following inventory, purchases, and sales data for the month of March:

Inventory, March 1	200 units @ $4.30	$ 860	
Purchases			
Mar. 10	500 units @ $4.50	2,250	
20	400 units @ $4.75	1,900	
30	300 units @ $5.00	1,500	
Sales			
Mar. 15	500 units @ $8.00	4,000	
25	400 units @ $8.00	3,200	

The physical inventory count on March 31 shows 500 units on hand.

Instructions

Under a periodic inventory system, determine the cost of the inventory on hand at March 31 and the cost of goods sold for March under (a) FIFO, (b) average, and (c) LIFO.

Solution to Demonstration Problem

The cost of goods available for sale is $6,510:

Beginning inventory	200	units @ $4.30	$ 860
Purchases			
Mar. 10	500	units @ 4.50	2,250
20	400	units @ 4.75	1,900
30	300	units @ 5.00	1,500
Total cost of goods available for sale	1,400		$6,510

(a) FIFO

	Units	Unit Cost	Total Cost
Ending inventory			
Mar. 30	300	$5.00	$1,500
20	200	4.75	950
	500		$2,450

Cost of goods sold: $6,510 − $2,450 = $4,060
Proof of cost of goods sold:

	Units	Unit Cost	Total Cost
Beginning inventory	200	$4.30	$ 860
Mar. 10	500	4.50	2,250
20	200	4.75	950
	900		$4,060

Check: $2,450 + $4,060 = $6,510

(b) Average
Weighted average unit cost: $6,510 ÷ 1,400 = $4.65
Ending inventory: 500 × $4.65 = $2,325
Cost of goods sold: $6,510 − $2,325 = $4,185
Proof of cost of goods sold: 900 × $4.65 = $4,185
Proof: $2,325 + $4,185 = $6,510

(c) LIFO

	Units	Unit Cost	Total Cost
Ending inventory:			
Beginning inventory	200	$4.30	$ 860
Mar. 10	300	4.50	1,350
	500		$2,210

Cost of goods sold: $6,510 − $2,210 = $4,300
Proof of cost of goods sold:

	Units	Unit Cost	Total Cost
Mar. 30	300	$5.00	$1,500
20	400	4.75	1,900
10	200	4.50	900
	900		$4,300

Check: $2,210 + $4,300 = $6,510

Action Plan

- Ignore the dates of sale in a periodic inventory system. Assume everything happens at the end of the period.

- Allocate costs to ending inventory. Subtract ending inventory from the cost of goods available for sale to determine the cost of goods sold.

- For FIFO, allocate the latest costs to the goods on hand.

- For average, calculate the weighted average unit cost (the cost of goods available for sale ÷ the number of units available for sale). Multiply this cost by the number of units on hand.

- For LIFO, allocate the oldest costs to the goods on hand.

- Prove the cost of goods sold separately and then check that ending inventory plus the cost of goods sold equals the cost of goods available for sale.

the navigator

Note: All questions, exercises, and problems below with an asterisk (*) relate to material in Appendix 6A.

Self-Study Questions

Study Tools (Self-Assessment Quizzes)

Answers are at the end of the chapter.

(SO 1) 1. A physical inventory count is normally taken:
    (a) in a periodic inventory system.
    (b) in a perpetual inventory system.
    (c) at the end of the company's fiscal year.
    (d) All of the above

(SO 1) 2. Which of the following should not be included in the physical inventory of a company?
    (a) Goods held on consignment from another company
    (b) Goods shipped on consignment to another company
    (c) Goods in transit that have been sold to another company and shipped FOB destination
    (d) Goods in transit that have been purchased from another company and shipped FOB shipping point

(SO 2) 3. Kam Ltd. has the following units and costs, and uses a periodic inventory system:

	Units	Unit Cost	Total Cost
Inventory, Jan. 1	8,000	$11	$ 88,000
Purchase, June 19	13,000	12	156,000
Purchase, Nov. 8	5,000	13	65,000
	26,000		$309,000

If 9,000 units are on hand at December 31, what is the cost of the ending inventory under FIFO?
    (a) $100,000   (c) $196,000
    (b) $113,000   (d) $209,000

(SO 2) 4. From the data in question 3, what is the cost of the goods sold (rounded to the nearest thousand dollars) under average?
    (a) $105,000   (c) $202,000
    (b) $107,000   (d) $204,000

(SO 3) 5. In periods of declining prices, the average cost flow assumption will produce:
    (a) higher net earnings than FIFO.
    (b) the same net earnings as FIFO.
    (c) lower net earnings than FIFO.
    (d) higher net earnings than LIFO.

(SO 3) 6. Lavigne Ltd.'s ending inventory is understated by $4,000. The effects of this error on the current year's cost of goods sold and net earnings, respectively, are:
    (a) understated and overstated.
    (b) overstated and understated.
    (c) overstated and overstated.
    (d) understated and understated.

(SO 4) 7. The lower of cost and market rule for inventory is an example of the application of:
    (a) the conservatism concept.
    (b) the cost principle.
    (c) the matching principle.
    (d) the economic entity assumption.

(SO 4) 8. Which of these would cause the inventory turnover ratio to increase the most?
    (a) Increasing the amount of inventory on hand
    (b) Keeping the amount of inventory on hand constant but increasing sales
    (c) Keeping the amount of inventory on hand constant but decreasing sales
    (d) Decreasing the amount of inventory on hand and increasing sales

(SO 5) *9. In a perpetual inventory system:
    (a) LIFO cost of goods sold will be the same as in a periodic inventory system.
    (b) average cost of goods sold will be the same as in a periodic inventory system.
    (c) FIFO cost of goods sold will be the same as in a periodic inventory system.
    (d) All of the above

(SO 5) *10. Mayerthorpe Inc. has the following units and costs in January, and uses a perpetual inventory system:

		Purchases			Cost of Goods Sold			Balance	
Date	Units	Unit Cost	Total Cost	Units	Unit Cost	Total Cost	Units	Unit Cost	Total Cost
Jan. 1							8,000	$11	$ 88,000
10	12,000	$12	$144,000				20,000	?	232,000
18				14,000	?	?	6,000	?	?
20	4,000	13	52,000				10,000	?	?

What was the moving average cost per unit after the last purchase on January 20?
    (a) $11.60   (c) $12.16
    (b) $12.00   (d) $13.00

Questions

(SO 1) 1. Your friend Tom Wetzel has been hired to help take the physical inventory in Kikujiro's Hardware Store. Explain to Tom how to do this job, giving him specific instructions for determining the inventory quantities that Kikujiro's has legal title over.

(SO 1) 2. What is internal control? How does it apply to taking a physical inventory count?

(SO 1) 3. Janine Ltd. ships merchandise to Fastrak Corporation on December 30. The merchandise reaches the buyer on January 5. Indicate the terms of sale (e.g., FOB shipping point or FOB destination) that will result in the goods being included in (a) Janine's December 31 inventory and (b) Fastrak's December 31 inventory.

(SO 1) 4. What are consigned goods? Which company, the consignee or the consignor, should include consigned goods in its inventory balance? Explain why.

(SO 2) 5. Dave Wier believes that the allocation of the cost of goods available for sale should be based on the actual physical flow of the goods. Explain to Dave why this may be both impractical and inappropriate.

(SO 2) 6. Distinguish between the three cost flow assumptions—FIFO, average, and LIFO.

(SO 2) 7. Which inventory cost flow assumption (a) Assumes that goods available for sale are identical? (b) Assumes that the last units purchased are the first to be sold? (c) Usually matches the actual physical flow of merchandise?

(SO 2) 8. Which inventory cost flow assumption—FIFO or LIFO—provides the best statement of earnings valuation? The best balance sheet valuation?

(SO 3) 9. Compare the financial effects of using the FIFO and average cost flow assumptions during a period of declining prices on (a) cash, (b) ending inventory, (c) cost of goods sold, and (d) net earnings.

(SO 3) 10. In a period of rising prices, the inventory reported in Plato Ltd.'s balance sheet is close to the replacement cost of the inventory, but York Ltd.'s inventory is considerably below its replacement cost. Identify the inventory cost flow assumption that is used by each company. Which company has probably been reporting the higher gross profit?

(SO 3) 11. Swift Corporation has been using the FIFO cost flow assumption during a prolonged period of inflation. During the same time period, Swift has been paying out a large amount of its net earnings as dividends. What adverse effects may result from this policy?

(SO 3) 12. Mila Ltd. discovers in 2007 that its ending inventory at December 31, 2006, was understated by $5,000. What effect will this error have on (a) 2006 net earnings, (b) 2007 net earnings, and (c) 2007 retained earnings?

(SO 3) 13. A customer took merchandise home on approval before deciding whether or not to purchase it. These goods were not included in the physical inventory count at year end. What effect will this error have on the components of the accounting equation: assets, liabilities, and shareholders' equity?

(SO 4) 14. Lucy Ritter is studying for her next accounting test. What should Lucy know about (a) when not to use the cost basis of accounting for inventories and (b) the usual meaning of market in the "lower of cost and market" method?

(SO 4) 15. Today's Music Inc. has five DVD players on hand at the balance sheet date that cost $400 each. The net realizable value is $320 per unit. Under the lower of cost and market basis of accounting for inventories, what value should be reported for the DVD players on the balance sheet? Why?

(SO 4) 16. Canadian Tire Corporation, Limited reports merchandise inventory of $620.6 million on its January 1, 2005, balance sheet. What additional disclosures about inventory are you likely to find in the notes to Canadian Tire's financial statements?

(SO 4) 17. Big Rock Brewery reports inventory in its December 31, 2004 financial statements as follows: raw materials and returnable glass containers $2,068,119; brews in progress $427,244; and finished products $1,770,495. Explain why Big Rock reports its inventory in these three components.

(SO 4) 18. Under what circumstances might the inventory turnover ratio be (a) too high and (b) too low? In other words, explain the negative consequences that might occur.

(SO 4) 19. Would an increase in the days in inventory ratio from one year to the next be viewed as an improvement or a deterioration in the company's efficiency in managing its inventory?

*20. Your classmate does not understand the difference (SO 5) between the perpetual and periodic inventory systems. "The same cost flow assumptions are used in both systems," he says, "and a physical inventory count is required in both systems—so what's the difference?" Explain to your confused classmate how the perpetual and periodic inventory systems differ.

*21. "When perpetual inventory records are kept, the (SO 5) results under the FIFO cost flow assumption is the same as it would be in a periodic inventory system." If this is the case, why should a company bother using a perpetual inventory system?

*22. How does the average cost flow assumption differ (SO 5) between a perpetual inventory system and a periodic inventory system?

Brief Exercises

Identify items in inventory.
(SO 1)

BE6–1   Helgeson Inc. identifies the following items as maybe belonging in the physical inventory count. For each item, indicate whether or not it should be included in the inventory.

(a) Goods shipped on consignment by Helgeson to another company
(b) Goods held on consignment by Helgeson from another company
(c) Goods sold to a customer, but being held for customer pickup
(d) Goods in transit to Helgeson from a supplier, shipped FOB destination
(e) Goods in transit to a customer, shipped FOB destination

Apply specific identification and
periodic cost flow assumptions.
(SO 2)

BE6–2   On January 3, Piano Corp. purchased three model EBS electronic pianos for $1,000 each. On January 20, it purchased two more model EBS electronic pianos for $1,200 each. An inventory count on January 31 revealed that three of the pianos were still on hand. Piano Corp. uses a periodic inventory system. Calculate the cost of the ending inventory and cost of goods sold on January 31 under (a) specific identification, (b) FIFO, (c) average, and (d) LIFO. Assume for (a) that one of the pianos sold during January was purchased on January 3 and the other was purchased on January 20.

Apply periodic cost flow
assumptions.
(SO 2)

BE6–3   In its first month of operations, Quilt Inc. made three purchases and two sales of merchandise in the following sequence: (1) 250 units purchased at $6, (2) 200 units sold at $9, (3) 400 units purchased at $7, (4) 400 units sold at $10, and (5) 350 units purchased at $8. Quilt uses a periodic inventory system. Calculate the cost of the ending inventory and cost of goods sold under (a) FIFO, (b) average, and (c) LIFO.

Compare financial statement
effects of inventory cost flow
assumptions.
(SO 3)

BE6–4   Interactive.com just started business and is trying to decide which inventory cost flow assumption to use. Assuming prices are falling, as they often do in the information technology sector, answer the following questions for Interactive.com:

(a) Which cost flow assumption will result in the highest ending inventory? Explain.
(b) Which cost flow assumption will result in the highest cost of goods sold? Explain.
(c) Which cost flow assumption will result in the highest pre-tax cash flow? Explain.
(d) What factors are important for Interactive.com to consider as it tries to select the most appropriate cost flow assumption?

Determine effect of inventory
error.
(SO 3)

BE6–5   Creole Ltd. reports net earnings of $90,000 in 2006. However, ending inventory was understated by $7,000. What is the correct net earnings for 2006? What effect, if any, will this error have on total assets and shareholders' equity reported in the balance sheet at December 31, 2006?

Determine effect of inventory
error for two years.
(SO 3)

BE6–6   DuPlessis Corporation counted and recorded its ending inventory as at December 31, 2006, incorrectly overstating its correct value by $25,000. Assuming that this misstatement was not later discovered and corrected, what is the impact of this error on assets, liabilities, and shareholders' equity at the end of 2006? At the end of 2007?

Determine LCM valuation.
(SO 4)

BE6–7   Hawkeye Video Centre Ltd. accumulates the following cost and market data at December 31:

Inventory Categories	Cost	Market
Cameras	$12,000	$11,200
Camcorders	9,000	9,500
DVD players	14,000	12,800

Calculate the lower of cost and market valuation for Hawkeye's total inventory.

Discuss inventory classifications.
(SO 4)

BE6–8   Maple Leaf Foods Inc. reports the following inventory components (in thousands):

	2004	2003	2002
Material held for production	$185,724	$142,739	$130,840
Finished products	199,404	117,019	136,049
	$385,128	$259,758	$266,889

Based on the above data, what guesses can you make about management's production plans?

Calculate inventory turnover and
days in inventory.
(SO 4)

BE6–9   At December 31, 2004, the following information (in millions) is available for paper products manufacturer Cascades Inc.: inventories, December 31, 2004, $559; inventories, December 31, 2003, $501; net sales $3,254; and cost of sales $2,691. Calculate the inventory turnover and days in inventory ratios for Cascades.

BE6–10 Indicate whether the following transactions would increase (+), decrease (−), or have no effect (NE) on the inventory turnover ratio:

Determine impact of transaction on inventory turnover.
(SO 4)

(a) ___ Beginning inventory was understated.

(b) ___ The cost of goods purchased was reduced by moving to a new, cheaper supplier.

(c) ___ Operating expenses increased.

(d) ___ Ending inventory was overstated.

*BE6–11 Berthiaume Inc. uses a perpetual inventory system. Data for product E2-D2 include the following purchases:

Apply perpetual cost flow assumptions.
(SO 5)

Date	Units	Unit Cost
May 7	50	$10
July 28	30	15

On June 1, Berthiaume sold 32 units for $20 each, and on August 27, Berthiaume sold 33 more units for $22 each. Calculate the cost of goods sold and ending inventory using (1) FIFO and (2) average.

*BE6–12 Data for Quilt Inc. are presented in BE6–3. Calculate the cost of the ending inventory and cost of goods sold under (a) FIFO, (b) average, and (c) LIFO, assuming Quilt uses a perpetual inventory system.

Apply perpetual cost flow assumptions.
(SO 5)

*BE6–13 At the beginning of the year, Seller Ltd. had 600 units with a cost of $3 per unit in its beginning inventory. The following inventory transactions occurred during the month of January:

Journalize transactions in periodic and perpetual inventory systems.
(SO 5)

Jan. 3 Sold 500 units on account for $6 each.
   9 Purchased 1,000 units on account for $4 per unit.
  15 Sold 800 units for cash at $8 each.

Prepare journal entries assuming that Seller Ltd. uses (a) FIFO under the periodic inventory assumption, and (b) FIFO under the perpetual inventory system.

Exercises

E6–1 Shippers Ltd. had the following inventory situations to consider at January 31, its year end:

Identify items in inventory.
(SO 1)

(a) Goods held on consignment for MailBoxes Corp. since December 22
(b) Goods shipped on consignment to Rinehart Holdings Ltd. on January 5
(c) Goods that are still in transit that were shipped to a customer FOB destination on January 29
(d) Goods that are still in transit and were shipped to a customer FOB shipping point on January 29
(e) Goods that are still in transit that were purchased FOB destination from a supplier on January 25
(f) Goods that are still in transit that were purchased FOB shipping point from a supplier on January 25
(g) Office supplies on hand at January 31

Instructions

Identify which of the above items should be included in inventory. If the item should not be included in inventory, state where it should be recorded.

E6–2 Gatineau Bank is considering giving Novotna Corporation a loan. Before doing so, it decides that further discussions with Novotna's accountant may be desirable. One area of particular concern is the inventory account, which has a year-end balance of $283,000. Discussions with the accountant reveal the following:

Determine correct inventory amount.
(SO 1)

1. Novotna sold goods costing $35,000 to India-based Moghul Company, FOB shipping point, on December 28. The goods are not expected to arrive in India until January 12. The goods were not included in the physical inventory because they were not in the warehouse.
2. The physical count of the inventory did not include goods costing $95,000 that were shipped to Novotna, FOB destination, on December 27 and were still in transit at year end.
3. Novotna received goods costing $28,000 on January 2. The goods were shipped FOB shipping point on December 26 by Cellar Corp. The goods were not included in the physical count.
4. Novotna sold goods costing $49,000 to UK-based Sterling of Britain Ltd., FOB destination, on December 30. The goods were received by Sterling on January 8. They were not included in Novotna's physical inventory.
5. Included in Novotna's ending inventory balance of $283,000 are $31,000 of goods held on consignment for Bras d'Or Limited.

Instructions

Determine the correct inventory amount on December 31.

Apply specific identification and periodic FIFO.
(SO 2)

E6–3   On December 1, Discount Electronics Ltd. has three DVD player/recorders left in stock. All are identical, and all are priced to sell at $750. One of the three DVD player/recorders, serial #1012, was purchased on June 1 at a cost of $500. Another, serial #1045, was purchased on November 1 for $450. The last player, serial #1056, was purchased on November 30 for $400. At year end, December 31, one player/recorder remained in inventory. Discount Electronics uses a periodic inventory system.

Instructions

(a) Calculate the cost of goods sold using the FIFO cost flow assumption.
(b) If Discount Electronics used the specific identification method instead of the FIFO cost flow assumption, how could Discount alter its earnings by "selectively choosing" which particular player/recorder to sell to the two customers? What would Discount Electronics' cost of goods sold be if the company wished to minimize earnings? To maximize earnings?
(c) Which inventory cost flow assumption do you recommend that Discount Electronics use? Explain why.

Apply periodic cost flow assumptions.
(SO 2)

E6–4   Mawmey Inc. uses a periodic inventory system. Its records show the following for the month of May, in which 70 units were sold:

Date	Explanation	Units	Unit Cost	Total Cost
May 1	Inventory	30	$ 8	$240
15	Purchase	45	11	495
24	Purchase	15	12	180
	Total	90		$915

Instructions

Calculate the cost of the ending inventory and cost of goods sold using (a) FIFO, (b) average, and (c) LIFO.

Apply periodic cost flow assumptions and assess financial statement effects.
(SO 2, 3)

E6–5   Lakshmi Ltd. reports the following inventory transactions in a periodic inventory system for the month of June. A physical inventory count determined that 180 units were on hand at the end of the month.

Date	Explanation	Units	Unit Cost	Total Cost
June 1	Inventory	150	$5	$ 750
12	Purchase	200	6	1,200
16	Purchase	480	8	3,840
23	Purchase	170	9	1,530

Instructions

(a) Calculate the ending inventory and cost of goods sold under (1) FIFO and (2) average.
(b) For part 2 of instruction (a), explain why the average unit cost is not $7.
(c) Which cost flow assumption gives the highest ending inventory? Why?
(d) Which cost flow assumption results in the highest cost of goods sold? Why?
(e) Which cost flow assumption results in the highest pre-tax cash flow? Why?

E6–6 Inventory data for Lakshmi Ltd. are presented in E6–5.

Apply periodic LIFO and assess financial statement effects.
(SO 2, 3)

Instructions

(a) Calculate the cost of the ending inventory and cost of goods sold using the LIFO cost flow assumption.
(b) Should the results in (a) be higher or lower than the results under (1) FIFO and (2) average? Explain why.

E6–7 Seles Hardware Limited reported its cost of goods sold as follows:

Determine effects of inventory errors.
(SO 3)

	2006	2005
Beginning inventory	$ 35,000	$ 30,000
Cost of goods purchased	160,000	175,000
Cost of goods available for sale	195,000	205,000
Ending inventory	45,000	35,000
Cost of goods sold	$150,000	$170,000

Seles made two errors: (1) ending inventory for 2005 was overstated by $3,000 and (2) ending inventory for 2006 was understated by $4,000.

Instructions

(a) Calculate the correct cost of goods sold for each year.
(b) Describe the impact of the error on each year, and in total for the two years.

E6–8 Aruba Inc. reported the following partial statement of earnings data for the years ended December 31, 2005 and 2006:

Correct partial statements of earnings.
(SO 3)

	2006	2005
Sales	$210,000	$250,000
Beginning inventory	52,000	44,000
Cost of goods purchased	173,000	202,000
Cost of goods available for sale	225,000	246,000
Ending inventory	64,000	52,000
Cost of goods sold	161,000	194,000
Gross profit	$ 49,000	$ 56,000

The inventories at January 1, 2005, and December 31, 2006, are correct. However, the ending inventory at December 31, 2005, is overstated by $5,000.

Instructions

(a) Prepare correct statements of earnings for the two years through to gross profit.
(b) What is the cumulative effect of the inventory error on total gross profit for the two years?
(c) Calculate the gross profit margin for each of the two years, before and after the correction.
(d) In a letter to the president of Aruba, explain what has happened—that is, explain the nature of the error and its effect on the financial statements.

E6–9 The Cody Camera Shop Ltd. uses the lower of cost and market basis for its inventory in a periodic inventory system. The following data are available at December 31:

Determine LCM valuation.
(SO 4)

	Units	Cost/Unit	Market Value/Unit
Cameras:			
Minolta	5	$175	$160
Canon	7	140	142
Light Meters:			
Vivitar	12	135	129
Kodak	10	115	120

Instructions

(a) Determine the total cost of the ending inventory.
(b) Determine the total market value of the ending inventory.
(c) What amount should be reported on Cody Camera Shop's financial statements, assuming the lower of cost and market rule is applied to total inventory?
(d) Prepare the journal entry to record any adjustment that is required when the lower of cost and market rule is applied.

Calculate inventory turnover, days in inventory, gross profit margin, and comment.
(SO 4)

E6–10   This information is available for Danier Leather Inc. for three recent years (in thousands):

	2004	2003	2002
Inventory	$ 29,915	$ 37,029	$ 38,662
Sales	178,115	175,487	179,977
Cost of sales	90,060	88,788	92,098

Instructions

Calculate the inventory turnover, days in inventory, and gross profit margin for 2004 and 2003. Comment on any trends.

Determine effect of cost flow assumption on inventory turnover.
(SO 4)

E6–11   Caterpillar Inc. values its inventories using the LIFO cost flow assumption. If it valued its inventories using FIFO, they would be reported at a higher value at December 31, 2004, as shown below (in U.S. millions):

	LIFO	FIFO
Cost of goods sold	$22,420	$17,143
Average inventory	3,861	5,854

Instructions

(a) Caterpillar's average inventory cost differs by U.S. $1,993 million (or more than 50 percent) when using the LIFO cost flow assumption, as opposed to the FIFO cost flow assumption. Why do you suppose there is such a significant difference between these two amounts?
(b) Calculate the inventory turnover under (1) LIFO and (2) FIFO.
(c) Which method gives you the highest inventory turnover?
(d) Does Caterpillar's inventory really turn over faster with one cost flow assumption than the other? Explain.

Apply perpetual cost flow assumptions.
(SO 5)

*E6–12   Inventory data for Lakshmi Ltd. are presented in E6–5.

Instructions

(a) Calculate the cost of goods sold and the cost of the ending inventory under (1) FIFO and (2) average, using a perpetual inventory system. Assume sales of 250 units on June 15 for $10 each and 570 units on June 27 for $12 each.
(b) How do the results in (a) differ from E6–5?
(c) Why is the average unit cost in part 2 of instruction (a) not $6 (simple average) or $6.30 (weighted average) with a perpetual system?

Apply periodic and perpetual cost flow assumptions.
(SO 2, 5)

*E6–13   Powder! sells an Xpert snowboard that is popular with snowboard enthusiasts. Below is information relating to Powder!'s purchases and sales of Xpert snowboards during September:

Date	Transaction	Units	Per Unit	Total Sales Price	Total Purchase Cost
Sept. 1	Beginning inventory	26	$297		$ 7,722
5	Purchase	28	302		8,456
12	Sale	(32)	449	$14,368	
19	Purchase	30	304		9,120
22	Sale	(50)	449	22,450	
25	Purchase	15	310		4,650
	Totals	17		$36,818	$29,948

Instructions

(a) Calculate the cost of the ending inventory and cost of goods sold using FIFO and average, assuming Powder! uses a perpetual inventory system.
(b) What would the cost of the ending inventory and cost of goods sold be if Powder! used each of these cost flow assumptions in a periodic inventory system?

Journalize transactions in perpetual and periodic inventory systems.
(SO 2, 5)

*E6–14   Refer to the data provided for Powder! in E6–13.

Instructions

(a) Prepare journal entries to record purchases and sales for Powder! in a perpetual inventory system under (1) FIFO and (2) average.
(b) Prepare journal entries to record purchases and sales for Powder! in a periodic inventory system under (1) FIFO and (2) average.

Problems: Set A

P6–1A Kananaskis Limited is trying to determine the amount of its ending inventory as at February 28, 2006, the company's year end. The accountant counted everything in the warehouse, which resulted in an ending inventory value of $95,000. However, the accountant was not sure how to treat the following transactions, so he did not record them. He asked for your help in determining whether they should be included in inventory or not:

Identify items in inventory. (SO 1)

1. On February 26, Kananaskis shipped goods costing $950 to a customer and charged the customer $1,300. The goods were shipped FOB destination. The receiving report indicates that the customer received the goods on March 3.
2. On February 26, Custom Inc. shipped goods to Kananaskis FOB shipping point. The invoice price was $375 plus $30 for freight. The receiving report indicates that the goods were received by Kananaskis on March 2.
3. Kananaskis had $630 of inventory isolated in the warehouse. The inventory is designated for a customer who has requested that the goods be shipped on March 10.
4. Also in Kananaskis' warehouse is $400 of inventory that Craft Producers Ltd. shipped to Kananaskis on consignment.
5. On February 26, Kananaskis purchased goods costing $750. The goods were shipped FOB destination. The receiving report indicates that Kananaskis received the goods on March 2.
6. On February 26, Kananaskis shipped goods to a customer FOB shipping point. The invoice price was $350 plus $25 for freight; the cost of the items sold was $280. The receiving report indicates that the goods were received by the customer on March 2.
7. Kananaskis shipped $875 of inventory on consignment to Banff Corporation on February 20. By February 28, Banff had sold $365 of this inventory for Kananaskis.

Instructions

(a) For each of the above transactions, specify whether the item should be included in ending inventory, and if so, at what amount. For each item that is not included in ending inventory, indicate who owns it and what account, if any, it should have been recorded in.
(b) What is the revised ending inventory amount?

P6–2A Kane Ltd. had a beginning inventory on January 1 of 100 units of Product SXL at a cost of $20 per unit. During the year, purchases were:

Apply periodic cost flow assumptions. (SO 2)

Mar. 15	300 units at $24	Sept. 4	300 units at $28
July 20	200 units at $25	Dec. 2	100 units at $30

Kane uses a periodic inventory system. At the end of the year, a physical inventory count determined that there were 150 units on hand.

Instructions

(a) Determine the cost of goods available for sale.
(b) Determine the cost of the ending inventory and the cost of the goods sold under each of the three cost flow assumptions: (1) FIFO, (2) average, and (3) LIFO.

P6–3A Data for Kane Ltd. were presented in P6–2A. Assume that Kane sold 850 units of product SXL for $40 each.

Prepare partial financial statements and assess financial statement effects. (SO 3)

Instructions

(a) Prepare a partial statement of earnings through to gross profit for each of the three cost flow assumptions: (1) FIFO, (2) average, and (3) LIFO.
(b) Show how inventory would be reported in the current assets section of the balance sheet for each of the three cost flow assumptions: (1) FIFO, (2) average, and (3) LIFO.
(c) Which cost flow assumption results in the highest inventory amount for the balance sheet? The highest cost of goods sold for the statement of earnings?

P6–4A The management of Tumatoe Inc. asks for your help in determining the comparative effects of the FIFO and average periodic inventory cost flow assumptions. For 2006, the accounting records show the following selected data:

Apply periodic cost flow assumptions; prepare statement of earnings and memo. (SO 2, 3)

Inventory, January 1 (10,000 units)	$ 35,000
Selling price of 100,000 units sold	700,000
Operating expenses	120,000

The costs of the goods purchased during the year are as follows:

Date	Units	Unit Cost	Total Cost
May 10	40,000	$4.00	$160,000
Aug. 15	50,000	4.25	212,500
Nov. 20	20,000	4.50	90,000
	110,000		$462,500

Instructions

(a) Calculate the cost of goods sold under the FIFO and average cost flow assumptions.
(b) Prepare comparative condensed statements of earnings for FIFO and average. Assume the company's income tax rate is 25%.
(c) Write a business memo to answer the following questions for management:
   1. Which inventory cost flow assumption produces the most meaningful inventory amount for the balance sheet? Why?
   2. Which inventory cost flow assumption produces the most meaningful net earnings? Why?
   3. How much cash will be available for management under each assumption?
   4. What factors should influence management's choice of cost flow assumption?

Determine effects of inventory errors.
(SO 3)

P6–5A   Appleby Corporation omitted to include inventory that was stored at an off-site warehouse in its physical inventory count at February 28, 2005, its year end. Its inventory was correctly stated at the end of 2006.

Instructions

Indicate the effect of this error (overstated, understated, or no effect) on the following:
(a) Cash at the end of 2005 and 2006
(b) The cost of goods sold for each of 2005 and 2006
(c) Net earnings for each of 2005 and 2006
(d) Retained earnings at the end of 2005 and 2006
(e) Ending inventory at the end of 2005 and 2006
(f) The gross profit margin for each of 2005 and 2006
(g) The inventory turnover ratio for each of 2005 and 2006

Determine effects of inventory errors.
(SO 3)

P6–6A   The records of Alyssa Inc. show the following data:

	2006	2005
Sales	$330,000	$320,000
Beginning inventory	31,000	24,000
Cost of goods purchased	230,000	240,000
Ending inventory	40,000	31,000
Operating expenses	66,000	64,000

After its July 31, 2006, year end, Alyssa discovers two errors:

1. Ending inventory at the end of 2005 was actually $33,000, not $31,000.
2. The cost of goods purchased for 2005 included $20,000 of merchandise that should have been recorded as a purchase in 2006.

Instructions

(a) Prepare incorrect and corrected statements of earnings for Alyssa Inc. for each of the two years. The income tax rate is 25%.
(b) What is the impact of these errors on retained earnings at July 31, 2006?

Prepare journal entries for buyer and seller using periodic average; apply LCM.
(SO 2, 4)

P6–7A   You are provided with the following information for Amelia Inc. Amelia purchases all items from Karina Inc. and makes sales to a variety of customers. All transactions are settled in cash. Returns are usually undamaged and are immediately restored to inventory for resale. Both Amelia and Karina use the periodic inventory method and the average cost flow assumption. Increased competition has reduced the price of the product.

Date		Description	Units	Unit Price	Total
July	1	Beginning inventory	25	$10	$250
	5	Purchase	60	9	540
	8	Sale	65	11	715
	10	Sale return	10	11	110
	15	Purchase	45	8	360
	16	Purchase return	5	8	40
	20	Sale	60	9	540
	25	Purchase	10	7	70

Instructions

(a) Prepare all journal entries for the month of July for Amelia Inc., the buyer.
(b) Prepare all journal entries for the month of July for Karina Inc., the seller.
(c) Determine the ending inventory amount for Amelia, using the average cost flow assumption.
(d) By July 31, Amelia learns that the product has a net realizable value of $8 per unit. What amount should ending inventory be valued at on the July 31 balance sheet?

P6–8A   The Tascon Corporation sells coffee beans, which are sensitive to market price fluctuations. The following inventory information is available for this product at December 31, 2006:

Apply LCM.
(SO 4)

Type of Bean	Quantity	Unit Cost	Net Realizable Value
Coffea arabica	13,000 bags	$5.30	$5.50
Coffea robusta	6,000 bags	3.50	3.00

Instructions

(a) Calculate Tascon's inventory value at cost and at net realizable value.
(b) At what value would Tascon's inventory be reported if it applied the LCM rule to individual items in its inventory? If it applied the LCM rule to its total inventory? Which do you recommend that Tascon use? Why?
(c) Applying the LCM rule to Tascon's total inventory, prepare the journal entry to adjust the inventory value. Assume Tascon uses a periodic inventory system.
(d) What accounting characteristic guides users in applying the LCM rule?

P6–9A   The following information (in thousands) is available for CoolBrands International Inc. for the year ended August 31:

Calculate ratios; comment on liquidity and effect of cost flow assumptions on ratios.
(SO 3, 4)

	2004	2003	2002
Cost of goods sold	$438,458	$207,870	$129,246
Inventory	64,618	55,604	25,361
Current assets	257,129	161,388	131,839
Current liabilities	97,774	75,654	74,485

The industry averages for the inventory turnover, days in inventory, and current ratios are as follows:

	2004	2003
Inventory turnover	13.4 times	12.1 times
Days in inventory	27 days	30 days
Current ratio	2.1:1	1.9:1

Instructions

(a) Calculate the inventory turnover, days in inventory, and current ratios for 2003 and 2004. Comment on CoolBrands' liquidity.
(b) If prices are rising, how would you expect the inventory turnover, days in inventory, and current ratios to change (e.g., increase or decrease) if CoolBrands used the average cost flow assumption instead of FIFO?

Apply periodic and perpetual
FIFO.
(SO 2, 5)

*P6–10A   You are provided with the following information for Danielle Inc. for the month ended June 30, 2004:

Date	Description	Units	Unit Price
June 1	Beginning inventory	25	$60
4	Purchase	85	64
10	Sale	90	90
18	Purchase	35	68
25	Sale	50	95
26	Sale return	5	95
28	Purchase	20	72

Instructions

(a) Calculate the cost of ending inventory and cost of goods sold under the FIFO cost flow assumption in (1) a perpetual inventory system, and (2) a periodic inventory system.
(b) Compare your results for parts 1 and 2 of instruction (a), commenting particularly on any differences or similarities between the two inventory systems.
(c) Would your results in (a) change if Danielle had experienced declining prices when purchasing additional inventory?

Apply perpetual cost flow
assumptions, and assess financial
statement effects.
(SO 3, 5)

*P6–11A   Save-Mart Centre Inc. began operations on July 1. It uses a perpetual inventory system. During July, the company had the following purchases and sales:

Date	Purchases Units	Unit Cost	Sales Units	Unit Price
July 1	5	$ 90		
4			2	$195
8	4	99		
12			4	225
15	3	103		
20			2	245
25			2	245

Instructions

(a) Determine the cost of ending inventory and cost of goods sold using (1) FIFO, (2) average, and (3) LIFO.
(b) Which cost flow assumption produces the highest gross profit and net earnings?
(c) Which cost flow assumption produces the highest ending inventory valuation?
(d) Which cost flow assumption produces the highest pre-tax cash flow?

Problems: Set B

Identify items in inventory.
(SO 1)

P6–1B   Banff Limited is trying to determine the value of its ending inventory as at February 28, 2006, the company's year end. The accountant counted everything that was in the warehouse, as at February 28, which resulted in an ending inventory valuation of $48,000. However, she did not know how to treat the following transactions so she chose not to include them in inventory:

1. On February 26, Banff shipped goods costing $800 to a customer. The goods were shipped FOB shipping point. The receiving report indicates that the customer received the goods on March 2.
2. On February 26, Seller Inc. shipped goods to Banff FOB destination. The invoice price was $350 plus $25 for freight. The receiving report indicates that the goods were received by Banff on March 1.
3. Banff had $620 of inventory at a customer's warehouse "on approval." The customer was going to let Banff know whether it wanted the merchandise by the end of the week, March 5.
4. Banff also had $570 of its inventory on consignment at a Jasper craft shop.
5. On February 25, Banff ordered goods costing $750. The goods were shipped FOB shipping point on February 27. The receiving report indicates that Banff received them on March 1.
6. On February 28, Banff packaged goods and had them ready for shipping to a customer FOB destination. The invoice price was $425 plus $20 for freight; the cost of the items was $360. The receiving report indicates that the goods were received by the customer on March 2.

7. On February 20, Banff received $875 of inventory on consignment from Kananaskis Limited. By February 28, Banff had sold $365 of this inventory for Kananaskis.

Instructions

(a) For each of the above transactions, specify whether the item should be included in ending inventory, and if so, at what amount. For each item that is not included in ending inventory, indicate who owns it and what account, if any, it should have been recorded in.
(b) What is the revised ending inventory amount?

P6–2B   Steward Inc. had a beginning inventory on January 1 of 200 units of Product MLN at a cost of $8 per unit. During the year, purchases were:

Apply periodic cost flow assumptions.
(SO 2)

Feb. 20	700 units at $9	Aug. 12	500 units at $11
May 5	500 units at $10	Dec. 8	100 units at $12

Steward uses a periodic inventory system. At the end of the year, a physical inventory count determined that there were 300 units on hand.

Instructions

(a) Determine the cost of goods available for sale.
(b) Determine the cost of goods sold and the ending inventory under each of the cost flow assumptions: (1) FIFO, (2) average, and (3) LIFO.

P6–3B   Data for Steward Inc. were presented in P6–2B. Assume that Steward sold 1,700 units of product MLN for $19 each.

Prepare partial financial statements and assess financial statement effects.
(SO 3)

Instructions

(a) Prepare a partial statement of earnings through to gross profit for each of the three cost flow assumptions: (1) FIFO, (2) average, and (3) LIFO.
(b) Show how inventory would be reported in the current assets section of the balance sheet for each of the three cost flow assumptions: (1) FIFO, (2) average, and (3) LIFO.
(c) Which cost flow assumption results in the lowest inventory amount for the balance sheet? The lowest cost of goods sold for the statement of earnings?

P6–4B   The management of Real Novelty Inc. is re-evaluating the appropriateness of using the average cost flow assumption, as it now does. The company requests your help in determining the results of operations for 2006 if the FIFO cost flow assumption had been used. For 2006, the accounting records show these data:

Apply periodic cost flow assumptions; prepare statement of earnings and memo.
(SO 2, 3)

Inventories		Purchases and Sales	
Beginning (15,000 units)	$33,750	Total net sales (225,000 units)	$900,000
Ending (20,000 units)	50,550	Total cost of goods purchased	585,500

The cost of goods purchased during the year are detailed as follows:

Quarter	Units	Unit Cost	Total Cost
1	60,000	$2.30	$138,000
2	50,000	2.50	125,000
3	50,000	2.60	130,000
4	70,000	2.75	192,500
	230,000		$585,500

Operating expenses were $147,000. The company's income tax rate is 30%.

Instructions

(a) Calculate cost of goods sold as though the FIFO cost flow assumption had been used, rather than the average cost flow assumption.
(b) Prepare comparative condensed statements of earnings for FIFO and average.
(c) Write a business memo to answer the following questions for management:
   1. Which cost flow assumption produces the most meaningful inventory amount for the balance sheet? Why?
   2. Which cost flow assumption produces the most meaningful net earnings? Why?
   3. Which assumption provides the most realistic gross profit figure?
   4. How much cash will be available for management under each assumption?
   5. What factors should influence management's choice of cost flow assumption?

Determine effects of inventory
errors.
(SO 3)

P6–5B   Handspring Corporation included inventory that it held on consignment in its physical inventory count at March 31, 2005. The inventory was correctly stated at the end of 2006.

Instructions

Indicate the effect of this error (overstated, understated, or no effect) on the following:
  (a) Cash at the end of 2005 and 2006
  (b) The cost of goods sold for each of 2005 and 2006
  (c) Net earnings for each of 2005 and 2006
  (d) Retained earnings at the end of 2005 and 2006
  (e) Ending inventory at the end of 2005 and 2006
  (f) The gross profit margin for each of 2005 and 2006
  (g) The days in inventory ratio for each of 2005 and 2006

Determine effects of inventory
errors.
(SO 3)

P6–6B   The records of Pelletier Inc. show the following data:

	2006	2005
Sales	$350,000	$330,000
Beginning inventory	46,000	27,000
Cost of goods purchased	320,000	260,000
Ending inventory	50,000	46,000
Operating expenses	63,000	60,000

After its July 31, 2005, year end, Pelletier discovers two errors:

  1. Ending inventory at the end of 2005 was understated by $3,000.
  2. The cost of goods purchased for 2006 included $25,000 of merchandise that should have been recorded as a purchase in 2005.

Instructions

  (a) Prepare incorrect and corrected statements of earnings for Pelletier Inc. for each of the two years. The income tax rate is 25%.
  (b) Calculate both the incorrect and corrected inventory turnover ratios for each of the two years.

Prepare journal entries for buyer
and seller using periodic FIFO;
apply LCM.
(SO 2, 4)

P6–7B   You are provided with the following information for the transactions of Leila G Inc. Leila G purchases all items from Pataki Inc. and makes sales to a variety of customers. All transactions are settled on account. Returns are normally undamaged and are immediately restored to inventory for resale. Both companies use the periodic inventory method and the FIFO cost flow assumption. Increased competition has reduced the price of the product.

Date		Description	Units	Unit Price
Oct.	1	Beginning inventory	60	$15
	5	Purchase	120	14
	8	Sale	150	24
	10	Sale return	25	24
	15	Purchase	40	13
	16	Purchase return	5	13
	20	Sale	75	18
	25	Purchase	10	11

Instructions

  (a) Prepare all journal entries for the month of October for Leila G Inc., the buyer.
  (b) Prepare all journal entries for the month of October for Pataki Inc., the seller.
  (c) Determine the ending inventory amount for Leila G, using the FIFO cost flow assumption.
  (d) By October 31, Leila G learns that the product has a net realizable value of $10 per unit. What amount should ending inventory be valued at on the October 31 balance sheet?

Apply LCM.
(SO 4)

P6–8B   Flin Flon Limited sells three products whose prices are sensitive to changes in market value. The following inventory information is available for these products at March 31, 2006:

Product	Quantity	Unit Cost	Net Realizable Value
A	60	$ 8	$9
B	35	6	5
C	20	10	8

Instructions

(a) Calculate Flin Flon's inventory value at cost and at net realizable value.
(b) At what value would Flin Flon's inventory be reported if it applied the LCM rule to individual items in its inventory? If it applied the LCM rule to its total inventory? Which do you recommend that Flin Flon use? Why?
(c) Prepare the journal entry (if any) required to adjust the inventory value to LCM. Assume Flin Flon uses a periodic inventory system.
(d) What accounting characteristic guides users in applying the LCM rule?

P6–9B The following information (in U.S. millions) is available for PepsiCo, Inc., for the year ended December 31:

Calculate ratios; comment on liquidity and effect of cost flow assumptions on ratios. (SO 3, 4)

	2004	2003	2002
Cost of goods sold	$13,406	$12,379	$11,497
Inventory	1,541	1,412	1,342
Current assets	8,639	6,930	6,413
Current liabilities	6,752	6,415	6,052

PepsiCo discloses the composition of its inventory, as follows:

	2004	2003	2002
Raw materials	$ 665	$ 618	$ 525
Work in process	156	160	214
Finished goods	720	634	603
	$1,541	$1,412	$1,342

Instructions

(a) Calculate the inventory turnover, days in inventory, and current ratios for 2003 and 2004. Comment on PepsiCo's liquidity.
(b) Comment on changes in the composition of PepsiCo's inventories over the last three years. Do these changes give you any insight into PepsiCo's production plans?
(c) Are the changes you observed in (b) consistent with the trends you observed in the inventory turnover ratio in (a)?

*P6–10B You are provided with the following information for Lahti Inc. for the month ended October 31, 2004:

Apply periodic and perpetual average. (SO 2, 5)

Date		Description	Units	Unit Price
Oct.	1	Beginning inventory	60	$25
	9	Purchase	120	26
	10	Purchase return	5	26
	15	Sale	150	35
	22	Purchase	70	27
	29	Sale	75	40

Instructions

(a) Calculate the cost of ending inventory and cost of goods sold under the average cost flow assumption in (1) a periodic inventory system, and (2) a perpetual inventory system.
(b) Compare your results for parts 1 and 2 of instruction (a), commenting specifically on any differences or similarities between the two inventory systems.

*P6–11B The Family Appliance Mart Ltd. began operations on May 1 and uses a perpetual inventory system. During May, the company had the following purchases and sales for one of its products:

Apply perpetual cost flow assumptions, and assess financial statement effects. (SO 3, 5)

Date	Purchases		Sales	
	Units	Unit Cost	Units	Unit Price
May 1	150	$17		
6	100	21		
11			200	$35
14	75	24		
21			100	40
27	50	28		

Instructions

(a) Determine the cost of the ending inventory and cost of goods sold using (1) FIFO, (2) average, and (3) LIFO.
(b) Which cost flow assumption produces the highest gross profit and net earnings?
(c) Which cost flow assumption produces the highest ending inventory valuation?
(d) Which cost flow assumption produces the highest pre-tax cash flow?

BROADENING YOUR PERSPECTIVE

Financial Reporting and Analysis

Analysis Tools

Financial Reporting Problem: *Loblaw*

BYP6–1   Refer to the financial statements of Loblaw in Appendix A.

Instructions

(a) What amounts did Loblaw report for inventories in its consolidated balance sheet at the end of fiscal 2003 and 2002?
(b) How does Loblaw value its inventories?
(c) Calculate the dollar amount of change and the percentage change in inventories between 2003 and 2002. Calculate inventory as a percentage of current assets for each of the two years. Comment on the results.
(d) Loblaw uses the FIFO cost flow assumption. Do you think that using a different cost flow assumption would change Loblaw's results significantly?

Comparative Analysis Problem: *Loblaw and Sobeys*

BYP6–2   The financial statements of Sobeys are presented in Appendix B, following the financial statements for Loblaw in Appendix A.

Instructions

(a) Based on the information in these statements, calculate the following values for Loblaw for fiscal 2003 and 2002 and for Sobeys for fiscal 2004 and 2003.
   1. Current ratio
   2. Inventory turnover, using "cost of sales, selling, and administrative expenses" instead of cost of goods sold, and using year-end inventory balances instead of averages.
   3. Days in inventory
(b) What conclusions about liquidity and the management of inventory, and about selling and administrative expenses can be drawn from your results in (a)?

Research Case

BYP6–3   The March 29, 2002, issue of *Report on Business Magazine* contains an article by Patrick Brethour entitled, "The Worst Is Not Over in Telecom: Billions More in Write-Offs Loom as Backlogs of Components Pile Up." This article discusses the inventory write-offs of communications equipment makers.

Instructions

Read the article and answer the following questions:

(a) Explain how writing down the value of inventory follows the lower of cost and market rule.
(b) How much was Nortel Networks' inventory write-off in 2001?
(c) What was Nortel's inventory turnover in 2001 and 2000? Explain how the inventory write-off contributed to the change in Nortel's inventory turnover.
(d) What is the danger sign to watch out for in the value of inventories?

Interpreting Financial Statements

BYP6–4   The following information was taken from the April 3, 2004, financial statements of Indigo Books & Music Inc. (in thousands):

	2004	2003	2002
Cost of product, purchasing, selling and administration	$761,300	$737,228	$698,660
Inventories	199,421	202,455	223,467

In its MD&A, the company stated that "Material improvements in shrink and labour productivity allowed the Company to invest in higher sales discounts to match market pricing on selected products... The Company reduces inventory for estimated shrinkage that has occurred between annual physical inventory counts. The net result is that inventory is valued at the lower of cost or net realizable value, less a normal profit margin." The company's inventory shrinkage as a percentage of sales was 2.3% in 2004, 3.0% in 2003, and 3.3% in 2002.

Instructions

(a) Calculate the company's inventory turnover and days in inventory ratios for 2004 and 2003. Use "cost of product, purchasing, selling and administration" in place of the cost of goods sold. Discuss the implications of any change in the ratios.
(b) What causes "inventory shrinkage"? Comment on the trend of the company's shrinkage as a percentage of sales—is this an improvement or a deterioration?
(c) To account for its inventories, Indigo uses the average cost flow assumption. Indigo's main competitor, Amazon.com, Inc., uses the FIFO cost flow assumption to account for its inventories. What difficulties would this create in comparing Indigo's financial results to those of Amazon.com? Explain.

A Global Focus

BYP6–5   Japan-based Fuji Photo Film and U.S.-based arch rival Eastman Kodak dominate the global market for film. The following information is from the financial statements of the two companies:

FUJI PHOTO FILM CO., LTD
Notes to the Financial Statements
March 31, 2004

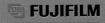

Note 2. Summary of significant accounting policies

The Company and its domestic subsidiaries maintain their records and prepare their financial statements in accordance with accounting practices generally accepted in Japan... Certain reclassifications and adjustments have been incorporated in the consolidated financial statements to conform them with accounting principles generally accepted in the United States of America

Inventories

Inventories are valued at the lower of cost or market, cost being determined principally by the moving average method.

Note 6. Inventories

Inventories at March 31, 2004 and 2003, consisted of the following (in yen millions):

	2004	2003
Finished goods	¥215,448	¥218,483
Work in process	63,558	65,273
Raw materials and supplies	69,303	67,992
	¥348,309	¥351,748

Additional information

2004 cost of goods sold, ¥1,362,672 million

EASTMAN KODAK COMPANY
Notes to the Financial Statements
December 31, 2003

Note 1. Summary of significant accounting policies

Inventories

Inventories are stated at the lower of cost or market. The cost of most inventories in the U.S. is determined by the last-in, first-out (LIFO) method. The cost of all of the Company's remaining inventories in and outside the U.S. is determined by the first-in, first-out (FIFO) or average cost method, which approximates current cost.

Note 3. Inventories

(in U.S. millions)	2003	2002
At FIFO or average cost (approximates current cost)		
Finished goods	$ 818	$ 831
Work in process	302	322
Raw materials and supplies	317	301
Total inventories at FIFO or average	$1,437	$1,454
At LIFO		
Total inventories at LIFO	$1,075	$1,062

Additional information

2003 cost of goods sold, U.S.$9,063 million (at FIFO) and U.S.$9,033 million (at LIFO)

Instructions

(a) Why do you suppose Fuji makes reclassifications and adjustments to its accounts so that they conform with U.S. accounting principles and currency when it reports its results?

(b) Does Fuji use a perpetual or periodic inventory method to account for its inventories?

(c) Why do you think Eastman Kodak would use a different cost flow assumption to account for its nondomestic inventories?

(d) What are the current period inventory turnover and days in inventory ratios of the two companies (use March 31, 2004, figures for Fuji and December 31, 2003, figures for Kodak using its FIFO or average cost flow assumption)? How does this comparison change when you use Kodak's inventory figures at LIFO to calculate the inventory turnover and days in inventory? Explain which comparison is the most relevant for decision-making purposes.

(e) Calculate, as a percentage of total inventory, the portion that each of the components of the current period's inventory (raw materials, work in process, and finished goods) represents (use March 31, 2004, figures for Fuji and December 31, 2003, figures for Kodak). Comment on your findings.

Financial Analysis on the Web

BYP6–6   In this activity, we use a company's annual report to calculate several key inventory-related ratios and to identify the company's inventory cost flow assumption.

Instructions

Specific requirements of this Web case can be found on the Toolkit website.

Analysis Tools
(Financial Analysis on the Web)

Critical Thinking

Collaborative Learning Activity

BYP6–7   Just-in-Time (JIT) Auto Parts Ltd. manufactures auto parts. The company's inventories reported on its balance sheet at July 31, 2006, total $1,094.7 million. Assume that the following transactions occurred during July and August:

1. Office supplies were shipped to JIT Auto Parts by Office Maxx, FOB destination. The goods were shipped July 31 and received August 3.
2. JIT Auto Parts purchased specialty plastic from DuPont Canada for use in the manufacture of door mouldings. The goods were shipped FOB shipping point July 31 and received August 3.
3. Ford Motor Company of Canada, Limited, purchased 3,000 rear liftgate assemblies to be used in the manufacture of the Ford Escape. They were shipped FOB shipping point July 29, and were received by Ford August 1.
4. Nadeau Furniture shipped office furniture to JIT Auto Parts, FOB destination, on July 27. The furniture was received August 3.
5. Inland Specialty Chemical shipped JIT Auto Parts chemicals that JIT Auto Parts uses in the manufacture of door mouldings and other items. The goods were sent FOB shipping point July 30 and received August 3.
6. JIT Auto Parts purchased new Lincoln Town Cars for its executives to drive. The cars were shipped FOB destination July 30 and received August 5.
7. To expand its manufacturing plant, JIT Auto Parts purchased steel from IPSCO, FOB Regina (shipping point). The steel was shipped July 30, arrived in Ontario August 2, and at JIT Auto Parts' plant in Aurora on August 3.
8. JIT Auto Parts shipped instrument panels to Jaguar, FOB destination. The panels were shipped July 31, and arrived at Jaguar's headquarters in England August 7.

Instructions

With the class divided into groups, answer the following:

(a) Determine which of the above transactions affect JIT Auto Parts' Inventory account. For each item that has an effect, would the transaction result in an increase or a decrease in the Inventory account at July 31, 2006?

(b) For each transaction that does not affect JIT Auto Parts' Inventory account, indicate who owns the relevant items and how they should be reported.

Communication Activity

BYP6–8   You are the controller of Small Toys Inc. Joy Small, the president, recently mentioned to you that she found an error in the 2005 financial statements which she believes has corrected itself. In discussions with the purchasing department, she determined that 2005 ending inventory was overstated by $1 million. Joy says that the 2006 ending inventory is correct, and she assumes that 2006 net earnings are correct. Joy says to you, "What happened has happened—there's no point in worrying about it anymore."

Instructions

You conclude that Joy is incorrect. Write a brief, tactful memo to her, clarifying the situation.

Ethics Case

Ethics In Accounting

BYP6–9   You are provided with the following information for Discount Diamonds Ltd. Discount only carries one brand and size of diamond—all are identical. Each batch of diamonds purchased is carefully coded and marked with its purchase cost.

Mar. 1 Beginning inventory is 140 diamonds at a cost of $300 per diamond.
      3 Purchased 200 diamonds at a cost of $340 each.
      5 Sold 170 diamonds for $600 each.
     10 Purchased 340 diamonds at a cost of $370 each.
     25 Sold 500 diamonds for $650 each.

Instructions

(a) Assuming that Discount Diamonds uses the specific identification cost flow method, do the following:
   1. Show how Discount Diamonds could maximize its gross profit for the month by selecting which diamonds to sell on March 5 and March 25.
   2. Show how Discount Diamonds could minimize its gross profit for the month by selecting which diamonds to sell on March 5 and March 25.
(b) Assume that Discount Diamonds uses the average cost flow assumption. How much gross profit would Discount Diamonds report under this assumption?
(c) Who are the stakeholders in this situation? Is there anything unethical in choosing which diamonds to sell in a month?
(d) Which cost flow assumption should Discount Diamonds select? Explain.

Serial Problem

(*Note*: This is a continuation of the serial problem from Chapters 1 through 5.)

BYP6–10   Natalie is busy establishing both divisions of Cookie Creations Ltd. (cookie classes and mixer sales) and completing her business degree. She has decided to concentrate her efforts on mixers for the next while, and try to sell at least one mixer a month.

The cost of the deluxe European mixers is expected to increase. New terms have just been negotiated with Kzinski that include shipping costs in the negotiated purchase price (mixers will be shipped FOB destination). The invoice price will be in Canadian dollars and will depend on the foreign exchange rate when Kzinski prepares its invoices for Cookie Creations Ltd. (Kzinski sets its mixer price in Euros). Natalie has chosen the FIFO cost flow assumption.

The following transactions occur between the months of February and May 2006:

Feb. 2 Two deluxe mixers are purchased on account from Kzinski Supply Co. for $1,100 ($550 each), FOB destination, terms n/30.
     16 One deluxe mixer is sold for $1,050 cash.
     24 Amounts owing to Kzinski are paid.
Mar. 2 One deluxe mixer is purchased on account from Kzinski for $567, FOB destination, terms n/30.
     30 Two deluxe mixers are sold for a total of $2,100 cash.
     31 Amounts owing to Kzinski are paid.

Apr. 3 Two deluxe mixers are purchased on account from Kzinski for $1,122 ($561 each), FOB destination, terms n/30.

13 Three deluxe mixers are sold on account for a total of $3,150 cash.

28 Amounts owing to Kzinski are paid.

May 4 Three deluxe mixers are purchased on account from Kzinski for $1,720 ($573.33 each), FOB destination, terms n/30.

25 One deluxe mixer is sold for $1,050 cash.

Natalie is finding it tedious to track the inventory information using FIFO in a perpetual inventory system. She wonders whether using FIFO in a periodic inventory system would save her both time and effort.

Instructions

(a) Using the FIFO cost flow assumption in a perpetual inventory system, prepare a schedule to track the purchases and sales of mixers, and the balance of the mixers inventory account. Use the format from Illustration 6A-1. Recall from Chapter 5 that at the end of January, Cookie Creations had three mixers on hand at a cost of $545 each.

(b) Using the FIFO cost flow assumption in a periodic inventory system, prepare a schedule to track the purchases and sales of mixers, and the balance of the mixers inventory account at the end of May. Use the format from Illustration 6-3. Recall from Chapter 5 that at the end of January, Cookie Creations had three mixers on hand at a cost of $545 each.

(c) Address Natalie's concerns. What are the differences in the results using each of these two inventory systems. What are the differences in information provided by each of these systems? Which inventory system—perpetual or periodic—would you recommend that Cookie Creations use and why?

Answers to Self-Study Questions

1. d   2. a   3. b   4. c   5. a   6. b   7. a   8. d   *9. c   *10. c

Answer to Loblaw Review It Question 2

Loblaw uses the FIFO (first-in, first-out) cost flow assumption to account for its inventories.

Remember to go back to the Navigator box at the beginning of the chapter to check off your completed work.

CHAPTER 7

Internal Control and Cash

Counting Out the Money

On any given evening at the Granite Brewery and Ginger's Tavern, you can find students and the after-work crowd enjoying pub snacks and quality ale brewed by owner Kevin Keefe.

The brewery and pub have become a Halifax institution since the brewery first opened in 1987. In fact, it was so popular that, in 1991, the Keefes opened a location in Toronto. In 2001, they added another in Halifax to house the brewing operations and a second restaurant, but have since disposed of the restaurant to focus on brewing and serving fine beer.

The Halifax brewery and pub take in approximately $300,000 in annual sales, all of which flows through the hands of the wait staff and bartenders. General manager Denise Avery has a detailed system to track it all.

"There are two cash registers," explains Ms. Avery, "and up to three people might use each one on any given shift. Each server has a private code number that they punch into the register when they ring up a sale, and it tracks their totals separately." Each bartender is given a float of $200. They are responsible for turning in that amount plus their total cash receipts at the end of the day.

What if there's a discrepancy between the cash register's total and the amount in the till? "The machine prints two tapes—one we can use as receipts and one that stays inside," says Ms. Avery, "so we can look for the error."

The Brewery also has internal controls in place at its two bars, where four bartenders work each day on two separate shifts. "When they come in to work in the morning, the first thing they do is count the inventory in the fridge and read the meters on each ale," explains Ms. Avery. "At the end of the shift, they do another count with the next bartender, who in turn rings off at closing." Everything must correspond to the cash register tape. For example, if three beers are missing from the fridge, three beers should have been rung in. If they weren't, the bartender is responsible.

"With a good system, discrepancies just don't happen often," she continues. "If ever there is one, it's usually pretty easy to find the problem by looking at the cash tapes."

Cash control is crucial to a business like the Granite Brewery. But, with a carefully thought-out system and the help of modern automation, cash can be controlled reliably and fairly easily.

the navigator

Granite Brewery: www.granitebrewery.ca

THE NAVIGATOR

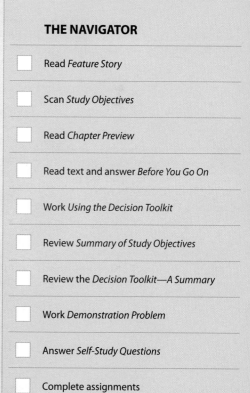

- [ ] Read *Feature Story*
- [ ] Scan *Study Objectives*
- [ ] Read *Chapter Preview*
- [ ] Read text and answer *Before You Go On*
- [ ] Work *Using the Decision Toolkit*
- [ ] Review *Summary of Study Objectives*
- [ ] Review the *Decision Toolkit—A Summary*
- [ ] Work *Demonstration Problem*
- [ ] Answer *Self-Study Questions*
- [ ] Complete assignments

STUDY OBJECTIVES

After studying this chapter, you should be able to:

1. Identify the principles of internal control.
2. Apply internal control to cash receipts and disbursements.
3. Prepare a bank reconciliation.
4. Explain the reporting of cash.
5. Identify ways to manage and monitor cash.

Cash is the lifeblood of any company. Large and small companies alike must guard it carefully. Even companies that are successful in every other way can go bankrupt if they fail to manage their cash well. Managers must know both how to use cash efficiently and how to control it, as described in the feature story. In this chapter, we explain the essential features of an internal control system and describe how these controls apply to cash receipts and disbursements. We then explain how cash is reported in the financial statements, and describe ways to manage and monitor cash.

The chapter is organized as follows:

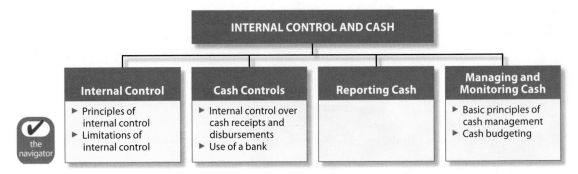

INTERNAL CONTROL AND CASH

Internal Control	Cash Controls	Reporting Cash	Managing and Monitoring Cash
▶ Principles of internal control ▶ Limitations of internal control	▶ Internal control over cash receipts and disbursements ▶ Use of a bank		▶ Basic principles of cash management ▶ Cash budgeting

the navigator

Internal Control

A 2004 report by the Association of Certified Fraud Examiners estimated that $4 billion is lost annually due to fraudulent activities committed within Canadian companies by their own employees. The Association also found that one-quarter of Canadian employees have either committed or witnessed fraudulent activity. Findings like these emphasize the need for a good system of internal control.

You were first introduced to the need for internal control in Chapter 6. As mentioned in that chapter, **internal control** consists of all the related methods and measures adopted within a business to:

1. **optimize the use of resources** to reduce inefficiencies and waste
2. **prevent and detect errors and irregularities** in the accounting process
3. **safeguard assets** from theft, robbery, and unauthorized use
4. **maintain reliable control systems** to enhance the accuracy and reliability of accounting records

The importance of internal control to the efficient and effective operation of a company cannot be overestimated. All federally incorporated companies are required, under the *Canada Business Corporations Act*, to maintain an adequate system of internal control. In addition, the Canadian Securities Administrators (CSA) have recently proposed that large publicly traded Canadian companies evaluate and report on the effectiveness of their internal control over financial reporting. The CSA believes that this proposal will help improve the quality and reliability of financial reporting, which had lost some of its credibility after many widely publicized corporate scandals.

ACCOUNTING MATTERS!   Ethics Perspective

Canadian securities regulators have been in a regulatory frenzy in the aftermath of corporate scandals such as those of Bre-X Minerals, Livent, Nortel Networks, and others. New requirements, including internal control reports, CEO/CFO certifications, independent audit committees, and other proposals, are coming fast and furious as regulators work to protect investors and rebuild confidence in Canada's capital markets. In addition, because many Canadian companies rely on U.S. capital, Canadian regulators have found that they simply have no choice but to keep pace with increasingly strict U.S. regulatory requirements, such as the *Sarbanes-Oxley Act* of 2002.

Principles of Internal Control

To optimize resources, prevent and detect errors and irregularities, safeguard assets, and maintain reliable systems, a company follows internal control principles. The specific control measures that are used vary with the size and nature of the business and with management's control philosophy. However, the six principles listed in Illustration 7-1 apply to most companies.

study objective 1

Identify the principles of internal control.

Illustration 7-1 ◀

Principles of internal control

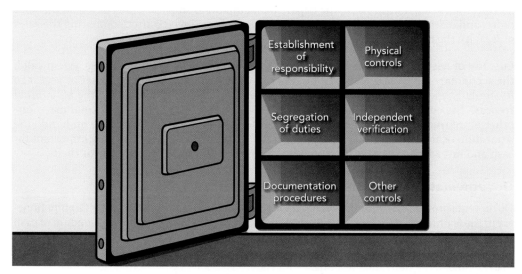

These principles are explained in the following sections.

Establishment of Responsibility

An essential characteristic of internal control is the assignment of responsibility to specific individuals. **Control is most effective when only one person is responsible for a specific task.** To illustrate, assume that the cash on hand at the end of the day is $10 short of the cash rung up on the cash register. If only one person has operated the register, responsibility for the shortage can be attributed quickly. If two or more individuals have worked the same register, it may be impossible to determine who is responsible for the error unless each person is given a separate cash drawer or code number, as is done at the Granite Brewery described in the feature story.

Responsibility must also be assigned for the authorization and approval of transactions. For example, the vice-president of sales should have the authority to establish policies for making credit sales. The policies that are established also typically require written credit department approval of credit sales.

Segregation of Duties

Segregation of duties is essential in a system of internal control. **The work of one employee should, without a duplication of effort, provide a reliable basis for evaluating the work of another employee.** There are two common applications of segregation of duties:

1. The responsibility for related activities should be assigned to different individuals.
2. The responsibility for accounting for an asset should be separate from the responsibility for physical custody of that asset.

Related Activities. When one individual is responsible for all of the related activities, the potential for errors and irregularities is increased. Consider related purchasing activities, for example, which include ordering merchandise, receiving goods, and paying (or authorizing payment) for merchandise. In purchasing, orders could be placed with friends or with suppliers who give kickbacks. In addition, payment might be authorized without a careful review of the invoice or, even worse, fictitious invoices might be approved for payment. When the responsibilities for ordering, receiving, and paying are assigned to different individuals, the risk of such abuses is much lower.

Related sales activities, such as making a sale, shipping (or delivering) the goods to the customer, and billing the customer, should also be assigned to different individuals. When one person is responsible for these related sales transactions, a salesperson could make sales at unauthorized prices to increase sales commissions, a shipping clerk could ship goods to himself or herself, or a billing clerk could understate the amount billed for sales made to friends and relatives. These abuses are less likely to occur when the sales tasks are divided: salespersons make the sale, shipping department employees ship the goods based on the sales order, and billing department employees prepare the sales invoice after comparing the sales order with the report of goods shipped.

Custody of Assets.   To make the accountability for an asset in an accounting system valid, the accountant (as record keeper) should not have physical custody of the asset or access to it. Similarly, the custodian of the asset should not maintain or have access to the accounting records. **The custodian of an asset is not likely to convert the asset to personal use if another employee maintains the record which states that the asset should be on hand.** The separation of accounting responsibility from the custody of assets is especially important for cash and inventories, because these assets are attractive for unauthorized use or theft.

Documentation Procedures

Documents provide evidence that transactions and events have occurred. At the Granite Brewery in the feature story, the cash register tape is documentation for a sale and the amount of cash received. Similarly, a shipping document indicates that goods have been shipped, and a sales invoice indicates that the customer has been billed for the goods. By adding a signature (or initials) to a document, the individual responsible for the transaction or event can be identified.

Procedures should be established for documents. **First, whenever possible, documents should be prenumbered and all documents should be accounted for.** Prenumbering helps to prevent a transaction from being recorded more than once or, conversely, from not being recorded at all. Second, documents that are source documents (the original receipts) for accounting entries should be promptly forwarded to the accounting department to help ensure timely recording of the transaction. This control measure contributes directly to the accuracy and reliability of the accounting records.

Physical Controls

Physical controls include mechanical and electronic controls to safeguard assets and enhance the accuracy and reliability of the accounting records. Examples of these controls are shown in Illustration 7-2.

Illustration 7-2 ▶

Physical controls

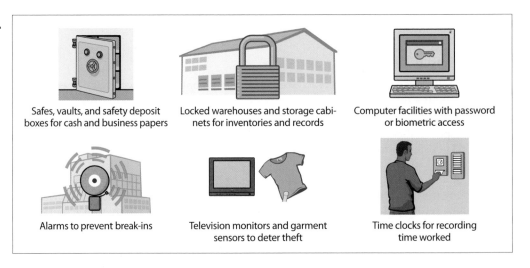

Safes, vaults, and safety deposit boxes for cash and business papers

Locked warehouses and storage cabinets for inventories and records

Computer facilities with password or biometric access

Alarms to prevent break-ins

Television monitors and garment sensors to deter theft

Time clocks for recording time worked

Independent Verification

Most systems of internal control provide for independent internal and external verification. This principle involves the review, comparison, and reconciliation of data prepared by employees. Three measures are recommended to benefit fully from independent verification:

1. The verification should be done periodically or on a surprise basis.
2. The verification should be done by an employee who is independent of the personnel responsible for the information.
3. Discrepancies and exceptions should be reported to a management level that can take appropriate corrective action.

Internal Verification. Independent internal verification is especially useful in comparing accounting records with existing assets. The inventory count by the two bartenders in the feature story about the Granite Brewery is an example. Another common example is the reconciliation by an independent person of the cash balance per books with the cash balance per bank. We will learn more about bank reconciliations later in this chapter.

In large companies, independent internal verification is often assigned to internal auditors. **Internal auditors** are employees of the company who evaluate the effectiveness of the company's system of internal control. They periodically review the activities of departments and individuals to determine whether prescribed internal controls are being followed. The importance of this function is illustrated by the fact that most fraud is discovered by companies through internal mechanisms, such as existing internal controls and internal audits.

External Verification. It is useful to contrast independent *internal* verification with independent *external* verification. **External auditors**, in contrast to internal auditors, are independent of the company. They are professional accountants hired by a company to report on whether or not the company's financial statements fairly present its financial position and results of operations. As part of the evaluation, they also examine and report on internal control.

Other Controls

Other control measures can include the following:

1. **Bonding of employees who handle cash.** Bonding means having insurance protection against the misappropriation of assets by dishonest employees. This measure contributes to the safeguarding of cash in two ways: First, the insurance company carefully screens all individuals before adding them to the policy and may reject risky applicants. Second, bonded employees know that the insurance company will vigorously prosecute all offenders.
2. **Rotating employees' duties and requiring employees to take vacations.** These measures are designed to deter employees from attempting any thefts, since they will not be able to permanently conceal their improper actions. Many embezzlements, for example, have been discovered when the perpetrator was on vacation or assigned to a new position.

Limitations of Internal Control

A company's system of internal control is generally designed to provide **reasonable assurance** that assets are properly safeguarded and that the accounting records are reliable—in other words, that a reliable control system is maintained. The concept of reasonable assurance rests on the idea that the costs of establishing control procedures should not be more than their expected benefit.

To illustrate, consider shoplifting losses in retail stores. Such losses could be completely eliminated by having a security guard stop and search customers as they leave the store. Store managers have concluded, however, that the negative effects of this procedure cannot be justified. Instead, stores have attempted to "control" shoplifting losses by using less costly procedures such as (1) posting signs saying, "We reserve the right to inspect all packages" and "All shoplifters will be prosecuted," (2) using hidden TV cameras and store detectives to monitor customer activity, and (3) using sensor equipment at exits.

The **human element** is an important factor in every system of internal control. A good system can become ineffective as a result of employee fatigue, carelessness, or indifference.

For example, a receiving clerk may not bother to count goods received or may just "fudge" the counts. Occasionally, two or more individuals may work together to get around prescribed controls. Such collusion can significantly lessen the effectiveness of a system because it eliminates the protection expected from segregating the employees' duties. If a supervisor and a cashier collaborate to understate cash receipts, the system of internal control may be defeated (at least in the short run).

The **size of the business** may impose limitations on internal control. In a small company, for example, it may be difficult to apply the principles of segregation of duties and independent internal verification because of the small number of employees. In situations such as this, it is often necessary for management to assume responsibility for, or to oversee, incompatible functions. For example, at a small gas station, it is not unusual for a cashier to receive the cash and also prepare and make the night deposit at the bank. If the cash register tape is locked so that the cashier cannot access it, internal control is strengthened when the manager later reconciles the bank deposit to the cash register tape.

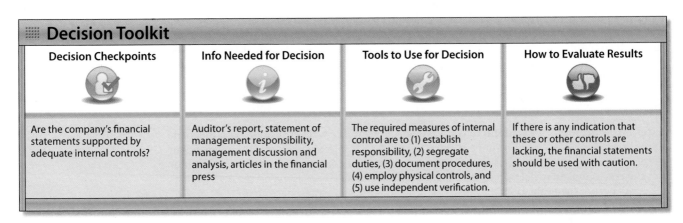

Decision Toolkit

Decision Checkpoints	Info Needed for Decision	Tools to Use for Decision	How to Evaluate Results
Are the company's financial statements supported by adequate internal controls?	Auditor's report, statement of management responsibility, management discussion and analysis, articles in the financial press	The required measures of internal control are to (1) establish responsibility, (2) segregate duties, (3) document procedures, (4) employ physical controls, and (5) use independent verification.	If there is any indication that these or other controls are lacking, the financial statements should be used with caution.

BEFORE YOU GO ON . . .

► Review It

1. What is internal control?
2. Identify and describe the principles of internal control.
3. What are the limitations of internal control?

► Do It

Identify the appropriate internal control principle and state whether it has been supported or violated in each of the following situations:

(a) The purchasing department orders, receives, and pays for merchandise.
(b) All cheques are prenumbered and accounted for.
(c) The internal auditor performs surprise cash counts.
(d) Extra cash is kept locked in a safe that can only be accessed by the head cashier.
(e) Each cashier has their own cash drawer.

Action Plan

• Understand the principles of internal control: establishment of responsibility, segregation of duties, documentation procedures, physical controls, and independent verification.

Solution

(a) Violation of segregation of duties
(b) Support of documentation procedures
(c) Support of independent verification
(d) Support of physical controls
(e) Support of establishment of responsibility

the navigator

Cash Controls

study objective 2

Apply internal control to cash receipts and disbursements.

Just as cash is the beginning of a company's operating cycle, it is usually the starting point for a company's system of internal control. Cash is easily concealed and transported, lacks owner identification, and is highly desired. Because of these characteristics, cash is highly susceptible to theft or misuse. In fact, the Association of Certified Fraud Examiners reports that cash is the asset targeted for theft 90 percent of the time. In addition, because of the large volume of cash transactions, errors may easily occur in executing and recording these transactions. To safeguard cash and to ensure the accuracy of the accounting records, effective internal control is essential.

Before we apply the internal control principles we learned in the last section to cash, let's look first at what cash is, and is not. **Cash** consists of coins, currency (paper money), cheques, money orders, and money on hand or on deposit in a bank or similar depository. The general rule is that if the bank will accept it for deposit, it is cash.

Debit card transactions and bank credit card receipts, such as VISA and MasterCard, are considered as cash but non-bank credit card receipts, such as Diner's Club, are not. In fact, debit and credit cards are used far more frequently than cash today. (We will learn more about accounting for debit and credit card transactions in Chapter 8.)

Cash does *not* include postdated (payable in the future) cheques, staledated (more than six months old) cheques, or returned cheques (due to insufficient funds). Nor are postage stamps or IOUs from employees cash, because these items are not the current medium of exchange or acceptable at face value on deposit.

Internal Control over Cash Receipts and Disbursements

Cash receipts come from a variety of sources: cash sales; collections on account from customers; the receipt of interest, rents, and dividends; investments by shareholders; bank loans; and proceeds from the sale of assets. Generally, internal control over cash receipts is more effective when **cash receipts are deposited intact into the bank account on a daily basis**. Bank deposits should be made by an authorized employee, such as the head cashier or general manager.

The internal control principles explained earlier apply to cash receipt transactions as shown in Illustration 7-3. As might be expected, companies vary considerably in how they apply these principles.

Illustration 7-3 ▼

Application of internal control principles to cash receipts

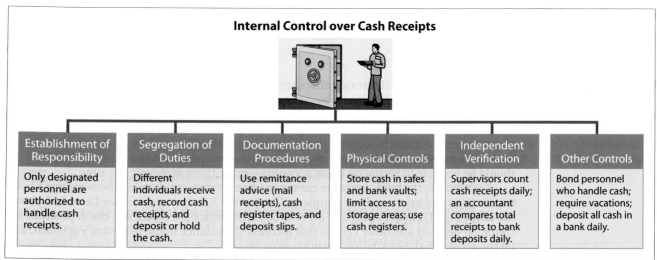

Internal Control over Cash Receipts

Establishment of Responsibility	Segregation of Duties	Documentation Procedures	Physical Controls	Independent Verification	Other Controls
Only designated personnel are authorized to handle cash receipts.	Different individuals receive cash, record cash receipts, and deposit or hold the cash.	Use remittance advice (mail receipts), cash register tapes, and deposit slips.	Store cash in safes and bank vaults; limit access to storage areas; use cash registers.	Supervisors count cash receipts daily; an accountant compares total receipts to bank deposits daily.	Bond personnel who handle cash; require vacations; deposit all cash in a bank daily.

Cash is disbursed for a variety of reasons, such as to pay expenses and liabilities or to purchase assets. Generally, internal control over cash disbursements is more effective when **payments are made by cheque rather than in cash**. Other control procedures (not discussed here) are put in place for the few payments that cannot be made by cheque (e.g., for postage).

Internal control over cheques includes the signing of cheques by an authorized person or persons (cheques often require two signatures). The cheque signer(s) should carefully review

Glossary

www.wiley.com/canada/kimmel

Study Tools (Glossary)

Cash   Resources that consist of coins, currency, cheques, money orders, and bank credit card slips that are acceptable at face value on deposit in a bank or similar institution. (p. 315)

Cash budget   A projection of anticipated cash flows, usually over a one- to two-year period. (p. 327)

Cash equivalents   Short-term, highly liquid investments that can be easily sold. (p. 324)

Compensating balances   Minimum cash balances required by a bank in support of bank loans. (p. 324)

Credit memoranda (CM)   Supporting documentation for increases (additions) that appear on the bank statement, such as interest earned. (p. 318)

Debit memoranda (DM)   Supporting documentation for charges (deductions) that appear on the bank statement, such as bank service charges. (p. 318)

Deposits in transit   Deposits recorded by the depositor that have not yet been recorded by the bank. (p. 319)

External auditors   Auditors who are independent of the organization. They examine internal control and attest to the presentation of the financial statements in accordance with generally accepted accounting principles. (p. 313)

Internal auditors   Company employees who evaluate the effectiveness of the company's system of internal control. (p. 313)

NSF (not sufficient funds) cheque   A cheque that is not paid by a bank because of insufficient funds in a customer's bank account. (p. 318)

Outstanding cheques   Cheques issued and recorded by a company that have not yet been paid by the bank. (p. 319)

Restricted cash   Cash that is not available for general use, but instead is restricted for a particular purpose. (p. 324)

Demonstration Problem

**Study Tools
(Demonstration Problems)**

Trillo Corporation reports the following condensed information from its general ledger Cash account and bank statement at June 30, 2006:

Cash				
June 1	Bal.	18,290		
June deposits		17,000	Cheques written	20,510
June 30	Bal.	14,780		

**TRILLO CORPORATION
Bank Statement
June 30, 2006**

	Cheques and Other Debits	Deposits and Other Credits	Balance
Balance, June 1			17,690
Deposits		15,248	32,938
Cheques cleared	18,100		14,838
EFT insurance payment	500		14,338
NSF cheque ($150 + $25)	175		14,163
Service charge	12		14,151
Interest earned		35	14,186

Additional information:

1. There was a deposit in transit of $600 at May 30, the preceding month, that cleared the bank in June. There were no outstanding cheques at the end of May.
2. The EFT payment for insurance is a pre-authorized monthly payment.
3. The NSF cheque was for $150, from Massif Corp., a customer, in payment of its account. The bank added a $25 processing fee.

Instructions

(a) Prepare a bank reconciliation at June 30.
(b) Journalize the entries required by the reconciliation.

Solution to Demonstration Problem

(a)

Action Plan
- Compare the deposits on the bank statement with the deposits recorded in the books to determine the deposits in transit.
- Compare the cheques that cleared the bank statement with the cheques recorded in the books to determine the outstanding cheques.
- Identify any items recorded on one side that are unrecorded on the other and adjust accordingly.
- All the journal entries should be based on the reconciling items per books.
- Make sure the Cash ledger account balance, after posting the reconciling items, agrees with the adjusted cash balance per books.

TRILLO CORPORATION
Bank Reconciliation
June 30, 2006

Cash balance per bank statement		$14,186
Add: Deposits in transit [$17,000 − ($15,248 − $600)]		2,352
		16,538
Less: Outstanding cheques ($20,510 − $18,100)		2,410
Adjusted cash balance per bank		$14,128
Cash balance per books		$14,780
Add: Interest earned		35
		14,815
Less: EFT insurance payment	$500	
NSF cheque ($150 + $25)	175	
Bank service charge	12	687
Adjusted cash balance per books		$14,128

(b)

June 30	Cash		35	
	Interest Revenue			35
	(To record bank interest earned)			
30	Insurance Expense		500	
	Cash			500
	(To record monthly insurance payment)			
30	Accounts Receivable		175	
	Cash			175
	(To re-establish accounts receivable for Massif Corp. for NSF cheque and related service charge)			
30	Bank Charges Expense		12	
	Cash			12
	(To record bank service charges)			

Check:

Cash				
June 30 Bal.	14,780	June 30	500	
	35		175	
			12	
June 30 Bal.	14,128			

the navigator

Self-Study Questions

Answers are at the end of the chapter.

(SO 1) 1. Which of the following is not an objective of internal control?
(a) Optimize resources
(b) Eliminate errors
(c) Safeguard assets
(d) Maintain reliable control systems

(SO 1) 2. The principles of internal control do not include:
(a) establishment of responsibility.
(b) documentation procedures.
(c) cost-benefit constraints.
(d) independent verification.

(SO 2) 3. Which of the following items in a cash drawer at November 30 is not cash?
(a) Debit card slips from sales to customers
(b) Unsubmitted bank credit card slips from sales to customers
(c) A customer cheque dated December 1
(d) A customer cheque dated November 28

(SO 2) 4. Permitting only designated personnel, such as cashiers, to handle cash receipts is an application of the principle of:
(a) segregation of duties.
(b) establishment of responsibility.
(c) independent verification.
(d) other controls.

(SO 2) 5. The use of prenumbered cheques in disbursing cash is an application of the principle of:
(a) establishment of responsibility.
(b) segregation of duties.
(c) physical controls.
(d) documentation procedures.

(SO 3) 6. Terriault Ltée reports an ending cash balance of $4,100 at the end of the month and $5,000 in its bank statement. Reconciling items include deposits in transit of $2,500, outstanding cheques of $3,500, and service charges of $100. What is the company's adjusted cash balance?
(a) $3,900   (c) $4,100
(b) $4,000   (d) $5,000

(SO 3) 7. A company erroneously recorded a $459 cheque written in payment of an account as $495. The adjusting journal entry required to correct this would be:
(a) debit Accounts Payable $36; credit Cash $36.
(b) debit Cash $36; credit Accounts Payable $36.
(c) debit Cash $36; credit Accounts Receivable $36.
(d) No journal entry is required.

(SO 4) 8. Which statement correctly describes the reporting of cash?
(a) Cash cannot be combined with cash equivalents.
(b) Restricted cash funds may be combined with cash.
(c) Cash is listed first in the current assets section.
(d) Compensating balances are reported as a current asset.

(SO 5) 9. The principles of cash management do not include:
(a) accelerating the collection of receivables.
(b) accelerating the payment of liabilities.
(c) keeping inventory low.
(d) investing idle cash.

(SO 5) 10. Which of the following is not one of the sections of a cash budget?
(a) Cash receipts section
(b) Cash disbursements section
(c) Financing section
(d) Cash from operating activities section

Questions

(SO 1) 1. In the corner grocery store, all the clerks make change out of the same cash register drawer. Is this a violation of internal control? Why?

(SO 1) 2. J. Duma is reviewing the principle of segregation of duties. What are the two common ways of applying this principle?

(SO 1) 3. How do documentation procedures contribute to good internal control?

(SO 1) 4. Explain the following internal control concepts: (a) the concept of reasonable assurance, and (b) the importance of the human factor.

(SO 2) 5. Dent Department Stores Ltd. has just installed new electronic cash registers with scanners in its stores.

How do these cash registers improve internal control over cash receipts?

(SO 2) 6. What internal control objectives are met by physical controls? Provide an example of how they apply to cash disbursements.

(SO 2) 7. At Allen Wholesale Ltd., two mail clerks open all mail receipts. How does this strengthen internal control?

(SO 2) 8. Why should the individual who receives cash not also be allowed to make cash payments or to record cash transactions?

(SO 2) 9. "To have maximum internal control over cash disbursements, all payments should be made by cheque." Is this true? Explain.

(SO 2) 10. Watch Central Ltd. is a small retail store. One of its employees, Wanda, is responsible for ordering the merchandise, receiving the goods, and paying for the goods. Describe the various ways Wanda could potentially commit a fraud with this arrangement.

(SO 3) 11. "The use of a bank contributes significantly to good internal control over cash." Is this true? Why?

(SO 3) 12. Paul Pascal is confused about the lack of agreement between the cash balance per books and the balance per bank. Explain the possible causes for the lack of agreement to Paul, and give an example of each cause.

(SO 3) 13. Mary Mora asks for your help concerning an NSF cheque. Explain to Mary (a) what an NSF cheque is, (b) how it is treated in a bank reconciliation, and (c) whether it will require an adjusting entry.

(SO 3) 14. The Diable Corporation wrote cheque #2375 for $1,325 on March 16. At March 31, the cheque had not cleared the company's bank account and was correctly listed as an outstanding cheque on the March 31 bank reconciliation. If the cheque has still not cleared the bank account on April 30, should it be included in the April bank reconciliation or not? Explain.

15. "Cash equivalents are the same as cash." Do you agree? (SO 4) Explain.

16. ⚬—⚬ The University of Western Ontario reported (SO 4) bank indebtedness on its April 30, 2004, balance sheet of $6.9 million. Would this amount be reported in the current assets or current liabilities section of the statement? Explain.

17. What is a compensating balance? How should com- (SO 4) pensating balances be reported in the financial statements?

18. Describe the basic principles of cash management. (SO 5)

19. ⚬—⚬ Talisman Energy Inc. generated a record high cash (SO 5) flow in 2004. In fact, the company has reported record cash flow amounts for the last six years. What cash management problems might this cause for Talisman?

20. What is a cash budget? Explain how a cash budget contributes to effective cash management. (SO 5)

Brief Exercises

BE7–1 Gina Milan is the new manager of Plenty Parking Ltd., a parking garage. She has heard about internal control but is not clear about its importance for the company. Explain to Gina the four purposes of internal control, and give her one application of each purpose for Plenty Parking.

Identify internal controls.
(SO 1)

BE7–2 West Inc. owns these assets at the balance sheet date:

Cash in bank—savings account	$ 6,000
Cash on hand	850
Income tax refund due from CRA	1,000
Cash in bank—chequing account	12,000
Bank credit card slips not yet submitted	2,500
Postdated cheques	500

Calculate cash.
(SO 2)

What amount should be reported as cash in the balance sheet?

BE7–3 Tene Ltd. has the following internal control procedures over cash receipts. Identify the internal control principle that is applicable to each procedure.

Identify internal controls for cash receipts.
(SO 2)

1. All over-the-counter receipts are recorded on cash registers.
2. All cashiers are bonded.
3. Daily cash counts are made by the head cashier.
4. The duties of receiving cash, recording cash, and maintaining custody of cash are assigned to different individuals.
5. Only cashiers may operate cash registers.
6. All cash is deposited intact in the bank account every day.

BE7–4 Rolling Hills Ltd. has the following internal control procedures over cash disbursements. Identify the internal control principle that is applicable to each procedure.

Identify internal controls for cash disbursements.
(SO 2)

1. Company cheques are prenumbered.
2. The bank statement is reconciled monthly by the assistant controller.
3. Blank cheques are stored in a safe in the controller's office.
4. Only the controller or assistant controller may sign cheques.
5. Cheque signers are not allowed to record cash disbursement transactions.
6. All payments are made by cheque.

Indicate location of items in bank reconciliation.
(SO 3)

BE7–5   For each of the items in the following list, identify where it is included on a bank reconciliation. Next to each item record the appropriate letter to indicate (a) an increase in the bank balance; (b) a decrease in the bank balance; (c) an increase in the book balance; (d) a decrease in the book balance; or (e) that the item would not be included in the bank reconciliation.

_____ A bank debit memorandum for service charges
_____ An EFT payment
_____ Outstanding cheques from the current month
_____ Outstanding cheques from a prior month that are still outstanding
_____ Outstanding cheques from a prior month that are no longer outstanding
_____ A bank error in recording a company cheque made out for $200 as $290
_____ A bank credit memorandum for interest revenue
_____ A company error in recording a $1,280 deposit as $1,680
_____ A bank debit memorandum for an NSF cheque
_____ A deposit in transit from the current month
_____ A company error in recording a cheque made out for $630 as $360
_____ A bank error in recording a $2,575 deposit as $2,755

Identify adjusting entries.
(SO 3)

BE7–6   Using the data in BE7–5, indicate (a) the items that will result in an adjustment to the depositor's records and (b) why the other items do not require adjustment.

Prepare bank reconciliation.
(SO 3)

BE7–7   At July 31, Dana Limited had an unadjusted cash balance of $9,125. An examination of the July bank statement shows a balance of $7,920 on July 31; outstanding cheques $1,144; deposits in transit $2,152; bank service charges $35; and an NSF cheque of $162. Prepare a bank reconciliation at July 31.

Prepare adjusting entries.
(SO 3)

BE7–8   Using the data in BE7–7, prepare the adjusting entries required on July 31 for Dana Limited.

Analyze outstanding deposits.
(SO 3)

BE7–9   For the months of January and February, Kahn Ltd. recorded cash deposits in its books of $2,800 and $2,500, respectively. For the same two months, the bank reported deposits totalling $2,000 and $2,300, respectively. Assuming that there were no outstanding deposits at the end of December, what was the amount of outstanding deposits at the end of January? At the end of February?

Analyze outstanding cheques.
(SO 3)

BE7–10   In the month of November, its first month of operations, Jayasinghe Inc. wrote cheques in the amount of $9,500. In December, cheques in the amount of $12,600 were written. In November, $8,700 of these cheques were presented to the bank for payment and $10,900 in December. What is the amount of outstanding cheques at the end of November? At the end of December?

Explain reporting of cash.
(SO 4)

BE7–11   Ouellette Ltée reports the following items: cash in bank $17,500; payroll bank account $6,000; short-term investments with maturity dates of less than 90 days $5,000; and plant expansion fund cash $25,000. Ouellette also maintains a $5,000 compensating bank balance in a separate bank account. Explain how each item should be reported on the balance sheet.

Discuss cash management.
(SO 5)

BE7–12   Identify and discuss the likely cash management issues faced by the following businesses:

(a) Toronto Maple Leafs hockey team   (d) Memorial University Bookstore
(b) Microsoft Corporation   (e) Tim Hortons
(c) WestJet Airlines Ltd.   (f) Pillar 'N Pine Christmas Tree Farm

Prepare cash budget.
(SO 5)

BE7–13   The following information is available for Marais Limited for the month of January: expected cash receipts $60,000; expected cash disbursements $65,000; and cash balance on January 1 $2,500. Management wants to keep a minimum cash balance of $4,000. Prepare a basic cash budget for the month of January.

Exercises

E7–1 The following control procedures are used in Tolan Ltd. for over-the-counter cash receipts:

Identify internal controls for cash receipts.
(SO 1, 2)

1. Cashiers are experienced, so they are not bonded.
2. All over-the-counter receipts are received by one of three clerks. The clerks share a cash register with a single cash drawer.
3. To minimize the risk of robbery, cash in excess of $100 is stored in an unlocked strongbox in the stockroom until it is deposited in the bank.
4. At the end of each day, the total receipts are counted by the cashier on duty and reconciled to the cash register total.
5. The company accountant makes the bank deposit and then records the day's receipts.

Instructions

(a) For each procedure, explain the weakness in internal control and identify the control principle that is violated.
(b) For each weakness, suggest a change in procedure that will result in good internal control.

E7–2 The following control procedures are used in Ann's Boutique Shoppe Ltd. for cash disbursements:

Identify internal controls for cash disbursements.
(SO 1, 2)

1. Blank cheques are stored in an unmarked envelope on a shelf behind the cash register.
2. The store manager personally approves all payments before signing and issuing cheques.
3. When the store manager has to go away for an extended period of time, she pre-signs a number of cheques to be used in her absence.
4. The company cheques are not prenumbered.
5. The company accountant prepares the bank reconciliation and reports any discrepancies to the store manager.

Instructions

(a) For each procedure, explain the weakness in internal control and identify the internal control principle that is violated.
(b) For each weakness, suggest a change in procedure that will result in good internal control.

E7–3 The following situations suggest either a strength or weakness in internal control:

Identify internal controls.
(SO 1, 2)

1. At Tingley's, Jill and John work alternate lunch hours. Normally Jill works the cash register at the checkout counter, but during her lunch hour, John takes her place. They both use the same cash drawer and jointly count cash at the end of the day.
2. The Do It Corporation accepts both cash and credit cards for its sales. Due to new privacy legislation, it shreds all credit card slips after they are processed.
3. The mail clerk of Mail Boxes prepares a daily list of all cash receipts. The cash receipts are forwarded to a staff accountant, who deposits the cash in the company's bank account. The list is sent to the accounts receivable clerk for recording.
4. The Candy Store can only afford a part-time bookkeeper. The bookkeeper's responsibilities include making the bank deposit, recording transactions, and reconciling the bank statement.
5. The Decorator Shoppe counts inventory at the end of each month. Two staff count the inventory together. It is then priced and totalled by the accounting department and reconciled to the perpetual inventory records. Any variances are investigated.

Instructions

(a) State whether each situation above is a strength or a weakness of internal control.
(b) For each weakness identified, suggest an improvement.

E7–4 On April 30, the bank reconciliation of Drofo Limited shows a deposit in transit of $1,437. A list of cash deposits recorded by the bank and the company in the month of May follows:

Calculate deposits in transit.
(SO 3)

Bank Statement Deposits and Other Credits		
Date	Description	Amount
May 2	Deposit	$1,437
10	Deposit	2,255
16	Deposit	3,218
20	Deposit	945
24	Deposit	1,298
31	IN	32

Drofo Limited Cash Receipts	
Date	Amount
May 6	$2,255
13	3,218
20	954
23	1,298
31	1,531

Additional information:

1. "IN" stands for interest earned.
2. The bank did not make any errors.

Instructions

(a) List the deposits in transit at May 31.
(b) List any other items that must be included in the bank reconciliation. Describe the impact of each item on the reconciliation.

Calculate outstanding cheques.
(SO 3)

E7–5   At April 30, the bank reconciliation of Drofo Limited shows three outstanding cheques: No. 254, $560; No. 255, $800; and No. 257, $410. A list of cheques recorded by the bank and the company in the month of May follows:

Bank Statement Cheques Paid and Other Debits May 31		
Date	Cheque No.	Amount
May 2	254	$560
4	257	410
12	258	159
17	259	275
20	260	500
29	263	840
30	262	750
31	SC	54

Drofo Limited Cash Disbursements May 31		
Date	Cheque No.	Amount
May 2	258	$159
5	259	275
10	260	500
15	261	867
22	262	750
24	263	440
29	264	650

Additional information:

1. "SC" stands for service charge.
2. The bank did not make any errors.

Instructions

(a) List the outstanding cheques at May 31.
(b) List any other items that must be included in the bank reconciliation. Describe the impact of each item on the reconciliation.

Calculate deposits in transit and outstanding cheques.
(SO 3)

E7–6   The cash records of Lejeune Inc. show the following situations:

Deposits in transit

1. The June 30 bank reconciliation indicated that deposits in transit total $1,050. During July, the general ledger account Cash shows deposits of $15,750, but the bank statement indicates that only $15,820 in deposits was received during the month.
2. In August, deposits per bank statement totalled $23,500 and deposits per books were $22,900.

Outstanding cheques

1. The June 30 bank reconciliation reported outstanding cheques of $970. During July, the Lejeune books show that $17,200 of cheques were issued, yet the bank statement showed that $16,660 of cheques cleared the bank in July.

2. In August, cash disbursements per books were $21,700 and cheques clearing the bank were $22,250.

Instructions

(a) What were the deposits in transit at July 31? At August 31?
(b) What were the outstanding cheques at July 31? At August 31?

E7–7 Refer to the data presented in E7–4 and E7–5. On May 31, Drofo Limited had an unadjusted cash balance of $6,023 in the general ledger. The bank statement showed a balance of $6,378 on May 31.

Prepare bank reconciliation and adjusting entries.
(SO 3)

Instructions

(a) Prepare a bank reconciliation for Drofo Limited on May 31.
(b) Prepare the adjusting journal entries required at May 31. Assume that all deposits were to record the collection of accounts receivable, and any cheques were for the payment of accounts payable.

E7–8 The following information is for Mohammed Ltd. in July:

Prepare bank reconciliation and adjusting entries.
(SO 3)

1. Cash balance per bank, July 31, $9,013
2. Cash balance per books, July 31, $7,190
3. Bank service charge, $24
4. Deposits in transit, $1,575
5. Electronic receipts from customers in payment of their accounts, $883
6. Outstanding cheques, $2,449
7. Cheque #373 was correctly written and recorded by the bank as $672. Mohammed recorded the cheque in the general journal as $762, in error. The cheque was written for the purchase of office supplies.

Instructions

(a) Prepare a bank reconciliation at July 31.
(b) Prepare the adjusting journal entries required at July 31.

E7–9 Reston Ltd.'s Cash account shows a balance of $17,933 at September 30. The September bank statement shows a balance of $17,292 at September 30 and the following memoranda:

Prepare bank reconciliation and adjusting entries.
(SO 3)

Credit Memoranda		Debit Memoranda	
Interest earned	$ 45	NSF cheque	$410
EFT collections on account	1,825	Safety deposit box fee	30

At September 30, deposits in transit were $4,910 and outstanding cheques totalled $3,839. The bank had incorrectly posted a cheque correctly written for $972 as $1,972. The cheque was payable to one of Reston's employees for his salary.

Instructions

(a) Prepare the bank reconciliation at September 30.
(b) Prepare the adjusting journal entries at September 30.

E7–10 A new accountant at La Maison Ltée is trying to identify which of the following amounts should be reported as the current asset "Cash and Cash Equivalents" in the year-end balance sheet, as at April 30, 2006:

Calculate cash and cash equivalents.
(SO 4)

1. Currency and coin totalling $57 in a locked box used for incidental cash transactions
2. A $10,000 guaranteed investment certificate, due May 31, 2006
3. April-dated cheques worth $300 that La Maison has received from customers but not yet deposited
4. An $85 cheque received from a customer in payment of its April account, but postdated to May 1
5. A balance of $2,575 in the Royal Bank chequing account
6. A balance of $4,000 in the Royal Bank savings account
7. Prepaid postage of $75 in the postage meter
8. A $25 IOU from the company receptionist
9. Debit card slips totalling $525
10. Bank credit card slips not yet submitted totalling $1,530

Instructions

(a) What amount should La Maison report as its "Cash and Cash Equivalents" balance at April 30, 2006?

(b) In which financial statement(s) and in what account(s) should the items not included in "Cash and Cash Equivalents" be reported?

Discuss cash management.
(SO 5)

E7–11   Tory, Hachey, and Wedunn, three young lawyers who have joined together to open a law practice, are struggling to manage their cash flow. They have not yet built up enough clientele and revenues to support the cost of running their legal practice. Initial costs, such as advertising, renovations to the premises, and so on, all result in outgoing cash flow at a time when little is coming in! Tory, Hachey, and Wedunn have not had time to establish a billing system since most of their clients' cases have not yet reached the courts and the lawyers did not think it would be right to bill them until "results were achieved." Unfortunately, Tory, Hachey, and Wedunn's suppliers do not feel the same way. Their suppliers expect them to pay their accounts payable within a few days of receiving their bills. So far, there has not even been enough money to pay the three lawyers, and they are not sure how long they can keep practising law without getting some money into their pockets!

Instructions

Can you provide any suggestions for Tory, Hachey, and Wedunn to improve their cash management practices?

Prepare cash budget.
(SO 5)

E7–12   Hanover Limited expects to have a cash balance of $46,000 on January 1, 2006. These are the relevant monthly budget data for the first two months of 2006:

1. Collections from customers: January, $70,000; February, $150,000
2. Payments to suppliers: January, $40,000; February, $75,000
3. Wages: January, $30,000; February, $40,000. Wages are paid in the month they are incurred.
4. Operating expenses: January, $35,000; February, $50,000. These costs include amortization of $1,000 per month. All other costs are paid as incurred.
5. Sales of short-term investments in January are expected to realize $10,000 in cash. Hanover has a line of credit at a local bank that enables it to borrow up to $25,000. The company wants to keep a minimum monthly cash balance of $20,000.

Instructions

Prepare a cash budget for January and February.

Problems: Set A

Identify internal controls for cash receipts.
(SO 1, 2)

P7–1A   Red River Theatre has a cashier's booth located near the entrance to the theatre. There are two cashiers: one works from 1:00 p.m. to 5:00 p.m., the other from 5:00 p.m. to 9:00 p.m. Each cashier is bonded. The cashiers receive cash from customers and operate a machine that ejects serially numbered tickets. The rolls of tickets are inserted and locked into the machine by the theatre manager at the beginning of each cashier's shift.

After purchasing a ticket, which may cost different amounts depending on the day of the week or the customer's age group, the customer takes the ticket to an usher stationed at the entrance to the theatre lobby, a few metres from the cashier's booth. The usher tears the ticket in half, admits the customer, and returns the ticket stub to the customer. The other half of the ticket is dropped into a locked box by the usher.

At the end of each cashier's shift, the theatre manager removes the ticket rolls from the machine and makes a cash count. The cash count sheet is initialled by the cashier. At the end of the day, the manager deposits the total receipts in a bank night deposit vault located in a nearby mall. In addition, the manager sends copies of the deposit slip and the initialled cash count sheets to the head cashier for verification and to the accounting department. Receipts from the first shift are stored in a safe located in the manager's office.

Instructions

(a) Identify the internal control principles and their application to the cash receipts transactions of Red River Theatre.
(b) If the usher and cashier decided to collaborate to steal cash, what actions might they take?

P7–2A The Art Appreciation Society operates a museum for its surrounding community's benefit and enjoyment. When the museum is open to the public, two clerks at the front entrance collect a $5.00 admission fee from each non-member patron. Members of the Art Appreciation Society enter free of charge by presenting their membership cards.

Identify internal controls for cash receipts.
(SO 1, 2)

At the end of each day, one of the clerks delivers the proceeds to the treasurer. The treasurer then counts the cash in front of the clerk and places it in a safe. Each Friday afternoon, the treasurer and one of the clerks deliver all cash in the safe to the bank and receive an authenticated deposit slip, which is the basis for the weekly entry in the general journal.

The society's board of directors would like to improve the internal control system over cash admission fees. The board has determined that the cost of installing turnstiles or sales booths, or of changing the museum's physical layout in some other way would be much higher than any benefits that might be derived. However, the board has agreed that a change in how admission tickets are sold must be an integral part of the improvement efforts.

Instructions

Identify any weaknesses in the existing internal control system over cash admission fees, and recommend one improvement for each of the weaknesses.

P7–3A Cedar Grove Middle School wants to raise money for a new sound system for its auditorium. The main fundraising event is a dance at which the famous disc jockey Obnoxious Al will play rap music. Roger DeMaster, the music teacher, has been given the responsibility for coordinating the fundraising efforts. This is Roger's first experience with fundraising. He decides to put the Student Representative Council (SRC) in charge of the event.

Identify internal controls for cash receipts and disbursements.
(SO 1, 2)

Roger had 500 unnumbered tickets printed for the dance. He left the tickets in a box on his desk and told the SRC students to take as many tickets as they thought they could sell for $10 each. To ensure that no extra tickets would be floating around, he told the students to get rid of any unsold tickets. When the students received payment for the tickets, they were to bring the cash back to Roger, and he would put it in a locked box in his desk drawer.

Some of the students were responsible for decorating the gymnasium for the dance. Roger gave each of them a key to the money box and told them that if they took money out to purchase materials, they should put a note in the box saying how much they took and what it was used for. After two weeks, the money box appeared to be getting full, so Roger asked Steve Stevens to count the money, prepare a deposit slip, and deposit the money in a bank account Roger had opened.

The day of the dance, Roger wrote a cheque from the account to pay Obnoxious Al. However, Al said that he accepted only cash and did not give receipts. So Roger took $200 out of the cash box and gave it to Al. At the dance, Roger had Sara Billings working at the entrance to the gymnasium, collecting tickets from students and selling tickets to those who had not prepurchased them. Roger estimated that 400 students attended the dance.

The following day, Roger closed out the bank account, which had $250 in it, and gave that amount plus the $180 in the cash box to Principal Skinner. Principal Skinner seemed surprised that, after generating roughly $4,000 in sales, the dance netted only $430 in cash. Roger did not know how to respond.

Instructions

Identify as many internal control weaknesses for the cash receipts and disbursements as you can in this fundraising effort. Suggest how each weakness could be addressed.

P7–4A Tarika Ltd. is a profitable small business. It has not, however, given much consideration to internal control. For example, in an attempt to keep clerical and office expenses to a minimum, the company has combined the jobs of cashier and bookkeeper. As a result, Rob Tang handles all cash receipts, keeps the accounting records, and prepares the monthly bank reconciliations.

Prepare bank reconciliation and identify internal controls.
(SO 1, 3)

The balance per bank statement on October 31, 2006, was $19,460. Outstanding cheques were #782 for $113.90, #783 for $160, #784 for $266.90, #789 for $170.70, #791 for $325.40, and

#792 for $173.10. Included with the statement was a credit memorandum for an electronic collection of $301 from a customer on account.

The company's general ledger showed the Cash account with a balance of $19,640. The balance included undeposited cash on hand. Because of the lack of internal controls, Tang took all of the undeposited receipts for personal use. He then prepared the following bank reconciliation to hide his theft of cash:

TARIKA LTD.
BANK RECONCILIATION
OCTOBER 31, 2006

Cash balance per books		$19,640
Less: Electronic collection from customer		301
Adjusted cash balance per books		$19,339
Cash balance per bank statement		$19,460
Less: Outstanding cheques		
#782	$11.39	
#783	16.00	
#784	26.69	
#789	17.07	
#791	32.54	
#792	17.31	121
Adjusted cash balance per bank		$19,339

Instructions

(a) Prepare a correct bank reconciliation. (*Hint*: The theft is the difference between the adjusted balance per books before the theft and the adjusted balance per bank.)

(b) Indicate the various ways that Tang tried to hide the theft and the dollar amount for each method.

(c) What principles of internal control were violated in this case?

Prepare bank reconciliation and adjusting entries.
(SO 3)

P7–5A   On July 31, 2006, Dubeau Ltd. had a cash balance per books of $7,393. The statement from the Caisse Populaire on that date showed a balance of $9,134. A comparison of the bank statement with the Cash account revealed the following:

1. The bank statement included a debit memo of $50 for bank service charges.
2. The bank statement included two credit memos. The first was for an electronic deposit of $2,031 received from customers on account. The second was for $24 of interest earned during the month.
3. The July 31 cash receipts of $1,393 were not included in the bank deposits for July. These receipts were deposited by the company in a night deposit vault on July 31.
4. Company cheque #2480 for $585, issued to J. Brokaw, a creditor, cleared the bank in July and was incorrectly entered in the general journal on July 10 as $855.
5. Cheques outstanding on June 30 totalled $922. Of these, $689 cleared the bank in July. There were $1,446 of cheques written in July that were still outstanding July 31.
6. On July 31, the bank statement showed an NSF charge of $820 for a cheque received by the company from a customer on account. This amount includes a $20 service charge by the bank.

Instructions

(a) Prepare the bank reconciliation at July 31.
(b) Prepare the adjusting journal entries required at July 31.

Prepare bank reconciliation and adjusting entries.
(SO 3)

P7–6A   The March bank statement showed the following for Yap Ltd.:

YAP LTD.
Bank Statement
March 31, 2006

Date	Deposits and Other Credits Amount	Cheques and Other Debits Number	Amount	Balance
Feb. 28				$14,368
Mar. 1	$2,530	3451	$2,260	14,638
2		3471	845	13,793
5	1,212			15,005
7		3472	1,427	13,578
10		NSF	550	13,028
15		3473	1,641	11,387
22		3474	2,130	9,257
27	2,567			11,824
31		SC	49	11,775
31	23	IN		11,798

Additional information:

1. The bank statement contained two debit memoranda:
   (a) An NSF cheque for $550 that had been deposited by Yap and was now returned due to insufficient funds in a customer's account. Yap believes it will be able to collect this amount from the customer in the future.
   (b) A service charge (SC) of $49 for bank services provided throughout the month
2. The bank statement contained one credit memorandum for $23 of interest (IN) earned on the account for the month.
3. No errors were made by the bank. The correction of any errors made by the company in the recording of cash disbursements should be made to Accounts Payable. The correction of any errors in the recording of cash receipts should be made to Sales.

Yap's cash receipts and disbursements for the month of March were as follows:

Cash Receipts Date	Amount
Mar. 4	$1,221
26	2,567
30	1,025
	$4,813

Cash Disbursements Date	Number	Amount
Mar. 7	3472	$1,427
15	3473	1,461
22	3474	2,130
29	3475	487
		$5,505

The bank portion of last month's bank reconciliation for Yap Ltd. at February 28, 2006, was as follows:

YAP LTD.
Bank Reconciliation
February 28, 2006

Cash balance per bank		$14,368
Add: Deposits in transit		2,530
		16,898
Less: Outstanding cheques		
#3451	$2,260	
#3470	1,535	
#3471	845	4,640
Adjusted cash balance		$12,258

Instructions

(a) Calculate Yap's unadjusted cash balance in its general ledger on March 31.
(b) What is the amount of the deposits in transit, if any, at March 31?
(c) What is the amount of the outstanding cheques, if any, at March 31?
(d) Prepare a bank reconciliation at March 31.
(e) Prepare any adjusting journal entries required at March 31.

Prepare bank reconciliation and
adjusting entries.
(SO 3)

P7–7A   The bank portion of the bank reconciliation for London Inc. at October 31, 2006, is
shown here:

LONDON INC.
Bank Reconciliation
October 31, 2006

Cash balance per bank		$12,444.70
Add: Deposits in transit		1,530.20
		13,974.90
Less: Outstanding cheques		
#2451	$1,260.40	
#2470	720.10	
#2471	844.50	
#2472	503.60	
#2474	1,050.00	4,378.60
Adjusted cash balance		$ 9,596.30

The November bank statement showed the following:

LONDON INC.
Bank Statement
November 30, 2006

Date	Deposits and Other Credits Amount	Cheques and Other Debits Number	Cheques and Other Debits Amount	Balance
Oct. 31				$12,444.70
Nov. 1	$1,530.20	2470	$ 720.10	13,254.80
2		2471	844.50	12,410.30
4	1,211.60	2475	1,640.70	11,981.20
5		2474	1,050.00	10,931.20
8	990.10	2476	2,830.00	9,091.30
10		2477	600.00	8,491.30
13	2,575.00			11,066.30
15		2479	1,750.00	9,316.30
18	1,472.70	2480	1,330.00	9,459.00
21	2,945.00			12,404.00
25	2,567.30	NSF	260.00	14,711.30
27		2481	695.40	14,015.90
28	1,650.00			15,665.90
29	EFT 2,479.00	2486	900.00	17,244.90
30	1,186.00	2483	575.50	17,855.40

The cash records per books for November showed the following:

Cash Receipts	
Date	Amount
Nov. 3	$ 1,211.60
7	990.10
12	2,575.00
17	1,472.70
20	2,954.00
24	2,567.30
27	1,650.00
29	1,186.00
30	1,338.00
	$15,944.70

Cash Disbursements		
Date	Number	Amount
Nov. 1	2475	$ 1,640.70
2	2476	2,380.00
2	2477	600.00
4	2478	538.20
8	2479	1,750.00
10	2480	1,330.00
15	2481	695.40
18	2482	612.00
20	2483	575.50
22	2484	829.50
23	2485	974.80
24	2486	900.00
29	2487	398.00
30	2488	1,200.00
		$14,424.10

Additional information:

1. The bank statement contained a credit memo of $2,479 for the electronic collection (EFT) of an account from a customer.
2. The bank statement contained a debit memo for an NSF cheque of $250 returned by a customer's bank for insufficient funds, plus a $10 service charge.
3. The bank did not make any errors.
4. Two errors were made by the company. The correction of any errors in the recording of cheques should be made to accounts payable. The correction of any errors in the recording of cash receipts should be made to accounts receivable.

Instructions

(a) Calculate the unadjusted cash balance per books as at November 30, prior to reconciliation.
(b) Prepare a bank reconciliation at November 30.
(c) Prepare any adjusting journal entries required at November 30.

P7–8A A first year co-op student is trying to determine the amount of cash that should be reported on a company's balance sheet. The following information was provided to the student at year end:

Calculate cash balance. (SO 4)

1. Cash on hand in the cash registers totals $5,000.
2. The balance in the commercial bank savings account is $100,000 and in the commercial bank chequing account, $25,000. The company also has a U.S. bank account, which contains the equivalent of $45,000 Canadian at year end.
3. A special bank account holds $150,000 cash that is restricted for equipment replacement.
4. A $50,000 line of credit is available at the bank on demand.
5. Amounts due from employees (travel advances) total $12,000.
6. Short-term investments held by the company include $32,000 in a money-market fund; $75,000 in treasury bills; and $40,000 of shares of Loblaw Companies Limited.
7. The company has a supply of unused postage stamps totalling $150.
8. The company has $1,750 of NSF cheques from customers that were returned by the bank.
9. The company has $9,250 of cash deposits (advances paid by customers) held in a special bank account.
10. The company keeps $5,000 as a compensating balance in a special account.

Instructions

(a) Calculate the cash balance that should be reported on the year-end balance sheet.
(b) Would your answer in (a) change if the company combines its cash and cash equivalents?
(c) Identify where any items that were not reported in the cash balance in (a) should be reported.

P7–9A　Wilfrid Laurier University reports the following selected information in its April 30, 2004, financial statements:

	2004	2003
Restricted cash	$　0	$3,062
Bank indebtedness	11,305	9,467
Cash provided by operating activities	8,461	5,944

Additional information: Cash was restricted for the construction of the King Street residence.

Instructions

(a) In which section of a classified balance sheet would the restricted cash most likely have been reported in 2003? Explain.
(b) In which section of a classified balance sheet would bank indebtedness most likely be reported in both years? Explain.
(c) How is it possible that Wilfrid Laurier University generated a positive cash flow from operating activities in each year but had no cash?

P7–10A　Hanover Ltd. expects to have a cash balance of $2,000 on January 1, 2006. Relevant monthly budget data for the first two months of 2006 are as follows:

1. Collections from customers: January $60,000; February $190,000
2. Payments to suppliers: January $50,000; February $75,000
3. Salaries: January $30,000; February $50,000. Salaries are paid in the month they are incurred.
4. Operating expenses: January $27,000; February $39,000. These costs do not include amortization and are paid as incurred.
5. Sales of short-term investments in January are expected to realize $8,000 in cash.
6. Hanover has a line of credit at a local bank that enables it to borrow up to $45,000. The company wants to keep a minimum monthly cash balance of $5,000. Any excess cash above the $5,000 minimum is used to pay off the line of credit.

Instructions

(a) Prepare a cash budget for January and February.
(b) Explain how a cash budget contributes to effective management.

Problems: Set B

P7–1B　You are asked to join the board of trustees of a local church to help with the internal controls for the offerings collection made at weekly services. At a meeting of the board of trustees, you learn the following:

1. The board of trustees has delegated responsibility for the financial management and audit of the financial records to the finance committee. This group prepares the annual budget and approves major disbursements but is not involved in collections or record keeping. No audit has been done in recent years because the same trusted employee has kept church records and served as financial secretary for 15 years. The church does not carry any fidelity insurance.
2. The collection at the weekly service is taken by a team of ushers who volunteer to serve for one month. The ushers take the collection plates to a basement office at the back of the church. They hand their plates to the head usher and return to the church service. After all plates have been turned in, the head usher counts the cash received. The head usher then places the cash in the church safe along with a notation of the amount counted. The head usher volunteers to serve for three months.
3. The morning after the service, the financial secretary opens the safe and recounts the collection. The secretary withholds $150 to $200 in cash, depending on the cash disbursements expected for the week, and deposits the remainder of the collection in the bank. To facilitate the deposit, church members who contribute by cheque are asked to make their cheques payable to "Cash."

4. Each month, the financial secretary reconciles the bank statement and submits a copy of the reconciliation to the board of trustees. The reconciliations have rarely revealed any bank errors and have never shown any errors per books.

Instructions

(a) Indicate the weaknesses in internal control in the handling of collections.
(b) List the improvements in internal control procedures that you plan to recommend at the next meeting of the board of trustees for the (1) head usher, (2) ushers, (3) financial secretary, and (4) finance committee.

P7–2B Segal Office Supply Limited recently changed its system of internal control over cash disbursements. The new system includes the following features:

Identify internal controls for cash disbursements.
(SO 1, 2)

1. All cheques are prenumbered and written by an electronic cheque-writing system.
2. Before a cheque can be issued, each invoice must have the approval of Cindy Morris, the purchasing agent, and Ray Mills, the receiving department supervisor.
3. Cheques must be signed by either controller Frank Malone or assistant controller Mary Arno. Before signing a cheque, the signer is expected to compare the amount of the cheque with the amount on the invoice.
4. After signing a cheque, the signer stamps the invoice "Paid" and writes in the date, cheque number, and amount of the cheque. The paid invoice is then sent to the accounting department for recording.
5. Blank cheques are stored in a safe in the controller's office. The combination to the safe is known by only the controller and assistant controller.
6. Each month the bank statement is reconciled by a staff accountant.

Instructions

Identify the internal control principles and their application to the cash disbursements at Segal Office Supply Limited.

P7–3B The president of a registered charity, the Helping Elderly Low-Income People Foundation (HELP), approaches you for help on a special project to set up the charity's accounting system. HELP is a relatively new organization, established in January 2005, and is regulated by both the federal and provincial governments. One requirement is that it maintain current financial records for the public to scrutinize. In other words, the records must be available to anyone who is interested in reviewing them. HELP must also spend 75 percent of all its revenues on charitable causes. It is now June 1, 2005, and HELP has come to you with a shoebox of receipts and bank statements. You notice that the bank statements are still in their envelopes—they have not been opened.

Identify internal controls for cash receipts and disbursements.
(SO 1, 2)

The charity's revenue is mostly from donations. A van driver takes volunteers around the city and they go door to door asking for donations. The volunteers give a donation receipt for amounts over $10. Since volunteering takes a lot of time, the charity has many short-term volunteers and anyone is welcome to be a volunteer.

Fortunately for HELP, two car companies generously donated minivans to the organization. The van drivers are paid $10 a day, which they take from the donations. Drivers keep a summary of the total donations collected by the volunteers, and at the end of the day the drivers take the money to a bank drop box and deposit it. Drivers also pay for their gas out of the donated funds.

HELP also held a fundraising dance last month. The president said he was disappointed with the project though, because it did not bring in much money. On the good side, it did raise public awareness. To keep costs down, the president made the dance tickets by photocopying tickets and cutting them up. He gave them out to volunteers to sell for $25 each. He estimates that he printed 500 tickets, but can only account for about $3,000 of revenues given in by his volunteers.

Instructions

Identify the internal control weaknesses over cash receipts and disbursements, and recommend improvements.

P7–4B Giant Inc. is a profitable small business. It has not, however, given much consideration to internal control. For example, in an attempt to keep clerical and office expenses to a minimum, the company has combined the jobs of cashier and bookkeeper. As a result, K.

Prepare bank reconciliation and identify internal controls.
(SO 1, 3)

Kilgora handles all cash receipts, keeps the accounting records, and prepares the monthly bank reconciliations.

The balance per bank statement on November 30, 2006, was $13,155. Outstanding cheques were #62 for $126.75, #83 for $180, #84 for $253.25, and #86 for $190. Included with the statement was a credit memorandum of $25 for interest earned during the month.

The company's general ledger showed the Cash account with a balance of $17,142. The balance included undeposited cash on hand. Because of the lack of internal controls, Kilgora took all of the undeposited receipts for personal use. She then prepared the following bank reconciliation to hide her theft of cash:

GIANT INC.
Bank Reconciliation
November 30, 2006

Cash balance per books			$17,142
Less: Interest expense			25
Adjusted cash balance per books			$17,117
Cash balance per bank statement			$13,155
Add: Deposit in transit			4,540
			17,695
Less: Outstanding cheques			
#62		$126.75	
#83		108.00	
#84		235.25	
#86		108.00	578
Adjusted cash balance per bank			$17,117

Instructions

(a) Prepare a correct bank reconciliation. (*Hint*: The theft is the difference between the adjusted balance per books before the theft and adjusted balance per bank.)

(b) Indicate the various ways that Kilgora tried to hide the theft and the dollar amount for each method.

(c) What principles of internal control were violated in this case?

Prepare bank reconciliation and adjusting entries.
(SO 3)

P7–5B   On May 31, 2006, Maloney Inc. had a cash balance per books of $6,760. The bank statement from Community Bank on that date showed a balance of $7,675. A comparison of the bank statement with the company's Cash account revealed the following:

1. The bank statement included a debit memo of $40 for the printing of additional company cheques.

2. The bank statement included two credit memos. The first was for an electronic deposit of $2,055 received from customers on account. The second was for $39 of interest earned during the month.

3. Cash sales of $836 on May 12 were deposited in the bank. The journal entry and the deposit slip were incorrectly made out and recorded by Maloney for $856. The bank detected the error and credited Maloney for the correct amount.

4. Outstanding cheques at April 30 totalled $1,450. Of these, $1,120 cleared the bank in May. There were $946 of cheques written in May that were still outstanding on May 31.

5. On May 18, the company issued cheque #1181 for $685 to a creditor in payment of its account. The cheque, which cleared the bank in May, was incorrectly journalized and posted by Maloney as being for $568.

6. Included with the cancelled cheques was a cheque issued by Baloney Inc. for $600 that was incorrectly charged to Maloney by the bank.

7. On May 31, the bank statement showed an NSF charge of $715 for a cheque issued by a customer in payment of its account. This amount included a $15 service fee charged by the bank.

8. The May 31 deposit of $963 was not included in the deposits on the May bank statement. The deposit had been placed in the bank's night deposit vault on May 31.

Instructions

(a) Prepare the bank reconciliation as at May 31.
(b) Prepare the adjusting journal entries required at May 31.

P7–6B The bank portion of last month's bank reconciliation showed the following for River Adventures Ltd.:

Prepare bank reconciliation and adjusting entries.
(SO 3)

RIVER ADVENTURES LTD.
Bank Reconciliation
April 30, 2006

Cash balance per bank			$9,008.53
Add: Deposits in transit			846.33
			9,854.86
Less: Outstanding cheques			
#526		$1,357.99	
#533		278.90	
#541		363.44	
#555		78.82	2,079.15
Adjusted cash balance			$7,775.71

The May bank statement showed the following:

RIVER ADVENTURES LTD.
Bank Statement
May 31, 2006

Date	Deposits and Other Credits Amount	Cheques and Other Debits Number	Amount	Balance
Apr. 30				$9,008.53
May 3	$ 846.33	526	$1,357.99	8,496.87
4		541	363.44	8,133.43
6		556	223.46	7,909.97
6	1,250.00	557	1,800.00	7,359.97
10	980.00			8,339.97
10		559	1,650.00	6,689.97
13	426.00			7,115.97
13	EFT 1,650.00			8,765.97
14		561	799.00	7,966.97
18		562	2,045.00	5,921.97
18	222.00			6,143.97
19		563	2,487.00	3,656.97
21		564	603.00	3,053.97
25		565	1,033.00	2,020.97
26	980.00			3,000.97
28	1,771.00	NSF	440.00	4,331.97
31		SC	25.00	4,306.97

River Adventure's cash receipts and disbursements for the month of May showed the following:

Cash Receipts	
Date	Amount
May 5	$1,250.00
8	980.00
12	426.00
18	222.00
25	890.00
28	1,771.00
31	1,286.00
	$6,825.00

Cash Disbursements		
Date	Number	Amount
May 4	556	$ 223.46
5	557	1,800.00
7	558	943.00
7	559	1,650.00
8	560	890.00
10	561	799.00
15	562	2,045.00
18	563	2,487.00
20	564	306.00
25	565	1,033.00
31	566	950.00
		$13,126.46

Additional information:

1. The bank statement contained two debit memos:
   (a) An NSF charge of $440 for a $425 cheque from a customer in payment of his account that was returned due to insufficient funds. It also includes a $15 service charge.
   (b) A service charge (SC) of $25 for bank services provided for the month.
2. The bank statement contained one credit memo for $1,650, from an electronic collection (EFT) of a customer's account.
3. The bank made an error when processing cheque #564. The company also made one error during the month.

Instructions

(a) Calculate River Adventure's unadjusted cash balance in its general ledger at May 31.
(b) What is the amount of the deposits in transit, if any, at May 31?
(c) What is the amount of the outstanding cheques, if any, at May 31?
(d) Prepare a bank reconciliation at May 31.
(e) Prepare the adjusting journal entries required at May 31.

Prepare bank reconciliation and adjusting entries. (SO 3)

P7–7B   The bank portion of the bank reconciliation for Racine Limited at November 30, 2006, is shown here:

RACINE LIMITED
Bank Reconciliation
November 30, 2006

Cash balance per bank		$14,367.90
Add: Deposits in transit		2,530.20
		16,898.10
Less: Outstanding cheques		
#3451	$2,260.40	
#3470	1,100.00	
#3471	844.50	
#3472	1,426.80	
#3474	1,050.00	6,681.70
Adjusted cash balance		$10,216.40

The December bank statement showed the following:

RACINE LIMITED
Bank Statement
December 31, 2006

Date	Deposits and Other Credits Amount	Cheques and Other Debits Number	Cheques and Other Debits Amount	Balance
Nov. 30				$14,367.90
Dec. 1	$2,530.20	3451	$2,260.40	14,637.70
2		3471	844.50	13,793.20
4	1,211.60	3475	1,640.70	13,364.10
7		3472	1,426.80	11,937.30
8	2,365.10	3476	1,300.00	13,002.40
10		3477	2,130.00	10,872.40
15	EFT 3,145.00	3479	3,080.00	10,937.40
16	2,672.70			13,610.10
21	2,945.00			16,555.10
26	2,567.30	NSF	1,027.10	18,095.30
27		3480	600.00	17,495.30
29	2,836.00	3483	1,140.00	19,191.30
30	1,025.00	3482	475.50	19,740.80
30		3485	540.80	19,200.00
31		SC	45.00	19,155.00

The cash records per books for December showed the following:

Cash Receipts Date	Amount
Dec. 3	$ 1,211.60
7	2,365.10
15	2,672.70
20	2,954.00
25	2,567.30
28	2,836.00
30	1,025.00
31	1,197.90
	$16,829.60

Cash Disbursements Date	Number	Amount
Dec. 1	3475	$ 1,640.70
2	3476	1,300.00
2	3477	2,130.00
4	3478	538.20
8	3479	3,080.00
10	3480	600.00
17	3481	807.40
20	3482	475.50
22	3483	1,140.00
23	3484	1,274.00
24	3485	440.80
30	3486	1,389.50
		$14,816.10

Additional information:

1. The bank statement contained a credit memo for the electronic collection (EFT) of an account from a customer in the amount of $3,145.
2. The bank statement contained two debit memos: one for an NSF cheque of $1,027.10 returned from a customer's bank for insufficient funds and another for $45 of bank service charges (SC) incurred for the month.
3. The bank did not make any errors.
4. Two errors were made by the company. The correction of any errors in recording cheques should be made to accounts payable. The correction of any errors in recording cash receipts should be made to accounts receivable.

Instructions

(a) Calculate the unadjusted cash balance per books at December 31, prior to reconciliation.
(b) Prepare a bank reconciliation at December 31.
(c) Prepare any adjusting journal entries required at December 31.

Calculate cash balance.
(SO 4)

P7–8B   A new CGA student has been asked to determine the balance that should be reported as cash and cash equivalents as at December 31, 2006, for one of the firm's clients. The following information is available:

1. Cash on hand in the cash registers on December 31 totals $1,600. Of this amount, $500 is kept on hand as a cash float.
2. The balance in the bank chequing account at December 31 is $7,460.
3. Short-term investments include $5,000 in a money-market fund and an investment of $2,500 in a six-month term deposit.
4. The company sold $250 of merchandise to a customer late in the day on December 31. The customer had forgotten her wallet and promised to pay the amount on January 2.
5. The company has a U.S. dollar bank account. At December 31, its U.S. funds were worth the equivalent of $2,241 Canadian.
6. At December 31, the company has Diner's Club credit card slips totalling $500 that have not yet been submitted to Diner's Club for payment.
7. The company received $500 of cash on December 31 as an advance deposit in trust on a property sale.
8. In order to hook up utilities, the company is required to deposit $1,000 in trust with Ontario Hydro. This amount must remain on deposit until a satisfactory credit history has been established. The company expects to have this deposit back within the year.

Instructions

(a) Calculate the cash and cash equivalents balance that should be reported on the year-end balance sheet.
(b) Identify where any items that were not reported in (a) should be reported.

Discuss reporting of cash.
(SO 4)

P7–9B   Royal Roads University reports the following selected information in its March 31, 2004, financial statements:

	2004	2003
Cash	$ 5,630,307	$ 1,566,575
Short-term investments	12,608,348	11,110,795
Restricted funds (net assets)	6,379,973	6,382,453
Cash provided by operating activities	5,656,704	5,362,128

Additional information:

1. Royal Roads' short-term investments consist of a money-market fund and an interest-bearing bank account at TD Canada Trust.
2. Restricted funds are for an infrastructure fund, a program development and research fund, and a marketing and market-research fund.

Instructions

(a) For reporting purposes, would Royal Roads' short-term investments be combined with cash and appear as cash equivalents in the current assets section of its balance sheet? Explain.
(b) Royal Roads has more than $6 million of restricted net assets (similar to restricted retained earnings) for a variety of funds. Is this the same as restricted cash? Explain.
(c) How is it possible that Royal Roads has $18,238,655 of cash and short-term investments at the end of 2004 but generated only $5,656,704 of cash flow from operating activities in the same year?

Prepare cash budget.
(SO 5)

P7–10B   You are provided with the following information taken from New Bay Inc.'s March 31, 2006, balance sheet:

Cash	$ 8,000
Accounts receivable	20,000
Inventory	36,000
Property, plant, and equipment, net of accumulated amortization	120,000
Accounts payable	21,750
Common shares	150,000
Retained earnings	12,250

Additional information:

1. The gross profit margin is 20% of sales.
2. Actual and budgeted sales data:

March (actual)	$50,000
April (budgeted)	60,000

3. Sales are 60% for cash and 40% on credit. Credit sales are collected in the month following the sale.
4. Half of each month's purchases are paid for in the month of purchase and half in the following month. Purchases of inventory totalled $44,000 for the month of March and are expected to total $52,000 for the month of April. Ending inventory is expected to be $43,000 at the end of April.
5. Cash operating expenses are expected to be $15,000 for the month of April.
6. Equipment costing $5,500 will be purchased for cash in April.
7. The company wants to keep a minimum cash balance of $5,000. An open line of credit is available at the bank. All borrowing is done at the beginning of the month and all repayments are made at the end of the month. The interest rate is 6% per annum. Interest expense is accrued at the end of the month and paid in the following month.

Instructions

(a) Calculate cash collections in April for March and April sales.
(b) Calculate the cash disbursements in April for March and April purchases.
(c) Prepare a cash budget for the month of April.
(d) Explain how a cash budget contributes to effective management.

BROADENING YOUR PERSPECTIVE

Financial Reporting and Analysis

Analysis Tools

Financial Reporting Problem: *Loblaw*

BYP7–1   Two reports are attached to the Loblaw financial statements presented in Appendix A of this book: (1) Management's Statement of Responsibility for Financial Reporting and (2) the Independent Auditors' Report.

Instructions

(a) What comments, if any, about the company's system of internal control are included in Management's Statement of Responsibility? In the Auditors' Report?
(b) What reference, if any, is made to internal and external auditors in each of the above reports?
(c) Explain how Loblaw can report both cash and cash equivalents and bank indebtedness on its balance sheet at the same time.
(d) Distinguish between Loblaw's cash equivalents and its short-term investments.

Comparative Analysis Problem: *Loblaw and Sobeys*

BYP7–2   The financial statements of Sobeys are presented in Appendix B, following the financial statements for Loblaw in Appendix A.

Instructions

(a) What is the balance in cash and cash equivalents reported by Sobeys and Loblaw's at the end of the current fiscal year? How much cash was provided by operating activities for each company for the current year?
(b) Does either company have any compensating balances?
(c) What conclusions about each company's ability to generate cash and its cash management can be made from the comparison of these results?

Research Case

BYP7–3   *Service Station and Garage Management* included an article by Bob Greenwood in the January 2005 edition, p. 24, entitled "Cash Management: A Necessity to Cope with Change."

Instructions

Read the article and answer these questions:

(a) What are the techniques designed to speed up cash inflow in the repair shop?
(b) Identify ways to control the outflow of cash from the repair shop.
(c) Why is it important for small and flexible businesses such as independent repair stations to measure liquidity?

Interpreting Financial Statements

BYP7–4   Below are selected account balances for Q9 Networks Inc., a Canadian provider of outsourced Internet infrastructure and managed services for companies with mission-critical Internet operations.

Q9 NETWORKS INC. Balance Sheet (partial) Years Ended October 31, 2004 and 2003 (in thousands)		
	2004	**2003**
Assets		
Current assets		
Cash and cash equivalents	$ 6,135	$ 2,195
Short-term investments (note 2)	64,023	39,638
Accounts receivable	1,846	1,959
Unbilled revenue	154	223
Prepaid expenses	646	378
	72,804	44,393
Restricted cash (note 3)	1,140	2,270
Capital assets (note 4)	38,212	38,572
Total assets	$112,156	$85,235

Instructions

(a) What are cash equivalents?
(b) What is meant by restricted cash?
(c) What percentage of the 2004 total assets is represented by short-term investments? What would be the characteristics of short-term investments that are not grouped with cash equivalents?

A Global Focus

BYP7–5 Shown below is selected information from Microsoft Corporation's balance sheet:

MICROSOFT CORPORATION Balance Sheet (partial) June 30, 2004 (in U.S. millions)		
	2004	2003
Current assets		
Cash and equivalents	$15,982	$ 6,438
Short-term investments	44,610	42,610
Other current assets	9,974	9,925
Total current assets	70,566	58,973
Total current liabilities	14,969	13,974

Additional information: Microsoft notes in its management discussion and analysis that the strengthening of most foreign currencies against the U.S. dollar in 2004 resulted in a net positive effect of more than $1 billion.

Instructions

(a) What is a cash equivalent? How do cash equivalents differ from other types of short-term investments?

(b) Calculate the (1) working capital and (2) current ratio for each year. The industry average for the current ratio was 3.5:1 in 2004 and 2.7:1 in 2003. Comment on your results.

(c) Is it possible to have too much cash? Explain why or why not.

(d) As an international company, Microsoft is affected by economic conditions in each of the countries in which it operates. For example, when the U.S. dollar devalues against other foreign currencies, as it did in 2004, Microsoft's financial results are affected. Explain how Microsoft's cash is affected by changes in foreign currency.

Financial Analysis on the Web

BYP7–6 Members of the Canadian Securities Administrators, other than British Columbia, have proposed regulations pertaining to the certification of and reporting on internal controls over financial reporting. This case will review these regulations and investigate how one Canadian company reports information about the integrity of its internal controls.

Analysis Tools
(Financial Analysis on the Web)

Instructions

Specific requirements of this Web case can be found on the Toolkit website.

Critical Thinking

Collaborative Learning Activity

BYP7–7 Think of your past or current employment and personal experiences, and identify situations in which cash was received and disbursed.

Instructions

With the class divided into groups, do the following:

(a) Identify the strengths and weaknesses in internal control used for cash receipts in the situations you have chosen.

(b) Identify the strengths and weaknesses in internal control used for cash disbursements in the situations you have chosen.

Communication Activity

BYP7–8   Landry Corporation is a small family-owned company selling office supplies. Guylaine Lavoie has been with the company from the beginning, doing all the clerical work, including recording and depositing cash, paying the bills, and reconciling the bank account monthly. The company has grown in size from three employees to twenty. Annual sales have increased from $200,000 to $7 million. Guylaine is still looking after the cash and says she does not need any help in completing her tasks.

Instructions

Write a letter to Lucette Landry, the president of Landry Corporation, explaining the weaknesses in internal control over cash and your recommendations for improving the system. In your answer, address the fact that the company used to be small but has now grown in both size and revenues.

Ethics In Accounting

Ethics Case

BYP7–9   Banks charge fees of up to $25 for bounced cheques—that is, NSF cheques that exceed the balance in the account. It has been estimated that processing bounced cheques costs a bank roughly $1.50 per cheque. Thus, the profit margin on bounced cheques is high. Recognizing this, banks process cheques from largest to smallest. By doing this, they maximize the number of cheques that bounce if a customer overdraws an account. One bank projected a $14-million increase in fee revenue as a result of processing the largest cheques first. In response to criticism, banks have responded that their customers prefer to have large cheques processed first, because those tend to be the most important. At the other extreme, some banks will cover their customers' bounced cheques, which is basically extending them overdraft protection.

Instructions

(a) Who are the stakeholders in this case?
(b) Freeman Corp. had a balance of $2,500 in its chequing account on a day when the bank received the following five cheques for processing against that account:

Cheque Number	Amount
3150	$ 35
3158	1,510
3162	400
3165	890
3169	180

Assuming a $25 fee is charged by the bank, how much fee revenue would the bank generate if it processed cheques from largest to smallest, (2) from smallest to largest, and (3) in the order of the cheque numbers?
(c) Do you think that processing cheques from largest to smallest is an ethical business practice?
(d) Besides ethical issues, what else must a bank consider in deciding whether to process cheques from largest to smallest?
(e) If you were managing a bank, what policy would you adopt on bounced cheques?

Serial Problem

(*Note*: This is a continuation of the serial problem from Chapters 1 through 6.)

BYP7–10   Natalie is struggling to keep up with the recording of the accounting transactions of Cookie Creations Ltd. She is spending a lot of time marketing and selling mixers and giving cookie-making classes. Her friend John is an accounting student who runs his own accounting service. He has asked Natalie if she would like to have him do the accounting for Cookie Creations Ltd.

John and Natalie meet and discuss the business. John suggests that he do the following for Natalie:

1. Hold onto cash until there is enough to be deposited. (He would keep Cookie Creation Ltd.'s cash locked up in his vehicle.) He would take all of the deposits to the bank at least twice a month.
2. Write and sign all of the cheques. He would review the invoices and send out cheques as soon as the invoices are received.
3. Record all of the deposits in the accounting records.
4. Record all of the cheques in the accounting records.
5. Prepare the monthly bank reconciliation.
6. Transfer all of Cookie Creations Ltd.'s accounting records to his computer accounting program. John maintains all of the accounting information that he keeps for his clients on his laptop computer.
7. Prepare Cookie Creations Ltd.'s monthly financial statements for Natalie to review.
8. Write himself a cheque each month for the work he has done for Cookie Creations Ltd.

Instructions

(a) Identify the weaknesses in internal control that you see in the system that John is recommending (consider the principles of internal control identified in the chapter).
(b) Can you suggest any improvements if John is hired to do the accounting for Cookie Creations Ltd.
(c) Identify the weaknesses in the way cash is being managed that you see in the system that John is recommending (consider the basic principles of cash management identified in the chapter).

Answers to Self-Study Questions

1. b   2. c   3. c   4. b   5. d   6. b   7. b   8. c   9. b   10. d

Answer to Loblaw Review It Question 2

Loblaw reported $618 million of cash and cash equivalents as at January 3, 2004. Loblaw's cash equivalents are defined in note 1 as "highly liquid investments with a maturity of 90 days or less."

Remember to go back to the Navigator box at the beginning of the chapter to check off your completed work.

CHAPTER 8

Reporting and Analyzing Receivables

Keeping Receivables Healthy

For any large company, managing receivables carefully is crucial to profitability. As Maria Cardoso knows, keeping tabs on the timely receipt of payments from hundreds of credit accounts can be a tough job.

Ms. Cardoso is supervisor of credit and collections at Mississauga-based Wyeth Consumer Healthcare, a Canadian subsidiary of global pharmaceutical company Wyeth. Wyeth distributes top-selling, name-brand, over-the-counter health-care products.

The company's sales terms are 1/15, n/30 (1% discount if paid within 15 days). Sometimes, if the customer pays several invoices—some under 15 days, some over—with one cheque, Ms. Cardoso might allow the discount for all of them. That's because smaller companies often write cheques only once a week, or even once a month. "We always consider each case individually," she says.

The process starts with a decision to grant a customer an account in the first place. A sales rep gives the customer a credit application, which Ms. Cardoso reviews. In addition to checking three good references, she screens prospective accounts with a credit agency. Once accepted, they are assigned a credit limit based on their size and history.

They are then supervised closely. "We get an aging report every morning that shows exactly what each customer owes and what category the account falls into—current, 1–30 days, 31–60 days, 61–90, and over 90," says Ms. Cardoso. "Fortunately, our receivables are always at 95% current or better." When an account is overdue, there's usually an explanation. Ms. Cardoso tends to call as soon as a payment is late. "If the invoice has gone missing, for example, you want to find out right away," she says.

The challenge with bigger customers is trying to reconcile accounts for short payments. Wyeth Consumer Healthcare often gives its customers vendor allowances for displaying its products prominently. "What occasionally happens is they just take the rebates off their payment," she says. "It would be a lot better if they waited for us to actually give it to them!" And, from time to time, payments are simply late.

Although the company's bad debts are minimal, Ms. Cardoso's boss, Terry Norton, records an estimate for them every year, based on a percentage of receivables and their current aging history. He and Ms. Cardoso know that keeping receivables healthy and customers happy are both good for business.

the navigator

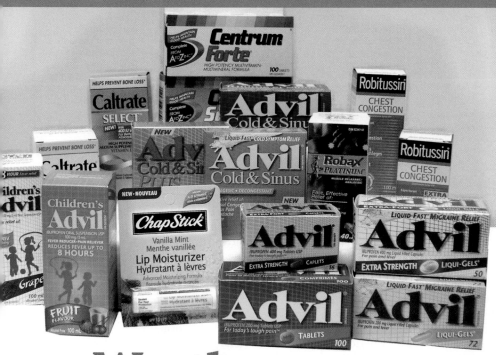

Wyeth
Consumer Healthcare

Wyeth: www.wyethconsumer.ca

THE NAVIGATOR

☐ Read *Feature Story*

☐ Scan *Study Objectives*

☐ Read *Chapter Preview*

☐ Read text and answer *Before You Go On*

☐ Work *Using the Decision Toolkit*

☐ Review *Summary of Study Objectives*

☐ Review the *Decision Toolkit—A Summary*

☐ Work *Demonstration Problem*

☐ Answer *Self-Study Questions*

☐ Complete assignments

STUDY OBJECTIVES

After studying this chapter, you should be able to:

1. Explain how accounts receivable are recognized in the accounts.
2. Account for bad debts.
3. Explain how notes receivable are recognized and valued in the accounts.
4. Explain the statement presentation of receivables.
5. Apply the principles of sound accounts receivable management.

the navigator

As indicated in our feature story, the management of receivables is important for any company that sells on credit, as Wyeth Consumer Healthcare does. In this chapter, we will learn how companies estimate, record, and then in some cases collect their uncollectible accounts. We will also discuss how receivables are reported on the financial statements and managed.

The chapter is organized as follows:

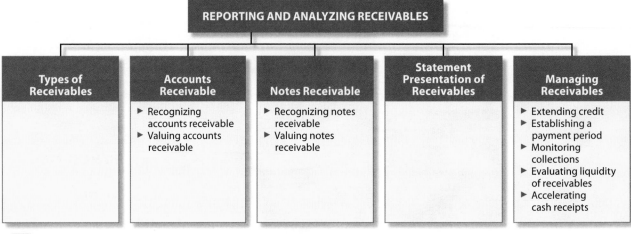

Types of Receivables

The term "receivables" refers to amounts that are due from individuals and other companies. Receivables are claims that are expected to be collected in cash and are frequently classified as (1) accounts receivable, (2) notes receivable, and (3) other receivables.

Accounts receivable are amounts owed by customers on account. They result from the sale of goods and services. These receivables generally are expected to be collected within 30 days or so, and are classified as current assets. They are usually the most significant type of claim held by a company.

Notes receivable are claims where formal instruments of credit—a written promise to repay—are issued as evidence of the debt. The credit instrument normally requires the debtor to pay interest and is for time periods of 30 days or longer. Notes receivable may be either current assets or noncurrent assets, depending on their due dates. Notes and accounts receivable that result from sales transactions are often called **trade receivables**.

Other receivables include interest receivable, loans to company officers, advances to employees, and recoverable sales taxes and income taxes. These receivables are generally classified and reported as separate items in the current or noncurrent assets section of the balance sheet, according to their due dates.

Accounts Receivable

We will now examine two accounting problems for accounts receivable: (1) recognizing accounts receivable and (2) valuing accounts receivable. A third issue, accelerating cash receipts from receivables, is discussed later in the chapter.

Recognizing Accounts Receivable

study objective 1

Explain how accounts receivable are recognized in the accounts.

The first step in recognizing an account receivable is straightforward. For a service company, a receivable is recorded when service is provided on account. For a merchandising company, a receivable is recorded at the point of sale of merchandise on account. Recall that we learned about the **revenue recognition principle** in Chapter 4. Revenue (and any related receivable) should be recognized when the sales effort is substantially complete. This normally occurs when the service is performed or at the point of sale when the good is delivered. In addition, collection must be reasonably certain. This will be discussed in the next section.

Receivables are reduced by sales discounts and sales returns. The seller may offer terms, such as providing a discount, that encourage early payment. For example, in the feature story, Wyeth's sales terms of 1/15, n/30 give the buyer a one-percent discount if the invoice is paid within 15 days. If the buyer chooses to pay within the discount period, the seller's accounts receivable are reduced by the amount of the sales discount. As well, product rebates sometimes reduce the amount due, as in Wyeth's case.

Finally, the buyer might find some of the goods unacceptable and choose to return them. This also results in a reduction of accounts receivable. For example, if $100 of merchandise purchased on account is returned, the seller reduces accounts receivable by $100 when the returned merchandise is received. We learned about the entries required to record sales discounts and sales returns in Chapter 5. You may find it helpful to return to Chapter 5 and refresh your memory about these.

Subsidiary Accounts Receivable Ledger

In Chapter 3, we learned about the general ledger. Using the Accounts Receivable account in the general ledger works well for companies that do not have many customer accounts. Imagine a company like Wyeth, however, recording the accounts receivable for each of its customers in only one general ledger account. If it did, it would be very difficult to determine the balance owed by any one customer at a specific point in time.

Instead, companies like Wyeth use a subsidiary ledger in addition to the general ledger. This helps the company organize and track individual customer balances. A **subsidiary ledger** is a group of accounts that share a common characteristic (e.g., all receivable accounts). The subsidiary ledger provides supporting detail to the general ledger, freeing it from excessive detail. It is common to have subsidiary ledgers for accounts receivable (to track individual customer balances), inventory (to track inventory quantities and balances), accounts payable (to track individual creditor balances), and payroll (to track individual employee pay records).

In the case of an accounts receivable subsidiary ledger, it contains all the individual customer receivables accounts—for example, a separate one for Adert Limited, Bortz Corporation, Mr. B. Carl, and so on. The general ledger contains only one receivables account—Accounts Receivable—which acts as a control account to the subsidiary ledger. A **control account** is a general ledger account that summarizes the subsidiary ledger data. At all times, the control account balance must equal the total of all the individual customer receivable account balances in the subsidiary ledger.

Consequently, each journal entry that affects accounts receivable must be posted twice—once to the subsidiary ledger account and once to the general ledger control account. Normally, entries to the subsidiary ledger are posted daily. You may recall that Ms. Cardoso mentioned in the feature story that she receives a report indicating what each customer owes daily. Entries to the general ledger are normally summarized and posted monthly in a manual accounting system. In a computerized accounting system, the posting to both ledgers occurs simultaneously.

Interest Revenue

At the end of each month, the company can use the subsidiary ledger to easily determine the transactions in each customer's account and then send the customer a statement of transactions that occurred that month. If the customer does not pay in full within a specified period of time (usually 30 days), most retailers add an interest (financing) charge to the balance due. Interest rates vary from company to company, but a common interest rate for retailers is 28.8 percent per year.

When financing charges are added, the seller recognizes interest revenue and increases the account receivable amount owed by the customer. Although Wyeth in our feature story does not charge interest on its overdue accounts, interest revenue is often a substantial amount for service and merchandising companies.

BEFORE YOU GO ON...

▶Review It

1. What types of receivables does Loblaw report on its balance sheet? (*Hint*: See Note 10 in addition to looking at the balance sheet.) The answer to this question is at the end of the chapter.
2. Explain the similarities and differences between a general ledger and a subsidiary ledger.
3. How is interest revenue on overdue accounts calculated and recorded?

Valuing Accounts Receivable

Account for bad debts.

Once receivables are recorded in the accounts, the next question is how these receivables should be reported in the financial statements. They are reported on the balance sheet as an asset. However, determining the amount to report is sometimes difficult because some receivables will become uncollectible.

Although each customer must satisfy the credit requirements of the seller before the credit sale is approved, inevitably some accounts receivable become uncollectible. For example, a corporate customer may not be able to pay because of a decline in sales due to a downturn in the economy. Similarly, individuals may be laid off from their jobs or faced with unexpected bills.

Credit losses are debited to bad debts expense. Such losses are considered a normal and necessary risk of doing business on a credit basis. The key issue in valuing accounts receivable is when to recognize these credit losses. If the company waits until it knows for sure that the specific account will not be collected, it could end up recording the bad debts expense in a different period than when the revenue was recorded.

Consider the following example. In 2005, the Quick Buck Computer Corporation decides it could increase its revenues by offering computers to students without requiring any money down, and with no credit approval process. It goes on campuses across the country and distributes one million computers with a selling price of $800 each. This increases Quick Buck's receivables and revenues by $800 million. The promotion is a huge success! The 2005 balance sheet and statement of earnings look wonderful. Unfortunately, during 2006, nearly 40 percent of the student customers default on their accounts. This makes the year 2006 balance sheet and statement of earnings look terrible. Illustration 8-1 shows that the promotion in 2005 was not such a great success after all.

Illustration 8-1 ▶

Effects of mismatching bad effects

Year 2005	Year 2006
Huge sales promotion. Sales increase dramatically. Accounts receivable increase dramatically.	Customers default on amounts owed. Bad debts expense increases dramatically. Accounts receivable plummet.

If credit losses are not recorded until they occur, no attempt is made to match bad debts expense to sales revenues in the statement of earnings. Recall that the matching principle requires expenses to be reported in the same period as the sales they helped generate. Quick Buck Computer Corporation's statement of earnings is skewed in both 2005 and 2006 because of mismatched sales and bad debts expense.

In addition, accounts receivable in the balance sheet are not reported at the amount actually expected to be collected. Consequently, Quick Buck Computer's receivables are overstated in 2005, misrepresenting its balance sheet.

The allowance method offers a solution to this problem. The **allowance method** of accounting for bad debts estimates the uncollectible accounts at the end of each period. This provides a better matching on the statement of earnings because credit losses that are expected to result from sales or service revenue in the accounting period are recorded in the same accounting period as when the revenue was generated. It also ensures that receivables are stated at their net realizable value on the balance sheet. **Net realizable value** is the amount expected to be received in cash. It does not include amounts that the company estimates it will not collect.

The allowance method is required for financial reporting purposes. It has three essential features:

1. **Recording estimated uncollectibles:** The amount of uncollectible accounts receivable is estimated. This estimate is treated as bad debts expense and matched against revenue in the accounting period in which the revenue was earned.
2. **Recording the write-off of an uncollectible account:** Actual uncollectibles are written off at the time the specific account is determined to be uncollectible.
3. **Recovery of an uncollectible account:** When an account that was previously written off is later collected, the original write-off is reversed and the collection is recorded. As neither the write-off nor the subsequent recovery affect the statement of earnings, matching is not distorted.

**Animated Tutorials
(Bad Debts)**

1. Recording Estimated Uncollectibles

To illustrate the allowance method, assume that Abrams Furniture Ltd. has net credit sales of $1.2 million in 2006. Of this amount, $200,000 remains uncollected at December 31. The credit manager estimates (using techniques we will discuss shortly) that bad debt expense is $10,000. The adjusting entry to record the bad debt expense for the year is:

Dec. 31	Bad Debts Expense	10,000	
	Allowance for Doubtful Accounts		10,000
	(To record estimate of uncollectible accounts)		

A	=	L	+	SE
−10,000				−10,000

Cash flows: no effect

Note that a new account, Bad Debts Expense, is used instead of debiting a contra sales account as we did for sales returns and allowances. An expense account is used because the responsibilities for granting credit and collecting accounts are normally separated from sales and marketing. You will recall from Chapter 7 that establishment of responsibility is an important feature of a good internal control system. In our feature story, each customer's application for credit is approved by Ms. Cardoso, Wyeth's supervisor of credit and collections, not by the sales representative.

Bad Debts Expense is reported in the statement of earnings as an operating expense. The estimated uncollectibles are matched with sales in 2006 because the expense is recorded in the same year that the sales are made.

Allowance for Doubtful Accounts is a contra asset account that shows the receivables that are expected to become uncollectible in the future. A contra account is used instead of a direct credit to Accounts Receivable for two reasons. First, we do not know which individual customers will not pay. If the company uses a subsidiary ledger, we are therefore unable to credit specific customer accounts. Recall that subsidiary ledger accounts must balance with the Accounts Receivable control account. This would not happen if the control account were credited and the subsidiary ledger accounts were not. Second, the estimate for uncollectibles is just an estimate. A contra account helps to separate estimates from actual amounts, such as those found in Accounts Receivable.

The balance in Allowance for Doubtful Accounts is deducted from Accounts Receivable in the current assets section of the balance sheet. Assuming that Abrams Furniture Ltd. has an opening balance of $1,000 in Allowance for Doubtful Accounts, its ending balance of $11,000 ($1,000 + $10,000) would be reported as follows:

ABRAMS FURNITURE LTD.
Balance Sheet (partial)
December 31, 2006

Current assets		
Cash		$ 14,800
Accounts receivable	$200,000	
Less: Allowance for doubtful accounts	11,000	189,000
Merchandise inventory		310,000
Prepaid expenses		25,000
Total current assets		$538,800

The $189,000 represents the expected net realizable value of the accounts receivable at the statement date. This can be represented by the following formula, shown in Illustration 8-2:

Illustration 8-2 ▶

Formula for calculating net realizable value

Accounts Receivable	−	Allowance for Doubtful Accounts	=	Net Realizable Value
$200,000	−	$11,000	=	$189,000

Estimating the Allowance.   For Abrams Furniture, the amount of the expected uncollectibles for the current period ($10,000) was given above. However, in actual practice, companies must estimate the amount of likely uncollectible accounts. While there are several acceptable ways to estimate uncollectible accounts, most companies use a percentage of their outstanding receivables to determine the allowance for doubtful accounts.

Under the **percentage of receivables basis**, management estimates what percentage of receivables will result in losses from uncollectible accounts. This percentage can be assigned to receivables in total, or stratified (divided further) by age of receivable. Stratifying the percentage classifies customer balances by the length of time they have been unpaid, which can improve the reliability of the estimate. Because of its emphasis on time, this is called **aging the accounts receivable**.

After the accounts are classified by age, the expected bad debt losses are determined by applying percentages, based on past experience, to the totals of each category. The longer a receivable is past due, the less likely it is to be collected. As a result, the estimated percentage of uncollectible debts increases as the number of days past due increases. An aging schedule for Abrams Furniture is shown in Illustration 8-3. Note the increasing uncollectible percentages from 2% to 50%.

Illustration 8-3 ▶

Aging schedule

Customer	Total	Number of Days Outstanding				
		0–30	31–60	61–90	91–120	Over 120
Adert Limited	$ 6,800	$3,800	$3,000			
Bortz Corporation	12,200	8,700	3,500			
B. Carl	9,400	6,400	3,000			
Diker Furnishings Ltd.	36,600	22,400	8,600	$4,000	$1,600	
T. Ebbet	2,500					$2,500
Others	132,500	70,200	23,300	34,000	5,000	
	$200,000	$111,500	$41,400	$38,000	$6,600	$2,500
Estimated percentage uncollectible		2%	5%	10%	25%	50%
Total estimated bad debts	$11,000	$2,230	$2,070	$3,800	$1,650	$1,250

The $11,000 total of estimated bad debts for Abrams Furniture is the amount of existing receivables that is expected to become uncollectible in the future. This amount is also the required balance in Allowance for Doubtful Accounts at the balance sheet date. Accordingly, **the amount of the bad debt adjusting entry is the difference between the required balance and the existing balance in the allowance account**. If the trial balance shows Allowance for Doubtful Accounts with a credit balance of $1,000, then, as we have seen, an adjusting entry for $10,000 ($11,000 − $1,000) is necessary, as follows:

Dec. 31	Bad Debts Expense	10,000	
	Allowance for Doubtful Accounts		10,000
	(To record estimate of uncollectible accounts)		

A = L + SE
−10,000   −10,000
Cash flows: no effect

After the adjusting entry is posted, the accounts of Abrams Furniture will show the following:

Bad Debts Expense		Allowance for Doubtful Accounts	
Dec. 31 Adj. 10,000		Jan. 1 Bal. 1,000	
		Dec. 31 Adj. 10,000	
		Dec. 31 Bal. 11,000	

Occasionally, the allowance account will have a debit balance before the adjustment. This occurs when write-offs during the year exceed previous estimates for bad debts. (We will discuss write-offs in the next section.) If there is an opening debit balance, the debit balance is added to the required balance when the adjusting entry is made. That is, if there had been a $1,000 debit balance in Abrams Furniture's allowance account before adjustment, the adjusting entry would have been for $12,000 to arrive at a credit balance in the allowance account of $11,000.

An important aspect of accounts receivable management is simply keeping a close watch on the accounts. Studies have shown that accounts that are more than 60 days past due lose approximately 50 percent of their value if no payment activity occurs within the next 30 days. For each additional 30 days that pass, the collectible value halves once again. As Wyeth does in our feature story, the majority of companies today use an aging schedule to closely monitor the collectibility of their accounts and to identify problem accounts.

2. Recording the Write-Off of an Uncollectible Account

Companies use various methods of collecting past-due accounts, such as letters, calls, collection agencies, and legal action. In the feature story, Wyeth calls its customers if payments are late. When all ways of collecting a past-due account have been tried and collection appears unlikely, the account should be written off.

To prevent premature or unauthorized write-offs, each write-off should be formally approved in writing by authorized management personnel. To keep good internal control, authorization to write off accounts should not be given to someone who also has daily responsibilities related to cash or receivables.

To illustrate a receivables write-off, assume that Abrams Furniture's vice-president of finance authorizes a write-off of the $2,500 balance owed by T. Ebbet, a customer, on March 1, 2007. The entry to record the write-off is:

Mar. 1	Allowance for Doubtful Accounts	2,500	
	Accounts Receivable—T. Ebbet		2,500
	(Write-off of T. Ebbet account)		

A = L + SE
+2,500
−2,500
Cash flows: no effect

Bad Debts Expense is not increased (debited) when the write-off occurs. **Under the allowance method, every bad debt write-off is debited to the allowance account and not to Bad Debts Expense.** A debit to Bad Debts Expense would be incorrect because the expense was already recognized when the adjusting entry was made for estimated bad debts last year.

Instead, the entry to record the write-off of an uncollectible account reduces both Accounts Receivable and Allowance for Doubtful Accounts. After posting, using an assumed Accounts Receivable opening balance of $227,500, the general ledger accounts will appear as follows:

Accounts Receivable				Allowance for Doubtful Accounts			
Feb. 28 Bal. 227,500	Mar. 1	2,500		Mar. 1	2,500	Jan. 1 Bal.	11,000
Mar. 1 Bal. 225,000						Mar. 1 Bal.	8,500

A write-off affects only balance sheet accounts. The write-off of the account reduces both Accounts Receivable and Allowance for Doubtful Accounts equally. Net realizable value in the balance sheet remains the same, as shown below:

	Before Write-Off	After Write-Off
Accounts receivable	$227,500	$225,000
Less: Allowance for doubtful accounts	11,000	8,500
Net realizable value	$216,500	$216,500

As mentioned earlier, the allowance account can sometimes end up with a debit balance after a write-off of an uncollectible account. This occurs if the write-offs during the period exceed the opening balance. This is only a temporary situation: it will be corrected when the adjusting entry for estimated uncollectible accounts is made at the end of the period.

3. Recovery of an Uncollectible Account

Occasionally, a company collects from a customer after the account has been written off as uncollectible. Two entries are required to record the recovery of a bad debt: (1) the entry made in writing off the account is reversed to reinstate the customer's account; and (2) the collection is journalized in the usual way.

To illustrate, assume that on July 1, T. Ebbet's fortunes have changed and he now wants to restore his credit with Abrams Furniture. In order to do so, he has to pay the $2,500 amount that had been written off on March 1. The entries are as follows:

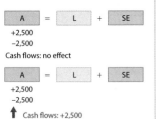

A = L + SE
+2,500
−2,500
Cash flows: no effect

A = L + SE
+2,500
−2,500
↑ Cash flows: +2,500

		(1)		
July	1	Accounts Receivable—T. Ebbet	2,500	
		Allowance for Doubtful Accounts		2,500
		(To reverse write-off of T. Ebbet account)		
		(2)		
	1	Cash	2,500	
		Accounts Receivable—T. Ebbet		2,500
		(To record collection from T. Ebbet)		

Note that the recovery of a bad debt, like the write-off of a bad debt, affects only balance sheet accounts. The net effect of the two entries is an increase (a debit) to Cash and an increase (a credit) to Allowance for Doubtful Accounts for $2,500. Accounts Receivable is debited and later credited for two reasons. First, the company must reverse the write-off. Second, T. Ebbet did pay, and the accounts receivable account in the subsidiary (and general) ledger should show this collection as it will need to be considered for future credit purposes.

Summary of Allowance Method

In summary, there are three types of transactions when accounts receivable are valued using the allowance method:

1. Uncollectible accounts receivable are recorded at the end of the period by debiting Bad Debts Expense and crediting Allowance for Doubtful Accounts. The amount to record can be determined by using a percentage of total receivables, or an aging schedule.
2. Actual uncollectibles, or write-offs, are then debited to Allowance for Doubtful Accounts and credited to an accounts receivable account.
3. Later recoveries, if any, are recorded in two separate entries. The first reverses the write-off by debiting Accounts Receivable and crediting Allowance for Doubtful Accounts. The second records the normal collection of the account by debiting Cash and crediting Accounts Receivable.

These entries are summarized and illustrated in the T accounts below:

Accounts Receivable		Allowance for Doubtful Accounts	
Beginning balance	Collections	Write-offs	Beginning balance
Credit sales	Write-offs		Subsequent recoveries
Subsequent recoveries			Bad debt adjustment
Ending balance			Ending balance

ACCOUNTING MATTERS!   Management Perspective

How can you tell if a company is selling too much on credit? You must watch not only the company's sales, but also changes in accounts receivable and allowance for doubtful accounts in order to assess the quality of a company's receivables.

For example, Nortel Networks saw its sales rocket 262 percent between 1995 and 2000. However, as these sales increased, the credit quality of the corresponding receivables deteriorated. During this same five-year period, Nortel's gross accounts receivable increased by 244 percent while its allowance for doubtful accounts increased by a staggering 494 percent.

The day of reckoning came in 2001. Nortel's accounts receivable decreased by 42 percent between 2000 and 2001 while its allowance increased by 65 percent. It was obvious that Nortel had loosened its credit policies in order to attract sales when, in 2001, it had to write off a large number of these accounts as uncollectible.

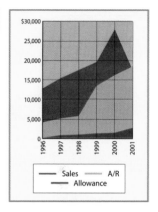

Decision Toolkit

Decision Checkpoints	Info Needed for Decision	Tools to Use for Decision	How to Evaluate Results
Is the amount of past-due accounts increasing? Which accounts require management's attention?	List of outstanding receivables and their due dates	Prepare an aging schedule showing the receivables in various stages: outstanding 0–30 days, 31–60 days, 61–90 days, 91–120 days, and over 120 days.	Accounts in the older categories require follow-up: letters, phone calls, e-mails, and possible renegotiations of terms.

BEFORE YOU GO ON . . .

▶ Review It

1. Explain how the allowance method respects the matching principle.
2. Distinguish between the journal entries required to record (a) estimated uncollectibles, (b) a write-off of an uncollectible account, and (c) a subsequent recovery of an uncollectible account.
3. To keep good internal control over receivables, who should authorize receivables write-offs?

▶ Do It

A partially prepared aging schedule for Woo Wholesalers Corporation at its year end, December 31, follows:

		Number of Days Outstanding			
	Total	0–30	31–60	61–90	Over 90
Accounts receivable	$230,000	$100,000	$60,000	$50,000	$20,000
Estimated percentage uncollectible		2%	5%	10%	20%
Total estimated bad debts					

Complete the aging schedule and prepare the journal entry required to record the estimated bad debts expense at December 31. Assume that Allowance for Doubtful Accounts has an opening credit balance of $4,000.

Action Plan

- Apply percentages to outstanding receivables in each age category to determine total estimated bad debts.
- The total estimated bad debts determined in the aging schedule is the ending balance required in the allowance account.
- Consider both the required ending balance and any existing balance in the allowance account to determine the adjustment amount.

Solution

Total estimated bad debts is $14,000 [($100,000 × 2%) + ($60,000 × 5%) + ($50,000 × 10%) + ($20,000 × 20%)]. The following entry should be made to adjust Allowance for Doubtful Accounts by $10,000 ($14,000 − $4,000) to reach the required ending balance of $14,000:

Dec. 31	Bad Debts Expense	10,000	
	Allowance for Doubtful Accounts		10,000
	(To record estimate of uncollectible accounts)		

Notes Receivable

study objective 3

Explain how notes receivable are recognized and valued in the accounts.

Credit may also be granted in exchange for a formal credit instrument known as a promissory note. A **promissory note** is a written promise to pay a specified amount of money on demand or at a definite time. Promissory notes may be used (1) when individuals and companies lend or borrow money, (2) when the amount of the transaction and the credit period exceed normal limits, and (3) in settlement of accounts receivable.

In a promissory note, the party making the promise to pay is called the maker; the party who will be paid is called the payee. For the maker of the note, the note would be classified as a note payable. For the payee of the note, the note would be classified as a note receivable.

The promissory note details the names of the maker and the payee, the principal or face value of the loan, the loan period, the interest rate, and whether interest is repayable monthly or at maturity (the note's due date) along with the principal amount. Other details might include whether any security is pledged as collateral for the loan and what happens if the maker defaults (does not pay).

Students often find it difficult to understand the difference between a note receivable and an account receivable. There are many differences, however. An account receivable is an informal promise to pay, while a note receivable is strengthened by a written promise to pay, which gives the payee a stronger legal claim. In addition, a note is a negotiable instrument (similar to a cheque), which means that it can be transferred to another party by endorsement (signature of the payee). An account receivable results from credit sales, while a note receivable can result from financing a purchase, lending money, or extending an account receivable beyond normal amounts or due dates. An account receivable is usually due within a short period of time (e.g., 30 days), while a note can extend for longer periods of time (e.g., 30 days to several years). An account receivable does not incur interest unless the account is overdue, while a note usually bears interest for an entire period.

There are also similarities between notes and accounts receivable. Both are credit instruments. Both can be sold to another party. And, as you will learn in the next section, both are valued at their net realizable value. The basic issues in accounting for notes receivable are the same as those for accounts receivable, as follows: (1) recognizing notes receivable and (2) valuing notes receivable.

Recognizing Notes Receivable

To illustrate the basic accounting for notes receivable, we will assume that on May 1, Tabusintac Inc. (the payee) accepts a note receivable in exchange for an account receivable from Raja Ltd. (the maker). The note is for $10,000, with 6 percent interest due in four months, on September 1.

We record this entry as follows for the receipt of the note by Tabusintac:

May	1	Notes Receivable—Raja Ltd.	10,000	
		Accounts Receivable—Raja Ltd.		10,000
		(To record acceptance of Raja Ltd. note)		

A	=	L	+	SE
+10,000				
−10,000				

Cash flows: no effect

If a note is exchanged for cash, the entry is a debit to Notes Receivable and a credit to Cash in the amount of the loan.

The note receivable is recorded at its principal value, the value shown on the face of the note. No interest revenue is reported when the note is accepted because the revenue recognition principle does not recognize revenue until it is earned. As we learned in Chapter 4, interest is earned (accrued) as time passes.

Contrary to accounts receivable, which only incur interest when the account is overdue, a note bears interest for the entire loan period. As you learned in Chapter 4, interest is calculated as follows:

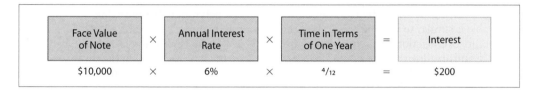

Face Value of Note	×	Annual Interest Rate	×	Time in Terms of One Year	=	Interest
$10,000	×	6%	×	$4/12$	=	$200

The interest rate specified on the note is an **annual** rate of interest. The time factor in the calculation represents the fraction of the year that the note is outstanding. As we did in past chapters, for simplicity we will continue to assume that interest is calculated in months, rather than days.

Interest on the Raja note will total $50 ($10,000 × 6% × $\frac{1}{12}$) a month, or $200 for the four-month period. This interest will be recorded as interest revenue for Tabusintac Inc. and interest expense for Raja Ltd. If Tabusintac Inc.'s year end was May 31, the following adjusting journal entry would be required to accrue interest for the month of May:

May	31	Interest Receivable	50	
		Interest Revenue		50
		(To accrue interest on Raja Ltd. note receivable)		

A	=	L	+	SE
+50				+50

Cash flows: no effect

Note that while interest on an overdue account receivable is debited to the Accounts Receivable account, interest on a note receivable is *not* debited to the Note Receivable account. Instead, a separate account for the interest receivable is used. Since the note is a formal credit instrument, its recorded principal must remain unchanged. In addition, it is useful for a company to track how much interest it is earning from notes receivable.

Notes are normally held to their maturity date, at which time the principal plus accrued interest is due. This is known as honouring (collecting) the note. In some situations, the maker of the note defaults and an appropriate adjustment must be made. This is known as dishonouring (not collecting) the note.

Honouring of Notes Receivable

A note is said to be honoured when it is paid in full at its maturity date. If Raja pays its note when it is due on September 1, the maturity date, the entry by Tabusintac to record the collection is:

Sept. 1	Cash	10,200	
	Notes Receivable—Raja Ltd.		10,000
	Interest Receivable		50
	Interest Revenue		150
	(To record collection of Raja Ltd. note and interest)		

Recall that one month of interest, $50, was previously accrued on May 31. Consequently, only three months of interest revenue, $150 ($10,000 × 6% × 3/12), is recorded in this period.

Dishonouring of Notes Receivable

A **dishonoured note** is a note that is not paid in full at maturity. A dishonoured note receivable is no longer negotiable. However, the payee still has a claim against the maker of the note for both the principal and any unpaid interest. Therefore, the Notes Receivable account balance is usually transferred to an account receivable by debiting Accounts Receivable for the total of the principal amount of the note and the interest due.

If there is no hope of collection, the principal and any accrued interest should be written off. No interest revenue would be recorded, because collection will not occur.

Valuing Notes Receivable

Like accounts receivable, notes receivable are reported at their **net realizable value.** Valuing notes receivable is similar to valuing accounts receivable. Each note must be analyzed to determine its probability of collection. If circumstances are such that eventual collection is in doubt, bad debts expense and an allowance for doubtful accounts (notes) must be recorded in the same way these are recorded for accounts receivable. Many companies use just the one account, Allowance for Doubtful Accounts, for all trade receivables (both accounts receivable and notes receivable).

BEFORE YOU GO ON . . .

▶Review It

1. Identify the similarities and differences between an account receivable and a note receivable.
2. How is interest recorded for a note receivable?
3. At what value are notes receivable reported on the balance sheet?
4. Explain the difference between honouring and dishonouring a note receivable.

▶Do It

Gambit Stores Ltd. accepts from Leonard Corp. a three-month, 6%, $3,400, note dated May 10 in settlement of Leonard's overdue account. What journal entries would be made by Gambit on May 10 and on August 10, the maturity date, assuming Leonard pays the note and interest in full at that time and no interest was previously accrued? What entry would be made on August 10, if Leonard could not pay the note? The note is expected to be collected in the future.

Action Plan

- Calculate the accrued interest. The formula is: face value × annual interest rate × time in terms of one year.
- If the note is honoured, record the collection of the note and any interest earned. Use separate accounts for the principal amount of the note and the interest.
- If the note is dishonoured, record the transfer of the note and any interest earned to an accounts receivable account if eventual collection is expected, or to an allowance account if collection is not expected.

Solution

May 10	Notes Receivable—Leonard Corp.	3,400	
	Accounts Receivable—Leonard Corp.		3,400
	(To replace account receivable with a 6% note receivable, due August 10)		

Note honoured:

Aug. 10	Cash		3,451	
	Notes Receivable—Leonard Corp.			3,400
	Interest Revenue ($3,400 × 6% × 3/12)			51
	(To record collection of Leonard note and interest)			

Note dishonoured:

10	Accounts Receivable—Leonard Corp.		3,451	
	Notes Receivable—Leonard Corp.			3,400
	Interest Revenue ($3,400 × 6% × 3/12)			51
	(To record transfer of dishonoured Leonard note and interest to accounts receivable)			

Statement Presentation of Receivables

Each of the major types of receivables should be identified in the balance sheet or in the notes to the financial statements. Short-term receivables are reported in the current assets section of the balance sheet, following cash and short-term investments. Although only the net realizable value of receivables must be disclosed, it is helpful to report both the gross amount of receivables and the allowance for doubtful accounts either in the statement or in the notes to the financial statements.

Illustration 8-4 shows the presentation of receivables for Bombardier Inc.

study objective 4

Explain the statement presentation of receivables.

Illustration 8-4 ◀

Balance sheet presentation of receivables

BOMBARDIER INC. Consolidated Balance Sheet (partial) January 31, 2005 (in U.S. millions)	BOMBARDIER
Current assets	
Cash and cash equivalents	$ 2,355
Receivables (Note 2)	1,622
Finance receivables (Note 3)	3,585
Assets under operating leases and other (Note 4)	474
Inventories (Note 5)	4,013
	12,049
Other assets (Note 8)	1,279

Bombardier discloses in Note 2 to its financial statements that its receivables consist of trade receivables, sales tax recoverable, and other receivables from which an allowance for doubtful accounts of U.S. $74 million was deducted.

In Note 3, Bombardier discloses that its finance receivables are notes receivable resulting from financing that the company made with its customers for sales of products and extensions of trade receivables. Bombardier also reports information about the average interest rates and maturity dates of these notes. It has deducted an allowance for doubtful notes of U.S. $46 million from its finance receivables. Although Bombardier reports its notes receivable (finance receivables) following accounts receivable, notes receivable are often listed before accounts receivable because they are usually more easily converted to cash.

In Note 8, Bombardier includes U.S. $316 million of long-term receivables from loans and leases as part of the other assets reported in the noncurrent section of its balance sheet.

In the statement of earnings, bad debts expense is reported in the operating expenses section. Interest revenue is shown under other revenues in the non-operating section of the statement of earnings. If a company has a significant risk of uncollectible accounts or other problems with its receivables, it is required to disclose this possibility in the notes to the financial statements.

BEFORE YOU GO ON . . .

▶Review It

1. Explain where accounts and notes receivable are classified on the balance sheet.
2. Where are bad debts expense and interest revenue reported on the statement of earnings?

Managing Receivables

study objective 5

Apply the principles of sound accounts receivable management.

There are five steps in managing accounts receivable:

1. Determine who to extend credit to.
2. Establish a payment period.
3. Monitor collections.
4. Evaluate the liquidity of receivables.
5. Accelerate cash receipts from receivables when necessary.

Extending Credit

A critical part of managing receivables is determining who should receive credit and who should not. Many companies increase sales by being generous with their credit policy, but they may end up extending credit to risky customers who do not pay. If the credit policy is too tight, the company will lose sales. If it is too loose, it may sell to those who will pay either very late or not at all.

Certain steps can be taken to help minimize losses as credit standards are relaxed. Risky customers might be required to provide letters of credit or bank guarantees. Then, if the customer does not pay, the bank that provided the guarantee will pay. Particularly risky customers might be required to pay cash on delivery.

In addition, companies should ask potential customers for references from banks and suppliers to determine their payment history. It is important to check these references on potential new customers, and to periodically check the financial health of existing customers. Many resources are available for investigating customers. For example, to aid in lending decisions, companies such as Equifax provide credit opinions on companies around the world.

Establishing a Payment Period

Companies that extend credit should determine a required payment period and inform their customers about it. It is important to make sure that your company's payment period is consistent with its competitors' policies. For example, if you decide to require payment within 15 days, but your competitors require payment within 45 days, you may lose sales to your competitors. One strategy, therefore, could be to allow up to 45 days to pay but also to offer a sales discount for people paying within 15 days. This matches your competitors' terms yet still encourages prompt payment of accounts.

Monitoring Collections

An accounts receivable aging schedule should be prepared often. In addition to its use in estimating the allowance for doubtful accounts, the aging schedule has other uses for management. It helps estimate the timing of future cash inflows, which is important information to know before preparing a cash budget. It also provides information about the overall collection experience of the company, and it identifies problem accounts. As we learned earlier in this chapter, problem accounts need to be vigorously pursued with phone calls, letters, and occasionally legal action.

Credit risk increases during periods of economic downturn. Credit policies and collection experience must always be monitored not only in comparison to past experience, but also in light of current economic conditions. This is especially important when a company has a high level of receivables from few customers.

If a company has significant concentrations of credit risk, it is required to discuss this risk in the notes to its financial statements. A **concentration of credit risk** is a threat of non-payment from a single customer or class of customers that could hurt the company's financial health. An excerpt from the credit risk note from the financial statements of Research in Motion is shown in Illustration 8-5.

Illustration 8-5 ◀

Concentration of credit risk

RESEARCH IN MOTION LIMITED
Notes to the Financial Statements
February 28, 2004

Note 20: Financial Instruments

The Company, in the normal course of business, monitors the financial condition of its customers and reviews the credit history of each new customer. The Company establishes an allowance for doubtful accounts that corresponds to the specific credit risk of its customers, historical trends, and economic circumstances...

While the Company sells its products and services to a variety of customers, two customers comprised 24% and 10% of trade receivables as at February 28, 2004 (2003—three customers comprised 17%, 16%, and 14%). Additionally, two customers comprised 15% and 13% of the Company's sales (March 1, 2003—one customer comprised 12%).

As the note states, Research in Motion has some credit risk concentrated in two customers. It is important for management to carefully monitor the collectibility of the receivables from these two customers.

Decision Toolkit

Decision Checkpoints	Info Needed for Decision	Tools to Use for Decision	How to Evaluate Results
Is the company's credit risk increasing?	Customer account balances and due dates	Accounts receivable aging schedule	Calculate and compare the percentage of receivables overdue in each age classification.
Does the company have significant concentrations of credit risk?	Note to the financial statements on concentrations of credit risk	If risky credit customers are identified, the financial health of those customers should be evaluated to gain an independent assessment of the potential for a material credit loss.	If a material loss appears likely, the potential negative impact of that loss on the company should be carefully evaluated, as well as how adequate the allowance for doubtful accounts is.

Evaluating Liquidity of Receivables

Investors and managers keep a watchful eye on the relationship between sales, accounts receivable, and cash collections. If sales increase, then accounts receivable are also expected to increase. But an unusually high increase in accounts receivable might signal trouble. Perhaps the company increased its sales by loosening its credit policy, and these receivables may be difficult or impossible to collect. Such receivables are considered less liquid. Recall that liquidity is measured by how quickly certain assets can be converted to cash.

The ratio used to assess the liquidity of the receivables is the **receivables turnover** ratio. This ratio measures the number of times, on average, that receivables are collected during the period. The receivables turnover is calculated by dividing net credit sales by the average gross accounts receivable during the year.

Unfortunately, companies seldom report the amount of net credit sales in their financial statements. In such instances, net sales (including both cash and credit sales) can be used as a substitute. In addition, because some companies do not publicly report their gross accounts receivable, net accounts receivable must be used. As long as one is consistent in choosing the components of any ratio, the resulting ratio will be useful for comparisons.

A popular variant of the receivables turnover is to convert it into an **average collection period** in terms of days. This is done by dividing 365 days by the receivables turnover. The average collection period is frequently used to assess the effectiveness of a company's credit and collection policies. The general rule is that the collection period should not greatly exceed the credit term period (i.e., the time allowed for payment).

The following data (in U.S. millions) are available for Wyeth. We have assumed that all sales are credit sales for the purposes of this illustration.

	2004	2003	2002
Net sales	$17,358.0	$15,850.6	$14,584.0
Accounts receivable (gross)	2,937.6	2,679.4	2,512.2
Allowance for doubtful accounts	139.1	149.8	132.3

The receivables turnover and average collection period for Wyeth are shown in Illustration 8-6, along with comparative industry data.

Illustration 8-6 ▶

Receivables turnover

$$\text{RECEIVABLES TURNOVER} = \frac{\text{NET CREDIT SALES}}{\text{AVERAGE GROSS ACCOUNTS RECEIVABLE}}$$

$$\text{AVERAGE COLLECTION PERIOD} = \frac{365 \text{ DAYS}}{\text{RECEIVABLES TURNOVER}}$$

(in U.S. millions)	Ratio	2004	2003
Wyeth	Receivables turnover	$\frac{\$17,358.0}{(\$2,937.6 + \$2,679.4) \div 2} = 6.2$ times	$\frac{\$15,850.6}{(\$2,679.4 + \$2,512.2) \div 2} = 6.1$ times
Wyeth	Average collection period	$\frac{365}{6.2} = 59$ days	$\frac{365}{6.1} = 60$ days
Industry average	Receivables turnover	5.6 times	6.0 times
Industry average	Average collection period	65 days	61 days

Wyeth's receivables turnover was 6.2 times in 2004, with an average collection period of 59 days. This was a slight improvement over its 2003 collection period of 60 days and compares favourably with the industry average collection period.

The receivables turnover is an important component of a company's overall liquidity. Ideally, it should be analyzed along with other information about a company's liquidity, including the current ratio and inventory turnover. Recall from earlier chapters that the receivables turnover and inventory turnover can distort a company's current ratio. In general, the faster the turnover, the more reliable the current ratio is for assessing liquidity.

Decision Toolkit

Decision Checkpoints	Info Needed for Decision	Tools to Use for Decision	How to Evaluate Results
Are collections being made in a timely fashion?	Net credit sales and average accounts receivable balance	$$\text{Receivables turnover} = \frac{\text{Net credit sales}}{\text{Average gross receivables}}$$ $$\text{Average collection period} = \frac{365 \text{ days}}{\text{Receivables turnover}}$$	The average collection period should be consistent with corporate credit policy. An increase may suggest a decline in the financial health of customers.

Accelerating Cash Receipts

In the normal course of events, receivables are collected in cash and then removed from the books. However, as credit sales and receivables grow in size and significance, waiting for receivables to be collected within the normal collection period results in increased costs and delays in being able to use the cash that is awaited. Two typical ways to accelerate the receipt of cash from receivables are using the receivables to secure a loan and selling the receivables.

Loans Secured by Receivables

One of the most common ways to speed up cash flow from receivables is to go to a bank and borrow money using receivables as collateral. While this does have a cost (interest has to be paid to the bank on the loan), the cash is available for company use earlier, and the loan can be repaid as the receivables are collected. Generally, banks are willing to provide financing for up to 75 percent of receivables that are less than 90 days old. Quite often, these arrangements occur through an **operating line of credit**.

Sale of Receivables

Companies also frequently sell their receivables to another company for cash, thereby shortening the cash-to-cash operating cycle. There are three reasons for the sale of receivables. The first is their size. For competitive reasons, **sellers (retailers, wholesalers, and manufacturers) often provide financing to purchasers of their goods**. For example, many major companies in the automobile, truck, equipment, computer, and appliance industries have created wholly owned captive financing companies that have the responsibility for accounts receivable financing. For example, Ford has Ford Credit Canada, Sears has Sears Acceptance Company Inc., and Bombardier has Bombardier Capital. The purpose of captive finance companies is to encourage the sale of a product by assuring financing to buyers without the parent companies that sell the product having to hold large amounts of receivables.

Second, **receivables may be sold because they may be the only reasonable source of cash**. When credit is tight, companies may not be able to borrow money in the usual credit markets. Even if credit is available, the cost of borrowing may be too high.

A final reason for selling receivables is that **billing and collection are often time-consuming and costly**. As a result, it is often easier for a retailer to sell the receivable to another party that has expertise in billing and collection matters. Credit card companies such as MasterCard and VISA specialize in billing and collecting accounts receivable.

Securitization of Receivables.   A common way to accelerate receivables collection is to transfer receivables to investors in return for cash through a process called securitization. In such cases, investors (usually a special-purpose entity or trust) issue securities as collateral for the securitized receivables. In certain cases, this transfer is treated as a sale of receivables; in other cases, it is treated as a secured loan. This topic is normally covered in detail in an intermediate accounting course.

Companies such as Sears Canada regularly securitize their accounts receivable to speed up collection. For the year ended January 1, 2005, Sears securitized more than 40 percent of its receivables.

Another way to accelerate receivables collection is by sale to a factor. A factor is a finance company or bank that buys receivables from businesses for a fee. If the customer does not pay, normally the company is responsible for reimbursing the factor for the uncollected amounts.

The differences between securitization and factoring are that securitization involves many investors, the cost is lower, the receivables are of a higher quality, and the seller usually continues to have some involvement with (e.g., responsibility to collect) the receivables. In factoring, the sale is usually to only one company, the cost is higher, the receivables quality is lower, and the seller does not normally have any involvement with the receivables.

Credit Card Sales.   It was recently estimated that in Canada more than 75 million credit cards were in use. Of these, about 65 percent are bank cards, such as VISA and MasterCard. The other 35 percent are cards issued by large department stores, gasoline companies, and other issuers, such as American Express and Diners Club.

Three parties are involved when credit cards are used in making retail sales: (1) the credit card issuer, who is independent of the retailer, (2) the retailer, and (3) the customer. A retailer's acceptance of a national credit card is another form of the retailer selling a receivable.

The issuer is responsible for performing the credit approval process. In addition, the issuer maintains and collects the customer accounts and absorbs any bad debts. The retailer receives cash more quickly from the credit card issuer than would have been the case in a normal credit situation. In exchange for these services, the retailer pays the credit card issuer a fee of 1 percent to 3 percent of the invoice price.

Sales resulting from the use of bank cards, such as VISA and MasterCard, are considered cash sales by the retailer. As soon as the credit card is electronically swiped, or when the bank that issued the card receives credit card sales slips from a retailer, the bank adds the amount to the seller's bank balance. These credit card sales slips are therefore recorded in the same way as cheques deposited from a cash sale, except for the additional service fee, which is normally deducted directly from the cash proceeds.

To illustrate, assume that MuchMusic Corp. sells $100 of CDs to Anita Ferreri on January 19. Anita pays for this purchase with her Royal Bank VISA card. The service fee that Royal Bank charges MuchMusic is 3 percent. The entry by MuchMusic to record this transaction is:

A	=	L	+	SE
+97				−3
				+100

↑ Cash flows: +97

Jan. 19	Cash ($100 − $3)	97	
	Service Charge Expense ($100 x 3%)	3	
	Sales		100
	(To record VISA credit card sale)		

Nonbank cards, such as American Express, Diners Club/enRoute, and Petro-Canada, are reported as credit sales, not cash sales. Conversion into cash does not occur until the financing company remits the net amount to the seller.

Debit Card Sales.   Canadians are the world's second most frequent users of debit cards, with only the inhabitants of the Netherlands using them more often. What is the difference between a debit card and a credit card? Debit cards allow customers to spend only what is in their bank account. Credit cards give a customer access to money made available by a bank or other financial institution, just like a loan. Credit cards are issued with the understanding that the amount charged will be repaid, with interest, if the account is not paid in full each month.

When a debit card sale occurs, the bank immediately deducts the cost of the purchase from the customer's bank account. This amount is electronically transferred into the retailer's bank account, less a service fee. The entries to record a debit card sale are identical to those shown earlier for bank credit card sales.

ACCOUNTING MATTERS! Management Perspective

The average interest rate on a bank credit card in Canada is 18 percent. Nonbank cards, such as Sears, can be as high as 28.8 percent. The Bank of Canada interest rate is 2.5 percent. Why are credit card rates so much higher than other interest rates?

The Bank of Canada interest rate is called the "risk-free" rate. This means that, theoretically, money can be borrowed at 2.5 percent if there is no other credit risk. The difference between the Bank of Canada rate and credit card rates is called a "risk premium." Banks justify this higher interest rate by saying that credit cards pose a greater risk. They argue that they have to cover their losses from fraud as well as their administrative costs. Given the amount of risk premium, the annual fee many consumers have to pay for their credit cards, and the service fee that banks charge retailers, banks appear to be well compensated for this risk.

BEFORE YOU GO ON . . .

▶Review It

1. What is meant by a concentration of credit risk?
2. What do the receivables turnover and the average collection period reveal?
3. Why do companies accelerate cash receipts from receivables?
4. What's the difference between a credit card sale and a debit card sale, if any?

the navigator

▦ Using the Decision Toolkit

Eli Lilly is one of Wyeth's top competitors. Selected financial information (in U.S. millions) taken from Eli Lilly's December 31, 2004, financial statements follows:

	2004	2003
Net sales	$13,857.9	$12,582.5
Accounts receivable (gross)	2,124.8	1,934.2
Total current assets	12,835.8	8,768.9
Total current liabilities	7,593.7	5,560.8

Instructions

Calculate Eli Lilly's current ratio, receivables turnover, and average collection period for 2004. Comment on the company's accounts receivable management and liquidity compared to that of Wyeth. Wyeth's current ratio was 1.7:1; the industry average, 1.7:1. Wyeth's receivables turnover and average collection period were calculated earlier in the chapter.

Solution

	Eli Lilly	Wyeth	Industry
Current ratio	$\dfrac{\$12,835.8}{\$7,593.7} = 1.7:1$	1.7:1	1.7:1
Receivables turnover	$\dfrac{\$13,857.9}{(\$2,124.8 + \$1,934.2) \div 2} = 6.8$ times	6.2 times	5.6 times
Average collection period	$\dfrac{365 \text{ days}}{6.8} = 54$ days	59 days	65 days

Eli Lilly, Wyeth, and the industry all have a strong, and similar, current ratio. However, a high current ratio does not always mean that a company has more liquidity. A current ratio could be artificially high because of uncollectible receivables or slow-moving inventory. So, further investigation is needed before we can fully compare Eli Lilly's and Wyeth's liquidity.

Eli Lilly's collection period of 54 days is better than both Wyeth and the industry. As all three have the same current ratio, but remembering that we have no information about inventory, we would have to conclude that Eli Lilly is the more liquid of the two companies.

Summary of Study Objectives

1. *Explain how accounts receivable are recognized in the accounts.* Accounts receivable are recorded at invoice price. They are reduced by sales returns and allowances. Sales discounts also reduce the amount received on accounts receivable. When interest is charged on a past-due receivable, this interest is added to the accounts receivable balance and is recognized as interest revenue.

2. *Account for bad debts.* The allowance method, using a percentage of receivables, is used to match bad debts expense against sales, in the period in which the sales occurred. A percentage of total receivables, or an aging schedule applying percentages to different categories of receivables, is used to estimate the allowance for doubtful accounts. The allowance is deducted from the receivables balance to report accounts receivable at their net realizable value on the balance sheet.

3. *Explain how notes receivable are recognized and valued in the accounts.* Notes receivable are recorded at their principal or face value. Interest is earned from the date the note is issued until it matures and is recorded in a separate interest receivable account. Like accounts receivable, notes receivable are also reported at their net realizable value.

Notes can be held to maturity, at which time the principal plus any unpaid interest is due and the note is removed from the accounts. In some situations, the maker of the note dishonours the note (defaults). If eventual collection is expected, an account receivable replaces the note receivable and any unpaid interest. If the amount is not expected to be repaid, the note is written off.

4. *Explain the statement presentation of receivables.* Each major type of receivable should be identified in the balance sheet or in the notes to the financial statements. It is desirable to report the gross amount of receivables and allowance for doubtful accounts. Bad debts and service charge expenses are reported in the statement of earnings as operating expenses, and interest revenue is shown as other revenues in the non-operating section of the statement.

5. *Apply the principles of sound accounts receivable management.* To properly manage receivables, management must (a) determine who to extend credit to, (b) establish a payment period, (c) monitor collections, (d) evaluate the liquidity of receivables by calculating the receivables turnover and average collection period, and (e) accelerate cash receipts from receivables when necessary.

Decision Toolkit—A Summary

Decision Checkpoints	Info Needed for Decision	Tools to Use for Decision	How to Evaluate Results
Is the amount of past-due accounts increasing? Which accounts require management's attention?	List of outstanding receivables and their due dates	Prepare an aging schedule showing the receivables in various stages: outstanding 0–30 days, 31–60 days, 61–90 days, 91–120 days, and over 120 days.	Accounts in the older categories require follow-up: letters, phone calls, e-mails, and possible renegotiations of terms.
Is the company's credit risk increasing?	Customer account balances and due dates	Accounts receivable aging schedule	Calculate and compare the percentage of receivables overdue in each age classification.
Does the company have significant concentrations of credit risk?	Note to the financial statements on concentrations of credit risk	If risky credit customers are identified, the financial health of those customers should be evaluated to gain an independent assessment of the potential for a material credit loss.	If a material loss appears likely, the potential negative impact of that loss on the company should be carefully evaluated, as well as how adequate the allowance for doubtful accounts is.
Are collections being made in a timely fashion?	Net credit sales and average accounts receivable balance	$\text{Receivables turnover} = \dfrac{\text{Net credit sales}}{\text{Average gross receivables}}$ $\text{Average collection period} = \dfrac{365 \text{ days}}{\text{Receivables turnover}}$	The average collection period should be consistent with corporate credit policy. An increase may suggest a decline in the financial health of customers.

www.wiley.com/canada/kimmel

Study Tools (Glossary)

Analysis Tools
(Decision Toolkit Summaries)

the navigator

Glossary

Accounts receivable Amounts owed by customers on account. (p. 360)

Aging the accounts receivable The analysis of customer balances by the length of time they have been unpaid. (p. 364)

Allowance method A method of accounting for bad debts that involves estimating uncollectible accounts at the end of each period. (p. 363)

Average collection period The average amount of time that a receivable is outstanding. It is calculated by dividing 365 days by the receivables turnover. (p. 374)

Concentration of credit risk The threat of nonpayment from a single customer or class of customers that could hurt the financial health of the company. (p. 373)

Control account An account in the general ledger that summarizes the detail for a subsidiary ledger and controls it. (p. 361)

Dishonoured note A note that is not paid in full at maturity. (p. 370)

Factor A finance company or bank that buys receivables from businesses for a fee. (p. 376)

Net realizable value The difference between gross receivables and the allowance for doubtful accounts. Net realizable value measures the net amount expected to be received in cash. (p. 363)

Notes receivable Claims for which formal instruments of credit are issued as evidence of the debt. (p. 360)

Percentage of receivables basis A percentage relationship established by management between the amount of receivables and the expected losses from uncollectible accounts. (p. 364)

Promissory note A written promise to pay a specified amount of money on demand or at a definite time. (p. 368)

Receivables turnover A measure of the liquidity of receivables, calculated by dividing net credit sales by the average gross accounts receivable. (p. 373)

Securitization The transfer of assets such as receivables to a company that issues securities as collateral for the receivables. (p. 376)

Subsidiary ledger A group of accounts that provide details of a control account in the general ledger. (p. 361)

Trade receivables Notes and accounts receivable that result from sales transactions. (p. 360)

Demonstration Problem

Presented here are selected transactions for O'Reilly Corp.:

Mar. 1 Sold $20,000 of merchandise to Potter Corporation, terms 2/10, n/30.

11 Received payment in full from Potter for balance due.

12 Accepted Juno Ltd.'s four-month, 6%, $20,000 note for its balance due. Interest is payable at maturity.

13 Made O'Reilly Corp. credit card sales for $13,200.

15 Made VISA credit sales totalling $6,700. A 3% service fee is charged by VISA.

Apr. 13 Received collections of $8,200 on O'Reilly credit card sales and added interest charges of 18% per annum (1.5% per month) to the remaining balances.

May 10 Wrote off as uncollectible $16,000 of accounts receivable.

June 30 The balance in Accounts Receivable at the end of the first six months is $200,000. Using an aging schedule, estimated uncollectible accounts are determined to be $20,000. At June 30, the credit balance in the allowance account before adjustment is $3,500.

July 12 Collected Juno note (see March 12 transaction).

16 One of the accounts receivable written off in May paid the amount due, $4,000, in full.

Instructions

Prepare the journal entries for the transactions.

Action Plan

- Record accounts receivable at invoice price.
- Recognize that sales returns and allowances and cash discounts reduce the amount received on accounts receivable.
- Record a service charge expense when credit cards are used.
- Calculate interest by multiplying the interest rate by the face value, adjusting for the portion of the year that has passed.
- Consider any existing balance in the allowance account when making the adjustment for uncollectible accounts.
- Record write-offs of accounts receivable only in balance sheet accounts.

Solution to Demonstration Problem

Date	Account	Debit	Credit
Mar. 1	Accounts Receivable—Potter	20,000	
	Sales		20,000
	(To record sales on account)		
11	Cash	19,600	
	Sales Discounts (2% × $20,000)	400	
	Accounts Receivable—Potter		20,000
	(To record collection of account receivable)		
12	Notes Receivable—Juno	20,000	
	Accounts Receivable—Juno		20,000
	(To record acceptance of Juno note)		
13	Accounts Receivable—O'Reilly	13,200	
	Sales		13,200
	(To record company credit card sales)		
15	Cash	6,499	
	Service Charge Expense (3% × $6,700)	201	
	Sales		6,700
	(To record credit card sales)		
Apr. 13	Cash	8,200	
	Accounts Receivable—O'Reilly		8,200
	(To record collection of accounts receivable)		
	Accounts Receivable [($13,200 − $8,200) × 18% × $^{1}/_{12}$]	75	
	Interest Revenue		75
	(To record interest charges on overdue receivables)		
May 10	Allowance for Doubtful Accounts	16,000	
	Accounts Receivable		16,000
	(To record write-off of accounts receivable)		
June 30	Bad Debts Expense ($20,000 − $3,500)	16,500	
	Allowance for Doubtful Accounts		16,500
	(To record estimate of uncollectible accounts)		

July	12	Cash	20,400	
		Notes Receivable—Juno		20,000
		Interest Revenue ($20,000 × 6% × ⁴/₁₂)		400
		(To record collection of Juno note receivable)		
	16	Accounts Receivable	4,000	
		Allowance for Doubtful Accounts		4,000
		(To reverse write-off of account receivable)		
	16	Cash	4,000	
		Accounts Receivable		4,000
		(To record collection of account receivable)		

Self-Study Questions

www.wiley.com/canada/kimmel

Study Tools (Self-Assessment Quizzes)

Answers are at the end of the chapter.

(SO 1) 1. On June 15, Patel Ltd. sells merchandise on account to Bullock Corp. for $1,000, terms 2/10, n/30. On June 20, Bullock returns merchandise worth $300 to Patel. On June 24, payment is received from Bullock for the balance due. What is the amount of cash received?
(a) $680   (c) $700
(b) $686   (d) $1,000

(SO 2) 2. Sanderson Corporation has a credit balance of $5,000 in its Allowance for Doubtful Accounts before any adjustments are made. Based on an aging of its accounts receivable at the end of the period, the company estimates that $60,000 of its receivables are uncollectible. The amount of bad debts expense which should be reported for this accounting period is:
(a) $5,000.   (c) $60,000.
(b) $55,000.   (d) $65,000.

(SO 2) 3. Sanderson Corporation has a debit balance of $5,000 in its Allowance for Doubtful Accounts before any adjustments are made. Based on an aging of its accounts receivable at the end of the period, the company estimates that $60,000 of its receivables are uncollectible. The amount of bad debts expense which should be reported for this accounting period is:
(a) $5,000.   (c) $60,000.
(b) $55,000.   (d) $65,000.

(SO 2) 4. On January 1, 2006, Allowance for Doubtful Accounts had a credit balance of $18,000. During 2006, $30,000 of uncollectible accounts receivable were written off. Aging indicates that uncollectible accounts are $20,000. What is the required adjustment in Bad Debts Expense at December 31, 2006?
(a) $2,000   (c) $20,000
(b) $8,000   (d) $32,000

(SO 3) 5. Sorenson Corp. accepts a three-month, 7%, $1,000 promissory note in settlement of Parton Ltd.'s account. The entry to record this transaction on Sorenson's books is:

(a)	Notes Receivable	1,017	
	Accounts Receivable		1,017
(b)	Notes Receivable	1,000	
	Accounts Receivable		1,000
(c)	Notes Receivable	1,000	
	Sales		1,000
(d)	Notes Receivable	1,070	
	Accounts Receivable		1,070

6. Schlicht Corp. holds Osgrove Inc.'s four-month, 9%, (SO 3) $10,000 note. The entry made by Schlicht Corp. when the note is collected, assuming no interest has previously been recorded, is:

(a)	Cash	10,300	
	Notes Receivable		10,300
(b)	Cash	10,000	
	Notes Receivable		10,000
(c)	Accounts Receivable	10,300	
	Notes Receivable		10,000
	Interest Revenue		300
(d)	Cash	10,300	
	Notes Receivable		10,000
	Interest Revenue		300

7. Accounts and notes receivable are reported in the (SO 4) asset section of the balance sheet at:
(a) net realizable value.
(b) invoice cost.
(c) lower of cost and market value.
(d) net book value.

8. The principles of sound accounts receivable (SO 5) management do not include:
(a) instituting a "cash only" policy.
(b) establishing a payment period.
(c) monitoring collections.
(d) evaluating the liquidity of receivables.

9. ⚒ Moore Corporation had net credit sales during the year of $800,000 and cost of goods sold of $500,000. The balance in Accounts Receivable at the beginning of the year was $100,000, and at the end of the year was $150,000. What were the receivables turnover and average collection period ratios, respectively?

(a) 4.0 and 91 days   (c) 6.4 and 57 days
(b) 5.3 and 69 days   (d) 8.0 and 46 days

10. ⚒ New Millennium Retailers Corp. accepted (SO 5) $50,000 of VISA credit card charges for merchandise sold on July 1. If the service charge is 4%, the entry to record this transaction will include a credit to Sales of $50,000 and a debit(s) to:

(a) Cash $48,000 and Service Charge Expense $2,000.
(b) Accounts Receivable $48,000 and Service Charge Expense $2,000.
(c) Cash $50,000.
(d) Accounts Receivable $50,000.

Questions

(SO 1) 1. What are the three major types of receivables? Where is each type of receivable generally classified on a balance sheet?

(SO 1) 2. When should a receivable be recorded for a service company? A merchandising company? Explain by referring to any relevant accounting principle(s).

(SO 1) 3. (a) What are the advantages of using an accounts receivable subsidiary ledger? (b) Describe the relationship between the general ledger control account and the subsidiary ledger.

(SO 1) 4. Under what circumstances is interest normally recorded for an account receivable?

(SO 2) 5. What are the essential features of the allowance method of accounting for bad debts? How does the allowance method respect the matching principle?

(SO 2) 6. Allowance for doubtful accounts is just one example of a contra account. Name one other contra asset and its related asset account. Name two contra revenue accounts and their related revenue accounts.

(SO 2) 7. Why is the bad debts expense that is reported in the statement of earnings usually not the same amount as the allowance for doubtful accounts amount reported in the balance sheet?

(SO 2) 8. Soo Eng cannot understand why the net realizable value does not change when an uncollectible account is written off under the allowance method. Clarify this for Soo Eng.

(SO 2) 9. What is the purpose of the account Allowance for Doubtful Accounts? Although the normal balance of this account is a credit balance, it can sometimes have a debit balance. Explain how this can happen.

(SO 2) 10. When an account receivable that was previously written off is later collected, two separate journal entries are usually made rather than one compound journal entry. Explain why.

(SO 3) 11. (a) Explain how accounts receivable and notes receivable are alike. (b) Explain how they differ.

(SO 3) 12. Danielle does not understand why a note receivable is not immediately recorded at its maturity value (principal plus interest), rather than its principal value. After all, you know you are going to collect both the principal and the interest and you know how much each will be. Explain to Danielle why notes are not recorded at their maturity value.

(SO 3) 13. Explain how recording interest revenue differs for accounts receivable and notes receivable.

(SO 3) 14. What is the difference between honouring a note receivable at maturity and dishonouring a note at maturity?

(SO 3) 15. How would the entries differ if a note receivable was dishonoured and eventual collection was expected compared to eventual collection not being expected?

(SO 4) 16. Saucier Ltd. has accounts receivable, notes receivable due in three months, notes receivable due in two years, an allowance for doubtful accounts, sales tax recoverable, and income tax receivable. How should the receivables be reported on the balance sheet?

(SO 5) 17. ⚒ What are the steps in having good receivables management?

(SO 5) 18. ⚒ What is meant by a concentration of credit risk?

(SO 5) 19. ⚒ CanWest Global Communications Corp.'s receivables turnover was 5.8 times in 2004 and 4.7 times in 2003. Has CanWest's receivables management improved or worsened?

(SO 5) 20. ⚒ The president of Ho Inc. proudly announces her company's improved liquidity since its current ratio has increased substantially. Does an increase in the current ratio always indicate improved liquidity? What other ratio or ratios might you review to determine whether or not the increase in the current ratio indicates an improvement in financial health?

(SO 5) 21. ⚒ During the year ended January 1, 2005, Canadian Tire Corporation, Limited transferred $2,209.3 million (79%) of its credit card receivables to an independent trust in a transaction known as securitization. Why might a company such as Canadian Tire securitize its receivables?

(SO 5) 22. ⚒ Sears accepts its own Sears credit card, bank credit cards, and debit cards. What are the advantages of accepting each type of card? Explain how the accounting is different for sales of each type.

Brief Exercises

BE8–1 Presented below are six receivables transactions. Indicate whether these receivables should be reported as accounts receivable, notes receivable, or other receivables on a balance sheet.

Identify types of receivables. (SO 1)

(a) Advanced $10,000 to an employee.
(b) Estimated $5,000 of income tax to be refunded.
(c) Received a promissory note of $5,000 for services performed.
(d) Sold merchandise on account to a customer for $6,000.
(e) GST of $2,500 is recoverable at the end of the quarter.
(f) Extended a customer's account for six months by accepting a note in exchange for the account.

BE8–2 Record the following transactions on the books of Essex Corp., which uses a perpetual inventory system:

Record receivables transactions. (SO 1)

(a) On July 1, Essex Corp. sold merchandise on account to Cambridge Inc. for $14,000, terms 2/10, n/30. The cost of the merchandise sold was $10,000.
(b) On July 8, Cambridge returned merchandise worth $2,400 to Essex. Its original cost was $1,440. The merchandise was restored to inventory.
(c) On July 10, Cambridge paid for the merchandise.
(d) Assume now that Cambridge did not pay on July 10, as indicated in part (c). At the end of August, Essex added one month's interest to Cambridge's account for the overdue receivable. Essex charges 24% on overdue accounts.

BE8–3 Massey Corp. estimates that 4% of total accounts receivable will become uncollectible at the end of December. Accounts receivable are $500,000 at the end of the year. Allowance for Doubtful Accounts has a credit balance of $3,000.

Record bad debts. (SO 2)

(a) Prepare the adjusting journal entry to record bad debts expense at December 31.
(b) If Allowance for Doubtful Accounts had a debit balance of $800 instead of a credit balance of $3,000, determine the amount to be reported for bad debts expense.

BE8–4 Refer to BE8–3. Massey Corp. decides to refine its estimate of uncollectible accounts by preparing an aging schedule. Complete the following schedule and prepare the adjusting journal entry at December 31 to record bad debts expense, assuming that the allowance account has a credit balance of $3,000.

Complete aging schedule and record bad debts. (SO 2)

Number of Days Outstanding	Accounts Receivable	Estimated Percentage Uncollectible	Estimated Bad Debts
0–30 days	$315,000	1%	
31–60 days	91,000	4%	
61–90 days	59,000	10%	
Over 90 days	35,000	20%	
Total	$500,000		

BE8–5 At the end of 2006, Searcy Corp. has accounts receivable of $700,000 and an allowance for doubtful accounts of $54,000. On January 24, 2007, it is learned that the company's $12,000 receivable from Hutley Inc. is not collectible. Management authorizes a write-off.

Record write-off, and compare net realizable value. (SO 2)

(a) Prepare the journal entry to record the write-off.
(b) What is the net realizable value of the accounts receivable (1) before the write-off and (2) after the write-off?

BE8–6 Assume the same information as in BE8–5. On March 4, 2007, Searcy Corp. receives payment of $12,000 in full from Hutley Inc., after the write-off. Prepare the journal entry (entries) required to record this transaction.

Record recovery of bad debt. (SO 2)

Calculate interest.
(SO 3)

BE8-7   Presented below are three promissory notes. Determine the missing amounts.

Date of Note	Term in Months	Principal	Interest Rate	Total Interest	Interest Revenue to Record for Year Ended December 31
Apr. 1	2	$900,000	10%	(c)	$15,000
July 2	6	79,000	(b)	$2,765	(d)
Nov. 1	18	(a)	6%	5,040	(e)

Record receivables transactions.
(SO 3)

BE8-8   On January 10, 2006, Kyiv Corp. sold merchandise on account to R. Opal for $12,000, terms n/30. The merchandise originally cost $8,000. On February 1, R. Opal gave Kyiv a five-month, 7% promissory note in settlement of this account. On July 1, R. Opal paid the note and accrued interest. Prepare the journal entries for Kyiv to record the above transactions. Kyiv has an April 30 year end and adjusts its accounts annually.

Record note receivable transactions.
(SO 3)

BE8-9   Lee Corporation accepts a three-month, 7%, $9,000 note receivable in settlement of an account receivable on April 1, 2006. Interest is due at maturity.

(a) Prepare the journal entries required to record the issue of the note on April 1, and the settlement of the note on July 1, assuming the note is honoured. No interest has previously been accrued.

(b) Repeat part (a) assuming that the note is dishonoured, but eventual collection is expected.

(c) Repeat part (a) assuming that the note is dishonoured, and eventual collection is not expected.

Prepare current assets section.
(SO 4)

BE8-10   Nias Corporation reported the following selected items at February 28, 2006:

Accounts payable	$469,000
Accounts receivable	235,000
Allowance for doubtful accounts	15,000
Bad debts expense	12,000
Cash	75,000
Inventory	190,000
Notes receivable—due November 1, 2006	150,000
Notes receivable—due April 1, 2009	200,000
Prepaid expenses	29,000
Recoverable sales taxes	19,000
Short-term investments	165,000

Prepare the current assets section of the balance sheet.

Identify principles of receivables management.
(SO 5)

BE8-11   The following is a list of activities that companies perform in relation to their receivables:

1. Accept bank credit cards.
2. Review company credit ratings.
3. Collect information about competitors' payment period policies.
4. Prepare the accounts receivable aging schedule.
5. Calculate the receivables turnover and average collection period.

Instructions

Match each of the activities above with a purpose listed below:

(a) ___ Determine who to extend credit to.

(b) ___ Establish a payment period.

(c) ___ Monitor collections.

(d) ___ Evaluate the liquidity of receivables.

(e) ___ Accelerate cash receipts from receivables when necessary.

Calculate ratios.
(SO 5)

BE8-12   The financial statements of Maple Leaf Foods Inc. report net sales of $6,365.0 million for the year ended December 31, 2004. Accounts receivable were $242.3 million at the beginning of the year, and $292.5 million at the end of the year. Calculate Maple Leaf's receivables turnover and average collection period.

BE8–13 St. Pierre Restaurant accepted a VISA card in payment of a $100 lunch bill. The bank charges a 2.5% fee. What entry should St. Pierre make to record the sale? How would this entry be different if payment had been made with an American Express credit card instead of a VISA card? A debit card instead of a VISA card? Assume that the same percentage fee applies for each type of card.

Record credit and debit card sales.
(SO 5)

Exercises

E8–1 On January 6, Nicklaus Corp. sells merchandise on account to Singh Inc. for $6,000, terms 2/10, n/30. The merchandise originally cost Nicklaus $4,000. On January 15, Singh pays the amount due. Both Nicklaus and Singh use a perpetual inventory system.

Record receivables and payables transactions.
(SO 1)

Instructions

(a) Prepare the entries on Nicklaus Corp.'s books to record the sale and related collection.
(b) Prepare the entries on Singh Inc.'s books to record the purchase and related payment.

E8–2 Presented below are the transactions for the Discovery Sports Ltd. store with four of its customers during the company's first month of business:

Record and post receivables transactions.
(SO 2)

Feb. 2 Sold $570 of merchandise to Andrew Noren on account, terms n/30.
      4 Andrew returned for credit $70 of the merchandise purchased on February 2.
      5 Sold $380 of merchandise to Dong Corporation on account, terms 2/10, n/30.
      8 Sold $421 of merchandise to Michael Collis for cash.
     14 The Dong Corporation paid its account in full.
     17 Andrew Noren purchased an additional $348 of merchandise on account, terms n/30.
     22 Sold $869 of merchandise to the Batstone Corporation, terms 2/10, n/30.
     28 Andrew Noren paid $500 on account.

Instructions

(a) Prepare journal entries to record each of the above transactions.
(b) Set up general ledger accounts for the Accounts Receivable control account and for the Accounts Receivable subsidiary ledger accounts. Post the journal entries to these accounts.
(c) Prepare a list of customers and the balances of their accounts from the subsidiary ledger. Prove the total of the subsidiary ledger balances is equal to the control account balance.

E8–3 Patillo Inc.'s general ledger reports a balance in Accounts Receivable of $90,000 at the end of December.

Record bad debts.
(SO 2)

Instructions

(a) If Allowance for Doubtful Accounts has a credit balance of $1,100, record the adjusting entry at December 31, assuming uncollectible accounts are determined to be $9,000 by aging the accounts.
(b) If Allowance for Doubtful Accounts has a credit balance of $1,100, record the adjusting entry at December 31, assuming uncollectible accounts are expected to be 10% of the accounts receivable.
(c) If Allowance for Doubtful Accounts has a debit balance of $600, journalize the adjusting entry at December 31, assuming uncollectible accounts are determined to be $9,000 by aging the accounts.

E8–4 Grevina Ltd. has accounts receivable of $92,500 at March 31, 2006. An analysis of the accounts shows these amounts:

Prepare aging schedule, record bad debts, and discuss implications.
(SO 2)

	March 31	
Month of Sale	2006	2005
March	$65,000	$75,000
February	12,600	8,000
January	8,500	2,400
October – December	6,400	1,100
	$92,500	$86,500

Credit terms are 2/10, n/30. At March 31, 2006, there is a $2,200 credit balance in the allowance account before adjustment. The company estimates its uncollectible accounts as follows:

Number of Days Outstanding	Estimated Percentage Uncollectible
0–30	2%
31–60	10%
61–90	30%
Over 90	50%

Instructions

(a) Prepare an aging schedule to determine the total estimated uncollectibles at March 31, 2006.
(b) Prepare the adjusting entry at March 31, 2006, to record bad debts expense.
(c) Discuss the implications of the changes in the age of receivables from 2005 to 2006.

Record bad debts, write-off, and recovery.
(SO 2)

E8–5   On December 31, 2006, when its Allowance for Doubtful Accounts had a debit balance of $1,000, Ceja Corp. estimated that $8,400 of its accounts receivable would become uncollectible, and it recorded the bad debts adjusting entry. On May 11, 2007, Ceja determined that Robert Worthy's account was uncollectible and wrote off $950. On November 12, 2007, Worthy paid the amount previously written off.

Instructions

Prepare the journal entries required to record each of the above transactions.

Record notes receivable transactions.
(SO 3)

E8–6   Passara Supply Corp. has the following selected transactions for notes receivable:

Nov. 1 Loaned $24,000 cash to A. Bouchard on a one-year, 8% note.
Dec. 1 Sold goods to Wright, Inc., receiving a two-month, 6%, $4,200 note. These goods cost $2,500.
      15 Received a six-month, 7%, $8,000 note on account from Barnes Corporation.
      31 Accrued interest on all notes receivable at year end. Interest is due at maturity.
Feb. 1 Collected the amount owing on the Wright note.

Instructions

Record the transactions for Passara Supply Corp.

Record notes receivable transactions.
(SO 3)

E8–7   The following selected transactions for notes receivable are for Rather Corp.:

May 1 Received a six-month, 5%, $6,000 note on account from Jioux Company. Interest is due at maturity.
June 30 Accrued interest on the Jioux note on this date, which is Rather's year end.
July 31 Lent $5,000 cash to an employee, issuing a three-month, 7% note. Interest is due at maturity.
Oct. 31 Received payment in full for the employee note.
Nov. 1 Wrote off the Jioux note as Jioux defaulted. Future payment is not expected.

Instructions

Record the transactions for Rather Corp.

Show presentation of receivables.
(SO 4)

E8–8   Deere & Company had the following balances in its short-term receivable accounts at October 31, 2004 (in U.S. millions): Allowance for Doubtful Trade Receivables $56; Allowance for Doubtful Financing Receivables $145; Financing Receivables $11,378; Other Receivables $663; Receivables from Unconsolidated Affiliates $17.6; and Trade Accounts and Notes Receivable $3,263.

Instructions

Show the presentation of Deere & Company's receivables in the current assets section of its balance sheet at October 31.

Discuss concentration of credit risk.
(SO 5)

E8–9   Refer to E8–8. Deere & Company reports in the notes to its financial statements that its trade accounts and notes receivable have significant concentrations of credit risk in the agricultural, commercial and consumer, and construction and forestry sections. However, it does not believe that it has a significant concentration of credit risk on a geographic basis.

Instructions

Why should the readers of Deere & Company's financial statements be concerned about credit risk?

E8–10   The following information (in millions) was taken from the December 31 financial statements of the Canadian National Railway Company:

Calculate ratios.
(SO 5)

	2004	2003	2002
Accounts receivable, gross	$ 863	$ 584	$ 781
Allowance for doubtful accounts	70	55	59
Accounts receivable, net	793	529	722
Revenues	6,548	5,884	6,110
Total current assets	1,654	1,092	1,163
Total current liabilities	2,259	1,977	2,134

Instructions

(a) Calculate the current ratio, receivables turnover, and average collection period for each of 2004 and 2003.
(b) Comment on any improvement or deterioration in CN's liquidity and management of accounts receivable.

E8–11   Refer to E8–10. In the notes to its financial statements, the Canadian National Railway Company reports that it has an accounts receivable securitization program under which it may sell, on a revolving agreement, a maximum of $450 million of eligible freight trade receivables and other receivables to an unrelated trust. As at December 31, the company had sold $445 million of these receivables.

Discuss sale of receivables.
(SO 5)

Instructions

Explain why CN, a financially stable company with positive cash flow, securitizes (sells) such a large portion of its receivables.

E8–12   Kasko Stores Ltd. accepts both its own credit cards and bank credit cards, in addition to debit cards. During the year, the following selected summary transactions occurred:

Record credit and debit card sales and indicate statement presentation.
(SO 4, 5)

Jan. 15 Made Kasko credit card sales totalling $17,000.
    20 Made VISA credit card sales (service charge fee, 3%) totalling $4,500.
    30 Made debit card sales (service charge fee, 2%) totalling $1,000.
Feb. 10 Collected $12,000 on Kasko credit card sales.
    15 Added interest charges of 28.8% to outstanding Kasko credit card balances.

Instructions

(a) Record the transactions for Kasko Stores.
(b) Indicate the statement presentation of the interest and credit and debit card service charges for Kasko Stores.

Problems: Set A

P8–1A   At January 1, 2006, Underwood Imports Inc. reported this information on its balance sheet:

Record receivables and bad debts transactions.
(SO 1, 2)

Accounts receivable	$995,000
Allowance for doubtful accounts	62,000

During 2006, the company had the following transactions for receivables:

1. Sales on account, $2,600,000
2. Sales returns and allowances, $40,000
3. Collections of accounts receivable, $2,700,000
4. Interest added to overdue accounts, $200,000
5. Write-offs of accounts receivable deemed uncollectible, $75,000
6. Recovery of accounts previously written off as uncollectible, $30,000

Instructions

(a) Prepare the journal entries to record each of the above summary transactions.
(b) Enter the January 1, 2006, balances in Accounts Receivable and Allowance for Doubtful Accounts, post the entries to the two accounts, and determine the balances.
(c) Prepare the journal entry to record bad debts expense at December 31, 2006, assuming that the aging of the accounts receivable indicates that the amount for estimated uncollectible accounts is $50,000.

Record receivables and bad debts transactions; show balance sheet presentation.
(SO 1, 2)

P8–2A   At the beginning of the current period, Fassi Corp. had balances in Accounts Receivable of $400,000 and in Allowance for Doubtful Accounts of $22,000 (credit). During the period, it had net credit sales of $950,000 and collections of $1,021,000. It wrote off accounts receivable of $29,000. However, a $2,000 account written off as uncollectible was recovered before the end of the current period. Uncollectible accounts are estimated to total $18,000 at the end of the period.

Instructions

(a) Prepare the entries to record sales and collections during the period.
(b) Prepare the entry to record the write-off of uncollectible accounts during the period.
(c) Prepare the entries to record the recovery of the uncollectible account during the period.
(d) Prepare the entry to record bad debts expense for the period.
(e) Determine the ending balance in Accounts Receivable and Allowance for Doubtful Accounts.
(f) Show the balance sheet presentation of the receivables at the end of the period.

Determine missing amounts.
(SO 1, 2)

P8–3A   Wilton Corporation reported the following information in its general ledger at December 31:

Accounts Receivable				Sales	
Beg. bal.	9,000	28,000			30,000
	(d)	(e)			
End. bal.	(f)				

Allowance for Doubtful Accounts				Bad Debts Expense	
		Beg. bal.	900	(c)	
	500	(b)			
		End. bal.	(a)		

All sales were on account. At the end of the year, uncollectible accounts were estimated to total $1,000 based on an aging schedule.

Instructions

Using your knowledge of receivables transactions, determine the missing amounts. (*Hint:* You may find it helpful to reconstruct the journal entries.)

Calculate bad debt amounts.
(SO 2)

P8–4A   Here is information for Aris Ltd. for the 2006 calendar year:

Total credit sales	$1,650,000
Accounts receivable at December 31	625,000
Accounts receivable written off	24,000
Accounts receivable later recovered	4,000

Instructions

(a) What amount of bad debts expense will Aris report if it does *not* use the allowance method of accounting for bad debts?
(b) Assume that Aris decides to estimate its uncollectible accounts using the allowance method and an aging schedule. Uncollectible accounts are estimated to total $52,000. What amount of bad debts expense will Aris record if Allowance for Doubtful Accounts has an opening credit balance of $20,000 on January 1?
(c) Assume the same facts as in part (b), except that there is a $2,000 opening debit balance in Allowance for Doubtful Accounts. What amount of bad debts expense will Aris record?
(d) What are the advantages of using the allowance method of reporting bad debts expense?

P8–5A The following is selected information taken from a company's aging schedule to estimate uncollectible accounts receivable at year end:

Record bad debts transactions.
(SO 2)

		Number of Days Outstanding			
	Total	0–30	31–60	61–90	Over 90
Accounts receivable	$260,000	$120,000	$60,000	$50,000	$30,000
Estimated percentage uncollectible		1%	5%	10%	25%
Estimated bad debts					

The unadjusted balance in Allowance for Doubtful Accounts is a credit of $10,000.

Instructions

(a) Complete the aging schedule and calculate the total estimated bad debts from the above information.
(b) Prepare the adjusting journal entry to record the bad debts using the information determined in (a).
(c) In the following year, $2,000 of the outstanding receivables is determined to be specifically uncollectible. Prepare the journal entry to write off the uncollectible amount.
(d) The company subsequently collects $850 of the $2,000 that was determined to be uncollectible in (c). Prepare the journal entries to restore the $2,000 account receivable and record the partial cash collection.
(e) Explain how establishing an allowance satisfies the matching principle.

P8–6A The following selected transactions occurred for Bleumortier Corporation. The company has a March 31 year end and adjusts its accounts annually.

Record receivables transactions.
(SO 1, 3)

Jan. 5 Sold $9,000 of merchandise to Brooks Limited, terms n/30. The cost of goods sold was $6,000.
Feb. 2 Accepted a four-month, 6%, $9,000 promissory note from Brooks for the balance due. Interest is payable at maturity.
  12 Sold $6,700 of merchandise costing $4,400 to Gage Company and accepted Gage's two-month, 6% note in payment. Interest is payable at maturity.
  26 Sold $4,000 of merchandise to Mathias Corp., terms n/30. The cost of the merchandise sold was $2,700.
Mar. 31 Accepted a two-month, 7%, $4,000 note from Mathias for the balance due. Interest is payable at maturity.
  31 Adjusted any accrued interest at year end.
Apr. 12 Collected the Gage note in full.
June 2 Collected the Brooks note in full.
   5 Mathias dishonours its note of March 31. It is expected that it will eventually pay the amount owed.

Instructions

Record the transactions.

P8–7A On November 1, 2006, a company accepted a three-month, 6%, $20,000 note from a customer in settlement of the customer's account. Interest is due at maturity. The company's year end is December 31. The company makes adjusting entries annually.

Record notes receivable transactions.
(SO 3)

Instructions

(a) Prepare all journal entries for the company over the life of the note. Assume that the customer settles the note in full on the maturity date.
(b) Assume that instead of honouring the note at maturity, the customer dishonours it. Prepare the necessary journal entry at the maturity date, February 1, 2007, assuming that eventual collection of the note is (1) expected, and (2) not expected.

Prepare assets section of balance sheet.
(SO 4)

P8–8A   Canadian Tire Corporation, Limited reports the following assets at January 1, 2005 (in millions):

Accounts receivable	$ 389.2
Accumulated amortization—buildings	652.5
Accumulated amortization—equipment and other	577.1
Allowance for doubtful accounts (assumed)	18.5
Buildings	1,987.5
Cash and cash equivalents	802.2
Credit card receivables	528.4
Equipment and other assets	1,155.2
Goodwill	41.7
Intangible assets	52.0
Land	672.1
Long-term receivables	65.6
Merchandise inventories	620.6
Other assets	64.1
Personal loans receivable (short-term)	64.0
Prepaid expenses and deposits	24.1

Instructions

Prepare the assets section of Canadian Tire's balance sheet.

Record receivables and credit and debit card transactions.
(SO 1, 5)

P8–9A   During July, the following selected transactions occurred for Bon Ton Limited:

July 1 Sold $2,800 of merchandise for cash. The cost of the goods sold was $1,700.

  5 Sold merchandise of $7,800 on Bon Ton credit cards. The cost of the goods sold was $4,700.

  14 Performed services for $700 on VISA credit cards. The credit card service charge was 3%.

  15 Sold merchandise for $1,200 on American Express credit cards. The cost of goods sold was $700 and the credit card service charge was 3%.

  16 Submitted American Express credit card slips received on July 15 to American Express for payment.

  17 Performed services for $1,000 on account, terms 2/10, n/30.

  20 Sold $1,800 of merchandise to customers who paid with their debit cards. The cost of goods sold was $1,000 and the bank service charge was 2%.

  26 Collected the amount owing from the July 17 transaction.

  31 Added $200 of interest to overdue Bon Ton credit card account holders.

  31 Submitted Bon Ton credit card slips accumulated to date to the credit card division for payment.

  31 Received the American Express cheque for the July 16 billing, less the service charge.

Instructions

Record the transactions.

Calculate and interpret ratios.
(SO 5)

P8–10A   Presented here is basic financial information (in U.S. millions) from the 2004 financial statements of Nike, Inc. and Reebok International Ltd.:

	Nike	Reebok
Net sales	$12,253.1	$3,785.3
Allowance for doubtful accounts, Jan. 1	81.9	70.8
Allowance for doubtful accounts, Dec. 31	95.3	81.3
Accounts receivable (gross), Jan. 1	2,165.8	603.1
Accounts receivable (gross), Dec. 31	2,215.5	741.9

Instructions

Calculate the receivables turnover and average collection period for both companies, assuming all sales are credit sales. The industry average for the receivables turnover was 7.3 times and the average collection period was 50 days. Comment on the difference in the two companies' collection experiences.

P8–11A The following selected ratios are available for Pampered Pets Inc. for the most recent three years:

Evaluate liquidity.
(SO 5)

	2006	2005	2004
Current ratio	2.6:1	2.4:1	2.1:1
Receivables turnover	6.7 times	7.4 times	8.2 times
Inventory turnover	7.5 times	8.7 times	9.9 times

Instructions

(a) Is Pampered Pets' liquidity improving or worsening? Explain.
(b) Do changes in turnover ratios affect cash flow? Explain.
(c) Identify any steps that the company may wish to take to improve its management of receivables and inventory.

Problems: Set B

P8–1B At January 1, 2006, Bordeaux Inc. reported this information on its balance sheet:

Record receivables and bad
debts transactions.
(SO 1, 2)

Accounts receivable	$960,000
Allowance for doubtful accounts	70,000

During 2006, the company had the following transactions for receivables:

1. Sales on account, $3,200,000
2. Sales returns and allowances, $50,000
3. Collections of accounts receivable, $3,000,000
4. Interest added to overdue accounts, $250,000
5. Write-offs of accounts receivable deemed uncollectible, $90,000
6. Recovery of accounts previously written off as uncollectible, $21,000

Instructions

(a) Prepare the journal entries to record each of the above summary transactions.
(b) Enter the January 1, 2006, balances in Accounts Receivable and Allowance for Doubtful Accounts, post the entries to the two accounts, and determine the balances.
(c) Prepare the journal entry to record bad debts expense at December 31, 2006, assuming that aging the accounts receivable indicates that the amount for estimated uncollectible accounts is $110,000.

P8–2B At the beginning of the current period, Huang Corp. had balances in Accounts Receivable of $200,000 and in Allowance for Doubtful Accounts of $14,000 (credit). During the period, it had net credit sales of $800,000 and collections of $723,000. It wrote off accounts receivable of $21,000. However, a $3,500 account written off as uncollectible was recovered before the end of the current period. Uncollectible accounts are estimated to total $16,000 at the end of the period.

Record receivables and bad
debts transactions; show balance
sheet presentation.
(SO 1, 2)

Instructions

(a) Prepare the entries to record sales and collections during the period.
(b) Prepare the entry to record the write-off of uncollectible accounts during the period.
(c) Prepare the entries to record the recovery of the uncollectible account during the period.
(d) Prepare the entry to record bad debts expense for the period.
(e) Determine the ending balances in Accounts Receivable and Allowance for Doubtful Accounts.
(f) Show the balance sheet presentation of the receivables at the end of the period.

Determine missing amounts.
(SO 1, 2)

P8–3B   Yasukuni Corporation reported the following information in its general ledger at June 30:

Accounts Receivable				Sales	
Beg. bal.	(f)	46,000			(d)
	45,000	(e)			
End. bal.	4,500				

Allowance for Doubtful Accounts				Bad Debts Expense	
		Beg. bal.	200	(c)	
	50	(b)			
		End. bal.	(a)		

All sales were on account. At the end of the year, uncollectible accounts were estimated to total $225 based on an aging schedule.

Instructions

Using your knowledge of receivables transactions, determine the missing amounts. (*Hint:* You may find it helpful to reconstruct the journal entries.)

Calculate bad debt amounts.
(SO 2)

P8–4B   Here is information for Volkov Ltd. for the year ended April 30, 2006:

Total credit sales	$2,000,000
Accounts receivable at April 30	800,000
Accounts receivable written off	35,000
Accounts receivable later recovered	5,000

Instructions

(a) What amount of bad debts expense will Volkov report if it does *not* use the allowance method of accounting for bad debts?

(b) Assume that Volkov decides to estimate its uncollectible accounts using the allowance method and an aging schedule. Uncollectible accounts are estimated to be $60,000. What amount of bad debts expense will Volkov record if Allowance for Doubtful Accounts has an opening credit balance of $4,000 on May 1, 2005?

(c) Assume the same facts as in part (b) except that there is a $4,000 opening debit balance in Allowance for Doubtful Accounts. What amount of bad debts expense will Volkov record?

(d) What are the advantages of using the allowance method of reporting bad debts expense?

Record bad debts transactions.
(SO 2)

P8–5B   Imagine Corporation produced the following aging schedule of its accounts receivable at year end:

	Total	Number of Days Outstanding			
		0–30	31–60	61–90	Over 90
Accounts receivable	$385,000	$220,000	$100,000	$40,000	$25,000
Estimated percentage uncollectible		1%	5%	10%	20%
Estimated bad debts					

The unadjusted balance in Allowance for Doubtful Accounts is a debit of $10,000.

Instructions

(a) Complete the aging schedule and calculate the total estimated bad debts from the above information.

(b) Prepare the adjusting journal entry to record the bad debts using the information determined in (a).

(c) In the following year, $6,500 of the outstanding receivables is determined to be specifically uncollectible. Prepare the journal entry to write off the uncollectible amount.

(d) The company subsequently collects $3,000 of the $6,500 that was determined to be uncollectible in (c). Prepare the journal entries to restore the $6,500 account receivable and record the partial cash collection.

(e) Comment on how your answers in (a) to (d) would change if Imagine used a percentage of total accounts receivable of 4%, rather than aging the accounts.

(f) What are the advantages to the company of aging the accounts receivable rather than applying a percentage to total accounts receivable?

P8–6B The following selected transactions are for Vu Ltd. Vu has a September 30 year end and adjusts its accounts annually.

Record receivables transactions.
(SO 1, 3)

Jan. 1 Loaned Emily Collis, an employee, $12,000 on a four-month, 8% note. Interest is due at maturity.

    5 Sold $16,000 of merchandise to Asiz Limited, terms n/15. The merchandise cost $9,600.

  20 Accepted Asiz Limited's two-month, 9%, $16,000 note for its balance due. Interest is due monthly.

Feb. 18 Sold $8,000 of merchandise costing $4,800 to Swaim Corp. Accepted Swaim's six-month, 7% note in payment. Interest is due at maturity.

  20 Collected interest on Asiz note.

Mar. 20 Collected principal and interest for the month on the Asiz note.

May 1 Received payment in full from Emily Collis.

  25 Accepted Avery Inc.'s three-month, 8%, $6,000 note in settlement of a past-due balance on account. Interest is due at maturity.

Aug. 18 Received payment in full from Swaim Corp. on its note due.

  25 The Avery note was dishonoured. Eventual payment is not expected.

Sept. 30 Adjusted any accrued interest at year end.

Instructions

Record the transactions.

P8–7B On July 31, 2006, a company accepted a two-month, 4%, $50,000 note from a customer in settlement of the customer's account. Interest is due at maturity. The company's year end is August 31. The company makes adjusting entries annually.

Record notes receivable transactions.
(SO 3)

Instructions

(a) Prepare all journal entries for the company over the life of the note. Assume that the customer settles the note in full on the maturity date.

(b) Assume that instead of honouring the note at maturity, the customer dishonours it. Prepare the necessary journal entry at the maturity date, September 30, 2006, assuming that eventual collection of the note is (1) expected, and (2) not expected.

P8–8B Hudson's Bay Company reports the following assets at January 31, 2004 (in millions):

Prepare assets section of balance sheet.
(SO 4)

Accumulated amortization—buildings	$ 158.5
Accumulated amortization—equipment and other	1,287.1
Allowance for doubtful credit cards	31.5
Buildings	318.0
Cash in stores	8.0
Credit card receivables	570.3
Equipment and other assets	2,162.9
Goodwill	152.3
Land	54.1
Merchandise inventories	1,485.1
Other accounts receivable	64.8
Other assets	517.7
Prepaid expenses and other current assets	78.7
Secured receivables (noncurrent)	7.1
Short-term deposits	168.9

Instructions

Prepare the assets section of the Hudson's Bay Company's balance sheet.

P8–9B During April, the following selected transactions occurred for the Orient Retail Corporation:

Record receivables and credit and debit card transactions.
(SO 1, 5)

Apr. 1 Sold $3,800 of merchandise for cash. The cost of the goods sold was $2,300.

  7 Sold merchandise of $6,800 on Orient Retail credit cards. The cost of the goods sold was $4,000.

  12 Performed services for $1,700, paid for with MasterCard credit cards. The credit card service charge was 3%.

  12 Sold merchandise for $2,200, paid for with American Express credit cards. The cost of goods sold was $1,320 and the credit card service charge was 3%.

Apr. 14 Submitted American Express credit card slips received on April 12 to American Express for payment.

18 Performed services for $2,000 on account, terms 1/10, n/30.

20 Sold $2,800 of merchandise to customers, who paid with their debit cards. The cost of goods sold was $1,700 and the bank service charge was 2%.

27 Collected amount owing from April 18 transaction.

29 Received the American Express cheque for the April 14 billing, less the service charge.

30 Added $150 of interest to overdue Orient Retail credit card account holders.

30 Submitted Orient Retail credit card slips accumulated to date to the credit card division for payment.

Instructions

Record the transactions.

Calculate and interpret ratios.
(SO 5)

P8–10B Presented here is basic financial information (in millions) from the 2004 annual reports of Rogers Communications Inc. and Shaw Communications Inc.:

	Rogers	Shaw
Net sales	$5,608.2	$2,079.7
Allowance for doubtful accounts, Jan. 1	75.7	22.7
Allowance for doubtful accounts, Dec. 31	94.9	23.0
Accounts receivable (gross), Jan. 1	626.5	166.7
Accounts receivable (gross), Dec. 31	768.0	142.5

Instructions

Calculate the receivables turnover and average collection period for both companies, assuming all sales are credit sales. The industry average for the receivables turnover was 12.8 times and the average collection period was 29 days. Comment on the difference in the companies' collection experiences.

Evaluate liquidity.
(SO 5)

P8–11B The following ratios are available for Tianjin Inc.:

	2006	2005	2004
Current ratio	1.5:1	1.5:1	1.5:1
Receivables turnover	6 times	7 times	8 times
Inventory turnover	8 times	7 times	6 times

Instructions

(a) Is Tianjin's short-term liquidity improving or worsening? Explain.

(b) Do changes in turnover ratios affect profitability? Explain.

(c) Identify any steps that the company may wish to consider to improve its management of its receivables or inventory.

BROADENING YOUR PERSPECTIVE

Financial Reporting and Analysis

Analysis Tools

Financial Reporting Problem: Loblaw

BYP8–1 Refer to the financial statements of Loblaw and the accompanying notes to its financial statements in Appendix A.

Instructions

(a) Assuming that all sales are credit sales, and using net receivables instead of gross receivables, calculate the receivables turnover and average collection period for 2003.

(b) What is Loblaw's policy on writing off uncollectible credit card receivables. (*Hint*: Review Note 1 to the financial statements.)

(c) Does Loblaw securitize any of its credit card receivables? If so, calculate the percentage of credit card receivables that it securitized in 2003. (*Hint*: Review Note 6 to the financial statements.)

(d) What conclusions can you draw about Loblaw's management of its receivables from parts (a) to (c)?

Comparative Analysis Problem: Loblaw and Sobeys

BYP8–2   The financial statements of Sobeys are presented in Appendix B, following the financial statements for Loblaw in Appendix A.

Instructions

(a) What types of receivables does each company report in its balance sheet?

(b) Calculate the following for each company for its most recent fiscal year. The industry average is shown in parentheses.
   1. Current ratio (1:1)
   2. Receivables turnover (21.9 times) (assume all sales were credit sales and use net receivables instead of gross receivables)
   3. Average collection period (17 days)

(c) What conclusions about each company's liquidity and management of accounts receivable can be drawn from your calculations in (b)?

Research Case

BYP8–3   The December 6, 2004, edition of *MacLean's* magazine includes an article on page 40 by Steve Maich entitled "Hip Deep in Hock." The article addresses the increase in personal debt and the consequential vulnerability to shifts in interest rates.

Instructions

Read the article and answer the following questions.

(a) According to the Bank of Canada, what is the collective debt of Canadian consumers? How does this compare to debt and disposable income levels ten years ago?

(b) How does the rate of savings in 2003 compare to that of 1985? How does the rate of savings help or hurt consumers and corporations deal with changes in interest rates and recessions?

(c) Why would companies looking to sell on credit be interested in consumers' personal income, savings, and debt levels?

Interpreting Financial Statements

BYP8–4   Suncor Energy Inc. reported the following information (in millions) in its 2004 financial statements:

	2004	2003	2002
Total current assets	$1,195	$1,279	$ 722
Total current liabilities	1,409	1,060	797
Operating revenues (assume all credit)	8,226	6,289	4,883
Accounts receivable (gross)	630	509	406
Allowance for doubtful accounts	3	4	3
Cost of goods sold	2,867	1,686	1,156
Inventory	423	371	266

Additional detail about Suncor's receivables includes the following:

The company has a securitization program in place to sell, on a revolving, fully serviced, and limited recourse basis, up to $170 million of accounts receivable having a maturity of 45 days or less, to a third party. As at December 31, 2004, $170 million in outstanding accounts receivable had been sold under the program.

Instructions

(a) Calculate the current ratio, receivables turnover, and inventory turnover for 2004 and 2003. Comment on Suncor's liquidity.
(b) In 2004, Suncor's dollar amount of its allowance for doubtful accounts was the same as it was in 2002. Comment on the relevance of this as a percentage of accounts receivable.
(c) Suncor regularly securitizes a portion of its accounts receivable. Comment on this practice as part of Suncor's management of its accounts receivable.

A Global Focus

BYP8–5 The Saskatchewan Wheat Pool is Canada's largest grain company. It reports the following information (in thousands) for its accounts receivables in its 2004 financial statements:

	2004	2003
Accounts receivable		
Trade accounts, net	$ 74,449	$ 72,710
The Canadian Wheat Board	71,266	137,624
Other accounts	18,519	11,803
	164,234	222,137
Total current assets	324,473	397,690

SASKATCHEWAN WHEAT POOL
Notes to the Consolidated Financial Statements
July 31, 2004

Note 23. **Financial and Other Instruments and Hedging**

a) Credit Risk

The company is exposed to credit risk from customers in all the business segments. In the Grain Handling and Marketing segment, a significant amount is receivable from The Canadian Wheat Board (see Note 6). The customer base in all other segments is diverse, which minimizes significant concentration of credit risk. Credit risk is limited due to the large number of customers in differing industries and geographic areas.

Instructions

(a) Is The Canadian Wheat Board's receivable amount a significant component of the company's total accounts receivable? Of total current assets?
(b) Evaluate the Saskatchewan Wheat Pool's credit risk.
(c) Comment on the information value of the Saskatchewan Wheat Pool's Note 23 (a) on credit risk.

Financial Analysis on the Web

Analysis Tools
(Financial Analysis on the Web)

BYP8–6 This case examines the Credit Card Costs Calculator, provided by the Office of Consumer Affairs, Industry Canada. Based on how a credit card is used, we will determine which cards cost the least in interest and fees over a year. The cost of borrowing from a bank is then compared to the cost of using a credit card.

Instructions

Specific requirements of this Web case can be found on the Toolkit website.

Critical Thinking

Collaborative Learning Activity

BYP8–7   From its inception, Campus Fashions Ltd. has sold merchandise for cash or on account, but no credit cards have been accepted. During the past several months, the management of Campus Fashions has begun to question its credit-sales policies. First, Campus Fashions has lost some sales because management refuses to accept credit cards. Second, representatives of two banks have convinced management to accept their national credit cards for a credit card fee of 3%.

Management decided that it should determine the cost of carrying its own in-house credit card. These data are from the accounting records of the past three years:

	2006	2005	2004
Net credit sales	$530,000	$650,000	$400,000
Collection agency fees for slow-paying customers	2,600	2,500	2,400
Salary of part-time accounts receivable clerk	4,500	4,300	4,100

Credit and collection expenses as a percentage of net credit sales are as follows: uncollectible accounts 1.6%; billing and mailing costs 0.5%; and credit investigation fee on new customers 0.1%. The company also determines that the average accounts receivable balance outstanding during the year is 5% of net credit sales. Management estimates that it could earn an average of 5% annually on cash invested in other business opportunities.

Instructions

With the class divided into groups, do the following:

(a) Prepare a table showing total credit and collection expenses in dollars and as a percentage of net credit sales for each year.
(b) Determine the net credit and collection expenses in dollars and as a percentage of sales after considering the revenue not earned from other investment opportunities.
(c) Discuss both the financial and non-financial factors that are relevant to the decision.

Communication Activity

BYP8–8   Toys for Big Boys sells snowmobiles, personal watercraft, ATVs, and the like. Recently, the credit manager of Toys for Big Boys retired. The sales staff threw him a big retirement party—they were glad to see him go, because they felt his credit policies restricted their selling ability. The sales staff convinced management that there was no need to replace the credit manager, since they could handle this responsibility in addition to their sales positions.

Management was thrilled at year end when sales doubled. However, gross accounts receivable also quadrupled and cash flow halved. Its average collection period increased from 30 days to 90 days.

Instructions

In a memo to management, explain the internal control and financial impact of allowing the sales staff to manage the credit function. Has the business assumed any additional credit risk? What would you recommend the company do to better manage its increasing accounts receivable?

Ethics Case

BYP8–9   The controller of Proust Corporation has completed an aging schedule, using the following percentages to estimate the uncollectible accounts: 0–30 days, 5%; 31–60 days, 10%; 61–90 days, 30%; and over 90 days, 50%. The president of the company, Suzanne Bros, is nervous because the bank expects the company to sustain its current growth rate of at least 5% over the next two years—the remaining term of its bank loan. President Bros suggests that

www.wiley.com/canada/kimmel

Ethics In Accounting

the controller increase the percentages, which will increase the amount of the required bad debts expense adjustment. The president thinks that the lower net earnings (because of the increased bad debts expense) will make it easier next year to show a better growth rate.

Instructions

(a) Who are the stakeholders in this case?

(b) Does the president's request pose an ethical dilemma for the controller?

(c) Should the controller be concerned with the company's growth rate in estimating the allowance? Explain.

Serial Problem

(*Note*: This is a continuation of the serial problem from Chapters 1 through 7.)

BYP8-10   Natalie has been approached by one of her friends, Curtis Lesperance. Curtis runs a coffee shop, Curtis's Coffee Ltd., where he sells specialty coffees, and prepares and sells muffins and cookies. He is anxious to purchase a deluxe European mixer from Cookie Creations Ltd. in order to prepare larger batches of muffins and cookies. Curtis's Coffee, however, cannot afford to pay for the mixer for at least 30 days. Curtis has asked Natalie if Cookie Creations would be willing to sell his company the mixer on credit.

Natalie comes to you for advice and asks the following questions:

1. Curtis has provided me with the most recent financial statements of Curtis's Coffee Ltd. What calculations should I do with the data from these statements and what questions should I ask him after I have analyzed the financial statements? How will this information help me decide if I should extend credit to Curtis's Coffee?

2. Is there another alternative other than extending credit to Curtis's Coffee for 30 days?

3. I am seriously thinking about allowing Cookie Creations's customers to use credit cards. What are some of the advantages and disadvantages of Cookie Creations' customers' paying by credit card?

Natalie continues to record the transactions of Cookie Creations Ltd. on her own. She did not hire her friend John to perform the accounting functions. The following transactions occurred between the months of June and August, 2006:

June 1 A mixer is sold on credit to Curtis's Coffee, for $1,025. The credit terms are n/30. The original cost of the mixer is $566.

        2 A credit card account with a bank is established for Cookie Creations. In payment, the bank will deduct from Cookie Creations' bank account a monthly equipment rental fee of $75, in addition to 3% of each credit card sales transaction.

       30 Natalie teaches 12 classes in June. Seven classes were paid for in cash, $875; the remaining five classes were paid for by credit card, $750.

       30 Curtis calls Natalie. Curtis's Coffee is unable to pay the amount outstanding for another month. The company converts its account receivable into a note receivable, signing a one-month, 8.25% promissory note.

       30 Natalie reconciles Cookie Creations' bank account. The bank account has been correctly charged for the rental of the credit card equipment, $75, and the 3% fee on all credit card transactions processed by the bank.

July 14 A mixer is sold to one of Curtis's friends for $1,025. The mixer is paid for by credit card. The cost of the mixer is $566.

       31 Natalie teaches 15 classes in July. Eight classes are paid for in cash, $1,000; and seven classes are paid for by credit card, $1,050.

       31 Natalie reconciles the bank account of Cookie Creations Ltd. The bank account has been correctly charged for the rental of the credit card equipment and the credit card sales.

       31 Curtis calls Natalie. Curtis's Coffee Ltd. is unable to pay its note receivable today but hopes to be able to pay by the end of the week. Natalie prepares the appropriate journal entry.

Aug. 10 Curtis calls again and promises that the outstanding account with Cookie Creations will be paid by the end of August, including interest for two months.

       31 A cheque is received from Curtis's Coffee in payment of the balance owed, including interest.

Instructions

(a) Answer Natalie's questions.

(b) Record the above transactions.

Answers to Self-Study Questions

1. b   2. b   3. d   4. d   5. b   6. d   7. a   8. a   9. c   10. a

Answer to Loblaw Review It Question 1

Loblaw reports accounts receivable in the current assets section of its balance sheet. In the noncurrent assets section of its balance sheet, Loblaw reports future income taxes recoverable. Within other assets, also in the noncurrent assets section of the balance sheet, Loblaw reports franchise investments and other receivables, unrealized equity forwards receivable, and unrealized cross currency basis swaps receivable.

Remember to go back to the Navigator box at the beginning of the chapter to check off your completed work.

CHAPTER 9

Reporting and Analyzing Long-Lived Assets

Tumult in the Skies

Air Canada has experienced a lot of turbulence in recent years. In 2000, things looked bright with the acquisition of insolvent Canadian Airlines. But, three years later, Air Canada itself was seeking bankruptcy protection, having suffered from increased competition from discount carriers like WestJet, as well as the fallout from the terrorist attacks of September 11, 2001, the Iraq war, and the SARS outbreak—all of which significantly reduced travel in general.

Canada's largest airline then re-emerged from bankruptcy protection in October 2004 as a restructured and streamlined air carrier. But the twists and turns this story has taken in the past five years have left everyone wondering what's going to happen next.

The 2004 restructuring plan focused on reducing operating costs, strengthening the balance sheet, and reorganizing the corporate structure. Air Canada had reduced its debt from approximately $12 billion to less than $5 billion. It also raised $1.1 billion in new equity capital and had approximately $1.9 billion of cash on hand.

Various businesses segments, including Air Canada Jazz, Destina.ca, Touram, Air Canada Technical Services, Air Canada Cargo, and Air Canada Groundhandling, now operate as separate legal entities under parent holding company ACE Aviation Holdings Inc.

The airline no longer flies older F-28, DC-9, B737, and B747 aircraft, having replaced them with newer, more fuel-efficient aircraft and aircraft better able to handle longer-range, nonstop flights. In doing so, it reduced the number of aircraft types to save on maintenance, spare parts inventory, and crew training.

Along with the restructuring came the unveiling of a new look for the airline, including an updated design and colour scheme for its fleet; new uniforms for its 6,700 flight attendants and 2,900 airport customer service agents; a new in-flight entertainment system; and lie-flat seats for international, executive-class passengers.

The changes were to be introduced over the course of 2005 both "strategically and economically" in order to minimize costs. Painting the airplanes would take place over two years, according to the airline's regular maintenance program. The marketing campaign was also produced within existing marketing budgets.

Air Canada has come a long way since Trans-Canada Airlines, its predecessor, was launched in 1937. And the company has been able to reposition itself several times since it changed from a Crown corporation to a public company in 1989. We'll have to keep an eye on the skies to see how well these latest developments fly for both the company and its shareholders.

Air Canada: www.aircanada.com

THE NAVIGATOR

- [ ] Read *Feature Story*
- [ ] Scan *Study Objectives*
- [ ] Read *Chapter Preview*
- [ ] Read text and answer *Before You Go On*
- [ ] Work *Using the Decision Toolkit*
- [ ] Review *Summary of Study Objectives*
- [ ] Review the *Decision Toolkit—A Summary*
- [ ] Work *Demonstration Problem*
- [ ] Answer *Self-Study Questions*
- [ ] Complete assignments

STUDY OBJECTIVES

After studying this chapter, you should be able to:

1. Describe how the cost principle applies to property, plant, and equipment.
2. Explain the concept of, and calculate, amortization.
3. Describe other accounting issues related to amortization.
4. Explain how to account for the disposal of property, plant, and equipment.
5. Identify the basic issues related to accounting for intangible assets.
6. Indicate how long-lived assets are reported in the financial statements.
7. Describe the methods for evaluating the use of assets.
8. Calculate amortization using the declining-balance method and the units-of-activity method (Appendix 9A).

the navigator

For airlines and many other companies, making the right decisions about long-lived assets is critical because these assets represent huge investments. These decisions include what assets to acquire and when, how to finance the acquisitions, how to account for the assets, and when to dispose of them, among others.

In this chapter, we address these and other issues surrounding long-lived assets. Our discussion of long-lived assets is presented in two parts: tangible assets and intangible assets. *Tangible* assets are the property, plant, and equipment (physical assets) that commonly come to mind when we think of a company. Tangible assets can also include natural resources, such as mineral deposits, oil and gas reserves, and timber. In addition to tangible assets, a company may have many important *intangible* assets. These are long-lived assets, such as goodwill, copyrights, and patents, that have no physical substance but are valuable and vital to a company's success.

The chapter is organized as follows:

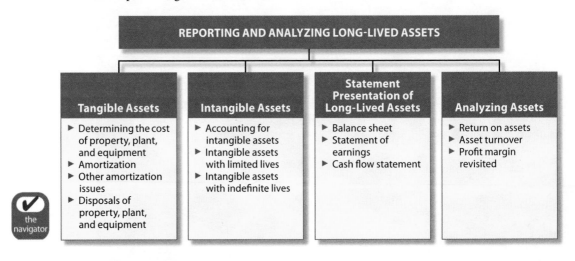

REPORTING AND ANALYZING LONG-LIVED ASSETS

Tangible Assets	Intangible Assets	Statement Presentation of Long-Lived Assets	Analyzing Assets
▶ Determining the cost of property, plant, and equipment ▶ Amortization ▶ Other amortization issues ▶ Disposals of property, plant, and equipment	▶ Accounting for intangible assets ▶ Intangible assets with limited lives ▶ Intangible assets with indefinite lives	▶ Balance sheet ▶ Statement of earnings ▶ Cash flow statement	▶ Return on assets ▶ Asset turnover ▶ Profit margin revisited

the navigator

Tangible Assets

Long-lived **tangible assets** are resources that have physical substance (a definite size and shape), are used in the operations of a business, and are not intended for sale to customers. Contrary to current assets, which are used or consumed in the current accounting period, long-lived tangible assets provide benefits over many years.

Tangible assets can be subdivided into two categories: (1) property, plant, and equipment, and (2) natural resources. With a few exceptions, the accounting for property, plant, and equipment and natural resources is similar. We will focus on property, plant, and equipment in this chapter and leave the discussion of natural resources for another accounting course.

Property, plant, and equipment are identifiable, long-lived tangible assets that the company owns and uses for the production and sale of goods or services to customers. These are critical to a company's success because they determine the company's production capacity and ability to satisfy customers. With too few planes, for example, Air Canada would lose customers to its competitors. With too many planes, it would be flying with a lot of empty seats. Management must constantly monitor its needs and adjust its assets accordingly. Not doing this can result in lost business opportunities or inefficient use of existing assets, and is likely to bring about poor financial results.

Many companies have large investments in property, plant, and equipment. Illustration 9-1 shows the percentages of net property, plant, and equipment in relation to total assets in several companies.

Alternative terminology
Property, plant, and equipment are also commonly known as *fixed assets, capital assets,* and *land, buildings, and equipment.*

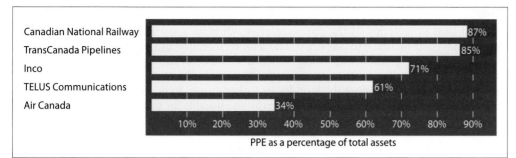

Canadian National Railway	87%
TransCanada Pipelines	85%
Inco	71%
TELUS Communications	61%
Air Canada	34%

PPE as a percentage of total assets

Illustration 9-1 ◀

Property, plant, and equipment (PPE) as a percentage of total assets

Determining the Cost of Property, Plant, and Equipment

The **cost principle** requires that property, plant, and equipment be recorded at cost. Thus, the new planes that Air Canada purchased are recorded at cost. Cost consists of all expenditures that are necessary to acquire an asset and make it ready for its intended use. For example, the purchase price, the freight costs, and any testing or installation costs paid by Air Canada are all considered part of the cost of the aircraft. All these costs are **capitalized** (recorded as property, plant, and equipment), rather than expensed, because they will provide benefits over more than one period.

Determining which costs to include in a long-lived asset account and which costs not to include is very important. Costs which benefit only the current period are expensed. Such costs are referred to as **operating expenditures**. Costs that benefit future periods are included in a long-lived asset account. These are referred to as **capital expenditures**.

This distinction is important because it has immediate, and often material, implications for the statement of earnings. In order to boost current earnings, some companies have been known to improperly capitalize expenditures that should have been expensed. For example, suppose that $10,000 of maintenance costs is improperly capitalized to a building account; that is, the costs are included in the asset account Buildings rather than being expensed immediately. If the cost of the building is being amortized over a 40-year life, then the maintenance cost of $10,000 will be incorrectly spread across 40 years instead of being expensed in the current year. Current-year expenses will be understated, and net earnings and total assets will be overstated. Future-year expenses will be overstated, and net earnings and total assets will be understated. Thus, determining which costs to capitalize and which to expense is very important.

study objective 1

Describe how the cost principle applies to property, plant, and equipment.

ACCOUNTING MATTERS! Ethics Perspective

In what is being heralded as one of the largest accounting frauds in history, WorldCom, a global communications company operating in more than 65 countries, improperly capitalized U.S. $7.2 billion of expenses. This accounting fraud artificially boosted WorldCom's net earnings by U.S. $5 billion for fiscal 2001 and the first quarter of 2002. If these expenses had been recorded properly as operating expenditures, WorldCom would have reported a net loss for 2001, as well as for the first quarter of 2002. Instead, WorldCom reported net earnings of $1.4 billion for 2001 and $130 million for the first quarter of 2002. Former WorldCom CEO Bernard Ebbers has since been indicted and found guilty on charges of fraud, conspiracy, and filing false documents with regulators.

Property, plant, and equipment is often subdivided into four classes:

1. **Land**, such as a building site
2. **Land improvements**, such as driveways, parking lots, fences, and underground sprinkler systems
3. **Buildings**, such as stores, offices, factories, and warehouses
3. **Equipment**, such as store checkout counters, cash registers, coolers, office furniture, factory machinery, and delivery equipment

How the cost principle is applied to each of the major classes of property, plant, and equipment is explained in the following sections.

Land

The cost of land includes (1) the purchase price, (2) closing costs such as survey and legal fees, and (3) costs incurred to prepare the land for its intended use, such as the removal of old buildings, clearing, grading, and filling. When land has been purchased to construct a building, all costs incurred up to the excavation for the new building are considered to be part of the costs necessary to prepare the land for its intended use. In other words, if the land has a building on it that must be removed to make the site suitable for construction of a new building, all demolition and removal costs, less any proceeds from salvaged materials, are recorded as capital expenditures in the Land account.

To illustrate, assume that the Brochu Corporation acquires real estate at a cost of $100,000. The property contains an old warehouse that is torn down at a net cost of $6,000 ($7,500 in costs less $1,500 in proceeds from salvaged materials). Additional expenditures are incurred for the legal fee of $1,000. Put together, these factors make the cost of the land $107,000, calculated as follows:

Cash price of property	$100,000
Net cost of removing warehouse	6,000
Legal fee	1,000
Cost of land	$107,000

When the acquisition is recorded, Land is debited for $107,000 and Cash is credited for $107,000 (assuming the expenditures were paid in cash). Once the land is ready for its intended use, recurring costs, such as annual property taxes, are recorded as operating expenditures—in other words, these costs are matched against the revenues the land helps generate.

Land Improvements

Land is a unique long-lived asset. Its cost is not amortized—allocated over its useful life—because land has an unlimited useful life. However, costs are often incurred for certain items related to land that do have limited useful lives. The costs of structural additions made to land, such as driveways, sidewalks, fences, and parking lots, are recorded separately as land improvements.

Land improvements decline in service potential over time, and require maintenance and replacement to keep their value. Because of this, these costs are recorded separately from land as land improvements and are amortized over their useful lives.

Buildings

All costs related to the purchase or construction of a building are charged to the Buildings account. When a building is **purchased**, such costs include the purchase price and closing costs. Costs to make the building ready for its intended use can include expenditures for re-modelling rooms and offices, and for replacing or repairing the roof, floors, electrical wiring, and plumbing.

When a new building is **constructed**, its cost consists of the contract price plus payments made for architect fees, building permits, and excavation costs. In addition, interest costs incurred to finance a construction project are included in the cost of the asset when a significant period of time is required to get the asset ready for use. In these circumstances, interest costs are considered as necessary as materials and labour. The inclusion of interest costs in the cost of a constructed building is limited to interest costs during the construction period. When construction has been completed, future interest payments on funds borrowed to finance the construction are recorded as operating expenditures by increases (debits) to Interest Expense.

Equipment

The "equipment" classification is a broad one that can include delivery equipment, office equipment, machinery, vehicles, furniture and fixtures, and other similar assets. The cost of such assets consists of the purchase price, freight charges, insurance during transit paid by the purchaser, and expenditures required in assembling, installing, and testing the equipment.

Annual costs such as licences and insurance are treated as operating expenditures as they are incurred, because they are recurring expenditures and do not benefit future periods. Two criteria apply in determining the cost of equipment: (1) the frequency of the cost (one-time or recurring) and (2) the benefit period (the life of the asset or less than one year).

To illustrate, assume that Lenard Ltd. purchases a used delivery truck for $32,000. Related expenditures are for painting and lettering, $500, motor vehicle licence, $80, and a one-year accident insurance policy, $1,600. The cost of the delivery truck is $32,500, calculated as follows:

Cash price	$32,000
Painting and lettering	500
Cost of delivery truck	$32,500

The cost of a motor vehicle licence is treated as an expense, and the cost of an insurance policy is considered a prepaid expense (a current asset). The entry to record the purchase of the truck and related expenditures, assuming all were paid in cash, is as follows:

Delivery Truck ($32,000 + $500)	32,500	
Licence Expense	80	
Prepaid Insurance	1,600	
Cash ($32,000 + $500 + $80 + $1,600)		34,180
(To record purchase of delivery truck and related expenditures)		

A = L + SE
+32,500
+1,600
−34,180   −80
↓ Cash flows: −34,180

Asset Retirement Costs

In some companies, there are significant costs for the eventual retirement of their long-lived assets. For example, a nuclear power plant must be decommissioned at the end of its useful life. The costs to decommission the Point Lepreau, New Brunswick, nuclear generating station are estimated at $478 million. Costs such as these are estimated in advance (using present-value concepts) and recorded as part of the asset cost. The other side of the entry records a liability for the asset retirement obligation.

While we will leave a more detailed discussion of asset retirement costs and their associated liabilities to a future accounting course, students should be aware that the cost of property, plant, and equipment will often include amounts for the retirement of the asset.

To Buy or Lease?

In this chapter, we focus on assets that are purchased, but we would like to give you a brief look at an alternative to purchasing—leasing. The Canadian Finance & Leasing Association estimated that nearly 25 percent of new property, plant, and equipment purchased in a recent year was financed by lease. In a lease, a party that owns an asset (the **lessor**) agrees to allow another party (the **lessee**) to use the asset for an agreed period of time at an agreed price.

Here are some advantages of leasing an asset versus purchasing it:

1. **Reduced risk of obsolescence.** Obsolescence is the process by which an asset becomes out of date before it physically wears out. Frequently, lease terms allow the party using the asset (the lessee) to exchange the asset for a more modern or technologically capable asset if it becomes outdated. This is much easier than trying to sell an obsolete asset.
2. **100-percent financing.** To purchase an asset, most companies must borrow money, which usually requires a down payment of at least 20 percent. Leasing an asset does not require any money down, which helps to conserve cash. In addition, interest payments are often fixed for the term of the lease, unlike other financing which often has a floating interest rate.
3. **Income tax advantages.** When a company owns an amortizable asset, it can only deduct the amortization expense (called capital cost allowance for income tax purposes) on its income tax return. (We will learn more about capital cost allowance in a later section of this chapter.) However, when a company leases an asset, it can deduct 100 percent of the lease payment on its income tax return.

4. **Off–balance sheet financing.** Many companies prefer to keep assets and, especially, liabilities off their books. Certain types of leases, called an **operating lease**, allow the lessee to account for the transaction as a rental with neither an asset nor a liability recorded. This is known as **off–balance sheet financing**, which is discussed in Chapter 10.

Under another type of lease, a **capital lease**, both the asset and the liability are shown on the balance sheet. On the lessee's balance sheet, the leased item is shown as an asset and the obligation owed to the lessor is shown as a liability. In addition, the leased asset is amortized by the lessee just as other long-lived assets are. Distinguishing between, and accounting for, operating and capital leases can be complex. Further detail will be deferred to an intermediate accounting course.

Companies often incur costs when they renovate leased property. These leasehold improvements are normally attached to the property and belong to the lessor at the end of the lease. These costs are charged to a separate account called Leasehold Improvements, and amortized over the remaining life of the lease or the useful life of the improvements, whichever is shorter.

Air Canada has made leasehold improvements to facilities it has under lease and reports a balance of $510 million for its buildings and leasehold improvements in its 2004 balance sheet. In addition, Air Canada leases the majority of its airplanes. In 2004, it reporting having 35 aircraft under capital lease. These aircraft appear on Air Canada's balance sheet as property and equipment in the amount of $1.7 billion. The majority of Air Canada's planes, however, are accounted for under operating leases. Because operating leases are accounted for as rentals, these planes do not appear on its balance sheet and are instead disclosed in the notes to the financial statements. That is one of the reasons why, in Illustration 9-1, Air Canada appears to have such a low percentage (34 percent) of property, plant, and equipment as a proportion of total assets in comparison to other companies.

BEFORE YOU GO ON . . .

▶Review It

1. What are long-lived assets? What are the major classes of property, plant, and equipment?
2. What types of costs are included in each major class of property, plant, and equipment?
3. Distinguish between operating expenditures and capital expenditures.
4. What are the main advantages of leasing?

▶Do It

Assume that $50,000 of factory machinery is purchased on February 4. A $20,000 down payment is made and a $30,000 note is issued for the balance. Cash expenditures that relate to this purchase include insurance during shipping, $100; the annual insurance policy, $750; and installation and testing costs, $500. Prepare the journal entry to record these expenditures.

Action Plan

- Capitalize expenditures that are made to get the machinery ready for its intended use.
- Expense operating costs that benefit only the current period, or which are recurring expenditures.

Solution

Feb. 3	Factory Machinery ($50,000 + $100 + $500)	50,600	
	Prepaid Insurance	750	
	Cash ($20,000 + $100 + $750 + $500)		21,350
	Note Payable		30,000
	(To record purchase of factory machinery and		
	related expenditures)		

the navigator

Amortization

As we learned in Chapter 4, **amortization is the process of allocating the cost of a long-lived asset to expense over the asset's useful (service) life in a rational and systematic way.** The cost is allocated in this way so that expenses are properly matched with revenues in accordance with the matching principle.

Let's briefly review what we've learned to date about amortization. Amortization is allocated through an adjusting journal entry which debits Amortization Expense and credits Accumulated Amortization. Amortization Expense is a statement of earnings account; Accumulated Amortization appears on the balance sheet as a contra asset account. This contra asset account is similar in purpose to the one used in Chapter 8 for the allowance for doubtful accounts. Both contra accounts reduce assets to their carrying values: the net realizable value for accounts receivable, and the net book value for tangible assets.

Recognizing amortization for an asset does not accumulate cash to replace the asset. The balance in Accumulated Amortization only represents the total amount of the asset's cost that has been allocated to expense to date: it is not a cash fund. Cash is not affected by the adjusting entry to record amortization.

It is important to understand that **amortization is a process of cost allocation, not a process of asset valuation**. No attempt is made to measure the change in an asset's market value while it is owned, because property, plant, and equipment are not held for resale. Current market values are not relevant (unless a permanent impairment loss has occurred, which we will discuss later in this chapter). So the net book value—cost less accumulated amortization—of property, plant, and equipment may be very different from its market value. In fact, if an asset is fully amortized, it can have zero book value but still have a large market value.

study objective 2

Explain the concept of, and calculate, amortization.

Animated Tutorials (Amortization)

Alternative Terminology
Amortization is also commonly known as *depreciation*.

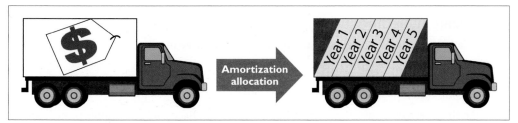

Illustration 9-2 ◀

Amortization as an allocation concept

Amortization applies to three classes of property, plant, and equipment: land improvements, buildings, and equipment. Each of these classes is considered an amortizable asset because the usefulness to the company and the revenue-producing ability of each class decrease over the asset's useful life. Amortization does not apply to land, because the usefulness and revenue-producing ability of land generally remain intact as long as the land is owned. In fact, in many cases, the usefulness of land increases over time because of the scarcity of good sites. Thus, land is not an amortizable asset.

During an amortizable asset's useful life, its revenue-producing ability declines because of **physical factors,** such as wear and tear. A delivery truck that has been driven 100,000 kilometres will be less useful to a company than one driven only 1,000 kilometres.

A decline in revenue-producing ability may also occur because of **economic factors,** such as obsolescence. For example, many companies replace their computers long before they wear out, because improvements in hardware and software make their old computers obsolete. It is important to understand that amortization only approximates the decline in revenue-producing ability. It cannot measure the true effects of physical or economic factors.

Factors in Calculating Amortization

Three factors affect the calculation of amortization:

1. **Cost.** Factors that affect the cost of an amortizable asset were explained earlier in this chapter. Remember that property, plant, and equipment are recorded at cost, in accordance with the cost principle. This includes all costs incurred to get the asset ready for use.
2. **Useful life.** Useful life is an estimate of the expected productive life, also called "service life," of the asset. Useful life may be expressed in terms of time, units of activity (such as machine hours), or units of output. Useful life is an estimate. In making the estimate, management

considers such factors as the intended use of the asset, repair and maintenance policies, and how vulnerable the asset is to wearing out or becoming obsolete. The company's past experience with similar assets is often helpful in determining expected useful life.

3. **Salvage value.** Salvage value is an estimate of the asset's value at the end of its useful life. The value may be based on the asset's worth as scrap or salvage, or on its expected trade-in value. Salvage value is not amortized, since the amount is expected to be recovered at the end of the asset's useful life. Like useful life, salvage value is an estimate. In making the estimate, management considers how it plans to dispose of the asset and its experience with similar assets.

Alternative Terminology
Salvage value is also known as *residual value*.

These factors are summarized in Illustration 9-3.

Illustration 9-3 ▶

Three factors in calculating amortization

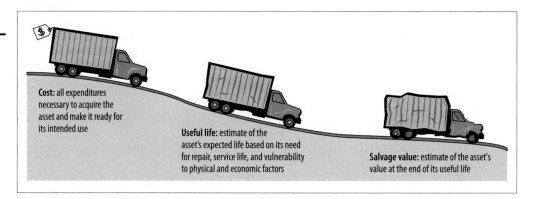

Cost: all expenditures necessary to acquire the asset and make it ready for its intended use

Useful life: estimate of the asset's expected life based on its need for repair, service life, and vulnerability to physical and economic factors

Salvage value: estimate of the asset's value at the end of its useful life

Amortization Methods

Amortization is generally calculated using one of these three methods:

1. Straight-line
2. Declining-balance
3. Units-of-activity

Like the alternative inventory cost flow assumptions discussed in Chapter 6, each amortization method is acceptable under generally accepted accounting principles. Management chooses the method that it believes will best measure an asset's contribution to revenue over its useful life. Once a method is chosen, it should be applied consistently over the useful life of the asset. Consistency makes it easier to compare financial statements.

Over 93 percent of Canadian public companies use the straight-line method of amortization. For this reason, we will present the procedures for straight-line amortization, and only briefly introduce the other two amortization methods in comparison. Detailed calculations for the other methods of amortization are presented in the chapter appendix.

Our illustration of amortization methods, both here and in the appendix, is based on the following data for a delivery van purchased by Perfect Pizzas Ltd. on January 1, 2006:

Cost	$33,000
Expected salvage value	$3,000
Estimated useful life (in years)	5
Estimated useful life (in kilometres)	100,000

Straight-Line.   Under the **straight-line method**, amortization expense is the same for each year of the asset's useful life. You learned how to calculate straight-line amortization, without the added complexity of salvage value, in Chapter 4. Now we will change our simplified calculation of straight-line amortization so that it includes the effects of salvage value. Salvage value is deducted from the cost of the asset to determine the asset's **amortizable cost**, the amount that can be amortized.

To calculate the annual amortization expense, we divide the amortizable cost by the estimated useful life. The calculation of amortization expense in the first year for Perfect Pizzas' delivery van is shown in Illustration 9-4.

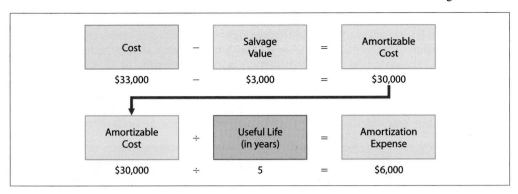

Illustration 9-4 ◀

Formula for straight-line method

Alternatively, we can calculate an annual rate at which the delivery truck is to be amortized. In this case, the amortization rate is 20 percent (100% ÷ 5 years). When an annual rate is used under the straight-line method, the amortizable cost of the asset is multiplied by the amortization rate to determine the amortization expense, as shown in the amortization schedule in Illustration 9-5.

					End of Year	
Year	Amortizable Cost	× Amortization Rate	= Amortization Expense		Accumulated Amortization	Book Value
						$33,000
2006	$30,000	20%	$ 6,000		$ 6,000	27,000
2007	30,000	20%	6,000		12,000	21,000
2008	30,000	20%	6,000		18,000	15,000
2009	30,000	20%	6,000		24,000	9,000
2010	30,000	20%	6,000		30,000	3,000
			$30,000			

PERFECT PIZZAS LTD.
Straight-Line Amortization Schedule

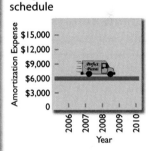

Illustration 9-5 ◀

Straight-line amortization schedule

Note that the amortization expense of $6,000 is the same each year, and that the book value at the end of the useful life is equal to the estimated $3,000 salvage value.

What happens when an asset is purchased during the year, rather than on January 1, as in our example? In that case, it is necessary to **prorate the annual amortization for the part of the year that is used**. If Perfect Pizzas had purchased the delivery van on April 1, 2006, the van would be used for nine months in 2006. The amortization for 2006 would be $4,500 ($30,000 × 20% × $^{9}/_{12}$). Note that amortization is normally rounded to the nearest month. Since amortization is an estimate only, calculating it to the nearest day gives a false sense of accuracy.

To keep things simple, some companies use a convention for partial-period amortization, rather than calculating amortization monthly. Companies may choose to allocate a full year's amortization in the year of acquisition and none in the year of disposal. Other companies record a half year's amortization in the year of acquisition, and a half year's amortization in the year of disposal. Whatever company policy is used for partial-year amortization, the impact is not significant in the long run if the policy is used consistently.

As indicated earlier, the straight-line method is what most companies use. It is simple to apply, and it matches expenses with revenues appropriately if the asset is used quite uniformly throughout its service life. Assets that give equal benefits over their useful lives generally are the kinds whose productivity is not affected by daily use. Examples are office furniture and fixtures, buildings, warehouses, and garages for motor vehicles.

Declining-Balance. The **declining-balance method** is called an "accelerated" method because it results in more amortization in the early years of an asset's life than does the straight-line method. However, as the total amount of amortization (the amortizable cost) taken over an asset's life is the same no matter what approach is used, the declining-balance method produces a decreasing annual amortization expense over the useful life of the asset. That is, in early years declining-balance amortization expense will be higher than the straight-line expense, but in later years it will be less than straight-line. Managers might choose an accelerated approach in order to match a higher cost with higher revenue-producing ability in the early years, or if the asset is expected to become less useful over time.

The declining-balance approach can be applied at different rates, which result in varying speeds of amortization. A common declining-balance rate is double the straight-line rate. If we apply the declining-balance method to Perfect Pizzas' delivery van using double the straight-line rate and a five-year life, we get the pattern of amortization shown in Illustration 9-6.

Illustration 9-6 ▶

Declining-balance amortization schedule

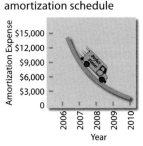

			End of Year	
Year	Amortization Expense		Accumulated Amortization	Book Value
				$33,000
2006	$13,200		$13,200	19,800
2007	7,920		21,120	11,880
2008	4,752		25,872	7,128
2009	2,851		28,723	4,277
2010	1,277		30,000	3,000
	$30,000			

PERFECT PIZZAS LTD.
Declining-Balance Amortization Schedule

The chapter's appendix presents the calculations that produce the numbers in the illustration. Again, note that total amortization over the life of the truck is $30,000, the amortizable cost.

Units-of-Activity. As indicated earlier, useful life can be expressed in ways other than a time period. Under the **units-of-activity method**, useful life is expressed in terms of either the total units of production or total use expected from the asset. The units-of-activity method works well for factory machinery: production can be measured in terms of units of output or machine hours used in operating the machinery. It is also possible to use the method for such items as motor vehicles (kilometres driven) and airplanes (hours in use). The units-of-activity method is generally not suitable for such assets as buildings or furniture, because activity levels are difficult to measure for these types of assets.

To apply the units-of-activity method to the delivery van owned by Perfect Pizzas, we first need to know some basic information. Perfect Pizzas expects to be able to drive the van a total of 100,000 kilometres. Assuming that the mileage occurs in the pattern given over its five-year life, amortization in each year is shown in Illustration 9-7. The calculations used to arrive at these results are presented in the chapter's appendix.

Illustration 9-7 ▶

Units-of-activity amortization schedule

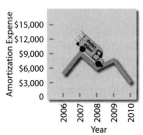

PERFECT PIZZAS LTD.
Units-of-Activity Amortization Schedule

				End of Year	
Year	Units of Activity (km)	Amortization Expense		Accumulated Amortization	Book Value
					$33,000
2006	15,000	$ 4,500		$ 4,500	28,500
2007	30,000	9,000		13,500	19,500
2008	20,000	6,000		19,500	13,500
2009	25,000	7,500		27,000	6,000
2010	10,000	3,000		30,000	3,000
	100,000	$30,000			

As the name implies, under units-of-activity amortization the amount of amortization is proportional to the activity that took place during the period. For example, the delivery van was driven twice as many kilometres in 2007 as in 2006, and amortization was exactly twice as much in 2007 as in 2006.

Comparison of Methods. The following schedule presents a comparison of annual and total amortization expense for Perfect Pizzas under the three amortization methods. In addition, if we assume that net earnings, before deducting amortization expense, were $45,000 for each of the five years, we can clearly see the impact the choice of method has on net earnings.

| | Straight-Line | | Declining-Balance | | Units-of-Activity | |
Year	Amortization Expense	Net Earnings	Amortization Expense	Net Earnings	Amortization Expense	Net Earnings
2006	$ 6,000	$ 39,000	$13,200	$ 31,800	$ 4,500	$ 40,500
2007	6,000	39,000	7,920	37,080	9,000	36,000
2008	6,000	39,000	4,752	40,248	6,000	39,000
2009	6,000	39,000	2,851	42,149	7,500	37,500
2010	6,000	39,000	1,277	43,723	3,000	42,000
	$30,000	$195,000	$30,000	$195,000	$30,000	$195,000

As discussed earlier, straight-line amortization results in the same amount of expense and earnings impact each year. Declining-balance results in a higher expense in the early years, and therefore lower earnings, and a lower expense in later years and higher earnings. Results for the units-of-activity method vary, depending on the actual usage each year. While periodic amortization and net earnings vary each year under the different methods, total amortization and total net earnings are the same for the five-year period.

Each method is acceptable in accounting because each one recognizes the decline in service potential of the asset in a rational and systematic way. Which method is preferable? There is no easy answer to this question.

The matching principle dictates that the cost of a long-lived asset should be matched to the revenue produced by that asset. Since the pattern of revenue production is different for each type of asset, each amortization method should be chosen based on the revenue pattern of the specific asset. For an asset that generates revenues fairly consistently over time, the straight-line method is appropriate. The declining-balance method best fits assets that are more productive (will generate greater revenue) in the earlier years of their life. The units-of-activity method applies well to assets whose usage varies over time.

BEFORE YOU GO ON . . .

▶ Review It

1. What is the relationship, if any, of amortization to (a) cost allocation, (b) asset valuation, and (c) cash accumulation?
2. Explain the factors that affect the calculation of amortization.
3. What range does Loblaw use as its estimated useful life for buildings? For its equipment and fixtures? For its leasehold improvements? The answers to these questions are at the end of the chapter.
4. How do annual amortization and net earnings differ annually, and in total, over the useful life of an asset under each of the three amortization methods?

▶ Do It

On October 1, 2006, Iron Mountain Ski Corporation purchased a new snow grooming machine for $50,000. The machine is estimated to have a 10-year life with a $2,000 salvage value. (a) What journal entry would Iron Mountain Ski Corporation make to record amortization at its year end, December 31, 2006, if it uses the straight-line method of amortization? (b) Would amortization expense and net earnings in 2006 be higher or lower if the declining-balance method had been used instead of the straight-line method of amortization?

Action Plan

- Calculate the amortizable cost (cost minus salvage value).
- Divide the amortizable cost by the asset's estimated useful life.
- Compare the effects of the straight-line and declining-balance amortization methods.

• Remember that amortization expense reduces net earnings, so the impact on net earnings is the opposite of the impact on the expense.

Solution

(a) The entry to record amortization expense would be:

Dec. 31	Amortization Expense	1,200[1]	
	Accumulated Amortization		1,200
	(To record amortization on snow grooming machine)		

[1] $\dfrac{\$50,000 - \$2,000}{10} \times {}^{3}\!/_{12} = \$1,200$

(b) The straight-line method of amortization results in an equal amount of amortization expense each year. The declining-balance method results in higher amortization expense in the early years than straight-line. This would result in a lower net earnings amount.

Other Amortization Issues

study objective 3

Describe other accounting issues related to amortization.

There are several other issues related to amortization that we will briefly introduce here. These include how assets are amortized for income tax purposes, how to account for the permanent impairment of assets when the market value declines, and how to revise amortization.

Amortization and Income Taxes

Helpful Hint Amortization for accounting purposes is usually different from amortization for income tax purposes.

The Canada Revenue Agency (CRA) allows companies to deduct a specified amount of amortization expense when they calculate their taxable income. As we have just learned, a company should choose the amortization method that best matches revenues to expenses for accounting purposes. However, the CRA does not permit a choice among the three amortization methods. Income tax regulations require the taxpayer to use a defined amortization method—single declining-balance—on the tax return, regardless of which method is used in preparing financial statements.

In addition, the CRA does not permit companies to estimate the useful lives, or amortization rates, of assets. It groups assets into various classes and provides maximum amortization rates for each asset class. Amortization allowed for income tax purposes is calculated on a class (group) basis, and is termed capital cost allowance (CCA). Capital cost allowance is an optional deduction from taxable income, so you may see some businesses deducting amortization for accounting purposes (required to fulfill the matching principle) while deducting no CCA for income tax purposes.

Impairments

International Note
Accounting for impairment is fundamentally different under international financial reporting standards than Canadian standards. These differences are likely to be lessened in the future as Canadian standards are aligned with international standards.

As noted earlier in the chapter, the book value of property, plant, and equipment is rarely the same as its market value. The market value is normally not relevant since property, plant, and equipment is not purchased for resale, but rather for use in operations over the long term. Consequently, the asset is carried at cost (reduced by accumulated amortization after its acquisition), in accordance with the cost principle.

In some instances, however, the market value of a long-lived asset falls substantially below its book value and is not expected to recover. This may happen because a machine has become obsolete, or the market for a product made by a machine has dried up or has become very competitive. A **permanent decline** in the market value of an asset is referred to as an **impairment loss**. The amount of the impairment loss is the amount by which the book value of an asset exceeds its market value. Obviously, if the market value is greater than the book value, no impairment has occurred. Air Canada reported in its 2004 financial statements that it had recorded an impairment loss of $75 million as a result of "the excess of net book value over fair value" for its non-operating aircraft and spare parts.

Unlike inventories, this application of the cost and market rule does not apply automatically to property, plant, and equipment. Because inventory is expected to be converted into cash within the year, it is important to value it annually at the lesser of its cost and market, or saleable, value. In contrast, property, plant, and equipment are used in operations over a longer term and are not available for resale. The going concern assumption assumes that a company will recover at least the cost of its long-lived assets. So, it is only when a permanent impairment occurs in the value of the asset that long-lived assets are written down to market. This does not happen often, and this write-down has to pass certain recoverability tests before it is done. Note also that if the value of the asset later increases, the book value is not then adjusted for any recovery in value.

To illustrate the write-down of a long-lived asset, assume that the Piniwa Corporation reviews its equipment for possible impairment. It owns equipment with a cost of $800,000 and accumulated amortization of $200,000. The equipment's market value is currently $550,000 and it is considered to be permanently impaired. The amount of the impairment loss is determined by comparing the asset's book value to its market value as follows:

Net book value ($800,000 − $200,000)	$600,000
Market value	550,000
Impairment loss	$ 50,000

The journal entry to record the impairment is:

Loss on Impairment	50,000	
Accumulated Amortization		50,000
(To record impairment loss on equipment)		

A	=	L	+	SE
−50,000				−50,000

Cash flows: no effect

Assuming that the asset will continue to be used in operations, the impairment loss is reported on the statement of earnings as part of income from continuing operations and not as an "other expense." Often the loss is combined and reported with amortization expense on the statement of earnings. An accumulated amortization account is credited for the impairment loss, rather than an asset account, in order to preserve the asset's original cost.

Companies are required to review their assets regularly for possible impairment or do so whenever a change in circumstances affects the market value of the asset. In the past, some companies delayed recording impairment losses until it was "convenient" to do so—that is, when the impact on the company's reported results was smaller. For example, if a company had record profits in one year, it could afford to write down some of its assets without hurting its reported results too much. Other companies chose instead to write down their assets in bad years, when they were going to report bad results anyway. This is known as taking a "big bath"—making poor results look even worse. Then, when the company recovers, its results look even better because of the lower amortization expense in later periods.

This practice of timing the recognition of losses to achieve certain earnings results is known as **earnings management**. Earnings management is no longer acceptable, and immediate recognition of impairment losses whenever they are known is now required.

ACCOUNTING MATTERS!   Investor Perspective

In December 2003, Alliance Atlantis Communications Inc. significantly reduced the size and scope of its production business. As a consequence, the company recorded a $210 million impairment loss related to its film and television library—a vast collection of programming that included such shows as *Da Vinci's Inquest* and *Traders*. Analysts commented that Alliance Atlantis's "cleaner" balance sheet positioned the company well for future deal making. Shareholders were essentially relieved about the company's plans to exit the costly production business, and share prices increased 7.4 percent to $24.15 on release of the news.

Decision Toolkit

Decision Checkpoints	Info Needed for Decision	Tools to Use for Decision	How to Evaluate Results
Does the company have impairment losses?	Impairment loss recorded on statement of earnings; book value of long-lived assets	Review the impairment losses recorded by the company. Compare book and market values in light of current business conditions and company performance.	If book value is higher than market value, assets and net earnings will be overstated in the current period. Watch for earnings management—the deliberate timing of the recognition of impairment losses.

Revising Periodic Amortization

Annual amortization expense should be reviewed periodically by management. If wear and tear or obsolescence indicates that annual amortization is either not enough or too much, the amortization expense amount should be changed. In addition, over the useful life of a long-lived asset, a company may incur additional capital expenditures for additions or improvements. These expenditures usually increase the operating efficiency, productive capacity, or expected useful life of the asset, which will change one or more of the factors (cost, salvage value, and useful life) affecting the calculation of amortization. And, as we learned in the last section, an impairment loss will result in a change to the amortizable cost of an asset, in which case future amortization calculations must be based on the revised amortizable cost.

Revising amortization is known as a **change in estimate**. Changes in estimates are made in **current and future years but not to prior periods**. Thus, when a change in amortization is made, (1) there is no correction of previously recorded amortization expense, and (2) amortization expense for current and future years is revised. The rationale for this treatment is that the original estimate was based on information known at the time the asset was purchased. The revision is based on new information which should only affect future periods. In addition, regular restatements of prior periods would make users feel less confident about financial statements. We will leave the detailed calculation of a change in an amortization estimate for another accounting course.

A significant change in an estimate must be disclosed in the notes to the financial statements so that financial statement users are aware of the financial impact. For example, extending an asset's useful life will reduce amortization expense and increase the current period net earnings. Remember that changes in amortization result in periodic effects only: total net earnings over the life of an asset will not be affected by any change in amortization.

BEFORE YOU GO ON . . .

▶Review It

1. How does amortization for accounting purposes differ from amortization for income tax purposes?
2. What is an impairment loss? How is it calculated?
3. What is earnings management?
4. Are revisions of periodic amortization made to prior periods, future periods, or both? Explain.

Disposals of Property, Plant, and Equipment

Companies dispose of property, plant, and equipment that is no longer useful to them. Illustration 9-8 shows three methods of disposal.

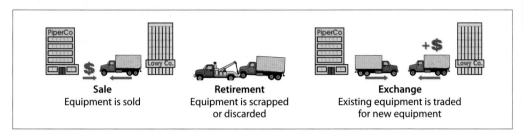

Sale
Equipment is sold

Retirement
Equipment is scrapped or discarded

Exchange
Existing equipment is traded for new equipment

Illustration 9-8 ◀

Methods of property, plant, and equipment disposal

Whatever the disposal method, the company must perform the following four steps to record the sale, retirement, or exchange of the property, plant, or equipment:

Step 1: Update amortization
If the disposal occurs in the middle of an accounting period, amortization must be updated for the fraction of the year since the last time adjusting entries were recorded to the date of disposal. Recall that amortization is recorded by debiting Amortization Expense and crediting Accumulated Amortization. Note that the update period would never exceed one year, since adjusting entries are made at least annually.

Step 2: Calculate the net book value
Calculate the net book value at the time of disposition:

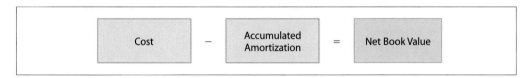

Step 3: Calculate the gain or loss
Determine the amount of the gain or loss on disposal, if any, by comparing the proceeds received to the net book value:

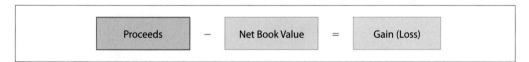

If the proceeds of the sale are more than the net book value of the property, plant, or equipment, there is a gain on disposal. If the proceeds of the sale are less than the net book value of the asset sold, there is a loss on disposal.

Step 4: Record the disposal
Record the disposal, removing the cost of the asset and the accumulated amortization from each affected account. Debit (decrease) Accumulated Amortization for the total amortization associated with that asset to the date of disposal, and credit (decrease) the specific asset account for the cost of the asset. Record the proceeds (if any) by debiting Cash and record the gain or loss on disposal (if any) by debiting a loss account or crediting a gain account.

Sale of Property, Plant, and Equipment

In the following sections, we will illustrate the recording of the sale of office furniture at both a gain and a loss.

Gain on Disposal. Assume that on July 1, 2006, Wright Ltd. sells office furniture for $25,000 cash. The office furniture was purchased January 1, 2003, at a cost of $60,000. At that time, it was estimated that the office furniture would have a salvage value of $5,000 and a useful life of five years. As at December 31, 2005, Wright's year end, it had accumulated amortization of $33,000 [($60,000 − $5,000) ÷ 5 = $11,000 × 3].

The first step is to update any unrecorded amortization. The entry to record amortization expense and update the accumulated amortization for the first six months of 2006 is as follows:

	July 1	Amortization Expense ($11,000 × $^{6}/_{12}$)	5,500	
		Accumulated Amortization—Office Furniture		5,500
		(To record amortization expense for the first six months of 2006)		

After the Accumulated Amortization balance is updated to $38,500 ($33,000 + $5,500), the net book value is calculated and compared to the proceeds to determine the gain on disposal of $3,500 as follows:

Cost of office furniture	$60,000
Less: Accumulated amortization ($33,000 + $5,500)	38,500
Net book value at date of disposal	21,500
Proceeds from sale	25,000
Gain on disposal	$ 3,500

The entry to record the sale of the office furniture is:

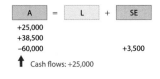

	July 1	Cash	25,000	
		Accumulated Amortization—Office Furniture	38,500	
		Office Furniture		60,000
		Gain on Disposal		3,500
		(To record sale of office furniture at a gain)		

A gain on disposal is reported in the "other revenues" section of the statement of earnings.

Loss on Disposal.   Assume that instead of selling the office furniture for $25,000, Wright sells it for $20,000. In this case, a loss of $1,500 is calculated as shown below:

Cost of office furniture	$60,000
Less: Accumulated amortization	38,500
Net book value at date of disposal	21,500
Proceeds from sale	20,000
Loss on disposal	$ 1,500

The entry to record the sale of the office furniture is:

	July 1	Cash	20,000	
		Accumulated Amortization—Office Furniture	38,500	
		Loss on Disposal	1,500	
		Office Furniture		60,000
		(To record sale of office furniture at a loss)		

A loss on disposal is reported in the "other expenses" section of the statement of earnings.

Retirement of Property, Plant, and Equipment

Some assets are simply retired by the company at the end of their useful lives rather than sold. For example, productive assets used in manufacturing may have very specific uses and consequently have no ready market when the company no longer needs them. In this case, the asset is simply retired. As noted in the feature story, Air Canada retired its F-28, DC-9, B737, and B747 aircraft, replacing them with a newer and more fuel-efficient fleet.

Retirement of an asset is recorded as a special case of a sale, one where no cash is received. As illustrated earlier, amortization is first updated for any partial period to the date of retirement. The net book value is then calculated. If the asset is retired before it is fully amortized, there is a loss on disposal that is equal to the asset's net book value at the date of retirement. Since no proceeds are received in a retirement, a gain will never occur.

Quite often the net book value will equal zero; however, a journal entry is still required to remove the asset and its related amortization from the books. Accumulated Amortization is decreased (debited) for the full amount of amortization taken over the life of the asset. The asset is reduced (credited) for the original cost of the asset. Any loss on disposal is recorded.

What happens if a company is still using a fully amortized asset? In this case, the asset and its accumulated amortization continue to be reported on the balance sheet, without further amortization, until the asset is retired. Reporting the asset and related amortization on the balance sheet informs the reader of the financial statements that the asset is still being used by the company. Once an asset is fully amortized, even if it is still being used, no additional amortization should be taken. Accumulated amortization on a piece of property, plant, and equipment can never be more than the asset's cost.

Exchanges of Property, Plant, and Equipment

In an exchange of assets, a new asset is typically purchased by trading in an old asset, and a **trade-in allowance** is given toward the purchase price of the new asset. An additional cash payment is usually also required for the difference between the trade-in allowance and the purchase price of the new asset.

Instead of being sold for cash, therefore, the old asset is sold for a trade-in allowance on the purchase of the new asset. The new asset is seen as being purchased for cash plus the value of the old asset. Accounting for exchange transactions is complex and further discussion of exchanges is left for future accounting courses.

BEFORE YOU GO ON . . .

▶Review It

1. What are the steps in accounting for sales and retirements of property, plant, and equipment?
2. What is the formula for calculating a gain or loss on disposal?

▶Do It

Overland Trucking Ltd. has a truck that cost $30,000 and has accumulated amortization of $16,000. Assume two different situations: (a) the company sells the truck for $17,000 cash, and (b) the truck is worthless, so the company simply retires it. What entry should Overland use to record each scenario?

Action Plan

- Update any unrecorded amortization for partial periods.
- Calculate the net book value.
- Compare the proceeds to the book value to determine whether any gain or loss has occurred.
- Record any proceeds that are received and any gain or loss. Remove both the asset and accumulated amortization accounts.
- Recall that a gain is not possible in a retirement of assets.

Solution

(a) Sale of truck for cash:

Cash	17,000	
Accumulated Amortization—Truck	16,000	
Truck		30,000
Gain on Disposal [$17,000 − ($30,000 − $16,000)]		3,000
(To record sale of truck at a gain)		

(b) Retirement of truck:

Accumulated Amortization—Truck	16,000	
Loss on Disposal [$0 − ($30,000 − $16,000)]	14,000	
Truck		30,000
(To record retirement of truck at a loss)		

Intangible Assets

study objective 5

Identify the basic issues related to accounting for intangible assets.

Both tangible and intangible long-lived assets benefit future periods and are used to produce products or provide services over these periods. **Intangible assets** are different from tangible assets as they involve rights, privileges, and competitive advantages that do not possess physical substance. In other words, they are not physical things. Many companies' most valuable assets are intangible. Some widely known intangibles are Alexander Graham Bell's patent on the telephone, the franchises of Tim Hortons, the trade name of President's Choice, and the trademark CBC.

There must be proof that an intangible exists. This proof can be a contract, licence, or other document. Intangibles may arise from the following sources:

1. Government grants such as patents, copyrights, trademarks, and trade names
2. Acquisition of another business in which the purchase price includes a payment for goodwill
3. Private monopolistic arrangements arising from contractual agreements, such as franchises and licences

As you will learn in this section, although financial statements do report many intangibles, many other significant intangibles are not reported. To give an example, according to its 2005 financial statements, Research in Motion had a net book value of U.S. $2.0 billion. But its *market* value—the total market price of all its shares on that same date—was U.S. $12.5 billion. Thus, its actual market value was more than six times greater than what its balance sheet said the company was worth at that time. It is not uncommon for a company's reported book value to differ from its market value, because balance sheets are reported at historical cost. But such an extreme difference seriously lessens the usefulness of the balance sheet to decision-makers. In the case of Research in Motion, the difference is due to unrecorded intangibles. For many high-tech or intellectual property companies, most of their value is from intangibles such as knowledge assets, and many of these are not reported under current accounting practices.

Accounting for Intangible Assets

Similar to tangible assets, **intangible assets are recorded at cost**. Cost includes all costs of acquisition and other costs that are needed to make the intangible asset ready for its intended use, including legal fees and similar charges.

Only certain types of intangible assets are amortized. To distinguish between those intangibles that are amortizable and those that are not, we categorize intangible assets as having either a limited life or an indefinite life.

If an intangible asset has a **limited life**, its amortizable cost (cost less salvage value) should be allocated over the shorter of the (1) estimated useful life and (2) legal life. Intangible assets, by their nature, rarely have any salvage value, so the amortizable cost is normally equal to the cost. In addition, the useful life of an intangible asset is usually shorter than its legal life, so useful life is most often used as the amortization period.

A company that has significant intangibles with a limited life should analyze the reasonableness of the estimated useful life it uses for these intangibles. When the company first determined the useful life, it should have considered obsolescence, inadequacy, and other factors that can make the intangible ineffective at helping earn revenue. For example, suppose a computer hardware manufacturer obtains a patent on a new computer chip that it has developed (we will discuss patents in the next section). The legal life of the patent is 20 years. From experience, we know that the useful life of a computer chip is not more than four to five years, and often less—because new, superior chips are developed so rapidly, existing chips quickly become obsolete. Consequently, we would question the amortization expense of a company if it amortized its patent on a computer chip for longer than five years. Amortizing an intangible over a period that is too long will understate amortization expense, overstate the company's net earnings, and overstate its assets.

What happens if the cost or useful life is changed? Similar to tangible assets, a revision of the amortization is then done and is treated as a change in estimate. As with tangible assets, intangible assets must be reviewed and tested for impairment whenever circumstances make this appropriate. Recall from earlier in this chapter that an impairment occurs if the asset's market value permanently falls below its book value. If any impairment is evident, the asset must be written down to its market value and an impairment loss must be recorded. If no impairment has occurred, the asset remains at its current value until the following year, when it is evaluated again.

If an intangible has an **indefinite life**, it is not amortized. Intangible assets with indefinite lives are tested more frequently for impairment than are tangible assets or intangible assets with limited lives. Indefinite-life assets should be tested for impairment at least annually.

At disposal, just as with tangible assets, the book value of the intangible asset is eliminated, and a gain or loss, if any, is recorded.

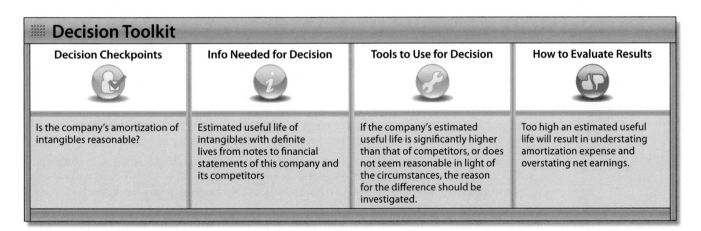

Decision Toolkit

Decision Checkpoints	Info Needed for Decision	Tools to Use for Decision	How to Evaluate Results
Is the company's amortization of intangibles reasonable?	Estimated useful life of intangibles with definite lives from notes to financial statements of this company and its competitors	If the company's estimated useful life is significantly higher than that of competitors, or does not seem reasonable in light of the circumstances, the reason for the difference should be investigated.	Too high an estimated useful life will result in understating amortization expense and overstating net earnings.

Intangible Assets with Limited Lives

Examples of intangible assets with limited lives include patents and copyrights. We also include research and development costs in this section because these costs often lead to the creation of patents and copyrights.

Patents

A **patent** is an exclusive right issued by the Canadian Intellectual Property Office of Industry Canada that allows the patent holder to manufacture, sell, or otherwise control an invention for a period of 20 years from the date of the application. A patent cannot be renewed. But the legal life of a patent can be extended if the patent holder obtains new patents for improvements or other changes in the basic design.

The initial cost of a patent is the price paid to acquire the patent. Subsequent to acquisition, legal costs are often incurred. The saying "A patent is only as good as the money you're prepared to spend defending it" is very true. An example is the U.S. $20 million that Research in Motion added to its patent account in 2005 when it settled a three-year patent dispute with NTP Inc. regarding RIM's wireless technology. Legal costs to successfully defend a patent in an infringement suit are considered necessary to prove the patent's validity. They are added to the patent account and amortized over the remaining life of the patent.

The cost of a patent should be amortized over its 20-year legal life or its useful life, whichever is shorter. As mentioned earlier, the useful life should be carefully assessed by considering whether the patent is likely to become ineffective at contributing to revenue before the end of its legal life.

Copyrights

A **copyright** is granted by the Canadian Intellectual Property Office, giving the owner the exclusive right to reproduce and sell an artistic or published work. Copyrights extend for the life of the creator plus 50 years. Generally, the useful life of a copyright is significantly shorter than its legal life, and the copyright is therefore amortized over its useful life.

The cost of the copyright consists of the cost of acquiring and defending it. The cost may be only the fee paid, or it may amount to a great deal more if a copyright infringement suit is involved.

ACCOUNTING MATTERS!   Ethics Perspective

Although the record industry won a copyright infringement case against Napster—an on-line music distribution company—the struggle to enforce copyright laws in the digital age continues to be an uphill battle. A recent survey found that 67 percent of those who download music from the Internet simply do not care if the files are copyrighted or not. This figure is striking given the flood of media coverage and legal cases aimed at educating the public about the damage that file-sharing can cause to the intellectual property industries.

Source: "Music Downloaders Remain Indifferent to Copyright," *Internet Magazine*, August 1, 2003.

Research and Development Costs

Research and development (R&D) costs are not intangible assets per se. But they may lead to patents, copyrights, new processes, and new products. Many companies spend very large sums of money on research and development in an ongoing effort to develop new products or processes. For example, in a recent year Research in Motion spent U.S. $101 million on research and development. Nortel Networks spent nearly $2 billion!

Research and development costs present two accounting problems: (1) It is sometimes difficult to determine the costs related to a specific project. (2) It is also hard to know the extent and timing of future benefits. As a result, accounting distinguishes between research costs and development costs.

Research is planned investigation that is done to gain new knowledge and understanding. **All research costs should be expensed when incurred.**

Development is the use of research findings and knowledge for a plan or design. **Development costs with reasonably certain future benefits can be capitalized.** Management must intend to produce and market the product or process, a future market must be defined, and adequate resources must exist to complete the project. Otherwise, development costs must also be expensed.

Illustration 9-9 ▶

Distinction between research and development.

Research	**Development**
Examples	Examples
• Laboratory research aimed at the discovery of new knowledge	• Testing in search or evaluation of product or process alternatives
• Searching for ways to use new research findings or other knowledge	• Design, construction, and testing of pre-production prototypes and models
• Forming concepts and designs of possible product or process alternatives	• Design of tools, jigs, moulds, and dies involving new technology

Other Intangible Assets

Other intangible assets sometimes found in corporate balance sheets include items such as customer lists, noncompetition agreements, sports contracts, startup costs, and rearrangement costs. These types of assets usually have a very short useful life, and are amortized over the shorter of their useful lives or legal lives. Of course, if any of these assets have an indefinite useful life, they are not amortized.

Some companies use the term "Deferred Charges" to classify these items. Others use the term "Other Assets." The trend has been toward listing these items separately, as neither term—Deferred Charges nor Other Assets—has much value as information.

Intangible Assets with Indefinite Lives

Examples of intangible assets with indefinite lives include trademarks and trade names, franchises and licences, and goodwill. Intangible assets do not always fit perfectly in a specific category. Sometimes trademarks, trade names, franchises, or licences do have limited lives. In such cases, they would be amortized over the shorter of their legal and useful lives. It is more usual, however, for these intangible assets, along with goodwill, to have indefinite lives.

Trademarks and Trade Names

A **trademark (trade name)** is a word, phrase, jingle, or symbol that distinguishes or identifies a particular enterprise or product. Trade names like Blue Jays, Big Mac, Nike, President's Choice, and TSN create immediate brand recognition and generally help the sale of the product or service. A 2005 national survey of readers of *Canadian Business* and *Marketing* magazines identified Tim Hortons as Canada's best-managed brand or trade name.

The creator or original user may obtain the exclusive legal right to the trademark or trade name by registering it with the Canadian Intellectual Property Office. This registration provides continuous protection and may be renewed every 15 years as long as the trademark or trade name is in use. In most cases, companies continuously renew their trademarks or trade names. In such cases, as long as the trademark or trade name continues to be marketable, it will have an indefinite useful life.

If the trademark or trade name is purchased, the cost is the purchase price. If it is developed internally rather than purchased, the cost includes legal fees, registration fees, design costs, and other expenditures that are directly related to securing it.

Franchises and Licences

When you purchase a Protegé from a Mazda dealer, fill up your tank at the corner Irving station, and order a double-double at Tim Hortons, you are dealing with franchises. A **franchise** is a contractual arrangement under which the franchisor grants the franchisee the right to sell certain products, to provide specific services, or to use certain trademarks or trade names, usually within a designated geographic area.

Another type of franchise, granted by a government body, permits the company to use public property in performing its services. Examples are the use of city streets for a bus line or taxi service; the use of public land for telephone, power, and cable television lines; and the use of airwaves for radio or TV broadcasting. Such operating rights are referred to as **licences**.

When costs can be identified with the acquisition of the franchise or licence, an intangible asset should be recognized. Air Canada reports $688 million on its 2004 balance sheet for route rights and landing and departure slot costs. These rights have indefinite lives and are not amortized.

Annual payments, often proportionate with sales, are sometimes required under a franchise agreement. These are called royalties and are recorded as **operating expenses** in the period in which they are incurred.

Goodwill

Usually the largest intangible asset that appears on a company's balance sheet is goodwill. **Goodwill** represents the value of all favourable attributes that relate to a company. These include exceptional management, a desirable location, good customer relations, skilled employees, high-quality products, fair pricing policies, and harmonious relations with labour unions. Unlike other assets, which can be sold *individually* in the marketplace—such as investments or property, plant, and equipment—goodwill can be identified only with the business *as a whole*.

If goodwill can only be identified with the business as a whole, how can it be determined? Certainly, a number of businesses have many of the factors cited above (exceptional management, a desirable location, and so on). However, to determine the value of these items would be difficult and very subjective. Subjective valuations would not contribute to the reliability of financial statements. Therefore, goodwill is recorded only when there is a purchase of an entire business, at which time an independent valuation can be determined.

In recording the purchase of a business, goodwill is the excess of cost over the market value of the net assets (assets less liabilities) acquired. Because goodwill has an indefinite life, just as the company has an indefinite life, it is not amortized.

Since goodwill is measured using the market value of a company—a subjective valuation which can easily change—it must be tested annually for impairment, just as other intangible assets with indefinite lives are. However, because of its nature, goodwill requires a write-down more often than any other type of intangible asset.

BEFORE YOU GO ON . . .

▶Review It

1. What are the main differences between accounting for intangible assets and for tangible assets?
2. Give some examples of intangible assets in your everyday surroundings.
3. Distinguish between the amortization policy for intangible assets with limited lives and the policy for those with indefinite lives.
4. Distinguish between the treatment of impairment losses for intangible assets with limited lives and the policy for those with indefinite lives.

▶Do It

The Dummies R' Us Corporation purchased a copyright on a new book series for $15,000 cash on August 1, 2006. The books are anticipated to have a saleable life of three years. One year later, the company incurs $6,000 of legal costs (paid in cash) to successfully defend this copyright in court. The company's year end is July 31. Record the purchase of the copyright on August 1, 2006; the year-end amortization, July 31, 2007; and the legal costs incurred at August 1, 2007.

Action Plan

- Amortize intangible assets with limited lives over the shorter of their useful life and legal life (the legal life of a copyright is the life of the author plus 50 years).
- Treat costs to successfully defend an intangible asset as capital expenditures because they benefit future periods.

Solution

Aug. 1, 2006	Copyright	15,000	
	Cash		15,000
	(To record purchase of copyright)		
July 31, 2007	Amortization Expense ($15,000 ÷ 3)	5,000	
	Accumulated Amortization—Copyright		5,000
	(To record amortization expense)		
Aug. 1, 2007	Copyright	6,000	
	Cash		6,000
	(To record costs incurred to defend copyright)		

the navigator

Statement Presentation of Long-Lived Assets

Long-lived assets have a major impact on all three financial statements: the balance sheet, statement of earnings, and cash flow statement.

study objective 6

Indicate how long-lived assets are reported in the financial statements.

Balance Sheet

Long-lived assets are normally reported in the balance sheet under the headings "Property, Plant, and Equipment," and "Intangible Assets." Goodwill must be separately disclosed; other intangibles can be grouped together for reporting purposes. Sometimes intangible assets are listed separately, following property, plant, and equipment, with no separate heading. Some companies combine property, plant, and equipment and intangible assets other than goodwill under the single heading "Capital Assets."

Either on the balance sheet or in the notes, the balances of the major classes of assets should be disclosed, as well as the accumulated amortization for assets that are amortized. In addition, the amortization methods used must be described.

Illustration 9-10 is an excerpt from the balance sheet of Air Canada (called ACE Aviation Holdings Inc. after the restructuring), which it calls its statement of financial position. Long-lived assets are summarized in the balance sheet and detailed in the notes.

ACE AVIATION HOLDINGS INC.
Consolidated Statement of Financial Position (partial)
December 31, 2004
(in millions)

Assets	
Property and equipment (note 8)	$3,696
Intangible assets (note 10)	2,691

Illustration 9-10 ◄

Balance sheet presentation of long-lived assets

Note 8 details the cost and accumulated amortization for flight equipment, buildings and leasehold improvements, ground equipment, and other property and equipment. Note 10 details the company's intangible assets, which have been separated into two categories: indefinite-life assets and finite-life assets. Accumulated amortization for the finite-life assets is also reported. The accounting policy note to the financial statements reports the amortization policy and period used for amortization.

Statement of Earnings

Amortization expense and impairment losses are presented in the operating section of the statement of earnings. Air Canada reported $397 million for "depreciation, amortization, and obsolescence" in the operating expenses section of its statement of earnings for the year ended December 31, 2004. Gains and losses on disposal are normally segregated and presented as "other revenues/expenses."

Companies must disclose their impairment policy in the notes to the financial statements. Air Canada states in the notes to its financial statements that "long-lived assets are tested for impairment whenever the circumstances indicate that the carrying value may not be recoverable," and that "indefinite lived assets are also subject to annual impairment tests." Air Canada found that the market value of its long-lived assets was higher than their book value in 2004, so no impairment loss was evident. If there is an impairment loss, companies must also disclose the circumstances that led to the impairment, how the market value was determined, and other information related to the impairment.

Cash Flow Statement

The cash flows from the purchase and sale of long-lived assets are reported in the investing activities section of the cash flow statement. For example, Illustration 9-11 shows the investing activities section of Air Canada's (ACE Aviation Holdings) cash flow statement.

Illustration 9-11 ▶

Cash flow statement presentation of long-lived assets

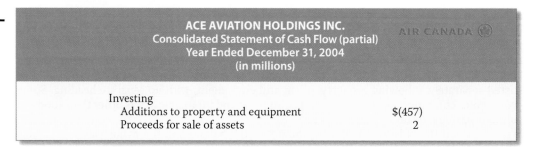

ACE AVIATION HOLDINGS INC. Consolidated Statement of Cash Flow (partial) Year Ended December 31, 2004 (in millions)		AIR CANADA
Investing		
Additions to property and equipment		$(457)
Proceeds for sale of assets		2

As indicated, Air Canada made significant investments in its property and equipment as part of its fleet modernization program. It would also be a good idea to examine the financing activities section of the statement to determine the amount of borrowing that was done for these acquisitions.

BEFORE YOU GO ON . . .

▶Review It

1. How are long-lived assets presented on the balance sheet? The statement of earnings? The cash flow statement?
2. What information about long-lived assets is disclosed in the notes to the financial statements?

Analyzing Assets

study objective 7

Describe the methods for evaluating the use of assets.

The presentation of financial statement information about long-lived assets allows decision-makers to analyze a company's use of its total assets. We will use two ratios to analyze assets: the return on assets and asset turnover.

Return on Assets

The **return on assets** ratio measures overall profitability. This ratio is calculated by dividing net earnings by average total assets. The return on assets ratio indicates the amount of net earnings generated by each dollar invested in assets. Thus, the higher the return on assets, the more profitable the company.

The following data (in millions) are provided for Air Canada and WestJet Airlines for the fiscal years 2004 and 2003:

	Air Canada		WestJet	
	2004	2003	2004	2003
Net sales	$8,900	$8,373	$1,053	$ 860
Net earnings (loss)	880	(1,867)	(17)	61
Total assets	9,386	6,910	1,877	1,477

Air Canada's statement of earnings is actually presented in two parts—the nine months ended September 30, 2004, before the restructuring, and the three months ended December 31,

2004, which occurred after the restructuring. Although these two periods are not totally comparable, we have combined them for this illustration. Total assets at the end of 2002 were $7,416 million for Air Canada and $784 million for WestJet.

The return on assets for Air Canada, WestJet, and the industry averages are shown in Illustration 9-12.

RETURN ON ASSETS = $\dfrac{\text{NET EARNINGS}}{\text{AVERAGE TOTAL ASSETS}}$		
($ in millions)	2004	2003
Air Canada	$\dfrac{\$880}{(\$9,386 + \$6,910) \div 2} = 10.8\%$	$\dfrac{(\$1,867)}{(\$6,910 - \$7,416) \div 2} = (26.1\%)$
WestJet	(1.0%)	5.4%
Industry average	(6.8%)	(4.0%)

Illustration 9-12 ◀

Return on assets

As shown from the information provided, Air Canada had a miserable year in 2003, reporting a negative 26.1-percent return on assets. This return was far below that of both WestJet and the industry. After its restructuring, Air Canada was able to significantly improve its return on assets in 2004 to a positive 10.8 percent, exceeding both WestJet and the industry.

The airline industry in general has been suffering over the last few years and many airlines have suffered financial distress like Air Canada's. WestJet's declining numbers in 2004 are not because of financial distress, however, but rather a conscious decision to speed up the replacement of its aircraft fleet. WestJet replaced many of its planes in 2004, incurring a $48-million impairment loss on its older fleet. Some observers believe that WestJet expanded too quickly in 2004 but that it will be able to regroup thanks to the reduced costs of its newer, more efficient fleet of aircraft.

Asset Turnover

The **asset turnover** ratio indicates how efficiently a company uses its assets—that is, how many dollars of sales are generated by each dollar invested in assets. It is calculated by dividing net sales by average total assets. When we compare two companies in the same industry, the one with the higher asset turnover ratio is operating more efficiently. It is generating more sales for every dollar invested in assets.

The asset turnover ratios for Air Canada and WestJet Airlines for 2004 and 2003 are calculated in Illustration 9-13.

ASSET TURNOVER = $\dfrac{\text{NET SALES}}{\text{AVERAGE TOTAL ASSETS}}$		
($ in millions)	2004	2003
Air Canada	$\dfrac{\$8,900}{(\$9,386 + \$6,910) \div 2} = 1.1 \text{ times}$	$\dfrac{\$8,373}{(\$6,910 + \$7,416) \div 2} = 1.2 \text{ times}$
WestJet	0.6 times	0.8 times
Industry average	0.7 times	0.6 times

Illustration 9-13 ◀

Asset turnover

The asset turnover ratios in the illustration mean that for each dollar invested in assets in 2004, Air Canada generated sales of $1.10 and WestJet $0.60. While Air Canada's return on assets improved in 2004, its asset turnover declined slightly—likely due to the continued effects of restructuring. Air Canada's asset turnover of 1.1 times in 2004 is nearly double that of WestJet and the industry. Air Canada's load factor (percentage of available seats filled) at 76.8 percent was better than WestJet's of 70 percent in 2004, which may partially explain the differing asset turnover ratios.

Asset turnover ratios vary considerably across industries. The average asset turnover for utility companies is 0.4 times, and the grocery store industry has an average asset turnover of 2.5 times. Asset turnover ratios, therefore, should only be compared within an industry, not between different industries.

Profit Margin Revisited

For a complete picture of the sales-generating ability of assets, one would also want to look at the company's profit margin ratio. In Chapter 5, you learned about profit margin. Profit margin is calculated by dividing net earnings by net sales. It tells how effective a company is in turning its sales into earnings—that is, how much earnings are generated by each dollar of sales.

Together, the profit margin and asset turnover explain the return on assets ratio. Illustration 9-14 shows how return on assets can be calculated from the profit margin and asset turnover ratios for Air Canada in 2004.

Illustration 9-14 ▶

Composition of Air Canada's 2004 return on assets

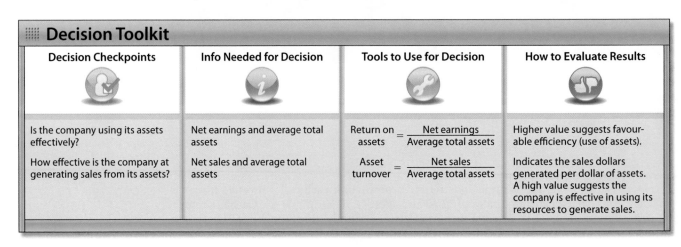

PROFIT MARGIN	×	ASSET TURNOVER	=	RETURN ON ASSETS
$\dfrac{\text{Net Earnings}}{\text{Net Sales}}$	×	$\dfrac{\text{Net Sales}}{\text{Average Total Assets}}$	=	$\dfrac{\text{Net Earnings}}{\text{Average Total Assets}}$
$\dfrac{\$880}{\$8,900} = 9.9\%$		$\dfrac{\$8,900}{(\$9,386 + \$6,910) \div 2} = 1.1 \text{ times}$		$\dfrac{\$880}{(\$9,386 + \$6,910) \div 2} = 10.8\%$

This relationship has important implications for management. From Illustration 9-14, we can see that if a company wants to increase its return on assets, it can do so either by increasing the margin it generates from each dollar of goods that it sells (profit margin), or by trying to increase the volume of goods that it sells (asset turnover).

Let's evaluate Air Canada's return on assets for 2004 again but this time by evaluating the ratio's components—the profit margin and asset turnover ratios. Air Canada has a profit margin of 9.89 percent. Compared to the industry average of a negative 9.9 percent, Air Canada has much better control of its costs than most of its industry competitors. And, as noted previously, Air Canada's asset turnover is also significantly better than the industry's.

Of course, Air Canada has a significant advantage compared to many of its competitors. It had the opportunity to make a "fresh start" with its recent restructuring. Nonetheless, it would appear that if Air Canada can increase its asset turnover by increasing the amount of sales it generates per dollar invested in planes, it could become one of the most profitable companies in the industry.

▦ Decision Toolkit

Decision Checkpoints	Info Needed for Decision	Tools to Use for Decision	How to Evaluate Results
Is the company using its assets effectively? How effective is the company at generating sales from its assets?	Net earnings and average total assets Net sales and average total assets	$\text{Return on assets} = \dfrac{\text{Net earnings}}{\text{Average total assets}}$ $\text{Asset turnover} = \dfrac{\text{Net sales}}{\text{Average total assets}}$	Higher value suggests favourable efficiency (use of assets). Indicates the sales dollars generated per dollar of assets. A high value suggests the company is effective in using its resources to generate sales.

BEFORE YOU GO ON . . .

►Review It

1. What is the purpose of the return on assets? Of the asset turnover? How are these ratios calculated?
2. How can the profit margin and asset turnover be used to explain the return on assets ratio?

the navigator

APPENDIX 9A ► CALCULATION OF AMORTIZATION USING OTHER METHODS

In this appendix, we show the calculation of the amortization expense amounts used in the chapter for the declining-balance and units-of-activity methods.

> **study objective 8**
>
> Calculate amortization using the declining-balance method and the units-of-activity method.

Declining-Balance

The **declining-balance method** produces a decreasing annual amortization expense over the useful life of the asset. It is called the "declining-balance" method because the calculation of periodic amortization is based on a declining book value of the asset (cost less accumulated amortization). Annual amortization expense is calculated by multiplying the **book value at the beginning of the year by the amortization rate. The amortization rate remains constant from year to year, but the book value that the rate is applied to declines each year.**

Book value for the first year is the cost of the asset, because the balance in Accumulated Amortization at the beginning of the asset's useful life is zero. In subsequent years, book value is the difference between cost and accumulated amortization at the beginning of the year. Unlike other amortization methods, the declining-balance method does not use amortizable cost. **Salvage value is not used in determining the amount that the declining-balance rate is applied to.** Salvage value does, however, limit the total amortization that can be taken. Amortization stops when the asset's book value equals its expected salvage value.

Varying rates of amortization may be used, depending on how fast the company wants to amortize the asset. You will find rates such as one time (single), two times (double), and even three times (triple) the straight-line rate of amortization. An amortization rate that is often used is double the straight-line rate. This method is referred to as the **double declining-balance method**.

Let's return to the illustration data used in the chapter for Perfect Pizzas. You will recall that Perfect Pizzas purchased a delivery van on January 1, 2006. The relevant data are shown again here:

> **Helpful Hint** The straight-line rate is determined by dividing 100% by the estimated useful life. In this case, it is 100% ÷ 5 = 20%.

Cost	$33,000
Expected salvage value	$3,000
Estimated useful life (in years)	5
Estimated useful life (in kilometres)	100,000

If Perfect Pizzas uses double the straight-line rate, the amortization rate is 40 percent (2 multiplied by the straight-line rate of 20 percent). Illustration 9A-1 presents the formula and calculation of the first year's amortization on the delivery van.

Book Value at Beginning of Year	×	Amortization Rate (Straight-Line Rate × Multiplier)	=	Amortization Expense
$33,000	×	20% × 2	=	$13,200

Illustration 9A-1 ◄

Formula for declining-balance method

The amortization schedule under this method is given in Illustration 9A-2.

Illustration 9A-2 ▶

Declining-balance
amortization schedule

PERFECT PIZZAS LTD.
Declining-Balance Amortization Schedule

Year	Book Value Beginning of Year	× Amortization Rate	= Amortization Expense	End of Year Accumulated Amortization	End of Year Book Value
					$33,000
2006	$33,000	40%	$13,200	$13,200	19,800
2007	19,800	40%	7,920	21,120	11,880
2008	11,880	40%	4,752	25,872	7,128
2009	7,128	40%	2,851	28,723	4,277
2010	4,277	40%	1,277ᵃ	30,000	3,000
			$30,000		

ᵃ Calculation of $1,711 ($4,277 × 40%) is adjusted to $1,277 so book value will equal salvage value.

You can see that the delivery equipment is 64-percent amortized ($21,120 ÷ $33,000) at the end of the second year. Under the straight-line method, it would be amortized 36 percent ($12,000 ÷ $33,000) at that time. Because the declining-balance method produces higher amortization expense in the early years than in the later years, it is considered an **accelerated amortization method**.

The declining-balance method respects the matching principle. The higher amortization expense in early years is matched with the higher benefits received in these years. Conversely, lower amortization expense is recognized in later years when the asset's contribution to revenue is less. Also, some assets lose their usefulness rapidly because of obsolescence. In these cases, the declining-balance method provides a more appropriate amortization amount.

When an asset is purchased during the year, it is necessary to prorate the declining-balance amortization in the first year, based on time. For example, if Perfect Pizzas had purchased the delivery equipment on April 1, 2006, amortization for 2006 would be $9,900 ($33,000 × 40% × 9/12) if amortization is calculated monthly. The book value for calculating amortization in 2007 then becomes $23,100 ($33,000 − $9,900), and the 2007 amortization is $9,240 ($23,100 × 40%). Future calculations would follow from these amounts until the book value equalled the salvage value.

While the declining-balance method is not as popular as the straight-line method, it is still used by a significant number of Canadian companies. In some cases, this method is chosen because it provides the best match of cost and benefit. In other cases, the single declining-balance method is chosen because it must be used for income tax purposes and it is simpler to use the same method for both accounting and tax purposes.

Units-of-Activity

Under the **units-of-activity method**, useful life is expressed in terms of the estimated total units of production or use expected from the asset, rather than as a time period. The units-of-activity method is ideal for equipment whose activity can be measured in units of output, kilometres driven, or hours in use. The units-of-activity method is generally not appropriate for assets such as buildings and furniture, because amortization for these assets is more a function of time than of use.

To use this method, the total units of activity for the entire useful life is estimated. This amount is divided into the amortizable cost (cost less salvage value) to determine the amortizable cost per unit. The amortizable cost per unit is then multiplied by the units of activity during the year and the result is the amortization expense.

To illustrate, assume that Perfect Pizzas' delivery truck is driven 15,000 kilometres in the first year of a total estimated useful life of 100,000 kilometres. Using this distance, Illustration 9A-3 presents the formula and calculation of amortization expense in the first year.

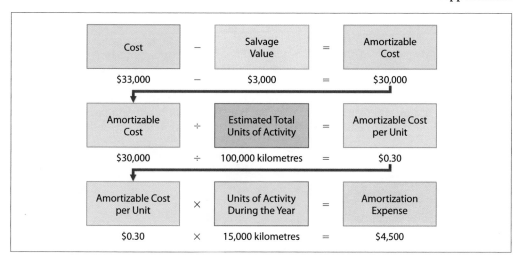

The amortization schedule, using assumed distance data for the later years, is shown in Illustration 9A-4.

| | | | | End of Year | |
| | Units of | Amortizable | Amortization | Accumulated | Book |
Year	Activity	Cost/Unit	Expense	Amortization	Value
					$33,000
2006	15,000	$0.30	$ 4,500	$ 4,500	28,500
2007	30,000	0.30	9,000	13,500	19,500
2008	20,000	0.30	6,000	19,500	13,500
2009	25,000	0.30	7,500	27,000	6,000
2010	10,000	0.30	3,000	30,000	3,000
			$30,000		

PERFECT PIZZAS LTD.
Units-of-Activity Amortization Schedule

This method is easy to apply when assets are purchased during the year. In such a case, the productivity of the asset for the partial year is used in calculating the amortization. The units of activity, therefore, do not need to be adjusted for partial periods as they already reflect how much the asset was used during the specific period.

Even though it is often difficult to make a reasonable estimate of total activity, about four percent of Canadian companies use this method for assets whose productivity varies significantly from one period to another. In this situation, the units-of-activity method results in the best matching of expenses with revenues.

▦ Using the Decision Toolkit

Research in Motion (RIM) Limited, headquartered in Waterloo, Ontario, manufactures and markets innovative wireless products (including the wildly popular BlackBerry) for the worldwide mobile communications market.

Many stock analysts have recommended purchasing RIM's shares. A friend of yours, Rafik Kurji, has an interest in buying RIM's shares and has asked you some questions about its financial statements. Excerpts from RIM's financial statements follow:

RESEARCH IN MOTION LIMITED
Balance Sheet (partial)
February 26, 2005
(in U.S. thousands)

Assets

Capital assets	$210,112
Intangible assets	83,740
Goodwill	29,026

RESEARCH IN MOTION LIMITED
Notes to the Consolidated Financial Statements
Year Ended February 26, 2005
(in U.S. thousands)

2. Summary of Significant Accounting Policies

(k) **Capital assets**

Capital assets are stated at cost less accumulated amortization... Amortization is provided using the following rates and methods:

Buildings, leaseholds and other	Straight-line over terms between 5 and 40 years
BlackBerry operations and other information technology	Straight-line over terms between 3 and 5 years
Manufacturing equipment, research and development equipment, and tooling	Straight-line over terms between 2 and 8 years
Furniture and fixtures	20% per annum declining balance

(l) **Intangible assets**

Intangible assets are stated at cost less accumulated amortization... Intangible assets are amortized as follows:

Acquired technology	Straight-line over 2 to 5 years
Licences	Lesser of 5 years or on a per unit basis based upon the anticipated number of units sold during the terms of the licence agreements
Patents	Straight-line over 17 years

6. Capital Assets

During fiscal 2004, the Company recorded additional amortization expense of $1,318 with respect to certain capital assets no longer used by the Company.

Instructions

1. Why does RIM report its intangible assets and goodwill separately on its balance sheet?
2. What methods and periods does the company use to amortize its capital assets (property, plant, and equipment)? Why does RIM use a different amortization method for its furniture and fixtures than it uses for its buildings and leaseholds?
3. What methods and periods does the company use to amortize its limited-life intangible assets?

4. Did RIM record any impairment losses in 2005? If so, explain why it was necessary to write down these assets.

5. Rafik was able to get the following information related to RIM:

	RIM	Industry average
Profit margin	15.8%	0.4%
Return on assets	9.4%	0.2%

Rafik knows that the profit margin and return on assets are related somehow. He thought that RIM's profit margin should be double its return on assets, similar to that of the industry average. Explain to Rafik why this is not so.

Solution

1. RIM's intangible assets consist of acquired technology, licences, and patents. These assets have a limited life and are amortized, whereas goodwill has an indefinite life and is not amortized.

2. RIM's capital assets are amortized as follows: Buildings, leaseholds, and other—straight-line amortization over 5 to 40 years; Blackberry operations and other information technology—straight-line amortization over 3 to 5 years; manufacturing equipment, research and development equipment, and tooling—straight-line over 2 to 8 years; and furniture and fixtures—declining-balance amortization over 5 years (20 percent rate).

   RIM likely uses a different amortization method for its furniture and fixtures because they have a different revenue producing pattern than its buildings and leaseholds. In the case of buildings, time is normally the most dominant factor affecting usage and therefore the straight-line method of amortization is often the most appropriate. In the case of furniture and fixtures, it may be that these are anticipated to be more productive in their early years than in their later years, and so the declining-balance method would be the most appropriate.

3. RIM's intangible assets are amortized as follows: acquired technology—straight-line amortization over 2 to 5 years; licences—the lesser of straight-line amortization over 5 years or units-of-activity amortization; and patents—straight-line amortization over 17 years.

4. RIM incurred an impairment loss of U.S. $1,318,000 on its capital assets. To ensure that the asset is not overstated on the books, it is written down to its new market value during the year in which a permanent decline in value occurs.

5. The return on assets is a function of two factors: profit margin and asset turnover. The formula to calculate return on assets is: return on assets = profit margin × asset turnover. The industry's asset turnover must be 0.5 times (0.2% ÷ 0.4%). RIM's asset turnover must be 0.6 times (9.4% ÷ 15.8%).

Summary of Study Objectives

1. Describe how the cost principle applies to property, plant, and equipment. The cost of property, plant, and equipment includes all expenditures necessary to acquire the assets and make them ready for their intended use.

2. Explain the concept of, and calculate, amortization. Amortization is the process of allocating the cost of a long-lived asset over the asset's useful (service) life in a rational and systematic way. Amortization is not a process of valuation, and it does not result in an accumulation of cash.

There are three amortization methods: straight-line, declining-balance, and units-of-activity. Each results in the same amount of total amortization over the useful life but they differ in how they allocate the amortization each year:

Method	Annual Amortization Pattern
Straight-line	Constant amount
Declining-balance	Decreasing amount
Units-of-activity	Varying amount

3. Describe other accounting issues related to amortization. Amortization for income tax purposes is known as capital cost allowance (CCA). The single declining-balance method is required and amortization rates are prescribed.

An impairment loss is recorded for long-lived assets when there is a permanent decline in market value below book value. Tangible and intangible assets with limited lives are tested for impairment as required and whenever circumstances make this appropriate. Intangible assets with indefinite lives are tested at least annually for impairment.

When circumstances change that affect the cost, salvage value, or useful life of an asset, a revision of amortization is required. Revisions are treated as changes in estimates and are adjusted in the present and future periods, not retroactively.

4. Explain how to account for the disposal of property, plant, and equipment. The procedure for accounting for the disposal of property, plant, and equipment through sale or retirement is:
(a) Update any unrecorded amortization.
(b) Calculate the net book value.
(c) Calculate any gain (proceeds less net book value) or loss (net book value less proceeds) on disposal.
(d) Eliminate the asset and accumulated amortization accounts at the date of disposal. Record the proceeds received and the gain or loss (if any).

5. Identify the basic issues related to accounting for intangible assets. The accounting for tangible and intangible assets is much the same. Intangible assets are reported at cost, which includes all expenditures necessary to prepare the asset for its intended use. Intangible assets with limited lives are amortized on a straight-line basis over the shorter of their useful lives or legal lives. Intangible assets with indefinite lives are not amortized.

6. Indicate how long-lived assets are reported in the financial statements. Amortization expense and any impairment losses are reported as operating expenses in the statement of earnings. Any gain or loss on disposal is reported in the "other revenue/expense" section of the statement of earnings.

In the balance sheet, land, land improvements, buildings, and equipment are usually combined and shown under the heading "Property, Plant, and Equipment." Intangible assets with limited lives are sometimes combined under the heading "Intangible Assets" or are listed separately. Goodwill is normally presented separately. Either on the balance sheet or in the notes, the balances of the major classes of amortizable assets are presented, and the accumulated amortization by major classes, or in total, is disclosed. The amortization methods must also be described. The company's impairment policy and any impairment losses should also be described and reported.

In the cash flow statement, any cash flows from the purchase or sale of long-lived assets are reported as investing activities.

7. Describe the methods for evaluating the use of assets. The use of assets may be analyzed using the return on assets and asset turnover ratios. Return on assets (net earnings ÷ average total assets) indicates how profitably assets are used to generate earnings. Asset turnover (net sales ÷ average total assets) indicates how efficiently assets are used to generate revenue. The components of the return on assets ratio can be further analyzed by multiplying the asset turnover and the profit margin.

8. Calculate amortization using the declining-balance method and the units-of-activity method (Appendix 9A). Amortization is calculated for the declining-balance method by multiplying the book value at the beginning of the year by the straight-line rate (100% divided by the useful life in years). The straight-line rate is often multiplied by a declining-balance multiplier (e.g., 2).

Amortization is calculated for the units-of-activity method by dividing the amortizable cost (cost less salvage value) by the total estimated useful life in units of activity. This result is multiplied by the actual units of activity in each period.

▦ Decision Toolkit—A Summary

Decision Checkpoints	Info Needed for Decision	Tools to Use for Decision	How to Evaluate Results
Does the company have impairment losses?	Impairment loss recorded on statement of earnings; book value of long-lived assets	Review the impairment losses recorded by the company. Compare book and market values in light of current business conditions and company performance.	If book value is higher than market value, assets and net earnings will be overstated in the current period. Watch for earnings management—the deliberate timing of the recognition of impairment losses.
Is the company's amortization of intangibles reasonable?	Estimated useful life of intangibles with definite lives from notes to financial statements of this company and its competitors	If the company's estimated useful life is significantly higher than that of competitors, or does not seem reasonable in light of the circumstances, the reason for the difference should be investigated.	Too high an estimated useful life will result in understating amortization expense and overstating net earnings.
Is the company using its assets effectively?	Net earnings and average total assets	$\text{Return on assets} = \dfrac{\text{Net earnings}}{\text{Average total assets}}$	Higher value suggests favourable efficiency (use of assets).
How effective is the company at generating sales from its assets?	Net sales and average total assets	$\text{Asset turnover} = \dfrac{\text{Net sales}}{\text{Average total assets}}$	Indicates the sales dollars generated per dollar of assets. A high value suggests the company is effective in using its resources to generate sales.

**Analysis Tools
(Decision Toolkit Summaries)**

the navigator

Glossary

Study Tools (Glossary)

Amortizable cost The cost of a long-lived asset less its salvage value. (p. 408)

Asset turnover A measure of how efficiently a company uses its total assets to generate sales. It is calculated by dividing net sales by average total assets. (p. 425)

Capital expenditures Expenditures that benefit future periods. They are recorded as long-lived assets. (p. 403)

Capital lease A long-term agreement allowing one party (the lessee) to use another party's (the lessor's) asset. The arrangement is accounted for as a purchase. (p. 406)

Copyright An exclusive right granted by the federal government allowing the owner to reproduce and sell an artistic or published work. (p. 420)

Declining-balance method An amortization method that applies a constant rate (the straight-line rate, which is 100% divided by the useful life) to the declining book value of an asset. This method produces a decreasing annual amortization expense over the useful life of the asset. (p. 409)

Franchise A contractual arrangement under which the franchisor grants the franchisee the right to sell certain products, to render specific services, or to use certain trademarks or trade names, usually within a designated geographic area. (p. 421)

Goodwill The amount paid to acquire another company that exceeds the market value of the company's net identifiable assets. (p. 421)

Impairment loss An impairment loss results when the market value of an asset permanently declines below its book value. (p. 412)

Intangible assets Rights, privileges, and competitive advantages that result from the ownership of long-lived assets that do not have physical substance. (p. 418)

Lessee A party that has made contractual arrangements to use another party's asset. (p. 405)

Lessor A party that has agreed contractually to let another party use its asset. (p. 405)

Licences Operating rights to use property, granted by a government agency to a company. (p. 421)

Off–balance sheet financing The intentional effort by a company to structure its financing arrangements so as to avoid showing liabilities on its books. (p. 406)

Operating expenditures Expenditures that benefit only the current period. They are immediately matched against revenues as an expense. (p. 403)

Operating lease An arrangement allowing one party (the lessee) to use the asset of another party (the lessor). The arrangement is accounted for as a rental. (p. 406)

Patent An exclusive right issued by the federal government that enables the recipient to manufacture, sell, or otherwise control an invention for a period of 20 years from the date of the application. (p. 419)

Property, plant, and equipment Identifiable, long-lived tangible assets, such as land, land improvements, buildings, and equipment, that support the production and sale of goods or services to customers. (p. 402)

Research and development (R&D) costs Expenditures that may lead to patents, copyrights, new processes, and new products. (p. 420)

Return on assets A profitability measure that indicates the amount of net earnings generated by each dollar invested in assets. It is calculated as net earnings divided by average total assets. (p. 424)

Straight-line method An amortization method in which the amortizable cost of an asset is divided by its estimated useful life. This method produces the same amortization expense for each year of the asset's useful life. (p. 408)

Tangible assets Long-lived resources that have physical substance, are used in the operations of the business, and are not intended for sale to customers. Tangible assets include property, plant, and equipment and natural resources. (p. 402)

Trademark (trade name) A word, phrase, jingle, or symbol that distinguishes or identifies a particular business or product. (p. 421)

Units-of-activity method An amortization method in which useful life is expressed in terms of the total units of production or total use expected from the asset. Amortization expense is calculated by multiplying the amortizable cost by actual activity during the year divided by estimated total activity. The method will produce an expense that will vary each period depending on activity. (p. 410)

Demonstration Problem

**Study Tools
(Demonstration Problems)**

DuPage Ltd. purchased a factory machine at a cost of $18,000 on January 1, 2006. The machine was expected to have a salvage value of $2,000 at the end of its four-year useful life. During its useful life, the machine was expected to be used 16,000 hours. Actual annual hourly use was as follows: 4,500 hours in 2006; 4,000 hours in 2007; 3,500 hours in 2008; and 4,000 hours in 2009.

Instructions

(a) Prepare an amortization schedule using the straight-line method.
(b) Prepare amortization schedules for the following methods: (1) units-of-activity and (2) declining-balance using double the straight-line rate (Appendix 9A).

Action Plan

- Deduct the salvage value in the straight-line and units-of-activity methods, but not the declining-balance method.
- In the declining-balance method, the straight-line amortization rate is applied to the net book value.
- Amortization should never reduce the book value of the asset below its expected salvage value.

Solution to Demonstration Problem

(a)

DUPAGE LTD.
Straight-Line Amortization Schedule

Year	Amortizable Cost	×	Amortization Rate	=	Amortization Expense	Accumulated Amortization	Book Value
							$18,000
2006	$16,000[a]		25%[b]		$4,000	$ 4,000	14,000
2007	16,000		25%		4,000	8,000	10,000
2008	16,000		25%		4,000	12,000	6,000
2009	16,000		25%		4,000	16,000	2,000

End of Year columns: Accumulated Amortization and Book Value.

[a] $18,000 − $2,000 = $16,000
[b] 100% ÷ 4 years = 25%

(b) (1)

DUPAGE LTD.
Units-of-Activity Amortization Schedule

Year	Units of Activity	×	Amortizable Cost/Unit	=	Amortization Expense	Accumulated Amortization	Book Value
							$18,000
2006	4,500		$1[a]		$4,500	$ 4,500	13,500
2007	4,000		1		4,000	8,500	9,500
2008	3,500		1		3,500	12,000	6,000
2009	4,000		1		4,000	16,000	2,000

End of Year column spans Accumulated Amortization and Book Value.

[a] $18,000 − $2,000 = $16,000 ÷ 16,000 hours = $1

(2)

DUPAGE LTD.
Declining-Balance Amortization Schedule

Year	Book Value Beginning of Year	×	Amortization Rate	=	Amortization Expense	Accumulated Amortization	Book Value
							$18,000
2006	$18,000		50%[a]		$9,000	$ 9,000	9,000
2007	9,000		50%		4,500	13,500	4,500
2008	4,500		50%		2,250	15,750	2,250
2009	2,250		50%		250[b]	16,000	2,000

End of Year column spans Accumulated Amortization and Book Value.

[a] 25% × 2 = 50%
[b] Adjusted to $250 because ending book value should not be less than expected value.

Note: All questions, exercises, and problems below with an asterisk (*) relate to material in Appendix 9A.

Self-Study Questions

Study Tools (Self-Assessment Quizzes)

Answers are at the end of the chapter.

(SO 1) 1. Corrieten Ltd. purchased equipment and incurred these costs:

Invoice price	$24,000
Freight—FOB shipping point	1,000
Insurance during transit	200
Installation and testing	400
Total costs	$25,600

What amount should be recorded as the cost of the equipment?
(a) $24,000   (c) $24,600
(b) $24,200   (d) $25,600

(SO 2) 2. Cuso Ltd. purchased equipment on January 1, 2005, at a total invoice cost of $400,000. The equipment has an estimated salvage value of $10,000 and an estimated useful life of five years. What is the amount of accumulated amortization at December 31, 2006, the second year of the asset's useful life, if the straight-line method of amortization is used?
(a) $78,000   (c) $156,000
(b) $80,000   (d) $160,000

3. Which amortization method would result in the high- (SO 2) est net earnings in the first year of an asset's life, if the asset's output was relatively high in its first year of operations?
(a) Straight-line
(b) Double declining-balance
(c) Units-of-activity
(d) Capital cost allowance

4. A piece of equipment has an original cost of $125,000, (SO 3) accumulated amortization of $25,000, and a market value of $80,000. If the decline in value is thought to be permanent, the impairment loss is:
(a) $0.   (c) $45,000.
(b) $20,000.   (d) $55,000.

5. Oviatt Ltd. sold equipment for $10,000 cash. At the time (SO 4) of disposition, the equipment had a cost of $45,000 and accumulated amortization of $30,000. Oviatt should record a:
(a) $5,000 loss on disposal.
(b) $5,000 gain on disposal.
(c) $15,000 loss on disposal.
(d) $15,000 gain on disposal.

(SO 5)   6. Pierce Inc. incurred $150,000 of research costs in its laboratory to develop a new product. It spent $20,000 in legal fees for a patent granted on January 2, 2006. On July 31, 2006, Pierce paid $15,000 for legal fees in a successful defence of the patent. What is the total amount that should be debited to Patents through July 31, 2006?
(a) $15,000   (c) $35,000
(b) $20,000   (d) $185,000

(SO 6)   7. Indicate which one of these statements is *true*:
(a) Since intangible assets lack physical substance, they need to be disclosed only in the notes to the financial statements.
(b) Goodwill should be combined and reported with the other intangible assets on the balance sheet.
(c) Intangible assets are typically combined with property, plant, and equipment and reported in the Property, Plant, and Equipment section of the balance sheet.
(d) Property, plant, and equipment, goodwill, and intangible assets should be separately reported on the balance sheet.

8. ⚙ Which of the following ratios helps determine   (SO 7) how efficiently a company uses its assets?
(a) Current ratio   (c) Debt to total assets
(b) Profit margin   (d) Asset turnover

*9. Kant Enterprises Ltd. purchases a truck for $32,000   (SO 8) on July 1, 2006. The truck has an estimated salvage value of $2,000, an estimated useful life of five years, and an estimated total mileage of 300,000 kilometres. If 50,000 kilometres are driven in 2006, what amount of amortization expense would Kant record at December 31, 2006, assuming it uses the units-of-activity method?
(a) $2,500   (c) $5,000
(b) $3,000   (d) $5,333

*10. Refer to the data provided for Kant Enterprises in   (SO 8) question 9. If Kant uses the double declining-balance method of amortization, what amount of amortization expense would be recorded at December 31, 2006?
(a) $6,000   (c) $12,000
(b) $6,400   (d) $12,800

Questions

(SO 1)   1. Susan Leung is uncertain about how the cost and matching principles apply to long-lived assets. Explain these principles to Susan.

(SO 1)   2. In 2005, Research in Motion Limited added $20 million of legal defence costs to its Patent account. Explain why the company recorded these as a capital expenditure and not an operating expenditure.

(SO 1)   3. What are the main advantages of leasing?

(SO 2)   4. In a recent press release, the president of Anwar Inc. stated that something has to be done about amortization. The president said, "Amortization does not come close to accumulating the cash needed to replace the asset at the end of its useful life." What is your response to the president?

(SO 2)   5. Contrast the effects of the three amortization methods on amortization expense, net earnings, and book value (1) in the early years of an asset's life, and (2) over the total life of the asset.

(SO 2)   6. Morgan Corporation and Petrunik Corporation both operate in the same industry. Morgan uses the straight-line method to account for amortization, whereas Petrunik uses the declining-balance method. Explain what complications might arise in trying to compare the results of these two companies.

(SO 3)   7. Lucien Corporation uses straight-line amortization for financial reporting purposes but CCA (the single declining-balance method) for income tax purposes. Is it acceptable to use different methods for these two purposes? Why is Lucien likely doing this?

8. ⚙ What is an impairment loss? Under what cir-   (SO 3) cumstances does it arise?

9. Explain the (a) similarities and (b) differences of the   (SO 3) application of the lower of cost and market rule for inventories and long-lived assets.

10. In the fourth year of an asset's five-year useful life, the   (SO 3) company decides that the asset will have a six-year total service life. Should prior periods be restated for the revised amortization? Explain why or why not.

11. If equipment is sold in the middle of a fiscal year, why   (SO 4) does amortization have to be updated for the partial period when the journal entry to record the sale subsequently removes the accumulated amortization from the books anyway?

12. How is a gain or a loss on the sale of property, plant, or   (SO 4) equipment calculated? Is the calculation the same for the retirement of property, plant, or equipment?

13. Rashid Corporation owns a machine that is fully amor-   (SO 4) tized but is still being used. How should Rashid account for this asset and report it in the financial statements?

14. Why are intangible assets with a limited life amortized   (SO 5) but intangible assets with an indefinite life are not?

15. Heflin Corporation hires an accounting student who   (SO 5) says that intangible assets with a limited life should always be amortized over their legal lives. Is the student correct? Explain.

16. Bob Leno, a business student, is working on a case for   (SO 5) one of his classes. In this case, the company needs to

raise cash to market a new product it developed. Saul Cain, an engineering student, takes one look at the company's balance sheet and says, "This company has an awful lot of goodwill. Why don't you recommend that they sell some of it to raise cash?" How should Bob respond to Saul?

(SO 6) 17. Explain how long-lived assets should be reported on the (a) balance sheet, (b) statement of earnings, and (c) cash flow statement.

(SO 6) 18. What information about long-lived assets should be disclosed in the notes to the financial statements?

(SO 7) 19. 🔧 Give an example of an industry that would be characterized by (a) a high asset turnover and a low profit margin, and (b) a low asset turnover and a high profit margin.

20. 🔧 Tim Hortons reported net sales of U.S. $995.6 (SO 7) million, operating earnings of U.S. $247.5 million, and average total assets of U.S. $997.6 million in a recent year. Using operating earnings as a substitute for net earnings, calculate Tim Hortons' return on assets and asset turnover ratios.

21. Explain how the profit margin and asset turnover (SO 7) ratios can be used to help explain return on assets.

*22. Why is amortizable cost (cost less salvage value) used (SO 8) in the straight-line and units-of-activity methods but not in the declining-balance method?

*23. Why must the calculation of amortization be adjusted (SO 8) for any fraction of a year since purchase when the straight-line and declining-balance methods are used, but no adjustment is needed when the units-of-activity method is used?

Brief Exercises

BE9–1 These expenditures were incurred by Shumway Ltd. in purchasing land: cash price $50,000; legal fees $2,500; clearing and grading $3,500; and installation of fence $3,000. What is the cost of the land?

Determine cost of land. (SO 1)

BE9–2 Basler Ltd. incurs these expenditures in purchasing a truck: invoice price $28,000; one-year accident insurance policy $2,000; motor vehicle licence $100; and painting and lettering $400. What is the cost of the truck?

Determine cost of truck. (SO 1)

BE9–3 Indicate whether each of the following items is an operating expenditure (O) or a capital expenditure (C). If the expenditure is neither, insert NA (not applicable) in the space provided.

Identify operating and capital expenditures. (SO 1)

(a) ___ Repaired building roof, $500

(b) ___ Replaced building roof, $7,500

(c) ___ Purchased building, $80,000

(d) ___ Purchased supplies, $350

(e) ___ Purchased truck, $35,000

(f) ___ Purchased oil and gas for truck, $75

(g) ___ Replaced tires on truck, $500

(h) ___ Anticipated retirement costs for plant, $5,000,000

(i) ___ Added a new wing to building, $250,000

(j) ___ Painted interior of building, $1,500

BE9–4 Cunningham Ltd. acquires a delivery truck on May 1, 2005, at a cost of $42,000. The truck is expected to have a salvage value of $2,000 at the end of its four-year useful life. Assuming the company's year-end is December 31, calculate the amortization expense for 2005 and 2006 using the straight-line method.

Calculate straight-line amortization. (SO 2)

BE9–5 The Fortune Cookie Corporation owns machinery that cost $90,000 and has accumulated amortization of $54,000. The machinery's market value is $30,000. Prepare the journal entry to record the impairment loss, assuming the decline in value is permanent.

Record impairment loss. (SO 3)

BE9–6 Wiley Inc. sells office equipment on September 30, 2006, for $21,000 cash. The office equipment originally cost $72,000 when purchased on January 1, 2003. It has an estimated salvage value of $2,000 and a useful life of five years. Amortization was last recorded on

Record sale of equipment. (SO 4)

December 31, 2005, the company's year end. Prepare the journal entries to (a) update amortization to September 30, 2006, and (b) record the sale of the equipment.

Record retirement of equipment.
(SO 4)

BE9–7   Ruiz Ltd. retires its delivery equipment which cost $42,000. Prepare journal entries to record the transaction if accumulated amortization is (a) $42,000, and (b) $40,000.

Evaluate value of goodwill.
(SO 5)

BE9–8   Royal Bank of Canada had, in its unadjusted trial balance, goodwill of $4,546 million at October 31, 2004. At year end, it was determined that goodwill attributable to RBC Mortgage Company was impaired by approximately $130 million. At what value should goodwill be reported on the Royal Bank's balance sheet at October 31, 2004? Explain why.

Record patent transactions; show balance sheet presentation.
(SO 5, 6)

BE9–9   The Surkis Corporation purchased a patent for $180,000 cash on January 2, 2006. Its legal life is 20 years and its estimated useful life is 10 years. (a) Prepare the journal entry to record the (1) purchase of the patent on January 2, 2006, and (2) amortization for the first year ended December 31, 2006. (b) Show how the patent would be reported on the balance sheet at December 31.

Classify long-lived assets.
(SO 6)

BE9–10   Indicate whether each of the following items should be recorded as property, plant, and equipment (PPE) or an intangible asset (I). If the asset does not fit one of these categories, insert NA (not applicable) in the space provided.

(a) ___ Building   (h) ___ Cash

(b) ___ Franchise   (i) ___ Goodwill

(c) ___ Inventory   (j) ___ Machinery

(d) ___ Common shares   (k) ___ Parking lot

(e) ___ Land   (l) ___ Patent

(f) ___ Land held for sale   (m) ___ Research costs

(g) ___ Licence right   (n) ___ Trademark

Prepare partial balance sheet.
(SO 6)

BE9–11   Canadian Tire Corporation, Limited reports the following selected information about long-lived assets at January 1, 2005 (in millions):

Accumulated amortization—buildings	$ 652.5
Accumulated amortization—fixtures and equipment	316.4
Accumulated amortization—leasehold improvements	69.0
Buildings	1,987.5
Fixtures and equipment	470.2
Goodwill	41.7
Land	672.1
Leasehold improvements	201.0
Mark's Work Wearhouse store brands and banners	50.0
Mark's Work Wearhouse franchise agreements	2.0
Other property, plant, and equipment, net	292.3

Mark's Work Wearhouse store brands, banners, and franchises are considered to have indefinite lives. Prepare a partial balance sheet for Canadian Tire.

Calculate ratios.
(SO 7)

BE9–12   Magna International Inc., a worldwide automotive supplier headquartered in Aurora, Ontario, reports the following in its 2004 financial statements (in U.S. millions): net sales $20,653; net earnings $692; total assets at December 31, 2003, $9,864; and total assets at December 31, 2004, $11,609. Calculate Magna's return on assets and asset turnover for 2004.

Calculate declining-balance amortization.
(SO 8)

*****BE9–13**   Amortization information for Cunningham Ltd. is given in BE9–4. Assuming the amortization rate is equal to (one times) the straight-line rate, calculate the amortization expense for 2005 and 2006 under the single declining-balance method.

Calculate units-of-activity amortization.
(SO 8)

*****BE9–14**   The Speedy Taxi Service uses the units-of-activity method to calculate amortization on its taxicabs. Each cab is expected to be driven 325,000 kilometres. Taxi 10 cost $33,000 and is expected to have a salvage value of $500. Taxi 10 was driven 125,000 kilometres in 2005 and 105,000 kilometres in 2006. Calculate the amortization expense for each year.

Exercises

E9–1 The following expenditures relating to property, plant, and equipment were made by Kosinki Ltd.:

Classify expenditures.
(SO 1)

1. Paid $45,000 for a new delivery truck.
2. Paid $250 to have the company name and advertising slogan painted on the new truck.
3. Paid a $75 motor vehicle licence fee on the new truck.
4. Paid $900 for a one-year accident insurance policy on the new truck.
5. Paid $100,000 for a plant site.
6. Paid $2,000 (net of proceeds) to demolish an old building on the plant site.
7. Paid $17,500 for paving the parking lot on the plant site.
8. Paid $4,000 of legal fees on the purchase of the plant site.
9. Paid $25,000 for new machinery.
10. Paid $800 for the installation of the machinery.

Instructions

(a) Explain the application of the cost principle in determining the acquisition cost of property, plant, and equipment.
(b) List the numbers of the preceding transactions, and beside each number indicate the account title that the expenditure should be debited in.

E9–2 Costello Limited purchased a new machine on April 1, 2005, at a cost of $90,000. The company estimated that the machine will have a salvage value of $12,000. The machine is expected to be used for 10,000 working hours during its five-year life.

Calculate straight-line amortization; compare methods.
(SO 2)

Instructions

(a) Calculate the amortization expense under the straight-line method for 2005 and 2006, assuming a December 31 year end.
(b) If Costello had used the declining-balance method instead of the straight-line method, which method would result in the highest book value for the first two years? The highest earnings? The highest cash flow?

E9–3 Lindy Weink, the new controller of Lafrenière Inc., reviewed the expected useful life and salvage value of the company's equipment at the beginning of 2006 and proposed changes as follows:

Record straight-line amortization; discuss revision of estimate.
(SO 2, 3)

Date Acquired	Cost	Useful Life (in years) Current	Proposed	Salvage Value Current	Proposed
Jan. 1, 2004	$120,000	5	4	$5,000	$3,600

Instructions

(a) Prepare the journal entry to record amortization for 2005 using the straight-line method and the current useful life and salvage value.
(b) Calculate the accumulated amortization on the equipment at December 31, 2005.
(c) If the company accepts Lindy's proposed changes in useful life and salvage value, will amortization expense in 2006 be higher or lower than amortization expense in 2005?

E9–4 The Penang Corporation purchased a piece of equipment on January 1, 2004, for $900,000. It had an estimated useful life of five years and a $50,000 salvage value. Penang uses straight-line amortization and has a December 31 year end. At December 31, 2006, the equipment had a permanent decline in its market value to $340,000.

Record impairment loss; discuss presentation.
(SO 3)

Instructions

(a) Calculate the equipment's book value at December 31, 2006.
(b) Prepare the journal entry to record any impairment loss.
(c) How should the impairment loss be reported in the financial statements?

E9–5 Presented here are selected transactions for Beck Corporation for 2006. Beck uses straight-line amortization.

Record disposal of equipment.
(SO 4)

Jan. 1 Retired a piece of machinery that was purchased on January 1, 1997. The machine cost $62,000 and had a useful life of 10 years with no salvage value.

June 30 Sold a computer that was purchased on January 1, 2004. The computer cost $5,475 and had a useful life of three years with no salvage value. The computer was sold for $500 cash.

Dec. 31 Sold a delivery truck for $10,000 cash. The truck cost $27,000 when it was purchased on January 1, 2004, and was amortized based on a four-year useful life with a $3,000 salvage value.

Instructions

Prepare all entries required to record the above transactions.

Record intangible asset transactions; show balance sheet presentation.
(SO 5, 6)

E9–6   Collins Ltd. has these transactions related to intangible assets in 2006, its first year of operations:

Jan.   2 Purchased a patent with an estimated useful life of five years and a legal life of 20 years for $40,000.
Apr.   1 Acquired another company, and recorded goodwill for $300,000 as part of a purchase.
July   1 Acquired a franchise for $250,000. The franchise agreement expires on July 1, 2016.
Sept. 1 Incurred research costs of $150,000.
       30 Incurred development costs of $50,000. No marketable product has been identified as yet.
Dec. 31 Recorded annual amortization.
      31 Tested the intangible assets for impairment. Market values exceeded book values in all cases.

Instructions

(a) Prepare the entries to record the above transactions. Assume all costs incurred were for cash.
(b) Show the balance sheet presentation of the intangible assets at December 31, 2006.

Discuss implication of amortization period.
(SO 5)

E9–7   Alliance Atlantis Communications Inc. changed its accounting policy to amortize a program's broadcast rights over the contracted exhibition period, which is based on the estimated useful life of the program. Previously, the company amortized broadcast rights over the lesser of two years or the contracted exhibition period.

Instructions

Write a short memo to your client explaining the implications this has for the analysis of Alliance Atlantis's results. Also discuss whether this change in amortization period looks reasonable.

Apply accounting concepts.
(SO 1, 2, 5)

E9–8   A co-op student encountered the following situations at Chin Chin Corporation:

1. The accounting co-op student learned that Chin Chin is amortizing its buildings and equipment, but not its land. The student could not understand why land was omitted, so she prepared journal entries to amortize all the company's property, plant, and equipment for the current year end.

2. The co-op student determined that Chin Chin's amortization policy on its intangible assets is wrong. The company is currently amortizing its patents but not its goodwill. The student fixed that for the current year end by adding goodwill to her adjusting entry for amortization. She told a fellow student that she felt she had improved the consistency of the company's accounting policies by making these changes.

3. Chin Chin has a building still in use that has a zero book value but a substantial market value. The co-op student felt that this practice did not benefit the company's users—especially the bank—and wrote the building up to its market value. After all, she reasoned, you can write down assets if market values are lower. Writing them up if market value is higher is yet another example of the improved consistency that her employment has brought to the company's accounting practices.

Instructions

Explain whether or not the accounting treatment in each of the above situations follows generally accepted accounting principles. Explain what accounting principle or assumption, if any, has been violated and what the appropriate accounting treatment should be.

E9–9 BCE Inc. reported the following selected information as at December 31, 2004 (in millions):

Classify long-lived accounts; show balance sheet presentation. (SO 6)

Accounts	Amounts
Accumulated amortization—buildings	$ 1,384
Accumulated amortization—finite-life intangible assets	1,418
Accumulated amortization—machinery and equipment	3,039
Accumulated amortization—other property, plant, and equipment	97
Accumulated amortization—satellites	758
Accumulated amortization—telecommunications assets	23,469
Amortization expense	3,108
Buildings	2,682
Cash paid for capital expenditures	3,364
Finite-life intangible assets	4,124
Goodwill	8,413
Indefinite-life intangible assets	2,916
Land	95
Machinery and equipment	5,529
Other property, plant, and equipment	278
Plant under construction	1,605
Satellites	1,769
Telecommunications assets	35,481

BCE's finite-life intangible assets include software and customer relationships. Its indefinite-life intangible assets include its brand name and licences.

Instructions

(a) Identify in which financial statement (balance sheet, statement of earnings, or cash flow statement) and which section (e.g., property, plant, and equipment) each of the above items should be reported.

(b) Prepare the tangible and intangible assets sections of the balance sheet as at December 31, 2004.

E9–10 Empire Company Limited reports the following information (in millions) at April 30, 2004: net sales $11,046.8; net earnings $173.1; total assets at April 30, 2004, $4,681.7; and total assets at April 30, 2003, $4,516.1.

Calculate ratios. (SO 7)

Instructions

(a) Calculate the (1) return on assets, (2) asset turnover, and (3) profit margin ratios for the year.

(b) Prove mathematically how the profit margin and asset turnover work together to explain return on assets, by showing the appropriate calculation.

(c) Empire Company owns Sobeys, Empire Theatres, Lawton Drugstores, and Wajax. It also manages commercial real estate, among other activities. Does this diversity of activities affect your ability to interpret the ratios you calculated in (a)? Explain.

*E9–11 Refer to the data provided in E9–2 for Costello Limited.

Calculate amortization using units-of-activity and declining-balance methods. (SO 8)

Instructions

(a) Calculate the amortization expense for each of the years ended December 31, 2005 and 2006, using the (1) units-of-activity method, assuming machine usage was 1,300 hours for 2005 and 1,800 hours for 2006, and (2) double declining-balance method.

(b) What factors should the company consider when deciding which amortization method to use?

*E9–12 Rahim Corporation purchased a computer for $5,000. The company planned to keep it for four years, after which it expected to sell it for $500.

Determine effect of choice of amortization method over life of asset. (SO 2, 8)

Instructions

(a) Calculate the amortization expense for each of the first three years under the (1) straight-line method, and (2) double declining-balance method.

(b) Assuming Rahim sold the computer for $1,225 at the end of the third year, calculate the gain or loss on disposal under each amortization method.

(c) Determine the impact on earnings (total amortization plus loss on disposal or less gain on disposal) of each method for use of the computer over the entire three-year period.

Problems: Set A

Analyze and record property transactions.
(SO 1)

P9–1A   Weiseman Ltd. incurred the following cash payments and receipts for the acquisition of property:

Payments	
1. Cost of real estate purchased as a plant site (land $235,000; building $45,000)	$280,000
2. Legal fees on real estate purchase in (1) above	3,800
3. Installation cost of fence around property while under construction	4,200
4. Cost of demolishing building to make land suitable for construction of new building	19,000
5. Excavation costs for new building	23,000
6. Architect's fees for building plans	18,000
7. Full payment to building contractor	600,000
8. Interest while under construction	15,000
9. Cost of parking lots and driveways	10,000
	$973,000

Receipts	
10. Proceeds from salvage of demolished building	$5,000

Instructions

(a) Analyze the above transactions, and determine the cost of land, land improvements, and building, and the impact on any other affected accounts.
(b) Prepare the journal entries to record the above transactions.

Classify operating and capital expenditures.
(SO 1)

P9–2A   The transactions below are expenditures related to property, plant, and equipment:

1. Operator controls on equipment were replaced for $7,000, because the original control devices were not adequate.
2. A total of $4,600 was spent for decorative landscaping (planting flowers and shrubs, etc.).
3. A new air conditioning system for the factory office was purchased for $16,000.
4. Windows broken in a labour dispute were replaced for $2,400.
5. A fee of $1,500 was paid for adjusting and testing new machinery before its use.
6. Machinery damaged by a forklift was repaired for $5,000.
7. The transmission in a delivery truck was repaired for $2,500.

Instructions

For each of the transactions listed above, indicate the title of the account that you think should be debited in recording the transaction. Briefly explain your reasoning.

Calculate straight-line amortization and compare effects of different methods.
(SO 2)

P9–3A   Mazlish Corporation purchased a machine on account on April 6, 2006, at an invoice price of $180,000. On April 7, 2006, it paid $900 for delivery of the machine. A one-year, $2,275 insurance policy on the machine was purchased on April 9, 2006. On April 22, 2006, Mazlish paid $3,300 for installation and testing of the machine. The machine was ready for use on April 30, 2006.

Mazlish estimates the useful life of the machine will be five years with a salvage value of $11,500. Mazlish uses straight-line amortization and has a December 31 year end.

Instructions

(a) Determine the cost of the machine.
(b) Calculate the amount of amortization expense that Mazlish should record during each year of the asset's life.
(c) Compare the impact of using the straight-line method to using the declining-balance method. State whether the result would be higher or lower for each year of the asset's life and in total over the five-year life for (1) amortization expense, (2) net earnings, and (3) net book value.
(d) Compare the impact of using the straight-line method to using the units-of-activity method. State whether the result would be higher or lower for each year of the asset's life and in total over the five-year life for (1) amortization expense, (2) net earnings, and (3) net book value.
(e) What factors should influence management's choice of amortization method for a machine such as this?

P9–4A At January 1, 2006, Hamsmith Corporation reported the following property, plant, and equipment accounts:

Record property, plant, and equipment transactions; prepare partial balance sheet.
(SO 2, 4, 6)

Accumulated amortization—buildings	$12,100,000
Accumulated amortization—equipment	5,000,000
Buildings	26,500,000
Equipment	40,000,000
Land	3,000,000

During 2006, the following selected transactions occurred:

Apr. 1 Purchased land for $2.2 million. Paid $440,000 cash and issued a three-year, 6% note for the balance.

May 1 Sold equipment that cost $600,000 when purchased on January 1, 1999. The equipment was sold for $200,000 cash.

June 1 Sold land for $1.8 million. Received $360,000 cash and accepted a three-year, 5% note for the balance. The land cost $500,000.

July 1 Purchased equipment for $1.1 million cash.

Dec. 31 Retired equipment that cost $500,000 when purchased on December 31, 1996.

Hamsmith uses straight-line amortization for buildings and equipment and its fiscal year end is December 31. The buildings are estimated to have a 40-year useful life and no salvage value; the equipment is estimated to have a 10-year useful life and no salvage value. Interest on the notes is payable or collectible annually on the anniversary date of the issue.

Instructions

(a) Record the above transactions.

(b) Record any adjusting entries required at December 31, 2006.

(c) Prepare the property, plant, and equipment section of Hamsmith's balance sheet at December 31, 2006.

P9–5A On January 1, 2004, Penaji Corporation acquired equipment costing $65,000. It was estimated at that time that this equipment would have a useful life of eight years and a salvage value of $3,000. The straight-line method of amortization is used by Penaji for its equipment, and its fiscal year end is December 31.

Calculate amortization; discuss revision of estimate.
(SO 2, 3)

At the beginning of 2006 (the beginning of the third year of the equipment's life), the company's engineers reconsidered their expectations. They estimated that the equipment's useful life would more likely be six years in total, instead of the previously estimated eight years.

Instructions

(a) Calculate the accumulated amortization and net book value of the equipment at the beginning of 2006, immediately before the change in useful life.

(b) Would you expect Penaji's amortization expense to increase or decrease in 2006, after the change in useful life? Explain why.

(c) Should Penaji treat the change in the useful life retroactively or only for current and future periods? Explain.

(d) If Penaji had *not* revised the equipment's remaining useful life at the beginning of 2006, what would its total amortization expense have been over the equipment's life? What would have been the accumulated amortization and net book value at the end of the equipment's useful life?

(e) Would you expect Penaji's total amortization expense to change after the useful life has been revised? Would there be changes to the accumulated amortization and net book value at the end of the equipment's useful life?

P9–6A Express Corp. purchased delivery equipment on July 1, 2004, for $65,000 cash. At that time, the equipment was estimated to have a useful life of five years and a salvage value of $5,000. The equipment was disposed of on September 30, 2006. Express uses the straight-line method of amortization and has a December 31 year end.

Record acquisition, amortization, and disposal of equipment.
(SO 2, 4)

Instructions

(a) Prepare the journal entry to record the acquisition of equipment on July 1, 2004.

(b) Record amortization for each of 2004, 2005, and 2006.

(c) Record the disposal of the equipment on September 30, 2006, under each of the following independent assumptions:

    1. It was sold for $37,000.

    2. It was sold for $40,000.

    3. It was retired.

Correct errors in recording intangible asset transactions.
(SO 5)

P9–7A   Due to rapid employee turnover in the accounting department, the following transactions involving intangible assets were recorded in a questionable way by Riley Corporation in the year ended December 31, 2006:

1. Riley developed a new manufacturing process at the beginning of the year, incurring research costs of $120,000. Of this amount, 45% was considered to be development costs that could be capitalized. Riley recorded the entire $120,000 in the Patents account and amortized it over a 15-year useful life.

2. On July 1, 2006, Riley purchased a small company and as a result recorded goodwill of $160,000. Riley recorded a half year's amortization for the goodwill in 2006, based on an estimated 40-year life.

3. The company purchased a trademark for $47,500. At the end of the year, Riley recorded an impairment loss of $2,500 because it believed that the trademark was only worth $45,000. Riley fully expects this value to recover next year after the conclusion of a legal case defending the company's right to use this trademark, but felt that it was better to err on the conservative side at this point in time.

4. The company made a $6,000 charitable donation on December 31, 2006, which it debited to goodwill.

Instructions

Prepare the journal entries necessary to correct any errors made in recording the above transactions.

Record intangible asset transactions; prepare partial balance sheet.
(SO 5, 6)

P9–8A   Selected information about Ghani Corporation's intangible assets at January 1, 2006, is presented here:

Trade name	$ 60,000
Copyright #1	36,000
Goodwill	125,000
	$221,000

The copyright was acquired January 1, 2004, and has a useful life of three years. The trade name was acquired January 1, 2002, and is expected to have an indefinite useful life. The company has a December 31 year end.

The following cash transactions may have affected intangible assets during 2006:

Jan. 5 Paid $7,000 in legal costs to successfully defend the trade name against infringement by another company.

July 1 Developed a new product, incurring $210,000 in research and $50,000 in development costs. A patent was granted for the product on July 1, and its useful life is equal to its legal life.

Sept. 1 Paid $60,000 to a popular hockey player to appear in commercials advertising the company's products. The commercials will air in September and October.

Oct. 1 Acquired another copyright for $180,000. The new copyright has a useful life of three years.

Dec. 31 The company determined the fair market value of goodwill to be $85,000. This is believed to represent a permanent impairment.

Instructions

(a) Prepare journal entries to record the above transactions.

(b) Prepare any adjusting journal entries required at December 31.

(c) Prepare the intangible assets section of the balance sheet at December 31, 2006.

P9–9A Green Mountain Coffee, Inc. and Starbucks Corporation reported the following information in 2004 (in U.S. millions):

Calculate and evaluate ratios. (SO 7)

	Green Mountain	Starbucks
Total assets, 2004	$ 78.3	$3,328.2
Total assets, 2003	60.0	2,729.7
Net sales	137.4	5,294.2
Net earnings	7.8	391.8

Industry averages are as follows: profit margin, 7.3%; return on assets, 11.7%; and asset turnover, 1.7 times.

Instructions

(a) For each company, calculate the profit margin, return on assets, and asset turnover ratios for 2004.
(b) Based on your calculations in part (a), comment on the effectiveness of each of the companies in using its assets to generate sales and produce net earnings. What, if anything, complicates your ability to compare the two companies?

P9–10A The following ratios are available for a company operating in the restaurant industry:

Evaluate ratios. (SO 7)

	Company	Industry Average
Return on assets	8.2%	7.0%
Profit margin	12.0%	6.4%
Asset turnover	0.7 times	1.2 times

Instructions

(a) The company's return on assets and profit margin are higher than that of the industry. Yet, its asset turnover is lower than the industry average. Explain what is mainly driving the company's return on assets, compared to that of the industry—margin (profit margin) or volume (asset turnover).
(b) Explain how the company might be able to improve its asset turnover ratio and what impact this might have on the profit margin and return on assets.

*P9–11A Whitley Corporation purchased machinery on January 1, 2006, at a cost of $170,000. The estimated useful life of the machinery is four years, with a salvage value of $20,000. The company is considering different amortization methods that could be used for financial reporting purposes.

Calculate and compare amortization under straight-line and declining-balance methods. (SO 2, 8)

Instructions

(a) Prepare separate amortization schedules for the life of the machinery using the straight-line method and the double declining-balance method.
(b) Which method would result in the higher net earnings for 2006? In the higher total net earnings over the four-year period?
(c) Which method would result in the higher net book value at the end of 2006? In the higher net book value at the end of the four-year period?
(d) Which method would result in the higher cash flow for 2006? In the higher total cash flow over the four-year period?
(e) What factors should management consider when it chooses an amortization method?

*P9–12A The Quai d'Valmy Inc. purchased a piece of high-tech equipment at a cost of $31,000. The equipment has an estimated useful life of three years with a salvage value of $1,000. Management is contemplating the merits of using the units-of-activity method of amortization, instead of the straight-line method which it currently uses.

Calculate and compare amortization under straight-line and units-of-activity methods. (SO 2, 8)

Under the units-of-activity method, management estimates a total production capacity of 30,000 units: 12,000 units in year 1; 10,000 units in year 2; and 8,000 units in year 3.

Instructions

(a) Prepare separate amortization schedules for the life of the equipment using the straight-line method and the units-of-activity method.

(b) Assume that the equipment is sold at the end of its second year for $10,000.
  1. Calculate the gain or loss on the sale of equipment, under (a) the straight-line method and (b) the units-of-activity method.
  2. Prepare a schedule to show the overall impact of the total amortization expense, combined with the gain or loss on sale for the two-year period, under each method of amortization (consider the total effect on net earnings over the two-year period). Comment on your results.

Problems: Set B

Analyze and record property transactions.
(SO 1)

P9–1B Kadlec Inc. incurred the following cash payments and receipts for the acquisition of property:

	Payments	
1.	Cost of real estate purchased as a plant site (land $170,000; building $50,000)	$220,000
2.	Legal fees on real estate purchase in (1) above	4,000
3.	Cost of demolishing building to make land suitable for construction of new building	21,000
4.	Excavation costs for new building	20,000
5.	Cost of filling and grading the land	7,000
6.	Architect's fees for building plans	15,000
7.	Full payment to building contractor	650,000
8.	Interest while under construction	16,000
9.	Cost of landscaping	34,000
		$987,000
	Receipts	
10.	Proceeds for salvage of demolished building	$10,500

Instructions

(a) Analyze the above transactions, and determine the cost of land, land improvements, and building, and the impact on any other affected accounts.

(b) Prepare the journal entries to record the above transactions.

Classify operating and capital expenditures.
(SO 1)

P9–2B The transactions below are expenditures for a forklift:

1. Rebuilding of a diesel engine, $10,000
2. New tires, $4,000
3. New safety cab, $5,000
4. Replacement of a windshield, $800
5. Training a new operator, $1,600
6. New paint job after the company changed its logo and colours, $2,000
7. One-year accident insurance policy, $1,110

Instructions

For each of the transactions listed above, indicate the title of the account that you think should be debited in recording the transaction. Briefly explain your reasoning.

Calculate straight-line amortization and compare effects of different methods.
(SO 2)

P9–3B The Moussaoui Corporation purchased a machine on September 3, 2006, at a cash price of $85,000. On September 4, 2006, it paid $400 for delivery of the machine. A one-year, $975 insurance policy on the machine was purchased September 6, 2006. On September 20, 2006, Moussaoui paid $2,500 for installation and testing of the machine. The machine was ready for use on September 30, 2006.

Moussaoui estimates the useful life of the machine will be four years with a salvage value of $6,000. Moussaoui uses straight-line amortization and has a November 30 year end.

Instructions

(a) Determine the cost of the machine.

(b) Calculate the amount of amortization expense that Moussaoui should record during each year of the asset's life.

(c) Compare the impact of using the straight-line method to using the declining-balance method. State whether the result would be higher or lower for each year of the asset's life and in total over the four-year life for (1) amortization expense, (2) net earnings, and (3) net book value.

(d) Compare the impact of using the straight-line method to using the units-of-activity method. State whether the result would be higher or lower for each year of the asset's life and in total over the four-year life for (1) amortization expense, (2) net earnings, and (3) net book value.

(e) What factors should influence management's choice of amortization method for a machine such as this?

P9–4B   At January 1, 2006, Yount Corporation reported the following property, plant, and equipment accounts:

Record property, plant, and equipment transactions; prepare partial balance sheet. (SO 2, 4, 6)

Accumulated amortization—buildings	$12,100,000
Accumulated amortization—equipment	15,000,000
Buildings	28,500,000
Equipment	48,000,000
Land	4,000,000

During 2006, the following selected transactions occurred:

Apr. 1 Purchased land for $2.63 million. Paid $630,000 cash and issued a 10-year, 6% note for the balance.

May 1 Sold equipment that cost $750,000 when purchased on January 1, 2002. The equipment was sold for $350,000 cash.

June 1 Sold land purchased on June 1, 1993, for $1.8 million. Received $180,000 cash and accepted a 6% note for the balance. The land cost $300,000.

July 1 Purchased equipment for $1 million on account, terms n/60.

Dec. 31 Retired equipment that cost $470,000 when purchased on December 31, 1996.

Yount uses straight-line amortization for buildings and equipment, and its fiscal year end is December 31. The buildings are estimated to have a 40-year life and no salvage value; the equipment is estimated to have a 10-year useful life and no salvage value. Interest on all notes is payable or collectible at maturity on the anniversary date of the issue.

Instructions

(a) Record the above transactions.

(b) Record any adjusting entries required at December 31, 2006.

(c) Prepare the property, plant, and equipment section of Yount's balance sheet at December 31, 2006.

P9–5B   On January 1, 2004, Bérubé Ltée acquired equipment costing $60,000. It was estimated at that time that this equipment would have a useful life of five years and a salvage value of $4,500. The straight-line method of amortization is used by Bérubé for its equipment, and its fiscal year end is December 31.

Calculate amortization; discuss revision of estimate. (SO 2, 3)

At the beginning of 2006 (the beginning of the third year of the equipment's life), the company's engineers reconsidered their expectations. They estimated that the equipment's useful life would more likely be six years in total, instead of the previously estimated five years.

Instructions

(a) Calculate the accumulated amortization and net book value of the equipment at the beginning of 2006, immediately before the change in useful life.

(b) Would you expect Bérubé's amortization expense to increase or decrease in 2006, after the change in useful life? Explain why.

(c) Should Bérubé treat the change in the useful life retroactively or only for current and future periods? Explain.

(d) If Bérubé had not revised the equipment's remaining useful life at the beginning of 2006, what would its total amortization expense have been over the equipment's life? What would have been the accumulated amortization and net book value at the end of the equipment's useful life?

(e) Would you expect Bérubé's total amortization expense to change after the useful life has been revised? Would there be changes to the accumulated amortization and net book value at the end of the equipment's useful life?

Record acquisition, amortization, and disposal of equipment.
(SO 2, 4)

P9–6B   Walker Corp. purchased office furniture on March 1, 2004, for $85,000 on account. At that time, the furniture was estimated to have a useful life of five years and a $1,000 salvage value. The furniture was disposed of on July 2, 2006, when the company relocated to new premises. Walker uses the straight-line method of amortization and has a December 31 year end.

Instructions

(a) Prepare the journal entry to record the acquisition of office furniture on March 1, 2004.
(b) Record amortization for each of 2004, 2005, and 2006.
(c) Record the disposal of the office furniture on July 2, 2006, under each of the following independent assumptions:
    1. It was sold for $50,000.   3. It was retired.
    2. It was sold for $45,000.

Correct errors in recording intangible asset transactions.
(SO 5)

P9–7B   Due to rapid employee turnover in the accounting department, the following transactions involving intangible assets were recorded in a questionable way by Baiji Ltd. in the year ended December 31, 2006:

1. Baiji developed an electronic monitoring device for running shoes. It incurred research costs of $60,000 and development costs of $35,000. It recorded all of these costs in the Patent account.
2. The company registered the patent for this "cyber shoe" device. Legal fees and registration costs totalled $21,000. These costs were recorded in the Legal Fees Expense account.
3. The company successfully fought off a competitor in court, defending its patent. It incurred $38,000 of legal fees. These costs were debited to the Legal Fees Expense account.
4. The company sold the rights to manufacture and distribute the "cyber shoe" device to Fleet Foot Inc. for an annual fee of $50,000. Baiji recorded the receipt of this fee as a credit to the Patent account.
5. The company recorded $2,250 annual amortization of the patent over its legal life of 20 years [$60,000 + $35,000 − $50,000 = $45,000 ÷ 20 years]. The expected useful life of the patent is five years. Assume that all costs occurred at the beginning of the year for amortization purposes.
6. Baiji tested the patent for impairment and found that its market value of $70,000 far exceeded its book value of $42,750 ($45,000 − $2,250).

Instructions

Prepare the journal entries to correct any errors made in recording the above transactions.

Record intangible asset transactions; prepare partial balance sheet.
(SO 5, 6)

P9–8B   Selected information about Ip Inc.'s intangible assets at January 1, 2006, is presented here:

Patent #1	$ 70,000
Copyright #1	48,000
Goodwill	210,000
	$328,000

Patent #1 was acquired in January 2004 and has a useful life of 10 years. Copyright #1 was acquired in January 2002 and also has a useful life of 10 years. The following cash transactions may have affected intangible assets during 2006:

Jan. 2 Paid $22,500 in legal costs to successfully defend Patent #1 against infringement by another company. Determined that the revised annual amortization for this patent will be $9,166.

July 1 Developed a new product, incurring $220,000 in research costs and $60,000 in development costs. Patent #2 was granted for the product on July 1, and its useful life is equal to its legal life.

Sept. 1 Paid $11,000 to an Olympic rower to appear in commercials advertising the company's products. The commercials will air in September.

Oct. 1 Acquired a second copyright for $16,000. Copyright #2 has a useful life of five years.

Dec. 31 The company determined the fair market value of the goodwill to be $175,000. Ip believes this to be a permanent impairment.

Instructions

(a) Prepare journal entries to record the above transactions.
(b) Prepare any adjusting journal entries required at December 31, the company's year-end.
(c) Prepare the intangible assets section of the balance sheet at December 31, 2006.

P9–9B Sleeman Breweries Ltd. and Big Rock Brewery Ltd. reported the following information in 2004 (in millions):

Calculate and evaluate ratios. (SO 7)

	Sleeman Breweries	Big Rock Brewery
Total assets, 2004	$300.2	$40.9
Total assets, 2003	242.8	40.8
Net sales	213.4	38.8
Net earnings	14.4	6.8

Industry averages are as follows: profit margin, 10.9%; return on assets, 7.8%; and asset turnover, 0.7 times.

Instructions

(a) For each company, calculate the profit margin, return on assets, and asset turnover ratios for 2004.
(b) Based on your calculations in part (a), comment on the effectiveness of each of the two companies in using its assets to generate sales and produce net earnings. What, if anything, complicates your ability to compare the two companies?

P9–10B The following ratios are available for a company operating in the computer industry:

Evaluate ratios. (SO 7)

	Company	Industry Average
Return on assets	7.5%	8.9%
Profit margin	8.5%	17.9%
Asset turnover	0.9 times	0.5 times

Instructions

(a) The company's return on assets and profit margin are lower than the industry averages. Yet, its asset turnover is higher than the industry average. Explain what is driving the company's return on assets compared to that of the industry: margin (profit margin) or volume (asset turnover).
(b) Speculate on this company's strategy for computer sales, compared to that of its competitors in the industry.

*P9–11B The Piper Corporation purchased machinery on January 1, 2006, at a cost of $260,000. The estimated useful life of the machinery is five years, with a salvage value of $20,000. The company is considering different amortization methods that could be used for financial reporting purposes.

Calculate and compare amortization under straight-line and declining-balance methods. (SO 2, 8)

Instructions

(a) Prepare separate amortization schedules for the life of the machinery using the straight-line method and the double declining-balance method.
(b) Which method would result in the higher net earnings for 2006? In the higher total net earnings over the five-year period?
(c) Which method would result in the higher net book value at the end of 2006? In the higher net book value at the end of the five-year period?
(d) Which method would result in the higher cash flow for 2006? In the higher total cash flow over the five-year period?
(e) What factors should the company consider when choosing an amortization method?

*P9–12B Rapid Transportation Ltd. purchased a new bus at a cost of $80,000. The bus has an estimated useful life of three years with a salvage value of $8,000. Management is contemplating the merits of using the units-of-activity method of amortization, instead of the straight-line method which it currently uses.

Calculate and compare amortization under straight-line and units-of-activity methods. (SO 2, 8)

Under the units-of-activity method, management estimates a total useful life of 300,000 kilometres: 120,000 kilometres driven in year 1; 100,000 kilometres in year 2; and 80,000 kilometres in year 3.

Instructions

(a) Prepare separate amortization schedules for the life of the bus using the straight-line method and the units-of-activity method.
(b) Assume that the bus is sold at the end of its second year for $25,000.
   1. Calculate the gain or loss on the sale of bus, under (a) the straight-line method and (b) the units-of-activity method.
   2. Prepare a schedule to show the overall impact of the total amortization expense, combined with the gain or loss on sale for the two-year period, under each method of amortization (consider the total effect on net earnings over the two-year period). Comment on your results.

BROADENING YOUR PERSPECTIVE

Financial Reporting and Analysis

Analysis Tools

Financial Reporting Problem: *Loblaw*

BYP9–1   Refer to the financial statements and the Notes to Consolidated Financial Statements of Loblaw in Appendix A.

Instructions

(a) What amortization method does Loblaw use?
(b) Identify the following amounts for the company's fixed assets at the end of fiscal 2003 and 2002: (1) cost, (2) accumulated depreciation (amortization), and (3) net book value.
(c) What was the amount of depreciation (amortization) expense reported in the statement of earnings for fiscal 2003? What is the difference between the accumulated depreciation reported at the end of fiscal 2003 and 2002 (see Note 8)? Why is this difference not the same as the depreciation expense reported in 2003?
(d) Using the cash flow statement, determine what amount of cash was received from fixed asset sales and what amount of cash was spent for fixed asset purchases in 2003.
(e) What types of intangible assets does Loblaw have?
(f) Did Loblaw report any impairment losses in 2003?

Comparative Analysis Problem: *Loblaw and Sobeys*

BYP9–2   The financial statements of Sobeys are presented in Appendix B, following the financial statements for Loblaw in Appendix A.

Instructions

(a) Based on the information in these financial statements, calculate the following values for each company for its most recent fiscal year:
   1. Profit margin
   2. Return on assets
   3. Asset turnover
(b) Industry averages for the above three ratios are as follows: profit margin, 0.6%; return on assets, 1.3%; and asset turnover, 2.5 times. What conclusions about the management of assets can be drawn from your results in (a) and these data?

Research Case

BYP9-3 The May 2005 issue of *CAmagazine* included the article "Value of the Brand" by Stephen Cole on page 39. The article discusses the fact that determining the value of a brand is more complicated than looking at the goodwill value on a company's balance sheet.

Instructions

Read the article and answer the following questions:

(a) List some examples of intangible assets. For each of the following three Canadian industries, what percentage of overall asset value do intangible asset values account for: (1) the technology, financial, communications and consumer non-cyclical sector; (2) the industrial, energy, base metal, and consumer cyclical sector; and (3) the utility sector.

(b) For each of the following companies, give the dollar amount of the company's brand value and what the brand value is as a percentage of that company's market value: Royal Bank of Canada; Canadian Tire; Molson; McCain Foods; and Sobeys.

(c) Which accounting principle governs how property, plant, and equipment, goodwill, and intangible assets are recorded? According to the *CAmagazine* article, how is brand "value" determined?

(d) Why are brand values relevant in buyouts or venture capital investments?

Interpreting Financial Statements

BYP9-4 Maple Leaf Foods Inc. is Canada's largest food processor. Recently, it spent $110 million to replace a 65-year-old pork-processing plant in Saskatoon. The old plant processed 17,000 hogs a week when operating at full capacity. The new plant can process 20,000 hogs a week on a single-shift, and has the capacity to expand to 40,000 hogs on a double-shift.

Instructions

(a) How should Maple Leaf account for the $110 million it spent to replace the 65-year-old pork-processing plant in Saskatoon?

(b) Identify and discuss the advantages and disadvantages of each amortization method for Maple Leaf Foods' pork-processing plant. Which method would you recommend Maple Leaf use to amortize its Saskatoon plant? Explain why you chose this method.

(c) Using the amortization method you chose in (b), explain how Maple Leaf's amortization expense will be affected if the plant moves to a double-shift operation and processes additional hogs.

A Global Focus

BYP9-5 Vivendi Universal S.A., with headquarters in France, is a world leader in entertainment. The following discussion of impairment of intangible assets was taken from the notes to the company's 2004 financial statements.

VIVENDI UNIVERSAL S.A.
Notes to the Financial Statements
December 31, 2004

4.4. Impairment Losses

In 2004, as consistently done since the end of 2001, Vivendi Universal re-assessed the value of goodwill and other intangible assets associated with its reporting units. Third-party appraisers assisted in the assessment of these intangible assets...

Total impairment losses recorded in 2004 amounted to €31 million and were recognized as a deduction from goodwill (€26 million) and other intangible assets (€5 million).

Instructions

(a) Vivendi follows generally accepted accounting principles for France. How does the company's treatment of the impairment losses compare with accounting practices in Canada?
(b) Reproduce the journal entry Vivendi would have made to record the impairment loss in 2004.
(c) How will this write-down affect Vivendi's balance sheet and statement of earnings in future years?

Financial Analysis on the Web

Analysis Tools
(Financial Analysis on the Web)

BYP9–6   SEDAR (System for Electronic Document Analysis and Retrieval) provides information about Canadian public companies and access to some of their documents. We will use SEDAR to select a public company, examine its financial statements, and identify the company's long-lived assets, profitability, amortization method, and current-year capital expenditures.

Instructions

Specific requirements of this Web case can be found on the Toolkit website.

Critical Thinking

Collaborative Learning Activity

*BYP9–7   Ty Corporation and Hamline Corporation are two companies that are similar in many ways except that Ty uses the straight-line method of amortization and Hamline the double declining-balance method. On January 2, 2004, both companies acquired the following assets:

Asset	Cost	Salvage Value	Useful Life
Building	$320,000	$20,000	30 years
Equipment	110,000	10,000	5 years

Net earnings for the companies in the years 2004, 2005, and 2006 and total earnings for the three years were as follows (the amounts include the appropriate amortization expense for each company):

	2004	2005	2006	Total
Ty Corporation	$84,000	$88,400	$90,000	$262,400
Hamline Corporation	68,000	76,000	85,000	229,000

At December 31, 2006, the balance sheets of the two companies are similar except that Hamline has lower assets and retained earnings than Ty.

Dawna Tucci is interested in investing in one of the companies, and she comes to you for advice.

Instructions

With the class divided into groups, do the following:

(a) Determine the annual and total amortization recorded by each company during the three years.
(b) Assuming that Hamline Corporation uses the straight-line method of amortization instead of the declining-balance method, prepare comparative earnings data for the three years.
(c) Which company should Dawna invest in? Why?

Communication Activity

BYP9–8   The chapter distinguishes between research and development (R&D) costs for accounting purposes. Research costs are always expensed and development costs are sometimes expensed.

Instructions

Assume that you are the president of a relatively new company that depends on ongoing research and development. Write a letter to the Accounting Standards Board complaining about the accounting for research and development. Your letter should address these questions, in addition to any other points you wish to raise:

(a) By requiring expensing of research costs, do you think companies will spend less on R&D? Why or why not?
(b) If a company makes a commitment to spend money on R&D, it must believe there is a future market for the product or process and that adequate resources exist to complete the project. Does that not imply that the expenditures represent a "probable future benefit" or an asset? What message does expensing some items send to external users about the merits of the R&D activities?

Ethics Case

BYP9–9 Imporia Container Ltd. is suffering declining sales of its main product, nonbiodegradable plastic cartons. The president, Benny Benson, instructs his controller, Yeoh Siew Hoon, to lengthen asset lives to reduce their amortization expense.

A processing line of automated plastic extruding equipment, purchased for $3 million in January 2004, was originally estimated to have a useful life of five years and a salvage value of $200,000. Amortization has been recorded for two years on that basis. Benny wants the estimated useful life changed to a total of seven years. Yeoh Siew is hesitant to make the change, believing it inappropriate to "manage earnings" in this way. Benny says, "Hey, the useful life is only an estimate, and I've heard that our competition uses a seven-year life on their production equipment."

Ethics in Accounting

Instructions

(a) Who are the stakeholders in this situation?
(b) Will Benny Benson's proposed change in useful life increase or decrease net earnings in 2006?
(c) What is earnings management? Is this proposed change an example of earnings management? Explain.
(d) Discuss whether the proposed change in useful life is unethical or simply a good business practice by an astute president.

Serial Problem

(*Note*: This is a continuation of the serial problem from Chapters 1 through 8.)

BYP9–10 Cookie Creations Ltd. is thinking about purchasing a van. The cost of the van is estimated to be $32,500. An additional $2,500 would be spent to have the van painted. As well, the back seat of the van would be removed to make more room for transporting mixer inventory and baking supplies. The cost of taking out the back seat and installing shelving units is estimated at $1,500. It is expected that the estimated useful life of the van will be five years or 200,000 kilometres. The annual cost of vehicle insurance will be $2,400. At the end of the van's useful life, it is expected that the van will sell for $6,500. It is anticipated that the van will be purchased on August 15, 2006, and will be ready for use on September 1.

Natalie is concerned about the impact of the van's cost on Cookie Creations Ltd.'s statement of earnings and balance sheet. She has come to you for advice on how the purchase of the van will affect her company's financial position.

Natalie is also concerned about how Cookie Creations Ltd. will finance the purchase of the van. She has come to you with questions on leasing rather than buying the van.

Instructions

(a) Determine the cost of the van.
*(b) Prepare schedules for each method of amortization: (1)straight-line (similar to the one in Illustration 9-5), (2) double declining-balance amortization (Illustration 9A-2), and (3)

units-of-activity (Illustration 9A-4). For units of activity, it is estimated that the van will be driven as follows: 15,000 km in 2006; 45,000 km in 2007; 50,000 km in 2008; 45,000 in 2009; 35,000 in 2010; and 10,000 km in 2011. Recall that Cookie Creations Ltd. has a December 31 year end.

(c) What impact will each method of amortization have on Cookie Creations' balance sheet at December 31, 2006? What impact will each method have on Cookie Creations' statement of earnings for the year ended December 31, 2006?

(d) What impact will each method of amortization have on Cookie Creations' statement of earnings in total over the van's five-year useful life?

(e) What impact will each method of amortization have on Cookie Creations' cash flow in total over the van's five-year useful life?

(f) Which method of amortization would you recommend Cookie Creations use?

(g) What are some of the advantages and disadvantages of leasing the van instead of buying it?

Answers to Self-Study Questions

1. d   2. c   3. a   4. b   5. a   6. c   7. d   8. d   *9. c   *10. b

Answer to Loblaw Review It Question 3

Loblaw amortizes its buildings over a period of 20 to 40 years and its equipment and fixtures over a period of 3 to 10 years. It amortizes its leasehold improvements over the lesser of the asset's useful life and the lease term plus one renewal period to a maximum of 10 years (see Note 1).

Remember to go back to the Navigator box at the beginning of the chapter to check off your completed work.

CHAPTER 10

Reporting and Analyzing Liabilities

ACCOUNTING MATTERS!

Borrowing Money to Make Money

"Neither a borrower nor a lender be," says Polonius in Shakespeare's Hamlet. But this philosophy wouldn't get him far in the modern business world! Take, for example, Pierre Péladeau, who borrowed $1,500 in 1950 to buy a small newspaper. At the time of his death 47 years later, Mr. Péladeau's shrewd management and aggressive acquisitions had turned this small business into a conglomerate operating on five continents, with more than 60,000 employees worldwide and annual sales in the billions.

Quebecor Inc. began with the purchase of the financially troubled *Le Journal de Rosemont* with that first loan. Mr. Péladeau turned the weekly community newspaper's finances around and soon purchased several others. He then acquired a printing firm to print his papers—and others—at a profit. In 1964, he founded *Le Journal de Montréal*, which became one of the largest newspapers in the country.

In the 1970s, Quebecor expanded beyond newspapers and printing into other communications media, and the company continued to grow through the 1980s and 1990s. By 1999, Quebecor was the largest commercial printer in the world, with major subsidiaries in several related markets: lumber, pulp, and newsprint marketing; DVD, CD, and Internet publishing; cable TV networks; magazine and book publishing; music retailing; and, of course, newspaper publishing.

With its diverse array of holdings, Quebecor has created a huge convergence-driven media group, placing it at the forefront of a sweeping trend that is changing the Canadian business landscape. Today, the activities of its two major subsidiaries span the globe.

Quebecor Media's operations are concentrated mostly in Quebec; however, the power of convergence is clearly illustrated in its production of the reality television show *Star Académie*. Every Quebecor company contributed to the success of the show, which drew record audiences in 2004 (reaching more than an 80-percent audience share). Meanwhile, Quebecor World, which oversees the company's worldwide printing activities, has more than 160 printing and related facilities in 17 countries.

Together, the revenue for Quebecor Inc. and its subsidiaries for 2004 was in excess of $11 billion. Its total liabilities, or debt, totalled $9.4 billion at the end of 2004.

Mr. Péladeau learned early that borrowing money can make good business sense. As the Quebecor story shows, strategic acquisitions can be a successful way of making a business grow quickly—and going into debt is one way to finance such acquisitions. If you invest only the cash you have on hand, you may miss out on significant opportunities for profit. Pierre Péladeau knew this at age 25 and turned this knowledge into a media empire.

the navigator

Quebecor: www.quebecor.com

- [ ] Read *Feature Story*
- [ ] Scan *Study Objectives*
- [ ] Read *Chapter Preview*
- [ ] Read text and answer *Before You Go On*
- [ ] Work *Using the Decision Toolkit*
- [ ] Review *Summary of Study Objectives*
- [ ] Review the *Decision Toolkit—A Summary*
- [ ] Work *Demonstration Problem*
- [ ] Answer *Self-Study Questions*
- [ ] Complete assignments

After studying this chapter, you should be able to:

1. Explain the accounting for current liabilities.
2. Explain the accounting for long-term notes payable.
3. Explain the accounting for bonds payable.
4. Identify the requirements for the financial statement presentation and analysis of liabilities.
5. Apply the straight-line and effective-interest methods of amortizing bond discounts and premiums (Appendix 10A).

the navigator

The feature story indicates that Quebecor has grown rapidly. It is unlikely that it could have grown so large without debt, but at times debt can threaten a company's very existence. Given this risk, why do companies borrow money? Why do they sometimes borrow for the short term and other times long-term? Aside from bank borrowings, what other kinds of debt might a company incur? In this chapter, we answer these questions.

This chapter is organized as follows:

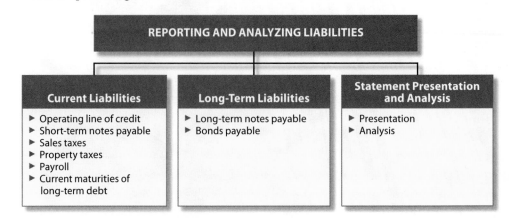

REPORTING AND ANALYZING LIABILITIES		
Current Liabilities	**Long-Term Liabilities**	**Statement Presentation and Analysis**
▸ Operating line of credit ▸ Short-term notes payable ▸ Sales taxes ▸ Property taxes ▸ Payroll ▸ Current maturities of long-term debt	▸ Long-term notes payable ▸ Bonds payable	▸ Presentation ▸ Analysis

the navigator

Current Liabilities

study objective 1

Explain the accounting for current liabilities.

In Chapter 2, we defined liabilities as obligations that result from past transactions. These obligations (debts) must be paid some time in the future by the transfer of assets or services. This future payment date (the maturity date) is the reason for the two basic classifications of liabilities: (1) current liabilities, and (2) long-term liabilities.

A **current liability** is a debt that will be paid within one year from existing current assets or through the creation of other current liabilities. Most companies pay current liabilities out of current assets (e.g., cash), rather than by creating other liabilities (e.g., paying an account payable by issuing a note payable). Debts that do not meet both criteria are classified as **long-term liabilities**.

Financial statement users want to know whether a company's obligations are current or long-term. A company, for example, that has more current liabilities than current assets often lacks liquidity, or short-term debt-paying ability. Users must also look at long-term liabilities in order to assess a company's solvency—its ability to pay its interest and debt when due. In addition, users want to know the types of liabilities a company has.

The different types of current liabilities include bank indebtedness arising from operating lines of credit; notes payable; accounts payable; unearned revenue; accrued liabilities such as taxes, salaries and wages, and interest; and the current portion of long-term debt. Entries for many of these liabilities have been explained in previous chapters. In this section, we discuss operating lines of credit, notes payable, sales taxes, property taxes, payroll, and current maturities of long-term debt in more detail.

Operating Line of Credit

Current assets (such as accounts receivable) do not always turn into cash at the exact time that current liabilities (such as accounts payable) must be paid. Consequently, most companies have an **operating line of credit** at their bank to help them manage temporary cash shortfalls. This means that the company has been pre-authorized by the bank to borrow money, up to a pre-set limit, when it is needed. Quebecor, for example, has access to nearly $2 billion as an operating line of credit.

Security, called **collateral**, is usually required by the bank as protection against a default on the loan. Collateral normally includes some, or all, of the company's current assets (e.g., accounts receivable or inventories), investments, or property, plant, and equipment.

Line of credit borrowings are normally on a short-term basis, and are repayable immediately upon request—that is, on demand—by the bank. In reality, repayment is rarely demanded without notice. A line of credit makes it very easy for a company to borrow money. It does not have to call or visit its bank to actually arrange the transaction. The bank simply covers any cheques written in excess of the bank account balance, up to the approved credit limit.

Some companies show a negative, or overdrawn, cash balance at year end as a result of using their line of credit. This amount is usually called **bank indebtedness**, **bank overdraft**, or **bank advances**. Quebecor reports $800,000 of bank indebtedness in the current liabilities section of its December 31, 2004, balance sheet.

No special entry is required to record the overdrawn amount. The normal credits to Cash will simply accumulate and are reported as a current liability on the balance sheet with a suitable note disclosure. Interest is usually charged on the overdrawn amount at a floating rate, such as prime plus a specified percentage rate. The prime rate is the interest rate that banks charge their best customers. This rate is usually increased by a specified percentage that matches the risk profile of the company.

Short-Term Notes Payable

Obligations in the form of written notes are recorded as **notes payable**. Notes payable are often used instead of accounts payable because they give the lender written documentation of the obligation, which helps if legal action is needed to collect the debt.

Notes are issued for varying periods. Notes that are due for payment within one year of the balance sheet date are classified as current liabilities. Most notes are interest-bearing, with interest due monthly or at maturity.

To illustrate the accounting for notes payable, assume that the HSBC Bank lends $100,000 to Williams Ltd. on March 1, 2006. Williams signs a four-month, 6%, $100,000 note payable. The note matures on July 1 and interest, along with the principal value of the note, is payable at maturity.

Williams makes the following journal entry when it receives the $100,000:

Mar. 1	Cash	100,000	
	Notes Payable		100,000
	(To record issue of four-month, 6% note to HSBC Bank)		

A = L + SE
+100,000   +100,000
↑ Cash flows: +100,000

Interest accrues over the life of the note and must be recorded periodically. If Williams has a March 31 year end, an adjusting entry is required to recognize the interest expense and interest payable of $500 ($100,000 × 6% × $1/12$) at March 31. The adjusting entry is:

Mar. 31	Interest Expense	500	
	Interest Payable		500
	(To accrue interest for one month on HSBC Bank note)		

A = L + SE
+500   −500
Cash flows: no effect

In the March 31 financial statements, the current liabilities section of the balance sheet will show notes payable of $100,000, and interest payable of $500. In addition, interest expense of $500 will be reported as an "other expense" in the statement of earnings.

At maturity (July 1), Williams Ltd. must pay the principal of the note ($100,000) plus $2,000 interest ($100,000 × 6% × $4/12$), $500 of which has already been accrued. The entry to record payment of the note and interest is:

July 1	Notes Payable	100,000	
	Interest Payable	500	
	Interest Expense ($100,000 × 6% × $3/12$)	1,500	
	Cash		102,000
	(To record payment of HSBC note and interest at maturity)		

A = L + SE
−102,000 −100,000 −1,500
          −500
↓ Cash flows: −102,000

Sales Taxes

As consumers, we are well aware that many of the products and services we purchase are subject to sales taxes. The taxes are expressed as a percentage of the sales price. Sales taxes may take the form of the Goods and Services Tax (GST), Provincial Sales Tax (PST), or Harmonized Sales Tax (HST). In Quebec, the PST is known as the Quebec Sales Tax (QST). Federal GST is assessed at 7%. Provincial sales tax rates vary from 0% to 10% across Canada. In Newfoundland and Labrador, Nova Scotia, and New Brunswick, the PST and GST have been combined into one 15% Harmonized Sales Tax.

The retailer collects the sales tax from the customer when the sale occurs, and periodically (normally monthly) remits (sends) the sales tax collected to the designated federal and provincial collecting authorities. In the case of GST and HST, collections may be offset against payments and only the net amount owing or recoverable will be paid or refunded.

The amount of the sale and the amount of the sales tax collected are usually rung up separately on the cash register. The cash register readings are then used to credit the two accounts Sales and Sales Taxes Payable. For example, assuming that the March 25 cash register readings for the Setthawiwat Corporation show sales of $10,000, federal sales taxes of $700 (GST rate of 7%), and provincial sales taxes of $800 (PST rate of 8%), the entry is:

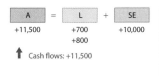

Mar. 25	Cash	11,500	
	Sales		10,000
	GST Payable ($10,000 × 7%)		700
	PST Payable ($10,000 × 8%)		800
	(To record sales and sales taxes)		

When the sales taxes are remitted, GST and PST (or HST) Payable is debited and Cash is credited. The company does not report sales taxes as an expense; it simply forwards the amount paid by the customer to the respective government. Thus, Setthawiwat Corporation is really only a collection agent for the governments.

In some provinces, PST is charged on GST. For example, in Quebec a $100 sale would result in $7 of GST (7%) and $8.03 of QST [($100 + $7) × 7.5%]. The increased sales tax rate is slightly over 15% [($7 + $8.03) ÷ $100] rather than 14.5% (7% GST + 7.5% QST). Because of the varying rate combinations that are used, it is important to be careful when recording sales tax amounts.

Property Taxes

Businesses that own property pay property taxes each year. These taxes are charged by the municipal and provincial governments, and are calculated at a specified rate for every $100 of the assessed value of the property (i.e., land and building). Property taxes are generally for a calendar year, although bills are not usually issued until the spring of each year.

To illustrate, assume that Tantramar Management Ltd. owns land and a building in the city of Regina. Tantramar's year end is December 31 and it makes adjusting entries annually. Tantramar receives its property tax bill of $6,000 on March 1, payable on May 31.

In March, when Tantramar receives the property tax bill, it records the liability owed for its property taxes. At this point in time, two months have passed in the year, so Tantramar also records the property tax expense for the months of January and February. The property tax for the remaining ten months of the year is recorded as a prepayment. The entry is as follows:

Mar. 1	Property Tax Expense [($6,000 ÷ 12) × 2]	1,000	
	Prepaid Property Tax [($6,000 ÷ 12) × 10]	5,000	
	Property Tax Payable		6,000
	(To record property tax expense for January and February, and amount owing)		

Note that Tantramar has both a current asset (Prepaid Property Tax) and a current liability (Property Tax Payable). In May, when Tantramar pays the property tax bill, the entry is a simple payment of the liability:

May 31	Property Tax Payable	6,000	
	Cash		6,000
	(To record payment of property tax)		

A = L + SE
−6,000   −6,000
↓ Cash flows: −6,000

At this point in time, Tantramar has a zero balance in its liability account but still has a prepayment. Since Tantramar only makes adjusting entries annually, it would not adjust the prepaid property tax until its year end, December 31:

Dec. 31	Property Tax Expense	5,000	
	Prepaid Property Tax		5,000
	(To record property tax expense for March through December)		

A = L + SE
−5,000   −5,000
Cash flows: no effect

At year end, the accounts Prepaid Property Tax and Property Tax Payable both have a zero balance. The Property Tax Expense account has a balance of $6,000. There are other ways to record and adjust property tax throughout the period; however, they should all result in the same ending balances.

Payroll

Every employer incurs liabilities related to employees' salaries or wages. One is the amount of salaries or wages owed to employees. The other is the amount of payroll deductions that by law have to be withheld from an employee's total, or gross, pay.

Assume that Linfang Wang works 40 hours this week for Pepitone Inc., earning $10 per hour. Will Linfang receive a cheque for $400 (40 x $10) at the end of the week? Definitely not. The reason: Pepitone has to withhold amounts known as payroll deductions from her wages, and pay these amounts to various other parties. Mandatory payroll deductions include amounts withheld for federal and provincial income taxes, Canada Pension Plan (CPP) contributions, and employment insurance (EI) premiums. Companies might also withhold voluntary deductions for charitable, insurance, and other purposes.

In addition to the liabilities incurred as a result of employee payroll deductions, employers also incur another liability related to these deductions. The employer is expected to pay various payroll costs that are charged on certain payroll deductions, such as the employer's share of CPP and EI. In addition, the provincial governments require employer funding of a Workplace Health, Safety and Compensation Plan. Each of these contributions, plus items such as paid vacations and employer-sponsored pensions, are referred to together as **employee benefits**. The employer's share of these costs is recorded as an employee benefits expense.

In summary, Pepitone must collect payroll deductions from its employees and itself on behalf of the government and other third parties. Until these payroll deductions are remitted to the third parties that Pepitone collected the amounts for, they are reported as a current liability in Pepitone's balance sheet.

Illustration 10-1, on the following page, summarizes the types of payroll deductions that most companies normally have.

Illustration 10-1 ▶

Payroll deductions

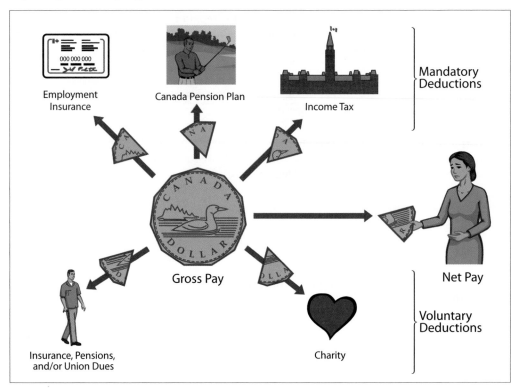

The following entries, using assumed amounts, show the accrual of a $100,000 weekly payroll for Pepitone Inc.:

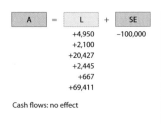

A	=	L	+	SE
+4,950				−100,000
+2,100				
+20,427				
+2,445				
+667				
+69,411				

Cash flows: no effect

Mar. 7	Wages Expense	100,000	
	CPP Payable		4,950
	EI Payable		2,100
	Income Taxes Payable		20,427
	United Way Payable		2,445
	Union Dues Payable		667
	Wages Payable		69,411
	(To record payroll and employee deductions for the week ending March 7)		

In this case, Pepitone records $100,000—the gross pay amount—as wages expense. In addition, Pepitone records liabilities to its employees for the wages payable as well as liabilities for payroll deductions withheld on behalf of others, such as the government, United Way, and the union. The difference between the gross pay and the payroll deductions is known as the **net pay**. It is this amount ($69,411 in this case) that is recorded as wages payable, and ultimately paid to employees.

The following entry must also be made to record the employer's share of the payroll deductions, or employee benefits:

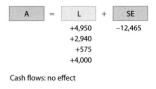

A	=	L	+	SE
+4,950				−12,465
+2,940				
+575				
+4,000				

Cash flows: no effect

Mar. 7	Employee Benefits Expense	12,465	
	CPP Payable		4,950
	EI Payable		2,940
	Worker's Compensation Payable		575
	Vacation Pay Payable		4,000
	(To record employer's payroll costs on March 7 payroll)		

The employer's payroll liability accounts are also classified as current liabilities. Similar to employee payroll deductions, they must either be paid to employees or remitted in the near term to government authorities or other third parties.

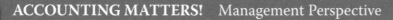

ACCOUNTING MATTERS! Management Perspective

The battle over employee benefits has grown as benefit increases outpace wages and salaries. Benefit costs now represent between 7 and 8 percent of payroll and are increasing by an average of 8 to 12 percent per year. In a recent survey of nearly 1,400 Canadian human resource professionals, limiting benefit costs was cited as their number one priority for 2005. Many companies have started to look at the impact of sharing benefit costs with employees, but they are moving slowly in order to measure its effect on employee relations.

Source: David Brown, "Employers Approach Benefits Cost Containment with Caution," *Canadian HR Reporter,* January 31, 2005, p. 2.

Current Maturities of Long-Term Debt

Companies often have a portion of long-term debt that is due in the current year. As an example, assume that Cudini Construction issues a five-year, interest-bearing, $25,000 note on January 1, 2006. This note specifies that each January 1, starting January 1, 2007, $5,000 of the note will be repaid. When financial statements are prepared on December 31, 2006, $5,000 should be reported as a current liability and $20,000 as a long-term liability.

It is not necessary to prepare an adjusting entry to recognize the current maturity of long-term debt. The proper statement classification of each balance sheet account is recognized when the balance sheet is prepared. At December 31, 2004, Quebecor reported $16.7 million as the "current portion of long-term debt and convertible notes" in the current liabilities section of its balance sheet.

BEFORE YOU GO ON . . .

▶Review It

1. What are the two criteria for classifying a debt as a current liability?
2. What are some examples of current liabilities?
3. Distinguish between (1) gross pay and net pay and (2) employee payroll deductions and employer payroll costs.
4. Identify the liabilities that Loblaw classifies as current. The answer to this question is at the end of the chapter.

▶Do It

Prepare the journal entries to record the following transactions:

1. Accrue interest on December 31 (the company's year end) for a three-month, 6%, $10,000 note payable issued November 1. Interest is payable at maturity.
2. Pre-tax sales totalled $256,000. The GST tax rate is 7% and the PST is 8%. Record the sales and sales taxes.
3. A property tax bill of $12,000 is received on May 1. Record this transaction, assuming the company has a January 31 year end.
4. A company's gross wages amount to $10,000. Amounts deducted from the employees' wages are CPP of $495, EI of $210, income tax of $3,965, and health insurance of $950. The employer's portion of CPP is $495 and of EI, $294. Record the weekly payroll.

Action Plan

- Remember the formula for interest: principal (face) value × annual interest rate × time.
- Record sales separately from sales taxes. Recall that sales taxes are a liability until they are remitted.
- Allocate the property tax bill between the expense (property tax expense) incurred to date and the asset (prepaid property tax) representing future benefit.
- Record both the employees' portion of the payroll and the benefits owed by the employer. Employee deductions are not an expense for the employer.

Solution

1.	Interest Expense ($10,000 × 6% × $^2/_{12}$)	100	
	Interest Payable		100
	(To accrue interest on note payable)		
2.	Cash ($256,000 + $17,920 + $20,480)	294,400	
	Sales		256,000
	GST Payable ($256,000 × 7%)		17,920
	PST Payable ($256,000 × 8%)		20,480
	(To record sales and sales taxes)		
3.	Property Tax Expense ($12,000 × $^3/_{12}$)	3,000	
	Prepaid Property Tax ($12,000 × $^9/_{12}$)	9,000	
	Property Tax Payable		12,000
	(To record property tax expense for February–April and amount owing)		
4.	Wages Expense	10,000	
	CPP Payable		495
	EI Payable		210
	Income Tax Payable		3,965
	Health Insurance Payable		950
	Wages Payable		4,380
	(To record payroll and employee deductions)		
4.	Employee Benefits Expense	789	
	CPP Payable		495
	EI Payable		294
	(To record employee benefits)		

the navigator

Long-Term Liabilities

study objective 2

Explain the accounting for long-term notes payable.

A **long-term liability** is an obligation that is expected to be paid after one year. In this section, we explain the accounting for the main types of obligations that are reported in the long-term liability section of the balance sheet. These obligations are often in the form of long-term notes or bonds. Notes payable are explained in the next section, followed by bonds.

Long-Term Notes Payable

Using long-term notes payable in debt financing is common. Long-term notes payable are similar to short-term notes payable except that the terms of the notes are for more than one year. In periods of unstable interest rates, the interest rate on long-term notes may follow changes in the market rate.

A long-term note may be **secured** or **unsecured**. A secured note pledges title (gives ownership) to specific assets as collateral or security for the loan. Quebecor had nearly $3.5 billion of secured notes payable at the end of 2004. Secured notes are also known as mortgages. A **mortgage note payable** is widely used by individuals to purchase homes. It is also used by many companies to acquire property, plant, and equipment.

Unsecured notes are issued against the general credit of the borrower. There are no assets used as collateral. Unsecured notes are also called **debentures**, and are used by large corporations with good credit ratings. Quebecor reported $876.9 million of debentures at the end of 2004.

Sometimes notes or other forms of long-term debt have a special feature that allows them to be converted into shares. These are called **convertible debt**. Convertible debt has features that are attractive to both debt holders and issuers. The conversion often gives the holder an opportunity to benefit if the market price of the borrower's common shares increases. Until conversion, though, the debt holder receives interest on the debt. For the issuer, the debt normally pays a lower rate of interest than comparable debt securities that have no conversion option. For example, Quebecor reported $135.4 million of convertible notes in 2004, with a

6-percent interest rate. Similar notes without the conversion feature that were issued at about the same time were paying an interest rate of 7.25 percent.

Convertible debt has two basic aspects. First, it is a liability because of the agreement to repay the principal upon maturity. Second, it is equity, since the debt holder has the right to convert the debt into shares. These two aspects—liability and equity—must be recorded and presented separately on the balance sheet. With debt like this, the distinction between debt financing and equity financing is less clear. For example, convertible notes are debt when they are originally issued. However, they can be converted into equity, which means that the company may never have to repay the debt. These and other innovative debt financing options are known as **financial instruments**. Accounting for financial instruments is complex and is discussed in more advanced accounting courses.

While short-term notes are normally repayable in full at maturity, most long-term notes are repayable in a series of periodic payments. These payments are known as **instalments** and are paid monthly, quarterly, semi-annually, or at another defined period. Each payment consists of (1) interest on the unpaid balance of the loan, and (2) a reduction of loan principal. Payments generally take one of two forms: (1) fixed principal payments plus interest, or (2) blended principal and interest payments. Let's look at each of these payment patterns in more detail.

Fixed Principal Payments

Instalment notes with fixed principal payments are repayable in **equal periodic amounts, plus interest**. Interest may be either **fixed** or **floating**. A fixed interest rate will be constant over the term of the note. A floating (or variable) interest rate will change with fluctuating market rates. Generally, floating rates are tied to changes in the prime rate. As explained earlier in the chapter, prime is the rate that banks use to loan money to their most creditworthy customers.

To illustrate, assume that on January 1, 2006, Belanger Ltée issues a five-year, 7%, $120,000 note payable to obtain financing for a new research laboratory. The entry to record the issue of the note payable is as follows:

Jan. 1	Cash	120,000	
	Notes Payable		120,000
	(To record five-year, 7% note payable)		

The terms of the note provide for equal monthly instalment payments of $2,000 ($120,000 ÷ 60 monthly periods) on the first of each month, plus interest of 7% on the outstanding principal balance.

Monthly interest expense is calculated by multiplying the outstanding principal balance by the interest rate. For the first payment date—February 1—interest expense is $700 ($120,000 × 7% × $\frac{1}{12}$). Note that the 7% is an annual interest rate and must be adjusted for the monthly time period. The cash payment of $2,700 for the month of February is the total of the instalment payment of $2,000, which is applied against the principal, plus the interest of $700.

The entry to record the first instalment payment on February 1 is as follows:

Feb. 1	Interest Expense ($120,000 × 7% × $\frac{1}{12}$)	700	
	Note Payable	2,000	
	Cash ($2,000 + $700)		2,700
	(To record monthly payment on note)		

An instalment payment schedule is a useful tool to help organize this information and to provide information that helps prepare journal entries. A partial instalment payment schedule for the first few months for Belanger Ltée, rounded to the nearest dollar, is shown in Illustration 10-2 on the following page.

Illustration 10-2 ▶

Instalment payment
schedule—fixed principal
payments

		(A) Cash Payment	(B) Interest Expense	(C) Reduction of Principal	(D) Principal Balance
	Interest Period	(B + C)	(D × 7% × ¹/₁₂)	($120,000 ÷ 60)	(D* − C)
	Jan. 1				$120,000
	Feb. 1	$2,700	$700	$2,000	118,000
	Mar. 1	2,688	688	2,000	116,000
	Apr. 1	2,677	677	2,000	114,000

BELANGER LTÉE
Instalment Payment Schedule—Fixed Principal Payments

* from the prior period

Column A, the cash payment, is the total of the instalment payment, $2,000, plus the interest. The cash payment changes each period because the interest changes. Column B determines the interest expense, which decreases each period because the principal balance, on which interest is calculated, decreases. Column C is the instalment payment of $2,000, which is applied against the principal. The instalment payment is constant each period in a "fixed principal payment plus interest" pattern. Column D is the principal balance, which decreases each period by the amount of the instalment payment.

In summary, with fixed principal payments, the interest decreases each period (as the principal decreases). The portion applied to the reduction of loan principal stays constant, but because of the decreasing interest, the total payment decreases.

Blended Principal and Interest Payments

Instalment notes with blended principal and interest payments are repayable in **equal periodic amounts, including interest**. Blended principal and interest payments result in changing amounts of interest and principal applied to the loan. As with fixed principal payments, the interest decreases each period (as the principal decreases). In contrast to fixed principal payments, the portion applied to the loan principal increases each period. Most consumer and mortgage loans use a blend of principal and interest payments rather than fixed principal payments.

To illustrate this option, assume that instead of fixed principal payments, Belanger Ltée repays its note in equal monthly instalments of $2,376. As with the fixed principal payments illustrated above, monthly interest expense is calculated by multiplying the outstanding principal balance by the interest rate. For the first payment date—February 1—interest expense is $700 ($120,000 × 7% × ¹/₁₂). The instalment payment of $2,376 is fixed for each month, and includes interest and principal amounts which will vary. In February, the principal balance will be reduced by $1,676, which is the difference between the instalment payment of $2,376 and the interest amount of $700.

The entry to record the issue of the note payable is the same as in the previous section. The entry to record the instalment payment uses the same accounts but different amounts. The first instalment payment on February 1 is recorded as follows:

Feb. 1	Interest Expense ($120,000 × 7% × ¹/₁₂)		700	
	Note Payable ($2,376 − $700)		1,676	
	Cash			2,376
	(To record monthly payment on note)			

An instalment payment schedule can also be prepared for blended principal and interest payments. Illustration 10-3 shows a partial instalment payment schedule for the first few months for Belanger Ltée, rounded to the nearest dollar.

BELANGER LTÉE
Instalment Payment Schedule—Blended Payments

Interest Period	(A) Cash Payment (B + C)	(B) Interest Expense (D × 7% × ¹/₁₂)	(C) Reduction of Principal (A − B)	(D) Principal Balance (D* − C)
Jan. 1				$120,000
Feb. 1	$2,376	$700	$1,676	118,324
Mar. 1	2,376	690	1,686	116,638
Apr. 1	2,376	680	1,696	114,942

* from the prior period

Column A, the cash payment, is specified and is the same for each period. The amount of this cash payment can actually be calculated mathematically. It can also be determined using the present value techniques discussed in the Study Tools section of the Toolkit website that accompanies this textbook. Column B determines the interest expense, which decreases each period because the principal balance that the interest is calculated on decreases. Column C is how much the principal is reduced by. This is the difference between the cash payment of $2,376 and the interest for the period. Consequently, this amount will increase each period. Column D is the principal balance, which decreases each period by a varying amount, that is, by the reduction of the principal amount from Column C.

With both types of instalment note payable, as with any other long-term note payable, the reduction in principal for the next year must be reported as a current liability. The remaining unpaid principal is classified as a long-term liability.

**Study Tools
(Present Value Concepts)**

BEFORE YOU GO ON . . .

► Review It

1. Distinguish between short-term and long-term notes payable.
2. Explain the accounting for long-term notes payable.
3. How does the reduction in principal differ in a note with fixed principal payments compared to a note with blended principal and interest payments?

► Do It

On December 31, 2005, Tian Inc. issued a 15-year, 8%, $500,000 mortgage note payable. The terms provide for semi-annual blended instalment payments of $28,915 (principal and interest) on June 30 and December 31. Prepare the journal entries required to record the issue of the note on December 31, 2005, and the first two payments on June 30, 2006, and December 31, 2006.

Action Plan

• Multiply the semi-annual interest rate by the principal balance at the beginning of the period to determine the interest expense.
• Record the mortgage payments, recognizing that each payment consists of (1) interest on the unpaid loan balance, and (2) a reduction of the loan principal.

Solution

Dec. 31, 2005	Cash	500,000	
	Mortgage Note Payable		500,000
	(To record issue of 15-year, 8% mortgage note payable)		
June 30, 2006	Interest Expense ($500,000 × 8% × 6/12)	20,000	
	Mortgage Note Payable ($28,915 − $20,000)	8,915	
	Cash		28,915
	(To record semi-annual mortgage payment)		
Dec. 31, 2006	Interest Expense [($500,000 − $8,915) × 8% × 6/12)]	19,643	
	Mortgage Note Payable ($28,915 − $19,643)	9,272	
	Cash		28,915
	(To record semi-annual mortgage payment)		

the navigator

Bonds Payable

study objective 3

Explain the accounting for bonds payable.

A **bond** is a form of interest-bearing note payable. Accounting for notes and bonds is quite similar. Both have a fixed maturity date and pay interest. The interest rate used to determine the amount of interest to pay to bondholders is known as the **contractual interest rate**. Usually, the contractual rate is stated as an annual rate and interest is paid semi-annually.

Similar to notes, bonds can have many different features. They may be **unsecured** or **secured**. They may also be **convertible** into shares. Both notes and bonds can be payable at maturity or in instalments. Bonds that mature (are due for payment) on a single specified future date are known as **term bonds**. The amount of principal due at maturity is usually called the **face value**. Bonds that mature in instalments are known as **serial bonds**.

Bond Trading

A significant difference between notes and bonds is that bonds are often traded on a stock exchange as shares are. Notes are seldom traded on the stock exchange. Small and large corporations issue notes, whereas only large corporations issue bonds. Bonds enable a company to borrow when the amount of financing needed is too large for one lender. Consequently, bonds are sold in small denominations (usually $1,000 or multiples of $1,000). As a result, similar to shares, they attract many investors.

Bond credit-rating agencies help investors assess the risk level or creditworthiness of bonds. The highest quality bonds are graded as AAA bonds; superior quality, AA; good quality, A; medium grade, BBB. Bonds rated below BBB are commonly referred to as "junk bonds." They are considered to be of higher credit risk; that is, the chance of default is higher for them than for bonds of better credit quality.

The following illustration shows a sample listing for Bell Canada bonds from the daily financial press:

Issuer	Coupon	Maturity Date	Bid Price	Ask Price	Bid Yld	Ask Yld	Yield Chg
Bell CDA	6.150	2009-Jun-15	106.89	106.95	4.75	4.74	+0.047

This bond listing indicates that Bell Canada's bonds have a contractual (coupon) interest rate of 6.15% per year. The bonds mature on June 15, 2009. **Bond prices are quoted as a percentage of the face value of the bonds, which is usually $1,000.** For example, if the bond price is stated as 100, this means that the bonds will sell at 100 percent of the face value. If the face value is $1,000, then the bonds will sell for $1,000 ($1,000 × 100%). If the bond price is quoted as 102, the bonds will sell at 102 percent of the face value, or $1,020 ($1,000 × 102%). Note that the percentage sign is not included in the quoted price, but must be implicitly assumed.

With respect to the Bell Canada bonds described in the above listing, $1,068.90 ($1,000 × 106.89%) was bid by an investor interested in purchasing these bonds. The amount $1,069.50 ($1,000 × 106.95%) was the asking price by an investor interested in selling these bonds. The yield, or market interest rate, on the bonds is 4.74% or 4.75%, depending on the ask or bid price. The **market interest rate** is the rate investors demand for lending their money. This rate is also commonly known as the yield, or effective interest rate. The yield change, 0.47%, is the change in the ask yield from the previous closing date. In this case, Bell Canada's bond asking yield is 0.047 points higher than yesterday's, which was 4.69%.

Transactions between a bondholder and other investors are not journalized by the issuing corporation. If Vinod Thakkar sells his Bell Canada bonds to Julie Tarrel, the issuing corporation, Bell Canada, does not journalize the transaction. While the issuer (or its trustee) does keep records of the names of bondholders, a corporation makes journal entries only when it issues or buys back bonds.

Determining the Market Value of Bonds

If you were an investor interested in purchasing a bond, how would you decide how much to pay? To be more specific, assume that Candlestick Inc. issues a zero-interest bond (pays no interest) with a face value of $1 million due in five years. For this bond, the only cash you receive is $1 million at the end of five years. Would you pay $1 million for this bond? We hope not, because $1 million received five years from now is not the same as $1 million received today.

You should not pay $1 million because of what is called the **time value of money**. If you had $1 million today, you would invest it and earn interest so that after five years your investment could be worth much more than $1 million. Thus, if someone is going to pay you $1 million five years from now, you would want to find its equivalent today. That amount—how much must be invested today at current interest rates to have $1 million in five years—is called the **present value**.

The present value of a bond is the value at which it sells in the marketplace. Market value (present value), therefore, depends on three factors: (1) the dollar amounts to be received, (2) the length of time until the amounts are received, and (3) the market rate of interest. The process of finding the present value is referred to as discounting the future amounts.

To illustrate, assume that on January 1, 2006, Candlestick Inc. issues $1 million of five percent bonds, due in five years, with interest payable semi-annually. The purchaser of the bonds would receive the following two cash inflows: (1) the face or principal amount of $1 million to be paid at maturity, and (2) ten $25,000 interest payments ($1,000,000 × 5% × $^{6}/_{12}$ months) over the term of the bonds. A time diagram for both cash flows is shown in Illustration 10-4.

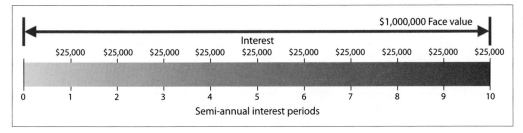

Illustration 10-4 ◀

Time diagram of cash flows

The current market value of a bond is equal to the present value of all the future cash payments promised by the bond. The present values of these amounts are shown below:

Present value of $1,000,000 received in 10 periods	
$1,000,000 × 0.78120 ($n = 10, i = 2.5$%)	$ 781,200
Present value of $25,000 received for each of 10 periods	
$25,000 × 8.75206 ($n = 10, i = 2.5$%)	218,800
Present value (market) price of bonds	$1,000,000
Where n = number of interest periods and i = interest rate	

Helpful Hint Bond prices vary inversely with changes in the market interest rate. As market interest rates decline, bond prices increase. When a bond is issued, if the market interest rate is below the contractual interest rate, the price will be higher than the face value.

Tables are available to provide the present value factors to be used (e.g., 0.78120 which is the present value factor of 1 and 8.75206 which is the present value factor of an annuity of 1), or these values can be determined mathematically. Further discussion of concepts and time value of money calculations is available on the Toolkit website accompanying this book.

Discount or Premium on Bonds

When the contractual interest rate and the market interest rate are the same, bonds will sell at their face value. Recall that the contractual interest rate is the rate applied to the face value to arrive at the interest paid in a year. The market interest rate is the rate investors demand for loaning funds to the corporation.

Market interest rates change daily. They are influenced by the type of bond issued, the state of the economy, current industry conditions, and the company's individual performance. As a result, the contractual and market interest rates often differ, and bonds therefore sell below or above their face value.

To illustrate, suppose that investors have one of two options: (1) purchase bonds that have just been issued with a contractual interest rate of six percent, or (2) purchase bonds issued at an earlier date with a lower contractual interest rate of five percent. If the bonds are of equal risk, investors will choose the six percent investment. To make the investments equal, and the option 2 bonds worth purchasing, investors would need a higher rate of interest for option 2 than the five percent contractual interest. But investors cannot change the contractual interest rate. What they can do is pay less than the face value for the bonds. By paying less for the bonds, investors can effectively obtain the market interest rate of six percent. When this happens, the bonds are said to sell at a **discount**.

On the other hand, the market interest rate may be lower than the contractual interest rate. In that case, investors will pay more than face value for the bonds. That is, if the market interest rate is four percent but the contractual interest rate on the bonds is five percent, everyone will want to buy the bonds and the price will rise above their face value. In these cases, the bonds are said to sell at a **premium**.

These relationships are shown in Illustration 10-5.

Illustration 10-5 ▶

Interest rates and bond prices

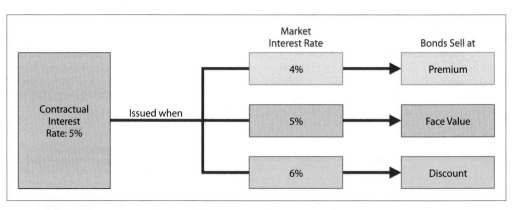

Issuing bonds at an amount different from face value is quite common. By the time a company prints the bond certificates (which provide the legal documentation for the bonds) and markets the bonds, it will be a coincidence if the market rate and the contractual rate are the same. Thus, the issue of bonds at a discount does not mean there is doubt about the financial strength of the issuer. Conversely, the sale of bonds at a premium does not indicate that the financial strength of the issuer is exceptional.

Accounting for Bond Issues

Bonds may be issued at face value, below face value (discount), or above face value (premium).

Issuing Bonds at Face Value.   To illustrate the accounting for bonds issued at face value, let's continue the example discussed in the last section where Candlestick Inc. issues five-year, 5%, $1-million bonds on January 1, 2006, for $1 million (100% of face value). The entry to record the sale is:

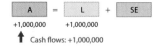

Jan. 1	Cash	1,000,000	
	Bonds Payable		1,000,000
	(To record sale of bonds at face value)		

These bonds payable are reported in the long-term liability section of the balance sheet because the maturity date is January 1, 2011 (more than one year away).

Over the term (life) of the bonds, entries are required for bond interest. Interest on bonds payable is calculated in the same manner as interest on notes payable, explained earlier. Interest is payable semi-annually on January 1 and July 1, so interest of $25,000 ($1,000,000 × 5% × $^6/_{12}$) must be paid on July 1, 2006. The entry for the payment is:

July 1	Bond Interest Expense	25,000	
	Cash		25,000
	(To record payment of bond interest)		

A	=	L	+	SE
−25,000				−25,000

↓ Cash flows: −25,000

At December 31, Candlestick's year end, an adjusting entry is required to recognize the $25,000 of interest expense incurred since July 1. The entry is:

Dec. 31	Bond Interest Expense	25,000	
	Bond Interest Payable		25,000
	(To accrue bond interest)		

A	=	L	+	SE
		+25,000		−25,000

Cash flows: no effect

Bond interest payable is classified as a current liability because it is scheduled for payment within the next year. When the interest is paid on January 1, 2007, Bond Interest Payable is decreased (debited) and Cash is also decreased (credited) for $25,000.

Issuing Bonds at a Discount. To illustrate the issue of bonds at a discount, assume that Candlestick sells its bonds for $957,345 (95.7345% of face value) rather than for $1 million (100% of face value) as we assumed above. The entry to record the issue is:

Jan. 1	Cash	957,345	
	Discount on Bonds Payable	42,655	
	Bonds Payable		1,000,000
	(To record sale of bonds at a discount)		

A	=	L	+	SE
+957,345		−42,655		
		+1,000,000		

↑ Cash flows: +957,345

Although Discount on Bonds Payable has a debit balance, it is not an asset. Rather, it is a **contra liability account** which is **deducted from Bonds Payable** on the balance sheet, as follows:

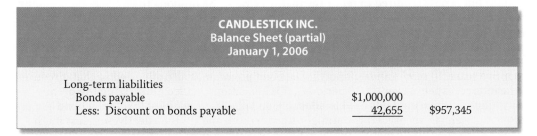

CANDLESTICK INC.
Balance Sheet (partial)
January 1, 2006

Long-term liabilities
  Bonds payable $1,000,000
  Less: Discount on bonds payable   42,655 $957,345

The $957,345 represents the **carrying (or book) value** of the bonds. On the date of issue, this amount equals the market price of the bonds.

The issue of bonds at a discount (below face value) makes the total cost of borrowing higher than the bond interest paid. That is, the issuing corporation must pay not only the contractual interest rate over the term of the bonds, but also the face value (rather than the issue price) at maturity. Therefore, the difference between the issue price ($957,345) and the face value ($1 million) of the bonds—the discount ($42,655)—is an **additional cost of borrowing**. That is, Candlestick must repay $1 million at maturity even though it only received $957,345 from the sale of the bonds.

To follow the matching principle, the bond discount should be allocated to expense over the life of the bonds. The $25,000 is recorded as interest expense every semi-annual period for five years (10 semi-annual periods). The bond discount is also allocated to interest expense over the 10 periods—this allocation is referred to as **amortizing the discount**.

Two methods are commonly used to allocate this discount to interest expense: (1) the straight-line method, and (2) the effective-interest method. The way to apply these methods is shown in Appendix 10A to this chapter.

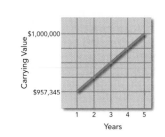

Whatever method is chosen to amortize the discount, amortization of the discount increases the amount of interest expense that is reported each period. That is, after amortizing the discount, the amount of interest expense reported in a period will exceed the contractual amount.

As the discount is amortized, its balance will decline. Therefore, the carrying value of the bonds will increase until at maturity the carrying value of the bonds equals their face value.

Issuing Bonds at a Premium.   The issue of bonds at a premium can be illustrated by assuming that the Candlestick bonds described earlier are sold for $1,044,915 (104.4915% of face value). The entry to record the sale is:

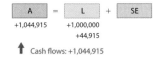

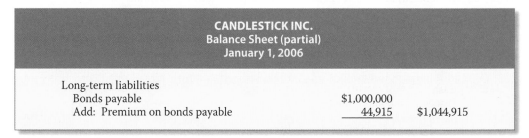

Premium on bonds payable is an adjunct account, which is added to bonds payable on the balance sheet. An adjunct account is the opposite of a contra account. A contra account reduces a related account. An adjunct account increases a related account, as shown below:

CANDLESTICK INC. Balance Sheet (partial) January 1, 2006		
Long-term liabilities		
Bonds payable	$1,000,000	
Add: Premium on bonds payable	44,915	$1,044,915

The sale of bonds above their face value causes the total cost of borrowing to be less than the bond interest paid because the borrower is not required to pay the bond premium at the maturity date of the bonds. That is, Candlestick received $1,044,915 from the sale of the bonds but is only required to repay the maturity value, $1 million. Thus, the bond premium is considered to be **a reduction in the cost of borrowing** that reduces bond interest expense over the life of the bonds.

To follow the matching principle, the bond premium should be allocated to expense over the life of the bonds. The $25,000 is recorded as interest expense every semi-annual period for five years (10 semi-annual periods). The bond premium is also allocated so that it reduces the interest expense over the 10 periods—this allocation is called **amortizing the premium**.

The same two methods used to allocate bond discounts are used to allocate bond premiums to interest expense: (1) the straight-line method, and (2) the effective-interest method. The way to apply these methods is shown in Appendix 10A to this chapter.

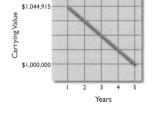

Whatever method is chosen to amortize the premium, amortization of the premium will decrease the amount of interest expense reported each period. That is, after amortizing the premium, the amount of interest expense reported in a period will be less than the contractual amount.

As the premium is amortized, its balance will decline until it reaches zero at maturity. Therefore, the carrying value of the bonds will decrease until at maturity the carrying value of the bonds equals their face value.

Accounting for Bond Retirements

Bonds are retired either (1) when they mature, or (2) when the issuing corporation purchases them on the open market before they mature. Some bonds have special redemption provisions that allow them to be retired before they mature. Bonds that can be retired at a stated dollar amount before maturity at the option of the company (the issuer) are known as **redeemable** (callable) bonds. To make the bonds more attractive to investors, the redemption or call price is usually a few percentage points above the face value.

Why would a company want to have the option to retire its bonds early? If interest rates drop, it can be financially advantageous to retire the bond issue and replace it with a new bond issue at a lower interest rate. Or a company may become financially able to repay its debt earlier than expected. Before a company does this, it should do an in-depth financial analysis to be sure it has enough cash resources to retire its bonds early. You will learn more about this type of analysis in a finance course.

Let's look now at the required entries for redeeming bonds at, or before, maturity.

Redeeming Bonds at Maturity. Regardless of the issue price of bonds, the carrying value of the bonds at maturity will equal their face value. By the time the bonds mature, any discount or premium will be fully amortized and will have a zero balance.

Assuming that the interest for the last interest payment period is recorded, the entry to record the redemption of the Candlestick bonds at maturity, on January 1, 2011, is:

Jan. 1	Bonds Payable		1,000,000	
	Cash			1,000,000
	(To record redemption of bonds at maturity)			

Since no proceeds are received, there is no gain or loss when bonds are retired at maturity.

Redeeming Bonds before Maturity. Redeeming bonds early is similar to disposing of property, plant, and equipment. To record a redemption of bonds, it is necessary to (1) update any unrecorded interest, (2) eliminate the carrying value of the bonds at the redemption date, (3) record the cash paid, and (4) recognize the gain or loss on redemption. The carrying value of the bonds is the face value of the bonds less the unamortized bond discount, or plus the unamortized bond premium, at the redemption date. So two accounts must be removed from the books in order to eliminate the carrying value: the Bonds Payable account and any related discount or premium account.

To illustrate, assume that Candlestick sells its bonds at a premium as described in the last section. It redeems the bonds at 103 at the end of the fourth year (eighth period), after paying the semi-annual interest. Assume that the carrying value of the bonds at the redemption date is $1,008,983. That is, the face value of the bonds is $1 million and the unamortized premium is $8,983. The entry to record the redemption on January 1, 2010 (end of the eighth period) is:

Jan. 1	Bonds Payable		1,000,000	
	Premium on Bonds Payable		8,983	
	Loss on Bond Redemption ($1,030,000 − $1,008,983)		21,017	
	Cash ($1,000,000 × 103%)			1,030,000
	(To record redemption of bonds at 103)			

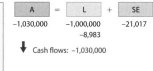

The loss of $21,017 is the difference between the cash paid of $1,030,000 and the carrying value of the bonds of $1,008,983 ($1,000,000 + $8,983). Calculating a loss or a gain on the redemption of bonds is similar to the calculation of a loss or gain on the sale of property, plant, and equipment. In both cases, the proceeds (cash) are compared to the carrying value. However, the determination of whether there is a loss or a gain is, of course, different. For example, when you sell an asset (such as property, plant, and equipment), you gain when the cash received is greater than the carrying value. When you retire a liability (such as bonds), you gain when the cash paid is less than the carrying value.

Property, Plant, and Equipment	Bonds Payable
Sale price	Purchase price
−Carrying (book) value	−Carrying value
Gain (loss)	Loss (gain)

Illustration 10-6 ◄

Comparison of asset and liability gain and loss

Losses and gains on bond redemption are reported in the statement of earnings as other expenses or revenues. Unlike the sale of property, plant, and equipment, which is considered part of earnings from operations, the redemption of bonds usually results in large and infrequent amounts which, because they are unusual, are reported separately.

ACCOUNTING MATTERS!　Management Perspective

University bonds are a relatively new phenomenon in Canada. Since 2001, six Canadian universities have issued bonds totalling nearly $1 billion. The bond issues range in size from $125 million (University of British Columbia) to $225 million (Concordia University).

Faced with increasing enrolments and decreasing financial resources from provincial governments, universities find bonds an attractive option to help finance the construction of new facilities and the repair of badly dated facilities. By issuing bonds, universities pay less interest than they would have to pay with a bank loan. And, unlike bank loans, which usually have to be renegotiated every few years, the interest rate for a bond offering is locked in for the duration of the term, which makes future budgets more stable.

BEFORE YOU GO ON . . .

▶Review It

1. What journal entry is made to record the issue of bonds payable of $500,000 at 100? At 96? At 102?
2. Why do bonds sell at face value? At a discount? At a premium?
3. Explain why bond discounts and premiums are amortized.
4. Explain the accounting for the redemption of bonds at maturity and before maturity.

▶Do It

On January 1, 2004, R & B Inc. issues $500,000 of 10-year, 4% bonds at 98. Before maturity, on June 30, 2008, when the carrying value of the bonds is $494,500, the company redeems the bonds at 101. Prepare the entry to record the (1) issue of the bonds on January 1, 2004, and (2) redemption of the bonds on June 30, 2008.

Action Plan

- Apply the issue price as a percentage (e.g., 98%) to the face value of the bonds to determine the proceeds received.
- Recall that discounts are debits, reducing the carrying value of the bonds. Premiums are credits, increasing the carrying value of the bonds.
- To record the redemption, first update any partial period interest and amortization, if required.
- Eliminate the carrying value of the bonds. Remove the balances from the Bonds Payable account and any discount or premium account.
- Record the cash paid.
- Calculate and record the gain or loss (the difference between the cash paid and the carrying value).

Solution

Jan. 1, 2004	Cash ($500,000 × 98%)	490,000	
	Discount on Bonds Payable	10,000	
	Bonds Payable		500,000
	(To record issue of bonds at 98)		
June 30, 2008	Bonds Payable	500,000	
	Loss on Bond Redemption ($505,000 − $494,500)	10,500	
	Discount on Bonds Payable ($500,000 − $494,500)		5,500
	Cash ($500,000 × 101%)		505,000
	(To record redemption of bonds at 101)		

the navigator

Statement Presentation and Analysis

Liabilities are a significant amount on the financial statements and they have to be disclosed in detail so they can be properly understood by creditors and investors. These and other users are very interested in assessing a company's liquidity and solvency in regard to its liabilities. We will look at the presentation and analysis of liabilities in the next sections.

study objective 4

Identify the requirements for the financial statement presentation and analysis of liabilities.

Presentation

The presentation of liabilities affects all three financial statements. In the statement of earnings, gains on bond redemption are reported as "other revenues" and losses on bond redemption and interest expense are reported as "other expenses." The balance sheet and cash flow statement presentations are a bit more involved, so we will look at each of these in more detail.

Balance Sheet Presentation

Current liabilities are reported as the first category in the liabilities section of the balance sheet. Each of the main types of current liabilities is listed separately in the category.

Similar to current assets, current liabilities are generally listed in their order of maturity. However, this is not always possible, because of the varying maturity dates that may exist for specific obligations such as notes payable. Long-term liabilities are reported separately, immediately following current liabilities. Quebecor's presentation of its liabilities is shown in Illustration 10-7.

Illustration 10-7 ◀

Quebecor liabilities

QUEBECOR INC.
Balance Sheet (partial)
December 31, 2004
(in millions)

QUEBECOR INC.

	2004	2003
Current liabilities		
Bank indebtedness	$ 0.8	$ 5.9
Accounts payable, accrued charges and deferred revenue	1,870.0	1,993.4
Income taxes (note 5)	73.3	50.8
Additional amount payable (note 13)	101.4	74.5
Current portion of long-term debt and convertible notes (notes 14 and 16)	16.7	98.2
Total current liabilities	2,062.2	2,222.8
Long-term debt (note 14)	4,888.2	5,286.4
Exchangeable debentures (note 15)	692.7	799.2
Convertible notes (note 16)	135.4	144.7
Other liabilities (note 17)	843.8	764.2
Future income taxes (note 5)	785.4	925.9
Total liabilities	$9,407.7	$10,143.2

Full disclosure of debt is very important. Summary data are usually presented in the balance sheet and detailed data (such as interest rates, maturity dates, conversion privileges, and assets pledged as collateral) are shown in the notes to the financial statements. Quebecor's disclosure about its debt fills more than eight pages in the notes to its financial statements.

Cash Flow Statement Presentation

The balance sheet presents the balances of a company's debt at a point in time. Information on cash inflows and outflows during the year that resulted from the principal portion of debt transactions is provided in the financing activities section of the cash flow statement. Interest expense is reported in the operating activities section even though it resulted from debt transactions.

Illustration 10-8, shown on the following page, presents selected debt items from the financing activities section of Quebecor's cash flow statement.

Illustration 10-8 ▶

Quebecor financing
activities

QUEBECOR INC. Statement of Cash Flows (partial) Year Ended December 31, 2004 (in millions)	QUEBECOR INC.

Cash flows related to financing activities	
Net repayments of bank indebtedness	$ (5.0)
Net borrowing (repayments) under revolving bank facilities and commercial paper	73.0
Issuance of long-term debt	389.2
Repayment of long-term debt	(658.4)

From this we learn that Quebecor reduced its bank indebtedness by $5 million. It increased its borrowing on its operating line of credit (revolving bank facilities) and commercial paper. It issued long-term debt of $389.2 million and repaid long-term debt of $658.4 million. It repaid more debt than it borrowed in 2004, so we would expect to see an improvement in its solvency ratios when we analyze the company's solvency in the next section.

Analysis

A careful examination of debt obligations makes it easier to assess a company's ability to pay its current obligations. It also helps to determine whether a company can obtain long-term financing in order to grow. To show the analysis of a company's liquidity and solvency, we will use the information presented in Illustration 10-7 about Quebecor's liabilities, and the following additional information about Quebecor's assets (in millions):

	2004	2003
Balance sheet		
Total current assets	$ 1,966.8	$ 2,008.6
Total noncurrent assets	12,437.7	13,171.6
Total assets	$14,404.5	$15,180.2
Statement of earnings		
Interest expense	$433.5	$513.7
Income tax expense	132.9	21.5
Net earnings	112.2	66.4

Liquidity

Liquidity ratios measure the short-term ability of a company to pay its maturing obligations and to meet unexpected needs for cash. A commonly used measure of liquidity was examined in Chapter 2: the **current ratio** (current assets ÷ current liabilities). Illustration 10-9 reviews this ratio, using Quebecor and industry data.

Illustration 10-9 ▶

Current ratio

$$\text{CURRENT RATIO} = \frac{\text{CURRENT ASSETS}}{\text{CURRENT LIABILITIES}}$$

($ in millions)	2004	2003
Current ratio	$\frac{\$1,966.8}{\$2,062.2} = 1.0\text{:}1$	$\frac{\$2,008.6}{\$2,222.8} = 0.9\text{:}1$
Industry average	1.5:1	1.1:1

Quebecor's current ratio increased slightly in 2004. Still, with a current ratio of 1:1 in 2004, Quebecor has not quite enough current assets to pay its current liabilities. Its current ratio is less than the industry average in both years, more significantly so in 2004.

Recall from earlier chapters that the current ratio can sometimes be misleading. For example, the current ratio's numerator can include some items in current assets that are not very liquid. When a company is having a difficult time selling its merchandise, its inventory and current ratio increase even though its liquidity has actually declined. Similarly, slow-moving accounts receivable increase assets but are not always collectible. Consequently, the current ratio should be supplemented by other ratios, such as the receivables turnover and inventory turnover. Both Quebecor's receivables turnover and inventory turnover (not presented here) improved in 2004, so we can be comfortable with our interpretation of the current ratio.

In recent years, many companies have intentionally reduced their liquid assets (such as accounts receivable and inventory) because they cost too much to hold. This is particularly true of large companies such as Quebecor. Companies that keep fewer liquid assets on hand must rely on other sources of liquidity. One such source is an **operating line of credit**, as discussed earlier in this chapter. If its low amount of liquid assets causes a cash shortfall, a company may borrow money on its available short-term lines of credit as necessary.

Quebecor and its subsidiary companies have access to an operating line of credit of nearly $2 billion of which only half has been used. Thus, while Quebecor's liquidity ratio is significantly below the industry average in 2004, its available lines of credit appear large enough to meet any short-term cash deficiency it might experience as its continues on its acquisition spree.

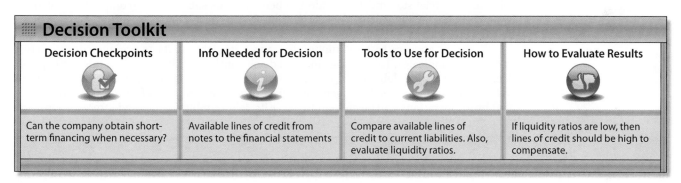

Decision Checkpoints	Info Needed for Decision	Tools to Use for Decision	How to Evaluate Results
Can the company obtain short-term financing when necessary?	Available lines of credit from notes to the financial statements	Compare available lines of credit to current liabilities. Also, evaluate liquidity ratios.	If liquidity ratios are low, then lines of credit should be high to compensate.

Solvency

Solvency ratios measure the ability of a company to repay its long-term debt and survive over a long period of time. As the feature story about Quebecor shows, going into debt is often necessary in order to grow the business. However, debt must be carefully monitored to ensure that it does not hurt a company's solvency.

In Chapter 2, you learned that one measure of a company's solvency is **debt to total assets**. It is calculated by dividing total liabilities by total assets. This ratio indicates how much of a company's debt could be repaid by liquidating the company's assets.

The debt to total assets ratio should be interpreted in light of the company's ability to handle its debt. That is, a company might have a high debt to total assets ratio, but still be able to easily cover its interest payments. Alternatively, a company may have a low debt to total assets ratio, and struggle to cover its interest payments.

The **times interest earned** ratio gives an indication of a company's ability to meet interest payments as they come due. It is calculated by dividing the sum of net earnings, interest expense, and income tax expense, by interest expense. It uses earnings before interest and taxes (often abbreviated as **EBIT**) because this number best represents the amount that is available to cover interest.

Alternative Terminology
The *times interest* earned ratio is also known as the *interest coverage ratio*.

We can use the balance sheet information presented in Illustration 10-7 and the additional information presented on the previous page to calculate solvency ratios for Quebecor. The debt to total assets and times interest earned ratios and averages for the industry are shown in Illustration 10-10 on the following page.

Illustration 10-10 ▶

Solvency ratios

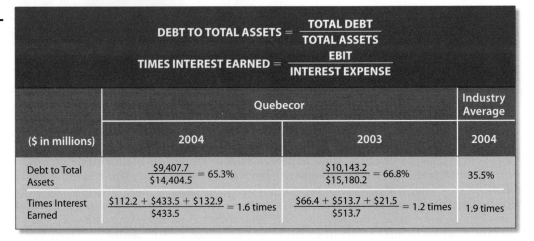

| ($ in millions) | Quebecor | | Industry Average |
	2004	2003	2004
Debt to Total Assets	$\frac{\$9,407.7}{\$14,404.5} = 65.3\%$	$\frac{\$10,143.2}{\$15,180.2} = 66.8\%$	35.5%
Times Interest Earned	$\frac{\$112.2 + \$433.5 + \$132.9}{\$433.5} = 1.6$ times	$\frac{\$66.4 + \$513.7 + \$21.5}{\$513.7} = 1.2$ times	1.9 times

Debt to total assets varies across industries, because different financing options are appropriate for different industries. The debt to total assets ratio for the communications and media industry is 35.5 percent—nearly half Quebecor's debt to total assets of 65.3 percent in 2004. Quebecor's debt to total assets did improve marginally from 2003 to 2004. One must be very careful when interpreting debt to assets ratios. For example, in Quebecor's case, its consolidated financial statements include 100 percent of its subsidiaries' (companies controlled by Quebecor) debt. Quebecor is not responsible for this debt if one of its subsidiary companies defaults on its loans.

Quebecor appears to be equipped to handle its debt, as its improving times interest earned ratio indicates. Its earnings increased substantially in 2004, and its interest expense declined as it repaid debt. Yet, Quebecor is still below the industry average in its ability to cover its interest charges. Management believes that the company's future cash flows generated by its operations will be enough to cover its debt reimbursement and interest payments.

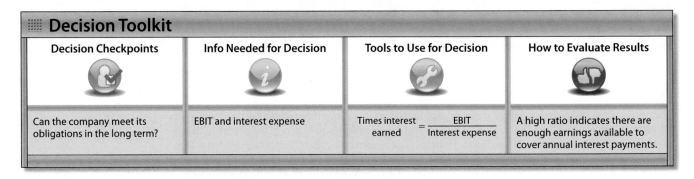

Decision Toolkit

Decision Checkpoints	Info Needed for Decision	Tools to Use for Decision	How to Evaluate Results
Can the company meet its obligations in the long term?	EBIT and interest expense	$\text{Times interest earned} = \frac{\text{EBIT}}{\text{Interest expense}}$	A high ratio indicates there are enough earnings available to cover annual interest payments.

Other Analysis Issues—Unrecorded Debt

A concern for analysts when they evaluate a company's liquidity and solvency is whether that company has properly recorded all of its obligations. The bankruptcy of Enron Corporation—the largest bankruptcy in corporate history—demonstrated how much damage can result when a company does not properly record or disclose all of its debts. Two examples are discussed here—contingencies and off–balance sheet financing.

Contingencies.   Sometimes a company's balance sheet does not fully disclose its actual obligations. One reason for this is that potential obligations which may result from contingencies are not always recorded. **Contingencies** are events with uncertain outcomes. A common type of contingency is a lawsuit. Suppose, for example, that you were analyzing the financial statements of a cigarette manufacturer and did not consider the possible negative implications of unsettled lawsuits. Your analysis of the company's financial position could be misleading if the company were to lose these suits. Other common types of contingencies are guarantees, product warranties, and environmental clean-up obligations.

Accounting rules require that contingencies either be disclosed in the notes to the financial statements or accrued as a liability. If the company can determine **a reasonable estimate** of the expected loss, and if it is **likely** to occur, then the company should accrue the potential loss and liability. If *both* of these conditions are not met, then the company must disclose the contingent loss in the notes to its financial statements.

Quebecor discloses two lawsuits against Vidéotron Ltée, one of its subsidiaries, in the notes to its financial statements. In one of the suits, it states that it is not possible to determine the outcome of the claim at this time. In the other suit, it states that "management claims the suit is not justified and intends to vigorously defend its case in Court."

Off–Balance Sheet Financing.   A second reason that a company's balance sheet might understate its actual obligations is that the company might have "off–balance sheet financing." **Off–balance sheet financing** refers to a situation where liabilities are not recorded on the balance sheet. This situation can occur when a company is able to obtain financing under certain terms that allow it to avoid recording the obligation. One common type of off–balance sheet financing results from leasing transactions, which you will recall were discussed in Chapter 9.

Critics of off–balance sheet financing argue that many operating leases are actually unavoidable obligations that meet the definition of a liability, and they should therefore be reported as liabilities on the balance sheet. To reduce these concerns, companies are required to report their operating lease obligations in a note to the financial statements. This allows analysts and other financial statement users to adjust ratios such as debt to total assets by adding leased assets and lease liabilities if they feel that this treatment is more appropriate.

Quebecor's obligations under operating leases total $655.8 million in 2004 and are disclosed in the notes to the financial statements. Illustration 10-11 presents Quebecor's 2004 debt to total asset ratios as calculated in Illustration 10-10, using the numbers presented in the balance sheet, and after adjusting the ratio for the off–balance-sheet debt and assets resulting from its operating leases.

Debt to Total Assets (using numbers as presented on the balance sheet)	Debt to Total Assets (adjusted for off–balance sheet leases)
$\dfrac{\$9,407.7}{\$14,404.5} = 65.3\%$	$\dfrac{\$9,407.7 + \$655.8}{\$14,404.5 + \$655.8} = 66.8\%$

Illustration 10-11 ◀

Debt to total assets adjusted for leases

Quebecor's operating leases are not very significant relative to its total assets of $14,404.5 million or total liabilities of $9,407.7 million. The inclusion of these operating leases increases Quebecor's debt to total assets ratio by only 1.5 percentage points.

▦ Decision Toolkit

Decision Checkpoints	Info Needed for Decision	Tools to Use for Decision	How to Evaluate Results
Does the company have any contingent liabilities?	Knowledge of events with uncertain negative outcomes	Financial statements and notes to financial statements	If negative outcomes are possible, determine the probability, the amount of loss, and the potential impact on financial statements.
Does the company have significant off–balance sheet financing, such as unrecorded lease obligations?	Information on unrecorded obligations, such as minimum lease payments from lease note	Compare liquidity and solvency ratios with and without unrecorded obligations included.	If ratios differ significantly after including unrecorded obligations, these obligations should not be ignored in analysis.

ACCOUNTING MATTERS!　Investor Perspective

New and innovative "off–balance sheet" financing arrangements are surfacing every day, all of them designed to help companies deal with deregulation, foreign exchange and interest rate volatility, income tax changes, and other factors. These types of arrangements include loan commitments, financial guarantees, options, synthetic leases, and asset securitizations. Accounting standard-setters are struggling to keep up with disclosure requirements for these evolving financial instruments as investors and regulators increasingly question the value of these transactions. One senior analyst noted, "I look at off–balance sheet financing from an investor's point of view. All material liabilities must be front and centre."

Source: "CFO Roundtable Webcast Debates the Future of Off–Balance Sheet Financing," *Business Wire*, January 21, 2003.

BEFORE YOU GO ON . . .

▶ Review It

1. How are liability transactions presented on the statement of earnings, balance sheet, and cash flow statement?
2. Distinguish between liquidity and solvency.
3. How does the times interest earned ratio help with the interpretation of the debt to total assets ratio?
4. What is off–balance sheet financing? Give some examples of off–balance sheet financing.

APPENDIX 10A ▶ AMORTIZATION OF BOND DISCOUNTS AND PREMIUMS

study objective 5

Apply the straight-line and effective-interest methods of amortizing bond discounts and premiums.

To follow the matching principle, bond discounts or premiums must be allocated to expense in each period in which the bonds are outstanding. There are two commonly used amortization methods to do this: the straight-line method and the effective-interest method.

Straight-Line Amortization

The **straight-line method of amortization** is the simpler of the two amortization methods. It allocates the same amount to interest expense in each interest period. The amount is determined as shown in Illustration 10A-1.

Illustration 10A-1 ▶

Formula for straight-line method of bond discount or premium amortization

Bond Discount/Premium	÷	Number of Interest Periods	=	Amortization Amount

Amortizing a Bond Discount

To illustrate the straight-line method of amortization, we will continue to use the Candlestick illustration presented earlier in the chapter. As you recall, Candlestick issued $1 million of five-year, 5% bonds for $957,345. Interest is payable semi-annually on July 1 and January 1.

In this example, the bond discount is $42,655 ($1,000,000 − $957,345). Semi-annual amortization of this discount is $4,265.50 ($42,655 ÷ 10 six-month periods), using the straight-line method. The entry to record the payment of bond interest and the amortization of bond discount on the first interest date (July 1, 2006) is as follows:

July 1	Bond Interest Expense	29,265.50	
	Discount on Bonds Payable ($42,655 ÷ 10)		4,265.50
	Cash ($1,000,000 × 5% × $^6/_{12}$)		25,000.00
	(To record payment of bond interest and amortization of bond discount)		

A	=	L	+	SE
−25,000.00		+4,265.50		−29,265.50

↓ Cash flows: −25,000

Note that it is the *interest payment*, and not the *interest expense*, that is calculated by applying the contractual interest rate for the period (5% × $^6/_{12}$) to the face value of the bonds. The interest expense includes both the interest payment ($25,000) and the bond discount amortization ($4,265.50). Recall from our chapter discussion that the bond discount is part of the cost of borrowing.

At December 31, Candlestick's year end, the adjusting entry is recorded as follows:

Dec. 31	Bond Interest Expense	29,265.50	
	Discount on Bonds Payable ($42,655 ÷ 10)		4,265.50
	Bond Interest Payable ($1,000,000 × 5% × $^6/_{12}$)		25,000.00
	(To record accrued bond interest and amortization of bond discount)		

A	=	L	+	SE
		+4,265.50		−29,265.50
		+25,000.00		

Cash flows: no effect

Over the term of the bonds, the balance in Discount on Bonds Payable will decrease semi-annually by the same amortization amount until it reaches zero at maturity. The carrying value of the bonds at maturity will be equal to the face value.

A bond discount amortization schedule, as shown in Illustration 10A-2, is a useful tool to organize and summarize this information. The schedule shows the interest payment, interest expense, discount amortization, and carrying value of the bond for each interest period. Note that the carrying value of the bond increases by $4,265.50 each period until it reaches its face value of $1 million at the end of period 10, its maturity date of January 1, 2011.

Illustration 10A-2 ▼

Bond discount amortization schedule—straight-line method

CANDLESTICK INC.
Bond Discount Amortization Schedule
Straight-Line Method

Semi-Annual Interest Period	(A) Interest Payment ($1,000,000 × 5% × $^6/_{12}$)	(B) Interest Expense (A + C)	(C) Discount Amortization ($42,655 × 10)	(D) Unamortized Discount (D − C)	(E) Bond Carrying Value ($1,000,000 − D)
Issue date				$42,655.00	$ 957,345.00
1	$ 25,000	$ 29,265.50	$ 4,265.50	38,389.50	961,610.50
2	25,000	29,265.50	4,265.50	34,124.00	965,876.00
3	25,000	29,265.50	4,265.50	29,858.50	970,141.50
4	25,000	29,265.50	4,265.50	25,593.00	974,407.00
5	25,000	29,265.50	4,265.50	21,327.50	978,672.50
6	25,000	29,265.50	4,265.50	17,062.00	982,938.00
7	25,000	29,265.50	4,265.50	12,796.50	987,203.50
8	25,000	29,265.50	4,265.50	8,531.00	991,469.00
9	25,000	29,265.50	4,265.50	4,265.50	995,734.50
10	25,000	29,265.50	4,265.50	0.00	1,000,000.00
	$250,000	$292,655.00	$42,655.00		

Column (A) remains constant because the face value of the bonds ($1,000,000) is multiplied by the semi-annual contractual interest rate each period.
Column (B) is calculated as the interest paid (Column A) plus the discount amortization (Column C).
Column (C) indicates the discount amortization each period.
Column (D) decreases each period by the same amount of discount amortization until it reaches zero at maturity.
Column (E) increases each period by the same amount of discount amortization until it equals the face value at maturity.

We have highlighted columns (A), (B), and (C) in the amortization schedule shown in 10A-2 to emphasize their importance. These three columns provide the numbers for each year's journal entries. They are the main reason for preparing the schedule. Column (A) provides the amount of the credit to Cash (or Interest Payable). Column (B) shows the debit to Bond Interest Expense. And column (C) is the credit to Discount on Bonds Payable.

Amortizing a Bond Premium

The amortization of a bond premium is like that of a bond discount. In the chapter example about a bond premium, Candlestick issued the bonds for $1,044,915. This resulted in a premium of $44,915 ($1,044,915 − $1,000,000). The premium amortization for each interest period is $4,491.50 ($44,915 ÷ 10). The entry to record the first payment of interest on July 1 is:

July 1	Bond Interest Expense	20,508.50	
	Premium on Bonds Payable ($44,915 ÷ 10)	4,491.50	
	Cash ($1,000,000 × 5% × 6/12)		25,000.00
	(To record payment of bond interest and amortization of bond premium)		

As we learned earlier in the chapter, the bond premium reduces the cost of borrowing. Consequently, the interest expense account is effectively increased (debited) for the interest payment ($25,000) and decreased (credited) for the premium amortization in the same entry. Note that interest expense is credited, rather than revenue or another account.

At December 31, the adjusting entry is:

Dec. 31	Bond Interest Expense	20,508.50	
	Premium on Bonds Payable ($44,915 ÷ 10)	4,491.50	
	Bond Interest Payable ($1,000,000 × 5% × 6/12)		25,000.00
	(To record accrued bond interest and amortization of bond premium)		

Over the term of the bonds, the balance in Premium on Bonds Payable will decrease semiannually by the same amount until it reaches zero at maturity. Carrying values *increase* to the maturity value with a bond discount and *decrease* to the maturity value with a bond premium.

A bond premium amortization schedule, as shown in Illustration 10A-3 on the following page, shows interest expense, premium amortization, and the carrying value of the bond for each interest period. The interest expense recorded each period for the Candlestick bond is $20,508.50 under the straight-line method. This is the amount of the interest payment ($25,000) reduced by the premium amortization ($4,491.50). Note also that the carrying value of the bond decreases by $4,491.50 each period until it reaches the face value of $1 million at the end of period 10, its maturity date of January 1, 2011.

CANDLESTICK INC.
Bond Premium Amortization Schedule
Straight-Line Method

Semi-Annual Interest Period	(A) Interest Payment ($1,000,000 × 5% × 6/12)	(B) Interest Expense (A − C)	(C) Premium Amortization ($44,915 ÷ 10)	(D) Unamortized Premium (D − C)	(E) Bond Carrying Value ($1,000,000 + D)
Issue date				$44,915.00	$1,044,915.00
1	$ 25,000	$ 20,508.50	$ 4,491.50	40,423.50	1,040,423.50
2	25,000	20,508.50	4,491.50	35,932.00	1,035,932.00
3	25,000	20,508.50	4,491.50	31,440.50	1,031,440.50
4	25,000	20,508.50	4,491.50	26,949.00	1,026,949.00
5	25,000	20,508.50	4,491.50	22,457.50	1,022,457.50
6	25,000	20,508.50	4,491.50	17,966.00	1,017,966.00
7	25,000	20,508.50	4,491.50	13,474.50	1,013,474.50
8	25,000	20,508.50	4,491.50	8,983.00	1,008,983.00
9	25,000	20,508.50	4,491.50	4,491.50	1,004,491.50
10	25,000	20,508.50	4,491.50	0.00	1,000,000.00
	$250,000	$205,085.00	$44,915.00		

Column (A) remains constant because the face value of the bonds ($1,000,000) is multiplied by the semi-annual contractual interest rate each period.
Column (B) is calculated as the interest paid (Column A) less the premium amortization (Column C).
Column (C) indicates the premium amortization each period.
Column (D) decreases each period by the same amount of premium amortization until it reaches zero at maturity.
Column (E) decreases each period by the same amount of premium amortization until it equals the face value at maturity.

Illustration 10A-3 ▲

Bond premium amortization schedule—straight-line method

Effective-Interest Amortization

We learned earlier in this chapter that bond discounts and premiums should be allocated to expense over the life of the bonds as required by the matching principle. However, to comply completely with the matching principle, interest expense as a percentage of carrying value should not change over the life of the bonds. This percentage, referred to as the market or effective interest rate, is established when the bonds are issued and remains constant in each interest period.

Under the **effective-interest method of amortization**, interest expense is calculated by multiplying the carrying value of the bonds by the effective interest rate at the time the bonds were issued. This method results in varying amounts of amortization and interest expense per period but in a constant percentage rate. The straight-line method results in constant amounts of amortization and interest expense per period but a varying percentage rate. The following illustration shows this by using data from selected interest periods of the bond premium amortization schedule shown in Illustration 10A-3.

CANDLESTICK INC.
Interest Expense Percentage
Straight-Line Method

Semi-Annual Interest Period	Interest Expense (B)	Bond Carrying Value (E)	Interest Expense as a Percentage of Carrying Value (B ÷ E)
1	$20,508.50	$1,044,915.00	1.96%
2	20,508.50	1,040,432.50	1.97%
3	20,508.50	1,035,932.00	1.98%
10	20,508.50	1,004,491.50	2.04%

Illustration 10A-4 ◀

Interest percentage rates under straight-line method

Both the straight-line and effective-interest methods of amortization result in the same total amount of interest expense over the term of the bonds. However, **when the amounts are materially different each interest period, the effective-interest method is required under generally accepted accounting principles**. The effective-interest method is considered better in theory than the straight-line method.

The following steps are required under the effective-interest method of amortization:

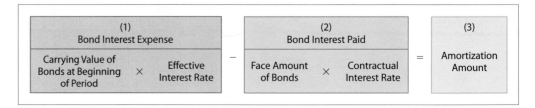

1. Calculate the **bond interest expense**: Multiply the carrying value of the bonds at the beginning of the interest period by the effective interest rate.
2. Calculate the **bond interest paid** (or accrued): Multiply the face value of the bonds by the contractual interest rate.
3. Calculate the **amortization amount**: Determine the difference between the amounts calculated in steps (1) and (2).

Amortizing a Bond Discount

To illustrate the effective-interest method of bond discount amortization, we will continue to use the Candlestick example illustrated earlier in the chapter. As you recall, Candlestick issued $1 million of 5%, five-year bonds. Interest is payable semi-annually on July 1 and January 1.

The bonds are issued to yield a market interest rate of six percent (the effective interest rate). Using time value of money techniques, we determine that the bonds will sell for $957,345 (95.7345% of face value).

Present value of $1,000,000 received in 10 periods	
$1,000,000 × 0.74409 ($n = 10, i = 3\%$)	$744,090
Present value of $25,000 received for each of 10 periods	
$25,000 × 8.53020 ($n = 10, i = 3\%$)	213,255
Present value (market) price of bonds	$957,345
Where n = number of interest periods and i = interest rate	

This market price results in a bond discount of $42,655 ($1,000,000 − $957,345).

For the first interest period, the bond interest expense is $28,720, calculated by multiplying the carrying value of the bonds by the effective interest rate ($957,345 × 6% × 6/12). The interest payment, $25,000, is the same under both methods. It is calculated by multiplying the face value of the bonds by the contractual interest rate ($1,000,000 × 5% × 6/12). The amortization in the effective-interest method is not a specific calculation, as it is in the straight-line amortization method. It is simply the difference between the interest expense and the interest paid ($28,720 − $25,000 = $3,720). The interest payment will remain constant each period while the interest expense and amortization will change with the carrying value.

A bond discount amortization schedule, as shown in Illustration 10A-5, makes it easier to record the interest expense and the discount amortization. For simplicity, amounts have been rounded to the nearest dollar in this schedule.

Semi-Annual Interest Period	(A) Interest Payment ($1,000,000 × 5% × $^6/_{12}$)	(B) Interest Expense (Preceding Bond Carrying Value × 6% × $^6/_{12}$)	(C) Discount Amortization (B − A)	(D) Unamortized Discount (D − C)	(E) Bond Carrying Value ($1,000,000 − D)
Issue date				$42,655	$ 957,345
1	$ 25,000	$ 28,720	$ 3,720	38,935	961,065
2	25,000	28,832	3,832	35,103	964,897
3	25,000	28,947	3,947	31,156	968,844
4	25,000	29,065	4,065	27,091	972,909
5	25,000	29,187	4,187	22,904	977,096
6	25,000	29,313	4,313	18,591	981,409
7	25,000	29,442	4,442	14,149	985,851
8	25,000	29,576	4,576	9,573	990,427
9	25,000	29,713	4,713	4,860	995,140
10	25,000	29,860*	4,860	0	1,000,000
	$250,000	$292,655	$42,655		

CANDLESTICK INC.
Bond Discount Amortization Schedule
Effective-Interest Method

Column (A) remains constant because the face value of the bonds ($1,000,000) is multiplied by the semi-annual contractual interest rate each period.
Column (B) is the bond carrying value at the end of the preceding period multiplied by the semi-annual market interest rate.
Column (C) indicates the discount amortization each period.
Column (D) decreases each period by the amortization amount until it reaches zero at maturity.
Column (E) increases each period by the amortization amount until it equals the face value at maturity.
* $6 difference due to rounding

Note that interest expense as a percentage of the carrying value remains constant at three percent (6% × $^6/_{12}$ mos.).

For the first interest period, the entry to record the payment of interest and amortization of bond discount by Candlestick is as follows:

Illustration 10A-5 ▲

Bond discount amortization schedule—effective-interest method

July 1	Bond Interest Expense ($957,345 × 6% × $^6/_{12}$)	28,720	
	Discount on Bonds Payable		3,720
	Cash ($1,000,000 × 5% × $^6/_{12}$)		25,000
	(To record payment of bond interest and amortization of bond discount)		

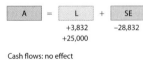

Recall from our chapter discussion that a bond discount increases the cost of borrowing. Consequently, the interest expense includes both the interest payment ($25,000) and the bond discount amortization ($3,720).

For the second interest period, at Candlestick's year end, the following adjusting entry is made:

Dec. 31	Bond Interest Expense ($961,065 × 6% × $^6/_{12}$)	28,832	
	Discount on Bonds Payable		3,832
	Bond Interest Payable ($1,000,000 × 5% × $^6/_{12}$)		25,000
	(To record accrued bond interest and amortization of bond discount)		

A = L + SE
+3,832 −28,832
+25,000

Cash flows: no effect

Amortizing a Bond Premium

The amortization of a bond premium by the effective-interest method is similar to the procedures for a bond discount. Assume that Candlestick issues its bonds to yield a market (effective) interest rate of 4%. Using time value of money techniques, we determine that the bonds will sell for $1,044,915.

Present value of $1,000,000 received in 10 periods	
$1,000,000 × 0.82035 (*n* = 10, *i* = 2)	$ 820,350
Present value of $25,000 received for each of 10 periods	
$25,000 × 8.98259 (*n* = 10, *i* = 2)	224,565
Present value (market) price of bonds	$1,044,915
Where *n* = number of interest periods and *i* = interest rate	

This market price results in a premium of $44,915 ($1,044,915 − $1,000,000).

The bond premium amortization schedule is shown in Illustration 10A-6. Figures have been rounded to the nearest dollar for simplicity.

CANDLESTICK INC.
Bond Premium Amortization Schedule
Effective-Interest Method

	(A)	(B)	(C)	(D)	(E)
		Interest Expense	Premium	Unamortized	Bond
Semi-Annual	Interest Payment	(Preceding Bond Carrying	Amortization	Premium	Carrying Value
Interest Period	($1,000,000 × 5% × ⁶/₁₂)	Value × 4% × ⁶/₁₂)	(A − B)	(D − C)	($1,000,000 + D)
Issue date				$44,915	$1,044,915
1	$ 25,000	$ 20,898	$ 4,102	40,813	1,040,813
2	25,000	20,816	4,184	36,629	1,036,629
3	25,000	20,733	4,267	32,362	1,032,362
4	25,000	20,647	4,353	28,009	1,028,009
5	25,000	20,560	4,440	23,569	1,023,569
6	25,000	20,471	4,529	19,040	1,019,040
7	25,000	20,381	4,619	14,421	1,014,421
8	25,000	20,288	4,712	9,709	1,009,709
9	25,000	20,194	4,806	4,903	1,004,903
10	25,000	20,097*	4,903	0	1,000,000
	$250,000	$205,085	$44,915		

Column (A) remains constant because the face value of the bonds ($1,000,000) is multiplied by the semi-annual contractual interest rate each period.
Column (B) is the bond carrying value at the end of the preceding period multiplied by the semi-annual market interest rate.
Column (C) indicates the premium amortization each period.
Column (D) decreases each period by the amortization amount until it reaches zero at maturity.
Column (E) decreases each period by the amortization amount until it equals the face value at maturity.
* $1 difference due to rounding

Note that interest expense as a percentage of the carrying value remains constant at two percent (4% × ⁶/₁₂).

The entry on the first interest date is as follows:

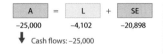

July 1	Bond Interest Expense ($1,044,915 × 4% × ⁶/₁₂)	20,898	
	Premium on Bonds Payable	4,102	
	Cash ($1,000,000 × 5% × ⁶/₁₂)		25,000
	(To record payment of bond interest and amortization of bond premium)		

As we learned earlier in the chapter, a bond premium reduces the cost of borrowing. Consequently, the interest expense account is effectively increased (debited) for the interest payment ($25,000) and decreased (credited) for the bond premium amortization ($4,102) in the same entry.

For the second period, the following adjusting entry is made. While the interest expense and amortization amounts vary, the cash payment is a constant $25,000 every interest period.

Dec. 31	Bond Interest Expense ($1,040,813 × 4% × 6/12)	20,816	
	Premium on Bonds Payable	4,184	
	Bond Interest Payable ($1,000,000 × 5% × 6/12)		25,000
	(To record accrued bond interest and amortization of bond premium)		

A = L + SE
−4,184 −20,816
+25,000

Cash flows: no effect

Note that the amount of periodic interest expense decreases over the life of the bond when the effective-interest method is applied to bonds issued at a premium. The reason is that a constant percentage is applied to a decreasing bond carrying value to calculate interest expense. The carrying value is decreasing because of the amortization of the premium.

Using the Decision Toolkit

CanWest Global Communications Corp. is the country's largest media conglomerate and one of Quebecor's biggest competitors. Selected financial information for CanWest is provided below as at August 31, 2004 and 2003:

CANWEST GLOBAL COMMUNICATIONS CORP.
Balance Sheet
August 31, 2004
(in millions)

	2004	2003
Assets		
Current assets		
Cash	$ 81.1	$ 121.9
Accounts receivable	398.5	391.7
Inventory	13.5	14.5
Other current assets	185.7	237.5
Total current assets	678.8	765.6
Noncurrent assets	4,203.3	4,553.2
Total assets	$4,882.1	$5,318.8
Liabilities and Shareholders' Equity		
Liabilities		
Current liabilities	$ 451.5	$ 648.9
Long-term liabilities	3,248.9	3,494.3
Total liabilities	3,700.4	4,143.2
Total shareholders' equity	1,181.7	1,175.6
Total liabilities and shareholders' equity	$4,882.1	$5,318.8
Other information		
Revenue	$2,113.0	$2,139.5
Net earnings (loss)	(13.5)	46.1
Interest expense	310.6	353.0
Income tax expense (recovery)	(10.2)	2.5

Available lines of credit: Credit facilities provide for revolving and term loans to the maximum amounts of $413.1 million and $665.0 million, respectively. As at August 31, 2004, none of the revolving loan had been utilized, but nearly all of the term loan had been used.

Instructions

(a) Evaluate CanWest's liquidity in 2004 using appropriate ratios, and compare the ratios to those of Quebecor and to industry averages.

(b) Evaluate CanWest's solvency in 2004 using appropriate ratios, and compare the ratios to those of Quebecor and to industry averages.

Solution

(a) CanWest's liquidity can be measured using the current and receivables turnover ratios. Cost of goods sold is not separately reported for CanWest Global so the inventory turnover ratio cannot be calculated.

Ratio	CanWest	Quebecor	Industry Average
Current	$\dfrac{\$678.8}{\$451.5} = 1.5{:}1$	1.0:1	1.3:1
Receivables turnover	$\dfrac{\$2{,}113.0}{[(\$398.5 + \$391.7) \div 2]} = 5.3 \text{ times}$	13.7 times	6.3 times

CanWest's current ratio is 1.5:1, which means that it has $1.50 of current assets to pay every $1 of current liabilities. Taken with its available line of credit, CanWest's liquidity appears to be good. It is also better than Quebecor's and the industry average in 2004. Its receivables turnover ratio is not as strong as Quebecor's or that of the industry's. CanWest's receivables turnover should be investigated further—perhaps CanWest has different terms of sale than Quebecor.

(b) CanWest's solvency can be measured with the debt to total assets and times interest earned ratios:

Ratio	CanWest	Quebecor	Industry Average
Debt to total assets	$\dfrac{\$3{,}700.4}{\$4{,}882.1} = 75.8\%$	65.3%	55.4%
Times interest earned	$\dfrac{\$(13.5) + \$310.6 + \$(10.2)}{\$310.6} = 0.9 \text{ times}$	1.6 times	15.4 times

CanWest's debt to total assets ratio of 75.8 percent is worse than Quebecor's. Both companies have more debt as a percentage of assets compared to the industry.

In addition, Quebecor was better able to handle its debt in 2004. Quebecor's times interest earned ratio of 1.6 times is better than CanWest's ratio of 0.9 times. CanWest's times interest earned ratio is difficult to properly interpret in 2004, since it is affected by a net loss. Both companies' times interest earned ratios are significantly lower than the industry average.

the navigator

Summary of Study Objectives

1. **Explain the accounting for current liabilities.** A current liability is a debt that will be paid (1) from existing current assets or through the creation of other current liabilities, and (2) within one year. An example of a current liability is an operating line of credit that results in bank indebtedness. Current liabilities also include sales taxes, payroll deductions, and employee benefits, all of which the company collects on behalf of third parties. Other examples include property taxes and interest on notes payable, which must be accrued until paid. The portion of long-term debt that is due within the next year must be deducted from the long-term liability and reported as a current liability.

2. **Explain the accounting for long-term notes payable.** Long-term notes payable are repayable in a series of payments. Each payment consists of (1) interest on the unpaid balance of the note, and (2) a reduction of the principal balance. These payments can be either (1) fixed principal payments or (2) blended principal and interest payments. With fixed principal payments, the reduction in principal is constant but the cash payment and interest decrease each period (as the principal decreases). Blended principal and interest payments result in a constant cash payment but changing amounts of interest and principal.

3. **Explain the accounting for bonds payable.** When bonds are issued, the Bonds Payable account is credited for the face value of the bonds. In addition, a contra liability account may exist for the bond discount (debit) if the bonds are issued for less than their face value, or an adjunct liability account may exist for the bond premium (credit) if the bonds are issued for more than their face value. Bond

discounts and bond premiums are amortized to interest expense over the life of the bond. The amortization of a bond discount increases interest expense. The amortization of a bond premium decreases interest expense.

When bonds are retired at maturity, Bonds Payable is debited and Cash is credited. There is no gain or loss at retirement. When bonds are redeemed before maturity, it is necessary to (a) update any unrecorded interest, (b) eliminate the carrying value of the bonds at the redemption date, (c) record the cash paid, and (d) recognize any gain or loss on redemption.

4. ***Identify the requirements for the financial statement presentation and analysis of liabilities.*** Interest expense and any gain or loss on the redemption of bonds is reported as an "other expense" or "other revenue" in the statement of earnings. In the balance sheet, current liabilities are reported first, followed by long-term liabilities. The nature of each liability should be described in the notes accompanying the financial statements. Inflows and outflows of cash related to the principal portion of long-term debt are reported in the financing activities section of the cash flow statement.

The liquidity of a company may be analyzed by calculating the current ratio, in addition to the receivables and inventory turnover ratios. The solvency of a company may be analyzed by calculating the debt to total assets and times interest earned ratios. Other factors to consider are unrecorded debt, such as contingent liabilities and operating lease obligations.

5. ***Apply the straight-line and effective-interest methods of amortizing bond discounts and premiums (Appendix 10A).*** Amortization is calculated under the straight-line method by dividing the bond discount or premium by the number of interest periods. Interest expense is calculated by multiplying the face value of the bonds by the contractual interest rate.

Amortization is calculated under the effective-interest method as the difference between the interest paid and the interest expense. Interest paid is calculated by multiplying the face value of the bonds by the contractual interest rate. Interest expense is calculated by multiplying the carrying value of the bonds at the beginning of the interest period by the effective interest rate.

The straight-line method of amortization results in a constant amount of amortization and interest expense each period, but a varying percentage rate. The effective-interest method of amortization results in varying amounts of amortization and interest expense each period, but a constant percentage rate of interest.

Decision Toolkit—A Summary

Decision Checkpoints	Info Needed for Decision	Tools to Use for Decision	How to Evaluate Results
Can the company obtain short-term financing when necessary?	Available lines of credit from notes to the financial statements	Compare available lines of credit to current liabilities. Also, evaluate liquidity ratios.	If liquidity ratios are low, then lines of credit should be high to compensate.
Can the company meet its obligations in the long term?	EBIT and interest expense	$$\text{Times interest earned} = \frac{\text{EBIT}}{\text{Interest expense}}$$	A high ratio indicates there is enough earnings available to cover annual interest payments.
Does the company have any contingent liabilities?	Knowledge of events with uncertain negative outcomes	Financial statements and notes to financial statements	If negative outcomes are possible, determine the probability, the amount of loss, and the potential impact on financial statements.
Does the company have significant off–balance sheet financing, such as unrecorded lease obligations?	Information on unrecorded obligations, such as minimum lease payments from lease note	Compare liquidity and solvency ratios with and without unrecorded obligations included.	If ratios differ significantly after including unrecorded obligations, these obligations should not be ignored in analysis.

**Analysis Tools
(Decision Toolkit Summaries)**

Glossary

Study Tools (Glossary)

Bond   A form of interest-bearing note payable issued by large corporations, universities, and governments. (p. 468)

Collateral   Assets pledged as security for the payment of a debt (e.g., land, buildings, and equipment in the case of a mortgage; accounts receivable or inventory in the case of a bank loan). (p. 458)

Contingencies   Events with uncertain outcomes, such as a potential liability that may become an actual liability sometime in the future. (p. 478)

Contractual interest rate   The rate used to determine the amount of interest the borrower pays and the investor receives. (p. 468)

Convertible debt   Debt such as notes or bonds that have the option of being converted into (exchanged for) common shares. (p. 464)

Current liability   A debt that will be paid (1) from existing current assets or through the creation of other current liabilities, and (2) within one year. (p. 458)

Debentures   Unsecured debt issued against the general credit of the borrower. (p. 464)

Discount (on a bond)   The difference between the face value of a bond and its selling price when a bond is sold for less than its face value. This occurs when the market interest rate is higher than the contractual interest rate. (p. 470)

EBIT   Earnings before interest expense and income tax expense. (p. 477)

Effective-interest method of amortization   A method of amortizing a bond discount or premium that results in a periodic interest expense that equals a constant percentage of the carrying value of the bond. (p. 483)

Long-term liability   An obligation expected to be paid more than one year in the future. (p. 464)

Market interest rate   The rate investors demand for loaning funds to a corporation. Also known as the effective interest rate. (p. 469)

Mortgage note payable   A long-term note secured by a mortgage that pledges title to property as collateral for the loan. (p. 464)

Notes payable   Obligations in the form of written notes. (p. 459)

Operating line of credit   A pre-arranged agreement to borrow money at a bank, up to an agreed-upon amount. (p. 458)

Premium (on a bond)   The difference between the selling price and the face value of a bond when a bond is sold for more than its face value. This occurs when the market interest rate is less than the contractual interest rate. (p. 470)

Present value   The value today of an amount to be received at some date in the future after taking interest rates into account. (p. 469)

Redeemable (callable) bonds   Bonds that are subject to retirement at a stated dollar amount before maturity at the option of the issuer. (p. 472)

Secured   Describes debt, such as notes or bonds, for which specific assets of the issuer have been pledged as collateral. (p. 464)

Straight-line method of amortization   A method of amortizing a bond discount or bond premium that allocates the same amount to interest expense in each interest period. (p. 480)

Times interest earned   A measure of a company's solvency, calculated by dividing earnings before interest expense and income tax expense (EBIT) by interest expense. (p. 477)

Unsecured   Describes debt, such as notes or bonds, that has been issued against the general credit of the borrower; also called debentures. (p. 464)

Demonstration Problem

Study Tools
(Demonstration Problems)

Snyder Software Inc. successfully developed a new spreadsheet program. To produce and market the program, the company needed to raise $500,000. On December 31, 2005, Snyder issued a 15-year, 6%, $500,000 mortgage note payable. The terms provide for semi-annual blended instalment payments of $25,510 (principal and interest) on June 30 and December 31.

Instructions

(a) Prepare a payment schedule for the first four instalment payments.
(b) Record the issue of the note on December 31, 2005.
(c) Record the first instalment payment on June 30, 2006.
(d) Indicate the current and noncurrent amounts that would be presented in the balance sheet for the mortgage note payable at December 31, 2006.

Solution

(a)

Semi-Annual Interest Period	Cash Payment	Interest Expense	Reduction of Principal	Principal Balance
Issue date (Dec. 31, 2005)				$500,000
1 (June 30, 2006)	$25,510	$15,000ᵃ	$10,510ᵇ	489,490ᶜ
2 (Dec. 31, 2006)	25,510	14,685	10,825	478,665
3 (June 30, 2007)	25,510	14,360	11,150	467,515
4 (Dec. 31, 2007)	25,510	14,025	11,485	456,030

a $500,000 × 6% × 6/12 = $15,000
b $25,510 − $15,000 = $10,510
c $500,000 − $10,510 = $489,490

(b)

Dec. 31, 2005	Cash	500,000	
	Mortgage Note Payable		500,000
	(To record issue of 15-year, 6% mortgage note payable)		

(c)

June 30, 2006	Interest Expense	15,000	
	Mortgage Note Payable	10,510	
	Cash		25,510
	(To record interest and instalment payment on mortgage note payable)		

(d) The current liability is $22,635 ($11,150 + $11,485).
The long-term liability is $456,030.
The total liability is $478,665, the balance at the end of the second period, December 31, 2006.

Action Plan

• Determine the interest expense for the mortgage by multiplying the semi-annual interest rate by the principal balance at the beginning of the period. The reduction of principal is the difference between the cash payment and the interest expense amounts.

• Recognize that as the principal amount decreases, so does the interest expense.

• Record mortgage payments, recognizing that each payment consists of (1) interest on the unpaid loan balance, and (2) a reduction of the loan principal.

the navigator

Note: All of the questions, exercises, and problems below with an asterisk (*) relate to material in Appendix 10A.

Self-Study Questions

www.wiley.com/canada/kimmel

Study Tools (Self-Assessment Quizzes)

Answers are at the end of the chapter.

(SO 1) 1. Reeves Ltd. has $4,515 of pre-tax sales. If Reeves collects 15% HST with each sale, what is the amount to be credited to Sales?
(a) $677   (c) $4,515
(b) $3,926   (d) $5,192

(SO 1) 2. On March 1, Swift Current Limited received its property tax assessment in the amount of $12,000 for the calendar year. The property tax bill is due May 1. If Swift Current prepares quarterly financial statements, how much prepaid property tax should the company report for the quarter ended March 31?
(a) $2,000   (c) $8,000
(b) $3,000   (d) $9,000

(SO 2) 3. Zhang Inc. issues a three-year, 7%, $497,000 instalment note payable on January 1. The note will be paid in three annual blended instalment payments of $189,383, each payable at the end of the year. What is the amount of interest expense that should be recognized by Zhang in the second year?
(a) $17,395   (c) $23,968
(b) $23,193   (d) $34,790

(SO 2) 4. Assume that the note issue by Zhang Inc. in question 3 above will be paid with fixed principal instalment payments of $165,667, each payable at the end of the year. What is the amount of interest expense that should be recognized by Zhang in the second year?
(a) $17,395   (c) $23,968
(b) $23,193   (d) $34,790

(SO 3) 5. On January 1, Scissors Corp. issues $200,000 of five-year, 7% bonds at 97. The entry to record the issue of the bonds would include a:
(a) debit to Cash for $200,000.
(b) debit to Bonds Payable for $200,000.
(c) debit to Discount on Bonds Payable for $6,000.
(d) credit to Premium on Bonds Payable for $6,000.

(SO 3) 6. Gester Corporation redeems its $100,000 of face value bonds at 105 on January 1. The carrying value of the bonds at the redemption date is $103,745. The entry to record the redemption will include a:
(a) debit of $1,255 to Loss on Bond Redemption.
(b) credit of $1,255 to Gain on Bond Redemption.
(c) credit of $3,745 to Premium on Bonds Payable.
(d) debit of $105,000 to Cash.

(SO 4) 7. 🔧 In a recent year, Kennedy Corporation had net earnings of $150,000, interest expense of $30,000, and income tax expense of $20,000. What was Kennedy's times interest earned ratio?
  (a) 5.0 times   (c) 6.0 times
  (b) 5.7 times   (d) 6.7 times

(SO 4) 8. 🔧 Which of the following items is not an example of off–balance sheet financing?
  (a) Contingent liabilities
  (b) Operating line of credit
  (c) Operating leases
  (d) Loan guarantee

(SO 5) *9. On January 1, Hurley Corporation issues $500,000 of five-year, 6% bonds at 96 with interest payable on July 1 and January 1. The entry on July 1 to record the payment of bond interest and the amortization of a bond discount using the straight-line method will include a:
  (a) debit to Interest Expense, $13,000.
  (b) debit to Interest Expense, $15,000.
  (c) debit to Discount on Bonds Payable, $2,000.
  (d) credit to Discount on Bonds Payable, $2,000.

*10. On January 1, Daigle Corporation issued $2 million of   (SO
five-year, 7% bonds with interest payable on January 1 and July 1. The bonds sold for $1,918,880, at a market interest rate of 8%. Assuming the effective-interest method is used, the debit entry to Bond Interest Expense (rounded to the nearest dollar) on July 1 is for:
  (a) $67,161.   (c) $76,755.
  (b) $70,000.   (d) $80,000.

Questions

(SO 1) 1. What is the difference between accounts payable and notes payable? Between notes payable and an operating line of credit?

(SO 1) 2. Jetsgo had $40.7 million from passengers for advance ticket sales when it filed for bankruptcy protection on March 11. Before seeking bankruptcy protection, how would this amount be reported on Jetsgo's financial statements?

(SO 1) 3. Your roommate says, "Sales taxes are part of the cost of doing business and should be reported as a deduction from sales in the sales revenue section of the statement of earnings." Do you agree? Explain.

(SO 1) 4. Explain how recording property taxes can result in both a liability (property tax payable) and an asset (prepaid property tax) in the same period.

(SO 1) 5. Where in the financial statements should a company report employee payroll deductions? Employee benefits?

(SO 2) 6. Identify the similarities and differences between accounts payable and notes payable.

(SO 2) 7. Identify the similarities and differences between short-term and long-term notes payable.

(SO 2) 8. Identify the similarities and differences between long-term notes payable and bonds payable.

(SO 2) 9. Distinguish between instalment notes payable with fixed principal payments and those with blended principal and interest payments.

(SO 2) 10. Doug Bareak, a friend of yours, has recently purchased a home for $200,000. He paid $20,000 down and financed the remainder with a 20-year, 5% mortgage, payable in blended payments of principal and interest of $1,290 per month. At the end of the first month, Doug received a statement from the bank indicating that only $390 of the principal was paid during the month. At this rate, he calculated that it would take over 38 years to pay off the mortgage. Explain why this is not the case.

11. La Mi and Jack Dalton are discussing how the mar- (SO
ket price of a bond is determined. La believes that the market price of a bond depends only on the amount of the principal payment at the end of the term of a bond. Is she right? Discuss.

12. Stoney Inc. sold bonds with a face value of $100,000 (SO
for $104,000. Was the market interest rate equal to, less than, or greater than the bonds' contractual interest rate? Explain.

13. How is the carrying value of a bond calculated if the (SO
bond is sold at a discount? At a premium? How does each of these amounts change over the life of the bond?

14. How will the total cost of borrowing be affected if a (SO
bond is sold (a) at a discount and (b) at a premium? Explain when this cost of borrowing should be recorded and identify the relevant generally accepted accounting principle.

15. Which accounts are debited and which are credited if (SO
a bond issue that was originally sold at a premium is redeemed before maturity at 97?

16. 🔧 In general, what are the requirements for the (SO
financial statement presentation of (a) current liabilities, and (b) long-term liabilities?

17. 🔧 Distinguish between liquidity and solvency. (SO
Provide an example of two ratios that are used to measure each.

18. 🔧 Explain why the debt to total assets ratio (SO
should never be interpreted without referring to the times interest earned ratio.

19. 🔧 How is the analysis of a company affected if it (SO
has significant operating leases?

(SO 4) 20. 🔧 What is a contingency? Why do investors need to know about something that might not even happen?

(SO 5) *21. Distinguish between the effective-interest and straight-line methods of amortizing discounts and premiums on bonds payable.

(SO 5) *22. Compare the effect of the straight-line and effective-interest methods of amortization on interest expense as a percentage of carrying value. Which method is considered to be better in theory? Explain why.

*23. Summit Corporation issues bonds at a premium. Will (SO 5) the annual interest expense increase, decrease, or remain unchanged over the life of the bonds if Summit uses the straight-line method of amortization? The effective-interest method of amortization?

Brief Exercises

BE10–1   Romez Limited borrows $55,000 on July 1 from the bank by signing a three-month, 5% note payable. Interest is due at maturity. Romez's year end is August 31. Prepare journal entries to record the (a) issue of the note on July 1, (b) accrual of interest on August 31, and (c) repayment of the note on October 1.

Record short-term note payable. (SO 1)

BE10–2   Centennial Property Ltd. collects $6,500 plus 15% HST for five months' rent paid in advance by Rikard's Menswear on October 1. Both companies have a December 31 year end. Prepare entries for both companies on October 1 and December 31.

Record unearned revenue and prepaid rent, with sales taxes. (SO 1)

BE10–3   Pierce Corp. has a June 30 year end. It received its property tax assessment of $25,200 on April 30 for the calendar year. The property tax bill is payable on July 15. How much property tax expense will Pierce report on its June 30 statement of earnings? How much property tax payable and/or prepaid property tax will Pierce report at June 30 on its balance sheet?

Determine amounts reported for property tax. (SO 1)

BE10–4   Zerbe Consulting Inc.'s gross salaries in August were $15,000. Deductions included $730 for CPP, $315 for EI, and $4,305 for income taxes. The company's payroll costs were $730 for CPP and $441 for EI. Prepare journal entries to record (a) the accrual and payment of salaries on August 31, and (b) the company's payroll costs for August.

Record payroll. (SO 1)

BE10–5   You qualify for a $10,000 loan from the Canada Student Loans Program to help finance your education. Once you graduate, you start repaying this 7% note payable with a monthly cash payment of $116.11, principal and interest, for 120 payments (10 years). Prepare an instalment payment schedule for the first three payments.

Prepare instalment payment schedule for long-term note payable. (SO 2)

BE10–6   Eyre Inc. issues a 10-year, 8%, $300,000 mortgage note payable on November 30, 2005, to obtain financing for a new building. The terms provide for monthly payments. Prepare the entries to record the mortgage loan on November 30, 2005, and the first two payments on December 31, 2005, and January 31, 2006, assuming the payment is (a) a fixed principal payment of $2,500, and (b) a blended principal and interest payment of $3,639.83.

Record mortgage note payable. (SO 2)

BE10–7   Keystone Corporation issued $1 million of five-year, 6% bonds dated March 1, 2006, at 100. Interest was payable semi-annually on September 1 and March 1. Keystone has a December 31 year end. (a) Record the issue of these bonds on March 1. (b) Record the first interest payment on September 1, 2006.

Record bond transactions. (SO 3)

BE10–8   Refer to the data presented in BE10–7 for Keystone Corporation's bond issue. (a) Prepare the journal entry to record the sale of these bonds on March 1, 2006, assuming that the bonds were issued at (1) 99 rather than 100, and (2) 101 rather than 100. (b) Show the balance sheet presentation of the bonds on March 1, 2006, assuming the bonds were issued at (1) 100, (2) 99, and (3) 101. (c) What will the carrying value be at maturity, March 1, 2011, under each of the three assumptions given in (b)?

Record bond issue; show balance sheet presentation. (SO 3)

BE10–9   Hathaway Ltd.'s general ledger reports the following account balances at November 30, 2006:

Record bond redemption. (SO 3)

Discount on bonds payable	$	60,000
Bonds payable		1,000,000

Hathaway decides to redeem these bonds on November 30 at 101. Prepare the journal entry to record the redemption.

Identify current liabilities.
(SO 4)

BE10–10   Identify which of the following transactions would be classified as a current liability. For those that are not current liabilities, identify where they should be classified.

1. A demand loan
2. Cash received in advance by WestJet Airlines for airline tickets
3. GST collected on sales
4. The current portion of long-term debt
5. Interest owing on an overdue account payable
6. Interest due on an overdue account receivable
7. A nuisance lawsuit pending against the company
8. Amounts withheld from the employees' weekly pay
9. Property tax payable
10. A mortgage payable with $5,000 due within one year

Prepare liabilities section of balance sheet.
(SO 4)

BE10–11   Presented here are liability items for Warner Ltd. at December 31, 2006. Prepare the liabilities section of Warner's balance sheet.

Accounts payable	$ 35,000	Mortgage note payable, due 2025	$400,000
Bank indebtedness	10,000	Notes payable, due 2007	80,000
Bonds payable, due 2016	500,000	Property tax payable	5,500
Current portion of long-term debt	40,000	Premium on bonds payable	5,000
Employee benefits payable	7,800	Sales taxes payable	1,400
Income tax payable	25,000	Salaries payable	135,000
Interest payable	40,000	Unearned revenue	2,500

Calculate liquidity and solvency ratios.
(SO 4)

BE10–12   Molson Coors' 2004 financial statements contain the following selected data (in millions):

Income tax expense	$ 95.2
Interest expense	72.4
Net earnings	196.7
Total assets	4,657.5
Total current assets	1,268.2
Total current liabilities	1,176.9
Total liabilities	3,019.5

Calculate Molson Coors' (a) current ratio, (b) debt to total assets ratio, and (c) times interest earned ratio.

Analyze solvency.
(SO 4)

BE10–13   The Canadian National Railway Company's (CN) total assets in 2004 were $19,271 million and its total liabilities were $11,924 million. That year, CN reported operating lease commitments for its locomotives, freight cars, and equipment totalling $992 million. Assume that if these assets had been recorded as capital leases, CN's assets and liabilities would have risen by approximately $992 million.

Calculate CN's debt to total assets ratio, first using the figures reported, and then after increasing assets and liabilities for the unrecorded operating leases. Discuss the potential effect of these operating leases on your assessment of CN's solvency.

Record bond transactions using straight-line amortization.
(SO 3, 5)

*BE10–14   On January 1, 2006, Dominic Ltd. issues $2 million of 10-year, 8% bonds at 96, with interest payable semi-annually on July 1 and January 1. The straight-line method of amortization is used. (a) Prepare the journal entry to record the sale of these bonds on January 1. (b) Prepare the journal entry to record the interest expense and bond discount amortization on the first interest payment date, July 1.

Record bond transactions using straight-line amortization.
(SO 3, 5)

*BE10–15   On January 1, 2006, Abela Inc. issues $5 million of five-year, 9% bonds at 103, with interest payable semi-annually on July 1 and January 1. The straight-line method of amortization is used. (a) Prepare the journal entry to record the sale of these bonds on January 1. (b) Prepare the journal entry to record the interest expense and bond premium amortization on the first interest payment date, July 1.

Record bond transactions using effective-interest amortization.
(SO 3, 5)

*BE10–16   On May 1, 2006, the Jianhua Corporation issued $120,000 of 15-year, 8% bonds, with interest payable semi-annually on November 1 and May 1. The bonds were issued to yield a market interest rate of 6%. Jianhua uses the effective-interest method of amortization. (a) Record the issue of the bonds on May 1. You will need to first calculate the issue price of the bonds using the following present value factors: Present value of 1, $n = 30$, $i = 3\%$ is 0.41199 and present value of an annuity of 1, $n = 30$, $i = 3\%$ is 19.60044. (b) Prepare the journal entry to record the payment of interest and amortization on the first interest payment date, November 1.

*BE10–17 Niagara Corporation issued $100,000 of five-year, 8.5% bonds on April 1, 2006, with interest payable semi-annually on October 1 and April 1. The bonds were issued at $106,237 to yield a market interest rate of 7%. How much interest expense would Niagara record on each of the first two interest payment dates if it used the (a) straight-line method of amortization, and (b) effective-interest method of amortization?

Compare interest expense using straight-line and effective-interest amortization. (SO 5)

Exercises

E10–1 MacDougald Construction Ltd. borrows $250,000 from the TD Bank on October 1, 2006, and signs a six-month, 5% note payable. Interest is payable at maturity. Both companies have a December year end.

Record short-term notes. (SO 1)

Instructions

(a) Prepare journal entries to record the acceptance of the note on October 1, and the accrual of interest on December 31 for MacDougald Construction.
(b) Prepare journal entries to record the issue of the note on October 1, and the accrual of interest on December 31 for the TD Bank. (Hint: You might find it helpful to review accounting for notes receivable in Chapter 8.)

E10–2 Jintao Ltd. incurred the following transactions related to current liabilities:

Record current liability transactions. (SO 1)

1. Jintao's cash register shows the following totals at the end of the day on April 10: pre-tax sales $25,000; GST $1,750; and PST $2,000.
2. Jintao receives its property tax bill for the calendar year for $26,400 on May 1, payable July 1.
3. On June 1, Jintao borrows $50,000 from First Bank on a 12-month, 8%, $50,000 note. Interest is payable at maturity.
4. Jintao's gross payroll for the week of August 15 is $40,500. The company deducted $1,715 for CPP, $850 for EI, and $8,010 for income taxes from the employees' earnings. Jintao's payroll costs for the week are $1,715 for CPP and $1,190 for EI.

Instructions

(a) Record the above transactions.
(b) Assuming that Jintao's year end is December 31, prepare any adjusting entries required for the property tax in transaction 2 and the interest in transaction 3.

E10–3 A list of transactions follows:

Determine impact of current liability transactions. (SO 1)

1. Purchased inventory (perpetual system) on account.
2. Extended payment terms of account payable in item 1 above by issuing a six-month, 5% note payable.
3. Recorded accrued interest on the note payable from item 2 above.
4. Recorded cash sales of $74,750, plus 15% HST.
5. Recorded wage expense of $35,000 and paid employees $25,000. The difference was due to various payroll deductions withheld.
6. Recorded employer's share of employee benefits.
7. Recorded property taxes payable.
8. Recorded the receipt of cash for services that will be performed in the future.

Instructions

Set up a table using the format shown below. Indicate the effect of each of the above transactions on the financial statement categories indicated: use "+" for increase, "–" for decrease, and "NE" for no effect. The first one has been done for you as an example.

	Assets	Liabilities	Shareholders' Equity	Revenues	Expenses	Net Earnings
1.	+	+	NE	NE	NE	NE

Record mortgage note payable.
(SO 2)

E10–4   Ste. Anne Corp. issues a 20-year, 6%, $150,000 mortgage note payable to finance the construction of a building at December 31, 2006. The terms provide for semi-annual instalment payments on June 30 and December 31.

Instructions

Prepare the journal entries to record the mortgage note payable and the first two instalment payments assuming the payment is (a) a fixed principal payment of $3,750, and (b) a blended principal and interest payment of $6,489.36.

Record long-term note payable.
(SO 2)

E10–5   On January 1, 2006, Wolstenholme Corp. borrows $9,000 by signing a three-year, 7% note payable. The note is repayable in three annual blended principal and interest instalments of $3,429.46 at the end of each year, December 31.

Instructions

(a) Prepare an instalment payment schedule for the note.
(b) Prepare the journal entries to record the note and the first instalment payment.
(c) What amounts would be reported as current and long-term in the liabilities section of Wolstenholme's balance sheet on December 31, 2006?

Analyze instalment payment
schedule.
(SO 2)

E10–6   The following instalment payment schedule is for a long-term note payable:

Interest Period	Cash Payment	Interest Expense	Reduction of Principal	Principal Balance
Issue date				$50,000
1	$13,500	$3,500	$10,000	40,000
2	12,800	2,800	10,000	30,000
3	12,100	2,100	10,000	20,000
4	11,400	1,400	10,000	10,000
5	10,700	700	10,000	0

Instructions

(a) Is this a fixed principal or blended principal and interest payment schedule?
(b) Assuming payments are made annually, what is the interest rate on the note?
(c) Prepare the journal entry to record the first instalment payment.
(d) What are the long-term and current portions of the note at the end of period 2?
(e) Suppose these are convertible notes. What circumstances would result in the note holders converting their notes into common shares?

Analyze and record bond issue.
(SO 3)

E10–7   The following information about two independent bond issues was reported in the financial press:

1. Bank of Montreal 7% bonds, maturing January 28, 2010, were issued at 111.12.
2. Bell Canada 7% bonds, maturing September 24, 2027, were issued at 99.08.

Instructions

(a) Were the Bank of Montreal bonds issued at a premium or a discount?
(b) Were the Bell Canada bonds issued at a premium or a discount?
(c) Explain how bonds, both paying the same contractual interest rate (7%), could be issued at different prices.
(d) Prepare the journal entry to record the issue of each of these two bonds, assuming $500,000 of bonds were issued in total.

Record bond transactions.
(SO 3)

E10–8   On September 1, 2006, Mooney Corporation issued $400,000 of 10-year, 5% bonds at 100. Interest is payable semi-annually on September 1 and February 1. Mooney's year end is December 31.

Instructions

(a) Prepare journal entries to record the following:
    1. The issue of the bonds on September 1, 2006
    2. The accrual of interest on December 31, 2006
    3. The payment of interest on February 1, 2007
(b) Show how the bonds would be presented in the liabilities section of Mooney's balance sheet at December 31, 2006.

E10−9 The following independent situations occurred on June 30, 2006:

Record bond redemption. (SO 3)

1. Ernst Corporation redeemed $120,000 of 7% bonds at 103. The carrying value of the bonds at the redemption date was $117,500.
2. Takase Corporation redeemed $150,000 of 8% bonds at 96. The carrying value of the bonds at the redemption date was $152,000.
3. Young, Inc. redeemed $150,000 of 9% bonds at their maturity date, June 30, 2006.

Instructions

Record the above transactions.

E10−10 Bombardier Inc. reports the following liabilities (in U.S. millions) in its January 31, 2005, financial statements:

Prepare liabilities section of balance sheet. (SO 4)

Accrued pension benefit liabilities	$ 897	Operating leases	$ 979
Accrued liabilities	1,277	Other current liabilities	3,182
Current portion of long-term debt	1,744	Payroll-related liabilities	334
Deferred (future) income taxes	41	Short-term borrowings	300
Income and other taxes payable	120	Trade accounts payable	2,112
Interest payable	73	Unused operating line of credit	2,199
Notes payable—long-term	5,160		

Instructions

(a) Identify which of the above liabilities are likely current and which are likely long-term. Say if an item fits in neither category. Explain the reasoning for your selections.
(b) Prepare the liabilities section of Bombardier's balance sheet.

E10−11 The following selected information (in thousands) was taken from the Calgary Exhibition & Stampede's December 31 balance sheet:

Analyze liquidity. (SO 4)

	2004	2003
Cash and short-term deposits	$ 1,634	$ 1,544
Total current assets	8,075	8,330
Bank indebtedness	4,482	4,467
Accounts payable and accrued liabilities	6,025	7,675
Total current liabilities	16,086	17,676

Instructions

(a) Calculate the current ratio for the Calgary Stampede for 2004 and 2003. Based only on this information, would you say that the Stampede's liquidity is strong or weak?
(b) Suppose that the Stampede used $500,000 of its cash and short-term deposits to pay off $500,000 of its bank indebtedness. Would this transaction change the current ratio?
(c) At December 31, 2004, the Stampede had an unused operating line of credit of $38 million. Does this information affect the assessment of the Stampede's short-term liquidity that you made in (a) above?

E10−12 Maple Leaf Foods Inc.'s financial statements contain the following selected data (in millions):

Analyze solvency. (SO 4)

	2004	2003
Total assets	$2,189.2	$2,148.7
Total liabilities	2,116.2	1,405.5
Net earnings	106.8	35.1
Income tax expense	58.9	22.9
Interest expense	83.5	68.4

Instructions

(a) Calculate the debt to total assets and times interest earned ratios for 2004 and 2003. Did Maple Leaf's solvency improve or deteriorate in 2004?
(b) The notes to Maple Leaf Foods' financial statements show that the company has future operating lease commitments totalling $279.5 million. Discuss how these unrecorded obligations affect the analysis of Maple Leaf Foods' solvency.

Record bond transactions using
straight-line amortization.
(SO 3, 5)

*E10–13   Blog Limited issued $300,000 of 20-year, 8% bonds on January 1, 2006, at 103. Interest is payable semi-annually on July 1 and January 1. Blog uses the straight-line method of amortization and has a December 31 year end.

Instructions

(a) Record the issue of the bonds on January 1, 2006.
(b) Record the payment of interest on July 1, 2006.
(c) Record the accrual of interest on December 31, 2006.
(d) Record the retirement of the bonds at maturity on January 1, 2026.

Record bond transactions using
straight-line amortization.
(SO 3, 5)

*E10–14   Cotter Ltd. issued $200,000 of 10-year, 6% bonds on January 1, 2006, at 96. Interest is payable semi-annually on July 1 and January 1. Cotter uses the straight-line method of amortization and has a December 31 year end.

Instructions

(a) Record the issue of the bonds on January 1, 2006.
(b) Record the payment of interest on July 1, 2006.
(c) Record the accrual of interest on December 31, 2006.
(d) Record the retirement of the bonds at maturity on January 1, 2016.

Record bond transactions using
effective-interest amortization.
(SO 3, 5)

*E10–15   Tagawa Corporation issued $650,000 of 10-year, 7% bonds on January 1, 2006, for $698,354. This price resulted in an effective interest rate of 6% on the bonds. Interest is payable semi-annually on July 1 and January 1. Tagawa uses the effective-interest method of amortization and has a December 31 year end.

Instructions

(a) Prove the calculation of the issue price of $698,354. The present value of 1 is 0.55368 and the present value of an annuity of 1 is 14.87747 for $n = 20$ and $i = 3\%$.
(b) Record the issue of the bonds on January 1, 2006.
(c) Record the payment of interest on July 1, 2006.
(d) Record the accrual of interest on December 31, 2006.

Record bond transactions using
effective-interest amortization.
(SO 3, 5)

*E10–16   Presented below is the partial bond amortization schedule for Chiasson Corporation, which uses the effective-interest method of amortization:

Semi-Annual Interest Periods	Interest Payment	Interest Expense	Discount/ Premium Amortization	Unamortized Discount/ Premium	Bond Carrying Value
Issue date				$62,311	$937,689
1	$45,000	$46,884	$1,884	60,427	939,573
2	45,000	46,979	1,979	58,448	941,552

(a) Prepare a journal entry to record the sale of the bonds at the issue date.
(b) Prepare the journal entry to record the payment of interest and the amortization at the end of period 1.
(c) Explain why interest expense is greater than interest paid.
(d) What will be the carrying value of the bonds on their maturity date?
(e) Outline the advantages of Chiasson's using the effective-interest method of amortization.

Problems: Set A

Record current liability
transactions; show balance sheet
presentation.
(SO 1, 4)

P10–1A   On February 28, 2006, Molega Software Ltd.'s general ledger contained the following liability accounts:

Accounts payable	$42,500
CPP payable	1,340
EI payable	756
GST payable	5,800
Income tax payable	2,515
PST payable	5,800
Unearned service revenue	15,000

During March, the following selected transactions occurred:

Mar. 1 Borrowed $15,000 on a four-month, 6% note. Interest is payable at maturity.

5 Sold merchandise for cash totalling $40,000, plus 7% GST and 7% PST. The cost of goods sold was $24,000. Molega Software uses a perpetual inventory system.

8 Received the property tax bill of $18,000 for the calendar year. It is payable on May 1.

12 Provided services for customers who had made advance payments of $8,500.

14 Paid $5,800 to the Receiver General and $5,800 to the Provincial Treasurer for sales taxes collected in February.

15 Paid $4,611 to the Receiver General for amounts owing from the February payroll for CPP, EI, and income tax ($1,340 + $756 + $2,515).

31 Paid monthly payroll. Gross salaries totalled $16,000 and payroll deductions included CPP of $720; EI of $336; and income tax of $3,215. Employee benefits included CPP of $720 and EI of $470.

Instructions

(a) Record the above transactions.
(b) Record any required adjusting entries at March 31.
(c) Prepare the current liabilities section of the balance sheet at March 31.

P10–2A Cling-on Ltd. sells rock-climbing products and also operates an indoor climbing facility for climbing enthusiasts. During the last part of 2006, Cling-on had the following transactions related to notes payable:

Record short-term note transactions; show balance sheet presentation. (SO 1, 4)

Sept. 1 Issued a three-month, 8%, $15,000 note to Black Diamond for the purchase of inventory. Interest is payable at maturity.

Oct. 2 Issued a 12-month, 8%, $25,000 note to Montpelier Bank to finance the building of a new climbing area for advanced climbers. Interest is payable monthly on the first of each month.

Nov. 1 Paid interest on the Montpelier Bank note.

2 Issued a one-month, 9%, $18,000 note to Auto Dealer Ltd. and paid $8,000 in cash to purchase a vehicle to transport clients to nearby climbing sites as part of a new series of climbing classes. Interest is payable at maturity.

Dec. 1 Paid principal and interest on the Black Diamond note (see Sept. 1 transaction).

1 Paid interest on the Montpelier Bank note.

2 Paid principal and interest on the Auto Dealer note (see Nov. 2 transaction).

31 Recorded accrued interest for the Montpelier Bank note at the company's year end.

Instructions

(a) Record the above transactions.
(b) Show the balance sheet presentation of notes payable and interest payable at December 31.
(c) Show the statement of earnings presentation of interest expense for the year.

P10–3A Elite Electronics issues a 10-year, 7.5%, $350,000 mortgage note on December 31, 2006. The proceeds from the note will be used to finance a new research laboratory. The terms of the note provide for fixed principal payments of $17,500, plus interest. Payments are due on June 30 and December 31.

Record long-term note transactions; show balance sheet presentation. (SO 2, 4)

Instructions

(a) Prepare an instalment payment schedule for the first two years. Round all calculations to the nearest dollar.
(b) Prepare the entries for (1) the mortgage loan, and (2) the first two instalment payments.
(c) Show the balance sheet presentation of the mortgage payable at December 31, 2006.

P10–4A Peter Furlong has just approached a venture capitalist for financing for his sailing school. The lender is willing to loan Peter $50,000 at a high-risk interest rate of 12%. The loan is payable over three years in blended principal and interest instalments of $3,335. Payments are due every other month (that is, six times per year). Peter receives the loan on May 1, 2006, the first day of his fiscal year. Peter makes the first payment on June 30.

Record long-term note transactions; show balance sheet presentation. (SO 2, 4)

Instructions

(a) Prepare an instalment payment schedule for the loan period.
(b) Prepare all related journal entries for the sailing school for the first six months of the 2006 fiscal year, beginning May 1 through to October 31.
(c) Show the balance sheet presentation of the note payable at October 31, 2006.

Record long-term note and bond transactions; show balance sheet presentation.
(SO 2, 3, 4)

P10–5A   On September 30, 2006, Atwater Corporation purchased a new piece of equipment for $550,000. The equipment was purchased with a $50,000 down payment and the issue of a three-year, 8%, $500,000 mortgage note payable for the balance. The terms provide for repayment of the mortgage with quarterly blended instalment payments of $47,280 starting on December 31.

Atwater is in the process of building a new, state-of-the-art production and assembly facility for $10 million. To finance the facility, it issued $10 million of five-year, 8% bonds at 102 on December 31, 2006. Atwater has a December 31 year end.

Instructions

(a) Record the purchase of equipment on September 30 and the first instalment payment on December 31.
(b) Record the issue of the bonds on December 31.
(c) Show the balance sheet presentation of these obligations at December 31.

Record bond transactions.
(SO 3)

P10–6A   On October 1, 2005, PFQ Corp. issued $600,000 of 10-year, 5% bonds at 100. The bonds pay interest semi-annually on October 1 and April 1. PFQ's year end is December 31.

Instructions

(a) Record the issue of the bonds on October 1, 2005.
(b) Prepare the adjusting entry to record the accrual of interest on December 31, 2005.
(c) Record the payment of interest on April 1, 2006.
(d) Assume that on April 1, 2006, immediately after paying the semi-annual interest, PFQ redeems all of the bonds at 103. Record the redemption of the bonds.

Record bond transactions.
(SO 3)

P10–7A   The following section is taken from Peppermint Patty Ltd.'s balance sheet at December 31, 2005:

PEPPERMINT PATTY LTD.	
Balance Sheet (partial)	
December 31, 2005	
Current liabilities	
Bond interest payable	$ 8,000
Long-term liabilities	
Bonds payable, 8%, due January 1, 2010	200,000

Interest is payable semi-annually on January 1 and July 1.

Instructions

(a) Record the payment of bond interest on January 1, 2006.
(b) Assume that on January 1, 2006, after paying interest, Peppermint Patty redeems bonds having a face value of $50,000 at 102. Record the redemption of the bonds.
(c) Record the payment of bond interest on July 1, 2006, on the remaining bonds.
(d) Prepare the adjusting entry on December 31, 2006, to accrue the interest on the remaining bonds.

Classify liabilities.
(SO 4)

P10–8A   The following transactions occurred in Wendell Corporation. Wendell's fiscal year end is December 31.

1. Wendell purchased goods for $120,000 on December 23, terms n/30.
2. Wendell made sales of $8,000 plus 15% HST on December 31.
3. Weekly salaries of $6,000 are paid every Friday for a five-day work week (Monday to Friday). This year, December 31 is a Wednesday. Payroll deductions include CPP of $297, EI of $126, and income tax of $1,800. Employee benefits include CPP of $297 and EI of $176.
4. Property taxes of $40,000 were assessed on March 1 for the calendar year. They are payable by May 1.
5. Wendell is the defendant in a negligence suit. Wendell's legal counsel estimates that Wendell may suffer a $75,000 loss if it loses the suit. In legal counsel's opinion, whether or not the case will be lost is not determinable at this time.

6. Wendell signed a 6%, $500,000 note payable on July 1. The note requires fixed principal instalment payments of $100,000 on each June 30 for the next five years. Interest is due monthly on the first of each month.

7. Wendell made income tax instalments of $60,000 throughout the year. After the preparation of its corporate income tax return at year end, it was determined that total income tax payable for the year was $50,000.

Instructions

(a) Identify which of the above transactions should be presented in the current liabilities section and which should be recorded in the long-term liabilities section of Wendell's balance sheet on December 31. Identify the account title(s) and amount(s) for each reported liability.

(b) Indicate any information that should be disclosed in the notes to Wendell's financial statements.

P10–9A   You have been presented with the following selected information taken from the financial statements of Magna International Inc. (in U.S. millions):

Analyze liquidity and solvency. (SO 4)

	2004	2003	2002
Balance sheet			
Accounts receivable	$ 3,276	$ 2,615	$ 2,094
Inventory	1,376	1,116	916
Total current assets	6,281	5,371	4,369
Total assets	11,609	9,864	10,153
Current liabilities	4,061	3,435	2,936
Total liabilities	6,167	4,946	4,732
Statement of earnings			
Net sales	20,653	15,345	12,422
Cost of goods sold	17,696	12,806	10,274
Interest expense	30	21	23
Income tax expense	398	373	326
Net earnings	692	520	552

Instructions

(a) Calculate each of the following ratios for 2004 and 2003. Industry ratios have been included in parentheses.
   1. Current ratio (1.3:1)
   2. Receivables turnover (6.4 times)
   3. Inventory turnover (13.3 times)
   4. Debt to total assets (45.1%)
   5. Times interest earned (2.9 times)
(b) Comment on Magna's liquidity and solvency.
(c) Magna has operating lease commitments totalling $2,360 million in 2004 and $2,080 million in 2003. Recalculate the debt to total assets ratio in light of this information, and discuss the implications for your analysis.

P10–10A   The following selected liquidity and solvency ratios are available for two companies operating in the petroleum industry:

Analyze liquidity and solvency. (SO 4)

Ratio	Petro-Zoom	Sun-Oil	Industry Average
Current ratio	0.7:1	0.9:1	1.4:1
Receivables turnover	11.9 times	13.3 times	11.0 times
Inventory turnover	15.8 times	9.5 times	19.0 times
Debt to total assets	21.1%	31.5%	34.2%
Times interest earned	23.9 times	171.5 times	12.1 times

Instructions

Assume that you are the credit manager of the local bank. Answer the following questions, using relevant ratios to justify your answer:

(a) Both Petro-Zoom and Sun-Oil have applied for a short-term loan from your bank. Which of the two companies is the most liquid and should get more consideration for a short-term loan? Explain.

(b) Both Petro-Zoom and Sun-Oil have applied for a long-term loan from your bank. Are you concerned with the solvency of either company? Explain why or why not.

Record bond transaction using straight-line amortization; show balance sheet presentation.
(SO 3, 4, 5)

*P10–11A   Max Music Inc. sold $1 million of 10-year, 8% bonds on April 1, 2006. The bonds pay interest semi-annually on April 1 and October 1. Max Music uses the straight-line method of amortization and has a December 31 year end.

Instructions

(a) Prepare all the necessary journal entries to record the issue of the bonds and bond interest expense for 2006, assuming that the bonds sold at (1) 102, and (2) 97.
(b) Show the balance sheet presentation at December 31, 2006, for each bond assumption.

Record bond transactions using straight-line amortization.
(SO 3, 5)

*P10–12A   The following section is taken from Bermuda Corporation's balance sheet:

BERMUDA CORPORATION
Balance Sheet (partial)
December 31, 2005

Current liabilities		
Bond interest payable		$ 96,000
Long-term liabilities		
Bonds payable, 8%, due January 1, 2015	$2,400,000	
Less: Discount on bonds payable	90,000	2,310,000

The bonds were originally issued January 1, 2005, at a discount of $100,000. Interest is payable semi-annually on January 1 and July 1. Bermuda uses straight-line amortization and has a December 31 year end.

Instructions

(a) Record the payment of bond interest on January 1 and July 1, 2006.
(b) Assume that on July 1, 2006, after paying interest, Bermuda redeems bonds having a face value of $800,000 at 102. Record the redemption of the bonds.
(c) Prepare the adjusting entry at December 31, 2006, to accrue interest on the remaining bonds.

Record bond transactions using effective-interest amortization; show balance sheet presentation.
(SO 3, 4, 5)

*P10–13A   On July 1, 2005, Global Satellites Corporation issued $1.2 million of 10-year, 7% bonds to yield an effective interest rate of 8%. Global uses the effective-interest method of amortization. The bonds pay semi-annual interest on July 1 and January 1. Global has a December 31 year end.

Instructions

(a) Calculate the issue price of the bonds. The present value factor of 1 is 0.45639 and the present value factor of an annuity of 1 is 13.59033 for $n = 20$ and $i = 4\%$. Round all calculations to the nearest dollar.
(b) Record the issue of the bonds on July 1, 2005.
(c) Prepare an amortization table through December 31, 2006 (three interest periods) for this bond issue.
(d) Show the balance sheet presentation of the liabilities at December 31, 2006.

Record bond transactions using effective-interest amortization; show balance sheet presentation.
(SO 3, 4, 5)

*P10–14A   On July 1, 2006, Imperial Ltd. issued $2 million of 10-year, 6% bonds at $2,155,890. This price resulted in a 5% effective interest rate on the bonds. Imperial uses the effective-interest method of amortization. The bonds pay semi-annual interest on each July 1 and January 1. Imperial has a December 31 year end.

Instructions

(a) Prepare the journal entries to record the following transactions:
    1. The issue of the bonds on July 1, 2006
    2. The accrual of interest and amortization on December 31, 2006
    3. The payment of interest on January 1, 2007
(b) Show the balance sheet presentation of the liabilities at December 31, 2006.
(c) Answer the following questions:
    1. What amount of interest expense is reported for 2006?

2. Would the bond interest expense reported in 2006 be the same as, greater than, or less than the amount that would be reported if the straight-line method of amortization were used?
3. Would the total bond interest expense be greater than, the same as, or less than the total interest expense that would be reported if the straight-line method of amortization were used?
4. Compare the advantages and disadvantages of the effective-interest and straight-line methods of amortization.

Problems: Set B

P10–1B   On December 31, 2005, Burlington Inc.'s general ledger contained these liability accounts:

Record current liability transactions; show balance sheet presentation.
(SO 1, 4)

Accounts payable	$52,000
CPP payable	1,905
EI payable	1,058
GST payable	7,500
Income tax payable	4,640
PST payable	8,570
Unearned service revenue	16,000

During January 2006, the following selected transactions occurred:

Jan. 5 Sold merchandise for cash totalling $15,820, plus 7% GST and 8% PST. The cost of goods sold was $9,500. Burlington uses a perpetual inventory system.
  13 Paid $7,500 to the Receiver General and $8,570 to the Minister of Finance for sales taxes collected in December.
  14 Paid $7,603 to the Receiver General for amounts owing from the December payroll for CPP, EI, and income tax ($1,905 + $1,058 + $4,640).
  15 Borrowed $18,000 from HSBC Bank on a three-month, 6% note. Interest is payable monthly on the 15th of each month.
  19 Provided services for customers who had made advance payments of $7,000.
  23 Paid $12,000 to creditors on account.
  31 Paid monthly payroll. Gross salaries totalled $22,500 and payroll deductions include CPP of $1,027; EI of $472; and income tax of $5,135. Employee benefits included CPP of $1,027 and EI of $661.

Instructions

(a) Record the above transactions.
(b) Record any required adjusting entries at January 31.
(c) Prepare the current liabilities section of the balance sheet at January 31.

P10–2B   MileHi Mountain Bikes Ltd. markets mountain-bike tours to clients vacationing in various locations in the mountains of British Columbia. In preparation for the upcoming summer biking season, MileHi carried out the following transactions related to notes payable:

Record short-term note transactions; show balance sheet presentation.
(SO 1, 4)

Mar. 2 Purchased Mongoose bikes for use as rentals by issuing a three-month, 7%, $8,000 note payable. Interest is payable at maturity.
Apr. 1 Issued a nine-month, 7%, $25,000 note to Mountain Real Estate for the purchase of mountain property on which to build bike trails. Interest is payable at the first of each month.
May 1 Paid interest on the Mountain Real Estate note.
  2 Borrowed $18,000 from the Western Bank on a four-month, 6% note. The funds will be used for working capital for the beginning of the season. Interest is payable at maturity.
June 1 Paid interest on the Mountain Real Estate note.
  2 Paid principal and interest on the Mongoose note (see March 2 transaction).
  30 Recorded accrued interest for the Mountain Real Estate and the Western Bank notes at the company's year end.

Instructions

(a) Record the above transactions.
(b) Show the balance sheet presentation of the note payable and interest payable at June 30.
(c) Show the statement of earnings presentation of interest expense for the year.

Record long-term note transactions; show balance sheet presentation.
(SO 2, 4)

P10–3B   Kinyae Electronics issues a 10-year, 7%, $500,000 mortgage note on December 31, 2006, to help finance a plant expansion. The terms of the note provide for fixed principal payments of $25,000, plus interest. Payments are due on June 30 and December 31.

Instructions

(a) Prepare an instalment payment schedule for the first two years. Round all calculations to the nearest dollar.
(b) Prepare the entries for (1) the mortgage loan, and (2) the first two instalment payments.
(c) Show the balance sheet presentation of the mortgage payable at December 31, 2006.

Record long-term note transactions; show balance sheet presentation.
(SO 2, 4)

P10–4B   A local ski hill has just approached a venture capitalist for financing for its new business venture, the development of a local ski hill. On April 1, 2005, the venture capitalist loaned the company $100,000 at an interest rate of 8%. The loan is repayable over four years in annual blended principal and interest instalments of $30,192, due each March 31. The first payment is due March 31, 2006. The ski hill's year end is March 31.

Instructions

(a) Prepare an instalment payment schedule for the loan period.
(b) Prepare all related journal entries for the ski hill for the first two fiscal years, beginning April 1, 2005 through March 31, 2007.
(c) Show the balance sheet presentation of the note payable as at March 31, 2007.

Record long-term note and bond transactions; show balance sheet presentation.
(SO 2, 3, 4)

P10–5B   On July 31, 2006, Myron Corporation purchased a piece of equipment for $750,000. The equipment was purchased with a $75,000 down payment and through the issue of a four-year, 6%, $675,000 mortgage note payable for the balance. The terms provide for the mortgage to be repaid with monthly blended instalment payments of $15,852 starting on August 31.

Myron is also in the process of building a new, state-of-the-art production and assembly facility for $12 million. To finance the facility, it issued $12 million of 10-year, 6% bonds at 98 on September 30, 2006. Myron has a September 30 year end.

Instructions

(a) Record the issue of the bonds on September 30.
(b) Record the purchase of equipment on July 31 and the first two instalment payments on August 31 and September 30.
(c) Show the balance sheet presentation of these obligations at September 30, 2006.

Record bond transactions.
(SO 3)

P10–6B   On May 1, 2005, MEM Corp. issued $800,000 of five-year, 4% bonds at 100. The bonds pay interest semi-annually on November 1 and May 1. MEM's year end is December 31.

Instructions

(a) Record the issue of the bonds on May 1, 2005.
(b) Record the first interest payment on November 1, 2005.
(c) Prepare the adjusting entry to record the accrual of interest on December 31, 2006.
(d) Record the second interest payment on May 1, 2005.
(e) Assume that on May 1, 2006, immediately after paying the semi-annual interest, MEM redeems all of the bonds at 98. Record the redemption of the bonds.

Record bond transactions.
(SO 3)

P10–7B   The following section is taken from Disch Corp.'s balance sheet at December 31, 2005:

DISCH CORP. **Balance Sheet (partial)** **December 31, 2005**	
Current liabilities	
Bond interest payable	$ 48,000
Long-term liabilities	
Bonds payable, 6%, due January 1, 2022	1,600,000

Interest is payable semi-annually on January 1 and July 1.

Instructions

(a) Record the payment of bond interest on January 1, 2006.
(b) Assume that on January 1, 2006, after paying interest, Disch redeems bonds having a face value of $400,000 at 99. Record the redemption of the bonds.
(c) Record the payment of bond interest on July 1, 2006, on the remaining bonds.
(d) Prepare the adjusting entry on December 31, 2006, to accrue the interest on the remaining bonds.

P10–8B The following transactions occurred in Iqaluit Ltd., which has an April 30 fiscal year end:

Classify liabilities. (SO 4)

1. Property taxes of $21,000 were assessed on March 1 for the calendar year. They are payable by May 1.
2. Iqaluit purchased goods for $12,000 on April 27, terms n/30.
3. Weekly salaries of $10,000 are paid every Friday for a five-day work week (Monday to Friday). This year, April 30 is a Thursday. Payroll deductions include CPP of $495, EI of $210, and income tax of $3,000. Employee benefits include CPP of $495 and EI of $294.
4. Iqaluit received $25,000 from customers on April 29 for services to be performed in May.
5. Iqaluit was named in a lawsuit alleging negligence for an oil spill that leaked into the neighbouring company's water system. Iqaluit's legal counsel estimates that the company will likely lose the suit. Restoration costs are expected to total $250,000.
6. The company purchased equipment for $35,000 on April 1. It issued a six-month, 7% note in payment. Interest is payable monthly on the first of each month.
7. Iqaluit paid income tax instalments of $225,000 throughout the year. After the preparation of its year-end corporate income tax return, it was determined that the total income tax payable for the year was $250,000.

Instructions

(a) Identify which of the above transactions should be presented in the current liabilities section and which should be recorded in the long-term liabilities section of Iqaluit's balance sheet on April 30. Identify the account title(s) and amount(s) for each reported liability.
(b) Indicate any information that should be disclosed in the notes to Iqaluit's financial statements.

P10–9B The following selected information was taken from Domtar Inc.'s financial statements (in millions):

Analyze liquidity and solvency. (SO 4)

	2004	2003	2002
Balance sheet			
Accounts receivable	$ 233	$ 197	$ 304
Inventory	723	670	736
Total current assets	1,124	1,026	1,176
Total assets	5,688	5,848	8,847
Current liabilities	716	704	854
Total liabilities	3,642	3,680	4,293
Statement of earnings			
Net sales	5,115	5,167	5,859
Cost of goods sold	4,381	4,335	4,686
Interest expense	160	158	185
Income tax expense (recovery)	(52)	(67)	56
Net earnings (loss)	(42)	(193)	141

Instructions

(a) Calculate each of the following ratios for 2004 and 2003. Industry ratios have been included in parentheses.
   1. Current ratio (1.3:1)
   2. Receivables turnover (5.1)
   3. Inventory turnover (6.3 times)
   4. Debt to total assets (52.4%)
   5. Times interest earned (2.3 times)
(b) Comment on Domtar's liquidity and solvency.

(c) Domtar has operating lease commitments totalling $106 million in 2004 and $114 million in 2003. Recalculate the debt to total assets ratio in light of this information and discuss the implications for your analysis.

Analyze liquidity and solvency.
(SO 4)

P10−10B   The following selected liquidity and solvency ratios are available for two companies operating in the fast food industry:

Ratio	Grab 'N Gab	Chick 'N Lick	Industry Average
Current ratio	0.8:1	0.7:1	0.9:1
Receivables turnover	25.8 times	27.7 times	33.8 times
Inventory turnover	59.1 times	49.6 times	31.1 times
Debt to total assets	39.4%	29.6%	39.4%
Times interest earned	9.9 times	4.9 times	7.3 times

Instructions

Assume that you are the credit manager of the local bank. Answer the following questions, using relevant ratios to justify your answer:

(a) Both Grab 'N Gab and Chick 'N Lick have applied for a short-term loan from your bank. Which of the two companies is the most liquid and should get more consideration for a short-term loan? Explain.

(b) Both Grab 'N Gab and Chick 'N Lick have applied for a long-term loan from your bank. Are you concerned with the solvency of either company? Explain why or why not.

Record bond transactions using
straight-line amortization; show
balance sheet presentation.
(SO 3, 4, 5)

*P10−11B   Diego Ltd. issued $1.5 million of 10-year, 7% bonds on July 1, 2006. The bonds pay interest semi-annually on July 1 and January 1. Diego uses the straight-line method of amortization and has a December 31 year end.

Instructions

(a) Prepare all the necessary journal entries to record the issue of the bonds and bond interest expense for 2006, assuming that the bonds sold at (1) 103, and (2) 96.

(b) Show the balance sheet presentation at December 31, 2006, for each bond assumption.

Record bond transactions using
straight-line amortization.
(SO 3, 5)

*P10−12B   The following section is taken from Walenda Oil Ltd.'s balance sheet:

WALENDA OIL LTD. Balance Sheet (partial) December 31, 2005		
Current liabilities		
Bond interest payable		$ 108,000
Long-term liabilities		
Bonds payable, due January 1, 2010	$3,600,000	
Add: Premium on bonds payable	24,000	3,624,000

The bonds were initially issued on January 1, 2000, at a $60,000 premium. Interest is payable semi-annually on January 1 and July 1. The interest payable of $108,000 reported on the balance sheet is for six months from July 1 to December 31. Walenda uses straight-line amortization and has a December 31 year end.

Instructions

(a) Calculate the contractual interest rate on the bonds.

(b) Record the payment of bond interest on January 1 and July 1, 2006.

(c) Assume on July 1, 2006, after paying interest, that Walenda redeems bonds having a face value of $1.8 million at 98. Record the redemption of the bonds.

(d) Prepare the adjusting entry at December 31, 2006, to accrue interest on the remaining bonds.

Record bond transactions using
effective-interest amortization;
show balance sheet presentation.
(SO 3, 4, 5)

*P10−13B   On July 1, 2005, Ponasis Corporation issued $1.5 million of 10-year, 6% bonds at $1,393,413. This price resulted in an effective interest rate of 7% on the bonds. Ponasis uses the effective-interest method of amortization. The bonds pay semi-annual interest on July 1 and January 1. Ponasis has a December 31 year end.

Instructions

(a) Calculate the issue price of the bonds. The present value factor of 1 is 0.50257 and the present value factor of an annuity of 1 is 14.21240 for $n = 20$ and $i = 3.5\%$. Round all calculations to the nearest dollar.

(b) Record the issue of the bonds on July 1, 2005.

(c) Prepare an amortization table through December 31, 2006 (three interest periods) for this bond issue.

(d) Show the balance sheet presentation of the liabilities at December 31, 2006.

*P10–14B   On July 1, 2006, Waubonsee Ltd. issued $2.2 million of 10-year, 5% bonds at $2,036,357. This price resulted in an effective interest rate of 6% on the bonds. Waubonsee uses the effective-interest method of amortization. The bonds pay semi-annual interest on July 1 and January 1. Waubonsee has a December 31 year end.

Record bond transactions using effective-interest amortization; show balance sheet presentation. (SO 3, 4, 5)

Instructions

(a) Prepare the journal entries to record the following transactions:
1. The issue of the bonds on July 1, 2006
2. The accrual of interest and amortization on December 31, 2006
3. The payment of interest on January 1, 2007

(b) Show the balance sheet presentation for the liabilities at December 31, 2006.

(c) Answer the following questions:
1. What amount of interest expense is reported for 2006?
2. Would the bond interest expense reported in 2006 be the same as, greater than, or less than the amount that would be reported if the straight-line method of amortization were used?
3. Would the total bond interest expense be greater than, the same as, or less than the total interest expense that would be reported if the straight-line method of amortization were used?
4. Compare the advantages and disadvantages of the effective-interest and straight-line methods of amortization.

BROADENING YOUR PERSPECTIVE

Financial Reporting and Analysis Analysis Tools

Financial Reporting Problem: *Loblaw*

BYP10–1   Refer to the financial statements of Loblaw and the Notes to Consolidated Financial Statements in Appendix A.

Instructions

(a) What current and long-term liabilities were reported in Loblaw's balance sheet at the end of fiscal 2003?

(b) What items related to liabilities were reported in Loblaw's statement of earnings for fiscal 2003?

(c) What financing activities related to liabilities were reported in Loblaw's cash flow statement for fiscal 2003?

(d) Does Loblaw disclose any off–balance sheet financing that could have a material impact on its financial position?

Comparative Analysis Problem: *Loblaw and Sobeys*

BYP10–2   The financial statements of Sobeys are presented in Appendix B, following the financial statements of Loblaw in Appendix A.

Instructions

(a) Based on the information contained in the financial statements, calculate the following ratios for each company for its most recent fiscal year. Industry ratios are shown in parentheses.

1. Current ratio (1.0:1)   3. Debt to total assets (37.1%)
2. Receivables turnover (20.6 times)   4. Times interest earned (1.3 times)

(b) What conclusions about the companies' liquidity and solvency can be drawn from the ratios calculated in (a)?

Research Case

BYP10–3   The May 4, 2002, issue of *The Economist* magazine contains an article on page 66 entitled "Company Accounts: Badly in Need of Repair."

Instructions

Read the article and answer the following questions:

(a) What are some examples of off–balance sheet financing? Can this be a risky practice? Explain.
(b) Operating leases make up most off–balance sheet financing. Why are operating leases so popular with the airline companies? What effect does using operating leases instead of capital leases have on net earnings? On the balance sheet?
(c) Is off–balance sheet financing in accordance with generally accepted accounting principles? What are standard-setters doing to try to limit abuses?

Interpreting Financial Statements

BYP10–4   Reitmans (Canada) Limited and La Senza Corporation are two specialty women's clothing merchandisers. Here are financial data for both companies at January 31, 2004 (in thousands):

	Reitmans	La Senza
Balance sheet data:		
Beginning accounts receivable	$ 5,089	$ 6,730
Ending accounts receivable	3,962	9,267
Total current assets	173,626	110,256
Beginning total assets	419,570	234,609
Ending total assets	453,467	224,137
Total current liabilities	90,942	55,279
Total liabilities	177,065	94,099
Statement of earnings data:		
Net sales	851,634	336,523
Interest expense	4,792	307
Income tax expense	15,655	7,094
Net earnings (loss) from continuing operations	40,035	(1,658)
Cash flow statement data:		
Cash provided by operating activities	102,522	15,017
Capital expenditures	40,064	14,209
Dividends paid	7,573	2,132
Notes to the financial statements:		
Operating lease commitments	359,530	185,199

Instructions

(a) Calculate the current ratio and receivables turnover for each company. Discuss their relative liquidity.
(b) Calculate the debt to total assets, times interest earned, and free cash flow for each company. Discuss their relative solvency.
(c) The notes to the financial statements indicate that many of the retail stores' furniture, fixtures, and similar items are leased using operating leases. Discuss the implications of these operating leases for each company's solvency.
(d) Calculate the profit margin, return on assets, and asset turnover for each company. Discuss their relative profitability.

A Global Focus

BYP10−5   Swedish Match AB is the world's largest maker of matches and the third largest producer of disposable lighters. It also produces a wide range of other tobacco products. Swedish Match reports the following selected information about contingencies in the notes to its financial statements:

SWEDISH MATCH AB
Notes to the Financial Statements (partial)
December 31, 2004
(in thousands of Swedish Kroner)

Note 22 Commitments and Contingent Liabilities

	2004	2003
Contingent liabilities		
Guarantees to subsidiaries	224	158
Guarantees to external companies	2	3
Other guarantees and contingent liabilities	185	280
Total contingent liabilities	411	441

Legal disputes

The Company is involved in a number of legal proceedings of a routine character. Although the outcome of these proceedings cannot be anticipated with any certainty, and accordingly no guarantees can be made, the view of management is that liabilities attributable to these disputes, if any, should not have any significant negative impact on the earnings or financial position of Swedish Match.

Instructions

(a) Why are guarantees considered to be contingent liabilities?
(b) Swedish Match is the defendant in more than 1,200 cases against tobacco companies. Management holds the view that there are good defences against all the claims and states that it will defend each case vigorously. In light of this statement, does it make sense to you that Swedish Match discloses information about its legal disputes rather than accruing the amounts of the lawsuits as liabilities? Explain.
(c) Swedish Match's debt to total assets ratio is lower than that of the industry. Its times interest earned ratio is higher than that of the industry. What implications do these contingent liabilities have for an analysis of Swedish Match's solvency?

Financial Analysis on the Web

BYP10−6   Bonds have complex terminology associated with them. In this case, we explore a glossary of bond and other terms available on the Globeinvestor website.

Analysis Tools
(Financial Analysis on the Web)

Instructions

Specific requirements of this Web case can be found on the Toolkit website.

Critical Thinking

Collaborative Learning Activity

BYP10–7   Every major airline has a frequent-flyer program to encourage passenger loyalty. Various types of awards are available for points accumulated under the program, including the right to free travel. There is great debate about how airlines should record the cost of this "free" seat when frequent-flyer points are redeemed.

Some airlines believe that frequent-flyer liabilities should be disclosed as contingent liabilities, arguing that the probability of the air miles being redeemed is not quantifiable.

Others believe that the liability should be estimated and accrued, but have different views on how the amount to be recorded should be determined. Some argue that only the increased or incremental cost of rewarding frequent-flyer members should be recorded. These costs would include food, drink, and ticket delivery costs. Other costs, such as fuel for the airplane and labour to staff it, are going to be incurred whether frequent flyers travel or not.

The other point of view is that the cost to be recorded should be a percentage of the ticket price originally eligible for point accumulation. This usually results in a cost allocation for each seat redeemed using frequent-flyer points that is roughly equivalent to a discounted or seat-sale price. Full fare is not usually a consideration, because it is unlikely that full-fare passengers will be displaced by passengers using free travel awards.

Instructions

With the class divided into groups, assign a debate position for the following issues:

(a) Recording the liability: One group should provide the arguments for disclosing the liability as a contingent liability, rather than recording it. Another group should provide the arguments for estimating and accruing the liability.

(b) Determining the amount of the liability: One group should provide the arguments in support of using incremental costs. Another group should provide the arguments for using a seat-sale fare. Another group should provide arguments for other cost allocations that should also be considered.

Communication Activity

BYP10–8   Financial statement users are interested in the obligations that a company has from past transactions. It is important to determine which liabilities are current and which are long-term. Yet some company obligations are not recorded on the balance sheet itself, but disclosed instead in the notes to the financial statements.

Instructions

Write a memorandum to a friend of yours who has inherited some money and is looking at investing in some companies. Your friend plans to get professional advice before investing but would like you to go over some basics with her. For instance, she is trying to determine the amount of cash that a company will have to pay within the next five years. She knows she should start with the liabilities that are on the balance sheet, but is wondering if any of those can be settled without the company having to write a cheque. She would also like to know what kinds of liabilities may exist but be buried somewhere in the notes to the financial statements.

Ethics Case

BYP10-9 Enron Corporation—formerly one of the world's largest electronic traders in natural gas and electricity—underwent one of the largest corporate bankruptcies in American history. Just weeks before it filed for bankruptcy, the company admitted that it had shifted billions of dollars in debt off its balance sheets and into a variety of complex partnerships.

One journalist wrote that "The Enron practice of shifting liabilities off the books to more than 3,500 subsidiaries raised so many red flags that you'd think you were in a military parade somewhere in China." Yet, Enron and its auditors argued vehemently that the "special purpose entity" partnerships they used were in accordance with U.S. GAAP and fully disclosed, even if not recorded in the books.

Ethics In Accounting

Instructions

(a) Who are the stakeholders in this situation?
(b) Explain how shifting debt off the balance sheet might mislead investors.
(c) Do you think that management has an obligation to ensure that its accounting and disclosure is relevant to users, even if doing this might not follow GAAP in some instances?

Serial Problem

(*Note*: This is a continuation of the serial problem from Chapters 1 through 9.)

BYP10-10 Recall that Cookie Creations Ltd. borrowed $2,000 on November 16, 2005, from Natalie's grandmother. Interest on the note is 6% per annum and the note plus interest was to be repaid in 24 months. A monthly adjusting journal entry was prepared for the months of November 2005 (half month); December 2005; and January 2006.

Instructions:

(a) Calculate the interest payable that was accrued and recorded from November 16, 2005, through January 31, 2006.
(b) Calculate the total interest expense from November 16, 2005, through August 31, 2006. Prepare the adjusting journal entry required at August 31, 2006, to update the interest.
(c) Cookie Creations repaid Natalie's grandmother on September 15, 2006—10 months after the loan was extended to Cookie Creations. Prepare the journal entry to record the loan repayment.

Answers to Self-Study Questions

1. c   2. d   3. c   4. b   5. c   6. a   7. d   8. b   *9. d   *10. c

Answer to Loblaw Review It Question 4

Loblaw has the following current liabilities, totalling $3,114 million at January 3, 2004: bank indebtedness; commercial paper; accounts payable and accrued liabilities; income taxes; and long-term debt due within one year.

the navigator

Remember to go back to the Navigator box at the beginning of the chapter to check off your completed work.

CHAPTER 11

Reporting and Analyzing Shareholders' Equity

ACCOUNTING MATTERS!

Wireless Winnings Bear Fruit

Until recently, the word "blackberry" would bring to mind images of the dark juicy fruit that grows wild on bushes. But the BlackBerry, a handheld wireless device that allows you to send and receive text messages and other data, has become a corporate mainstay with more than two million subscribers worldwide. The word has certainly taken on new meaning.

"When you say 'blackberry,' a lot of people automatically think of our unit... There are verbs now like 'Berry me,'" says Angelo Loberto, vice-president, finance, of Waterloo, Ontario-based Research In Motion Ltd. (RIM), maker of the BlackBerry.

Engineering students Mike Lazaridis (president and co-CEO) and Douglas Fregin (vice-president, operations) founded RIM in 1984. During the 1990s, the company was making Type II radio modem cards for laptop computers. "We thought, hey, can we slap some plastic and a keyboard around this and make it a two-way pager?" says Mr. Loberto. Thus the Interactive Pager was born in 1996.

RIM's initial public offering took place a year later. The company has had three rounds of financing through share offerings since then. The last round, the issue of 12.1 million shares in January 2004, raised U.S. $905.2 million. Shareholders' equity for the fiscal year ending Feb. 28, 2004, was U.S. $1.7 billion, compared to U.S. $0.7 billion in 2003, a significant increase due mainly to the share issue.

Then, in May 2004, RIM had a two-for-one stock split, in which the price of a single share was cut in half.

At the time of the January 2004 financing, RIM's stock was trading at U.S. $78. A year later, its value was again up in the U.S. $75 range, despite the stock split in April. "We've basically doubled since our last round of financing," says Mr. Loberto. "We're happy because we've got more money to finance the company's needs, and the shareholders are really happy because they've doubled their money in a year."

RIM's three-pronged business approach includes service, software, and the device itself. Service providers worldwide provide RIM's BlackBerry products and software to corporate clients. The company also licenses its software to other companies that download it onto their handhelds. Their carrier then pays RIM a subscriber fee. "We don't get the handheld sale, but we get the other two pieces, instead of not getting the sale at all," Mr. Loberto points out.

RIM's ultimate goal? To be the global standard for wireless solutions, says Mr. Loberto— which is something RIM shareholders would also likely welcome.

the navigator

RIM: www.rim.com

THE NAVIGATOR

☐ Read *Feature Story*

☐ Scan *Study Objectives*

☐ Read *Chapter Preview*

☐ Read text and answer *Before You Go On*

☐ Work *Using the Decision Toolkit*

☐ Review *Summary of Study Objectives*

☐ Review the *Decision Toolkit—A Summary*

☐ Work *Demonstration Problem*

☐ Answer *Self-Study Questions*

☐ Complete assignments

STUDY OBJECTIVES

After studying this chapter, you should be able to:

1. Identify and discuss the major characteristics of a corporation and its shares.
2. Record share transactions.
3. Prepare the entries for cash dividends, stock dividends, and stock splits, and understand their financial impact.
4. Indicate how shareholders' equity is presented in the financial statements.
5. Evaluate dividend and earnings performance.

the navigator

Companies can start out small and grow large, as Research in Motion has. It should not be surprising, then, that corporations are the dominant form of business organization. In this chapter, we look at the essential features of a corporation. The accounting for, and reporting of, shareholders' equity is explained. We conclude by reviewing various measures of corporate performance.

The chapter is organized as follows:

REPORTING AND ANALYZING SHAREHOLDERS' EQUITY				
The Corporate Form of Organization	**Share Capital**	**Retained Earnings**	**Financial Statement Presentation of Shareholders' Equity**	**Measuring Corporate Performance**
▶ Characteristics of a corporation ▶ Share issue considerations	▶ Common shares ▶ Preferred shares	▶ Dividends ▶ Retained earnings restrictions	▶ Balance sheet ▶ Cash flow statement	▶ Dividend record ▶ Earnings performance

the navigator

The Corporate Form of Organization

A **corporation** is a legal entity that is separate and distinct from its owners, who are known as shareholders. As a legal entity, a corporation has most of the rights and privileges of a person. It must respect laws and it must pay income tax. The major exceptions are privileges that only a living person can exercise, such as the right to vote or to hold public office.

Corporations may be classified in a variety of ways. Two common classifications are by purpose and by ownership. A corporation may be organized for the purpose of making a **profit** (such as Research in Motion), or it may be **not-for-profit** (such as the Canadian Cancer Society or Carleton University).

Classification by ownership distinguishes between public and private corporations. A **public corporation** may have thousands of shareholders, and its shares are regularly traded on a securities market, such as the Toronto Stock Exchange. Most of the largest Canadian companies are publicly held. Examples are George Weston Ltd., Magna International Inc., and Bombardier Inc.

In contrast, a **private corporation**—often called a closely held corporation—usually has only a few shareholders. It does not offer its shares for sale to the general public. Private companies are generally much smaller than public companies, although there are some big exceptions, such as McCain Foods, The Jim Pattison Group, and the Irving companies. Research in Motion, in our feature story, was a privately held corporation until it offered its shares for sale to the public in 1997.

A relatively new form of corporation in Canada is the income trust. An **income trust** is a special or limited purpose company, set up specifically to invest in income-producing assets. The trust pays out most of its earnings to investors, called unitholders, and there is no income tax payable for the trust itself. Instead the unitholders pay income tax on the cash they receive. Except for the distribution of earnings and the equity structure, there is no significant difference in accounting for income trusts than for other types of corporations. Currently, there are more than 200 income trusts in Canada, including well-known companies such as Big Rock Brewery, Enbridge, Sleep Country Canada, and A&W.

Characteristics of a Corporation

study objective 1

Identify and discuss the major characteristics of a corporation and its shares.

Many characteristics distinguish corporations from proprietorships and partnerships. Recall from Chapter 1 that a proprietorship is a business owned by one person, and a partnership is owned by two or more people who are associated as partners. A corporation has the following distinguishing characteristics:

Separate Legal Existence

As an entity that is separate and distinct from its owners, the corporation acts under its own name rather than in the name of its shareholders. RIM, for example, may buy, own, and sell property, borrow money, and enter into legally binding contracts in its own name. It may also sue or be sued. It also pays income taxes as a separate entity.

In contrast to a proprietorship or partnership, where the owners' actions bind the proprietorship or partnership, the acts of a corporation's owners (shareholders) do not bind the corporation unless these owners are also agents of the corporation. For example, if you owned RIM shares, you would not have the right to purchase a new production facility for the company unless you were designated as an agent of the corporation.

Limited Liability of Shareholders

The liability of shareholders is limited to their investment in the corporation, and ownership is represented by the number of shares owned. This means that creditors only have access to corporate assets to satisfy their claims: shareholders cannot be made to pay for the company's liabilities out of their personal assets.

Limited liability is a significant advantage for the corporate form of organization. However, in certain situations, creditors may demand a personal guarantee from a controlling shareholder. This has the effect of making the controlling shareholder's personal assets available, if required, to satisfy the creditor's claim—which, of course, eliminates or reduces the advantage of limited liability.

Transferable Ownership Rights

Ownership of a corporation is held in shares of capital, which are transferable units. Shareholders can let go of part or all of their interest in a corporation simply by selling their shares. The transfer of shares is entirely up to the shareholder. It does not require the approval of either the corporation or other shareholders.

The transfer of ownership rights among shareholders has no effect on the operating activities of the corporation. Nor does it affect the corporation's assets, liabilities, or shareholders' equity. The transfer of ownership rights is a transaction between individual shareholders. The corporation does not participate in the transfer of these ownership rights; it is only involved in the original sale of the share capital.

Ability to Acquire Capital

It is fairly easy for a corporation to obtain capital by issuing shares. Buying shares in a corporation is often attractive to an investor because a shareholder has limited liability and shares are readily transferable. Also, because only small amounts of money need to be invested, many individuals can become shareholders. In sum, the ability of a successful corporation to obtain capital is almost unlimited.

Note that the "almost unlimited" ability of a corporation to acquire capital is only true for large, publicly traded corporations. Small, or closely held, corporations can have as much difficulty in acquiring capital as do proprietorships or partnerships.

Continuous Life

Corporations have an unlimited life. Since a corporation is a separate legal entity, its continuance as a going concern is not affected by the withdrawal, death, or incapacity of a shareholder, employee, or officer. As a result, a successful corporation can have a continuous and indefinite life. For example, the Hudson's Bay Company, Canada's oldest corporation, was founded in 1670 and is still going strong. In contrast, proprietorships end if anything happens to the proprietor and partnerships normally reform if anything happens to one of the partners.

Corporation Management

Although shareholders legally own the corporation, they manage it indirectly through a board of directors they elect. The board, in turn, decides the operating policies for the company. The board also selects officers, such as a president and one or more vice-presidents, to execute policy and to perform daily management functions. As mentioned in the feature story, Mike Lazaridis is the president and co-CEO of Research in Motion and Douglas Fregin is one of the company's vice-presidents.

The organizational structure of a corporation enables a company to hire professional managers to run the business. However, some critics see this separation as a weakness. The separation of ownership and management prevents owners from having an active role in managing the company, which some owners would prefer to have.

Government Regulations

Canadian companies may be incorporated federally, under the terms of the *Canada Business Corporations Act*, or provincially, under the terms of a provincial business corporations act. Federal and provincial laws usually state the requirements for issuing and reacquiring shares and distributing earnings. Similarly, the regulations of provincial securities commissions control the sale of share capital to the general public. When a corporation's shares are listed and traded on foreign securities markets, the corporation must also respect the reporting requirements of these exchanges. For example, Research in Motion's shares are listed on both the Toronto Stock Exchange in Canada and the Nasdaq Stock Market in the U.S. Complying with federal, provincial, and securities regulations increases the cost and complexity of the corporate form of organization.

Income Taxes

Neither proprietorships nor partnerships pay income tax as separate entities. Instead, each owner's share of earnings from these organizations is reported on his or her personal income tax return. Taxes are then paid on this amount by the individual.

Corporations, on the other hand, must pay income taxes as separate legal entities (with the exception of income trusts). These taxes can be substantial and can amount to as much as 45 to 50 percent of taxable income.

There are, however, income tax rate reductions available to some corporations. With eligible reductions, or other corporate tax incentives, a corporation's tax rate may be reduced to between 15 and 25 percent on certain kinds of active small business income. This tax rate is much lower than the tax rate for the same amount of income earned by an individual.

In some circumstances, an advantage of incorporation is being able to delay personal income tax. The shareholders of a corporation do not pay tax on the corporate earnings until the earnings are distributed to them as dividends. Many people argue that corporate earnings are taxed twice, once at the corporate level and again at the individual level. This is not exactly true, however, as individuals receive a dividend tax credit to reduce this tax burden.

It is wise to get expert advice to determine whether incorporating will result in more or less income tax than operating as a proprietorship or partnership. Income tax laws are complex, and careful tax planning is essential for any business venture.

ACCOUNTING MATTERS!　International Perspective

Corporations in North America are identified by "Ltd.," "Inc.," "Corp.," or in some cases, "Co." following their names. These abbreviations can also be spelled out. In Brazil and France, the letters used are "SA" (Sôciedade Anonima, Société Anonyme); in Japan, "KK" (Kabushiki Kaisha); in the Netherlands, "NV" (Naamloze Vennootschap); in Italy, "SpA" (Società per Azioni); and in Sweden, "AB" (Aktiebolag).

In the UK, public corporations are identified by "Plc" (Public limited company), while private corporations are denoted by "Ltd." The same designations in Germany are "AG" (Aktiengesellschaft) for public corporations and "GmbH" (Gesellschaft mit beschränkter Haftung) for private corporations.

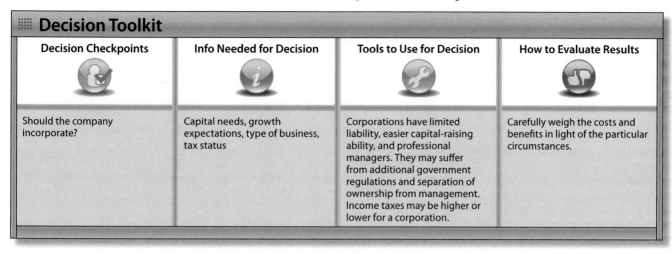

Decision Toolkit

Decision Checkpoints	Info Needed for Decision	Tools to Use for Decision	How to Evaluate Results
Should the company incorporate?	Capital needs, growth expectations, type of business, tax status	Corporations have limited liability, easier capital-raising ability, and professional managers. They may suffer from additional government regulations and separation of ownership from management. Income taxes may be higher or lower for a corporation.	Carefully weigh the costs and benefits in light of the particular circumstances.

Share Issue Considerations

After incorporation, a corporation sells ownership rights as shares. The shares of the company are divided into different classes, such as Class A, Class B, and so on. The rights and privileges for each class of shares are stated in articles of incorporation, which form the "constitution" of the company. The different classes are usually identified by the generic terms *common shares* and *preferred shares*. When a corporation has only one class of shares, that class has the rights and privileges of **common shares**. Research in Motion has only one class of shares, called common shares.

Each common share gives the shareholder the ownership rights shown in Illustration 11-1.

Shareholders have the right to:

1. Vote in the election of the board of directors at the annual meeting. Vote on actions that require shareholder approval.

2. Share the corporate earnings through the receipt of dividends.

3. Share in the company's assets if it is liquidated, and in proportion to the shareholder's holdings. This is called a residual claim because shareholders are paid with assets that remain after all other claims have been paid.

Illustration 11-1 ◀

Ownership rights of shareholders

When Research in Motion first issued common shares in 1997, it had to make several decisions. How many shares should be authorized for sale? At what price should the shares be issued? What value should be assigned to the shares? These questions are answered in the following sections.

Authorized Share Capital

The amount of share capital that a corporation is authorized to sell is indicated in its articles of incorporation. It may be specified as an unlimited amount or a certain number (e.g., 500,000 shares authorized). More than 75 percent of public companies in Canada have an unlimited amount of authorized shares. Research in Motion has an unlimited number of shares authorized. If a number is specified, the amount of **authorized shares** normally anticipates a company's initial and later capital needs. **Issued shares** are authorized shares that have been sold.

The authorization of share capital does not result in a formal accounting entry, because the event has no immediate effect on either corporate assets or shareholders' equity. However, the number of shares authorized and issued must be disclosed in the shareholders' equity section of the balance sheet.

Issue of Shares

A corporation can issue common shares directly to investors or indirectly through an investment dealer (brokerage house) that specializes in bringing securities to the attention of potential investors. Direct issue is typical in closely held companies. Indirect issue is customary for a publicly held corporation, such as Research in Motion in our feature story.

The first time a corporation's shares are offered to the public, the offer is called an **initial public offering (IPO)**. The company receives the cash (less any financing or issue fees) from the sale of the IPO shares whether it is done by a direct or indirect issue. The company's assets (cash) increase, and its shareholders' equity (share capital) also increases.

Once these shares have been issued and sold, they continue trading on the **secondary market**. That is, investors buy and sell shares from each other, rather than from the company. When shares are sold among investors, there is no impact on the company's financial position. The company receives no additional assets, and it issues no additional shares. The only change in the company records is the name of the shareholder, not the number of shares issued.

Market Value of Shares

After the initial issue of new shares, the market price per share changes according to the interaction between buyers and sellers. In general, the price follows the trend of a company's earnings and dividends. Factors that are beyond a company's control (such as an embargo on oil, changes in interest rates, the outcome of an election, and war) also influence market prices.

For each listed security, the financial press reports the high and low share prices for the year, the annual dividend rate, the high and low prices for the day, and the net change over the previous day. The total volume of shares traded on a particular day, the dividend yield, and price-earnings ratios are also reported. A recent listing for Research in Motion's common shares on the Toronto Stock Exchange (TSX) is shown below:

365-day		stock	sym	div	high	low	close	chg	Vol (h)	yld	p/e ratio
high	low										
127.91	69.24	Research in Motion	RIM		99.63	95.56	96.49	−2.16	732.9		67.3

Research in Motion's shares have traded as high as $127.91 and as low as $69.24 during the past year. The stock's ticker symbol is "RIM." Research in Motion does not pay an annual dividend, which is indicated by the blank space in the "div" column. The high and low prices for the date shown were $99.63 and $95.56 per share, respectively. The closing share price was $96.49, a decrease of $2.16 from the previous day. The trading volume was 732,900 shares (the number shown is given in hundreds "(h)"). Since Research in Motion does not pay any dividend, there is no dividend yield ("yld"). The dividend yield reports the rate of return an investor earned from dividends, calculated by dividing the dividend by the share price. We will learn more about this ratio later in the chapter. Research in Motion's shares are currently trading at a price-earnings ("p/e") ratio (share price divided by earnings per share) of 67.3 times earnings. The dividend yield and price-earnings ratios are often interpreted together to determine how highly investors favour a company.

Legal Capital

When shares are issued, they form the share capital of the corporation. You will recall that the shareholders' equity section of a corporation's balance sheet includes both share capital and retained earnings. The distinction between retained earnings and share capital is important from both a legal and an economic point of view. Retained earnings can be distributed to shareholders as dividends or retained in the company for operating needs. On the other hand, share capital is **legal capital** that cannot be distributed to shareholders. It must remain invested in the company for the protection of corporate creditors.

Years ago, a value—known as par or stated value—was assigned to shares to predetermine the amount of legal capital. Today, the use of par or stated values for shares is either not required or prohibited in Canada. Instead, **no par value shares**, or shares that have not been assigned a predetermined value, are issued. When no par value shares are issued, all of the proceeds received are considered to be legal capital. Whenever shares are issued in this chapter, you can assume that they are no par value shares.

BEFORE YOU GO ON . . .

▶Review It

1. What are the advantages and disadvantages of a corporation compared to a proprietorship or a partnership?
2. To a corporation, what is the significance of the amount of authorized shares? Of the amount of issued shares?
3. How does the sale of shares affect a company in an initial public offering? And afterwards when they are sold in the secondary market?
4. How is the legal capital of shares determined?

Share Capital

Share capital is the amount contributed to the corporation by shareholders in exchange for shares of ownership. Other amounts can also be contributed by, or accrue to, shareholders. Together, these other amounts and the share capital form the total **contributed capital** of the corporation. Recall that share capital can consist of both common shares and preferred shares. We will look at common shares in this section and preferred shares in the next. We will also learn more about other sources of contributed capital.

study objective 2

Record share transactions.

Common Shares

Common shares may be issued (sold) to investors, who then become shareholders of the corporation. Common shares can also be reacquired from shareholders. We will look at each of these types of transactions in more detail.

Issue of Shares

To illustrate the issue of common shares, assume that Hydro-Slide, Inc. is authorized to issue an unlimited number of no par value common shares. It issues 1,000 of these shares for $6 per share on January 12.

As mentioned earlier, when no par value common shares are issued, the entire proceeds from the sale become legal capital. That means that the proceeds are credited to the Common Shares account. The entry to record this transaction is:

Jan. 12	Cash	6,000	
	Common Shares		6,000
	(To record issue of 1,000 common shares)		

A	=	L	+	SE
+6,000				+6,000

↑ Cash flows: +6,000

If Hydro-Slide has retained earnings of $27,000, the shareholders' equity section of the balance sheet is as shown in Illustration 11-2.

HYDRO-SLIDE, INC.
Balance Sheet (partial)
December 31, 2006

Shareholders' equity	
Common shares	$ 6,000
Retained earnings	27,000
Total shareholders' equity	$33,000

Illustration 11-2 ◀

Shareholders' equity

Common shares are most commonly issued in exchange for cash. However, they may also be issued for other considerations than cash, such as services (e.g., compensation to lawyers or consultants) or noncash assets (e.g., land, buildings, or equipment). To comply with the cost principle in a noncash transaction, **cost is the cash equivalent price**. Thus, cost is the market value of the consideration (common shares) given up. If the common shares do not have a ready market, we then use the market value of the consideration received to determine cost.

Reacquisition of Shares

Companies can purchase their own shares on the open market. A corporation may acquire its own shares to meet any of the following objectives:

1. To increase trading of the company's shares in the securities market in the hope of enhancing the company's market value
2. To reduce the number of shares issued and so increase the earnings per share
3. To eliminate hostile shareholders by buying them out
4. To have additional shares available for issue to employees under bonus and stock compensation plans, or for use in acquiring other companies

When a company reacquires its own shares, the repurchased shares must be retired and cancelled. This effectively restores the shares to the status of authorized but unissued shares. Reacquisition of shares is a common practice and the financial press often contains announcements of "normal course issuer bids" which inform the public that the company plans to repurchase shares.

The Canadian Imperial Bank of Commerce (CIBC) recently announced its intention to repurchase up to 17 million (about five percent) of its common shares in a normal course issuer bid to boost the bank's share price. By buying back some of its own shares, the bank will reduce the number of common shares, and this has the effect of increasing demand. In addition, with fewer shares issued, earnings per share may increase.

To illustrate the accounting for reacquired shares, assume that Hydro-Slide, Inc. now has a total of 25,000 common shares issued and a balance in its Common Shares account of $50,000. On September 23, Hydro-Slide purchases and cancels 5,000 of its common shares. Recall that when a long-lived asset is retired, the cost of the asset must be credited. Any difference between the proceeds received and the original cost is recorded as a gain or loss. Similarly, the cost of the common shares that are reacquired and retired must be determined, and that amount is then deleted (debited) from the Common Shares account.

The difference between the price paid to reacquire the shares and their original cost is, in essence, a "gain" or a "loss" on reacquisition. However, companies cannot realize a gain or suffer a loss from share transactions with their own shareholders, so these amounts are not reported on the statement of earnings. They are seen instead as an excess or deficiency that belongs to the original shareholders and is reported as an increase or decrease in contributed capital.

To determine the cost of the common shares reacquired, the average cost per share must first be calculated. As it is impractical, and often impossible, to determine the cost of each individual common share that has been reacquired, an average cost per common share is instead calculated by dividing the balance in the Common Shares account by the number of shares issued. In the case of Hydro-Slide, the average cost of the common shares, immediately before the reacquisition, is $2 per share ($50,000 ÷ 25,000).

The accounting for the reacquisition of shares is different depending on whether the shares are reacquired by paying less than average cost or more than average cost.

Reacquisition below Average Cost.   To illustrate the reacquisition of common shares at a price less than their average cost, assume that Hydro-Slide reacquired its 5,000 common shares at a price of $1.50 per share. Since the average cost of the shares was $2 per share, a $0.50 ($2.00 − $1.50) addition to contributed capital results, as shown below:

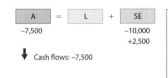

A	=	L	+	SE
−7,500				−10,000
				+2,500

↓ Cash flows: −7,500

Sept. 23	Common Shares (5,000 × $2)	10,000	
	Contributed Capital—Reacquisition of Common Shares		2,500
	Cash (5,000 × $1.50)		7,500
	(To record reacquisition and retirement of 5,000 common shares)		

After this entry, Hydro-Slide still has an unlimited number of shares authorized, but only 20,000 (25,000 − 5,000) shares issued, and a balance of $40,000 ($50,000 − $10,000) in its Common Shares account. The difference between the average cost of the shares and the amount paid to repurchase them is credited to a new shareholders' equity account, one that is specifically for the contributed capital realized from the reacquisition of shares. The cash in the entry was paid to the shareholders who the shares were repurchased from.

Reacquisition above Average Cost. If Hydro-Slide had paid $2.50 per share to reacquire 5,000 of its common shares, rather than the $1.50 per share assumed above, it would result in a debit to a contributed capital account for the difference between the price paid to reacquire the shares and their average cost. If there is any balance in the contributed capital account from previous reacquisitions, this amount would first be reduced (debited). However, contributed capital cannot be reduced beyond any existing balance. In other words, contributed capital can never have a negative, or debit, balance. Instead, any excess deficiency amount would be debited to Retained Earnings.

The journal entry to record the reacquisition and retirement of Hydro-Slide's common shares at a price of $2.50 per share is as follows:

Sept. 23	Common Shares (5,000 × $2)	10,000	
	Retained Earnings	2,500	
	Cash (5,000 × $2.50)		12,500
	(To record reacquisition and retirement of 5,000 common shares)		

A = L + SE
−12,500   −10,000
               −2,500

↓ Cash flows: −12,500

In this entry, Hydro-Slide is assumed to have no previous balance in the contributed capital account. After this entry, Hydro-Slide still has 20,000 (25,000 − 5,000) shares issued and a balance of $40,000 ($50,000 − $10,000) in its Common Shares account.

The only difference in the accounting for reacquisitions at prices below or above the average cost has to do with recording the difference between the amount paid to repurchase the shares and their average cost. If the shares are reacquired at a price below the average cost, the difference is credited to a contributed capital account. If the shares are reacquired at a price above the average cost, the difference is debited first to the contributed capital account used in prior reacquisitions below cost of the same class of shares, and second, to the Retained Earnings account if there is no credit balance remaining in the contributed capital account.

Preferred Shares

A corporation may issue preferred shares in addition to common shares. Like common shares, preferred shares may be issued for cash or for noncash considerations. They can also be reacquired. The entries for these transactions are similar to the entries for common shares, so they are not repeated here. When a company has more than one class of shares, separate account titles should be used (e.g., Preferred Shares, Common Shares).

Preferred shares have contractual provisions that give them a preference, or priority, over common shares in certain areas. Typically, preferred shareholders have priority over the payment of dividends and, in the event of liquidation, over the distribution of assets. However, they do not usually have the voting rights that the common shares have. A recent survey indicated that more than one-half of Canadian companies have preferred shares.

Dividend Preference

As indicated above, **preferred shareholders have the right to share in the distribution of dividends before common shareholders do**. For example, if the dividend rate on preferred shares is $5 per share, common shareholders will not receive any dividends in the current year until preferred shareholders have received $5 per share. The first claim to dividends does not, however, guarantee dividends. Dividends depend on many factors, such as adequate retained earnings and the availability of cash. In addition, all dividends must be formally approved by the board of directors.

Preferred shares may contain a **cumulative dividend** feature. This right means that preferred shareholders must be paid both current-year dividends and any unpaid prior-year dividends before common shareholders receive dividends. Preferred shares without this feature are called **noncumulative**. The majority of preferred shares issued today are noncumulative.

When preferred shares are cumulative, preferred dividends that are not declared in a period are called **dividends in arrears**. To illustrate, assume that Stine Corporation has 10,000 $3 cumulative preferred shares. The per share dividend amount is usually given as an annual amount, similar to interest rates. So, Stine's annual total dividend is $30,000 (10,000 × $3 per share). If dividends are two years in arrears, preferred shareholders are entitled to receive the following dividends:

Dividends in arrears ($30,000 × 2)	$60,000
Current-year dividends	30,000
Total preferred dividends	$90,000

No distribution can be made to common shareholders until this entire preferred dividend is paid. In other words, dividends cannot be paid to common shareholders while any preferred share dividends are in arrears.

Dividends in arrears are not considered a liability. No obligation exists until a dividend is declared by the board of directors. However, the amount of dividends in arrears should be disclosed in the notes to the financial statements. This allows investors to evaluate the potential impact of this commitment on the corporation's financial position.

Even though there is no requirement to pay an annual dividend, companies that are unable to meet their dividend obligations—whether cumulative or noncumulative—are not looked upon favourably by the investment community. As a financial officer noted in discussing one company's failure to pay its preferred dividend for a period of time, "Not meeting your obligations on something like that is a major black mark on your record."

Liquidation Preference

Most preferred shares have a preference on corporate assets if the corporation fails. This feature provides security for the preferred shareholder. The preference on assets may be for the legal value of the shares or for a specified liquidating value. The liquidation preference is used in bankruptcy lawsuits involving the respective claims of creditors and preferred shareholders.

Other Preferences

The attractiveness of preferred shares as an investment is sometimes increased by adding a conversion privilege. **Convertible preferred shares** allow the exchange of preferred shares for common shares at a specified ratio, at the shareholder's option. Convertible preferred shares are purchased by investors who want the greater security of preferred shares, but who also desire the added option of conversion if the market value of the common shares increases significantly.

Many preferred shares are also issued with a redemption or call feature. **Redeemable (or callable) preferred shares** give the issuing corporation the right to purchase the shares from shareholders at specified future dates and prices. The redemption feature offers some flexibility to a corporation by enabling it to eliminate this type of equity security when it is advantageous to do so.

Retractable preferred shares are similar to redeemable or callable preferred shares, except that it is at the *shareholder's* option, rather than the corporation's option, that the shares are redeemed. This usually occurs at an arranged price and date.

When preferred shares are redeemable or retractable, the distinction between equity and debt is less clear. Redeemable and retractable preferred shares are similar in some ways to debt. They both offer a rate of return to the investor, and with the redemption of the shares, they both offer a repayment of the principal investment.

Contractual arrangements of this sort are known as **financial instruments**. A **financial instrument** is a contract that creates a financial instrument for one company and a financial liability or equity instrument for another company. Financial instruments must be presented in accordance with their economic substance rather than their form. That is, redeemable and retractable preferred shares are usually presented in the *liabilities* section of the balance sheet rather than in the equity section. This is because they often have more of the features of debt than of equity.

Companies are issuing an increasing number of shares with innovative preferences. Some have the attributes of both debt and equity; others have the attributes of both common and preferred shares. Accounting for such financial instruments presents unique challenges for accountants. Further detail is left for an intermediate accounting course.

BEFORE YOU GO ON . . .

▶Review It

1. Explain the accounting for the issue of shares.
2. Distinguish between the accounting for a repurchase of shares at a price less than average cost and more than average cost.
3. Did Loblaw repurchase and cancel any of its own shares in fiscal 2003? The answer to this question is at the end of the chapter.
4. Compare the normal rights and privileges of common and preferred shares.

▶Do It

The Assiniboia Corporation begins operations on March 1 by issuing 100,000 common shares for $12 per share. On March 15, it issues an additional 20,000 common shares at $15 per share. On June 1, Assiniboia repurchases 10,000 of its own common shares at $10 per share. On September 1, the company issued 25,000 preferred shares at $50 per share. Record the share transactions.

Action Plan

• Credit the appropriate share capital account for the proceeds received in a share issue.
• Calculate the average cost per share by dividing the balance in the shares account by the number of shares issued.
• Debit the shares account for the average cost of the reacquired shares. If the reacquisition cost is below the average cost, credit the difference to a contributed capital account. If the reacquisition cost is above the average cost, debit the difference to Retained Earnings unless there is already a balance in a contributed capital account from previous reacquisitions and retirements.

Solution

Mar. 1	Cash (100,000 × $12)	1,200,000	
	Common Shares		1,200,000
	(To record issue of 100,000 common shares at $12 per share)		
15	Cash (20,000 × $15)	300,000	
	Common Shares		300,000
	(To record issue of 20,000 common shares at $15 per share)		
June 1	Common Shares (10,000 × $12.50)	125,000	
	Contributed Capital—Reacquisition of Shares		25,000
	Cash (10,000 × $10)		100,000
	(To record reacquisition and retirement of 10,000 common shares at an average cost of $12.50 [$1,500,000 ÷ 120,000])		
Sept. 1	Cash (25,000 × $50)	1,250,000	
	Preferred Shares		1,250,000
	(To record issue of 25,000 preferred shares at $50 per share)		

Retained Earnings

As we have learned in past chapters, retained earnings are the cumulative net earnings since incorporation that have been retained in the company (i.e., that have not distributed to shareholders). Each year, net earnings are added to (or a net loss is deducted) and dividends are deducted from the opening Retained Earnings account balance to determine the ending retained earnings amount. We have looked at the components of net earnings in prior chapters. We will focus on the impact of dividends on retained earnings in this section.

study objective 3

Prepare the entries for cash dividends, stock dividends, and stock splits, and understand their financial impact

Dividends

A **dividend** is a pro rata (equal) distribution of a portion of a corporation's retained earnings to its shareholders. "Pro rata" means that if you own, say, 10 percent of the common shares, you will receive 10 percent of the dividend. In 2004, Canadian companies paid out $62 billion dollars in dividends to shareholders—an all-time record. So it should not be surprising that investors are very interested in a company's dividend practices.

Many high-growth companies, such as Research in Motion in our feature story, do not pay dividends. Their policy is to retain all of their earnings to make it easier to grow. Investors purchase shares in companies like RIM in the hope that the share price will increase in value and they will realize a profit when they sell their shares. Other investors purchase shares of established companies in hope of earning dividend revenue (and maybe also in profiting from some share price appreciation when they sell their shares). The Bank of Montreal has the longest unbroken dividend record in Canadian history, having begun paying dividends in 1829.

In the financial press, **dividends are generally reported as an annual dollar amount per share**, even though it is usual to pay dividends quarterly. For example, the Bank of Montreal has an annual dividend rate of $1.84 on its common shares. This dividend is paid quarterly at a rate of $0.46 ($1.84 ÷ 4) per share.

Cash dividends are the most common in practice but stock dividends are also declared fairly often. We will look at each of these types of dividends in the next two sections.

Cash Dividends

A **cash dividend** is a distribution of cash to shareholders. For a corporation to pay a cash dividend, it must have the following:

1. **Enough retained earnings.**   Dividends are distributed from (reduce) retained earnings, so a company must have enough retained earnings in order to pay a dividend. Companies seldom pay out dividends equal to their retained earnings, however. They must retain a certain portion of retained earnings (i.e., net assets) to finance their operations. In addition, some level of retained earnings must be maintained to provide a cushion or buffer against possible future losses.

2. **Enough cash.**   The fact that a company has enough retained earnings does not necessarily mean that it has enough cash. There is no direct relationship between the balance in the Retained Earnings account and the balance in the Cash account at any one point in time. So, in addition to having enough retained earnings, a company must also have enough cash before it can pay a dividend.

    How much cash is enough? That is hard to say but a company must keep enough cash on hand to pay for its ongoing operations and to pay its bills as they come due. Under the *Canada Business Corporations Act*, a corporation cannot pay a dividend if it would subsequently be unable to pay its liabilities.

    For example, RIM had U.S. $1.2 billion of cash at the end of February 2004. Even if it had wanted to, it would not have been able to declare a U.S. $1.2-billion cash dividend to its shareholders because that would not have left the company with enough cash to pay its bills. Before declaring a cash dividend, a company's board of directors must carefully consider current and future demands on the company's cash resources. In some cases, current (or planned future) liabilities may make a cash dividend inappropriate.

3. **A declaration of dividends.**   A company does not pay dividends unless its board of directors decides to do so, at which point the board "declares" the dividend to be payable. The board of directors has full authority to determine the amount of retained earnings to be distributed in the form of dividends and the amount to be retained in the company. Dividends do not accrue like interest on a note payable, and they are not a liability until they are declared.

The amount and timing of a dividend are important issues for management to consider. The payment of a large cash dividend could lead to liquidity problems for the company. On the other hand, a small dividend or a missed dividend may cause unhappiness among shareholders. Many shareholders purchase shares with the expectation of receiving a reasonable cash payment from the company on a periodic basis.

In order to remain in business, companies must honour their interest payments to creditors, bankers, and debt holders. But the payment of dividends to shareholders is another matter.

Many companies can survive, and even thrive, without such payouts. Research in Motion is a case in point.

Investors must keep an eye on the company's dividend policy and understand what it may mean. For most companies, for example, regular dividend increases when the company has irregular earnings can be a warning signal. Companies with high dividends and rising debt may be borrowing money to pay shareholders. On the other hand, low dividends may not be a negative sign. This could mean that higher returns will be earned through share price appreciation rather than through the receipt of dividends. Presumably, investors for whom regular dividends are important tend to buy shares in companies that pay periodic dividends, and those for whom growth in the share price is more important tend to buy shares in companies that retain earnings.

ACCOUNTING MATTERS!   Investor Perspective

Bombardier Inc.—the Montreal-based plane and train maker—recently asked the federal government for financial assistance. Claude Lamoureux, head of the Ontario Teachers Pension Plan and well-known shareholder activist, suggested that Bombardier should abolish its $0.09 annual per share dividend. He argued that before a company asks the government for "help," it should cut payments to its own shareholders. Bombardier's dividend had already been reduced to $0.09 from $0.18 a share in 2003. Subsequently, for the first time in more than 20 years, Bombardier did end up suspending its annual dividend in order to keep some much-needed cash.

Source: Jim Stanford, "Bombardier's Dividends: The Case for Tied Aid," *The Globe and Mail*, March 28, 2005, A13.

Entries for Cash Dividends.   Three dates are important in connection with dividends: (1) the declaration date, (2) the record date, and (3) the payment date. Normally, there are several weeks between each date and the next one. For example, on May 25, 2005 (declaration date), the Bank of Montreal declared a dividend of $0.46 per share payable to its common shareholders. These dividends were paid on August 30, 2005 (payment date) to the shareholders of record at the close of business on August 5, 2005 (record date). Accounting entries are required on two of the dates—the declaration date and the payment date.

On the **declaration date**, the board of directors formally authorizes the cash dividend and announces it to shareholders. The declaration of a cash dividend commits the corporation to a binding legal obligation. An entry is therefore required to recognize the increase in Cash Dividends (which results in a decrease in retained earnings) and the increase in the liability Dividends Payable.

Cash dividends can be paid to preferred or common shareholders (preferred have to be paid before common, though). To illustrate a cash dividend to preferred shareholders, assume that on December 1, 2006, the directors of IBR Inc. declare a $0.50 per share cash dividend on the company's 100,000 preferred shares, payable on January 20 to shareholders of record on December 22. The dividend is $50,000 (100,000 × $0.50), and the entry to record the declaration is:

	Declaration Date		
Dec. 1	Cash Dividends	50,000	
	Dividends Payable		50,000
	(To record declaration of cash dividend)		

Cash flows: no effect

Helpful Hint Between the declaration date and the record date, the number of shares remains the same. The purpose of the record date is to identify the persons or companies that will receive the dividend, not to determine the total amount of the dividend liability.

Dividends Payable is a current liability: it will normally be paid within the next month or so.

On the **record date**, ownership of the shares is determined so that the company knows who to pay the dividend to. The shareholder records give this information. In the interval between the declaration date and the record date, the company updates its share ownership record. For IBR, the record date is December 22. No entry is required on the record date because the corporation's liability recognized on the declaration date is unchanged.

On the **payment date**, dividend cheques are mailed to the shareholders and the payment of the dividend is recorded. The entry on January 20, the payment date, is:

	Payment Date		
Jan. 20	Dividends Payable	50,000	
	Cash		50,000
	(To record payment of cash dividend)		

Cash flows: −50,000

Note that the declaration of a cash dividend increases liabilities and reduces shareholders' equity. The payment of a dividend reduces both assets and liabilities, but it has no effect on shareholders' equity. The cumulative effect of the declaration and payment of a cash dividend on a company's financial statements is to **decrease both assets (through cash) and shareholders' equity (through retained earnings)**.

Stock Dividends

A **stock dividend** is a distribution of the corporation's own shares to shareholders. Whereas a cash dividend is paid in cash, a stock dividend is distributed (paid) in shares. And, while a cash dividend decreases assets and shareholders' equity, a stock dividend does not change either assets or shareholders' equity. **A stock dividend results in a decrease in retained earnings and an increase in share capital** but it does not change *total* shareholders' equity.

Note that since a stock dividend neither increases nor decreases the assets in the company, investors are not receiving anything they did not already own. In a sense, it is like ordering a piece of pie and cutting it into smaller pieces. You are no better or worse off, as you have your same amount of pie.

To illustrate a stock dividend for common shareholders, assume that you have a 2% ownership interest in IBR Inc. You own 1,000 of its 50,000 common shares. If IBR declares a 10% stock dividend, 5,000 (50,000 × 10%) additional shares would be issued. You would receive 100 (5,000 × 2%) new common shares. Would your ownership interest change? No, it would remain at 2% (1,100 ÷ 55,000). You now own more shares, but your ownership interest has not changed.

Illustration 11-3 shows the effect of a stock dividend for shareholders:

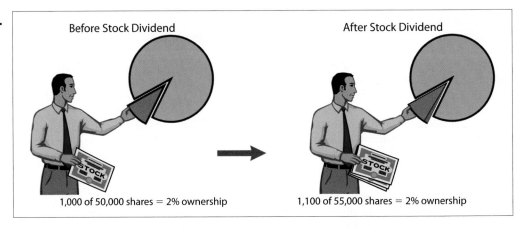

From the company's point of view, no cash has been paid, and no liabilities have been assumed. What, then, are the purposes and benefits of a stock dividend? A corporation generally issues a stock dividend for one or more of the following reasons:

1. To satisfy shareholders' dividend expectations while conserving cash.
2. To increase the marketability of the shares. When the number of shares increases, the market price per share decreases. Decreasing the market price of the shares makes it easier for investors to purchase the shares.
3. To emphasize that a portion of shareholders' equity has been permanently reinvested in the business and is unavailable for cash dividends.

The size of the stock dividend and the value to be assigned to each dividend share are determined by the board of directors when the dividend is declared. The *Canada Business Corporations Act* recommends that stock dividends be valued using the **market value per share** at the declaration date, which is what companies generally do.

Entries for Stock Dividends.   To illustrate the accounting for stock dividends, assume that IBR Inc. has a balance of $300,000 in Retained Earnings. On June 30, it declares a 10% stock dividend on its 50,000 common shares, to be distributed to shareholders on August 5. The market value of its shares on that date is $15 per share. The number of shares to be issued is 5,000 (50,000 × 10%). The total amount to be debited to stock dividends is $75,000 (5,000 × $15). The entry to record the declaration of the stock dividend is as follows:

June 30	Stock Dividends—Common	75,000	
	Common Stock Dividends Distributable		75,000
	(To record declaration of 10% stock dividend)		

A = L + SE
−75,000
+75,000
Cash flows: no effect

Helpful Hint Note that the dividend account title uses the word "Distributable," not "Payable."

At the declaration date, the Stock Dividends account is increased by the market value of the shares issued, and Common Stock Dividends Distributable is increased by the same amount. Common Stock Dividends Distributable is a shareholders' equity account. It is not a liability, because assets will not be used to pay the dividend. Instead, it will be "paid" with common shares. If a balance sheet is prepared before the dividend shares are issued, the distributable account is reported as share capital in the shareholders' equity section of the balance sheet.

As with cash dividends, no entry is required at the record date. When the dividend shares are issued on August 5, the account Common Stock Dividends Distributable is decreased (debited) and the account Common Shares is increased (credited), as follows:

Aug. 5	Common Stock Dividends Distributable	75,000	
	Common Shares		75,000
	(To record issue of 5,000 common shares in a 10% stock dividend)		

A = L + SE
−75,000
+75,000
Cash flows: no effect

Note that neither of the above entries changes shareholders' equity in total. However, the composition of shareholders' equity changes because a portion of retained earnings is transferred to the common shares account. These effects are shown below for IBR Inc.:

	Before Stock Dividend	After Stock Dividend
Shareholders' equity		
Common shares	$500,000	$575,000
Retained earnings	300,000	225,000
Total shareholders' equity	$800,000	$800,000
Number of shares	50,000	55,000

In this example, the Common Shares account increased by $75,000 and Retained Earnings decreased by the same amount. Note also that total shareholders' equity remains unchanged at $800,000, the total both before and after the stock dividend.

Stock Splits

We discuss stock splits in this section because of their similarities to stock dividends. A **stock split**, like a stock dividend, involves the issue of additional shares to shareholders according to their percentage ownership. However, a stock split is usually much larger than a stock dividend. The purpose of a stock split is to increase the marketability of the shares by lowering the market value per share. A lower market value increases investor interest and makes it easier for the corporation to issue additional shares.

The effect of a stock split on market value is generally inversely proportional to the size of the split—i.e., the larger the split, the lower the market value per share. Sometimes, due to increased investor interest, the share price then rises more rapidly beyond its original split value. For example, as mentioned in the feature story, Research in Motion split its stock two-for-one in May 2004. Before the stock split, the company's shares were trading at U.S. $78. One year later, despite the stock split, its shares continued to trade around this value. As Mr. Loberto, the vice-president of finance, said, however, "the shareholders are really happy because they've doubled their money in a year."

In a stock split, the number of shares is increased by a specified proportion. For example, in a two-for-one split, one share is exchanged for two shares. Research in Motion had 92.4 million common shares before its two-for-one stock split, and 184.8 million after. **A stock split does not have any effect on total share capital, retained earnings, or total shareholders' equity.** Only the number of shares increases.

These effects are shown below for IBR Inc., assuming that instead of issuing a 10 percent stock dividend, it split its 50,000 common shares on a two-for-one basis.

	Before Stock Split	After Stock Split
Shareholders' equity		
Common shares	$500,000	$500,000
Retained earnings	300,000	300,000
Total shareholders' equity	$800,000	$800,000
Number of shares	50,000	100,000

Because a stock split does not affect the balances in any shareholders' equity accounts, **it is not necessary to journalize a stock split**. Only a memo entry explaining the effect of the split is needed.

ACCOUNTING MATTERS!   Investor Perspective

Google Inc., which operates the world's most powerful on-line search engine, has no interest in splitting its stock. The stock split is a widely used market manoeuvre designed to make shares more affordable. In fact, stock splits have become so commonplace that investors almost automatically expect them whenever a company's share price approaches $100. However, despite Google's shares crossing the U.S. $200 threshold recently, Google's management continues to defy stock market convention and show no interest in a stock split. Yahoo Inc., Google's biggest rival, has split its stock four times. If not for the split, Yahoo's shares would be trading at U.S. $866 rather than their current price of U.S. $36.

Source: Michael Liedtke, "Stock Split Might Not Be in Google's Future," *Canadian Press Newswire,* November 11, 2004.

Comparison of Effects

Significant differences between the financial effects of cash dividends, stock dividends, and stock splits are shown in Illustration 11-4. In the illustration, "+" means increase, "−" means decrease, and "NE" means "no effect."

Illustration 11-4 ▶

Effects of cash dividends, stock dividends, and stock splits

	Assets	Liabilities	Shareholders' Equity	
			Share Capital	Retained Earnings
Cash dividend	−	NE	NE	−
Stock dividend	NE	NE	+	−
Stock split	NE	NE	NE	NE

In addition, a stock dividend and a stock split increase the number of shares issued.

Retained Earnings Restrictions

The balance in Retained Earnings is generally available for dividend declarations. In some cases, however, there may be **retained earnings restrictions**. These make a portion of the balance unavailable for dividends. Restrictions result from one or more of these types of causes: legal or contractual obligations, or voluntary choices. Retained earnings restrictions are generally disclosed in the notes to the financial statements. Only about four percent of Canadian companies reported retained earnings restrictions in a recent year.

Remember that retained earnings are part of the shareholders' claim on the corporation's total assets. The balance in Retained Earnings does not, however, represent a claim on any one specific asset. For example, restricting $100,000 of retained earnings does not necessarily mean that there will be $100,000 of cash set aside. All that a restriction does is to inform users that a portion of retained earnings (and correspondingly, net assets) is not available for dividend payments.

BEFORE YOU GO ON . . .

▶Review It

1. What entries are made for cash dividends on the (a) declaration date, (b) record date, and (c) payment date?
2. Distinguish between stock dividends and stock splits.
3. Contrast the effects of a stock dividend and a stock split on (a) assets, (b) liabilities, (c) shareholders' equity, and (d) the number of shares.
4. What is a retained earnings restriction?

▶Do It

Sing CD Corporation has had five years of record earnings. Due to this success, the market price of its 500,000 common shares tripled from $15 per share to $45. During this period, the Common Shares account remained the same at $2 million. Retained Earnings increased from $1.5 million to $10 million. President John Horne is considering either a (1) 10-percent stock dividend or (2) two-for-one stock split. He asks you to show the before-and-after effects of each option on shareholders' equity and on the number of shares.

Action Plan

- Calculate the stock dividend effects on retained earnings by multiplying the stock dividend percentage by the number of existing shares to determine the number of new shares to be issued. Multiply the number of new shares by the market price of the shares.
- A stock dividend increases the number of shares and affects both Common Shares and Retained Earnings.
- A stock split increases the number of shares but does not affect Common Shares or Retained Earnings.

Solution

1. With a 10% stock dividend, the stock dividend amount is $2,250,000 [(500,000 × 10%) × $45]. The new balance in Common Shares is $4,250,000 ($2,000,000 + $2,250,000) and in Retained Earnings is $7,750,000 ($10,000,000 − $2,250,000).
2. With a stock split, the account balances in Common Shares and Retained Earnings after the stock split are the same as they were before: $2 million and $10 million, respectively.

The effects in the shareholders' equity accounts of each option are as follows:

	Original Balances	After Stock Dividend	After Stock Split
Common shares	$ 2,000,000	$ 4,250,000	$ 2,000,000
Retained earnings	10,000,000	7,750,000	10,000,000
Total shareholders' equity	$12,000,000	$12,000,000	$12,000,000
Number of shares	500,000	550,000	1,000,000

the navigator

Financial Statement Presentation of Shareholders' Equity

Shareholders' equity transactions are reported in the balance sheet and cash flow statement. Equity transactions are not reported in the statement of earnings, although the statement of earnings is linked to shareholders' equity indirectly through retained earnings.

study objective 4

Indicate how shareholders' equity is presented in the financial statements

Balance Sheet

In the shareholders' equity section of the balance sheet, the following are reported: (1) contributed capital, (2) retained earnings, and (3) accumulated other comprehensive income. We have already learned about the first two categories and will review them briefly here. Accumulated other comprehensive income is a new concept that we will discuss in more detail later in this chapter and the next one.

Contributed Capital

Within contributed capital, two classifications are recognized:

1. **Share capital.**   This category consists of preferred and common shares. Because of the additional rights they give, preferred shares are shown before common shares. Information about the legal capital, number of shares authorized, number of shares issued, and any particular share preferences (e.g., cumulative) is reported for each class of shares. Note also that any stock dividends distributable are also reported under share capital if they exist at year end.
2. **Additional contributed capital.**   This category includes amounts contributed from re-acquiring and retiring shares. Other situations not discussed in this textbook can also result in additional contributed capital. If a company has a variety of sources of additional contributed capital, it is important to distinguish each one by source. For many companies, however, there is no additional contributed capital.

Retained Earnings

Retained earnings in the balance sheet are derived from the statement of retained earnings. Recall that it is only the end-of-period balance of retained earnings that is presented in the shareholders' equity section of the balance sheet, not the detailed changes that are presented in the statement of retained earnings. Notes to the financial statements are required to explain any restricted retained earnings and any dividends that may be in arrears.

Retained Earnings is a shareholders' equity account whose normal balance is a credit. If a deficit (debit balance) exists, it is reported as a deduction from shareholders' equity, rather than as the usual addition.

Accumulated Other Comprehensive Income

Most revenues, expenses, gains, and losses are included in net earnings. However, certain gains and losses bypass net earnings and are recorded as direct adjustments to shareholders' equity. **Comprehensive income** includes all changes in shareholders' equity during a period except for changes that result from the sale or repurchase of shares or from the payment of dividends. This means that it includes (1) the revenues, expenses, gains, and losses included in net earnings, *and* (2) the gains and losses that bypass net earnings but affect shareholders' equity. This latter category is referred to as "other comprehensive income."

There are several examples of other comprehensive income. One example, that we will learn about in more detail in the next chapter, is unrealized gains and losses on certain types of investments. If a company has debt or equity securities available for sale, they must be adjusted up or down to their market value at the end of each accounting period. This results in an unrealized gain or loss. We say "unrealized" to distinguish it from the "realized" gains and losses that occur when the investment is actually sold.

Of course, not all companies will have examples of other comprehensive income. However, if they do, they must report comprehensive income separately in a statement of comprehensive income or another acceptable format, and as a separate component of shareholders' equity.

Reporting other comprehensive income separately from net earnings and retained earnings is done for two important reasons: (1) it protects earnings from sudden changes that would simply be caused by fluctuations in market value, and (2) it informs the financial statement user of the gain or loss that would have occurred if the securities had actually been sold at year end.

Comprehensive income is a recent concept in Canada, although it has been used in the United States and internationally for many years. These new rules are part of the standards harmonization efforts we learned about in Chapter 2. They are mandatory for interim and annual financial statements related to any fiscal year beginning on or after October 1, 2006, although earlier adoption was permitted.

Presentation

Research in Motion reports common shares, retained earnings, and accumulated other comprehensive income in the shareholders' equity section of its balance sheet, as shown in Illustration 11-5.

Illustration 11-5 ◀

RIM shareholders' equity section

RESEARCH IN MOTION LIMITED
Balance Sheet (partial)
February 28, 2004
(in U.S. thousands)

	2004	2003
Shareholders' equity		
Capital stock		
Authorized—unlimited number of non-voting, cumulative, redeemable, retractable preferred shares; unlimited number of non-voting, redeemable, retractable Class A common shares and unlimited number of voting common shares		
Issued—92,415,066 common shares (2003—77,172,597)	$1,829,388	$874,377
Retained earnings (accumulated deficit)	(119,206)	(177,240)
Accumulated other comprehensive income	11,480	7,597
	$1,721,662	$704,734

Research in Motion has an unlimited number of preferred and common shares authorized. Two different classes of common shares are authorized to be issued—non-voting and voting. Although some companies have what is called a dual-common-share structure (shares that vote and some that do not), non-voting common shares are unusual. There has been significant pressure recently for companies to eliminate dual-share structures. Regardless, Research in Motion has no preferred shares or non-voting common shares issued. Only voting common shares have been issued: 92,415,066 at February 28, 2004.

RIM reported a deficit in both years, which is deducted from shareholders' equity as indicated earlier in this section. RIM also reported accumulated other comprehensive income due to net unrealized gains on its investments. Note that comprehensive income is identified as *accumulated* other comprehensive income because it is a balance sheet account that builds on prior period balances, just as other balance sheet accounts do.

Cash Flow Statement

The balance sheet presents the balances of a company's shareholders' equity accounts at a point in time. Information about cash inflows and outflows during the year that result from equity transactions is reported in the financing activities section of the cash flow statement. Illustration 11-6 presents the cash flows from financing activities from RIM's cash flow statement.

Illustration 11-6 ◀

RIM's cash flow statement

RESEARCH IN MOTION LIMITED
Cash Flow Statement (partial)
Year Ended February 28, 2004
(in U.S. thousands)

	2004	2003
Cash flows from financing activities		
Issuance of share capital and warrants	$994,640	$ 1,155
Financing costs	(39,629)	–
Buyback of common shares	–	(24,502)
Repayment of long-term debt	(6,130)	(614)
	$948,881	$(23,961)

From the equity-related information presented in the financing activities section of the cash flow statement, we learn that the company issued a significant amount of new shares in 2004. As mentioned in the feature story, RIM raised more than U.S. $905.2 million by issuing 12.1 million shares in January 2004. The remainder came from the issue of stock options and warrants: these are special rights to purchase shares that are discussed in intermediate accounting courses. Note that there were financing costs related to this share issue. We also learn from the above information that in 2003 the company's repurchase of shares exceeded its issues of new shares. Note that no dividends were paid.

BEFORE YOU GO ON . . .

▶Review It

1. Identify the classifications within the shareholders' equity section of a balance sheet.
2. Why is accumulated other comprehensive income reported separately from retained earnings?
3. Where are shareholders' equity transactions reported in the cash flow statement?

Measuring Corporate Performance

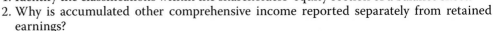

study objective 5

Evaluate dividend and earnings performance.

Investors are interested in both a company's dividend record and its earnings performance. Although they are often parallel, sometimes they are not. Thus, each item should be investigated separately.

Dividend Record

One way that companies reward investors for their investment is to pay them dividends. The **payout ratio** measures the percentage of earnings distributed as cash dividends. It is calculated by dividing the cash dividends by net earnings.

We are unable to calculate a payout ratio for RIM because it does not pay dividends. Companies that have high growth rates like RIM are usually characterized by low payout ratios because they reinvest most of their net earnings in the business. Thus, no, or a low, payout ratio is not necessarily bad news. However, low dividend payments, or a cut in dividend payments, might also signal that a company has liquidity or solvency problems and is trying to free up cash by not paying dividends. In other words, the reason for low dividend payments should always be investigated and understood.

To illustrate the calculation of the payout ratio, we will use the Bank of Montreal (BMO). BMO pays dividends on both its preferred and common shares. We will look at the payout ratios for its common shares for the years ended October 31, 2004 and 2003. In this particular case, since we are calculating the payout ratio for only the common shares, we use **net earnings available to common shareholders** rather than net earnings. Net earnings available to common shareholders are calculated by subtracting any preferred dividends from net earnings. This is done because preferred shareholders have a preferential right to receive this dividend before the common shareholders can share in any remaining amounts.

The following selected information (in millions, except for share price) is used in the calculation of the payout ratio shown in Illustration 11-7:

	2004	2003
Net earnings	$2,351	$1,825
Dividends—common shares	797	666
—preferred shares	76	82
Dividends per common share	$1.59	$1.34
Common share price	$57.55	$49.33

Illustration 11-7 ◄

BMO payout ratio

$$\text{PAYOUT RATIO} = \frac{\text{CASH DIVIDENDS}}{\text{NET EARNINGS}}$$		
(in millions)	2004	2003
Payout ratio	$\frac{\$797}{\$2{,}351 - \$76} = 35.0\%$	$\frac{\$666}{\$1{,}825 - \$82} = 38.2\%$
Industry average	40.5%	34.8%

Banks traditionally have high payout ratios. In 2004, BMO paid 35 percent of its earnings back to its common shareholders, a decline from 2003 when it paid 38.2 percent. Its payout ratio fell below that of the industry in 2004, although it exceeded the industry payout ratio in 2003. It is actually difficult to compare a specific company's payout ratio to industry averages because so many factors affect a company's dividend policy.

Another dividend measure that interests shareholders is the dividend yield. You may recall that earlier in the chapter the dividend yield was mentioned when we looked at stock market information presented for RIM. The **dividend yield** is calculated by dividing the dividend per share by the market price per share as shown in Illustration 11-8.

Illustration 11-8 ◄

BMO dividend yield

$$\text{DIVIDEND YIELD} = \frac{\text{DIVIDEND PER SHARE}}{\text{MARKET PRICE PER SHARE}}$$		
(in millions)	2004	2003
Dividend yield	$\frac{\$1.59}{\$57.55} = 2.8\%$	$\frac{\$1.34}{\$49.33} = 2.7\%$
Industry average	3.1%	3.0%

The dividend yield is a measure of the earnings generated by each share for the shareholder, based on the market price of the shares. Mature companies like BMO tend to have relatively higher dividend yields. BMO's dividend yield was 2.8 percent at the end of 2004 and 2.7 percent at the end of 2003, lower than that of the industry but following the same general trend year-to-year. You will note that both BMO's share price and its dividend per share increased in 2004. Share prices often follow dividend changes. That is why the dividend yield is often reviewed together with the price-earnings ratio, as mentioned earlier in the chapter.

Illustration 11-9 shows the top five companies in terms of dividend yield in Canada in 2004.

Illustration 11-9 ◄

Highest dividend yields

Rank	Company	Dividend Yield (%)
1	First Capital Realty	6.9
2	Trizec Canada	6.3
3	TransAlta	5.5
4	Rothmans	5.4
5	Emera	4.8

Earnings Performance

The earnings performance of a company is measured in several different ways. In an earlier chapter, we learned about the earnings per share ratio. In this section, we will revisit the calculation of this ratio and introduce a new return ratio, the return on common shareholders' equity.

Earnings per Share

You will recall that we learned how to calculate earnings per share in Chapter 2. In that chapter, the formula for earnings per share was presented as shown in Illustration 11-10.

Illustration 11-10 ▶

Earnings per share formula

Net Earnings Available to Common Shareholders	÷	Weighted Average Number of Common Shares	=	Earnings per Share

At that time, we gave the information for you to calculate the earnings per share and said that you would learn how to calculate the numerator (net earnings available to common shareholders) and the denominator (weighted average number of common shares) in Chapter 11. As we learned above, the net earnings available to the common shareholders used in the numerator of this calculation is easily determined by deducting any preferred dividends from net earnings. The weighted average number of common shares used in the denominator requires more explanation.

You will recall that whenever we calculate a ratio with a period figure (e.g., net earnings) and an end-of-period figure (e.g., the number of common shares), we always average the end-of-period figure so that the numerator and denominator in the calculation are for the same period of time. However, we do not use a straight average in the calculation of the number of common shares as we do in some other ratio calculations. For example, we do not take the beginning and ending balances of the number of common shares, add them together, and divide the result by two.

Instead, we use a **weighted average number of common shares** as this considers the impact of shares issued at different times throughout the year. This is done because the issue of shares changes the amount of net assets on which earnings can be generated. Consequently, shares issued or purchased during each current period must be weighted by the fraction of the year (or period) that they have been issued. If there is no change in the number of common shares issued during the year, the weighted average number of shares will be the same as the ending balance. If new shares are issued throughout the year, then these shares are adjusted for the fraction of the year they are outstanding to determine the weighted average number of shares.

To illustrate the calculation of the weighted average number of common shares, assume that a company had 100,000 common shares on January 1, and issued an additional 10,000 shares on October 1. The weighted average number of shares for the year would be calculated as follows:

Date	Actual Number		Weighted Average
Jan. 1	100,000	$\times\ ^{12}/_{12} =$	100,000
Oct. 1	10,000	$\times\ ^{3}/_{12} =$	2,500
	110,000		102,500

As illustrated, 110,000 shares were actually issued by the end of the year. Of these, 100,000 were outstanding for the full year and are allocated a full weight, or 12 months of 12 months. The other 10,000 shares have only been outstanding for three months (from October 1 to December 31) and are weighted for $^{3}/_{12}$ of the year, to result in 2,500 weighted shares. In total, the company's weighted average number of shares is 102,500 for the year. In the next calendar year, the 110,000 shares would receive full weight (unless some of these shares are repurchased) because all 110,000 shares would be outstanding for the entire year.

Calculating the weighted average number of shares becomes more complicated again when stock dividends and splits are issued. This topic, and more information about other types of earnings per share calculations, is presented in intermediate accounting courses.

Return on Equity

A widely used ratio that measures profitability from the common shareholders' viewpoint is the **return on common shareholders' equity**. This ratio shows how many dollars were earned for each dollar invested by common shareholders. It is calculated by dividing net earnings available to common shareholders by average common shareholders' equity. You will recall that the net earnings available to common shareholders is net earnings less any preferred dividends. Common shareholders' equity is total shareholders' equity less the legal capital of any preferred shares.

We can calculate a return on common shareholders' equity for Research in Motion using the information (in U.S. thousands) presented below. In RIM's particular case, its common shareholders' equity is the same as its total shareholders' equity since it does not have any preferred shares.

	2004	2003	2002
Net earnings (loss)	$ 51,829	$(148,857)	$ (28,479)
Shareholders' equity	1,721,622	704,734	948,157

RIM's return on common shareholders' equity ratios are calculated for 2004 and 2003 in Illustration 11-11.

Illustration 11-11 ◄

RIM return on common shareholders' equity

RETURN ON COMMON SHAREHOLDERS' EQUITY =	NET EARNINGS AVAILABLE TO COMMON SHAREHOLDERS / AVERAGE COMMON SHAREHOLDERS' EQUITY	
(in U.S. thousands)	**2004**	**2003**
Return on common shareholders' equity	$\dfrac{\$51,829 - \$0}{(\$1,721,622 + \$704,734) \div 2} = 4.3\%$	$\dfrac{\$(148,857) - \$0}{(\$704,734 + \$948,157) \div 2} = (18.0\%)$
Industry average	1.5%	(48.0%)

In 2004, RIM's return on common shareholders' equity was a respectable 4.3 percent, much higher than the industry average. Its return in 2003 was negative, which is really not very meaningful. The year 2003 was dismal for the whole industry.

Return on equity is a widely published figure. Recently, the highest return on equity among Canada's top 500 corporations was reported by A.W.A.R.D. Wholesale & Retail Distributors Ltd.—182 percent.

BEFORE YOU GO ON . . .

►Review It

1. What measures can be used to evaluate a company's dividend record, and how are they calculated?
2. Why are net earnings available to common shareholders not always the same as net earnings?
3. How is the weighted average number of common shares calculated?
4. How is the return on common shareholders' equity calculated?

►Do It

The Shoten Corporation reported net earnings of $249,750 for the year ended October 31, 2006. The shareholders' equity section of its balance sheet reported 3,000 $2 cumulative preferred shares issued and 50,000 common shares issued. Of the common shares, 40,000 had been outstanding since the beginning of year, 15,000 shares were issued on March 1, and 5,000 shares were repurchased on August 1. Calculate Shoten's earnings per share.

Action Plan

• Subtract any preferred dividends from net earnings to determine the earnings available for common shareholders.

- Adjust the shares for the fraction of the year outstanding to determine the weighted average number of common shares.
- Divide the earnings available for common shareholders by the weighted average number of common shares to calculate earnings per share.

Solution

Weighted average number of common shares:

Date	Actual Number		Weighted Average
Nov. 1	40,000	$\times$ $^{12}/_{12}$ =	40,000
Mar. 1	15,000	$\times$ $^{8}/_{12}$ =	10,000
Aug. 1	(5,000)	$\times$ $^{3}/_{12}$ =	(1,250)
	50,000		48,750

Earnings per share: $\dfrac{\$249{,}750 - \$6{,}000\ (3{,}000 \times \$2)}{48{,}750} = \$5$

Decision Toolkit

Decision Checkpoints	Info Needed for Decision	Tools to Use for Decision	How to Evaluate Results
What portion of its earnings does the company pay out in dividends?	Net earnings and total cash dividends	Payout ratio = $\dfrac{\text{Cash dividends}}{\text{Net earnings}}$	A low ratio suggests that the company is retaining its earnings for investment in future growth.
What percentage of the share price is the company paying in dividends?	Dividends and market price, expressed on a per share basis	Dividend yield = $\dfrac{\text{Dividends per share}}{\text{Market price per share}}$	A high dividend yield is considered desirable for investors. It also means that the company is paying out its earnings rather than retaining them.
What is the company's return on its common shareholders' investment?	Earnings available to common shareholders and average common shareholders' equity	Return on common shareholders' equity = $\dfrac{\text{Net earnings} - \text{Preferred share dividends}}{\text{Average common shareholders' equity}}$	A high measure suggests a strong earnings performance from the common shareholders' perspective.

Using the Decision Toolkit

palmOne, Inc. is RIM's closest competitor. Both palmOne and RIM are leading providers of wireless handheld computers. The following selected information (in U.S. thousands, except share data) is available for palmOne. Note that palmOne has no preferred shares.

	2004	2003	2002
Net earnings (loss)	$(21,849)	$(442,582)	$(82,168)
Shareholders' equity	$491,534	$255,786	$690,848
Proceeds from issue of common shares	$56,447	$2,477	$3,288
Weighted average number of common shares	84,035	30,778	36,309
Share price	$21.23	$8.09	$21.48

Instructions

(a) Calculate the earnings per share, price-earnings ratio, and return on common shareholders' equity for palmOne for 2004 and 2003. Contrast palmOne's earnings performance with that of RIM, which is given in the chapter. RIM's earnings per share was $0.33 in 2004 and $(0.96) in 2003. Its price-earnings ratio was 150 times in 2004.

As RIM's earnings per share was negative in 2003, its P-E ratio cannot be calculated for that year.

(b) Both companies, palmOne and RIM, had a large share issue in 2004. Why do you suppose investors were interested in purchasing shares of these companies, given their dismal earnings performance?

Solution

(a)

	2004	2003
Earnings (loss) per share	$\dfrac{\$(21,849) - \$0}{84,035} = \$(0.26)$	$\dfrac{\$(442,582) - \$0}{30,778} = \$(14.38)$
Price-earnings ratio	n/a	n/a
Return on common shareholders' equity	$\dfrac{\$(21,849) - \$0}{(\$491,534 + \$255,786) \div 2} = (5.8)\%$	$\dfrac{\$(442,582) - \$0}{(\$255,786 + \$690,848) \div 2} = (93.5)\%$

RIM's earnings per share was at least positive in 2004, while palmOne's continued to show negative values in each year. Nonetheless, palmOne's loss per share did improve in 2004 to $0.26 from a loss per share of $14.38 in 2003. The price-earnings ratio is not meaningful, given the loss per share, and could not be calculated for palmOne.

RIM's return on common shareholders' equity was also positive in 2004 at 4.3 percent—much higher than palmOne's negative 5.8 percent. However, similar to its loss per share, palmOne's return on equity has improved significantly in 2004.

(b) Perhaps surprisingly, despite RIM's small earnings per share value of $0.33 (positive for the first time in 2004), investors are still willing to pay 150 times earnings to purchase RIM's shares. Many would say that these shares are overpriced. Even palmOne's shares sold at $21.23 per share despite continuing, although lesser, losses. Investors purchase shares in companies like RIM and palmOne not for the dividend income (neither company pays dividends) but for future profitable resale. Investors believe in both companies' products and are counting on their future profitability.

the navigator

Summary of Study Objectives

1. **Identify and discuss the major characteristics of a corporation and its shares.** The major characteristics of a corporation are separate legal existence, limited liability of shareholders, transferable ownership rights, the ability to acquire capital, continuous life, corporation management, government regulations, and corporate income taxes.

Companies issue shares for sale to the public. After the initial share offering, the shares trade among investors and do not affect the company's financial position. A company can also reacquire its own shares from investors, but it must then cancel the shares.

2. **Record share transactions.** When no par value shares are issued for cash, the entire proceeds from the issue become legal capital and are credited to the Preferred Shares or Common Shares account, depending on what class of shares is issued. Preferred shares have contractual provisions that give them priority over common shares in certain areas. Typically, preferred shareholders have a preference over (a) dividends and (b) assets in the event of liquidation. However, only common shares have voting rights.

When shares are reacquired, the average cost is debited to the shares account. If the shares are reacquired at a price below the average cost, the difference is credited to a contributed capital account. If the shares are reacquired at a price above the average cost, the difference is debited first to the Contributed Capital account if it has a balance, and secondly to the Retained Earnings account.

3. **Prepare the entries for cash dividends, stock dividends, and stock splits, and understand their financial impact.** Entries for both cash and stock dividends are required at the declaration date and the payment or distribution date. There is no entry (other than a memo entry) for a stock split. Cash dividends reduce assets (cash) and shareholders' equity (retained earnings). Stock dividends increase common shares and decrease retained earnings but do not affect assets, liabilities, or shareholders' equity in total. Stock splits also have no impact on assets, liabilities, or shareholders' equity. The number of shares increases with both stock dividends and stock splits.

4. *Indicate how shareholders' equity is presented in the financial statements.* In the shareholders' equity section of the balance sheet, share capital, retained earnings, and accumulated other comprehensive income are reported separately. If additional contributed capital exists, then the caption "Contributed capital" is used for share capital (preferred and common shares) and additional contributed capital that may have been created from the reacquisition of shares or from other sources. Cash inflows and outflows for the issue or reacquisition of shares, or a payment of dividends, are reported in the financing section of the cash flow statement.

Notes to the financial statements explain restrictions on retained earnings, and dividends in arrears, if there are any.

5. *Evaluate dividend and earnings performance.* A company's dividend record can be evaluated by looking at what percentage of net earnings it chooses to pay out in dividends, as measured by the dividend payout ratio (dividends divided by net earnings) and the dividend yield (dividends per share divided by the share price). Earnings performance is measured with the return on common shareholders' equity ratio (earnings available to common shareholders divided by average common shareholders' equity).

Decision Toolkit—A Summary

Decision Checkpoints	Info Needed for Decision	Tools to Use for Decision	How to Evaluate Results
Should the company incorporate?	Capital needs, growth expectations, type of business, tax status	Corporations have limited liability, easier capital-raising ability, and professional managers. They may suffer from additional government regulations and separation of ownership from management. Income taxes may be higher or lower for a corporation.	Carefully weigh the costs and benefits in light of the particular circumstances.
What portion of its earnings does the company pay out in dividends?	Net earnings and total cash dividends	$$\text{Payout ratio} = \frac{\text{Cash dividends}}{\text{Net earnings}}$$	A low ratio suggests that the company is retaining its earnings for investment in future growth.
What percentage of the share price is the company paying in dividends?	Dividends and market price, expressed on a per share basis	$$\frac{\text{Dividend}}{\text{yield}} = \frac{\text{Dividends per share}}{\text{Market price per share}}$$	A high dividend yield is considered desirable for investors. It also means that the company is paying out its earnings rather than retaining them.
What is the company's return on its common shareholders' investment?	Earnings available to common shareholders and average common shareholders' equity	$$\frac{\text{Return on}}{\text{common}} = \frac{\text{Net earnings} - \text{Preferred share dividends}}{\text{Average common shareholders' equity}}$$	A high measure suggests a strong earnings performance from the common shareholders' perspective.

**Analysis Tools
(Decision Toolkit Summaries)**

Glossary

Authorized shares The amount of share capital that a corporation is authorized to sell. The amount may be unlimited or specified. (p. 517)

Cash dividend A pro rata (proportional) distribution of cash to shareholders. (p. 524)

Comprehensive income All changes in shareholders' equity during a period except those changes resulting from the sale or repurchase of shares, or from the payment of dividends. Comprehensive income includes (1) the revenues, expenses, gains, and losses included in net earnings, *and* (2) the gains and losses that bypass net earnings but affect shareholders' equity. (p. 530)

Contributed capital The total amount contributed by shareholders, or reacquired from them, in exchange for share capital. (p. 519)

Convertible preferred shares Preferred shares that the shareholder can convert into common shares at a specified ratio. (p. 522)

Corporation A company organized as a separate legal entity, with most of the rights and privileges of a person. Shares are evidence of ownership. (p. 514)

Cumulative dividend A feature of preferred shares that entitles the shareholder to receive current and unpaid prior-year dividends before common shareholders receive any dividends. (p. 521)

Declaration date The date the board of directors formally declares (approves) a dividend and announces it to shareholders. (p. 525)

Dividend A distribution of cash or shares by a corporation to its shareholders on a pro rata (proportional) basis. (p. 524)

Dividends in arrears Preferred dividends that were not declared during a period. (p. 522)

Dividend yield A measure of the percentage of the share price that is paid in dividends. It is calculated by dividing dividends per share by the share price. (p. 533)

Financial instrument A contract that creates a financial instrument for one company and a financial liability or equity instrument for another company. (p. 522)

Initial public offering (IPO) The initial offering of a corporation's shares to the public. (p. 518)

Issued shares The portion of authorized shares that has been sold. (p. 517)

Legal capital The amount per share that must be retained in the business for the protection of corporate creditors. (p. 518)

Net earnings available to common shareholders Net earnings less the annual preferred dividend. (p. 532)

Noncumulative Preferred shares that are entitled to the current dividend, but not to any unpaid amounts from prior years. (p. 521)

No par value shares Share capital that has not been pre-assigned a legal capital value. The total proceeds from the sale of no par value shares becomes the legal capital. (p. 518)

Payment date The date dividend cheques are mailed to shareholders. (p. 525)

Payout ratio A measure of the percentage of earnings distributed in the form of cash dividends to common shareholders. It is calculated by dividing cash dividends by net earnings. (p. 532)

Preferred shares Share capital that has contractual preferences over common shares in certain areas. (p. 521)

Record date The date when ownership of shares is determined for dividend purposes. (p. 525)

Redeemable (callable) preferred shares Preferred shares that grant the issuer the right to purchase the shares from shareholders at specified future dates and prices. (p. 522)

Retained earnings restrictions Circumstances that make a portion of retained earnings currently unavailable for dividends. (p. 528)

Retractable preferred shares Preferred shares that grant the shareholder the right to redeem the shares at specified future dates and prices. (p. 522)

Return on common shareholders' equity A measure of profitability from the shareholders' point of view. It is calculated by dividing net earnings minus preferred dividends by average common shareholders' equity. (p. 534)

Share capital The amount paid to the corporation by shareholders in exchange for shares of ownership. It can consist of preferred and common shares. (p. 519)

Stock dividend A pro rata (proportional) distribution of the corporation's own shares to shareholders. (p. 526)

Stock split The issue of additional shares to shareholders accompanied by a reduction in the legal capital per share. (p. 527)

Weighted average number of common shares A weighted average of the number of common shares outstanding during the year. Shares issued or purchased during the year are weighted by the fraction of the year for which they have been outstanding. (p. 534)

Demonstration Problem

The Rolman Corporation is authorized to issue an unlimited number of no par value common shares and 100,000 no par value $6 cumulative preferred shares. In its first year, the company has the following share transactions:

Jan. 10 Issued 400,000 common shares at $8 per share.
July 1 Issued 20,000 preferred shares at $50 per share.
Sept. 1 Declared a 5% stock dividend to common shareholders of record on September 15, distributable September 30. The market value of the common shares on this date was $10 per share.
Nov. 1 Reacquired 5,000 preferred shares at $40 per share.
Dec. 24 Declared the preferred cash dividend to shareholders of record on January 15, payable January 31.

Instructions

(a) Journalize the transactions.
(b) Prepare the shareholders' equity section of the balance sheet assuming the company had net earnings of $392,000 for the year ended December 31, 2006.

Action Plan

- Keep a running total of the number of shares issued to date.
- Apply the stock dividend percentage to the number of common shares issued. Multiply the new shares to be issued by the market value of the shares.
- Record the reacquisition of shares at the average cost.
- Note that the preferred dividend rate is an annual rate. Adjust for any partial periods.
- Disclose the share details in the shareholders' equity section of the balance sheet.
- Recall that the Stock Dividends Distributable account is not a liability.

Solution to Demonstration Problem

(a)

Date	Account	Debit	Credit
Jan. 10	Cash (400,000 × $8)	3,200,000	
	Common Shares		3,200,000
	(To record issue of 400,000 common shares)		
July 1	Cash (20,000 × $50)	1,000,000	
	Preferred Shares		1,000,000
	(To record issue of 20,000 preferred shares)		
Sept. 1	Stock Dividends (400,000 × 5% = 20,000 × $10)	200,000	
	Stock Dividends Distributable		200,000
	(To record declaration of 5% stock dividend)		
Sept. 30	Stock Dividends Distributable	200,000	
	Common Shares		200,000
	(To record issue of 20,000 common shares in a 5% stock dividend)		
Nov. 1	Preferred Shares (5,000 × $50)	250,000	
	Cash (5,000 × $40)		200,000
	Contributed Capital—Reacquisition of Preferred Shares		50,000
	(To record reacquisition of 5,000 preferred shares at an average cost of $50 [$1,000,000 ÷ 20,000] per share)		
Dec. 24	Cash Dividends—Preferred		
	(20,000 − 5,000 = 15,000 × $6 × $6/_{12}$)	45,000	
	Dividends Payable		45,000
	(To record declaration of semi-annual preferred cash dividend)		

(b)

ROLMAN CORPORATION		
Balance Sheet (partial)		
December 31, 2006		

Shareholders' equity
  Contributed capital
    Share capital

Preferred shares, 100,000 no par value $6 cumulative authorized, 15,000[a] shares issued	$ 750,000[b]	
Common shares, unlimited number of no par value shares authorized, 420,000[c] shares issued	3,400,000[d]	$4,150,000
Additional contributed capital		
Contributed capital—reacquisition of preferred shares		50,000
Total contributed capital		4,200,000
Retained earnings		147,000[e]
Total shareholders' equity		$4,347,000

Calculations:
[a] 20,000 − 5,000 = 15,000
[b] $1,000,000 − $250,000 = $750,000
[c] 400,000 + 20,000 = 420,000
[d] $3,200,000 + $200,000 = $3,400,000
[e] $392,000 − $200,000 − $45,000 = $147,000

the navigator

www.wiley.com/canada/kimmel

Self-Study Questions

Answers are at the end of the chapter.

(SO 1) 1. Which of these is *not* a major advantage of a corporation?
  (a) Separate legal existence
  (b) Continuous life
  (c) Government regulations
  (d) Transferable ownership rights

(SO 1) 2. The Saint Simeon Corporation has 100,000 common shares authorized and 75,000 common shares issued. How many more common shares can Saint Simeon sell?
  (a) 0   (c) 75,000
  (b) 25,000   (d) 100,000

(SO 2) 3. ABC Corporation issues 1,000 preferred shares at $12 per share. In recording the transaction, a credit is made to:
  (a) Equity Investments for $12,000.
  (b) Preferred Shares for $12,000.
  (c) Retained Earnings for $12,000.
  (d) Gain on Sale of Shares for $12,000.

(SO 2) 4. A company will buy back its own shares:
  (a) to force the share price up.
  (b) to force the share price down.
  (c) to increase the number of shares available for dividends.
  (d) to save cash.

(SO 3) 5. Entries for cash dividends are required on the:
  (a) declaration date and record date.
  (b) record date and payment date.
  (c) declaration date, record date, and payment date.
  (d) declaration date and payment date.

(SO 3) 6. Which of the following statements about stock dividends and stock splits is true?
  (a) A stock dividend and stock split increase total shareholders' equity.
  (b) A stock dividend and stock split decrease total shareholders' equity.
  (c) A stock dividend and stock split have no effect on total shareholders' equity.
  (d) A stock dividend and stock split have no effect on the number of common shares.

(SO 4) 7. Which of the following is *not* reported in a statement of retained earnings?
  (a) Cash dividend
  (b) Stock dividend
  (c) Net earnings
  (d) Accumulated other comprehensive income

(SO 4) 8. The cash received on issuing shares would be reported in what section of the cash flow statement?
  (a) Operating activities
  (b) Investing activities
  (c) Financing activities
  (d) It is not reported in the cash flow statement.

(SO 5) 9. If a company's net earnings are $50,000, its preferred dividends $15,000, its common share capital $500,000, its retained earnings $200,000, and its net sales $800,000, its return on common shareholders' equity is:

(a) 5%.
(b) 6.25%.
(c) 7.1%.
(d) 10%.

10. For the year ended June 30, 2006, Dupuis Inc. reported net earnings of $90,000. It had 5,000 common shares outstanding since the beginning of the year, July 1, 2005, and 2,000 shares issued on January 1, 2006. In addition, it paid dividends of $3 per share during the year and had a share price of $60. It had no preferred shares. What were its earnings per share and dividend yield? (SO 5)

(a) $12.86 and 5%
(b) $12.86 and 23%
(c) $15 and 5%
(d) $15 and 20%

Questions

(SO 1) 1. Corporations can be classified in a number of ways. For example, they may be classified as profit, not-for-profit, public, private, or as income trusts. Explain the difference between each of these types of corporations.

(SO 1) 2. Pat Kabza, a student, asks for your help in understanding the different corporation characteristics. Explain each of these to Pat: (a) separate legal existence, (b) limited liability of shareholders, (c) transferable ownership rights, (d) ability to acquire capital, (e) continuous life, (f) separation of management and ownership, (g) government regulations, and (h) income taxation.

(SO 1) 3. CoolBrands International Inc. markets frozen novelty and dessert products. Its share price was $4.03 recently. Earlier in the same year, its share price was $25.60. What kind of factors influence a change such as this in a company's share price? How do changes in share prices affect a company's financial position?

(SO 1) 4. What is legal capital? How is the value of the legal capital determined? Why is legal capital reported separately from retained earnings in the shareholders' equity section of the balance sheet?

(SO 1, 2) 5. What are the basic ownership rights of common shareholders? Of preferred shareholders?

(SO 1, 2) 6. Letterman Corporation is authorized to issue 100,000 common shares. During its first two years of operation, Letterman issued 60,000 shares to shareholders and reacquired and cancelled 7,000 of these shares. After these transactions, how many shares are authorized and issued?

(SO 2) 7. On November 1, 2004, the Canadian National Railway Company (CN) began a one-year share reacquisition program to repurchase up to 14 million, or five percent, of its shares. Immediately after the announcement about the repurchase plan, CN's share price increased by $1.33 to $65.90. Why did CN's share price likely increase?

(SO 2) 8. Explain how the accounting for the reacquisition of shares changes depending on whether the reacquisition price is greater or lower than average cost.

(SO 2) 9. Yip wonders why dividends in arrears are not reported as a liability in the balance sheet. "After all," he says, "the company will have to pay these dividends to its cumulative preferred shareholders at some future date."

Explain to Yip where dividends in arrears are presented in the financial statements and why.

10. What is the difference between cumulative and non-cumulative preferred shares? Redeemable and retractable preferred shares? (SO 2)

11. What three conditions must be met before a cash dividend is paid? (SO 3)

12. Contrast the effects of a cash dividend, stock dividend, and stock split on a company's (a) assets, (b) liabilities, (c) share capital, (d) retained earnings, and (e) number of shares. (SO 3)

13. George Karygiannis has heard that a company in which he owns shares is thinking of declaring either a cash dividend or a stock dividend. He is hoping that the company decides to pay a cash dividend, since he has heard that a stock dividend does not change anything. Is George right in thinking that it is better for shareholders to receive a cash dividend than a stock dividend? (SO 3)

14. Bella Corporation has 500,000 common shares authorized and 10,000 common shares issued when it announces a two-for-one split. Before the split, the shares had a market price of $140 per share. After the split, how many shares will be authorized and issued? What will be the approximate market price per share? (SO 3)

15. What is the purpose of a retained earnings restriction? How are retained earnings restrictions reported in the financial statements? (SO 3)

16. Indicate how each of the following should be reported in the shareholders' equity section of the balance sheet: (a) common shares, (b) preferred shares, (c) stock dividends distributable, (d) contributed capital—reacquisition of shares, (e) retained earnings, and (f) accumulated other comprehensive income. (SO 4)

17. Distinguish between share capital and additional contributed capital. Indicate how each is reported in the balance sheet. (SO 4)

18. What is comprehensive income? Why is comprehensive income reported separately from net earnings? (SO 4)

19. Explain where share transactions and dividend transactions are reported in the (a) balance sheet and (b) cash flow statement. (SO 4)

(SO 5) 20. 🔧 Indicate whether each of the following is generally considered favourable or unfavourable by a potential investor:
(a) A decrease in the payout ratio
(b) An increase in the dividend yield
(c) A decrease in the return on common shareholders' equity
(d) An increase in earnings per share

(SO 5) 21. 🔧 Coca-Cola recently reported dividends per share of U.S. $1.04 and a dividend yield of 2.3%. Pepsico reported dividends per share of U.S. $2.51 and a dividend yield of 1.7% for the same period. Which company had the higher share price?

22. In the calculation of earnings per share, why is the (SO 5) weighted average number of common shares used instead of the number of common shares at the end of the year?

23. Why do the earnings per share and return on common shareholders' equity ratios use net earnings available to common shareholders in their numerator rather than net earnings? (SO 5)

Brief Exercises

BE11–1 Nortel Networks' share price has dropped significantly over the last five years. For example, its share price was $124.50 in July 2000. In July 2005, it was $3.60. What is the impact of this drop in share price on (a) Nortel's financial position and (b) its shareholders' financial position?

Evaluate share price impact.
(SO 1)

BE11–2 On May 10, Armada Corporation issued 1,000 common shares for $15 per share. On June 15, Armada issued an additional 500 shares for $17 per share. On November 1, Armada issued 100 preferred shares for $50 per share. Journalize the share transactions.

Record issue of shares.
(SO 2)

BE11–3 On June 12, Dieppe Corporation issued 60,000 common shares for $300,000. On July 11, it issued an additional 15,000 common shares for $90,000. On November 28, it repurchased 25,000 shares for $100,000. Journalize the share transactions.

Record issue and reacquisition of shares.
(SO 2)

BE11–4 The Quebec-based international paper company Cascades Inc. repurchased 238,400 of its own common shares in 2002 and cancelled them. The share reacquisition resulted in a debit of $1 million to the Common Shares account and a debit of $3 million to the Retained Earnings account. How much did Cascades pay, on average, to reacquire its shares? What was the initial issue price of the shares, on average? Why do you think Cascades likely reacquired some of its own shares?

Discuss share reacquisition.
(SO 2)

BE11–5 The Seabee Corporation has 10,000 common shares. It declares a $0.50 per share cash dividend on November 1 to shareholders of record on December 1. The dividend is paid on December 31. Prepare the entries on the appropriate dates to record the cash dividend.

Record cash dividend.
(SO 3)

BE11–6 Satina Corporation has 100,000 common shares. It declares a 5% stock dividend on December 1, when the market value of the shares is $5, to shareholders of record on December 20. The dividend shares are issued on January 10. Prepare the entries on the appropriate dates to record the stock dividend.

Record stock dividend.
(SO 3)

BE11–7 The shareholders' equity section of Chew Corporation's balance sheet consists of 100,000 common shares for $1 million, and retained earnings of $400,000. A 10% stock dividend is declared when the market value per share is $8. Show the before-and-after effects of the dividend on (a) share capital, (b) retained earnings, (c) total shareholders' equity, and (d) the number of shares.

Analyze impact of stock dividend.
(SO 3)

BE11–8 In May 2005, Enbridge Inc. announced a two-for-one stock split. Immediately before the split, Enbridge had 174 million common shares trading at $64 per share. (a) How many shares will it have after the stock split? (b) What will be the most likely price of the shares after the stock split? (c) How would Enbridge record this stock split?

Analyze impact of stock split.
(SO 3)

BE11–9 Kaposi Corporation reported the following selected information at December 31, 2006: Common shares, no par value, unlimited number of shares authorized, 5,000 shares issued, $50,000; preferred shares, $8 cumulative, no par value, unlimited number of shares authorized, 800 shares issued, $20,000; contributed capital—reacquisition of common shares, $5,000; and retained earnings, $29,000. Prepare the shareholders' equity section of the balance sheet.

Prepare shareholders' equity section.
(SO 4)

BE11–10 Cameco Corporation reported the following selected information (in thousands) at December 31, 2004: unlimited number of preferred shares authorized and none issued; unlimited number of common shares authorized and 173,040 issued; common shares

Prepare shareholders' equity section with comprehensive income.
(SO 4)

$750,559; contributed capital $511,674; retained earnings $938,809; and accumulated other comprehensive loss $40,522. Prepare the shareholders' equity section of the balance sheet.

Evaluate dividend record.
(SO 5)

BE11–11   Paul Schwartz, president of Schwartz Corporation, believes that it is good practice to maintain a constant payout of dividends relative to earnings. Last year, net earnings were $600,000, and the corporation paid $60,000 in dividends. This year, due to some unusual circumstances, the corporation had net earnings of $2 million. Paul expects next year's net earnings to be about $700,000. What was Schwartz Corporation's payout ratio last year? If it is to maintain the same payout ratio, what amount of dividends would it pay this year? Is this a good idea—that is, what are the pros and cons of maintaining a constant payout ratio?

Calculate weighted average number of shares.
(SO 5)

BE11–12   Messier Inc. has 40,000 common shares on January 1, 2006. On April 1, 8,000 shares were repurchased. On August 31, 12,000 shares were issued. Calculate the number of common shares at December 31, 2006, and the weighted average number of common shares for 2006.

Calculate return on equity.
(SO 5)

BE11–13   Sleeman Breweries Ltd. reported the following selected information (in thousands) for the year ended January 1, 2005: net earnings, $14,426; beginning shareholders' equity, $103,800; and ending shareholders' equity, $121,784. Sleeman has no preferred shares. Calculate the return on common shareholders' equity..

Exercises

Interpret stock market listing.
(SO 1)

E11–1   Presented below is a recent stock market listing for Canadian Pacific Railway Limited (CP) common shares:

365-day		stock	sym	div	high/ bid	low/ ask	close	chg	vol 100s	yld	p/e ratio
high	low										
46.88	31.11	CP Railway	CP	0.60	45.99	44.53	44.53	−0.97	11845	1.4	15.0

Instructions

(a) What is the highest price CP's shares traded for during the last year? The lowest?
(b) What is the annual per share dividend paid on these shares?
(c) If you had purchased 1,000 common shares at CP's closing price of the day in the above listing, what would be the total cost of your share purchase?
(d) What was the closing price of CP's common shares on the previous day?
(e) How many CP common shares were sold on the trading day of the listing?
(f) What would be your likely motivation for purchasing these shares—future dividend income or future price increase? Explain.

Record issue of shares.
(SO 2)

E11–2   Santiago Corp. had the following share transactions during the year:

June 12 Issued 50,000 common shares for $5 per share.
July 11 Issued 1,000 preferred shares for $105 per share.
Oct. 1 Issued 10,000 common shares in exchange for land. The common shares had a market value of $6 per share on that date. The fair market value of the land was estimated to be $65,000.
Nov. 15 Issued 1,500 preferred shares for $100 per share.

Instructions

(a) Journalize the share transactions.
(b) Calculate the average cost for each of the common and preferred shares.

Record reacquisition of shares.
(SO 2)

E11–3   Enviro Corporation reported the following on its January 31, 2006, balance sheet: common shares, no par value, unlimited number of shares authorized, 35,000 shares issued, $122,500. On February 15, 2006, it reacquired 5,000 of these shares. This is the first time Enviro has reacquired any of its shares.

Instructions

(a) Journalize the reacquisition of the shares, assuming the company paid $14,500 to reacquire them.
(b) Repeat part (a), assuming instead that the company paid $18,750 to reacquire the shares.

E11–4 Moosonee Ltd. was incorporated on January 5, 2006, and is authorized to issue an unlimited number of common and preferred shares. The company had the following share transactions in its first month of operations:

Jan. 6 Issued 200,000 common shares for $1.50 per share.
      12 Issued 50,000 common shares for $1.75 per share.
      17 Issued 1,000 $7 cumulative preferred shares for $105 per share.
      18 Issued 1 million common shares for $2 per share.
      24 Reacquired 200,000 common shares for $1.95 per share.
      30 Reacquired 150,000 common shares for $1.80 per share.

Instructions

(a) Journalize the above transactions.
(b) What is the number of common shares remaining, and their average cost, at the end of January?

E11–5 On January 1, Tarow Corporation had 75,000 common shares. During the year, the following transactions occurred:

Apr.   1 Issued 5,000 common shares at $10 per share.
June 15 Declared a cash dividend of $0.25 per share to shareholders of record on June 30, payable on July 10.
July 10 Paid the $0.25 cash dividend.
Aug. 21 Declared a 5% stock dividend to shareholders of record on September 5, distributable on September 20. The market value of the shares was $12 at this time.
Dec.   1 Issued 3,000 common shares at $15 per share.
      15 Declared a cash dividend of $0.25 per share to shareholders of record on December 31, payable on January 10.

Instructions

(a) Journalize the above transactions.
(b) Explain where the (1) common shares, (2) dividends, (3) dividends payable, (4) cash received from the issue of common shares, and (5) cash paid for dividends would be reported in the December 31 financial statements.

E11–6 Kalyani Corporation has 100,000 $8 cumulative preferred shares issued. In its first year of operations, it paid $450,000 of dividends to its preferred shareholders. In its second year, the company paid dividends of $1.15 million to its preferred shareholders.

Instructions

(a) Calculate any dividends in arrears in years 1 and 2.
(b) Explain how dividends in arrears are reported in the financial statements.
(c) If the preferred shares were noncumulative rather than cumulative, how much dividend would the company likely have paid its preferred shareholders in year 2?
(d) Why do companies issue preferred shares in addition to common shares?

E11–7 Laine Inc. is considering following one of three courses of action: (1) paying a $1 cash dividend; (2) distributing a 5% stock dividend, or (3) effecting a two-for-one stock split. The current market price is $14 per share.

Instructions

Help Laine make its decision by completing the following chart (treat each possibility independently):

	Before Action	After Cash Dividend	After Stock Dividend	After Stock Split
Total assets	$1,250,000			
Total liabilities	$ 50,000			
Common shares	800,000			
Retained earnings	400,000			
Total shareholders' equity	1,200,000			
Total liabilities and shareholders' equity	$1,250,000			
Number of common shares	80,000			

Prepare correcting entries for
dividends and stock split.
(SO 3)

E11–8   Before preparing financial statements for the current year, the auditors for Koo Ltd. discovered the following errors in the accounts:

1. Koo has 10,000 $5 cumulative preferred shares issued. It paid the preferred shareholders a $25,000 cash dividend, which was recorded as a debit to Dividends Expense for $50,000, a credit to Cash for $25,000, and a credit to Dividends Payable of $25,000.
2. A 10% common stock dividend (1,000 shares) was declared when the market price per share was $5. The transaction was recorded by debiting Investment in Equity Securities for $5,000 and crediting Dividends Payable for $5,000. The shares have not yet been distributed.
3. A four-for-one stock split involving the issue of 400,000 new common shares in exchange for 100,000 old common shares was recorded as a debit to Cash for $2 million and a credit to Common Shares for $2 million. The market price per share was $5 on the date of the split.

Instructions

Prepare any correcting entries required.

Classify financial statement
accounts.
(SO 4)

E11–9   The general ledger of Val d'Or Corporation contains the following selected accounts and information:

1. Cash
2. Common shares
3. Unrealized gain on investments
4. Patents
5. Preferred shares
6. Retained earnings
7. Contributed capital
   —reacquisition of common shares
8. Dividends
9. Stock dividends distributable
10. Cash paid for dividends

Instructions

Using the table headings below, indicate whether or not each of the above accounts should be reported in the shareholders' equity section of the balance sheet. If yes, indicate whether the account should be reported as share capital, additional contributed capital, retained earnings, or accumulated other comprehensive income. If not, indicate in which financial statement (balance sheet, statement of earnings, or cash flow statement) and in which section the account should be reported. The first account has been done for you as an example.

		Shareholders' Equity				
	Share	Additional	Retained	Accumulated Other	Financial	
Account	Capital	Contributed Capital	Earnings	Comprehensive Income	Statement	Classification
1. Cash					Balance sheet	Current assets

Prepare shareholders' equity
section.
(SO 4)

E11–10   The following accounts appear in the ledger of Ozabal Inc. after the books are closed at December 31, 2006:

Common shares (no par value, unlimited number of shares authorized, 300,000 shares issued)	$300,000
Common stock dividends distributable	75,000
Preferred shares ($4 noncumulative, no par value, 100,000 shares authorized, 30,000 shares issued)	150,000
Contributed capital—reacquisition of common shares	25,000
Retained earnings	900,000

Instructions

Prepare the shareholders' equity section of Ozabal's balance sheet, assuming $100,000 of retained earnings is restricted for a plant expansion.

Prepare statement of retained
earnings and shareholders'
equity section.
(SO 4)

E11–11   Intrawest Corporation reported the following selected accounts and information (dollars in U.S. thousands), as at June 30, 2004:

Accumulated other comprehensive income (foreign currency translation adjustment)	$ 4,941
Common shares, unlimited number without par value authorized, 47,604,562 shares issued	460,534
Contributed capital	2,951
Dividends	5,706
Net earnings	59,949

Preferred shares, unlimited number without
 par value authorized, nil shares issued $ 0
Retained earnings, July 1, 2003   264,640

Instructions

Prepare a statement of retained earnings and the shareholders' equity section of the balance sheet for Intrawest.

E11–12   The following selected information (in U.S. dollars) is available for two competitors, Nike, Inc. and Reebok International Ltd.:

Evaluate dividend yield and price-earnings ratios. (SO 5)

	Nike	Reebok
Share price	$84.80	$41.70
Dividends per share	0.85	0.30
Earnings per share	4.32	3.12

Instructions

(a) Calculate the dividend yield and price-earnings ratios for each company.
(b) Which company do investors favour?

E11–13   Chinook Corporation reported net earnings of $343,125 for its November 30, 2006, year end. During the year, cash dividends of $75,000 were paid on the common shares and $45,000 on the preferred shares. The following changes in common shares occurred during the year:

Calculate earnings per share. (SO 5)

Dec. 1, 2005   The opening balance in the number of common shares was 60,000.
Feb. 28, 2006   Sold 10,000 common shares for $200,000 cash.
May 31, 2006   Reacquired 5,000 shares for $90,000 cash.
Nov. 1, 2006   Issued 15,000 common shares in exchange for land with a market value of $310,000.

Instructions

(a) Calculate the earnings available for the common shareholders.
(b) Calculate the weighted average number of common shares for the year.
(c) Calculate the earnings per share for the year.
(d) Why is it necessary to calculate a weighted average number of shares? Why not use the number of shares at the end of the year?

E11–14   Selected financial information (in millions, except per share information) is available for CIBC at October 31:

Evaluate corporate performance. (SO 5)

	2004	2003	2002
Total dividends paid to common shareholders	$781	$591	$577
(Per share)	$2.20	$1.64	$1.60
Total dividends paid to preferred shareholders	$208	$188	$161
Net earnings	$2,199	$2,063	$653
Weighted average number of common shares	356	360	361
Common shareholders' equity	$10,397	$10,421	$9,245
Price per common share	$73.90	$59.21	$38.75

Instructions

Calculate the dividend yield, payout, earnings per share, and return on common shareholders' equity ratios for the common shareholders for 2004 and 2003. Comment on your findings.

Problems: Set A

P11–1A   Remmers Corporation was organized on January 1, 2006. It is authorized to issue an unlimited number of $3 noncumulative no par value preferred shares and an unlimited number of no par value common shares. The following share transactions were completed during the company's first year of operations:

Record and post share transactions; prepare contributed capital section. (SO 2, 4)

Jan. 10   Issued 100,000 common shares for $2 per share.
Mar. 1   Issued 10,000 preferred shares for $42 per share.

May 1 Issued 75,000 common shares for $3 per share.
July 24 Issued 16,800 common shares for $60,000 cash and used equipment. The equipment originally cost $10,000. It now has a net book value of $4,000 and a market value of $5,000. The market value of the common shares was $4 per share on this date.
Sept. 1 Issued 5,000 common shares for $5 per share.
Nov. 1 Issued 2,000 preferred shares for $48 per share.
Dec. 12 Repurchased 50,000 common shares for $3 per share.

Instructions

(a) Journalize the above transactions.
(b) Open general ledger accounts and post to the shareholders' equity accounts.
(c) Prepare the contributed capital portion of the shareholders' equity section of the balance sheet at December 31, 2006.

Show impact of transactions on accounts.
(SO 2, 3, 4)

P11–2A   The following shareholders' equity accounts are reported by Talty Inc. on January 1, 2006:

Common shares (500,000 issued)	$4,000,000
Preferred shares ($6 cumulative, 4,000 issued)	600,000
Retained earnings	1,958,000
Accumulated other comprehensive income	25,000

The following selected transactions occurred during the year:

1. Issued 10,000 common shares for $10 per share.
2. Issued 500 common shares in exchange for equipment. The market value of the shares was $11 per share; of the equipment, $6,000.
3. Issued 1,000 preferred shares for $160 per share.
4. Reacquired 500 preferred shares for $150 each.
5. The annual preferred share dividend was declared and paid during the year.
6. Determined that the company had an unrealized loss on its investments of $5,000.

Instructions

For each of the above transactions, indicate its impact on the items in the table below. Indicate if the item will increase (I) or decrease (D), and by how much, or if it will not be affected (n/a). The first transaction has been done for you as an example.

				Shareholders' Equity			
	Assets	Liabilities	Preferred Shares	Common Shares	Other Contributed Capital	Retained Earnings	Accumulated Other Comprehensive Income
1.	$100,000	n/a	n/a	$100,000	n/a	n/a	n/a

Record and post equity transactions; prepare shareholders' equity section.
(SO 2, 3, 4)

P11–3A   Largent Corporation is authorized to issue 200,000 no par value $6 cumulative preferred shares and an unlimited number of no par value common shares. On January 1, 2006, the general ledger contained the following shareholders' equity accounts:

Preferred shares (5,000 shares issued)	$ 525,000
Common shares (70,000 shares issued)	1,050,000
Retained earnings	300,000

The following equity transactions occurred in 2006:

Jan. 10 Repurchased 20,000 common shares for $240,000.
Feb. 6 Issued 10,000 preferred shares for $1.1 million.
Apr. 14 Issued 40,000 common shares for $560,000.
May 29 Declared a semi-annual dividend to the preferred shareholders of record at June 12, payable July 1.
Aug. 22 Issued 10,000 common shares in exchange for a building. At the time of the exchange, the building was valued at $165,000 and the common shares at $150,000.
Nov. 29 Declared a semi-annual dividend to the preferred shareholders of record at December 12, payable January 1.
Dec. 31 Net earnings for the year were $582,000.

Instructions

(a) Journalize the 2006 transactions.
(b) Open general ledger accounts and post to the shareholders' equity accounts.
(c) Prepare the shareholders' equity section of the balance sheet at December 31, 2006.

P11–4A On December 31, 2005, Conway Ltd. had the following shareholders' equity accounts:

Record and post equity transactions; prepare shareholders' equity and financing activities sections.
(SO 2, 3, 4)

Common shares, no par value, unlimited number authorized, 1.5 million issued	$16,500,000
Retained earnings	900,000
Accumulated other comprehensive income	25,000

The following selected transactions occurred during 2006:

Jan. 2 Issued 100,000 no par value $6 noncumulative preferred shares at $110 per share.
Mar. 5 Declared the quarterly cash dividend to preferred shareholders of record on March 20, payable April 1.
Apr. 18 Issued 250,000 common shares at $13 per share.
June 5 Declared the quarterly cash dividend to preferred shareholders of record on June 20, payable July 1.
Sept. 5 Declared the quarterly cash dividend to preferred shareholders of record on September 20, payable October 1.
Dec. 15 Declared the quarterly cash dividend to preferred shareholders of record on December 20, payable January 1.
    31 Net earnings for the year were $3.6 million.

Instructions

(a) Journalize the 2006 transactions.
(b) Open general ledger accounts and post to the shareholders' equity accounts.
(c) Prepare the shareholders' equity section of the balance sheet at December 31.
(d) Prepare the financing activities section of the cash flow statement for the year.

P11–5A After the books have been closed at Robichaud Corporation on December 31, 2006, the general ledger contains the following shareholders' equity accounts:

Reproduce retained earnings account; prepare shareholders' equity section.
(SO 3, 4)

Preferred shares (10,000 shares issued)	$1,000,000
Common shares (420,000 shares issued)	3,700,000
Common stock dividends distributable	252,000
Retained earnings	3,558,000

A review of the accounting records reveals the following information:

1. Preferred shares are $5 noncumulative no par value shares. An unlimited number are authorized.
2. Common shares are no par value. An unlimited number are authorized.
3. The January 1 balance in Retained Earnings was $2.98 million.
4. On October 1, 100,000 common shares were sold for cash at $10 per share.
5. The preferred shareholders' dividend was declared and paid in cash in 2006. No dividends were paid to preferred shareholders in 2005.
6. On December 31, a 5% common stock dividend was declared on common shares when the market price per share was $12. The stock dividend is distributable on January 20.
7. Net earnings for the year were $880,000.
8. On December 31, the board of directors authorized a $125,000 restriction on retained earnings for a plant expansion.

Instructions

(a) Reproduce the Retained Earnings general ledger account for the year.
(b) Prepare the shareholders' equity section of the balance sheet at December 31, including any required note disclosure.

Compare impact of cash
dividend, stock dividend, and
stock split.
(SO 3)

P11–6A   The condensed balance sheet of Laporte Corporation reports the following amounts:

LAPORTE CORPORATION
Balance Sheet (partial)
June 30, 2006

Total assets		$15,500,000
Total liabilities		$5,500,000
Shareholders' equity		
Common shares, unlimited number authorized,		
400,000 issued	$2,000,000	
Retained earnings	8,000,000	10,000,000
Total liabilities and shareholders' equity		$15,500,000

Laporte wants to assess the impact of three possible alternatives on the corporation and its shareholders:

1. Payment of a $1.50 per share cash dividend.
2. Distribution of a 5% stock dividend. The market price of the common shares is currently $30 per share.
3. A two-for-one stock split.

Instructions

(a) Determine the impact on assets, liabilities, shareholders' equity (common shares and retained earnings), and the number of shares under each of the three alternatives for Laporte Corporation.
(b) Assume a Laporte shareholder currently owns 1,000 common shares for which she paid $28,000. What is the impact of each alternative for the shareholder? Which one is best for her?

Record and post dividend
transactions, prepare
shareholders' equity section, and
calculate ratios.
(SO 3, 4, 5)

P11–7A   On January 1, 2006, Wirth Corporation had these shareholders' equity accounts:

Common shares (no par value, unlimited number of	
shares authorized, 90,000 shares issued)	$1,100,000
Retained earnings	540,000

During the year, the following transactions occurred:

Jan. 15 Declared a $1 per share cash dividend to shareholders of record on January 31, payable February 15.
Apr. 15 Declared a 10% stock dividend to shareholders of record on April 30, distributable May 15. On April 15, the market price of each share was $15.
July   1 Effected a two-for-one stock split. The market price of each share was $20 immediately before the announcement of the split.
Dec. 31 Determined that net earnings for the year were $250,000.
      31 The market price of each share was $15 on this date.

Instructions

(a) Journalize the above transactions.
(b) Open general ledger accounts as required and post to the shareholders' equity accounts.
(c) Prepare the shareholders' equity section of the balance sheet at December 31.
(d) Calculate the dividend payout, dividend yield, and return on common shareholders' equity ratios.

Evaluate dividend policy.
(SO 5)

P11–8A   The following summary of the earnings per share (in U.S. dollars), price-earnings, payout, and dividend yield ratios is available for the five years ended January 31 for Bombardier Inc.:

	Earnings per Share	Price-Earnings Ratio	Payout Ratio	Dividend Yield
2001	$0.70	62.7 times	19.3%	0.67%
2002	0.27	29.0	66.7	1.07
2003	(0.47)	n/a	n/a	1.93
2004	(0.13)	n/a	n/a	2.07
2005	(0.06)	n/a	n/a	2.03

Instructions

(a) What are some possible reasons that Bombardier's dividend payout ratio jumped to 66.7% and its dividend yield ratio jumped to 1.07% in 2002? Note that payout ratios could not be calculated for the last three years because dividends cannot be meaningfully compared to net losses.

(b) Why do you think Bombardier's price-earnings ratio fell in 2002 even though its dividend yield increased? Note that the price-earnings ratios could not be calculated for the last three years because of the loss per share.

(c) If you were an investor looking for dividend income, would you be happy with Bombardier's dividend policy? Explain.

(d) If you were one of Bombardier's creditors, what would you think about the company continuing to pay dividends regardless of whether it reports net earnings or a net loss?

P11–9A Gualtieri Inc.'s shareholder's equity accounts were as follows at the beginning of the current fiscal year, August 1, 2005:

Calculate earnings per share. (SO 5)

$4 noncumulative preferred shares (25,000 shares issued)	$1,250,000
Common shares (350,000 shares issued)	3,750,000
Retained earnings	2,250,000
Total shareholders' equity	$7,250,000

During the year, the following selected transactions occurred:

Dec. 1 Issued 40,000 common shares for $12 per share.
Feb. 1 Reacquired 6,000 common shares for $10 per share.
June 20 Declared the annual preferred dividend to shareholders of record on July 10, payable on July 31.
July 31 Net earnings for the year ended July 31, 2006, were $1,025,000.

Instructions

(a) Calculate the weighted average number of common shares for the year.
(b) Calculate the earnings per share.
(c) Why is it important to use a weighted average number of shares in the calculation of earnings per share? Why not just use the number of shares issued at year end?

P11–10A The following selected information (in millions, except for per share information) is available for the Canadian National Railway Company (CN) for the year ended December 31:

Evaluate corporate performance. (SO 5)

	2004	2003
Weighted average number of common shares	285.1	287.8
Net earnings	$1,297	$734
Total common cash dividends (per share)	222 (0.78)	191 (0.67)
Total preferred cash dividends	0	0
Average common shareholders' equity	6,914	6,553.5
Price per common share	72.59	53.42

Industry averages were as follows:

	2004	2003
Payout ratio	20.8%	n/a
Dividend yield	0.9%	1.1%
Earnings per share	n/a	n/a
Price-earnings ratio	11.3 times	16.2 times
Return on common shareholders' equity	9.8%	(6.4%)

Instructions

(a) Calculate the following ratios for each fiscal year:
  1. Payout ratio   4. Price-earnings ratio
  2. Dividend yield   5. Return on common shareholders' equity
  3. Earnings per share

(b) Comment on the above ratios for 2004 in comparison to the prior year, and in comparison to the industry.

Evaluate corporate performance.
(SO 5)

P11–11A Selected ratios for two companies operating in the petroleum industry follow, along with the industry averages:

Ratio	Petro-Boost	World Oil	Industry Average
Profit margin	9.0%	8.4%	5.7%
Return on common shareholders' equity	15.1%	29.6%	18.1%
Return on assets	7.0%	13.4%	6.1%
Asset turnover	0.9 times	1.7 times	1.1 times
Earnings per share	$4.06	$4.38	n/a
Price-earnings ratio	14.2 times	17.1 times	11.8 times
Payout ratio	12.3%	11.9%	17.0%
Dividend yield	0.9%	0.7%	n/a

Instructions

(a) Compare the profitability of Petro-Boost to that of World Oil, and to the industry average. Which company is more profitable? Explain.

(b) You would like to invest in the shares of one of the two companies. Your goal is to have regular income from your investment that will help pay your tuition fees for the next few years. Which of the companies is a better choice for you? Explain.

(c) Assume that instead of looking for regular income, you are looking for growth in the share value so that you can resell the shares at a gain in the future. Now which of the two companies is better for you? Explain.

Problems: Set B

Record and post share transactions; prepare contributed capital section.
(SO 2, 4)

P11–1B Wetland Corporation was organized on June 1, 2006. It is authorized to issue an unlimited number of no par value $4 cumulative preferred shares and an unlimited number of no par value common shares. The following share transactions were completed during the company's first year of operations:

June 5 Issued 80,000 common shares for $4 per share.
Aug. 21 Issued 5,000 preferred shares for $115 per share.
Sept. 15 Issued 22,000 common shares in exchange for land. The asking price of the land was $100,000. The market value of the common shares was $4.25 per share on this date.
Nov. 20 Issued 78,000 common shares for $4.50 per share.
Jan. 12 Repurchased 80,000 common shares for $4 per share.
Mar. 9 Issued 10,000 common shares for $4.50 per share.
Apr. 16 Issued 2,000 preferred shares for $120 per share.

Instructions

(a) Journalize the above transactions.

(b) Open general ledger accounts and post to the shareholders' equity accounts.

(c) Prepare the contributed capital portion of the shareholders' equity section of the balance sheet at May 31, 2007.

Show impact of transactions on accounts.
(SO 2, 3, 4)

P11–2B The following shareholders' equity accounts are reported by Branch Inc. on January 1, 2006:

Common shares (150,000 issued)	$2,400,000
Preferred shares ($4 noncumulative, 5,000 issued)	350,000
Retained earnings	1,276,000
Accumulated other comprehensive income	15,000

The following selected transactions occurred during the year:

1. Issued 1,000 common shares for $18 per share.
2. Issued 100 preferred shares for $75 per share.
3. Reacquired 10,000 common shares for $20 per share.
4. Issued 1,000 common shares in exchange for land. The market value of each common share was $25; of the land, $23,500.
5. Determined that the company had an unrealized gain on its investments of $5,000.
6. Declared and paid the preferred shareholders a $2 per share dividend.

Instructions

For each of the above transactions, indicate its impact on the items in the table below. Indicate if the item will increase (I) or decrease (D), and by how much, or if it will not be affected (n/a). The first transaction has been done for you as an example.

| | | | Shareholders' Equity | | | |
| | | Preferred | Common | Other | Retained | Accumulated Other |
Assets	Liabilities	Shares	Shares	Contributed Capital	Earnings	Comprehensive Income
1. $18,000	n/a	n/a	$18,000	n/a	n/a	n/a

P11–3B Cattrall Corporation is authorized to issue an unlimited number of no par value $5 noncumulative preferred shares and an unlimited number of no par value common shares. On February 1, 2006, the general ledger contained the following shareholders' equity accounts:

Preferred shares (4,000 shares issued)	$ 440,000
Common shares (70,000 shares issued)	1,050,000
Contributed capital—reacquisition of shares	58,000
Retained earnings	300,000

Record and post equity transactions; prepare shareholders' equity section. (SO 2, 3, 4)

The following equity transactions occurred during the year ended January 31, 2007:

Feb. 28 Issued 1,200 preferred shares for $150,000.
Apr. 12 Issued 200,000 common shares for $3,200,000.
May 25 Issued 5,000 common shares in exchange for land. At the time of the exchange, the land was valued at $75,000 and the common shares at $80,000.
Sept. 12 Repurchased 75,000 common shares for $1,275,000.
Dec. 29 Declared a $2 per share dividend to the preferred shareholders of record at January 15, payable February 1.
Jan. 31 A net loss of $5,000 was incurred for the year.

Instructions

(a) Journalize the above transactions.
(b) Open general ledger accounts and post to the shareholders' equity accounts.
(c) Prepare the shareholders' equity section of the balance sheet at January 31, 2007.

P11–4B On January 1, 2006, Schipper Ltd. had the following shareholders' equity accounts:

Common shares, no par value, unlimited number authorized, 1.5 million issued	$1,000,000
Retained earnings	1,700,000
Accumulated other comprehensive loss	18,000

Record and post equity transactions; prepare shareholders' equity and financing activities sections. (SO 2, 3, 4)

The following selected transactions occurred during 2006:

Jan. 2 Issued 100,000 no par value $4 noncumulative preferred shares for $25 per share.
Mar. 10 Declared the quarterly cash dividend to preferred shareholders of record on March 22, payable April 1.
June 10 Declared the quarterly cash dividend to preferred shareholders of record on June 22, payable July 1.
Aug. 12 Issued 100,000 common shares for $0.75 per share.
Oct. 1 Declared the quarterly cash dividend to preferred shareholders of record on October 22, payable November 1. Also declared a $0.25 cash dividend per share to the common shareholders of record on October 22, payable November 1.
Dec. 10 Due to a temporary shortfall of cash, was unable to declare or pay the quarterly cash dividend to preferred shareholders.
      31 Net loss for the year was $100,000.

Instructions

(a) Journalize the 2006 transactions.
(b) Open general ledger accounts and post to the shareholders' equity accounts.
(c) Prepare the shareholders' equity section of the balance sheet at December 31.
(d) Prepare the financing activities section of the cash flow statement for the year.

Reproduce retained earnings account; prepare shareholders' equity section.
(SO 3, 4)

P11–5B The post-closing trial balance of Maggio Corporation at December 31, 2006, contains these shareholders' equity accounts:

Preferred shares (12,000 shares issued)	$ 850,000
Common shares (233,200 shares issued)	3,200,000
Contributed capital—reacquisition of common shares	55,000
Retained earnings	787,000

A review of the accounting records reveals the following information:

1. Preferred shares are $6 cumulative, no par value shares. An unlimited number of preferred shares is authorized.
2. Common shares are no par value. An unlimited number are authorized.
3. The January 1 balance in Retained Earnings was $980,000.
4. On March 1, 20,000 common shares were sold for $15 per share.
5. On August 18, a 6% common stock dividend was declared for 13,200 shares when the share price was $20. The stock dividend was distributed on September 25.
6. The preferred shareholders' dividend was declared and paid in 2006 for three quarters. Due to a cash shortage, the last quarter's dividend was not paid.
7. Net earnings for the year were $125,000.
8. On December 31, the directors authorized a $200,000 restriction on retained earnings in accordance with a debt covenant.

Instructions

(a) Reproduce the Retained Earnings general ledger account for the year.
(b) Prepare the shareholders' equity section of the balance sheet at December 31, including any required note disclosure.

Compare impact of cash dividend, stock dividend, and stock split.
(SO 3)

P11–6B The condensed balance sheet of Erickson Corporation reports the following amounts:

ERICKSON CORPORATION
Balance Sheet (partial)
January 31, 2007

Total assets		$9,000,000
Total liabilities		$2,500,000
Shareholders' equity		
Common shares, unlimited number		
authorized, 500,000 issued, no par value	$3,000,000	
Retained earnings	3,500,000	6,500,000
Total liabilities and shareholders' equity		$9,000,000

Erickson wants to assess the impact of three possible alternatives on the corporation and its shareholders. The alternatives are:

1. Payment of a $1.20 per share cash dividend.
2. Distribution of a 6% stock dividend. The market price of the common shares is currently $20 per share.
3. A two-for-one stock split.

Instructions

(a) Determine the impact on assets, liabilities, shareholders' equity (common shares and retained earnings), and the number of shares under each of the three alternatives.
(b) Assume an Erickson shareholder currently owns 2,000 common shares for which he paid $35,000. What is the impact of each alternative for the shareholder? Which one is best for him?

Record and post dividend transactions, prepare shareholders' equity section, and calculate ratios.
(SO 3, 4, 5)

P11–7B On January 1, 2006, Stengel Corporation had these shareholders' equity accounts:

Common shares (no par value, unlimited number of shares authorized, 60,000 shares issued)	$1,700,000
Retained earnings	600,000

During the year, the following transactions occurred:

Feb. 1 Declared a $2 per share cash dividend to shareholders of record on February 15, payable March 1.

Apr. 1 Effected a three-for-one stock split. The market price of each share was $36 immediately before the announcement of the split.

July 1 Declared a 5% stock dividend to shareholders of record on July 15, distributable July 31. On July 1, the market price was $20 per share.

Dec. 31 Determined that net earnings for the year were $410,000.

31 The market price of the common shares on this date was $25.

Instructions

(a) Journalize the above transactions.
(b) Open general ledger accounts and post to the shareholders' equity accounts.
(c) Prepare the shareholders' equity section of the balance sheet at December 31.
(d) Calculate the dividend payout, dividend yield, and return on common shareholders' equity ratios.

P11–8B The following summary of the earnings per share, price-earnings, payout, and dividend yield ratios is available for the five years ended December 31 for TransAlta Corporation:

Evaluate dividend policy.
(SO 5)

	Earnings per Share	Price-Earnings Ratio	Payout Ratio	Dividend Yield
2000	$1.66	16.7 times	75.8%	4.6%
2001	1.27	17.3	78.5	4.6
2002	1.12	41.7	241.8	5.8
2003	1.26	14.7	79.0	5.4
2004	0.88	21.7	120.0	5.5

Instructions

(a) What are some possible reasons that TransAlta's dividend payout ratio jumped to 241.8% in 2002. What does this mean?
(b) Why do you think TransAlta's price-earnings ratio declined by nearly 65% while its dividend yield only declined by 7% in 2003?
(c) What are some possible reasons that TransAlta's payout and dividend yield ratios increased in 2004 at a time when its earnings per share decreased substantially?
(d) If you were an investor looking for dividend income, would you be happy with TransAlta's dividend policy? Explain.

P11–9B Blue Bay Logistics Ltd.'s shareholder's equity accounts were as follows at the beginning of the current fiscal year, April 1, 2006:

Calculate earnings per share.
(SO 5)

$4 cumulative preferred shares (20,000 shares issued)	$1,800,000
Common shares (500,000 shares issued)	3,750,000
Contributed capital—reacquisition of common shares	50,000
Retained earnings	1,500,000
Total shareholders' equity	$7,100,000

During the year, the following selected transactions occurred:

June 1 Reacquired 12,000 common shares for $7 per share.
July 1 Issued 50,000 common shares for $8 per share.
Feb. 28 Declared the annual preferred dividend to shareholders of record on March 12, payable on April 1.
Mar. 31 Net earnings for the year ended March 31, 2007, were $975,000.

Instructions

(a) Calculate the weighted average number of common shares for the year.
(b) Calculate the earnings per share.
(c) Why is it important to use net earnings available for the common shareholders in the calculation of earnings per share? Why not just use net earnings?

P11–10B The following selected information (in millions, except for per share information) is available for the National Bank of Canada for the year ended October 31:

Evaluate corporate performance.
(SO 5)

	2004	2003
Weighted average number of common shares	171	178
Net earnings	$725	$624
Total common cash dividends (per share)	243 (1.42)	193 (1.08)
Total preferred cash dividends	23	25
Average common shareholders' equity	3,776	3,662
Price per common share	48.78	40.91

Industry averages were as follows:

	2004	2003
Payout ratio	36.6%	n/a
Dividend yield	3.1%	3.0%
Earnings per share	n/a	n/a
Price-earnings ratio	13.6 times	12.6 times
Return on common shareholders' equity	16.2%	15.0%

Instructions

(a) Calculate the following ratios for the common shareholders for each fiscal year:
  1. Payout ratio   4. Price-earnings ratio
  2. Dividend yield   5. Return on common shareholders' equity
  3. Earnings per share
(b) Comment on the above ratios for 2004 in comparison to the prior year, and in comparison to the industry.

Evaluate corporate performance. (SO 5)

P11–11B   Selected ratios for two retailers follow, along with the industry averages:

Ratio	Bargain Hunters	Discount Paradise	Industry Average
Profit margin	6.8%	3.5%	3.7%
Return on common shareholders' equity	24.9%	22.4%	20.8%
Return on assets	10.4%	8.6%	8.7%
Asset turnover	1.5 times	2.5 times	2.5 times
Earnings per share	$3.30	$2.49	$2.33
Price-earnings ratio	16.3 times	19.2 times	18.5 times
Payout ratio	9.4%	21.7%	19.3%

Instructions

(a) Compare the profitability of Bargain Hunters to that of Discount Paradise and to the industry. Which company is more profitable? Explain.
(b) You would like to invest in the shares of one of the two companies. Your goal is to have regular income from your investment that will help pay your tuition fees for the next few years. Which of the two companies is a better choice for you? Explain.
(c) Assume that instead of looking for regular income, you are looking for growth in the share value so that you can resell the shares at a gain in the future. Now which of the two companies is better for you? Explain.

BROADENING YOUR PERSPECTIVE

Financial Reporting and Analysis

www.wiley.com/canada/kimmel/ **Analysis Tools**

Financial Reporting Problem: *Loblaw*

BYP11–1   The shareholders' equity section of Loblaw's balance sheet is shown in the Consolidated Balance Sheet in Appendix A. You will also find data for this problem in the Notes to the Consolidated Financial Statements and in the Eleven-Year Summary (share price).

Instructions

(a) How many common shares has Loblaw authorized? How many common shares were issued at the end of the 2003 and 2002 fiscal years? What was the weighted average number of common shares each fiscal year?
(b) Did Loblaw repurchase any shares in 2003 and 2002? If so, how much cash did it spend on this activity in each year?
(c) How much cash did Loblaw pay out in dividends in each of 2003 and 2002?
(d) Calculate the payout, dividend yield, and return on common shareholders' equity ratios for 2003 and 2002. Loblaw's shareholders' equity was $3,569 million at the end of 2001.

Comparative Analysis Problem: *Loblaw and Sobeys*

BYP11–2 The financial statements of Sobeys are presented in Appendix B, following the financial statements for Loblaw in Appendix A.

Instructions

(a) Calculate the payout ratios for each company for the most recent fiscal year. Which company pays out a higher percentage of its earnings to shareholders?

(b) Calculate or find the earnings per share and return on common shareholders' equity ratios for each company for the most recent fiscal year. Based on these measures, which company is more profitable?

Research Case

BYP11–3 The April 2003 issue of *CMA Management* magazine included the article "The REIT Revisited" by Olev Edur. The article examines the growth in income trusts, particularly real estate income trusts (REITs).

Instructions

Read the article and answer the following questions:

(a) This chapter introduced you to a relatively new form of corporation in Canada: the income trust. This article expands the discussion to include real estate income trusts. According to the article, how is this form of business repackaged to create tax savings for investors?

(b) Do the earnings of income trusts tend to be stable or volatile? Are they heavily taxed?

(c) Do interest rate changes affect the value of income trusts?

(d) Are REITs more or less risky than other kinds of income trusts?

Interpreting Financial Statements

BYP11–4 Talisman Energy Inc. explores for, develops, and produces crude oil, natural gas, and natural gas liquids. Talisman's authorized share capital includes an unlimited number of common shares. During the 2004 fiscal year, Talisman repurchased 8,987,400 common shares for a total of $286 million. Also during 2004, Talisman effected a three-for-one common stock split after its share price reached an all-time high of more than $84.

The following additional information is available for the year ended December 31 (in millions of dollars, except per share data). For comparative purposes, all relevant information in 2003 has been restated for the effects of the stock split.

	2004	2003
Net earnings	$ 663	$1,012
Preferred dividends	32	22
Common dividends	114	90
Cash dividend per common share	0.30	0.23
Weighted average number of common shares	383	386
Average common shareholders' equity	4,709	4,329
Price per common share	32.22	24.28

Instructions

(a) What are some of the reasons why management repurchases its own shares? Talisman debited Retained Earnings for $222 million when it repurchased 8,987,400 common shares in 2004. Did the company repurchase its shares at more than or less than average cost?

(b) Why did Talisman likely split its shares?

(c) Calculate the dividend payout, dividend yield, earnings per share, price-earnings, and return on common shareholders' ratios for 2004 and 2003. Discuss the implications of your findings for investors.

A Global Focus

BYP11–5   UK-based cosmetics retailer The Body Shop International plc operates more than 2,000 stores in 52 countries. The Body Shop reported the following selected information (in millions of £, except per share data, which is stated in pence) for fiscal 2005 and 2004:

	2005	2004
Net sales	£419.0	£381.1
Average total assets	233.6	219.0
Average common shareholders' equity	141.2	130.7
Total dividends	11.9	11.6
Net earnings	27.0	21.7
Weighted average number of common shares	206.6	202.1
Cash dividend per share	5.7	5.7
Price per share	208.25	130.37

The Body Shop has no preferred shares.

Instructions

(a) Calculate the asset turnover, return on assets, and return on common shareholders' equity ratios for each fiscal year. Evaluate The Body Shop's change in profitability.

(b) Calculate the earnings per share, price-earnings, dividend payout, and dividend yield ratios for each fiscal year. Discuss the implications of your findings for investors.

Financial Analysis on the Web

www.wiley.com/canada/kimmel

Analysis Tools
(Financial Analysis on the Web)

BYP11–6   The Toronto Stock Exchange (TSX) is Canada's premier stock exchange and one of the top ten exchanges in the world. The TSX is Canada's largest capital market, accounting for over 80 percent of the value of shares traded on Canadian exchanges. This case explores the information available on the TSX website.

Instructions

Specific requirements of this Web case can be found on the Toolkit website.

Critical Thinking

Collaborative Learning Activity

BYP11–7   The annual meeting for the Mantle Corporation has been in progress for some time. Mantle's chief financial officer is reviewing the company's financial statements and explaining the items that make up the shareholders' equity section of the balance sheet for the current year. The shareholders' equity section for Mantle Corporation is as follows:

MANTLE CORPORATION
Balance Sheet (partial)
December 31, 2006

Shareholders' equity	
Contributed capital	
Share capital	
Preferred shares, 1 million shares authorized, $8 cumulative, no par value, 6,000 shares issued	$ 600,000
Common shares, unlimited number authorized, no par value, 3 million shares issued	28,000,000
Total share capital	28,600,000
Additional contributed capital	
Contributed capital—reacquisition of shares	50,000
Total contributed capital	28,650,000
Retained earnings	900,000
Accumulated other comprehensive income	5,000
Total shareholders' equity	$29,555,000

Several people at the meeting have now raised questions about the above shareholders' equity section.

Instructions

With the class divided into groups, answer the following questions that the chief financial officer has been asked:

(a) "What does the cumulative provision for the preferred shares mean? How much total annual dividend does the company have to pay?"

(b) "I thought the common shares were presently selling at $12 per share. Yet the shares have an average cost of $9.33 ($28,000,000 ÷ 3,000,000). How can that be?"

(c) "You mentioned that the company repurchased 300,000 common shares during 2004. Why is the company buying back its common shares? Did the company pay more or less than the average cost when it repurchased them?"

(d) "You mentioned that $50,000 of the retained earnings is restricted for a plant expansion. I know that retained earnings aren't cash. How can retained earnings finance a plant expansion?"

(e) "What is accumulated other comprehensive income? If it's income, why isn't it reported on the statement of earnings?"

Communication Activity

BYP11–8 Your parents, who have been financing your university education, come to you looking for some advice. They explain that an investment broker made a presentation at their social club and was trying to convince club members to purchase certain investments. Some of the terms sounded confusing and it was only after the broker left that members thought of a few more things to ask. For example, they wondered what is the significance of the terms price-earnings ratio and dividend yield and what magic number should they look for with each measure. Your parents bragged—yet again—to their friends about your brilliant knowledge of all matters related to accounting and promised to return to next week's meeting with an explanatory memo.

Instructions

Prepare a memo for your parents to use at their social group.

Ethics Case

BYP11–9 Flambeau Corporation has paid 60 consecutive quarterly cash dividends (15 years' worth). The last six months have been a real cash drain on the company, however, as profit margins have been greatly narrowed by increasing competition. With a cash balance that is only enough to meet day-to-day operating needs, the president, Vince Ramsey, has decided that a stock dividend instead of a cash dividend should be declared. He tells Flambeau's financial vice-president, Janice Rahn, to issue a press release stating that the company is extending its consecutive dividend record with the declaration of a 5% stock dividend. "Write the press release convincing the shareholders that the stock dividend is just as good as a cash dividend," he orders. "Just watch our share price rise when we announce the stock dividend; it must be a good thing if that happens."

Ethics In Accounting

Instructions

(a) Who are the stakeholders in this situation?

(b) Is there anything unethical about President Ramsey's intentions or actions?

(c) What is the effect of a stock dividend on a corporation's shareholders' equity accounts? As a shareholder, would you prefer to receive a cash dividend or a stock dividend? Why?

Serial Problem

(*Note:* This is a continuation of the serial problem from Chapters 1 through 10.)

BYP11–10   Natalie's friend Curtis Lesperance has operated a coffee shop for the past two years as a sole proprietorship. He buys coffee, muffins, and cookies from a local supplier. He now meets with Natalie to discuss the possibility of combining her business, Cookie Creations Ltd., with his. As you know, Natalie's business consists of giving cookie-making classes and selling fine European mixers. The plan is for Natalie to use the premises Curtis currently rents as a place to give her cookie-making classes and demonstrations of the mixers that she sells. Natalie will also hire, train, and supervise staff hired to bake cookies and muffins sold in the coffee shop. By offering her classes on the premises, Natalie will save on travel time going from place to place. The coffee shop will also provide one central location for selling the mixers.

Because Natalie has been so successful with Cookie Creations and Curtis has been just as successful with his coffee shop, they both conclude that they could benefit from each other's business expertise. Curtis will transfer two of his assets (inventory and equipment) into Cookie Creations in exchange for common shares of Cookie Creations Ltd.

The share capital and retained earnings of Cookie Creations Ltd. at December 31, 2006, before the transfer takes place, are as follows:

Share capital	
$6 cumulative preferred shares, no par value,	
10,000 shares authorized, none issued	
Common shares, no par value, unlimited number	$ 1,800
of shares authorized, 1,800 shares issued	
Retained earnings	$12,500

On January 1, 2007, Curtis transfers his assets to Cookie Creations at their current market value as follows: merchandise inventory $400, and equipment $2,500. In exchange, Curtis receives 1,450 Cookie Creations common shares.

Natalie and Curtis are very excited about combining their two companies. They come to you with the following questions:

1. Curtis's Dad and Natalie's grandmother are interested in investing $5,000 each in Cookie Creations Ltd. We are considering issuing the preferred shares. What would be the advantage of issuing the preferred shares instead of common shares?
2. Our lawyer has sent us a bill for $750. When we talked the bill over with her, she said that she would be willing to receive common shares in our corporation instead of cash. We would be happy to issue her shares, but we are a bit worried about accounting for this transaction. Can we do this? If so, how do we determine how many shares to give her?

Instructions

(a) Answer their questions.
(b) Prepare the journal entry required on January 1, 2007, the date when Curtis transfers his two assets into Cookie Creations Ltd.
(c) Assume the Cookie Creations Ltd. issues 1,000 $6 cumulative preferred shares to Curtis's Dad and the same number to Natalie's grandmother for $5,000 each. Also assume that Cookie Creations Ltd. issues 375 common shares to its lawyer. Prepare the journal entries required for each of these transactions that also occurred on January 1, 2007.
(d) Prepare the shareholders' equity section for Cookie Creations Ltd. as at January 1, 2007, after the transactions are recorded in (b) and (c) above.
(e) For the year ended December 31, 2006, Cookie Creations Ltd.'s earnings per share was $11.75. Explain whether you expect Cookie Creations' earnings per share to increase, decrease, or not change in the upcoming year because of the transactions that occurred on January 1, 2007.

Answers to Self-Study Questions

1. c   2. b   3. b   4. a   5. d   6. c   7. d   8. c   9. a   10. c

Answer to Loblaw Review It Question 3

Loblaw repurchased and cancelled 1,282,900 common shares in 2003 (see Note 14).

Remember to go back to the Navigator box at the beginning of the chapter to check off your completed work.

CHAPTER 12

Reporting and Analyzing Investments

ACCOUNTING MATTERS!

Birth of a Giant

Hundreds of mergers and acquisitions take place every year in Canada, and many are in the oil and gas industry. The biggest deal that took place in the second quarter of 2004 was Calgary-based EnCana Corporation's $3.6-billion acquisition of Tom Brown, Inc. Although impressive, this falls short of the $9.2-billion merger between Alberta Energy Co. (AEC) and PanCanadian Energy Corp. that created EnCana in 2002. The story behind this mega-merger underlines the role that strategic acquisitions play in the growth of corporations.

AEC was launched in 1975 as a Crown corporation, with half of its shares owned by the Alberta government and the rest held by the public. Over the years, AEC invested in other industries, including coal and steel, forest products, and petrochemicals. By 1993, however, the provincial government no longer held shares and it became a 100-percent publicly owned company. Between 1995 and 2001, the company doubled in size by acquiring Conwest Exploration, Amber Energy, and McMurray Oil. By 2001, it was the largest independent gas storage operator in North America.

PanCanadian Energy's history dates back to 1881 and the federal government's commissioning of the Canadian Pacific Railway (CPR) to build a cross-country railroad. As partial payment, CPR received 25 million acres of land, on which it discovered natural gas. CPR created Canadian Pacific Oil and Gas Company in 1958. When the company amalgamated with Central-Del Rio Oils in 1971, its name changed to PanCanadian Energy.

Fast-forward to April 2002. AEC and PanCanadian exchanged shares in a "friendly merger" to create a company with a combined value of $30 billion. By the end of 2003, EnCana had one of the largest proven reserve bases among independent oil and gas companies—8.4 trillion cubic feet of natural gas and 960 million barrels of oil and natural gas liquid reserves.

In addition to offshore activities along Canada's eastern coast, the company has had major operations in the U.S. Rockies, Ecuador, the Gulf of Mexico, and the UK's North Sea. However, in late 2004, EnCana sold its equity investments in a number of UK ventures to Nexen Inc. for U.S. $2.1 billion. It has also deemed its Ecuador and Gulf of Mexico assets to be noncore and has started a divestiture process for them. The company intends to focus on its North American natural gas and oil sands projects.

Which other companies will EnCana buy or sell? Much will depend, of course, on oil and gas prices. In the meantime, investors and competitors alike will be watching closely as this story unfolds.

the navigator

EnCana Corporation www.encana.com

THE NAVIGATOR

- [ ] Read *Feature Story*

- [ ] Scan *Study Objectives*

- [ ] Read *Chapter Preview*

- [ ] Read text and answer *Before You Go On*

- [ ] Work *Using the Decision Toolkit*

- [ ] Review *Summary of Study Objectives*

- [ ] Review the *Decision Toolkit—A Summary*

- [ ] Work *Demonstration Problem*

- [ ] Answer *Self-Study Questions*

- [ ] Complete assignments

STUDY OBJECTIVES

After studying this chapter, you should be able to:

1. Identify the reasons corporations invest in short- and long-term debt and equity securities.
2. Explain the accounting for debt investments.
3. Explain the accounting for equity investments.
4. Describe how investments are valued and performance is evaluated.
5. Indicate how investments are reported in the financial statements.

the navigator

EnCana grew through a policy of aggressive growth by investing in the equity securities (shares) of other companies. Equity investments can be purchased as a passive investment or with the intention to control another company, as was the case when EnCana acquired Tom Brown, Inc. by purchasing 100 percent of its common shares.

In addition to purchasing equity securities, companies also purchase other securities, such as debt securities issued by corporations, governments, or other institutions. Investments can be purchased for a short or long period of time. As you will see later in the chapter, the way in which a company accounts for its investments is determined by several factors.

The chapter is organized as follows:

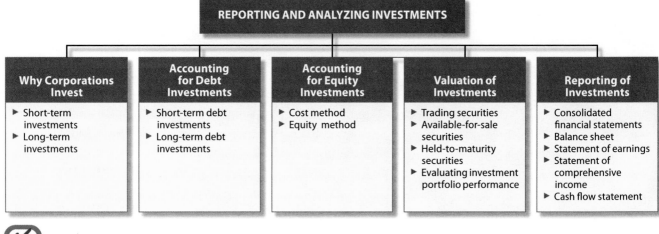

the navigator

Why Corporations Invest

Corporations generally purchase investments in debt securities (money-market instruments, bonds, commercial paper, or similar items) and equity securities (preferred and common shares) for one of three reasons. First, a corporation may have **excess cash** that it does not immediately need. For example, many companies have seasonal fluctuations in their sales levels which can lead to idle cash until purchases are made for the next busy season. Until the cash is needed, the excess funds may be invested to earn a greater return than would be realized by just holding the funds in the company's chequing account.

When investing excess cash for short periods of time, corporations generally invest in money-market instruments, which are short-term debt securities of low risk and high liquidity. Examples include money-market funds, bankers acceptances, term deposits, and treasury bills. It is not wise to invest short-term excess cash in equity securities. If the price of the shares drops just before the company needs the cash again, it will be forced to sell its investment at a loss. Money-market instruments do not change in market value. Their value arises from the interest they generate.

A second reason that some companies purchase investments is to **generate investment revenue**. Companies generate interest revenue from debt securities and dividend revenue from some equity securities. Recall from Chapter 11 that there is no obligation for a company to pay dividends on its shares. Most companies buy preferred shares of companies that have a stable dividend policy if they are trying to generate dividend revenue. A company can also invest in debt and equity securities hoping it can sell them at a higher price than it originally paid for them. It speculates that the investment will increase in value and result in a gain when it is sold.

A third reason that companies invest is for **strategic purposes**. A company may purchase a noncontrolling (less than 50 percent) ownership interest in another company in a related industry in which it wants to establish a presence. Alternatively, a company can exercise some influence over one of its customers or suppliers by purchasing a significant, but not controlling, interest in that company. For example, EnCana owns 36 percent of the shares of Oleoducto Trasandino, the owner of a crude oil pipeline that ships crude oil from the producing areas of Argentina to the refineries in Chile. Then again, a company may choose to purchase a controlling interest in another company as EnCana did when it purchased 100 percent of Tom Brown, Inc.'s common shares.

In summary, businesses invest in other companies for the reasons shown in Illustration 12-1.

Illustration 12-1 ◄

Why corporations invest

Reason	Typical Investment
To house excess cash until needed	Low-risk, high-liquidity, short-term debt securities (money-market instruments)
To generate investment revenue *I want to buy a two-year certificate of deposit.* BANK	Debt securities (money-market instruments, bonds, commercial paper) and equity securities (preferred and common shares)
To meet strategic goals	Common shares of companies in a related industry or an unrelated industry that the company wants to enter

Short-Term Investments

Short-term investments can include investments in either debt or equity securities, or both. In order to be classified as a short-term investment and reported as a current asset, investments must be (1) **readily marketable** and (2) **intended to be converted into cash** in the near future.

Alternative Terminology
Short-term investments are also called *marketable securities* or *temporary investments*.

Readily Marketable

An investment is "readily marketable" if it can easily be sold whenever there is a need for cash. Money-market instruments meet this criterion, as they can be sold readily to other investors. Shares and bonds traded on organized securities markets, such as the Toronto Stock Exchange, are readily marketable because they can be bought and sold daily.

Intent to Convert

"Intent to convert" means that management intends to sell the investment whenever the need for cash arises. It is the intention to sell that determines whether or not the investment is classified as short-term, not the length of time it is actually held. For example, a ski resort may invest idle cash during the summer months and intend to sell the securities to buy supplies and equipment shortly before the next winter season. This investment is considered to be a short-term investment even if a lack of snow cancels the next ski season and eliminates the need to convert the securities into cash as intended.

Short-term investments can be further designated as either trading securities or available-for-sale securities. **Trading securities** are debt or equity securities purchased and held for resale in the short term, hopefully at a gain. For the most part, this type of investment is found in financial institutions, who frequently buy and sell trading securities in the normal course of business. However, any marketable security can be designated by management as a trading security when purchased, as long as the intent to sell is present.

Available-for-sale securities are debt or equity securities that are held with the intention of selling them sometime in the future. This category includes money-market investments, but also debt and equity securities of other companies that can be sold if the need for cash arises. While available-for-sale securities are held, they will generate investment revenue. When they are sold, they will generate a gain or loss on sale.

While trading securities are always considered to be short-term investments, available-for-sale securities can be either short- or long-term, depending on management's intent.

Long-Term Investments

Long-term investments can also consist of debt securities and equity securities. To determine whether a debt or equity security is short-term or long-term, we test the investment against the short-term investment criteria. Investments that do not meet **both** short-term investment criteria—readily marketable and intent to convert—are long-term investments.

As we discussed in the previous section, **available-for-sale securiti**es are classified as long-term investments if management does not have the intent to sell them if the need for cash arises. **Held-to-maturity securities** are debt securities that the investor has the intention and ability to hold to maturity. Naturally, held-to-maturity securities are always long-term investments, except when they are within one year from maturity.

In addition, certain equity securities purchased for the purpose of significant influence or control are also long-term investments. These types of investments are not purchased for trading purposes, and are not available for sale. EnCana's equity investments in Tom Brown, Inc. and Oleoducto Trasandino are examples of long-term investments in equity securities.

The classification of investments as trading, available-for-sale, and held-to-maturity is part of sweeping new standards affecting the recognition and measurement of financial instruments. Financial instruments include debt and equity investments, among other items reported on the balance sheet. While we discuss debt and equity investments here, discussion of other types of financial instruments is deferred to an intermediate accounting course.

ACCOUNTING MATTERS!   International Perspective

The Accounting Standards Board issued new standards for financial instruments that will affect nearly every company in Canada, small and large, no later than fiscal year ends beginning on or after October 1, 2006. The new standards are extensive, and the result of many years of consultation with Canadian users and international standard setters. New standards on recognizing and measuring financial instruments will move companies away from reporting certain types of investments on their balance sheets at historical cost, or at the lower of cost and market. Investments purchased for the purpose of resale will now be reported at their market value, which many observers believe is far more relevant to decision-makers. With the implementation of this new accounting standard, Canadian accounting practices for investments will agree with those used internationally and in the U.S.

BEFORE YOU GO ON . . .

▶Review It

1. What are the reasons that corporations invest in debt and equity securities?
2. What criteria must be met for an investment to be classified as short-term? Long-term?
3. Distinguish between trading securities, available-for-sale securities, and held-to-maturity securities.

Accounting for Debt Investments

study objective 2

Explain the accounting for debt investments.

Debt investments include investments in money-market instruments, as well as investments in bonds, commercial paper, and a large variety of other debt securities available for purchase. As we just learned, these investments may be classified as short-term or long-term. The accounting for debt investments differs depending on their classification.

Short-Term Debt Investments

In accounting for short-term debt investments, entries are required to record the (1) acquisition, (2) interest revenue, and (3) maturity or sale.

Money-Market Instruments

As we have learned, money-market instruments are relatively safe, short-term investments that allow a company to earn a higher rate of interest than would otherwise be earned if the money was kept in a regular bank account. Companies often buy and sell money-market instruments as a way to manage their cash flow.

Recording Acquisition of Money-Market Instruments.   Assume that Cheung Corporation has excess cash on hand. On November 30, 2006, it purchases a three-month, $5,000 term deposit which pays an annual interest rate of 2 percent. The entry to record Cheung's short-term investment is as follows:

Nov. 30	Debt Investment—Term Deposit	5,000	
	Cash		5,000
	(To record purchase of three-month, 2% term deposit)		

A = L + SE
+5,000
−5,000

↓ Cash flows: −5,000

Recording Interest Revenue.   Cheung Corporation's year end is December 31. Most term deposits pay a fixed interest rate on maturity, although variable interest rates are also possible. Assuming that Cheung Corporation's term deposit pays a fixed interest rate at maturity, it is necessary to accrue $8 ($5,000 × 2% × $\frac{1}{12}$, rounded to the nearest dollar) interest for the month of December:

Dec. 31	Interest Receivable	8	
	Interest Revenue		8
	(To accrue interest on term deposit)		

A = L + SE
+8   +8

Cash flows: no effect

Recording Maturity of Money-Market Instruments.   On February 28, 2007, when the term deposit matures, it is necessary to (1) update the interest, and (2) record the receipt of cash and elimination of the term deposit. Most banks credit the company's bank account directly for the interest and principal amounts when a term deposit matures, unless they have been advised to do otherwise. The entry to record the maturity of the term deposit is as follows:

Feb. 28	Cash	5,025	
	Interest Receivable		8
	Interest Revenue ($5,000 × 2% × $\frac{2}{12}$)		17
	Debt Investment—Term Deposit		5,000
	(To record maturity of term deposit)		

A = L + SE
+5,025   +17
−8
−5,000

↑ Cash flows: +5,025

If the company does not require the money when the term deposit matures, it may reinvest the term deposit for a further period of time. In such cases, two separate entries should be recorded. One entry, as above, records the maturation of the term deposit and interest earned. The second entry records the acquisition of the new term deposit, which will have a different maturity date, and may very well also have a different interest rate.

If a term deposit, or other money-market instrument, is sold before it matures, it typically does not result in any gain or loss—just less interest revenue. Some term deposits are not cashable before the maturity date and some are. It is wise to look carefully at any penalties or conditions attached to money-market instruments that are purchased for short-term use.

Bonds

We learned about bonds in Chapter 10 from the liability side—i.e., the issuer's perspective. Corporations, governments, and universities issue bonds, which are purchased by investors. The issuer of the bonds is known as the **investee**. The purchaser of the bonds, or the bondholder, is known as the **investor**. The recording of short-term investments in bonds differs from money-market instruments in three ways: the determination of cost, the timing of the receipt of interest, and the sale of the bond.

First, the cost of the bond often includes additional costs, such as brokerage fees, whereas money-market instruments rarely do since they are usually purchased directly from a bank.

Second, bond investments receive interest semi-annually, while money-market investments normally receive interest only at maturity. Finally, bonds are issued for a much longer term than money-market instruments. This means that when bonds are purchased as a short-term investment, they will be sold before they mature and will likely result in a gain or loss.

Recording Acquisition of Bonds.   At acquisition, the **cost principle** applies. Cost includes all expenses to acquire these investments, such as the price paid plus brokerage fees (commissions), if any.

Assume that Kuhl Corporation acquires 50 Doan Inc. 10-year, 6-percent, $1,000 bonds on January 1, 2006, for $51,000, including brokerage fees of $1,000. The bonds pay interest semi-annually, on July 1 and January 1. The entry to record the investment is as follows:

+51,000
–51,000

↓ Cash flows: –51,000

Jan. 1	Debt Investments—Doan Bonds ($50,000 + $1,000)	51,000	
	Cash		51,000
	(To record purchase of 50 Doan Inc. bonds)		

ACCOUNTING MATTERS!   Investor Perspective

Corporate bonds, like shares, are traded on securities exchanges. They can be bought and sold at any time. Bond prices and trading activity are published daily in the financial press, in the format shown below:

	Coupon	Maturity	Price	Yield
Hydro One	5.77	Nov. 15/12	100.50	5.70

This information indicates that Hydro One Inc. has issued 5.77-percent, $1,000 bonds (default amount), maturing November 15, 2012. These bonds are currently yielding a 5.70-percent effective interest rate. Investors are willing to pay 100.50 percent of face value, or $1,005 ($1,000 × 100.5%) for each bond, on this particular day. Note that since the coupon (contractual) interest rate is higher than the market interest rate, Hydro One's bonds are trading at a premium.

Recording Interest Revenue.   Kuhl's investment in Doan bonds pays interest of $1,500 ($50,000 × 6% × $6/12$) semi-annually on July 1 and January 1. Note that interest is calculated using the face value of the bonds, $50,000, and not the cost of the bonds, $51,000. The entry for the receipt of interest on July 1 is:

+1,500   +1,500

↑ Cash flows: +1,500

July 1	Cash	1,500	
	Interest Revenue		1,500
	(To record receipt of interest on Doan bonds)		

Recording Sale of Bonds.   In recording the sale of bonds in advance of their maturity date, it is necessary to (1) update any unrecorded interest, (2) debit Cash for the net proceeds received, (3) credit the investment account for the cost of the bonds, and (4) record any gain or loss on the sale. Any difference between the net proceeds from the sale (sales price less brokerage fees) and their original cost is recorded as a gain or loss.

Assume, for example, that Kuhl receives net proceeds of $53,000 ($54,000 less $1,000 brokerage fees) on the sale of the Doan bonds on July 1, 2006, after receiving the interest due. Since the debt securities cost $51,000, a gain of $2,000 has been realized. The entry to record the sale is:

+53,000   +2,000
–51,000

↑ Cash flows: +53,000

July 1	Cash ($54,000 − $1,000)	53,000	
	Debt Investments—Doan Bonds		51,000
	Gain on Sale of Debt Investment		2,000
	(To record sale of Doan bonds)		

A gain on the sale of debt investments is reported as other revenue in the statement of earnings.

Recording for Investor and Investee

Recording a debt investment in bonds (an asset) for an investor is essentially the opposite of recording bonds payable (a liability) for an investee, which was discussed in Chapter 10. Using the Kuhl Corporation example introduced earlier, Illustration 12-2 compares the recording of the bonds as an investment for Kuhl (the investor) and the recording of the bonds as a liability for Doan (the investee). For this illustration, we have assumed that the bonds have been issued at face value.

Illustration 12-2 ▼

Comparison of short-term bond investment and liability

Kuhl Corporation—Investor			
Jan. 1	Debt Investment—Doan Bonds	51,000	
	Cash		51,000
	(To record purchase of 10-year, 6% Doan bonds)		
July 1	Cash ($50,000 × 6% × 6/12)	1,500	
	Interest Revenue		1,500
	(To record receipt of semi-annual interest)		

Doan Inc.—Investee			
Cash		50,000	
Bonds Payable			50,000
(To record issue of 10-year, 6% bonds)			
Interest Expense		1,500	
Cash ($50,000 × 6% × 6/12)			1,500
(To record payment of semi-annual interest)			

Long-Term Debt Investments

The accounting for short-term debt investments and for long-term debt investments is similar. The major exception is when there is a debt investment in bonds and the bonds are purchased at a premium or a discount. As we learned in Chapter 10, this happens when a bond is purchased above its face value (at a premium) or below its face value (at a discount).

For both short- and long-term debt investments, any bond premium or discount is usually combined and recorded along with the face value of the investment. That is, a bond premium or discount is not separately recorded and the Debt Investment account is reported net of any premium or discount.

For short-term bond investments, the premium or discount is not amortized. This is because the bonds are held for a short period of time and any misstatement of interest is not considered to be significant. In contrast, for long-term bond investments, if there is any bond premium or discount, it must be amortized over the remaining term of the bonds.

Recall from Chapter 10 that premiums or discounts on long-term bonds payable are amortized to the Interest Expense account. In contrast, premiums or discounts on long-term bond investments are amortized to the Interest Revenue account. If there is a bond premium on a long-term bond investment, the Interest Revenue account is *reduced* by the amortization amount. If there is a bond discount, the Interest Revenue account is *increased* by the amortization amount. The effective-interest method of amortization is applied to long-term bond investments as is described in Chapter 10 for the issuer of the bonds.

The accounting for financial instruments such as long-term debt investments is complicated and further discussion is left to a future accounting course.

BEFORE YOU GO ON . . .

►Review It

1. What entries are required for a short-term investment in money-market instruments? In bonds?
2. Compare the accounting for short-term bond investments and liabilities.
3. How does the recording of a long-term bond investment differ from the recording of a short-term bond investment?

►Do It

The Wang Corporation had the following transactions for short-term debt investments:

Jan. 1 Purchased 30 5%, $1,000 Hillary Corp. bonds for $30,000, plus brokerage fees of $900. Interest is payable semi-annually on July 1 and January 1.

July 1 Received semi-annual interest on the Hillary bonds.
    1 Sold 15 Hillary bonds for $15,000, less $400 of brokerage fees.

(a) Journalize the transactions.
(b) Prepare the adjusting entry for the accrual of interest on December 31, Wang's year end.

Action Plan

- Record the bond investment at cost, including brokerage fees.
- When bonds are sold, (1) update any unrecorded interest and (2) credit the investment account for the cost of the bonds.
- Record any difference between the cost of the bonds and the net proceeds as a gain or loss: Gain = proceeds > cost. Loss = proceeds < cost.

Solution

(a)

Jan. 1	Debt Investments—Hillary Bonds ($30,000 + $900)	30,900	
	Cash ($30,000 + $900)		30,900
	(To record purchase of 5% Hillary Corp. bonds)		
July 1	Cash	750	
	Interest Revenue ($30,000 × 5% × $6/12$)		750
	(To record receipt of semi-annual interest on Hillary bonds)		
1	Cash ($15,000 − $400)	14,600	
	Loss on Sale of Debt Investments	850	
	Debt Investments—Hillary Bonds ($30,900 × $15/30$)		15,450
	(To record sale of 15 Hillary bonds)		

(b)

Dec. 31	Interest Receivable	375	
	Interest Revenue ($15,000 × 5% × $6/12$)		375
	(To accrue semi-annual interest on Hillary bonds)		

Accounting for Equity Investments

study objective 3

Explain the accounting for equity investments.

Equity investments are investments in the share capital—common and/or preferred—of other corporations. As we learned earlier in the chapter, preferred shares are usually held to earn dividend income. Either common or preferred shares can also be held for share price increases. Common shares can also be held to influence relationships between companies.

The accounting for equity investments in common shares is based on how much influence the investor has over the operating and financial affairs of the issuing corporation (the investee). Illustration 12-3 shows the guidelines for the levels of influence.

Illustration 12-3 ◀

Accounting guidelines for equity investments

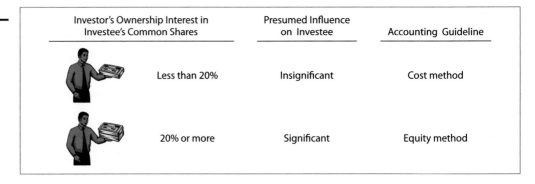

Investor's Ownership Interest in Investee's Common Shares	Presumed Influence on Investee	Accounting Guideline
Less than 20%	Insignificant	Cost method
20% or more	Significant	Equity method

All short-term equity investments are accounted for using the cost method. Long-term equity investments are accounted for by either the cost method or the equity method, depending on the amount of influence the investor can exert on the investee.

When an investor owns 20 percent or more of the common shares of another company, the investor is generally presumed to have a significant influence over the decisions of the investee company. The presumed influence may be cancelled by other circumstances, however. For example, a company that acquires a 25-percent interest in another company in a "hostile" takeover may not have any significant influence over the investee.

Among the questions that should be considered in determining an investor's influence are whether (1) the investor has representation on the investee's board of directors, (2) the investor participates in the investee's policy-making process, (3) there are material transactions between the investor and the investee, and (4) the common shares held by other shareholders are concentrated or dispersed. Companies are required to use judgment instead of blindly following the guidelines. We now explain and illustrate the application of each guideline.

Cost Method

In accounting for equity investments of less than 20 percent, the cost method is used. Under the **cost method**, the investment is recorded at cost, and revenue is only recognized when cash dividends are received (or declared). The entries for equity investments using the cost method are explained next. They are identical regardless of whether the investment is short-term or long-term.

Recording Acquisitions of Shares

Similar to debt investments, cost includes all expenses to acquire the equity securities, such as the price paid plus brokerage fees, if any. Assume, for example, that on July 1, 2006, Passera Corporation (the investor) acquires 1,000 common shares of Beal Corporation (the investee) at $40 per share, plus brokerage fees of $500. If Beal has a total of 10,000 common shares, then Passera has a 10-percent ownership interest in Beal. This investment would be recorded using the cost method, since significant influence is unlikely to exist.

The entry to record the equity investment is:

July 1	Equity Investments—Beal Common [(1,000 × $40) + $500]	40,500	
	Cash		40,500
	(To record purchase of 1,000 common shares of Beal)		

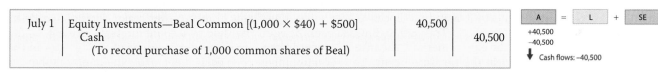

While the investor, Passera Corporation, must make an entry to record this acquisition, no entry is required by Beal Corporation. Recall that after shares have been issued, they are traded among investors. Passera did not purchase these shares directly from Beal. It purchased them from investors on organized stock exchanges, such as the Toronto Stock Exchange.

Recording Dividend Revenue

During the time the shares are held, entries are required for any cash dividends that are received. If a $2-per-share dividend is received by Passera Corporation on December 1, the entry is:

Dec. 1	Cash (1,000 × $2)	2,000	
	Dividend Revenue		2,000
	(To record receipt of cash dividend)		

Dividend revenue is reported as other revenue in the statement of earnings. Recall that, unlike interest, dividends do not accrue before they are declared. Therefore, adjusting entries are not required to accrue dividend revenue.

Recording Sales of Shares

When shares are sold, the difference between the net proceeds from the sale (sales price less brokerage fees) and the cost of the shares is recognized as a gain or loss. We call this a *realized* gain or loss because the sale has actually happened. This is to distinguish it from an *unrealized* gain or loss, which we will discuss later in the chapter when we learn how to value investments for reporting purposes.

Assume that Passera Corporation receives net proceeds of $39,500 on the sale of its Beal Corporation shares on February 10, 2007. Because the shares cost $40,500, there has been a loss of $1,000. The entry to record the sale is:

+39,500
−40,500   −1,000

⬆ Cash flows: +39,500

Feb. 10	Cash	39,500	
	Loss on Sale of Equity Investments	1,000	
	Equity Investments—Beal Common		40,500
	(To record sale of Beal common shares)		

The loss is reported as other expenses in the statement of earnings, whereas a gain on sale is shown as other revenues.

Equity Method

When an investor owns only a small portion of the common shares of another company, the investor cannot control the investee in any way. But when an investor owns at least 20 percent of the common shares of a corporation, it is presumed that the investor has significant influence over the investee's financial and operating activities and plans to hold this investment for the long term. The investor probably has a representative on the investee's board of directors. Through that representative, the investor begins to exercise some control over the investee. The investee company, to some extent, becomes part of the investor company.

Of course, when an investor owns more than 50 percent of the common shares of a corporation, it has more than significant influence—it has control. Either way, when an investor owns 20 percent or more of the common shares of another company, unless there is other evidence to the contrary, it will be able to exercise significant or total influence over the investee.

As mentioned earlier in the chapter, EnCana has a 36-percent equity investment in Oleoducto Trasandino. Because it exercises significant influence over major decisions made by Oleoducto Trasandino, EnCana uses the equity method to account for its investment. Under the **equity method, the investor records its share of the net earnings of the investee in the year the earnings occur.** An alternative might be to delay recognizing the investor's share of net earnings until a cash dividend is received or declared. But that approach would ignore the fact that the investor and investee are, in some sense, one company, which means the investor benefits from, and can influence the timing of, the distribution of the investee's earnings.

Under the equity method, the investment in common shares is initially recorded at cost. After that, the investment account is adjusted annually to show the investor's equity in the investee. Each year, the investor increases (debits) its investment account and increases (credits) revenue for its share of the investee's net earnings. Conversely, when the investee has a net loss the investor increases (debits) a loss account and decreases (credits) the investment account for its share of the investee's net loss. The investor also decreases (credits) the investment account for the amount of any dividends received. The investment account is reduced for dividends received because the net assets of the investee are decreased when a dividend is paid.

Recording Acquisitions of Shares

Assume that Milar Corporation (the investor) acquires 30 percent of the common shares of Beck Inc. (the investee) for $120,000 on January 1, 2006. Milar is assumed to have significant influence over Beck and will use the equity method to account for this transaction. The entry to record this investment is:

Jan. 1	Equity Investments—Beck Common	120,000	
	Cash		120,000
	(To record purchase of Beck common shares)		

A	=	L	+	SE
+120,000				
−120,000				

↓ Cash flows: −120,000

Recording Investment Revenue

For the year ended December 31, 2006, Beck reports net earnings of $100,000. It declares and pays a $40,000 cash dividend. Milar is required to record (1) its share of Beck's earnings, $30,000 (30% × $100,000), and (2) the reduction in the investment account for the dividends received, $12,000 ($40,000 × 30%). The entries are as follows:

	(1)		
Dec. 31	Equity Investments—Beck Common	30,000	
	Revenue from Investment in Beck		30,000
	(To record 30% equity in Beck's net earnings)		

A	=	L	+	SE
+30,000				+30,000

Cash flows: no effect

	(2)		
Dec. 31	Cash	12,000	
	Equity Investments—Beck Common		12,000
	(To record dividends received)		

A	=	L	+	SE
+12,000				
−12,000				

↑ Cash flows: +12,000

After the transactions for the year are posted, the investment and revenue accounts show the following:

Equity Investments—Beck Common				Revenue from Investment in Beck	
Jan. 1	120,000	Dec. 31	12,000	Dec. 31	30,000
Dec. 31	30,000				
Bal.	138,000				

During the year, the investment account has increased by $18,000 ($30,000 − $12,000). This $18,000 is Milar's 30-percent equity in the $60,000 increase in Beck's retained earnings ($100,000 − $40,000). In addition, Milar will report $30,000 of revenue from its investment, which is 30 percent of Beck's net earnings of $100,000.

The difference between reported earnings under the cost method and under the equity method can be significant. For example, Milar would report only the $12,000 of dividend revenue (30% × $40,000) if the cost method were used.

Illustration 12-4 ompares the journal entries used to record these investment transactions under the cost and equity methods. On the left-hand side of the illustration, we assume that Milar had no significant influence over Beck and used the cost method instead of the equity method. On the right-hand side of the illustration, we assume that Milar did have significant influence over Beck and used the equity method (as we just illustrated in this section).

Illustration 12-4 ▼

Comparison of cost and equity methods

Cost Method			Equity Method		
Acquisition			**Acquisition**		
Equity Investments—Beck	120,000		Equity Investments—Beck	120,000	
Cash		120,000	Cash		120,000
Investee reports earnings					
No entry			Equity Investments—Beck	30,000	
			Revenue from Investment		30,000
Investee pays dividends					
Cash	12,000		Cash	12,000	
Dividend Revenue		12,000	Equity Investments—Beck		12,000

BEFORE YOU GO ON . . .

▶Review It

1. Compare the accounting for short-term and long-term equity investments.
2. Compare the accounting for equity investments in common shares with ownership of (a) less than 20 percent with no significant influence, and (b) more than 20 percent with significant or total influence.

▶ Do It

CJW, Inc., purchased 20 percent of North Sails Ltd.'s 60,000 common shares for $10 per share on January 1, 2006. On April 15, North Sails paid a cash dividend of $45,000. On December 31, North Sails reported net earnings of $120,000 for the year. Prepare all necessary journal entries assuming (a) there is no significant influence and (b) there is significant influence.

Action Plan

- Use the cost method when there is no significant influence (normally less than 20 percent ownership of the common shares of another corporation).
- Under the cost method, recognize investment revenue when dividends are declared.
- Use the equity method when there is significant influence (normally 20 percent or more ownership of the common shares of another corporation).
- Under the equity method, recognize investment revenue when the investee declares net earnings. The distribution of dividends is not revenue; rather, it reduces the equity investment.

Solution

(a) Cost Method

Jan. 1	Equity Investments—North Sails Common	120,000	
	(20% × 60,000 × $10)		
	Cash		120,000
	(To record purchase of 12,000 [20% × 60,000] North Sails shares)		
Apr. 15	Cash	9,000	
	Dividend Revenue (20% × $45,000)		9,000
	(To record receipt of cash dividend)		

(b) Equity Method

Jan. 1	Equity Investments—North Sails Common	120,000	
	(20% × 60,000 × $10)		
	Cash		120,000
	(To record purchase of 12,000 [20% × 60,000] North Sails shares)		
Apr. 15	Cash	9,000	
	Equity Investments—North Sails Common		9,000
	(20% × $45,000)		
	(To record receipt of cash dividend)		
Dec. 31	Equity Investments—North Sails Common	24,000	
	(20% × $120,000)		
	Revenue from Investment in North Sails		24,000
	(To record 20% equity in North Sails' net earnings)		

the navigator

Valuation of Investments

study objective 4

Describe how investments are valued and performance is evaluated.

The value of debt and equity investments may rise and fall greatly during the time they are held. Bond and share prices may jump dramatically with favourable economic events and drop drastically with unfavourable economic developments. For example, EnCana's share price rose more than 50 percent in 2005 and more than doubled over the preceding three years in response to rapidly increasing natural gas prices.

If prices can change so much, how should investments be valued at the balance sheet date? Valuation could be at cost or at market value. If investments are valued at cost, changes in the market value of an investment would have no effect on the balance sheet or statement of earnings until the investment is actually sold. When the investment is sold, the difference between its cost and market value would be recognized as a **realized gain or loss**.

If investments are valued at market value, changes in the market value would change the asset value reported on the balance sheet, with a corresponding gain or loss. The difference between cost and market value while an investment is held is called an **unrealized gain or loss**.

Whether market or cost is used depends on the classification of the security. You will recall that we learned earlier in the chapter that there are three categories of securities:

1. **Trading securities** are securities held mainly for sale in the near term to generate earnings on short-term price differences.
2. **Available-for-sale securities** are securities that are held with the intention of selling them sometime in the future.
3. **Held-to-maturity securities** are debt securities that the investor has the intention and ability to hold to maturity.

Trading and available-for-sale securities are valued at market value. Because these investments are purchased for the purpose of resale, it makes sense to value them at the amount of cash that could be received from selling them. In addition, the market values of these types of investments are easily determined. This is not to say that the market values will not change, but, at any specific point in time, market value can be objectively determined. And market value enables users to better assess the impact of changing prices on a company's liquidity and solvency.

Because held-to-maturity securities are not purchased for the purpose of resale, they are valued at cost. The valuation guidelines for the three categories of securities are summarized in illustration 12-5.

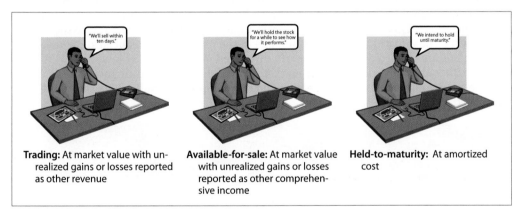

Trading: At market value with unrealized gains or losses reported as other revenue

Available-for-sale: At market value with unrealized gains or losses reported as other comprehensive income

Held-to-maturity: At amortized cost

Illustration 12-5 ◄

Valuation guidelines

Note that the above guidelines apply to all debt investments but only to equity investments for which there is no significant influence (ownership is less than 20 percent).

Trading Securities

Since trading securities are purchased with the intention of selling them in the near future, it is not surprising that they are valued at market value, as shown in Illustration 12-5. This valuation approach is also referred to as mark-to-market accounting.

To illustrate the valuation of trading securities, assume that on December 31, 2006, Plano Corporation has the following costs and market values:

Trading Securities	Cost	Market Value	Unrealized Gain (Loss)
Bell Canada bonds	$ 50,000	$ 48,000	$(2,000)
Norbord shares	90,000	95,000	5,000
Total	$140,000	$143,000	$3,000

Plano has an unrealized gain of $3,000 because the total market value ($143,000) is $3,000 greater than the total cost ($140,000). Its trading securities would be reported at their market value of $143,000 at December 31 in the current assets section of the balance sheet. In addition, Plano would report an unrealized gain of $3,000 as other revenue in its statement of earnings. **Note that unrealized gains and losses for trading securities are reported in exactly the same way as realized gains and losses.**

The adjustment of the trading securities to market value and the recognition of any unrealized gain or loss is usually done through an adjusting journal entry at year end. The adjusting entry for Plano is:

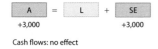

+3,000   +3,000

Cash flows: no effect

Dec. 31	Allowance to Adjust Trading Securities to Market Value	3,000	
	Unrealized Gain—Trading Securities		3,000
	(To record unrealized gain on trading securities)		

In this entry, a valuation allowance account, Allowance to Adjust Trading Securities to Market Value, is used to record the difference between the total cost and the total market value of the securities. Note that it is the entire portfolio of securities that is adjusted—not individual securities. The valuation allowance enables the company to keep a record of the actual investment cost, which is needed to determine the gain or loss realized when the securities are sold.

The allowance account is an **adjunct account**, a debit, if the market value is greater than cost. It is a **contra account**, a credit, if the market value is less than cost. The allowance account is adjusted at each balance sheet date and is reported with the trading securities on the balance sheet. Quite often, just the market value is reported on the balance sheet, with any allowance or valuation adjustment detailed in the notes to the financial statements. For example, EnCana reported $190 million of "unrealized mark-to-market losses" in 2004 from adjusting its trading securities to their market value in the notes to its financial statements.

The following is one example of how Plano might report its trading securities in its balance sheet:

Illustration 12-6 ▶

Presentation of trading securities

PLANO CORPORATION
Balance Sheet (partial)
December 31, 2006

Assets

Current assets
Trading securities, at cost	$140,000
Add: Allowance to adjust trading securities to market value	3,000
Trading securities, at market	143,000

Available-for-Sale Securities

As indicated earlier, available-for-sale securities are held with the intention of selling them sometime in the future. They are also valued at market value at year end. The procedure for determining and recording any change in market value and resulting unrealized gain or loss on these securities is the same as that used for trading securities.

However, the reporting of an unrealized gain or loss differs for available-for-sale securities. There is a reporting difference because while trading securities will be sold in the near term, available-for-sale securities may or may not be sold in the near term. Thus, before the actual sale, it is more likely that changes in market value may reverse any unrealized gain or loss at a specific point in time. Consequently, an unrealized gain or loss on available-for-sale securities is not reported as part of net earnings. Instead, it is separately reported as other comprehensive income.

As we learned in Chapter 11, **comprehensive income** includes all changes to shareholders' equity during a period, except changes resulting from investments by shareholders and dividends. There are a number of alternative formats for reporting comprehensive income, including presenting it in a separate statement of comprehensive income, a combined statement of earnings and comprehensive income, or a statement of equity. We will assume the use of a simple statement of comprehensive income in this chapter. Other formats will be illustrated in senior accounting courses. The following presents a sample statement of comprehensive income for Plano Corporation, using assumed data:

PLANO CORPORATION Statement of Comprehensive Income Year Ended December 31, 2006	
Net earnings	$651,000
Other comprehensive income	
Unrealized gains and losses on available-for-sale securities	1,144
Comprehensive income	$652,144

Illustration 12-7 ◄

Statement of comprehensive income

Recall that comprehensive income is also presented on the balance sheet as a separate component of shareholders' equity as illustrated in Chapter 11. In the case of Plano, the changes in comprehensive income for the period, $1,144, would be added to the opening balance of accumulated other comprehensive income to determine the ending balance of accumulated other comprehensive income reported on the balance sheet.

Held-to-Maturity Securities

Only debt securities are classified as held-to-maturity, because equity securities have no maturity date. A debt security is classified as held-to-maturity if the investor has the intention and ability to hold the investment until it matures. If the company intends to hold the security until it matures and has no plans to sell it, then market values are irrelevant. Consequently, these investments are valued at cost, and their values are not adjusted to reflect changes in market value. We usually say that held-to-maturity investments are valued at *amortized* cost, because any premiums or discounts included in the investment accounts must be amortized, as we have previously learned.

If the market value falls substantially below cost, and the decline is considered permanent, then (and only then) will a held-to-maturity debt security be adjusted to its market value. This value becomes the debt investment's new cost base. Any write-down to market value is directly credited to the investment account because no future recovery in value is expected. This write-down results in an impairment loss and applies to equity investments as well as to other long-lived assets. You will recall that we learned about impairment losses in Chapter 9.

Evaluating Investment Portfolio Performance

We have learned that whether market or cost is used to value investments depends on the classification of the security. For example, companies can choose which of the three categories of securities—trading, available-for-sale, or held-to-maturity—to use for an investment. These classifications require a substantial amount of management judgement and can have a significant impact on the financial position and performance of the company. For example, trading and available-for-sale securities are valued at market. Realized and unrealized gains and losses for trading securities are reported in the statement of earnings while only realized gains and losses are reported for available-for-sale and held-to-maturity securities.

Although it may be tempting to think about how one could manage earnings by reclassifying investments from one category to another, moving securities from one classification to another at whim would call into question the credibility of financial reporting. Consequently, there are specified restrictions to minimize this possibility. For example, reclassification of trading and held-to-maturity securities is generally prohibited.

In addition, whether an available-for-sale security is classified as short- or long-term depends primarily on management intent—another subjective determination and one fraught with risk. Management can change, or even misrepresent, their intentions. Or, economic circumstances can change for the company. Consequently, the intent and ability to hold an investment must be reassessed at least annually.

Nonetheless, the potential for earnings management with respect to investments still exists. Companies can easily "window dress" their reported earnings results—that is, make net earnings look better or worse than they really are—if they want to do so. If a company wanted to increase its reported earnings, it could simply sell its available-for-sale securities that have unrealized gains, and not sell its available-for-sale securities that have unrealized losses. By doing this, the company would realize its gains and report them in the statement of earnings, thus increasing net earnings. It would report its unrealized losses in the statement of comprehensive income, thus deferring the recognition of the losses until a later period.

You may wonder why it matters whether a gain or loss is reported as a component of net earnings in the statement of earnings or as a component of other comprehensive income in the statement of comprehensive income. After all, the information is fully reported and disclosed—whether it is realized or unrealized. Unfortunately, investors do not usually pay as much attention to comprehensive income as they do to net earnings. And ratio analyses, such as the ones that we have learned so far in this textbook, use net earnings and not comprehensive income in their formulas.

Sometimes unrealized losses on available-for-sale securities can be significant. For example, for the year ended February 26, 2005, Research in Motion Limited reported net earnings of U.S. $213.4 million. It also reported U.S. $18.4 million in unrealized losses on its available-for-sale securities as a reduction to other comprehensive income. If these securities had been sold before year end, net earnings would have declined by U.S. $18.4 million, or nine percent. Clearly, when the performance of a company's investment portfolio is being evaluated, it is important to consider the impact of actual and potential gains and losses on current and future earnings.

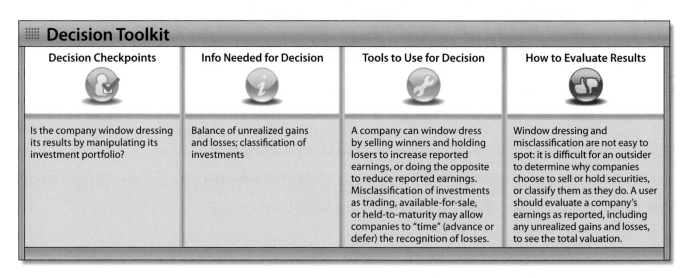

Decision Toolkit

Decision Checkpoints	Info Needed for Decision	Tools to Use for Decision	How to Evaluate Results
Is the company window dressing its results by manipulating its investment portfolio?	Balance of unrealized gains and losses; classification of investments	A company can window dress by selling winners and holding losers to increase reported earnings, or doing the opposite to reduce reported earnings. Misclassification of investments as trading, available-for-sale, or held-to-maturity may allow companies to "time" (advance or defer) the recognition of losses.	Window dressing and misclassification are not easy to spot: it is difficult for an outsider to determine why companies choose to sell or hold securities, or classify them as they do. A user should evaluate a company's earnings as reported, including any unrealized gains and losses, to see the total valuation.

BEFORE YOU GO ON . . .

▶Review It

1. What is the proper valuation for (a) trading securities, (b) available-for-sale securities, and (c) held-to-maturity securities?
2. Distinguish between the reporting of unrealized gains and losses for trading securities and available-for-sale securities.
3. How might a company window dress its reported earnings using its available-for-sale securities?

the navigator

Reporting of Investments

In this section, we will learn how equity investments are reported when one company controls another company. We will also review the presentation of investments in the balance sheet, statement of earnings, statement of comprehensive income, and cash flow statement.

study objective 5

Indicate how investments are reported in the financial statements.

Consolidated Financial Statements

Earlier in the chapter, we learned that when a company has significant influence over another company it uses the equity method of accounting. This is true whether a company owns 20 percent or 100 percent of another company. If a company owns between 20 percent and 50 percent of the common shares of another company, the investment is reported as a long-term equity investment in the investor's financial statements.

However, when a company owns more than 50 percent, or controls the common shares of another company, an additional set of financial statements is required. Note that control can occur with share ownership of less than 50 percent, depending on how widely dispersed the share ownership is, and other factors mentioned previously.

When one company (known as the **parent company**) controls another company (known as the **subsidiary company**), consolidated financial statements must be prepared for financial reporting purposes. Consolidated financial statements present the assets and liabilities that are controlled by the parent company and the total revenues and expenses of the subsidiary companies. They indicate the size and scope of operations of the companies under common control. Most publicly traded Canadian companies present consolidated financial statements.

Consolidated financial statements are prepared as an addition to the financial statements for the parent company and each subsidiary company. For example, as indicated in the feature story, EnCana recently acquired 100 percent of the common shares of Tom Brown, Inc. EnCana uses the equity method to account for its investment in Tom Brown in its own accounting records and internal financial statements. But, for external reporting, EnCana consolidates Tom Brown's results with its own. Under this approach, the individual assets and liabilities of Tom Brown are included with those of EnCana.

Consolidation is a complex topic which is usually dealt with in advanced accounting courses.

ACCOUNTING MATTERS! Management Perspective

The top five subsidiary companies in Canada, ranked by revenue, are listed below. In all cases, the major shareholder controls (owns more than 50 percent) of the subsidiary's shares. The percentage ownership is indicated in parentheses.

Rank	Subsidiary	Parent
1	Loblaw, Toronto	George Weston (61%)
2	Bell Canada, Montreal	BCE (100%)
3	Power Financial, Montreal	Power Corp. of Canada (67%)
4	Great-West Lifeco, Winnipeg	Power Financial (83%)
5	Sobeys, Stellarton	Empire (65%)

Balance Sheet

In the balance sheet presentation, investments are classified as short-term or long-term.

Short-Term Investments

Investments that are held for trading purposes are always classified as short-term. Available-for-sale securities may be classified as short- or long-term, depending on management's intent. Short-term investments—whether trading or available-for-sale—are reported in the current assets section of the balance sheet at their market value. The valuation allowance to adjust cost to market value may be added or deducted directly on the balance sheet, or it can be disclosed in the notes to the financial statements.

Long-Term Investments

Whether classified as short- or long-term, available-for-sale securities are reported on the balance sheet at their market value. The valuation allowance to adjust cost to market value may be added or deducted directly on the balance sheet, or disclosed in the notes to the financial statements.

Held-to-maturity securities are debt securities that are classified as long-term investments until they are about to mature. Any portion that is expected to mature within the year is classified as a current asset. Held-to-maturity securities are reported at their amortized cost.

Equity investments that give significant influence are reported separately as long-term investments, and supporting details provided in the notes to the financial statements. And, as we just learned in the previous section, if control exists, consolidated financial statements must be prepared. For reporting purposes, in the consolidated financial statements the equity investment would be eliminated because you cannot own an investment in yourself.

No distinction is usually made between debt and equity securities for financial reporting purposes. These securities are usually combined and reported as one portfolio amount for each classification in the balance sheet.

Illustration 12-8 ▶

Comprehensive balance sheet

XYZ CORPORATION
Balance Sheet
December 31, 2006

Assets

Current assets			
Cash and cash equivalents			$ 21,000
Trading securities, at market			60,000
Accounts receivable		$84,000	
Less: Allowance for doubtful accounts		4,000	80,000
Merchandise inventory			130,000
Prepaid insurance			23,000
Total current assets			314,000
Investments			
Available-for-sale securities, at market		$100,000	
Held-to-maturity securities, at amortized cost		50,000	
Equity investments, at equity		150,000	
Total long-term investments			300,000
Property, plant, and equipment			
Land		$200,000	
Buildings	$800,000		
Less: Accumulated amortization	200,000	600,000	
Equipment	$180,000		
Less: Accumulated amortization	54,000	126,000	
Total property, plant, and equipment			926,000
Intangible assets			
Goodwill			170,000
Total assets			$1,710,000

Liabilities and Shareholders' Equity

Current liabilities			
Accounts payable			$ 185,000
Bond interest payable			10,500
Income tax payable			60,000
Total current liabilities			255,500
Long-term liabilities			
Bonds payable, 7%, due 2016			300,000
Total liabilities			555,500
Shareholders' equity			
Common shares, no par value, unlimited number			
authorized, 80,000 issued		$900,000	
Retained earnings		265,000	
Accumulated other comprehensive loss		(10,500)	
Total shareholders' equity			1,154,500
Total liabilities and shareholders' equity			$1,710,000

Illustration 12-8, shown on the previous page, presents a comprehensive balance sheet, using assumed data. In this illustration, we have highlighted in red the presentation of its short- and long-term investments. We have shown the presentation of the trading and available-for-sale securities net of the allowance to adjust them to their respective market values. Further detail about this disclosure would be reported in the notes to the financial statements. Compare this type of presentation to that shown earlier in Illustration 12-6 where the allowance details were reported directly on the balance sheet.

Note also the addition of an accumulated other comprehensive loss in the shareholders' equity section of the balance sheet. Just as net earnings increase retained earnings, the amount of comprehensive income or loss reported in the statement of comprehensive income becomes part of the accumulated other comprehensive income (or loss) in the shareholders' equity section of the balance sheet.

Statement of Earnings

Gains and losses on investments, whether they are realized or unrealized, must be presented in the financial statements. Realized gains and losses are presented in the statement of earnings. Unrealized gains and losses from trading securities are also presented in the statement of earnings.

These gains and losses, as well as other investment-related accounts such as those for interest and dividend revenue, are reported in the non-operating section of the statement of earnings. Illustration 12-9 presents examples of other revenue and other expenses that relate to investments.

Other Revenue	Other Expenses
Dividend revenue	Loss on sale of investment
Gain on sale of investment	Unrealized loss—trading securities
Interest revenue	
Investment revenue	
Unrealized gain—trading securities	

Illustration 12-9 ◄

Non-operating items related to investments

Statement of Comprehensive Income

Unrealized gains and losses from available-for-sale securities are presented in the statement of comprehensive income as shown in Illustration 12-7 and are not illustrated again here.

Cash Flow Statement

Information on the cash inflows and outflows that resulted from investment transactions during the period is reported in the investing activities section of the cash flow statement. Illustration 12-10 presents the cash flows from investing activities from EnCana's 2004 cash flow statement, with activities related to investments highlighted in red.

Illustration 12-10 ◄

Cash flow statement presentation of investments

ENCANA CORPORATION
Cash Flow Statement (partial)
Year Ended December 31, 2004
(in millions)

ENCANA.

Investing activities	
Business combinations	$(2,335)
Capital expenditures	(4,817)
Proceeds on disposal of assets	1,144
Dispositions (acquisitions)	386
Equity investments	47
Net change in investments and other	45
Net change in noncash working capital from continuing operations	(21)
Discontinued operations	1,292
	$(4,259)

From this information, we learn that EnCana spent a total of $4,259 million on investing activities in 2004. These activities included spending $2,335 to acquire Tom Brown, Inc. This cash outflow was offset by $386 million received from corporate dispositions, which included EnCana selling its 53.3-percent ownership interest in Petrovera Resources. In addition, $47 million was received from revenue earned from equity investments and $45 million was received from other investments.

BEFORE YOU GO ON . . .

▶Review It

the navigator

1. Are Loblaw's financial statements consolidated? If yes, what percentage of its subsidiaries does Loblaw own? (*Hint*: Note 1 provides useful information to help you with these questions). The answers to these questions are provided at the end of this chapter.
2. Are trading securities normally classified as short-term or long-term on the balance sheet? What about available-for-sale securities? Held-to-maturity securities?
3. How are investments reported on the balance sheet? On the statement of earnings? On the statement of comprehensive income? On the cash flow statement?

▦ Using the Decision Toolkit

The Royal Bank of Canada reports the following selected information related to its investments:

ROYAL BANK OF CANADA
Consolidated Balance Sheet (partial)
December 31, 2004
(in millions)

	2004	2003
Trading securities	$ 87,635	$ 86,719
Available-for-sale securities	39,861	41,619
	127,496	128,338
Accumulated other comprehensive income (loss)	(1,632)	(1,374)

Additional information:

1. Trading and available-for-sale securities include both debt and equity securities. The maturity dates of the debt securities vary from within three months to more than 10 years in each category.
2. A net realized and unrealized gain of $1,526 million was reported for trading securities.
3. A net realized gain of $82 million ($146 million of gains less $64 million of losses) and a net unrealized gain of $361 million ($488 million of gains less $127 million of losses) were reported for available-for-sale securities

Instructions

(a) What reason does the Royal Bank likely have for purchasing investments rather than only making loans? Why does it purchase investments that vary in terms of both their maturities and their type (debt and equity)?
(b) In what section of a classified balance sheet do you think the Royal Bank reports its trading securities, available-for-sale securities, and accumulated other comprehensive

loss? At what value are trading and available-for-sale securities reported in the balance sheet?

(c) Where would the Royal Bank report the net realized and unrealized gain of $1,526 million for trading securities, the net realized gain of $82 million for available-for-sale securities, and the net unrealized gain of $361 million reported for available-for-sale securities?

(d) Suppose that the management of the Royal Bank was not happy with its net earnings. What step could it have taken with its investment portfolio that would have increased its net earnings? What were management's likely reasons for not doing this?

Solution

(a) Although banks are mainly in the business of lending money, they need to balance their portfolio through investments. For example, a bank may have cash on hand from depositors that it has not yet loaned which it wants to invest in short-term liquid assets. Or it may believe that it can earn a higher rate of interest by buying certain investments rather than by making new loans. Or it may purchase investments for speculation because it believes these investments will increase in value. Banks purchase a variety of investments with a variety of terms to match the duration of their loans.

(b) Trading securities are reported at market value in the current assets section. Even though there are varying terms within the trading securities category, it is management's intention to sell these securities if the need for cash arises, and they are therefore classified as short-term investments. Available-for-sale securities are reported at market value as a short- or long-term investment, depending on management's intention. Accumulated other comprehensive loss is reported in the shareholders' equity section.

(c) The net realized and unrealized gain for trading securities is presented in the other revenue section of the statement of earnings. The net realized gain for available-for-sale securities is presented in the other revenue section of the statement of earnings. The net unrealized gain for available-for-sale securities is presented as other comprehensive income in the statement of comprehensive income.

(d) The Royal Bank could have sold its shares with an unrealized gain in the available-for-sale portfolio at year end and increased its net earnings by $488 million. The company chose not to "manage earnings" by selling these securities for the following possible reasons: (a) it felt that the securities had additional room for price appreciation, (b) it did not want to pay the additional income tax associated with selling shares at a gain, or (c) it wanted to hold the securities because they were needed to provide the proper asset balance in the bank's total asset portfolio.

the navigator

Summary of Study Objectives

1. *Identify the reasons corporations invest in short- and long-term debt and equity securities.*   Corporations invest for three common reasons: (1) They have excess cash. (2) They view investments as a revenue source. (3) They have strategic goals such as gaining control of a competitor, promoting strategic alliances, or moving into a new line of business.

Short-term investments are debt or equity securities held by a company that are readily marketable and intended to be converted to cash in the near future when cash is needed. Investments that do not meet both criteria are classified as long-term investments.

2. *Explain the accounting for debt investments.*   Debt investments include investments in money-market instruments, bonds, commercial paper, and similar items. Entries are required to record the (1) acquisition, (2) interest revenue, and (3) maturity or sale.

3. *Explain the accounting for equity investments.*   Equity investments are investments in the share capital of other corporations. Entries are required to record the (1) acquisition, (2) investment revenue, and (3) sale.

When the investor company is not able to exert significant influence (share ownership usually 20 percent or less) over the investee company, the cost method should be used. The cost method records investment revenue when dividends are received. When significant influence exists (share ownership usually 20 percent or more), the equity method should be used. The equity method records investment revenue when net earnings are reported by the investee and increases its investment account accordingly. Dividends received reduce the value of the investment account.

4. *Describe how investments are valued and performance is evaluated.*   Investments in debt and equity securities are classified as trading, available-for-sale, or held-to-maturity securities for valuation purposes. Trading securities are reported at market value; and unrealized gains and losses resulting from adjusting cost to market value are reported as other revenue in the statement of earnings. Available-for-sale securities are reported at market value; and unrealized gains and losses resulting from adjusting cost to market value are reported as other comprehensive income in the statement of comprehensive income. Held-to-maturity securities are reported at amortized cost. Care must be taken to classify securities appropriately and evaluate the impact of both realized and unrealized gains and losses on current and future earnings.

5. *Indicate how investments are reported in the financial statements.*   When a company controls (ownership usually greater than 50 percent) the common shares of another company, consolidated financial statements that detail the financial position of the combined entity must also be prepared. Trading securities are presented in the current assets section of the balance sheet. Available-for-sale securities may be classified as short-term or long-term, depending on management's intention. Held-to-maturity securities and equity investments of significant influence are classified as long-term investments. Accumulated other comprehensive income, which includes unrealized gains or losses from available-for-sale securities, is presented in the shareholders' equity section of the balance sheet.

Realized gains and losses are presented as other revenue and other expenses in the statement of earnings. Unrealized gains and losses for trading securities are presented in the statement of earnings, while unrealized gains and losses for available-for-sale securities are presented as comprehensive income in the statement of comprehensive income. The purchase and sale of investments are reported in the investing activities section of the cash flow statement.

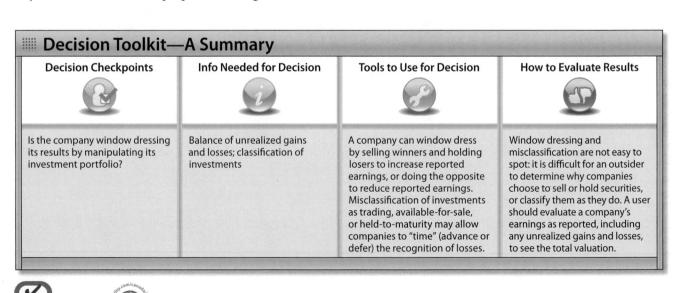

▦ Decision Toolkit—A Summary

Decision Checkpoints	Info Needed for Decision	Tools to Use for Decision	How to Evaluate Results
Is the company window dressing its results by manipulating its investment portfolio?	Balance of unrealized gains and losses; classification of investments	A company can window dress by selling winners and holding losers to increase reported earnings, or doing the opposite to reduce reported earnings. Misclassification of investments as trading, available-for-sale, or held-to-maturity may allow companies to "time" (advance or defer) the recognition of losses.	Window dressing and misclassification are not easy to spot: it is difficult for an outsider to determine why companies choose to sell or hold securities, or classify them as they do. A user should evaluate a company's earnings as reported, including any unrealized gains and losses, to see the total valuation.

the navigator

www.wiley.com/canada/kimmel

**Analysis Tools
(Decision Toolkit Summaries)**

Glossary

Study Tools (Glossary)

Available-for-sale securities Debt or equity securities that may be sold in the future. Reported at market value on the balance sheet. (p. 565)

Consolidated financial statements Financial statements that present the assets and liabilities controlled by the parent company and the total profitability of the combined companies. (p. 579)

Cost method An accounting method in which the equity investment is recorded at cost. Investment revenue is recognized only when cash dividends are received. (p. 571)

Debt investments Investments in money-market instruments, bonds, commercial paper, or similar items. (p. 566)

Equity investments Investments in the common and/or preferred shares of other corporations. (p. 570)

Equity method An accounting method in which the investment in common shares is initially recorded at cost. The investment account is then adjusted (increased for the investor's share of the investee's net earnings and decreased for dividends received) to show the investor's equity in the investee. (p. 572)

Held-to-maturity securities Debt securities that the investor has the intention and ability to hold to their maturity date. Reported at amortized cost on the balance sheet. (p. 566)

Investee The corporation that issues (sells) the debt or equity securities. (p. 567)

Investor The corporation that buys (owns) the debt or equity securities. (p. 567)

Long-term investments Investments that are not readily marketable or that management does not intend to convert into cash in the near future. (p. 566)

Realized gain or loss The difference between market value and cost when an investment is actually sold. (p. 575)

Short-term investments Investments that are readily marketable and intended to be converted into cash in the near future when cash is needed. (p. 565)

Trading securities Debt or equity securities that are bought and held for sale in the near term, and mainly to generate earnings from short-term price differences. Reported at market value on the balance sheet. (p. 565)

Unrealized gain or loss The difference between market value and cost for an investment still on hand (not sold). Sometimes referred to as a "paper" gain or loss because it has not been realized. (p. 575)

Demonstration Problem

Study Tools
(Demonstration Problems)

In 2006, its first year of operations, the Northstar Finance Corporation. had the following transactions in trading securities:

Mar. 14 Purchased $10,000 of treasury bills.

June 1 Purchased 600 Sanburg common shares for $24 per share, plus $300 of brokerage fees.

June 29 Sold treasury bills for $10,000, plus $50 interest.

July 1 Purchased 800 Cey common shares for $33 per share, plus $600 of brokerage fees.

Sept. 1 Received a $1-per-share cash dividend from Cey Corporation.

Nov. 1 Sold 200 Sanburg common shares for $27 per share, less $150 of brokerage fees.

Dec. 15 Received a $0.50-per-share cash dividend on Sanburg common shares.

31 At December 31, the market values per share were Sanburg, $25, and Cey, $30.

Instructions

(a) Journalize the above transactions.

(b) Prepare the adjusting entry required to report the securities at their market value.

(c) Show the presentation of the trading securities, and related accounts, in the balance sheet and statement of earnings

Solution to Demonstration Problem

(a)

Mar. 14	Debt Investments—Treasury Bills	10,000	
	Cash		10,000
	(To record purchase of treasury bills)		
June 1	Equity Investments—Sanburg Common	14,700	
	Cash [(600 × $24) + $300]		14,700
	(To record purchase of 600 Sanburg common shares)		
29	Cash	10,050	
	Debt Investments—Treasury Bills		10,000
	Interest Revenue		50
	(To record sale of treasury bills)		
July 1	Equity Investments—Cey Common	27,000	
	Cash [(800 × $33) + $600]		27,000
	(To record purchase of 800 Cey common shares)		
Sept. 1	Cash (800 × $1)	800	
	Dividend Revenue		800
	(To record receipt of $1-per-share cash dividend from Cey)		
Nov. 1	Cash [(200 × $27) − $150]	5,250	
	Equity Investments—Sanburg Common (200 ÷ 600 × $14,700)		4,900
	Gain on Sale of Equity Investments		350
	(To record sale of 200 Sanburg common shares)		
Dec. 15	Cash [(600 − 200) × $0.50]	200	
	Dividend Revenue		200
	(To record receipt of $0.50-per-share dividend from Sanburg)		

(b)

Dec. 31	Unrealized Loss—Trading Securities	2,800	
	Allowance to Adjust Trading Securities to Market Value		2,800
	(To record unrealized loss on trading securities)		

Trading Security	Cost	Market Value	Unrealized Gain (Loss)
Sanburg common shares (400)	$ 9,800	$10,000	$ 200
Cey common shares (800)	27,000	24,000	(3,000)
Total	$36,800	$34,000	$(2,800)

(c)

NORTHSTAR FINANCE CORPORATION
Balance Sheet (partial)
December 31, 2006

Assets

Current assets	
Trading securities, at cost	$36,800
Less: Allowance to adjust trading securities to market value	2,800
Trading securities, at market	34,000

Note: This information could also be presented in the current assets section net of the allowance, with details disclosed in the notes to the financial statements.

| NORTHSTAR FINANCE CORPORATION | | |
| Statement of Earnings (partial) | | |
Year Ended December 31, 2006		
Other revenue		
Unrealized loss on trading securities		$2,800
Dividend revenue ($800 + $200)		1,000
Interest revenue		50
		3,850

the
navigator

Self-Study Questions

www.wiley.com/canada/kimmel

Study Tools (Self-Assessment Quizzes)

Answers are at the end of the chapter.

(SO 1) 1. Which of the following is *not* a reason that corporations invest in debt and equity securities?
  (a) They have excess cash.
  (b) They want to lose money and generate losses to reduce taxable income.
  (c) They want to generate investment revenue.
  (d) They invest to meet strategic goals.

(SO 1) 2. Short-term investments must be readily marketable and expected to be sold:
  (a) within three months.
  (b) within six months.
  (c) within one year.
  (d) when cash is needed.

(SO 2) 3. Zundel Corporation purchased bonds as a short-term debt investment for $100,000, plus brokerage fees of $5,000. Assuming the bonds were issued by Plaza Ltd. at face value, this transaction would be recorded on the books of the investor and investee, as follows:
  (a) Debt Investment $100,000 (investor); Bonds Payable $100,000 (investee)
  (b) Debt Investment $105,000 (investor); Bonds Payable $100,000 (investee)
  (c) Bonds Payable $105,000 (investor); Debt Investment $100,000 (investee)
  (d) Bonds Payable $100,000 (investor); Debt Investment $105,000 (investee)

(SO 2) 4. Boisclair Ltée sells short-term debt investments costing $26,000 for $28,000. The gain or loss on this transaction should be reported in the statement of earnings as a:
  (a) realized loss of $2,000 under other expenses.
  (b) unrealized loss of $2,000 under other expenses.
  (c) realized gain of $2,000 under other revenues.
  (d) unrealized gain of $2,000 under other revenues.

(SO 3) 5. The equity method of accounting for long-term equity investments should be used when the investor owns:
  (a) more than zero percent of the investee's common shares

  (b) less than 20 percent of the investee's common shares.
  (c) 20 percent or more of the investee's common shares.
  (d) more than 20 percent but less than 50 percent of the investee's common shares.

6. The Big K Ranch owns 20 percent of the Little L Ranch. (SO 3) The Little L Ranch reported net earnings of $150,000 and paid dividends of $40,000 this year. How much investment revenue would the Big K Ranch report if it used the cost method to account for this investment? The equity method?
  (a) $8,000 under both methods
  (b) $8,000 cost method; $22,000 equity method
  (c) $8,000 cost method; $30,000 equity method
  (d) $40,000 cost method; $110,000 equity method

7. At the end of the first year of operations, the total cost (SO 4) of the trading securities portfolio is $120,000 and the total market value is $115,000. What should the financial statements show?
  (a) A reduction in a current asset of $5,000 reported in the balance sheet, and a realized loss of $5,000 reported in the statement of earnings
  (b) A reduction in a current asset of $5,000 reported in the balance sheet, and an unrealized loss of $5,000 reported in the statement of earnings
  (c) A reduction in a current asset of $5,000 reported in the balance sheet, and an unrealized loss of $5,000 reported in the statement of comprehensive income
  (d) No reduction and no loss

8. If a company wants to increase its earnings by (SO 4) manipulating its investment accounts, which should it do?
  (a) Sell its "winner" trading securities and hold its "loser" trading securities
  (b) Hold its "winner" trading securities and sell its "loser" trading securities
  (c) Sell its "winner" available-for-sale securities and hold its "loser" available-for-sale securities
  (d) Hold its "winner" available-for-sale securities and sell its "loser" available-for-sale securities

(SO 5) 9. Consolidated financial statements do not:
(a) determine the profitability of specific subsidiaries.
(b) determine the total profitability of entities under common control.
(c) determine the extent of a parent company's operations.
(d) determine the full extent of the collective obligations of companies under common control.

10. In the balance sheet, when the market value of available-for-sale securities is less than cost, the Allowance to Adjust Available-for-Sale Securities to Market Value is reported as a: (SO 5)
(a) contra asset account.
(b) adjunct asset account.
(c) contra shareholders' equity account.
(d) adjunct shareholders' equity account.

Questions

(SO 1) 1. What are the reasons that corporations invest in debt and equity securities?

(SO 1) 2. Distinguish between short-term investments and long-term investments.

(SO 1) 3. Distinguish between trading securities, available-for-sale securities, and held-to maturity securities.

(SO 1) 4. The Cumby Corporation, a golf equipment retailer, owns common shares in EnCana Corporation, which it intends to sell if it needs cash. Should the investment in EnCana be classified as (a) a short-term investment or a long-term investment, and (b) a trading security, available-for-sale security, or held-to-maturity security? Explain your reasoning.

(SO 2) 5. How is the cost of a debt or equity investment determined? Which accounting principle guides this determination?

(SO 2) 6. Distinguish between the accounting for short-term debt investments in money-market instruments and bonds.

(SO 2) 7. Dugas Ltd. paid $65,000, plus $1,300 of brokerage fees, to acquire a short-term investment in bonds. It later sold them for $70,000, less $1,400 of brokerage fees. How much is the gain or loss on sale? Where should this amount be reported?

(SO 2) 8. Compare the accounting for a debt investment in bonds to that for a bond liability.

(SO 3) 9. When should a long-term equity investment be accounted for using (a) the cost method and (b) the equity method?

(SO 3) 10. What constitutes "significant influence?" Is it safe to conclude that there is significant influence when a company owns 20 percent of the common shares of another company?

(SO 3) 11. Identify what is included in the carrying value of an equity investment using (a) the cost method and (b) the equity method.

(SO 3) 12. Explain how, and why, the investment revenue differs when an equity investment is accounted for using (a) the cost method and (b) the equity method.

13. At what value are each of the following reported on a balance sheet: (a) trading securities, (b) available-for-sale securities, and (c) held-to-maturity securities? (SO 4)

14. BCE Inc. reports available-for-sale securities at December 31, 2004, with a cost of $261 million and a market value of $265 million. How should the difference between these two amounts be recorded and reported? Would your answer differ if these were trading securities rather than available-for-sale securities? (SO 4)

15. ⚲ In what ways does classifying investments of the Royal Bank as trading or available-for-sale help investors evaluate the bank's profitability? (SO 4)

16. ⚲ Identify two ways a company might be able to "manage its earnings" with respect to its investment portfolio. (SO 4)

17. What are consolidated financial statements? When must they be prepared? (SO 5)

18. Onex Corporation owns 100 percent of the common shares of Cineplex-Galaxy. (a) What method—cost or equity—should Onex use to account for this investment? (b) Which company is the parent? The subsidiary? (c) How should this investment be reported in Onex's consolidated financial statements? (SO 5)

19. Where are cash inflows and outflows related to investments presented in the cash flow statement? (SO 5)

20. China Mobile (Hong Kong) Limited reported the following selected data (in RMB millions) at December 31, 2004: investment securities 77; equity investments, at cost 468,222; term deposits with banks within three months of maturity 7,100; term deposits with banks 20,264; cash paid for the acquisition of subsidiaries 12,238; cash received from dividends 84; interest income 1,014; and cash received from interest 939. Identify on which financial statement each of these amounts should be reported and give the most likely classification. (SO 5)

Brief Exercises

BE12–1 On March 1, Toyworks Ltd. invested $100,000 in the ADR Canadian Money-Market Fund. On March 31, it received notification that $200 of interest had been earned for the month and added to the fund. On April 30, it cashed in the fund and received $100,401 cash, which included $201 of interest earned in April. Record each of these transactions.

Record debt investment transactions. (SO 2)

BE12–2 On January 1, Phelps Corporation purchased a debt investment for $41,500, plus brokerage fees of $800. On July 1, Phelps received interest of $1,245. On October 1, it sold the investment for $43,000, less brokerage fees of $850. Record each of these transactions.

Record debt investment transactions. (SO 2)

BE12–3 On June 30, Erb Inc. issued 10-year, 5% bonds at their face value of $50,000. Interest is payable semi-annually each June 30 and December 31. (a) Record the purchase of the debt investment on June 30 and the receipt of the first interest payment on December 31 in the books of the investor. (b) Record the issue of the debt on June 30 and the first interest payment in December 31 in the books of the investee (issuer).

Record debt investment transactions for investor and investee. (SO 2)

BE12–4 On August 1, McLellan Ltd. purchased 1,000 Datawave common shares for $36,000 cash, plus brokerage fees of $725. On October 15, it received a cash dividend of $1 per share on the Datawave shares. On December 1, McLellan sold the shares for $35,000, less brokerage fees of $700. Record the purchase and sale of the Datawave shares, assuming McLellan does not have significant influence over Datawave.

Record equity investment transactions. (SO 3)

BE12–5 On January 1, Crook Corporation purchased 25% of Hook Ltd. for $150,000. At December 31, Hook paid a $10,000 dividend and reported net earnings of $200,000. Record each of these transactions, assuming Crook has significant influence over Hook. How much revenue was reported by Crook?

Record transactions under equity method. (SO 3)

BE12–6 Using the data presented in BE12–5, assume that Crook Corporation does not have significant influence over Hook Ltd. Record each of the transactions under this assumption. How much revenue was reported by Crook? Explain why this differs from the answer in BE12–5.

Record transactions under cost method. (SO 3)

BE12–7 Chan Inc. owns 20% of Dong Ltd.'s common shares. During the year, Dong reported net earnings of $250,000 and paid a $15,000 dividend. Indicate whether using the equity method instead of the cost method would result in an increase (+), a decrease (−), or no effect (NE) in each of the following categories:

Compare impact of cost and equity methods. (SO 3)

Balance Sheet			Statement of Earnings		
Assets	Liabilities	Shareholders' Equity	Revenues	Expenses	Net Earnings

BE12–8 Indicate whether each of the following transactions would increase, decrease, or have no effect on earnings:

Identify impact of earnings manipulation. (SO 4)

(a) Classification of available-for-sale securities as short-term rather than long-term
(b) Classification of short-term investments as available-for-sale rather than trading at a time when the market value was lower than cost
(c) Sale of an available-for-sale security with a market value greater than cost
(d) Reclassification of an investment in bonds with an unrealized loss from an available-for-sale security to a held-to-maturity security

BE12–9 Cost and market data for the trading securities of Deal.com Ltd. at December 31, 2006, are $64,000 and $65,000, respectively. Prepare the adjusting entry to record the securities at market value. Show the financial statement presentation of the trading securities and any gain or loss.

Record adjusting entry for trading securities; show statement presentation. (SO 4, 5)

BE12–10 Cost and market data for the available-for-sale securities of Leafblower Ltd. at December 31, 2006, are $72,000 and $65,000, respectively. Prepare the adjusting entry to record the securities at market value. Show the financial statement presentation of the available-for-sale securities and any gain or loss. It is not management's intent to sell the securities in the short term, if the need for cash arises.

Record adjusting entry for available-for-sale securities; show statement presentation. (SO 4, 5)

Prepare investments section of balance sheet.
(SO 5)

BE12–11   Sabre Corporation has the following investments at November 30, 2006:

- Trading securities: common shares of National Bank, cost $25,000, market value $26,000
- Available-for-sale securities (short-term): common shares of Sword Corp., cost $108,000, market value $105,000
- Equity investment: common shares of Epee Inc. (30% ownership), cost $210,000, equity $250,000
- Held-to-maturity securities: bonds of Ghoti Ltd., amortized cost $150,000, market value $175,000

Prepare the investments section of the balance sheet.

Discuss presentation of unrealized gain.
(SO 5)

BE12–12   Cameco Corporation reported an unrealized gain of $36.8 million on its available-for-sale securities for the year ended December 31, 2004, and an accumulated unrealized gain of $60.7 million on available-for-sale securities as at December 31, 2004. Discuss how each of these gains should be reported in Cameco's financial statements.

Exercises

Record debt investment transactions.
(SO 2)

E12–1   The Happy Valley Corporation has a policy of investing excess cash in money-market instruments. During the year ended November 30, 2006, it had the following transactions for money-market instruments:

Jan. 2 Purchased a 90-day treasury bill maturing on April 1 for $9,938.
Apr. 1 The treasury bill matured. Happy Valley received $10,000 cash, which included the interest earned.
June 1 Invested $40,000 in a money-market fund.
     30 Received notification that $75 of interest had been earned and added to the fund.
July 31 Received notification that $75 of interest had been earned and added to the fund.
Aug. 15 Cashed the money-market fund and received $40,188.
Oct. 31 Purchased a three-month, 2.5% term deposit for $24,000.

Instructions

(a) Record the above transactions.
(b) Prepare any required adjusting entries at November 30.

Record debt investment transactions.
(SO 2)

E12–2   Piper Corporation had the following transactions for short-term debt investments:

Jan. 1 Purchased 60 Harris Corp. 6%, $1,000 bonds for $60,000, plus brokerage fees of $1,200. Interest is payable semi-annually on July 1 and January 1.
July 1 Received semi-annual interest on Harris bonds.
     1 Sold 30 Harris bonds for $32,000, less $650 of brokerage fees.
Dec. 31 Accrued interest at Piper's year end.

Instructions

Record the above transactions.

Record debt investment transaction for investor and investee.
(SO 2)

E12–3   On June 30, 2006, Imperial Inc. purchased $250,000 of Acme Corp. 5% bonds at 98 as a held-to-maturity security. The bonds pay interest semi-annually and mature June 30, 2016.

Instructions

(a) Record the purchase of the bonds for Imperial, the investor.
(b) Record the issue of the bonds for Acme, the investee (issuer).
(c) Explain how the amortization of any bond premium or discount would affect each company.

Record equity investment transactions.
(SO 3)

E12–4   During the year ended December 31, 2006, McCormick Inc. had the following transactions for its available-for-sale securities:

Jan. 1 Purchased 1,000 Starr Corporation 5% noncumulative preferred shares for $105,000 cash, plus a $2,000 brokerage fee.
Apr. 1 Received quarterly cash dividend.

July 1 Received quarterly cash dividend.
 2 Sold 500 Starr shares for $57,000 cash, less a $1,000 brokerage fee.
Oct. 1 Received quarterly cash dividend.

Instructions

(a) Record the above transactions.
(b) Starr declared its usual quarterly dividend on November 22, to preferred shareholders of record on December 15, payable on January 1. Prepare any required adjusting entry at December 31 for this dividend. If no adjusting entry is required, explain why.

E12–5 Visage Cosmetics Ltd. acquired 45% of Diner Corporation's 30,000 common shares for $9 per share on January 1, 2006. On June 15, Diner paid a cash dividend of $35,000. On December 31, Diner reported net earnings of $75,000 for the year.

Visage Cosmetics also acquired 10% of the 200,000 common shares of Bell Fashion Ltd. for $12 per share on March 18, 2006. On June 30, Bell paid a $75,000 dividend. On December 31, Bell reported net earnings of $122,000 for the year.

Record transactions under cost and equity methods.
(SO 3)

Instructions

Record the above transactions for the year ended December 31, 2006.

E12–6 On November 1, 2005, as a short-term equity investment, Lajeunesse Lteé purchased 1,000 Lyman Corporation common shares for $60 per share and 200 Kaur Inc. preferred shares for $90 per share. On December 15, Lajeunesse sold 400 Lyman shares for $80 per share. At December 31, the company's year end, the market value of the Lyman shares is $70 per share and the market value of the Kaur shares is $75 per share. On March 31, 2006, Lajeunesse sold the remaining Lyman shares for $65 per share. On December 31, 2006, the market value of the Kaur shares is $80 per share.

Record equity investment transaction.
(SO 3, 4)

Instructions

Record the above transactions, including any required adjusting entries, for 2005 and 2006.

E12–7 Brascan Corporation, an asset management company, reports the following selected long-term equity investments at December 31, 2004:

Identify method of accounting for equity investments.
(SO 3, 5)

Investment	Percentage Ownership	Method
Louisiana HydroElectric Power	75%	_____
Brookfield Properties Corp.	51%	_____
Noranda Inc.	42%	_____
Fraser Papers Inc.	42%	_____
Norbord Inc.	36%	_____
Canary Wharf Group plc	17%	_____

Instructions

(a) Indicate whether each of the above investments should be accounted for using the cost method or the equity method by writing the words "cost" or "equity" in the space provided.
(b) Which of the above investments, if any, should be consolidated with Brascan's operations?

E12–8 Kouchibouguac Inc. reports the following cost and market values for its investment portfolio of available-for-sale securities:

Record adjusting entries for available-for-sale securities for multiple years.
(SO 4)

	Cost	Market Value
June 30, 2004	$275,000	$263,500
June 30, 2005	325,600	354,000
June 30, 2006	475,700	589,500

Instructions

For each year, prepare the required adjusting entry to report the investment portfolio at market value.

E12–9 At December 31, 2006, the trading securities for Louden Financial, Inc., are as follows:

Record adjusting entry for trading securities; show statement presentation.
(SO 4, 5)

Trading Security	Cost	Market Value
A	$17,500	$16,000
B	12,500	14,000
C	23,000	19,000
Total	$53,000	$49,000

Instructions

(a) Prepare the adjusting entry to report the investment portfolio at market value at December 31.

(b) Show the balance sheet and statement of earnings presentation at December 31.

Record adjusting entry for available-for-sale securities; show statement presentation. (SO 4, 5)

E12–10   Data for equity investments classified as trading securities are presented in E12–9. Assume that the investments are classified as short-term available-for-sale securities with the same cost and market value data.

Instructions

(a) Prepare the adjusting entry to report the investment portfolio at market value at December 31.

(b) Show the balance sheet and statement of comprehensive income presentation at December 31.

Indicate statement presentation. (SO 5)

E12–11   Shaw Communications Inc. reports the following selected information related to investments in its financial statements for the year ended August 31, 2004 (in thousands):

Account	Amount	Financial Statement	Classification
Investments in private technology companies, at cost	$ 4,063	_____	_____
Investments in specialty channel networks, at equity	702	_____	_____
Write-down of investments	651	_____	_____
Equity loss on investees	250	_____	_____
Gain on sale of investments	356	_____	_____
Cash paid for acquisition of investments	495	_____	_____
Unrealized gains on investments	23,880	_____	_____
Accumulated other comprehensive income	9,809	_____	_____

Instructions

Indicate on which financial statement (i.e., balance sheet, statement of earnings, statement of comprehensive income, or cash flow statement) each of the above accounts would be reported. Also note the appropriate classification (e.g., long-term investments, other revenue, investing activities, etc.).

Problems: Set A

Record debt investment transactions for investor and investee. (SO 2)

P12–1A   On January 1, 2006, CASB Incorporated issued $1 million of 10-year, 7% bonds at face value. The bonds pay interest semi-annually on June 30 and December 31. On July 1, Densmore Consulting Ltd. purchased $100,000 of CASB bonds on the TSX Venture Exchange at 98 as a short-term investment. On December 31, after receiving the bond interest, Densmore Consulting sold its CASB bonds on the TSX Venture Exchange at 99. Both companies have a December 31 year end.

Instructions

(a) Prepare all required entries for Densmore Consulting, the investor, for 2006.

(b) Prepare all required entries for CASB, the investee, for 2006.

(c) Comment on the differences in recording that you observe between the investor and the investee.

Record debt investment transactions; show statement presentation. (SO 2, 4, 5)

P12–2A   The following Liu Corporation transactions are for bonds purchased as a short-term available-for-sale security during the year ended December 31, 2006:

Jan.   1   Purchased $50,000 RAM Corporation 6% bonds at 100. Interest is paid semi-annually on July 1 and January 1.

July   1   Received interest on RAM bonds.

     2   Sold $25,000 of RAM bonds at 110.

Dec. 31   Accrued interest on remaining RAM bonds.

   31   The market value of the bonds was $24,000 on this date.

Instructions

(a) Record the above transactions.

(b) Prepare the adjusting entry required at December 31 to adjust the bonds to market value.

(c) Show the financial statement presentation of the bonds and any related accounts at December 31.

P12–3A During 2006, Money Mart Ltd. purchased the following trading securities:

Record debt and equity investment transactions; show statement presentation. (SO 2, 3, 4, 5)

Feb. 1 Purchased 1,000 IBF common shares for $40,000.

Mar. 1 Purchased 500 RST common shares for $18,000.

Apr. 1 Purchased 6% CRT bonds for $70,000, plus $1,200 of brokerage fees. Interest is payable semi-annually on April 1 and October 1.

July 1 Received a cash dividend of $1.50 per share on the IBF common shares.

Aug. 1 Sold 350 IBF common shares at $42 per share.

Sept. 1 Received a cash dividend of $1 per share on the RST common shares.

Oct. 1 Received the semi-annual interest on the CRT bonds.

1 Sold the CRT bonds for $68,000, less $1,000 of brokerage fees.

Dec. 31 The market values of the IBF and RST common shares were $39 and $40 per share, respectively.

Instructions

(a) Record the above transactions.

(b) Prepare the adjusting entry required at December 31 to adjust the trading securities to market value.

(c) Show the balance sheet presentation of the trading securities at December 31, 2006.

(d) Identify the statement of earnings accounts involved and give the statement classification of each account.

P12–4A Olsztyn Inc. had the following investment transactions:

Identify statement impact of investment transactions. (SO 2, 3, 4, 5)

1. Purchased Arichat Corporation common shares as a trading security.

2. Received a cash dividend on Arichat common shares.

3. Purchased Bombardier bonds as an available-for-sale security.

4. Received interest on Bombardier bonds.

5. Sold half of the Bombardier bonds at a price greater than originally paid.

6. Purchased 40% of LaHave Ltd.'s common shares as a long-term equity investment.

7. Received LaHave's financial statements, which reported net earnings for the year.

8. LaHave paid a cash dividend.

9. The market value of Arichat's common shares was higher than cost at year end.

10. The market value of Bombardier's bonds was lower than cost at year end.

Instructions

Using the following table format, indicate whether each of the above transactions would result in an increase (+), a decrease (−), or no effect (NE). The first one has been done for you as an example.

	Balance Sheet			Statement of Earnings			Statement of Comprehensive Income	Cash Flow Statement
	Assets	Liabilities	Shareholders' Equity	Revenues	Expenses	Net Earnings	Other Comprehensive Income	Investing Activities
1.	NE	NE	NE	NE	NE	NE	NE	−

P12–5A On December 31, 2005, Hi-Tech Limited's portfolio of short-term available-for-sale investments was as follows:

Record equity investment transactions; show statement presentation. (SO 3, 4, 5)

	Quantity	Cost
Awixa Corporation common shares	500	$26,000
HAL Corporation common shares	700	42,000
Renda Corporation preferred shares	400	16,800
		$84,800

On December 31, 2005, the total cost of the investment portfolio equalled the total market value. Hi-Tech had the following transactions related to the securities during 2006:

Jan.   7 Sold all of the Awixa common shares at $56 per share.
        10 Purchased 200 Mintor Corporation common shares at $78 per share.
        26 Received a cash dividend of $1.20 per share on the HAL common shares.
Feb.   2 Received a cash dividend of $1 per share on the Renda preferred shares.
        10 Sold all of the Renda preferred shares at $40 per share.
Apr. 30 Received 700 additional HAL common shares as a result of a two-for-one stock split.
July   1 Received a cash dividend of $0.60 per share on the HAL common shares.
Aug. 23 Received 20 Mintor common shares as a result of a 10% stock dividend when the price
          was $75 per share.
Sept. 1 Purchased an additional 400 Mintor common shares at $70 per share.
Dec. 31 The market value of HAL's common shares was $31 per share and the market value of
          Mintor's common shares was $72 per share.

Instructions

(a) Record the above transactions.
(b) Prepare the adjusting entry required at December 31 to adjust the available-for-sale securities to market value.
(c) Show the balance sheet presentation at December 31.
(d) Explain how any unrealized gain or loss would be reported for Hi-Tech. Would your answer change if the investment portfolio was classified as trading securities rather than as available-for-sale securities?

Record transactions under cost and equity methods; prepare memo explaining differences. (SO 3)

P12–6A   Cardinal Concrete Corp. acquired 20% of Edra Inc.'s common shares on January 1, 2006, by paying $1.2 million for 50,000 shares. Edra paid a $0.50-per-share cash dividend on June 30 and again on December 31. Edra reported net earnings of $750,000 for the year.

Instructions

(a) Prepare the journal entries for Cardinal Concrete for 2006, assuming Cardinal cannot exercise significant influence over Edra.
(b) Prepare the journal entries for Cardinal Concrete for 2006, assuming Cardinal can exercise significant influence over Edra.
(c) The board of directors of Cardinal Concrete is confused about the differences between the cost and equity methods. Write a memo to the board that (1) explains each method, and (2) shows the investment and revenue account balances under each method at December 31, 2006.

Record transactions under cost and equity methods; show statement presentation. (SO 3, 5)

P12–7A   Sub Corporation has 500,000 common shares. On January 10, 2006, Par Inc. purchased a block of these shares in the open market at $10 per share to hold as a long-term equity investment. At the end of 2006, Sub Corporation reported net earnings of $260,000 and paid a $0.25-per-share dividend.

This problem assumes three independent situations related to the accounting for this investment by Par.:

Situation 1: Par purchased 50,000 Sub common shares.
Situation 2: Par purchased 150,000 Sub common shares.
Situation 3: Par purchased 500,000 Sub common shares.

Instructions

(a) For each situation, identify whether Par should use the cost or equity method to account for its investment in Sub.
(b) For each situation, record all transactions related to the investment in Par's books for the year ended December 31, 2006.
(c) Compare Par's nonconsolidated balance sheet and statement of earnings accounts for these investments at December 31 for each of the three situations.
(d) In situation 3, what kind of financial statements should be prepared to report the combined operations of Par and Sub? Whose name will be on the financial statements?

Analyze cost and equity methods. (SO 3)

P12–8A   On January 2, 2006, Haidey Inc. purchased shares of Jordan Cycles Corp. for $10 per share. Haidey intends to hold these shares as a long-term equity investment. During 2006, Jordan Cycles reported net earnings of $400,000 and paid cash dividends of $100,000.

Haidey's accountant prepared a trial balance as at December 31, 2006, under the assumption that Haidey could exercise significant influence over Jordan Cycles. Under this assumption, the trial balance included the following accounts and amounts:

Long-term equity investment—Jordan Cycles	$575,000
Investment revenue—Jordan Cycles	100,000

Instructions

(a) What percentage of the Jordan Cycles shares does Haidey own?

(b) How many shares of Jordan Cycles did Haidey purchase on January 2?

(c) What was the amount of the cash dividend that Haidey received from Jordan Cycles during 2006?

(d) Upon closer examination of the situation, Haidey's auditors determine that Haidey does not have significant influence over Jordan Cycles. If that is the case, what amount should be reported on Haidey's balance sheet at December 31 for its investment in Jordan Cycles? What will be reported on Haidey's statement of earnings for 2006?

P12–9A   On January 1, 2006, Sturge Enterprises Inc. held the following equity investments:

Determine valuation of equity investments.
(SO 3, 4)

Security	Quantity	Cost Per Share
X	1,500	$11
Y	2,000	8

During the year, Sturge made the following purchases:

Security	Quantity	Cost Per Share
X	1,500	$10
X	1,000	8
X	1,000	7
Y	500	9
Z	3,000	12

The market values of the various securities at year end, December 31, 2006, were as follows: X, $6; Y, $10; and Z, $12.

Instructions

(a) Calculate the cost and market values of Sturge Enterprises' equity investment portfolio at December 31.

(b) If Sturge Enterprises considers its entire portfolio to be trading securities, at what value should the equity investments be reported on the balance sheet at December 31? At what amount, and where, should any unrealized gains or losses be reported?

(c) If Sturge Enterprises considers its entire portfolio to be available-for-sale securities, at what value should the equity investments be reported on the balance sheet at December 31? At what amount, and where, should any unrealized gains or losses be reported?

(d) If Sturge Enterprises decides to classify the X shares as available-for-sale securities and the Y and Z shares as trading securities, what would be the impact on the statement of earnings? On the balance sheet?

P12–10A   The following data, presented in alphabetical order, are taken from the general ledger of Stinson Corporation at December 31, 2006:

Prepare balance sheet.
(SO 5)

Accounts payable	$ 200,000
Accounts receivable	90,000
Accumulated amortization—building	180,000
Accumulated amortization—equipment	72,000
Accumulated other comprehensive income	20,000
Allowance for doubtful accounts	6,000
Allowance to adjust available-for-sale securities to market value	
(adjunct account)	10,000
Available-for-sale securities (short-term), at cost	350,000
Bonds payable (6%, due 2012)	400,000
Buildings	900,000
Cash and cash equivalents	100,000
Common shares (no par value, unlimited authorized, 300,000 issued)	1,000,000
Discount on bonds payable	20,000

Dividends payable	$ 70,000
Equipment	275,000
Goodwill	200,000
Held-to-maturity securities, at amortized cost	24,000
Income tax payable	120,000
Interest payable	12,000
Land	500,000
Long-term equity investment—Indira common shares, at equity	270,000
Merchandise inventory, at average cost	170,000
Notes payable (due 2007)	70,000
Preferred shares (no par value, $5 cumulative, 5,000 shares authorized and issued)	200,000
Retained earnings	665,000
Supplies	6,000
Trademark	100,000

Instructions

Prepare a balance sheet.

Problems: Set B

Record debt investment transactions for investor and investee.
(SO 2)

P12–1B   The following bond transactions occurred during 2006 for the University of Higher Learning (UHL) and Otutye Ltd.:

Feb. 1 UHL issued $10 million of five-year, 6% bonds at face value which pay interest semi-annually on August 1 and February 1.
   1 Otutye Ltd. purchased $3 million of UHL's bonds on the TSX Venture Exchange at 98 as a short-term investment.
Mar. 31 UHL and Otutye Ltd. both have a March 31 year end and accrue the bond interest.
Aug. 1 The semi-annual interest on the bonds was paid.
   1 After paying the semi-annual interest on the bonds on this date, UHL decided to repurchase $3 million of its bonds and retire them. UHL repurchased all $3 million of the bonds from Otutye at 103.

Instructions

(a) Prepare all required journal entries for Otutye Ltd., the investor, to record the above transactions.
(b) Show how the investment would be presented on Otutye's March 31, 2006, balance sheet.
(c) Prepare all required entries for UHL, the investee, to record the above transactions.
(d) Show how the bond liability would be presented on UHL's March 31, 2006, balance sheet.

Record debt investment transactions; show statement presentation.
(SO 2, 4, 5)

P12–2B   The following Givarz Corporation transactions are for bonds purchased as a long-term available-for-sale security during the year ended December 31, 2006:

Feb. 1 Purchased $100,000 Leslye Corporation 5% bonds at 100. Interest is paid semi-annually on August 1 and February 1.
Aug. 1 Received interest on Leslye bonds.
   2 Sold $40,000 of the Leslye bonds at 95.
Dec. 31 Accrued interest on the Leslye bonds.
   31 The market value of the bonds was $61,000 on this date.

Instructions

(a) Record the above transactions
(b) Prepare the adjusting entry required at December 31 to adjust the bonds to market value.
(c) Show the financial statement presentation of the bonds and any related accounts at December 31.

Record debt and equity investment transactions; show statement presentation.
(SO 2, 3, 4, 5)

P12–3B   During 2006, the Kakisa Financial Corporation purchased the following trading securities:

Feb. 1 Purchased 600 CBF common shares for $32,000, plus brokerage fees of $650.

Mar. 1 Purchased 800 RSD common shares for $20,000, plus brokerage fees of $400.

Apr. 1 Purchased 6% MRT bonds for $50,000. Interest is payable semi-annually on April 1 and October 1.

July 1 Received a cash dividend of $2 per share on the CBF common shares.

Aug. 1 Sold 200 CBF common shares at $50 per share, less brokerage fees of $200.

Sept. 1 Received a $1-per-share cash dividend on the RSD common shares.

Oct. 1 Received the semi-annual interest on the MRT bonds.

1 Sold the MRT bonds for $53,000.

Dec. 31 The market values of the CBF and RSD common shares were $45 and $27 per share, respectively.

Instructions

(a) Record the above transactions.

(b) Prepare the adjusting entry required at December 31 to adjust the trading securities to market value.

(c) Show the balance sheet presentation of the trading securities at December 31, 2006.

(d) Identify the statement of earnings accounts that are used and give the statement classification of each account.

P12–4B Lai Inc. had the following investment transactions:

Identify statement impact of investment transactions.
(SO 2, 3, 4, 5)

1. Purchased Chang Corporation preferred shares as an available-for-sale security.
2. Received a stock dividend on the Chang preferred shares.
3. Purchased Government of Canada bonds for cash as a trading security.
4. Accrued interest on the Government of Canada bonds.
5. Sold half of the Chang preferred shares at a price less than originally paid.
6. Purchased 25% of Xing Ltd.'s common shares as a long-term equity investment.
7. Received Xing's financial statements, which reported a net loss for the year.
8. Xing paid a cash dividend.
9. The market value of Chang's preferred shares was lower than cost at year end.
10. The market value of the Government of Canada bonds was higher than cost at year end.

Instructions

Using the following table format, indicate whether each of the above transactions would result in an increase (+), a decrease (−), or no effect (NE). The first one has been done for you as an example.

	Balance Sheet			Statement of Earnings			Statement of Comprehensive Income	Cash Flow Statement
	Assets	Liabilities	Shareholders' Equity	Revenues	Expenses	Net Earnings	Other Comprehensive Income	Investing Activities
1.	NE	NE	NE	NE	NE	NE	NE	−

P12–5B On December 31, 2005, the Head Financial Corporation's portfolio of trading securities was as follows:

Record equity investment transaction; show statement presentation.
(SO 3, 4, 5)

	Quantity	Cost
Aglar Corporation common shares	500	$26,000
BAL Corporation common shares	700	42,000
Hicks Corporation preferred shares	400	16,800
		$84,800

On December 31, 2005, the total cost of the portfolio equalled its total market value. Head Financial had the following transactions for the securities during 2006:

Jan. 7 Sold all of the Aglar common shares at $56 per share.

10 Purchased 400 Miley Corporation common shares at $78 per share.

Feb. 2 Received a cash dividend of $2 per share on the Hicks preferred shares.

10 Sold all the Hicks preferred shares at $40 per share.

Mar. 15 Received 70 BAL common shares as a result of a 10% stock dividend when the price was $55 per share.

June 23 Received 800 additional Miley common shares as a result of a three-for-one stock split.

Sept. 1 Purchased an additional 300 Miley common shares at $30 per share.

Dec. 15 Received a cash dividend of $1 per share on the Miley common shares.

31 The market value of BAL's common shares was $50 per share and the market value of Miley's common shares was $33 per share.

Instructions

(a) Record the above transactions.
(b) Prepare the adjusting entry required at December 31 to adjust the trading securities to market value.
(c) Show the balance sheet presentation at December 31.
(d) Explain how any unrealized gain or loss would be reported for Head Financial. Would your answer change if the investment portfolio was classified as available-for-sale securities rather than as trading securities?

Record transactions under cost and equity methods; compare balances.
(SO 3)

P12–6B   DFM Services Ltd. acquired 25% of the common shares of BNA Ltd. on January 1, 2006, by paying $800,000 for 50,000 shares. BNA paid a $0.25-per-share cash dividend on each of March 15, June 15, September 15, and December 15. BNA reported net earnings of $350,000 for the year.

Instructions

(a) Prepare the journal entries for DFM Services for 2006, assuming DFM cannot exercise significant influence over BNA.
(b) Prepare the journal entries for DFM Services for 2006, assuming DFM can exercise significant influence over BNA.
(c) Compare the investment and revenue account balances at December 31, 2006, under each method of accounting.
(d) What factors help determine whether a company has significant influence over another company?

Record transactions under cost and equity methods; show statement presentation.
(SO 3, 5)

P12–7B   Hat Limited has 200,000 common shares. On October 1, 2005, Cat Inc. purchased a block of these shares in the open market at $40 per share to hold as a long-term equity investment. Hat reported net earnings of $375,000 for the year ended September 30, 2006, and paid a $0.20-per-share dividend.

This problem assumes three independent situations related to the accounting for this investment by Cat:

Situation 1: Cat purchased 20,000 Hat common shares.
Situation 2: Cat purchased 60,000 Hat common shares.
Situation 3: Cat purchased 200,000 Hat common shares.

Instructions

(a) For each situation, identify whether Cat should use the cost or equity method to account for its investment in Hat.
(b) For each situation, record all transactions related to the investment in Cat's books for the year ended September 30, 2006.
(c) Compare Cat's nonconsolidated balance sheet and statement of earnings accounts related to these investments at September 30 for each of the three situations.
(d) In situation 3, what kind of financial statements should be prepared to report the combined operations of Cat and Hat? Whose name will be on the financial statements?

Analyze cost and equity methods.
(SO 3)

P12–8B   Khalil Travel Agency Ltd. has 500,000 common shares authorized and 180,000 shares issued on December 31, 2005. On January 2, 2006, Stewart Inc. purchased shares of Khalil Travel Agency for $15 per share. Stewart intends to hold these shares as a long-term equity investment.

Stewart's accountant prepared a trial balance as at December 31, 2006, under the assumption that Stewart could not exercise significant influence over Khalil Travel Agency. Under this assumption, the trial balance included the following accounts and amounts:

Long-term equity investment—Khalil Travel Agency	$540,000
Investment revenue—Khalil Travel Agency	72,000

Instructions

(a) How many shares of Khalil Travel Agency did Stewart purchase on January 2?

(b) What percentage of Khalil Travel Agency shares does Stewart own?

(c) What was the amount of the cash dividend per share that Stewart received from Khalil Travel Agency during 2006?

(d) Upon closer examination of the situation, Stewart's auditors determine that Stewart does have significant influence over Khalil Travel Agency. Accordingly, the investment account balance was adjusted to $600,000 at December 31, 2006. What were the net earnings reported by Khalil Travel Agency for the year ended December 31, 2006?

(e) Assuming that Stewart does have significant influence over Khalil Travel Agency, what amount will Stewart report on its statement of earnings for 2006 for this investment?

P12–9B On December 31, 2006, Val d'Or Ltée held the following debt and equity investments:

Determine valuation of equity investments.
(SO 3, 4)

	Quantity	Cost Per Unit	Market Value per Unit
Debt Securities			
Money-market instruments	10,000	$ 1	$ 1
CIBC bonds	2,000	98	100
Government of Canada bonds	1,000	100	140
Equity Securities			
Bank of Montreal	1,000	$31	$57
Bombardier	5,000	15	3
Nortel Networks	5,000	55	3

Instructions

(a) Calculate the total cost and total market values of Val d'Or's investment portfolio at December 31.

(b) If Val d'Or considers its entire portfolio to be trading securities, at what value should the investments be reported on the balance sheet at December 31? At what amount, and where, should any unrealized gains or losses be reported?

(c) If Val d'Or considers its entire portfolio to be available-for-sale securities, at what value should the investments be reported on the balance sheet at December 31? At what amount, and where, should any unrealized gains or losses be reported?

(d) If Val d'Or decides to classify the Bombardier and Nortel shares as available-for-sale securities and the Bank of Montreal and debt securities as trading securities, what would be the impact on the statement of earnings? On the balance sheet?

P12–10B The following data, presented in alphabetical order, are taken from the general ledger of the Yeung Finance Corporation at June 30, 2007:

Prepare balance sheet.
(SO 5)

Accounts payable	$231,000
Accounts receivable	140,000
Accumulated amortization—buildings	180,000
Accumulated amortization—equipment	52,000
Accumulated other comprehensive loss	97,000
Allowance for doubtful accounts	14,000
Allowance to adjust trading securities to market value (contra account)	20,000
Bond interest payable	5,000
Bonds payable (4%, due 2010)	250,000
Buildings	950,000
Cash	72,000
Common shares (no par value, unlimited authorized, 220,000 issued)	817,000
Current portion of mortgage payable	27,000
Dividends payable	40,000
Equipment	275,000
Held-to-maturity securities, at amortized cost	100,000
Income tax payable	53,000
Interest receivable	8,000
Land	500,000
Long-term equity investment—Huston common shares, at equity	330,000
Merchandise inventory, at FIFO cost	170,000
Mortgage payable	670,000

Patent	$200,000
Premium on bonds payable	40,000
Prepaid insurance	10,000
Retained earnings	660,000
Unearned service revenue	15,000
Trading securities, at cost	195,000

Instructions

Prepare a balance sheet.

BROADENING YOUR PERSPECTIVE

Financial Reporting and Analysis

Analysis Tools

Financial Reporting Problem: *Loblaw*

BYP12–1 Refer to the financial statements and accompanying notes for Loblaw presented in Appendix A.

Instructions

(a) What information about investments is reported in the consolidated balance sheet?
(b) Note 1 to the financial statements identifies Loblaw's ownership interest in the voting share capital of its subsidiaries. What is this percentage?
(c) Based on the information in Note 5 to Loblaw's financial statements, how much interest income was earned on short-term investments in 2003? In 2002?
(d) Judging from the cash flow statement, were more short-term investments acquired than sold, or vice versa, in 2003? In 2002?

Comparative Analysis Problem: *Loblaw and Sobeys*

BYP12–2 The financial statements of Sobeys are presented in Appendix B, following the financial statements for Loblaw in Appendix A.

Instructions

Compare the investing activities sections of the cash flow statements of the two companies for the two most recent fiscal years.

Research Case

BYP12–3 The January 2005 issue of *CAmagazine* includes the article "Financial Instruments—Filling the Gap in GAAP," by Ian P. Hague. The article provides information on the new accounting standards for reporting investments, and other financial instruments, at market value.

Instructions

Read the article and answer these questions:

(a) What gap in GAAP will the new accounting standards fill?
(b) What are financial assets?
(c) How does the market, or fair, value of financial assets relate to the concept of the relevance of financial statement items?

(d) How will gains and losses on financial assets be reported under the new accounting standards?

(e) How will the new accounting standards affect the recording of straight forward items such as accounts receivable and accounts payable?

Interpreting Financial Statements

BYP12–4 Stratos Global Corporation provides mobile and fixed telecommunication services to customers operating in remote areas of the world. Although headquartered in the U.S., Stratos' accounting operations are located in Canada. It reports its financial statements using Canadian GAAP, but in U.S. dollars. On January 13, 2005, Stratos acquired a 49-percent ownership interest for U.S. $6.1 million in Navarino Telecom SA and NTS Maritime Limited, Stratos' largest maritime distributor.

Instructions

(a) Assuming cash was paid for this investment, prepare the journal entry that Stratos made to record the acquisition of Navarino.

(b) What method would Stratos use to account for its investment in Navarino?

(c) During the first quarter of 2005, Stratos recorded earnings of U.S. $100,000 related to its investment in Navarino. Prepare the journal entry that Stratos would have recorded.

(d) Would Stratos prepare consolidated financial statements for its investment in Navarino?

A Global Focus

BYP12–5 American Express Company is the world's #1 travel company, with operations in more than 200 countries. The company reported the following selected information for its investment portfolio for the year ended December 31, 2004 (in U.S. millions):

	2004	2003
Trading securities, at market value	$ 1,098	$ 995
Available-for-sale securities, at market value	56,188	51,848
Held-to-maturity securities, at amortized cost	3,523	3,794
	$60,809	$56,637

The following additional information was available for the company's available-for-sale investment portfolio:

	Cost	Unrealized Gains	Unrealized Losses	Market Value
2004	$54,878	$1,570	$260	$56,188
2003	50,356	1,763	271	51,848

Instructions

(a) Why does American Express most likely have an investment portfolio consisting of three different types of securities?

(b) American Express has a significant amount invested in an available-for-sale portfolio in relation to its total investment portfolio. Why do you suppose it has such a high percentage of its portfolio invested in available-for-sale securities?

(c) American Express' net earnings were $3,445 million in 2004. How much, and by what percentage, could the company have increased its net earnings in 2004 by selling its "winners" while holding its "losers?"

(d) Why should a company not engage in earnings management, such as that described in (c) above?

Financial Analysis on the Web

**Analysis Tools
(Financial Analysis on the Web)**

BYP12–6   The Ontario Securities Commission (OSC) is the regulatory agency of Canada's largest capital market. Its job is to administer and enforce securities legislation in the province of Ontario. We will explore this site and learn about the OSC's mandate and other stock-related information.

Instructions

Specific requirements for this Web case can be found on the Toolkit website.

Critical Thinking

Collaborative Learning Activity

BYP12–7   At the beginning of the question and answer portion of the annual shareholders' meeting of Réno-Déco Corporation, shareholder Carol Finstrom asks, "Why did management sell its equity investment in AHM Limited at a loss when this company was very profitable during the period its shares were held by Réno-Déco?"

Since president Nathalie Clément has just concluded her speech on the recent success and bright future of Réno-Déco, she is taken aback by this question and responds, "I remember we paid $1 million for those shares some years ago, and I am sure we sold the shares at a higher price. You must be mistaken."

Finstrom retorts, "Well, right here in note number seven to the financial statements, it shows that 240,000 shares, a 30% interest in AHM, were sold on the last day of the year. Also, it states that AHM earned $550,000 this year and paid out $150,000 in cash dividends. Further, a summary statement indicates that in past years, while Réno-Déco held AHM shares, AHM earned $1.2 million and paid out $500,000 in dividends. Finally, the statement of earnings for this year shows a loss on the sale of AHM shares of $180,000. So, I doubt that I am mistaken."

Red-faced, president Clément turns to you, the vice-president of finance, for answers.

Instructions

With the class divided into groups, answer the following:

(a) What dollar amount did Réno-Déco receive for the sale of the AHM shares?
(b) Explain why both shareholder Finstrom and president Clément are correct.

Communication Activity

BYP12–8   In 2006, accounting standards changed so that trading securities and available-for-sale securities are reported at market values, rather than at cost or the lower of cost and market.

Instructions

Discuss whether reporting investments at their market value rather than cost provides better information for investors to evaluate the performance of a company's investment portfolio. Outline the advantages and disadvantages of this approach. Describe any additional data that investors would need to have to properly evaluate investment performance

Ethics Case

Ethics In Accounting

BYP12–9   Kreiter Financial Services Ltd. holds a large portfolio of debt and equity investments. The total market value of the portfolio at December 31, 2006, is greater than its total cost, with some securities having increased in value and others having decreased. Financial vice-president Vicki Lemke and controller Ula Greenwood are in the process of classifying the securities in the portfolio in accordance with the new accounting standard.

Lemke suggests classifying the securities that have increased in value as trading securities in order to increase net earnings for the year. She wants to classify the securities that have decreased in value as available-for-sale securities so that the decreases in value will not affect the 2006 net earnings.

Greenwood disagrees. She recommends classifying the securities that have decreased in value as trading securities and those that have increased in value as available-for-sale securities. Greenwood argues that the company is having a good earnings year and that recognizing the losses now will help to smooth earnings for this year. Moreover, for future years, when the company may not be as profitable, the company will have built-in gains "held in reserve."

Instructions

(a) Will classifying the investments as Lemke and Greenwood suggest actually affect earnings as each says it will?

(b) Is there anything unethical in what Lemke and Greenwood propose? Who are the stakeholders affected by their proposals?

(c) Assume that Lemke and Greenwood classify the portfolio properly. Now, at year end, Lemke proposes to sell the securities that will increase net earnings for 2006, and Greenwood proposes to sell the securities that will decrease net earnings for 2006. Is this unethical?

Serial Problem

(*Note:* This is a continuation of the serial problem from Chapters 1 through 11.)

BYP12–10   Natalie and Curtis have been approached by Ken Thornton, a shareholder of The Beanery Coffee Ltd. Ken wants to retire and would like to sell his 1,000 shares in The Beanery Coffee Ltd., which represents 20 percent of all common shares issued. The Beanery is currently operated by Ken's twin daughters, who each own 40 percent of the common shares. The Beanery not only operates a coffee shop but also roasts and sells beans to retailers, under the name "Rocky Mountain Beanery."

The business has been operating for approximately five years, and in the last two years Ken has lost interest and left the day-to-day operations to his daughters. Both daughters at times find work at the coffee shop overwhelming. They would like to have a third shareholder to take over some of the responsibilities of running a small business. Both feel that Natalie and Curtis are entrepreneurial in spirit and that their expertise would be a welcome addition to the business operation. The twins have also said that they plan to operate this business for another ten years and then retire.

Ken has met with Curtis and Natalie to discuss the operations of The Beanery. All have concluded that there would be many advantages if Cookie Creations Ltd. acquired an interest in The Beanery. One of the major advantages would be volume discounts for purchases of coffee bean inventory.

Despite the apparent advantages, Natalie and Curtis are still not convinced that Cookie Creations should participate in this business venture. They come to you with the following questions:

1. We are a little concerned about how much influence we would have in the decision-making process for The Beanery Coffee Ltd. Would the amount of influence we have affect how we would account for this investment in the accounting records of Cookie Creations Ltd.?

2. Can you think of other advantages of going ahead with the purchase of this investment?

3. Can you think of other disadvantages of going ahead with the purchase of this investment?

Instructions

(a) Answer their questions.

(b) Assume that Ken wants to sell his 1,000 shares of The Beanery Coffee Ltd. for $12,500. Prepare the journal entry required if Cookie Creations Ltd. buys Ken's shares.

(c) Assume that Cookie Creations Ltd. buys the shares, and in the following year The Beanery Coffee Ltd. earns $50,000 and pays $40,000 in dividends. Prepare the journal entries required under both the cost method and the equity method of accounting for this investment.

(d) Identify where this investment would be classified on the balance sheet of Cookie Creations Ltd. and explain why. What amount would appear on the balance sheet under (1) the cost method and (2) the equity method of accounting for this investment?

Answers to Self-Study Questions

1. b   2. d   3. b   4. c   5. c   6. b   7. b   8. c   9. a   10. a

Answer to Loblaw Review It Question 1

Loblaw's financial statements are indeed consolidated, as indicated in the title of each statement. Note 1 outlines the basis of consolidation, and states that the company owns 100 percent of its subsidiaries' common shares.

Remember to go back to the Navigator box at the beginning of the chapter to check off your completed work.

CHAPTER 13

Cash Flow Statement

You Have to Spend Money to Make Money

Big-ticket leisure travel has become big business. And perhaps no company has tapped into this market more thoroughly than Vancouver-based Intrawest Corporation. Intrawest is the world's largest developer and operator of destination resorts, whose flagship Whistler/Blackcomb resort will play host to the Winter Olympic Games in 2010.

The secret to the company's success is its growth formula: Start with a resort. Build a village so people stay longer. This attracts more visitors who come more often and spend more money. Build more real estate attractions, drawing in more people. This leads to the creation of shops, hotels, convention centres, and restaurants. The result: a year-round destination resort that puts the company into a financial position where it can invest in more locations. It's a fine balance of spending money to make money and making sure there is enough cash flow to cover debt.

In 2003, Intrawest's formula needed a bit of tweaking. While resort operations were cash flow–positive, the real estate business was cash flow–negative. To solve this problem, the company formed two partnerships with outside investors to create Leisura Developments, which takes on the most capital-intensive development projects. "As a result, the amount of capital that we are required to invest in new real estate projects is significantly reduced," says David Blaiklock, Intrawest's vice president and corporate controller.

The initial result was indeed significant. Cash flow from operating activities for the 2004 fiscal year was U.S. $422.9 million, compared to a negative cash flow of U.S. $20.9 million in 2003. Intrawest generated U.S. $303.1 million in free cash flow in 2004, which it used to reduce debt.

"A significant component of that cash flow was the one-time impact of introducing this partnership structure," Mr. Blaiklock stresses. Still, by selling real estate projects to Leisura, the company's cash flow requirements will be reduced.

As for the 2010 Olympics, their impact on cash flow can only be positive. Since Whistler/Blackcomb already hosts World Cup alpine ski events, no infrastructure investment is required. The federal and provincial governments are spending millions on improvements to the highway from Vancouver to Whistler, which will increase real estate values and the number of resort visitors. The new athletes' village will provide affordable housing for resort employees. And then there's the prestige that comes with having been an Olympic host city. Although Whistler/Blackcomb is already a world-class destination, the Olympics will only generate more interest and more visitors, and thus more cash.

the navigator

ntrawest: www.intrawest.com

THE NAVIGATOR

- [ ] Read *Feature Story*
- [ ] Scan *Study Objectives*
- [ ] Read *Chapter Preview*
- [ ] Read text and answer *Before You Go On*
- [ ] Work *Using the Decision Toolkit*
- [ ] Review *Summary of Study Objectives*
- [ ] Review *Decision Toolkit—A Summary*
- [ ] Work *Demonstration Problem*
- [ ] Answer *Self-Study Questions*
- [ ] Complete assignments

STUDY OBJECTIVES

After studying this chapter, you should be able to:

1. Describe the purpose and format of the cash flow statement.
2. Prepare a cash flow statement using one of two approaches: (a) the indirect method or (b) the direct method.
3. Use the cash flow statement to evaluate a company's liquidity and solvency.

The balance sheet, statement of earnings, and statement of retained earnings do not always show the whole picture of the financial condition of a company. In fact, looking at the financial statements of some well-known companies, a thoughtful investor might ask questions like these: How did Andrés Wines pay $3 million of dividends in a year when it had no cash but bank indebtedness instead? How did the Wilfrid Laurier University Students' Union increase its cash balance by more than $400,000 in a year in which it only earned a little more than $100,000? How did Rogers Communications finance its $25-million purchase of the SkyDome (now called the Rogers Centre)? Answers to these and similar questions can be found in this chapter, which presents the cash flow statement.

The chapter is organized as follows:

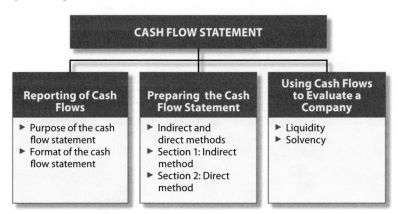

the navigator

Reporting of Cash Flows

The three financial statements that we have studied so far present only partial information about a company's cash flows (cash receipts and cash payments). For example, comparative balance sheets show the increase in property, plant, and equipment during the year, but they do not show how the additions were financed or paid for. The statement of earnings shows net earnings, but it does not indicate the amount of cash generated by operating activities. The statement of retained earnings shows cash dividends declared, but not the cash dividends paid during the year. None of these statements reports the change in cash as a result of operating, investing, and financing activities during the period.

Purpose of the Cash Flow Statement

study objective 1

Describe the purpose and format of the cash flow statement.

The main purpose of the cash flow statement is to provide information about cash receipts, cash payments, and the net change in cash that result from the operating, investing, and financing activities of a company during a specific period. Reporting the causes of changes in cash is useful because investors, creditors, and other interested parties want to know what is happening to a company's most liquid resource—its cash. As the feature story about Intrawest demonstrates, to understand a company's financial position, it is essential to understand its cash flows.

The information in a cash flow statement should help investors, creditors, and others assess the following aspects of a company's financial position:

1. **The investing and financing transactions during the period.** By examining a company's investing and financing activities, a financial statement reader can better understand why assets and liabilities increased or decreased during the period.
2. **The company's ability to generate future cash flows.** Investors and others examine the relationships between items in the cash flow statement. From these, they can better predict the amounts, timing, and uncertainty of future cash flows than they can from accrual-based data.
3. **The company's ability to pay dividends and meet obligations.** If a company does not have enough cash, it cannot pay employees, settle debts, or pay dividends. Employees,

creditors, shareholders, and customers are particularly interested in this statement because it alone shows the flow of cash in a business.

4. **The reasons for the difference between net earnings and cash provided (used) by operating activities.** Net earnings provide information on the success or failure of a business. However, some people are critical of accrual-based net earnings because these earnings require estimates, allocations, and assumptions. As a result, the reliability of net earnings is often doubted.

Cash flow is less susceptible to earnings management than net earnings. Although we suggest that relying on cash flows only and ignoring accrual accounting is inappropriate, comparing cash provided or used by operating activities to net earnings can reveal important information about the "quality" of the reported net earnings—that is, this comparison can show how good net earnings are as a measure of actual performance.

ACCOUNTING MATTERS!   Investor Perspective

During the 1990s, analysts increasingly used cash-based measures, such as cash provided by operating activities, instead of, or in addition to, net earnings. The reason for the change was that they had lost faith in accrual-based measures. Sadly, nowadays even cash flow is not always what it seems to be.

Take, for example, Alliance Atlantis Communications Inc. The company reported cash flow provided by operating activities of $686.5 million in 2001. Looks impressive, right? However, in 2002, the company's cash flow statement for 2001 was restated to report cash used by operating activities of $59.9 million. What happened? Accounting standard-setters decided that money spent to acquire, develop, and produce films and television programs was an operating expense, not an investment. In other words, Atlantis' cash flow did not actually change, but its reporting did. The moral of this story is that accounting principles can alter not only reported earnings, but also cash flow.

Source: Fabrice Taylor, "Show Me the Real Money," *Report on Business Magazine*, November 2002, 109.

Format of the Cash Flow Statement

The general format of the cash flow statement is organized around the three activities of operating, investing, and financing. Transactions within each activity are as follows:

1. **Operating activities** include the cash effects of transactions that create revenues and expenses. They affect net earnings.
2. **Investing activities** include (a) purchasing and disposing of investments and long-lived assets and (b) lending money and collecting the loans. They affect short-term investments that are not cash equivalents, and they affect long-term asset accounts.
3. **Financing activities** include (a) obtaining cash from issuing debt and repaying the amounts borrowed and (b) obtaining cash from shareholders and paying them dividends. They affect short-term notes payable, and long-term liability and shareholders' equity accounts.

Illustration 13-1 lists typical cash receipts and cash payments in each of the three activities.

Illustration 13-1 ▶

Cash receipts and payments
classified by activity

Operating activities—statement of earnings items and changes in noncash working capital
   Cash inflows:
      From the sale of goods or services
      From returns on debt investments (interest) and on equity investments (dividends)
   Cash outflows:
      To suppliers for inventory
      To employees for services
      To governments for taxes
      To lenders for interest
      To others for expenses
Investing activities—changes in short-term investments and long-term assets
   Cash inflows:
      From the sale of property, plant, and equipment
      From the sale of debt or equity investments
      From the collection of principal on loans to other companies
   Cash outflows:
      To purchase property, plant, and equipment
      To purchase debt or equity investments
      To make loans to other companies
Financing activities—changes in short-term notes payable, long-term liabilities, and equity
   Cash inflows:
      From the sale of shares (preferred and common)
      From the issue of debt (notes and bonds)
   Cash outflows:
      To shareholders as dividends
      To redeem long-term debt or reacquire share capital

As you can see, some cash flows relating to investing or financing activities are classified as operating activities. For example, receipts of investment revenue (interest and dividends) are classified as operating activities. So are payments of interest to lenders. Why are these considered operating activities? Because these items are reported in the statement of earnings, where results of operations are shown.

Note the following general guidelines: (1) Operating activities involve items that determine income (statement of earnings and noncash working capital items). (2) Investing activities involve cash flows that result from changes in short-term investments and long-term asset items. (3) Financing activities involve cash flows that result from changes in short-term notes payable, and long-term liability and shareholders' equity items.

Illustration 13-2 shows these general guidelines. There are exceptions, of course, but these relationships between operating, investing, and financing activities and the statement of earnings and balance sheet are the most common.

Illustration 13-2 ▼

Operating, investing, and
financing activities

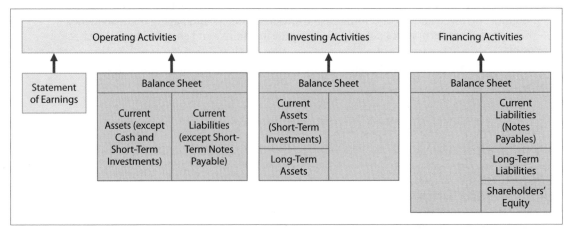

A sample cash flow statement, presenting operating, investing, and financing activities, is shown in Illustration 13-3 in condensed format.

Illustration 13-3 ◄

Format of cash flow
statement

COMPANY NAME Cash Flow Statement Period Covered		
Operating activities		
(List of individual inflows and outflows)	$x	
Net cash provided (used) by operating activities		$x
Investing activities		
(List of individual inflows and outflows)	$x	
Net cash provided (used) by investing activities		x
Financing activities		
(List of individual inflows and outflows)	$x	
Net cash provided (used) by financing activities		x
Net increase (decrease) in cash		x
Cash, beginning of period		x
Cash, end of period		$x

Alternative Terminology
The *cash flow statement* is
also commonly known as
the *statement of changes in
financial position.*

The cash flow statement covers the same period of time as the statements of earnings and retained earnings. The section that reports cash flows from operating activities always appears first. It is followed by the investing activities section and then the financing activities section. Note also that the individual inflows and outflows from investing and financing activities are reported separately. Thus, the cash outflow for the purchase of equipment is reported separately from the cash inflow from the sale of equipment. Similarly, the cash inflow from the issue of debt securities is reported separately from the cash outflow for the retirement of debt. If a company did not report the inflows and outflows separately, some of the investing and financing activities would be hidden. This would make it more difficult for the user to assess future cash flows.

The reported operating, investing, and financing activities result in net cash either provided or used by each activity. The amounts of net cash provided or used by each activity are then totalled. The result is the net increase or decrease in cash for the period. This amount is then added to or subtracted from the beginning-of-period cash balance to obtain the end-of-period cash balance. The end-of-period cash balance should agree with the cash balance reported on the balance sheet.

Definition of Cash

The cash flow statement is often prepared using **cash and cash equivalents** as its basis rather than just cash. You will recall from Chapter 7 that cash equivalents are short-term, highly liquid investments that are readily convertible to cash within a very short period of time. Generally, only money-market instruments due within three months qualify by this definition. Sometimes short-term or demand loans are also deducted from this amount. Because of the varying definitions of "cash" that can be used in this statement, companies must clearly define *cash equivalents* when they are included.

Since cash and cash equivalents are viewed as the same, transfers between the cash account and the cash equivalent accounts are not treated as cash receipts and cash payments. These transfers are therefore not reported in the cash flow statement.

Significant Noncash Activities

In addition, it is important to recognize that not all of a company's significant activities involve cash. The following are examples of noncash activities:

1. Issues of common shares to purchase assets
2. Conversions of debt into equity
3. Issues of debt to purchase assets
4. Exchanges of property, plant, and equipment

Significant investing and financing activities that do not affect cash are not reported in the body of the cash flow statement. However, these activities are reported in a note to the financial statements. The reporting of these activities in a note satisfies the **full disclosure principle**.

BEFORE YOU GO ON . . .

▶Review It

1. What is the main purpose of a cash flow statement?
2. How does the cash flow statement help users understand a company's financial position?
3. What amounts does Loblaw report in its 2003 cash flow statement for (a) operating activities, (b) investing activities, and (c) financing activities? The answers to these questions are provided at the end of this chapter.
4. What is a cash equivalent?
5. Where are significant noncash activities reported? Give an example.

▶Do It

Plano Moulding Corp. had the following cash transactions:

(a) Issued common shares.
(b) Sold an available-for-sale debt security.
(c) Purchased a tractor-trailer truck. Made a cash down payment and financed the remainder with a mortgage note payable.
(d) Paid interest on the mortgage note payable.
(e) Collected cash for services provided.

Classify each of these transactions by type of cash flow activity. Indicate whether the transaction would be reported as a cash inflow or cash outflow, or as a noncash activity.

Action Plan

- Identify the three types of activities used to report all cash inflows and outflows.
- Report as operating activities the cash effects of transactions that create revenues and expenses and are used to determine net earnings.
- Report as investing activities the transactions that (a) acquire and dispose of investments and long-lived assets, and (b) lend money and collect loans.
- Report as financing activities the transactions that (a) obtain cash by issuing debt or repay the amounts borrowed, and (b) obtain cash from shareholders or pay them dividends.

Solution

(a) Financing activity, cash inflow
(b) Investing activity, cash inflow
(c) Investing activity, cash outflow for down payment. Remainder is noncash investing (tractor-trailer truck) and financing (mortgage note payable) activity
(d) Operating activity, cash outflow
(e) Operating activity, cash inflow

Preparing the Cash Flow Statement

study objective 2

Prepare a cash flow statement using one of two approaches: (a) the indirect method or (b) the direct method.

The cash flow statement is prepared differently from the other three financial statements. First, it is not prepared from an adjusted trial balance. The statement requires detailed information on the changes in account balances that occurred between two periods of time. An adjusted trial balance does not provide the necessary data. Second, the cash flow statement deals with cash receipts and payments. As a result, **the accrual concept is not used in the preparation of a cash flow statement**.

The information to prepare this statement usually comes from three sources:

1. The **comparative balance sheet** indicates the amounts of the changes in assets, liabilities, and shareholders' equity from the beginning to the end of the period.
2. The **statement of earnings** helps the reader determine the amount of cash provided or used by operating activities during the period.
3. **Additional information** includes transaction data that are needed to determine how cash was provided or used during the period.

There are four steps to prepare the cash flow statement from these data sources, as shown in Illustration 13-4.

Illustration 13-4 ◄

Steps in preparing the cash flow statement

Step 1: Determine the net cash provided (used) by operating activities by converting net earnings from an accrual basis to a cash basis.

The current year's statement of earnings is analyzed, as are the comparative balance sheet and selected additional information.

Step 2: Determine the net cash provided (used) by investing activities by analyzing changes in short-term investment and long-term asset accounts.

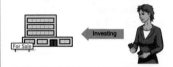

Comparative balance sheet data and selected additional information are analyzed for their effects on cash.

Step 3: Determine the net cash provided (used) by financing activities by analyzing changes in short-term notes payable and long-term liability and equity accounts.

Comparative balance sheet data and selected additional information are analyzed for their effects on cash.

Step 4: Determine the net increase (decrease) in cash. Compare the net change in cash with the change in cash reported on the balance sheet to make sure the amounts agree.

The difference between the beginning and ending cash balances can easily be calculated from the comparative balance sheet.

Indirect and Direct Methods

In order to perform step 1 and determine the cash provided (used) by operating activities, **net earnings must be converted from an accrual basis to a cash basis**. This conversion may be done by either of two methods: indirect or direct. The **indirect method** converts total net earnings from an accrual basis to a cash basis. The **direct method** converts each individual revenue and expense account to a cash basis, identifying specific cash receipts and payments. **Both methods arrive at the same total amount** for "net cash provided (used) by operating activities." The only difference is which items they disclose. Note that the two methods only produce differences in the operating activities section. The investing activities and financing activities sections are not affected by the choice of the indirect or direct method.

Most companies use the indirect method. They prefer this method for three reasons: (1) it is easier to prepare; (2) it focuses on the differences between net earnings and net cash flow from operating activities; and (3) it tends to reveal less company information to competitors.

The CICA allows the use of both the indirect and direct methods, but encourages companies to use the direct method of reporting operating activities. Despite the CICA's preference for the direct method, it is rarely used in Canadian practice. Less than one percent of the companies in Canada use the direct method. The authors of *Financial Reporting in Canada* state, "We continue to be surprised by the failure to use the direct method for presenting this important figure. It is difficult to believe that investors would not find information on the various functional cash flows (e.g., payments to employees) more useful than the information on the adjustments required to convert net income into cash flows from operating activities (e.g., amortization expense)."

ACCOUNTING MATTERS!   Investor Perspective

The cash flow statement ought to be one of the most important tools for any investor. But, all too often, this statement provides little insight into a company's operations. Take, for example, Hudson's Bay Company. The Bay's business is pretty simple. It buys clothes, housewares, and other products, puts them in its stores, and sells them.

When you look at the operating activities section of The Bay's cash flow statement, however, you find references to amortization and "net change in operating working capital." Nowhere does it tell you how much cash The Bay received from its customers or how much it paid its suppliers.

So why do companies choose not to report this information in their cash flow statement? "It gives material information, so managements don't want to use it," says Richard Rooney, president of Burgundy Asset Management. Rooney would like to see the direct method of preparing the operating activities section of the cash flow statement become mandatory. "Something like this is comprehensible, easy to understand, and I think it would be harder to fudge—though where there's a will, there's a way."

Source: Derek DeCloet, "Show Investors the Cash Flow," *Financial Post*, March 28, 2002, IN3.

On the following pages, in two separate sections, we describe the use of the indirect and direct methods of preparing the cash flow statement. Section 1 illustrates the indirect method. Section 2 illustrates the direct method. These sections are independent of each other. When you have finished the section(s) assigned by your instructor, turn to the concluding section of the chapter—"Using Cash Flows to Evaluate a Company."

SECTION 1 ▶ INDIRECT METHOD

To explain and illustrate the indirect method, we will use financial information from Computer Services Corporation to prepare a cash flow statement. Illustration 13-5 presents Computer Services' current- and previous-year balance sheet, its current-year statement of earnings, and related financial information.

Illustration 13-5 ◀

Comparative balance sheet, statement of earnings, and additional information

COMPUTER SERVICES CORPORATION
Balance Sheet
December 31

Assets	2006	2005	Change Increase/Decrease
Current assets			
Cash	$ 55,000	$ 33,000	$ 22,000 Increase
Accounts receivable	20,000	30,000	10,000 Decrease
Inventory	15,000	10,000	5,000 Increase
Prepaid expenses	5,000	1,000	4,000 Increase
Property, plant, and equipment			
Land	130,000	20,000	110,000 Increase
Building	160,000	40,000	120,000 Increase
Accumulated amortization—building	(11,000)	(5,000)	6,000 Increase
Equipment	27,000	10,000	17,000 Increase
Accumulated amortization—equipment	(3,000)	(1,000)	2,000 Increase
Total	$398,000	$138,000	
Liabilities and Shareholders' Equity			
Current liabilities			
Accounts payable	$ 28,000	$ 12,000	$ 16,000 Increase
Income tax payable	6,000	8,000	2,000 Decrease
Long-term liabilities			
Bonds payable	130,000	20,000	110,000 Increase
Shareholders' equity			
Common shares	70,000	50,000	20,000 Increase
Retained earnings	164,000	48,000	116,000 Increase
Total	$398,000	$138,000	

COMPUTER SERVICES CORPORATION
Statement of Earnings
Year Ended December 31, 2006

Sales revenue		$507,000
Cost of goods sold		150,000
Gross profit		357,000
Operating expenses (excluding amortization)	$111,000	
Amortization expense	9,000	
Loss on sale of equipment	3,000	123,000
Earnings from operations		234,000
Interest expense		42,000
Earnings before income tax		192,000
Income tax expense		47,000
Net earnings		$145,000

> Additional information for 2006:
>
> 1. The company paid a $29,000 cash dividend.
> 2. The company obtained land by issuing $110,000 of long-term bonds.
> 3. Equipment costing $25,000 was purchased for cash.
> 4. The company sold equipment with a book value of $7,000 (cost of $8,000, less accumulated amortization of $1,000) for $4,000 cash.
> 5. Amortization expense consisted of $6,000 for the building and $3,000 for equipment.

We will now apply the four steps to the information provided for Computer Services Corporation.

Step 1: Operating Activities

Determine the Net Cash Provided (Used) by Operating Activities by Converting Net Earnings from an Accrual Basis to a Cash Basis

To determine the net cash provided (or used) by operating activities under the indirect method, net earnings is adjusted for items that did not affect cash.

A useful starting point is to understand why net earnings must be converted to net cash provided by operating activities. Under generally accepted accounting principles, companies use the accrual basis of accounting. As you have learned, this basis requires that revenue be recorded when it is earned and that expenses be matched against the revenue they helped generate. Earned revenues may include credit sales that have not been collected in cash. Expenses incurred, such as amortization or cost of goods sold, may not have been paid in cash. Consequently, under the indirect method, accrual-based net earnings must be adjusted to convert certain items to the cash basis.

The indirect method starts with net earnings and converts it to net cash provided or used by operating activities. Illustration 13-6 shows three types of adjustments that are made to adjust net earnings for items that affect accrual-based net earnings but do not affect cash. The first two types of adjustments are found on the statement of earnings. The last type of adjustment—changes to current asset and current liability accounts—is found on the balance sheet.

Illustration 13-6 ▶

Adjustments to convert net earnings to net cash provided by operating activities

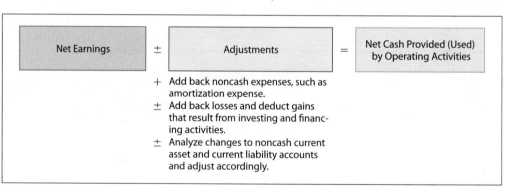

The next three sections explain each type of adjustment.

Amortization Expense

Computer Services' statement of earnings shows an amortization expense of $9,000. Although amortization expense reduces net earnings, it does not reduce cash. Recall that the entry to record amortization is:

Cash flows: no effect

	9,000	
Amortization Expense	9,000	
Accumulated Amortization		9,000

This entry has no effect on cash, so amortization expense is added back to net earnings in order to arrive at net cash provided by operating activities:

Operating activities	
Net earnings	$145,000
Adjustments to reconcile net earnings to net cash provided by operating activities:	
Amortization expense	9,000
Net cash provided by operating activities	154,000

Amortization is often listed in the cash flow statement as the first adjustment to net earnings. It is important to understand that amortization expense is not added to operating activities as if it were a source of cash. As shown in the journal entry above, amortization does not involve cash. It is added to cancel the deduction created by the amortization expense in the determination of net earnings.

Gains and Losses on the Sale of Assets

Computer Services' statement of earnings reports a $3,000 loss on the sale of equipment. With the additional information provided, we can reconstruct the journal entry to record the sale of equipment:

Cash	4,000	
Accumulated Amortization	1,000	
Loss on Sale of Equipment	3,000	
Equipment		8,000

A = L + SE
+4,000 −3,000
+1,000
−8,000
↑ Cash flows: +4,000

Illustration 13-1 states that cash received from the sale of long-lived assets should be reported in the investing activities section of the cash flow statement. Consequently, **all gains and losses from investing activities must be eliminated from net earnings to arrive at cash from operating activities**.

In our example, Computer Services' $3,000 loss should not be included in the operating activities section of the cash flow statement. This amount is eliminated by adding the $3,000 back to net earnings to arrive at net cash provided by operating activities:

Operating activities		
Net earnings		$145,000
Adjustments to reconcile net earnings to net cash provided by operating activities:		
Amortization expense	$9,000	
Loss on sale of equipment	3,000	12,000
Net cash provided by operating activities		157,000

If a gain on sale occurs, the gain is deducted from net earnings in order to determine net cash provided by operating activities. For both a gain and a loss, the actual amount of cash received from the sale is reported as a source of cash in the investing activities section of the cash flow statement.

If we did not eliminate gains and losses and remove them from net earnings, they would be counted twice—once in the operating activities section (as part of net earnings), and again in the investing activities section (as part of the cash proceeds from the sale).

Gains and losses are also possible in other circumstances, such as when debt is retired. The same adjustment guidelines apply as described for gains and losses on the sale of assets, except that the other side of the transaction is reported in financing activities, rather than investing activities.

Changes in Noncash Current Asset and Current Liability Accounts

A final adjustment in converting net earnings to net cash provided by operating activities involves examining all changes in current asset and current liability accounts. Most current asset and current liability accounts result from operating activities. For example, accounts receivable indicate credit sales that have been recorded as revenue but for which cash collections have not yet been received. Prepaid expenses, such as insurance, reflect insurance that has been paid for, but which has not yet expired and therefore has not been recorded as an expense. Similarly, income tax payable reflects income tax expense incurred by the company but not yet paid.

As a result, we need to adjust net earnings for these accruals and prepayments to determine net cash provided by operating activities. We do this by analyzing the change in each current asset and current liability account to determine each change's impact on net earnings and cash.

There are situations when current asset and current liability accounts do not result from operating activities. Short-term investments are an example of a current asset that does not relate to operating activities. Short-term investments are shown in the investing activities section of the cash flow statement if they are not part of cash equivalents. Short-term notes payable are an example of a current liability that does not relate to operating activities. These are shown instead in the financing section of the cash flow statement.

Changes in Noncash Current Assets

The adjustments required for changes in noncash current asset accounts are as follows: increases in current asset accounts are deducted from net earnings and decreases in current asset accounts are added to net earnings, to arrive at net cash provided by operating activities. We will observe these relationships by analyzing Computer Services' current asset accounts.

Decrease in Accounts Receivable.   When accounts receivable decrease during the year, revenues on an accrual basis are lower than revenues on a cash basis. In other words, more cash was collected during the period than was recorded as revenue. Computer Services' accounts receivable decreased by $10,000 (from $30,000 to $20,000) during the year. For Computer Services, this means that cash receipts were $10,000 higher than revenues.

Illustration 13-5 shows that Computer Services had $507,000 in sales revenue reported on its statement of earnings. To determine how much cash was collected in connection with this revenue, it is useful to analyze the Accounts Receivable account:

	Accounts Receivable			
Jan. 1 Balance	30,000			
Sales on account	507,000	Receipts from customers		517,000
Dec. 31 Balance	20,000			

$10,000 net decrease

If sales revenue (assumed to be sales on account) journalized during the period was $507,000 (Dr. Accounts Receivable; Cr. Sales Revenue), and the change in Accounts Receivable during the period was a decrease of $10,000, then cash receipts from customers must have been $517,000 (Dr. Cash; Cr. Accounts Receivable).

Consequently, revenues reported on the accrual-based statement of earnings were lower than cash collections. To convert net earnings to net cash provided by operating activities, the $10,000 decrease in accounts receivable must be added to net earnings because $10,000 more cash was collected than was reported as accrual-based revenue in the statement of earnings.

When the Accounts Receivable balance increases during the year, revenues on an accrual basis are higher than cash receipts. Therefore, the amount of the increase in accounts receivable is deducted from net earnings to arrive at net cash provided by operating activities.

Increase in Inventory.   Assuming a perpetual inventory system is being used, the Merchandise Inventory account is increased by the cost of goods purchased. It is decreased by the cost of goods sold. When inventory increases during the year, the cost of goods purchased is greater than the cost of goods sold expense recorded in the statement of earnings. Any increase in the Inventory account must be deducted from net earnings, in a manner similar to the increase in the Accounts Receivable account explained above.

Inventory increased by $5,000 for Computer Services Corporation. Because the Inventory account is increased by the purchase of goods (Dr. Inventory; Cr. Accounts Payable) and is decreased by the cost of goods sold (Dr. Cost of Goods Sold; Cr. Inventory), Computer Services must have purchased $5,000 more inventory than it sold. Therefore, because the cost of goods sold reported on the statement of earnings is $150,000, purchases of merchandise during the year must have been $155,000:

Inventory			
Jan. 1 Balance	10,000		
Purchases	155,000	Cost of goods sold	150,000
Dec. 31 Balance	15,000		

} $5,000 net increase

To convert net earnings to net cash provided by operating activities, the $5,000 increase in inventory must be deducted from net earnings. The increase in inventory means that the cash-based expense must be increased, which has the effect of reducing net earnings.

This deduction does not completely convert an accrual-based figure to a cash-based figure. It does not tell us how much cash was paid for the goods purchased. It just converts the cost of goods sold to the cost of goods purchased during the year. The analysis of accounts payable—shown later—completes this analysis by converting the cost of goods purchased from an accrual basis to a cash basis.

Increase in Prepaid Expenses.   Prepaid expenses increased during the period by $4,000. This means that the cash paid for expenses is higher than the expenses reported on the accrual basis. In other words, cash payments were made in the current period, but expenses have been deferred to future periods. To determine how much cash was paid relative to the operating expenses, it is useful to analyze the Prepaid Expenses account. Operating expenses, as reported on the statement of earnings, are $111,000. Accordingly, payments for expenses must have been $115,000:

Prepaid Expenses			
Jan. 1 Balance	1,000		
Payments for expenses	115,000	Operating expenses	111,000
Dec. 31 Balance	5,000		

} $4,000 net increase

To adjust net earnings to net cash provided by operating activities, the $4,000 increase in prepaid expenses must be deducted from net earnings to determine the cash paid for expenses. If prepaid expenses decrease, reported expenses are higher than the expenses paid. therefore, the decrease in prepaid expenses is added to net earnings to arrive at net cash provided by operating activities.

These adjustments may not completely convert accrual-based expenses to cash-based expenses. For example, if Computer Services Corporation had any accrued expenses payable, these would also have to be considered before we could completely determine the amount of cash paid for operating expenses.

Computer Services does not have any accrued expenses payable related to operating expenses. However, if it did, they would be treated in the same manner as income tax payable, which will we look at in the next section when we adjust for the changes in the current liability accounts. Income tax payable is actually an example of an accrued expense payable; however, it is dealt with separately because income tax expense is reported by itself on the statement of earnings.

The following partial cash flow statement shows the impact on operating activities of changes in noncash current asset accounts, in addition to those adjustments described earlier:

Operating activities		
Net earnings		$145,000
Adjustments to reconcile net earnings to net cash		
provided by operating activities:		
Amortization expense	$ 9,000	
Loss on sale of equipment	3,000	
Decrease in accounts receivable	10,000	
Increase in inventory	(5,000)	
Increase in prepaid expenses	(4,000)	13,000
Net cash provided by operating activities		158,000

Changes in Current Liabilities

The adjustments required for changes in current liability accounts are as follows: increases in current liability accounts are added to net earnings, and decreases in current liability accounts are deducted from net earnings, to arrive at net cash provided by operating activities. We will observe these relationships by analyzing Computer Services' current liability accounts, Accounts Payable and Income Tax Payable.

Increase in Accounts Payable. The Accounts Payable account is increased by purchases of merchandise (Dr. Inventory; Cr. Accounts Payable) and decreased by payments to suppliers (Dr. Accounts Payable; Cr. Cash). We determined the amount of purchases made by Computer Services in the analysis of the Inventory account earlier: $155,000. Using this figure, we can now determine that payments to suppliers must have been $139,000:

$16,000 net increase

Accounts Payable			
		Jan. 1 Balance	12,000
Payments to suppliers	139,000	Purchases	155,000
		Dec. 31 Balance	28,000

To convert net earnings to net cash provided by operating activities, the $16,000 increase in accounts payable must be added to net earnings. The increase in accounts payable means that less cash was paid for the purchases than was deducted in the accrual-based expenses section of the statement of earnings. The addition of $16,000 completes the adjustment required to convert the cost of goods purchased to the cash paid for these goods.

In summary, the conversion of the cost of goods sold on the accrual-based statement of earnings to the cash paid for goods purchased involves two steps: First, the change in the Inventory account adjusts the cost of goods sold to the accrual-based cost of goods purchased. Second, the change in the Accounts Payable account adjusts the accrual-based cost of goods purchased to the cash-based payments to suppliers:

Cost of goods sold	$150,000
Add: Increase in inventory	5,000
Cost of goods purchased	155,000
Less: Increase in accounts payable	16,000
Cash payments to suppliers	$139,000

Remember that adjustments to accrual-based expense accounts result in an adjustment in the opposite direction to net earnings. That is, when an expense account such as Cost of Goods Sold is increased because of an increase in inventory, this amount must be *deducted* from net earnings. This is because expenses reduce net earnings. Likewise, when Cost of Goods Sold is decreased because of an increase in accounts payable, this amount must be *added* to net earnings.

If a periodic inventory system was in use, the accounts for purchases and related expenses, rather than Cost of Goods Sold, would be adjusted in a similar way for any change in accounts payable. There would be no change in the Inventory account throughout the period in a periodic inventory system.

Decrease in Income Tax Payable. When a company incurs income tax expense but has not yet paid its taxes, it records income tax payable. A change in the Income Tax Payable account reflects the difference between the income tax expense incurred and the income tax actually paid during the year.

Computer Services' Income Tax Payable account decreased by $2,000. This means that the $47,000 of income tax expense reported on the statement of earnings was $2,000 less than the $49,000 of taxes paid during the period, as shown in the following T account:

Income Tax Payable				
		Jan. 1 Balance	8,000	
Payments for income tax	49,000	Income tax expenses	47,000	$2,000 net decrease
		Dec. 31 Balance	6,000	

To adjust net earnings to net cash provided by operating activities, the $2,000 decrease in income tax payable must be deducted from net earnings. If the amount of income tax payable had increased during the year, the increase would be added to net earnings to reflect the fact that income tax expense deducted on the accrual-based statement of earnings was higher than the cash paid during the period.

The partial cash flow statement in Illustration 13-7 shows the impact on operating activities of the changes in current liability accounts, and also shows the adjustments described earlier for amortization expense, gains and losses, and changes in noncash current asset accounts. The operating activities section of the cash flow statement is now complete.

COMPUTER SERVICES CORPORATION
Cash Flow Statement—Indirect Method (partial)
Year Ended December 31, 2006

Operating activities		
Net earnings		$145,000
Adjustments to reconcile net earnings to net cash provided by operating activities:		
Amortization expense	$ 9,000	
Loss on sale of equipment	3,000	
Decrease in accounts receivable	10,000	
Increase in inventory	(5,000)	
Increase in prepaid expenses	(4,000)	
Increase in accounts payable	16,000	
Decrease in income tax payable	(2,000)	27,000
Net cash provided by operating activities		172,000

Illustration 13-7 ◄

Net cash provided by operating activities—indirect method

Helpful hint Whether the indirect or direct method (Section 2) is used, net cash provided by operating activities will be the same.

In summary, Illustration 13-7 shows that the accrual-based net earnings of $145,000 resulted in net cash provided by operating activities of $172,000, after adjustments for noncash items.

Summary of Conversion to Net Cash Provided by Operating Activities—Indirect Method

As shown in the previous pages, the cash flow statement prepared by the indirect method starts with net earnings. It then adds or deducts items to arrive at net cash provided (or used) by operating activities. The adjustments generally take one of three forms: (1) noncash expenses such as amortization, (2) gains and losses on the sale of assets, and (3) changes in noncash current asset and current liability accounts.

Illustration 13-8 summarizes these changes.

Illustration 13-8 ▶

Adjustments required to
convert net earnings to net
cash provided by operating
activities

		Adjustment Required to Convert Net Earnings to Net Cash Provided (Used) by Operating Activities
Noncash charges	Amortization expense	Add
Gains and losses	Gain on sale of asset	Deduct
	Loss on sale of asset	Add
Changes in noncash current asset and current liability accounts	Increase in current asset account	Deduct
	Decrease in current asset account	Add
	Increase in current liability account	Add
	Decrease in current liability account	Deduct

Step 2: Investing Activities

Determine the Net Cash Provided (Used) by Investing Activities by Analyzing Changes in Short-term Investment and Long-Term Asset Accounts

Helpful hint Investing and
financing activities are
measured and reported in
the same way under the
direct and indirect methods.

Investing activities affect long-term asset accounts, such as property, plant, and equipment, and intangible assets. Short-term investments (other than those classified as cash equivalents) are also reported as investing activities. To determine the investing activities, the balance sheet and additional information provided in Illustration 13-5 must be examined.

The change in each noncurrent account (and short-term investments and notes payable) is analyzed to determine what effect, if any, the change had on cash. Computer Services has three long-term asset accounts that must be analyzed: Land, Buildings, and Equipment.

Increase in Land.   Land increased by $110,000 during the year, as reported in Computer Services' balance sheet. The additional information states that this land was purchased by issuing long-term bonds. Issuing bonds for land has no effect on cash, but it is a significant noncash investing activity that must be disclosed in a note to the statement.

Increase in Building.   The Building account increased by $120,000 during the year. What caused this increase? No additional information has been provided regarding this change. Whenever unexplained differences in noncurrent accounts occur, we assume the transaction was for cash. That is, we would assume in this case that a building was acquired, or expanded, for $120,000 cash.

Increase in Accumulated Amortization—Building.   Accumulated Amortization increased by $6,000 during the year. As explained in the additional information, this increase resulted from the amortization expense reported on the statement of earnings for the building:

$6,000 net increase

Accumulated Amortization—Building		
	Jan. 1 Balance	5,000
	Amortization expense	6,000
	Dec. 31 Balance	11,000

Amortization expense is a noncash charge and was added back to net earnings in the operating activities section of the cash flow statement to cancel this charge. No further adjustment or reporting is necessary for amortization related to the building.

Increase in Equipment.   Computer Services' Equipment account increased by $17,000. The additional information explains that this was a net increase resulting from two different transactions: (1) a purchase of equipment for $25,000 cash, and (2) a sale of equipment that cost $8,000 for $4,000 cash. The T account that follows shows the reasons for the change in this account during the year:

The following entries show the details of the equipment transactions:

Equipment	25,000	
Cash		25,000

A = L + SE
+25,000
−25,000

Cash flows: −25,000

Cash	4,000	
Accumulated Amortization	1,000	
Loss on Sale of Equipment	3,000	
Equipment		8,000

A = L + SE
+4,000   −3,000
+1,000
−8,000

Cash flows: +4,000

Each transaction should be reported separately on the cash flow statement. When a net change in a noncurrent balance sheet account has occurred during the year, the individual items that cause the net change should be reported separately. Note that this is different from our practice with working capital (current asset and current liability) accounts, where we report only the net change.

In this particular case, the purchase of equipment should be reported as a $25,000 outflow of cash. The sale of equipment should be reported as a $4,000 inflow of cash. Note that it is the cash proceeds that are reported on the cash flow statement, not the cost of the equipment sold.

Increase in Accumulated Amortization—Equipment. The accumulated amortization for equipment increased by $2,000. This change does not represent the overall amortization expense for the year. The additional information in Illustration 13-5 helps us determine the details of this change.

Accumulated Amortization—Equipment			
		Jan. 1 Balance	1,000
Sale of equipment	1,000	Amortization expense	3,000
		Dec. 31 Balance	3,000

$2,000 net increase

This account was decreased (debited $1,000) as a result of the sale of equipment, as described earlier. The account was also increased by $3,000 of amortization expense for the current period.

As we have seen, there are two accounts affected by the sale of the equipment on Computer Services' statement of earnings (Amortization Expense and Loss on Sale of Equipment) and two accounts on the balance sheet (Equipment and Accumulated Amortization). In the cash flow statement, it is important to combine the effects of this sale in one place—in the investing activities section.

The amortization expense and loss on sale reported in the statement of earnings are shown as additions to net earnings in the operating activities section of the cash flow statement. As we learned earlier in the chapter, they are added back to net earnings not because they are sources of cash but because they are noncash charges that must be added to net earnings to cancel the deduction from operating cash flows.

So, no cash impact of the sale of the equipment ends up being included in the operating activities section. Rather, the cash proceeds received from the sale of the equipment are shown in their entirety in the investing activities section.

The investing activities section of Computer Services' cash flow statement follows. It reports the changes in the accounts Land, Building, and Equipment.

Investing activities		
Purchase of building	$(120,000)	
Purchase of equipment	(25,000)	
Sale of equipment	4,000	
Net cash used by investing activities		$(141,000)
Note x: Significant noncash investing and financing activities		
Issue of bonds to purchase land		$110,000

Step 3: Financing Activities

Determine the Net Cash Provided (Used) by Financing Activities by Analyzing Changes in Short-Term Notes Payable and Long-Term Liability and Equity Accounts

The third step is to analyze the changes in long-term liability and equity accounts, including changes involving short-term notes payable. Computer Services has one long-term liability account, Bonds Payable, and two shareholders' equity accounts: Common Shares and Retained Earnings.

Increase in Bonds Payable.   Bonds Payable increased by $110,000. As indicated earlier, land was acquired by issuing these bonds. This noncash transaction is reported as a note to the cash flow statement because it is a significant financing activity.

Increase in Common Shares.   Computer Services' Common Shares account increased by $20,000. Since no additional information is provided about any reacquisition of shares, we assume that this change relates solely to the issue of additional common shares for cash. This cash inflow is reported in the financing activities section of the cash flow statement.

Increase in Retained Earnings.   What caused the net increase of $116,000 in Retained Earnings? This increase can be explained by two factors. First, net earnings increased retained earnings by $145,000. Second, the additional information provided in Illustration 13-5 indicates that a cash dividend of $29,000 was paid. This information could also have been deduced by analyzing the T account:

	Retained Earnings		
		Jan. 1 Balance	48,000
Cash dividend	29,000	Net earnings	145,000
		Dec. 31 Balance	164,000

$116,000 net increase {

As noted earlier, these two changes must be reported separately. The net earnings is therefore reported in the operating activities section of the cash flow statement (and adjusted to a cash basis). The cash dividend paid is reported as a cash outflow in the financing activities section of the statement.

The financing activities section of Computer Services' cash flow statement is shown below and reports the issue of common shares and payment of a dividend:

Financing activities		
Issue of common shares	$ 20,000	
Payment of cash dividend	(29,000)	
Net cash used by financing activities		$(9,000)
Note x: Significant noncash investing and financing activities		
Issue of bonds to purchase land		$110,000

Cash Flow Statement

Using the previous information, we can now combine the sections and present a complete cash flow statement for Computer Services Corporation in Illustration 13-9. The statement starts with operating activities, follows with investing activities, and continues with financing activities. It concludes with the net change in cash, reconciled to the beginning- and end-of-period cash balances. Finally, a significant noncash investing and financing activity is reported in the note to the statement.

Illustration 13-9 ◄

Cash flow statement—indirect method

COMPUTER SERVICES CORPORATION
Cash Flow Statement—Indirect Method
Year Ended December 31, 2006

Operating activities		
Net earnings		$145,000
Adjustments to reconcile net earnings to net cash provided by operating activities:		
Amortization expense	$ 9,000	
Loss on sale of equipment	3,000	
Decrease in accounts receivable	10,000	
Increase in inventory	(5,000)	
Increase in prepaid expenses	(4,000)	
Increase in accounts payable	16,000	
Decrease in income tax payable	(2,000)	27,000
Net cash provided by operating activities		172,000
Investing activities		
Purchase of building	$(120,000)	
Purchase of equipment	(25,000)	
Sale of equipment	4,000	
Net cash used by investing activities		(141,000)
Financing activities		
Issue of common shares	$ 20,000	
Payment of cash dividend	(29,000)	
Net cash used by financing activities		(9,000)
Net increase in cash		22,000
Cash, January 1		33,000
Cash, December 31		$ 55,000
Note x: Significant noncash investing and financing activities		
Issue of bonds to purchase land		$110,000

Helpful hint Note that in the investing and financing activities sections, positive numbers indicate cash inflows (receipts) and negative numbers indicate cash outflows (payments).

Computer Services' cash flow statement shows the following: Operating activities provided $172,000 of cash. Investing activities used $141,000 of cash. Financing activities used $9,000 of cash. There was a significant noncash investing and financing activity for $110,000.

Step 4: Net Change in Cash

Determine the Net Increase (Decrease) in Cash. Compare the Net Change in Cash with the Change in Cash Reported on the Balance Sheet to Make Sure the Amounts Agree

The comparative balance sheets in Illustration 13-5 indicate that the net change in cash during the period was an increase of $22,000. The $22,000 net increase in cash reported in the cash flow statement above agrees with this change.

Notice how the cash flow statement links the statement of earnings with the beginning and ending balance sheet amounts. Net earnings from the statement of earnings is the starting point in determining operating activities. The changes in the balance sheet accounts are explained in terms of their impact on cash. These changes lead to the end-of-period cash balances on the balance sheet and on the cash flow statement.

BEFORE YOU GO ON . . .

▶Review It

1. What is the format of the operating activities section of the cash flow statement using the indirect method?
2. Where is amortization expense shown on a cash flow statement using the indirect method?
3. Where are significant noncash investing and financing activities shown in a cash flow statement? Give some examples.

▶Do It

Presented below is information for Reynolds Ltd. Use the indirect method to prepare a cash flow statement.

REYNOLDS LTD.
Balance Sheet
December 31

Assets	2006	2005	Change Increase/Decrease	
Cash	$ 54,000	$ 37,000	$ 17,000	Increase
Accounts receivable	68,000	26,000	42,000	Increase
Inventories	54,000	10,000	44,000	Increase
Prepaid expenses	4,000	6,000	2,000	Decrease
Land	45,000	70,000	25,000	Decrease
Buildings	200,000	200,000	0	
Accumulated amortization—buildings	(21,000)	(11,000)	10,000	Increase
Equipment	193,000	68,000	125,000	Increase
Accumulated amortization—equipment	(28,000)	(10,000)	18,000	Increase
Totals	$569,000	$396,000		
Liabilities and Shareholders' Equity				
Accounts payable	$ 23,000	$ 50,000	$ 27,000	Decrease
Accrued expenses payable	10,000	0	10,000	Increase
Bonds payable	110,000	150,000	40,000	Decrease
Common shares	220,000	60,000	160,000	Increase
Retained earnings	206,000	136,000	70,000	Increase
Totals	$569,000	$396,000		

REYNOLDS LTD.
Statement of Earnings
Year Ended December 31, 2006

Sales revenue		$890,000
Cost of goods sold	$465,000	
Operating expenses	221,000	
Loss on sale of equipment	2,000	688,000
Earnings from operations		202,000
Interest expense		12,000
Earnings before income tax		190,000
Income tax expense		65,000
Net earnings		$125,000

Additional information:

1. Operating expenses include an amortization expense of $33,000.
2. Equipment with a cost of $166,000 was bought for cash. Equipment with a cost of $41,000 and a net book value of $36,000 was sold for $34,000 cash.
3. Bonds of $40,000 were redeemed at their face value for cash.

Action Plan

- Determine the net cash provided (used) by operating activities. Operating activities generally relate to revenues and expenses, which are affected by changes in noncash current assets and current liabilities in the balance sheet, and noncash items in the statement of earnings.
- Determine the net cash provided (used) by investing activities. Investing activities generally relate to changes in noncurrent assets.
- Determine the net cash provided (used) by financing activities. Financing activities generally relate to changes in noncurrent liabilities and shareholders' equity accounts.
- Determine the net increase (decrease) in cash. Reconcile to the end-of-period cash balance reported on the balance sheet.

Solution

REYNOLDS LTD.
Cash Flow Statement—Indirect Method
Year Ended December 31, 2006

Operating activities		
Net earnings		$ 125,000
Adjustments to reconcile net earnings to net cash provided		
by operating activities:		
Amortization expense	$ 33,000	
Loss on sale of equipment	2,000	
Increase in accounts receivable	(42,000)	
Increase in inventories	(44,000)	
Decrease in prepaid expenses	2,000	
Decrease in accounts payable	(27,000)	
Increase in accrued expenses payable	10,000	(66,000)
Net cash provided by operating activities		59,000
Investing activities		
Sale of land	$ 25,000	
Sale of equipment	34,000	
Purchase of equipment	(166,000)	
Net cash used by investing activities		(107,000)
Financing activities		
Redemption of bonds	$ (40,000)	
Issue of common shares	160,000	
Payment of dividends	(55,000)[a]	
Net cash provided by financing activities		65,000
Net increase in cash		17,000
Cash, January 1		37,000
Cash, December 31		$ 54,000

[a] $136,000 + $125,000 − $206,000 = $55,000

the navigator

Note: This concludes Section 1 on the preparation of the cash flow statement using the indirect method. Unless your instructor assigns Section 2, you should turn to the concluding section of the chapter, "Using Cash Flows to Evaluate a Company."

SECTION 2 ▶ DIRECT METHOD

study objective 2b

Prepare a cash flow statement using the direct method.

To illustrate the direct method, we will use financial information from Computer Services Corporation to prepare a cash flow statement. Illustration 13-10 presents Computer Services' current- and previous-year balance sheet, its current-year statement of earnings, and related financial information.

Illustration 13-10 ▶

Comparative balance sheet, statement of earnings, and additional information

COMPUTER SERVICES CORPORATION
Balance Sheet
December 31

Assets	2006	2005	Change Increase/Decrease
Current assets			
Cash	$ 55,000	$ 33,000	$ 22,000 Increase
Accounts receivable	20,000	30,000	10,000 Decrease
Inventory	15,000	10,000	5,000 Increase
Prepaid expenses	5,000	1,000	4,000 Increase
Property, plant, and equipment			
Land	130,000	20,000	110,000 Increase
Building	160,000	40,000	120,000 Increase
Accumulated amortization—building	(11,000)	(5,000)	6,000 Increase
Equipment	27,000	10,000	17,000 Increase
Accumulated amortization—equipment	(3,000)	(1,000)	2,000 Increase
Total	$398,000	$138,000	
Liabilities and Shareholders' Equity			
Current liabilities			
Accounts payable	$ 28,000	$ 12,000	$ 16,000 Increase
Income tax payable	6,000	8,000	2,000 Decrease
Long-term liabilities			
Bonds payable	130,000	20,000	110,000 Increase
Shareholders' equity			
Common shares	70,000	50,000	20,000 Increase
Retained earnings	164,000	48,000	116,000 Increase
Total	$398,000	$138,000	

COMPUTER SERVICES CORPORATION
Statement of Earnings
Year Ended December 31, 2006

Sales revenue		$507,000
Cost of goods sold		150,000
Gross profit		357,000
Operating expenses (excluding amortization)	$111,000	
Amortization expense	9,000	
Loss on sale of equipment	3,000	123,000
Earnings from operations		234,000
Interest expense		42,000
Earnings before income tax		192,000
Income tax expense		47,000
Net earnings		$145,000

Additional information for 2006:

1. The company paid a $29,000 cash dividend.
2. The company obtained land through the issue of $110,000 of long-term bonds.
3. Equipment costing $25,000 was purchased for cash.
4. The company sold equipment with a book value of $7,000 (cost of $8,000, less accumulated amortization of $1,000) for $4,000 cash.
5. Amortization expense consisted of $6,000 for the building and $3,000 for equipment.

We will now apply the four steps to the information provided for Computer Services Corporation.

Step 1: Operating Activities

Determine the Net Cash Provided (Used) by Operating Activities by Converting Net Earnings from an Accrual Basis to a Cash Basis

Under the direct method, net cash provided (or used) by operating activities is calculated by adjusting each item in the statement of earnings from the accrual basis to the cash basis. To simplify and condense the operating activities section, only major classes of operating cash receipts and cash payments are reported. The difference between the cash receipts and cash payments for these major classes is the net cash provided by operating activities. These relationships are shown in Illustration 13-11.

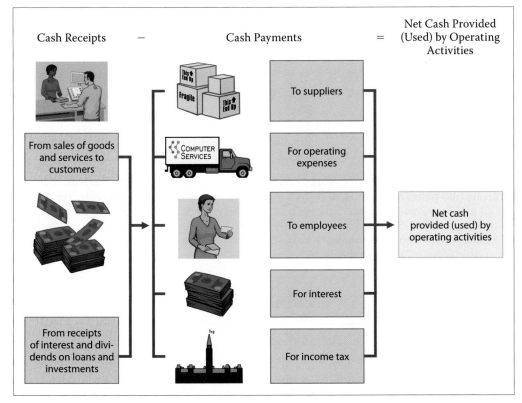

Illustration 13-11 ◄

Major classes of cash receipts and payments

An efficient way to apply the direct method is to analyze the items reported in the statement of earnings in the order in which they are listed. Cash receipts and cash payments related to these revenues and expenses are then determined by adjusting for changes in the related balance sheet accounts. Most current asset and current liability accounts result from operating activities. For example, accounts receivable indicate credit sales that have been recorded as revenue but for which cash has not yet been received. Prepaid expenses, such as insurance, reflect insurance that has been paid for, but which has not yet expired and therefore has not been recorded as an expense. Similarly, income tax payable reflects income tax expense incurred by the company but not yet paid.

As a result, we need to adjust revenues and expenses reported on the statement of earnings for these accruals and prepayments to determine the net cash provided by operating activities. To do this, increases in current asset accounts are deducted from revenues and added to expenses to convert accrual-based statement of earnings amounts to cash-based amounts. Conversely, decreases in current asset accounts are added to revenues and deducted from expenses. Increases in current liability accounts are added to revenues and deducted from expenses to convert accrual-based statement of earnings amounts to cash-based amounts. Conversely, decreases in current liability accounts are deducted from revenues and added to expenses.

We explain the reasoning behind these adjustments for Computer Services Corporation, first for cash receipts and then for cash payments, in the following sections.

Cash Receipts

Computer Services has only one source of cash receipts—customers.

Cash Receipts from Customers.   The statement of earnings for Computer Services reported sales revenue from customers of $507,000. How much of that was cash receipts? To answer that, it is necessary to consider the change in accounts receivable during the year.

When accounts receivable decrease during the year, revenues on an accrual basis are lower than revenues on a cash basis. In other words, more cash was collected during the period than was recorded as revenue. Computer Services' accounts receivable decreased by $10,000 (from $30,000 to $20,000) during the year. This means that cash receipts were $10,000 higher than revenues. To determine the amount of cash receipts, the decrease in accounts receivable is added to sales revenue.

Thus, cash receipts from customers were $517,000, calculated as in Illustration 13-12.

Illustration 13-12 ▶

Formula to calculate cash receipts from customers—direct method

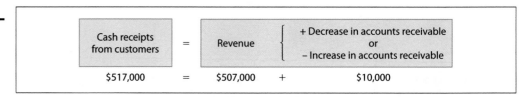

Alternatively, when the Accounts Receivable balance increases during the year, revenues on an accrual basis are higher than cash receipts. In other words, revenues have increased, but not all of these revenues resulted in cash receipts. Therefore, the amount of the increase in accounts receivable is deducted from sales revenues to arrive at cash receipts from customers.

Cash receipts from customers can also be determined from an analysis of the Accounts Receivable account, as shown below:

		Accounts Receivable			
Jan.	1 Balance	30,000			
	Sales on account	507,000	Receipts from customers		517,000
Dec. 31 Balance		20,000			

$10,000 net decrease

Cash Receipts from Interest and Dividends.   Computer Services does not have cash receipts from any source other than customers. If a statement of earnings details other revenue, such as interest and/or dividend revenue, these amounts must be adjusted for any accrued amounts receivable to determine the actual cash receipts. As in Illustration 13-12, increases in accrued receivables would be deducted from accrual-based revenues. Decreases in accrued receivable accounts would be added to accrual-based revenues.

Cash Payments

Computer Services has many sources of cash payments—suppliers, operating expenses, interest, and income taxes. We will analyze each of these in the next sections.

Cash Payments to Suppliers. Using the perpetual inventory system, Computer Services reported a cost of goods sold of $150,000 on its statement of earnings. How much of that was cash payments to suppliers? To answer that, it is necessary to find the cost of goods purchased for the year by adjusting the cost of goods sold for changes in inventory. When inventory increases during the year, the cost of goods purchased exceeds the cost of goods sold. To determine the cost of goods purchased, the increase in inventory is added to the cost of goods sold. Any decrease in inventory would be deducted from the cost of goods sold. Computer Services' inventory increased by $5,000 so its cost of goods purchased is $155,000 ($150,000 + $5,000).

After the cost of goods purchased is calculated, cash payments to suppliers can be determined. This is done by adjusting the cost of goods purchased for the change in accounts payable. When accounts payable increase during the year, purchases on an accrual basis are higher than they are on a cash basis. To determine cash payments to suppliers, an increase in accounts payable is deducted from the cost of goods purchased. On the other hand, there may be a decrease in accounts payable. That would occur if cash payments to suppliers exceeded purchases. In that case, the decrease in accounts payable is added to the cost of goods purchased.

For Computer Services, cash payments to suppliers were $139,000 ($150,000 + $5,000 − $16,000), as calculated in Illustration 13-13.

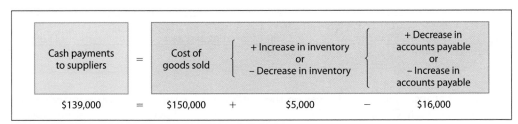

Illustration 13-13 ◄

Formula to calculate cash payments to suppliers—direct method

Cash payments to suppliers can also be determined from an analysis of the Inventory and Accounts Payable accounts below:

Inventory			
Jan. 1 Balance	10,000		
Purchases	155,000	Cost of goods sold	150,000
Dec. 31 Balance	15,000		

$5,000 net increase

Accounts Payable			
		Jan. 1 Balance	12,000
Payments to suppliers	139,000	Purchases	155,000
		Dec. 31 Balance	28,000

$16,000 net increase

Cash Payments for Operating Expenses. Operating expenses of $111,000 were reported on Computer Services' statement of earnings. To determine the cash paid for operating expenses, we need to adjust this amount for any changes in prepaid expenses and accrued liabilities.

If prepaid expenses increase during the year, the cash paid for operating expenses will be higher than the operating expenses reported on the statement of earnings. To adjust operating expenses to cash payments for services, any increase in prepaid expenses must be added to operating expenses. On the other hand, if prepaid expenses decrease during the year, the decrease must be deducted from operating expenses.

Operating expenses must also be adjusted for changes in accrued liability accounts (e.g., Accrued Expenses Payable). While some companies record accrued liabilities separately, others combine them with accounts payable. In a merchandising company, such as Computer Services, the Accounts Payable account is often used only for purchases of merchandise inventory on account. Accrued liability accounts are used for all other payables.

At this point in time, Computer Services does not have any accrued expenses payable related to its operating expenses. If it did, any changes in the Accrued Expenses Payable account would affect operating expenses as follows. When accrued expenses payable increase during the year, operating expenses on an accrual basis are higher than they are on a cash basis. To determine cash payments for operating expenses, an increase in accrued expenses payable is deducted from operating expenses. On the other hand, a decrease in accrued expenses payable is added to operating expenses because the cash payments exceed the operating expenses.

Computer Services' cash payments for operating expenses were $115,000, calculated as in Illustration 13-14.

Illustration 13-14 ▶

Formula to calculate cash payments for operating expenses—direct method

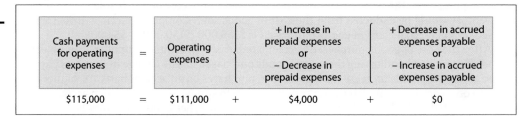

Cash payments for operating expenses can also be determined from an analysis of the Prepaid Expenses account, as shown below:

Prepaid Expenses			
Jan. 1 Balance	1,000		
Payments for expenses	115,000	Operating expenses	111,000
Dec. 31 Balance	5,000		

$4,000 net increase

Noncash Charges.   Noncash charges on the statement of earnings are not reported on the cash flow statement. Computer Services reports two noncash expenses: amortization expense and a loss on the sale of equipment.

Computer Services' amortization expense in 2006 was $9,000. Recall that the entry to record the amortization would be as follows:

Cash flows: no effect

Amortization Expense	9,000	
Accumulated Amortization		9,000

This entry has no impact on cash.

Amortization expense was shown separately on Computer Services' statement of earnings. Sometimes amortization expense is included in operating expenses. If the amount for operating expenses includes amortization expense, operating expenses must be reduced by the amount of amortization to determine the cash payments for operating expenses. Other charges to expense that do not require the use of cash, such as bad debt expense, are treated in the same manner as amortization.

The $3,000 loss on the sale of equipment is also a noncash charge. The loss on the sale of equipment reduces net earnings, but it does not reduce cash. Thus, the loss on the sale of equipment is not reported on the cash flow statement. If there were a gain, it would not be reported either.

Cash Payments to Employees.   Some companies report payments to employees separately, removing these payments from their operating expenses. To determine payments to employees, you would have to know the salary expense amount on the statement of earnings and any salaries payable on the balance sheet. Cash payments to employees would equal the salary expense plus any decrease (or less any increase) during the period in salaries payable.

Some companies condense their statements of earnings in such a manner that cash payments to suppliers and employees cannot be separated from cash payments for operating expenses (i.e., they do not disclose cost of goods sold or salary expense separately). Although the disclosure will not be as informative, for reporting purposes it is acceptable to combine these sources of cash payments.

Cash Payments for Income Tax.   The statement of earnings for Computer Services shows an income tax expense of $47,000 and a decrease in income tax payable of $2,000. When a company incurs income tax expense but has not yet paid its taxes, it records income tax payable. A change in the Income Tax Payable account reflects the difference between income tax expense incurred and income tax actually paid during the year.

The relationship among cash payments for income tax, income tax expense, and changes in income tax payable is shown in Illustration 13-15.

Cash payments for income tax	=	Income tax expense	{	+ Decrease in income tax payable or – Increase in income tax payable
$49,000	=	$47,000	+	$2,000

Illustration 13-15 ◄

Formula to calculate cash payments for income tax—direct method

Computer Services' Income Tax Payable account decreased by $2,000. This means that the $47,000 of income tax expense reported on the statement of earnings was $2,000 less than the $49,000 of taxes paid during the period, as detailed in the following T account:

Income Tax Payable			
		Jan. 1 Balance	8,000
Payments for income tax	49,000	Income tax expense	47,000
		Dec. 31 Balance	6,000

$2,000 net decrease

All of the revenues and expenses in the statement of earnings have now been adjusted to a cash basis. The operating activities section of the cash flow statement is shown in Illustration 13-16.

COMPUTER SERVICES CORPORATION
Cash Flow Statement—Direct Method (partial)
Year Ended December 31, 2006

Operating activities		
Cash receipts from customers		$517,000
Cash payments		
To suppliers	$139,000	
For operating expenses	115,000	
For interest	42,000	
For income tax	49,000	(345,000)
Net cash provided by operating activities		172,000

Illustration 13-16 ◄

Net cash provided by operating activities—direct method

Helpful hint Whether the direct or indirect method (Section 1) is used, net cash provided by operating activities will be the same.

Step 2: Investing Activities

Determine the Net Cash Provided (Used) by Investing Activities by Analyzing Changes in Short-term Investment and Long-Term Asset Accounts

Investing activities affect long-term asset accounts, such as property, plant, and equipment, and intangible assets. Short-term investments (other than those classified as cash equivalents) are also reported as investing activities. To determine the investing activities, the balance sheet and additional information provided in Illustration 13-10 must be examined.

The change in each noncurrent account (and short-term investments and notes payable) is analyzed to determine what effect, if any, the change had on cash. Computer Services has three long-term asset accounts that must be analyzed: Land, Buildings, and Equipment.

Helpful hint Investing and financing activities are measured and reported in the same way under the direct and indirect methods.

Increase in Land.   Land increased by $110,000 during the year, as reported in Computer Services' balance sheet. The additional information states that this land was purchased by issuing long-term bonds. This transaction has no effect on cash, but it is a significant noncash investing activity that must be disclosed in a note to the statement.

Increase in Building.   The Building account increased by $120,000 during the year. What caused this increase? No additional information has been provided regarding this change. Whenever unexplained differences in noncurrent accounts occur, we assume the transaction was for cash. That is, we would assume in this case that a building was acquired, or expanded, for $120,000 cash.

Increase in Accumulated Amortization—Building.   Accumulated Amortization increased by $6,000 during the year. As explained in the additional information, this increase resulted from the amortization expense reported on the statement of earnings for the building:

$6,000 net increase {

Accumulated Amortization—Building			
	Jan. 1	Balance	5,000
		Amortization expense	6,000
	Dec. 31	Balance	11,000

As explained earlier, amortization expense is a noncash charge and does not affect the cash flow statement.

Increase in Equipment.   Computer Services' Equipment account increased by $17,000. The additional information explains that this was a net increase resulting from two different transactions: (1) a purchase of equipment for $25,000 cash, and (2) a sale of equipment that cost $8,000 for $4,000 cash. The T account below shows the reasons for the change in this account during the year:

$17,000 net increase {

Equipment				
Jan. 1	Balance	10,000		
	Purchase of equipment	25,000	Cost of equipment sold	8,000
Dec. 31	Balance	27,000		

The following entries show the details of the equipment transactions:

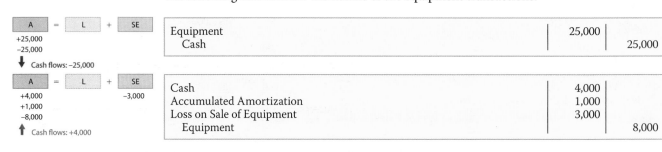

Equipment	25,000	
Cash		25,000

Cash	4,000	
Accumulated Amortization	1,000	
Loss on Sale of Equipment	3,000	
Equipment		8,000

Each transaction should be reported separately on the cash flow statement. When a net change in a noncurrent balance sheet account has occurred during the year, the individual items that cause the net change should be reported separately. The sale of equipment should be reported as a $4,000 inflow of cash. The purchase of equipment should be reported as a $25,000 outflow of cash. Note that it is the cash proceeds that are reported on the cash flow statement, not the cost of the equipment sold.

Increase in Accumulated Amortization—Equipment.   The accumulated amortization for equipment increased by $2,000. This change does not represent the overall amortization expense for the year. The T account below helps us determine the details of this change.

$2,000 net increase {

Accumulated Amortization—Equipment				
			Jan. 1 Balance	1,000
Sale of equipment		1,000	Amortization expense	3,000
			Dec. 31 Balance	3,000

As previously noted, amortization has no impact on cash and does not affect the cash flow statement. The impact of the sale of the equipment was reported as indicated above.

The investing activities section of Computer Services' cash flow statement is shown below and reports the changes in the accounts Land, Building, and Equipment:

Investing activities		
Purchase of building	$(120,000)	
Purchase of equipment	(25,000)	
Sale of equipment	4,000	
Net cash used by investing activities		$(141,000)
Note x: Significant noncash investing and financing activities		
Issue of bonds to purchase land		$110,000

Step 3: Financing Activities

Determine the Net Cash Provided (Used) by Financing Activities by Analyzing Changes in Short-Term Notes Payable and Long-Term Liability and Equity Accounts

The third step is to analyze the changes in long-term liability and equity accounts, including changes involving short-term notes payable. Computer Services has one long-term liability account, Bonds Payable, and two shareholders' equity accounts: Common Shares and Retained Earnings.

Increase in Bonds Payable.   Bonds Payable increased by $110,000. As indicated earlier, land was acquired by issuing these bonds. This noncash transaction is reported as a note to the cash flow statement because it is a significant financing activity.

Increase in Common Shares.   Computer Services' Common Shares account increased by $20,000. Since no additional information is provided about any reacquisition of shares, we assume that this change relates solely to the issue of additional common shares for cash. This cash inflow is reported in the financing activities section of the cash flow statement.

Increase in Retained Earnings.   What caused the net increase of $116,000 in Retained Earnings? This increase can be explained by two factors. First, net earnings increased retained earnings by $145,000. Second, the additional information provided in Illustration 13-10 indicates that a cash dividend of $29,000 was paid. This information could also have been deduced by analyzing the T account:

Retained Earnings				
		Jan. 1 Balance	48,000	
Cash dividend	29,000	Net earnings	145,000	$116,000 net increase
		Dec. 31 Balance	164,000	

Net earnings is not reported separately in the cash flow statement under the direct method. Rather, the cash components of the items (revenues and expenses) comprising net earnings are reported in the operating activities section, as we learned earlier. The cash dividend paid is reported as a cash outflow in the financing activities section of the statement.

The financing activities section of Computer Services' cash flow statement is shown below and reports the issue of common shares and payment of a dividend:

Financing activities		
Issue of common shares	$ 20,000	
Payment of cash dividend	(29,000)	
Net cash used by financing activities		$(9,000)
Note x: Significant noncash investing and financing activities		
Issue of bonds to purchase land		$110,000

Cash Flow Statement

Using the previous information, we can now combine the sections and present a complete cash flow statement for Computer Services Corporation in Illustration 13-17. The statement starts with operating activities, follows with investing activities, and continues with financing activities. It concludes with the net change in cash, reconciled to the beginning- and end-of-period cash balances. Finally, a significant noncash investing and financing activity is reported in the note to the statement.

Illustration 13-17 ►

Cash flow statement—direct method

Helpful hint Note that in the investing and financing activities sections, positive numbers indicate cash inflows (receipts) and negative numbers indicate cash outflows (payments).

COMPUTER SERVICES CORPORATION
Cash Flow Statement—Direct Method
Year Ended December 31, 2006

Operating activities		
Cash receipts from customers		$517,000
Cash payments		
To suppliers	$ 139,000	
For operating expenses	115,000	
For interest	42,000	
For income tax	49,000	(345,000)
Net cash provided by operating activities		172,000
Investing activities		
Purchase of building	$(120,000)	
Purchase of equipment	(25,000)	
Sale of equipment	4,000	
Net cash used by investing activities		(141,000)
Financing activities		
Issue of common shares	$ 20,000	
Payment of cash dividend	(29,000)	
Net cash used by financing activities		(9,000)
Net increase in cash		22,000
Cash, January 1		33,000
Cash, December 31		$ 55,000
Note x: Significant noncash investing and financing activities		
Issue of bonds to purchase land		$110,000

Computer Services' cash flow statement shows the following: Operating activities provided $172,000 of cash. Investing activities used $141,000 of cash. Financing activities used $9,000 of cash. There was a significant noncash investing and financing activity for $110,000.

Step 4: Net Change in Cash

Determine the Net Increase (Decrease) in Cash. Compare the Net Change in Cash with the Change in Cash Reported on the Balance Sheet to Make Sure the Amounts Agree

The comparative balance sheets in Illustration 13-10 indicate that the net change in cash during the period was an increase of $22,000. The $22,000 net increase in cash reported in the cash flow statement agrees with this change.

BEFORE YOU GO ON . . .

▶Review It

1. What is the format of the operating activities section of the cash flow statement using the direct method?
2. Where is amortization expense shown on a cash flow statement using the direct method?
3. Where are significant noncash investing and financing activities shown on a cash flow statement? Give some examples.

▶Do It

Information for Reynolds Ltd. follows. Use the direct method to prepare a cash flow statement.

REYNOLDS LTD.
Balance Sheet
December 31

Assets	2006	2005	Change Increase/Decrease
Cash	$ 54,000	$ 37,000	$ 17,000 Increase
Accounts receivable	68,000	26,000	42,000 Increase
Inventories	54,000	10,000	44,000 Increase
Prepaid expenses	4,000	6,000	2,000 Decrease
Land	45,000	70,000	25,000 Decrease
Buildings	200,000	200,000	0
Accumulated amortization—buildings	(21,000)	(11,000)	10,000 Increase
Equipment	193,000	68,000	125,000 Increase
Accumulated amortization—equipment	(28,000)	(10,000)	18,000 Increase
Totals	$569,000	$396,000	
Liabilities andShareholders' Equity			
Accounts payable	$ 23,000	$ 50,000	$ 27,000 Decrease
Accrued expenses payable	10,000	0	10,000 Increase
Bonds payable	110,000	150,000	40,000 Decrease
Common shares	220,000	60,000	160,000 Increase
Retained earnings	206,000	136,000	70,000 Increase
Totals	$569,000	$396,000	

REYNOLDS LTD.
Statement of Earnings
Year Ended December 31, 2006

Sales revenue		$890,000
Cost of goods sold	$465,000	
Operating expenses	221,000	
Loss on sale of equipment	2,000	688,000
Earnings from operations		202,000
Interest expense		12,000
Earnings before income tax		190,000
Income tax expense		65,000
Net earnings		$125,000

Additional information:

1. Operating expenses include an amortization expense of $33,000.
2. Equipment with a cost of $166,000 was bought for cash. Equipment with a cost of $41,000 and a net book value of $36,000 was sold for $34,000 cash.
3. Bonds of $40,000 were redeemed at their face value for cash.
4. Accounts payable pertain to merchandise suppliers.

Action Plan

- Determine the net cash provided (used) by operating activities. Operating activities generally relate to revenues and expenses shown on the statement of earnings, which are affected by changes in noncash current assets and current liabilities shown on the balance sheet.
- Determine the net cash provided (used) by investing activities. Investing activities generally relate to changes in noncurrent assets.
- Determine the net cash provided (used) by financing activities. Financing activities generally relate to changes in noncurrent liabilities and shareholders' equity accounts.
- Determine the net increase (decrease) in cash. Reconcile to the end-of-period cash balance reported on the balance sheet.

REYNOLDS LTD.
Cash Flow Statement—Direct Method
Year Ended December 31, 2006

Operating activities		
Cash receipts from customers		$ 848,000 [a]
Cash payments		
To suppliers	$(536,000) [b]	
For operating expenses	(176,000) [c]	
For interest	(12,000)	
For income tax	(65,000)	(789,000)
Net cash provided by operating activities		59,000
Investing activities		
Sale of land	$ 25,000	
Sale of equipment	34,000	
Purchase of equipment	(166,000)	
Net cash used by investing activities		(107,000)
Financing activities		
Redemption of bonds	$ (40,000)	
Issue of common shares	160,000	
Payment of dividends	(55,000) [d]	
Net cash provided by financing activities		65,000
Net increase in cash		17,000
Cash, January 1		37,000
Cash, December 31		$ 54,000

Calculations:
[a] Cash receipts from customers: $890,000 − $42,000 = $848,000
[b] Payments to suppliers: $465,000 + $44,000 + $27,000 = $536,000
[c] Payments for operating expenses: $221,000 − $33,000 − $2,000 − $10,000 = $176,000
[d] Payment of dividends: $136,000 + $125,000 − $206,000 = $55,000

the navigator

Note: This concludes Section 2 on the preparation of the cash flow statement using the direct method. You should now continue with the next—and concluding—section of the chapter, "Using Cash Flows to Evaluate a Company."

Using Cash Flows to Evaluate a Company

study objective 3

Use the cash flow statement to evaluate a company's liquidity and solvency.

Previous chapters have presented ratios that are used to analyze a company's liquidity and solvency. Most of those ratios used accrual-based numbers from the statement of earnings and balance sheet. Analysts often have doubts about accrual-based numbers because they feel that the adjustment process allows management too much discretion. These analysts like to supplement accrual-based analysis with measures that use information from the cash flow statement. In this section, we will introduce liquidity and solvency ratios that are *cash-based* rather than accrual-based. That is, instead of using numbers from the statement of earnings, we will use numbers from the cash flow statement.

We will use the following selected information (in U.S. thousands) for Intrawest Corporation in our analysis:

	2004	2003
Cash provided (used) by operating activities	$ 422,865	$ (20,879)
Current liabilities	406,371	645,886
Total liabilities	1,468,441	1,804,583

Liquidity

Liquidity is the ability of a company to meet its immediate obligations. In Chapter 2, you learned that one measure of liquidity is the current ratio (current assets divided by current liabilities). One disadvantage of the current ratio is that it uses year-end balances of current asset and current liability accounts. These year-end balances may not be representative of the company's position during most of the year. Another disadvantage is that current assets and current liabilities include accrual-based numbers.

A ratio that partially corrects this problem is the **cash current debt coverage** ratio. It is calculated by dividing cash provided by operating activities by average current liabilities. We say "partially corrects this problem" because even though the numerator uses cash-based numbers, the denominator, current liabilities, does not.

The cash current debt coverage ratio for Intrawest is shown in Illustration 13-18, along with comparative information given for Vail Resorts, Inc. Intrawest is North America's #1 ski resort, Vail #2. We have also provided each company's current ratio. Unfortunately, although there are industry averages for the more commonly used accrual-based measures, no averages are readily available for cash-based measures.

Illustration 13-18 ◄

Cash current debt coverage

$$\text{CASH CURRENT DEBT COVERAGE} = \frac{\text{CASH PROVIDED (USED) BY OPERATING ACTIVITIES}}{\text{AVERAGE CURRENT LIABILITIES}}$$

(in U.S. thousands)	Cash Current Debt Coverage	Current Ratio
Intrawest	$\dfrac{\$422,865}{(\$406,371 + \$645,886) \div 2} = 0.8$ times	1.9:1
Vail Resorts	0.9 times	0.8:1

Intrawest's cash provided by operating activities is less than its average current liabilities. Intrawest's cash current debt coverage ratio of 0.8 times means that only $0.80 of cash flow from operating activities has been generated to cover each dollar of current liabilities. The higher the cash current debt coverage ratio is, the better a company's liquidity is.

Intrawest's current ratio is much stronger than its cash current debt coverage ratio. However, with the amount of the difference between the two measures, it is likely that Intrawest's current assets include a large amount of accruals (e.g., from revenue billed but not yet collected, from merchandise purchased on account, prepayments, etc.). This is not a problem, however, as long as the receivables are collectable and the inventory is saleable.

Intrawest's cash current debt coverage ratio is slightly lower than that of Vail Resorts, even though its current ratio is much higher. As we have learned in previous chapters, additional ratios such as receivables turnover and inventory turnover must be calculated in order to properly assess a company's liquidity.

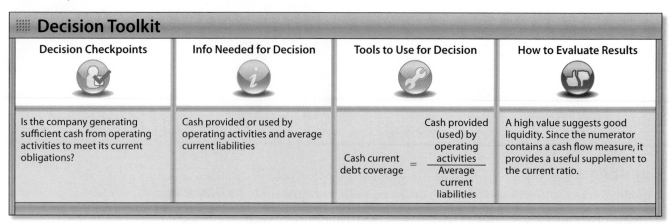

Decision Toolkit

Decision Checkpoints	Info Needed for Decision	Tools to Use for Decision	How to Evaluate Results
Is the company generating sufficient cash from operating activities to meet its current obligations?	Cash provided or used by operating activities and average current liabilities	$$\text{Cash current debt coverage} = \frac{\text{Cash provided (used) by operating activities}}{\text{Average current liabilities}}$$	A high value suggests good liquidity. Since the numerator contains a cash flow measure, it provides a useful supplement to the current ratio.

Solvency

Solvency is the ability of a company to survive over the long term. In Chapter 2, you learned about one cash-based measure of solvency, free cash flow. **Free cash flow** describes the cash remaining from operating activities after adjusting for capital expenditures and dividends. As indicated in our feature story, Intrawest generated U.S. $303.1 million of free cash flow in 2004. This compares favourably to a negative free cash flow of U.S. $68.8 million in 2003 and is a benefit of Intrawest's partnership venture in Leisura Developments.

Another cash-based measure of solvency is the **cash total debt coverage** ratio. It is similar to the cash current debt coverage ratio except that it uses total liabilities instead of current liabilities. The cash total debt coverage ratio is calculated by dividing cash provided by operating activities by average total liabilities. This ratio indicates a company's ability to repay its liabilities from cash generated from operating activities without having to liquidate productive assets such as property, plant, and equipment. The higher the cash total debt coverage ratio is, the more solvent a company is.

The cash total debt coverage ratios for Intrawest and Vail Resorts are given in Illustration 13-19. For comparative purposes, the accrual-based counterpart, the debt to total assets ratio, is also provided for each company. You will recall from Chapter 2 that the debt to total assets ratio is calculated by dividing total liabilities by total assets.

Illustration 13-19 ▶

Cash total debt coverage

CASH TOTAL DEBT COVERAGE =	CASH PROVIDED (USED) BY OPERATING ACTIVITIES / AVERAGE TOTAL LIABILITIES	
(in U.S. thousands)	Cash Total Debt Coverage	Debt to Total Assets
Intrawest	$$\frac{\$422,865}{(\$1,468,441 + \$1,804,583) \div 2} = 0.3 \text{ times}$$	65.1%
Vail Resorts	0.2 times	68%

Both companies have similar solvency positions, although Intrawest's solvency is slightly better than that of Vail Resorts. Its cash total debt coverage ratio of 0.3 times means that it is generating $0.30 to cover each dollar of total liabilities. This ratio is significantly less than its cash current debt coverage ratio of 0.8 times, so we know that Intrawest has a considerable amount of long-term liabilities.

Intrawest's cash total debt coverage ratio is better than Vail Resorts', as is its debt to total assets ratio. Recall that the *higher* the cash total debt coverage ratio, the better the result, while the *lower* the debt to total assets ratio, the better the result. Since both ratios are moving in the same direction (i.e., both are better), we can conclude that there is no significant difference between the cash and accrual measures for the two companies.

It is difficult to reach a conclusion about either company's solvency position without also knowing more about each company's ability to handle its debt (e.g., its times interest earned ratio). However, although both companies appear to be low on operating cash flow, it is reasonable to expect both of them to have a high debt to total assets ratio because of the amount of total liabilities that companies like these usually have.

Decision Toolkit

Decision Checkpoints	Info Needed for Decision	Tools to Use for Decision	How to Evaluate Results
Is the company generating sufficient cash from operating activities to meet its total obligations?	Cash provided or used by operating activities and average total liabilities	$$\text{Cash total debt coverage} = \frac{\text{Cash provided (used) by operating activities}}{\text{Average total liabilities}}$$	A high value suggests the company is solvent; that is, it will meet its obligations in the long term.

ACCOUNTING MATTERS!   Investor Perspective

Another commonly used cash-based measure is EBITDA. It is an abbreviation for "earnings before interest, tax, depreciation, and amortization." EBITDA is frequently cited in annual reports and in the financial press as a cash-based measure of earnings. Both Intrawest and Vail Resorts reported record amounts of EBITDA in fiscal 2004. For Vail Resorts, its 2004 EBITDA was the best reported in its 42-year history. Banks and other creditors prefer EBITDA over net earnings because it eliminates the effects of many accounting and financing decisions.

BEFORE YOU GO ON . . .

▶ Review It

1. Why might an analyst want to supplement accrual-based ratios with cash-based ratios?
2. What are some cash-based ratios to measure liquidity and solvency?
3. What accrual-based ratio does the cash current debt coverage ratio compare to?
4. What accrual-based ratio does the cash total debt coverage ratio compare to?

the navigator

▦ Using the Decision Toolkit

The American Skiing Company is North America's #3 ski resort operator, after Intrawest and Vail Resorts. Selected financial statement data for the company follow (in U.S. thousands):

	2004	2003
Cash used by operating activities	$ (1,092)	$ (7,999)
Current assets	31,544	31,211
Total assets	475,305	430,800
Current liabilities	202,873	176,886
Total liabilities	413,901	671,762

Instructions

Calculate the following cash- and accrual-based ratios for the American Skiing Company for 2004, and compare them to those provided in the chapter for Intrawest:

(a) Cash current debt coverage and current ratio
(b) Cash total debt coverage and debt to total assets.

Solution

(a) Cash current debt coverage and current ratio

(in U.S. thousands)	Cash Current Debt Coverage	Current Ratio
American Skiing	$\dfrac{\$(1,092)}{(\$202,873 + \$176,886) \div 2} = (0.1)$ times	$\dfrac{\$31,544}{\$202,873} = 0.2{:}1$
Intrawest	0.8 times	1.9:1

The American Skiing Company's liquidity, as shown by the cash current debt coverage and current ratio, is weak. It has only $0.20 of current assets to cover each $1 of current liabilities. Its cash flow from operating activities is negative, which means that the company basically has no cash flow to cover its current liabilities. Intrawest's liquidity is significantly stronger by comparison.

(b) Cash total debt coverage and debt to total assets.

(in U.S. thousands)	Cash Total Debt Coverage	Debt to Total Assets
American Skiing	$\dfrac{\$(1,092)}{(\$413,901 + \$671,762) \div 2} = (0.0)$ times	$\dfrac{\$413,901}{\$475,305} = 87.1\%$
Intrawest	0.3 times	65.1%

The American Skiing Company's solvency, as shown by the cash total debt coverage and debt to total assets ratios, is weak, similar to its liquidity. It has $0.87 of debt for each $1 of assets. Its cash flow from operating activities is negligible and negative so that it essentially has no cash flow to cover any of its liabilities.

The American Skiing Company appears to have an "avalanche of debt." A few winters with very little snow resulted in repeated and heavy losses. American Skiing now plans to limit expansion except in the golf and convention businesses, and will focus on improving its results at existing resorts.

Obviously, Intrawest's solvency is significantly stronger by comparison. As we learned in the feature story, Intrawest has worked very hard to diversify its resorts into year-round destination.

the navigator

Summary of Study Objectives

1. ***Describe the purpose and format of the cash flow statement.*** The cash flow statement provides information about the cash receipts and cash payments resulting from the operating, investing, and financing activities of a company during a specific period. In general, operating activities include the cash effects of transactions that are used in the determination of net earnings. Investing activities involve cash flows resulting from changes in investments and long-term asset items. Financing activities involve cash flows resulting from changes in short-term notes payable, long-term liabilities, and shareholders' equity items.

2a. ***Prepare a cash flow statement using the indirect method.*** The preparation of a cash flow statement involves four steps: (1) Determine the net cash provided (used) by operating activities by converting net earnings from an accrual basis to a cash basis. (2) Analyze changes in short-term investment and noncurrent asset accounts and record them either as investing activities or as significant noncash transactions. (3) Analyze changes in short-term liability, noncurrent liability, and equity accounts and record them either as financing activities or as significant noncash transactions. (4) Compare the net change in cash with the change in cash reported on the balance sheet to make sure the amounts agree.

2b. ***Prepare a cash flow statement using the direct method.*** The preparation of the cash flow statement involves four steps: (1) Determine the net cash provided (used) by operating activities by converting net earnings from an accrual basis to a cash basis. (2) Analyze changes in short-term investment and noncurrent asset accounts and record them either as investing activities or as significant noncash transactions. (3) Analyze changes in short-term liability, noncurrent liability, and equity accounts and record them either as financing activities or as significant noncash transactions. (4) Compare the net change in cash with the change in cash reported on the balance sheet to make sure the amounts agree.

3. ***Use the cash flow statement to evaluate a company's liquidity and solvency.*** Liquidity can be measured by the cash-based cash current debt coverage ratio (cash provided [used] by operating activities divided by average current liabilities) and compared to the accrual-based current ratio (current assets divided by current liabilities). Solvency can be measured by the cash-based cash total debt coverage ratio (cash provided [used] by operating activities divided by average total liabilities) and compared to the accrual-based debt to total assets ratio (total liabilities divided by total assets).

Decision Toolkit—A Summary

Decision Checkpoints	Info Needed for Decision	Tools to Use for Decision	How to Evaluate Results
Is the company generating sufficient cash from operating activities to meet its current obligations?	Cash provided or used by operating activities and average current liabilities	$\text{Cash current debt coverage} = \dfrac{\text{Cash provided (used) by operating activities}}{\text{Average current liabilities}}$	A high value suggests good liquidity. Since the numerator contains a cash flow measure, it provides a useful supplement to the current ratio.
Is the company generating sufficient cash from operating activities to meet its total obligations?	Cash provided or used by operating activities and average total liabilities	$\text{Cash total debt coverage} = \dfrac{\text{Cash provided (used) by operating activities}}{\text{Average total liabilities}}$	A high value suggests the company is solvent; that is, it will meet its obligations in the long term.

Analysis Tools
(Decision Toolkit Summaries)

Glossary

Study Tools (Glossary)

Cash current debt coverage   A cash-based ratio used to evaluate liquidity. It is calculated by dividing cash provided (used) by operating activities by average current liabilities. (p. 639)

Cash total debt coverage   A cash-based ratio used to evaluate solvency. It is calculated by dividing cash provided (used) by operating activities by average total liabilities. (p. 640)

Direct method   A method of determining net cash provided by operating activities by adjusting each item in the statement of earnings from the accrual basis to the cash basis. (p. 613)

Financing activities   Cash flow activities from short-term notes payable and noncurrent liability and equity items. These include (a) obtaining cash by issuing debt and repaying the amounts borrowed and (b) obtaining cash from shareholders and providing them with a return on their investment. (p. 609)

Indirect method   A method of determining net cash provided by operating activities in which net earnings are adjusted for items that do not affect cash. (p. 613)

Investing activities   Cash flow activities from short-term investments and noncurrent assets. These include (a) purchasing and disposing of investments and long-lived assets and (b) lending money and collecting on those loans. (p. 609)

Operating activities   Cash flow activities from transactions which create revenues and expenses and therefore are included in the determination of net earnings. (p.609)

Demonstration Problem

Study Tools
(Demonstration Problems)

The statement of earnings for Kosinski Manufacturing Inc. contains the following condensed information:

KOSINSKI MANUFACTURING INC.
Statement of Earnings
Year Ended December 31, 2006

Sales		$6,583,000
Cost of goods sold		3,427,000
Gross profit		3,156,000
Operating expenses	$1,469,000	
Amortization expense	880,000	2,373,000
Loss on sale of machinery	24,000	
Earnings before income taxes		783,000
Income tax expense		353,000
Net earnings		$ 430,000

The $24,000 loss resulted from the sale of old machinery for $270,000 cash. New machinery was purchased during the year at a cost of $750,000. Dividends paid in 2006 totalled $200,000.

The following current asset and current liability balances are reported on Kosinski's comparative balance sheet at December 31:

	2006	2005	Increase (Decrease)
Cash	$672,000	$130,000	$542,000
Accounts receivable	775,000	610,000	165,000
Inventories	834,000	867,000	(33,000)
Accounts payable	521,000	501,000	20,000

Instructions

(a) Prepare the cash flow statement using the indirect method.
(b) Prepare the cash flow statement using the direct method.

Solution to Demonstration Problem

(a)

KOSINSKI MANUFACTURING INC.
Cash Flow Statement—Indirect Method
Year Ended December 31, 2006

Operating activities		
Net earnings		$ 430,000
Adjustments to reconcile net earnings to net cash provided by operating activities		
Amortization expense	$ 880,000	
Loss on sale of machinery	24,000	
Increase in accounts receivable	(165,000)	
Decrease in inventories	33,000	
Increase in accounts payable	20,000	792,000
Net cash provided by operating activities		1,222,000
Investing activities		
Sale of machinery	$ 270,000	
Purchase of machinery	(750,000)	
Net cash used by investing activities		(480,000)
Financing activities		
Payment of cash dividends	$(200,000)	
Net cash used by financing activities		(200,000)
Net increase in cash		542,000
Cash, January 1		130,000
Cash, December 31		$ 672,000

(b)

KOSINSKI MANUFACTURING INC.
Cash Flow Statement—Direct Method
Year Ended December 31, 2006

Operating activities		
Cash receipts from customers		$ 6,418,000 [a]
Cash payments to suppliers		(3,374,000) [b]
Cash payments for operating expenses		(1,469,000)
Cash payment for income taxes		(353,000)
Net cash provided by operating activities		1,222,000
Investing activities		
Sale of machinery	$ 270,000	
Purchase of machinery	(750,000)	
Net cash used by investing activities		(480,000)
Financing activities		
Payment of cash dividends	$(200,000)	
Net cash used by financing activities		(200,000)
Net increase in cash		542,000
Cash, January 1		130,000
Cash, December 31		$ 672,000

Direct Method Calculations

[a] Cash receipts from customers:	
Sales per the statement of earnings	$6,583,000
Deduct: Increase in accounts receivable	165,000
Cash collections from customers	$6,418,000
[b] Cash payments to suppliers:	
Cost of goods sold per the statement of earnings	$3,427,000
Deduct: Decrease in inventories	33,000
Increase in accounts payable	20,000
Cash payments to suppliers	$3,374,000

Action Plan

- Apply the same data to the cash flow statement under both the indirect and direct methods.
- Note the similarities of the two methods: Both methods report the same information in the investing and financing sections.
- Note the difference between the two methods: The cash flows from operating activities sections report different information (however, the *amount* of net cash provided by operating activities is the same for both methods).

the navigator

Self-Study Questions

(SO 1) 1. A cash flow statement does *not* help readers understand which of the following aspects of a company's financial position?
   (a) The ability to pay dividends and meet obligations
   (b) The ability to generate future cash flows
   (c) Reasons for the difference between net earnings and cash provided or used by operating activities
   (d) Reasons for the difference between net earnings and comprehensive income

(SO 1) 2. Which is an example of a cash flow from an operating activity?
   (a) A payment of cash to lenders for interest
   (b) A receipt of cash from the sale of common shares
   (c) A payment of cash dividends to shareholders
   (d) A receipt of cash from the issue of a short-term note payable

(SO 1) 3. Which is an example of a cash flow from an investing activity?
   (a) A receipt of cash from the issue of bonds payable
   (b) A payment of cash to repurchase common shares
   (c) A receipt of cash from the sale of equipment
   (d) A payment of cash to suppliers of inventory

(SO 2) 4. Which of the following is incorrect about the cash flow statement?
   (a) The direct method may be used to report cash provided by operating activities.
   (b) The indirect method may be used to report cash provided by operating activities.
   (c) The statement shows the cash provided (used) by operating, investing, and financing activities.
   (d) Significant noncash investing and financing activities are reported in the body of the statement.

(SO 2a) 5. Net earnings are $132,000. During the year, accounts payable increased by $10,000, inventory decreased by $6,000, and accounts receivable increased by $12,000. Under the indirect method, what is net cash provided by operating activities?
   (a) $102,000   (c) $124,000
   (b) $112,000   (d) $136,000

6. In determining cash provided by operating activities (SO 2) under the indirect method, noncash items that are added back to net earnings do not include:
   (a) amortization expense.
   (b) a decrease in inventory.
   (c) a gain on the sale of equipment.
   (d) a loss on the sale of equipment.

7. The beginning balance in Accounts Receivable is (SO 2) $44,000. The ending balance is $42,000. Sales during the period are $129,000. What are the cash receipts from customers?
   (a) $127,000   (c) $131,000
   (b) $129,000   (d) $141,000

8. Which of the following items is reported in the oper- (SO 2) ating activities section of a cash flow statement prepared by the direct method?
   (a) A loss on the sale of a building
   (b) An increase in accounts receivable
   (c) Amortization expense
   (d) Cash payments to suppliers

9. ⚒ The cash current debt coverage ratio is a cash- (SO 3) based counterpart to the accrual-based:
   (a) current ratio.
   (b) receivables turnover.
   (c) debt to total assets.
   (d) free cash flow

10. ⚒ Which of the following is not a measure of sol- (SO 3) vency?
   (a) Free cash flow
   (b) Cash current debt coverage
   (c) Cash total debt coverage
   (d) Debt to total assets

the navigator

Questions

(SO 1) 1. What is a cash flow statement and why is it useful?

(SO 1) 2. Distinguish among the three categories of activities reported in the cash flow statement.

(SO 1) 3. What are "cash equivalents?" How do cash equivalents affect the cash flow statement?

(SO 1) 4. Darren and Adriana were discussing where they should report significant noncash transactions in Rock Candy Corp.'s cash flow statement. Give two examples of noncash transactions and describe where they should be reported.

(SO 2) 5. Why is it necessary to use a comparative balance sheet, a statement of earnings, and certain transaction data in preparing a cash flow statement?

(SO 2) 6. Contrast the advantages and disadvantages of the direct and indirect methods of preparing the cash flow statement. Are both methods acceptable? Which method is preferred by the CICA? Which method is more popular? Why?

(SO 2) 7. In 2004, The Brick Group, one of Canada's largest retailers of household furniture, reported $22.3 million of net earnings. Yet, during the same period of time, its cash provided by operating activities decreased by $11.6 million. Explain how this could occur.

(SO 2) 8. Goh Corporation changed its method of reporting operating activities from the indirect method to the direct method in order to make its cash flow statement more informative to its readers. Will this change increase, decrease, or not affect the net cash provided by operating activities?

(SO 2a) 9. Describe the indirect method for determining net cash provided or used by operating activities.

(SO 2a) 10. Identify four adjustments required under the indirect method to convert net earnings to net cash provided by operating activities.

(SO 2a) 11. Why and how is amortization expense reported in a cash flow statement prepared using the indirect method?

(SO 2a) 12. Explain how the sale of equipment at a gain is reported on a cash flow statement using the indirect method.

(SO 2b) 13. Describe the direct method for determining net cash provided or used by operating activities.

(SO 2b) 14. Give the formulas under the direct method for calculating (a) cash receipts from customers, and (b) cash payments to suppliers.

(SO 2b) 15. Under the direct method, why is amortization expense not reported in the operating activities section?

(SO 2b) 16. Explain how the sale of equipment at a gain is reported on a cash flow statement using the direct method.

(SO 3) 17. ⚒ Give examples of cash- and accrual-based ratios that measure (a) liquidity, and (b) solvency.

(SO 3) 18. ⚒ In 2004, Leon's Furniture Limited reported a current ratio of 1.9:1 and a cash current debt coverage ratio of 0.5 times. Explain why Leon's cash current debt coverage is likely so much lower than its current ratio.

(SO 3) 19. ⚒ In 2004, Rogers Communications Inc. reported a debt to total assets ratio of 78.3% and a cash total debt coverage ratio of 0.2 times. Its competitor, Shaw Communications Inc., reported a debt to total assets ratio of 67.0% and a cash total debt coverage ratio of 0.1 times in the same year. Which company is more solvent?

(SO 3) 20. ⚒ A company's cash total debt coverage ratio and free cash flow have been declining steadily over the last five years. What does this decline likely mean to creditors and investors?

Brief Exercises

BE13–1 For each of the following transactions, indicate whether it will result in an increase (+), decrease (−), or have no effect (NE) on cash flows:

Indicate impact of transaction on cash flow.
(SO 1)

(a) ___ Repayment of short-term notes payable

(b) ___ Sale of land for cash, at a gain

(c) ___ Reacquisition of common shares

(d) ___ Purchase of a trading security

(e) ___ Issue of preferred shares

(f) ___ Collection of accounts receivable

(g) ___ Payment of dividend

(h) ___ Purchase of equipment

(i) ___ Purchase of inventory

(j) ___ Recording of amortization expense

BE13–2 Classify each of the transactions listed in BE13-1 as an operating, investing, or financing activity.

Classify transactions by activity.
(SO 1)

Calculate cash received from sale
of equipment.
(SO 2)

BE13–3   The T accounts for equipment and accumulated amortization for Trevis Ltd. are shown here:

Equipment				Accumulated Amortization—Equipment			
Beg. Bal.	80,000	Disposals	22,000	Disposals	5,500	Beg. Bal.	44,500
Acquisitions	41,600					Amortization	12,000
End Bal.	99,600					End Bal.	51,000

In addition, Trevis' statement of earnings reported a $4,900 loss on the sale of equipment. What amount was reported on the cash flow statement as "cash provided by sale of equipment"?

Calculate dividends paid.
(SO 2)

BE13–4   Canadian Tire Corporation, Limited reported net earnings of $291.5 million for the year ended January 1, 2005. Its retained earnings were $1,318.0 million at the beginning of the year and $1,546.9 million at the end of the year. It also repurchased shares, which resulted in a $22.1-million reduction to retained earnings during the year. What amount of dividends was paid by Canadian Tire during the year ended January 1, 2005?

Indicate impact on operating
activities using indirect method.
(SO 2a)

BE13–5   Indicate whether each of the following transactions would be added to (+) or subtracted from (−) net earnings in calculating cash provided or used by operating activities using the indirect method:

(a) ___ Amortization expense

(e) ___ Decrease in income tax payable

(b) ___ Increase in accounts receivable

(f) ___ Gain on sale of equipment

(c) ___ Decrease in inventory

(g) ___ Loss on sale of trading security

(d) ___ Increase in accounts payable

Calculate cash from operating
activities using indirect method.
(SO 2a)

BE13–6   Crystal, Inc. reported net earnings of $2.5 million. Amortization expense for the year was $260,000, accounts receivable decreased by $350,000, prepaid expenses increased by $95,000, accounts payable decreased by $280,000, and the company incurred a $10,000 gain on the sale of equipment. Calculate cash provided or used by operating activities using the indirect method.

Calculate cash from operating
activities using indirect method.
(SO 2a)

BE13–7   The comparative balance sheet for Dupigne Corporation shows the following non-cash current asset and liability accounts at March 31:

	2007	2006
Accounts receivable	$60,000	$40,000
Merchandise inventory	64,000	70,000
Prepaid expenses	6,000	4,000
Accounts payable	35,000	40,000
Income tax payable	22,000	12,000

Dupigne's statement of earnings reported the following selected information for the year ended March 31, 2007: net earnings were $250,000 and amortization expense was $60,000. Calculate net cash provided or used by operating activities using the indirect method.

Calculate cash receipts from
customers using direct method.
(SO 2b)

BE13–8   Idol Corporation has accounts receivable of $14,000 at January 1, 2006, and of $24,000 at December 31, 2006. Sales revenues were $470,000 for the year. What amount of cash was received from customers in 2006?

Calculate cash payments to
suppliers using direct method.
(SO 2b)

BE13–9   Columbia Sportswear Company reported cost of goods sold of U.S. $578.7 million on its 2004 statement of earnings. It also reported an increase in inventory of U.S. $38.6 million and an increase in accounts payable of U.S. $15.9 million. What amount of cash was paid to suppliers in 2004, assuming accounts payable relate only to merchandise creditors?

Calculate cash payments for
operating expenses using direct
method.
(SO 2b)

BE13–10   Excel Corporation reports operating expenses of $100,000, including amortization expense of $15,000 for 2006. During the year, prepaid expenses decreased by $6,600 and accrued expenses payable increased by $2,400. Calculate the cash paid for operating expenses in 2006.

Calculate cash-based ratios.
(SO 3)

BE13–11   Jain Corporation reported cash provided by operating activities of $300,000, cash used by investing activities of $250,000, and cash provided by financing activities of $70,000. In addition, cash spent for capital expenditures during the period was $200,000. No dividends were paid. Average current liabilities were $150,000 and average total liabilities were $225,000. Calculate these values: (a) free cash flow, (b) cash current debt coverage, and (c) cash total debt coverage.

BE13–12 Fairmont Hotels & Resorts Inc. reported the following selected liquidity ratios:

	2004	2003
Current ratio	1.3:1	0.5:1
Cash current debt coverage	0.3 times	0.5 times

Evaluate liquidity.
(SO 3)

How is it possible that Fairmont's current ratio improved in 2004 but its cash current debt coverage ratio deteriorated? What does this mean?

BE13–13 Fairmont Hotels & Resorts Inc. reported the following selected solvency ratios:

	2004	2003
Debt to total assets	31.3%	38.2%
Cash total debt coverage	0.1 times	0.1 times

Evaluate solvency.
(SO 3)

Has Fairmont's solvency improved or deteriorated? Explain.

Exercises

E13–1 He Corporation had the following transactions:

Transaction	Net Earnings	Cash Provided (Used) by Operating Activities
1. Sold merchandise inventory for cash at a higher price than cost.	+	+
2. Sold merchandise inventory on account at a price less than cost.		
3. Purchased merchandise inventory on account.		
4. Paid a cash dividend.		
5. Paid salaries.		
6. Accrued salaries payable.		
7. Accrued interest receivable.		
8. Recorded amortization expense.		
9. Paid an amount owing on account.		
10. Collected an amount owing from a customer.		

Indicate impact of transactions on net earnings and operating activities.
(SO 1)

Instructions

Complete the above table indicating whether each transaction will increase (+), decrease (−) or have no effect (NE) on net earnings and cash provided or used by operating activities. The first one has been done for you as an example.

E13–2 Eng Corporation had the following transactions:

Transaction	(a) Classification	(b) Cash Inflow or Outflow
1. Issued common shares for $50,000.	F	+$50,000
2. Purchased a machine for $30,000. Made a $5,000 down payment and issued a long-term note for the remainder.		
3. Collected $16,000 of accounts receivable.		
4. Paid a $25,000 cash dividend.		
5. Sold an available-for-sale security with a cost of $15,000 for $10,000.		
6. Repurchased bonds for $175,000. The bonds had a carrying value of $200,000 at the time of the repurchase.		
7. Paid $18,000 on account.		
8. Purchased a trading security for $100,000.		
9. Purchased merchandise inventory for $28,000 on account.		
10. Collected $1,000 in advance from customers.		

Classify transactions by activity.
(SO 1)

Instructions

Complete the above table indicating whether each transaction (a) should be classified as an operating activity (O), investing activity (I), financing activity (F), or noncash transaction (NC); and (b) represents a cash inflow (+), cash outflow (−), or has no effect (NE) on cash. If the transaction results in a cash inflow or outflow, state the amount. The first one has been done for you as an example.

Prepare operating activities
section using indirect method.
(SO 2a)

E13–3   Pesci Ltd. reported net earnings of $195,000 for the year ended July 31, 2007. Pesci also reported amortization expense of $45,000 and a gain of $5,000 on the sale of equipment on its statement of earnings. The comparative balance sheet shows a decrease in accounts receivable of $15,000, an increase in accounts payable of $10,000, a decrease in prepaid expenses of $4,000, and a decrease in accrued liabilities of $3,500 for the year.

Instructions

Prepare the operating activities section of the cash flow statement, using the indirect method.

Prepare operating activities
section using indirect method.
(SO 2a)

E13–4   The current assets and liabilities sections of Barth Inc.'s comparative balance sheet at December 31 are presented here:

BARTH INC.
Balance Sheet (partial)
December 31, 2006

	2006	2005
Current assets		
Cash	$105,000	$ 99,000
Accounts receivable	120,000	89,000
Inventory	161,000	186,000
Prepaid expenses	27,000	32,000
Total current assets	$413,000	$406,000
Current liabilities		
Accounts payable	$ 85,000	$ 92,000
Accrued expenses payable	15,000	5,000
Total current liabilities	$100,000	$ 97,000

Barth's net earnings for 2006 were $153,000. Amortization expense was $19,000.

Instructions

Prepare the operating activities section of Barth Inc.'s cash flow statement, using the indirect method.

Classify transactions by activity
using indirect method.
(SO 2a)

E13–5   The following is a list of transactions that occurred during the year.

Transaction	Operating Activities	Investing Activities	Financing Activities	Noncash Investing and Financing Activities
1. Purchased inventory for cash.	—	NE	NE	NE
2. Sold inventory on account.				
3. Sold equipment for cash at a loss.				
4. Purchased equipment by issuing a short-term note payable.				
5. Paid a cash dividend.				
6. Sold a trading security at a gain.				
7. Collected an account from a customer.				
8. Issued bonds payable.				
9. Reacquired common shares at a price less than the average cost.				
10. Purchased land by issuing common shares.				

Instructions

For each transaction, indicate (a) in which category each transaction would appear in a cash flow statement prepared using the indirect method, and (b) whether the transaction should be added (+), deducted (−), or has no effect (NE) in the category you have chosen. The first transaction has been done for you as an example.

Calculate cash flows using
indirect method.
(SO 2a)

E13–6   The following selected accounts are from Dupré Corp.'s general ledger:

Equipment

Date		Debit	Credit	Balance
Jan. 1	Balance			160,000
July 31	Purchase of equipment	70,000		230,000
Sept. 2	Purchase of equipment	53,000		283,000
Nov. 10	Cost of equipment sold		39,000	244,000

Accumulated Amortization—Equipment

Date		Debit	Credit	Balance
Jan. 1	Balance			71,000
Nov. 10	Accumulated amortization on equipment sold	30,000		41,000
Dec. 31	Amortization for year		28,000	69,000

Notes Payable

Date		Debit	Credit	Balance
Jan. 1	Balance			0
Sept. 2	Issue of note to purchase equipment		53,000	53,000

Retained Earnings

Date		Debit	Credit	Balance
Jan. 1	Balance			105,000
Aug. 23	Dividends (cash)	14,000		91,000
Dec. 31	Net earnings		67,000	158,000

Instructions

From the postings in the above accounts, indicate how the information would be reported on a cash flow statement using the indirect method. The loss on the sale of equipment was $3,000.

E13–7 The following is a list of transactions that must be converted from the accrual basis to the cash basis in order to calculate cash provided or used by operating activities using the direct method:

Indicate impact of transactions on operating activities using direct method.
(SO 2b)

Transaction	(a) Related Statement of Earnings Account	(b) Add to (+) or Deduct from (−) Statement of Earnings Account	(c) Related Cash Receipt or Payment
1. Increase in accounts receivable	Sales revenue	−	Cash receipts from customers
2. Increase in accounts payable (related to merchandise purchases)			
3. Decrease in interest payable			
4. Increase in prepaid insurance			
5. Increase in inventory			
6. Increase in income tax payable			
7. Decrease in accounts receivable			
8. Decrease in inventory			

Instructions

For each transaction, (a) identify the related statement of earnings account, (b) indicate if the transaction should be added to or deducted from the statement of earnings account you identified in (a) in order to convert the accrual-based number to a cash-based number, and (c) state the title of the resulting cash receipt or payment on the cash flow statement. The first transaction has been done for you as an example.

E13–8 The following selected information is available:

Calculate cash flows using direct method.
(SO 2b)

Sales:	Revenue from sales	$190,000
	Accounts receivable, January 1	12,000
	Accounts receivable, December 31	7,000
Rent:	Rent expense	31,000
	Prepaid rent, January 1	5,900
	Prepaid rent, December 31	9,000
Salaries:	Salaries expense	54,000
	Salaries payable, January 1	10,000
	Salaries payable, December 31	8,000

Instructions

Using the direct method, calculate (a) cash receipts from customers, (b) cash paid for rent, and (c) cash paid for salaries.

Calculate cash payments using direct method.
(SO 2b)

E13–9   Clearly Canadian Beverage Corporation reports the following information (in U.S. thousands) for the year 2004: The statement of earnings shows cost of goods sold of $8,048, and operating expenses (exclusive of amortization) of $5,587. The comparative balance sheet for the year shows that inventory decreased by $106, prepaid expenses increased by $15, and trade accounts payable (merchandise suppliers) increased by $513.

Instructions

Using the direct method, calculate (a) cash payments to suppliers and (b) cash payments for operating expenses.

Prepare operating activities section using direct method.
(SO 2b)

E13–10   McGillis Ltd. completed its first year of operations on December 31, 2006. Its statement of earnings showed revenues of $182,000, operating expenses of $88,000, and income tax expense of $21,000. Accounts receivable, accounts payable, and income tax payable at year end were $42,000, $33,000, and $1,500, respectively. Assume that accounts payable related to operating expenses.

Instructions

Prepare the operating activities section of the cash flow statement, using the direct method.

Prepare operating activities section using direct method.
(SO 2b)

E13–11   The accounting records of Flypaper Airlines Inc. reveal the following for the year ended March 31, 2007:

Payment of interest	$ 10,000	Payment of operating expenses	$ 28,000
Cash sales	48,000	Collection of accounts receivable	192,000
Receipt of dividend revenue	18,000	Payment of salaries	53,000
Payment of income taxes	12,000	Amortization expense	16,000
Net earnings	38,000	Proceeds from sale of aircraft	812,000
Payment of accounts payable for		Purchase of equipment for cash	22,000
merchandise	110,000	Loss on sale of aircraft	3,000
Payment for land	74,000	Payment of dividends	14,000

Instructions

Prepare the operating activities section of the cash flow statement, using the direct method. (*Note*: Not all of the above items will be used.)

Prepare cash flow statement using indirect and direct methods.
(SO 2a, 2b)

E13–12   The comparative balance sheet for Puffy Ltd. is presented below:

PUFFY LTD.
Balance Sheet
December 31

Assets	2006	2005
Cash	$ 63,000	$ 22,000
Accounts receivable	85,000	76,000
Inventories	180,000	189,000
Land	75,000	100,000
Equipment	260,000	200,000
Accumulated amortization	(66,000)	(32,000)
Total assets	$597,000	$555,000
Liabilities and Shareholders' Equity		
Accounts payable	$ 39,000	$ 47,000
Bonds payable	150,000	200,000
Common shares	209,000	174,000
Retained earnings	199,000	134,000
Total liabilities and shareholders' equity	$597,000	$555,000

Additional information:

1. Net earnings were $105,000.
2. Sales were $978,000.
3. Cost of goods sold was $751,000.
4. Accounts payable relate only to purchases of merchandise.
5. Operating expenses were $43,000, exclusive of amortization expense.
6. Income tax expense was $50,000.
7. Land was sold at a gain of $5,000.
8. No equipment was sold during 2006.
9. Bonds payable amounting to $50,000 were redeemed for $50,000.
10. Common shares were issued for $35,000.

Instructions

Prepare a cash flow statement for the year ended December 31, 2006, using (1) the indirect method, and (2) the direct method.

E13–13   Condensed cash flow statements are as follows for two companies operating in the same industry:

Compare cash flows for two companies.
(SO 3)

	Company A	Company B
Cash provided (used) by operating activities	$100,000	$(90,000)
Cash provided (used) by investing activities	(10,000)	(10,000)
Cash provided (used) by financing activities	(30,000)	160,000
Increase in cash	60,000	60,000
Cash, beginning of period	15,000	15,000
Cash, end of period	$ 75,000	$ 75,000

Instructions

Which company is in better financial shape? Explain why.

E13–14   Information for two companies in the same industry, Ria Corporation and Les Corporation, is presented here:

Calculate and assess cash-based ratios.
(SO 3)

	Ria Corporation	Les Corporation
Cash provided by operating activities	$200,000	$200,000
Average current liabilities	50,000	100,000
Average total liabilities	200,000	250,000
Capital expenditures	20,000	35,000
Dividends paid	14,000	18,000

Instructions

(a) Calculate the cash current debt coverage ratio, cash total debt ratio, and free cash flow for each company.
(b) Compare the liquidity and solvency of the two companies.

E13–15   Presented here are selected ratios for PepsiCo, Inc. and The Coca-Cola Company:

Evaluate liquidity and solvency.
(SO 3)

	PepsiCo	Coca-Cola
Current ratio	1.3:1	1.1:1
Cash current debt coverage	0.8 times	0.6 times
Debt to total assets	51.5%	49.1%
Cash total debt coverage	0.4 times	0.4 times
Free cash flow (in U.S. millions)	$2,338	$2,517

Instructions

Evaluate the liquidity and solvency of the two companies.

Problems: Set A

Classify transactions by activity; indicate impact on cash flow and net earnings.
(SO 1)

P13–1A   The following is a list of transactions that took place during the year:

Transaction	(a) Classification	(b) Cash Inflow or Outflow	(c) Net Earnings
1. Paid wages to employees.	O	–	–
2. Sold equipment for cash, at a gain.			
3. Sold land for cash, at a loss.			
4. Purchased a building by paying 10% in cash and signing a mortgage payable for the balance.			
5. Made principal repayments on the mortgage.			
6. Issued common shares for cash.			
7. Purchased shares of another company to be held as a long-term equity investment.			
8. Paid dividends to common shareholders.			
9. Purchased inventory on account. The company uses a perpetual inventory system.			
10. Sold inventory on account, at a price greater than cost.			

Instructions

Complete the above table for each of the following requirements. The first one has been done for you as an example.

(a) Classify each transaction as an operating activity (O), investing activity (I), financing activity (F), or noncash transaction (NC).
(b) Specify if the transaction will result in a cash inflow (+), cash outflow (−), or have no effect on cash (NE).
(c) Indicate if the transaction will increase (+), decrease (−), or have no effect (NE) on net earnings.

Calculate and classify cash flows for property, plant, and equipment.
(SO 2)

P13–2A   The following selected account balances relate to the property, plant, and equipment accounts of Trudeau Inc.:

	2006	2005
Accumulated amortization—buildings	$337,500	$300,000
Accumulated amortization—equipment	144,000	96,000
Amortization expense	101,500	85,500
Land	100,000	60,000
Buildings	750,000	750,000
Equipment	300,000	240,000
Gain on sale of equipment	1,000	0

Additional information:

1. Trudeau purchased $40,000 of land for cash.
2. The company purchased $80,000 of equipment for cash.

Instructions

(a) Calculate any cash inflows or outflows related to the property, plant, and equipment accounts in 2006.
(b) Indicate where each of the cash inflows or outflows identified in (a) would be reported on the cash flow statement.

Calculate and classify cash flows for shareholders' equity.
(SO 2)

P13–3A   The following selected account balances relate to the shareholder's equity accounts of Valerio Corp.:

	2006	2005
Preferred shares	$275,000	$225,000
Common shares	550,000	410,000
Retained earnings	300,000	100,000
Cash dividends	65,000	50,000
Dividends payable	0	15,000

The company did not reacquire any shares in 2006.

Instructions

(a) What was the amount of net earnings reported by Valerio in 2006?

(b) Calculate any cash inflows or outflows related to the share capital and dividend accounts in 2006.

(c) Indicate where each of the cash inflows or outflows identified in (b) would be classified on the cash flow statement.

P13–4A   This comparative balance sheet is for Tommy's Toys Ltd. as at December 31:

Prepare cash flow statement using indirect method. (SO 2a)

TOMMY'S TOYS LTD.
Balance Sheet
December 31

Assets	2006	2005
Cash	$ 81,000	$ 45,000
Accounts receivable	47,500	62,000
Inventory	151,450	142,000
Prepaid expenses	16,780	21,000
Land	90,000	130,000
Building	200,000	200,000
Accumulated amortization—building	(60,000)	(40,000)
Equipment	228,000	155,000
Accumulated amortization—equipment	(45,000)	(35,000)
Total assets	$709,730	$680,000
Liabilities and Shareholders' Equity		
Accounts payable	$ 53,730	$ 40,000
Mortgage note payable	260,000	300,000
Common shares	200,000	160,000
Retained earnings	196,000	180,000
Total liabilities and shareholders' equity	$709,730	$680,000

Additional information:

1. Net earnings were $38,000.
2. Land was sold for its carrying value.
3. Amortization expense of $22,000 was recorded on the equipment.
4. Equipment was purchased for $95,000 cash. In addition, equipment costing $22,000 with a book value of $10,000 was sold for $8,100 cash.
5. A repayment of $40,000 was made on the mortgage note payable.

Instructions

Prepare a cash flow statement for the year, using the indirect method.

P13–5A   The statement of earnings for Breckenridge Ltd. is presented here:

Prepare operating activities section using indirect and direct methods. (SO 2a, 2b)

BRECKENRIDGE LTD.
Statement of Earnings
Year Ended November 30, 2006

Sales		$8,200,000
Cost of goods sold		
Beginning inventory	$1,900,000	
Purchases	4,400,000	
Goods available for sale	6,300,000	
Ending inventory	1,400,000	4,900,000
Gross profit		3,300,000
Operating expenses	$2,075,000	
Amortization expense	75,000	2,150,000
Earnings before income taxes		1,150,000
Income tax expense		300,000
Net earnings		$ 850,000

Additional information:

1. Accounts receivable increased by $200,000 during the year.
2. Prepaid expenses increased by $150,000 during the year.
3. Accounts payable to suppliers of merchandise decreased by $300,000 during the year.
4. Accrued expenses payable decreased by $100,000 during the year.
5. Income tax payable increased by $20,000 during the year.

Instructions

(a) Prepare the operating activities section of the cash flow statement for the year, using the indirect method.
(b) Prepare the operating activities section of the cash flow statement for the year, using the direct method.

Prepare operating activities section using indirect and direct methods.
(SO 2a, 2b)

P13–6A   The statement of earnings for Vail Limited is presented here:

VAIL LIMITED		
Statement of Earnings		
Year Ended December 31, 2006		
Revenues		$900,000
Operating expenses	$624,000	
Amortization expense	60,000	
Interest expense	5,000	
Loss on sale of equipment	26,000	715,000
Earnings before income taxes		185,000
Income tax expense		46,250
Net earnings		$138,750

Vail's balance sheet contained the following selected data at December 31:

	2006	2005
Accounts receivable	$47,000	$57,000
Accounts payable	41,000	36,000
Income tax payable	4,000	9,250
Interest payable	1,000	550
Unearned revenue	12,000	9,000

Instructions

(a) Prepare the operating activities section of the cash flow statement for the year, using the indirect method.
(b) Prepare the operating activities section of the cash flow statement for the year, using the direct method.

Prepare cash flow statement using indirect and direct methods.
(SO 2a, 2b)

P13–7A   Financial statements for E-Perform, Inc. follow:

E-PERFORM, INC.
Balance Sheet
December 31

Assets	2006	2005
Cash	$ 97,800	$ 48,400
Accounts receivable	95,800	33,000
Inventories	112,500	102,850
Prepaid expenses	28,400	26,000
Available-for-sale investments	128,000	114,000
Property, plant, and equipment	270,000	242,500
Accumulated amortization	(50,000)	(52,000)
Total assets	$682,500	$514,750
Liabilities and Shareholders' Equity		
Accounts payable	$102,000	$ 67,300
Accrued expenses payable	16,500	17,000
Notes payable	110,000	150,000
Common shares	220,000	175,000
Retained earnings	234,000	105,450
Total liabilities and shareholders' equity	$682,500	$514,750

E-PERFORM, INC.
Statement of Earnings
Year Ended December 31, 2006

Sales		$392,780
Cost of goods sold		135,460
Gross profit		257,320
Operating expenses	$12,410	
Amortization expense	46,500	
Interest expense	4,730	
Loss on sale of equipment	7,500	71,140
Earnings before income tax		186,180
Income tax expense		45,000
Net earnings		$141,180

Additional information:

1. New equipment costing $85,000 was purchased for cash during the year.
2. Old equipment having an original cost of $57,500 was sold for $1,500.
3. Accounts payable relate only to merchandise creditors.

Instructions

(a) Prepare a cash flow statement for the year, using the indirect method.
(b) Prepare a cash flow statement for the year, using the direct method.

P13−8A   The financial statements of Resolute Inc. are presented here:

RESOLUTE INC.
Balance Sheet
December 31

Assets	2006	2005
Cash	$ 13,000	$ 5,000
Money-market instruments	16,000	5,000
Accounts receivable	38,000	24,000
Merchandise inventory	27,000	20,000
Property, plant, and equipment	80,000	78,000
Accumulated amortization	(30,000)	(24,000)
Total assets	$144,000	$108,000

Liabilities and Shareholders' Equity		
Accounts payable	$ 17,000	$ 15,000
Income taxes payable	1,000	8,000
Notes payable	47,000	33,000
Common shares	18,000	14,000
Retained earnings	61,000	38,000
Total liabilities and shareholders' equity	$144,000	$108,000

RESOLUTE INC.
Statement of Earnings
Year Ended December 31, 2006

Sales		$242,000
Cost of goods sold		180,000
Gross profit		62,000
Operating expenses		24,000
Earnings from operations		38,000
Gain on sale of equipment	$1,000	
Interest expense	2,000	1,000
Earnings before income taxes		37,000
Income tax expense		9,250
Net earnings		$ 27,750

Additional data:

1. During the year, equipment was sold for $9,500 cash. The equipment originally cost $12,000 and had a book value of $8,500 at the time of sale.
2. Equipment costing $14,000 was purchased in exchange for a note payable.
3. Amortization expense is included in operating expenses.
4. Accounts payable relate only to merchandise suppliers.
5. Resolute's money-market instruments are highly liquid and should be considered a cash equivalent for this statement.

Instructions

(a) Prepare a cash flow statement for the year, using the indirect method.
(b) Prepare a cash flow statement for the year, using the direct method.

P13−9A   You are provided with the following transactions for Great Big Sea Inc. during the year ended July 31, 2007:

1. Sold 1,000 common shares for $75 per share.
2. Purchased recording equipment by signing a four-year, 6%, $200,000, note payable at the beginning of the fiscal year. Interest is due annually.
3. Recorded amortization for the year on the recording equipment assuming a four-year life, $20,000 salvage value, and use of the straight-line method of amortization.
4. Paid the amount of interest owing on the note payable for the year, plus $50,000 on the principal of the note.

5. Purchased an inventory of DVDs on account for $75,000.
6. Sold DVDs to customers for $200,000. Of that amount, $150,000 was paid in cash and the remainder was on account. The cost of the DVDs that were sold was $50,000.
7. Collected $18,000 on account.
8. Sold for $7,000 cash a piece of equipment with a cost of $10,000 and accumulated amortization of $2,250.
9. Paid $45,000 of operating expenses.
10. Paid income tax of $12,000.

Instructions

(a) Prepare a statement of earnings for the year.
(b) Prepare a cash flow statement for the year, using the direct method.
(c) Compare the results of the accrual-based statement and the cash-based statement. Which do you think is more useful to decision-makers?

P13–10A Selected information (in thousands) for Reitmans (Canada) Limited and La Senza Corporation for fiscal 2005 follow:

Calculate and assess cash-based ratios.
(SO 3)

	Reitmans	La Senza
Cash provided by operating activities	$117,104	$46,674
Average current liabilities	95,348	53,228
Average total liabilities	164,499	90,788
Capital expenditures	45,503	9,180
Dividends paid	14,171	2,149

Instructions

(a) Calculate the cash current debt coverage ratio, cash total debt coverage ratio, and free cash flow for each company.
(b) Using the ratios calculated in (a), compare the liquidity and solvency of the two companies.

P13–11A Selected ratios for two companies are as follows:

Evaluate liquidity and solvency.
(SO 3)

	Grenville	Robson
Current ratio	1.7:1	1.2:1
Receivables turnover	10 times	20 times
Inventory turnover	4 times	2 times
Cash current debt coverage	0.4 times	0.3 times
Debt to assets	60%	20%
Times interest earned	5 times	20 times
Cash total debt coverage	0.2 times	0.1 times

Instructions

(a) Which company is more liquid? Explain.
(b) Which company is more solvent? Explain.

P13–12A Sleeman Breweries Ltd.'s January 1, 2005, balance sheet reported current assets of $90.2 million and current liabilities of $60.8 million, including bank indebtedness (a negative cash balance) of $9.6 million. On a more positive note, Sleeman increased its earnings by 18 percent in 2004, from $12.3 million in 2003 to $14.4 million in 2004. In addition, its cash flow statement indicates that Sleeman generated $13.2 million of cash from operating activities in 2004.

Discuss cash position.
(SO 3)

Instructions

(a) Do you believe that Sleeman's creditors should be worried about the bank indebtedness? Explain why or why not.
(b) Why do you think Sleeman generated $13.2 million cash from operating activities but has no cash?
(c) If you were a creditor of Sleeman, what additional information could you ask for that would help you assess the company's liquidity and solvency?

Problems: Set B

Classify transactions by activity; indicate impact on cash flow and net earnings.
(SO 1)

P13–1B   The following is a list of transactions that took place during the year:

Transaction	(a) Classification	(b) Cash Inflow or Outflow	(c) Net Earnings
1. Collected an account receivable.	O	+	NE
2. Sold a patent for cash, at a loss.			
3. Sold land for cash, at a gain.			
4. Acquired land by issuing common shares.			
5. Reacquired common shares at a price in excess of average cost.			
6. Paid dividends to preferred shareholders.			
7. Purchased a trading security.			
8. Issued preferred shares for cash.			
9. Purchased inventory for cash. The company uses a perpetual inventory system.			
10. Provided services on account.			

Instructions

Complete the above table for each of the following requirements. The first one has been done for you as an example.

(a) Classify each transaction as an operating activity (O), investing activity (I), financing activity (F), or noncash transaction (NC).

(b) Specify if the transaction will result in a cash inflow (+), cash outflow (−), or have no effect on cash (NE).

(c) Indicate if the transaction will increase (+), decrease (−), or have no effect (NE) on net earnings.

Calculate and classify cash flows for property, plant, and equipment.
(SO 2)

P13–2B   The following selected account balances relate to the property, plant, and equipment accounts of Cretien Corp. at year end:

	2006	2005
Accumulated amortization—buildings	$ 675,000	$ 600,000
Accumulated amortization—equipment	288,000	192,000
Amortization expense	203,000	171,000
Land	250,000	200,000
Buildings	1,250,000	1,250,000
Equipment	500,000	480,000
Loss on sale of equipment	5,000	0

Additional information:

1. Cretien acquired land in exchange for common shares.
2. The company purchased $80,000 of equipment for cash.

Instructions

(a) Calculate any cash inflows or outflows related to the property, plant, and equipment accounts in 2006.

(b) Indicated where each of the cash inflows or outflows identified in (a) would be classified on the cash flow statement.

Calculate and classify cash flows for shareholders' equity.
(SO 2)

P13–3B   The following selected account balances relate to the shareholders' equity accounts of Mathur Corp. at year end:

	2006	2005
Preferred shares	$125,000	$125,000
Common shares	168,000	140,000
Contributed capital—reacquired common shares	1,500	0
Cash dividends	10,000	10,000
Retained earnings	300,000	240,000

The company reacquired common shares in 2006, with an average cost of $32,000.

Instructions

(a) What was the amount of net earnings reported by Mathur in 2006?
(b) Determine the amounts of any cash inflows or outflows related to the share capital and dividend accounts in 2006.
(c) Indicate where each of the cash inflows or outflows identified in (b) would be classified on the cash flow statement.

P13–4B Presented here is the comparative balance sheet for Cortina Limited at December 31:

Prepare cash flow statement using indirect method.
(SO 2a)

CORTINA LIMITED
Balance Sheet
December 31

Assets	2006	2005
Cash	$ 30,000	$ 57,000
Accounts receivable	77,000	64,000
Inventory	192,000	140,000
Prepaid expenses	12,140	16,540
Land	105,000	150,000
Building	250,000	250,000
Accumulated amortization—building	(75,000)	(50,000)
Equipment	200,000	175,000
Accumulated amortization—equipment	(60,000)	(42,000)
Total assets	$731,140	$760,540
Liabilities and Shareholders' Equity		
Accounts payable	$ 33,000	$ 45,000
Bonds payable	235,000	265,000
Common shares	280,000	250,000
Retained earnings	183,140	200,540
Total liabilities and shareholders' equity	$731,140	$760,540

Additional information:

1. Net earnings were $26,890.
2. Amortization expense of $70,000 was recorded on the buildings and equipment.
3. Land was sold for its carrying value.
4. Equipment was purchased for $65,000 cash. In addition, equipment costing $40,000 with a book value of $13,000 was sold at a gain of $1,000.
5. Bonds were retired for $30,000, resulting in a loss of $2,500.

Instructions

Prepare a cash flow statement for the year, using the indirect method.

P13–5B The statement of earnings of Gum San Ltd. is presented here:

Prepare operating activities section using indirect and direct methods.
(SO 2a, 2b)

GUM SAN LTD.
Statement of Earnings
Year Ended December 31, 2006

Sales		$5,400,000
Cost of goods sold		3,290,000
Gross profit		2,110,000
Operating expenses	$925,000	
Amortization expense	145,000	1,070,000
Earnings before income taxes		1,040,000
Income tax expense		260,000
Net earnings		$ 780,000

Additional information:

1. Accounts receivable increased by $510,000 during the year.
2. Prepaid expenses increased by $170,000 during the year.
3. Inventory decreased by $220,000 during the year.
4. Accounts payable to merchandise suppliers increased by $50,000 during the year.
5. Accrued expenses payable decreased by $165,000 during the year.
6. Income taxes payable decreased by $16,000 during the year.

Instructions

(a) Prepare the operating activities section of the cash flow statement for the year, using the indirect method.
(b) Prepare the operating activities section of the cash flow statement for the year, using the direct method.

Prepare operating activities
section using indirect and direct
methods.
(SO 2a, 2b)

P13−6B   The statement of earnings for Hanalei International Inc. is presented here:

HANALEI INTERNATIONAL INC.
Statement of Earnings
Year Ended December 31, 2006

Fee revenue		$545,000
Operating expenses		370,000
Earnings from operations		175,000
Gain on sale of equipment	$ 25,000	
Interest expense	(10,000)	15,000
Earnings before income taxes		190,000
Income tax expense		47,500
Net earnings		$142,500

Hanalei's balance sheet contained these comparative data at December 31:

	2006	2005
Accounts receivable	$50,000	$60,000
Prepaid insurance	8,000	5,000
Accounts payable	30,000	41,000
Interest payable	2,000	750
Income tax payable	8,000	4,000

Additional information:

1. Hanalei has no amortizable assets.
2. Accounts payable relate to operating expenses.

Instructions

(a) Prepare the operating activities section of the cash flow statement for the year, using the indirect method.
(b) Prepare the operating activities section of the cash flow statement for the year, using the direct method.

P13–7B Financial statements for Nackawic Inc. follow:

Prepare cash flow statement using indirect and direct methods.
(SO 2a, 2b)

NACKAWIC INC.
Balance Sheet
December 31

Assets	2006	2005
Cash	$ 92,700	$ 47,250
Accounts receivable	90,800	37,000
Inventories	121,900	102,650
Available-for-sale securities	84,500	107,000
Property, plant, and equipment	290,000	205,000
Accumulated amortization	(49,500)	(40,000)
Total assets	$630,400	$458,900
Liabilities and Shareholders' Equity		
Accounts payable	$ 52,700	$ 48,280
Accrued expenses payable	12,100	18,830
Notes payable	140,000	70,000
Common shares	250,000	200,000
Retained earnings	175,600	121,790
Total liabilities and shareholders' equity	$630,400	$458,900

NACKAWIC INC.
Statement of Earnings
Year Ended December 31, 2006

Revenues		
Sales		$297,500
Gain on sale of equipment		8,750
		306,250
Expenses		
Cost of goods sold	$99,460	
Amortization expense	58,700	
Operating expenses	14,670	
Interest expense	2,940	
Loss on sale of available-for-sale security	7,500	183,270
Earnings before income taxes		122,980
Income tax expense		32,670
Net earnings		$ 90,310

Additional information:

1. Available-for-sale securities were sold for $15,000, resulting in a loss of $7,500.
2. New equipment costing $141,000 was purchased for cash during the year.
3. Equipment costing $56,000 was sold for $15,550, resulting in a gain of $8,750.
4. Accounts payable relate only to merchandise suppliers.

Instructions

(a) Prepare a cash flow statement for the year, using the indirect method.
(b) Prepare a cash flow statement for the year, using the direct method.

Prepare cash flow statement
using indirect and direct
methods.
(SO 2a, 2b)

P13–8B   The financial statements of Wetaskiwin Limited are presented here:

WETASKIWIN LIMITED
Balance Sheet
December 31

Assets	2006	2005
Cash	$ 12,000	$ 10,000
Money-market instruments	14,000	23,000
Accounts receivable	28,000	14,000
Merchandise inventory	38,000	25,000
Property, plant, and equipment	70,000	78,000
Accumulated amortization	(30,000)	(24,000)
Total assets	$132,000	$126,000
Liabilities and Shareholders' Equity		
Accounts payable	$ 34,000	$ 43,000
Income taxes payable	15,000	20,000
Notes payable	15,000	10,000
Common shares	25,000	25,000
Retained earnings	43,000	28,000
Total liabilities and shareholders' equity	$132,000	$126,000

WETASKIWIN LIMITED
Statement of Earnings
Year Ended December 31, 2006

Sales		$286,000
Cost of goods sold		194,000
Gross profit		92,000
Operating expenses		34,000
Earnings from operations		58,000
Loss on sale of equipment	$2,000	
Interest expense	5,000	7,000
Earnings before income taxes		51,000
Income tax expense		15,000
Net earnings		$ 36,000

Additional information:

1. During the year, equipment was sold for $8,000 cash. This equipment originally cost $18,000 and had a book value of $10,000 at the time of sale.
2. Equipment costing $10,000 was purchased in exchange for $5,000 cash and a note payable for the balance.
3. Amortization expense is included in operating expenses.
4. Accounts payable relate only to merchandise suppliers.
5. Wetaskiwin's money-market instruments are highly liquid and should be considered a cash equivalent for this statement.

Instructions

(a) Prepare a cash flow statement for the year, using the indirect method.
(b) Prepare a cash flow statement for the year, using the direct method.

Prepare statement of earnings
and cash flow statement using
direct method.
(SO 2b)

P13–9B   DesRoches Inc. incorporated a repair business on January 1, 2006. You are provided with the following transactions for the month of January:

1. Issued common shares for $5,000.
2. Borrowed $15,000 from a local bank on a two-year, 7% note payable. Interest is repayable at maturity.
3. Rented space, paying rent in advance for three months—January, February, and March—at $1,000 a month.

4. Purchased a one-year insurance policy, effective January 1, for $1,200.
5. Rented repair and office equipment for $750 a month. Paid January's rent and hopes to purchase this equipment at a later date when its cash flow improves.
6. Purchased $1,000 of supplies on account. The cost of the supplies remaining at the end of the month was $300.
7. Cash paid on accounts payable during the month totalled $800.
8. Provided repair services for $2,500 cash and $15,000 on account.
9. Cash collected from customers on account was $12,200.
10. Other operating expenses paid totalled $2,000.
11. Unpaid salaries at the end of the month were $500.
12. Income taxes of $3,000 are owed.

Instructions

(a) Prepare a statement of earnings for the month.
(b) Prepare a cash flow statement for the month, using the direct method.
(c) Compare the results of the accrual-based statement and the cash-based statement. Which do you think is more useful to decision-makers?

P13–10B   Selected information (in U.S. millions) for Google Inc. and Yahoo! Inc. for 2004 follows:

Calculate and assess cash-based ratios.
(SO 3)

	Google	Yahoo!
Cash provided by operating activities	$977	$1,090
Average current liabilities	288	944
Average total liabilities	333	1,822
Capital expenditures	344	1,001
Dividends	0	0

Instructions

(a) Calculate the cash current debt coverage ratio, cash total debt coverage ratio, and free cash flow for each company.
(b) Using the ratios calculated in (a), compare the liquidity and solvency of the two companies.

P13–11B   Selected ratios for two companies are as follows:

Evaluate liquidity and solvency.
(SO 3)

	Burrard	Pender
Current ratio	1:1	0.8:1
Receivables turnover	6 times	4 times
Inventory turnover	5 times	4 times
Cash current debt coverage	0.5 times	0.4 times
Debt to total assets	75%	50%
Times interest earned	6 times	2 times
Cash total debt coverage	0.4 times	0.3 times

Instructions

(a) Which company is more liquid? Explain.
(b) Which company is more solvent? Explain.

P13–12B   Ontario Power Generation (OPG) Inc.'s cash flow statement reported cash provided by operating activities of $226 million, a significant increase over the $97 million reported in 2003. It reported net earnings of $42 million in 2004, also a significant increase over a net loss of $491 million reported in 2003. Yet, cash and cash equivalents reported on the balance sheet declined to $2 million in 2004 from $286 million in 2003.

Discuss cash position.
(SO 3)

Instructions

(a) How is it possible that OPG can have $226 million of cash provided by operating activities but only have $42 million of net earnings in 2004?
(b) Explain how OPG increased its cash provided by operating activities by $129 million ($226 − $97) from 2003 to 2004, when net earnings increased by $533 million ($42 + $491) over the same period.
(c) Explain how OPG can have an increase in its cash provided by operating activities of $129 million ($226 − $97) from 2003 to 2004, but experience a decrease in its cash and cash equivalents of $284 million ($286 − $2) over the same period.

Financial Reporting and Analysis

Analysis Tools

Financial Reporting Problem: *Loblaw*

BYP13–1   Refer to the financial statements of Loblaw presented in Appendix A.

Instructions

(a) How does Loblaw define "cash" for the purpose of its cash flow statement?
(b) What was the amount of the increase or decrease in cash for fiscal 2003? Fiscal 2002?
(c) What was the amount of cash flows from operating activities for 2003? For 2002? What was the main reason for any change in cash flows from operating activities?
(d) Does Loblaw use the indirect or direct method of calculating operating activities?
(e) From your analysis of the 2003 cash flow statement, what were the most significant investing activities? Financing activities?
(f) Did Loblaw report any significant noncash investing and financing activities?

Comparative Analysis Problem: *Loblaw and Sobeys*

BYP13–2   The financial statements of Sobeys are presented in Appendix B, following the financial statements for Loblaw in Appendix A.

Instructions

(a) Based on the information in the financial statements, calculate the following ratios for Loblaw for the year ended January 3, 2004, and Sobeys for the year ended May 1, 2004:
  1. Cash current debt coverage   3. Cash total debt coverage
  2. Current ratio   4. Debt to total assets
(b) What conclusions about liquidity and solvency can be drawn from the ratios calculated in (a)?

Research Case

BYP13–3   The November 2002 issue of *Report on Business Magazine* includes an article by Fabrice Taylor entitled "Show Me the Real Money" on page 109. This article discusses whether cash flow or earnings is a better indicator of a company's performance.

Instructions

Read the article and answer these questions:

(a) What are the three major components of a company's financial results?
(b) Cash flow from operating activities can be altered by accounting assumptions. What did Alliance Atlantis do in the year 2002 to alter its cash flow from operating activities in the years 2000 and 2001?
(c) Bombardier's 2002 cash flow statement showed an $88.5-million contribution to the company's pension and benefit plan. The statement of earnings showed an expense of $179.7 million. Why would the two amounts differ?
(d) Do consolidated financial statements of a holding company reflect the same percentage share of profits and losses as the cash flow provided by operating activities?
(e) Cash flow is often thought of as a more reliable indicator of a company's performance than earnings are. Would you agree with this statement? Why or why not?

Interpreting Financial Statements

BYP13–4 The following information was available from WestJet Airlines Ltd.'s financial statements (in thousands):

	2004	2003	2002
Total current assets	$ 195,075	$ 276,857	$143,015
Total assets	1,877,354	1,476,858	784,205
Total current liabilities	304,449	238,077	175,064
Total liabilities	1,287,462	896,046	428,449
Cash provided by operating activities	144,072	192,417	161,624
Capital expenditures	584,842	596,287	344,668
Dividends paid	0	0	0

Instructions

(a) Calculate the current and cash current debt coverage ratios for WestJet for 2004 and 2003 and discuss the airline's liquidity

(b) Calculate the debt to total assets and cash total debt coverage ratios for WestJet for 2004 and 2003 and discuss the airline's solvency.

(c) Calculate free cash flow for WestJet for 2004 and 2003 and discuss the airline's ability to finance expansion from internally generated cash.

A Global Focus

BYP13–5 The format of the cash flow statement varies from country to country throughout the world. The following cash flow statement is from the 2004 financial statements of tire manufacturer Compagnie Générale des Établissements Michelin (Michelin). Michelin is headquartered in France and sells tires worldwide.

COMPAGNIE GÉNÉRALE DES ÉTABLISSEMENTS MICHELIN Cash Flow Statement Year Ended December 31, 2004 (in thousands of euros)		
	2004	2003
Cash flows from operating activities		
Net income before minority interests	527,163	328,862
Adjustments to reconcile net income before minority interests to net cash provided by operating activities:		
Depreciation and amortization	839,851	1,162,520
Allowances, provisions and deferred taxes	(38,321)	(87,145)
Net gains on disposals of assets	39,454	8,371
Other	(15,228)	(5,240)
Cash flow	1,352,919	1,407,368
Change in inventories	(175,035)	(43,059)
Change in receivables	(9,484)	14,081
Change in payables	59,679	44,420
Other changes in working capital	108,862	119,342
Net change in working capital	(15,978)	134,784
Cash flows from operating activities	1,336,941	1,542,152

Cash flows from investing activities		
Additions to property, plant, and equipment and intangible assets	(1,116,781)	(1,117,798)
Additions to investments	(170,807)	(305,199)
Total	(1,287,588)	(1,422,997)
Proceeds from disposal of property, plant, and equipment and intangible assets	91,958	100,586
Proceeds from disposal of investments	64,947	76,333
Total	156,905	176,919
Impact of changes in Group structure	(11,839)	14,884
Net change in working capital	31,916	(11,469)
Cash flows from investing activities	(1,110,606)	(1,242,663)
Cash flows from financing activities		
Employee share ownership plan	0	20,739
Expenses related to the stock-for-stock offer	0	(645)
Dividends paid to parent company shareholders	(133,312)	(130,692)
Other dividends paid	(51,994)	(49,669)
Total	(185,306)	(160,267)
Change in long- and short-term debt	(187,629)	513,936
Net change in working capital	33,252	(46,811)
Net cash (used) provided by financing activities	(339,683)	306,858
Effect of exchange rate changes on cash and cash equivalents	(4,910)	(41,759)
Change in cash and cash equivalents	(118,258)	564,588
Cash and cash equivalents at beginning of period	1,773,656	1,209,068
Cash and cash equivalents at the period-end	1,655,398	1,773,656
Including—Cash	1,420,140	1,234,168
—Cash equivalents	235,258	539,488

Instructions

(a) What similarities to Canadian cash flow statements do you notice in the general format and terminology?

(b) What differences do you notice in the general format and terminology?

(c) Using the data in the cash flow statement, calculate free cash flow. Do the differences in format and terminology make it harder for you to calculate this measure?

Financial Analysis on the Web

Analysis Tools
(Financial Analysis on the Web)

BYP13–6 The film and video industry in Canada can present some interesting challenges because of the high costs of producing and distributing television shows and movies. In 2005, Alliance Atlantis Communications Inc. celebrated its 10th anniversary as a leading specialty broadcaster, continuing to offer Canadians recognizable, high-quality brands boasting targeted, high-quality programming across 13 specialty channels. In this case, we will learn how Alliance Atlantis meets the challenges of managing cash flow in the capital-intensive film industry.

Instructions

Specific requirements of this Web case can be found on the Toolkit website.

Critical Thinking

Collaborative Learning Activity

BYP13–7 Greg Nord and Debra Gee are examining the following cash flow statement for Tuktoyaktuk Trading Company Limited for the year ended January 31, 2007:

TUKTOYAKTUK TRADING COMPANY LIMITED		
Cash Flow Statement		
Year Ended January 31, 2007		
Cash inflows		
From sale of merchandise	$390,000	
From sale of common shares	420,000	
From sale of investment (purchased below)	80,000	
From amortization	55,000	
From issue of note for truck	25,000	
From interest on investment	6,000	
Total sources of cash		$976,000
Cash outflows		
For purchase of fixtures and equipment	$320,000	
For merchandise purchased for resale	268,000	
For operating expenses	160,000	
For purchase of investment	75,000	
For purchase of truck by issue of note	25,000	
For interest on note payable	3,000	
Total uses of cash		851,000
Net increase in cash		$125,000

Greg claims that Tuktoyaktuk's cash flow statement is an excellent portrayal of a superb first year, with cash increasing by $125,000. Debra replies that it was not a superb first year. Rather, she says that the year was an operating failure, that the statement is presented incorrectly, and that $125,000 is not the actual increase in cash. The cash balance at the beginning of the year was $40,000.

Instructions

With the class divided into groups, answer the following:

(a) Who do you agree with, Greg or Debra? Explain your position.
(b) Using the data provided, prepare a cash flow statement using the indirect method. Assume that there were no changes in any current accounts other than cash.
(c) Prepare a cash flow statement in proper form using the direct method.
(d) Would you recommend the payment of a dividend this year?

Communication Activity

BYP13–8 Many investors today prefer the cash flow statement over the statement of earnings. These people believe that cash-based data are a better measure of performance than accrual-based data because the former are less susceptible to possible earnings management.

Instructions

Write a brief memo explaining whether or not cash-based data is less susceptible to earnings management than accrual-based data. In your answer, state which financial statement, if any, you believe is the better measure of a company's performance and explain why.

Ethics Case

BYP13–9 The Onwards and Upwards Corporation has paid cash dividends to its shareholders for eight consecutive years. The board of directors' policy requires that in order for a dividend to be declared, cash provided by operating activities as reported in the current year's cash flow statement must exceed $1 million. The job of president Phil Monat is secure so long as Phil produces annual operating cash flows to support the usual dividend.

At the end of the current year, controller Leland Yee informs president Monat of some disappointing news. The cash provided by operating activities is only $970,000. The president

www.wiley.com/canada/kimmel

Ethics In Accounting

says to Leland, "We must get that amount above $1 million. Isn't there some way to increase cash from operating activities by another $30,000?" Leland answers, "These figures were prepared by my assistant. I'll go back to my office and see what I can do." The president replies, "I know you won't let me down, Leland."

Upon close scrutiny of the cash flow statement, Leland concludes that he can get cash from operating activities above $1 million by reclassifying a two-year, $60,000 note payable listed in the financing activities section as "Proceeds from bank loan—$60,000." Leland will prepare the operating activities section of the cash flow statement using the indirect method and report the note as an adjustment to net earnings called "increase in payables—$60,000." He returns to the president, saying, "You can tell the board to declare their usual dividend. Our cash flow provided by operating activities is $1,030,000." The president is excited and states, "Good man, Leland! I knew I could count on you."

Instructions

(a) Who are the stakeholders in this situation?
(b) Was there anything unethical about the president's actions? Was there anything unethical about the controller's actions?
(c) Are the board members or anyone else likely to discover the misclassification?

Serial Problem

(*Note*: This is a continuation of the serial problem from Chapters 1 through 12.)

BYP13–10   Natalie has prepared the balance sheet and statement of earnings of Cookie Creations Ltd. for the year ended December 31, 2008, but she does not understand how to prepare the cash flow statement. The balance sheet and the statement of earnings follow:

COOKIE CREATIONS LTD.		
Balance Sheet		
December 31, 2008		

	2008	2007
Assets		
Cash	$ 16,344	$ 3,050
Accounts receivable	3,250	1,710
Inventory	7,897	5,450
Prepaid expenses	6,300	3,050
Furniture and fixtures	12,500	5,000
Accumulated amortization—furniture and fixtures	(2,000)	(1,000)
Computer equipment	4,000	4,500
Accumulated amortization—computer equipment	(600)	(1,500)
Kitchen equipment	80,000	66,000
Accumulated amortization—kitchen equipment	(22,600)	(6,600)
Total assets	$105,091	$79,660
Liabilities and Shareholders' Equity		
Accounts payable	$ 3,650	$ 6,930
Income taxes payable	10,251	11,200
Dividends payable	28,000	25,000
Salaries payable	2,250	1,280
Interest payable	188	0
Note payable–current portion	3,000	0
Note payable–long-term portion	4,500	0
Preferred shares ($6 cumulative, 3,000 in 2008 and 2,500 in 2007)	15,000	10,000
Common shares (3,625 shares issued)	5,450	5,450
Retained earnings	32,802	19,800
Total liabilities and shareholders' equity	$105,091	$79,660

COOKIE CREATIONS LTD.
Statement of Earnings
Year Ended December 31, 2008

Sales	$485,625
Cost of goods sold	222,694
Gross profit	262,931
Operating expenses	
Amortization expense	17,600
Salaries and wage expense	147,979
Other operating expenses	43,186
Total operating expenses	208,765
Earnings from operations	54,166
Other expenses	
Interest expense	413
Loss on sale of computer equipment	2,500
Total other expenses	2,913
Earnings before income tax	51,253
Income tax expense	10,251
Net earnings	$ 41,002

Additional information:

1. All of the computer equipment was disposed of at the beginning of the year for $500 cash. New computer equipment was then bought for $4,000 cash.
2. Additional kitchen equipment was bought for $14,000 on January 1, 2008. A $9,000 note payable was signed. The terms provide for equal semi-annual instalment payments of $1,500 on July 1 and January 1 of each year, plus interest of 5% on the outstanding principal balance.
3. Additional furniture was bought for $7,500 cash.
4. Dividends were declared to the preferred and common shareholders on December 15, 2008, to be paid January 15, 2009.
5. Accounts payable relate only to merchandise creditors.
6. Prepaid expenses relate only to other operating expenses.

Instructions

(a) Prepare a cash flow statement, using the indirect method or the direct method, as required by your instructor.
(b) Calculate and compare the cash current debt coverage ratio to the current ratio, and the cash total debt coverage ratio to the debt to total assets ratio.

Answers to Self-Study Questions

1. d 2. a 3. c 4. d 5. d 6. c 7. c 8. d 9. a 10. b

Answer to Loblaw Review It Question 3

In 2003, Loblaw reported (a) $1,032 million provided by operating activities, (b) $1,448 million used by investing activities, and (c) $386 million provided by financing activities

Remember to go back to the Navigator box at the beginning of the chapter to check off your completed work.

CHAPTER 14

Performance Measurement

Corporate Reporting
Proves to Be Fertile Ground

Launched as a Crown Corporation by the Province of Saskatchewan in 1975, Potash Corporation of Saskatchewan Inc. (PotashCorp) became a public company in 1989. With the world's largest integrated production capacity for the three primary nutrients (potash, phosphate and nitrogen)—their products are used by fertilizer, feed and industrial customers on six continents—PotashCorp takes the transparency and accountability that comes with being a public company very seriously.

The Saskatoon-based company took the Overall Award of Excellence at the Canadian Institute of Chartered Accountants' 2004 Corporate Reporting Awards. PotashCorp also won in the mining industry sector, and received awards of excellence for electronic disclosure and sustainable reporting, and an honourable mention for excellence in annual reporting.

Like all annual reports, PotashCorp's document presented the year's financial results, a message from the president and CEO, management discussion and analysis (MD&A), and information on the company's directors. The report also stated what the company's goals for the current year were and how well it had met them, and listed targets for the next year. What impressed the judges was the fact that environmental policies, as well as social and economic issues being faced, were included in the MD&A section.

The annual report is the most important document a company produces. It is a crucial tool for investors, creditors, and regulators to gather the information they require. To help them, PotashCorp's annual report includes a 10-year review of its financial performance, including production statistics, and detailed explanations of risks and how the company manages them.

PotashCorp also addresses corporate governance and sustainable development issues. The judges described the Board/Governance/Responsibility section of the company's website as "outstanding," providing all the information you could need on the corporate mission and governance. PotashCorp was the first publicly traded fertilizer company in North America to produce a separate sustainability report to document its economic impact, social involvement, and progress in safety, health, and the environment.

These accolades came from a year that was in fact poor in terms of financial performance. "We are especially proud to earn recognition for our reporting [this year]," said Chief Financial Officer Wayne Brownlee. "The fertilizer industry endured the sixth year of a down cycle and our company had the lowest financial returns in our history. We tackled that head on in our reporting."

By communicating effectively with its shareholders and other parties, the company demonstrates its commitment to keeping investors and other stakeholders informed—one of the most important issues in corporate governance today.

Potash: www.potashcorp.com

THE NAVIGATOR

☐ Read *Feature Story*

☐ Scan *Study Objectives*

☐ Read *Chapter Preview*

☐ Read text and answer *Before You Go On*

☐ Work *Using the Decision Toolkit*

☐ Review *Summary of Study Objectives*

☐ Review *Decision Toolkit—A Summary*

☐ Work *Demonstration Problem*

☐ Answer *Self-Study Questions*

☐ Complete assignments

STUDY OBJECTIVES

After studying this chapter, you should be able to:

1. Understand the concept of sustainable earnings and indicate how irregular items are presented.
2. Explain and apply horizontal analysis.
3. Explain and apply vertical analysis.
4. Identify and calculate ratios used to analyze liquidity, solvency, and profitability.
5. Understand the concept of quality of earnings.

the navigator

An important lesson can be learned from PotashCorp's annual report described in our feature story. Effective communication is the key to understanding. This has become even more important as a result of corporate scandals that have left a strong feeling of doubt about the usefulness of financial reporting.

The purpose of this chapter is to give you a comprehensive review of financial statements—a company's most important means of communication. We will examine the impact of certain irregular items on financial results and analyses. In addition, we show how difficult it can be to develop high-quality financial numbers because of the complexities of financial reporting. Finally, we will review all of the decision tools presented in this text and use them to analyze PotashCorp's financial statements.

The chapter is organized as follows:

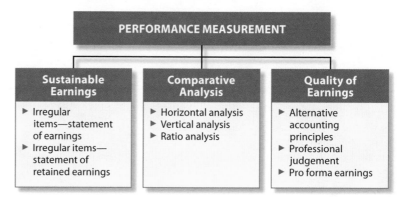

the navigator

Sustainable Earnings

study objective 1

Understand the concept of sustainable earnings and indicate how irregular items are presented.

Sustainable earnings are the most likely level of earnings to be obtained in the future. In other words, they indicate how accurately the most recent year's net earnings predict future years' net earnings. Sustainable earnings differ from actual net earnings by the amount of irregular, or non-typical, revenues, expenses, gains, and losses that are included in net earnings. Users are interested in sustainable earnings because the amount helps them estimate future earnings without the "noise" of irregular items. For example, suppose Rye Corporation reports that this year's net earnings are $500,000, but this amount includes a once-in-a-lifetime gain of $400,000. In estimating next year's net earnings for Rye Corporation, we would likely ignore this $400,000 gain and estimate that next year's net earnings will be in the neighbourhood of $100,000, plus or minus any expected changes. That is, based on this year's results, the company's sustainable earnings are roughly $100,000.

In earlier chapters, you learned that earnings are presented on both the statement of earnings and the statement of retained earnings. In this chapter, we will explain how irregular items affect the presentation of these two financial statements.

Irregular Items—Statement of Earnings

To help determine sustainable earnings, irregular items are identified by type on the statement of earnings. Two types of irregular items are reported: (1) discontinued operations and (2) extraordinary items.

Irregular items are reported net of income taxes; that is, the applicable income tax expense or tax savings is shown for earnings before income taxes and for each of the irregular items. The general concept is "Let the tax follow the earnings or loss."

Discontinued Operations

Discontinued operations refer to the disposal of an identifiable reporting or operating segment of the business. An **identifiable business segment** can be a separate subsidiary company, an operating division within the company, or even a group of assets, as long as it is a separate business that can be clearly distinguished from the company as a whole.

Most large corporations have multiple business segments or divisions. PotashCorp, from our feature story, has three business segments that it reports financial and operating information about: potash, phosphate, and nitrogen. The company states that "these business segments are differentiated by the chemical nutrient contained in the product that each produces."

If a company sells a segment of its business, the sale is reported separately on the statement of earnings as a nonrecurring item called discontinued operations. Note that discontinued operations relate only to the disposal of an identifiable business segment, such as the elimination of an entire line of business or a product group. The phasing out of a model or part of a line of business is *not* considered a disposal of a business segment.

When the disposal of an identifiable business segment occurs, the statement of earnings should report both the earnings (or loss) from continuing operations and the earnings (or loss) from discontinued operations. The earnings (loss) from discontinued operations consists of two parts: the earnings (loss) from operations and the gain (loss) on the disposal of the segment.

To illustrate, assume that Rozek Inc. has sales of $2.5 million, cost of goods sold of $1.3 million, and operating expenses of $400,000 for the year ended December 31, 2006. The company therefore has earnings before income tax of $800,000. If we assume that Rozek has a 30-percent income tax rate, it would report $240,000 ($800,000 × 30%) income tax on these earnings, resulting in $560,000 of earnings from continuing operations. Also during 2006, Rozek discontinues and sells its unprofitable chemical division. The loss from chemical operations is $140,000 ($200,000 less $60,000 income tax savings). The loss on disposal of the chemical division is $70,000 ($100,000 less $30,000 income tax savings). The statement of earnings is presented below:

ROZEK INC.
Statement of Earnings
Year Ended December 31, 2006

Sales		$2,500,000
Cost of goods sold		1,300,000
Gross profit		1,200,000
Operating expenses		400,000
Earnings before income taxes		800,000
Income tax expense		240,000
Earnings from continuing operations		560,000
Discontinued operations		
Loss from operations of chemical division, net of $60,000		
income tax savings	$140,000	
Loss from disposal of chemical division, net of $30,000		
income tax savings	70,000	(210,000)
Net earnings		$ 350,000

Note that the caption "earnings from continuing operations" is used and the section "discontinued operations" is added. Within the new section, both the operating loss and the loss on disposal are reported net of applicable income taxes. In addition, the impact of the discontinued operations on cash flow must also be reported separately on the cash flow statement. This presentation clearly indicates the separate effects of continuing operations and discontinued operations on net earnings. Discontinued operations are quite common. In a recent year, nearly 30 percent of the companies surveyed by *Financial Reporting in Canada* reported discontinued operations.

Extraordinary Items

Extraordinary items are events and transactions that meet three conditions. They are (1) not expected to occur frequently, (2) not typical of normal business activities, and (3) not subject to management's discretion.

To be infrequent, the item should not be expected again in the foreseeable future. To be atypical, the item should be only incidentally related to normal activities. To be outside of management's discretion, the item should not depend on decisions by management.

All three criteria must be evaluated in terms of the environment in which the business operates. Thus, Alcan Aluminium Limited reported the government cancellation of a contract to supply power to B.C. Hydro as an extraordinary item because the event was infrequent, unusual, and not determined by management. In contrast, Canada West Tree Fruits Ltd. of the Okanagan Valley does not report frost damage to its fruit crop as an extraordinary item because frost damage is somewhat frequent there.

Illustration 14-1 shows the appropriate classification of extraordinary and ordinary items.

Illustration 14-1 ▶

Classification of extraordinary and ordinary items

Extraordinary Items	Ordinary Items
1. Effects of major casualties (acts of God), if rare in the area 	1. Effects of major casualties (acts of God), not uncommon in the area 
2. Expropriation (takeover) of property by a foreign government 	2. Write-down of inventories or write-off of receivables 
3. Effects of a newly enacted law or regulation, such as a condemnation action 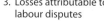	3. Losses attributable to labour disputes 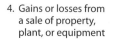
4. Destruction of property	4. Gains or losses from a sale of property, plant, or equipment 

In reality, extraordinary items are rare. *Financial Reporting in Canada* notes that no public company has reported an extraordinary item since 2001. If a company does have an extraordinary item, it should be reported net of taxes in a separate section of the statement of earnings, immediately below discontinued operations. Further information about the extraordinary item is given in a note to the financial statement. As extraordinary items are rare, they are not illustrated here.

If a transaction or event meets one but not all of the criteria for an extraordinary item, it should be reported in a separate line item in the upper half of the statement of earnings, rather than in the bottom half as an extraordinary item. Usually, these items are reported under either "other revenues" or "other expenses" at their gross amount (not net of tax). This is true, for example, of gains (losses) resulting from the sale of property, plant, and equipment, as explained in Chapter 9.

We have shown in this section that irregular items can have a significant impact on net earnings. In general, in evaluating a company, it makes sense to eliminate all irregular items from net earnings when estimating future sustainable earnings.

ACCOUNTING MATTERS!   International Perspective

The criteria used to determine whether an item is extraordinary or not differ across countries. For example, in the United States extraordinary items do not rule out management involvement. Consequently, in the U.S., extraordinary items are far more frequent than in Canada and can include items such as losses from the retirement of debt that involve decisions by management.

Canada, Australia, the U.S., and the UK report extraordinary items (they are called "exceptional" in the UK) separately from ordinary items. Many other countries, however, do not distinguish extraordinary and ordinary items.

Irregular Items—Statement of Retained Earnings

Another type of irregular item, one that affects earnings of prior periods, is a change in accounting principle. A **change in accounting principle** occurs when the principle used in the current year is different from the one used in the preceding year.

Alternative Terminology
Accounting principles are also known as *accounting policies* and *accounting standards*.

To ensure comparability, accounting principles should be applied consistently from period to period. This does not mean, however, that changes can never be made. A change in accounting principle is permitted when management can show that the new accounting principle results in a more appropriate presentation of events or transactions in the financial statements.

This type of change affects financial reporting in four ways:

1. The cumulative effect of the change in accounting principle should be reported (net of income tax) as an adjustment to opening retained earnings. Since prior-period earnings are affected, a change in accounting principle must be reported on the statement of retained earnings, rather than on the current period's statement of earnings.
2. The new principle should be used for reporting the results of operations in the current year.
3. All prior-period financial statements should be restated to make comparisons easier.
4. The effects of the change should be detailed and disclosed in a note.

Examples of a change in accounting principle include a change in amortization methods (such as declining-balance to straight-line) and a change in inventory costing methods (such as FIFO to average cost). Often a change in accounting principle is required by the CICA. For example, in the notes to its 2004 financial statements, PotashCorp states that the company retroactively adopted the new *CICA Handbook* section "Accounting for Asset Retirement Obligations." This new accounting principle requires companies to record an asset and related liability for the costs associated with the retirement of long-lived tangible assets.

We will use our earlier illustration of Rozek Inc. to illustrate how changes in accounting principles are reported. Assume that at the beginning of 2006 Rozek changes from the straight-line method to the declining-balance method of amortization for equipment which had been purchased on January 1, 2002. This change results in increased amortization expense and accumulated amortization for the years 2002 to 2005.

Retained earnings are reduced by the cumulative effect of the change in amortization expense for the prior periods. Assume that the total increase in amortization expense for the years 2002 through 2005 amounts to $24,000. Rozek has a 30-percent income tax rate, so the after-tax effect of the change on prior-period net earnings would be $16,800 ($24,000 − $7,200 [$24,000 × 30%]).

The presentation of this change in the statement of retained earnings is shown in the following illustration. The opening retained earnings balance is assumed to be $500,000.

ROZEK INC. Statement of Retained Earnings Year Ended December 31, 2006	
Retained earnings, January 1, as previously reported	$500,000
Deduct: Cumulative effect on prior years of change in amortization method, net of $7,200 income tax savings	(16,800)
Retained earnings, January 1, as adjusted	483,200
Add: Net earnings	350,000
Retained earnings, December 31	$833,200

A financial statement from any prior year which is presented for comparative purposes would be restated using the declining-balance method of amortization. Rozek's statement of earnings will also show amortization expense for the current year, 2006, on a declining-balance basis (i.e., using the new method of amortization). Accumulated amortization on the balance sheet will be calculated as though declining-balance had always been used. An appropriately cross-referenced note to the statements should give details about the impact of the change and the fact that statements from prior years have been restated.

Decision Toolkit

Decision Checkpoints	Info Needed for Decision	Tools to Use for Decision	How to Evaluate Results
Has the company sold an identifiable business segment?	Discontinued operations section of statement of earnings	Anything reported in this section indicates that the company has discontinued an identifiable business segment.	If an identifiable business segment has been discontinued, its results in the current period should not be included in estimates of future net earnings.
Has the company experienced any extraordinary events or transactions?	Extraordinary item section of statement of earnings	Anything reported in this section indicates that the company experienced an event that was infrequent, unusual, and not determined by management.	These items should be ignored in estimating future net earnings.
Has the company changed any of its accounting principles?	Cumulative effect of change in accounting principle in statement of retained earnings	Anything reported in this manner indicates that the company has changed an accounting principle during the current year.	Financial statements are restated using the new principle to make them easy to compare.

BEFORE YOU GO ON . . .

▶Review It

1. What are sustainable earnings?
2. What irregular items affect the statement of earnings? What effect do they have on estimating future earnings?
3. What irregular item affects the statement of retained earnings? What impact does this item have on the comparability of prior-period earnings?
4. Did Loblaw report any irregular items in 2003? The answer to this question is at the end of this chapter.

Comparative Analysis

As mentioned earlier, in assessing financial performance, investors and creditors are interested in the sustainable earnings of a company. In addition to this, they are also interested in making comparisons from period to period. Throughout this book, we have relied on three types of comparisons to improve the usefulness of financial information for decision-making:

1. **Intracompany basis.** Comparisons within a company are often useful to detect changes in financial relationships and significant trends. For example, a comparison of PotashCorp's current-year cash amount with its prior-year cash amount shows either an increase or a decrease. Likewise, a comparison of PotashCorp's year-end cash amount with the amount of its total assets at year end shows the proportion of total assets that is cash.
2. **Intercompany basis.** Comparisons with other companies give insight into a company's competitive position. For example, PotashCorp's net sales for the year can be compared with the net sales of Agrium Inc., one of its competitors in the agricultural chemicals industry.
3. **Industry averages.** Comparisons with industry averages give information about a company's relative position within the industry. For example, PotashCorp's financial data can be compared with the averages for its industry that are calculated by financial ratings organizations such as Dun & Bradstreet, the *Financial Post*, and Statistics Canada, or with information provided on the Internet by organizations such as Yahoo!, on its finance site.

In assessing a company's financial performance, we usually start with the financial statements. But, it is important to also review other financial and non-financial information included in the company's annual report. Other financial information includes a management discussion and analysis (MD&A) of the company's financial position and a summary of historical key financial figures and ratios.

Non-financial information includes a discussion of the company's mission, goals and objectives, market position, people, and products. Understanding a company's goals and objectives is important when interpreting financial performance. As mentioned in our feature story, PotashCorp's annual report not only presents the company's goals but also compares its performance to those goals and identifies its targets for the upcoming year.

We must also consider the economic circumstances a company is operating in. Economic measures such as the rate of interest, inflation, unemployment, and changes in demand and supply can have a significant impact on a company's performance. For example, it would be difficult to properly interpret PotashCorp's performance without knowing that potash prices are at an all-time high due to increasing demand and tight supply.

Financial analysis must also include non-financial measures in addition to financial measures, such as those we have calculated in this textbook. Some analysts argue that non-financial, or qualitative, measures are even more important than financial, or quantitative, measures in assessing success. Financial measures can only evaluate past performance. Non-financial measures may be better predictors of future performance. Non-financial performance measures include factors such as customer satisfaction, employee satisfaction, product reputation, innovation, knowledge resources, sustainable development, and so on. As mentioned in our feature story, PotashCorp's annual report received an award of excellence for its non-financial reporting (in addition to its financial reporting). It was the first fertilizer producer in North America to include a sustainability report documenting the company's economic impact, social involvement, and progress in safety, health, and the environment.

While non-financial measures are important, the focus of this chapter is on financial measures. Various tools are used to evaluate the significance of financial data. Three commonly used tools follow:

1. **Horizontal analysis.** This tool evaluates a series of financial statement data over a period of time.
2. **Vertical analysis.** This tool evaluates financial statement data by expressing each item in a financial statement as a percentage of a base amount for the same period of time.
3. **Ratio analysis.** This tool expresses relationships among selected items of financial statement data.

Horizontal analysis is mostly used in intracompany comparisons. Two features in published financial statements make this type of comparison easier. First, each of the financial statements is presented on a comparative basis for a minimum of two years. Second, a summary of selected financial data is presented for a series of 5 to 10 years or more.

Vertical analysis is used in both intracompany and intercompany comparisons. Ratio analysis is used in all three types of comparisons.

Horizontal Analysis

Horizontal analysis, also called **trend analysis**, is a technique for evaluating a series of financial statement data over a period of time. Its purpose is to determine the increase or decrease that has taken place, and this is expressed as either an amount or a percentage. For example, net sales for the last five years for PotashCorp are shown below in dollars (U.S. millions) and percentages:

study objective 2

Explain and apply horizontal analysis.

2004	2003	2002	2001	2000
$2,901.4	$2,465.8	$1,913.8	$2,072.7	$2,231.6
130.0%	110.5%	85.8%	92.9%	100.0%

In the above illustration, we have assumed that 2000 is the base year, and have expressed net sales in each year as a percentage of the base-period amount. This is done by dividing the amount for the specific year we are analyzing by the base-year amount. For example, we can determine that net sales in 2004 are 130 percent of net sales in 2000 by dividing U.S. $2,901.4 million by U.S. $2,231.6 million. In other words, net sales in 2004 are 30 percent greater than sales five years earlier, in 2000. From this horizontal analysis, we can easily see PotashCorp's sales trend. Net sales declined in 2001 and 2002, before turning around and increasing in 2003 and 2004.

We can also measure the percentage change for each specific period by dividing the dollar amount of the change between the specific year and the base year by the base-year amount. For example, if we set 2003 as our base year, we can see that net sales increased by U.S. $435.6 million ($2.901.4 − $2,465.8) between 2004 and 2003. This increase can then be expressed as a percentage, 17.7 percent, by dividing the amount of the change between the two years, U.S. $435.6 million, by the amount in the base year, U.S. $2,465.8. That is, in 2004 net sales increased by 17.7 percent compared to 2003.

Balance Sheet

To further illustrate horizontal analysis, we will use PotashCorp's financial statements. Condensed balance sheets for 2004 and 2003, showing dollar and percentage changes for the two-year period, are shown in Illustration 14-2.

Illustration 14-2

Horizontal analysis of balance sheet

POTASH CORPORATION OF SASKATCHEWAN INC.
Balance Sheet
December 31
(in U.S. millions)

	2004	2003	Increase (Decrease) Amount	Increase (Decrease) Percent
Assets				
Current assets				
Cash and cash equivalents	$ 458.9	$ 4.7	$454.2	9,663.8%
Accounts receivable	352.6	305.0	47.6	15.6%
Inventories	396.8	395.2	1.6	0.4%
Prepaid expenses and other current assets	35.3	29.0	6.3	21.7%
Total current assets	1,243.6	733.9	509.7	69.5%
Property, plant, and equipment	3,098.9	3,108.1	(9.2)	(0.3)%
Intangible and other assets	784.3	725.3	59.0	8.1%
Total assets	$5,126.8	$4,567.3	$559.5	12.3%
Liabilities and Shareholders' Equity				
Liabilities				
Current liabilities	$ 703.7	$ 557.8	$145.9	26.2%
Long-term liabilities	2,037.5	2,035.7	1.8	0.1%
Total liabilities	2,741.2	2,593.5	147.7	5.7%
Shareholders' equity	2,385.6	1,973.8	411.8	20.9%
Total liabilities and shareholders' equity	$5,126.8	$4,567.3	$559.5	12.3%

Note that, in a horizontal analysis, while the amount column of the increase or decrease is additive (the total change is an increase of U.S. $559.5 million), the percentage column is not additive (12.3 percent is *not* a total).

The horizontal analysis of PotashCorp's comparative balance sheet shows that several changes occurred between 2003 and 2004. In the current assets section, cash and cash equivalents appear to have increased by a whopping 9,663.8 percent! This number appears disproportionately large because we are calculating a percentage change based on a very small number in 2003 (U.S. $4.7 million). Accounts receivable increased by U.S. $47.6 million, or 15.6 percent. We will look at the statement of earnings in the next section to determine if sales increased proportionately to the receivables increase. If not, this may be an indicator of slow-moving receivables. Prepaid expenses and other current assets increased by U.S. $6.3 million, or 21.7 percent.

In the long-term assets section, intangible and other assets increased by U.S. $59 million, or 8.1 percent. The notes to PotashCorp's financial statements explain that this increase is mostly due to its long-term investments, which have increased by the amount of equity investees' earnings.

PotashCorp's current liabilities rose by U.S. $145.9 million, or 26.2 percent. Details in the notes to the financial statements about the company's current liabilities indicate that its accounts payable and income taxes payable both increased significantly in 2004. Its long-term liabilities increased only marginally.

In the shareholders' equity section, increased earnings accounted for most of the U.S. $411.8-million increase. We can see that PotashCorp is financing its business by retaining earnings, rather than by assuming additional long-term debt.

Statement of Earnings

Illustration 14-3 presents a horizontal analysis of PotashCorp's condensed statement of earnings for the years 2004 and 2003.

Illustration 14-3 ◄

Horizontal analysis of statement of earnings

POTASH CORPORATION OF SASKATCHEWAN INC.
Statement of Earnings
Year Ended December 31
(in U.S. millions)

	2004	2003	Increase (Decrease) Amount	Percent
Net sales	$2,901.4	$2,465.8	$435.6	17.7%
Cost of goods sold	2,220.0	2,085.4	134.6	6.5%
Gross profit	681.4	380.4	301.0	79.1%
Selling and administrative expenses	130.6	96.1	34.5	35.9%
Other operating expenses	115.9	373.1	(257.2)	(68.9%)
Earnings from operations	434.9	(88.8)	523.7	n/a
Interest expense	84.0	91.3	(7.3)	(8.0%)
Other revenue	79.4	33.2	46.2	139.2%
Earnings (loss) before income tax	430.3	(146.9)	577.2	n/a
Income taxes	131.7	(20.6)	152.3	n/a
Net earnings (loss)	$ 298.6	$ (126.3)	$424.9	n/a

A horizontal analysis of the statement of earnings shows that net sales increased by U.S. $435.6 million, or 17.7 percent. This appears to be reasonably consistent with the 15.6 percent increase in accounts receivable we noted in the balance sheet. That is, if sales increase, it is not surprising to also have an increase in receivables. The fact that the increase in accounts receivables is less than the increase in sales reassures us about how collectible the receivables are. Interestingly, while net sales increased by 17.7 percent, cost of goods sold increased by only 6.5 percent.

PotashCorp's selling and administrative expenses increased by U.S. $34.5 million, or 35.9 percent—a higher percentage increase than net sales. However, its other expenses decreased by U.S. $257.2 million, or 68.9 percent. This was due to expenses incurred in 2003 related to plant shutdowns in Tennessee, Louisiana, North Carolina, and Chile that were not incurred in 2004. Note that these expenses are not reported as discontinued operations because only a few plants were shut down, not all. That is, PotashCorp did not discontinue operations of an entire business segment.

Its other revenue increased by U.S. $46.2 million, or 139.2 percent, mainly due to a gain on the sale of long-term investments. Note that the gain on sale of long-term investments is not an irregular item. It may be unusual, but it is not irregular. PotashCorp did not report any irregular items in 2004 or 2003. If it had, these items should be excluded from our comparisons.

The measurement of changes from period to period in percentages is fairly straightforward and quite useful. However, the calculations can be affected by complications. As mentioned earlier about the change in cash and cash equivalents, if an item has a small value in a base year and a large value in the next year, the percentage change may not be meaningful. In addition, if an item has no value in a base year and a value in the next year, no percentage change can be determined. And, if a negative amount appears in the base year, and a positive amount in the following year, or vice versa, no percentage change can be calculated. For example, no percentage could be calculated for PotashCorp's earnings figures because it incurred a net loss in 2003.

We have not done a horizontal analysis of PotashCorp's statement of retained earnings and cash flow statement as this is not as useful as horizontal analyses done on the balance

Helpful Hint When using horizontal analysis, both dollar amount changes and percentage changes need to be examined. It is not necessarily bad if a company's earnings are growing at a declining rate. The **amount** of increase may be the same as or more than the base year, but the **percentage** change may be less because the base is greater each year.

sheet and statement of earnings. The amounts presented in the statement of retained earnings and cash flow statement already give details of the changes between two periods (the opening and ending balance sheet dates).

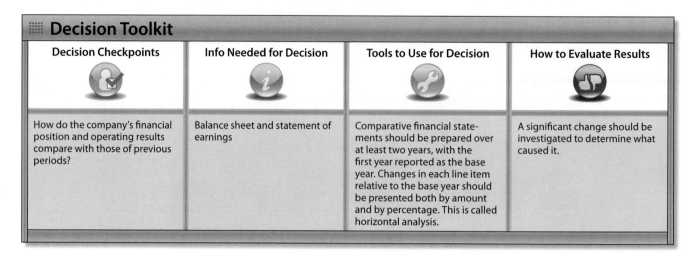

Decision Toolkit

Decision Checkpoints	Info Needed for Decision	Tools to Use for Decision	How to Evaluate Results
How do the company's financial position and operating results compare with those of previous periods?	Balance sheet and statement of earnings	Comparative financial statements should be prepared over at least two years, with the first year reported as the base year. Changes in each line item relative to the base year should be presented both by amount and by percentage. This is called horizontal analysis.	A significant change should be investigated to determine what caused it.

BEFORE YOU GO ON . . .

▶Review It

1. Distinguish between intracompany, intercompany, and industry comparisons.
2. What are the different tools that are used to compare financial information?
3. How is a percentage change from a base period calculated?

▶Do It

Summary financial information for Bonora Ltd. is as follows:

	2006	2005
Current assets	$234,000	$180,000
Noncurrent assets	756,000	420,000
Total assets	$990,000	$600,000

Calculate the amount and percentage changes for 2006, using horizontal analysis.

Action Plan

- Find the percentage change by dividing the amount of the increase by the 2005 (base year) amount.

Solution

the navigator

		Increase in 2006
	Amount	Percent
Current assets	$ 54,000	30% [($234,000 − $180,000) ÷ $180,000]
Noncurrent assets	336,000	80% [($756,000 − $420,000) ÷ $420,000]
Total assets	$390,000	65% [($990,000 − $600,000) ÷ $600,000]

Vertical Analysis

Vertical analysis is a technique for evaluating financial statement data that expresses each item in a financial statement as a percentage of a base amount. For example, on a balance sheet we might say that current assets are 24.3 percent of total assets (total assets being the base amount). Or, on a statement of earnings we might say that cost of goods sold is 76.5 percent of net sales (net sales being the base amount).

Balance Sheet

Illustration 14-4 presents a vertical analysis of PotashCorp's comparative balance sheet. The base for the asset items is **total assets**, and the base for the liability and shareholders' equity items is **total liabilities and shareholders' equity**, which equals total assets.

Illustration 14-4 ◄

Vertical analysis of a balance sheet

POTASH CORPORATION OF SASKATCHEWAN INC. ⟋⟍ PotashCorp
Balance Sheet
December 31
(in U.S. millions)

	2004		2003	
	Amount	Percent	Amount	Percent
Assets				
Current assets				
Cash and cash equivalents	$ 458.9	9.0%	$ 4.7	0.1%
Accounts receivable	352.6	6.9%	305.0	6.7%
Inventories	396.8	7.7%	395.2	8.7%
Prepaid expenses and other current assets	35.3	0.7%	29.0	0.6%
Total current assets	1,243.6	24.3%	733.9	16.1%
Property, plant, and equipment	3,098.9	60.4%	3,108.1	68.1%
Intangible and other assets	784.3	15.3%	725.3	15.8%
Total assets	$5,126.8	100.0%	$4,567.3	100.0%
Liabilities and Shareholders' Equity				
Liabilities				
Current liabilities	$ 703.7	13.7%	$ 557.8	12.2%
Long-term liabilities	2,037.5	39.8%	2,035.7	44.6%
Total liabilities	2,741.2	53.5%	2,593.5	56.8%
Shareholders' equity	2,385.6	46.5%	1,973.8	43.2%
Total liabilities and shareholders' equity	$5,126.8	100.0%	$4,567.3	100.0%

Vertical analysis shows the relative size of each category in the balance sheet. It also allows us to compare the percentage sizes of the individual asset, liability, and shareholders' equity items. For example, we can see that even though accounts receivable increased by 15.6 percent from 2003 to 2004 in our horizontal analysis in Illustration 14-2, they remained relatively constant as a percentage of total assets at 6.7 percent in 2003 and 6.9 percent in 2004.

Property, plant, and equipment changed very little (0.3 percent) between 2003 and 2004, according to our horizontal analysis in Illustration 14-2. However, it decreased as a percentage of total assets, from 68.1 percent in 2003 to 60.4 percent in 2004. Intangible and other assets increased by 8.1 percent in our horizontal analysis, but it changed very little as a percentage of total assets, from 15.8 percent in 2003 to 15.3 percent in 2004. As the increase was mostly due to an increase in its investee's equity earnings, it makes sense that total assets would also increase proportionately.

Current liabilities increased only slightly from 12.2 percent to 13.7 percent as a percentage of total liabilities and shareholders' equity from 2003 to 2004, despite reporting a 26.2-percent horizontal increase in Illustration 14-2. Long-term liabilities actually decreased from 44.6 percent in 2003 to 39.8 percent in 2004 as a percentage of total liabilities and shareholders' equity. Shareholders' equity increased from 43.2 percent in 2003 to 46.5 percent in 2004 as a percentage of total liabilities and shareholders' equity.

Statement of Earnings

Illustration 14-5 presents a vertical analysis of PotashCorp's comparative statement of earnings on the following page. The base for this analysis is **net sales**.

Illustration 14-5 ▶

Vertical analysis of
statement of earnings

POTASH CORPORATION OF SASKATCHEWAN INC.
Statement of Earnings
Year Ended December 31
(in U.S. millions)

	2004 Amount	2004 Percent	2003 Amount	2003 Percent
Net sales	$2,901.4	100.0%	$2,465.8	100.0%
Cost of goods sold	2,220.0	76.5%	2,085.4	84.6%
Gross profit	681.4	23.5%	380.4	15.4%
Selling and administrative expenses	130.6	4.5%	96.1	3.9%
Other operating expenses	115.9	4.0%	373.1	15.1%
Earnings from operations	434.9	15.0%	(88.8)	(3.6%)
Interest expense	84.0	2.9%	91.3	3.7%
Other revenue	79.4	2.7%	33.2	1.3%
Earnings (loss) before income tax	430.3	14.8%	(146.9)	(6.0%)
Income taxes	131.7	4.5%	(20.6)	(0.9%)
Net earnings (loss)	$ 298.6	10.3%	$ (126.3)	(5.1%)

Although cost of goods sold increased by 6.5 percent in 2004 in our horizontal analysis in Illustration 14-3, it actually declined as a percentage of sales from 84.6 percent in 2003 to 76.5 percent in 2004. As we found in our horizontal analysis, selling and administrative expenses increased and other operating expenses decreased. And, of course, net earnings increased significantly to 10.3 percent of sales in 2004, compared to a net loss of 5.1 percent reported in 2003.

Although vertical analysis can also be performed on the statement of retained earnings and the cash flow statement, this is seldom done. As mentioned earlier, the value of these statements comes from the analysis of the changes during the year, and not from percentage comparisons of these changes against a base amount.

Vertical analysis also make it easier to compare different companies. For example, one of PotashCorp's main competitors is Agrium Inc. Using vertical analysis, we can make a more meaningful comparison of the condensed statements of earnings of PotashCorp and Agrium, as shown in Illustration 14-6.

Illustration 14-6 ▶

Intercompany comparison
by vertical analysis

POTASHCORP AND AGRIUM
Statement of Earnings
Year Ended December 31, 2004
(in U.S. millions)

	PotashCorp Amount	PotashCorp Percent	Agrium Amount	Agrium Percent
Net sales	$2,901	100.0%	$2,838	100.0%
Cost of goods sold	2,220	76.5%	1,928	67.9%
Gross profit	681	23.5%	910	32.1%
Selling and administrative expenses	130	4.5%	301	10.6%
Other operating expenses	116	4.0%	142	5.0%
Earnings from operations	435	15.0%	467	16.5%
Interest expense	84	2.9%	55	2.0%
Other revenue	79	2.7%	0	0.0%
Earnings before income tax	430	14.8%	412	14.5%
Income taxes	132	4.5%	136	4.8%
Net earnings	$ 298	10.3%	$ 276	9.7%

PotashCorp's cost of goods sold is a higher percentage of net sales at 76.5 percent than Agrium's at 67.9 percent. PotashCorp's selling and administrative expenses, however, are significantly lower than Agrium's, while its interest expense is slightly higher. PotashCorp's net earnings are also slightly higher at 10.3 percent of net sales than Agrium's at 9.7 percent of net sales.

Although PotashCorp and Agrium are roughly the same size, vertical analysis clearly shows the differences between the two companies. Vertical analysis is also useful in comparing companies of different sizes, reducing each financial statement item to a comparable percentage.

Decision Toolkit

Decision Checkpoints	Info Needed for Decision	Tools to Use for Decision	How to Evaluate Results
How do the relationships between items in this year's financial statements compare with last year's relationships or those of competitors?	Balance sheet and statement of earnings	Each line item on the balance sheet should be presented as a percentage of total assets (total liabilities and shareholders' equity). Each line item on the statement of earnings should be presented as a percentage of net sales. This is called vertical analysis.	Any difference, either across years or between companies, should be investigated to determine the cause.

BEFORE YOU GO ON . . .

▶ Review It

1. What is vertical analysis?
2. What base is used to calculate the percentage size of an amount reported in a balance sheet? In a statement of earnings?
3. How can vertical analysis be used to compare two companies of differing sizes?

▶ Do It

Summary financial information for Bonora Ltd. is as follows:

	2006	2005
Current assets	$234,000	$180,000
Noncurrent assets	756,000	420,000
Total assets	$990,000	$600,000

Calculate the percentage sizes of each category for each year, using vertical analysis.

Action Plan

- Find the relative percentage by dividing the specific asset amount by total assets for each year.

Solution

	2006		2005	
	Amount	Percent	Amount	Percent
Current assets	$234,000	23.6% ($234,000 ÷ $990,000)	$180,000	30% ($180,000 ÷ $660,000)
Noncurrent assets	756,000	76.4% ($756,000 ÷ $990,000	420,000	70% ($420,000 ÷ $600,000)
Total assets	$990,000	100.0%	$600,000	100%

the navigator

Ratio Analysis

Ratio analysis expresses the relationship between selected financial statement items. Ratios are generally classified into three types:

1. **Liquidity ratios.** These measure the short-term ability of the company to pay its maturing obligations and to meet unexpected needs for cash.
2. **Solvency ratios.** These measure the ability of the company to survive over a long period of time.
3. **Profitability ratios.** These measure the earnings or operating success of a company for a specific period of time.

In previous chapters, we presented liquidity, solvency, and profitability ratios to evaluate the financial position and performance of a company. In this section, we provide a summary listing of these ratios. Chapter and page references to earlier discussions are included so you can review any individual ratio. In addition, there is an example of a comprehensive financial analysis using these ratios in the appendix to this chapter. This analysis uses three categories of comparisons: (1) **intracompany**, comparing two years of data for PotashCorp, (2) **intercompany**, comparing PotashCorp and Agrium, and (3) **industry**, comparing both companies to industry averages for the fertilizer industry.

Liquidity Ratios

Liquidity ratios measure the short-term ability of a company to pay its maturing obligations and to meet unexpected needs for cash. Short-term creditors, such as bankers and suppliers, are particularly interested in assessing liquidity. Illustration 14-7 lists the liquidity ratios we have seen in this textbook. It is important to remember that these are only examples of commonly used liquidity ratios. You will find more examples as you learn more about financial analysis.

Illustration 14-7 ▶

Summary of liquidity ratios

Ratio	Formula	Purpose	Discussion
Working capital	Current assets − Current liabilities	Measures short-term debt-paying ability	Ch. 2, p. 65
Current ratio	$\dfrac{\text{Current assets}}{\text{Current liabilities}}$	Measures short-term debt-paying ability	Ch. 2, p. 65
Inventory turnover	$\dfrac{\text{Cost of goods sold}}{\text{Average inventory}}$	Measures liquidity of inventory	Ch. 6, p. 280
Days in inventory	$\dfrac{365 \text{ days}}{\text{Inventory turnover}}$	Measures the of number days inventory is on hand	Ch. 6, p. 280
Receivables turnover	$\dfrac{\text{Net credit sales}}{\text{Average gross accounts receivable}}$	Measures liquidity of receivables	Ch. 8, p. 374
Average collection period	$\dfrac{365 \text{ days}}{\text{Receivables turnover}}$	Measures number of days receivables are outstanding	Ch. 8, p. 374
Cash current debt coverage	$\dfrac{\text{Cash provided (used) by operating activities}}{\text{Average current liabilities}}$	Measures short-term debt-paying ability (cash basis)	Ch. 13, p. 639

Solvency Ratios

Solvency ratios measure the ability of a company to survive over a long period of time. Long-term creditors and shareholders are interested in a company's long-run solvency, particularly its ability to pay interest as it comes due and to repay the face value of debt at maturity. Illustration 14-8 lists the solvency ratios we have seen in this textbook.

Illustration 14-8 ▶

Summary of solvency ratios

Ratio	Formula	Purpose	Discussion
Debt to total assets	$\dfrac{\text{Total liabilities}}{\text{Total assets}}$	Measures percentage of total assets provided by creditors	Ch. 2, p. 66
Free cash flow	Cash provided (used) by operating activities − Net capital expenditures − Dividends paid	Measures cash available for expanding operations or paying more dividends	Ch. 2, p. 68
Times interest earned	$\dfrac{\text{Earnings before interest expense and income tax expense (EBIT)}}{\text{Interest expense}}$	Measures ability to meet interest payments	Ch. 10, p. 478
Cash total debt coverage	$\dfrac{\text{Cash provided (used) by operating activities}}{\text{Average total liabilities}}$	Measures long-term debt-paying ability (cash basis)	Ch. 13, p. 640

Profitability Ratios

Profitability ratios measure the earnings or operating success of a company for a specific period of time. A company's earnings, or lack of them, affect its ability to obtain debt and equity financing, its liquidity position, and its growth. As a result, both creditors and investors are interested in evaluating profitability. Profitability is frequently used as the ultimate test of management's operating effectiveness. Illustration 14-9 lists the profitability ratios we have seen in this textbook.

Ratio	Formula	Purpose	Discussion
Earnings per share	$\dfrac{\text{Net earnings available to common shareholders}}{\text{Weighted average number of common shares}}$	Measures net earnings earned on each common share	Ch. 2, p. 62
Price-earnings ratio	$\dfrac{\text{Market price per share}}{\text{Earnings per share}}$	Measures relationship between market price per share and earnings per share	Ch. 2, p. 63
Gross profit margin	$\dfrac{\text{Gross profit}}{\text{Net sales}}$	Measures margin between selling price and cost of goods sold	Ch. 5, p. 225
Profit margin	$\dfrac{\text{Net earnings}}{\text{Net sales}}$	Measures net earnings generated by each dollar of sales	Ch. 5, p. 226
Return on assets	$\dfrac{\text{Net earnings}}{\text{Average total assets}}$	Measures overall profitability of assets	Ch. 9, p. 425
Asset turnover	$\dfrac{\text{Net sales}}{\text{Average total assets}}$	Measures how efficiently assets are used to generate sales	Ch. 9, p. 425
Payout ratio	$\dfrac{\text{Cash dividends}}{\text{Net earnings}}$	Measures percentage of earnings distributed as cash dividends	Ch. 11, p. 533
Dividend yield	$\dfrac{\text{Dividend per share}}{\text{Market price per share}}$	Measures earnings generated by each share, based on the market price per share	Ch. 11, p. 533
Return on common shareholders' equity	$\dfrac{\text{Net earnings available to common shareholders}}{\text{Average common shareholders' equity}}$	Measures profitability of shareholders' investment	Ch. 11, p. 535

Illustration 14-9 ◀

Summary of profitability ratios

As analysis tools, ratios can give clues about underlying conditions that may not be seen from an inspection of the individual components of a particular ratio. But a single ratio by itself is not very meaningful. Accordingly, ratios must be interpreted along with the information gained from a detailed review of the financial information, including horizontal and vertical analyses, and non-financial information described earlier in the chapter.

ACCOUNTING MATTERS!   Investor Perspective

Al and Mark Rosen recommend the following five steps in analyzing a company: (1) force yourself to read the company's quarterly and annual financial statements, including all the notes and the management discussion and analysis, (2) watch for too-good-to-be-true situations, (3) be careful about who you trust, (4) watch for specific accounting games and poor financial statement disclosures, and (5) look out for executive compensation schemes that base management performance bonuses on slippery accounting figures.

Source: Al Rosen and Mark Rosen, "Dig Deeper," *Canadian Business,* January 17–30, 2005, 27.

BEFORE YOU GO ON . . .

▶Review It

1. What are liquidity ratios? Explain working capital, the current ratio, inventory turnover, days in inventory, receivables turnover, average collection period, and cash current debt coverage.
2. What are solvency ratios? Explain debt to total assets, free cash flow, times interest earned, and cash total debt coverage.
3. What are profitability ratios? Explain earnings per share, the price-earnings ratio, gross profit margin, profit margin, return on assets, asset turnover, the payout ratio, dividend yield, and return on common shareholders' equity.

the navigator

Quality of Earnings

study objective 5

Understand the concept of quality of earnings.

In evaluating the financial performance of a company, the quality of earnings is extremely important to analysts. A company that has a high **quality of earnings** provides full and transparent information that will not confuse or mislead users of the financial statements. PotashCorp, described in our feature story, has a high quality of earnings, as the information it gives users is thorough and clear. Some of the factors that can affect the quality of earnings include the choice of accounting principles, the use of professional judgement, and pro forma earnings. These topics are discussed in the next sections.

Alternative Accounting Principles

Variations among companies in their use of generally accepted accounting principles may lessen comparability and reduce the quality of earnings. For example, Agrium, one of PotashCorp's competitors, chose to adopt the new accounting principle for asset retirement obligations early, effective January 1, 2003. PotashCorp adopted this principle effective January 1, 2004. Consequently, Agrium would have higher assets and liabilities than PotashCorp in 2003 simply because of the early inclusion of asset retirement costs in Agrium's property, plant, and equipment and long-term liabilities. It would also have a higher amortization expense and lower net earnings in comparison to PotashCorp.

Companies may choose from a large number of acceptable accounting principles, such as different inventory cost flow assumptions (FIFO or average) or amortization methods (straight-line, declining-balance, or units-of-activity). Different choices result in differing financial positions, which again affect comparability. All of these are what we call "artificial," or timing, differences. Although there may be differences year by year, in total, over the life of the asset, there is no difference.

As well, in more and more industries, competition is global. To evaluate a company's standing, an investor must make comparisons to companies from other countries. For example, although both PotashCorp and Agrium are Canadian, other competitors include Yara International, of Norway, and the Mosaic Company in the United States. Although differences in accounting principles might be detectable from reading the notes to the financial statements, adjusting the financial data to compensate for the different principles is difficult, if not impossible, in some cases.

Professional Judgement

We must accept that management has to use professional judgement in choosing the most appropriate principle for the circumstances. So, different accounting principles are likely to be used by different companies. In addition, many estimates are required in preparing financial information. Estimates are used, for example, in determining the allowance for uncollectible receivables, periodic amortization, and market values of trading and available-for-sale securities.

When managers choose accounting principles and estimates to manage earnings, the quality of the earnings will decrease. Fortunately, the chief executive officer and chief financial officer of publicly traded companies must ensure, and personally declare, that the reported financial information is accurate, relevant, and understandable. In addition, audit committees are held responsible for quizzing management on the degree of aggressiveness or conservatism that has been applied and on the quality of underlying accounting principles, key estimates, and judgements.

A strong corporate governance process, including an active board of directors and audit committee, is essential to ensure the quality of earnings. As mentioned in our feature story, PotashCorp won an award for its corporate governance disclosure. Following best practices in corporate governance helps a company commit to transparency and accountability. Betty-Ann Heggie, senior vice-president of corporate relations at PotashCorp, says, "Reputation is the most valuable asset any business can have and only by disclosing entirely transparent corporate information can we hope to win people's trust and, in the course of events, enhance our value with investors."

Pro Forma Earnings

Publicly traded companies are required to present their earnings in accordance with generally accepted accounting principles. Many companies also report another measure of earnings in addition to GAAP earnings. This measure is called pro forma earnings. **Pro forma earnings** are a non-GAAP earnings measure that excludes items which the company thinks are unusual or nonrecurring.

Different companies use different definitions of pro forma earnings. These definitions have been known to exclude costs such as interest expense, stock compensation expenses, and impairment losses. For example, fibre-optics manufacturer JDS Uniphase Corporation, with headquarters in Ottawa and San Jose, reported U.S. $67 million of pro forma earnings in a recent year. These pro forma earnings excluded things like goodwill, stock-option charges, and losses on investments. Once these costs were added back, they resulted in a staggering U.S. $50.6 billion loss—a difference of nearly U.S. $50.7 billion! Such a large difference in earnings between GAAP numbers and pro forma numbers is not all that unusual. At one time, the 100 largest companies on the Nasdaq stock exchange reported total pro forma earnings of U.S. $19.1 billion. This was U.S. $101.4 billion more than GAAP-based numbers, which added up to a loss of U.S. $82.3 billion.

Since there are no rules as to how to prepare pro forma earnings, companies have free rein to exclude any items they consider inappropriate for measuring their performance. Consequently, comparisons of pro forma earnings among companies can be tricky.

Recently, Canadian securities regulators have cracked down on companies that abuse the flexibility that pro forma numbers allow. Publicly traded companies are now expected to give GAAP numbers alongside non-GAAP earnings, explain how pro forma numbers are calculated, and detail why they exclude certain items required by GAAP. Everyone seems to agree that pro forma numbers can be useful and can provide insights into a company's sustainable earnings, as long as they are clearly detailed and explained.

ACCOUNTING MATTERS!   Investor Perspective

Biovail Corporation, a Mississauga-based pharmaceutical company, reported three different net earnings figures in a recent set of financial statements. It reported U.S. $89 million of net earnings using U.S. GAAP, which was significantly lower than the U.S. $468 million of net earnings it reported using Canadian GAAP. In addition, Biovail also reported $757 million of pro forma earnings, which excluded one-time items as well as some research and development expenses.

Which of these widely different numbers should investors use? There is no easy answer to that question. However, an educated investor who understands the differences between these numbers is the best informed investor.

Source: Al Rosen, "All's Fair in Accounting," *Canadian Business*, November 23, 2003, 27.

Decision Toolkit

Decision Checkpoints	Info Needed for Decision	Tools to Use for Decision	How to Evaluate Results
Are efforts to evaluate the company helped or hampered by the quality of earnings?	Financial statements as well as other information disclosed	Review accounting principles, estimates, and pro forma earnings for reasonableness. Assess strength of corporate governance processes.	If there are any irregularities, the analysis should be relied on with caution.

BEFORE YOU GO ON . . .

▶ Review It

1. Describe some of the factors that may reduce the quality of earnings.
2. Explain how alternative accounting principles can affect the comparability and quality of earnings.
3. How can corporate governance help the quality of earnings?
4. Explain what is meant by "pro forma earnings."

APPENDIX 14A ▶ COMPREHENSIVE ILLUSTRATION OF RATIO ANALYSIS

In previous chapters, we calculated many ratios that are used to evaluate the financial health and performance of a company. In this appendix, we give a comprehensive review of these ratios and discuss some important relationships among them. In this review, we use the following comparisons:

1. **Intracompany comparisons** covering two years (2003 and 2004) for the Potash Corporation of Saskatchewan Inc. (PotashCorp)
2. **Intercompany comparisons** for the year ended December 31, 2004, for Agrium Inc., one of PotashCorp's competitors
3. **Industry average comparisons** for 2004 for the agricultural chemicals industry. For some of the ratios that we use, industry comparisons are not available. These are marked "n/a."

You will recall that PotashCorp's balance sheet was presented earlier in the chapter in Illustration 14-2 and its statement of earnings in Illustration 14-3. We will use the information in these two financial statements, in addition to the following data, to calculate PotashCorp's ratios:

(in U.S. millions, except for per share information)	2004	2003
Cash provided by operating activities	$649.6	$381.5
Net capital expenditures	218.0	150.7
Total dividends paid	56.1	52.3
Dividends per share	0.55	0.50
Market price per share	83.06	43.24
Weighted average number of shares	108.0	104.5

Although the calculations are not shown, you can use these data to calculate each ratio yourself to make sure you understand where the numbers came from. Detailed financial data are not shown for either Agrium or the industry.

Liquidity Ratios

Liquidity ratios measure the ability of a company to pay its current liabilities. Consequently, liquidity ratios focus mainly on the relationships between current assets and current liabilities reported on the balance sheet and related accounts on the statement of earnings. Cash provided by operating activities, reported on the cash flow statement, is also useful in assessing liquidity. Liquidity ratios include working capital, the current ratio, cash current debt coverage, receivables turnover, average collection period, inventory turnover, and days in inventory.

Working Capital

Working capital is the difference between current assets and current liabilities. It is one measure of liquidity. However, as we learned in Chapter 2, the current ratio—which expresses current assets and current liabilities as a ratio rather than as an amount—is a more useful indicator of liquidity. Consequently, we will not illustrate working capital again here, and will focus instead on the current ratio.

Current Ratio

The current ratio expresses the relationship of current assets to current liabilities, and is calculated by dividing current assets by current liabilities. It is widely used for evaluating a company's liquidity and short-term debt-paying ability. The 2004 and 2003 current ratios for PotashCorp and comparative data are shown in Illustration 14A-1.

Illustration 14A-1 ▼

Current ratio

Ratio	Formula	Indicates	PotashCorp 2004	2003	Agrium 2004	Industry 2004
Current ratio	Current assets / Current liabilities	Short-term debt-paying ability	1.8:1	1.3:1	2.5:1	1.9:1

What does the ratio actually mean? The 2004 ratio of 1.8:1 means that for every dollar of current liabilities, PotashCorp has $1.80 of current assets. PotashCorp's current ratio increased between 2003 and 2004, mainly because of a significant increase in its cash and cash equivalents. Recall from Illustration 14-2 that current assets increased by 69.5 percent, while current liabilities increased by only 26.2 percent.

PotashCorp's current ratio is less than Agrium's, but it is consistent with the industry average. However, it is too early in our analysis to draw any conclusions about PotashCorp's liquidity because the current ratio is only one measure of liquidity. It does not take into account the composition of the current assets. For example, a satisfactory current ratio could hide the fact that a portion of current assets may be tied up in uncollectible accounts receivable or slow-moving inventory.

Cash Current Debt Coverage

One disadvantage of the current ratio is that it uses year-end balances of current asset and current liability accounts. These year-end balances may not reflect the company's position during most of the year. A ratio that partially corrects this problem is the cash current debt coverage ratio. Because it uses cash provided by operating activities, which covers a period of time, rather than current assets, which represent a balance at a point in time, it may be a better indicator of liquidity.

PotashCorp's cash current debt coverage ratio is shown in Illustration 14A-2 on the following page.

Ratio	Formula	Indicates	PotashCorp 2004	PotashCorp 2003	Agrium 2004	Industry 2004
Cash current debt coverage	$\dfrac{\text{Cash provided (used) by operating activities}}{\text{Average current liabilities}}$	Short-term debt-paying ability (cash basis)	1.0 times	0.6 times	0.8 times	n/a

Illustration 14A-2 ▲

Cash current debt coverage

PotashCorp's cash provided by operating activities increased from U.S. $381.5 million in 2003 to U.S. $649.6 million in 2004. This represents an increase of 70.3 percent! However, its current liabilities only increased by 26.2 percent during the same period. Consequently, the cash current debt coverage increased in 2004 to 1.0 time from 0.6 times in 2003.

PotashCorp's cash current debt coverage is higher than Agrium's. Industry averages are not available for cash-based ratios.

Receivables Turnover

We mentioned earlier that a high current ratio is not always a good indication of liquidity. The high result could be because of increased receivables resulting from uncollectible accounts. The ratio used to assess the liquidity of the receivables is the receivables turnover. It measures the number of times, on average, that receivables are collected during the period. The receivables turnover is calculated by dividing net credit sales (sales on account less sales returns and allowances and discounts) by average gross accounts receivable (before the allowance for doubtful accounts is deducted) during the year.

Illustration 14A-3 ▼

Receivables turnover

The receivables turnover ratio for PotashCorp is shown in Illustration 14A-3.

Ratio	Formula	Indicates	PotashCorp 2004	PotashCorp 2003	Agrium 2004	Industry 2004
Receivables turnover	$\dfrac{\text{Net credit sales}}{\text{Average gross accounts receivable}}$	Liquidity of receivables	8.8 times	5.5 times	8.1 times	8.5 times

Since companies do not normally disclose the proportion of their sales that were made for cash and for credit, we normally assume that all sales are credit sales. In addition, not all companies report gross and net accounts receivable separately. In such cases, it is appropriate to use net accounts receivable. The important thing is to be consistent in your input data to ensure that the resulting ratios are comparable.

PotashCorp's receivables turnover increased significantly in 2004. PotashCorp states in its annual report that its goal is to become "the preferred supplier to high-volume, high margin customers with the lowest credit risk." Its receivables turnover is consistent with Agrium's and the industry average for 2004.

Average Collection Period

A popular variant of the receivables turnover is calculated by converting it into a collection period stated in days. This is done by dividing 365 days by the receivables turnover.

Illustration 14A-4 ▼

Average collection period

The average collection period for PotashCorp is shown in illustration 14A-4.

Ratio	Formula	Indicates	PotashCorp 2004	PotashCorp 2003	Agrium 2004	Industry 2004
Average collection period	$\dfrac{365 \text{ days}}{\text{Receivables turnover}}$	Number of days receivables are outstanding	42 days	66 days	45 days	43 days

PotashCorp's 2004 receivables turnover of 8.8 times is divided into 365 days to obtain an average collection period of 42 days. Analysts frequently use the average collection period to assess the effectiveness of a company's credit and collection policies. The general rule is that the collection period should not greatly exceed the credit period (i.e., the time allowed for payment). PotashCorp's customer credit policies have remained fairly consistent with 2003. That being said, the company has done a better job at collecting accounts receivable in 2004 than in 2003.

PotashCorp's collection period is similar to that of Agrium and the industry. The company's receivables management appears to be in good shape, which makes the increased current ratio look more reliable.

Inventory Turnover

Slow-moving inventory can also distort the current ratio. The liquidity of a company's inventory is measured by the inventory turnover ratio. This ratio measures the number of times on average that the inventory is sold during the period, and is calculated by dividing the cost of goods sold by the average inventory. Unless seasonal factors are significant, average inventory can be calculated from the beginning and ending inventory balances.

PotashCorp's inventory turnover is shown in Illustration 14A-5.

Illustration 14A-5 ▼

Inventory turnover

Ratio	Formula	Indicates	PotashCorp 2004	PotashCorp 2003	Agrium 2004	Industry 2004
Inventory turnover	Cost of goods sold / Average inventory	Liquidity of inventory	5.6 times	4.7 times	4.7 times	4.8 times

PotashCorp's inventory turnover increased in 2004. PotashCorp's strategy is to match supply to demand to minimize excess inventory. Its inventory turnover is better than both Agrium's and the industry average.

Days in Inventory

A variant of the inventory turnover ratio is days in inventory, which measures the average number of days it takes to sell the inventory. It is calculated by dividing 365 days by the inventory turnover.

The days in inventory for PotashCorp is shown in Illustration 14A-6.

Illustration 14A-6 ▼

Days in inventory

Ratio	Formula	Indicates	PotashCorp 2004	PotashCorp 2003	Agrium 2004	Industry 2004
Days in inventory	365 days / Inventory turnover	Number of days inventory is on hand	65 days	78 days	78 days	76 days

PotashCorp's 2004 inventory turnover of 5.6 times is divided into 365 days to obtain 65 days in inventory. This means that, on average, it takes PotashCorp 65 days to sell its inventory. This average is better than that of Agrium and the industry. Generally, the faster inventory is sold, the less cash there is tied up in inventory and the less chance there is of inventory becoming obsolete.

It is now safe to conclude that the increase in Potash Corp's current ratio indicates improved liquidity, since we have learned nothing to the contrary in our analysis of the receivables and inventory turnover ratios. It is worth noting here that the above interpretations are based not only on the financial data, but also on the knowledge gained from an understanding of PotashCorp and Agrium, their businesses, and their activities over the last year. As mentioned in the chapter, non-financial information is important in interpreting the financial results.

Liquidity Conclusion

In an intracompany comparison, all of PotashCorp's liquidity ratios improved from 2003 to 2004. In an intercompany and industry comparison, PotashCorp's current ratio was lower than both Agrium's and the industry average. However, all of its other liquidity ratios were better than both Agrium's and the industry average. Agrium's current ratio and the industry average were likely inflated because of slower-moving receivables and inventory.

To conclude, PotashCorp's liquidity is fine. Its current ratio is greater than one and its cash current debt coverage is 1.0. It has a strong collection record and its inventory is moving. It also has access to an operating line of credit.

Solvency Ratios

While liquidity ratios measure the ability of a company to pay its current liabilities, solvency ratios measure the ability of a company to pay its total liabilities. The debt to total assets, times interest earned, and cash total debt coverage ratios give information about debt-paying ability. In addition, free cash flow gives information about the company's ability to expand operations or pay additional dividends.

Debt to Total Assets

The debt to total assets ratio measures the percentage of the total assets that is provided by creditors. It is calculated by dividing total liabilities (both current and long-term) by total assets. This ratio indicates the company's reliance on debt. The higher the percentage of debt to total assets, the greater the risk that the company may be unable to meet its maturing obligations. The lower the ratio, the more equity "buffer" there is for creditors if the company becomes insolvent. So, from the creditors' point of view, a low ratio of debt to total assets is good.

Illustration 14A-7 ▼

Debt to total assets

PotashCorp's debt to total assets is shown in Illustration 14A-7.

Ratio	Formula	Indicates	PotashCorp 2004	PotashCorp 2003	Agrium 2004	Industry 2004
Debt to total assets	$\dfrac{\text{Total liabilities}}{\text{Total assets}}$	Percentage of total assets provided by creditors	53.5%	56.8%	57.6%	57.0%

PotashCorp's debt to total assets ratio of 53.5 percent means that creditors have provided financing to cover 53.5 percent of the company's total assets. PotashCorp's solvency improved during the year, from 56.8 percent to 53.5 percent. According to Illustration 14-2, presented earlier in the chapter, total assets increased by 12.3 percent in 2004 and total liabilities increased by 5.7 percent. It appears that PotashCorp is financing additional assets by using retained earnings rather than by adding additional debt. PotashCorp's debt to total assets ratio is better than both Agrium's 57.6 percent and the industry average of 57 percent.

Another ratio with a similar meaning is the **debt to equity ratio**. It shows the use of borrowed funds relative to the investments by shareholders. The debt to equity ratio is calculated by dividing total liabilities by total shareholders' equity. When the debt to total assets ratio equals 50 percent, the debt to equity ratio is 100 percent (because total liabilities plus shareholders' equity equals total assets).

Using this definition, PotashCorp's debt to equity ratio for 2004 is 114.9 percent (U.S. $2,741.2 million ÷ U.S. $2,385.6 million). This means that PotashCorp has financed its operations with 1.149 times as much debt as equity.

Times Interest Earned

The debt level of a company is not as important as its ability to service the debt—that is, pay the interest. The times interest earned ratio (also called interest coverage) indicates the company's ability to meet interest payments as they come due. It is calculated by dividing earnings before interest expense and income taxes by interest expense. This is often abbreviated as EBIT, which stands for earnings before interest and tax. EBIT represents the amount that is available to cover interest.

Illustration 14A-8 ▼

Times interest earned

PotashCorp's times interest earned ratio is shown in Illustration 14A-8.

Ratio	Formula	Indicates	PotashCorp 2004	PotashCorp 2003	Agrium 2004	Industry 2004
Times interest earned	$\dfrac{\text{Earnings before interest expense and income tax expense (EBIT)}}{\text{Interest expense}}$	Ability to meet interest payments	6.1 times	(0.6) times	8.5 times	7.2 times

PotashCorp's 2004 times interest earned was 6.1 times. That is, earnings before interest and taxes were 6.1 times the amount needed for interest expense. PotashCorp's times interest earned ratio improved substantially from 2003 to 2004. However, it is still less than the industry average of 7.2 times, and less than Agrium's ratio of 8.5 times.

Times interest earned should always be interpreted along with the debt to total assets ratio. Since PotashCorp's debt to total assets improved in 2004, as did its times interest earned ratio, its solvency is in good shape.

Cash Total Debt Coverage

A cash-based equivalent to the debt to total assets ratio is the cash total debt coverage ratio. This ratio indicates a company's ability to repay its liabilities from cash provided by operating activities, without having to liquidate the assets used in its operations. It is calculated by dividing cash provided (or used) by operating activities (from the cash flow statement) by average total liabilities.

Illustration 14A-9 shows PotashCorp's cash total debt coverage.

Illustration 14A-9 ▼

Cash total debt coverage

Ratio	Formula	Indicates	PotashCorp 2004	PotashCorp 2003	Agrium 2004	Industry 2004
Cash total debt coverage	Cash provided (used) by operating activities / Average total liabilities	Long-term debt-paying ability (cash basis)	0.2 times	0.1 times	0.3 times	n/a

An industry ratio for this measure is not available, but PotashCorp's cash total debt coverage ratio increased from 0.1 times in 2003 to 0.2 times in 2004. One way of interpreting the cash total debt coverage ratio is to say that cash provided from PotashCorp's 2004 operating activities would be enough to pay off 20 percent of its total liabilities. If 20 percent of liabilities were retired each year, it would take approximately four more years to retire all debt. PotashCorp's cash total debt coverage ratio was slightly below Agrium's 0.3 times.

This ratio improved, similar to the debt to total assets ratio. Both are moving in the same direction, which lessens concerns about cash- and accrual-based accounting differences.

Free Cash Flow

Another indication of a company's solvency is the amount of excess cash that it generates after investing to maintain its current productive capacity and after paying current dividends. This amount is referred to as free cash flow.

PotashCorp's free cash flow (in U.S. millions) is shown in Illustration 14A-10:

Illustration 14A-10 ▼

Free cash flow

Ratio	Formula	Indicates	PotashCorp 2004	PotashCorp 2003	Agrium 2004	Industry 2004
Free cash flow	Cash provided (used) by operating activities − net capital expenditures − dividends paid	Cash available for expanding operations or paying more dividends	$375.5	$178.5	$363.0	n/a

PotashCorp's free cash flow has improved considerably from 2003 to 2004. Cash provided by operating activities increased in 2004 by 70.3 percent or U.S. $268.1 million. This huge increase, as discussed in the management discussion and analysis section of the company's annual report, was attributed mostly to the higher gross margin earned in potash sales and a decrease in working capital requirements.

PotashCorp's free cash flow is consistent with Agrium's U.S. $363 million. There is no amount available for the industry.

Solvency Conclusion

In an intracompany comparison, all of PotashCorp's solvency ratios improved in 2004. Although it improved greatly in 2004, in an intercompany and industry comparison, Potash-Corp's solvency was fairly consistent overall with that of Agrium and the industry: although its debt to total assets ratio was better, its interest coverage was worse.

Profitability Ratios

For a company to be successful, assets must be used to generate revenue efficiently and expenses must be controlled effectively. Consequently, profitability ratios focus mainly on the relationships between statement of earnings items and balance sheet items. Understanding these relationships can help management determine where to focus efforts on improving profitability.

Illustration 14A-11 diagrams these relationships and will guide our discussion of Potash-Corp's profitability. Profitability ratios include the return on common shareholders' equity, return on assets, profit margin, asset turnover, and gross profit margin ratios, as shown in Illustration 14A-11.

Illustration 14A-11 ▶

Relationship among profitability measures

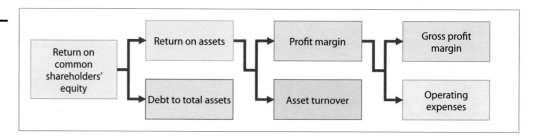

As shown in the above illustration, the return on common shareholders' equity ratio is affected by the return on assets and debt to total assets ratios. If a company wants to increase its return on common shareholders' equity, it can either increase its return on assets or increase its reliance on debt financing. In fact, as long as the return on assets is higher than the interest rate paid on debt, the return on common shareholders' equity will always be increased by the use of debt.

The return on assets ratio is affected by the profit margin and asset turnover. If a company wants to increase its return on assets, it can do this by either increasing its operating efficiency (profit margin), or trying to increase its asset utilization (asset turnover).

And, of course, the profit margin is affected by the gross profit margin and the amount, or percentage, of operating expenses (assuming there are no other revenues or other expenses). If a company wants to increase its profit margin, it can increase its gross profit margin by either raising selling prices, reducing its cost of goods sold, or reducing its operating expenses.

We will now look at each of these ratios in turn and examine their relationships. In addition, we will review four other commonly used profitability measures that are of specific interest to investors—earnings per share, price-earnings ratio, payout ratio, and dividend yield.

Return on Common Shareholders' Equity

A widely used measure of profitability from the common shareholders' viewpoint is the return on common shareholders' equity. This ratio shows how many dollars of net earnings were earned for each dollar invested by the shareholders. It is calculated by dividing net earnings available to common shareholders by average common shareholders' equity.

Illustration 14A-12 ▼

Return on common shareholders' equity

The return on common shareholders' equity for PotashCorp is shown in Illustration 14A-12.

Ratio	Formula	Indicates	PotashCorp 2004	PotashCorp 2003	Agrium 2004	Industry 2004
Return on common shareholders' equity	$\dfrac{\text{Net earnings available to common shareholders}}{\text{Average common shareholders' equity}}$	Profitability of shareholders' investment	13.7%	(6.2%)	27.4%	11.0%

PotashCorp's return on shareholders' equity improved significantly in 2004. Recall that the company reported a net loss in 2003, and a net profit in 2004. Even with this improvement, however, it is still much lower than Agrium's. Both companies' ratios are better than the industry average.

Return on Assets

The return on common shareholders' equity is affected by two factors: the return on assets ratio and the debt to total assets ratio. We looked earlier in this appendix at PotashCorp's debt to total assets ratio and noted a significant improvement. We will now look at its return on assets.

Return on assets measures the overall profitability of assets in terms of how much is earned on each dollar invested in assets. It is calculated by dividing net earnings by average total assets. PotashCorp's return on assets is shown in Illustration 14A-13.

Illustration 14A-13 ◀

Return on assets

Ratio	Formula	Indicates	PotashCorp 2004	PotashCorp 2003	Agrium 2004	Industry 2004
Return on assets	Net earnings / Average total assets	Overall profitability of assets	6.2%	(2.8%)	10.4%	7.1%

PotashCorp's return on assets of 6.2 percent in 2004 is much higher than its negative return of 2.8 percent in 2003. This change is once again influenced by the switch from a net loss in 2003 to a net profit in 2004. Although its return on assets is significantly below Agrium's, it is fairly consistent with the industry average.

Note that PotashCorp's rate of return on common shareholders' equity (13.7 percent) is much higher than its rate of return on assets (6.2 percent). The reason is that PotashCorp has made effective use of leverage. **Leveraging** or **trading on the equity** means that the company has borrowed money at a lower rate of interest than the rate of return it earns on the assets it purchased with the borrowed funds. Leverage enables management to use money supplied by non-shareholders (non-owners) to increase the return to shareholders.

PotashCorp's return on shareholders' equity is higher than its return on assets because of the positive benefit of leverage. Recall from our earlier discussion that PotashCorp's percentage of debt financing as measured by the ratio of debt to total assets was 53.5 percent in 2004 (see Illustration 14A-7). In contrast, Agrium had a slightly higher debt to total assets ratio of 57.6 percent. It appears that Agrium's higher return on shareholders' equity, compared to PotashCorp's, is mostly because it uses more leverage.

Profit Margin

Return on assets is affected by two factors, and the first of these is the profit margin. The profit margin measures the percentage of net earnings that each dollar of sales produces. It is calculated by dividing net earnings by net sales for the period.

PotashCorp's profit margin is shown in Illustration 14A-14.

Illustration 14A-14 ◀

Profit margin

Ratio	Formula	Indicates	PotashCorp 2004	PotashCorp 2003	Agrium 2004	Industry 2004
Profit margin	Net earnings / Net sales	Net earnings generated by each dollar of sales	10.3%	(5.1%)	9.7%	5.4%

PotashCorp reported a 10.3-percent profit margin in 2004. This profit margin was of course greater than that of 2003, given the change in earnings between the two years. It also exceeded Agrium's and the industry average.

Asset Turnover

The other factor that affects the return on assets ratio is asset turnover. The asset turnover ratio measures how efficiently a company uses its assets to generate sales. It is calculated by dividing net sales by average total assets for the period. The resulting number shows the dollars of sales produced by each dollar invested in assets.

Illustration 14A-15 shows the asset turnover for PotashCorp on the following page.

Ratio	Formula	Indicates	PotashCorp 2004	PotashCorp 2003	Agrium 2004	Industry 2004
Asset turnover	Net sales / Average total assets	How efficiently assets are used to generate sales	0.6 times	0.5 times	1.1 times	1.1 times

The asset turnover ratio shows that PotashCorp generated $0.60 of sales in 2004 for each dollar it had invested in assets. Although the asset turnover increased only slightly from 2003, it is lower than Agrium's and that of the industry.

In summary, PotashCorp's return on assets changed a lot from 2003 to 2004, increasing from a negative 2.8 percent to a positive 6.2 percent. Underlying this large change was an increased profitability of each dollar of sales, which we will discuss further in the next section.

Gross Profit Margin

We saw in Illustration 14A-14 that the profit margin increased in 2004 from a negative 5.1 percent to a positive 10.3 percent. Two factors influence the profit margin. One is the gross profit margin. The other is the company's ability to control its operating expenses.

The gross profit margin is calculated by dividing gross profit (net sales less cost of goods sold) by net sales. This ratio indicates a company's ability to maintain an adequate selling price above its cost of goods sold. Illustration 14A-16 shows PotashCorp's gross profit margin.

Ratio	Formula	Indicates	PotashCorp 2004	PotashCorp 2003	Agrium 2004	Industry 2004
Gross profit margin	Gross profit / Net sales	Margin between selling price and cost of goods sold	23.5%	15.4%	32.1%	24.3%

PotashCorp's gross profit margin increased from 15.4 percent in 2003 to 23.5 percent in 2004. This gross profit margin is lower than Agrium's 32.1 percent and slightly lower than the industry average of 24.3 percent.

There were several reasons for the increased gross profit in 2004 for PotashCorp. First, the gross margin of U.S. $422.8 million in the potash business segment was more than twice that of 2003. Secondly, the gross margin in the nitrogen business segment was pushed to a record high in 2004 of U.S. $242.8 million, a 26-percent increase over 2003 because of the tight supply and demand for nitrogen.

PotashCorp's increase in its gross profit margin was a significant factor that contributed to the increase in its profit margin. As mentioned above, the other factor affecting the profit margin is operating expenses. PotashCorp had 23.5 percent of each dollar of sales remaining in 2004 to cover its operating expenses and generate a profit. The company was not as effective in controlling its operating expenses in 2004 as it was in controlling its cost of goods sold. As shown in Illustration 14-3, selling and administrative expenses increased by 35.9 percent, a much faster rate than the 17.7 percent increase in sales. This increase was attributed by the company to increases in compensation tied to its stock option program. The company's other operating expenses declined significantly though, by 68.9 percent, which resulted in an overall net decline in operating expenses. The decline in operating expenses occurred simply because operating expenses in the preceding year, 2003, were abnormally high because of costs related to plant shutdowns.

Earnings per Share

The next four ratios that we will discuss are earnings per share, the price-earnings ratio, the payout ratio, and dividend yield. These ratios are also measures of profitability, but are often of more interest to investors than to management.

Earnings per share is a measure of the net earnings realized on each common share. It is calculated by dividing net earnings available to common shareholders by the weighted average number of common shares. Shareholders usually think in terms of the number of shares they own or plan to buy or sell. Expressing net earnings on a per share basis provides a useful perspective for determining profitability. This measure is widely used and reported. Because of the ratio's importance, companies are required to present it directly on their statement of earnings.

PotashCorp's earnings per share is shown in Illustration 14A-17.

Ratio	Formula	Indicates	PotashCorp 2004	PotashCorp 2003	Agrium 2004	Industry 2004
Earnings per share	Net earnings available to common shareholders / Weighted average number of common shares	Net earnings earned on each common share	$2.77	$(1.21)	$2.04	n/a

Illustration 14A-17 ▲

Earnings per share

Note that no industry average is presented in Illustration 14A-17. Comparisons to the industry average, or to Agrium's earnings per share, are not meaningful, because of the wide variations in numbers of shares among companies. The only meaningful earnings per share comparison is an intracompany one. PotashCorp's earnings per share increased a lot in 2004, now reporting net earnings instead of the previous year's net loss.

Price-Earnings Ratio

The price-earnings ratio is an often-quoted statistic that measures the ratio of the market price of each common share to the earnings per share. The price-earnings ratio reflects investors' assessments of a company's future earnings. It is calculated by dividing the market price per share by earnings per share. PotashCorp's price-earnings ratio is shown in Illustration 14A-18.

Illustration 14A-18 ▼

Price-earnings ratio

Ratio	Formula	Indicates	PotashCorp 2004	PotashCorp 2003	Agrium 2004	Industry 2004
Price-earnings ratio	Market price per share / Earnings per share	Relationship between market price per share and earnings per share	30.0 times	n/a	8.3 times	24.8 times

In 2004, each PotashCorp common share sold for 30 times the amount that was earned on each share. In 2003, no meaningful price-earnings ratio can be calculated for PotashCorp because its earnings per share had a negative value in 2003. PotashCorp's price-earnings ratio is much higher than both Agrium's and the industry average.

In general, a higher price-earnings ratio means that investors favour the company. They are willing to pay more for the shares because they believe the company has prospects for growth and earnings in the future.

Some investors carefully study price-earnings ratios over time to help them determine when to buy or sell shares. If the highs and lows of a particular share's price-earnings ratio remain constant over several operating cycles, then these highs and lows can indicate selling and buying points for the shares. They could also mean other things, however, including that the share is over- or under-priced. Investors should be very cautious in interpreting price-earnings ratios.

Payout Ratio

The payout ratio measures the percentage of earnings distributed as cash dividends. It is calculated by dividing cash dividends by net earnings. Companies that have high growth rates usually have low payout ratios because they reinvest most of their net earnings back into the company.

The payout ratio for PotashCorp is shown in Illustration 14A-19.

Illustration 14A-19 ▼

Payout ratio

Ratio	Formula	Indicates	PotashCorp 2004	PotashCorp 2003	Agrium 2004	Industry 2004
Payout ratio	Cash dividends / Net earnings	Percentage of earnings distributed as cash dividends	18.8%	n/a	8.3%	26.5%

In 2004, PotashCorp's payout ratio was significantly higher than Agrium's, but lower than the industry average. Management has some control over the amount of dividends paid each year, and companies are generally reluctant to reduce a dividend below the amount paid in a previous year. Therefore, the payout ratio will actually decrease if a company's net earnings increase but the company keeps its total dividend payment the same or more. PotashCorp has historically paid a quarterly dividend of $0.125 per share. It did increase its dividend in November 2004, to $0.15 per share.

A payout ratio was not calculated for PotashCorp in 2003 as the company reported a net loss and the ratio would not have been meaningful.

Dividend Yield

Illustration 14A-20 ▼

Dividend yield

The dividend yield supplements the payout ratio. The dividend yield reports the rate of return a shareholder earned from dividends during the year. It is calculated by dividing the dividend per share by the market price per share, as shown in Illustration 14A-20.

Ratio	Formula	Indicates	PotashCorp 2004	PotashCorp 2003	Agrium 2004	Industry 2004
Dividend yield	Dividend per share / Market price per share	Earnings generated by each share, based on the share price	0.7%	1.2%	0.6%	n/a

PotashCorp's dividend yield declined in 2004 compared to 2003. Share prices increased significantly from $43.24 in 2003 to $83.06 in 2004. PotashCorp's dividend yield is slightly higher than Agrium's. A dividend yield is not available for the industry as share prices are not comparable. As with the payout ratio, companies that are expanding rapidly can be expected to have lower dividend yields.

Profitability Conclusion

In an intracompany comparison, PotashCorp's profitability measures have improved from 2003 to 2004, except for the price-earnings ratio and dividend yield. However, share prices increased substantially in 2004 and this affected the calculation of both price-earnings and dividend yield.

In an intercompany comparison, PotashCorp's profitability ratios are below Agrium's, except for the profit margin, price-earnings ratio, payout ratio, and dividend yield. Investors favour PotashCorp over Agrium, likely because of its improved profitability and larger payout ratio.

Agrium had better results than the industry in all ratios except for the price-earnings and payout ratios. PotashCorp exceeded the industry ratios as well, except for its return on assets, asset turnover, gross profit margin, and payout ratio.

This ends our comprehensive analysis illustration using PotashCorp. What can be practically covered in a textbook gives you only the tip of the iceberg when it comes to the types of financial information available and the ratios used by various industries. The availability of information is not a problem. The real trick is to be discriminating enough to do relevant analyses and choose pertinent data for comparisons.

▦ Using the Decision Toolkit

When analyzing a company, financial data for an extended period of time should be reviewed, as this helps determine whether the condition and performance of the company are changing. The condensed financial statements of PotashCorp for 2001 and 2002 follow. They supplement the data presented earlier in the chapter for 2003 and 2004, giving us a four-year period for preparing a vertical analysis.

POTASH CORPORATION OF SASKATCHEWAN INC.   ℞ PotashCorp
Balance Sheet
December 31
(in U.S. millions)

Helping Nature Provide

	2002 Amount	2002 Percent	2001 Amount	2001 Percent
Assets				
Current assets				
Cash and cash equivalents	$ 24.5		$ 45.3	
Accounts receivable	267.8		256.7	
Inventories	499.3		481.1	
Prepaid expenses and other current assets	40.4		36.5	
Total current assets	832.0		819.6	
Property, plant, and equipment	3,269.9		3,245.6	
Intangibles and other assets	583.7		532.1	
Total assets	$4,685.6		$4,597.3	
Liabilities and Shareholders' Equity				
Liabilities				
Current liabilities	$ 823.4		$ 772.5	
Long-term liabilities	1,769.7		1,738.3	
Total liabilities	2,593.1		2,510.8	
Shareholders' equity	2,092.5		2,086.5	
Total liabilities and shareholders' equity	$4,685.6		$4,597.3	

POTASH CORPORATION OF SASKATCHEWAN INC.   ℞ PotashCorp
Statement of Earnings
Year Ended December 31
(in U.S. millions)

Helping Nature Provide

	2002 Amount	2002 Percent	2001 Amount	2001 Percent
Net sales	$1,913.8		$2,072.7	
Cost of goods sold	1,612.2		1,673.5	
Gross profit	301.6		399.2	
Selling and administrative expenses	91.7		99.7	
Other operating expenses	73.5		56.3	
Earnings from operations	136.4		243.2	
Interest expense	83.1		80.3	
Other revenue	30.5		26.5	
Earnings before income tax	83.8		189.4	
Income taxes	30.2		68.2	
Net earnings	$ 53.6		$ 121.2	

Instructions

(a) Prepare a vertical analysis of PotashCorp's balance sheet and statement of earnings, inserting the appropriate percentages in the spaces provided above.

(b) Comment on any relevant trends between 2001 and 2002, and in comparison to the vertical analysis for 2003 and 2004 presented earlier in the chapter in Illustrations 14-4 and 14-5.

Solution

(a) Vertical analysis: The following lists the percentages for each of the four years—2001 and 2002 that you calculated above, and 2003 and 2004 presented in Illustrations 14-4 and 14-5 in the chapter—in a side-by-side format for easier reference.

POTASHCORP
Percentage Balance Sheet
December 31

	2004	2003	2002	2001
Assets				
Current assets				
Cash and cash equivalents	9.0%	0.1%	0.5%	0.9%
Accounts receivable	6.9%	6.7%	5.7%	5.6%
Inventories	7.7%	8.7%	10.7%	10.5%
Prepaid expenses and other current assets	0.7%	0.6%	0.8%	0.8%
Total current assets	24.3%	16.1%	17.7%	17.8%
Property, plant, and equipment	60.4%	68.1%	69.8%	70.6%
Intangibles and other assets	15.3%	15.8%	12.5%	11.6%
Total assets	100.0%	100.0%	100.0%	100.0%
Liabilities and Shareholders' Equity				
Liabilities				
Current liabilities	13.7%	12.2%	17.6%	16.8%
Long-term liabilities	39.8%	44.6%	37.7%	37.8%
Total liabilities	53.5%	56.8%	55.3%	54.6%
Shareholders' equity	46.5%	43.2%	44.7%	45.4%
Total liabilities and shareholders' equity	100.0%	100.0%	100.0%	100.0%

POTASHCORP
Percentage Statement of Earnings
Year Ended December 31

	2004	2003	2002	2001
Net sales	100.0%	100.0%	100.0%	100.0%
Cost of goods sold	76.5%	84.6%	84.2%	80.7%
Gross profit	23.5%	15.4%	15.8%	19.3%
Selling and administrative expenses	4.5%	3.9%	4.9%	4.8%
Other operating expenses	4.0%	15.1%	3.8%	2.7%
Earnings from operations	15.0%	(3.6%)	7.1%	11.8%
Interest expense	2.9%	3.7%	4.3%	3.9%
Other revenue	2.7%	1.3%	1.6%	1.3%
Earnings (loss) before income tax	14.8%	(6.0%)	4.4%	9.2%
Income taxes	4.5%	(0.9%)	1.6%	3.3%
Net earnings (loss)	10.3%	(5.1%)	2.8%	5.9%

(b) Current assets have remained relatively constant from 2001 to 2003. An increase in cash and cash equivalents increased current assets in 2004. PotashCorp's current assets were fairly consistent with current liabilities from 2001 to 2003, and in 2004 current assets were much higher than current liabilities. PotashCorp's property, plant, and equipment has been decreasing as a percentage of total assets each year from 2001. Long-term liabilities have decreased between 2003 and 2004.

PotashCorp's liquidity and solvency would appear to be improving over the four years, with decreasing percentages of liabilities. We would have to do further analysis (e.g., ratio analysis as detailed in Appendix 14A) to determine whether this is actually the case and, if so, the reasons for this decline.

In terms of profitability, PotashCorp appears to be controlling its costs and expenses in 2004. The selling and administrative expenses are consistent with 2001 and 2002. Other operating expenses in 2003 were high due to provisions for plant shutdowns. The gross profit margin has increased significantly in 2004, due in part to the efficiency of maintaining control over inventory and thus over the cost of goods sold. The company's profitability also appears to be on the increase in 2004, especially after a decline in 2003 and 2002.

Summary of Study Objectives

1. **Understand the concept of sustainable earnings and indicate how irregular items are presented.** Sustainable earnings refer to a company's ability to sustain its profits from operations. Irregular items—discontinued operations and extraordinary items—are presented on the statement of earnings, net of tax, below "Earnings from continuing operations" to highlight their infrequent nature. Another irregular item—the cumulative effect on prior-period earnings of a change in accounting principle—is presented on the statement of retained earnings, net of tax, as an adjustment to opening retained earnings. For comparability, all prior-period financial statements that are presented are restated using the new principle.

2. **Explain and apply horizontal analysis.** Horizontal analysis is a technique for evaluating a series of data over a period of time to determine the increase or decrease that has taken place, expressed as either an amount or a percentage.

3. **Explain and apply vertical analysis.** Vertical analysis is a technique that expresses each item in a financial statement as a percentage of a relevant total (base amount).

4. **Identify and calculate ratios used to analyze liquidity, solvency, and profitability.** The formula and purpose of each ratio is presented in Illustration 14-7 (liquidity), Illustration 14-8 (solvency), and Illustration 14-9 (profitability).

5. **Understand the concept of quality of earnings.** A high quality of earnings means giving full and transparent information that will not confuse or mislead users of the financial statements. Issues related to quality of earnings are (1) alternative accounting principles, (2) professional judgement, and (3) pro forma earnings.

▦ Decision Toolkit—A Summary

Decision Checkpoints	Info Needed for Decision	Tools to Use for Decision	How to Evaluate Results
Has the company sold an identifiable business segment?	Discontinued operations section of statement of earnings	Anything reported in this section indicates that the company has discontinued an identifiable business segment.	If an identifiable business segment has been discontinued, its results in the current period should not be included in estimates of future net earnings.
Has the company experienced any extraordinary events or transactions?	Extraordinary item section of statement of earnings	Anything reported in this section indicates that the company experienced an event that was infrequent, unusual, and not determined by management.	These items should be ignored in estimating future net earnings.
Has the company changed any of its accounting principles?	Cumulative effect of change in accounting principle in statement of retained earnings	Anything reported in this manner indicates that the company has changed an accounting principle during the current year.	Financial statements are restated using the new principle to make them easy to compare.
How do the company's financial position and operating results compare with those of previous periods?	Balance sheet and statement of earnings	Comparative financial statements should be prepared over at least two years, with the first year reported as the base year. Changes in each line item relative to the base year should be presented both by amount and by percentage. This is called horizontal analysis.	A significant change should be investigated to determine what caused it.
How do the relationships between items in this year's financial statements compare with last year's relationships or those of competitors?	Balance sheet and statement of earnings	Each line item on the balance sheet should be presented as a percentage of total assets (total liabilities and shareholders' equity). Each line item on the statement of earnings should be presented as a percentage of net sales. This is called vertical analysis.	Any difference, either across years or between companies, should be investigated to determine the cause.
Are efforts to evaluate the company helped or hampered by the quality of earnings?	Financial statements as well as other information disclosed	Review accounting principles, estimates, and pro forma earnings for reasonableness. Assess strength of corporate governance processes.	If there are any irregularities, the analysis should be relied on with caution.

**Analysis Tools
(Decision Toolkit Summary)**

Glossary

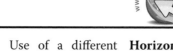

Study Tools (Glossary)

Change in accounting principle   Use of a different accounting principle in the current year compared to what was used in the preceding year. (p. 677)

Discontinued operations   The disposal of an identifiable segment of a business. (p. 674)

Extraordinary items   Events and transactions that meet three conditions: they are (1) not expected to occur frequently, (2) not typical of normal business activities, and (3) not subject to management's discretion. (p. 675)

Horizontal analysis   A technique for evaluating a series of financial statement data over a period of time to determine the increase (decrease) that has taken place. This increase (decrease) is expressed as either an amount or a percentage. (p. 679)

Pro forma earnings   A measure of earnings that is not GAAP-based and which excludes items that a company thinks are unusual or nonrecurring. (p. 689)

Quality of earnings An indicator of the level of full and transparent information that is provided to users of the financial statements. (p. 688)

Sustainable earnings The most likely level of earnings to be obtained in the future, determined by adjusting net earnings for irregular items. (p. 674)

Vertical analysis A technique for evaluating financial statement data that expresses each item in a financial statement as a percentage of a base amount. (p. 682)

Demonstration Problem

Study Tools
(Demonstration Problems)

The events and transactions of Dever Corporation for the year ending December 31, 2006, resulted in these data:

Cost of goods sold	$2,600,000
Net sales	4,400,000
Operating expenses	1,100,000
Other expenses	9,600
Other revenues	5,600
Earnings from operations of plastics division (discontinued operations)	70,000
Gain on sale of plastics division (discontinued operations)	500,000
Cumulative effect of changing from straight-line amortization to double declining-balance (increase in amortization expense)	300,000
Retained earnings, January 1	3,926,000
Dividends	40,000

All items are before the applicable income tax rate of 30%.

Instructions

Prepare statements of earnings and retained earnings for the year.

Solution to Demonstration Problem

DEVER CORPORATION
Statement of Earnings
Year Ended December 31, 2006

Net sales		$4,400,000
Cost of goods sold		2,600,000
Gross profit		1,800,000
Operating expenses		1,100,000
Earnings from operations		700,000
Other revenues	$ 5,600	
Other expenses	(9,600)	(4,000)
Earnings before income taxes		696,000
Income tax expense ($696,000 × 30%)		208,800
Earnings from continuing operations		487,200
Discontinued operations		
Earnings from operations of plastics division, net of $21,000 income taxes ($70,000 × 30%)	$ 49,000	
Gain on sale of plastics division, net of $150,000 income taxes ($500,000 × 30%)	350,000	399,000
Net earnings		$ 886,200

Action Plan

- Remember that items not typical of operations are reported in separate sections, net of income tax.

- Cumulative effects from changes in accounting principles affect prior periods and are adjusted through opening retained earnings, not current earnings.

DEVER CORPORATION
Statement of Retained Earnings
Year Ended December 31, 2006

Retained earnings, January 1	$3,926,000
Cumulative effect on prior years of change in amortization method, net of $90,000 income tax savings ($300,000 × 30%)	(210,000)
Retained earnings, January 1, as restated	3,716,000
Add: Net earnings	886,200
	4,602,200
Less: Dividends	40,000
Retained earnings, December 31	$4,562,200

Self-Study Questions

Answers are at the end of the chapter. ⟨━━⟩ All self-study questions in this section use decision tools.

(SO 1) 1. Sustainable earnings means:
(a) net earnings.
(b) net earnings adjusted for irregular items.
(c) earnings from operations.
(d) retained earnings.

(SO 1) 2. The Dhillon Corporation has net earnings of $400,000, including a pre-tax loss from discontinued operations of $100,000. If Dhillon's income tax rate is 25%, the statement of earnings should show earnings from continuing operations of:
(a) $325,000.   (c) $475,000.
(b) $400,000.   (d) $500,000.

(SO 2) 3. In a horizontal analysis, each item is expressed as a percentage of the:
(a) net sales amount.
(b) total assets amount.
(c) total liabilities and shareholders' equity amount.
(d) base-year amount.

(SO 2) 4. The Rankin Inlet Corporation reported net sales of $300,000, $330,000, and $360,000 in the years 2004, 2005, and 2006, respectively. If 2004 is the base year, what is the horizontal percentage for 2006?
(a) 9%   (b) 100%   (c) 110%   (d) 120%

(SO 3) 5. In a vertical analysis, the base amount for amortization expense is generally:
(a) net sales.
(b) amortization expense in a previous year.
(c) total assets.
(d) total property, plant, and equipment.

(SO 3) 6. The following schedule shows what type of analysis?

	Amount	Percent
Current assets	$200,000	25%
Noncurrent assets	600,000	75%
Total assets	$800,000	100%

Study Tools (Self-Assessment Quizzes)

www.wiley.com/canada/kimmel

(a) Horizontal analysis (c) Vertical analysis
(b) Differential analysis (d) Ratio analysis

7. Which of the following is *not* a liquidity ratio?   (SO
(a) Current ratio
(b) Cash total debt coverage
(c) Inventory turnover
(d) Receivables turnover

8. Which of the following situations would be the most   (SO
likely indicator that Wang Corporation might have a
solvency problem?
(a) Increasing debt to total assets and times interest
earned ratios
(b) Increasing debt to total assets and decreasing times
interest earned ratios
(c) Decreasing debt to total assets and times interest
earned ratios
(d) Decreasing debt to total assets and increasing
times interest earned ratios

9. Which of the following situations is a likely indicator   (SO
of profitability?
(a) Increasing price-earnings ratio
(b) Increasing return on assets, asset turnover, and
profit margin ratios
(c) Decreasing return on common shareholders' equity
and payout ratios
(d) Decreasing gross profit margin and increasing profit
margin

10. Which situation might indicate that a company has a   (SO
low quality of earnings?
(a) The same accounting principles are used each year.
(b) Revenue is recognized when earned.
(c) Management tries to record as many impairment
losses as possible in a year when it is going to report
a net loss anyway.
(d) Best corporate governance practices are followed.

Questions

🔧 All of the questions in this section use decision tools.

(SO 1) 1. Explain the concept of sustainable earnings. What is the relationship between this concept and the treatment of irregular items on the statement of earnings?

(SO 1) 2. What are discontinued operations? Why is it important to report the results of discontinued operations separately from those of continuing operations?

(SO 1) 3. Distinguish between ordinary and extraordinary items.

(SO 1) 4. How does a change in accounting principle affect financial reporting?

(SO 2) 5. Distinguish among the following bases of comparison: intracompany, intercompany, and industry average.

(SO 2) 6. Explain how the percentage increase or decrease from a base-period amount is calculated in horizontal analysis.

(SO 2) 7. If The Forzani Group Limited had net earnings of $28 million for fiscal 2004, and it experienced a 23% decrease in net earnings for fiscal 2005, what are its net earnings for 2005?

(SO 2, 3) 8. Two methods of financial statement analysis are horizontal analysis and vertical analysis. Explain the difference between these two methods.

(SO 3) 9. What items are usually assigned a 100% value in a vertical analysis of (a) the balance sheet and (b) the statement of earnings?

(SO 3) 10. Can vertical analysis be used to compare two companies of different sizes and using different currencies, such as InBev, the world's largest brewer, headquartered in Belgium, and the Molson Coors Brewing Company, the fifth largest brewer, headquartered in the U.S.? Explain.

(SO 3) 11. Tim Hortons reported U.S. $995.6 million of revenue in 2004. If its cost of goods sold is 47.5% in a vertical analysis, what is the dollar amount of its cost of goods sold?

(SO 4) 12. What does each of the following types of ratios measure: (a) liquidity, (b) solvency, and (c) profitability?

(SO 4) 13. Is a high current ratio always a good indicator of a company's liquidity? Describe two situations in which a high current ratio might be hiding liquidity problems.

(SO 4) 14. Bullock Ltd., a retail store, has a receivables turnover of 4.5 times. The industry average is 6.5 times. Does Bullock have a collection problem with its receivables?

(SO 4) 15. Laser Corp.'s cash provided by operating activities in 2006 was double the amount in 2005. Its free cash flow in 2006 was half the amount in 2005. Does the decline in free cash flow indicate a decline in the company's solvency?

(SO 4) 16. McDonald's Corporation reported a debt to total assets ratio of 37% in 2004. The industry average is 39%. Is McDonald's solvency better or worse than that of the industry?

(SO 4) 17. Recently, the price-earnings ratio of the Bank of Nova Scotia was 13.6 times, and the price-earnings ratio of the Bank of Montreal was 12.3 times. Which company did investors favour? Explain.

(SO 4) 18. CIBC's return on assets is 0.8%. During the same year, CIBC reported a return on common shareholders' equity of 12.8%. What is the explanation for the difference in the two ratios?

(SO 4) 19. Which ratios should be used to help answer each of these questions?
(a) How efficient is the company in using its assets to produce sales?
(b) How near to sale is the inventory on hand?
(c) How many dollars were earned for each dollar invested by shareholders?
(d) How able is the company to pay interest charges as they come due?
(e) How able is the company to repay a short-term loan?

(SO 5) 20. Identify and explain the factors that can affect the quality of earnings.

(SO 5) 21. Explain how changing from one generally accepted accounting principle to another can affect the quality of earnings.

(SO 5) 22. Explain how earnings management can affect the quality of earnings.

(SO 5) 23. What are pro forma earnings? Can comparisons of pro forma earnings be useful to decision-makers?

Brief Exercises

⚲═══ All of the brief exercises in this section use decision tools.

Indicate reporting of regular and irregular items.
(SO 1)

BE14–1   Indicate how each of the following items would be reported on a statement of earnings:

(a) A loss from the sale of trading securities
(b) A loss caused by a labour strike
(c) A loss caused when the Canadian Food Inspection Agency prohibited the manufacture and sale of a product
(d) A loss of inventory from flood damage to a warehouse located on a flood plain that floods every few years
(e) A loss on the write-down of obsolete inventory
(f) A loss from a foreign government's expropriation of a production facility
(g) A loss from damage to a warehouse caused by a major earthquake

Prepare discontinued operations section.
(SO 1)

BE14–2   The Osborn Corporation discontinued a business segment of its operations in 2006. The operating loss from the discontinued operations was $300,000 before income tax. The loss on the disposal of these operations was $160,000 before income tax. Osborn's earnings from continuing operations are $950,000 for the year ended December 31, 2006. Its income tax rate is 25%. Prepare a partial statement of earnings for the year, starting with "earnings from continuing operations."

Prepare statement of retained earnings.
(SO 1)

BE14–3   On July 2, 2006, Unisource Inc. changed from the straight-line method of amortization to the declining-balance method. The cumulative effect of the change was to increase the prior years' accumulated amortization by $40,000 before income tax of 30%. Unisource's retained earnings on July 1, 2006, were $335,000. It reported net earnings of $195,000 and paid a dividend of $47,000 during the year. Prepare Unisource's statement of retained earnings for the year ended June 30, 2007.

Prepare horizontal analysis.
(SO 2)

BE14–4   Using the following selected data from the comparative balance sheet of Rioux Ltd., prepare a horizontal analysis:

	2006	2005
Cash	$ 150,000	$ 175,000
Accounts receivable	600,000	400,000
Inventory	780,000	600,000
Property, plant, and equipment	3,130,000	2,800,000
Total assets	$4,660,000	$3,975,000

Use horizontal analysis to determine change in net earnings.
(SO 2)

BE14–5   Horizontal analysis percentages from Coastal Ltd.'s statement of earnings are listed here:

	2006	2005	2004
Sales	96%	107%	100%
Cost of goods sold	102%	97%	100%
Operating expenses	111%	95%	100%
Income tax expense	76%	132%	100%

Assuming that Coastal did not have any non-operating or irregular items, did its net earnings increase, decrease, or remain unchanged over the three-year period? Explain.

Prepare vertical analysis.
(SO 3)

BE14–6   Using the data presented in BE14–4 for Rioux Ltd., prepare a vertical analysis.

Use vertical analysis to determine change in net earnings.
(SO 3)

BE14–7   Vertical analysis percentages from Waubon Corp.'s statement of earnings are listed here:

	2006	2005	2004
Sales	100%	100%	100%
Cost of goods sold	59%	62%	64%
Operating expenses	25%	27%	28%
Income tax expense	3%	2%	2%

Assuming that Waubon did not have any non-operating or irregular items, did its net earnings as a percentage of sales increase, decrease, or remain unchanged over the three-year period? Explain.

BE14–8 For each of the following factors, indicate whether it generally signals good or bad news about a company. Assume all other factors stay constant.

(a) An increase in the profit margin
(b) A decrease in inventory turnover
(c) An increase in the current ratio
(d) A decrease in earnings per share

(e) An increase in the price-earnings ratio
(f) An increase in debt to total assets
(g) A decrease in times interest earned
(h) A decrease in the dividend yield

Interpret changes in ratios.
(SO 4)

BE14–9 Holysh Inc. reported a current ratio of 1.5:1 in the current fiscal year, which is higher than last year's current ratio of 1.3:1. It also reported a receivables turnover of 8 times, which is less than last year's receivables turnover of 12 times, and an inventory turnover of 6 times, which is about the same as last year's inventory turnover. Is Holysh's liquidity improving or deteriorating? Explain.

Evaluate liquidity.
(SO 4)

BE14–10 The following selected data were reported by Maple Leaf Foods Inc. at December 31 (in millions):

Calculate and evaluate receivables ratios.
(SO 4)

	2004	2003	2002
Accounts receivable	$ 292.5	$ 242.3	$ 243.1
Sales*	6,365.0	5,041.9	5,075.9

*Assume that all sales are on account, with credit terms of n/45.

Calculate, for 2004 and 2003, the (a) receivables turnover and (b) average collection period. What conclusions about the management of accounts receivable can be drawn from these data?

BE14–11 The following selected data were reported by Danier Leather Inc. at June 30 (in millions):

Calculate and evaluate inventory ratios.
(SO 4)

	2005	2004	2003
Sales revenue	$166.4	$175.3	$175.5
Cost of goods sold	82.9	88.7	88.8
Inventory	29.0	29.5	37.0

Calculate, for 2005 and 2004, the (a) inventory turnover and (b) days in inventory. What conclusions about the management of the inventory can be drawn from these data?

BE14–12 The Brick Group Income Fund, one of Canada's largest retailers of home furniture, began operations in 2004. It reported the following selected data at December 31, 2004 (in millions):

Calculate and evaluate solvency ratios.
(SO 4)

Net earnings	$ 22.3
Interest expense	1.9
Income tax expense	2.1
Total assets	860.5
Total liabilities	219.3

Calculate the debt to total assets and times interest earned ratios for Brick. The industry average for debt to total assets is 23% and for times interest earned is 12.1 times. How does Brick's solvency compare to that of its industry?

BE14–13 The Topps Company, Inc. is a trading-card and bubble gum company, whose products are sold in more than 50 countries. Selected measures are available for 2005 and 2004:

Evaluate solvency.
(SO 4)

	2005	2004
Debt to total assets	24.6%	23.3%
Cash total debt coverage	0.3 times	0.2 times
Free cash flow (in U.S. millions)	$13.8	$(36.4)

Is Topps' solvency improving or deteriorating? Explain.

BE14–14 Haymark Products Corporation has shareholders' equity of $400,000 and net earnings of $56,000. It has a payout ratio of 20% and a return on assets of 16%. How much did Haymark Products pay in cash dividends, and what were its average total assets?

Calculate amounts from profitability ratios.
(SO 4)

BE14–15 Staples, Inc. reported the following ratios for 2005 and 2004:

Evaluate profitability.
(SO 4)

	2005	2004
Asset turnover	2.2 times	2.2 times
Return on assets	10.8%	8.0%
Gross profit margin	30.3%	29.6%
Profit margin	5.0%	3.7%

Is Staples' profitability improving or deteriorating? Explain.

Exercises

⚙━━ All of the exercises in this section use decision tools.

Prepare discontinued operations
section.
(SO 1)

E14–1   Davis Ltd. reports earnings from continuing operations of $270,000 for the year ended December 31, 2006. It also has the following pre-tax items: (1) a net gain of $40,000 from a discontinued division, which includes a $110,000 gain from the operation of the division and a $70,000 loss on its disposal, and (2) a cumulative change in accounting principle that resulted in a $30,000 increase in the prior years' amortization. Assume all items are subject to a 40% income tax rate.

Instructions

(a) Prepare a partial statement of earnings for the year, starting with "earnings from continuing operations."
(b) Indicate the statement presentation of any items not included in (a).

Prepare statement of retained
earnings.
(SO 1)

E14–2   Vinh Corporation changed its method of inventory costing from average to FIFO in 2006. The cumulative effect of this change on prior years' earnings was $25,000 before income tax of 25%. Vinh's opening retained earnings on January 1, 2006, was $800,000. The company reported net earnings of $225,000 and distributed stock dividends of $50,000 for the year ended December 31, 2006.

Instructions

(a) If inventory prices have been rising each year since Vinh began operations, will the change from average to FIFO result in an increase or decrease to prior years' earnings? Explain.
(b) Prepare a statement of retained earnings for the year.

Prepare horizontal analysis.
(SO 2)

E14–3   Condensed data from the comparative balance sheet of Dressaire Inc. are presented below:

	2006	2005
Current assets	$128,000	$100,000
Noncurrent assets	400,000	350,000
Current liabilities	91,000	70,000
Long-term liabilities	144,000	95,000
Common shares	150,000	115,000
Retained earnings	143,000	170,000

Instructions

Prepare a horizontal analysis.

Prepare vertical analysis.
(SO 3)

E14–4   Condensed data from the statement of earnings for Fleetwood Corporation are presented below:

	2006	2005
Sales	$800,000	$600,000
Cost of goods sold	500,000	390,000
Operating expenses	200,000	156,000
Income tax expense	25,000	13,500
Net earnings	75,000	40,500

Instructions

Prepare a vertical analysis for each year.

E14–5 The statement of earnings for the Gap Inc. is presented below:

Prepare horizontal and vertical analyses of statement of earnings.
(SO 2, 3)

GAP INC.
Statement of Earnings
Year Ended January 29, 2005
(in U.S. millions)

	2005	2004
Net sales	$16,267	$15,854
Cost of goods sold	9,886	9,885
Gross profit	6,381	5,969
Operating expenses	4,296	4,068
Earnings from operations	2,085	1,901
Other expense	272	255
Other revenue	(59)	(38)
Earnings before income taxes	1,872	1,684
Income tax expense	722	653
Net earnings	$ 1,150	$ 1,031

Instructions

(a) Prepare a horizontal analysis.
(b) Prepare a vertical analysis for each year.
(c) Comment on any significant changes from 2004 to 2005.

E14–6 The condensed comparative balance sheet for Mountain Equipment Co-operative is presented below:

Prepare horizontal and vertical analyses of balance sheet.
(SO 2, 3)

MOUNTAIN EQUIPMENT CO-OPERATIVE
Balance Sheet
December 31
(in thousands)

	2004	2003
Assets		
Current assets	$58,150	$43,074
Property, plant, and equipment	39,225	39,868
Deferred store pre-opening costs	296	1,063
Total assets	$97,671	$84,005
Liabilities and Members' Equity		
Current liabilities	$18,873	$16,203
Long-term liabilities	4,113	5,330
Total liabilities	22,986	21,533
Members' equity	74,685	62,472
Total liabilities and members' equity	$97,671	$84,005

Instructions

(a) Prepare a horizontal analysis.
(b) Prepare a vertical analysis for each year.
(c) Comment on any significant changes from 2003 to 2004.

E14–7 The following is a list of the ratios and values we have calculated in this text:

Classify ratios.
(SO 4)

___ Asset turnover	___ Free cash flow
___ Average collection period	___ Inventory turnover
___ Cash current debt coverage	___ Payout ratio
___ Cash total debt coverage	___ Price-earnings ratio
___ Current ratio	___ Profit margin
___ Days in inventory	___ Receivables turnover
___ Debt to total assets	___ Return on assets

___ Dividend yield   ___ Return on common shareholders' equity
___ Gross profit margin   ___ Times interest earned
___ Earnings per share   ___ Working capital

Instructions

Classify each of the ratios as a liquidity (L), solvency (S), or profitability (P) ratio.

Calculate and evaluate liquidity ratios.
(SO 4)

E14–8   Carleton University had the following selected financial statement data as at April 30 of each year (in thousands):

	2005	2004
Current assets		
Cash and cash equivalents	$87,504	$ 85,773
Accounts receivable	22,003	15,603
Prepaid expenses	1,838	1,967
Total current assets	111,345	103,343
Total current liabilities	83,930	72,584
Revenues	361,837	337,711
Cash provided by operating activities	40,625	46,576

Instructions

(a) Calculate Carleton's current ratio, cash current debt coverage, receivables turnover, and average collection period for 2005. Use total revenues as a substitute for credit sales in the receivables turnover ratio.

(b) Comment on Carleton's liquidity.

Evaluate liquidity.
(SO 4)

E14–9   The following selected ratios are available for Pampered Pets Inc. for the three most recent years:

Ratio	2006	2005	2004
Current ratio	2.6:1	2.4:1	2.1:1
Receivables turnover	6.7 times	7.4 times	8.2 times
Inventory turnover	7.5 times	8.7 times	9.9 times

Instructions

(a) Has the company's collection of its receivables improved or deteriorated over the last three years?

(b) Is the company selling its inventory faster or slower than in past years?

(c) Overall, has the company's liquidity improved or deteriorated over the last three years? Explain.

Evaluate solvency.
(SO 4)

E14–10   The following selected ratios are available for Ice-T Inc. for the three most recent years:

Ratio	2006	2005	2004
Debt to total assets	50%	45%	40%
Times interest earned	2.0 times	1.5 times	1.0 times
Cash total debt coverage	0.8 times	0.6 times	0.4 times

Instructions

(a) Has the company's solvency improved or deteriorated over the last three years? Explain.

(b) How should you interpret accrual- and cash-based ratios that move in opposite directions? For example, what does it mean when an accrual-based solvency ratio, such as debt to total assets, indicates a deterioration of solvency and a cash-based solvency ratio, such as cash total debt coverage, indicates an improvement of solvency?

Calculate solvency and profitability ratios.
(SO 4)

E14–11   Selected financial data for Shoppers Drug Mart Corporation are presented below (in millions):

	2004	2003
Revenue	$4,723	$4,415
Cost of goods sold and other operating expenses	4,087	3,847
Interest expense	47	76
Income tax expense	174	152
Net earnings	316	257
Total assets	3,500	3,276
Total liabilities	1,342	1,446
Total common shareholders' equity	2,157	1,830
Cash provided by operating activities	377	365
Weighted average number of common shares	208	207

Instructions

Calculate the following ratios for 2004 and indicate whether each one is a measure of profitability or solvency:

(a) Profit margin
(b) Debt to total assets
(c) Asset turnover
(d) Return on assets

(e) Return on common shareholders' equity
(f) Times interest earned
(g) Earnings per share
(h) Cash total debt coverage

E14–12 Live Ltd. reported the following comparative balance sheet data:

Calculate ratios.
(SO 4)

LIVE LTD.
Balance Sheet
December 31

	2006	2005
Assets		
Cash	$ 20,000	$ 30,000
Accounts receivable	65,000	60,000
Inventories	60,000	50,000
Property, plant, and equipment	200,000	180,000
	$345,000	$320,000
Liabilities and Shareholders' Equity		
Accounts payable	$ 50,000	$ 60,000
Mortgage payable	100,000	100,000
Common shares	140,000	120,000
Retained earnings	55,000	40,000
	$345,000	$320,000

Additional information for 2006:

1. Net earnings were $21,000.
2. Sales on account were $420,000. Sales returns and allowances amounted to $20,000.
3. Cost of goods sold was $198,000.
4. The allowance for doubtful accounts was $8,500 at the end of 2006, and $8,000 at the end of 2005.
5. Cash provided by operating activities was $41,000.

Instructions

Calculate the following ratios for 2006:

(a) Current ratio
(b) Receivables turnover
(c) Average collection period
(d) Inventory turnover
(e) Days in inventory

(f) Cash current debt coverage
(g) Cash total debt coverage
(h) Debt to total assets
(i) Return on common shareholders' equity
(j) Return on assets

Evaluate profitability.
(SO 4)

E14–13 Nexen Inc. and Petro-Canada reported the following investor-related information recently:

	Nexen	Petro-Canada
Earnings per share	$2.47	$6.40
Price-earnings ratio	16.8 times	12.7 times
Dividend yield	0.5%	0.7%

Instructions

(a) Based on the above information, can you tell which company is more profitable?

(b) Which company do investors favour?

(c) Would investors purchase shares in these companies mainly for growth or for dividend income?

Evaluate liquidity, solvency, and profitability.
(SO 4)

E14–14   The following selected ratios are available for a recent year for Four Seasons Hotels Inc. and Fairmont Hotels & Resorts Inc., two large hotel chains headquartered in Toronto:

	Four Seasons	Fairmont	Industry Average
Liquidity			
Current ratio	5.6:1	1.0:1	1.0:1
Receivables turnover	3.8 times	10.9 times	8.5 times
Solvency			
Debt to total assets	30.6%	21.9%	42.9%
Times interest earned	327.7 times	8.0 times	3.5 times
Profitability			
Profit margin	7.2%	19.8%	7.2%
Return on assets	2.5%	6.3%	4.6%
Return on common shareholders' equity	3.8%	9.4%	11.0%

Instructions

(a) Which company is more liquid? Explain.

(b) Which company is more solvent? Explain.

(c) Which company is more profitable? Explain.

Determine effect of transactions on ratios.
(SO 4)

E14–15   Mahat Corporation started the year with the following ratios. During the year, these transactions occurred:

Transaction	Current ratio (1.5:1)	Cash current debt coverage (0.4 times)	Debt to total assets (30%)	Return on assets (20%)
(a) Purchased merchandise inventory on account. Mahat uses a perpetual inventory system.	D	D	I	D
(b) Paid cash on account				
(c) Sold merchandise on account.				
(d) Collected an account from a customer.				
(e) Purchased equipment, issuing a long-term note payable in payment.				
(f) Paid salaries.				

Instructions

Complete the above table, indicating whether the transaction causes each ratio to improve (I) or deteriorate (D), or if the transaction has no effect (NE). The first one has been done for you as an example.

Problems: Set A

🔧 All of the problems in this section use decision tools.

Prepare statements of earnings and retained earnings.
(SO 1)

P14–1A   Hyperchip Corporation reports the following summary data for the year ended July 31, 2007:

Net sales	$1,500,000	Other expenses	$ 30,000
Cost of goods sold	800,000	Retained earnings, August 1, 2006	1,225,000
Operating expenses	240,000	Dividends	50,000
Other revenues	40,000		

Your review of the transactions reveals the following additional information that is not included in the above data:

1. The ceramics division was discontinued during the year. The pre-tax loss from operations for this division was $150,000. The division was sold at a pre-tax gain of $70,000.
2. At the end of June, Hyperchip recorded a $28,000 pre-tax impairment loss on its goodwill.
3. Hyperchip changed its amortization method from straight-line to declining-balance during the year. The cumulative effect of the change on prior years' net earnings was a decrease of $30,000 before income tax.
4. The income tax rate is 30%.

Instructions

(a) Prepare a statement of earnings for the year.
(b) Prepare a statement of retained earnings for the year.

P14–2A Sleeman Breweries Ltd. has seen a significant amount of growth over the last three years. The following selected information is available for this craft brewer:

Prepare horizontal analysis.
(SO 2)

SLEEMAN BREWERIES LTD.
Balance Sheet
December 31
(in thousands)

	2004	2003	2002
Assets			
Current assets	$ 90,158	$ 73,118	$ 54,074
Noncurrent assets	209,994	169,637	167,359
Total assets	$300,152	$242,755	$221,433
Liabilities and Shareholders' Equity			
Current liabilities	$ 60,823	$ 55,512	$ 48,980
Noncurrent liabilities	117,545	83,443	82,256
Total liabilities	178,368	138,955	131,236
Shareholders' equity	121,784	103,800	90,197
Total liabilities and shareholders' equity	$300,152	$242,755	$221,433

SLEEMAN BREWERIES LTD.
Statement of Earnings
Year Ended December 31
(in thousands)

	2004	2003	2002
Net revenue	$213,354	$185,036	$157,053
Cost of goods sold	106,207	96,703	79,059
Gross profit	107,147	88,333	77,994
Operating expenses	85,019	67,330	59,483
Earnings before income taxes	22,128	21,003	18,511
Income tax expense	7,702	8,750	6,190
Net earnings	$ 14,426	$ 12,253	$ 12,321

Instructions

(a) Prepare a horizontal analysis of the balance sheet and statement of earnings.
(b) What components in Sleeman's balance sheet and statement of earnings have been the main drivers of the company's growth?

P14–3A The Big Rock Brewery has seen a significant number of changes in its financial position since it reorganized as an income trust in 2003. The following condensed information is available for this craft brewer:

Prepare vertical analysis.
(SO 3)

BIG ROCK BREWERY INCOME TRUST
Balance Sheet
December 31

	2004	2003
Assets		
Current assets	$ 9,980,068	$10,006,747
Noncurrent assets	30,948,400	30,804,429
Total assets	$40,928,468	$40,811,176
Liabilities and Unitholders' Equity		
Current liabilities	$ 4,014,186	$ 4,958,338
Noncurrent liabilities	7,394,131	9,166,319
Total liabilities	11,408,317	14,124,657
Unitholders' equity	29,520,151	26,686,519
Total liabilities and unitholders' equity	$40,928,468	$40,811,176

BIG ROCK BREWERY INCOME TRUST
Statement of Earnings
December 31

	2004 (12 months)	2003 (9 months)
Net sales	$38,789,564	$28,503,840
Cost of sales	13,696,549	10,298,575
Gross profit	25,093,015	18,205,265
Operating expenses	17,397,249	12,757,866
Earnings before income taxes	7,695,766	5,447,399
Income tax expense	928,858	891,543
Net earnings	$ 6,766,908	$ 4,555,856

Instructions

(a) Prepare a vertical analysis of the balance sheet and statement of earnings for each year.
(b) What components in Big Rock Brewery's balance sheet and statement of earnings have been the main drivers of the change between the two years?
(c) Is it possible to realistically compare the results for 2003 and 2004 using vertical analysis, given that 2003 covers only a nine-month period, and 2004 covers a twelve-month period? Explain.

Calculate and evaluate profitability ratios with discontinued operations. (SO 1, 4)

P14–4A   Montreal-based Alcan Inc. is one of the world's largest aluminum producers. It reported the following selected information for the last five years (in U.S. millions):

	2004	2003	2002	2001	2000
Revenues	$24,885	$13,850	$12,483	$12,545	$ 9,237
Average common shareholders' equity	10,342	9,124	8,271	8,495	7,060
Average total assets	32,644	24,854	17,656	17,698	13,848
Earnings (loss) from continuing operations	$252	$262	$421	$(60)	$582
Discontinued operations	6	(159)	(21)	(6)	
Net earnings (loss)	$258	$103	$400	$(66)	$582
Earnings (loss) per share from continuing operations	$0.67	$0.79	$1.29	$(0.01)	$2.42
Earnings (loss) per share	0.69	0.30	1.22	(0.02)	2.42

Instructions

(a) Calculate Alcan's profit margin, return on common shareholders' equity, and return on assets ratios before and after discontinued operations for each of the last five years.
(b) Evaluate Alcan's profitability over the last five years before and after discontinued operations.
(c) Which analysis is more relevant to investors? Explain.

P14–5A Fly-by-Night Inc. is in its first year of operations. The president of the company is debating which generally accepted accounting principles to use. She would like you to advise her about the impact that certain accounting principles will have on the various company ratios listed below:

Determine effects of alternative accounting principles on ratios. (SO 1, 4)

Accounting Principle	Current ratio (1.5:1)	Debt to total assets (25%)	Times interest earned (5×)	Gross profit margin (40%)	Earnings per share ($1.50)
(a) The company will be leasing automobiles and is thinking about setting the lease up as a capital lease. Interest expense and amortization expense under a capital lease will be higher than rent expense would be under an operating lease.	D	I	D	NE	D
(b) The company is considering using double declining-balance amortization, which will result in a higher expense than other methods.					
(c) It is a period of inflation and the president would like to use the FIFO inventory cost flow assumption, instead of average cost.					

Instructions

Indicate whether the above accounting principles will increase (I), decrease (D), or have no effect (NE) on each of the ratios presented. The first one has been done for you as an example.

P14–6A Selected ratios for two different real companies are presented below. One of the companies is in the retail industry, the other in the construction industry.

Identify industry from ratio analysis. (SO 4)

	Company A	Company B
Receivables turnover	51.9 times	12.8 times
Inventory turnover	17.4 times	8.3 times
Debt to total assets	31.2%	51.9%
Gross profit margin	24.5%	15.5%
Profit margin	3.6%	6.1%
Return on assets	8.6%	4.7%
Asset turnover	2.5 times	0.8 times

Instructions

Identify which company operates in which industry. Explain your reasoning for each choice.

P14–7A The management of Bella Coola Inc. would like to better understand the impact of the following transactions on specific ratios:

Determine effect of transactions on ratios. (SO 4)

Transaction	Ratio
(a) Issue notes payable to finance an expansion	Debt to total assets; times interest earned
(b) Issue common shares to finance an expansion	Return on common shareholders' equity
(c) Pay dividends	Payout ratio; dividend yield
(d) Purchase inventory on credit in a perpetual inventory system	Current ratio; inventory turnover
(e) Sell inventory on credit in a perpetual inventory system	Receivables turnover; gross profit margin
(f) Write off an uncollectible account	Current ratio; receivables turnover
(g) Purchase a new building	Return on assets; asset turnover

Instructions

Indicate whether each of the above transactions will increase (I), decrease (D), or have no effect (NE) on the ratio(s) listed next to the transaction. Explain your reasoning.

Calculate and evaluate ratios.
(SO 4)

P14–8A   Condensed balance sheet and statement of earnings data for Pitka Corporation are presented here:

PITKA CORPORATION
BALANCE SHEET
December 31

	2006	2005	2004
Assets			
Cash	$ 40,000	$ 20,000	$ 18,000
Accounts receivable (net)	50,000	45,000	48,000
Available-for-sale securities (short-term)	55,000	70,000	45,000
Inventory	90,000	85,000	64,000
Property, plant, and equipment	500,000	370,000	258,000
	$735,000	$590,000	$433,000
Liabilities and Shareholders' Equity			
Current liabilities	$ 85,000	$ 80,000	$ 30,000
Long-term liabilities	165,000	85,000	20,000
Common shares	340,000	300,000	300,000
Retained earnings	145,000	125,000	83,000
	$735,000	$590,000	$433,000

PITKA CORPORATION
Statement of Earnings
Year Ended December 31

	2006	2005
Sales	$640,000	$500,000
Less: Sales returns and allowances	40,000	50,000
Net sales	600,000	450,000
Cost of goods sold	425,000	300,000
Gross profit	175,000	150,000
Operating expenses	113,000	84,000
Earnings from operations	62,000	66,000
Interest expense	8,000	4,000
Earnings before income taxes	54,000	62,000
Income tax expense	10,800	12,400
Net earnings	$ 43,200	$ 49,600

Additional information:

1. The allowance for doubtful accounts was $5,000 in 2006, $4,500 in 2005, and $4,800 in 2004.
2. All sales were credit sales.
3. The market prices of Pitka's common shares were $8 at the end of 2006 and $5 at the end of 2005.
4. All dividends were paid in cash. (*Hint*: Analyze retained earnings to calculate dividends.)
5. On July 1, 2006, 4,000 common shares were issued, bringing the total number of shares to 34,000.

Instructions

(a) Calculate the following ratios for 2005 and 2006:

1. Current ratio	8. Gross profit margin
2. Receivables turnover	9. Profit margin
3. Inventory turnover	10. Return on assets
4. Debt to total assets	11. Asset turnover
5. Times interest earned	12. Payout ratio
6. Earnings per share	13. Dividend yield
7. Price-earnings	

(b) Based on the ratios calculated, discuss the improvement or lack of improvement in the financial position and operating results from 2005 to 2006.

P14–9A Condensed balance sheet and statement of earnings data for Click and Clack Ltd. are presented here:

Calculate and evaluate ratios. (SO 4)

CLICK AND CLACK LTD.
Balance Sheet
December 31

	2006	2005
Assets		
Cash	$ 70,000	$ 65,000
Accounts receivable (net of allowance for doubtful		
accounts of $5,000 in 2006 and $4,000 in 2005)	94,000	90,000
Inventories	230,000	125,000
Prepaid expenses	25,000	23,000
Available-for-sale securities (long-term)	45,000	40,000
Property, plant, and equipment	390,000	305,000
Total assets	$854,000	$648,000
Liabilities and Shareholders' Equity		
Notes payable	$170,000	$100,000
Accounts payable	45,000	42,000
Accrued liabilities	40,000	40,000
Bonds payable	250,000	150,000
Common shares (20,000 shares)	200,000	200,000
Retained earnings	149,000	116,000
Total liabilities and shareholders' equity	$854,000	$648,000

CLICK AND CLACK LTD.
Statement of Earnings
Year Ended December 31

	2006	2005
Sales	$900,000	$840,000
Cost of goods sold	620,000	575,000
Gross profit	280,000	265,000
Operating expenses	194,000	180,000
Earnings before income taxes	86,000	85,000
Income tax expense	30,000	30,000
Net earnings	$ 56,000	$ 55,000

Additional information:
1. Accounts receivable at the beginning of 2005 were $88,000, net of an allowance for doubtful accounts of $3,000.
2. Inventories at the beginning of 2005 were $115,000.
3. Total assets at the beginning of 2005 were $630,000.
4. Shareholders' equity at the beginning of 2005 was $315,000.
5. Seventy-five percent of the sales were on account.

Instructions

Indicate, by using ratios, the change in Click and Clack's liquidity, solvency, and profitability from 2005 to 2006. (*Note*: Not all ratios can be calculated.)

Evaluate liquidity, solvency, and profitability.
(SO 4)

P14–10A   Best Buy Co., Inc., the #1 consumer electronics retailer, distributes its goods in Canada through Future Shop Ltd. Circuit City Stores, Inc., the #3 consumer electronics retailer, distributes its goods in Canada through InterTAN, Inc. The following ratios are available for each company, and their industry, for a recent year:

	Best Buy	Circuit City	Industry Average
Liquidity			
Current ratio	1.4:1	2.1:1	1.6:1
Receivables turnover	76.4 times	27.8 times	44.6 times
Inventory turnover	7.5 times	5.2 times	5.5 times
Solvency			
Debt to total assets	11.5%	0.1%	42.9%
Times interest earned	n/a	47.4 times	19.9 times
Profitability			
Gross profit margin	25.4%	27.1%	29.0%
Profit margin	3.6%	0.5%	2.8%
Asset turnover	2.9 times	2.8 times	2.4 times
Return on assets	9.6%	1.4%	6.1%
Return on common shareholders' equity	22.1%	2.6%	13.4%
Price-earnings ratio	23.4 times	59.9 times	28.4 times
Payout ratio	14.3%	31.0%	7.9%

Instructions

(a) Which company is more liquid? Explain.
(b) Which company is more solvent? Explain.
(c) Which company is more profitable? Explain.
(d) Which company do investors favour? Is your answer consistent with your analysis in (c)?

Evaluate liquidity, solvency, and profitability.
(SO 4)

P14–11A   The following ratios are available for fast-food competitors McDonald's Corporation and Wendy's International, Inc., and their industry, for a recent year:

	McDonald's	Wendy's	Industry Average
Liquidity			
Current ratio	1.0:1	0.7:1	0.9:1
Receivables turnover	29.0 times	29.9 times	31.7 times
Inventory turnover	65.0 times	47.3 times	29.7 times
Solvency			
Debt to total assets	37.1%	28.6%	39.4%
Times interest earned	10.2 times	9.3 times	6.3 times
Profitability			
Gross profit margin	56.6%	24.4%	39.3%
Profit margin	12.8%	1.4%	6.6%
Return on common shareholders' equity	17.0%	2.9%	15.8%
Return on assets	9.2%	1.6%	7.4%
Asset turnover	0.7 times	1.2 times	1.2 times
Payout ratio	28.2%	111.1%	20.7%
Price-earnings ratio	14.3 times	105.9 times	19.2 times

Instructions

(a) Which company is more liquid? Explain.
(b) Which company is more solvent? Explain.
(c) Which company is more profitable? Explain.
(d) Which company do investors favour? Is your answer consistent with your findings in (c)?

Evaluate ratios.
(SO 4)

P14–12A   You are the chief financial officer for a major office supply company called Paperclip Inc. You have been asked to prepare a report for the board of directors on the financial condition and performance of the company. To that end, you have assembled the following ratios for Paperclip Inc., and its competitor Stapler Ltd.:

	Paperclip	Stapler	Industry Average
Asset turnover	2.5 times	2.2 times	2.5 times
Average collection period	31 days	35 days	36 days
Cash current debt coverage	0.3 times	0.1 times	0.2 times
Current ratio	1.7:1	3.0:1	1.6:1
Debt to total assets	50%	33%	50%
Earnings per share	$3.50	$0.40	n/a
Gross profit margin	23%	40%	27%
Inventory turnover	7 times	3 times	5 times
Payout ratio	8.5%	22%	10%
Price-earnings ratio	29 times	45 times	38 times
Profit margin	5%	4%	4%
Return on common shareholders' equity	25%	13%	16%
Times interest earned	4.2 times	8.6 times	7.1 times

Instructions

(a) You want to start the presentation to the board by commenting on Paperclip's overall corporate performance compared to Stapler and industry averages. Specifically, what ratio would you choose to assess overall corporate performance for the current fiscal year? Why? Explain how the result for Paperclip compares to Stapler and the industry average.

(b) Paperclip offers its customers credit terms of net 30 days. Indicate the ratio(s) to use to assess Paperclip's accounts receivable management. Comment on how well Paperclip appears to be managing its accounts receivable.

(c) Which company, Paperclip or Stapler, is more solvent? Identify the ratio(s) used to determine this and explain the significance of Paperclip's result. Is Paperclip more or less solvent than the industry?

(d) To your surprise, you notice that Paperclip's gross profit margin is less than both Stapler's and the industry average. Identify two possible reasons for this.

(e) How well does Paperclip appear to be managing its inventory? Indicate the ratio(s) used to assess the company's inventory management. How well is Paperclip managing its inventory compared to Stapler and the industry average?

(f) Paperclip's payout ratio is lower than Stapler's and the industry average. Indicate one possible reason for this.

(g) What is the market price per share of Paperclip's common shares?

(h) Which company—Paperclip or Stapler—do investors appear to believe has greater prospects for growing its earnings and dividends? Indicate the ratio(s) you used to reach this conclusion and explain your reasoning.

P14–13A Presented here are an incomplete statement of earnings and balance sheet for Schwenke Corporation:

Calculate missing information using ratios.
(SO 4)

SCHWENKE CORPORATION
Statement of Earnings
Year Ended December 31, 2006

Sales	$ (a)
Cost of goods sold	(b)
Gross profit	(c)
Operating expenses	322,833
Earnings from operations	(d)
Interest expense	10,500
Earnings before income taxes	(e)
Income tax expense	(f)
Net earnings	$125,000

SCHWENKE CORPORATION
Balance Sheet
December 31, 2006

Assets

Current assets	
Cash	$ 54,000
Accounts receivable	(g)
Inventory	(h)
Total current assets	(i)
Property, plant, and equipment	(j)
Total assets	$ (k)
Liabilities	
Current liabilities	$ (l)
Long-term liabilities	210,000
Total liabilities	(m)
Shareholders' Equity	
Common shares	320,000
Retained earnings	330,000
Total shareholders' equity	650,000
Total liabilities and shareholders' equity	$ (n)

Additional information:

1. The profit margin is 10%.
2. The gross profit margin is 40%.
3. The income tax rate is 25%.
4. The asset turnover is 1.25 times.
5. The current ratio is 2:1.
6. The inventory turnover is 6 times.

Instructions

Calculate the missing information using the ratios. Use ending balances instead of average balances, where averages are required for ratio calculations. Show your calculations. (*Hint*: Start with one ratio and get as much information as possible from it before trying another ratio. You will not be able to calculate the missing amounts in the same sequence as they are presented above.)

Problems: Set B

🔧 All of the problems in this section use decision tools.

Prepare statements of earnings and retained earnings.
(SO 1)

P14–1B   The Fox Harbour Corporation reports the following summary data for the year ended December 31, 2006:

Net sales	$1,700,000
Cost of goods sold	1,100,000
Operating expenses	260,000
Other revenues	20,000
Other expenses	8,000
Retained earnings, January 1	940,000
Dividends	25,000

Your review of the transactions reveals the following additional information that is not included in the above data:

1. The communications division was discontinued during the year. The pre-tax gain from operations for this division was $20,000. The division was sold at a pre-tax loss of $70,000.

2. Fox Harbour incurred a pre-tax loss from winter storm damage of $28,000. The company is located on the Northumberland Shore of Nova Scotia where strong winds and waves frequently occur.

3. Fox Harbour changed its amortization method from declining-balance to straight-line during the year. The cumulative effect of the change on prior years' net earnings was an increase of $60,000 before income tax.

4. The income tax rate is 25%.

Instructions

(a) Prepare a statement of earnings for the year.
(b) Prepare a statement of retained earnings for the year.

P14–2B ClubLink Corporation is Canada's largest golf course and resort owner with about 25 private courses, four daily fee courses (including Glen Abbey, one of the country's top public courses), and five golf resorts. The following selected information is available for ClubLink:

Prepare horizontal analysis.
(SO 2)

CLUBLINK CORPORATION
Balance Sheet
December 31
(in thousands)

	2004	2003	2002
Assets			
Current assets	$ 8,902	$ 9,350	$ 12,132
Noncurrent assets	532,116	516,938	480,109
Total assets	$541,018	$526,288	$492,241
Liabilities and Shareholders' Equity			
Current liabilities	$ 32,294	$ 90,534	$ 27,605
Noncurrent liabilities	330,055	246,588	189,515
Total liabilities	362,349	337,122	217,120
Shareholders' equity	178,669	189,166	275,121
Total liabilities and shareholders' equity	$541,018	$526,288	$492,241

CLUBLINK CORPORATION
Statement of Earnings
Year Ended December 31
(in thousands)

	2004	2003	2002
Revenue	$129,728	$117,310	$109,912
Operating expenses	112,336	103,763	95,373
Earnings from operations	17,392	13,547	14,539
Other revenues	2,533	3,071	2,874
Other expenses	22,383	16,607	14,713
Earnings (loss) before income taxes	(2,458)	11	2,700
Income tax expense (recovery)	(170)	822	1,878
Net earnings (loss)	$ (2,288)	$ (811)	$ 822

Instructions

(a) Prepare a horizontal analysis of the balance sheet and statement of earnings.
(b) How has ClubLink financed its growth in assets during a time of increasing losses?

P14–3B The Yellow Pages Income Fund started operations August 1, 2003. The following condensed information is available for Canada's largest telephone directories publisher:

Prepare vertical analysis.
(SO 3)

YELLOW PAGES INCOME FUND
Balance Sheet
December 31
(in thousands)

	2004	2003
<u>Assets</u>		
Current assets	$ 351,620	$ 386,331
Capital assets	58,082	40,834
Intangible assets	1,199,196	1,307,601
Goodwill	3,268,927	2,681,579
Other assets	62,621	46,399
Total assets	$4,940,446	$4,462,744
<u>Liabilities and Unitholders' Equity</u>		
Current liabilities	$ 135,870	$ 309,765
Noncurrent liabilities	1,292,905	1,730,498
Total liabilities	1,428,775	2,040,263
Unitholders' equity	3,511,671	2,422,481
Total liabilities and unitholders' equity	$4,940,446	$4,462,744

YELLOW PAGES INCOME FUND
Statement of Earnings
December 31
(in thousands)

	2004 (12 months)	2003 (5 months)
Revenues	$637,346	$25,416
Operating expenses	484,120	21,377
Earnings from operations	153,226	4,039
Other revenues		2,106
Other expenses	79,820	5,175
Earnings before income taxes	73,406	970
Income tax expense (recovery)	(33,583)	(2,191)
Net earnings	$106,989	$ 3,161

Instructions

(a) Prepare a vertical analysis of the balance sheet and statement of earnings for each year.
(b) What is the probable reason that the Yellow Pages has such a large and increasing proportion of intangible assets and goodwill?
(c) How has the Yellow Pages financed its asset growth—through debt or equity?
(d) Is it possible to realistically compare the results for 2003 and 2004 using vertical analysis, given that 2003 covers only a 5-month period and 2004 covers a 12-month period? Explain.

Calculate and evaluate profitability ratios with discontinued operations.
(SO 1, 4)

P14–4B   Nexen Inc. is a globe-trotting oil and gas and chemicals company. It reported the following selected information for the last five years (in millions):

	2004	2003	2002	2001	2000
Revenues	$ 3,905	$3,454	$2,837	$3,073	$2,967
Average common shareholders' equity	2,471	1,832	1,362	932	1,264
Average total assets	10,050	7,138	5,995	5,543	4,880
Earnings from continuing operations	$780	$550	$356	$411	$565
Discontinued operations	13	28	53		
Net earnings	$793	$578	$409	$411	$565
Earnings per share from continuing operations	$6.07	$4.45	$2.91	$3.40	$4.52
Earnings per share	6.17	4.67	3.34	3.40	4.52

Instructions

(a) Calculate Nexen's profit margin, return on common shareholders' equity, and return on assets ratios before and after discontinued operations for each of the last five years.

(b) Evaluate Nexen's profitability over the last five years before and after discontinued operations.

(c) Which analysis is more relevant to investors? Explain.

P14–5B The president of Dot.Com Inc. is debating which generally accepted accounting principles to use. He would like you to advise him about the impact that selected accounting principles will have on the various company ratios listed below:

Determine effects of alternative accounting principles on ratios.
(SO 1, 4)

Accounting Principle	Current ratio (1.5:1)	Debt to total assets (25%)	Times interest earned (5×)	Gross profit margin (40%)	Earnings per share ($1.50)
(a) The company will be leasing equipment and is thinking about setting it up as an operating lease. Rent expense under an operating lease will be lower than interest and amortization expense would be under a capital lease.	NE	D	I	NE	I
(b) The company is considering using straight-line amortization, which will result in a lower expense than other methods.					
(c) It is a period of deflation and the president would like to use the FIFO inventory cost flow assumption, instead of average cost.					

Instructions

Indicate whether the above accounting principles will increase (I), decrease (D), or have no effect (NE) on each of the ratios presented. The first one has been done for you as an example.

P14–6B Selected ratios for two different real companies are presented below. One of the companies is in the brewing industry, the other in the energy industry.

Identify industry from ratio analysis.
(SO 4)

	Company A	Company B
Receivables turnover	16.5 times	11.2 times
Inventory turnover	11.2 times	n/a
Debt to total assets	36.7%	62.0%
Gross profit margin	45.5%	31.6%
Profit margin	14.7%	8.4%
Return on assets	13.3%	2.6%
Asset turnover	0.9 times	0.3 times

Instructions

Identify which company operates in which industry. Explain your reasoning for each choice.

P14–7B The management of Konotopsky Inc. would like to better understand the impact of the following transactions on specific ratios:

Determine effect of transactions on ratios.
(SO 4)

Transaction	Ratio
(a) Issued bonds payable to finance an expansion	Debt to total assets; cash total debt coverage
(b) Paid interest on bonds	Times interest earned
(c) Reacquired common shares	Return on common shareholders' equity
(d) Performed services on account	Receivables turnover; profit margin
(e) Sold inventory for cash in a perpetual inventory system	Inventory turnover; gross profit margin
(f) Collected a previously written-off account receivable	Current ratio; receivables turnover
(g) Sold a piece of land at a gain	Return on assets; asset turnover

Instructions

Indicate whether each of the above transactions will increase (I), decrease (D), or have no effect (NE) on the ratio(s) listed next to the transaction. Explain your reasoning.

Calculate and evaluate ratios.
(SO 4)

P14–8B   Condensed balance sheet and statement of earnings data for Colinas Corporation are presented here:

COLINAS CORPORATION
Balance Sheet
December 31

	2006	2005	2004
Assets			
Cash	$ 40,000	$ 24,000	$ 20,000
Accounts receivable (net)	73,000	55,000	48,000
Inventory	55,000	40,000	45,000
Other current assets	80,000	75,000	62,000
Available-for-sale securities (long-term)	90,000	76,000	50,000
Property, plant, and equipment	595,000	360,000	315,000
	$933,000	$630,000	$540,000
Liabilities and Shareholders' Equity			
Current liabilities	$ 98,000	$ 75,000	$ 70,000
Long-term liabilities	250,000	75,000	65,000
Common shares	400,000	340,000	300,000
Retained earnings	185,000	140,000	105,000
	$933,000	$630,000	$540,000

COLINAS CORPORATION
Statement of Earnings
Year Ended December 31

	2006	2005
Sales	$800,000	$750,000
Less: Sales returns and allowances	40,000	50,000
Net sales	760,000	700,000
Cost of goods sold	420,000	400,000
Gross profit	340,000	300,000
Operating expenses	266,000	237,000
Earnings before income taxes	74,000	63,000
Income tax expense	22,200	18,900
Net earnings	$ 51,800	$ 44,100

Additional information:

1. The allowance for doubtful accounts was $3,650 in 2006, $2,750 in 2005, and $2,400 in 2004.
2. All sales were credit sales.
3. The market price of Colinas' common shares was $10 and $11 for 2006 and 2005, respectively.
4. All dividends were paid in cash. (*Hint*: Analyze retained earnings to determine dividends.)
5. On July 1, 2005, 4,000 common shares were issued, and on July 1, 2006, 7,500 shares were issued. At the end of 2006, 40,000 shares have been issued in total.
6. Cash provided by operating activities was $51,800 in 2006 and $29,000 in 2005.

Instructions

(a) Calculate the following ratios for 2005 and 2006:
   1. Current ratio
   2. Receivables turnover
   3. Inventory turnover
   4. Debt to total assets
   5. Cash total debt coverage
   8. Gross profit margin
   9. Profit margin
   10. Return on assets
   11. Asset turnover
   12. Payout ratio

6. Earnings per share 13. Dividend yield
7. Price-earnings

(b) Based on the ratios calculated, discuss the improvement or lack of improvement in the financial position and operating results from 2005 to 2006.

P14–9B Condensed balance sheet and statement of earnings data for Star Track Ltd. are presented here:

Calculate and evaluate ratios. (SO 4)

STAR TRACK LTD. BALANCE SHEET DECEMBER 31		
	2006	2005
Assets		
Cash and cash equivalents	$ 50,000	$ 42,000
Accounts receivable (net of allowance for doubtful accounts of $5,000 in 2006 and $4,000 in 2005)	100,000	87,000
Inventories	440,000	300,000
Prepaid expenses	25,000	31,000
Available-for-sale securities (long-term)	80,000	50,000
Land	75,000	75,000
Buildings and equipment	570,000	400,000
Total assets	$1,340,000	$985,000
Liabilities and Shareholders' Equity		
Notes payable	$ 125,000	$ 25,000
Accounts payable	160,000	90,000
Current portion of mortgage payable	48,750	25,000
Mortgage payable	200,000	125,000
Common shares (100,000 shares)	500,000	500,000
Retained earnings	306,250	220,000
Total liabilities and shareholders' equity	$1,340,000	$985,000

STAR TRACK LTD. Statement of Earnings Year Ended December 31		
	2006	2005
Sales	$1,000,000	$940,000
Cost of goods sold	650,000	635,000
Gross profit	350,000	305,000
Operating expenses	235,000	215,000
Earnings before income taxes	115,000	90,000
Income tax expense	28,750	22,500
Net earnings	$ 86,250	$ 67,500

Additional information:

1. Inventories at the beginning of 2005 were $350,000.
2. Accounts receivable at the beginning of 2005 were $80,000, net of an allowance for doubtful accounts of $3,000.
3. Total assets at the beginning of 2005 were $1,175,000.
4. Current liabilities at the beginning of 2005 were $200,000.
5. Total liabilities at the beginning of 2005 were $835,000.
6. Total shareholders' equity at the beginning of 2005 was $340,000.
7. All sales were on account.
8. Cash provided by operating activities was $80,000 in 2006, and $65,000 in 2005.

Instructions

Indicate, by using ratios, the change in Star Track's liquidity, solvency, and profitability from 2005 to 2006. (*Note*: Not all ratios can be calculated.)

Evaluate liquidity, solvency, and
profitability.
(SO 4)

P14–10B   The following ratios are available for tool-makers Black & Decker Corporation
and Snap-On Incorporated, and their industry, for a recent year:

	Black & Decker	Snap-On Tools	Industry Average
Liquidity			
Current ratio	1.5:1	1.8:1	1.9:1
Receivables turnover	5.9 times	4.3 times	5.0 times
Inventory turnover	3.8 times	3.6 times	3.4 times
Solvency			
Debt to total assets	44.1%	23.7%	28.6%
Times interest earned	41.2 times	6.5 times	15.7 times
Profitability			
Gross profit margin	38.5%	47.6%	40.0%
Profit margin	8.9%	3.6%	7.4%
Asset turnover	1.2 times	1.1 times	1.1 times
Return on assets	9.5%	3.9%	7.5%
Return on common shareholders' equity	34.5%	8.1%	16.6%
Price-earnings ratio	14.3 times	23.2 times	16.8 times
Payout ratio	14.4%	67.1%	23.1%

Instructions

(a) Which company is more liquid? Explain.
(b) Which company is more solvent? Explain.
(c) Which company is more profitable? Explain.
(d) Which company do investors favour? Is your answer consistent with your analysis in (c)?

Evaluate liquidity, solvency, and
profitability.
(SO 4)

P14–11B   The following ratios are available for two paper products companies, Domtar Inc.
and Cascades Inc., and their industry, for a recent year:

	Domtar	Cascades	Industry Average
Liquidity			
Current ratio	1.6:1	1.8:1	1.3:1
Receivables turnover	23.8 times	6.4 times	5.3 times
Inventory turnover	5.9 times	5.1 times	6.5 times
Solvency			
Debt to total assets	50.5%	54.5%	51.5%
Times interest earned	0.4 times	1.3 times	3.0 times
Profitability			
Gross profit margin	15.5%	17.3%	27.7%
Profit margin	(0.8)%	0.7%	3.9%
Return on common shareholders' equity	(2.1)%	2.2%	8.9%
Return on assets	0.4%	3.0%	2.9%
Asset turnover	0.9 times	1.0 times	0.7 times
Payout ratio	(1.3)%	0.6%	67.3%
Dividend yield	1.5%	1.2%	n/a
Price-earnings ratio	n/a	46.4 times	20.9 times

Instructions

(a) Which company is more liquid? Explain.
(b) Which company is more solvent? Explain.
(c) Which company is more profitable? Explain.
(d) Which company do investors favour? Is your answer consistent with your findings in (c)?

Evaluate ratios.
(SO 4)

P14–12B   Selected ratios for the current year for two companies in the beverage industry,
Refresh Corp. and Flavour Limited, follow:

	Refresh	Flavour	Industry Average
Asset turnover	1.0 times	1.0 times	0.9 times
Cash total debt coverage	32%	20%	n/a
Current ratio	0.6:1	1.1:1	0.8:1
Debt to total assets	56%	72%	81%
Earnings per share	$0.98	$1.37	$1.08
Gross profit margin	74%	60%	58%
Inventory turnover	5.8 times	9.9 times	8.3 times
Price-earnings ratio	50.3 times	24.3 times	32.2 times
Profit margin	12%	11%	8%
Receivables turnover	11.4 times	9.8 times	9.3 times
Return on assets	11%	9%	7%
Return on common shareholders' equity	26%	30%	26%
Times interest earned	15.3 times	7.9 times	5.3 times

Instructions

(a) Both companies offer their customers credit terms of net 30 days. Indicate the ratio(s) to use to assess accounts receivable management. Comment on how well each company appears to be managing its accounts receivable.

(b) Which company, Refresh or Flavour, is more solvent? Identify the ratio(s) used to determine this and defend your choice.

(c) To your surprise, you notice that Refresh's gross profit margin is much higher than both Flavour's and the industry average. Identify two possible reasons for this.

(d) How well does each company appear to be managing its inventory? Indicate the ratio(s) used to assess inventory management.

(e) What is mostly driving Refresh's higher return on assets—profit margin or asset turnover? Explain.

(f) What is the market price per share of each company's common shares?

(g) Which company do investors appear to believe has greater prospects for growing its earnings and dividends? Indicate the ratio(s) you used to reach this conclusion and explain your reasoning.

P14–13B Presented here are an incomplete statement of earnings and balance sheet for Vienna Corporation:

Calculate missing information using ratios.
(SO 4)

VIENNA CORPORATION
Statement of Earnings
Year ended December 31, 2006

Sales	$11,000,000
Cost of goods sold	(a)
Gross profit	(b)
Operating expenses	1,500,000
Earnings from operations	(c)
Interest expense	(d)
Earnings before income taxes	(e)
Income tax expense	560,000
Net earnings	$ (f)

VIENNA CORPORATION
Balance Sheet
December 31, 2006

Assets

Current assets

Cash	$	(g)
Accounts receivable		(h)
Inventory		(i)
Total current assets		(j)
Available-for-sale securities		430,000
Property, plant, and equipment		4,620,000
Total assets	$	(k)

Liabilities

Current liabilities	$	(l)
Long-term liabilities		(m)
Total liabilities		(n)

Shareholders' Equity

Common shares		2,500,000
Retained earnings		900,000
Total shareholders' equity		3,400,000
Total liabilities and shareholders' equity	$	(o)

Additional information:

1. The receivables turnover is 10 times.
2. All sales are on account.
3. The gross profit margin is 36%.
4. The profit margin is 14.5%.
5. The return on assets is 22%.
6. The current ratio is 2:1.
7. The inventory turnover is 8 times.

Instructions

Calculate the missing information using the ratios. Use ending balances instead of average balances, where averages are required for ratio calculations. Show your calculations. (*Hint:* Start with one ratio and get as much information as possible from it before trying another ratio. You will not be able to calculate the missing amounts in the same sequence as they are presented above.)

BROADENING YOUR PERSPECTIVE

Financial Reporting and Analysis

 Analysis Tools

Financial Reporting Problem: *Loblaw*

BYP14–1   Refer to the financial statements of Loblaw presented in Appendix A.

Instructions

(a) Prepare a horizontal analysis for 2003 and 2002.
(b) Prepare a vertical analysis for 2003 and 2002.
(c) Comment on any significant changes you observe from your calculations in (a) and (b).

Comparative Analysis Problem: *Loblaw and Sobeys*

BYP14–2   The financial statements of Sobeys are presented in Appendix B, following the financial statements for Loblaw in Appendix A.

Instructions

(a) Calculate or find liquidity ratios that you believe are relevant for each company. Which company is more liquid?
(b) Calculate or find solvency ratios that you believe are relevant for each company. Which company is more solvent?
(c) Calculate or find profitability ratios that you believe are relevant for each company. Which company is more profitable?
(d) What information that is not included in the financial statements might also be useful for comparing Sobeys and Loblaw?

Research Case

BYP14–3   The March 14–27, 2005, issue of *Canadian Business* includes an article by Al Rosen on page 45 entitled "Artful Figures: How Companies Can Mislead Investors with Annual Reporting."

Instructions

Read the article and answer these questions:

(a) The article gives several examples of poor or deceptive financial reporting. Choose any two examples and explain why they have been included in this list of examples.
(b) Which company does Al Rosen call "one of the worst in Canada" when it comes to financial reporting? Why?

Interpreting Financial Statements

BYP14–4   Selected ratios for the Coca-Cola Company and PepsiCo, Inc., and their industry, are presented here for a recent year:

	Coca-Cola	PepsiCo	Industry
Liquidity			
Current ratio	1.2:1	1.2:1	1.1:1
Receivables turnover	10.7 times	9.5 times	10.5 times
Inventory turnover	4.7 times	8.0 times	8.4 times
Solvency			
Debt to total assets	29.6%	23.1%	45.9%
Times interest earned	29.0 times	32.3 times	8.2 times
Profitability			
Gross profit margin	69.4%	58.0%	55.0%
Profit margin	21.3%	14.5%	11.1%
Return on common shareholders' equity	28.6%	30.9%	24.9%
Return on assets	14.9%	15.1%	9.4%
Asset turnover	0.7 times	1.1 times	0.9 times
Price-earnings ratio	21.3 times	21.6 times	20.1 times

Instructions

(a) Comment on the relative liquidity of the two companies.
(b) Comment on the relative solvency of the two companies.
(c) Comment on the relative profitability of the two companies.

A Global Focus

BYP14–5 Tire manufacturer Compagnie Générale des Établissements Michelin (Michelin) is headquartered in France and manufactures and distributes tires globally. According to its 2004 annual report, Michelin has a 20-percent share of the tire market and labels itself "the world's No. 1 tire manufacturer." One of Michelin's main competitors, The Goodyear Tire & Rubber Company makes similar claims: "the world's largest tire company, with operations in most regions of the world." The following data were taken from the December 31, 2004 financial statements of each company:

	Michelin (in millions of Euros)		Goodyear (in U.S. millions)	
	2004	2003	2004	2003
Cash and cash equivalents	€ 1,655.4	€ 1,773.7	$ 1,967.9	$ 1,546.3
Accounts receivable	2,920.2	2,984.5	3,427.4	2,616.3
Total current assets	9,390.6	9,565.5	8,631.7	6,959.6
Total assets	16,170.5	16,166.9	16,533.3	14,701.1
Total current liabilities	8,505.2	8,751.5	5,113.1	3,666.5
Total shareholders' equity	4,601.9	4,327.4	72.8	(32.2)
Net sales	15,688.8	15,369.8	18,370.4	15,122.1
Operating expenses	14,997.1	14,831.6	2,833.1	2,374.2
Interest expense	213.2	224.9	368.8	296.3
Income tax expense	315.8	261.4	207.9	117.1
Net earnings	515.1	317.5	114.8	(807.4)
Cash provided by operating activities	1,336.9	1,542.2	719.8	(288.8)
Capital expenditures	1,116.8	1,117.8	518.6	375.4
Dividends	185.3	180.4	28.9	38.6

Instructions

Where available, industry averages are shown in parentheses next to each ratio below.
(a) Calculate the following liquidity ratios for 2004 and discuss the relative liquidity of the two companies and the tire manufacturing industry:
   1. Current ratio (2.0:1)
   2. Cash current debt coverage (n/a)
   3. Receivables turnover (5.8 times)
(b) Calculate the following solvency ratios for 2004 and discuss the relative solvency of the two companies and of the tire manufacturing industry:
   1. Debt to total assets (59.5%)
   2. Times interest earned (3.1 times)
   3. Cash total debt coverage (n/a)
   4. Free cash flow (n/a)
(c) Calculate the following profitability ratios for 2004 and discuss the relative profitability of the two companies and the tire manufacturing industry:
   1. Asset turnover (1.1 times)
   2. Profit margin (2.8%)
   3. Return on assets (3.0%)
   4. Return on common shareholders' equity (14.3%)
(d) What factors might be causing the differences you found?

Financial Analysis on the Web

Analysis Tools
(Financial Analysis on the Web)

BYP14–6   In this problem, comparative data and industry data are used to evaluate the performance and financial position of two integrated oil and gas companies, Petro-Canada and Suncor.

Instructions

Specific requirements of this Web case can be found on the Kimmel website.

Critical Thinking

Collaborative Learning Activity

BYP14–7 You are a loan officer for a bank in Hamilton, Ontario. Ted Bourcier, president of Bourcier Corporation, has just left your office. His company is looking for a five-year loan for an expansion, as the borrowed funds would be used to purchase new equipment. As evidence of the company's creditworthiness, Bourcier provided you with the following facts.

	2006	2005
Current ratio	1.8:1	1.2:1
Receivables turnover	12 times	10 times
Asset turnover	2.8 times	2.2 times
Cash total debt coverage	0.1 times	0.2 times
Net earnings	Up 32%	Down 8%
Earnings per share	$2.00	$1.50

Ted Bourcier is a very insistent (some would say pushy) man. When you told him that you would need additional information before making your decision, he acted offended and said, "What more could you possibly want to know?"

Instructions

(a) Discuss the implications of the ratios that Bourcier provided for the lending decision you need to make. That is, does the information paint a favourable picture? Are these ratios relevant to the decision?

(b) List other ratios that you would want to calculate for this company, and explain why you would use each of them.

(c) What additional information would you like to see that would help you make this credit decision?

Communication Activity

BYP14–8 You are a new member of the board of directors of Shifty Inc. You are preparing for your first meeting of the audit committee and want to reassure yourself about the quality of the company's earnings.

Instructions

Write a memo to yourself, listing questions that you should raise at the audit committee meeting to satisfy any concerns you may have about Shifty's earnings quality.

Ethics Case

BYP14–9 Vern Fairly, president of Flex Industries Inc., wants to issue a press release to boost the company's image and its share price, which has been gradually falling. As controller, you have been asked to provide a list of financial ratios and other operating statistics for Flex Industries' first-quarter operations.

Two days after you provide the ratios and data requested, you are asked by Anne Saint-Onge, Flex's public relations director, to review the accuracy of the financial and operating data contained in the press release written by the president and edited by Anne. In the news release, the president highlights the sales increase of 25% over last year's first quarter and the positive change in the current ratio from 1.5:1 last year to 3:1 this year. He also emphasizes that production was up 50% over last year's first quarter.

You note that the release contains only positive or improved ratios and none of the negative or worsening ratios. For instance, there is no mention of the fact that the debt to total assets ratio has increased from 35% to 55%, or that inventories are up 89%. There is also no indication that the reported earnings for the quarter would have been a loss if the estimated lives of Flex's machinery had not been increased by 30%.

www.wiley.com/canada/kimmel/

Ethics In Accounting

Instructions

(a) Who are the stakeholders in this situation?

(b) Is there anything unethical in President Fairly's actions?

(c) As controller, should you remain silent? Does Anne have any responsibility?

Serial Problem

(*Note:* This is a continuation of the serial problem from Chapters 1 through 13.)

BYP14–10   Cookie Creations' comparative balance sheets and statements of earnings for the years ended December 31, 2008 and 2007 are presented below:

COOKIE CREATIONS LTD.
Balance Sheet
December 31, 2008

	2008	2007
Assets		
Cash	$ 16,344	$ 3,050
Accounts receivable	3,250	1,710
Inventory	7,897	5,450
Prepaid expenses	6,300	3,050
Furniture and fixtures	12,500	5,000
Accumulated amortization—furniture and fixtures	(2,000)	(1,000)
Computer equipment	4,000	4,500
Accumulated amortization—computer equipment	(600)	(1,500)
Kitchen equipment	80,000	66,000
Accumulated amortization—kitchen equipment	(22,600)	(6,600)
Total assets	$105,091	$79,660
Liabilities and Shareholders' Equity		
Accounts payable	$ 3,650	$ 6,930
Income taxes payable	10,251	11,200
Dividends payable	28,000	25,000
Salaries payable	2,250	1,280
Interest payable	188	0
Note payable—current portion	3,000	0
Note payable—long-term portion	4,500	0
Preferred shares ($6 cumulative, 3,000 in 2008 and 2,500 in 2007)	15,000	10,000
Common shares (3,625 shares issued)	5,450	5,450
Retained earnings	32,802	19,800
Total liabilities and shareholders' equity	$105,091	$79,660

COOKIE CREATIONS LTD.
Statement of Earnings
Year Ended December 31, 2008

	2008	2007
Sales	$485,625	$462,500
Cost of goods sold	222,694	208,125
Gross profit	262,931	254,375
Operating expenses		
Amortization expense	17,600	9,100
Salaries and wage expense	147,979	146,350
Other operating expenses	43,186	42,925
Total operating expenses	208,765	198,375
Earnings from operations	54,166	56,000
Other expenses		
Interest expense	413	0
Loss on sale of computer equipment	2,500	0
Total other expenses	2,913	0
Earnings before income tax	51,253	56,000
Income tax expense	10,251	11,200
Net earnings	$ 41,002	$ 44,800

Instructions:

(a) Calculate the following ratios for 2007 and 2008:
  1. Current ratio
  2. Debt to total assets
  3. Gross profit margin
  4. Profit margin
  5. Return on assets (Total assets at the beginning of 2007 were $33,180.)
  6. Return on common shareholders' equity (Total common shareholders' equity at the beginning of 2007 was $17,200.)
  7. Payout ratio ($18,000 dividends were paid to the preferred shareholders and $10,000 to the common shareholders in 2008. $15,000 dividends were paid to the preferred shareholders and $10,000 to the common shareholders in 2007.)
(b) Prepare a horizontal analysis of the statement of earnings, using 2007 as a base year.
(c) Prepare a vertical analysis of the statement of earnings for 2008 and 2007.
(d) Comment on your findings from parts (a) to (c).

Answers to Self-Study Questions

1. b   2. c   3. d   4. d   5. a   6. c   7. b   8. b   9. b   10. c

Answer to Loblaw Review It Question 4

Loblaw did not report any discontinued or extraordinary items on its statement of earnings in 2003. However, it did report a change in accounting principle on its 2002 statement of retained earnings due to implementing the new CICA standard on goodwill and other intangible assets. This resulted in a $25-million decrease in opening retained earnings.

Remember to go back to the Navigator box at the beginning of the chapter to check off your completed work.

Specimen Financial Statements: Loblaw Companies Limited

In this appendix, and the next, we illustrate current financial reporting with two comprehensive sets of corporate financial statements that are prepared in accordance with generally accepted accounting principles. We are grateful for permission to use the actual financial statements of Loblaw Companies Limited in Appendix A and Sobeys Inc. in Appendix B.

The financial statement package for each company includes the statement of earnings, statement of retained earnings, balance sheet, cash flow statement, and notes to the financial statements. The financial statements are preceded by two reports: management's statement of responsibility for the financial statements and the auditors' report on these statements.

Loblaw's complete annual report, including the financial statements, is reviewed in detail on the companion Toolkit website accompanying this textbook. We encourage students to use these financial statements in conjunction with relevant material in the textbook, and to solve the Review It questions in the Before You Go On section of you chapter and the Financial Reporting Problems and Comparative Analysis Problems in the Broadening Your Perspective section of the end of chapter material.

www.wiley.com/canada/kimmel

Animated Tutorials
(Annual Report Walkthrough)

MANAGEMENT'S STATEMENT OF RESPONSIBILITY FOR FINANCIAL REPORTING

The management of Loblaw Companies Limited is responsible for the preparation, presentation and integrity of the accompanying consolidated financial statements, Management's Discussion and Analysis and all other information in this Annual Report. This responsibility includes the selection and consistent application of appropriate accounting principles and methods in addition to making the judgments and estimates necessary to prepare the consolidated financial statements in accordance with Canadian generally accepted accounting principles. It also includes ensuring that the financial information presented elsewhere in this Annual Report is consistent with the consolidated financial statements.

To provide reasonable assurance that assets are safeguarded and that relevant and reliable financial information is produced, management maintains a system of internal controls reinforced by the Company's standards of conduct and ethics set out in written policies. Internal auditors, who are employees of the Company, review and evaluate internal controls on management's behalf, coordinating this work with the independent auditors. KPMG LLP, whose report follows, were appointed as independent auditors by a vote of the Company's shareholders to audit the consolidated financial statements.

The Board of Directors, acting through an Audit Committee comprised solely of directors who are unrelated to and independent of the Company, is responsible for determining that management fulfills its responsibilities in the preparation of the consolidated financial statements and the financial control of operations. The Audit Committee recommends the independent auditors for appointment by the shareholders. The Audit Committee meets regularly with financial management, internal auditors and the independent auditors to discuss internal controls, auditing activities and financial reporting matters. The independent auditors and internal auditors have unrestricted access to the Audit Committee. These consolidated financial statements and Management's Discussion and Analysis have been approved by the Board of Directors for inclusion in this Annual Report based on the review and recommendation of the Audit Committee.

Toronto, Canada
March 9, 2004

John A. Lederer
PRESIDENT

Richard P. Mavrinac
EXECUTIVE VICE PRESIDENT

Stephen A. Smith
EXECUTIVE VICE PRESIDENT

INDEPENDENT AUDITORS' REPORT

To the Shareholders of Loblaw Companies Limited:

We have audited the consolidated balance sheets of Loblaw Companies Limited as at January 3, 2004 and December 28, 2002 and the consolidated statements of earnings, retained earnings and cash flow for the 53 week and 52 week years then ended, respectively. These consolidated financial statements are the responsibility of the Company's management. Our responsibility is to express an opinion on these consolidated financial statements based on our audits.

We conducted our audits in accordance with Canadian generally accepted auditing standards. Those standards require that we plan and perform an audit to obtain reasonable assurance whether the consolidated financial statements are free of material misstatement. An audit includes examining, on a test basis, evidence supporting the amounts and disclosures in the consolidated financial statements. An audit also includes assessing the accounting principles used and significant estimates made by management, as well as evaluating the overall consolidated financial statement presentation.

In our opinion, these consolidated financial statements present fairly, in all material respects, the financial position of the Company as at January 3, 2004 and December 28, 2002 and the results of its operations and its cash flow for the years then ended in accordance with Canadian generally accepted accounting principles.

KPMG

KPMG LLP

Toronto, Canada
March 9, 2004

Chartered Accountants

Consolidated Statements of Earnings

For the years ended January 3, 2004 and December 28, 2002
($ millions except where otherwise indicated)

	2003 (53 weeks)	2002 (52 weeks)
SALES	$ 25,220	$ 23,082
OPERATING EXPENSES		
Cost of sales, selling and administrative expenses	23,360	21,425
Depreciation	393	354
	23,753	21,779
OPERATING INCOME	1,467	1,303
Interest Expense (note 3)	196	161
EARNINGS BEFORE INCOME TAXES	1,271	1,142
Income Taxes (note 7)		
Provision	419	414
Other	7	
	426	414
NET EARNINGS	$ 845	$ 728
NET EARNINGS PER COMMON SHARE ($) (note 4)		
Basic	$ 3.07	$ 2.64
Diluted	$ 3.05	$ 2.62

See accompanying notes to the consolidated financial statements.

Consolidated Statements of Retained Earnings

For the years ended January 3, 2004 and December 28, 2002
($ millions except where otherwise indicated)

	2003 (53 weeks)	2002 (52 weeks)
RETAINED EARNINGS, BEGINNING OF YEAR	$ 2,929	$ 2,375
Impact of implementing new accounting standard (note 1)		(25)
Net earnings	845	728
Premium on common shares purchased for cancellation (note 14)	(71)	(16)
Dividends declared per common share – 60¢ (2002 – 48¢)	(165)	(133)
RETAINED EARNINGS, END OF YEAR	$ 3,538	$ 2,929

See accompanying notes to the consolidated financial statements.

Consolidated Balance Sheets

As at January 3, 2004 and December 28, 2002
($ millions)

	2003	2002
ASSETS		
Current Assets		
Cash and cash equivalents (note 5)	$ 618	$ 823
Short term investments (note 5)	378	304
Accounts receivable (note 6)	588	571
Inventories	1,778	1,702
Future income taxes (note 7)	92	68
Prepaid expenses and other assets	31	24
Total Current Assets	3,485	3,492
Fixed Assets (note 8)	6,422	5,587
Goodwill (note 9)	1,607	1,599
Future Income Taxes (note 7)	7	15
Other Assets (note 10)	656	417
TOTAL ASSETS	$ 12,177	$ 11,110
LIABILITIES		
Current Liabilities		
Bank indebtedness	$ 38	
Commercial paper	603	$ 533
Accounts payable and accrued liabilities	2,227	2,336
Income taxes	140	179
Long term debt due within one year (note 12)	106	106
Total Current Liabilities	3,114	3,154
Long Term Debt (note 12)	3,956	3,420
Future Income Taxes (note 7)	138	68
Other Liabilities (note 13)	237	344
TOTAL LIABILITIES	7,445	6,986
SHAREHOLDERS' EQUITY		
Common Share Capital (note 14)	1,194	1,195
Retained Earnings	3,538	2,929
TOTAL SHAREHOLDERS' EQUITY	4,732	4,124
TOTAL LIABILITIES AND SHAREHOLDERS' EQUITY	$ 12,177	$ 11,110

See accompanying notes to the consolidated financial statements.

Approved on behalf of the Board

W. Galen Weston
DIRECTOR

T. Iain Ronald
DIRECTOR

Consolidated Cash Flow Statements

For the years ended January 3, 2004 and December 28, 2002 ($ millions)	2003 (53 weeks)	2002 (52 weeks)
OPERATING ACTIVITIES		
Net earnings	$ 845	$ 728
Depreciation	393	354
Future income taxes	50	37
Change in non-cash working capital	(250)	(163)
Other	(6)	42
CASH FLOWS FROM OPERATING ACTIVITIES	1,032	998
INVESTING ACTIVITIES		
Fixed asset purchases	(1,271)	(1,079)
Short term investments	(114)	135
Proceeds from fixed asset sales	35	63
Credit card receivables, after securitization (note 6)	(16)	(100)
Franchise investments and other receivables	(48)	(10)
Other	(34)	(4)
CASH FLOWS USED IN INVESTING ACTIVITIES	(1,448)	(995)
FINANCING ACTIVITIES		
Bank indebtedness	38	(95)
Commercial paper	70	342
Long term debt (note 12)		
– Issued	655	200
– Retired	(102)	(77)
Common share capital		
– Issued (note 15)	2	2
– Retired (note 14)	(76)	(17)
Dividends	(198)	(127)
Other	(3)	(2)
CASH FLOWS FROM FINANCING ACTIVITIES	386	226
Effect of foreign currency exchange rate changes on cash and cash equivalents (note 5)	(175)	19
Change in Cash and Cash Equivalents	(205)	248
Cash and Cash Equivalents, Beginning of Year	823	575
CASH AND CASH EQUIVALENTS, END OF YEAR	$ 618	$ 823

See accompanying notes to the consolidated financial statements.

Notes to the Consolidated Financial Statements

For the years ended January 3, 2004 and December 28, 2002
($ millions except where otherwise indicated)

NOTE 1. SUMMARY OF SIGNIFICANT ACCOUNTING POLICIES

The consolidated financial statements were prepared in accordance with Canadian generally accepted accounting principles ("GAAP").

Basis of Consolidation The consolidated financial statements include the accounts of Loblaw Companies Limited and its subsidiaries, collectively referred to as the "Company". The Company's interest in the voting share capital of its subsidiaries is 100%.

Fiscal Year The fiscal year of the Company ends on the Saturday closest to December 31. As a result, the Company's fiscal year is usually 52 weeks in duration but includes a 53rd week every 5 to 6 years. The years ended January 3, 2004 and December 28, 2002 contained 53 weeks and 52 weeks, respectively.

Revenue Recognition Sales include revenues from customers through corporate stores operated by the Company and sales to and service fees from its franchised stores, associated stores and independent account customers. The Company recognizes revenue at the time the sale is made to its customers.

Earnings per Share ("EPS") Basic EPS is calculated by dividing the net earnings available to common shareholders by the weighted average number of common shares outstanding during the year. Diluted EPS is calculated using the treasury stock method, which assumes that all outstanding stock options with an exercise price below the average market price are exercised and the assumed proceeds are used to purchase the Company's common shares at the average market price during the year.

Cash, Cash Equivalents and Bank Indebtedness Cash balances which the Company has the ability and intent to offset are used to reduce reported bank indebtedness. Cash equivalents are highly liquid investments with a maturity of 90 days or less.

Short Term Investments Short term investments are carried at the lower of cost or quoted market value and consist primarily of United States government securities, commercial paper and bank deposits.

Credit Card Receivables The Company, through President's Choice Bank ("PC Bank"), a wholly owned subsidiary of the Company, has credit card receivables that are stated net of an allowance for credit losses. Credit card receivables are fully written off when payments are contractually 180 days in arrears or when the likelihood of collection is considered remote. Interest income on credit card receivables is recorded when billed to customers and is recognized in operating income.

Allowance for Credit Losses PC Bank maintains a general allowance for credit losses which, in management's opinion, is adequate to absorb all credit-related losses in its credit card receivables portfolio, based upon a statistical analysis of past performance and management's judgment. The allowance for credit losses is deducted from the credit card receivables balance. The net credit loss experience for the year is recognized in operating income.

Securitization PC Bank securitizes credit card receivables through the sale of a portion of the total interest in these receivables to an independent trust and does not exercise any control over the trust's management, administration or assets. When PC Bank sells credit card receivables in a securitization transaction, it has a retained interest in the securitized receivables represented by a cash reserve account and the right to future cash flows after obligations to investors have been met. Although PC Bank remains responsible for servicing all credit card receivables, it does not receive additional compensation for servicing those credit card receivables sold to the trust. Any gain or loss on the sale of these receivables depends, in part, on the previous carrying amount of receivables involved in the securitization, allocated between the receivables sold and the retained interest, based on their relative fair values at the date of securitization. The fair values are determined using a financial model. Any gain or loss on a sale is recognized in operating income at the time of the securitization. The carrying value of retained interests is periodically reviewed and when a decline in value is identified that is other than temporary, the carrying value is written down to fair value.

Inventories Retail store inventories are stated at the lower of cost and estimated net realizable value less normal gross profit margin. Wholesale inventories are stated at the lower of cost and estimated net realizable value. Cost is determined substantially using the first-in, first-out method.

Fixed Assets Fixed assets are recorded at cost including capitalized interest. Depreciation commences when the assets are put into use and is recognized principally on a straight-line basis to depreciate the cost of these assets over their estimated useful lives. Estimated useful lives range from 20 to 40 years for buildings and from 3 to 10 years for equipment and fixtures. Leasehold improvements are depreciated over the lesser of the applicable useful life and the term of the lease plus one renewal period to a maximum of 10 years.

Fixed assets are written-down to their net recoverable amount when their estimated future cash flows are less than their net carrying value. A write-down is recognized in operating income.

Goodwill Goodwill represents the excess of the purchase price of a business acquired over the fair value of the underlying net assets acquired at the date of acquisition. Goodwill is not amortized and its carrying value is tested at least annually for impairment. Any impairment in the carrying value of goodwill is recognized in operating income. The Company performed the annual impairment test for goodwill and determined that there was no impairment to the carrying value of goodwill.

Foreign Currency Translation Assets and liabilities denominated in foreign currencies are translated into Canadian dollars at the foreign currency exchange rate in effect at each year end date. Exchange gains or losses arising from the translation of these balances denominated in foreign currencies are recognized in operating income. Revenues and expenses denominated in foreign currencies are translated into Canadian dollars at the average foreign currency exchange rate for the year.

Financial Derivative Instruments The Company uses financial derivative agreements in the form of cross currency basis swaps, interest rate swaps and equity forwards to manage its current and anticipated exposure to fluctuations in foreign currency exchange rates, interest rates and the market price of the Company's common shares. The Company does not enter into financial derivative agreements for trading or speculative purposes.

The Company enters into cross currency basis swaps and interest rate swaps as a hedge against its exposure to fluctuations in foreign currency exchange rates and interest rates on a portion of its United States dollar denominated assets, principally cash, cash equivalents and short term investments. Realized and unrealized foreign currency exchange rate adjustments on cross currency basis swaps are offset by realized and unrealized foreign currency exchange rate adjustments on a portion of the Company's United States dollar denominated assets and are recognized in operating income. The cumulative unrealized foreign currency exchange rate receivable or payable is recorded in other assets or other liabilities, respectively. The exchange of interest payments on the cross currency basis swaps and interest rate swaps is recognized on an accrual basis in interest expense. Unrealized gains or losses on the interest rate swaps are not recognized.

Equity forwards are used to manage exposure to fluctuations in the Company's stock-based compensation cost because they change in value as the market price of the underlying common shares changes. The market price adjustments on the equity forwards are recognized in operating income as gains or losses and the cumulative unrealized gains or losses are recorded in other assets or liabilities, respectively. Interest on the equity forwards is recognized on an accrual basis in interest expense.

The Company entered into an electricity forward contract to minimize price volatility and to maintain a portion of the Company's electricity costs in Ontario, Canada at approximately 2001 rates. This contract is identified as a hedge of an anticipated transaction as it partially offsets the volatility in the price of electricity.

Income Taxes The Company uses the asset and liability method of accounting for income taxes. Under the asset and liability method, future income tax assets and liabilities are recognized for the future income tax consequences attributable to differences between the financial statement carrying values of existing assets and liabilities and their respective income tax bases. Future income tax assets and liabilities are measured using enacted or substantively enacted income tax rates expected to apply to taxable income in the years in which those temporary differences are expected to be recovered or settled. The effect on future income tax assets and liabilities of a change in income tax rates is recognized in income taxes expense when enacted or substantively enacted. Future income tax assets are evaluated and a valuation allowance, if required, is recorded against any future income tax asset if it is more likely than not that the asset will not be realized.

Pension, Post-Retirement and Post-Employment Benefits The cost of the Company's defined benefit pension plans, post-retirement and post-employment benefits is accrued based on actuarial valuations, which are determined using the projected benefit method pro-rated on service and management's best estimate of the expected long term rate of return on plan assets, salary escalation, retirement ages and expected growth rate of health care costs. Market values are used to value benefit plan assets. The obligation related to employee future benefits is measured using current market interest rates, assuming a portfolio of Corporate AA bonds with terms to maturity that, on average, match the terms of the obligation. Past service costs from plan amendments and the excess net actuarial gain or loss over 10% of the greater of the accrued benefit plan obligation and the market value of the benefit plan assets are amortized on a straight-line basis over the average remaining service period of the active employees, ranging from 6 to 17 years with a weighted average of 12 years at year end. The cost of pension benefits for defined contribution plans and multi-employer pension plans are expensed as contributions are paid.

Stock-Based Compensation Effective December 30, 2001, the Company implemented the standard issued by the Canadian Institute of Chartered Accountants ("CICA") on stock-based compensation and other stock-based payments. The standard was implemented retroactively without restatement of the prior period consolidated financial statements. The cumulative effect of implementation was a decrease to retained earnings of $25 ($80 less $23 of future income tax recoverable and the $32 fair value impact of the equity forwards).

The Company recognizes a compensation cost in operating income and a liability related to employee stock options that allow for settlement in shares or in the share appreciation value in cash at the option of the employee, which is accounted for using the intrinsic value method. Under the intrinsic value method, the stock-based compensation liability is the amount by which the market price of the common shares exceeds the exercise price of the stock options. A year over year change in the stock-based compensation liability is recognized in operating income.

The Company accounts for stock options issued prior to December 30, 2001 that will be settled by issuing common shares as capital transactions. Consideration paid by employees on the exercise of this type of stock option is credited to common share capital. This type of option was last issued in 2001 and represents approximately 3% of all options outstanding.

The Company maintains an Employee Share Ownership Plan for its employees which allows employees to acquire the Company's common shares through regular payroll deductions of up to 5% of their gross regular earnings. The Company contributes an additional 15% of each employee's contribution to the plan, which is recognized in operating income as a compensation cost when the contribution is made.

Outside members of the Company's Board of Directors may elect annually to receive all or a portion of their annual retainer(s) and fees in the form of deferred share units. The deferred share units obligation is accounted for using the intrinsic value method and the year over year change in the deferred share units obligation is recognized as a compensation expense in operating income and as a liability.

Use of Estimates and Assumptions The preparation of the consolidated financial statements in conformity with Canadian GAAP requires management to make estimates and assumptions that affect the reported amounts and disclosures made in the consolidated financial statements and accompanying notes. These estimates and assumptions are based on management's historical experience, best knowledge of current events and conditions and activities that the Company may undertake in the future. Actual results could differ from these estimates.

Comparative Information Certain prior year's information was reclassified to conform with the current year's presentation.

NOTE 2. SPECIAL VOLUNTARY EARLY RETIREMENT PROGRAM

As a result of union negotiations, certain employees of Locals 1000A, 1977 and 175 of the United Food and Commercial Workers union in Ontario became eligible to receive a voluntary early retirement offer. Employees of Locals 1000A and 1977 were required to indicate their acceptance of this voluntary offer in writing by October 31, 2003 and employees of Local 175 had to respond by January 31, 2004. At year end, 541 employees had accepted the voluntary early retirement offer which resulted in a charge of $25 recognized in operating income. Approximately $5 of this charge had been paid by the end of 2003. The remaining accrual is expected to be paid during the first half of fiscal 2004. Subsequent to year end, an additional 94 employees of Local 175 had accepted the voluntary early retirement offer. Therefore, an additional charge of $2 will be recognized in operating income in fiscal 2004.

NOTE 3. INTEREST EXPENSE

	2003	2002
Interest on long term debt	$ 269	$ 246
Other long term interest	(45)	(38)
Net long term interest	224	208
Net short term interest	5	(17)
Capitalized to fixed assets	(33)	(30)
Interest expense	$ 196	$ 161

Net interest paid in 2003 was $211 (2002 – $185).

NOTE 4. BASIC AND DILUTED NET EARNINGS PER COMMON SHARE

	2003	2002
Net earnings	$ 845	$ 728
Weighted average common shares outstanding (in millions)	275.4	276.2
Dilutive effect of stock-based compensation (in millions)	1.7	1.7
Diluted weighted average common shares outstanding (in millions)	277.1	277.9
Basic net earnings per common share ($)	$ 3.07	$ 2.64
Dilutive effect of stock-based compensation per common share ($)	(0.02)	(0.02)
Diluted net earnings per common share ($)	$ 3.05	$ 2.62

NOTE 5. CASH, CASH EQUIVALENTS AND SHORT TERM INVESTMENTS

At year end, the Company had $991 (2002 – $1.1 billion) in cash, cash equivalents and short term investments held by Glenhuron Bank Limited ("Glenhuron"), a wholly owned subsidiary of the Company in Barbados. The $14 (2002 – $24) of income from cash, cash equivalents and short term investments was recognized in net short term interest.

The Company recognized an unrealized foreign currency exchange rate loss of $215 (2002 – gain of $32) as a result of translating its United States dollar denominated cash, cash equivalents and short term investments of which $175 (2002 – gain of $19) related to cash and cash equivalents. The resulting loss on cash, cash equivalents and short term investments is offset in operating income by the unrealized foreign currency exchange rate gain on the cross currency basis swaps. A cumulative unrealized foreign currency exchange rate receivable of $96 (2002 – payable of $131) relating to these swaps is recorded in other assets on the balance sheet.

NOTE 6. CREDIT CARD RECEIVABLES

During 2003, the Company through PC Bank securitized $202 (2002 – $244) of credit card receivables, yielding a minimal loss (2002 – minimal gain) on the initial sale, inclusive of a $2 (2002 – $2) servicing liability. Servicing liabilities expensed during the year were $9 (2002 – $4) and the fair value of recognized servicing liabilities was $6 (2002 – $4). The trust's recourse to PC Bank's assets is limited to PC Bank's retained interests and is further supported by the Company through a standby letter of credit for 15% of the securitized amount.

	2003	2002
Credit card receivables	$ 711	$ 502
Amount securitized	(558)	(356)
Net credit card receivables	$ 153	$ 146
Net credit loss experience	$ 9	$ 6

The following table shows the key economic assumptions used in measuring the retained interests at the date of securitization for securitizations completed in 2003. The table also displays the sensitivity of the current fair value of retained interests to an immediate 10% and 20% adverse change in the 2003 key economic assumptions.

		Change in Assumptions	
	2003	(10%)	(20%)
Carrying value of retained interests	$ 9		
Payment rate (monthly)	45.0%		
Weighted average life (years)	0.6		
Expected credit losses (annual)	3.4%	$ (0.3)	$ (0.7)
Discounted residual cash flows (annual)	14.0%	$ (1.2)	$ (2.4)

The details on the cash flows from securitization are as follows:

	2003	2002
Proceeds from new securitizations	$ 202	$ 244
Net cash flows received on retained interests	$ 53	$ 24

NOTE 7. INCOME TAXES

The Company's effective income tax rate in the consolidated statements of earnings is reported at a rate less than the weighted average basic Canadian federal and provincial statutory income tax rate for the following reasons:

	2003	2002
Weighted average basic Canadian federal and provincial statutory income tax rate	36.5%	38.6%
Net decrease resulting from:		
Earnings in jurisdictions taxed at rates different from the Canadian statutory income tax rates	(3.8)	(2.9)
Non-taxable amounts (including capital gains/losses)	(0.3)	(0.1)
Large corporation tax	0.6	0.7
Enacted changes in income tax rates	0.5	
Effective income tax rate	33.5%	36.3%

Net income taxes paid in 2003 were $399 (2002 – $313).

In 2003, the Ontario government enacted both the repeal of the income tax rate reductions of 1.5% scheduled for each of 2004, 2005 and 2006 and the increase in the provincial income tax rate to 14% in 2004 from 12.5% in 2003. Therefore, future income tax balances were adjusted resulting in a $7 charge to future income tax expense in 2003.

The income tax effects of temporary differences that gave rise to significant portions of the future income tax assets (liabilities) were as follows:

	2003	2002
Accounts payable and accrued liabilities	$ 85	$ 62
Long term debt (including amounts due within one year)	7	11
Other liabilities	78	55
Losses carried forward (expiring 2007)	3	20
Fixed assets	(183)	(132)
Other assets	(39)	(19)
Other	10	18
Net future income tax assets (liabilities)	$ (39)	$ 15

	2003	2002
PRESENTED ON THE CONSOLIDATED BALANCE SHEETS AS:		
Future income tax assets		
Current	$ 92	$ 68
Non-current	7	15
	99	83
Future income tax liabilities		
Non-current	(138)	(68)
Net future income tax assets (liabilities)	$ (39)	$ 15

NOTE 8. FIXED ASSETS

	2003			2002		
	Cost	Accumulated Depreciation	Net Book Value	Cost	Accumulated Depreciation	Net Book Value
Properties held for development	$ 433		$ 433	$ 336		$ 336
Properties under development	248		248	234		234
Land	1,387		1,387	1,201		1,201
Buildings	3,484	$ 638	2,846	2,983	$ 552	2,431
Equipment and fixtures	2,724	1,612	1,112	2,421	1,415	1,006
Leasehold improvements	651	264	387	599	233	366
	8,927	2,514	6,413	7,774	2,200	5,574
Capital leases –						
buildings and equipment	83	74	9	83	70	13
	$ 9,010	$ 2,588	$ 6,422	$ 7,857	$ 2,270	$ 5,587

NOTE 9. BUSINESS ACQUISITIONS

In the normal course of business, the Company acquires franchisee stores and converts them to corporate stores. In 2003, the Company acquired 15 franchisee businesses. The acquisitions were accounted for using the purchase method of accounting with the results of the businesses acquired included in the Company's consolidated financial statements from the date of acquisition. The fair value of the net assets acquired consisted of fixed assets of $7, other assets, principally inventory, of $6 and goodwill of $8 for cash consideration of $11, net of accounts receivable due from the franchisees of $10.

NOTE 10. OTHER ASSETS

	2003	2002
Franchise investments and other receivables	$ 315	$ 300
Accrued pension and other benefit plans (note 11)	87	37
Unrealized equity forwards receivable (note 16)	92	34
Deferred charges and other	66	46
Unrealized cross currency basis swaps receivable (note 16)	96	
	$ 656	$ 417

NOTE 11. PENSION, POST-RETIREMENT AND POST-EMPLOYMENT BENEFITS

The Company has a number of defined benefit and defined contribution plans providing pension and other retirement and post-employment benefits to certain employees. The Company also contributes to various multi-employer pension plans providing pension benefits.

Information about the Company's defined benefit plans, in aggregate, was as follows:

	2003		2002	
	Pension Benefit Plans	Other Benefit Plans	Pension Benefit Plans	Other Benefit Plans
BENEFIT PLAN ASSETS				
Fair value, beginning of year	$ 628	$ 23	$ 690	$ 16
Actual return on plan assets	94	1	(19)	4
Employer contributions	93	20	13	13
Employees' contributions	2		2	
Benefits paid	(45)	(14)	(51)	(10)
Other	(1)		(7)	
Fair value, end of year	$ 771	$ 30	$ 628	$ 23
ACCRUED BENEFIT PLAN OBLIGATIONS				
Balance, beginning of year	$ 817	$ 166	$ 692	$ 103
Current service cost	30	5	21	2
Interest cost	54	10	52	7
Benefits paid	(45)	(14)	(51)	(10)
Actuarial loss	28	23	106	64
Plan amendments	4		(1)	
Other	(1)		(2)	
Balance, end of year	$ 887	$ 190	$ 817	$ 166
DEFICIT OF PLAN ASSETS VERSUS PLAN OBLIGATIONS	$ (116)	$ (160)	$ (189)	$ (143)
Unamortized past service costs	6		3	
Unamortized net actuarial loss	143	75	168	56
Net accrued benefit plan asset (liability)	$ 33	$ (85)	$ (18)	$ (87)
Accrued benefit plan asset included in other assets	$ 68	$ 19	$ 31	$ 6
Accrued benefit plan liability included in other liabilities	(35)	(104)	(49)	(93)
Net accrued benefit plan asset (liability)	$ 33	$ (85)	$ (18)	$ (87)

At year end 2003, the deficit of plan assets versus plan obligations for those pension benefit plans and post-employment benefit plans where the accrued benefit plan obligations exceeded the fair value of benefit plan assets were $118 and $12, respectively (2002 – $193 and $14). There are no plan assets in non-registered pension plans. The Company's post-retirement benefit plans also had no plan assets and, at year end 2003, had an aggregate accrued benefit plan obligation of $148 (2002 – $129).

The significant annual weighted average actuarial assumptions used in measuring the Company's accrued benefit plan obligations as of the end of the year were as follows:

	2003		2002	
	Pension Benefit Plans	Other Benefit Plans	Pension Benefit Plans	Other Benefit Plans
Discount rate	6.25%	6.0%	6.5%	6.2%
Rate of compensation increase	3.5%		3.5%	

The significant annual weighted average actuarial assumptions used in calculating the Company's net defined benefit plan expense for the year were as follows:

	2003		2002	
	Pension Benefit Plans	Other Benefit Plans	Pension Benefit Plans	Other Benefit Plans
Discount rate	6.5%	6.2%	7.5%	6.9%
Expected long term rate of return on plan assets	8.0%	5.0%	8.0%	6.0%
Rate of compensation increase	3.5%		3.5%	

The Company's growth rate of health care costs, primarily drug costs, was estimated at 9.0% (2002 – 9.0%) and assumed to decrease gradually to 5.0% in 2011 and remain at that level thereafter.

The accrued benefit plan obligations and the fair value of the benefit plan assets were determined using a September 30 measurement date.

The total net expense for the Company's benefit plans and the multi-employer pension plans was as follows:

	2003		2002	
	Pension Benefit Plans	Other Benefit Plans	Pension Benefit Plans	Other Benefit Plans
Current service cost, net of employee contributions	$ 28	$ 5	$ 19	$ 2
Interest cost on plan obligations	54	10	52	7
Expected return on plan assets	(50)	(1)	(54)	(1)
Amortization of net actuarial loss	9	4		
Other			1	
Net defined benefit plan expense	41	18	18	8
Defined contribution plan expense	6		5	
Multi-employer pension plan expense	37		33	
Net benefit plan expense	$ 84	$ 18	$ 56	$ 8

NOTE 12. LONG TERM DEBT

	2003	2002
PROVIGO INC. DEBENTURES		
Series 1997, 6.35%, due 2004	$ 100	$ 100
Series 1996, 8.70%, due 2006	125	125
Other (i)	9	13
LOBLAW COMPANIES LIMITED NOTES		
6.60%, due 2003 (ii)		100
6.95%, due 2005	200	200
6.00%, due 2008	390	390
5.75%, due 2009	125	125
7.10%, due 2010	300	300
6.50%, due 2011	350	350
5.40%, due 2013 (ii)	200	
6.00%, due 2014	100	100
7.10%, due 2016	300	300
6.65%, due 2027	100	100
6.45%, due 2028	200	200
6.50%, due 2029	175	175
11.40%, due 2031		
– principal	151	151
– effect of coupon repurchase	(11)	(4)
6.85%, due 2032	200	200
6.54%, due 2033 (ii)	200	
8.75%, due 2033	200	200
6.05%, due 2034 (ii)	200	
6.45%, due 2039	200	200
7.00%, due 2040	150	150
5.86%, due 2043 (ii)	55	
Other at a weighted average interest rate of 10.64%, due 2004 to 2040	43	51
Total long term debt	4,062	3,526
Less amount due within one year	106	106
	$ 3,956	$ 3,420

The five year schedule of repayment of long term debt based on maturity is as follows: 2004 – $106; 2005 – $215; 2006 – $129; 2007 – $5; 2008 – $393.

(i) Other of $9 (2002 – $13) represents the unamortized portion of the adjustment to fair value the Provigo Inc. Debentures. This adjustment was recorded as part of the Provigo purchase equation and was calculated using the Company's average credit spread applicable to the remaining life of the Provigo Inc. Debentures. The adjustment is being amortized over the remaining term of the Provigo Inc. Debentures.

(ii) During 2003, the Company issued $200 of 5.40% Medium Term Notes ("MTN") due 2013, $200 of 6.54% MTN due 2033, $200 of 6.05% MTN due 2034 and $55 of 5.86% MTN due 2043. The Company also repaid its $100 of 6.60% MTN as it matured.

(iii) Subsequent to year end 2003, the Company issued $200 of 6.15% MTN due 2035.

NOTE 13. OTHER LIABILITIES

	2003	2002
Accrued pension and other benefit plans (note 11)	$ 139	$ 142
Unrealized cross currency basis swaps payable (note 16)		131
Stock-based compensation	82	54
Other	16	17
	$ 237	$ 344

NOTE 14. COMMON SHARE CAPITAL (authorized – unlimited)

The changes in the common shares issued and outstanding during the year were as follows:

	2003		2002	
	Number of Common Shares	Common Share Capital	Number of Common Shares	Common Share Capital
Issued and outstanding, beginning of year	276,018,714	$ 1,195	276,252,714	$ 1,194
Issued for stock options exercised (note 15)	93,200	4	75,000	2
Purchased for cancellation	(1,282,900)	(5)	(309,000)	(1)
Issued and outstanding, end of year	274,829,014	$ 1,194	276,018,714	$ 1,195
Weighted average outstanding	275,405,585		276,209,323	

Normal Course Issuer Bids ("NCIB") During 2003, the Company purchased for cancellation 1,282,900 (2002 – 309,000) of its common shares for $76 (2002 – $17) and entered into equity forwards to buy 1,103,500 (2002 – 390,100) of its common shares, pursuant to its NCIB. In addition, the Company intends to renew its NCIB to purchase on the Toronto Stock Exchange or enter into equity forwards to purchase up to 5% of its common shares outstanding. The Company, in accordance with the rules and by-laws of the Toronto Stock Exchange, may purchase its shares at the then market price of such shares.

Subsequent to year end, the Company purchased for cancellation 132,400 of its common shares for $8, pursuant to its NCIB.

NOTE 15. STOCK-BASED COMPENSATION ($)

The Company maintains three types of stock-based compensation plans, which are described below.

Stock Option Plan The Company maintains a stock option plan for certain employees. Under this plan, the Company may grant options for up to 20.4 million common shares, however the Company has set a guideline which limits the number of stock option grants to a maximum of 5% of outstanding common shares at any time. Stock options have up to a seven-year term, vest 20% cumulatively on each anniversary date of the grant and are exercisable at the designated common share price, which is 100% of the market price of the Company's common shares on the last trading day prior to the effective date of the grant. Each stock option is exercisable into one common share of the Company at the price specified in the terms of the option, or option holders may elect to receive in cash the share appreciation value equal to the excess of the market price at the date of exercise over the specified option price.

During 2003, the Company granted 2,367,746 stock options to 196 employees with an exercise price of $53.60 per common share and 20,000 stock options with an exercise price of $61.95 per common share under its existing stock option plan, which allows for settlement in shares or in the share appreciation value in cash at the option of the employee.

In 2003, the Company recognized in operating income a compensation cost related to its stock option plan of $62 million (2002 – $21 million) and a gain on the fair value impact of the equity forwards of $66 million (2002 – $7 million). The share appreciation value of $28 million (2002 – $22 million) was paid on the exercise of 802,701 (2002 – 685,447) stock options. The Company issued 93,200 common shares on the exercise of stock options for cash consideration of $2 million for which it had recorded a stock-based compensation liability of $4 million. In 2002, the Company issued 75,000 common shares for cash consideration of $2 million on the exercise of stock options issued prior to December 30, 2001 that will be settled by issuing common shares.

At year end, a total of 5,407,026 (2002 – 4,055,237) stock options were outstanding, and represented approximately 2.0% (2002 – 1.5%) of the Company's issued and outstanding common shares, which was within the Company's guideline of 5%. Of the 5,407,026 outstanding options, 5,253,286 relate to stock option grants that allow for settlement in shares or in the share appreciation value in cash at the option of the employee and 153,740 relates to stock option grants, issued prior to December 30, 2001 that will be settled by issuing common shares.

A summary of the status of the Company's stock option plan and activity was as follows:

	2003		2002	
	Options (number of shares)	Weighted Average Exercise Price/Share	Options (number of shares)	Weighted Average Exercise Price/Share
Outstanding options, beginning of year	4,055,237	$ 32.029	4,832,900	$ 30.680
Granted	2,387,746	$ 53.670	80,000	$ 55.400
Exercised	(895,901)	$ 24.570	(760,447)	$ 25.857
Forfeited/cancelled	(140,056)	$ 43.173	(97,216)	$ 32.477
Outstanding options, end of year	5,407,026	$ 42.533	4,055,237	$ 32.029
Options exercisable, end of year	2,016,552	$ 37.527	1,491,119	$ 28.192

	2003 Outstanding Options			2003 Exercisable Options	
Range of Exercise Prices	Number of Options Outstanding	Weighted Average Remaining Contractual Life (years)	Weighted Average Exercise Price/Share	Number of Exercisable Options	Weighted Average Exercise Price/Share
$ 24.500 – $ 35.600	2,615,146	3	$ 31.399	1,384,538	$ 30.790
$ 43.800 – $ 49.050	394,190	4	$ 48.294	156,476	$ 48.100
$ 53.600 – $ 61.950	2,397,690	6	$ 53.730	475,538	$ 53.661

Employee Share Ownership Plan ("ESOP") The Company maintains an ESOP for their employees, which allows employees to acquire the Company's common shares through regular payroll deductions of up to 5% of their gross regular earnings. The Company contributes an additional 15% of each employee's contribution to the plan. The ESOP is administered through a trust, which purchases the Company's common shares on the open market on behalf of employees. A compensation cost of $2 million (2002 – $2 million) related to this plan was recognized in operating income.

Deferred Share Units Plan Outside members of the Company's Board of Directors may elect annually to receive all or a portion of their annual retainer(s) and fees in the form of deferred share units, the value of which is determined by the market price of the Company's common shares at the time of payment of the director's annual retainer(s) or fees. Upon termination of Board service, the common shares due to the director, as represented by the deferred share units, will be purchased on the open market on the director's behalf. At year end, 21,489 (2002 – 12,941) deferred share units were outstanding. The year over year change in the deferred share units obligation was minimal and was recognized in operating income.

NOTE 16. FINANCIAL INSTRUMENTS

A summary of the Company's outstanding financial derivative instruments is as follows:

	Notional Amounts Maturing in						2003 Total	2002 Total
	2004	2005	2006	2007	2008	Thereafter		
Cross currency basis swaps	$ 331		$ 11	$ 68	$ 227	$ 577	$ 1,214	$ 1,118
Interest rate swaps	$ 282	$ 161	$ (43)		$ 240	$ 40	$ 680	$ 867
Equity forwards						$ 233	$ 233	$ 150
Electricity forward contract	$ 47	$ 16					$ 63	$ 106

Cross Currency Basis Swaps The Company enters into cross currency basis swaps to hedge its exposure to fluctuations in the foreign currency exchange rate on a portion of its United States dollar denominated assets, principally cash, cash equivalents and short term investments.

Loblaw Companies Limited 2003 Annual Report 61

The Company entered into cross currency basis swaps to exchange United States dollars for $1.2 billion (2002 – $1.1 billion) Canadian dollars, which mature by 2016. Currency adjustments receivable or payable arising from these swaps may be settled in cash on maturity or the term may be extended. At year end, a cumulative unrealized foreign currency exchange rate receivable of $96 was recorded in other assets (2002 – $131 payable recorded in other liabilities).

Interest Rate Swaps The Company enters into interest rate swaps to hedge a portion of its exposure to fluctuations in interest rates.

The Company entered into interest rate swaps converting a net notional $680 (2002 – $867) of its floating rate investments to fixed rate investments at 6.72% (2002 – 6.88%), which mature by 2013.

Equity Forwards ($) The Company enters into equity forwards to manage its exposure to fluctuations in its stock-based compensation cost as a result of changes in the market price of its common shares.

In 2003, the Company entered into equity forwards to buy 1,103,500 (2002 – 390,100) of its common shares at an average forward price of $56.39 (2002 – $55.65) per common share, with an average initial term of 10 years (2002 – 10 years). At year end, the Company had cumulative equity forwards to buy 4.8 million (2002 – 3.7 million) of its common shares at an average forward price of $48.56 (2002 – $44.88) including $3.69 (2002 – $3.47) per common share of interest expense net of dividends that will be paid at redemption. The equity forwards allow for settlement in cash, common shares or net settlement. The Company has included a cumulative unrealized market gain of $92 million (2002 – $34 million) in other assets relating to these equity forwards.

Electricity Forward Contract The Company entered into an electricity forward contract to minimize price volatility and to maintain a portion of the Company's electricity costs in Ontario, Canada at approximately 2001 rates. This electricity forward contract has an initial term of three years and expires in May 2005.

Counterparty Risk The Company may be exposed to losses should any counterparty to its financial derivative agreements fail to fulfill its obligations. The Company has sought to minimize potential counterparty risk and losses by conducting transactions for its derivative agreements with counterparties that have at minimum a long term A credit rating and by placing risk adjusted limits on its exposure to any single counterparty for its financial derivative agreements. The Company has internal policies, controls and reporting processes, which require ongoing assessment and corrective action, if necessary with respect to its derivative transactions. In addition, principal amounts on cross currency basis swaps and equity forwards are each netted by agreement and there is no exposure to loss of the original notional principal amounts on the interest rate swaps and equity forwards.

Fair Value of Financial Instruments The fair value of a financial instrument is the estimated amount that the Company would receive or pay to terminate the instrument agreement at the reporting date. The following methods and assumptions were used to estimate the fair value of each type of financial instrument by reference to various market value data and other valuation techniques as appropriate.

The fair values of cash, cash equivalents, short term investments, accounts receivable, bank indebtedness, commercial paper, accounts payable and accrued liabilities approximated their carrying values given their short term maturities.

The fair value of the cross currency basis swaps was estimated based on the market spot exchange rates and forward interest rates and approximated carrying value.

The fair value of long term debt issues was estimated based on the discounted cash flows of the debt at the Company's estimated incremental borrowing rates for debt of the same remaining maturities.

The fair value of the interest rate swaps was estimated by discounting net cash flows of the swaps at market and forward interest rates for swaps of the same remaining maturities.

The fair value of the equity forwards, which approximated carrying value, was estimated by multiplying the number of the Company's common shares outstanding under the equity forwards by the difference between the market price of its common shares and the average forward price of the outstanding forwards at year end.

The fair value of the electricity forward contract was provided by the counterparty based on expected future electricity prices.

	2003		2002	
	Carrying Value	Estimated Fair Value	Carrying Value	Estimated Fair Value
Long term debt liability	$ 4,062	$ 4,457	$ 3,526	$ 3,890
Interest rate swaps net asset		$ 12		$ 32
Electricity forward contract net asset		$ 2		$ 15

NOTE 17. CONTINGENCIES, COMMITMENTS AND GUARANTEES

The Company is involved in and potentially subject to various claims and litigation arising out of the normal course and conduct of its business including product liability, labour and employment, environmental and tax. Although such matters cannot be predicted with certainty, management considers the Company's exposure to such claims and litigation, to the extent not provided for through insurance or otherwise, not to be material to these consolidated financial statements.

The Company is committed to various operating leases. Future minimum lease payments relating to these operating leases are as follows:

	Amounts Maturing in							
	2004	2005	2006	2007	2008	Thereafter to 2049	2003 Total	2002 Total
Operating lease payments	$ 159	$ 147	$ 132	$ 117	$ 103	$ 626	$ 1,284	$ 1,260
Expected sub-lease income	(38)	(37)	(35)	(31)	(24)	(40)	(205)	(258)
Net operating lease payments	$ 121	$ 110	$ 97	$ 86	$ 79	$ 586	$ 1,079	$ 1,002

At year end, the Company has committed approximately $370 with respect to capital investment projects such as the construction, expansion and renovation of buildings and the purchase of real property.

The Company establishes standby letters of credit used in connection with certain obligations mainly related to real estate transactions and benefit and insurance programs. The aggregate gross potential liability related to these standby letters of credit is approximately $82. Other standby letters of credit related to the financing program for the Company's franchisees and securitization of PC Bank's credit card receivables have been identified as guarantees and are discussed further in the Guarantees section below.

In connection with the purchase of Provigo, the Company committed to support Quebec small business and farming communities as follows: for a period of seven years commencing in 1999 and, subject to business dispositions, the aggregate amount of goods and services purchased from Quebec suppliers in the normal course of business will not fall below those of 1998. The Company has fulfilled its commitment in each year from 1999 to and including 2003.

Guarantees Effective December 29, 2002, the Company implemented Accounting Guideline 14, "Disclosure of Guarantees", issued by the CICA, which requires a guarantor to disclose in its notes to the consolidated financial statements significant information about guarantees it has provided. Under this Guideline, a guarantee is defined as a contract or indemnification agreement, which requires the Company to make payments (cash, financial instruments, other assets, the Company's own shares or the provision of services) to a third party contingent on future events (a "Guarantee"). These payments are contingent on one of the following: (i) a change in an underlying interest rate, security price, commodity price, foreign currency exchange rate or other variable that is related to an asset, liability or an equity security of the guaranteed party, (ii) the failure of another entity to perform under an obligating agreement or (iii) the failure of another party to pay
its indebtedness when due. The disclosures are required even when the likelihood of the guarantor having to make any payment under the Guarantee is remote.

The Company has provided to third parties the following significant Guarantees:

Standby Letters of Credit A standby letter of credit for the benefit of an independent trust with respect to the credit card receivables securitization program of PC Bank has been provided by a major Canadian bank. This standby letter of credit could be drawn upon in the event of a major decline in the income flow from or in the value of the securitized credit card receivables after the cash reserve account established pursuant to the securitization agreement has been depleted. The Company has agreed to reimburse the issuing bank for any amount drawn on the standby letter of credit. The Company believes that the likelihood of this occurrence is remote. The aggregate gross potential liability under this arrangement, which represents 15% of the securitized credit card receivables amount, is approximately $84.

A standby letter of credit has been provided by a major Canadian bank in the amount of $35 for the benefit of an independent trust which provides loans to the Company's franchisees for their purchase of inventory and fixed assets, mainly fixturing and equipment. In the event that a franchisee defaults on its loan and the Company has not, within a specified time period, (i) assumed the loan, (ii) purchased the assets of the defaulting franchisee over which security has been taken by the trust, or (iii) provided for an increase of the amount of the standby letter of credit by the outstanding amount under the loan, the trust may draw upon this standby letter of credit or realize on its security. The Company has agreed to reimburse the issuing bank for any amount drawn on the standby letter of credit.

Lease Obligations In connection with historical dispositions of certain of its assets, the Company has assigned leases to third parties. The Company remains contingently liable for these lease obligations in the event any of the assignees are in default of their lease obligations. The estimated amount for minimum rent, which does not include other lease related expenses such as property tax and common area maintenance charges, is $173 (2002 – $204).

Indemnification Provisions The Company from time to time enters into agreements in the normal course of its business, such as service arrangements and leases, in connection with business or asset acquisitions or dispositions. These agreements by their nature may provide for indemnification of counterparties. These indemnification provisions may be in connection with breaches of representation and warranty or with future claims for certain liabilities, including liabilities related to tax and environmental matters. The terms of these indemnification provisions vary in duration and may extend for an unlimited period of time. Given the nature of such indemnification provisions, the Company is unable to reasonably estimate its total maximum potential liability as certain indemnification provisions do not provide for a maximum potential amount and the amounts are dependent on the outcome of future contingent events, the nature and likelihood of which cannot be determined at this time. Historically, the Company has not made any significant payments in connection with these indemnification provisions.

NOTE 18. OTHER INFORMATION

Segment Information The Company's only reportable operating segment is food distribution. All sales to external parties were generated in Canada and all fixed assets and goodwill were attributable to Canadian operations.

Related Party Transactions The Company's majority shareholder, George Weston Limited, its subsidiaries and its affiliates are related parties. It is the Company's policy to conduct all transactions and settle balances with related parties on normal trade terms. Total purchases from related parties represented approximately 3% (2002 – 3%) of the cost of sales, selling and administrative expenses.

Pursuant to an investment management agreement, the Company, through Glenhuron, manages certain United States cash, cash equivalents and short term investments on behalf of wholly owned non-Canadian subsidiaries of George Weston Limited. Management fees were based on market rates and were included in interest expense.

Eleven Year Summary (1)

Year (2)

($ millions except where otherwise indicated)	2003	2002	2001	2000
OPERATING RESULTS				
Sales	25,220	23,082	21,486	20,121
EBITDA (3)	1,860	1,657	1,451	1,259
Operating income	1,467	1,303	1,136	976
Interest expense	196	161	158	143
Net earnings	845	728	563	473
FINANCIAL POSITION				
Working capital	371	338	290	(291)
Fixed assets	6,422	5,587	4,931	4,174
Goodwill	1,607	1,599	1,599	1,641
Total assets	12,177	11,110	10,025	9,025
Net debt (3)	3,707	2,932	2,699	2,216
Shareholders' equity	4,732	4,124	3,569	3,124
CASH FLOW				
Cash flows from operating activities	1,032	998	818	785
Capital investment	1,271	1,079	1,108	943
PER COMMON SHARE ($)				
Basic net earnings	3.07	2.64	2.04	1.71
Basic earnings before goodwill charges	3.07	2.64	2.20	1.87
Dividend rate at year end	.60	.48	.40	.40
Cash flows from operating activities	3.75	3.61	2.96	2.84
Capital investment	4.62	3.91	4.01	3.42
Book value	17.22	14.94	12.92	11.31
Market price at year end	67.85	54.00	51.85	50.50
FINANCIAL RATIOS				
EBITDA margin (%) (3)	7.4	7.2	6.8	6.3
Operating margin (%)	5.8	5.6	5.3	4.9
Net earnings margin (%)	3.4	3.2	2.6	2.4
Return on average total assets (%) (3)	13.9	13.7	13.4	12.8
Return on average shareholders' equity (%)	19.1	18.9	16.8	15.7
Interest coverage	7.5	8.1	7.2	6.8
Net debt to equity (3)	.78	.71	.76	.71
Cash flows from operating activities to net debt (3)	.28	.34	.30	.35
Price/net earnings ratio at year end	22.1	20.5	25.4	29.5
Market/book ratio at year end	3.9	3.6	4.0	4.5

(1) For financial definitions and ratios refer to the Glossary of Terms on page 66.
(2) 2003 and 1997 contained 53 weeks.
(3) See Non-GAAP Financial Measures on page 44.

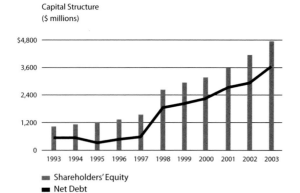

Capital Structure
($ millions)

- Shareholders' Equity
- Net Debt

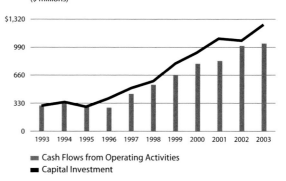

Cash Flows from Operating Activities and Capital Investment
($ millions)

- Cash Flows from Operating Activities
- Capital Investment

1999	1998	1997	1996	1995	1994	1993
18,783	12,497	11,008	9,848	9,854	10,000	9,356
1,077	712	573	481	449	410	326
811	529	428	361	322	274	203
112	68	44	46	54	63	54
376	261	213	174	147	126	90
(397)	(707)	202	154	179	29	148
3,549	3,194	2,093	1,738	1,491	1,603	1,414
1,685	1,363	38	40	42	44	49
7,979	7,105	4,013	3,531	3,197	3,042	2,743
1,999	1,842	513	435	287	525	506
2,904	2,595	1,495	1,311	1,160	1,105	985
656	530	426	262	270	328	279
802	599	517	389	302	339	315
1.37	1.06	.88	.72	.60	.50	.36
1.52	1.06	.88	.73	.61	.50	.37
.24	.20	.16	.12	.12	.09	.08
2.38	2.15	1.76	1.08	1.12	1.35	1.15
2.92	2.43	2.14	1.62	1.25	1.41	1.34
10.56	9.46	6.08	5.35	4.74	4.27	3.79
35.25	37.40	26.00	14.25	10.29	7.96	7.63
5.7	5.7	5.2	4.9	4.6	4.1	3.5
4.3	4.2	3.9	3.7	3.3	2.7	2.2
2.0	2.1	1.9	1.8	1.5	1.3	1.0
11.9	10.9	14.2	13.6	12.3	10.6	8.6
13.7	12.8	15.3	14.2	13.4	12.5	9.7
7.2	7.8	9.7	7.9	6.0	4.3	3.7
.69	.71	.34	.33	.25	.48	.51
.33	.29	.83	.60	.94	.62	.58
25.8	35.3	29.6	19.8	17.2	15.9	21.2
3.3	4.0	4.3	2.7	2.2	1.9	2.0

Basic Earnings before Goodwill Charges per Common Share
($)

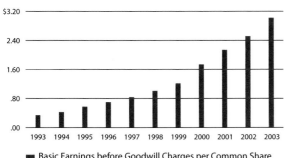

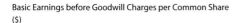

■ Basic Earnings before Goodwill Charges per Common Share

Common Share Market Price Range
($)

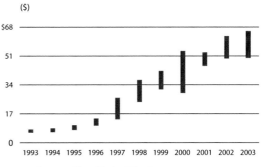

■ Common Share Market Price Range

Specimen Financial Statements: Sobeys Inc.

In this appendix, we illustrate current financial reporting with a comprehensive set of corporate financial statements that are prepared in accordance with generally accepted accounting principles. We are grateful for permission to use the actual financial statements of Canada's second largest food distributor: Sobeys Inc.

The financial statement package includes the balance sheet, statement of retained earnings, statement of earnings, cash flow statement, and notes to the financial statements. The financial statements are preceded by two reports: a statement summarizing management's responsibility for the financial statements and the auditors' report on these statements.

We encourage students to use these financial statements in conjunction with relevant material in the textbook, and to solve the Comparative Analysis Problems in the Broadening Your Perspective section of the end of chapter material.

Management's Responsibility for Financial Reporting

Preparation of the consolidated financial statements accompanying this annual report and the presentation of all other information in the report is the responsibility of management. The consolidated financial statements have been prepared in accordance with appropriate Canadian generally accepted accounting principles and reflect management's best estimates and judgements. All other financial information in the report is consistent with that contained in the consolidated financial statements.

Management of the Company has established and maintains a system of internal control that provides reasonable assurance as to the integrity of the consolidated financial statements, the safeguarding of Company assets, and the prevention and detection of fraudulent financial reporting.

The Board of Directors, through its Audit Committee, which is comprised solely of directors who are unrelated to, and independent of, the Company, meets regularly with financial management and external auditors to satisfy itself as to the reliability and integrity of financial information. The Audit Committee reports its findings to the Board of Directors for consideration in approving the annual consolidated financial statements to be issued to the shareholders. The external auditors have full and free access to the Audit Committee.

Bill McEwan
President &
Chief Executive Officer
June 23, 2004

R. Glenn Hynes, C.A.
Executive Vice President &
Chief Financial Officer
June 23, 2004

Auditors' Report

To the Shareholders of Sobeys Inc.
We have audited the consolidated balance sheets of Sobeys Inc. as at May 1, 2004 and May 3, 2003, and the consolidated statements of earnings, retained earnings, and cash flows for the fiscal years then ended. These consolidated financial statements are the responsibility of the Company's management. Our responsibility is to express an opinion on these consolidated financial statements based on our audits.

We conducted our audits in accordance with Canadian generally accepted auditing standards. Those standards require that we plan and perform an audit to obtain reasonable assurance whether the consolidated financial statements are free of material misstatement. An audit includes examining, on a test basis, evidence supporting the amounts and disclosures in the financial statements. An audit also includes assessing the accounting principles used and significant estimates made by management, as well as evaluating the overall consolidated financial statement presentation.

In our opinion, these consolidated financial statements present fairly, in all material respects, the financial position of the Company as at May 1, 2004 and May 3, 2003, and the results of its operations and its cash flows for the fiscal years then ended in accordance with Canadian generally accepted accounting principles.

Grant Thornton LLP
Chartered Accountants
New Glasgow, Canada
June 7, 2004

43

Consolidated Balance Sheets

(in millions)

	May 1, 2004	May 3, 2003
Assets		
Current		
Cash and cash equivalents (Note 2)	$ 164.6	$ 123.1
Temporary investments, at cost (quoted market value May 2003 – $191.4)	–	191.4
Receivables	272.4	285.4
Inventories	455.0	444.0
Prepaid expenses	40.9	30.5
Future tax assets (Note 8)	1.5	2.7
Mortgages and loans receivable	15.4	15.4
Assets of discontinued operations (Note 3)	–	1.9
	949.8	1,094.4
Mortgages and loans receivable (Note 4)	150.1	134.6
Deferred costs (Note 5)	143.8	135.5
Future tax assets (Note 8)	33.7	28.5
Property and equipment (Note 6)	1,350.1	1,243.9
Assets for realization (Note 3)	16.3	–
Intangibles (less accumulated amortization of $0.5) (Note 18)	13.1	–
Goodwill	617.8	555.6
	$ 3,274.7	$ 3,192.5
Liabilities		
Current		
Accounts payable and accrued liabilities	$ 1,051.1	$ 971.9
Income taxes payable	6.7	37.4
Future tax liabilities (Note 8)	47.8	21.1
Long term debt due within one year	31.9	150.1
	1,137.5	1,180.5
Long term debt (Note 9)	410.9	435.3
Employee future benefit obligation (Note 17)	88.4	75.5
Future tax liabilities (Note 8)	55.8	57.7
Deferred revenue	6.6	6.7
	1,699.2	1,755.7
Shareholders' equity		
Capital stock (Note 10)	907.6	903.4
Retained earnings	667.9	533.4
	1,575.5	1,436.8
	$ 3,274.7	$ 3,192.5

See accompanying notes to the consolidated financial statements.

Approved on behalf of the Board

Bill McEwan
Director

Sir Graham Day
Director

Consolidated Statements of Retained Earnings

Year Ended (in millions)

	May 1, 2004	May 3, 2003
Balance, beginning of year	$ 533.4	$ 382.0
Net earnings	167.5	179.0
	700.9	561.0
Dividends declared	29.0	23.8
Premium on common shares purchased for cancellation (Note 10)	4.0	3.8
Balance, end of year	$ 667.9	$ 533.4

See accompanying notes to the consolidated financial statements.

Consolidated Statements of Earnings

Year Ended (in millions)

	May 1, 2004	May 3, 2003
Sales	$ 11,046.8	$ 10,414.5
Gain on sale of assets (Note 11)	14.6	–
Operating expenses		
Cost of sales, selling and administrative expenses	10,615.4	9,964.4
Depreciation	150.4	124.0
Intangible amortization	0.5	–
Operating income	295.1	326.1
Interest expense		
Long-term debt	39.2	41.7
Short-term debt	3.2	–
	42.4	41.7
Earnings before income taxes	252.7	284.4
Income taxes (Note 8)	85.2	105.4
Net earnings	$ 167.5	$ 179.0
Net earnings per share basic and diluted (Note 12)	$ 2.54	$ 2.72
Basic and diluted weighted average number of common shares outstanding, in millions	65.9	65.9

See accompanying notes to the consolidated financial statements.

Consolidated Statements of Cash Flows

Year Ended (in millions)

	May 1, 2004	May 3, 2003
Operations		
Net earnings	$ 167.5	$ 179.0
Items not affecting cash (Note 13)	193.1	187.6
	360.6	366.6
Net change in non-cash working capital	3.8	(18.5)
Cash flows from operating activities	364.4	348.1
Investment		
Property and equipment purchases	(316.1)	(342.3)
Proceeds on disposal of property and equipment	80.1	48.0
Long term investments and advances	(15.5)	(9.8)
Increase in deferred costs	(33.9)	(41.6)
Business acquisitions, net of cash acquired	(53.6)	(2.5)
Cash flows used in investing activities	(339.0)	(348.2)
Financing		
Issue of long term debt	14.9	118.6
Repayment of long term debt	(162.7)	(56.8)
Decrease (increase) of share purchase loan	1.3	(2.5)
Issue of capital stock	5.4	6.7
Repurchase of capital stock	(6.5)	(5.9)
Dividends	(29.0)	(23.8)
Cash flows from (used in) financing activities	(176.6)	36.3
Increase (decrease) in cash from continuing operations	(151.2)	36.2
Discontinued operations (Note 3)	1.3	3.9
Increase (decrease) in cash	(149.9)	40.1
Cash, beginning of year	314.5	274.4
Cash, end of year	$ 164.6	$ 314.5

Cash is defined as cash, treasury bills, guaranteed investments, and temporary investments.

See accompanying notes to the consolidated financial statements.

Notes to the Consolidated Financial Statements

May 1, 2004 (In millions, except share capital)

1. Summary of significant accounting policies

Principles of consolidation

These consolidated financial statements include the accounts of the Company and all subsidiary companies. All of the Company's subsidiaries are wholly owned.

Depreciation

Property and equipment are recorded at cost.

Depreciation is recorded on a straight line basis over the estimated useful lives of the assets as follows:

Equipment and vehicles	3–20 years
Buildings	10–40 years
Leasehold improvements	7–10 years

Cash and cash equivalents

Cash and cash equivalents are defined as cash, treasury bills, and guaranteed investments.

Inventories

Warehouse inventories are valued at the lower of cost and net realizable value with cost being determined substantially on a first-in, first-out basis. Retail inventories are valued at the lower of cost and net realizable value less normal profit margins as determined by the retail method of inventory valuation.

Leases

Leases meeting certain criteria are accounted for as capital leases. The imputed interest is charged against income and the capitalized value is depreciated on a straight line basis over its estimated useful life. Obligations under capital leases are reduced by rental payments net of imputed interest. All other leases are accounted for as operating leases with rental payments being expensed as incurred.

Goodwill

Goodwill represents the excess of the purchase price of the business acquired over the fair value of the underlying net tangible and intangible assets acquired at the date of acquisition.

Goodwill and intangible assets with indefinite useful lives are subject to an annual impairment review. Any permanent impairment in the book value of goodwill or intangible assets will be written off against earnings. The Company has completed its review and has determined the book value of existing goodwill is not impaired.

Intangibles

Intangibles arise on the purchase of new businesses, existing franchises, and the acquisition of pharmacy prescription files. Amortization is on a straight-line basis, over 10–15 years.

Stock-based compensation

At the beginning of fiscal 2003, the Company adopted, on a prospective basis, CICA Handbook section 3870 "Stock-Based Compensation and Other Stock-Based Payments." There was no effect on the Company upon implementation of this standard. In fiscal 2004, the Emerging Issues Committee issued Abstract 132 "Share Purchase Financing". This Abstract requires Share Purchase Loans that are not treated as assets on the balance sheet to be accounted for as stock-based compensation. Accordingly, pro-forma fair-value-based net income and earnings per share information is disclosed in Note 19 for Share Purchase Loans issued in the 2004 fiscal year.

Revenue recognition

Sales are recognized at the point-of-sale. Sales include revenues from customers through corporate stores operated by the Company, and revenue from sales to franchised stores, associated stores and independent accounts.

Interest capitalization

Interest related to the period of construction is capitalized as part of the cost of the related property and equipment. The amount of interest capitalized to construction in progress in the current year was $0.6 (May 3, 2003 $1.3).

Deferred revenue

Deferred revenue consists of long term supplier purchase agreements, and rental revenue arising from the sale of subsidiaries. Deferred revenue is being taken into income over the term of the related agreements and leases.

Store opening expenses

Store opening expenses of new stores and store conversions are written off during the first year of operation.

Financial instruments

The Company uses interest rate instruments to manage exposure to fluctuations in interest rates. The realized gain or loss arising from the instruments is included in interest expense.

Accounting estimates

The preparation of consolidated financial statements, in conformity with Canadian generally accepted accounting principles, requires management to make estimates and assumptions that affect the amounts reported in the consolidated financial statements and accompanying notes. These estimates are based on management's best knowledge of current events and actions that the Company may undertake in the future.

Future income taxes

The difference between the tax basis of assets and liabilities and their carrying value on the balance sheet is used to calculate future tax assets and liabilities. The future tax assets and liabilities have been measured using substantially enacted tax rates that will be in effect when the differences are expected to reverse.

Net earnings per share

Net earnings per share is calculated by dividing the earnings available to common shareholders by the weighted average number of common shares outstanding during the year.

Long-lived assets

At the beginning of fiscal 2004, the Company adopted two new CICA Handbook sections. Section 3063, "Impairment of Long-Lived Assets", provides guidance with regards to the measurement, recognition and disclosure of the impairment of long-lived assets. There was no impact of the application of Section 3063 on the financial statements. Section 3475, "Disposal of Long-Lived Assets and Discontinued Operations", provides guidance with regards to the identification, measurement and disclosure of any long-lived assets not held for use and discontinued operations (see Note 3).

Foreign currency translation

Assets and liabilities denominated in foreign currencies are translated into Canadian dollars at the foreign currency exchange rate in effect at each year end date. Exchange gains or losses arising from the translation of these balances denominated in foreign currencies are recognized in operating income. Revenues and expenses denominated in foreign currencies are translated into Canadian dollars at the average foreign currency exchange rate for the period.

NOTES TO THE CONSOLIDATED FINANCIAL STATEMENTS

2. Cash and cash equivalents

Included in cash and cash equivalents is restricted cash of $24.9 relating to the sale of assets in the fourth quarter of fiscal 2004, which is being held in trust for 28 days.

3. Assets for realization

Certain land and buildings have been listed for sale and reclassified as "Assets for realization" in accordance with CICA Handbook section 3475. These assets are expected to be sold within a twelve month period and are no longer productive assets and there is no longer an intent to develop for future use. Assets for realization are valued at the lower of cost and fair value less cost of disposal.

Cash flow from discontinued operations for the 52 weeks ended May 1, 2004 and May 3, 2003 include cash generated by disposal of assets of discontinued operations of $1.3, and $3.9, respectively.

4. Mortgages and loans receivable

	May 1, 2004	May 3, 2003
Loans receivable	$ 156.9	$ 140.4
Mortgages receivable	7.9	9.0
Other	0.7	0.6
	$ 165.5	$ 150.0
Less amount due within one year	15.4	15.4
	$ 150.1	$ 134.6

Loans receivable
Loans receivable represent long-term financing to certain retail associates. These loans are primarily secured by inventory, fixtures and equipment, bear various interest rates and have repayment terms up to ten years. The carrying amount of the loans receivable approximates fair value based on the variable interest rates charged on the loans and the operating relationship of the associates with the Company.

5. Deferred costs

	2004 Net Book Value	2003 Net Book Value
Deferred store marketing costs	$ 55.2	$ 40.1
Deferred financing costs	4.5	7.0
Deferred purchase agreements	17.4	16.7
Transitional pension asset	33.9	38.1
Other	32.8	33.6
	$ 143.8	$ 135.5

Deferred costs are amortized as follows:
Deferred store marketing – 7 years
Deferred financing – over the term of the debt
Deferred purchase agreements – over the term of the franchise agreement

NOTES TO THE CONSOLIDATED FINANCIAL STATEMENTS

6. Property and equipment

	May 1, 2004		
	Cost	Accumulated Depreciation	Net Book Value
Land	$ 72.3	$ –	$ 72.3
Land held for development	81.4	–	81.4
Buildings	492.1	100.6	391.5
Equipment and vehicles	1,567.2	937.5	629.7
Leasehold improvements	278.9	169.0	109.9
Construction in progress	55.4	–	55.4
Assets under capital leases	15.7	5.8	9.9
	$ 2,563.0	$ 1,212.9	$ 1,350.1

	May 3, 2003		
	Cost	Accumulated Depreciation	Net Book Value
Land	$ 83.4	$ –	$ 83.4
Land held for development	81.4	–	81.4
Buildings	451.3	96.3	355.0
Equipment and vehicles	1,320.3	774.7	545.6
Leasehold improvements	263.9	146.7	117.2
Construction in progress	50.9	–	50.9
Assets under capital leases	15.4	5.0	10.4
	$ 2,266.6	$ 1,022.7	$ 1,243.9

7. Bank loans and bankers' acceptances

Under the terms of a credit agreement entered into between the Company and a banking syndicate arranged by the Bank of Nova Scotia, a revolving term credit facility of $300.0 was established. This 364-day revolving unsecured facility was renewed on June 1, 2004. Various provisions of the agreement provide the Company with the ability to extend the facility for a minimum period of two years.

Interest payable on this facility fluctuates with changes in the prime interest rate.

8. Income taxes

Income tax expense varies from the amount that would be computed by applying the combined federal and provincial statutory tax rate as a result of the following:

	May 1, 2004	May 3, 2003
Income tax expense according to combined statutory rate of 33.7% (2003 – 36.5%)	$ 85.1	$ 103.9
Increase (reduction) in income taxes resulting from:		
Non-taxable gains	(1.4)	(0.3)
Large corporation tax	1.5	1.8
Total income taxes	$ 85.2	$ 105.4

May 1, 2004 income tax expense attributable to net income consists of:

	Current	Future	Total
Operations	$ 64.4	$ 20.8	$ 85.2

NOTES TO THE CONSOLIDATED FINANCIAL STATEMENTS

May 3, 2003 income tax expense attributable to net income consists of:

	Current	Future	Total
	$ 64.6	$ 40.8	$ 105.4

The tax effect of temporary differences that give rise to significant portions of the future tax liability are presented below:

	May 1, 2004	May 3, 2003
Employee future benefit obligation	$ 31.0	$ 24.3
Restructuring provisions	1.5	2.7
Pension contributions	(16.2)	(12.3)
Deferred costs	(18.8)	(14.9)
Deferred credits	(47.8)	(34.9)
Goodwill	(6.3)	(4.4)
Fixed assets	(11.4)	(5.5)
Other	(0.4)	(2.6)
	$ (68.4)	$ (47.6)
Current future tax assets	$ 1.5	$ 2.7
Non-current future tax assets	33.7	28.5
Current future tax liabilities	(47.8)	(21.1)
Non-current future tax liabilities	(55.8)	(57.7)
	$ (68.4)	$ (47.6)

9. Long-term debt

	May 1, 2004	May 3, 2003
First mortgage loans, average interest rate 9.8%, due 2008–2021	$ 23.3	$ 25.1
Bank loans, average interest rate 6.4%, due September 30, 2004	20.0	60.0
Medium Term Note, interest rate of 7.6%, due November 1, 2005	175.0	175.0
Medium Term Note, interest rate of 7.0%, due October 2, 2003	–	100.0
Medium Term Note, interest rate of 7.2%, February 26, 2018	100.0	100.0
Debentures, average interest rate 10.7%, due 2008–2013	73.3	78.3
Notes payable and other debt at interest rates fluctuating with the prime rate	38.6	37.6
	430.2	576.0
Capital lease obligations, 2004–2011, net of imputed interest	12.6	9.4
	442.8	585.4
Less amount due within one year	31.9	150.1
	$ 410.9	$ 435.3

The Company has fixed the interest rate on $11.8 of its long-term debt at 6.4% by utilizing interest exchange agreements.

First mortgage loans are secured by land, buildings, and specific charges on certain assets. Sobeys Group Inc., an indirect subsidiary of Sobeys Inc., has provided the debenture holders with a floating charge over all its assets, subject to permitted encumbrances, a general assignment of book debts, and the assignment of proceeds of insurance policies.

During fiscal 2001, the Company negotiated a new unsecured $550.0 credit facility consisting of $250.0 of non-revolving debt to be repaid over five years, plus a $300.0 revolving line of credit. As of May 1, 2004, $230.0 of the non-revolving debt had been retired. On December 20, 2002 (amended on February 17, 2003) the Company filed a final short form prospectus providing for the issuance of up to $500.0 of unsecured medium term notes over the next two years.

NOTES TO THE CONSOLIDATED FINANCIAL STATEMENTS

On October 2, 2003, Medium Term Notes of $100.0 were repaid in accordance with their terms. Debt retirement payments and capital lease obligations in each of the next five fiscal years are:

	Long-Term Debt	Capital Leases
2005	$ 28.1	$ 3.8
2006	183.4	3.4
2007	7.8	2.1
2008	8.6	1.0
2009	5.9	0.7

Operating leases

The net aggregate, annual, minimum rent payable under operating leases for fiscal 2005 is approximately $119.9 ($246.0 gross less expected sub-lease income of $126.1). The net commitments over the next five fiscal years are:

	Net Lease Obligation
2005	$ 119.9
2006	112.5
2007	101.4
2008	89.4
2009	87.7

10. Capital stock

Authorized

	Number of Shares
Preferred shares, par value of $25 each, issuable in series as a class	500,000,000
Preferred shares, without par value, issuable in series as a class	500,000,000
Common shares, without par value	499,438,543

Issued and outstanding

	Number of Shares		Capital Stock (in millions)	
	May 1, 2004	May 3, 2003	May 1, 2004	May 3, 2003
Common shares, without par value	65,860,719	65,893,168	$ 925.6	$ 922.7
Loans receivable from officers and employees under share purchase plan	–	–	(18.0)	(19.3)
Total capital stock	65,860,719	65,893,168	$ 907.6	$ 903.4

During the current fiscal year, the Company purchased for cancellation 187,572 (2003 – 151,965) of its common shares from employees, and as part of a normal course issuer bid announced on December 13, 2002. The purchase price for the shares was $6.5 (2003 – $5.9) and $4.0 (2003 – $3.8) of the purchase price (representing the excess of the purchase price over the average paid-up value of common shares purchased for cancellation) was charged to retained earnings.

During the year 155,123 (2003 – 169,387) common shares of Sobeys Inc. were issued under the Company's share purchase plan to certain officers and employees for $5.4 (2003 – $6.7).

NOTES TO THE CONSOLIDATED FINANCIAL STATEMENTS

Loans receivable from officers and employees of $18.0 under the Company's share purchase plan are classified as a reduction of capital stock. Loan repayments will result in a corresponding increase in capital stock. The individual loans are non-interest bearing, non-recourse, and are secured by the individual's common shares of Sobeys Inc. (580,782 combined total).

11. Gain on sale of assets

During the fourth quarter, the Company sold several redundant real estate assets. These assets were not considered strategic for the long-term plans of the Company. The gain realized on the sales of these assets was $14.6.

12. Net earnings per share

	May 1, 2004	May 3, 2003
Net earnings	$ 167.5	$ 179.0
Weighted average common shares outstanding	65,877,959	65,928,308
Net earnings per common share	$ 2.54	$ 2.72

13. Supplementary cash flow information

a) Items not affecting cash:	May 1, 2004	May 3, 2003
Depreciation	$ 150.4	$ 124.0
Future tax provision	20.8	40.8
Loss (gain) on disposal of assets	(15.7)	0.7
Amortization of intangibles	0.5	–
Amortization of deferred items	25.5	17.0
Employee future benefit obligation	11.6	5.1
	$ 193.1	$ 187.6

b) Other items:		
Interest paid	$ 42.4	$ 40.7
Taxes paid	$ 111.0	$ 66.5

14. Related party transactions

The Company leased certain real property from related parties, at formula determined rates that approximate fair market value over the life of the leases. The aggregate net payments under these leases amounted to approximately $52.2 (2003 - $49.8). The Company was charged expenses of $0.4 (2003 - $0.5) by related parties.

In the current year the Company sold real property to related parties, at fair market value with aggregate proceeds of $3.3 and a resulting gain of $0.6.

In the prior fiscal year, the Company received $1.6 from the sale of marketable securities to its parent company. The marketable securities were sold at fair market value and resulted in a gain of $1.4.

At May 1, 2004, mortgage receivables of $2.2 were owing from related parties.

Related party transactions are with the parent company Empire Company Limited and any of its subsidiaries. Empire Company Limited is a majority shareholder of Sobeys Inc., holding 65% of Sobeys Inc. common shares.

15. Financial instruments

Credit risk

There is no significant concentration of credit risk. The credit risk exposure is considered normal for the business.

Fair value of financial instruments

The book value of cash and cash equivalents, temporary investments, receivables, mortgages and loans receivable, and accounts payable and accrued liabilities approximate fair values at May 1, 2004.

The total fair value of long-term debt is estimated to be $480.2. The fair value of variable rate long term-debt is assumed to approximate its carrying amount. The fair value of other long-term debt has been estimated by discounting future cash flows at a rate offered for debt of similar maturities and credit quality.

Interest rate risk

The majority of the Company debt is at fixed rates. Accordingly, there is limited exposure to interest rate risk.

16. Contingent liabilities

Guarantees and commitments

The Company has undertaken to provide cash to meet any obligations which Sobey Leased Properties Limited (a wholly owned subsidiary of Empire Company Limited) is unable or fails to meet until all of its debentures have been paid in full in accordance with their terms. Any deficiency payment made by the Company will be by purchase of fully-paid non-assessable 5% redeemable, non-voting preference shares of that company. The aggregated outstanding principal amounts of these debentures at May 1, 2004 is $38.6 (2003 - $40.6). Sobey Leased Properties Limited's principal business relates to leasing real estate locations to Sobeys Capital Incorporated (a subsidiary of Sobeys Inc.) and its subsidiary companies.

At May 1, 2004, the Company was contingently liable for letters of credit issued in the aggregate amount of $22.0 (2003 – $27.4).

The Company has guaranteed certain bank loans contracted by franchisees. As at May 1, 2004, these loans amounted to approximately $5.0 (2003 – $7.3).

Upon entering into the lease of its new Mississauga distribution centre, in March 2000, Sobeys Capital Incorporated guaranteed to the landlord a performance, by SERCA Foodservice Inc., of all its obligations under the lease. The remaining term of the lease is 16 years with an aggregate obligation of $48.8. At the time of the sale of assets of SERCA Foodservice Inc. to Sysco Corp., the lease of the Mississauga distribution centre was assigned to and assumed by the purchaser and Sysco Corp. agreed to indemnify and hold Sobeys Capital Incorporated harmless from any liability it may incur pursuant to its guarantee.

On March 26, 2003 the Shareholders of IGA Canada Limited approved a resolution terminating the operations of the IGA Canada Buying Group effective December 31, 2003. On April 14, 2003 the members of the Buying Group were notified of the shareholders intention to terminate the operations of the Buying Group. The buying group operations ceased effective December 31, 2003. The cross guarantees for members of the Buying Group have been eliminated with the wind-up of the Buying Group as of December 31, 2003.

There are various claims and litigation, which the Company is involved with, arising out of the ordinary course of business operations. The Company's management does not consider the exposure to such litigation to be material, although this cannot be predicted with certainty.

NOTES TO THE CONSOLIDATED FINANCIAL STATEMENTS

17. Employee future benefits

The Company has a number of defined benefit and defined contribution plans providing pension and other retirement benefits to many of its employees.

Defined contribution plans

The total expense for the Company's defined contribution plans is as follows:

	2004	2003
Defined benefit plans	$ 11.2	$ 11.0

Information about the Company's defined benefit plans, in aggregate, is as follows:

	Pension Benefit Plans 2004	Pension Benefit Plans 2003	Other Benefit Plans 2004	Other Benefit Plans 2003
Accrued benefit obligation				
Balance at beginning of year	$ 231.6	$ 204.2	$ 87.3	$ 88.0
New incidence (post-employment benefits)	–	–	7.7	–
Current service cost	2.3	2.8	2.2	3.1
Interest cost	14.8	14.8	6.0	6.1
Employee contributions	0.5	0.5	–	–
Special termination benefits	1.3	–	–	–
Plan amendments	–	–	1.3	–
Benefits paid	(16.5)	(17.1)	(4.4)	(4.6)
Plan merger	–	11.8	–	–
Actuarial loss	14.0	14.6	8.0	(5.3)
Balance at end of year	$ 248.0	$ 231.6	$ 108.1	$ 87.3
Plan assets				
Market value at beginning of year	$ 199.8	$ 203.5	$ –	$ –
Actual return on plan assets	36.8	(13.3)	–	–
Employer contributions	2.9	15.0	4.4	4.6
Employee contributions	0.5	0.5	–	–
Plan merger	–	11.2	–	–
Benefits paid	(16.5)	(17.1)	(4.4)	(4.6)
Market value at end of year	$ 223.5	$ 199.8	$ –	$ –
Funded status				
Surplus (deficit)	$ (24.5)	$ (31.8)	$ (108.1)	$ (87.3)
Unamortized past service cost	0.3	0.3	1.2	–
Unamortized actuarial loss	52.0	64.7	18.5	11.8
Accrued benefit asset (liability)	$ 27.8	$ 33.2	$ (88.4)	$ (75.5)
Expense				
Current service cost	$ 2.3	$ 2.8	$ 2.2	$ 3.1
Interest cost	14.8	14.8	6.0	6.1
Amortization	3.5	0.2	1.4	0.5
Special termination benefits	1.3	–	–	–
New incidence (post-employment benefits)	–	–	7.7	–
Expected return on plan assets	(13.6)	(15.1)	–	–
	$ 8.3	$ 2.7	$ 17.3	$ 9.7

Included in the accrued benefit obligation at year-end are the following amounts in respect of plans that are not funded:

	Pension Benefit Plans 2004	Pension Benefit Plans 2003	Other Benefit Plans 2004	Other Benefit Plans 2003
Accrued benefit obligation	$ 15.7	$ 14.9	$ 88.4	$ 75.5

The significant actuarial assumptions adopted in measuring the Company's accrued benefit obligations are as follows (weighted-average assumptions as of May 1, 2004):

	Pension Benefit Plans 2004	Pension Benefit Plans 2003	Other Benefit Plans 2004	Other Benefit Plans 2003
Discount rate	6.00%	6.50%	6.00%	6.50%
Expected long-term rate of return on plan assets	7.00%	7.00%		
Rate of compensation increase	4.00%	4.00%		

For measurement purposes, a 9% fiscal 2004 annual rate of increase in the per capita cost of covered health care benefits was assumed. The cumulative rate expectation to 2010 is 6%. The average remaining service period of the active employees covered by the pension benefit plans and other benefit plans is 12 and 18 years, respectively.

18. Business Acquisitions

Other Acquisitions

The Company acquires franchisee stores, and prescription files as part of its normal operations. The results of these acquisitions have been included in the consolidated financial results of the Company, and were accounted for through the use of the purchase method. The method of amortization is on a straight-line basis, over 10–15 years.

Franchisees		
Inventory	$	2.4
Property and equipment		3.0
Intangibles		8.0
Other Assets		0.1
Cash consideration	$	13.5
Prescription Files		
Intangibles	$	0.2
Cash consideration	$	0.2

NOTES TO THE CONSOLIDATED FINANCIAL STATEMENTS

Commisso's Food Markets Limited and Commisso's Grocery Distributors Limited

During the fiscal year, the Company acquired substantially all of the assets and trade liabilities of Commisso's Food Markets Limited and Commisso's Grocery Distributors Limited which are located in Southern Ontario. The acquisition included 15 grocery stores, six cash-and-carry outlets, and a wholesale business and distribution centre. The acquisition was completed February 1, 2004, and was accounted for using the purchase method, with operating results being included in the consolidated financial statements at this date. Due to the size and complexity of the acquisition, the determination of fair value of certain net assets is still being finalized. To the extent that estimates need to be adjusted, they will be adjusted accordingly.

Inventory	$ 16.2
Property and equipment	13.6
Goodwill	62.5
Intangibles	5.4
Other assets	3.1
Accounts payable	(32.1)
Long term liabilities	(6.5)
Other liabilities	(21.2)
	$ 41.0
Expenses	(0.8)
Cash consideration	$ 40.2

19. Stock-Based Compensation

Deferred Share Units

Members of the Board of Directors may elect to receive all or any portion of their fees in Deferred Share Units (DSU's) in lieu of cash. The number of DSU's received is determined by the market value of Sobeys Inc. common shares on each directors' fee payment date. Additional DSU's are received as dividend equivalents. DSU's cannot be redeemed for cash until the holder is no longer a director of the Company. The redemption value of a DSU equals the market value of a Sobeys Inc. common share at the time of the redemption. On an ongoing basis, the Company values the DSU obligation at the current market value of a common share and records any increase in the DSU obligation as an operating expense. At May 1, 2004 there were 38,813 (May 3, 2003 26,617) DSU's outstanding. During the year, the stock-based compensation expense was $0.6 (2003 – $0.6).

Share Purchase Loans

The Company has a Share Purchase Loan plan for employees of the company whereby loans are granted to purchase common stock. On a pro-forma basis, if the loans had been treated as stock-based compensation in accordance with Emerging Issues Committee Abstract 132, and the compensation cost was amortized on a straight-line basis over the period that the underlying shares are expected to be released to the employees, the effect would have been as follows:

Net Earnings	
As reported	$ 167.5
Pro-forma	$ 167.2
Diluted Net Earnings per Share	
As reported	$ 2.54
Pro-forma	$ 2.54

NOTES TO THE CONSOLIDATED FINANCIAL STATEMENTS

The compensation cost relating to the 2004 Share Purchase Loans was determined to be $1.5 million with amortization of the cost over 5 years. The cost was calculated using the Black-Scholes model with the following assumptions:

Expected life	5 years
Risk-free interest rate	4.2%
Expected volatility	26.5%
Dividend yield	1.2%

20. Comparative figures

Comparative figures have been reclassified, where necessary, to reflect the current year's presentation, including required disclosure for discontinued operations.

Glossary of Terms

Adjusted debt – funded debt plus capitalized value of operating lease payments, which is calculated as six times net annual operating lease payments

Adjusted debt to capital – adjusted debt divided by the sum of adjusted debt and shareholders' equity

Capital expenditure / investment – payments made for the acquisition of property and equipment

Company-wide capital expenditures – total investment in property and equipment, which includes investment financed by the Company, third party operating leases, landlords and franchise affiliates

EBITDA – earnings before interest, taxes, depreciation and amortization

EBITDA margin – EBITDA divided by sales

Expanded stores – stores that undergo construction resulting in square footage increase during the year

Funded debt – all interest bearing debt, which includes bank loans, bankers' acceptances and long–term debt

Hedge – a financial instrument used to manage foreign exchange or interest rate risk by making a transaction which offsets the existing position

Interest coverage – EBITDA divided by interest expense

Letters of credit – financial instruments issued by a financial institution to guarantee the Company's payments to a third party

Managed working capital – the net amount of accounts receivable and inventories less accounts payable

National share of requirements – measurement (percentage) of all Sobeys shopping households' total grocery requirements that are satisfied by the Company's retail stores

On balance sheet investment – the Company's investment in property and equipment that is recorded on the balance sheet

Operating earnings – net earnings before gain on sale of discontinued operations, and net capital loss & other items

Operating Income (EBIT) – earnings before interest and taxes

Operating margin (EBIT) – EBIT divided by sales

Renovated stores – stores that undergo construction, resulting in no increase in square footage

Retail Brands – a brand of products that is marketed, distributed and owned by the Company

Return on equity – operating earnings divided by average shareholders' equity

Same store sales – sales from stores in the same locations in both reporting periods

Total capital – funded debt plus shareholders' equity

Weighted average number of shares – number of common shares outstanding adjusted to take into account the time the shares are outstanding in the reporting period

Working capital – total current assets less total current liabilities

Photo Credits

All images are copyright © Photo Disc, Inc./Getty Images unless otherwise noted.

Logos are registered trademarks of the respective companies and are reprinted with permission.

Chapter 1
Opener: Loblaw Companies Ltd.

Chapter 2
Opener: Frank Gunn/Canadian Press CP. Page 52: Sears Canada Inc. logo is a registered Trade Mark of Sears licensed for use in Canada. All rights reserved. Page 69: Elaine Thompson/Associated Press AP.

Chapter 3
Opener: BeaverTails Canada Inc. Page 111: The Goodyear Tire & Rubber Co.

Chapter 5
Opener: Wal-Mart Stores, Inc. Page 223: Nell Redmond/Associated Press AP.

Chapter 6
Opener: Syncrude Canada Inc. Page 274: Getty/Digital Vision. Page 280: Brand X Pictures.

Chapter 7
Opener: Granite Brewery. Page 310: Getty/Digital Vision. Page 317: Bank of Montreal.

Chapter 8
Opener: Wyeth Consumer Healthcare. Page 375: Sears Canada Inc.

Chapter 9
Opener: Air Canada. Page 403: Suzanne Plunkett/Associated Press AP. Page 413: Frank Gunn/Canadian Press CP.

Chapter 10
Opener: Quebecor Inc. Page 463: Corbis Images. Page 474: Concordia University.

Chapter 11
Opener: Research In Motion Ltd. Page 525: Ian Barrett/Canadian Press CP. Page 528: Paul Sakuma/Associated Press CP.

Chapter 12
Opener: Encana Corporation. Page 579: Loblaw Companies Ltd.

Chapter 13
Opener: Intrawest Corporation. Page 609: Digital Vision.

Chapter 14
Opener: Potash Corporation of Saskatchewan Inc. Page 687: © IT Stock. Page 689: Corbis Digital Stock.

Company Index

Subject Index